02/09/2017
31/10/2017

LYM

www.hants.gov.uk/library

Hampshire
County Council

Love YOUR LIBRARY

Tel: 0300 555 1387

Da...
sin...
be...
Aw...
Belfast Journalist of the Year.

David McVea graduated in politics and modern history from Queen's University, Belfast, and has an MA from Sussex University. He was head of the politics department of a Belfast grammar school where he taught both history and political studies.

They were among the authors of the landmark million-word book *Lost Lives*, detailing all those who died in the troubles, which received the Christopher Ewart-Biggs Memorial Prize for the promotion of peace and understanding in Ireland.

KU-750-957

C016385559

Making Sense of the Troubles

A History of the Northern Ireland Conflict

DAVID McKITTRICK
DAVID McVEA

VIKING
an imprint of
PENGUIN BOOKS

VIKING

Published by the Penguin Group

Penguin Books Ltd, 80 Strand, London WC2R 0RL, England

Penguin Group (USA) Inc., 375 Hudson Street, New York, New York 10014, USA

Penguin Group (Canada), 90 Eglinton Avenue East, Suite 700, Toronto, Ontario, Canada M4P 2Y3
(a division of Pearson Penguin Canada Inc.)

Penguin Ireland, 25 St Stephen's Green, Dublin 2, Ireland (a division of Penguin Books Ltd)

Penguin Group (Australia), 250 Camberwell Road,
Camberwell, Victoria 3124, Australia (a division of Pearson Australia Group Pty Ltd)

Penguin Books India Pvt Ltd, 11 Community Centre,
Panchsheel Park, New Delhi – 110 017, India

Penguin Group (NZ), 67 Apollo Drive, Rosedale, Auckland 0632, New Zealand
(a division of Pearson New Zealand Ltd)

Penguin Books (South Africa) (Pty) Ltd, Block D, Rosebank Office Park,
181 Jan Smuts Avenue, Parktown North, Gauteng 2193, South Africa

www.penguin.com

Penguin Books Ltd, Registered Offices: 80 Strand, London WC2R 0RL, England

First published by The Blackstaff Press 2000
First published in Penguin Books 2001
This revised edition published by Viking 2012

006

Copyright © David McKittrick and David McVea, 2000, 2001, 2012
All rights reserved

The moral right of the authors has been asserted

Set in Dante 12/14.75pt
Typeset by Palimpsest Book Production Limited, Falkirk, Stirlingshire
Printed in England by Clays Ltd, St Ives plc

Except in the United States of America, this book is sold subject
to the condition that it shall not, by way of trade or otherwise, be lent,
re-sold, hired out, or otherwise circulated without the publisher's
prior consent in any form of binding or cover other than that in
which it is published and without a similar condition including this
condition being imposed on the subsequent purchaser

ISBN: 978-0-241-96265-7

www.greenpenguin.co.uk

MIX
Paper from
responsible sources
FSC www.fsc.org FSC™ C018179

Penguin Books is committed to a sustainable
future for our business, our readers and our planet.
This book is made from Forest Stewardship
Council™ certified paper.

To our wives
and families

Contents

Introduction

This book is a fully updated version of our original work published in 2000 at a time of much uncertainty in Northern Ireland. The years that followed have been both highly eventful and mostly positive, witnessing a decline in violence and much political progress, producing a more stable political settlement than most had dared to hope for. While that settlement certainly has its critics, practically everyone regards it as preferable to what went before. There are still occasional crises but most of these tend to be political rather than violent, and are generally settled by negotiation. Politics has become the order of the day: and who would have guessed that, by 2012, one of the grumbles about the Stormont administration was that its proceedings had come to seem dull.

People did not celebrate in the streets in 2007 when two of the principal warriors of the troubles, loyalist Ian Paisley and republican Martin McGuinness, became joint heads of a new cross-community administration amid affirmations that the war was over and that a new era of cooperation was at hand. It flew in the face of history, experience and intuition to think of Paisley and McGuinness promising to run Northern Ireland together for the benefit of all. Paisley, as Northern Ireland's new First Minister, spoke of 'a time when hate will no longer rule'. McGuinness, the ex-IRA commander, spoke of peace and reconciliation. Almost four decades of death, destruction and distrust had left Northern Ireland such a tight, closed and wary society that the event brought few spontaneous eruptions of joy or celebration.

And yet there was a near-universal sense – not quite a certainty, but much more than a hope – that Northern Ireland's long nightmare was finally coming to an end after more than 3,700 deaths and after generations of discord. It felt over. The general desire for peace was so strong that it would be easy to be complacent and to assert that Northern Ireland would never experience war again. That error has certainly been made in the past: an eminent historian had airily written in the 1930s, for example, that while political and religious difficulties had left their marks on Ireland 'they have been dissolved in the light of modern reasonableness'. This serves as a warning that it is dangerous to declare that peace has broken out in Ireland, especially Northern Ireland. The earlier history, and above all the troubles, left so many scars and so many divisions that the future is hardly likely to be a tranquil one. Yet the 2007 surge of 'modern reasonableness', together with the predominant feeling that decades of conflict had demonstrated that no one element was going to achieve victory over the others, seemed to indicate that a return to full-scale violence was scarcely imaginable. There will certainly be conflict ahead, but the betting is that it will for the most part be confined to the political arena rather than the streets of Belfast and the border lanes of south Armagh. That is probably as much as can be hoped for: Northern Ireland is never going to be a utopia, but nor is it fated to continue in violence.

For very many people the troubles were a terrible time in which a generation grew up not knowing peace or stability. They represented a lethal but fascinating time in Northern Ireland's history, witnessing as they did not only death, injury and destruction but also huge political and social change. While some might argue that it may be too early for a full account of these years, there is so much material available, and so many memories are so fresh, that we believe a proper attempt can be made to make some sense of the troubles.

Many secrets doubtless remain to be revealed, and there is important information which may not emerge for many years, if ever. Some events and interpretations are destined to be disputed for decades, yet much of the course of the troubles is already reasonably clear. The main political events are there for all to see, as are the main characters. So too, tragically, are the more than 3,700 deaths of the troubles, deaths whose consequences are all too evident to the relatives and friends affected.

Both of the authors are acutely aware of this last, since we were among the five authors of *Lost Lives*, the book which gives an account of every troubles death. In writing this book it was always at the forefront of our minds that the troubles should not be regarded simply as a period of political upheaval but also as a time when so many lives were lost and so many people injured or bereaved. For this reason the reader will find here a greater than usual emphasis on the deaths as well as the major political events.

Hundreds of books and millions of words have been written on the troubles: *Lost Lives* alone, for example, contains almost a million of them. The aim of this book is to provide an overview, excising a great many details. When the choice was between giving intricate detail or a broad-brush overview, we almost always opted for the latter. There were many points where we were tempted to pause and indulge in lengthier analysis but for the most part we aimed instead for maintaining narrative momentum. To complement this approach, the substantial chronology gives greater detail on many events.

Our research involved consulting many of the hundreds of books on various aspects of this period, as well as going through primary source material in newspaper libraries and at the Public Record Office of Northern Ireland. We also consulted a vast collection of clippings and notes in addition to having journalistic access to many of the participants, ranging from those responsible for governing in London, Belfast and Dublin to those responsible for carrying out killings, covering the spectrum from politicians and officials to republicans and loyalists and all points in between. Our original brief was for 'a clear, concise, authoritative history' and we have adhered as closely as possible to that. This book was published first by Blackstaff of Belfast in 2000, in the following year by Penguin and in 2002 in the US by Ivan R. Dee of Chicago. Two new chapters bring the story up to 2012 while fresh analysis is presented of the major events. In addition to this we have also made various modifications, mostly minor, to the original text. For this version we have provided an updated chronology and statistical tables.

In the first edition we concluded: 'There is a widespread sense that a corner has been decisively turned. It can be forecast with some confidence that the future will bring much improvement on the last three turbulent decades.' Much of this has been borne out with the virtual, though not complete, ending of troubles-related deaths. The political scene has improved beyond recognition, making advances which no one predicted and few dared to hope for.

A new political dispensation has emerged while British–Irish relations have entered a golden age. Soldiers have all but disappeared from the streets. The IRA has departed and Sinn Féin endorses new policing arrangements. Loyalist paramilitary activity has plummeted while unionist leaders have developed constructive new relations with the Irish Republic. This settlement has received overwhelming endorsement in a number of elections. The world, and almost everyone in Northern Ireland, now simply wants the new political axis to provide stable government, to secure the peace, and to consign the troubles to the past.

The static society
1921–63

Protestants and Catholics

The troubles which broke out in the late 1960s had roots going back many decades, for Northern Ireland never resembled a place at peace with itself. In what are today assumed to be quiet and uneventful periods, even a cursory glance at the records of the time reveals a most unsettled society. A stream of incidents, large and small, testified to deep and dangerous fault lines in the society. Viewed from this perspective, the troubles can be seen as a more violent expression of existing animosities and unresolved issues of nationality, religion, power and territorial rivalry. They can be viewed in fact simply as a new phase in a continuum of division. With hindsight the seeds of the later violence can be seen with some clarity.

In the 1960s, as in later decades, four basic elements were present in the Northern Ireland equation. First there were the Protestants, who made up roughly two-thirds of the population of a million and a half. The vast majority of Protestants were Unionists, favouring the existing link with Britain. Although they always had criticisms of London governments, they emphatically regarded themselves as British and not Irish. They not only treasured the link with Britain but dreaded the alternative, which they envisaged as a united Ireland in which Irish nationalists would attack their political, religious and economic interests.

Almost all Protestants voted Unionist but scarcely any Catholics did. Catholics, the second major element of the equation, made up the other one-third of the population and in the main viewed themselves not as British but as Irish. Most of them regarded Northern Ireland as an unsatisfactory and even illegitimate state, believing that an independent united Ireland was the natural political unit for the island. The heart of the Northern Ireland problem lies in this clash between two competing national aspirations. This basic competition is complicated by issues of power, territory and justice.

The third and fourth elements involved were the British and Irish governments. The word 'involved' is largely a misnomer, since until the late 1960s both attempted, generally successfully, to keep the Northern Ireland issue at arm's length. With the onset of the troubles, however, both were drawn ever more deeply into the problem.

The roots of that problem lay deep in history. As the twentieth century began the population of Ireland, which was a part of the United Kingdom of Great Britain and Ireland, was four and a quarter million, made up of three and a quarter million Catholics and just over one million Protestants. Most of the Protestants were descendants of settlers who emigrated from England and Scotland to various parts of Ireland with the encouragement of English governments, mainly in the sixteenth and seventeenth centuries. A major aim of the settlements was to plant a loyal British garrison community to establish control in the face of periodic Irish uprisings which at times threatened English security by linking up with England's traditional Catholic enemies, France and Spain.

At times some Protestants identified with Irish causes against the English, but these were the exceptions. Although there was some inter-marriage between the Catholic natives and Protestant settlers, the two communities, especially in the north-east, continued down through the years to regard themselves as largely separate entities. The Protestant settler community enjoyed political and economic ascendancy. The communities were differentiated primarily on the basis of conflicting national identities, but the various other important points of difference kept communal divisions fresh and potent.

As the nineteenth century ended there was increasing pressure in Ireland for what was known as Home Rule, whose supporters

advocated a new Dublin parliament under Westminster's authority. At this stage the demand for complete Irish independence did
not have significant support, but Home Rule seemed a real possibility. Unionists were opposed to the concept, organising themselves to fight against the attempts of Liberal governments to bring
it into being in the last two decades of the nineteenth century.
Unionists feared Home Rule as a threat to the Union with Britain,
and as a prelude to complete Irish independence and the ending of
Protestant and British domination of Irish affairs.

Unionist resistance was strongest in the north-eastern counties
where the largest concentration of Protestants lived. In the nineteenth century, especially around Belfast, a prosperous economy
had been developed based on industries such as linen, shipbuilding
and engineering. This north-eastern region was very much part of
the British industrial economy, Belfast having closer ties and economic similarities with Glasgow and Liverpool than with Dublin.

Protestants mobilised formidable bodies such as the Ulster
Unionist Council and the Orange Order, a long-established
Protestant grouping, to oppose any weakening of the link with
Britain and to safeguard Protestant interests. (There is much continuity here: the UUC was the forerunner of the Ulster Unionist
party, which together with the Orange Order remains in existence
to this day.)

Between 1912 and 1914 the British government again introduced
a Home Rule Bill which this time seemed certain to become law.
The response of Unionists was to pledge their determination to
oppose Home Rule by 'all means which may be found necessary'.
In the spring of 1914 Unionist leaders organised the smuggling in of
25,000 rifles and 3 million rounds of ammunition from Germany.
These were used to arm an unofficial Protestant militia, the Ulster
Volunteer Force. With vast rallies and drilling exercises, Unionism
openly proclaimed its readiness to act outside the law. But just as a
major military confrontation seemed inevitable, the outbreak of
World War One intervened and the issue was put on ice for its
duration.

1916 saw the Easter Rising in Dublin, with a small number of republicans staging an armed rebellion against British rule. The rising itself was quickly put down, but the action of the British government of the day in executing many of its leaders rebounded: London was deemed to have overreacted and a huge swell of sympathy for the republicans ensued. By the time World War One ended in 1918, the Irish desire for Home Rule had been swept away and replaced by the demand for an independent Irish republic. The newly formed Irish Republican Army, known as the IRA, began a violent campaign against Britain which is today referred to in the south as the War of Independence. After lengthy negotiations, Westminster in 1920 passed the Government of Ireland Act in an attempt to satisfy the conflicting demands of the two traditions.

In essence this act hoped to solve the problem by keeping all of Ireland in British hands while providing for a Home Rule parliament in the twenty-six southern counties, together with a separate devolved parliament for the six north-eastern counties. As well as having its own parliament Northern Ireland would continue to send MPs to Westminster. Aware of the rising nationalist tide, Ulster Unionists reluctantly accepted this and Northern Ireland came into existence. Irish nationalists rejected the plan and their war for independence continued until a treaty in 1921 created a twenty-six-county Irish Free State.

The new state

Northern Ireland was born in violence. From the first months of its existence there were occasional IRA raids from across the new border as well as major outbreaks of sectarian violence, especially in Belfast. In the two years from June 1920 until June 1922, 428 people were killed, two-thirds of them Catholic, fourteen people dying in one weekend. The communal violence in Belfast, which was on a scale and ferocity not equalled until August 1969, left a deep and bitter imprint on many in both communities.

The creation of Northern Ireland did not bring security for the Protestants despite their comfortable majority, for it was clear that London was never as committed to the Union as they were. They lived in a state of political nervousness, constantly fearing British policy might move to support a united Ireland. They also remained deeply suspicious of the almost half-million Catholics who found themselves within the boundaries of the new Northern Ireland.

Those Catholics considered themselves trapped in this new state, denied their Irish identity, cut off from their co-religionists in the Free State and politically powerless. To this was quickly added another complaint: that the Unionist establishment, which was to run the state on the basis of Protestant majority rule for the following half-century, actively discriminated against Catholics in the allocation of jobs and housing, over political rights and in other areas.

The boundaries of Northern Ireland which came into being in 1921 were essentially worked out between Westminster and the Ulster Unionist party. The six north-eastern counties of Ireland made up the new state, with Belfast as its capital. Unionists used the word 'Ulster' to describe the new entity, though nationalists objected to this. Catholics who use the term 'Ulster' generally mean one of the four ancient provinces into which Ireland was quartered, the others being Leinster, Munster and Connaught. This Ulster had nine counties, Antrim, Armagh, Down, Derry (only Unionists tended to call it Londonderry), Fermanagh, Tyrone, Cavan, Donegal and Monaghan. Although Northern Ireland consisted of only the first six of these, Unionists appropriated the word 'Ulster' and made extensive use of it. The defining feature of the new entity was its demographics: it was two-thirds Protestant and one-third Catholic, the guiding concept in deciding its borders having been that it should have a decisive Protestant majority.

In the early days many people, both Protestant and Catholic, were unsure whether the new state would survive. Some nationalists believed it to be too small to form the basis of a feasible state, and assumed it would prove unworkable. Some thought the promised review by a Boundary Commission would end its existence by reducing its size even further, although when the commission's report emerged in 1925 no changes to the border resulted. Many Protestants wondered whether Northern Ireland could hold out in the face of an apparently lukewarm British commitment, as well as hostility from nationalists both within its boundaries and from the new and almost entirely Catholic state to the south.

In the event, however, Britain attempted no withdrawal, the south attempted no invasion, and the northern Catholic minority proved politically impotent. Britain hoped the Irish question, as the issue had been known during the nineteenth century, had been settled by the partition of Ireland. The Free State was aggrieved by the loss of what it regarded as its rightful territory, but concentrated its attention on making a success of its own fledgling state.

Northern Ireland settled down, within a perhaps surprisingly few years, into what looked like stability. There was violence, but it was contained; there was a great deal of communal tension, but it too was contained; and after some troubled years a sullen form of peace descended. It was however a peace achieved at a high cost, for the new state had an imbalance at its heart. Most Unionist politicians had not wanted their own devolved parliament in Belfast, preferring to remain more closely integrated with Britain. But once the 1920 settlement had handed almost all political power into their hands, they realised they could make effective use of it to buttress and protect the new Northern Ireland.

This aim took precedence over all other considerations, including any thought of building bridges between Protestants and Catholics. Catholic representatives of the time tended to hope not for some new shared system, but for its collapse. They often resorted to boycotting the new institutions, both political leaders and Catholic bishops making no secret of their hope that Northern Ireland would not last.

The prevailing attitudes were aptly described decades later, in 1998, by Ulster Unionist party leader David Trimble, when he said in his speech accepting the Nobel peace prize: 'Ulster Unionists, fearful of being isolated on the island, built a solid house, but it was a cold house for Catholics. And northern nationalists, although they had a roof over their heads, seemed to us as if they meant to burn the house down.'

The Unionist party spoke for the overwhelming majority of Protestant voters, and since Protestants were in a majority it automatically became the new government. It was to hold this position for half a century, wielding virtually complete and certainly uninterrupted power. The Northern Ireland system was closely modelled on the House of Commons at Westminster, but crucially it lacked the element of alternation in government: the 1920 settlement had ensured that nationalists were forever excluded from power and that Unionists forever wielded it in unbroken one-party rule. The steps the Unionist party took in the 1920s to strengthen its own power, and to defend the existence of the state, created a system of extraordinary longevity which was to preserve and reinforce many of the attitudes of the 1920s.

The system survived for so long because of Unionism's monolithic strength, aided by divisions within nationalism and by Westminster indifference. It turned out not to be a fair arrangement, but in London's terms it worked, and a potentially vexatious state remained reasonably quiet.

The collective self-image of Unionists today is not far removed from that of their ancestors as they arrived in Ireland, or from that of the founding fathers of Northern Ireland. They saw themselves as a frontier community facing wily and violent enemies, and backed by only half-hearted allies. Unionists were for the most part an inward-looking people, conservative, cautious and suspicious of change. In this they followed the model of their forebears who, moving from England and Scotland and given territory in a hostile land, developed a defensive attitude evident in the later Unionist slogans of 'No Surrender' and 'What we have we hold' and 'Not an inch'. Socially Unionists could be warm-hearted and tremendously hospitable: politically they were fated to be eternally on the defensive.

The government system put in place in the 1920s is one of the keys to explaining the later troubles, since there was such extraordinary continuity in its workings over the decades, and since the outbreak of the troubles was so directly related to it. The Catholic civil rights movement would take to the streets in 1968 with complaints which related directly to the arrangements of the 1920s.

Consolidating control

From the start the Unionist party's leaders believed that the new state could only survive if the levers of power were firmly in reliable Protestant hands. The first instincts of Unionists, having been put in charge by Westminster, were to ensure that their power should be both undiluted and permanent. Thus one of the new government's earliest acts was to set about changing the voting system and local council boundaries inherited by the new Unionist government.

This was a key measure since the seventy-three local authorities were important as sources of power and patronage in areas such as housing and education. In the first council elections after partition the Unionist party had won control of around two-thirds of them, but some of those in nationalist hands were troublesome. A number of western councils had symbolically voted to secede from Northern Ireland and join the south, while others refused to acknowledge the authority of the new government. Northern Ireland's first prime minister, James Craig, responded quickly by revising the voting system and later altering boundaries so that Unionists could deal with such mutinous councils by simply assuming control of them.

In 1922 the voting system known as proportional representation (PR) was abolished. Its removal was by no means simply a technical adjustment, since it had been built in both as an actual safeguard for Catholic and Protestant minorities in the two parts of Ireland and also a symbol of respect for their views. The first-past-the-post system introduced in its place, together with the highly partisan redrawing of local government boundaries, was of huge benefit to the Unionist party. As a result of the changes nationalists lost their majorities in thirteen of twenty-four councils they had originally controlled. Surveying the electoral consequences decades later, Professor John Whyte concluded: 'Nationalists were manipulated out of control in a number of councils where they had a majority of electors. This is one of the clearest areas of discrimination in the whole field of controversy.'

Northern Ireland's second city, Londonderry, moved from nationalist to Unionist control even though it had a clear nationalist majority. Another adjustment was made there years later in 1936, when local Unionist party leaders feared they might lose control of the city. One of Craig's cabinet ministers wrote to him: 'Unless something is done now, it is only a matter of time until Derry passes into the hands of the Nationalist and Sinn Féin parties for all time. On the other hand, if proper steps are taken now, I believe Derry can be saved for years to come.'

The government did indeed take such steps, in the form of an ingenious new arrangement designed to ensure that around 7,500 Unionist voters returned twelve councillors while 10,000 nationalist voters returned only eight. Nationalists branded this boundary manipulation as 'gerrymandering', a term which was to have a prominent place in the political lexicon for many decades. In public Unionist party representatives denied its existence in Londonderry and elsewhere, but in private some were more candid, one Unionist MP describing the new arrangements as a 'shameless and obvious gerrymander'. Another senior Unionist was to write to the Unionist cabinet in 1968, against the background of the civil rights campaign, saying:

> If ever a community had a right to demonstrate against a denial of
> civil rights, Derry is the finest example. A Roman Catholic and
> nationalist city has for three or four decades been administered (and
> none too fairly administered) by a Protestant and Unionist majority
> secured by a manipulation of the ward boundaries for the sole pur-
> pose of retaining Unionist control. I was consulted by Sir James

Craig at the time it was done. Craig thought that the fate of our constitution was on a knife edge at the time and that, in the circumstances, it was defensible on the basis that the safety of the State is the supreme law. It was most clearly understood that the arrangement was to be a temporary measure – five years was mentioned.

The original abolition of PR in local government was so successful in enhancing the Unionist party's power that in the late 1920s Craig did the same thing for the Belfast parliament. Again PR was dropped and again constituency boundaries were redrawn. The first election to the parliament, in 1921, had produced a comfortable majority for the Unionist party but Craig put much effort into increasing its grip by weeding out the handful of independent Unionists who were not subject to his party's direct control. The Unionist government carried out an intricate micromanagement of the new system. It carefully calculated that under a first-past-the-post system and with the new boundaries, nationalists could expect to keep a dozen of the fifty-two seats, a figure it considered as respectable while offering no real threat to Unionist control. The new voting system meant that nearly every contest pitted a Unionist party candidate against an anti-Unionist. Independent Unionist candidates who thought of standing were denounced as renegades who were liable to 'split the vote', risking a nationalist victory by dividing Protestant support.

In Craig's terms the ending of PR in elections to parliament worked beautifully, his party winning thirty-seven of the fifty-two seats in 1929. While the exercise had been aimed at wiping out independent Unionists, the 37 to 15 majority it delivered to Craig was so overwhelming that most of the Catholic opposition simply gave up. Most nationalists rarely attended and debates became much shorter, the votes which followed becoming mere formalities. In 1933, in fact, the entire general election became a formality since twenty-seven seats were uncontested by non-Unionists. As a result the Unionist party won the election before a vote was cast.

Craig's was a vision of the politics of permanent confrontation. His model was one of trench warfare of the kind he had personally experienced as a soldier in World War One, with rival forces in perpetual and often static enmity. He succeeded in constructing a political version of the western front, though in this instance the outcome of the war was pre-ordained as a victory for Unionism. Northern Ireland's demographic make-up and the governing set-up and other factors left Unionists in permanent possession of the citadels of power. The trench warfare model was to endure for decades.

Nationalists regarded all this as deeply undemocratic. The only element with the power to intervene was Westminster itself, which had laid down in Section 75 of the 1920 Government of Ireland Act that, notwithstanding devolution, it retained supreme authority over Northern Ireland matters. The British government of the day disapproved of the abolition of PR in local government and asked Craig not to proceed, but when he and his cabinet threatened to resign, British ministers backed down. This confrontation, which took place in private, set a far-reaching precedent in that Westminster conceded that Unionism was effectively in charge. That same Section 75 would, in the late 1960s, reappear on the political agenda when debates broke out on exactly what influence Westminster could wield over the Unionist government.

But in the 1920s London politicians, who in any case tended to have a strong instinct to keep matters Irish at arm's length, accepted these realities. Nationalists and others who journeyed to London to complain about practices in Belfast started then to hear a response that would become familiar over the decades: such things were the concern of the Belfast parliament itself, which was the proper place in which to raise them. Thus a Conservative Home Secretary in London, receiving in 1928 a delegation complaining of the abolition of PR, told them it was a matter for Craig. The Home Secretary then wrote to Craig: 'I don't know whether you would care at any time to discuss the matter with me; of course I am always at your disposal. But beyond that "I know my place", and don't propose to interfere.' This was also the attitude of the Westminster Commons, where as early as 1922 a convention was established prohibiting parliamentary questions or debates on matters within the Belfast parliament's jurisdiction. This convention was to prevail for almost half a century.

The absence of Westminster supervision, the establishment of what was in effect a permanent Unionist government and the Unionist party's domination of local government represented the top strata of Unionist power in Northern Ireland. That power had, however, many other aspects which, taken together, amounted to a remarkable degree of control over most aspects of government and society. This control extended to the fields of justice and law and order. Judges and magistrates were almost all Protestants, many of them closely associated with the Unionist party. Between 1937 and 1968, for example, thirteen sitting Unionist MPs were appointed judges, moving effortlessly from making laws to enforcing them.

The Ulster Special Constabulary, the heavily armed auxiliary force later known more often as the B Specials, was exclusively Protestant. Although it seemed for a fleeting moment that the new police force, the Royal Ulster Constabulary (RUC), might become religiously integrated, it remained throughout its history more than 90 per cent Protestant. The police had no real operational independence, responding directly to directions from ministers, with senior police officers sometimes attending cabinet meetings. The political, legal and policing worlds were thus inextricably linked: one community governed, judged and policed the other.

RUC officers carried revolvers and sometimes heavier weaponry, while the armament of the B Specials included handguns, rifles and submachine guns. The police had at their disposal the Special Powers Act, a sweeping piece of legislation which allowed arrests without warrant, internment without trial, unlimited search powers and bans on meetings and publications, as well as providing far-reaching catch-all clauses. Most of these provisions were used sparingly but their existence, together with the large numbers of police and B Specials, brought Catholic complaints that policing had a military character and very often an intimidating effect. These security forces, once pointedly described as the armed wing of Unionism, not only maintained law and order but also provided jobs for Protestants.

This was one of many points of Protestant advantage in the field of employment. The civil service was predominantly Protestant, with perhaps 10 per cent Catholic representation in its lower reaches. A 1943 survey established that there were no Catholics in the 55 most senior jobs, with only 37 Catholics in the 600 middle-ranking posts. The picture was similar in most local authorities and other parts of the public sector, with only occasional exceptions. There were no Catholics among the cabinet, the senior staff in the Stormont Commons, the top ranks of the RUC, the Civil Service Commission and other important public bodies.

In the private sector many large firms, and indeed whole industries, commonly had workforces that were more than 90 per cent Protestant, while Catholics tended to predominate in some lower-status occupations such as the drinks trade. The jewels in Northern Ireland's industrial crown, such as its shipyards and heavy engineering concerns, employed few Catholics. Moreover there were, at times of high tension, periodic purges in which Catholic workers were forcibly expelled from some of the big companies. Unsurprisingly, Catholic unemployment was generally more than double Protestant unemployment, partly because of these patterns and partly because a higher proportion of Catholics lived in areas of high unemployment such as the west.

Part of this picture was the result of apparently innocuous practices such as recruitment of staff by word of mouth or on the recommendation of a friend or a relative. Usually this meant the hiring of another Protestant since most employers, particularly those with large concerns, were Protestant. Such habits, though seeming to be the natural run of things in the eyes of those who benefited from them, nonetheless played a part in perpetuating employment differentials.

Housing was another area that produced much Catholic complaint, especially after World War Two when a major building programme was introduced to improve the very poor housing standards. Housing was largely in the hands of local councils, and although many councils functioned in a non-controversial manner, in others policy was distorted for political ends. What made house building and allocation so sensitive was that voting in local government elections was limited to ratepayers and their spouses. A new house would thus often carry two votes, a matter that could be of great political significance in areas where the Unionist and nationalist votes were evenly balanced. The most frequent criticisms were of councils in western counties where battles for control were the hardest fought.

Votes had an extra significance in local government, where the electorate was a full one-quarter smaller than that for the Belfast parliament. Since only ratepayers and their spouses had the vote, others such as subtenants, lodgers and anyone living at home with their parents could not vote. This restriction, which most affected the poorer sections of the population, was later to provide one of the most potent slogans for the civil rights movement with its demand for 'one man – one vote'. Paradoxically, the acceleration in house building after 1945 heightened the potential for controversy by providing local councils with many more houses to assign. This was a heavily politicised activity: in some cases individual dwellings were allocated at council meetings, though more often allocations were decided by small groups of councillors on housing committees. In 1963 the Unionist chairman of Enniskillen housing committee made clear their approach: 'The council will decide what wards the houses are to be built in. We are not going to build houses in the South Ward and cut a rod to beat ourselves later on. We are going to see that the right people are put in these houses, and we are not going to apologise for it.'

The record of the Unionist government, particularly in its early decades, contains many instances of senior government ministers not only condoning similar practices but approving of them. The tone was set by Craig when, in response to criticism of the Orange Order, he told the Belfast parliament: 'I have always said I am an Orangeman first and a politician and member of this parliament afterwards. All I boast is that we are a Protestant parliament and a Protestant state.' Down the years this, slightly misquoted, entered political folklore as 'a Protestant parliament for a Protestant people'.

The Orange Order

The Orange Order, a Protestant organisation viewed by Catholics as bigoted and anti-Catholic but regarded by most Protestants as an important guardian of their heritage, held a significant place in political life. The Unionist community contained in its ranks people who differed widely in terms of class, outlook and geography. While Catholics had only one church, Protestants were splintered into dozens of denominations, large and small, from high-church Anglicans to Presbyterians with a history of independence and dissent. The Orange Order played a key role in providing the political cement to hold them all together.

The Order was founded in 1795 following clashes between Protestant and Catholic factions in County Armagh. This mêlée, known now as the Battle of the Diamond, is one of the major events in Orange folk history, together with two incidents in the seventeenth century when Protestants prevailed over Catholics, the Siege of Derry in 1689 and the Battle of the Boyne in 1690. In later years the Orange Order established what came to be known as the marching season, holding hundreds of parades during the summer months. In the nineteenth century these gave rise to recurring riots, particularly in Belfast. One official report said: 'The celebration of that (Orange July) festival is plainly and unmistakably the originating cause of these riots.' It added that the occasion was used 'to remind one party of the triumph of their ancestors over those of the other, and to inculcate the feelings of Protestant superiority over their Roman Catholic neighbours'.

The Orange culture was separatist and anti-ecumenical. Although its regulations told its members to abstain from uncharitable words or deeds against Catholics, they were also pledged to 'resist the ascendancy of that church' by all lawful means. They were further warned not to attend 'any act or ceremony of Popish worship'. One observer summed it up: 'The Orange Order ensures that the majority of the majority maintain a rigid stance. It articulates their underlying fears in such a way as to suggest that there is only one way of guarding against the dangers: obstinate resistance rather than mutual accommodation.' Orange lodges provided the framework for the Ulster Volunteer Force, and from the start the new state took on a distinctly Orange hue. An Orange lodge was established within the RUC, while Orangemen made up the bulk of the B Specials, who in some areas were based in Orange halls.

Politically too, Orangeism became an integral part of the state. Between 1921 and 1969 only three of fifty-four Unionist cabinet ministers were not members of the Order. Three others left the Order while in office: one was expelled for attending a Catholic service as part of his public duties, while another resigned when his daughter married a Catholic. Eighty-seven of the ninety-five Unionist backbenchers during the same period were members of the Order. The Order was institutionally linked to the Unionist party, occupying a substantial proportion of the seats on the Ulster Unionist Council, the party's ruling body. Many Unionist party meetings were held in Orange halls, with ministers using Orange platforms to deliver important speeches.

The power of the Orange Order during those years has been described by two senior Methodists: 'Membership was an indispensable condition of political advancement. It protected the employment of Protestants by its influence over employers, which is a polite way of saying that it contrived systematic discrimination against Catholics. Local authorities were dominated by members of the local lodges.' Orange marches became part of the fabric of Unionist government while at the same time nationalist parades were subject to severe restriction. The Twelfth of July celebrations, the climax of the Orange marching season, effectively became a ritual of state.

In essence Orange culture set the tone for Unionist rule at Stormont. One classic instance of the Orange Order's influence prevailing over other considerations was seen in 1934 when the Order complained that a Catholic was working as a gardener in the grounds of Stormont, the large east Belfast estate where a new parliament building had been erected. The fact that the man had a distinguished war record and a personal reference from the Prince of Wales himself was not enough to overcome the Orange objection to his religion.

On numerous occasions over the decades complaints from hardliners within the Unionist party and the Orange Order galvanised the Stormont government into reassuring them. In 1933, for example, the Minister of Labour (and later prime minister) J. M. Andrews reacted quickly to rumours that the porters at Stormont included many Catholics. He told MPs: 'Another allegation made against the government, and which was untrue, was that, of 31 porters at Stormont, 28 were Roman Catholic. I have investigated the matter, and I find that there are 30 Protestants, and only one Roman Catholic there temporarily.'

This excess of populism was a familiar feature of the Unionist party leadership both before and during the troubles: again and again leaders were nervous of the Protestant grassroots and often reluctant to stand up to extremists. Their actions mirrored to an extraordinary extent, either through conviction or ambition, the views of their grassroots. Some ministers were personally frankly anti-Catholic; others did not necessarily hold extreme views, but regarded voicing them as a political necessity.

Ministers and MPs regularly made statements directed against Catholics. One minister, Basil Brooke, who was later to become prime minister, declared: 'Many in the audience employ Catholics, but I have not one about my place. Catholics are out to destroy Ulster with all their might and power. They want to nullify the Protestant vote and take all they can out of Ulster, and then see it go to hell.' When the then prime minister, James Craig, was asked to disown this statement he responded not with condemnation but endorsement, declaring in Stormont: 'He spoke entirely on his own when he made the speech, but there is not one of my colleagues who does not entirely agree with him, and I would not ask him to withdraw one word he said.' Other ministers transmitted the same unmistakable message. The Minister of Agriculture, Sir Edward Archdale, said: 'I have 109 officials, and so far as I know there are four Roman Catholics, three of whom were civil servants turned over to me, whom I had to take when we began.' Nationalist critics chronicled dozens of similar statements.

Craig and Brooke and many of their closest associates were from the upper strata of society. Craig was the son of a millionaire whiskey distiller, while Brooke came from a landowning family which had centuries earlier settled in rich Fermanagh farmland. The Unionist party was firmly in the hands of men from big business and the landed gentry, many of them well-educated and well-travelled. Yet very often they appeared to share the most basic sentiments of their grassroots. One cabinet minister would not use the telephone for sensitive conversations after he discovered 'with a great deal of surprise, that a Roman Catholic telephonist has been appointed to Stormont'. Craig's personal feelings were described by Dame Enid Lyons, wife of Joseph Lyons, who was prime minister of Australia in the 1930s. She recalled in her memoirs:

> Lord Craigavon, the fiercely anti-Catholic prime minister of Northern Ireland, asked Joe at a banquet: 'Lyons, have you got many Catholics in Australia?' 'Oh, about one in five,' Joe had replied. 'Well watch them, Lyons, watch them,' Craigavon had urged. 'They breed like bloody rabbits.'

Catholics were not actively persecuted by the authorities; they were not deported to the south; only a comparatively small number, nearly all active republicans, ever experienced internment without trial. The Catholic Church was free to go about its business, and to run its own schools and hospital facilities, though there was much wrangling about whether the Unionist government was adequately contributing to their upkeep. Nationalist newspapers, in particular the Belfast-based *Irish News*, were generally free to criticise the government and unceasingly did so. (That newspaper provided a daily reminder of Catholic disapproval of the state: for decades it refused to use the title 'Northern Ireland', referring instead to 'the Six County State'.)

But Catholics and nationalists were clearly regarded as second-class citizens, as intrinsically dangerous to the state, and as being less deserving of houses and jobs than their Protestant neighbours. A very few Catholics reached high office in the judiciary, the civil service and other spheres, but it was always clear these were to be exceptions to the general rule. The representatives of Catholics and nationalists were deliberately and efficiently excluded from political power or influence. This was not Nazi Germany or anything like it. But it was institutionalised partiality, and there was no means of redress for Catholic grievances, no avenue of appeal against either real or imagined discrimination. Freed from any effective oversight the Unionist machine was able to function without any checks or balances or mechanisms which might have curbed excesses.

The Catholic minority

In these circumstances most Catholic representatives resorted to the politics of bitter but ineffectual complaint, and indulgence in an often monotonous rehearsal of familiar grievances. Many stayed away from Stormont for long periods of time, maintaining that attendance was a humiliating travesty of parliamentary practice. The Catholic Church firmly hung on to its control of the education of its flock: this was a familiar stance of the Church in many countries, but in Northern Ireland there seemed an extra determination to keep young Catholics out of the clutches of Stormont. Some Unionists were to claim that Catholic children should take their places in the state-run schools attended by Protestants, but in truth neither side favoured religious integration in schools. Both were more comfortable with their 'own sort'.

The Catholic Church was not enthusiastic about integration, forbidding Catholics from attending Protestant church services. Many of the better-educated Catholics went on to the priesthood but overall the Catholic middle class was unusually small. Its members tended to service the Catholic community in areas such as the law, medicine, education, construction, shops and pubs. It was not until the introduction of UK-wide education reforms in the late 1940s that third-level education came within the grasp of working-class students, both Catholic and Protestant.

With Catholic unemployment at high levels and many of the better jobs regarded as the preserve of Protestants, the Catholic emigration rate was higher than that of Protestants. Many Catholic schools advised pupils not to apply to the civil service or local authorities for jobs, regarding such applications as pointless. Those few Catholics who did reach senior posts in areas such as the civil service tended to be viewed by their co-religionists as rare and faintly unpatriotic creatures. One of the most senior Catholic civil servants wrote in his memoirs that to other Catholics, people like him 'were lost souls'.

While there had always been a large measure of segregation between Protestants and Catholics, particularly in Belfast, the Stormont system helped ensure that such patterns would continue. The two communities mixed in some fields, but in their housing, education, and very often in their employment they kept apart. The situation was summed up in 1971 by a Catholic observer who said: 'If there is one thing which I have learned in my 30–40 odd years as a community social worker it is this: that, broadly speaking, two communities have lived side by side in Northern Ireland without really knowing each other, or without making any real honest, sincere and conscious effort to bridge the communications gap.'

Politics atrophied in both communities. Many nationalists simply did not vote or voted only rarely, succumbing to apathy brought on by the realisation that the Unionist voting machine was invincible.

In contrast to the highly effective communication skills which it would develop during the troubles, the Catholic community was able to attract little attention or sympathy from outsiders. It often came across as negative, backward-looking and incessantly complaining.

When they did vote, a number of options were available to Catholics. The main Catholic voice in Stormont was provided by the Nationalist party, though the word 'party' is probably a misnomer for a body so disorganised and lacking in either central control or agreement on policy. The party's representatives frequently went their own individual ways, often resorting to boycotting Stormont. Its nominal leader in the 1960s, Londonderry accountant Eddie McAteer, was an early exponent of the ear-catching soundbite, but failed to develop a coherent philosophy or plan of action. He and his colleagues were often characterised as rural, old, staid, conservative and unimaginative. They tended not to be held in high esteem, even by their own voters. 'They were the boys who huffed in the corner,' a Catholic politician of a later age remarked. Another Catholic observer, who was a young teacher in the 1950s, recalled:

> Unionists could despise the Nationalist MPs, as they did – almost as much as the nationalist population who voted for them despised them. It was because of the pointlessness of their political programme: they had none, except to say that in an ideal world this state wouldn't exist. But they had no programme to bring about this ideal world, no function other than to protest. There was nothing the Nationalists could do.

While Nationalists tended to dominate in country areas, Belfast was different. Here a number of canny representatives emerged from the backstreets to act as local champions. Some founded micro-parties whose titles included designations such as 'Republican', 'Socialist' or 'Labour'. The most successful of these was to be Gerry Fitt, a one-time merchant seaman and Belfast councillor who was

elected to Westminster in 1966 on a Republican Labour party platform. In many Westminster elections, seats were contested by Sinn
Féin on an abstentionist ticket, its candidates pledging not to take
their seats if elected. The Sinn Féin of the 1950s bore little resem-
blance to the republican party that would emerge as an electoral
force in the 1980s, its earlier approach being largely confined to the
politics of the defiant gesture.

The IRA stayed in being throughout Northern Ireland's history,
though it remained tiny and ineffectual before its rapid expansion in
the early 1970s. Its sporadic campaigns were dealt with reasonably
easily by the authorities: its most determined effort, in the 1950s,
was crushed by the use of internment without trial on both sides of
the border, and ignominiously petered out.

While internment and other security measures were the immediate causes of the IRA's periodic defeats, a much more telling factor
lay in the judgement of the Catholic population as a whole that its
violence was futile. Although most Catholics held the aspiration to
one day see a united Ireland, this did not extend to enthusiasm for
the bomb and the bullet. A major 1960s opinion poll found, in fact,
that more Protestants than Catholics indicated they were ready to
condone violence in support of political ends. The judgement of
the *New York Times* following the fizzling out of the 1950s campaign
seemed to be shared by most nationalists: 'The IRA belongs to history, and it belongs to better men in times that are gone. So does the
Sinn Féin. Let us put a wreath of red roses on their grave and move
on.'

Most Catholics looked to the south as, if not quite the promised
land, at least an example of a society in which their national and
civil rights would be recognised. The fact was, however, that while
Catholic northerners looked fondly to Dublin, Dublin tended to
regard them as an unwelcome nuisance. The south was absorbed
with building its own structures and coping with the long-lasting
after-effects of a bitter civil war.

Southern political leaders produced a fair amount of rhetoric
concerning the north, generally denouncing partition as unnatu-

ral and unjust. Unionism was condemned for its discriminatory policies, and Britain was urged to solve the Northern Ireland problem. The suggested remedy was simplistic in the extreme: London, which had created partition and the border, was simply to announce plans to withdraw and thus bring about a united Ireland. This was clearly more of a slogan than a policy, in that it took no account of the likely Unionist reaction to such a move. The rights of Unionists, or the potential they had for resisting such a move, were barely contemplated. Irish nationalism became even fuzzier when the future of Unionists was concerned. It was sometimes suggested that many Protestants would withdraw with the British, returning to the English and Scottish homelands vacated centuries earlier by their ancestors. Alternatively, it was suggested that a British withdrawal would cause the scales to fall from Protestant eyes, allowing them to realise that they were not really British but Irish, at which point they would embrace a new future as part of the Irish nation.

Rhetoric was plentiful but in reality southern ministers had to accept there was little practical to be done. Northern Ireland and its Catholic minority were in a sense standing affronts to southern self-esteem, representing as they did constant reminders that the south's nation-building efforts were deeply imperfect. Politically, northern nationalist leaders were unwelcome ghosts at the feast in Dublin. Eddie McAteer recalled: 'I made many trips to Dublin for talks and consultations with Dublin ministers. I got hospitality but little real support. There was less than enthusiasm to get involved.' He was particularly disappointed in Seán Lemass, the Fianna Fáil leader who became Taoiseach (Irish prime minister) in 1959. McAteer wrote of meeting him:

I got neither the encouragement nor understanding of our position that I expected. Lemass said that it appeared to him that the Catholics in the north were just as intractable as the Protestants. It was hardly the reaction that I expected from a Taoiseach with his republican background to the representative of the oppressed Irish minority in the Six Counties. I came away with the conviction that as far as Seán Lemass was concerned, the northern Irish were very much on their own.

Far from being acclaimed in Dublin, northern nationalist politicians were sidelined. They regularly pressed for invitations to state occasions in the south but were not particularly welcomed. They were invited to a presidential inauguration in Dublin in 1945 only after writing to complain that they had been excluded. In 1956, when McAteer asked for a chance to address the Dáil, as the Dublin parliament is known, he was refused. In Lemass's case the lack of sympathy went further and extended to active distaste for northern nationalists. After his retirement he said his impression of them was that 'for them the day partition ended would be the day that would get their foot on the throat of the Orangeman across the road'.

Such chilly receptions did not kill off northern dreams and the attraction of the south. One elderly Catholic woman recalled in the 1990s, 'I never thought of myself as being part of Northern Ireland. When you went across the border, you felt you were in a different atmosphere, relaxed, at home.' This was echoed by a Catholic teacher: 'Even in the fifties, when the southern state was a ramshackle affair, nothing to be admired, the state in Northern Ireland still lacked legitimacy. There was no emotional identification with it, and you ultimately didn't recognize its right to tell you what to do. You obeyed the law but that sort of commitment was not there in the mildest of nationalists.' An anecdote related by a Catholic woman helps explain why even an only theoretically welcoming south seemed preferable to northern realities. She recalled how, as a teenager in a small and predominantly Protestant County Armagh town, she was asked by a local Protestant doctor why she did not play table tennis with young Protestants in the local Orange hall. When she said she did not believe she would be welcome he persuaded her to go along, saying, 'Nonsense, you're being silly.' She recounted, 'I had a great evening, enjoyed myself very much, but the next day the doctor came to me, all embarrassed, and said: "I'm really sorry about this, but they've asked me to tell you not to come back. They were going to tell you this but I said I'd tell you." He was shocked and embarrassed. I never forgot that.'

Political stagnation

In both communities, social exclusion went hand in hand with political stagnation. The unchanging realities of politics can be illustrated by the electoral history of one constituency. Dehra Parker held the Londonderry City and County seat from 1921 until 1929 when she stood down to allow her relative Captain James Lenox-Conyngham Chichester-Clark, a member of the local gentry, to replace her in the new South Londonderry constituency. After his death in 1933 the seat returned, again uncontested, to Dehra Parker. She was returned uncontested in the elections of 1938 and 1945. Four years later she defeated a nationalist candidate and was subsequently returned uncontested in 1953 and 1958. In 1960 she resigned, handing over the seat to Major James Dawson Chichester-Clark, son of the earlier Chichester-Clark. He was elected unopposed and held the seat in uncontested elections in 1962 and 1965. He finally faced a nationalist challenge in 1969, and won. The seat was thus contested only twice in twelve elections over forty years. And the votes cast in the two contested elections, held twenty years apart, were uncannily alike: Dame Dehra won in 1949 by 9,193 votes to 5,909; Major Chichester-Clark won in 1969 by 9,195 votes to 5,812. The figures give some sense of the political stasis.

Unopposed elections were a feature of the Stormont system. Since elections were essentially decided on a religious headcount, the side which was in the minority in a constituency often simply gave up and stopped fielding a candidate there. In the South Antrim constituency, for example, the Unionist majority was so secure that for nine consecutive elections no nationalist went forward, a

Unionist candidate being returned unopposed each time. This meant that no polling took place there in Stormont elections between 1929 and 1965.

The almost stultifying continuity was emphasised by the remarkable longevity of Unionist prime ministers. The first, Sir James Craig, held the post from 1921 until 1940. Although the second, J. M. Andrews, stayed only three years, the third, Sir Basil Brooke, lasted for twenty years. Those who served in their cabinets also tended to have a long political life span: by 1939 not only Craig but four of his seven ministers had been in the cabinet for eighteen years. Nor was this an era for young men: Craig was sixty-nine years old when he left office, Andrews seventy-two, Brooke seventy-four.

Although there were major economic changes over the decades, the basic elements of Unionist dominance, Catholic powerlessness and Westminster disregard survived relatively untouched even an event as cataclysmic as World War Two. The war years did produce one episode capable of shaking Northern Ireland to its political foundations, but the fact that it took place in private meant it had little effect on public opinion. This occurred in 1940 when the Churchill government approached the Dublin Taoiseach, Eamon de Valera, with an offer to explore the option of declaring in favour of Irish unity in return for Irish wartime assistance. The Unionist government, on learning of this, was appalled and furious, but the initiative came to nothing. Wartime censorship kept the episode from the public, but it helped reinforce in Stormont ministers the awareness that Britain always meant more to Northern Ireland than Northern Ireland meant to Britain.

However, the fact that Northern Ireland was involved in the war effort while the south remained neutral meant that Unionism's stock rose in London while sympathy for the nationalist cause decreased. This was useful to the Unionist party when a post-war British Labour government was elected, and when in 1948 the Dublin government unexpectedly announced that Ireland, though effectively independent for many years, was formally declaring a republic and leaving the Commonwealth. This major constitutional change meant Labour needed new legislation to regularise Northern Ireland's position. Up to that point the Labour government had exhibited what one of its junior ministers, the pro-nationalist Lord Longford, described as 'a rather hazy benevolence' towards southern Ireland. This was very much a traditional Labour approach, for expatriate Irishmen and their descendants had played a significant role in the labour movement since its early days.

When it came to brass tacks, however, such sentiment went by the board. The government headed by Clement Attlee inserted a clause in the new Ireland Bill laying down that Northern Ireland would remain in the UK so long as a majority in the Stormont parliament in Belfast wanted it. Given Stormont's inbuilt Unionist majority, nationalists protested that the clause copper-fastened the partition of Ireland. But Attlee's cabinet tended to lean towards the Unionists, partly because his deputy Herbert Morrison was sympathetic to the Unionist cause, and partly because that cause had been much strengthened by Northern Ireland's war role.

Against this background the cabinet took a hard look at Northern Ireland and made some key political judgements. The first of these concerned the reality of Protestant power, with ministers delving back into the 1914 period and the Ulster Volunteer Force gunrunning. The 1949 cabinet minutes record Labour's conclusion: 'Unless the people of Northern Ireland felt reasonably assured of the support of the people of this country, there might be a revival of the Ulster Volunteers and of other bodies intending to meet any threat of force by force; and this would bring nearer the danger of an outbreak of violence in Ireland.'

A second issue was closer to home: that of the UK's wider strategic defence considerations. These were set out by the cabinet secretary, Lord Normanbrook, who wrote that the south's departure from the Commonwealth meant that keeping Northern Ireland within the United Kingdom had become 'a matter of first-class strategic importance to this country'. The issue was so vital, he argued, that even if Northern Ireland wanted to leave the UK it was unlikely that any British government could allow it to do so. The perpetual

Protestant majority meant that Normanbrook's view was never put to the test.

What went by the board in 1949 was the issue which two decades later would give rise to the civil rights movement: the question of the fairness of the Stormont system. When Lord Longford protested that Catholics were being discriminated against he was allowed to address the cabinet which received him, he recalled, with 'chilly indifference'. The young Michael Foot supported the Ireland Act but at the same time called for a commission of inquiry into Stormont's 'monstrously undemocratic methods'. The minutes show, however, that the cabinet decided to keep its distance: 'It was the general view of ministers that the UK government would be ill-advised to appear to be interesting themselves in this matter.'

The remarks made by Foot and others in the Commons, together with the evidence of cabinet papers, show that the government was fully aware of the allegations that Stormont was being run in an unfair manner. It is clear that Attlee had few illusions about Stormont's record, for he turned down a request from the Unionist government to have the power to appoint Supreme Court judges transferred from London to Belfast. Attlee privately noted 'my impression that they would allow political considerations to influence their appointments'. Normanbrook agreed, writing to Attlee that the powers asked for 'certainly have the appearance of being directed to a much more sinister purpose'.

When in 1955 Conservative ministers turned their attentions to Northern Ireland, they took a view similar to that of Labour. One minister noted that the Union 'creates particularly tiresome problems' for the government and was 'apt to be a nuisance', in that it generated criticism from those of Irish descent abroad. But again defence considerations prevailed, the minister concluding: 'Nevertheless it must be recognised that the possession of Northern Ireland is of capital importance in the defence of Great Britain.' The advantages of retaining Northern Ireland, he wrote, 'are overwhelming'.

Thus the 1940s and 1950s came and went, with not even the war changing the basic grammar of Northern Ireland political life, and with the Unionist system as strong as ever. After World War One Churchill had written thus of the longevity of the Irish question, saying in an often-quoted purple passage:

> Then came the Great War. Every institution, almost, in the world was strained. Great empires have been overturned. The whole map of Europe has been changed. The position of countries has been violently altered. The modes of thought of men, the whole outlook on affairs, the grouping of parties, all have encountered violent and tremendous change in the deluge of the world. But as the deluge subsides and the waters fall short we see the dreary steeples of Fermanagh and Tyrone emerging once again. The integrity of their quarrel is one of the few institutions that have been unaltered in the cataclysm which has swept the world.

During World War Two Churchill's own offer on Irish unity could have changed the course of Irish history. It did not, however, and in 1945 he could have repeated every word of his earlier assessment. Not until the 1960s would the Northern Ireland system first begin to tremble, disintegrate, and then descend into violence.

2.

The O'Neill years
1963–69

The years between 1963 and 1969 are often referred to as 'the O'Neill era'. This is entirely appropriate in that the personality and approach of the Stormont prime minister of the time, Captain Terence O'Neill, represented a striking departure from tradition. From the start there was a sense of generational change as he took over from the ageing Brooke, who had been in office for a full two decades. O'Neill's six-year term represented a turning point in Northern Ireland's history. The O'Neill years might be regarded as a tragic missed opportunity in that with hindsight they appear to have been the last chance to tackle, by political means and in a time of relative peace, Northern Ireland's structural problems. Opinions will differ on whether more skill and more luck could have averted the troubles. Terence O'Neill sought to change the entire tone of government, introducing the rhetoric of Protestant–Catholic reconciliation in place of the unapologetically Protestant stance of Craig and Brooke. In retrospect it was an inadequate attempt to brush away decades of division without tackling the underlying problems. These eventually produced a tidal wave of conflicting forces which swept O'Neill from office.

When O'Neill took charge of Northern Ireland it seemed, on the surface at least, reasonably tranquil. From the start of his premiership he asserted that he would be in the business of making changes and of producing 'bold and imaginative measures'. His proposition was that Northern Ireland could be reformed and modernised without endangering either the Union with Britain or his own party's unbroken run in government. The O'Neill government set about building new links with the trade union movement and attracting new investment from abroad to replace ailing existing industries. While such moves were initially generally uncontroversial, much debate was generated by his new emphasis on improving community relations. He became the first Unionist prime minister to pay regular visits to Catholic schools and to offer handshakes to nuns.

Northern Ireland was unused to all this, its first three prime ministers having been men of the laager who defined nationalists, and indeed Catholics in general, as hostile to the state. O'Neill, only the fourth prime minister in more than forty years, presented himself not just as open to change but as an enthusiastic advocate of reform. It was a time when the winds of change were sweeping through many parts of the western world. It was the decade when John F. Kennedy became US president, associated with the themes of youth, equality and new American frontiers. Closer to home, Harold Wilson and the Labour party came to power in Britain, again stressing modernisation. In the Irish Republic too change was the order of the day. There was even a reforming Pope, John XXIII, who instituted widespread reforms within Catholicism and encouraged ecumenical activity.

Terence O'Neill was far from being a dangerous radical. His background was Anglo-Irish, he was Eton-educated and he had served with the Irish Guards in World War Two, during which both his brothers were killed. Retaining his wartime rank as many Unionist politicians did, he was known throughout his political career as Captain O'Neill, entering Stormont in 1946 and spending seven years as finance minister before becoming prime minister. To the Unionist party he seemed a reasonably safe pair of hands, though he was sometimes prone to flights of fancy such as his 1958 whimsy of draining Lough Neagh and thus increasing Northern Ireland's six counties to seven. To the Unionist establishment which chose him as leader, after private consultations, he was above all else one of them, being a member of the gentry which dominated the party at its top levels.

In selecting O'Neill the party had passed over a more able and much more ambitious rival in the cabinet in the form of businessman Brian Faulkner. Faulkner's sense that he had lost because he was from the merchant class rather than the landed gentry would damage the relationship between the two men and undermine O'Neill's authority. Within months there was talk of moves to get rid of O'Neill, with Faulkner publicly denying involvement in any plot. But during O'Neill's time hardly a year went by without rumoured or actual attempts to unseat him, with Faulkner invariably suspected of complicity.

Economic pressures

O'Neill had practical reasons for pursuing modernisation, certainly in the economic sphere. Traditional industries such as shipbuilding and linen were in steep decline, shedding tens of thousands of jobs and forcing unemployment up to levels generally more than double the UK average. O'Neill set about planning a transformation of the economy, accepting ideas such as the creation of a new town, a second university and a new housing programme. His major drive to attract outside industry by improving the infrastructure and offering generous financial incentives worked to some extent, with the arrival of such big names as Grundig, Goodyear and Michelin. But unemployment remained high in a number of districts as the creation of new jobs barely kept pace with the loss of jobs from the older industries. It is scarcely a coincidence that some of the areas which were to feature prominently in the troubles, such as north and west Belfast and Londonderry city, were among those where poor housing and high unemployment persisted.

O'Neill's economic difficulties were accompanied by political problems. The sharp drop in economic activity towards the end of the 1950s coincided with the emergence of a new political challenge in the form of the Northern Ireland Labour party. This was a left-leaning party which, though it had both Catholics and Protestants in its ranks, supported the Union with Britain and attracted largely Protestant support. The NILP twice won four of Stormont's fifty-two seats, winning 26 per cent of the total vote in the 1962 election. For O'Neill it posed a double challenge. Just as Sir James Craig had feared in the early years of the state that the Unionist party might be faced by pro-Union rivals, so O'Neill was concerned that Protestant support might drain away to the NILP. Second, the surge in support for the NILP happened just before Labour came to power in Britain. Harold Wilson's 1964 arrival in Downing Street thus meant that the NILP had ready-made and very powerful friends across the Irish Sea. For Unionism, this dangerous conjunction meant it made even more political sense for O'Neill to stress industrial modernisation and religious bridge-building, since in doing so he was both stealing some of the NILP's clothes and in effect echoing the approach of the Wilson government.

All this had major implications since Wilson was instinctively anti-Unionist and was not well-disposed towards the Stormont regime. This meant that O'Neill was the first Unionist prime minister to be faced with a British counterpart unfriendly to his government. It was thus highly desirable, for a whole series of reasons, to project Northern Ireland as a modern state, at ease with itself and with its neighbours. The NILP was to be warded off; Wilson was to be persuaded that both Northern Ireland's economy and its politics were being updated in a progressive manner; and investors were to be presented with an attractive investment proposition. O'Neill was the first Unionist leader with a keen sense of public relations and the importance of image, grasping from the start that attracting new investment meant working to avoid any appearance of instability and of unresolved ancient quarrels. As part of his campaign he looked south, with an initiative aimed at ending the long cold war between Belfast and Dublin.

The Lemass visit

A similar economic evolution was already taking place across the border in Dublin, where Lemass was jettisoning the inward-looking, protectionist economics of his predecessor de Valera. North–south relations had been so glacial that prime ministers of the two states had not met since the 1920s, and there was virtually no co-ordination between the two governments. Years later a southern civil servant recalled that one of the few channels of communication was provided by rugby matches in Dublin, where Belfast and Dublin officials would meet discreetly to sort out mutual problems.

By the mid-1960s the common aim of O'Neill and Lemass of attracting new investment led them to think of normalising relations. This brought O'Neill to take the initiative for which he is best remembered, inviting Lemass to Belfast in 1965. The visit was a political sensation since no Taoiseach had ever before made the journey to Stormont, and it was a gamble for both men. O'Neill later recounted that Lemass had remarked to him in a Stormont toilet, 'I shall get into terrible trouble for this.' O'Neill said he replied, 'No, Mr Lemass, it is I who will get into trouble for this.' O'Neill was correct, though at the time the visit was viewed as a great success for both men, many people north and south feeling that regularising relations should be added to the other 1960s innovations. For southerners the visit was a welcome move. O'Neill's standing remained high among sections of southern opinion through the years that followed and in 1969 he was voted Man of the Year by readers of a Dublin newspaper.

Most of Unionism voiced approval of the visit, though protests were staged by the Reverend Ian Paisley, a hardline young fundamentalist clergyman with a talent for self-publicity. Some Unionist ministers grumbled that the visit had taken place in strict secrecy, and that they had known of it only after Lemass was actually at Stormont, but overall the initiative was seen as a great success. O'Neill followed it up by twice visiting Dublin, and even the staid Nationalist party was stirred into uncharacteristic action, agreeing at Lemass's urging to assume the role of official Stormont opposition. This was seen as a significant political thaw. There was much talk of new dawns and new eras and bridge-building, especially in the Unionist *Belfast Telegraph*, which enthusiastically backed O'Neill's innovations. Its strong-minded editor, Jack Sayers, was influential with O'Neill and crusaded strongly on his behalf.

O'Neill's rhetorical tone was striking and even visionary: he appealed for 'a new pride in the province' and for 'all sections of the community to feel committed to the task'. He felt it essential 'to convince more and more people that the government is working for the good of all and not only those who vote Unionist'. This was stirring rhetoric, well in tune with the expansive modernising mood of the heady 1960s. The Unionist party did well in the 1965 election, with opinion polls of the time indicating a high degree of Protestant support for such initiatives.

Unionist opposition

Yet for a substantial minority of Protestants even these limited gestures seemed too much too soon, and too drastic a departure from Unionist tradition. The scornful Paisley verdict on O'Neill's bridge-building summed up what one end of the Unionist spectrum thought: 'A traitor and a bridge are very much alike, for they both go over to the other side.' The constant Unionist fear of the traitor within was to prove a fertile seam for Paisley to exploit in the years to come.

Unionists had been raised in a culture which defined the primary aim as preservation of the citadel. This, originally defined as defence of the Union, evolved into a defence of Stormont, with the Unionist party defined as the key instrument. The idea was ingrained in many in the Unionist community that Catholics *per se* were enemies of the state; indeed Craig and Brooke had defined them almost literally in those terms. Yet O'Neill was a Unionist prime minister with an outreach programme apparently designed to bring Catholics within the fold. Those who thought that Unionism was about preserving Protestant unity and control and keeping Catholics at arm's length were dismayed.

On one point these hardliners were certainly right, though

whether it was a self-fulfilling prophecy remains open to argument. They viewed O'Neill's talk of winning Catholic support for Unionism as sheer fantasy, and indeed the decades that followed produced no real evidence of any appreciable Catholic support for Unionist parties. The fault line within Unionism between reformers and traditionalists was to remain visible throughout the troubles. One segment in effect would flatly refuse to contemplate striking a deal with Catholics and nationalists. At the other pole were Unionist party leaders and followers who hoped that such a deal could be done; and in between has been a volatile third segment, vacillating uncertainly between the two positions.

In the years which followed the Reverend Ian Paisley would grow from a semi-comical and apparently insignificant pantomime demon into a formidable figure in Unionist politics. He went on to build a vote which see-sawed between 10 per cent and a high point of more than 30 per cent of all votes cast. O'Neill's party in the decades ahead would remain the primary political voice of Ulster Protestants, but there would be many internal battles and defections, generally to groupings which viewed its policies as insufficiently hardline. The shadow of Paisleyism would forever hang over it, with the tactically astute cleric ever ready to poach its voters. The Unionist party itself would continue to encompass within its ranks dealers, non-dealers and the undecided, destined to remain in a permanent state of flux.

The recurring rumours of leadership challenges culminated in 1966 in a serious effort by some backbenchers to dislodge O'Neill in favour of Faulkner. Although the attempt was unsuccessful, it served to illustrate O'Neill's vulnerability inside even the parliamentary party. In essence he lacked not just standing in the party but also the personal and political skills necessary to see through even the modest changes he had embarked upon. Brooke had been a gruff old frontiersman who had helped create and run the B Specials in a perilous border area; O'Neill was a gentleman from a safe part of County Antrim.

O'Neill's brand of Unionism set him apart from many: he was an unconditional Unionist, identifying absolutely with Britain, while many of his critics were Ulster Unionists first and British second. His wife was English; he often seemed more comfortable in the English country-house world; and it came as little surprise when after his retirement he moved to Hampshire.

Although Unionists proclaimed the strength of their attachment to Britain, many of them instinctively found O'Neill to be too English. Anglican and English-educated, he possessed a nasal, aristocratic voice which made him sound as much an Englishman as an Ulsterman. This had considerable political significance, in that an important component of Unionism has been a distrust of the English and a suspicion of English motives. This derives in part from the fact that many Protestants come from Scottish Dissenting stock, a tradition which has its reservations about the English, and in part from the psychology of the settler who is forever nervous about sentiments back in the homeland. O'Neill, who projected complete faith in Britain, worried many Protestants in that he did not appear to share their almost genetic unease about London.

He also lacked the social and personal skills which were of much importance in a parliament of only fifty-two members: in this field, friend and foe agree, he was frankly terrible. One of his strongest cabinet supporters recalled: 'He lacked the common touch. He found it difficult to communicate warmth and friendliness. I found him distant and uninspiring: I would not, I confess, have felt like dying in a ditch for him.' A Unionist MP described him as 'the most egotistical man I have ever met, and altogether quite the most unpleasant personality I have ever encountered'. A Unionist political journalist commented: 'O'Neill was a disaster. Every time you met him you would have to be introduced to him all over again, whereas Faulkner might not have seen you for a year but would instantly know you.'

Rather than attempting to develop contacts with political colleagues, O'Neill fuelled widespread resentment by spending much time closeted with a small group of officials. The ablest of these was civil servant Ken Bloomfield, who was described by British prime minister James Callaghan as 'the brains of the outfit'. Bloomfield wrote later that O'Neill had no regular practice of talking things over with senior political colleagues, adding that 'his rather shy, lonely and not very communicative nature held him back from cultivating political intimates'. As early as 1965 the *Observer* newspaper reported:

> He is better liked outside his party than in it. Captain O'Neill brings his crises on himself by his brusque and ruthless handling of people. He has made enemies in politics and in the civil service, where his reshuffles and dismissals have been equally brutal. With a small coterie of advisers, his administration sometimes resembles a medieval court, and the roots of his personal power are perilously shallow.

Ian Paisley

In addition to internal party problems there were also destabilising splinters from the mainstream, one of them the politically insatiable and highly divisive Reverend Ian Paisley. Paisley's extraordinary career encompassed politics, the pulpit, marches and rallies, and two spells in jail. It was a career packed with incident and drama, with innumerable demonstrations, diatribes, walkouts and much incendiary rhetoric. But the most extraordinary thing about the career was its climax in 2007 when he astounded the world by agreeing to form a government with Sinn Féin. Overnight he left behind the oratory of division, speaking instead of 'a time when hate will no longer rule'. This was nothing short of sensational. The astonishment came from the fact that he had spent so many decades in the forefront of conflict. In the 1960s there was certainly no inkling that he would eventually end up cordially sharing power with republicans.

O'Neill never could cope with him, and nor could any of his successors. Other figures might have been bought off by being brought inside the fold, but Paisley showed himself uninterested in joining any team.

Ordained a minister by his father, he was installed as moderator of his own sect, the Free Presbyterian Church, a post he held until 2008. In the 1960s he became a formidable street demagogue before turning to party politics: when O'Neill gave up his Stormont seat in 1970 it was Paisley who won it. He did not create the fundamentalist and uncompromising strand in Unionism, but previously it had been largely contained within the Unionist party and the Orange Order. His flair for not just articulating but amplifying the deepest fears of many Protestants meant he harvested votes in large numbers. He formed first the Protestant Unionist party and later the Democratic Unionist party, the latter constituting a force in Unionist politics throughout the troubles and eventually eclipsing the Unionist party.

Paisley was a permanent thorn in the flesh of both the Unionist party and the major Protestant churches, harrying those he denounced as too soft, too ecumenical and too accommodating. Throughout the O'Neill years he staged an almost ceaseless series of demonstrations and stunts, for example protesting against the lowering of the flag at Belfast City Hall to mark the death of Pope John XXIII. He and a thousand supporters complained about 'the lying eulogies now being paid to the Roman anti-Christ'. In 1964 he was involved in the Divis Street riots, the worst Belfast street disturbances for thirty years. During the general election campaign of that year he protested at the display of an Irish tricolour in the window of the republican headquarters in the Catholic Falls Road district of Belfast. When the RUC removed the flag to forestall a Paisley threat to do so, the result was two days of serious rioting and many injuries.

In 1966 Paisley launched the *Protestant Telegraph* weekly newssheet and the associated organisations which took part in many of his demos. In the same year there were disturbances during his protest at the Presbyterian General Assembly meeting in Belfast attended by the Governor of Northern Ireland, Lord Erskine.

Although it has often been asserted that the civil rights movement was the first body in Northern Ireland to exploit the new media age with skill, the fact is that Paisley was the first to make use of newspaper and television publicity. That the media were universally antagonistic towards both his beliefs and his methods was in the end of little moment to him: he realised at an early stage that any publicity was good publicity. Although the media in general initially portrayed him as an anachronistic crank, it gradually became obvious that he had substantial support within a section of rural and working-class Protestants. His mix of religious fundamentalism, political opportunism, personal charisma and talent for self-publicity was a potent one.

1966: loyalist violence

Just as this Protestant extremist was the first to exploit the opportunities of the media, other Protestant extremists were the first to take life. A rise in tension in 1966, as republicans celebrated the fiftieth anniversary of the 1916 rising, led to three killings carried out by a group styling itself the Ulster Volunteer Force. The UVF, though named after the organisation that had helped bring Northern Ireland into being, was a far cry from the original body of that name. It was instead made up of at most a couple of dozen men who met in backstreet pubs, many in the Shankill Road district, to discuss over drinks means of combating the practically nonexistent IRA. A series of attacks carried out in a two-month period in 1966, many of which were drunken escapades, claimed three lives.

None of those killed was remotely connected with the IRA. The first victim was a 77-year-old Protestant widow who was fatally injured in a fire started by a petrol bomb aimed at a Catholic-owned bar. Their second was a Catholic man on his way home in the Falls Road district after a night's drinking: the gang shot him after hearing him shout 'Up the Republic, up the rebels'. Their third victim was a teenage Catholic barman who strayed into a bar in Malvern

Street in the Shankill Road district. He was shot as he left the bar, the shooting becoming known as the Malvern Street murder.

Most people were aghast at such incidents, which were condemned from every quarter. The RUC quickly rounded up members of the gang, some of whom were given lengthy prison sentences. The events were an unwelcome reminder that for all the talk of modernisation, old enmities continued to simmer not far below the surface. The *Belfast Telegraph*, in a remarkably prescient editorial, gave this warning:

> Violence has been smouldering in Belfast and district for weeks past, and the point has been reached at which a united effort is called for to prevent crazy people leading the province on a path to self-destruction. No longer may any Protestant wonder where his loyalties lie. They lie on the side of law and order and public decency. They can have nothing to do with those who have been sowing dragon's teeth, and can now see how terrible the harvest can be. Ulster is in danger of being thrown back into a dark past by sectarian forces which have too long been winked at by many who should know better.

But although most Unionists were against violence, a substantial number were also very much against Terence O'Neill. By 1967 sections of the Orange Order were in open revolt against him, critics at the main Twelfth of July demonstration passing out leaflets condemning his 'tottering leadership'. When a senior Orange official attempted to read out a resolution praising O'Neill his words were drowned by hecklers. An MP who was due to speak at a Fermanagh Orange demonstration withdrew when it became clear that the O'Neill resolution would not even be proposed. At another Orange demonstration a Westminster Unionist MP was dragged from the stage and beaten unconscious when he remonstrated with anti-O'Neill hecklers. Early the next year the prime minister himself was attacked with stones, flour and eggs by Paisleyite demonstrators while attending a Unionist party meeting in Belfast: his immediate sin had been to visit a convent school some days earlier. All of this meant that O'Neill was preaching a new accommodation against an increasingly unsettled background.

The civil rights campaign

Just as Unionism was showing signs of coming apart, Catholics and nationalists were breaking new ground in politics. They were finding novel means of making their political voice heard as British post-war educational reforms produced a Catholic middle class which was both larger and much more assertive than ever before. This new generation regarded the Nationalist party as outmoded and ineffectual, and viewed the IRA and Sinn Féin as belonging to a past age.

During the 1960s a number of Catholic voices emerged that not only criticised Unionism, as was traditional, but also argued for greater Catholic participation in the state. One of these was John Hume's. In 1964, as a 27-year-old teacher and credit union organiser, Hume urged Catholics in a newspaper article to be more outgoing, writing, 'There has been no attempt to be positive, to encourage the Catholic community to develop the resources which they have in plenty, to make a positive contribution in terms of community service.' His words were evidence of increasing Catholic restlessness with existing structures. A significant organisation emerged from Tyrone in the form of the Campaign for Social Justice. Consisting of thirteen Catholic professionals who included four doctors, it assembled and circulated detailed statistics in support of its allegations of discrimination.

A turning point came with the election of a Labour government in 1964. The Unionist party had not come into serious conflict with Conservative governments, and the post-war Attlee Labour government had offered no threat to the Unionist cause. But Harold Wilson as prime minister presented a very different figure since, instinctively anti-Unionist and representing a largely Irish Catholic constituency in Liverpool, he made no secret of his disdain for the Unionist party.

He was pressed into paying attention to Northern Ireland issues when in 1965 a Campaign for Democracy in Ulster (CDU) was formed at Westminster, attracting the support of around a hundred Labour backbenchers. With MP Paul Rose as its leading figure, the CDU took a lively and continuing interest in Northern Ireland affairs, campaigning against the long-standing convention which ruled out discussion of Northern Ireland affairs at Westminster.

An important figure arrived at Westminster in 1966 when Gerry Fitt, who was to have a long-running career in Northern Ireland politics, won the West Belfast seat for the Republican Labour party. An affable ex-seaman who enlivened every bar he visited, Fitt won many friends among Labour MPs with his endless flow of patter which effectively mixed anecdotes, jokes and shrewd political points. A cute backstreet politician with a power base in the rough Docks area of Belfast, he ran rings round the staid Unionists with his natural flair for publicity, his talent for impressing journalists, and his ready identification with many of Wilson's backbenchers. The *Belfast Telegraph* outlined the dangers Fitt posed to Unionism, noting a year after his election: 'He enjoys the friendly recognition of ministers and Labour backbenchers alike. He is an astute politician – one of the most effective non-Unionists who have been sent to Westminster by Northern Ireland – and his presence has materially helped to alter the climate of the Ulster Unionists.'

Wilson and his colleagues pressed O'Neill for reform. Minutes of 1966 and 1967 ministerial meetings reveal Home Secretary Roy Jenkins urging, ominously for Unionists, that 'a real effort should be made to meet some of the grievances which had been expressed: otherwise Westminster would be forced to act'. O'Neill told his cabinet that there was 'an underlying sense of pressure' coming from London. Many in Unionism, conditioned as they were to view criticism and opposition as conspiracy, were ill-equipped to respond to this new situation. O'Neill himself was clearly well aware that the game had changed and that pressure from London could not be dismissed, but many in his party were slow to grasp this.

It was against this background that Catholics and nationalists chanced upon a powerful new political instrument in the form of the civil rights movement. This was not a party but an umbrella group wide enough to embrace every anti-Unionist element in the land. It was amorphous in the sense that it had no coherent central leadership and no formal membership. In 1967 a committee emerged styling itself the Northern Ireland Civil Rights Association (NICRA), but from the start activists in many districts organised themselves with little or no reference to the supposed leadership. While NICRA was never more than the notional directing force, the theme of civil rights was to catch the imagination of the very many Catholics who were not members of any organised body. In 1968 it was to galvanise the Catholic community politically.

NICRA had a shopping list of demands which included one man – one vote, the redrawing of electoral boundaries, anti-discrimination legislation, a points system for housing allocation, the repeal of the Special Powers Act, and the disbanding of the B Specials. The most potent of these was the demand for one man – one vote, a reference to the different voting arrangements in Stormont and council elections. In council elections subtenants, lodgers and anyone living at home with their parents could not vote, so that around a quarter of Stormont voters had no say in local government elections. Opinions differ on the exact effect the introduction of one man – one vote might have had, though an unpublished Unionist government study concluded that nationalists would have benefited significantly in Tyrone, Fermanagh and Londonderry city. This might have led to a loss of Unionist party control over much of the west, which explains why Unionists were so strongly opposed to one man – one vote.

It was a touchstone issue but there were many other rallying points, and many reasons why even the more moderate civil rights figures were not inclined to give O'Neill the benefit of the doubt. By 1968 he had been in office for five years, yet his reform proposals still seemed largely confined to the realms of rhetoric. Nationalists debated whether he was a genuine reformer, a cunningly disguised unreconstructed Unionist of the old sort, or perhaps a well-intentioned man who was simply not in control of his own party. Many Catholics saw

O'Neillism as a distinctly conditional advance in that at its heart lay an attempt to give the Unionist party a more accommodating aspect without affecting its hold on power. Complete success for O'Neill's project would have meant a continuation and in fact a consolidation of Unionist rule. Nationalists therefore wondered what they had to gain from the architect of a scheme designed to create a more intelligent form of Unionism rather than sponsor a genuine breakthrough on their behalf.

In any event, many of what O'Neill presented as reforms did little to better the lot of nationalists. Many of the new companies attracted to Northern Ireland wound up either in Belfast or in its satellite towns, often in mainly Protestant areas with mainly Protestant workforces. Catholics complained that the largely Catholic west lost out and was bypassed by the much-vaunted industrial modernisation. When a new city was planned, it was placed in a mostly Protestant area and pointedly named Craigavon in commemoration of the old Unionist prime minister. A second university was established but there was political uproar in the north-west when mainly Catholic Londonderry was passed over in favour of Protestant Coleraine. Londonderry's Catholics, and indeed many of its Protestants, claimed this was a perverse decision explicable only in sectarian terms.

Catholic politicians complained that while the Unionist rhetoric was new, the effect was the old discrimination under a new name. It was argued that in his five years in office O'Neill had hardly made a dent in the ingrained practices in fundamental areas such as schools, housing, jobs and local government. As late as 1967, for example, when three public boards were reconstituted, the seventy-nine members included only seven Catholics. It was also obvious enough that whether or not O'Neill was a genuine reformer there was a great deal of Protestant opposition to change, both inside and outside his party.

The civil rights movement encompassed supporters of the Nationalist party, members and supporters of the IRA, communists, liberals, trade unionists, assorted left-wingers and radicals, exuberant students, middle-class professionals and many more, united in a fluid coalition which was not to last for long before splitting back into its constituent components. Although Gerry Fitt and other prominent Catholic public figures were there too, it was a new breed of better educated representatives who came to the fore, including John Hume and psychology student Bernadette Devlin. The movement's principal activity was the staging of marches designed to generate media coverage and publicise the cause. The movement was much influenced by the model of Martin Luther King and the black civil rights movement in America, though it was also to draw inspiration from the street activities of students and others in Paris, Prague and elsewhere. This was to be the new politics which would break the old mould, and it was seized on with heady excitement.

1968: *the mould breaks*

The movement's first manifestation, in terms of generating publicity and highlighting an issue, came in 1968 when Austin Currie, a young Nationalist MP, staged a protest by squatting in a house in the County Tyrone village of Caledon near Dungannon. The episode has come to be regarded as a seminal moment in Northern Ireland's history, some even regarding it as the start of the troubles, or at least as the spark which ignited the bonfire.

County Tyrone had over the years generated many allegations of unfair housing allocation, and this particular case led to much local Catholic indignation. The facts were regarded by local Catholics as a clear example of politics and religion taking precedence over housing need. The house at the centre of the controversy was allocated, by a local Unionist party councillor, to a nineteen-year-old unmarried Protestant girl. She was secretary to the councillor's solicitor, who was also a Unionist parliamentary candidate. The girl was given the house in preference to two Catholic families, who had squatted for a time in the district, and who had complained that the same councillor had opposed the building of houses for Catholic tenants in the Dungannon area. A few days after the girl moved in, Catholic squatters in the house next door were evicted by police, with full television coverage.

Currie, an energetic MP who was to have a long political career, raised the matter unsuccessfully both with the local council and at Stormont. Following a heated debate he was ordered to leave the Commons chamber. He then symbolically occupied the girl's house, remaining in it for some hours before being evicted by the RUC. One of the policemen who removed him was the girl's brother, who himself later moved into the same house.

The incident became a *cause célèbre*. Thousands attended a public rally addressed by Currie a few days after the squatting incident, and in August the civil rights movement staged its first protest march, from the village of Coalisland to the town of Dungannon. In a pattern which was to be repeated many times, a thousand members and supporters of Paisley's Ulster Protestant Volunteers gathered to confront them in Dungannon. The marchers, consciously emulating American civil rights protesters, sang 'We Shall Overcome'. Confrontation was avoided, but the pattern of demonstration and counter-demonstration was set.

It is no exaggeration to say that the next civil rights march made history, for the violence which accompanied it transformed Northern Ireland politics. The march, in the city of Londonderry on 5 October 1968, was organised by a left-wing group which was hopeful of provoking the authorities into confrontation. That strategy worked. First William Craig, O'Neill's particularly hardline Minister for Home Affairs, banned the march, a move which swelled the numbers attending it. Then the RUC spectacularly overreacted, using water cannon and batons on an obviously peaceful group of marchers.

Crucially, a Dublin television cameraman was on hand to capture the RUC actions on film. In particular he recorded the scene as a senior RUC officer uninhibitedly used a long blackthorn stick, the official symbol of his authority, to rain heavy blows indiscriminately on a number of marchers. The pictures of the officer fiercely laying about the demonstrators, then turning towards the camera, wild-eyed and almost out of control, were shown repeatedly at the time. In the years that followed the film clip was broadcast on television hundreds and perhaps thousands of times, making an appearance in almost all accounts of how the troubles broke out.

Local hospitals later reported treating seventy-seven civilian casualties, most of whom had bruises and lacerations to the head. The most important of those heads belonged to Gerry Fitt, who had taken three Labour MPs with him to Londonderry to witness the march, and had been in the front line when the police moved in. An official report later concluded that he had been struck 'wholly without justification or excuse' and that RUC men had used their batons indiscriminately. Fitt later recounted:

> A sergeant grabbed me and pulled my coat down over my shoulders to prevent me raising my arms. Two other policemen held me as I was batoned on the head. I could feel the blood coursing down my neck and on to my shirt. As I fell to my knees I was roughly grabbed and thrown into a police van. At the police station I was shown into a room with a filthy wash basin and told to clean up but I was not interested in that. I wanted the outside world to see the blood which was still flowing strongly down my face.

The images of Fitt's bloody head and shirt and of the incensed police officer flashed around the world and at a stroke rewrote the basic grammar of Northern Ireland politics. Disastrously for the RUC and the Unionist government, the film was to provide a world-wide audience with a vivid and endlessly repeated record of events which inflicted huge damage on O'Neill's government.

The events in Londonderry on 5 October caused an explosion of anger within the wider Catholic community. It guaranteed the civil rights movement a level of support in Northern Ireland and far beyond that was to prove irresistible. In the days and weeks afterwards, marches, sit-ins, demonstrations, protests and court appearances became almost daily occurrences. For its part the O'Neill government struggled to find ways to respond. O'Neill's instinct was that concessions had to be made quickly, but as he sought support for this many in the party demanded an old-style Unionist response to challenges by rebels. Even years later William Craig revealed a breathtaking ignorance of public relations considerations when he said: 'I thought the way the police acted on the day was fair enough. I would have intensified it. I wouldn't have given two hoots for the Labour MPs who were present, or the TV pictures.'

Comment in the British and world press and at Westminster was overwhelmingly critical, and the Westminster convention of not discussing Northern Ireland affairs evaporated. Wilson summoned O'Neill to Downing Street. The Stormont cabinet minutes for 14 October, nine days after the Londonderry march, record O'Neill as saying:

> Within the next month or so we must face Harold Wilson again. Now I ask my colleagues to be realistic about the situation we are likely, indeed in my view certain, to face there. We shall be told that unless we can give a definite undertaking that we will introduce further reforms, Her Majesty's Government will no longer be able to stand aloof from the situation. Let's face the fact – HMG do not have to do something openly spectacular to make us feel the pinch: they merely have to be unwilling in the future to do any more exceptional things for us.

He told his ministers: 'Of course there are anti-partitionist agitators prominently at work, but can any of us truthfully say in the confines of this room that the minority has no grievance calling for remedy?' He added:

> Believe me, I realise the appalling political difficulties we face. The first reaction of our own people to the antics of Fitt and Currie and the abuse of the world's press is to retreat into old hardline attitudes. But if this is all we can offer, we face a period when we govern Ulster

by police power alone, against a background of mounting disorder. Are we ready, and would we be wise, to face up to this? We would have a very hard job to sell concessions to our people: but in this critical moment may this not be our duty?

William Craig was particularly opposed to concessions, warning of 'disastrous political repercussions' in the party if one man – one vote was conceded. According to the minutes, Craig 'could not agree that Mr Wilson should be allowed to tell them how to act. Although they should go to the meeting in a cooperative spirit, clearly they must be responsible to their own electorate, and Mr Wilson could be relied upon to appreciate this. Intervention would provoke a constitutional crisis and a massive uprising in the loyalist community.'

The cabinet discussed a number of reforms, but significantly could only agree on a few largely inconsequential measures and above all would not give the go-ahead for one man – one vote. A number of Unionists advocated reform, including backbencher Richard Ferguson who said, 'So long as this state of affairs continues it inhibits our progress and provides material for our opponents. Let us at least get the credit for putting our own house in order.' But such sentiments were unpopular messages to many in the Unionist community. One reason for this was the fact that to some Unionists the civil rights movement was simply the IRA and other anti-partitionists in a different guise, ostensibly asking for civil rights but actually intent on attacking the British connection. This analysis led many Unionists to oppose any concessions to the movement.

William Craig and others frequently alleged that the IRA was intimately involved in the civil rights movement, and in this they were correct. It was certainly the case that prominent IRA figures and other republicans had been present at the birth of the movement, but this was by no means the whole story. The IRA itself had had a major rethink since the abject failure of its 1950s campaign, and in the process had swung sharply to the left with prominent Marxists taking control. It moved away from the idea of using violence as its only tactic and became a left-wing pressure group agitating on issues such as housing, particularly in the south.

The civil rights banner gave the new-style IRA the chance to operate on another front and it enthusiastically backed the new phenomenon. Unionists like Craig were right when they said there were many republicans in the ranks of the civil rights movement, but wrong in thinking that the IRA was using the movement to foment trouble as a prelude to a new campaign of violence. They were also wrong in assuming that the IRA was a dominant force in the movement, since it was simply one component among many others, and never came close to taking charge of it. As an official report later put it, 'While there is evidence that members of the IRA are active in the civil rights organisation, there is no sign that they are in any sense dominant or in a position to control or direct policy.'

In a final memo to his cabinet before going to Downing Street O'Neill again unsuccessfully pushed for an agreed plan of significant reform, writing, 'It is not weakness but commonsense to go into the conference chamber with some weapons in our own hands, rather than be placed entirely on the defensive.' He was unsuccessful, however, in getting agreement for anything other than modest moves and promises to consider other reforms at some future stage.

Westminster pressure

O'Neill knew this was never going to be enough, and so it proved. The reception which he, Craig and Faulkner received at Downing Street on 4 November can only be described as a mauling at the hands of Harold Wilson and Home Secretary James Callaghan. The minutes show that in the wake of the 5 October march London–Belfast relations had changed utterly. Wilson pitched straight in, opening the meeting with a reminder that Stormont was subordinate to Westminster and following up with a direct threat to cut off some of Northern Ireland's money: some of London's subsidies, he said, 'would clearly be at risk in any situation in which the United Kingdom government needed to bring pressure to bear'. He went on to complain about the lack of one man – one vote and about Stormont emergency legislation.

Then Callaghan stepped in to warn that 'if there was any thought of just stringing the UK government along it had better be forgotten'. Agitation at Westminster for change was 'clearly about to grow on a massive scale', he said, pressing for early movement on voting reform and housing. Wilson returned to the attack with an even more overt financial threat, saying that if reform was not accelerated 'they would feel compelled to propose a radical course involving the complete liquidation of all financial agreements with Northern Ireland'.

It fell to O'Neill to reply to this onslaught, which was of a type none of his predecessors had ever had to face. Previous UK governments might have grumbled at the size of the subsidies required by Northern Ireland, but never had a prime minister directly threatened to take such drastic action. And while Wilson had previously pressed O'Neill to move faster on reform, such demands had never before been couched in terms of a financially menacing ultimatum. O'Neill responded by saying he had resolved to do everything he could to break down old animosities, adding he had been successful to the extent that the RUC had advised him that his personal safety was at risk, not from the IRA but from extreme loyalists. He argued that he had made considerable headway, with movement in terms of providing jobs for Catholics, housing, education and voting, pressing ahead in the face of opposition within his own party.

Craig added that local government reform was being energetically pursued even though this was, he said, a difficult and highly unpopular task. Disregarding Callaghan's strictures against any thought of delay, he said a review of local government which had started in 1966 would take another three years to complete. He went on at some length, saying many more houses for Catholics were planned, defending emergency legislation, and asserting that the IRA was behind the civil rights movement.

In the discussion which followed Callaghan and Wilson continued to push for speedy reforms, especially one man – one vote. Wilson illustrated the new influence of the media when he asserted: 'The television media could not be accused of falsifying their reportage of the occurrences. Opinion among moderate members, not by any means normally ill-disposed towards Northern Ireland, had been very critical of the police action at Londonderry.' Craig stoutly defended the RUC, saying that 'police action in the Londonderry riot had been examined exhaustively and minutely and there was no justification for the aspersions cast on the RUC'. His examination had completely vindicated the police, he said; Wilson's idea of holding an inquiry into the event would be 'quite disastrous' in undermining police morale.

Callaghan pointedly returned to the money issue, rehearsing in detail the financial benefits Northern Ireland received and again warning against delay in reform. Wilson summed up by saying that what the Stormont ministers had said 'could not be considered in any sense as satisfactory' and ordering them to draw up and send him a reform plan.

This very tense meeting ended with a final display of what can only be described as political obtuseness when Craig, in spite of the repeated threats to cut off money, asked for additional financial help for a large Belfast company. This caused Wilson to snap, in what may have been a loss of prime ministerial temper, that he was 'fed up with this firm which had become a kind of soup kitchen and was no good to anybody'.

With those angry words ringing in their ears the Unionists took the plane back to Stormont to consider the new realities of politics, and to ponder on whether Wilson was serious about his threat to cut off the money. O'Neill was convinced he meant it though Craig took the view that Wilson was bluffing, and that his bluff should be called. The Stormont cabinet as a whole concluded it was not a bluff and set about assembling a set of reforms which it hoped might satisfy London while proving acceptable to the Unionist party. In fact such a balancing act was never to be achieved. Ken

Bloomfield summed up in his memoirs the pattern of events of the next four years as one of 'pressure for reform constantly increasing, agonising debate about further concession, and the announcement too late of compromises no longer acceptable to anyone. In a rising market, Unionism constantly tried, unsuccessfully, to buy reform at last year's prices.'

Within weeks the O'Neill government produced a five-point reform package which included establishment of a commission to run Londonderry, changes in housing policy, limited voting reform, and a future review of emergency legislation. One week later, however, William Craig threw down the gauntlet both to O'Neill and to Wilson by questioning many of the proposed reforms and declaring at a rally: 'There is all this nonsense about civil rights, and behind it all there is our old traditional enemy exploiting the situation. The civil rights movement is bogus and is made up of ill-informed people who see in unrest a chance to renew the campaign of violence.' When O'Neill said in Stormont that he regretted the tone of these remarks Craig defiantly delivered the same speech again.

The temperature rose still further with a menacing confrontation between civil rights demonstrators and Paisley supporters in the city of Armagh. With an increasing sense that events were spinning out of control, O'Neill made a television appeal in December in an attempt to calm the situation. The Belfast Chamber of Trade called on shops to close early to enable people to watch the appeal, which was broadcast by both local television channels, with the *Belfast Telegraph* producing a special edition carrying what became known as 'the crossroads speech'.

Declaring that Northern Ireland was at a crossroads, O'Neill called for restraint from all citizens, saying a minority of agitators was responsible for starting the trouble in Londonderry 'but the tinder for that fire in the form of grievances, real or imaginary, had been building up for years'. To civil rights campaigners and the Catholic community he said, 'Your voice has been heard.' To Unionists he said: 'Unionism armed with justice will be a stronger cause than Unionism armed merely with strength.' Addressing both sides, he asked, 'What kind of Ulster do you want? A happy and respected province, in good standing with the rest of the UK, or a place continually torn apart by riots and demonstrations, and regarded as a political outcast?'

Within days, however, O'Neill's differences with Craig came to a head and the prime minister sacked his Home Affairs minister. This followed a speech in which Craig directly challenged Westminster's authority, declaring: 'I would resist any effort by any government in Great Britain, whatever its complexion might be, to exercise that power in any way to interfere with the proper power and jurisdiction of the parliament and government of Northern Ireland.' In the letter sacking him O'Neill referred to Craig's 'attraction to ideas of a UDI [unilateral declaration of independence] nature. Your idea of an Ulster which can go it alone is a delusion.' Craig joined the ranks of the disaffected on the backbenches, where important figures such as former minister Harry West were already calling for O'Neill's resignation.

After the speech, moderate elements in the civil rights campaign agreed to a pause in demonstrations to lower the temperature and test the government's reform promises. By this stage, however, O'Neill himself had become profoundly pessimistic. He wrote in a private letter on Christmas Eve, 'What a year! I fear 1969 will be worse. The one thing I cannot foresee in 1969 is peace. As I look in the glass darkly I see demonstrations, counter-demonstrations, meetings, rows, and general misery. In such an atmosphere of hatred would one in fact wish to continue this job – I doubt it.'

1969: end of the O'Neill era

O'Neill's pessimism was well-founded. Even as he spent Christmas in England, the People's Democracy (PD), a radical, mainly student civil rights group impatient with calls for restraint, set out on a march from Belfast to Londonderry which was to pass through a number of strongly loyalist areas. The PD regarded O'Neill's reforms as too little too late, particularly as they did not include one man – one vote. The march was challenged by groups of loyalists, many of them mobilised by eccentric Paisley ally Ronald Bunting, and there were a number of tense moments. Eventually, on 4 January 1969, it flared into open violence at Burntollet Bridge, in what would be regarded as one of the key events of the civil rights era. The march was ambushed by hundreds of loyalists at the bridge, a rural location in County Londonderry, with large numbers of attackers throwing stones and assaulting both male and female marchers with cudgels.

Once again the world's television screens were filled with images of demonstrators with blood flowing from head wounds; once again the episode was a public relations disaster for the Unionist government and the RUC. The police were accused of standing by as the ambush took place, and even of helping to engineer it, while a number of off-duty members of the B Specials were said to be among the attackers. The PD marchers themselves, who before the incident had been criticised by other civil rights campaigners as irresponsible and provocative, instantly won the sympathy of almost the entire Catholic community. The weeks which followed brought more and more demonstrations, with the RUC struggling to cope with so much unrest and street activity. The force, which had just over 3,000 members, was unused to dealing with so many marches and so much appalling publicity.

Desperately seeking to recapture the initiative, O'Neill announced the setting up of a commission to inquire into the causes of the events of 5 October in Londonderry. Such a move had been resisted by Unionists but now was seen as a way of buying time. Lord Cameron, the Scottish judge who headed the commission, would eventually produce a report highly critical of the Unionist government, but by the time he did so far worse disturbances had broken out. The decision to appoint Cameron was denounced by leading backbenchers Harry West and William Craig, but worse for O'Neill was the resignation of Brian Faulkner, which led to a bitter exchange of letters.

By the end of January Ian Paisley was in prison as a result of events during a demonstration in Armagh. In mid-February twelve hardline Unionist MPs met to demand O'Neill's resignation. It was becoming clear that the prime minister had few cards left to play, and in a final gamble he called an election in late February. It was a messy election campaign with a messy result. Most of the Ulster Unionist candidates were pro-O'Neill but a number made no secret of their opposition to him. Others were not official party nominees but nonetheless stood on a pro-O'Neill ticket. The result was a bitter and divisive campaign with much Unionist infighting.

When the votes were counted O'Neill had a bare majority in Stormont, but the Unionist vote had splintered in a way that was the stuff of Sir James Craig's nightmares. The party which had often been described as a monolith was a monolith no longer, and never would be one again. Far from delivering the decisive vote of confidence for which O'Neill had hoped, the election starkly illustrated the depth of divisions. It was a further blow to O'Neill's prestige and authority. The election was also highly significant on the Catholic side, where a number of Nationalist MPs were replaced by younger civil rights candidates, among them John Hume.

In the following weeks a number of bombings at electricity and water facilities increased the sense of instability. A thousand B Specials were mobilised to guard public utilities, together with a number of troops. The attacks were attributed by the RUC to the IRA, though much later it emerged that the devices were the work of the loyalist UVF, which was successfully attempting to bring down O'Neill. He was later to write that he was 'blown out of office' by the bombings.

A by-election in March added to O'Neill's woes when the death of a Unionist MP led to the arrival at Westminster of Bernadette Devlin, a student who was one of the most colourful and radical of the emerging civil rights figures. Her election and her particularly striking maiden speech in the Commons generated huge world-wide publicity, all of it adding to general Unionist frustration and to O'Neill's problems. In a final irony, just before he left office O'Neill managed to push one man – one vote through the cabinet, but the divisions in his party were too deep to allow him to continue. In the last days a relative, James Chichester-Clark, resigned from the cabinet. In a retirement address on television O'Neill referred to his gamble in calling an election, concluding that 'in many places, old fears, old prejudices and old loyalties were too strong'. In some areas loyalists celebrated his departure by lighting bonfires.

Opinions of his premiership differ. The nationalist *Irish News* said on his departure: 'The judgement of history will certainly be kinder to him than to his predecessors, who did nothing at all to bridge the chasm that divides our society and which Unionism of the anti-O'Neill variety still seems unwilling to attempt. At least Mr O'Neill tried.' Student leader Michael Farrell dismissed him however as 'a colourless figure who was largely a mouthpiece for technocrats in the civil service'. Maurice Hayes, a Catholic observer who later became a senior civil servant, praised O'Neill but listed his shortcomings as 'his lack of personal warmth, his difficulty with personal relationships, his inability to communicate, even with his friends, his defensiveness in the face of criticism and his inability to mend fences within the party'. The *Belfast Telegraph* concluded:

> Basically, his mistake was that as prime minister he never managed to establish a working relationship with his party. The leaders at grassroots level did not understand, or want to understand, his new brand of liberal Unionism, and in the end he probably had more friends outside the party than inside it. Not only had he to deal with a slumbering party, lulled by 40 years' unchallenged rule, but he had to try to modernise a province that was temperamentally unsuited and physically unprepared for change.

A Unionist journalist summed him up:

> He was essentially an Englishman. He was desperately out of touch with everything. I remember reporting on a speech he made at an Orange hall somewhere in County Down. First you had a speaker

who got them all fired up with 'no surrender' stuff. Then you had another who told a lot of anti-Catholic jokes. Then you had Terence, stiffly reading out a 20-minute speech about the successes of a Belfast factory. Then you had another speaker and you were back to the good old Orange stuff again.

If O'Neill had difficulty in his relations with other Unionists, he also had little success in connecting with Catholics. A much-quoted remark he made after leaving office is cited as evidence of a super-cilious and patronising attitude: 'It is frightfully hard to explain to Protestants that if you give Roman Catholics a good job and a good house they will live like Protestants, because they will see neigh-bours with cars and television sets. They will refuse to have eight-een children, but if a Roman Catholic is jobless and lives in the most ghastly hovel, he will rear eighteen children on National Assistance.'

Looking back on contemporary assessments, it is striking to note how much emphasis was placed on what was seen as O'Neill's unfortunate personality and his lack of personal and man-management skills. The clear implication is that a Unionist leader with greater talent might have enjoyed greater success. With hind-sight it is fairly obvious that O'Neill's way of working made even more difficult what he described as a difficult and lonely office. By the time the crises of 1968 and 1969 arrived, the Stormont back-benches were stacked with disgruntled former ministers who felt unfairly treated, together with Unionist MPs who felt little personal loyalty to him. Many Unionists were prepared to go along with him, but many others simply said no, in the same way as, nearly three decades later, many would say no to the 1998 Good Friday Agreement. The Unionist machine was beginning to splinter into its constituent parts: O'Neill had not put the machine together, and did not know how to fix it.

The events of 1968 and 1969 tended to show O'Neill as a figure-head who was unable to bring Unionism into line with his own updated rhetoric. Although few now doubt that he genuinely wanted a fresh start, the gap between the rhetoric and the actual record is striking. Much of Unionism seemed impervious to the talk of change. Events such as the handling of the 5 October Londonderry march, which was first banned and then became the occasion for an intimidating display of police violence, seemed to show that the state could not cope with even peaceful protest.

O'Neill faced a nationalism reinvigorated by the civil rights movement and enlivened by a new generation of bright young leaders. From the Unionist side came not fresh thinking but Ian Paisley, a highly disruptive and destructive element, as well as opposition from within his own party. O'Neill also faced a demanding British prime minister in the person of Harold Wilson, who was not only generally unsympathetic to Unionism but also under pressure from Labour backbenchers. One of the great ironies of O'Neill's career was that he was in 1963 the first significant figure to start talking of change and reform, and in 1969 he was brought down when the debate over change spiralled out of control. He was the first Unionist leader to realise that Northern Ireland could not forever go on as it was, but he did not manage to convince Unionism as a whole of the need for change, or convince nationalists that he could deliver it. With hindsight, the notion that he might have persuaded Unionism to change its ways was as improbable as his scheme for draining Lough Neagh.

3.

Descent into violence
1969–71

O'Neill's successor was his distant relative James Chichester-Clark, who was first and foremost a County Londonderry farmer and only secondarily a politician. A former Irish Guards officer, he was not only landed gentry but had an almost hereditary claim on his Stormont seat, members of his family having held it since partition. Most of the early assessments were that he was a basically decent man but not a natural politician. A Protestant official sympathetically described him as slow, phlegmatic, honest and sensible; a Catholic official called him, with less charity, 'a very limited and extremely wooden man who had been far out of his depth as a minister and was a cruel caricature as a prime minister'.

Such assessments were to be borne out, for he lasted less than two unhappy years before resigning and returning to political obscurity. He appeared to do so with a sense of relief rather than any sense of ambition thwarted. He never had much ambition to begin with, and in office soon concluded that like O'Neill he could not reconcile the competing pressures from Unionism, nationalism and London.

He had little in the way of a political honeymoon. He pressed ahead with one man – one vote and other reforms, but the focus was moving to the streets. The crunch came in August 1969, the crisis sparked off by controversy over a parade. The Apprentice Boys of Derry, an organisation similar to the Orange Order, wished to stage its traditional march in Londonderry. Both Stormont and the Wilson government debated for some time on whether the march should be allowed, concerned that there could be a major flare-up in the tinderbox atmosphere of the time. In the end permission was given and the feared eruption duly took place, as early skirmishes between Catholics and Protestants escalated into what came to be known as the Battle of the Bogside. This amounted to something close to a full-scale uprising on the part of residents of the Bogside, a Catholic enclave close to Londonderry city centre.

It took the form of pitched battles between police and local men and youths using petrol bombs, bricks and any other missiles they could find to prevent the RUC from entering the district. Police replied with tear gas and by throwing stones back at the rioters. Fierce rioting went on for days, with many injuries on both sides: of one RUC unit of 59 men, 43 were treated for injuries.

When police vehicles at one stage breached barricades, Protestant mobs charged in after the RUC, smashing windows in Catholic houses. By all accounts the police had not planned this, but its effect was nonetheless galvanising. A local priest commented that this incursion 'brushed aside any hope of moderation or any hope of restoring calm. There was an apparent unanimity in opposition to the police force. Over the next few days the determination was so unanimous that I would only regard it as a community in revolt rather than just a street disturbance or a riot.'

In effect the authorities had, despite the deployment of a large proportion of the entire RUC, lost control of a substantial part of Londonderry city. The running street battles meant that the police eventually became exhausted. Instead of abating, however, the trouble spread to other places including Belfast. This took place after a number of civil rights leaders called for diversionary activities outside Londonderry to 'take the heat' off the Bogsiders. Although most of those who made the call did not mean to stir up violence it broke out on a large scale, in particular in north and west Belfast. The city of Belfast had always had higher sectarian tensions than Londonderry, with large numbers of working-class Protestants and Catholics living in close but uneasy proximity in places such as the Shankill and the Falls. A recurring history of violent clashes between such districts meant that outbreaks of trouble had an almost historical sanction.

The result was violence involving large numbers of Protestants and Catholics, centring on the Falls and in the Ardoyne–Crumlin Road area of north Belfast. Ancient guns came out of their attic hiding places, sending rifle and pistol shots ringing down the back-streets. Hundreds of houses were set on fire. Thousands of stones and other missiles were thrown, and barricades were erected across streets. The RUC staged baton charges, crowds surging back and forward between Protestant and Catholic areas.

Evidence given to the Scarman tribunal, the inquiry headed by a senior English judge to look into the disturbances, gives a flavour of the time. Describing the scene in Ardoyne its report said:

> The street lights in Hooker Street had been deliberately extinguished during earlier disturbances and the street was plunged in darkness, relieved only by fires burning in houses and other adjacent premises. In the Crumlin road and the side streets were to be found, and stumbled over, all the clutter of urban rioting – barricades, debris, flame, and liquid petrol. Normal traffic movement had stopped: the noise of hostile, jeering crowds, the crackle and explosions of burning buildings, and the shattering of glass had enveloped the area. But, save where the fighting was in progress, the streets were empty.

Amid all the chaos and destruction eight people lay dead, four of them killed by the RUC and another by B Specials. The police force, which was then only 3,000-strong, had reached its limits and with its men exhausted and in many cases injured Chichester-Clark asked London to send in troops to restore order. He did so with the greatest reluctance, since Wilson and Callaghan had already made it clear that they did not wish to deploy the military. They had also made it clear that if troops did go in, the political balance between Belfast and London would change fundamentally, since they would not place the army under Stormont control. When the first troops marched nervously on to the streets of Londonderry and Belfast, therefore, they did so with many political strings attached.

Soldiers on the streets

Callaghan was travelling in an RAF plane when the formal request for troops came through. He recorded in his memoirs that he was given a message on a signal pad: 'It tersely informed us that an official request for the use of troops had been made. I immediately scribbled "permission granted" on the pad and handed it back to the navigator. A few minutes later troops began to relieve the police in the Bogside amid loud jubilation from the inhabitants.' The arrival of the soldiers was welcomed by Catholics and brought a temporary respite from the violence, but as the smoke cleared the extent of the damage became all too clear. In addition to the eight deaths at least 750 people were injured, 150 of them having suffered gunshot wounds. 180 homes and other buildings were demolished, and 90 required major repair. Compensation was estimated to cost at least £2.25 million.

Around 1,800 families had fled their homes in the disturbances: the sight of their pathetic belongings being heaped on to lorries provided one of the abiding images of the troubles. Belfast had a long history of sectarian clashes; now it was permanently and phys- ically scarred by ugly barricades across many of its mean streets. The original unofficial improvised barriers made of commandeered cars, corrugated iron and whatever else came to hand were replaced, as the years passed and violence continued, by larger and more sub- stantial permanent brick and metal structures erected by the author- ities. These 'peacelines' were to last into the twenty-first century.

The damage caused by the violence of August 1969 was not con- fined to the strictly physical. It deepened community divisions and increased bitterness, and it wrecked whatever relationship existed between a large proportion of the Catholic community and the RUC. Part of the Bogside became a 'no-go area', sealed off by bar- ricades which remained in position until 1972.

Some of those who had been killed by the RUC died in controversial circumstances. In one incident an eight-year-old boy was killed in his Falls Road bedroom when a bullet from a heavy machine gun fired from an RUC armoured car ripped through walls and hit him in the head. In addition to the four Catholics killed on and around 14 August, three other men died following other brushes with the police in July and August. There were many stories of B Specials and on occasion RUC officers acting in concert with loyalist rioters during battles with Catholics. These reports sealed the fate of the B Specials, who were to be disbanded within months, and represented another grievous blow to the credibility of the RUC.

The relationship between the Westminster and Stormont governments also changed, Wilson and Callaghan taking a much more hands-on approach and the latter immersing himself in policy details. London officials were stationed in Belfast to act as London's eyes and ears, to pass on instructions to Stormont and, in Callaghan's words, to 'put some stiffening into the administration'. The most senior official sent over to Belfast reported back to London on the Stormont cabinet: 'In my view they were not evil men bent on maintaining power at all costs. They were decent but bewildered men, out of their depth in the face of the magnitude of their problem. I was convinced that not only did they want to do the right thing; they also wanted to be told what was the right thing to do.'

Senior Belfast civil servant Ken Bloomfield wrote that Stormont became 'a client regime, under constant supervision both at ministerial and official levels'. Faulkner wrote in his memoirs that Callaghan became 'Big Brother', adding, 'I increasingly felt that he was pressurizing and bullying Chichester-Clark into taking hasty decisions'. Faulkner was to write scornfully of Callaghan's trips to Belfast as 'superficial circuses and messianic visits'. Unionists objected both to Callaghan's close involvement and to the fact that in their eyes he took the nationalist side. When he visited the Bogside he was given a hero's welcome by Catholics who felt his presence signified an end to Unionist rule.

He and Wilson pressed Unionists hard for more and more

movement on the reform front. Within a short time London had pushed through a reform package which included the end of the B Specials, an overhaul of policing and other measures. Less than two months after the mid-August violence the committee investigating policing, headed by Lord Hunt, recommended a thorough-going reform of the RUC, including its disarming, together with the abolition of the B Specials. A few months later an English policeman, Sir Arthur Young, was appointed head of the RUC with a brief to modernise the force.

Publication of the Hunt report was the occasion not just for political controversy but serious violence. Loyalists rioted on the Shankill Road in protest against the reforms, the irony being that when the Protestant guns came out they killed a member of the RUC. Constable Victor Arbuckle, the first member of the force to die in the troubles, was shot by loyalists protesting in defence of the RUC.

An important player arrived on the stage at this point in the form of the Irish Republic. Some in the south viewed the events of August 1969 as a valuable political opportunity, while others saw them as a grave danger to the stability of the southern state. When the explosion of violence took place the Taoiseach was Jack Lynch, a mild-mannered politician who had replaced Seán Lemass as leader of Fianna Fáil, the most republican-leaning of the southern parties. Lynch had met Terence O'Neill on several occasions but had not made a great priority of the Northern Ireland question. However, the violent upheaval and the first deaths posed the most fundamental of challenges to the south, which was suddenly confronted with the thorny unfinished business of partition. As one writer put it: 'The violence started and within a week set the ghosts of 50 years on the march.' A series of prominent northern nationalists streamed to Dublin asking for help. Many of them, including some leading political figures, asked for guns, arguing that force was the only way to prevent loyalists rampaging into the Falls and Ardoyne. The southern public had much sympathy with their northern co-religionists, though many would have drawn the line at sending them weaponry. Some of Lynch's ministers are believed to have favoured despatching not only guns but also Irish soldiers to the north.

Sending in troops would have been more of a token gesture than an actual invasion, since the Irish army was tiny in comparison to its British counterpart, with the capacity to hold perhaps a town or two for a very short time. Lynch opted for a less drastic line, though it was one which enraged Unionists. In a broadcast during the August 1969 crisis he declared: 'It is clear that the Irish government can no longer stand by and see innocent people injured and perhaps worse.' (This has gone down in popular folklore as the 'not stand idly by' speech, though Lynch did not use the adverb.) He also announced the setting up of field hospitals close to the border to treat injured northerners.

This hugely important intervention from a Taoiseach who could no longer remain inactive as the north exploded on his doorstep took Dublin policy further than it had ever gone before. But it also defined its limitations. There was support for northern nationalists but first and foremost the aim was to protect the southern state against becoming physically embroiled in the northern conflagration. Unionists condemned the broadcast, Faulkner accusing Lynch of 'pouring fuel on the northern flame in the hope that out of the chaos he would reap some benefits in terms of progress towards a united Ireland'. The broadcast caused Callaghan to wonder whether the field hospitals 'might conceivably be a blind for further troop movements'. Although Callaghan said in his memoirs that he did not really believe the south would invade, he added that officials discussed deploying British troops on the border, just in case.

Lynch made other moves. Some men from Londonderry were given arms training by Irish soldiers in Donegal, while at one point 500 rifles were moved up to the border. The government allocated £100,000 for 'the relief of distress', some of which would mysteriously vanish. Whether those in power in London, Belfast or Dublin liked it or not, and most did not, the violence of August 1969 brought the southern state into the northern political equation. In the years that followed, Dublin never again extricated itself from the Northern Ireland issue, though the south's private position was very different from its public position that Irish unity was the only solution. One of Harold Wilson's aides would later describe a lunch at which the British Labour leader floated a plan for a united Ireland: 'The fascinating moment at the Taoiseach's lunch came when Harold Wilson put forward the plan for turning the dream of unity into reality. I had thought they would jump for joy, but their reaction was more akin to falling through the floor.'

The northern violence also brought about hugely important changes within republicanism. Of the 1,800 families who fled their homes, the Catholic community had very much come off worst. 1,500 of those who moved were Catholic, which meant that more than 5 per cent of all Catholic households in Belfast were displaced. More than 80 per cent of the premises damaged were occupied by Catholics, and six of the eight people killed in mid-August were Catholics. Since one of the roles of the IRA was supposed to be the defence of such areas against incursions by the security forces or loyalists, much criticism was directed against the organisation for its evident ineffectiveness. The bitter phrase 'IRA – I ran away' is famously said to have appeared on a wall in the Falls Road area, reflecting the feelings of working-class nationalists in west and north Belfast that the IRA had failed them.

The first great hero of republicanism was Wolfe Tone, who was associated with the 1798 rebellion and the aspiration of bringing together Catholics and Protestants in the common name of Irishman. Although that was the high mythic theory of republicanism, the practical reality was that the majority of Catholics did not support the IRA, and looked to them only in times of high tension. In such times, and August 1969 was one of them, the IRA was supposed to protect areas such as the Falls and Ardoyne against attack. The death toll, the pattern of destruction of property and the high number of Catholic refugees provided the starkest testimony that the IRA had not been organised or armed when the crisis came. The consensus in the Catholic ghetto backstreets was that an effective defence force was needed, and so a new IRA came into being. This new group may have emerged to defend the ghettos, but it would before long develop into an aggressive killing machine.

By 1969 the IRA was guided by left-wing theory and essentially led from the south of Ireland. It was so strongly wedded to the theory of forging working-class unity between Protestants and Catholics that even the August 1969 spasm of sectarian violence was not enough to shift its leadership from this quixotic notion. It was against this background that the fateful split occurred, late in 1969, which brought into being the Official and Provisional wings of the IRA. Broadly speaking the Officials were Marxists while the Provisionals were republican traditionalists, many of whom had been unhappy for some time with the IRA's direction. (They took their name from the proclamation used in the 1916 rising, which referred to a provisional government for a new Republic. The Officials technically retained leadership of the organisation, but the Provisionals were quickly to become the more numerous.)

The split took place following a series of tense and angry meetings of both the IRA and Sinn Féin. As the Officials continued to edge towards conventional politics the Provisionals cut their links, establishing the Provisional IRA and Provisional Sinn Féin. They dismissed what they viewed as the fanciful and unrealistic notions of the Officials and instead prepared for battle. Within months their approach was being described as 'combined defence and retaliation'.

On the Protestant side too men were forming vigilante groups and defence organisations, some of which would in time mutate into fully fledged paramilitary groups. More deaths followed those of August 1969 as tensions remained at a high level. In September a Protestant vigilante was shot dead following a dispute with Catholic counterparts in Belfast; some weeks later a Londonderry Protestant was kicked to death by Catholics during a confrontation between rival groups. On the night of the Arbuckle killing two Shankill Road Protestants were killed by army bullets. One, who was hit by a ricochet, was said 'to have been wandering about to see what was going on that night'. Then a UVF member blew himself up while attempting to set off a bomb in the Republic. Next came the first IRA fatality of the troubles, killed in a car crash while on active service: with him in the car at the time was the future president of Sinn Féin, Gerry Adams. On the surface, calm had been restored by the arrival of troops, but in the backstreets both republicans and loyalists were readying themselves for future bouts of confrontation.

1970–71: *the violence increases*

The year 1970 was to see continuing deterioration rather than any new stability. Callaghan kept up the pressure to maintain momentum in the reform programme. Chichester-Clark complied, though always against a background of grumbling and dissatisfaction from Unionist hardliners. This dissension in the grassroots was evident when votes drained away from the main Unionist party to Ian Paisley, who in this year was elected first to Stormont and then to Westminster. On the streets the situation degenerated as one deadly milestone after another was passed. Republicans and loyalists exchanged shots while the army came more and more into conflict with republicans and large sections of working-class Catholics, particularly in Belfast.

In June three Protestant men were shot dead by the IRA in north Belfast during large-scale rioting following an Orange march. Gerry Adams later noted: 'In this instance the IRA were ready and waiting and in the ensuing gun battle three loyalists were killed.' On the same day two more Protestants and a Catholic man died during clashes in and around the grounds of a Catholic church, St Matthew's, on the edge of the small Catholic enclave of Short Strand in east Belfast. A senior Belfast IRA leader of the time, Billy McKee, who was seriously injured in the St Matthew's church clashes, entered republican folklore by reputedly holding off Protestant gunmen almost single-handed and preventing a loyalist invasion of the Short Strand. His action did much to restore the ghetto credibility of the IRA as defenders of Catholic districts.

In early July came the Falls Road curfew, which can be seen as a final poisoning of the initially good relationship between Catholics and British troops. Following a confrontation between soldiers and locals, a large area of the Lower Falls district was sealed off by the army for several days while soldiers were sent in to conduct rigorous house-to-house searches. The exercise entailed ordering perhaps 20,000 people not to leave their homes. The searches uncovered more than one hundred weapons but in the process considerable damage was done to hundreds of households as soldiers prised up floorboards and ransacked rooms. In addition to such personal indignities there were four deaths, all caused by the army: three men were shot dead by troops while a fourth was crushed by a military vehicle. None of those killed had any IRA or other extreme connections. The sense that the army was being deployed against the general Catholic population was compounded when troops brought in two Unionist ministers to tour the area in armoured cars.

A senior civil servant recalled: 'It is hard to remember any other incident that so clearly began the politicisation and alienation of a community.' A moderate local councillor wrote: 'Overnight the population turned from neutral or even sympathetic support for the military to outright hatred of everything related to the security forces. I witnessed voters and workers turn against us to join the Provisionals. Even some of our most dedicated workers and supporters turned against us.'

Later in July came another violent landmark when the army shot dead a Catholic teenager in disputed circumstances during a riot in north Belfast. The army claim that he was a petrol-bomber was denied by local people. The tougher military line coincided with a change of government at Westminster. Labour lost the general election in June, with Wilson and Callaghan replaced by Conservative leader Edward Heath as prime minister and Reginald Maudling as Home Secretary.

Maudling, who had a reputation for being bright but lazy,

provided a marked contrast to Callaghan, who had been a direct and powerful presence, pushing hard for reforms. Maudling was both less forceful and less absorbed by the conflict than Callaghan had been. He also assumed responsibility at a less promising time, at a point when violence, though by no means reaching the heights it would later touch, had become a background constant. A local civil servant later wrote: 'What you got from Maudling was the impression of a massive intelligence, only partly in gear, which moved sideways towards the problem, like a crab, and then scuttled back into its hole without actually coming to grips with it.'

The two quotations with which Maudling will forever be associated both speak to a Tory sense of pessimism and lack of firm ideas. First he created a political storm when he spoke of the concept of 'an acceptable level of violence', which was taken as a fatalistic acknowledgement that violence might never come to an end. And, second, he is said to have said to a stewardess, while flying back to London after a fruitless round of meetings in Belfast, 'What a bloody awful country. For God's sake bring me a large Scotch.' (Some versions render this as a gin and tonic, but the spirit remains the same.)

With a less forceful sense of direction coming from the government, some of the initiative seeped across to the army who, with the enthusiastic backing of the Chichester-Clark administration, employed more aggressive tactics such as the curfew. But the tougher line did nothing to halt the general deterioration, and in August the first two RUC officers to be killed by the IRA died in south Armagh.

Politically Chichester-Clark found himself caught in the same permanently uncomfortable position as had O'Neill. On the one hand London continued to press for more and more political change; on the other Unionism, as Paisley's electoral successes showed, was becoming more hardline. And all this took place against a difficult background of continuing violence. Chichester-Clark's reforms included the introduction of one man – one vote and important changes in policing and housing. The Unionist grass-

roots were either unenthusiastic or downright hostile to this programme, but most of all they demanded tougher security. Since
Unionists believed in a military solution, the demands were to 'Stop
the army fighting with one hand behind its back', and to 'Go in
there after them', meaning that the army should pursue the IRA
into republican areas. Internment without trial, sealing the border,
and flooding republican areas with troops were among the popular
Unionist solutions. Chichester-Clark tried in vain to persuade the
grassroots that the army should be subject to political restrictions,
saying later, 'They were making it very difficult for me, at meeting
after meeting. They could not grasp the fact that the army could
not go in with enormous force.'

He also tried with equal lack of success to persuade the grassroots, as O'Neill had before him, that final authority rested with
Westminster rather than Stormont. At one party gathering he
opposed the motion 'That we will be masters in our own house',
telling delegates that soon he would be in London seeking more
money. He posed the question: 'Am I to go to London and say, "We
want all this support and oh, by the way, my party ask you to keep
your noses out of our business"?' He warned that unless the Unionist
party could deliver 'reasonable policies of fairness and justice for
everyone' then it might face direct rule from London. But he had
neither the skills nor the opportunity to balance the competing
forces or to seize the political initiative; the general feeling during
his premiership was that he was out of his depth.

Important developments took place within nationalism, north
and south, in the second half of 1970. The civil rights movement
faded in importance, to be superseded by a new grouping, the Social
Democratic and Labour party (SDLP), as the principal voice of
nationalism in the north. The party consisted principally of anti-
Unionist Stormont MPs, some from the labour tradition and some
who had come to prominence in the civil rights movement. With
Gerry Fitt as leader and John Hume as its chief strategist, the party
would remain the largest northern nationalist grouping for most of
the troubles.

In the south, meanwhile, politically sensational events took place. Following reports of an illegal attempt to import arms for the north, Taoiseach Jack Lynch had sacked two of his most senior ministers, Neil Blaney and the highly ambitious Charles Haughey. A third minister resigned in protest. Soon afterwards Haughey and Blaney were charged with conspiring to import arms and ammunition into Ireland. The case against Blaney was dropped at an early stage but Haughey went on trial, together with an Irish army intelligence officer, a senior republican from Belfast, and a Belgian businessman. All were acquitted by a Dublin jury following a trial in which Haughey and another cabinet minister flatly contradicted each other's testimony. When the verdicts came in, Haughey directly challenged Lynch, saying those responsible 'for this debacle should do the honourable thing'. Lynch, however, pointedly observed that he still believed there had been an attempt to bring in guns, and faced Haughey down. The episode remains a mysterious one, with few believing that the whole truth emerged. It did nothing to lessen Unionist suspicions of southern politicians, especially Haughey, who was later to become Taoiseach.

In Belfast the sense of crisis grew with an escalation of violence in early 1971. In February the deaths took place, on the same night in north Belfast, of the first soldier to be shot by the IRA, and the first IRA member to be shot by the army. Three days later an IRA bomb placed on a County Tyrone mountain for members of the security forces instead killed five civilians on their way to service a BBC transmitter. Later in the same month two policemen were shot dead, again in north Belfast.

In March came an incident which was regarded as a new low point. Three Scottish soldiers who had been drinking off-duty in a Belfast bar were lured to a lonely road on the outskirts of the city and shot dead by the IRA. The huge impact of their killings is still remembered by many as one of the key points in Northern Ireland's descent into full-scale violence. Three soldiers had already died in the troubles, but the Scottish soldiers were the first to be killed off-duty; two of them were brothers who were aged only seventeen and eighteen. A newspaper editorial commented, 'After all the horrors of recent weeks and months, Ulster people have almost lost the capacity for feeling shock. But the ruthless murder of three defenceless young soldiers has cut to the quick. These were cold-blooded executions for purely political reasons.'

As their funerals took place in Scotland, an estimated 30,000 people attended rallies in Belfast and elsewhere. Four thousand shipyard workers marched in Belfast demanding internment. A few days later Chichester-Clark flew to London to ask Heath for tougher security measures. When Heath offered only extra troops, Chichester-Clark returned to Belfast and resigned, stepping down from office with an almost visible sense of relief.

Faulkner becomes prime minister

Chichester-Clark was succeeded as Stormont prime minister by Brian Faulkner, who was easily the most talented Unionist politician of the time. Faulkner won the leadership election comfortably, defeating William Craig by twenty-six votes to four. It was widely said, correctly as it turned out, that he was probably Unionism's last chance to save the Stormont system. After O'Neill and Chichester-Clark, both of whom had the whiff of being amateurs in politics, Faulkner looked every inch the professional politician. He brought to the post of prime minister his obvious ability, both as an administrator and as a communicator and in both fields he was probably the finest Unionism had ever produced. He was credited with putting down the IRA's 1950s campaign, principally through the use of internment, and in the 1960s had been conspicuously successful in attracting new industry from abroad.

An ambitious man, Faulkner thought he should have had the premiership instead of O'Neill in 1963. He believed it was his again in 1969, only to be pipped by one vote by Chichester-Clark. Within the Unionist party he had moved tactically over the years from his early days as a stalwart traditionalist to a less distinct standpoint in the O'Neill years. But although his abilities were too obvious to be denied, he had also acquired a reputation for shiftiness and lack of loyalty. O'Neill and many others believed that during his premiership Faulkner had repeatedly tried to undermine him. During one leadership rumble against O'Neill, Faulkner had studiously and skilfully equivocated, causing one political journalist to accuse him of 'speaking in conundrums' and to comment: 'His attempts to keep out of trouble become more and more devious and unacceptable to those who above all respect a politician who talks straight from the shoulder.' This was the politician who now attempted to master the balancing act that had defeated both O'Neill and Chichester-Clark. London had a healthy respect for his talents and hoped he might succeed where his predecessors had failed, thus avoiding a resort to direct rule from Westminster.

From the start Faulkner attempted to strike a balance which would reassure both the Unionist grassroots and the British government through a combination of security and political measures. He first constructed a government which encompassed both wings of the Unionist party, the liberal and the hardline, as well as the first-ever non-Unionist cabinet minister in the form of an NILP politician. While it was true that the NILP man was neither a Catholic nor a nationalist and that the appointment was for only six months, this was nonetheless seen as an imaginative step.

Faulkner made his big political move in June 1971 by offering a shake-up of Stormont. Under his proposals three new committees would be introduced to review policy and advise on legislation, with opposition members chairing two of them. At first sight these appeared to be influential posts, and the SDLP gave the idea an initial welcome and entered talks on the proposals. Within weeks, however, politics was overtaken by events on the streets. To balance his political concessions, Faulkner had successfully pressed London for a tougher army approach, himself announcing in Stormont: 'Any soldier seeing any person with a weapon or acting suspiciously may, depending on the circumstances, fire to warn or with effect without waiting for orders.'

One result of this was seen in July when soldiers shot dead two Catholics, a man and a teenager, during disturbances in Londonderry. The authorities said the man had a gun and the teenager had a bomb, while local people insisted both were unarmed. The incident disrupted the political talks as the SDLP warned it would withdraw from Stormont unless an independent inquiry was established to investigate the deaths. When no inquiry was set up, the SDLP walked out of Stormont never to return, and Faulkner's committee offer became academic.

Internment

Faulkner was intent on balancing his Stormont committees offer with a radical security initiative in the form of internment without trial. Having helped build his own reputation with the use of internment in the 1950s, he saw it as a panacea which would halt the violence and in time provide a more peaceful atmosphere in which political progress would be easier. Others saw it as a measure of last resort and even desperation. Internment meant stepping outside the rule of law and abandoning legal procedures in favour of simply rounding up suspects and putting them behind bars without benefit of trial. It was bound to attract strong condemnation from nationalist and human rights bodies both at home and internationally.

The feeling which prevailed in both the Unionist and British governments was simply that the steady deterioration could not be allowed to continue. Maudling wrote later of internment: 'No one could be certain what would be the consequences, yet the question was simply this: what other measures could be taken?' He added, 'I think if we hadn't introduced internment there was the danger of the Protestant backlash. What we were always worried about was if people did not think the British government were doing all they could to deal with violence, they might take the law into their own hands.' As this indicates, the government had an eye not just to the rising tide of IRA activity but also to the possibility of an eruption of loyalist violence. The steadily rising graph of shootings and bombings, as well as the street rioting in republican districts, contributed to the sense that something had to be done.

It was for Faulkner something close to a last throw of the dice. Success would have meant he might go down in history as the man who ended the troubles and led Northern Ireland into a bright new future. And London fervently hoped he could pull it off, for he looked like the last best chance to stave off direct rule. A Northern Ireland official later wrote that all involved knew how high the stakes were, with London making it clear that if internment failed 'very fundamental questions could arise'.

So it was that in the early hours of 9 August 1971 a large-scale arrest operation, codenamed Operation Demetrius, was launched, with thousands of troops and police despatched to round up the IRA. The first swoops resulted in around 340 arrests, but almost immediately it became clear that little was going according to plan. It quickly emerged that the RUC Special Branch had not kept pace with the rapidly expanding Provisional IRA and that its files were out of date and inaccurate. In any event many IRA men, suspecting that internment was on the way, had already gone on the run. The troops who were sent to make the arrests often found themselves at the wrong house, or finding not an IRA suspect but his father, or brother. Many of these were nonetheless arrested and taken in for 'screening'. Allegations that soldiers had in the process often used brutal methods were denied by the authorities but often substantiated by later inquiries and court proceedings. Many of those held were released within hours or days, often traumatised, radicalised and infuriated by the experience. It later emerged that more than a dozen suspects had been given special experimental interrogation treatment. They were subjected to sensory deprivation techniques which included the denial of sleep and food and being forced to stand spreadeagled against a wall for long periods. Taped electronic 'white noise' sounds were continuously played to complete the disorientation. Years later the European Court of Human Rights characterised this episode as 'inhuman and degrading' treatment.

Within two days more than a hundred of those detained were released, a pattern which was to be repeated in the months that followed: in the first six months of internment over 2,400 people were arrested, and most of them were freed after a short time in custody. The fact that this was clearly a highly inefficient operation was demonstrated both by the number of early releases and, most of all, by an eruption of violence on the streets. In the immediate aftermath of the first arrests widespread violence broke out in many areas, with major gun battles between the army and the IRA sometimes lasting for hours.

One author gave a flavour of the disruption in Belfast:

The city was in turmoil, with confusion, distress and fear on all sides. Local people were erecting improvised barricades to seal off entry to Catholic areas, which were becoming increasingly isolated and cut off. Public transport had broken down, and there was increasingly a breakdown in services. There was ominous rattling of hundreds of bin-lids as communities sent out a call to arms and for defenders to man the ramparts. Buses were being hijacked on all sides, cars were dragged from burned-out showrooms, builders' skips, rubble, anything was being used to make barriers. Milk vans were being commandeered and the bottles used to make petrol bombs, pavements were being ripped up for missiles and to build barricades. Smoke, fire, disorder, noise and impending disaster were everywhere.

A great deal of property was destroyed, while there was large-scale evacuation and flight by families. According to one official estimate at least 2,000 and possibly more than 2,500 families moved home around August 1971. Far from halting the violence, internment increased it tremendously. In 1971, before 9 August 31 people were killed; in the rest of August 35 died. Between 9 August and the end of the year around 150 people were killed. The dead included soldiers, members of the IRA and many civilians.

For Faulkner and for the rest of society this was not deliverance but something close to disaster, the opening of a new phase with a

much higher level of violence. Confronted with this sharp deterioration Faulkner and Heath decided to press on in the hope of an
eventual breakthrough against the IRA; but it was a breakthrough
that never came. As the deaths continued Faulkner defiantly
defended his policy, proclaiming: 'You can no more deal with such
deep rooted terror without toughness and determination than you
can excise a deep seated tumour without cutting the flesh. It is not
a pleasant business. Sometimes innocent people will suffer.' He
argued that internment was working: 'The army is fighting back,
not only fighting back but taking the offensive, and now, loud and
clear, we hear the squeal of the increasingly cornered rat.'

The use of internment was to continue for another four years,
during which time it attracted much condemnation of Britain and
never looked like defeating the IRA. It came to be almost universally
regarded as a misjudgement of historic proportions which inflicted
tremendous damage both politically and in terms of fatalities. It
was also seen by nationalists as a cynical weapon, since they regarded
Faulkner's primary motive not as a concern to reduce violence but
as the partisan purpose of propping up his government and preserving Stormont. The internment process was an openly political one,
Faulkner personally signing each individual internment order.

The ineptitude of the RUC Special Branch was compounded by
the casual brutality used by troops during and after the arrest operations, often on people who were not members of the IRA. Internees
were mostly held in poor conditions, some of them on an ageing
ship in Belfast Lough and later at Long Kesh near Belfast. This was
a former airfield whose rusty Nissen huts and barbed wire, smacking as they did of a World War Two prison camp, constituted
another long-running public relations setback for the authorities.

Faulkner was heavily criticised for the fact that not a single loyalist had been detained, leading to charges of blatant partiality.
Faulkner recorded that Maudling had said to him, 'Lift some
Protestants if you can', a remark which if accurately reported
reveals much cynicism but also some grasp of public relations considerations. The failure to use internment against loyalists seemed

to many to confirm that it was as much a political device as a security measure. Sir John Peck, then British ambassador to Dublin, wrote later: 'Internment attacked the Catholic community as a whole. What was worse, it was directed solely against the Catholics, although there were many Protestants who provided just as strong grounds for internment.'

The mood across the Catholic and nationalist community was thus one of communal outrage against a measure they viewed as the essence of injustice. In physical terms many Catholic working-class areas of Belfast were for months afterwards convulsed by gun battles and killings on the streets, while thousands of homes were searched by the army. In 1971 more than 170 people were killed; a further 2,600 were injured and 17,000 homes were searched. Unsurprisingly, there was massive alienation from authority. To the outside world internment might be seen as a response to IRA violence, but many Catholics in areas such as west Belfast regarded IRA activity as a response to violence from the authorities.

The upsurge in IRA violence demonstrated the underlying support the organisation could command among working-class Catholics. The Stormont and British rhetoric of the time commonly spoke of a handful of men of violence holding communities to ransom. The prevailing Unionist theory was that there was a military solution to the troubles and that the IRA could be isolated and defeated almost without reference to the wider political picture: hence Faulkner's image of 'excising a deep seated tumour'.

The fact that the IRA was able to escalate its violence in the wake of internment showed that in its strongholds it had a substantial and indeed rapidly expanding reservoir from which to draw recruits and other support. The official rhetoric had it that the time had come for ordinary Catholics to choose between terrorists and the men of peace, the security forces. The flaw in this projection was that, at ghetto street level, the security forces looked not so much like men of peace as agents of a state intent on attacking their neighbourhoods. The government had imperfect control over the squaddies on the street, who could often look on all Catholics as the enemy.

There were innumerable cases of Catholic youths being kicked and punched, and sometimes arrested and ill-treated for no good reason; at the time these were airily dismissed as republican propaganda. The many thousands of house searches, often carried out as routine rather than as a result of information, similarly generated much bitterness. The authorities said they were a military necessity but the inevitable disruption and indignities generated great resentment among those inconvenienced, many of whom had no republican connections.

Another source of grievance was the considerable number of Catholics who died at the hands of troops. This is a largely disregarded phenomenon but it was especially evident in the second half of 1971. Of the 150 people who died in that period, almost half were Catholic civilians; and of these around 29 were killed by soldiers. In some cases the army acknowledged that its men were at fault and apologised for causing deaths. In other cases, including the deaths of teenagers as young as thirteen who were killed during riots, the army denied that disproportionate force had been used.

But in many other instances they said that men and youths they had shot dead had been armed when soldiers had shot them. In some cases this may have been true, but in most it was not. The non-involvement of many of those killed became evident later, at inquests or when the authorities quietly paid out substantial compensation to relatives of the dead. At the time, however, the army insisted that many of those shot were gunmen. Local claims that this was untrue were generally dismissed, the outside world tending to accept the word of officialdom rather than that of Falls Road residents. But locals had a fair idea of who was and who was not a gunman among their neighbours, and in some districts the feeling was universal that the army had not only shot without justification but had then denigrated those killed as gunmen when they were not. This sense was captured by John Hume in a case when a soldier shot dead in Londonderry a man said to be aiming a rifle at an army post. Saying that the army's statement was 'without the slightest shred of truth', Hume asked:

Can the army not in this case at least tell the full truth about what happened? He was not armed, nor had he any association with any sort of political body in this city. He was walking in the street with some friends at the time. He was shot down by an army bullet. Army statements about incidents in Derry have lost all credibility among people because they have been proved incorrect so often.

All of this meant that many non-republicans and their families became radicalised and often became republicans. But in the wake of internment Catholic alienation was almost complete, stretching well beyond republican districts. The SDLP, which had already withdrawn from Stormont over the two Londonderry killings, announced that it would not return until internment was ended. The party gave its support to a rent and rates strike which was so widely supported that the authorities estimated that 20 per cent of the entire population had joined it. In some areas more than 90 per cent of tenants were involved. Many Catholics withdrew from public life, while most nationalist representatives ceased to attend local councils. Some 200 Catholic members left the Ulster Defence Regiment (UDR), the force which had replaced the B Specials in 1970.

Anglo-Irish relations took a severe battering. Jack Lynch had cautioned strongly against internment, as Sir John Peck recorded in his memoirs. The Taoiseach had delivered to him, he wrote, 'the most serious and solemn warning that the consequences in the north would be catastrophic: for every man put behind the wire a hundred would volunteer'. Heath and Lynch took part in an extraordinarily angry public exchange of messages in the days after internment, momentarily flinging diplomatic convention to the wind. Lynch said that internment and military solutions had failed and that he supported 'the policy of passive resistance now being pursued by the non-Unionist population'. Heath in reply said his message was 'unjustifiable in its contents and unacceptable in its attempt to interfere in the affairs of the United Kingdom'. There was much more in this vein.

Within a few weeks, the two premiers had calmed down and Lynch flew to London to meet Heath. Personal contacts did not remove the difficulties, however, since Heath continued to put much store in a security solution while Lynch held that the problem was at root political. There was little or no personal affinity between them, Peck recording dryly that 'it would be an abuse of the English language to describe the talks as negotiations'. The ambassador noted in his memoirs: 'For the first half of my term of duty in Dublin I thought it very important that the prime minister and the Taoiseach should get together. For the second half I rather hoped that they could be kept apart. It was not quite a dialogue of the deaf but I sometimes felt that a pair of powerful hearing aids would come in handy.'

There were many matters on which the two premiers were never to agree, in particular in the security field, with Lynch saying internment should be ended and Heath retorting that the Irish government should take much stronger action against the IRA south of the border. Many even worse Anglo-Irish spats lay ahead, yet in one area, the shape of future government in Northern Ireland, London and Dublin were gradually converging.

Although Faulkner, like Chichester-Clark before him, brought a raft of incremental reforms into effect, the policy of both London and Dublin was evolving. Crucially, they both moved away from the idea that a solution lay in the model of a Unionist government delivering a stream of concessions to nationalists. Both Chichester-Clark and Faulkner had produced reform after reform, to disapproving mutterings from the Protestant grassroots; but now the idea took hold that what was needed was not reforms but participation.

London and Dublin found common ground in the concept that Catholics had to be brought into government. They would never wholly identify with the state, the theory ran, if they remained in perpetual opposition, and so had to become part of the fabric of administration. This idea gained currency, giving rise to the emergence of terms such as 'community government'. The initials 'PAG' made an appearance, signifying what was defined as a 'permanent, active and guaranteed role for the majority and minority alike'.

Dublin wanted the abolition of Stormont and remained formally committed to the traditional goal of Irish unity. But Lynch was also thinking in terms of nationalist involvement in government, through SDLP participation in a new administration and through new north–south links. Heath did not want to abolish Stormont but he too was thinking of a powersharing arrangement, as he later wrote: 'In order to give Catholics a real stake in society, it was not enough for them to be protected from discrimination. They also had to be given a positive role in governing the country in which they lived. I also believed that the Republic of Ireland had to be brought into the relationship once more.'

In September Heath took pride in staging a meeting involving himself, Lynch and Faulkner, which he described as one of the historic events of his premiership. Faulkner attracted criticism from hardliners for agreeing to take part in the meeting but felt he could not turn down Heath's invitation. Internment had delivered not peace but increased violence and in doing so had comprehensively wiped out the possibility of any new agreement on Faulkner's terms. The SDLP was adamant it would not return to Stormont while internment lasted. From Faulkner's point of view, however, his fate depended on persisting with internment until it began to produce positive results. Heath was impatiently casting around for new ideas, and was clearly thinking in terms of involving Dublin, an idea bound to stir strong Unionist opposition.

Even worse, from the point of view of Faulkner and other Unionists, was the fact that Harold Wilson, as leader of the opposition, was attempting to put a united Ireland on the British political agenda. In November he presented in the Commons a convoluted scheme which envisaged Irish unity in fifteen years, with the south rejoining the Commonwealth. This was to come to nothing, but it was unsettling to Unionists, showing as it did that major British political figures were beginning to think the previously unthinkable. In response Faulkner persisted with his ideas for new Stormont committees chaired by nationalist politicians, and took the unprec-edented step of appointing to his cabinet G. B. Newe, a respected Catholic community worker who was active in public life but attached to no political party. He thus became the first ever Catholic Stormont minister. Nationalists criticised Newe for swimming against the abstentionist nationalist tide, denouncing the appoint-ment as gimmickry.

In the wake of internment the problem had become one of battling simply to keep the administration functioning. The serious-ness of the situation was evident in a meeting between Heath and Faulkner in October 1971, the minutes of which were released in 2000 in advance of the normal thirty-year rule as part of documen-tation for the Bloody Sunday inquiry. The meeting began with Heath saying that 'the situation was now grave socially, economic-ally and politically, and the British public was losing patience'. Faulkner agreed, pointing out that a high-level British official had concluded that the economic situation was 'desperate'. He also revealed that senior Belfast civil servants had, 'in a review of the economic and social position, indicated that a breakdown in gov-ernment might occur in a matter of weeks'. Such apocalyptic assess-ments give an indication of the overall sense of rapid deterioration. The option of closing down Stormont might have had more attrac-tion at this point had London not been receiving the warnings from the army about the possible consequences of doing so. A Ministry of Defence document, released during the Bloody Sunday inquiry, revealed that the army had advised 'that in the event of direct rule the cooperation to be expected from the civil service, the public utility services etc would be less than has hitherto been assumed in London'. The memo added:

> This renders the direct rule option even less palatable than we have always suggested. Moreover it is at least possible that a situation in which the army was either fighting both sides in the middle of a civil war or (with whatever help was available from GB police, prison service etc) having virtually to run Northern Ireland, would, quite

apart from its military implications, be very difficult to sustain in British political terms.

December brought an incident with one of the highest civilian death tolls in the troubles: a small Catholic bar in north Belfast, McGurk's, was blown up with the loss of fifteen lives. A powerful explosion caused the old building to collapse, reducing it to smouldering rubble. Local people, members of the security forces and emergency crews pulled away the debris with their bare hands.

The attack was the work of the UVF which, together with the UDA, was growing in strength in areas such as the Shankill as loyalists became more and more anxious about the army's evident inability to defeat or even contain the IRA. UVF involvement was confirmed years later when a member of the organisation confessed and was jailed for life. At the time, however, both Stormont government and army sources flatly denied that loyalists were responsible, claiming that both forensic and intelligence evidence showed that the IRA was to blame. They alleged the bombing was not an attack on the pub but the premature explosion of a device which was being stored inside it. These false claims, disputed at the time by the IRA and nationalist representatives, fuelled nationalist alienation from the authorities, who had of course argued that no loyalists were dangerous enough to be interned. Much more loyalist violence lay ahead.

4.

The end of Stormont
1972–73

1972: the most violent year

The worst year of the troubles was 1972, its death toll of almost five hundred far exceeding that of any other year. Fourteen of those deaths occurred in Londonderry on 30 January, in what was to be remembered as one of the key events of the troubles, Bloody Sunday. What happened on that day was to drive even more men and youths into paramilitary groups. Thirteen people were killed and another thirteen were injured, one fatally, when soldiers of the Parachute Regiment and other units opened fire following a large illegal civil rights march in Londonderry city.

Both the Provisional and Official IRA denied that any of their units were involved. Soldiers claimed they came under intensive attack from gunmen and from nailbombers but local residents disputed their account, saying they had opened fire without justification. No soldiers were either killed or injured by gunfire or nailbombs, and no weapons were recovered by the army.

Catholic priest Father Edward Daly, who later became Bishop of Derry and will always be associated with Bloody Sunday, witnessed the death of a seventeen-year-old youth as both ran away from soldiers. He said he saw the youth laughing at the sight of a priest running: 'The next thing he suddenly gasped and threw his hands up in the air and fell on his face. He asked me: "Am I going to die?" and I said no, but I administered the last rites. I can remember him holding my hand and squeezing it. We all wept. We got him to the top of the street. I knelt beside him and told him, "Look son, we've got to get you out", but he was dead. He was very youthful looking, just in his seventeenth year but he only looked about twelve.' The shootings produced one of the lasting images of the troubles in photographs and television film of Father Daly waving a white handkerchief while helping carry a fatally wounded youth out of the killing zone.

Father Daly said later: 'A lot of the younger people in Derry who may have been more pacifist became quite militant as a result of it. People who were there on that day and who saw what happened were absolutely enraged by it and just wanted to seek some kind of revenge for it. In later years many young people I visited in prison told me quite explicitly that they would never have become involved in the IRA but for what they witnessed, and heard of happening, on Bloody Sunday.' In his memoirs Gerry Adams wrote: 'Money, guns and recruits flooded into the IRA.'

The incident had enormous ramifications, taking a place in Irish history as a formative moment which not only claimed fourteen lives but also hardened attitudes, increased paramilitary recruitment, helped generate more violence, and convulsed Anglo-Irish relations. In 1998 Tony Blair, as prime minister, announced the establishment of a full-scale judicial inquiry.

The effect at the time was a dramatic increase in nationalist alienation. In the aftermath of the shootings Irish nationalists, north and south, erupted in shock, the Irish government recalling its ambassador from London. Bernadette Devlin rushed across the floor of the Commons and scratched Maudling's face. Most of those Catholics who had not yet left public life now did so, while in the Republic a day of national mourning was held on the day of the funerals. After some days of protests a large crowd cheered as the British embassy in Dublin was set alight and destroyed. In his memoirs, ambassador Sir John Peck wrote:

Bloody Sunday had unleashed a wave of fury and exasperation the like of which I had never encountered in my life, in Egypt or Cyprus or anywhere else. Hatred of the British was intense. Someone had summed it up: 'We are all IRA now.' The already shaky position of Jack Lynch, the Irish Taoiseach, was now extremely precarious, and the threat posed by the IRA to democratic institutions in the Republic would now be far more serious.

More violence followed three weeks later when the Official IRA staged a revenge attack on the Parachute Regiment's headquarters in Aldershot. Their attempt to kill paratroopers instead killed a Catholic chaplain, a gardener and five women members of the domestic staff. A fresh wave of nationalist indignation followed publication of the report into Bloody Sunday carried out by the Lord Chief Justice, Lord Widgery. His conclusion that the firing of some paratroopers had 'bordered on the reckless' brought a deluge of criticism and allegations that it was a 'whitewash' and a cover-up rather than an honest attempt to find out how fourteen people came to be shot dead by soldiers.

Early March brought a particularly shocking IRA attack when a bomb went off in a popular Belfast city centre bar, the Abercorn, on a busy Saturday afternoon. Two young women were killed and seventy others were injured. Some of the horror was conveyed in a newspaper report: 'Two sisters have both been seriously maimed. One, who planned to marry, has lost both legs, an arm and an eye. Her sister has lost both legs. Last night their mother was under sedation. A male victim lost two legs, and a female lost one leg and one arm. Another female lost one limb and three of the injured have lost eyes.' The Royal Victoria Hospital used a disaster plan for the first time. A senior doctor recalled, 'We were seeing injuries we had never seen before. The victims were black from the dirt and dust that was thrown up by the bombing. There was also a powerful smell of burning. The high proportion of young people struck everybody.'

Two weeks later came another horrendous incident when seven people were killed by a 200lb IRA car bomb left in Donegall Street, close to Belfast city centre, following contradictory telephoned warnings. The explosion injured 150 people, including many who were fleeing from a bomb scare in an adjoining street. The *Belfast Telegraph* reported:

> Donegall Street looked like a battlefield. When the smoke and dust from the blast cleared, injured people were seen lying in pools of blood on the roadway. Some of the casualties lay in agony with glass splinters embedded in their wounds. A body was blown to pieces by the force of the explosion, which rocked the entire city centre. An old man was comforted on the footpath. As he lay barely conscious, he was unaware that half his leg had been blown off in the explosion.

The final weeks of Stormont

All of this increased the sense of crisis and galvanised the British government. Heath noted in his memoirs: 'The atmosphere had now grown more poisoned than ever and I feared that we might, for the first time, be on the threshold of complete anarchy.' He, Maudling and other ministers had already considered a wide range of options, some of which would have greatly alarmed Unionists had they known of them. One idea was for a repartition which would divide Northern Ireland into Protestant and Catholic districts, with the latter being allowed to join the Republic. Another was to have Northern Ireland governed jointly by Britain and the Republic, its citizens having dual citizenship. Heath seems to have considered and rejected these options, though intriguingly the minutes of one meeting of ministers, released in the spring of 2000, mention the possibility of Irish unity. Recording the gist of ministerial discussions, this document said: 'If the object were to preserve the option of creating a united Ireland at some time in the future, it might be better to seek first for a political solution in which the minority were persuaded to participate in government.'

But many other ideas were in the air and when, five days after Bloody Sunday, Faulkner went to Downing Street he found, in his words, questions coming at him thick and fast. Discussion touched, among other things, on handing over some areas to the Republic; on a referendum on Northern Ireland's constitutional position; on what would happen if troops were removed from Catholic areas; on ways of involving Catholics in government, and on transferring control of security to London.

Faulkner urged Heath to persevere with internment, arguing that if violence could be ended then he 'would be in a strong position to urge magnanimity upon the majority'. He spoke against most of Heath's ideas, making clear his two main sticking points. The first was opposition to guaranteeing Catholics a place in government. He argued strongly against a new coalition involving Unionists and nationalists, saying it was unworkable and would result in 'a bedlam cabinet, a kind of fragmentation bomb virtually certain to fly apart at the first meeting'. He also refused to contemplate a Westminster takeover of security powers, saying this would 'reduce our govern-ment to a mere sham'.

Heath and his ministers were unconvinced by Faulkner and had lost confidence in the ability of the Stormont regime to restore order, though Faulkner did not appear to realise this. He wrote later that he had several times asked if direct rule was in prospect and was assured that it was not.

Within the Unionist community, however, many did not believe that Stormont was secure or that the IRA was on the road to defeat. This was put most forcibly by William Craig, who had been roundly beaten by Faulkner for leadership of the Unionist party. He formed an organisation called the Ulster Vanguard movement, and, while remaining a member of the Unionist party, used Vanguard as his own power base, designing it as an umbrella group to enlist as many supporters as possible from the various loyalist groupings which were springing up in response to the mounting tension.

He associated with some loyalist paramilitary organisations such as the UDA. Advocating a semi-independent Northern Ireland he staged a series of Oswald Mosley-style 'monster rallies', arriving complete with motorcycle outriders to inspect thousands, and sometimes tens of thousands, of men drawn up in military-style formation. What Craig said at the rallies and elsewhere was even more alarming. In a series of what became known as the 'shoot-to-kill' speeches he openly threatened the use of force, declaring: 'We must build up dossiers on those men and women in this country who are a menace to this country because one of these days, if and when the politicians fail us, it may be our job to liquidate the enemy.'

Part of the message here was a warning to Britain not to bring down Stormont, but Heath was undeterred. When Faulkner received another summons to go to London on 22 March, it was for a meeting which would spell the end of Unionist government. He appears to have been totally surprised when Heath announced that he wanted to begin phasing out internment, to take over control of security, and to move towards powersharing with Catholics. Faulkner was to write: 'We were more puzzled than angry. We decided that Heath was bluffing.' Heath in turn was to write of Faulkner: 'Initially he seemed to think that we were bluffing.' But nine hours of argument failed to shake Heath, and when Faulkner returned to Belfast to talk it over with his cabinet they unanimously voted to resign. Heath had apparently expected this.

One of the few points of substance on which the memoirs of Heath and Faulkner differ is on the prospect of direct rule. Faulkner accused the British prime minister of misleading him, writing: 'The rug was pulled out from under my feet, and it came to me personally as a bitter blow. I was shaken and horrified and felt completely betrayed.' Heath by contrast wrote that he had specifically made it clear to Faulkner when he became Stormont prime minister 'that if significant progress was not made in the next year or so, we would have to introduce direct rule. He did not like the prospect and later claimed he had been duped by us. This is not so. He was aware, from the day he took office, that his premiership was Stormont's last chance.'

A two-day protest strike which was called by Craig and Vanguard brought Northern Ireland to a virtual standstill in late March with up to 200,000 workers downing tools, most motivated by indignation, some by intimidation. Industry, commerce and most public services ground to a halt as electricity production was cut to one-third of its usual level. Around 100,000 people made their way to Stormont for a rally at which Ulster flags outnumbered Union Jacks, a sign of Protestant anger with London. Faulkner and Craig both addressed the crowd, though those who thought this an indication of a new Unionist unity were to be proved wrong. Stormont adjourned for the last time at 4.15 p.m. on 28 March, ending an existence of just over half a century.

The ending of Stormont rule was an emotional and traumatic time for Protestants and Unionists, involving as it did the demise of the institution which they regarded as their chief bulwark against nationalists and republicans. Brian Faulkner had been prime minister for just a year, the sixth and last person to hold that office. His premiership had indeed been Stormont's last chance. The irony was that the man regarded as Unionism's most professional politician had in the space of a year made two major miscalculations. First he thought internment would significantly improve the security situation, and second he thought Heath would not abolish Stormont. He was not just wrong but spectacularly wrong in each case. He further overestimated the RUC and underestimated the IRA.

For his part, Edward Heath had travelled a considerable political distance in a short time. To begin with he regarded Northern Ireland as more of a security problem than a political problem, and was prepared to give Faulkner the chance to proceed with heavy emphasis on security. By March 1972 Heath still believed in strong security measures, but he had come to place much greater importance on political initiatives, which included the involvement of Dublin and moves towards powersharing. In the process he came to conclude that Stormont as then constituted was irreformable, that a cross-community government had to be fashioned and that, in his words, 'only direct rule could offer us the breathing-space necessary for building it'.

Stormont fell because, with Northern Ireland locked in serious crisis, Heath came to conclude that Faulkner could deliver neither security success nor political progress. Internment, as well as being disastrously counterproductive on the streets, had also destroyed all hope of early political advance. Faulkner had made it clear that he would not relinquish certain areas of Unionist power to London, especially responsibility for security, and would not agree to powersharing with nationalist parties. Although he had invited two non-Unionists into his cabinet, both were there at his personal invitation: he drew the line at having representatives of nationalist parties in it.

It is certainly true that violence increased greatly in August 1971, though it is also probably true that it would have gone up in any case, given that both the IRA and loyalist groups were becoming bigger and more organised, as the increase in IRA violence and the bombing of McGurk's bar testified. Nonetheless, three events taken together – the introduction of internment, Bloody Sunday and the fall of Stormont – served to trigger the worst violence ever seen in Northern Ireland. Faulkner portrayed Stormont's end as primarily the achievement of the IRA, declaring: 'Chief amongst those who have sought the emasculation and ultimately the downfall of Stormont have been the IRA terrorists themselves.' Heath also admitted that he was shaken by the violence, and that he feared complete anarchy.

It seems unlikely, however, that violence alone would have brought Stormont down. The pressure came not just from IRA violence, but from rejection of Stormont by the entire Catholic community. The writing may have been on the wall as early as the summer of 1971, for Heath was to write that the SDLP walkout had 'deprived Stormont of any remaining legitimacy'. The rent-and-rates strike, the withdrawal of many nationalists from public life, and the poor state of Anglo-Irish relations were all signs of complete and apparently irreversible nationalist alienation from the old Stormont system. IRA bombs were the most dramatic manifestation of this, but the sense was strong that the Catholic community, whose expectations had been raised so much, had rejected the old system once and for all. And Heath, having concluded that Stormont was part of the problem rather than part of the solution, thus consigned it to history.

The 1972 figure of almost 500 killings stands as a vivid illustration of the lethal depths to which the troubles descended. There were almost 2,000 explosions and over 10,000 shooting incidents, an average of around 30 shootings per day. Almost 5,000 people were injured. Almost 2,000 armed robberies netted £800,000, most of it going into paramilitary coffers. In the worst month of the entire troubles, July 1972, almost a hundred people died as both republican and loyalist groups went on an uninhibited rampage. As the year opened, 17,000 soldiers were available for duty; when it ended a series of hasty reinforcements had brought the figure to 29,000.

The car bomb, a terrifying and often entirely indiscriminate weapon, was introduced by the IRA, causing many deaths, terrible injuries and enormous damage. Violence from loyalists increased significantly from the spring of 1972 when working-class Protestants turned in their thousands to paramilitarism as insecurity and uncertainty soared. Furtive meetings between the IRA and British politicians, first Harold Wilson and later the Tories, reinforced Unionist fears that Britain was attempting to negotiate with republicanism behind Unionist backs. Any hopes that the closure of Stormont and the end of Unionist rule would lead to a reduction of violence were soon dashed. In the twelve months up to direct rule, 250 died; in the twelve months which followed, the killing rate doubled.

It is also worth remarking however on what did not happen. Despite being fearful and insecure about their future, the Protestant community did not attempt to oppose the imposition of direct rule. Although there was deep resentment at the removal of Stormont, there were no serious signs of mutiny among the Protestants who predominated in the civil service and the RUC. The acceptance of direct rule may have been surly, but it was nonetheless acceptance.

Talks and violence

Direct rule was intended as very much a temporary system while a cross-community successor to the Stormont system was devised. In

London, responsibility was transferred from the Home Office to a new department, the Northern Ireland Office (NIO). Its first head, who was known as the Northern Ireland Secretary, or more often in Belfast as the Secretary of State, was William Whitelaw. Whitelaw, who in later years would go on to become deputy leader of the Conservative party, was a wealthy landowner whose political skills lay in the field of conciliation. A natural consensus politician in the high Tory mould, he was adept at personal relations and maintained contact with a wide range of opinion.

His task was to kick-start politics and open negotiations with the parties. In the early months of direct rule he attempted to placate both Unionists and nationalists against the background of steadily worsening violence and continual security crises. Many of the main parties and other elements were not speaking to each other, while the SDLP had for many months refused to meet British ministers. Whitelaw moved quickly to improve his relations with nationalists and republicans by releasing a number of internees and making other conciliatory moves. One of the most important of these, which was to have significant long-term consequences, was to defuse a republican hungerstrike by conceding 'special category status' to prisoners associated with paramilitary groups. This amounted to an acceptance of the IRA argument that its prisoners were different from other inmates jailed for criminal as opposed to paramilitary offences. It was a later attempt to withdraw this concession which led to the republican hungerstrikes and political upheavals of 1980 and 1981.

Anxious to explore the minds of IRA leaders, Whitelaw arranged for senior republicans to be flown, in the strictest of secrecy, to a government minister's home in Chelsea in July. The republicans included veterans and younger elements such as Gerry Adams and Martin McGuinness. The importance of Adams was emphasised by the fact that he was released from prison to make the trip. McGuinness later recalled: 'I was 22 years of age, and I couldn't be anything but impressed by the paraphernalia surrounding that whole business, and the cloak and dagger stuff of how we were transported from Derry to London. I was on the run at the time. There were contacts with the British government and we insisted on a written note from them which would guarantee our safety in the event of us agreeing to go to London. That we were given, and it was held by a lawyer acting on our behalf.

'We assembled in Derry, six of us, and we were taken in a blacked-out van to a field in which a helicopter landed. We were put in the helicopter and brought to the military end of Aldergrove airport near Belfast. We were brought then on by RAF plane to a military airfield in England, where we were met by a fleet of limousines. They were the fanciest cars I had ever seen in my life: it was a most unreal experience. We were escorted by the Special Branch through London to Cheyne Walk and there we met Willie Whitelaw. We were offered drinks at the meeting and we all refused.' McGuinness added: 'The only purpose of the meeting with Whitelaw was to demand a British declaration of intent to withdraw. All of us left the meeting quite clear in our minds that the British government were not yet at a position whereby we could do serious business.'

Whitelaw was as unimpressed with the republicans as they were with him. He recorded in his memoirs: 'The meeting was a non-event. The IRA leaders simply made impossible demands which I told them the British government would never concede. They were in fact still in a mood of defiance and determination to carry on until their absurd ultimatums were met.' The very fact that the meeting took place, however, was of great psychological importance in both political and paramilitary circles, being regularly cited in support of the argument that Britain might someday not rule out doing a deal with violent groupings.

Unionists were appalled when news of the exercise broke, stirring as it did their traditional fear that Britain might betray them. Others too disapproved, such as Garret FitzGerald, later Fine Gael Taoiseach and for years a major influence in Anglo-Irish relations. He wrote: 'The contacts that had taken place had the effect merely of prolonging the violence by deluding the IRA into believing that a British government would eventually negotiate a settlement with them.' As the troubles developed, a sporadic channel of communication was to remain open between the British and the IRA, even as the republican campaign of violence went on. In the 1990s this channel would play an important role in the developing peace process, but Whitelaw concluded after the Chelsea encounter that the new political structures he hoped to construct had no place in them for republicans.

He sounded out loyalist paramilitaries too, on one occasion meeting loyalists wearing masks and sunglasses in his Stormont Castle office. But a few days after his encounter with republicans a brief IRA ceasefire broke down. The IRA and the British government had met face to face, each concluding that the other was unreasonable and in effect beyond political reach. The IRA stepped up its violence with a vengeance, while loyalist groups also began killing on a large scale.

By this stage it was clear that working-class Protestants were flocking to unofficial defence organisations in their tens of thousands. The huge rise in violence following internment meant many Protestants lost confidence in the security forces, with the result that vigilante organisations sprang into being in Protestant areas. They felt politically insecure, wondering who would prevail in the fierce battles between the army and the IRA, while many of those who lived close to republican areas also felt physically insecure.

At first the authorities did not display serious concern about the groups of men who barricaded districts and patrolled them, sometimes carrying sticks and clubs. According to official minutes Faulkner had told Heath in late 1971: 'Their purpose was to identify and exclude terrorists in places where the security forces could not guarantee protection. It was worth considering whether they could be employed as an "eyes and ears" force on a regular basis.' Heath turned down the idea.

It soon became obvious that this was more than simple vigilantism. The majority of those who joined such groupings were not necessarily extremists, but within their ranks were some hundreds prepared to resort to open violence. The bombing of McGurk's bar was one example of this, but as 1972 went on there were more and more killings of Catholics, carried out in particular by militant pockets within the UDA. By the end of the year loyalists had killed 120 people.

The UDA also made its point in a more public way by staging large marches in Belfast with thousands of men parading in semi-military uniforms including combat jackets, bush hats, sunglasses and sometimes masks. These were not openly violent occasions, although there were occasional confrontations with the army; but the message that Protestants were if necessary prepared to fight for their cause was unmistakable.

Horror piled on horror in July 1972. The restlessness of the mid-1960s had first degenerated into the violent clashes of August 1969 and now descended further into killings at a rate of three a day. That month had many of the features which were to become all too familiar as the troubles went on. Republicans killed Protestants while loyalists claimed Catholic lives, often with particular savagery. On 11 July a number of drunken loyalists broke into the home of a Catholic family, killing a mentally handicapped youth and raping his mother. At the resulting murder trial a lawyer told the court: 'The restraints of civilisation on evil human passions are in this case totally non-existent. You may well think that in this case we have reached the lowest level of human depravity.'

Republicans meanwhile set off bombs which killed large numbers of people. Nine died in Belfast on what came to be known as Bloody Friday, as the IRA detonated twenty devices in just over an hour, injuring 130 others and producing widespread confusion and fear in many parts of the city. According to one account: 'In many places there was panic and pandemonium as shoppers and others heard bombs going off all over the city. The carnage, with some people blown to pieces, was such that the number of dead was unclear for some time, newspapers at first reporting that eleven people had been killed.' A police officer who went to a bomb scene in Oxford Street said: 'You could hear people screaming and crying and moaning. The first thing that caught my eye was a torso of a human being lying in the middle of the street. It was recognisable as a torso because the clothes had been blown off and you could actually see parts of the human anatomy.' In his memoirs Brian Faulkner wrote: 'Few Ulster people will forget seeing on television young policemen shovelling human remains into plastic bags in Oxford Street.'

Yet still the horror continued. On the last day of the month nine people, including a child and old people, were killed by IRA car bombs left in the previously peaceful County Londonderry village of Claudy. Apart from the human tragedy involved, both Bloody Friday and Claudy were seen at the time as major political setbacks for the IRA. The security forces were able to capitalise by moving into Londonderry, in a massive exercise known as Operation Motorman, to remove the 'no-go areas' which had been controlled by the IRA. But although this was a short-term setback for the republicans their campaign of violence went on regardless. At the beginning of 1972 the IRA had predicted imminent victory: by the middle of the year, both they and the authorities were geared up for a conflict that both rightly suspected could be long and bloody.

New proposals

It was against a background of such unremitting violence that Whitelaw turned to the task of finding a new political settlement. The SDLP was at that point recommending that sovereignty over Northern Ireland should be shared by London and Dublin. Brian Faulkner meanwhile called for a return of Stormont though with nationalist influence on some committees and some new links with the south, approaches that were viewed as modest concessions to Catholics.

In November 1972 Whitelaw published a discussion document, *The Future of Northern Ireland*, which set out the government's approach in general terms. It was important in that it laid out many ideas which were to form the basis of the approach of both this government and future administrations. The discussion document stressed Northern Ireland's financial dependence on Britain, pointedly adding that membership of the United Kingdom 'carries with it the obligations of membership including acceptance of the sovereignty of parliament as representing the people as a whole'. But in a major departure the document formally conceded that Dublin had a legitimate interest in Northern Ireland affairs, declaring: 'A settlement must recognise Northern Ireland's position within Ireland as a whole. It is therefore clearly desirable that any new arrangements should, whilst meeting the wishes of Northern Ireland and Great Britain, be so far as possible acceptable to and accepted by the Republic of Ireland.' The document introduced to the political lexicon the phrase 'Irish dimension' in acknowledgement of the south's interest.

In his memoirs Heath explained the rationale for this: 'It was no good just pretending that nationalist aspirations did not exist and that Irish nationalism in Northern Ireland would either be contained or burn itself out. The strength of feeling in the Catholic community had to be addressed, and that meant finding some way of involving the government of the Republic directly in the affairs of the province.' The document continued the gradual redrafting of London's approach to Northern Ireland and the possibility of a united Ireland. It said: 'No UK government for many years has had any wish to impede the realisation of Irish unity, if it were to come about by genuine and freely given mutual agreement and on conditions acceptable to the distinctive communities.'

The discussion document laid down that unfettered majority rule was a thing of the past and that future devolution would be on a basis of partnership. New institutions, it stipulated, must 'seek a much wider consensus than has hitherto existed. As a minimum it would mean assuring minority groups of an effective voice and a real influence; but there are strong arguments that the objective of real participation should be achieved by giving minority interests a share in the exercise of executive power.' In putting the concepts of powersharing and an Irish dimension on the table as the pillars of a future settlement, London had defined what were to be the main constitutional battlegrounds for the next three decades.

These ideas held no attraction for the IRA, which saw them as desperate attempts to shore up crumbling British rule. It remained intent on fighting on in the hope of wearing down the British will and bringing about a British withdrawal. But the new concepts were much welcomed by the SDLP and the Irish government, both of which had been lobbying for such an approach.

The proposals were much more problematic for Unionists, representing as they did a radical departure from the old system of majority rule. Faulkner did not consort with paramilitary groups, but others on the Unionist side were less fastidious. The most outspoken Unionist politician was William Craig, whose Vanguard movement continued to hold rallies and threatened a range of protests which included a Protestant rent-and-rates strike, a boycott of council elections and a refusal to pay gas and electricity bills. These generally came to nothing, but what really raised the temperature were Craig's fiery speeches. Addressing a meeting of the Monday Club group of far-right Conservatives in London he said, 'I am prepared to come out and shoot and kill. Let us put the bluff aside. I am prepared to kill and those behind me will have my full support. When we say force we mean force. We will only assassinate our enemies as a last desperate resort when we are denied our democratic rights.' There were calls for Craig's prosecution: some argued he was giving voice to legitimate Protestant anger, while others accused him of recklessly fanning the flames of violence.

But if the authorities were alarmed by Craig they were relieved by an unexpected new tack taken by Paisley, who during 1972 temporarily switched from incendiary demagoguery to an uncharacteristically moderate note. Instead of stirring Protestant anxieties he suddenly sought to soothe them, taking the line that the loss of Stormont was not the end of the world. 'Stormont is a thing of the past and there is no good use for Unionists to think that, by some way or other, Stormont shall return,' he declared. Denouncing Craig's threats, he told supporters, 'The voice of Mr Craig and the advice of Mr Craig are the voice and advice of folly. Do not be misled. Do not wreck your country and bring it to an end by self-inflicted wounds. Do not copy the deplorable tactics your enemies have adopted.'

Paisley's approach at this stage was to advocate stern security policies, including twenty-four-hour curfews in republican areas, but instead of calling for the return of Stormont he become an integrationist, one of those rare Unionists who believed a new Stormont would tend to separate Northern Ireland from the rest of the UK. It was an interesting theory but at the time there were few Unionist takers for it, and eventually Paisley would quietly abandon it and return to more familiar ground.

By this point Unionism had splintered, with Faulkner prepared to negotiate, Paisley pressing for integration, and Craig apparently bent on confrontation. Prominent Unionist former ministers such as Harry West and John Taylor demanded a return to the old Stormont system, while many other politicians added to the general confusion by changing their minds and their political lines, sometimes several times. Faulkner found it difficult to hold his party together, particularly since he was advancing the problematic policy of negotiating with a British government which had, in the eyes of most Unionists, been guilty of a betrayal in removing the Stormont system. Some liberal Unionists drifted away from politics entirely, depriving Faulkner of potentially useful support.

1973

At the beginning of 1973 the United Kingdom and the Irish Republic became members of the European Economic Community (EEC), a development which over time had a major effect on Anglo-Irish relations. Disparity in the wealth of the two countries had added to the historical distance between coloniser and colonised, with Irish dependence on British trade reinforcing this. Their simultaneous entry to the EEC, however, helped alter some of the fundamentals of the relationship and increased the south's international standing. Joining Europe also markedly increased the Republic's sense of national self-esteem as Irish ministers, and some talented Dublin civil servants, were seen to perform well on the international stage. British and Irish officials also formed useful working relationships which would later be important in developing greater understanding and mutual respect.

But meanwhile the violence continued. Security force arguments that loyalist violence was too unplanned to be susceptible to internment became steadily less tenable, and in February the first loyalists were interned. The move was followed by a one-day strike, backed by a range of loyalist paramilitary and political groupings, which was marked by considerable loyalist violence and five deaths. On the republican side the IRA gradually changed the emphasis from open confrontations and car bombings to more carefully planned sniping attacks, together with bombing attacks in England. Bombs planted in London in March 1973 led to one death and almost two hundred injuries, the first of many sporadic but often spectacular IRA attacks in England which in the course of the troubles would take more than a hundred lives. This figure was low in relation to the overall death toll, but the political impact of attacks in Britain was often great.

On the political front, 1973 saw Whitelaw continuing to draw the parties into talks on a settlement. A referendum or border poll was held in March, with voters asked whether they wanted Northern Ireland to remain part of the United Kingdom or join a united Ireland. The exercise was supposed to reassure Unionists that, whatever other changes might be on the way, their place in the UK was secure. In the event all shades of nationalist opinion boycotted the exercise, resulting in an almost entirely Unionist turnout. On a 59 per cent poll, 99 per cent voted to stay in the UK, only 1 per cent favouring a united Ireland. Unionists drew some fleeting cheer from the result, though there was no sign that it gave them any lasting reassurance.

By the spring of 1973 London's thinking had crystallised and was laid out in a government white paper entitled *Northern Ireland Constitutional Proposals*. This proposed the introduction of proportional representation, the same system James Craig had abolished in the 1920s, to elect a new assembly to replace Stormont. A new devolved government or executive would be made up from the major parties, including both Unionists and nationalists. The white paper reaffirmed Northern Ireland's constitutional status within the UK but envisaged new north–south links. It also made it clear that London intended keeping control over sensitive matters such as security, the legal system, emergency powers and elections.

The white paper reaffirmed that the concepts of powersharing and an Irish dimension were to be the mainstays of a new settlement. It said that government 'can no longer be solely based upon any single party, if that party draws its support and its elected representatives virtually entirely from only one section of a divided community'. The white paper advocated the creation of a Council of Ireland for consultations and cooperation with the south.

Faulkner accepted the white paper as a basis for negotiation, though his party's council endorsed his line without enthusiasm. William Craig meanwhile broke with the Unionist party, converting his movement into the Vanguard party. Others within Unionism, including Ian Paisley and the Orange Order, flatly denounced the white paper as unacceptable. There was much confusion in Unionist ranks as prominent figures toyed with alternatives such as forcing a return to Stormont, integration with Britain, independence from Britain, and even the idea of negotiating a new federal Ireland with nationalists. But none of these notions took root, partly because they seemed unrealistic or undesirable to mainstream Unionists, and partly because there were so many personality differences between leading Unionist figures. In the end the central divide within Unionism came down to those headed by Faulkner who found the white paper an acceptable basis for talks, and those, such as Craig and Paisley, who did not.

Although the rejectionist Unionists were against Faulkner and against Whitelaw, personality and political differences meant they were clearly not united in leadership, aims, methods or alternatives. Political groupings, and sometimes loyalist paramilitary groups, from time to time formed umbrella groups but these tended to be shifting, unstable and suspicious coalitions which knew what they stood against but disagreed on what they stood for.

All parties had difficulties with Whitelaw's proposals. For many Unionists, powersharing with nationalists and a Council of Ireland were objectionable, for all Whitelaw's stress on Northern Ireland's guaranteed status within the UK. For the SDLP the initiative was in most aspects a huge advance, even though it fell well short of the London–Dublin joint authority the party had advocated. The continuing use of internment also posed a major problem for the SDLP.

Elections to the new assembly were held in June 1973. During the campaign the wily Faulkner repeated that his party would not share power with any party 'whose primary objective was to break the link with Great Britain'. Some Unionists appear to have voted for him on the assumption that this meant he would not share power with the SDLP. Afterwards, when it emerged he was indeed prepared to sit in government with the SDLP, opponents accused him of misleading voters. His reasoning was that ending the Union, while perhaps the ultimate ambition of the SDLP, was not its primary objective.

The election result was yet another illustration of Unionist divisions. Thirty-nine of the Unionist party candidates gave their allegiance to the Faulkner approach but, in an echo of O'Neill's 1969 crossroads election, ten others refused to do so. Unionist rejectionists won 27 of the 78 assembly seats with 235,000 votes, while Unionists supporting the initiative won 22 seats with 211,000 votes. Faulkner thus emerged from the election leading a bitterly divided party and without a majority among Unionist voters. His best hope was that, if a working system of government could be set up, its successful functioning would gradually attract more Unionist popular support.

The powersharing project that was to follow was based on the idea of combining the more moderate parties in a new coalition which would run Northern Ireland on a partnership basis. Both republican and Unionist extremes were to be excluded from this centrist idea – in fact they excluded themselves by refusing to take part in it – but as time went by, the theory ran, support for the extremes would dwindle.

While this scheme was politically coherent, two sets of statistics, concerning electoral support and the level of violence, help show just how formidable were the forces ranged against it. A majority of Unionist voters were against the proposition, while perhaps 30,000 or more of them were so opposed to accommodation that they joined loyalist paramilitary groups prepared to use force to resist what they saw as any further erosion of Protestant rights. There was a certain overlap of the political and paramilitary within the assembly itself, where half a dozen or more anti-deal Unionists had connections with shadowy loyalist groups. In the political centre only a small number of voters supported cross-community parties, the non-sectarian Alliance party being the most prominent, with 9 per cent of the vote.

On the nationalist side the SDLP dominated, having taken 22 per cent of the overall vote and representing in one party virtually all of constitutional nationalism. Nationalism had by this stage regrouped into two very distinct and opposing positions, most Catholics voting for the SDLP. Republicans were not, however, represented, having boycotted the elections: in the 1980s they would build a significant vote but during the 1970s they did not contest elections. Most of those who opted for a violent path came together in the IRA, known in those days as the Provisional IRA, which believed in an eventual republican victory achieved through force. Only a few individuals and organisations, such as Bernadette Devlin, the rump of the Civil Rights Association, and the Official IRA, did not align themselves with either of the two large nationalist groupings.

Republicans made their presence felt not in the assembly but by means of the continuing IRA campaign of violence. The death toll fell substantially in 1973, almost halving from the previous year's figure of 498. The number of victims in almost every category roughly halved. In round figures during the year 130 civilians were killed as

well as 80 members of the security forces. Republicans were responsible for 140 deaths, loyalists for 90 and the security forces for 30. The
year also had fewer horrors than 1972, though there were some multiple death tolls, as in Coleraine in County Londonderry where an
IRA bomb killed six people. There were also fewer loyalist torture
killings, though UDA members killed an SDLP politician and a
woman friend by stabbing them dozens of times. Although taken
overall the year was a clear improvement on 1972, the continuing
violence provided an unhelpful backdrop to attempts to build a new
politics based on harmony and partnership. The total figure of 265
killings meant that hardly a newspaper or evening television programme did not bring news of either a killing or a funeral.

When the assembly met it turned into a forum for division rather
than for a new start. Its first meeting in July set a pattern of repeated
unruly gatherings, with hours of rowdy and rancorous debate,
many obstructive points of order and a great deal of personal abuse.
Yet even as the assembly chamber became a byword for acrimony,
real negotiation was going on behind the scenes as Whitelaw, the
Unionist party, the SDLP and Alliance argued out the details of a
new settlement. In October Faulkner won the support of his party's
standing committee for powersharing with the SDLP, though only
by the narrow majority of 132 votes to 105.

A new element of inter-party trust appeared as the negotiations
went on, helped by the SDLP's position on one touchstone issue,
when the party indicated it would call for an end to the rent-and-
rates strike which it had previously endorsed as a protest against
internment. But such thorny subjects as the composition and powers
of the new executive and the Council of Ireland, together with
issues such as policing and internment, were difficult areas which
required many months of negotiation.

Faulkner was forced to fight major battles within his own party as
senior figures such as John Taylor fought a strong rearguard action
against the emerging new settlement. Faulkner eventually won the
backing of his party's ruling council, though by the ominously
small majority of 379 votes to 369.

By November the talks had achieved agreement on most of the major issues but were stalled on the composition of the eleven-man executive (no women were in line for office) and had yet to settle the form of the Irish dimension. Faulkner insisted that his party should have a majority in the executive while the SDLP and Alliance pointed out that he did not command a majority within Unionism and certainly not within the assembly. Whitelaw told Edward Heath that he expected the talks to fail and made plans to return to London to make a statement in the Commons on 22 November. On the day before, however, he piled the pressure on the parties to reach agreement by having his helicopter land, visibly and very noisily, on the lawn outside Stormont Castle where the talks were taking place.

A last-minute breakthrough was achieved with the aid of the ingenious device of creating a new category of extra ministers. Faulkner would have a majority within the eleven-strong executive, which was to be made up of six Unionists, four SDLP and one Alliance. But four extra non-voting ministers were to be appointed, so that the full executive would consist of seven Unionists, six SDLP and two Alliance members. This piece of sleight-of-hand meant that Faulkner could claim he had a Unionist majority while non-Unionists could simultaneously claim he had not.

Sunningdale

The next step was to assemble the three parties which would form the executive, together with the London and Dublin governments. They met at a civil service training centre at Sunningdale in Berkshire in late 1973, the deal which emerged from it becoming known thereafter as the Sunningdale Agreement. Whitelaw, the principal architect of the new settlement, was promoted to a senior post in London, Heath believing that he needed his talents for his government's confrontation with trade unions in Britain. He was replaced by the less experienced Francis Pym only four days before the Sunningdale conference took place.

The principal tasks of the gathering were to agree on the Council of Ireland's composition and functions, to deal with the subject of greater north–south security cooperation, and to attempt to settle the constitutional status of Northern Ireland. After high-pressure late-night sessions, with Heath personally taking a leading role, the shape of the Council of Ireland was eventually hammered out. It would consist of seven northern and seven southern ministers, a consultative tier with thirty members of the Irish parliament and thirty members of the assembly, and a permanent secretariat. It was to have 'executive and harmonising functions'.

All of this was alarming to Unionism, smacking as it did of a dangerous and potentially growing Dublin foothold in Northern Ireland affairs. Faulkner thus tried hard to water down the powers of the Council of Ireland but in the end had to accept much more than he had bargained for. He later defended his concessions on the council's functions and powers on the basis that they were 'nonsense' that 'meant nothing in practice' because executive ministers and the assembly would have to agree to anything proposed by the new body.

Although London and Dublin were able to reach agreement on most issues, they had to agree to differ on a number of points and especially on one hugely important issue. In the absence of an agreed single statement on the status of Northern Ireland, the governments agreed that separate statements should be printed side by side in the final conference communiqué. This was seen both as an oddity and as a sign of continuing British–Irish differences. The Irish government statement 'fully accepted and solemnly declared that there could be no change in the status of Northern Ireland until a majority of the people of Northern Ireland desired a change in their status'. Dublin did not, however, propose to delete or change Articles 2 and 3 of the Irish constitution, which Unionists regarded as an offensive claim to jurisdiction over Northern Ireland. Some in Dublin favoured such a move, but the problem was that the constitution could only be changed by a referendum. If a referendum had been held and lost, the entire initiative would have been undermined.

On the issue of cross-border security cooperation there was also much division. Faulkner's main demand was for the extradition of suspects to Northern Ireland, but Dublin resisted this, proposing instead the creation of a single all-Ireland court and a common law enforcement area, allowing terrorist offenders to be tried in whichever jurisdiction they were arrested. The fact that the issue was referred to a London–Dublin commission was a significant blow to Faulkner. He had hoped to return from Sunningdale with a southern guarantee of Northern Ireland's status and a new extradition deal which he could present as political and security gains.

The Sunningdale conference dealt also with the issue of policing. John Hume held that it would be difficult for SDLP members to take their places in a Northern Ireland executive if they were not able to give support to the police force. He argued however that this support would be almost impossible to sell to nationalists unless the police force was tied in some way to the Council of Ireland, a link which could offer the nationalist community some guarantees on policing. Although the SDLP had reluctantly conceded that there would be no change to the name of the RUC, at Sunningdale they were insistent that the Council of Ireland must have some policing oversight role. In his memoirs the Irish Foreign Minister, Garret FitzGerald, recalled that the Dublin delegation privately concluded that the Unionists had fared badly on most of the major issues, and thus it decided that on policing Faulkner should be allowed to prevail. The result was that the council's role in policing was largely cosmetic. Faulkner would later insist that this role was 'tenuous and totally meaningless', but for many Unionists the mere existence of a council was objectionable.

The Sunningdale conference was something of a cultural clash: the Unionist delegation decided not to use the drinks cabinet provided in their room in case their judgement should be affected. Other delegations laboured under no such inhibitions, first exhausting their own supplies and then gladly accepting the Unionist supplies. Faulkner's team instead sent out for Polo mints. However, the hours of intense negotiations engendered growing understanding and respect. Faulkner would later write: 'There was a feeling of comradeship and trust between those of us who had been through hundreds of hours of negotiations, and a sense almost of moral purpose.'

As the parties returned to Northern Ireland, Unionists could point to a reassuring Irish declaration on Northern Ireland's status, a law commission to tackle cross-border security problems and a Council of Ireland which they argued was largely toothless. The SDLP could claim victories in securing a role at the highest level of government, together with new all-Ireland institutions with the potential to evolve. Both the SDLP and the Faulkner Unionists claimed success, but as one historian pointed out: 'They were contradictory arguments. The success of the agreement depended on neither side listening to what their allies were saying about it.'

5.

Sunningdale, strike & stalemate
1974–76

Powersharing

The first day of January 1974 was intended to be a historic day for Northern Ireland as the powersharing executive took office. With Brian Faulkner as chief minister and SDLP leader Gerry Fitt as his deputy, the administration brought together ministers from the Unionist party, the SDLP and Alliance. Billed as a chance for a fresh start, the powersharing executive was hailed as a momentous new departure. Politically it was certainly light years away from the Stormont majority rule system, for instead of the traditional all-Unionist cabinet the executive included prominent nationalists. John Hume was minister for commerce while Austin Currie, who had led the well-remembered Caledon squat, became housing minister. This new arrangement had the goodwill of almost the whole world; certainly the fervent good wishes of Britain and the Republic went with it.

But right from the start it was beleaguered, facing as it did opposition both from the IRA and from a majority of the Protestant population. The IRA sought outright victory, while many Unionists simply would not accept the new deal. Some Unionists feared the new arrangements were the start of a slippery slope towards a united Ireland; others simply could not abide the thought of having Catholics in government. All this meant that while the new arrangements had majority support within the assembly, and indeed within Northern Ireland as a whole, they had the support of fewer than half of Unionist voters and politicians.

The Unionist party itself was the scene of internal running battles. Three days after the executive came into being, a meeting of the Ulster Unionist Council was called to discuss a motion condemning the Council of Ireland. The Ulster Unionist Council's eccentric structure meant it included delegates from affiliated organisations such as the Orange Order; some delegates were not even members of the party, and some were actually members of rival parties such as Vanguard. When Faulkner's opponents won the vote by 427 votes to 374 he resigned as party leader, to be replaced by the uncompromising Harry West. Faulkner would eventually establish a new grouping to be known as the Unionist Party of Northern Ireland, with the backing of around twenty members of the assembly.

Thus after only one week of the new Northern Ireland executive's existence its head had effectively lost his party, which meant that all three major Unionist parties – the UUP, DUP and Vanguard – were opposed to the entire initiative. Paisley and the other anti-Sunningdale Unionists, who had already formed an umbrella United Ulster Unionist Council (UUUC), were now joined by West and the main Unionist party.

A further problem for the executive was that the Sunningdale Agreement was in reality an agreement to reach an agreement, with much remaining to be finalised. With the details of the Council of Ireland still to be worked out, Faulkner found it difficult to answer the wilder allegations of Unionist opponents. He was unable to gain political cover by pointing to significant gains in cross-border security, while the whole Sunningdale project was not helped by the fact that during the executive's existence violence rose. The increase on the republican side was fairly modest, but loyalist killings trebled.

Issues which Sunningdale was supposed to settle refused to go away. In a newspaper interview within days of the conference the Taoiseach, Liam Cosgrave, said, 'There is no question of changing our constitution with regard to our claim of sovereignty over all of Ireland.' This was damaging to Faulkner's claim to have won a significant concession from the Republic in recognising Northern Ireland's status. He suffered a further blow when in January a legal challenge was mounted in the Dublin courts, charging that the Irish government's Sunningdale declaration on the status of Northern Ireland was unconstitutional. To win the case the Irish government was obliged to argue that nothing they had agreed affected the south's claim of jurisdiction over Northern Ireland contained in Articles 2 and 3. This was seen as confirming the accusation of the anti-Faulkner Unionists that he had not managed to dilute the south's claim.

Later in January the first meeting of the assembly since Sunningdale reached a new peak of unpleasantness as scenes of open violence broke out. Rejectionist Unionists attacked Faulkner supporters, with five RUC officers injured in the disturbances. One newspaper described the scene:

> The loyalists entered at 2:30 in the afternoon, prayed, and rushed forward to seize the seats designated for the executive. There were shouts and howls. Some climbed up and danced on desks. Other loyalists leaped upon the table beside the dispatch box, removed the mace, and began a parade about the chamber. One danced upon the speaker's table and shouted, 'We have driven the money-changers from the temple.' He then chained and padlocked himself to a bench.

Despite such histrionics members of the executive attempted to get on with running their new departments, quickly developing a perhaps surprising spirit of cooperation among traditional opponents. But although in administrative terms the executive made a promising start, political events in Britain were to undermine its standing. Heath, who was locked in a struggle with the miners and other trade unions which resulted in strikes and widespread disruption, called a general election for the end of February. The outcome of the contest was a major blow for the executive since the rejectionist Unionists, organised together in the UUUC, cooperated to nominate agreed candidates on a single straightforward anti-Sunningdale ticket. One of their more potent slogans was 'Dublin is just a Sunningdale away.'

Every circumstance seemed to conspire against Faulkner. He was attempting to have Unionists actively endorse a system radically different from anything that had gone before, and one that was susceptible to charges that it might weaken the link with Britain. The UUUC representatives by contrast had the reassuring tone of being unity candidates intent on maximising the Unionist vote. In some constituencies UUUC candidates looked such obvious winners that Faulkner did not even field candidates against them. Instead, the executive parties found themselves standing against each other in many constituencies. The tribal imperative worked in favour of the UUUC since in most constituencies they seemed the men most likely to avert a nationalist victory. Just when Faulkner was trying to sell the proposition of a new partnership across the divide, the venerable Unionist duty of preventing nationalists from winning seats reasserted itself.

When the votes were counted, the anti-Sunningdale Unionists had won eleven of the twelve Northern Ireland seats. Gerry Fitt was now the sole pro-Sunningdale MP. The leaders of the three main Unionist rejectionist parties, Paisley, Craig and West, were all elected in a harmful blow to the executive's credibility and authority. Nowhere in the statistics was there any comfort for the pro-Sunningdale camp. UUUC candidates amassed over 300,000 votes while Faulkner's supporters managed only 94,000. The charge that Faulkner spoke for less than half of Unionists had received irrefutable electoral proof.

In Britain Heath lost the election, Harold Wilson returned to power with a minority Labour government, and Merlyn Rees arrived in Belfast as a new and inexperienced Northern Ireland Secretary. Labour inherited an initiative which was not of their making, and which had been badly wounded by the rejectionist Unionists. Perhaps it was not surprising that the new government would later be accused of not giving its all in defence of the new deal.

Following the disastrous election result, Faulkner insisted on a secret renegotiation of the Council of Ireland, arguing that the election had shown that the council as it stood was unacceptable to Unionists. He said of the general election vote: 'It represents the fears of the Unionists, fears about the unknown and the unknowns expressed in that term Sunningdale. People don't know what Sunningdale is and they fear a sell-out on the constitutional position.'

The April announcement that there was not to be extradition of IRA suspects from the south to the north handed the UUUC another weapon to use against Faulkner, the common loyalist charge being that the south was soft on the IRA. Relations within the assembly remained acrimonious, with the UUUC members making it clear they did not accept the legitimacy of the new executive. Sometimes they boycotted the proceedings, sometimes they attempted to snarl them up with obstructive tactics, and sometimes a roughhouse developed. Some UUUC members were courteous individuals but many were not. One assembly official recalled in his memoirs: 'Ministers, especially Faulkner, were abused verbally on every occasion and sometimes even physically. Faulkner was spat upon, jostled, reviled and shouted down. It was sad to see him spat upon by lesser men, political pygmies and procedural bullies and wild men of the woods and the bogs.'

The disruption and occasional fisticuffs poisoned the atmosphere but showed no sign of bringing down the fledgling institutions. That was soon to be achieved however by a loose coalition of loyalist politicians, groups of workers and, above all, paramilitary groups. They did it not through political means but by a Protestant general strike which saw aggressive picketing, threats and intimidation, and widespread power cuts.

The UWC strike

Although loyalist one-day strikes had been staged on a number of occasions in 1972 and 1973, the fact that they almost invariably degenerated into violence meant the tactic was generally looked on as discredited. The strike of May 1974 was different in that it had an obvious and vulnerable target to attack in the form of the Sunningdale Agreement and the executive, featuring as it did such Unionist hate-figures as Fitt and Currie.

A number of elements were involved in the organisation of the strike. The nucleus was a group styling itself the Ulster Workers Council (UWC), consisting of trade unionists and others, some based in key industries with predominantly Protestant workforces. These included shipbuilding, heavy engineering and, above all, electric power generation. In May 1974 hardly anyone had heard of the UWC, and hardly anyone took them seriously when, in response to an assembly vote endorsing the Sunningdale Agreement, the organisation announced a general strike. The UWC had approached a number of loyalist politicians for support, but most of these were unenthusiastic, doubting the organisation's capacity to deliver. Some of the paramilitary groups, in particular the Ulster Defence Association, were much more interested in the idea.

On the first day of the strike, 15 May, the vast majority of workers travelled to work as usual. UDA leader Andy Tyrie later recalled arriving at the almost deserted strike headquarters: 'I suddenly realised that the UWC did not really exist as an organisation. And there was no strike in existence either.' Tyrie and the UDA took the initiative and by the middle of the day UDA members were, as Tyrie put it, 'persuading' workers that they should not be working. It was not long before the strike ceased to be merely a concept and became an organised campaign.

This meant blocked roads, hijacked cars, and visits by masked men to factories. In many areas barricades became a familiar sight, with cars, lorries and other obstacles slung across roads in makeshift obstructions. Bands of men and youths, sometimes carrying clubs and staves, were often in attendance. There was relatively little overt violence but then there did not have to be: motorists were not about to tackle groups of loyalists, risking perhaps a beating and the loss of their vehicle. It was intimidation on a huge scale. Another highly effective strike weapon arose from loyalist control over the power stations: within a short time electricity output was reduced to 60 per cent and power cuts forced workplaces to close. This pattern continued for the course of the two-week strike, so that for many workers it was a lockout rather than a strike.

The lack of electricity was one vital point; another was that the army and RUC did not set about keeping the roads open in a determined fashion. In a few instances blockades were dismantled and the pickets were dispersed, but very often if a road was blocked it stayed blocked. Security force patrols continued, but soldiers and pickets generally kept their distance from each other.

The army took the straightforward position that their job was to combat terrorism and not to curb street protests, an approach outlined years later in an interview by the late General Sir Frank King, who was then General Officer Commanding of troops in Northern Ireland. He related:

When the strike started I remember having a conference and deciding not to get mixed up in it. What amazed us at the time was that we never had any aggro at all with the strikers. They never once stopped an army vehicle – as far as we were concerned it was almost as if the strike was not on at all. Dealing with intimidation was a police job. The fact that the RUC didn't do too much about it was no concern of ours. We were angry at the time but it wasn't our job. If Rees had ordered us to move against the barricades we would have said, 'With great respect, this is a job for the police. We will assist them if you wish, but it's not terrorism.'

During the strike there was, in fact, a bombing attack which claimed more lives than almost any other single incident in the troubles, but it took place not in the north but south of the border. This was what came to be known as the Dublin and Monaghan bombings, which on the third day of the strike killed twenty-five people in Dublin and a further seven in the border town of Monaghan. Three separate car bombs went off without warning in Dublin, causing carnage during the evening rush hour. One newspaper report described the scene: 'Dozens of people lay on the pavements and in the road and in front of broken shops, dead, dying or screaming with pain and shock. A newspaper photographer was sick when he saw a gutter literally running with blood. A few feet away was a human leg and next to it a head.' A report on the inquest said: 'Horrifying head wounds, loss of limbs, enormous lacerations and the presence of debris and shrapnel in the victims' bodies were described to the court. Most of the victims died from multiple injuries, shock and haemorrhage.' Loyalist sources said the UVF was responsible for the attacks, but some years later it was alleged that British intelligence had played a part, a claim which led to a long-running campaign by relatives for an inquiry into the episode.

Back in Belfast the strike revealed daily the impotence of both the British government and the fledgling executive. Since the executive had no power over security and law and order its members could only complain bitterly to Rees that control of the streets had been conceded to the UWC and their paramilitary allies. UDA leader Tyrie would admit later that a major show of force by the RUC and the army at the start might have destroyed the momentum of the strike, but it is clear that Rees and the army had serious doubts about the possibility of defeating the strike through open confrontation. On one day it was said that 2,000 soldiers and police were required simply to keep five main roads into Belfast open. By the second week of the strike, power seemed to have shifted from Rees and the executive to the loyalist strikers.

General King was influenced in his stance by his judgement that the executive was already dead in the water. He said in the interview: 'Although armies are non-political, we were a fairly sensitive barometer of feeling. Every time a patrol went out they were debriefed by an intelligence officer or intelligence sergeant, and they repeated every little bit of gossip they heard along the way. It was clear even before the strike that the executive was already dead as a doornail. For months it had been losing support and power. One could feel them losing power.'

The army was insistent that its engineers could not move into the power stations and crank up electricity generation to a level which would end the daily power cuts. It said they could generate only a small amount of power but could not distribute it. The army also warned that other workers would walk out if they moved in, and that loyalists might sabotage generators with, as the general portrayed it, disastrous results – 'sewage bubbling in the streets, perhaps cholera, no bread, no milk, no power for the hospitals'.

Whatever the initial reactions of the Protestant middle class to an exercise so clearly enforced by paramilitaries, many of its members came to endorse the strike. In his memoirs Rees recalled returning late one evening to the Culloden hotel in affluent north Down. Describing walking through the plush lounge largely occupied by Protestant customers, he remembered: 'The cry of "traitor" came in unison, a spontaneous response of anger. We the Brits were the outsiders.'

Throughout the strike the executive continued to function. It eventually announced the postponement of much of the implementation of the Council of Ireland until after the next assembly election: some weeks earlier this might have had a major impact, but with virtually all attention now focused on the streets the move seemed barely relevant. A reluctant decision by the Wilson government to use the army to break the loyalist control of petrol and oil supplies, largely at the insistence of executive members, made things worse. In a petulant television broadcast known thereafter as the 'spongers speech', Wilson referred to loyalists as 'people who spend their lives sponging on Westminster and British democracy and then systematically assault democratic methods'. He asked contemptuously: 'Who do they think they are?' The description infuriated almost all Unionists, one senior assembly official describing it as 'catastrophically unhelpful'. In the days that followed many loyalists proudly and defiantly sported pieces of sponge in their lapels.

After two weeks of the strike, and after Rees had refused Faulkner's call to him to open talks with the strike leaders,

Faulkner concluded that there was no help for the executive and resigned. It was the end of a unique constitutional experiment which had taken almost two years of hard work to construct, but which survived for only five months. Following Faulkner's resignation, Rees announced the winding-up of the executive, and the two governments and the powersharing parties trudged dispiritedly back to square one.

In the years since then, debates have continued about whether the authorities could have handled the strike better and prevented the rejectionist Unionists from winning such a victory. As usual, there have been allegations of both conspiracy and cock-up. There have been allegations that military or intelligence elements opposed to the Sunningdale Agreement, or disinclined to make efforts to support it, helped ensure its downfall. It is certainly the case, on General King's own admission, that he could hardly have done less in support of the executive.

The argument is that more vigorous action by the authorities, in terms of propaganda and publicity, in terms of giving the army stronger direction, in terms of keeping the roads open and in terms of preserving power supplies, might have preserved Sunningdale. Rees was certainly an inexperienced minister whom a number of commentators have criticised as too indecisive a man for a post which, at that moment of emergency, called for swift and resolute action. A newspaper quoted one of his officials as saying, 'I don't mind Merlyn wrestling with his conscience for ages over every issue. What I mind is that the result always seems to be a draw.'

Rees himself would later argue in a television documentary: 'I didn't let them win. They were going to win anyway. It could not be done, that's the short answer. The police were on the brink of not carrying out their duties and the middle class were on the strikers' side. This wasn't just an industrial dispute. This was the Protestant people of Northern Ireland rising up against Sunningdale and it could not be shot down.'

It was certainly the case that the Sunningdale initiative had already run into severe problems, and that the strength of loyalist opposition to it might well eventually have brought it down. On the other hand, no one can know whether a defeat for the strikers might have provided a boost for the new government which might have seen it through to eventual success. Robert Fisk's book on the strike, *The Point of No Return*, is highly critical of the inactivity of the NIO and the security forces but significantly concludes: 'Even if the police had chosen to act against the men who wanted to overthrow the state was this option open to them? The evidence is that it was not.'

The agreement's basic unpopularity in the Unionist community was made worse by Faulkner's loss of the leadership of the Unionist party, the Dublin constitutional court case, the damaging February elections, and the continuing violence. Rees wrote of Faulkner: 'British governments had expected too much of him. He had been obliged to go into no-man's-land with his troops left far behind.' Senior official Maurice Hayes agreed:

> There is now plenty of evidence that he was pushed farther than he should have been, and beyond his power to deliver. The general consensus now is that the nationalist side overbid their hands, and won. It is clear that Faulkner was saddled with a load which he could not carry and which eventually brought him down, and with him the whole power-sharing experiment.

Another continuing debate concerned whether the sharpest loyalist opposition to Sunningdale had been generated by the Irish dimension or by powersharing. Most commentators held that the Dublin connection had been the more potent, though others disagreed. One Catholic official concluded: 'I believe that the fundamental, gut objection all along was to sharing power with Catholics, and that opposition to the Council of Ireland was a smokescreen to conceal a much deeper and atavistic historic antagonism which had not been put to rest.'

Strike aftermath

While loyalists celebrated their victory with a huge rally at Stormont, much of the rest of the world viewed the downfall of Sunningdale as politically catastrophic and profoundly depressing. The new system had appeared to offer the possibility of eventually settling the troubles by giving moderate Unionists and nationalists a chance to work together. The theory had been that the old Stormont Unionism had failed to preserve order through its insistence on excluding Catholics from power. It seemed obvious that the way to stabilise the state was to reassemble Stormont with a Catholic component. Thus a coalition of the two religions would isolate the extremists on both sides and Catholics could be brought to identify with the state as they never had before.

But a great many Protestants had never subscribed to this proposition, and scepticism in their community rose steadily as the months passed with no let-up in violence. The sense grew that Sunningdale offered not a new beginning but a dangerous threat to their interests. Furthermore the partnership concept was shattered by the harsh reality of the strike, which demonstrated that Protestants collectively had both the determination and the ability to bring down a system they opposed. They had a clear numerical majority in Northern Ireland; they held the key jobs in the key industries; and they had shown they could bring Northern Ireland to a standstill. Although some argued that Rees had been at fault, the general moral drawn was that Unionists had demonstrated their power of veto.

This was accepted, however reluctantly, in the Republic as well as in Britain. Until May 1974 many in the south had airily assumed that northern Protestants would come to see that they had been simply wrongheaded in opposing partnership and eventual Irish unity. But the strike, coupled with the carnage of the Dublin and Monaghan bombings, brought home the extent of loyalist determination to oppose what they regarded as dangerous.

The theory that only some form of partnership government would work continued to hold sway in London and Dublin and within the SDLP, but the success of the strike was taken as demonstrating that it was impossible to put that theory into practice. A collective nationalist rejection of the old Stormont had eventually brought that institution down; now Unionists had managed to destroy its successor. The analysis that there appeared to be a double veto, with Unionists and nationalists able to deny the other what they wanted, caused a great many to conclude that this was a problem without a solution. That element of Unionism which had been prepared to share power virtually disappeared overnight. Rees went back to the drawing board in search of some new avenue of progress. He found none, since Unionists and loyalists, suffused with the glow of their victory, were in no mood to accept anything other than a return to majority rule.

The schizophrenic Unionist attitude towards law and order and legitimate protests had rarely been seen in a more illuminating light than in the strike's aftermath. The part of the Unionist psychology which held that protest was legitimate and sometimes essential meant that there was widespread Protestant support for the stoppage, despite the obvious use of violence and intimidation. During the strike senior politicians, who would later express horror at any idea of contacts with 'IRA terrorists', routinely sat in meetings with representatives of paramilitary groups which had many members serving prison sentences for murder. Yet once the collapse of the executive had been achieved, the law-and-order strand of the Unionist psyche reasserted itself.

Everyone went quietly back to work and waited to see what the government would do next. Politically Rees felt he could do little. His best effort, after much tortured thought, was to decide to establish a 'constitutional convention' to bring local politicians together in the hope that they might find a new agreement among themselves. Rees was criticised for allegedly abdicating governmental responsibility and putting the onus on local parties to find a solution. He refused however to take any more serious political initiative though he did make a move in another direction, which was towards the paramilitary groups and in particular the IRA.

The IRA's killing rate had halved, from 280 in 1972 to 280 in the following two years, but it remained the major taker of life. Although Whitelaw had concluded in 1972 that his meeting with the IRA had been useless, Rees again put out feelers towards the republicans. In this he appears to have been encouraged by the NIO's most senior civil servant, Sir Frank Cooper, who had a reputation for being both forceful and devious. In 1974 Rees legalised both Sinn Féin, the IRA's political wing, and the UVF, partly to facilitate the business of talking to them. Republicans and loyalists were regularly invited to Laneside, a large government-owned house in a plush area of County Down, for informal chats with officials.

The talks which ensued, there and elsewhere, helped lead to IRA ceasefires in 1974 and 1975. There are many conflicting accounts about what was conveyed and why, with allegations that the officials involved in the discussions led republicans to believe that their goal of British withdrawal was a distinct possibility. It was certainly an era of furtive contacts and murmured assurances: many mysteries persist about what was said and what was meant. There is no real evidence however that a British withdrawal was ever intended, whatever was discussed at Laneside.

The contacts did not at first result in a reduction of IRA violence. In the autumn of 1974 the IRA maintained a concerted campaign not just in Northern Ireland but also in England with a number of bombings which were to have lengthy legal sequels. Explosions at bars in Birmingham killed 21 people and injured almost 200 more, while 7 people died in the bombings of pubs in Guildford and Woolwich. While the IRA inflicted much damage on people and property it also suffered numerous casualties. By the beginning of 1974, almost 150 of its members had been killed, and hundreds more were behind bars.

In 1974, as contacts between the IRA and the government developed, there was no shortage of official and unofficial go-betweens. In one unprecedented move a group of senior northern Protestant churchmen travelled south to meet IRA leaders at Feakle in County Clare, reporting back to NIO officials on their talks. IRA demands which included a British declaration of intent to withdraw were conveyed to Rees, the IRA promising a cessation of violence in return. The organisation next delivered a brief ceasefire over the 1974 Christmas period. Rees responded by signing no new internment orders and giving an assurance that security force activity would be scaled down. He also sanctioned official contacts with the republicans to supplement the many unofficial contacts.

The IRA ceasefire survived into 1975 and, despite IRA complaints that the British were not responding to their proposals, it was extended and in February declared indefinite. Rees responded by continuing to release detainees, by scaling down army operations in nationalist areas, and by setting up 'incident centres' from which republicans could report on events in particular districts. In a formulation which would be important in later years, Rees also signalled that the British government had no territorial or political interests in Ireland beyond its obligations to the citizens of Northern Ireland. The SDLP and the Irish government strenuously objected to all of this, complaining that such moves enhanced the credibility of the IRA and Sinn Féin at their expense. While Rees insisted that there were no secret deals with the IRA, rumours were rife that the continuing contact between the government and republicans might lead to a British withdrawal.

The formal ceasefire lasted for much of 1975 but was often breached. A number of members of the security forces were killed in attacks which the IRA characterised as retaliations for official breaches of the ceasefire. Overall in 1975, 33 security force personnel died, exactly half the toll of the previous year.

Loyalist violence remained at a high level with both the UDA and UVF highly active. The IRA responded by becoming embroiled in what were described as sectarian 'tit-for-tat' exchanges, with more than forty Protestants killed in 1975 and January 1976. A few of them had loyalist connections but most were chosen at random. The attacks included an attack on an Orange Order meeting in south Armagh in which five were killed, a bombing and shooting attack on a Shankill Road pub which also killed five, and the killings of ten Protestant workmen, again in south Armagh, in retaliation for loyalist killings. Republican theorists, who say that loyalist groups are sectarian but insist that the IRA is not, look back on this particular period with some embarrassment. A violent Provisional IRA feud with the Official IRA in the autumn of 1975 added to the death toll.

By early November the ceasefire existed only in name and the incident centres were closed. In December Rees released the final internees and declared internment to be over, but was able to tell the Commons that in 1975 more than 1,100 people had been charged with paramilitary offences, and that the prison population had risen by 40 per cent. Meanwhile, of course, no steps towards British withdrawal had been taken. In fact, during the ceasefire period the authorities had been carefully planning a new security phase.

The mid-1970s ceasefire period is remembered in republican folklore as a disaster which brought the IRA close to defeat. It was said to have reduced morale and recruiting, and in republican terms it diverted the IRA's energies away from the security forces and into overtly sectarian killing and internecine feuding. Most republicans came to believe that the episode was essentially an exercise in deception, with officials promising the earth to a gullible republican leadership, which was headed at that time by southern veterans Ruairí Ó Brádaigh and Dáithí Ó Conaill. Northern republicans such as Gerry Adams and Martin McGuinness would later take control of the republican movement, arguing that the mid-1970s leaders had been duped. Years later McGuinness declared: 'The former leadership of this movement has never been able to come to terms with this leadership's criticism of the disgraceful attitude adopted by them during the disastrous ceasefire in the mid-1970s.'

The Rees convention

On the party political front, the constitutional convention produced only one moment of real interest. The whole exercise looked unpromising from the start, since in the wake of the UWC strike neither Unionists nor nationalists were in any mood to make concessions. Nationalists tended to feel that the British government had abdicated its fundamental governmental responsibilities and had caved in to intimidation. The general Unionist sense was that Sunningdale-style powersharing and the Irish dimension had been banished and that majority rule should now be re-established. This majoritarian sentiment was reinforced in the Westminster election of October 1974, when the UUUC MPs held ten of their eleven seats.

The elections to the convention in May 1975 produced a result which practically ensured that the new body would not reach agreement, since UUUC candidates won 47 of the 78 seats with 55 per cent of the vote. Support for Faulkner collapsed, with his UPNI taking less than 8 per cent of the vote. In the assembly in 1974 he had around twenty supporters but in 1975 he had only five. The man who had been close to the centre of power for so many years now cut a forlorn figure on the convention's backbenches, where his much-depleted band of supporters served as a daily reminder of the eclipse of moderate Unionism.

Before convention members got together at Stormont, Rees ordered workmen into the chamber to rearrange the furniture in the hope of encouraging them to think in terms of consensus rather than confrontation. Curved cross-benches were installed to make the point that Unionists and nationalists should aim to meet each other in the middle. The UUUC's overall majority ensured, however, that the creative carpentry was in vain.

It was true that there were many stresses and strains and personality differences within the UUUC, encompassing as it did West, Craig and Paisley and some independents. In the aftermath of the strike there had been a brief tussle between Unionist politicians and loyalist paramilitants who argued that their efforts during the stoppage entitled them to political representation. Although the politicians won these exchanges fairly easily, perhaps half a dozen of the 47 Unionist members had some form of paramilitary associations.

Most of these were linked not to the UDA or UVF, groups actively engaged in assassination campaigns, but to what were called 'doomsday' or 'respectable' groups, who saw themselves as being in the business of preparing for a possible civil war.

The fact that they, and many others, thought in such apocalyptic terms illustrates that the first half of the 1970s was a highly uncertain time in which many believed the worst might happen. Northern Ireland, after its first four decades of sullen stability, had gone through the political unrest of the 1960s followed by large-scale violence and constitutional upheavals: nobody was really sure what might come next, and many feared the worst. A common observation in shops and pubs at the time was, 'It'll get worse before it gets better.'

There were many in both Unionism and nationalism who suspected that in the wake of the strike Britain, feeling even less loyalty to the Unionist community than previously, was tempted by the withdrawal option. The SDLP urged the Irish government to prepare contingency plans for a doomsday scenario, a prospect Dublin took seriously. Dublin minister Garret FitzGerald, worried that Wilson might opt for British withdrawal, lobbied Henry Kissinger who was then US Secretary of State. He told Kissinger that Dublin might seek American assistance 'in persuading Britain not to embark on a course of action that could be so fraught with dangers'. FitzGerald's fears, as he later acknowledged, were groundless.

In the convention meanwhile Unionist members, whatever their differences, came together for key votes, their combined strength meaning that they always won on the important issues. There was no repeat of the unruly scenes of the assembly, since Unionists now regarded themselves as being in control. Yet even as Unionists flexed their majoritarian muscles in the chamber, surreptitious talks went on behind the scenes with the SDLP. These talks produced one intriguing idea known as 'voluntary coalition'. The idea, advanced primarily by William Craig, who had undergone a remarkable change since his 'shoot-to-kill' days a few years earlier, suggested the establishment of a new Unionist-dominated administration, with a prime minister who would invite SDLP members into his cabinet. The model was primarily based on the type of emergency coalition which had governed Britain during World War Two. The concept appears to have been discussed by leading members of the major Unionist parties, but all of them except Craig hurriedly backed away from it.

He not only failed to carry the UUUC with him, but failed to convince his own Vanguard party. He and a few assembly members, including future Unionist party leader David Trimble, were banished from the UUUC, which even without them still had an overall majority in the convention. There was no agreement between the UUUC and the rest of the assembly's members. The UUUC drew up a report which was essentially a Unionist wish-list, seeking a return to majority rule and ruling out any new Council of Ireland. The report wanted a new Stormont with even greater powers, a doubling of Northern Ireland seats at Westminster, and the introduction of an oath of allegiance to the Queen for all major appointments. Nationalists were offered little more than the prospect of chairing some committees.

The other parties, complaining their views had been ignored, boycotted the final debates and submitted minority reports. Rees asked the Unionists to reconsider but they stuck to their original report and in March 1976 he wound up the convention. Realistically, there was no chance of the British government accepting the convention report. Its underlying philosophy was simple: the restoration of Unionist majority rule, with a coalition headed by West, Paisley and Craig's successor, Ernest Baird.

The government was in a double bind. The display of loyalist strength in the UWC strike had led the government to conclude that it could not impose powersharing and an Irish dimension on an unwilling Protestant population. But at the same time it was not about to agree to the UUUC's demands to turn the clock back and revert to majority rule. The idea of Catholics and nationalists accepting a rebirth of Stormont was equally out of the question. The problem was what political policy the government might pursue if both powersharing and majority rule were non-starters. Its answer was to move away from the idea of finding political agreement and to concentrate instead on the security and economic fields. This new approach was personified in a new Northern Ireland Secretary, Roy Mason, who replaced Rees in September 1976.

The violence continues

The years 1975 and 1976 were a time of major violence which claimed almost six hundred lives. The IRA was as ever the highest single taker of life though loyalist groups were highly active. The army suffered far fewer casualties in 1975–76, losing 30 men compared to 250 killed during the previous four years. Killings attributed to the army were also well down: 20 people died at the hands of troops in these two years compared to 170 in the years from 1971 to 1974. But the civilian casualty rate remained high as the IRA and loyalists, particularly the UVF, carried out many attacks that resulted in civilian casualties. These included many bombings and shootings which caused multiple deaths. The IRA attacked a number of Protestant bars, while the UVF and UDA targeted many Catholic pubs.

A few incidents stand out. One was the January 1976 IRA attack, at Kingsmills in south Armagh, on a coachload of Protestant workmen, following a wave of anti-Catholic attacks by the UVF. IRA gunmen lined up the workmen at the side of the road and opened fire with at least four weapons, killing ten men. Also well-remembered are the actions of the IRA unit which became known as the Balcombe Street gang in and around London. They carried out up to fifty bombings and shootings in the London area during 1974 and 1975, especially an intense burst of violent activity in late 1975 which included no-warning bomb attacks on pubs and other premises. Fifteen people were killed.

Loyalists were more unabashedly and consistently sectarian than the IRA. Republicans often denied the IRA was involved in sectarian killings and sometimes used a cover name to claim responsibility for attacks. The UVF and UDA, by contrast, made little secret of the fact that they regarded the Catholic population in general as legitimate targets, and made no bones about attacking Catholic bars and other targets with the aim of killing as many as possible. In one UVF killing spree on a single day in October 1975 twelve people died in an unprecedented wave of shootings and bombings. Most of those killed were Catholic, though the death toll included four UVF members killed when their own bomb exploded prematurely. Thirteen UVF bombs went off during the day.

One of the UVF members involved in the killings was Lenny Murphy, who was later to be killed by the IRA. He was leader of the Shankill Butchers gang, a collection of UVF members responsible for a large number of murders which together make up what are probably the most notorious sequence of killings in Northern Ireland. The deaths, which stretched over many years, included both sectarian killings and many loyalist feud deaths. They included shootings, bombings and in particular killings carried out with knives and by savage beatings. The most infamous were those of seven Catholics who between 1975 and 1977 were picked up at random during the hours of darkness. The victims were selected solely for their religion. They were then killed with implements such as cleavers, axes and the butchers' knives which earned the gang their nickname. Some had their throats cut and others were tortured. In a statement to police about one victim a member of the gang said: 'When he was lying on the ground I cut his throat. It was a butcher's knife I had, sharp as a lance. I just slit his throat right open.'

While Murphy himself did not take part in all of the killings he was regarded as the gang's leader and driving force, even while in prison. During an inquest a detective said of him: 'He was a ruthless, dedicated terrorist with a sadistic streak, regarded by those who knew him well as a psychopath. He inflicted terror on those around him.' The ferocity of some of the killings meant that the gang's actions remained fresh in the public consciousness years after the actual events. Many of the group were jailed in a large-scale trial in 1979. Eleven gang members were sentenced on more than a hundred charges which included nineteen murders, receiving a total of 42 life sentences, along with sentences of imprisonment amounting to almost 2,000 years. Passing sentence the judge said: 'Many of the murders you have pleaded guilty to were carried out in a manner so cruel and so ruthless as to be beyond the comprehension of any normal person.' Murphy was himself already in jail serving a sentence for lesser offences. He was not charged in the Shankill Butchers trial and was never convicted of murder.

One incident which sent shock waves through Anglo-Irish relations was the IRA assassination of the British ambassador to the Republic, Christopher Ewart-Biggs, in Dublin in July 1976. The attack took place just beyond the gates of his County Dublin official residence: his car was blown up by a landmine, killing him and his secretary. He had been ambassador for only twelve days before his death. It later emerged that Merlyn Rees had at the last minute been forced to cancel plans which would have meant that he too would have been travelling in the convoy. Garret FitzGerald, then Irish foreign minister and later Taoiseach, wrote of the ambassador: 'He was to pay his first official visit to me at 10 a.m. Just as I had finished clearing my desk to receive him, I was told there had been an explosion near his residence. I was filled with horror at the atrocity, with shame that Irishmen had murdered the envoy of a neighbouring country, and with shock at our failure to protect him.'

A month later, in August 1976, came another terrible incident which, at the same time as taking the lives of innocents, momentarily seemed to hold out the hope of helping bring an end to the violence. It would prove to be a false dawn. The incident began when a member of the IRA was shot dead by troops at the wheel of a car during a car chase in west Belfast. The vehicle careered out of control and mounted the pavement at a school where a Catholic woman, Anne Maguire, was walking with her three children. The car crushed them all against railings.

The crash killed eight-year-old Joanne Maguire and her brothers John, aged two, and Andrew who, only six weeks old, was being pushed in a pram. Anne Maguire was unconscious for two weeks before awakening to discover that three of her four children were dead. As one account put it, 'When the wrecked car, pram and bicycle were removed local residents set up a little shrine at the mangled railings. Flowers and candles marked the scene of a tragedy that cut through the emotional defences of a community inured to all manner of atrocity.'

The wave of anger and grief generated by the deaths gave rise to the Peace People movement, led by two Belfast women, Mairead Corrigan, the children's aunt, and local woman Betty Williams. The movement quickly snowballed, its early rallies attracting tens of thousands of people and huge international publicity. As the months passed, however, the movement suffered from outside criticism, internal bickering and personality clashes. The award of the Nobel Peace Prize to its two leaders did nothing to halt the arguments and the slide in its credibility and popularity, critics accusing them of mercenary motives. The movement eventually petered out, a transient phenomenon with powerful initial impetus but which in the end did not deliver peace.

In a tragic postscript Anne Maguire took her own life some years later, leaving a note for her surviving children which said, 'Forgive me – I love you.' Although she regained her health she never recovered psychologically from the loss of her children. Her sister Mairead Corrigan later wrote: 'Anne never saw her children buried. In her own mind she refused to accept their deaths. She would often talk about seeing them playing in the garden. Their deaths and the brain bruising she suffered resulted in psychotic depression. Anne became a troubled soul, knowing no peace of mind. She seemed to lock herself in a private world with her dead babies.'

No one could know it at the time, but late 1976 and early 1977 were to mark the end of the most violent phase of the troubles. These months were followed by no new political agreement, but the killing rate dropped dramatically. The statistics tell the story. Of the more than 3,700 troubles deaths, almost exactly half took place in the period of five years and four months which began when internment was introduced in August 1971. In the final months of

1971 the total killed was 149; the total deaths for the five years which followed were, in rough terms, 500, 260, 300, 260 and 300. In the quarter-century which followed, deaths would never exceed 125 in a single year. But the deaths, though fewer, were to continue for a quarter of a century and more.

6.

From Castlereagh to Warrenpoint
1977–79

The second strike

Roy Mason, who took over as Northern Ireland Secretary in September 1976, was very different from Merlyn Rees in both style and substance. Rees's two and a half years in Belfast had been a harrowing time for him, as Harold Wilson's press secretary Joe Haines observed: 'Northern Ireland wore out Merlyn Rees. He ached, and looked as if he ached, with tiredness after his first 15 months in office.' Haines saw him as 'a good, kind and able minister who had become trapped by his office and was too exhausted to realise he had little more to offer'.

Roy Mason was a very different character. A tough Barnsley ex-miner who was short in physical stature but long on self-confidence, he was as decisive as Rees had been tentative. He arrived in Belfast following a spell as defence minister, a job which encouraged him to think in terms of a military approach. Where Rees had rambled, Mason was blunt; where Rees had anguished about the complexities of office, Mason tended to reduce policy to brass tacks.

Almost from the start he made a number of strategic choices. While Rees had maintained contact with republicans with the aim of gaining ceasefires, Mason quickly made it clear that he was in the more straightforward business of defeating the IRA. At his first press conference he described the IRA as 'reeling', and within months had closed down Laneside, the NIO residence associated with suspicions of underhand deals. This sent out a signal that the days of secret conversations were over. Many had not trusted Merlyn Rees when he declared that a British withdrawal was not in prospect. When Mason gave such assurances, which he did with regularity, he tended to be believed. This was largely because he was so clearly determined, in the language of the day, to 'take on the terrorists'.

He also made it clear that the days of political initiatives, on the scale of Sunningdale or even the constitutional convention, were over. He spoke of steering clear of 'dramatic initiatives that might lead to failure and leave people in deep despair again'. He remarked later in his autobiography: 'I thought it futile to barge in with great plans and programmes and proposals for constitutional change.' This approach dismayed many local politicians, who saw it as a declaration that they were redundant and were to be sidelined. Concluding that a search for political agreement among the parties was pointless, Mason instead concentrated on security and the economy in the hope that militant republicanism could be defeated by a mixture of security force activity and job creation.

Unionists meanwhile approached the late 1970s with a mixture of satisfaction and frustration: satisfaction that they had comprehensively defeated the Sunningdale powersharing initiative, but frustration at Westminster's flat refusal to bring back majority rule. The 1974 UWC strike had shown muscle, while the Unionist strength in numbers was also evident in the convention and Westminster elections which had established beyond doubt that anti-deal Unionist parties were very much dominant. But while they were clearly in the ascendant they could not deliver a new Protestant ascendancy. While Unionism had the negative power of being able to prevent powersharing, it conspicuously lacked the power of persuasion. No significant body of opinion in the Commons supported the convention report's demand for a return to majority rule; in fact in all the years that followed, Unionism failed to persuade any significant section of opinion of the merits of simple majority rule.

May 1977 brought an attempt by some sections of Unionism to extract by coercion what could not be achieved by persuasion, via an attempt to stage a rerun of the 1974 UWC strike. Although the UUUC was still in existence at this stage as a political co-ordinating body, it divided and fell apart on the issue of a second strike. Ian Paisley and Ernest Baird were enthusiastic, but major elements such as Harry West's Ulster Unionist party and the Orange Order stayed aloof. Paisley and Baird became involved, together with the UWC and paramilitary groups including the UDA, in a new organisation styling itself the United Unionist Action Council (UUAC).

In April this body announced that an indefinite strike would be launched the following month, with the aims of pressurising Westminster into a stronger security policy and the return of majority rule. From the start the odds seemed to be against the success of the strike, with little real appetite for it within the general Protestant community. There was a clear division in Unionist ranks on the tactic; Mason was more to the liking of most Unionists than Rees, and the early months of the year had seen a reduction of violence. There were also no unpopular targets around, as there had been in 1974 in the form of the Sunningdale Agreement. The move was opposed by almost the entire business community, trade unions and the main Protestant churches. Paisley and Baird did their best to stir up feelings with over-the-top rhetoric, Baird accusing Westminster politicians of losing their sense of British identity and having 'maybe more in common with Communist Russia or anarchy than they have with the British way of life'. Paisley too condemned British politicians: 'When I consider the drunkenness, lewdness, immorality and filthy language of many MPs, I care absolutely nothing for their opinions. Ulster Protestants are not interested in gaining the goodwill of such reprobates.'

When the strike was launched on 2 May, widespread intimidation was evident from the outset, the RUC receiving 400 complaints on its first day. Although many workplaces opened normally there was a steady stream of closures during the day. Gangs of up to a hundred UDA men appeared on main roads in loyalist areas of Belfast, vehicles were hijacked and roads strewn with broken glass, and many businesses reported threatening telephone calls.

Within days, however, a drift back to work was reported. A crucial factor was that the authorities performed very differently in 1977 than they had in 1974. They had clearly absorbed many lessons from the previous stoppage and had made contingency plans. Mason also proved to be a much more determined figure than Rees. When loyalists blocked a main road in east Belfast, police and troops in riot gear were sent in to move them on, and after a brief skirmish the loyalists took to their heels. Thus while intimidation and road-blocks had some effect, the security forces were seen to be working to keep roads open.

Another vital factor was that there were virtually no power cuts. Some power workers co-operated with the strike leaders, but a majority resented being dragooned into the front line of a strike which lacked widespread support. Some of them stopped work but most stayed at their posts, supplying enough electricity to avoid widespread cuts. The only interruptions to supply came in a few areas where loyalists set off explosive devices.

Behind the scenes Mason and Paisley were locked in intense efforts to lobby the power workers, oil tanker drivers and other key workers. The turning point came when workers at the principal power station, Ballylumford, voted by 286 to 171 in a secret ballot not to support the stoppage. By this stage, leaders of the three main Protestant churches were protesting against what they described as 'extensive intimidation and brutality'.

Increasingly desperate, the loyalist paramilitary groups escalated their violence, and there were three deaths in one day as they blew up a filling station and shot dead a bus driver. None of this helped the strikers' cause and the stoppage was ignominiously called off soon afterwards, Paisley declining to stand by a pledge to retire from political life if the strike failed. Although the strike collapsed, Mason acknowledged in his memoirs that it was a close-run thing, writing: 'At any moment during the ten days of crisis, the balance could so easily have tilted against the government. Intimidation might have worked; Paisley might have succeeded in rallying the great mass of Protestants.'

It seemed a humiliating defeat for Paisley, yet within a week of the strike's end came local council elections which offered a telling insight into the Protestant attitude towards protests in general and

Paisley in particular. In the poll, Paisley's party vote dropped only slightly. It was a demonstration of his own extraordinary resilience and a demonstration too that the Unionist electorate did not punish those representatives whom it felt had protested too much. Those such as Brian Faulkner who were considered too accommodating could be heavily penalised at the polls, but those whose line was thought too hard were not.

Because it petered out, the second strike has received little attention in accounts of the troubles. The fact is that the stoppage took place exactly as one phase of the troubles was ending and another was beginning. How much this watershed was due to the strike and its outcome, and how much may have been sheer coincidence are matters for debate. What is not in question is that the level of violence plummeted so dramatically around this time that 1977 can only be regarded as an important turning point in the troubles.

Violence and changing security policy

The 308 deaths of 1976 were followed by only 116 in 1977. The troubles would drag on for a further quarter of a century, but the early months of 1977 mark the halfway point in terms of lives lost. The most dramatic change in the casualty figures was the decline in the number of civilians killed, from 220 in 1976 to 55 the following year.

Violence by loyalists decreased from 127 killings in 1976 to just 28 in 1977. In the five years prior to 1977 the loyalist toll was 590; in the five years from 1977 on it was only 84. Most immediately this was attributed to the defeat suffered by the UDA, the largest of the Protestant paramilitary organisations, in the UUAC strike. In the years that followed membership of such groups as the UDA dropped sharply, while many other less active paramilitary organisations, such as the Orange Volunteers, virtually disappeared from the scene.

There were deeper reasons for this than simply the failure of the strike. For one thing, Mason's approach caused many loyalists to conclude that it was simply no longer necessary for them to involve themselves in paramilitarism. Mason's political line, which he pursued with ever-greater confidence following the strike, was to go after the IRA and loyalist paramilitants with tougher security policies. As this policy became clear and the overall level of violence fell, many working-class Protestants concluded that the IRA was being tackled with determination, that the Union looked safe, and that their presence in the paramilitary ranks was not needed.

The Rees administration had made various plans aimed at putting security policy on a more logical and rational basis, and Mason and the new Chief Constable of the RUC, a shrewd Englishman called Kenneth Newman, built on these to produce a coherent if often controversial strategy. Among important strategic changes to security and political policy were the concepts of 'criminalisation' and 'Ulsterisation'. The first meant that the IRA and other paramilitary groups were to be denied any acknowledgement of political motivation, and were to be treated in exactly the same way as those the authorities sarcastically called 'ordinary decent criminals'. Mason and others spoke regularly of the IRA as a mafia-style organisation headed by 'godfathers' who were said to care more for money than for patriotism. The policy was partly motivated by a desire to change perceptions of the conflict from the colonial war of republican propaganda to that of a campaign against criminal gangs. The battle over criminalisation would later come to a head in the prisons. Ulsterisation was a play on the word 'Vietnamisation', the process by which the US army in Vietnam had recruited and trained locals to take the place of US troops in the front line. In a Belfast context this involved planning a gradual decrease in the number of regular troops and their replacement by an expanded RUC and UDR. It also meant what was known as 'police primacy', giving the RUC the lead in security matters and placing the army largely under its direction.

The policy brought about striking changes in casualty patterns. In 1972, 110 regular soldiers and 40 locally recruited personnel were killed. For 1976 the corresponding figures were 14 and 40, with local deaths out-numbering the deaths of regular troops in almost every year of the decade that followed. In spite of the high casualty rates, large numbers of local men, almost all of them Protestants, were ready to join the RUC and UDR, both of which consistently had more applications than vacancies. Ulsterisation also made broad political sense in that the drop in regular army casualties helped prevent any build-up of sentiment in Britain for a withdrawal from Northern Ireland.

Internment had been ended at the end of 1975, and an alternative approach was developed to put paramilitants and especially IRA members behind bars using the criminal courts. Since the early 1970s the trials of defendants charged with troubles-related offences had taken place not before a jury but before a single judge. Juries had been abolished following the 1972 Diplock report which had highlighted the fear of paramilitary intimidation of jurors. For the same reason witnesses were in short supply and very often refused to testify. Forensic evidence was of some use, but the authorities realised that the most effective way of securing convictions was to extract confessions from the accused.

This simple fact became the new central plank of the RUC's battle with the IRA and loyalist groups. Its detective ranks were reorganised, with specialist collators appointed, in the largely pre-computer age, to amass and analyse every scrap of evidence. Trained teams of interrogators were then put to work in new specially designed interrogation centres, most notably at Castlereagh in east Belfast. IRA and loyalist suspects were rounded up by the score and subjected to intense interrogations, with many of them subsequently charged with serious offences. As this system, which functioned with the regularity of a conveyor belt, got under way, it was found that although violence was decreasing, the number of people being charged stayed at more than a thousand a year. Lengthy remand periods meant that even those eventually acquitted were often taken off the streets for more than a year.

Before long, most cases heard by the non-jury courts consisted of the prosecution producing an incriminating statement or statements which the defendant was said to have made voluntarily while in Castlereagh or one of the other interrogation centres. The classic defence in such cases was for the defendant to say that the statement was not admissible in evidence because it had been extracted through either physical or psychological ill-treatment. The outcome of the trial would then turn on whether the judge ruled that the statement had been extracted by fair and legal means or whether detectives had extracted it through threats or by beatings. Both republicans and loyalists claimed brutality had become routine within Castlereagh and that convictions were being secured 'through the systematic application of torture techniques'. There were also stirrings of concern among civil liberties groups and other bodies. Garret FitzGerald records that leaders of the Presbyterian Church privately asked him to use his influence on the British government because they believed a number of loyalist suspects had been beaten during interrogation.

Other aspects of security policy also became decidedly tougher, with increased use of the army's undercover SAS regiment to stage ambushes in which IRA members were shot. During 1978 four members of the IRA were killed in this way, the SAS also accidentally killing three uninvolved civilians in the same year.

Party differences

Dublin and the SDLP quietly applauded Mason's performance in the UUAC strike, lamenting only that he had not been in office during the 1974 strike instead of Rees. Nevertheless, the constitutional nationalists were much against Mason's approach of downplaying politics and concentrating on security, since to them it was an article of faith that there was no military solution and that the troubles could only be ended by political means.

The SDLP came out of the experiences of Sunningdale, the UWC strike and the constitutional convention a greatly disillusioned party. Until the 1974 strike, things had seemed to be going well for constitutional nationalism: first Wilson and Callaghan had pushed for reforms, and then Heath had gone further and decided that nationalists needed to be in government. Heath had also come to support the existence of a strong Irish dimension, and Dublin had become established as a major element in the Northern Ireland question. Things had fallen apart, however, with the UWC strike, the resurgence of hardline Protestant power, and Labour's subsequent unwillingness to consider taking on the loyalists again. Brian Faulkner's untimely death in a horse-riding accident in 1977 seemed to epitomise the demise of moderate Unionism. From this viewpoint the convention had achieved little beyond confirming that with West, Paisley and Baird in control of Unionism there was no prospect of accommodation. One newspaper columnist wrote of the SDLP: 'Since the convention's failure the party has clung to a position which more and more of its members see as entirely honourable and yet completely nonsensical – offering partnership to parties who don't want it. The Unionists don't want to know them.'

The SDLP and in particular John Hume, its chief strategist, reacted to these unwelcome but unmistakable facts of life by moving to internationalise the question. Hume gradually shifted the focus away from the search for powersharing in Belfast and into an Anglo-Irish context, pressing London and Dublin to work together on a new approach. He also went further afield, cultivating the American political and media establishment to great effect. As early as 1977 he played a major part in persuading the most significant Irish-American politicians, who included Senator Edward Kennedy and the Speaker of the House of Representatives, Tip O'Neill, to unite as an Irish-American political force.

One motive for this was to wrest Irish-American influence away from the republican movement, for many Irish-Americans simplistically viewed the conflict in Northern Ireland as a classic colonial struggle between British occupying forces and the gallant freedom-fighters of the IRA. In this romantic version of events many complicating factors, including the very existence of the Unionist population, simply did not exist when viewed from across the Atlantic. This enabled the IRA to obtain both money and guns from Irish-Americans. Hume and the Irish government, which was represented in Washington by some exceptionally able Irish diplomats, sought to deny Irish-American influence to the republicans and instead harness it as a resource for constitutional nationalism.

Nationalist disenchantment with London increased as the belief grew that the Unionist party was gaining fresh influence at Westminster, not through force of argument but because James Callaghan's government had a dwindling majority and was anxious to persuade Unionists not to help bring it down. Callaghan supplied Unionists with a number of modest concessions including an increase in the number of Northern Ireland seats in the Commons. Nationalists accused Callaghan, who had been seen as being pro-nationalist in the late 1960s, of involvement in a sordid deal with Unionists.

Although there was never any question of Callaghan agreeing to the return of majority rule, by this stage some Unionists were themselves questioning whether this would be a good idea. Harry West as party leader and indeed the vast bulk of Unionist voters were still wedded to traditional devolution, but the alternative idea of integration with Britain was quietly gaining ground. The concept, which had been espoused briefly by Paisley around 1972, never found widespread support among the Unionist grassroots but it did take root in some important sections of the party. Among its devotees were MP James Molyneaux, who in 1979 was to succeed West as party leader, and his close associate Enoch Powell, the one-time Tory minister who had become a Unionist MP after splitting with the Conservative party on the race issue. Part of the attraction of integration was that, since majority rule seemed unattainable, it might be the next best thing and would be easier to achieve. It received philosophical underpinning from Powell, who had constructed intricate theories on why it, rather than devolution, was the best way of securing the Union. The notion grew that direct rule, which was not strictly integration but was leaning in that direction, was not a regrettable necessity but a system which could itself have beneficial effects and might be built upon.

Mason meanwhile strove as far as possible to present a normal face to the world, paying close attention to measures to strengthen the local economy. He staked a great deal of credibility, and a very great deal of public money, on a flagship project designed to provide a dramatic kickstart. In an attempt which was simultaneously imaginative, desperate and foolish, Mason announced a £56 million government subsidy to glamorous American car maker John De Lorean to establish a new plant to produce futuristic luxury sports cars on the outskirts of west Belfast. Years later the venture was to end in a costly fiasco, the plant eventually closing with much of the money unaccounted for, no cars being produced for sale and no lasting jobs.

Republican evolution

Meanwhile significant changes were taking place within the republican movement with a younger northern element, most importantly Gerry Adams and Martin McGuinness, taking power from the older southerners Ruairí Ó Brádaigh and Dáithí Ó Conaill in a bloodless coup. Adams emerged from behind bars in the spring of 1977 following a spell in prison where he had built a reputation as a formidable theorist. Once back on the outside he deftly eased the old guard aside. The northerners argued that the ceasefire of the mid-1970s had been disastrous for the IRA and that not enough was being done to counteract the Castlereagh interrogation system. Once in charge, the new leaders made many significant changes in terms of both republican politics and of the structure of the IRA.

They set out to dispel among republicans the idea that an IRA victory was just around the corner, a belief that had lingered since the 1975 ceasefire. The new orthodoxy was set out in a speech, largely drafted by Adams, which was delivered in 1977 by respected republican veteran Jimmy Drumm. This declared: 'The British government is not withdrawing from the Six Counties. It is committed to stabilising the Six Counties and is pouring in vast amounts of money to assure loyalists and secure from loyalists support for a long haul against the IRA.' Adams later explained in his autobiography: 'We had not yet developed an integrated or strategic overview, but our entire struggle was at a crucial juncture, a defining moment, and we were convinced that the struggle needed to sort itself out and to go on.'

To cope with the British long haul the IRA would develop what came to be known as the 'long war', a war of attrition which it accepted would have to go on for years. The IRA fell back on hoping that political stalemate, continued violence, occasional attacks in Britain, international pressure, the enormous cost and the apparent insolubility of the problem would ultimately sap Britain's will to stay in Northern Ireland. To the republican mind, Unionists were not a major problem, being merely puppets of British imperialism. In republican theory the real enemy was Britain; and once Britain had been defeated Unionist resistance would simply collapse.

There was increasing internal republican debate on future tactics. Adams in particular argued the need for the IRA campaign to be augmented by political action, a notion in which can be seen the germ of his later emphasis on building up Sinn Féin into an organisation in its own right. Adams, who in this deeply militaristic movement always thought in conspicuously political terms, was to write: 'There is now a realisation in republican circles that armed struggle on its own is inadequate and that non-armed forms of political struggle are at least as important.' More than a few republicans noted the similarities with the road taken into politics by the old IRA in the 1960s. The difference this time was that entry into the political arena was being advocated by republicans whose continued commitment to the armed struggle was beyond doubt, and who saw the politics as part of the war.

The same northern leadership that was urging more emphasis on politics was simultaneously reshaping the IRA into a more effective killing machine. The IRA was partly reorganised into a cell structure in order to guard against the effects of informers and interrogation. It also widened its range of targets, killing a number of senior business figures and explaining in statements that such individuals were attempting to stabilise the economy and were therefore 'part of the British war machine'. Prison staff also became what the IRA termed 'legitimate targets', with many killings of off-duty officers. A new threat to the security forces emerged with the appearance of what was known as 'the M60 gang', a group of IRA members armed with heavy M60 machine guns smuggled in from America where they had been stolen from US armed forces. The weapon, which was capable of firing 600 shots a minute, proved devastating in urban ambushes, claiming the lives of eight members of the security forces. The IRA also kept up its attacks on the locally recruited security forces, causing the deaths of many RUC and UDR members.

February 1978 brought another of those events which recurred periodically during the republican campaign, in which the IRA both inflicted great human tragedy and damaged its own interests. This was the bombing of La Mon House, a small hotel on the outskirts of east Belfast. IRA members attached a bomb to a grille on a window, as they had done at several other business premises, and made off. But unlike other occasions the warning given was inadequate and the premises had not been evacuated when the device went off. The result was devastating.

The device produced an effect similar to napalm, sending a fireball rushing through the window and through a room containing dozens of people attending the annual dinner-dance of the Irish Collie Club. A waitress said later: 'People were on fire, actually burning alive. I watched men pulling long curtains off the rails and wrapping people up in them to try to put out the flames. I could smell the burning flesh. I didn't realise at the time what I was smelling but I realised later what that dreadful stench was.'

The explosion killed twelve people, seven of them women, and injured more than thirty others. Those who died included three married couples; all the victims were Protestants. A local paper reported: 'For those who were there to see this holocaust it was sickening. Sickening to see pieces of a human body, limbs and other parts of the body being lifted. Many of them were just pure red flesh so indistinguishable that even forensic science experts found difficulty in sifting out their identification.' Thousands of posters showing a charred and incinerated body, so burnt as to be unrecognisable, were distributed by the RUC.

In his memoirs Adams claimed the incident left him despondent, depressed and deeply affected by the deaths and injuries, adding: 'I could also feel two years of work go down the drain.' Up until the La Mon bomb the IRA had been causing fewer civilian casualties, partly because the drop in loyalist violence had brought a sharp decrease in tit-for-tat killings, and partly because it knew how counterproductive civilian deaths were.

For the IRA the almost unimaginable horror of the La Mon attack was a disastrous setback, since although it regarded itself as an army, almost the entire world regarded La Mon as sheer terrorism, indefensible on any basis. In IRA terms this was one of the lowest points of the troubles, giving the authorities great scope to move against them. The security forces duly took the initiative, making twenty-five arrests in west Belfast in the aftermath of the explosion. Among those arrested was Adams, who was not charged in connection with the attack but was accused of IRA membership. He was acquitted, though only after spending months back behind bars.

It soon became apparent, however, that although the world at large had recoiled from the horror of La Mon the republican core support had remained loyal. But it was clear that the IRA was at a low ebb, the La Mon attack demoralising its members and the Castlereagh system sending a steady stream of them behind bars, either for lengthy periods on remand or for even lengthier sentences following conviction.

There were rumours that the IRA, which was undoubtedly much weakened, might be forced into declaring a ceasefire. The difference between this ceasefire and the 1975 one, it was said, was that this would be unilateral rather than as a result of an agreement with the government. It would, in other words, signal a defeat rather than a deal. Emboldened by intelligence reports to this effect Mason made several highly optimistic statements forecasting that the IRA was on its last legs, saying at one point: 'My view is that their strength has waned to the point where they cannot sustain a campaign.'

The anticipated ceasefire never arrived, and things began to go wrong for the authorities in terms of the Castlereagh system. This was producing results in putting republicans behind bars, but in the process it was attracting more and more criticism. The government issued blanket denials of any wrongdoing, Mason describing criticisms as 'wild allegations'. In his autobiography he listed a series of killings and summed up: 'Words cannot express the disgust I felt when the people responsible for such evils bleated about the alleged erosion of their human rights.'

Interrogation was not a gentle business. Questioning, by rotating teams of detectives, could go on for six to eight hours a day with few breaks, and even long into the night. The courts threw out some cases, but for the most part allowed detectives a great degree of latitude, one senior judge ruling that a blow to the face which left the nose 'swollen and caused it to bleed' did not necessarily mean a subsequent confession was inadmissible as evidence. The assumption was widespread that fists were being freely used in Castlereagh and elsewhere. As one newspaper columnist summed up: 'Hardly anyone believes that members of the RUC do not rough up suspects. The only things in question, in the minds of most, are how frequently such treatment occurs, whether it is sanctioned at top level, and whether it is justified.'

Mason was to recall in his memoirs: 'I had been harassing the IRA with as much vigour as was legally acceptable in a liberal democracy. I was being as tough as I could be; and though my policy was undeniably a ruthless business, it at least meant that the level of violence was beginning to come down.' The government found itself locked in a propaganda firestorm with republicans, one denying ill-treatment in Castlereagh while the other claimed it was routine and rife. The problem for the authorities was that the republican claims were at least partly backed by non-republican sources.

A 1978 Amnesty International report concluded that 'maltreatment of suspected terrorists by the RUC has taken place with sufficient frequency to warrant the establishment of a public inquiry to investigate it'. Under pressure from this and numerous other allegations the government established a judicial committee to investigate. In the meantime a leading police doctor caused a major stir when he said he had seen a large number of people who had been physically ill-treated while in custody. When it appeared in 1979 the official report judiciously steered away from making direct accusations against the police, but made dozens of recommendations which taken together amounted to a programme for a complete overhaul of interrogation safeguards and complaints procedures. Once these were enacted the level of complaints dropped dramatically.

Hopes for an IRA ceasefire faded as Mason's assessments were shown up as unrealistic. While he had talked enthusiastically of rolling the IRA up 'like a tube of toothpaste', a leaked 1979 army document written by a senior army officer painted a very different picture of the organisation. He wrote:

> There is a stratum of intelligent, astute and experienced terrorists who provide the backbone of the organization. Our evidence of the calibre of rank-and-file terrorists does not support the view that they are merely mindless hooligans drawn from the unemployed and unemployable. The IRA will probably continue to recruit the men it needs. They will still be able to attract enough people with leadership talent, good education and manual skills to continue to enhance their all-around professionalism. By reorganizing on cellular lines, PIRA has become much less dependent on public support than in the past and is less vulnerable to penetration by informers. The campaign is likely to continue while the British remain in Northern Ireland.

The IRA was not the only danger on the republican side, for the much smaller Irish National Liberation Army (INLA) claimed an increasing number of lives from the late 1970s on. This group began life in the mid-1970s as a Marxist grouping to the left of the IRA, but as the years went by it became much more republican than socialist. It carried out a high-profile attack during the Westminster general election campaign in the spring of 1979. Airey Neave, who was the shadow Northern Ireland Secretary and one of Conservative party leader Margaret Thatcher's closest aides, died when members of the INLA planted a booby-trap bomb which exploded underneath his car as he drove out of the House of Commons. He had been in charge of Thatcher's successful campaign for the Tory leadership against Heath in 1975, and was expected to become Northern Ireland Secretary after the general election.

The election of the Thatcher government in May brought a new Northern Ireland Secretary in the shape of Humphrey Atkins, who is remembered as a less forthright and less forceful minister than Mason. The Thatcher government had only been in office a few months when two events on a single day, 27 August, created a major security crisis. These were the assassination of the Queen's cousin, Lord Mountbatten, and the deaths of eighteen soldiers at Warrenpoint in County Down.

Mountbatten died in the Irish Republic, together with three other people, when an IRA device exploded on board his pleasure craft in the sea off County Sligo, where he regularly holidayed. A great-grandson of Queen Victoria, he had served in the Royal Navy in both world wars, subsequently acting as the last British viceroy in India, overseeing the ending of British rule.

Within hours of his death came the Warrenpoint bombing, a two-stage IRA attack which inflicted on the army its worst casualty toll during the troubles by killing eighteen soldiers, sixteen of them members of the Parachute Regiment. The attack began as a convoy of two army trucks led by a Land Rover made its way along a road running parallel to Carlingford Lough, which at that point marks the boundary between Northern Ireland and the Republic. At this spot the Republic is only a few hundred yards away across the inlet.

An 800lb IRA bomb hidden in a trailer by the side of the road, concealed among bales of straw, was set off, killing six soldiers. When other troops arrived at the scene there was gunfire across the lough from IRA members in the Republic. The surviving paratroopers and the other soldiers who had gone to the scene established a defensive position behind nearby gates and a wall, not realising that the IRA, guessing that they would do so, had concealed a second device there. This large bomb was detonated half an hour after the first explosion, killing a dozen more soldiers. The incident was described as the Parachute Regiment's worst setback since Arnhem in World War Two. The deaths of the soldiers and Mountbatten had a huge impact, sparking a major Anglo-Irish political crisis and marking out that day as one of the most dramatic of the troubles.

The Mason era was a true turning-point in that violence fell dramatically, and would never again rise to the scale experienced in the 1971–76 period. But the highest hopes of the Mason era were dashed: the theories that the De Lorean project could help turn round the economy, that Castlereagh would crush the IRA, that a military solution was possible without the need for political action. August 1979 cruelly shattered hopes that the troubles might be tailing off, leaving Northern Ireland to face the unpalatable fact that violent conflict looked set to continue indefinitely, and that the long war still had a long way to run.

7.

The hungerstrikes
1980–81

This was a year of comparative calm before the storm which was to break in 1981. It was a year when violence continued at a fairly low level while a half-hearted attempt at making political progress petered out within months. On the political front, in late 1979, Humphrey Atkins had announced plans for a conference of the major parties on devolution. The fact that the government made little attempt to apply serious pressure to the participants meant that from the start expectations were low. *The Economist*, for example, in an article entitled 'An initiative born to fail', declared, 'Even before the launch it was clear that the move stood little or no chance of success. Not a single Northern Ireland politician expects any real gains to come from the exercise.'

The conference precipitated an important personnel change at the highest level of Northern Ireland politics. Gerry Fitt, leader of the SDLP since its formation in 1970, believed his party was wrong in its decision to boycott the conference and resigned from it. More generally he complained that the SDLP was becoming less socialist and too nationalist. The party's other most prominent socialist, Paddy Devlin, had already gone, citing similar reasons.

Fitt and Devlin had been among Northern Ireland's best-known political personalities since the 1960s, providing much of the SDLP's early socialist character. Devlin had once declared, in a statement which also reflected Fitt's approach: 'I am basically a trade unionist and a socialist. I am not a Catholic or an Irish nationalist.' Both disapproved of the SDLP's increasing commitment to a stronger Irish dimension and its move away from the idea of powersharing.

As the years went by, however, the SDLP became greener and less leftwing, a process which was mirrored within the republican movement and within northern nationalism in general. The move away from the left was also in line with the trend in Britain, where Thatcherism was becoming the order of the day. Fitt and Devlin had thus tended to become isolated as nationalism shifted in a direction they disliked. When they eventually left, the fact that no one of note followed their lead illustrated the sense that they were figures who had not evolved in line with the rest of the party.

Fitt's natural successor as leader was John Hume, who as deputy leader had always been seen as the party's dominant theorist and strategist. The unique feature of Hume, who was already a well-known figure in both Europe and the US, was seen as his ability to combine theory with practical politics. He was among those who challenged the traditional nationalist assertion that the root of the problem was the British presence in Northern Ireland. He argued that the heart of the Irish question was not the British but the Protestants, that the problem was the divisions between Unionist and nationalist, and that partition was not the cause of division but a symptom of it. The mission of nationalism, he contended, was not to drive out the British but to convince Unionism that its concerns could be accommodated in an agreed Ireland.

The agenda for the Atkins conference illustrated that significant changes had taken place in London's thinking in ways which struck out in the opposite direction to the SDLP's progressively greener line. An official working paper set out a number of models, most of which were variations on the theme of powersharing. Some of its models envisaged having nationalists in government; others did not. The working paper specifically ruled out any return to either the old Stormont system or any revival of the Sunningdale Agreement, saying there was no prospect of agreement on either scheme. In a major change of policy, it flatly ruled out any Irish dimension, Atkins saying that, if the Irish dimension was raised at the conference, 'I shall rule it out of order, I shall say that it is out of order'.

This was clearly a major retreat from the approach of the last Conservative government which had insisted on the Irish dimension and whose preferred solution had been Sunningdale. At the same time the fact that a return to majority rule was firmly ruled out meant the conference held little attraction for Unionist politicians. While the SDLP eventually agreed to attend, to the surprise of many the conference was boycotted by the Ulster Unionist party, which had also acquired a new leader in the person of James Molyneaux.

Molyneaux took over in 1979 from Harry West, who had been trounced by Paisley in a European election. The party's official policy remained that of devolution, but it was an open secret that Molyneaux's personal preference was for integration. Seen in this light, his decision to stay away from the Atkins conference on devolution was perhaps predictable.

Although he was to serve as leader of the Unionist party for more than a decade and a half, until 1995, Molyneaux was such a quiet, reserved figure that he hardly became known to the British public. While his long-time rival Ian Paisley was noisy and obstreperous, Molyneaux was unfailingly courteous, the most low-key of politicians. What he had in common with Paisley was that he was simply not in the business of making a deal with nationalists. His belief, unshaken during his long years as Unionist leader, was that Unionism was best served by adopting a defensive posture to fend off all new initiatives and attempts at finding inter-party agreement. He once compared his role to that of 'a general with an army that isn't making anything much in terms of territorial gains but has the satisfaction of repulsing all attacks on the citadel'.

The models put forward by Atkins had included one which had evidently been designed to attract Molyneaux's interest, but the Unionist leader decided to steer well clear of the whole exercise in the hope that it would fizzle out and pave the way for a new integrationist approach. The government never would come round to an integrationist approach, but the Atkins conference certainly did rapidly peter out.

Violence and the prisons

The death toll for 1980 was 86, a considerable drop from the previous year's toll of 125. The year brought a new tack in loyalist violence, as the UDA expanded its activities from the random killing of Catholics to attacks on a number of prominent nationalist and republican figures. These included Protestant nationalist politician John Turnly, university lecturer Miriam Daly, and INLA activist Ronnie Bunting. In another attack in January 1981, Bernadette McAliskey, who as Bernadette Devlin had been MP for Mid-Ulster, had a near-miraculous escape from death when she and her husband were repeatedly shot by UDA gunmen.

What all these targets had in common was their prominence in what was known as 'the H-blocks campaign', which was waged in support of the continuing protests by republicans inside the Maze, the new name for Long Kesh prison. This dispute had been going on since 1976, though attracting little attention from the outside world. In late 1980 and in 1981, however, it developed into a fierce battle which is seen as one of the most important watersheds of the troubles.

In 1972 William Whitelaw had granted what was known as 'special category status' to prisoners associated with paramilitary groups. He had done so to defuse a hungerstrike by republican prisoners, at a time when he was anxious to open exploratory links to the IRA. The prisoners demanded to be treated differently from inmates jailed for criminal as opposed to paramilitary offences. Whitelaw would in later years admit that he had made a mistake in introducing special category status, or 'political status' as it was called by republicans, and subsequent Labour administrations worked on ways of bringing it to an end.

In the absence of adequate cell accommodation, internment and the special category system had given rise at Long Kesh to what in many respects resembled a World War Two prisoner-of-war camp. The internees and convicted prisoners lived in wartime Nissen huts within barbed-wire compounds. The continuation of special category status was a logical affront to the approach of criminalisation developed by Rees and later put into effect by Roy Mason, in that it was taken as an affirmation that jailed paramilitary inmates were in a sense political prisoners.

Republican and loyalist internees and 'special cats', as they were nicknamed, served their time in compounds inside Long Kesh, where they responded to orders not from warders but from their paramilitary 'OC', or Officer Commanding. To a large extent they controlled their own compounds. They wore their own clothes, were not forced to work, and were allowed additional visits and parcels. Prisoners and prison officers went their parallel but largely separate ways, with soldiers guarding the perimeter. The prisoners, divided into compounds by organisation, basically ran their own lives. It was this semblance of prisoner-of-war status which Rees had decided should end.

The authorities shied away from the idea of removing special category status from those inmates who already had it, correctly surmising that any such attempt would result in major disturbances. In late 1975 Rees announced that from early 1976 special category status would be phased out, with newly convicted prisoners expected to wear prison uniform, carry out prison work and have only limited association with other prisoners. These prisoners would be held not in the compounds but in newly built cell blocks in another part of the prison. These became known, because of their shape, as the H-blocks. Furthermore, there was to be an end to the segregation of paramilitary and non-paramilitary inmates. The H-blocks, as the authorities would repeatedly insist, provided some of the most modern prison conditions in western Europe. Loyalist prisoners initially objected to the changes and briefly staged protests but reluctantly accepted the new circumstances.

Many republican prisoners by contrast determinedly resisted the

changes, seeing prison uniform in particular as a badge of criminality they refused to acknowledge. A republican song became the
unofficial anthem of the protest, summing up their attitude:

> I'll wear no convict's uniform,
> Nor meekly serve my time,
> That England might
> Brand Ireland's fight
> Eight hundred years of crime.

From the autumn of 1976 on, republican prisoners refused to put on
prison clothes, and were punished by being kept in their cells
wrapped only in a blanket. A refusal to wear prison uniform left
prisoners naked, confined almost permanently to cells and regularly
punished for non-conforming by three days 'on the boards' when all
cell furniture was removed. Without uniform there were no family
visits and remission was lost, which in practice could double the
time spent in prison.

By mid-1977 almost 150 prisoners were refusing to cooperate with
the authorities. Mason had approached the issue with characteristic
grit, declaring in his memoirs: 'Whatever happened I was determined not to budge. The prisoners were criminals and as far as I
was concerned would always be treated as criminals.' Relations
between prisoners and prison officers, which in the compounds
were largely remote, rapidly became bitter. Prisoners complained
of beatings by groups of warders, while outside the prison the IRA
went on a systematic offensive against prison officers. Nineteen
were killed between 1976 and 1980, with ten dying in 1979, one of
whom was deputy governor of the Maze with particular responsibility for the H-blocks.

Adams wrote in his biography: 'Bitterness between prisoners and
screws was extreme. The screws were implementing a criminalisation regime, which included the violence and indignity of forced
washing. The IRA meanwhile were carrying out a policy on the
outside of shooting members of prison staffs.' After prisoners

stepped up the protest by smashing cell furniture they were each left with only a mattress and blankets. By 1978 there were already 300 'on the blanket'. As early as 1977 senior IRA members inside and outside the prison were suggesting to them that the protest was going nowhere, but the advice to drop it was rejected.

A frequent Unionist, and sometimes government, misconception throughout the years of protest was that these prisoners were unfortunate victims who were being sacrificed by a ruthless IRA leadership. In fact all the evidence points to an IRA leadership opposed to and frustrated by the tactics of the prisoners. These formed the one group within republicanism which was in a position to act against the wishes of the leadership in that they were accorded a freedom of action not normally permitted to others. They also had strength of numbers, for at any given time there were probably more IRA members in prison than outside: in 1980 for example there were over 800 republican prisoners.

The problem for the 'blanket men' was that by 1978 the protest was in its third year, the prison system appeared to be containing it, and outside the prison they had little support apart from the rest of the republican movement. A newspaper reported in early 1978: 'The current campaign has been going on for 18 months, with no sign of abating but equally no sign of success. Public support is minimal.' With their morale low, the prisoners stepped up the protest by resorting to a tactic which was simultaneously repulsive and, in Mason's later words, 'a brilliant stroke'. They launched what was initially a 'no wash' protest. As one prisoner wrote later: 'The pressure was on for movement. So we decided to escalate the protest and embark on the no wash protest. On hearing this, morale rose again. The lads were on a high.'

Up to that point they had left their cells to wash, empty their chamber pots, have showers and attend mass. Now they refused to leave the cells at all, leaving prison officers to empty the chamber pots. The clashes this led to meant that excrement and urine literally became weapons in the war between prisoners and prison officers. The no wash protest quickly became the 'dirty protest' with the remains of food and the overflowing chamber pots left in cells. Soon the protest was again escalated, prisoners spreading their excrement on the cell walls. As conditions reached dangerous levels with maggot infestations and the threat of disease, the prison authorities forcibly removed prisoners to allow cells to be steam-cleaned with special equipment. The prison authorities also responded with forcible baths, shaves and haircuts of protesting prisoners.

The dirty protest succeeded in its aim of winning publicity for the prisoners. The leader of the Catholic Church in Ireland, Cardinal Tomás Ó Fiaich, brought the issue to the fore when he paid a much-publicised visit to the jail and emerged to say he had found conditions similar 'to the plight of people living in sewer-pipes in the slums of Calcutta'. While he stopped short of calling for the reintroduction of special category status, he said republican prisoners must be looked upon as different from ordinary prisoners. He declared: 'No one could look on them as criminals. These boys are determined not to have criminal status imposed on them.'

Mason, like Unionist politicians, was outraged by what he later described as the cardinal's 'emotive and grossly biased' words. The Northern Ireland Secretary had until that point regarded the protest as embarrassing but containable, but the cardinal's visit received worldwide coverage. Mason later wrote: 'The image of prisoners naked in their cells with nothing for company but their own filth is undeniably potent, and it was being trumpeted round the world. But despite the adverse publicity I couldn't give in. To do so would give the IRA its biggest victory in years. It would mean the abandonment of the policy of police primacy and the rule of law.'

Although a major propaganda war raged between the republicans and the government from then on, there was still only minimal sympathy for the protesters. By 1980 even this extraordinary protest had become part of the prison routine, republican veteran Joe Cahill reluctantly concluding that 'the main demonstrations on the H-block issue have remained within the nationalist ghetto areas'.

The first hungerstrike

In 1980 the prisoners decided to employ what was seen as their ultimate weapon: a hungerstrike. It was a tactic with a chequered but
revered place in republican history, being regarded as close to the
ultimate in self-sacrifice and possible martyrdom. Although special
category status had first been won in 1972 with a hungerstrike, other
uses of the tactic had not proved effective. In the light of this record
the overall republican leadership was very much against the idea,
Adams recording that he wrote to the prisoners: 'We are tactically,
strategically, physically and morally opposed to a hungerstrike.'
One prisoner who was to spend seventy days on hungerstrike later
wrote that if the IRA had forbidden the move 'it would have been
an absolute disaster because people would have gone on hungerstrike anyway, and it would have caused a major split within the
IRA'.

Seven prisoners, who included one member of the INLA, went
on hungerstrike in October 1980. Republicans abandoned their
other protests, ending the killing of prison officers and winding
down the dirty protest. There were five demands: the right to wear
their own clothes; no prison-dictated work; free association; weekly
letters, visits and parcels, and the restoration of all remission lost as
a result of the protests.

Their adversary in chief was Margaret Thatcher, whose reputation
as the Iron Lady was partly to stem from her stance during this period.
At the time however she was a relatively untested prime minister who
had not yet established her full authority. She saw the prison confrontation as one between good and evil, democracy and terrorism. She
had lost a close friend and associate, in Airey Neave, to republican
violence, and as prime minister had been shaken by the Mountbatten
assassination and the deaths of eighteen soldiers at Warrenpoint. As
the hungerstrike began she stated: 'I want this to be utterly clear – the
government will never concede political status to the hungerstrikers
or to any others convicted of criminal offences.'

Through intermediaries the Northern Ireland Office indicated to republicans that concessions on matters such as clothes and the nature of work would be possible, but only once the hungerstrike was ended and prisoners conformed to the prison regime. Previous clandestine IRA links with MI6 were reactivated and a government document making some proposals was circulated. In December 1980, when one of the hungerstrikers lost his sight and was removed to a Belfast hospital, by all accounts on the point of death, the prisoners called off the hungerstrike amid much confusion. Although Sinn Féin initially claimed victory, it soon emerged that the prisoners had not triumphed. Exactly what concessions had been promised, how they were supposed to be implemented, and whose fault the breakdown was has been the subject of much debate. What was clear, however, was that prisoners had not won their demands, and as this became clear plans were laid for a second hungerstrike.

The second hungerstrike

The second hungerstrike began on 1 March 1981: this was to be a phased exercise, with the first republican to go on hungerstrike being joined at intervals by other inmates from both the IRA and INLA. The first to refuse food was the IRA OC in the Maze, Bobby Sands, whose name was to become known all over the world. Sands was to be joined on hungerstrike after two weeks by another inmate and then another each week thereafter, with the purpose of creating ever-increasing pressure on the government. In launching the second hungerstrike Sands and the others again rejected the advice of the outside IRA leadership. The IRA felt the hungerstrikes represented a serious diversion of resources of all kinds from their main campaign of violence, and feared another damaging and divisive failure.

From the beginning of the second hungerstrike it was judged highly likely that this time there would be deaths, for Sands and the others believed the fiasco of the first strike had to be avenged. His own reputation for determination was evident in his nickname Geronimo. He grew up in the mainly Protestant Rathcoole estate on the outskirts of north Belfast, but his family were among a large number of Catholics forced to leave the area by a systematic campaign of loyalist intimidation. The family moved to west Belfast where he became an active member of the IRA, serving a short prison sentence in the early 1970s before being sentenced in 1977 to fourteen years' imprisonment after being arrested in possession of a gun in a car while on an IRA operation.

Tensions mounted to an extraordinary degree as the strike went on amid a major propaganda battle, with polarisation between ordinary Protestants and Catholics reaching new levels. For many nationalists the brutal clarity of the issue left no room for ambiguity, and many who did not support the IRA nonetheless reacted against what they saw as British inflexibility.

In propaganda terms Sands benefited from the fact that he developed an aura of victimhood and self-sacrifice. He was a convicted member of the IRA yet his personal image was highly media friendly. He had been jailed for having a gun rather than for murder, and the photograph of him which appeared thousands of times in newspapers and on television projected a good-looking young man with long hair, sporting a fetching grin. The fact that he looked more like a drummer in a rock band than a ruthless terrorist was important in the propaganda battle that raged all around the world.

As the days passed, numerous groups and individuals sought to mediate in the dispute, but they made little progress with either the prisoners or the authorities. The IRA suspected such groups were likely to confuse the issues, bypass the IRA itself or be manipulated by the authorities. The fact that IRA violence continued, including the killing of a young mother in Londonderry, merely hardened the characteristic Thatcher resolve. She observed that 'if Mr Sands persisted in his wish to commit suicide, that was his choice'.

Although Adams and the republican leadership had been against the hungerstrike, sheer chance delivered them a golden political opportunity. Five days after Sands began refusing food, independent nationalist MP Frank Maguire died suddenly, creating a by-election in the Fermanagh–South Tyrone Westminster constituency. Maguire's brother was dissuaded by republicans from going forward, and Sands became the sole nationalist candidate. In the election he beat Harry West, the former Unionist party leader who was attempting a come-back, to win the seat by 30,492 votes to 29,046 on an 87 per cent poll. It was a propaganda victory of huge proportions for the IRA, made possible by the widespread nationalist sense that Thatcher was adopt-ing altogether too rigid a stance. Since Sands's victory was one of the key events in the development of Sinn Féin as an electoral force, some observers regard it as the genesis of what would eventually become the peace process. At the time, however, it made no difference to the government's attitude, and the stalemate continued.

Sands died at 1.17 a.m. on 5 May, instantly becoming one of repub-licanism's most revered martyrs. Thatcher coldly informed the Commons that 'Mr Sands was a convicted criminal. He chose to take his own life. It was a choice his organisation did not allow to many of its victims.' But although there was little sympathy in Britain, his death generated a huge wave of emotion and anger among republicans and nationalists, an estimated 100,000 people attending his funeral. From the wider world came much interna-tional criticism of Britain and of Thatcher, who was widely con-demned for inflexibility. World attention was focused on Belfast, Adams later recalling that the death of Sands 'had a greater interna-tional impact than any other event in Ireland in my lifetime'.

The widespread street disturbances arising from the hungerstrike helped drive the death toll for 1981 up to 117 from the previous year's total of 86. Deaths caused by the security forces increased as troops and police used large numbers of plastic bullets in response to street disturbances. As a result seven Catholics were killed, two of them young girls. Although the security forces usually maintained that those killed had been active rioters, it often emerged afterwards that this was not so. In five of the seven cases, inquests later specifically found that those who died had been innocents, and more than £75,000 was paid out in compensation cases.

James Prior, who replaced Humphrey Atkins as Northern Ireland Secretary in the autumn of 1981, recalled in his memoirs: 'The police and army were firing prodigious numbers of plastic bullets. A number of innocent people, including children, were killed or maimed, their deaths adding to all the bitterness.' One example of this was the death of an innocent fourteen-year-old girl, Julie Livingstone, who was killed when she was struck by a plastic bullet. She had not been involved in rioting and her family later received compensation. Her mother recalled: 'She was a lively wee girl, into everything, keeping the wee lads going. The despair would hurt you now and again. Most days you get it some part of the day. I'll never get rid of her name – she wrote it anywhere, inside the airing cupboard and on books. I was changing a pillow and she had written her name on the inside of it. In the kitchen, just under the cooker under the wallpaper, she must have lifted a brush and written her name on the bare wall.'

Such tragedies were not confined to the nationalist side. In the same month as the Julie Livingstone killing, during rioting which followed the death of Sands, a crowd in north Belfast stoned a milk lorry. The vehicle went out of control in a hail of missiles and crashed into a lamppost, killing Protestant milkman Eric Guiney and his fourteen-year-old son Desmond who was helping on the milk round. After the deaths Mrs Guiney said: 'Everyone loved Desmond – he was always such a jolly wee boy and would have given you the coat off his back. Once when they changed part of the milk round, the customers phoned the dairy to ask them to put Desmond back.'

The months that followed are remembered as being particularly grim and destabilising as the confrontation continued, with neither the government nor the hungerstrikers prepared to give way. With hindsight, it is clear that each deeply misunderstood the other: Thatcher never came close to grasping the IRA's psychology, while some republicans persisted in believing that she was bound to give in eventually. Even after six hungerstrike deaths Brendan McFarlane, who had taken over from Sands as the IRA OC in the Maze, wrote in a smuggled message to Adams, 'I do feel we can break the Brits.'

The unyielding attitude of both sides resulted, between May and August 1981, in the deaths of a total of ten hungerstrikers, seven from the IRA and three from the INLA. As the summer progressed and prisoners died, numerous mediators tried to resolve the problem with no success: the Red Cross, a European Human Rights Commission delegation, the Catholic Church in Ireland, a Vatican representative, John Hume, Irish government representatives, the IRA–MI6 secret link.

Prior visited the Maze and had a glimpse through a window of a prisoner on the forty-sixth day of his hungerstrike. Prior recalled later: 'He was just sitting there, staring into space. There was no great sense of agony, of emaciation, nor any sign of pain. I was struck by how much this man looked at peace with himself.' Prior said he began to realise that there were on both sides 'a number of people of utter determination and conviction, prepared to commit acts of violence and in a stubborn, yet courageous, way to accept the inevitable and to die'.

The ending of the hungerstrike came soon afterwards, largely through the intervention of the families of prisoners, encouraged by prison chaplain Father Denis Faul. The families began to realise that the government would not concede, and to conclude that the deaths of their husbands and sons were both inevitable and futile. An increasing number of families took action once their sons had lapsed into the coma which normally preceded death, asking the authorities to medically revive them. In October the hungerstrikers called off the protest, thwarted by their families rather than by the government or the prison authorities. Within days Prior eased regulations to allow prisoners to wear their own clothes at all times and made limited concessions on the other demands.

The original feeling among republicans was that they had suffered a huge defeat in the hungerstrike. One prisoner wrote: 'Despite my relief that no one else would die, I still felt gutted because ten men had died and we had not won our demands. My morale was never as low.' Thatcher had taken on the IRA head-on and in the end their willpower cracked while hers did not. She said at one point,

'Faced with the failure of their discredited cause the men of violence have chosen in recent months to play what might be their last card.'

Yet hers was a Pyrrhic victory. One newspaper recorded:

> This has been one of the best times the IRA has ever had. The Northern Ireland problem is seen worldwide as the IRA has always wanted it to be: the hammer and the anvil, the Brits versus the Provos, nothing in between and nobody else relevant. The paradox at the centre of all this success for the Provisionals is that their gains have come through an election won by the very opposite of a Provo campaign, a campaign based on an appeal to save life, and through the self-sacrifice of their men. Somebody somewhere among the Provos has finally come to accept the truth of the old saying that it is not those who inflict the most who ultimately win, but those who endure the most.

The hungerstrikes had lasting effects, most of which were bad for the authorities and for almost everyone apart from the republican movement. For one thing, the extended trauma of the months of confrontation seared deep into the psyches of large numbers of people, stirring many troubling emotions. Community divisions had always been deep, but now they had a new rawness. Prior said he arrived in Belfast to find 'an embittered and totally polarised society'.

Aftermath

In November 1981, IRA gunmen assassinated the Reverend Robert Bradford, a Unionist MP and Methodist minister who had advocated a tougher security line against the IRA. At the funeral James Prior was jostled and verbally abused by angry loyalists, several hundred surging forward to bang on the roof of his car. He was hissed as he walked into the church, and as he left he was again surrounded, some members of the crowd calling, 'Kill him, kill him'. The day of the funeral was marked by a widespread work stoppage by Protestants as memorial services were held in many towns. Paisley threatened to organise tax and rent strikes as part of a protest campaign to make Northern Ireland 'ungovernable', and loyalists staged a day of action at which members of a 'third force' were paraded.

Those who had already viewed Northern Ireland as a dysfunctional society whose people could never be brought to live amicably together seemed confirmed in their view, while many others sadly concluded that they were probably correct. Certainly the fact that an apparently modern society had been so convulsed for so long left the lasting impression of structural political instability.

As far as IRA prisoners were concerned the 1981 hungerstrike had ended in defeat. Although they were subsequently allowed to wear their own clothes, this was granted as a concession from a government which appeared to have won the exchange. As the IRA prisoners saw it, ten colleagues had given their lives, apparently in vain. Describing the hungerstrike as 'an Everest amongst the mountains of traumatic events which the Irish people have experienced', Gerry Adams would write a decade and a half later, 'I cannot yet think with any intensity of the death of Bobby Sands and the circumstances of his passing without crying.'

Yet the hungerstrike was to bring republicans many gains. The ten deaths effectively put an end to the criminalisation argument. The hungerstrike had not technically achieved special category status but in effect it had achieved something much more potent: political status. There could have been no more definitive display of political motivation than the spectacle of ten men giving their lives in an awesome display of self-sacrifice and dedication. It was possible to view this as outlandish fanaticism, and many did; but it was not possible to claim that these were indistinguishable from ordinary criminals. The hungerstrikers thus won political status in the eyes of the world.

Radicalised recruits flocked to the IRA and Sinn Féin, swelling the ranks of both and laying the foundations for both further violence and an infiltration of the political system. The republican electoral advances pointed to a new potential in the north and possibly south. Ahead lay more violence and a regular vote for Sinn Féin.

This fired sweeping new ambitions among the republican leadership. Three weeks after the end of the hungerstrike, Adams aide Danny Morrison outlined to the Sinn Féin ard fheis (annual conference) a grandiose new vision, declaring: 'Who here really believes we can win the war through the ballot box? But will anyone here object if, with a ballot box in one hand and the Armalite in the other, we take power in Ireland?' Adams would later sum up the paradoxical outcome of the hungerstrike which he had never wanted: 'Physically, emotionally and spiritually, the hungerstrike was intensely draining; yet we derived immense new energy, commitment and direction from the extraordinary period during which our ten comrades slowly and painfully sacrificed their lives.'

8.

Anglo-Irish accord
1982–85

Men of violence

The years after 1981 saw a variety of political and security initiatives as London and Dublin sought to cope with the aftermath of the traumatic hungerstrike period. The IRA once again returned to bombing targets in England, while the security forces attempted to counter them with new military and legal measures. Loyalist killings went on at a relatively low level, while 1982 saw the violent end to the violent career of one of the most notorious loyalist killers. This was Lenny Murphy, who as leader of the UVF Shankill Butchers gang had been involved in at least eighteen killings over a full two decades. Murphy met his own death at the hands of IRA gunmen who shot him twenty-two times as he drew up in his car outside his girlfriend's home.

Although attention has tended to be concentrated on such well-remembered incidents, the sobering fact is that over the years of the troubles tens of thousands of men became involved with violent republican and loyalist groups. 600 or more men were convicted of murder, while many times that number were jailed for lesser offences. Republican groups estimate that there are 15,000 republican ex-prisoners while at a rough guess around the same number of loyalists also served sentences. In other words, more than 30,000 men were involved with groups that have carried out killings and a great deal of other violence, a statistic which illustrates how deeply society was permeated by paramilitarism.

Although the number of IRA killings fell slightly, the organisation carried out major attacks in Britain. Two attacks on a single day in July 1982 killed a total of eleven soldiers in two London parks, one of the highest military casualty tolls of the troubles. The first device was detonated as a troop of soldiers in full regalia made their way on horseback through Hyde Park on their way from their Knightsbridge barracks to Whitehall. Four soldiers died. In Britain an extra dimension of condemnation arose from the fact that a number of horses were also killed in the Hyde Park explosion. One horse which survived numerous injuries, Sefton, became an equine symbol of British defiance of the IRA and something close to a national hero. A newspaper reported: 'The horror of the incident was brought home to the public through gruesome pictures broadcast on lunchtime television, showing a scene of carnage and devastation. Eye-witnesses gave graphic accounts of charred bodies and people and horses with terrible injuries.' A few hours later a bomb went off in Regent's Park as military bandsmen performed a lunchtime concert at an open-air bandstand. The device, which had been placed under the bandstand, killed seven soldiers.

Another IRA attack in London came in December 1983, when a bomb left in a car outside Harrods department store exploded seven days before Christmas while the area was thronged with shoppers. The explosion, which killed six people, was generally regarded as a setback for the IRA because of its civilian death toll.

The IRA was not the only dangerous republican group in these years, since the smaller INLA was also intermittently active. This group, which had come into being in the mid-1970s, showed over the years an extraordinary capacity to revive itself after setbacks and once again flare into violent life. Many of the setbacks were self-inflicted: time and again internal feuds broke out, claiming the lives of many of its members. The years 1981 to 1983 were its most lethal with fifty-three people dying at its hands. Although it had initially had a left-wing ideology it degenerated over the years into a collection of local gangs often dominated by personalities who had parted company from the IRA, usually because they were considered too erratic.

Two of the best-known of these were Dessie 'Border Fox' O'Hare and Dominic 'Mad Dog' McGlinchey, who were both active in these years. O'Hare revelled in his reputation as a fearsome killer, claiming in a newspaper interview that he had killed approximately twenty-six people, an estimate security sources did not contest. His victims included many members of the security forces as well as a number of INLA members killed in the spasms of feuding which periodically racked the organisation. In his interview he said of one INLA member he had killed: 'I would have burned him alive if I had the chance.' In the case of another INLA man, O'Hare and his associates used bolt cutters to sever an earlobe and a finger. O'Hare commented chillingly, 'We just wanted to kill him, to give him a hard death. They were a bad crowd. I had a deep hate for him and all those guys. I did not want him to die lightly.' O'Hare was regarded as such a menace to society that he was eventually jailed for forty years, the longest jail sentence ever handed down by a court in the Republic, even though he was convicted of lesser offences than murder.

Dominic McGlinchey was one of the most feared gunmen to emerge in the troubles, first as a member of the IRA before being expelled for 'indiscipline', and then as leader of the INLA. In a newspaper interview he boasted of killing around thirty people, saying: 'I like to get in close to minimise the risk for myself. We were involved mainly in the killing of UDR men and policemen, and we did a fair few bombings of police barracks and towns.' McGlinchey and his wife were both to die in feud shootings.

The highest death toll inflicted by the INLA came in December 1982, when seventeen people were killed in an attack on a bar at Ballykelly in County Londonderry. Eleven of the dead were soldiers based in the garrison town. The others were civilians, four of them women, who were attending a disco in the bar. The bomb used in the incident was a comparatively small device but it was placed near a support pillar in a function room. Over 150 people were in the room when the bomb exploded, bringing down the roof. An army officer who rushed to the scene spoke of finding bodies 'like dominos, one on top of the other'. The majority of the dead were not killed by the blast but were crushed by fallen masonry.

In his memoirs James Prior wrote: 'As we flew in, the white ribbons cordoning off the area marked a scene of total devastation. The bar and dance hall had been reduced to smouldering remains, completely flattened by the bomb. The whole roof collapsed on to the crowded dance floor. It is a miracle that more were not killed.' An INLA spokesman declared: 'We believe that it is only attacks of such a nature that bring it home to the people in Britain and the British establishment. The shooting of an individual soldier, for the people of Britain, has very little effect in terms of the media or in terms of the British administration.' In his newspaper interview McGlinchey admitted he was involved in the incident.

The INLA argued that the disco constituted a military target, but another of its attacks in this period, in November 1983, was capable of no such interpretation. This took place at a small Pentecostal church at Darkley close to the border in County Armagh. Members of the sixty-strong congregation, made up mainly of farming families, were singing 'Are you washed in the blood of the lamb?' when gunmen arrived and sprayed the building with bullets, killing three of the church elders. At least three gunmen stood outside the hall and strafed it, wounding seven more people as up to forty bullets passed through the thin wooden walls.

Accounts of the troubles inevitably concentrate on major incidents such as these, partly because of the death tolls, partly because such attacks often had political significance and in part because many of them are among the best-remembered incidents of the troubles. Over the years, however, the majority of those who were killed died singly, in individual incidents. The following are representative or at least illustrative of the vast majority of troubles victims.

Francis McCluskey, aged forty-six, was among the many Catholics killed by loyalists, in particular in the north Belfast area. In August 1982 he was walking to work when two masked men chased him and shot him six times. His wife, who was pregnant at the time of his death, later gave birth to their ninth child, whom she named Francine in memory of her husband. Detectives told the inquest he was the victim of a loyalist sectarian attack; a relative said he was murdered for no other reason than his religion.

Some months after his death his wife said: 'He was so happy that morning. When he was up and about the whole house joined in. He was a terrible one for playing jokes, an innocent man whose life revolved around me and the children. I remember him asking me for another kiss but I laughed that he had already had his share of two that morning. Those were the last words he said. Francis went out full of fun. That night he came home in a coffin. Francine will know that her daddy loved us all very much. I hold no bitterness towards my husband's murderers. I can just feel sorry for them and their parents. The baby will grow up without any hatred or malice, but love for the father she never knew.' In the course of the troubles loyalists were responsible for the deaths of just over one thousand people, most of them civilians.

Hugh Cummings, thirty-nine, was one of two hundred UDR members who died, many of them while off-duty, meeting his death like Francis McCluskey in August 1982. A part-time member of the UDR, he was shot by the IRA in the town of Strabane as he got into his car, the fourth member of the local UDR company to be killed in a seven-month period. His family refused to accept a letter of sympathy from James Prior which was delivered to them on the day of the funeral, sending it back with a message that 'the hands of the security forces should be freed'. A spokesman for the family said: 'Nothing is being done. Feelings are running very high on this issue here. Innocent, defenceless people are being mown down and no action is being taken against the godfathers who are walking the streets. They are getting away with murder.'

Security reactions

The security forces reacted to the continuing violence in a number of ways. The RUC created its own SAS-style unit, training its men for violent encounters with the IRA and INLA. Known as E4A its approach was based, in the words of a senior police officer, on 'speed, firepower and aggression'. All these characteristics were on display when, in three separate incidents in a period of a month, E4A members shot and killed five men and a youth, all in County Armagh. Three were IRA members, two were in the INLA and one was a civilian. Some of these were clearly dangerous men, but all those killed were unarmed when shot.

In the first incident three IRA members were killed when police fired 109 shots at their car. In the second a teenager who was a civilian was shot dead and another was seriously injured. In the third incident two members of the INLA were shot dead in a car. These events, which came to be known as 'shoot-to-kill' incidents, were surrounded by controversy which persists to the present day. They also gave rise to long-running legal sequels. In the case of the three IRA men, three policemen were charged with murder. In acquitting them a senior judge generated further controversy when in congratulating them he added: 'I regard each of the accused as absolutely blameless in this matter. That finding should be put in their record along with my own commendation for their courage and determination in bringing the three deceased men to justice, in this case the final court of justice.'

The controversy which followed the killings led to the appointment of the Deputy Chief Constable of the Greater Manchester Police, John Stalker, to investigate the incidents. Stalker, who claimed his inquiries had been obstructed, was later removed from the inquiry in controversial circumstances when disciplinary charges were brought against him in Manchester. These were later dropped. A final report of the inquiries was not published but in 1988 it was announced in the Commons that although evidence had been found of attempts by police officers to pervert the course of justice, there would be no prosecutions on the grounds of national security. The inquest into the IRA deaths became a protracted affair, with five different coroners appointed to handle the hearing at various stages. Eventually in 1994 a coroner said he was abandoning the proceedings, which had become the longest-running inquest of its kind in British legal history. These circumstances gave rise to continuing nationalist and republican allegations of a cover-up.

Another significant development in the first half of the 1980s was the police use of supergrasses, which for several years inflicted considerable damage to both republican and loyalist groups. The supergrass system entailed persuading former members of such groups to testify against their alleged former associates, in exchange for a new life outside Northern Ireland. Immunity from prosecution was sometimes granted, along with payment of substantial sums of money.

Although the system gave rise to human rights concerns, on a practical level it took large numbers of active republicans and loyalists off the streets. In some cases thirty or more defendants were charged on the word of one supergrass. Some were sentenced to long terms of imprisonment, and even those who were eventually acquitted generally spent many months behind bars while awaiting trial. The remand record was held by an INLA member who was held on the evidence of five separate supergrasses. All the cases against him eventually collapsed, but in the meantime he spent four years and four months on remand. (The irony in his case was that shortly after his release he was shot dead in an INLA feud.)

Campaigns against the practice were waged by republicans, loyalists and human rights groups. One of the main criticisms was that large numbers of people were being convicted sometimes on the word of a single person, who admitted he had himself been involved in paramilitary activity and sometimes pleaded guilty to murder. In most cases there was no corroborating evidence. The practice caused much disruption to both republican and loyalist organisations, and may have been one of the causes of the comparatively low level of loyalist violence around this time.

At least twenty-five supergrasses emerged during this period, providing information which led to the arrests of nearly 600 suspects. At one stage around 230 men were held in prison on their evidence. The courts were initially enthusiastic about the supergrass phenomenon. In one case a judge described aspects of a supergrass's testimony as 'unreliable, false, bizarre and incredible' but then went on to convict defendants on the basis of other parts of his evidence.

The classic security force problem throughout the troubles was that they believed that through their intelligence agencies they knew a great deal about who the leaders of paramilitary groups were, and who had ordered or carried out many killings and other offences. As in other countries, however, their difficulty lay in converting intelligence into evidence which would stand up in a court of law. The supergrass tactic seemed to offer a mechanism for achieving this. As time passed, however, the legal and political controversy grew and judges became more cautious about convicting. In a key IRA case a senior judge cleared thirty-five defendants. He said that while there was more than a trace of probability that many of the defendants were members of an illegal organisation, the supergrass was 'a selfish and self-regarding man to whose lips a lie invariably came more naturally than the truth'.

One of those taken out of circulation by the supergrass system was Gerard Steenson, a highly active INLA gunman with the nickname Doctor Death, who was convicted of sixty-seven offences and given six life sentences for murder. The judge in the case was clearly correct in saying of him: 'Of all those who have appeared before me he is undoubtedly the most dangerous and sinister terrorist – a ruthless and highly dedicated, resourceful and indefatigable planner of criminal exploits who did not hesitate to take a leading part in assassinations and other crimes.'

Yet the system began to fall apart as judges signalled their dissatisfaction with it, and most of those charged, including Steenson, eventually walked free. Appeal courts overturned a number of verdicts, and as more and more cases collapsed the system was eventually abandoned.

It is hardly surprising, given her reputation for combativeness, that approaches such as the creation of E4A and the use of the supergrass tactic should have been deployed during Margaret Thatcher's years as prime minister. Described by James Prior as 'a natural sympathiser with the Unionists', she had briefly toyed with the idea of a majority-rule government with strong guarantees for the minority. In her own words, however, 'it was not long before it became clear to me that this model was not going to work, at least for the present'. She explained: 'There was no getting away from the fact that, with some justice, the long years of Unionist rule were associated with discrimination against Catholics.'

Her first stab at a political approach had taken the form of the abortive Atkins conference. The next came in 1980, when she made an effort to form a working relationship with Charles Haughey, Jack Lynch's successor as Taoiseach. Despite their very different nationalist instincts, she was prepared to do business with him and, to the surprise of most, this unlikely couple at first got on well. A Thatcher biographer attributed this to 'a certain roguish mutual admiration', while Prior described it as 'apparently a great love match'.

Two summit meetings went exceptionally well, in particular one which came to be known as 'the teapot summit' because of Haughey's gift to Thatcher of an elegant Georgian teapot. An eyewitness said: 'She was charmed by the teapot. He was an extraordinarily charming man when he wanted to be and he exercised all his charm on her. The relationship just grew from there.' But disillusion set in very quickly. Haughey suggested their meetings had led to a constitutional breakthrough and did not set 'any limits on the arrangements that might be agreed'. His Foreign Minister made things worse by adding that 'all options are open' and that 'everything is on the table'. This was taken as implying that Thatcher had agreed radical solutions which might even include moves towards Irish unity. She was furious.

She wanted closer Anglo-Irish relations but a united Ireland was not on her horizon, and she felt betrayed by what she regarded as a gross distortion of her position. When she and Haughey next met she delivered what was described as 'a monologue, a diatribe' by one of those present. This source added, 'She couldn't speak coherently, she was in such a rage. She just said in no uncertain terms what she thought.' Haughey had overplayed his hand and his relations with Thatcher never recovered, and in fact deteriorated even further when differences developed during the 1981 hungerstrike and the Falklands war.

The next political initiative originated not with Thatcher but with James Prior whom she had despatched to Belfast as a form of exile after he proved too moderate and too 'wet' in handling industrial relations as Employment Secretary. The Belfast post was described by Prior in a disgruntled moment as 'the dustbin of British politics', a cabinet colleague saying Thatcher's motivation was 'to get him out of the prime minister's hair'. The initiative he designed took the form of an idea known as rolling devolution. He had modest ambitions for the scheme, seeing it as an attempt 'to narrow the differences, to try to bring the disagreement within proportions which are at least manageable'. His plan was for an elected assembly to which powers would be transferred as and when the parties reached a certain level of agreement in particular areas: the greater the agreement, the more power would be transferred. Prior described it as 'the same step-by-step approach that I had applied with some success to the changes in industrial relations legislation'.

But approaches useful in dealings with British trade unions turned out to be less effective in Belfast. Few were enthusiastic about his plan, and there was open opposition from many quarters. The critics included many in his own party, up to and including the prime minister herself. She allowed Prior to put legislation for the assembly through Westminster but, as he later testified, 'She made her views abundantly clear, saying that she thought it was a rotten Bill.' Several dozen Tory backbenchers agreed, harassing Prior with filibustering tactics in the Commons.

Nationalists were also against the scheme, Haughey condemning it as 'one of the most disastrous things that has ever happened in Anglo-Irish relations'. Prior was instructed by Thatcher to tone down the modest Irish dimension he had envisaged. In his memoirs he described this move as 'probably our great mistake' in that it led to the SDLP refusing to take its seats in his new assembly. Sinn Féin took a similar position, which meant that from the start the assembly was a nationalist-free zone, serving only as a platform for Unionist speeches and never offering any real hope of political progress.

The rise of Sinn Féin

The next initiative of the Thatcher years was much more far-reaching, more carefully thought out and in the end would come to be seen as a watershed, both in terms of Anglo-Irish relations and in changing the course of the troubles. It would produce the Anglo-Irish Agreement of 1985, which in many ways broke the mould of London–Dublin relations.

The new initiative had its roots largely in the reaction of first Dublin and later London to the rise of Sinn Féin as an electoral force in the wake of the 1981 hungerstrike. Within republicanism Adams and others had always been wary of what they pejoratively referred to as 'electoralism', suspecting that entering the political processes would blunt the IRA's revolutionary edge. But when they saw the many thousands who had voted for Bobby Sands they realised that they had stumbled on a basis for broadening their campaign.

As a result they transformed Sinn Féin from little more than a flag of convenience for the IRA into a political organisation with a life of its own. Many republican sympathisers who baulked at joining the IRA, or had been through its ranks and did not wish to return, were prepared to work for it politically. Republicans thus turned to contesting elections in earnest, with spectacular initial success which was enhanced to some extent by the ancient art of vote-stealing. In four elections between 1982 and 1985 Sinn Féin averaged around 12 per cent of the total vote and 40 per cent of the nationalist vote, establishing itself as the fourth largest party and a political force which could not be ignored. Its best performance came in 1983 when it took more than 100,000 votes and, in a victory of great symbolic significance, had Gerry Adams elected as Westminster MP for West Belfast. Adams's election victory won him new allies among the British Labour left and he made several trips to England, attracting saturation publicity as he met figures such as Ken Livingstone. The subsequent election of almost sixty Sinn Féin representatives to local councils brought widespread Unionist protests and often disruption at council meetings. Sinn Féin was the focus of all attention and there was much worried talk that its foray into politics was poisoning the wells of political processes.

Emboldened by their advances in the north, the republicans turned their eyes south. At the height of the hungerstrikes a number of republican prisoners put themselves forward in southern elections and two of them were elected to the Dáil. This was taken as a sign that a great potential for republican growth existed in the south, with Sinn Féin well placed to pick up votes in border counties and from the disaffected Dublin poor.

Party politics in the south was particularly fragmented at that stage, as a decline in the fortunes of the largest party, Fianna Fáil, prevented it from securing an overall majority. This created the possibility that a handful of Sinn Féin members could find themselves in a pivotal position in the Dáil. All of this was alarming for southern politicians, who feared their political system was about to be invaded by republican revolutionaries intent on overthrowing it from within. One Irish minister spoke fearfully of the prospect of 'IRA army council deputies (members of the Dáil) stalking the corridors of Dáil Eireann, holding the balance of power'. At that moment many republicans believed that the new strategy of combining IRA violence and political activity offered a route to victory, and enthusiastically set about building up Sinn Féin.

One of the southern figures most perturbed by the Sinn Féin advance was Fine Gael leader Dr Garret FitzGerald, who during the 1970s and much of the 1980s played a central role both in domestic southern politics and Anglo-Irish relations. He was significant both in terms of his actions during his two spells as Taoiseach, and intellectually as one of the key thinkers who helped redefine Irish nationalism. FitzGerald's nightmare was that Sinn Féin might actually overtake John Hume's SDLP as the principal voice of nationalism in the north. He viewed Sinn Féin as a malignant dry rot which threatened to spread south. He feared, as he later explained in his memoirs, that 'the situation there could get out of control and threaten the whole island, for in those circumstances the IRA might seek a violent confrontation with the Unionists and try to follow this by an attempt to destabilise the Republic'.

Some in the British government shared his concern, Prior warning a private Conservative meeting that the island of Ireland could become 'a Cuba off our western coast'. If that happened, he said, one could foresee the whole of Ireland being taken over by the Marxists of Sinn Féin. The main British aim at this time was to contain a dangerous situation and restore as much stability as possible. The lack of success of the Prior assembly put paid to the idea of making progress through the devolution of power to Northern Ireland politicians. Attempting to integrate Northern Ireland with Britain, as advocated by Molyneaux and some other Unionists, was rejected. Withdrawal was not favoured because it would inevitably be viewed as a defeat for Britain at the hands of terrorism, and because in any event it could result in a level of violence worse than anything yet experienced.

Constitutional nationalists, meanwhile, went back to basics. Acting on an idea put forward by Hume, FitzGerald convened a New Ireland Forum to act as a think-tank for all shades of constitutional

nationalist opinion. Senior figures from all the major constitutional nationalist parties debated the way ahead for months. Its
1984 report reproached the British government for allegedly insensitive security policies and for concentrating on crisis management. Calling for a major reassessment by Britain, it warned:
'Constitutional politics are on trial. This requires priority attention and urgent action to halt and reverse the constant drift into
more violence, anarchy and chaos.' The report put forward
options such as a united Ireland, a federal Ireland and joint
London–Dublin authority over Northern Ireland, also mentioning, in what looked like a throwaway line, that 'the parties in the
forum also remain open to discuss other views which may contribute to political development'.

All shades of Unionist opinion summarily rejected the three
main forum options. So too did Thatcher, and with such brusque-
ness that she caused a crisis in Anglo-Irish relations. A unitary
state, she told the media, was out; a federal Ireland was out; and
joint authority was out. Her response, which became known as
'Out, out, out', was taken as an affront by all sections of opinion
in the Republic. A senior British minister would later describe this
as 'a humiliating episode' for FitzGerald.

Thatcher had hoped to work with FitzGerald to improve London–
Dublin relations and to increase cross-border security cooperation,
but the 'Out, out, out' furore looked like jeopardising her hopes.
Taken aback, she asked FitzGerald how she could made amends.
With hindsight it can be seen that this was a crucial moment in
Anglo-Irish relations. Over the years one of the specialities of Irish
diplomacy has been to turn apparent reverses to Dublin's advan-
tage, and this is what happened.

In fact the two governments had for some time been exploring
the possibility of a far-reaching new agreement designed to bolster
constitutional nationalism against the menace of Sinn Féin and the
IRA. This now intensified. The initiative had the support not only
of Hume but also, more unusually, of a number of key British civil
servants. The move thus originated in Dublin but was endorsed and

jointly crafted by senior British civil servants and diplomats. Chief among these was Sir Robert (now Lord) Armstrong, who was then cabinet secretary. He and other formidable mandarins, all of whom were convinced something needed to be done, were put to work on an Anglo-Irish committee with an equally formidable and experienced team of Irish diplomats including Seán Donlon and Dermot Nally. They had the support of Foreign Secretary Sir Geoffrey Howe, who described the officials as a 'galaxy of skill'. The approach of containment and crisis management was left behind as the team went to work in a determined attempt to seize the initiative from the republicans.

Thatcher's motivation in approving the new negotiation sprang primarily from security considerations and the desire to reduce violence. Howe later wrote: 'It was this point that always drove Margaret most strongly – security, success against the men of violence, was her main preoccupation.' FitzGerald argued primarily from a political point of view. He pressed the need to reduce nationalist 'alienation' so much that, according to Howe, Thatcher would cry, 'I do wish you would stop using that dreadful word, Garret.' One of the British negotiating team later said privately:

Perhaps Mrs Thatcher had a less than comprehensive grasp of Irish history but she's an intensely pragmatic politician. She was conscious of the need to do something – not to solve the situation, but to move it forward from the impasse which it had reached. It was logical to explore the possibilities of the Anglo-Irish dimension.

Those of us negotiating were under a clear political direction to reach an agreement. We were aware of history but we were not cowed by it. We met on equal terms. We were able to meet with a degree of personal commitment to achieving something, and in an atmosphere of trust and friendship. We were aware of national obligations but we shared a common commitment and a common sense that we were engaged in a very important and very exciting and rather new stage in the long history of relations between Britain and Ireland.

A complex negotiation followed, civil servants in all taking part in thirty-six meetings. British and Irish ministers, including Thatcher and FitzGerald, met regularly to review progress. Among the many ideas considered and rejected were joint authority, the placing of an Irish minister in Belfast, and a joint north–south policing zone on the border. This negotiation was ultimately successful, in the eyes of both governments, in that it produced the Anglo-Irish Agreement of November 1985. But the process of negotiation was itself important in that key figures in London and Dublin developed relationships of trust and friendship. Anglo-Irish relations had often been difficult and many more rocky periods lay ahead; but the mid-1980s represented an important turning point in that Dublin, and important figures in London, came to see the Northern Ireland question as a common problem which was best managed jointly. FitzGerald would later explain:

> In the 1970s London and Dublin were thought to be pursuing different policies with different attitudes, because the focus of attention in people's minds was on Irish unity versus Northern Ireland remaining part of the UK. It was therefore thought to be a conflict of interest. But the reality, because of the IRA, has been that that long term divergence of interest has been subordinated to the common concern, the restoration of peace. That change from a position of polarised attitudes to one of common purpose has been the fundamental change of Anglo-Irish relations in the last twenty years.

While constitutional nationalism was intent on making progress through peaceful negotiations, the IRA went on prosecuting its war. In one of many incidents nine RUC officers, two of them women, were killed when an IRA mortar made a direct hit on an RUC canteen in the grounds of the police station in Newry, County Down.

Then in October 1984 a bomb meant for Margaret Thatcher exploded at the Grand Hotel in Brighton during the Conservative party conference. The blast, which took place in the early hours of the morning, demolished much of the façade of the old building. It missed its primary target, the prime minister, but killed five other people including an MP and the wives of three more Conservatives. A chilling IRA statement addressed to Thatcher said: 'Today we were unlucky, but remember, we have only to be lucky once. You will have to be lucky always. Give Ireland peace and there will be no war.' It was the closest the IRA had come to striking at the heart of the British political establishment, and the shock waves reverberated throughout Britain and Ireland; but the long, careful Anglo-Irish negotiation kept inching painstakingly forward. Howe would write that the Brighton attack did not perceptibly alter Thatcher's approach 'save to reinforce the dominant importance which she already attached to closer security cooperation'.

Anglo-Irish Agreement

The document Thatcher and FitzGerald formally signed in Hillsborough, County Down, in November 1985 was by any standards a historic one, giving the Republic as it did a significant consultative role in the running of Northern Ireland. The agreement opened with a statement by the two governments that any change in Northern Ireland's status could only come about with the consent of a majority of its people. For the governments, this was clearly an advance on the separate statements printed side by side in the Sunningdale Agreement.

The agreement then unveiled intricately crafted new structures, at the heart of which was an intergovernmental conference to be jointly chaired by London and Dublin ministers. This was to be serviced by a small secretariat of British and Irish civil servants based at Maryfield, a closely guarded office building on the outskirts of east Belfast. At the intergovernmental conference the Irish government could put forward views and proposals on almost any subject. The Republic was given no executive power, but the agreement committed the two governments to making 'determined efforts' to resolve their differences within the conference.

Almost everyone was surprised that Thatcher was prepared to sign such a document. Howe wrote later that the personal chemistry between herself and FitzGerald was decisive, saying that the Taoiseach's 'manifest sincerity over meeting after meeting could not have been more effective'. Thatcher had a reputation of being one of the few British politicians to retain any personal commitment to the Union between Britain and Ireland; moreover, as European and other countries had ample cause to know, she was famously jealous and protective of British sovereignty. That sovereignty was technically untouched by the Anglo-Irish Agreement, yet its nationalist tone was obvious to everyone. It was certainly evident to Unionists, who were unanimously appalled by its contents, believing that it weakened the Union. It was a nightmare for Protestants in general in that they felt spurned and abandoned by a government whose leader was supposed to have strong Unionist instincts.

The Unionist party's approach had been to leave things to James Molyneaux, who was said to have the ear of the people who mattered at Westminster. He had early on opted out of any negotiations, believing that by doing so he was ensuring that no real deal would be possible: his theory was that Britain and Dublin could not formulate an agreement without the input and consent of Unionist politicians. It was a historic mistake, in that London examined Molyneaux's integrationist approach and found it wanting. His suggestions of modest local government reform and procedural changes at Westminster did not begin to address the central question of what was to be done to improve relations with Dublin and to tackle Catholic alienation and the joint menace of the IRA and Sinn Féin.

Since many Unionists had initially relaxed on being reassured by Molyneaux that their interests were safe, the trauma of the agreement was all the deeper for being unexpected. They saw it as striking at their own sense of Britishness, and saw it too as Britain entering a compact with their ancient opponents. They regarded it as a deal done in an underhand way, with the prime minister taking far-reaching steps without consulting Unionist leaders. Thatcher herself tended to regard the accord as a security initiative rather than a historic new beginning. Howe later reflected: 'It took a gigantic struggle by many far-sighted people to persuade her; but although her head was persuaded, her heart was not.'

Unionists saw the agreement as a victory for constitutional nationalism, and constitutional nationalism agreed with them. It represented in fact an unprecedented new partnership between London and Dublin: in the years which followed that partnership had tense and difficult moments during many political and security crises, but though battered it was not broken. The agreement greatly reduced the practice of megaphone diplomacy, Irish politicians no longer stomping the US censuring Britain. London, for its part, seemed glad to have the south as an active ally in running the north.

This was partly because important sections of the British establishment had come to appreciate that constitutional nationalism had essentially redefined itself. This process was first seen in the civil rights campaign, which represented a major departure from old-style nationalist politics, and from the traditional nationalist assumption that the heart of the problem was the British presence. The previous nationalist recipe for solving the problem had therefore been to persuade the British to leave – or, in the view of the IRA, to force them to do so. The assumption was that Unionists, faced with an imminent British withdrawal, would embrace a new destiny as a minority in a united Ireland.

The new nationalist theory, as evolved by Hume, FitzGerald and others, rejected many of the old assumptions. In this revised view the key to the problem was not Britain but the Protestant community. The import was that the British presence was not imperialist but neutral, that the border was maintained not because of British interests but at the insistence of the Unionists, and that Irish unity could only come about with Protestant consent. The real border, it was now said, was not geographical but in men's minds. Though very different from conventional Irish nationalism, this doctrine by no means jettisoned the idea that a united Ireland was the ultimate solution. Unity, the rhetoric had it, would come through reconciliation rather than coercion.

As the years of violence dragged on there was a steady convergence of London and Dublin opinions, and of interests. The Republic no longer saw itself as warring with the British over the fate of the north: instead, the two governments came to view it as a difficult and dangerous problem for both. The emphasis thus switched to joint management and containment. The agreement reflected the fact that constitutional nationalism had shifted its emphasis away from simple separatism and towards accommodation. Dublin accepted, if grudgingly, that a united Ireland was not on the horizon, but in the meantime the accord was to give Irish nationalists a say in the formulation of British policy.

As it became clear that Molyneaux had been wrong about an agreement, Unionists threatened large-scale protests for more than a month before its signing. In apocalyptic terms Paisley's deputy Peter Robinson predicted confrontations with the security forces, demanding, 'What is Mrs Thatcher going to do after she has shot the first thousand Unionists in the streets of Belfast?' Paisley himself said that the proposals would be 'resisted to the very death' and accused the prime minister of being prepared 'to wade knee-deep in the blood of loyalists for this document of treachery and deceit'.

In an emotional speech Unionist MP Harold McCusker told the Commons that he 'never knew what desolation felt like until he read the Agreement', adding that now his constituents would be 'Irish-British hybrids'. In the immediate aftermath of the signing of the agreement most attention was focused on Protestant attempts to bring it down. Unionists flocked to a huge rally at Belfast City Hall, some estimates putting the attendance at well over 100,000 people. Unionist-controlled councils adjourned their meetings in protest. The Northern Ireland Secretary, Tom King, who had taken over when James Prior's successor Douglas Hurd had been moved on after only a year, was physically attacked by loyalists when he visited Belfast City Hall.

Unionist opposition to the agreement was so deep that it lasted for years, with protests ranging from political boycotts to mass rallies, demonstrations, and an increase in loyalist killings. Unionists objected not just to the text of the agreement but also to what a Protestant clergyman described as 'all the stuff in there between the lines'. Many nationalists also believed, or at least hoped, that they detected a barely concealed agenda on the British side, with London signalling that it did not forever expect to be in charge of Northern Ireland.

There were violent clashes between protesters and police, in one of which a Portadown loyalist was killed by a plastic bullet fired by a police officer, the first and only Protestant plastic bullet death. Loyalist paramilitants launched a systematic campaign of intimidation against RUC personnel, petrol-bombing the homes of police officers: more than 500 police homes were attacked, and 150 officers were forced to move house. Unionist politicians boycotted government ministers, and there was much rhetoric threatening the use of force. The fifteen Unionist MPs resigned their seats to force by-elections, a move that backfired when one of the seats was lost to the SDLP. A loyalist 'day of action' brought much of Northern Ireland to a standstill, but many Protestants disapproved of the widespread intimidation and riots which accompanied it.

Unionist politicians tried a range of approaches. At one point Peter Robinson joined a gang of loyalists who staged a late-night incursion into County Monaghan to demonstrate, they claimed, inadequate border security. Security was however sufficient to effect the MP's arrest, a second humiliation coming when he pleaded guilty in a southern court and paid a £15,000 fine for unlawful assembly.

The agreement survived it all. Historian Alvin Jackson summed up: 'The Unionists had once again backed themselves into a tactical dead-end in order to demonstrate the intensity of their convictions.

Unionist tardiness and negativism had led inexorably towards marginalisation and humiliation.' The Unionist trauma was obvious, but the agreement posed great challenges for republicans too. They recognised it as a major departure in British policy, but debated long and hard about its exact significance.

9.

Enniskillen, Libya & bombs in England
1986–93

When republicans contemplated the Anglo-Irish Agreement they were in the first instance most worried about its security aspects. The agreement was accompanied by new moves such as the erection of a string of watchtowers aimed at curbing IRA activities along the border, particularly in south Armagh. Republicans worried too that friendlier London–Dublin relations would bring a new level of isolation for republicanism and perhaps an erosion in the Sinn Féin vote. Britain was clearly intent on forging a new deal with constitutional nationalism and in doing so was prepared to stand up to fierce Unionist opposition. The IRA had seen itself as engaged in an anti-colonial, anti-imperialist freedom struggle. Suddenly, however, the supposed imperialist power had made an important move which cast it in a new light. This raised the issue, in more thoughtful republican minds, of whether a continuation of violent action represented the best way ahead. A senior Sinn Féin source later said privately: 'We saw the coming together of Dublin and London, and this proved London could be shifted. The fact that Britain moved unilaterally was pivotal. They hit the Unionists a kick in the balls, saying to them, "We've tried to work with you but that failed." That didn't go unrecorded in republicanism.'

In November 1986, the desire to modernise republicanism to keep abreast of such developments brought Sinn Féin to drop its age-old policy of refusing to take seats in the Dáil. The old guard, led by Ruairí Ó Brádaigh, fiercely resisted this, warning that dropping abstentionism from Sinn Féin's constitution would spell the beginning of the end for republican militancy. At a highly charged special conference debate, Sinn Féin thrashed out an issue which would be critical in setting the future direction of republicanism. For more than six decades it had been an article of faith that Sinn Féin members should not actually take their seats in the Dáil. The more traditional republicans regarded themselves as the keepers of the sacred republican abstentionist flame, while the Adams faction argued that the time had come for a change.

This faction believed there was a substantial vein of support to be tapped in the south, Martin McGuinness predicting that Sinn Féin could win up to five Dáil seats if abstentionism were abandoned. He swung opinion at the conference with a decisive speech in which he declared: 'They tell you that it is inevitable certainty that the war against British rule will be run down. These suggestions deliberately infer that the present leadership of Sinn Féin and the IRA are intent on edging the republican movement on to a constitutional path. Shame – shame – shame. I reject the notion that entering the Dáil would mean an end to Sinn Féin's unapologetic support for the right of the Irish people to oppose in arms the British forces of occupation. Our position is clear and it will never, never, never change: the war against British rule must continue until freedom is achieved.'

It is interesting to wonder whether the militant republican ever envisaged that he would one day take office first as education minister and later as Ian Paisley's Deputy First Minister in a Stormont administration. The vote in favour of dropping abstentionism was 429 to 161: a new era was in prospect.

The late 1980s and early 1990s were not a good time for politics either within Northern Ireland or in terms of Anglo-Irish relations. Political Unionism remained in protest mode for years after the Anglo-Irish Agreement, for some time refusing to meet government ministers, who would venture out of their heavily fortified offices only furtively and under heavy escort. The Unionist goal was defined, if it was defined at all, as the negative aim of bringing down the agreement rather than producing a positive alternative.

Nationalists initially regarded the agreement as a major and

possibly historic advance, but gradually disillusion and disappointment set in. Their general assumption that the accord would give
rise to a series of significant reforms which would be to the nationalist advantage proved unfounded. Margaret Thatcher and Tom
King, who were unnerved by the furious Unionist response to the
agreement, and disappointed that greater security gains did not follow, decided that the priority was to soothe Protestant fears and
opted for consolidation rather than any evolution of the agreement.
As a result the accord did not prove to be an engine providing the
sort of development which Unionists had feared and nationalists
had anticipated.

London–Dublin relations, which had been so good at the time
the Anglo-Irish Agreement was signed, deteriorated as the south
became dismayed by the British decision to apply the brake to the
reform process. They were also made more difficult by a series of
sometimes heated disagreements between the governments on
legal and human rights issues including the Stalker affair and the
long-running cases of the Birmingham Six, Guildford Four and
Maguire family. In these three cases Irish people had been jailed for
lengthy terms, sometimes for life, in connection with bombings in
England during the 1970s. In each case Britain resisted Dublin's
arguments that miscarriages of justice had taken place. It was not
until the 1990s that all the sentences were quashed, proving Dublin's
point.

Britain was in turn highly critical of the Republic for the recurring complications in extradition cases which generally resulted in
the failure of London's attempts to have republican suspects handed
over from the south.

For a brief moment, at the time of the Anglo-Irish Agreement,
nationalists had delightedly thought that Thatcher had been
convinced that any solution would be political rather than
military, the old issue over which Edward Heath and Jack Lynch
had disagreed so strenuously. The standard British justification
for heavier security measures was that the state had the duty to
take exceptional measures to protect itself and its citizens. The

standard Irish rejoinder was that injustices had counterproductive consequences for public confidence in the security forces, the
courts and eventually the whole system of government. The
bottom line for both governments was that the Anglo-Irish
Agreement was worthwhile and should be maintained, but both
felt it failed to deliver its full potential.

The Libyan connection

Republicans meanwhile pursued a double strategy, attempting to
penetrate the political system while at the same time rearming
themselves with an arsenal so large that it converted them into one
of the world's best-equipped underground organisations. They did
so with the help of the Libyan ruler, Colonel Gaddafi, who gave the
IRA an unprecedented amount of weaponry.

Gaddafi had provided guns and money to the IRA in the early
1970s but his interest appeared to have cooled until 1984, when his
relations with Britain sharply deteriorated. As a result he renewed
the relationship, giving the IRA large stocks of modern military
hardware. Four separate shipments of arms made their way from
Libya to Ireland in the mid-1980s, bringing the IRA around a thousand rifles together with fearsome weapons such as Semtex plastic
explosives, heavy machine guns firing armour-piercing rounds
which could cut through even protected police vehicles, SAM-7 missiles and anti-aircraft guns capable of downing helicopters and
planes, and even flame-throwers.

The authorities knew nothing of the Libyan link, which amounted
to the worst British intelligence lapse for decades. Both the IRA and
Libya itself were under surveillance from a battery of security agencies, yet all the resources of the RUC, military intelligence, MI5 and
MI6 had failed to uncover the Libyan connection. In the meantime
the authorities at first mistakenly believed that the fight against the
IRA was going fairly well, for the death toll was down and republicans seemed if anything to be short of weapons. No one realised

that the organisation was simply keeping its powder dry by not using any of the heavy weaponry in case its appearance should disclose its Libyan source and cut the supply route.

The new weapons meant the IRA was able to step up its violence, not just in Northern Ireland but also in England and Europe. The Libyan armament was brought into play only gradually, but as it came into greater use the IRA killing rate rose from thirty-seven in 1986 to fifty-eight in 1987 and sixty-six the following year. The IRA aim was to reverse the pattern of security force casualties, for more RUC and UDR personnel, sometimes called the 'Ulsterised' security forces, were being killed than were regular British troops. In the years 1985 to 1987, for example, nine regular soldiers were killed compared to seventy-one police and UDR members. The republicans coldly set out to kill more British troops, calculating that this was the way to increase the impact of their violence.

The IRA thus stepped up violence in England, attempting to move from the previous pattern, which was generally one of hit-and-run, and instead establish an ongoing presence in Britain, with IRA members and supporters waging a sustained and in effect continuous offensive. They attacked a wide range of targets including military personnel, who tended to be more relaxed in Britain than in Northern Ireland. This approach was further extended to mainland Europe, where British troops came under attack in Germany and neighbouring countries. This expanded IRA campaign was to prove such a danger that the Ministry of Defence was forced to spend £126 million on anti-terrorist security measures at military bases in Britain and West Germany.

In Northern Ireland the IRA staged a series of what they termed 'spectaculars', in which prominent people or large numbers of security force personnel were killed. These included the 1985 incident in which nine RUC officers were killed by a mortar bomb which landed inside the grounds of Newry police station in County Down, and the 1987 assassination of a senior judge and his wife in a border landmine attack.

At the same time the security forces hit back against the IRA with

SAS ambushes. The most notable of many such incidents took place in May 1987 when eight IRA members were killed as they attacked a small RUC station in the County Armagh village of Loughgall. The heavily armed IRA unit was attempting to blow up the part-time station when waiting SAS soldiers opened fire on them, inflicting what was in terms of lives lost the worst single setback during the modern history of the IRA. Several of those killed were regarded as being among the IRA's most proficient and most dangerous members.

November 1987 brought an even more crushing shock to the republican cause. No IRA members died in the incident, but the eleven civilian fatalities represented a hammer blow to the IRA's support and Sinn Féin's prospects for political expansion. This was the Enniskillen bombing, which took place on the morning of Remembrance Day as large numbers of Protestants gathered in the Fermanagh town in readiness for the annual parade and service. A large IRA device hidden in a community hall just behind them exploded without warning, demolishing a wall and bringing down tons of masonry. A man who lived nearby said, 'The explosion itself seemed to last about fifteen seconds. Then there was a dead silence for ten seconds. Then there was sobbing and crying.' As the dust cleared the disbelieving survivors made frantic efforts to dig victims from the rubble.

A local man, Gordon Wilson, gave an account of how he lay trapped in the debris holding his daughter's hand, in a radio interview which is remembered as one of the most poignant and affecting moments of the troubles. They talked for a while but then Marie said, 'Daddy, I love you very much', and fell silent. Mr Wilson survived the ordeal but his daughter did not. After her death he summoned the strength of character to say, 'She was a great wee lassie. She was a pet, and she's dead. But I bear no ill will, I bear no grudge.' The final death toll was eleven but more than sixty other people, aged from 2 to 75, were injured. Five of the dead were women. The IRA had desecrated an occasion set aside for the remembrance of the dead, and the world condemned them for it. Two themes flashed round the world in the wake of the bombing: one was that the IRA had killed eleven Protestant civilians as they gathered on Remembrance Day; the second was the almost superhuman display of Christian charity and forgiveness shown by Gordon Wilson.

A few days after the bombing a senior IRA source acknowledged the damage it had inflicted on his movement, saying:

> Politically and internationally it is a major setback. Our central base can take a hell of a lot of jolting and crises with limited demoralisation, but the outer reaches are just totally devastated. It will hurt us really badly in the Republic more than anywhere else. We were trying to convince people there that what's happening in the north is a legitimate armed struggle. But the obloquy we've attracted cuts the ground from under us. It allows the Brits to slot us into the category of terrorists and that's bad. People in the IRA just feel sick. This is probably the worst year the IRA has had for five years.

Enniskillen was clearly a grave setback for the republican movement, but two other almost simultaneous events combined to make the month of November 1987 a watershed. First a French customs patrol intercepted a trawler off the coast of France, finally alerting the authorities to the Libyan arms connection. For the first time the authorities north and south of the border realised the scale of the threat posed by the IRA. The Dublin government was particularly alarmed by the revelation, realising that the IRA now possessed weapons which might even match those available to the Irish army itself.

This sense of alarm in the south was heightened even more by an extraordinary episode over which the IRA had no control. Dessie O'Hare, the renegade INLA member, and a small gang kidnapped a Dublin dentist. They held him for several weeks until, in an action that appalled the entire country, O'Hare hacked off two of his captive's fingers with a chisel. Shortly afterwards the dentist was rescued, but for the following three weeks O'Hare and other gang members were pursued by police over large stretches of Ireland, twice shooting their way out of roadblocks and injuring several Gardaí before their eventual capture. The fact that he had been able to remain at large for weeks, and his ability to outgun Gardaí in their clashes, sapped public confidence in the police.

The combination of the Enniskillen bomb, the Libyan guns and the O'Hare dragnet created widespread alarm that the northern conflict was spilling across the border and threatening the stability of the entire island. For years afterwards, Sinn Féin expansion would not be a possibility in the south: the republican ambition of having up to five members holding the balance of power in the Dáil was set back for many years.

Violence 1988–90

The year 1988 brought no statistical rise in violence, but it included some terrible incidents which have remained in the memory of many who lived through them. One sequence in particular, in March of that year, will always be associated with one of the darkest and most traumatic periods of the troubles, when for a time violence seemed to be spiralling completely out of control. The sequence began not in Northern Ireland but in the British possession of Gibraltar. In the first week of March three IRA members, one of them a woman, were shot dead in disputed circumstances by the SAS in what came to be regarded as one of the most controversial incidents of the troubles. Although the IRA unit was intent on staging a bomb attack against British soldiers, the fact that they were unarmed when killed led to widespread criticism of the authorities. Controversy stemmed from claims by witnesses that the IRA members may have been attempting to surrender, and that they were shot while lying on the ground. The SAS members involved said the three had been given a chance to surrender but had failed to freeze immediately and had made suspicious movements.

The three shot dead were elevated to instant republican martyr-dom. Hundreds gathered at Dublin airport as their bodies were flown to Ireland, thousands lining the route as the coffins were driven to Belfast. The killings not only sparked off intense international controversy but also led on to an unprecedented cycle of death and brutality. Many thousands more attended the funerals in west Belfast, but in Milltown cemetery mayhem broke out when to general amazement a lone loyalist gunman, Michael Stone, launched an attack on mourners. After much initial confusion Stone, a stockily built man with long hair and a moustache, was to be seen firing a handgun and throwing hand grenades towards the gravesides.

He then jogged towards a motorway several hundred yards away, pursued by hundreds of men and youths. On his way he periodically stopped, firing shots and throwing grenades to hold back his pursuers, killing three of them. He eventually reached the motorway, but by that stage had apparently exhausted his supply of grenades and ammunition. An incensed crowd overpowered him and beat him unconscious before police arrived and saved his life. Most of this extraordinary scene was televised.

More was to follow. One of those killed by Stone was a member of the IRA, and as his subsequent funeral made its way to Milltown a car carrying two British army corporals unaccountably drove into the cortège. Mourners besieged the car, assuming that its occupants were loyalists intent on a repeat attack. Dozens of them rushed forward, kicking the car and attempting to open its doors. Both the soldiers inside the car were armed, and one climbed partly out of a window, firing a shot in the air which briefly scattered the crowd. The crowd surged back, however, again attacking the vehicle, and the corporals were eventually pulled from the car and punched and kicked to the ground. They were then dragged into a nearby sports ground where they were again beaten and partially stripped. Finally they were driven to a patch of waste ground and shot dead. The sequence of events is still remembered, often with a shudder, as an almost unreal period of instability and polarisation.

The violence was unremitting. For one thing the loyalist killing rate rose sharply, from only 5 deaths in 1985 to a total of 62 in the following three years, as both the UDA and UVF increased their activity in the wake of the Anglo-Irish Agreement. Their victims were mainly civilians, 40 of them Catholics and 8 Protestants. Although loyalists always harboured the ambition to kill active republicans, they rarely managed to do so, with only half a dozen Sinn Féin or IRA members or supporters among the dead in this three-year period. More republicans were to be targeted in subsequent years but at this stage Catholic civilians bore the brunt of the loyalist violence. As in previous bouts of loyalist violence the victims were often chosen at random or because they were convenient targets.

As always, however, republican violence attracted more attention than did loyalist killings. The IRA was active on many fronts, causing the deaths of a substantial number of Protestants whom it claimed were loyalist extremists involved in violence. Some were but some were not. The IRA also stepped up its killings of regular soldiers, particularly in 1988, causing the deaths of fourteen soldiers in two incidents by blowing up coaches in Lisburn in County Antrim and Ballygawley in Tyrone.

These attacks spurred Thatcher into a legal clampdown on republicans. A high-level review led to a series of measures which included banning Sinn Féin voices from the airwaves, a loss of remission for paramilitary prisoners, and a partial withdrawal of the right to silence of paramilitary suspects. The authorities were also clearly concerned by the new IRA campaign in Britain and mainland Europe. While the attempt to attack troops in Gibraltar had failed, in the following year an IRA bomb killed eleven army bandsmen at a military music school at Deal in Kent. There was also a series of lucky escapes for troops at barracks in England and Germany as the IRA attempted to inflict large-scale loss of life by placing bombs at army sleeping quarters during the night. A further major tightening of security was ordered following the IRA assassination in 1990 of Ian Gow, a Conservative MP who had been both a personal friend of Thatcher and a strong supporter of the Unionist cause. He died in a car booby-trap explosion at his home in Sussex.

But even as the IRA celebrated such deaths as successes, the organisation's members were also killing substantial numbers of civilians, generally by accident. So many were being killed that Adams as Sinn Féin president publicly appealed to IRA volunteers in 1989 to avoid such incidents, saying: 'At times the fate of this struggle is in your hands. You have to be careful and careful again. The morale of your comrades in jail, your own morale and of your comrades in the field, can be raised or dashed by your actions. You can advance or retard the struggle.' The lesson to be drawn from the pattern of deaths, however, was that the waging of high-level campaigns of violence made civilian deaths an inevitability. The pattern was different on the republican and loyalist sides, in that the latter's main target grouping was Catholic men.

Republicans during this period hotly denied any sectarian motivation to their actions, saying they wished to kill only those who were part of the 'British war machine'. In pursuit of this they targeted, among others, prison officers, legal figures, and civilian contractors who carried out building work and other jobs for the security forces. The different viewpoints of the two communities led to radically different perspectives on the IRA campaign. Republicans would say they deliberately killed only those involved with the security forces, but many Protestants pointed out that most of the victims, deliberate or accidental, were Protestants, and alleged that all or part of the motivation was sectarian. Many Catholics tended to accept the republican explanation, but very many Protestants did not.

1989 brought one of the numerous incidents which over the years raised human rights concerns, and produced republican allegations that the authorities were engaged in dirty tricks and underhand activity of various kinds. In this instance Pat Finucane, a Belfast solicitor who had represented republican clients in a series of high-profile cases, was shot dead in his home by loyalist gunmen.

The case, like many others throughout the troubles, led to long-running controversy, with allegations about the incident still being levelled by human rights groups decades after his death. The accusation was that he had been such a thorn in the side of the authorities that they had urged loyalists to attack him, and had probably helped them to do so.

The controversy surrounding his death arose from a number of sources, one of which was the statement by a junior government minister, three weeks before the shooting, that a number of solicitors were 'unduly sympathetic to the cause of the IRA'. Another aspect of the controversy arose from allegations that detectives interrogating loyalist prisoners in Castlereagh holding centre had urged loyalists to shoot the solicitor. A judge and senior police officer both concluded there had been collusion in the attack, but in 2011 the government set up a review of the case by a lawyer rather than a full inquiry.

Late in 1990 the IRA produced a new tactic which came to be known as the 'human bomb'. In the first instance of its use a Londonderry Catholic man, Patsy Gillespie, who worked in a local army canteen, was taken from his home by IRA members. While his wife and family were assured he would be returned safely, he was chained into a hijacked vehicle and ordered to drive to an army border checkpoint. When he arrived there the IRA detonated a large bomb which had been concealed in the vehicle. The checkpoint was heavily fortified but little defence was possible against such a powerful device, and five soldiers were killed. For many hours the security forces were unsure whether Gillespie himself had escaped or not, for no trace of his body could be found. Even after all the years of the troubles the incident, and several similar attacks, still managed to generate a fresh sense of horror.

1991

Some months later, in February 1991, the IRA staged one of its most audacious attacks in England. The target was originally Margaret Thatcher, but by the time the incident took place she had been replaced as prime minister by John Major. He was chairing a meeting of ministers during the first Gulf War when a number of mortar bombs rained down in the vicinity of 10 Downing Street. Major described hearing 'a tremendous explosion' but no one was killed or injured even though damage was caused in the back garden of Number 10. The IRA had succeeded in exploding a substantial mortar bomb within yards of the prime minister, one of the most closely guarded people in Britain. The attack achieved major international publicity for the IRA and represented a serious embarrassment to the British security services. Major wrote later, 'If it had been ten feet closer half the cabinet could have been killed.'

The rest of 1991 brought more IRA attacks in Britain, more killings of IRA members by the SAS and an increase in loyalist activity. Much loyalist violence emanated from the County Armagh town of Portadown, where the local UVF was headed by a number of particularly violent leaders including Billy Wright, a local man who came to be known as King Rat. In March four Catholic men were killed in a UVF gun attack at a bar in the County Tyrone village of Cappagh. Although the UVF gunmen did not know it at the time, three of those killed were IRA members. In the same month the UVF killed two teenage girls and a man, all Catholics, in an attack on a mobile shop in a housing estate in Craigavon, County Armagh. In November two Catholics and a Protestant were killed as they left a factory near Lurgan in the same county.

The sluggish political scene had been enlivened a little in mid-1989 by the replacement of Tom King by Peter Brooke. King's years in Belfast had been dominated by the furious loyalist reaction to the Anglo-Irish Agreement, the frigid political atmosphere offering little hope of finding agreement among the parties. By the time Peter Brooke took his place something of a thaw had set in, with the political parties, in particular the Unionists, adopting a less confrontational stance.

The widespread early impression of Brooke was that he was a descendant of the old Anglo-Irish ascendancy, a quasi-aristocrat who would be out of his depth in the shark-infested waters he had been despatched to manage. His upbringing had been the picture of establishment orthodoxy: he was educated at Marlborough and

Oxford, and his father had been a Tory Home Secretary. In fact, he would turn out to be one of the most thoughtful and imaginative, if not always the most deft, of the many politicians given the task of running Northern Ireland.

The first major stir of his tenure came in November 1989, when a journalist asked him whether he could ever imagine a British government talking to Sinn Féin. Instead of the standard ministerial response that there was no question of the government talking to terrorists, he gave a long and thoughtful answer. In the course of it he remarked:

> Let me remind you of the move towards independence in Cyprus, and a British Minister stood up in the House of Commons and used the word 'never' in a way which within two years there had been a retreat from that word. All I'm saying is that I would hope that the British government on a long-term basis would be sufficiently flexible, that if flexibility were required it could be used, but I am in no way predicating or predicting what those circumstances would be.

His mention of Cyprus also excited much republican interest in that it presented an example of an island which had been a British possession, but which in 1959 had achieved independence following a campaign which combined political agitation and violence.

A year later, in November 1990, Brooke delivered a speech which was to have far-reaching effects. In part of it he declared: 'The British government has no selfish strategic or economic interest in Northern Ireland: our role is to help, enable and encourage. Britain's purpose, as I have sought to describe it, is not to occupy, oppress or exploit, but to ensure democratic debate and free democratic choice. That is our way.' His words, like his earlier reference to Cyprus, aroused intense interest within the republican movement.

When he took an initiative to try to get politics rolling again, however, Sinn Féin were excluded from it. He believed he saw a window of opportunity, and although none of the major parties was particularly keen to get round the table, he nonetheless embarked on a long process of nudging and persuading them towards talks. Many months of intricate political activity followed. He began the effort in January 1990, and it took more than a year to get agreement from all sides to sit down together.

The talks were conducted within parameters which would become a familiar formula in the years that followed. They were divided into three 'strands', originally formulated by John Hume, dealing with internal Northern Ireland matters, north–south relations and overall Anglo-Irish relations. The discussions were useful in exploring some political details, but they never looked like providing a solution to the troubles; indeed they never looked like producing even an agreement among the parties at the table. Despite the close attentions of London and Dublin the talks ran into the sands after a few months.

1992 violence

1992 was again marred by violence. Only seventeen days into the year an IRA bomb planted at the side of a County Tyrone road blew apart a van, killing eight Protestant workers travelling home after carrying out building work at an army base. The vehicle took the full force of the blast. The van's upper part was torn asunder, but instead of being blown into a field its momentum kept it tumbling along the road for thirty yards. Seven men were killed outright, an eighth dying shortly afterwards. The scene at that point was hellish, with dead, dying and injured bodies scattered on the road, in a field, and trapped under wreckage. Some passers-by who stopped to help were sent into shock by the sight of terrible mutilations. It took the emergency services a considerable time to work out how many had been killed. Yet another Northern Ireland place-name, that of Teebane Crossroads, would forever afterwards be associated with violent death.

One of the survivors later described his ordeal: 'I looked and all I could see was fire. I was yelling, I was screeching and it was an experience I had never come through before. A flash came through my mind that overhead lines had fallen – the big overhead power lines. I thought we had been electrocuted because of the pain. I have experienced getting an electric shock, but fire was coming out of my eyes. I just squealed for breath and I seemed to be heading away. I seemed to be literally going to float away. I felt I was going backwards. I was lying on the broad of my back and I couldn't see down to see my legs and I couldn't feel them. I was trying to get up. I had plenty of power in my two arms but no power anywhere else. I saw a fella who had been sitting beside me on the bus staggering about and I yelled and shouted at him but he never heard me. I said to a man: "Are my legs on?" and he said, "You're all right", and he shook my legs but I couldn't feel them. I said: "Get me up", and part of my kneecap came off but I knew my leg was there and I thanked God that I was living.'

Just over two weeks later came another shocking and unprecedented attack. An off-duty RUC constable, Allen Moore, arrived in plain clothes at the Sinn Féin press office on the Falls Road in Belfast, posing as a journalist. Once admitted to the building he produced a pump-action shotgun and turned it on three men in a ground-floor office, killing them all. Constable Moore then drove out of Belfast to a secluded spot and shot himself dead.

The following day came yet more violence as loyalists exacted revenge for the Teebane attack. Two members of the UDA walked into a Catholic betting shop on the Ormeau Road in south Belfast and systematically shot as many men as they could. The attack only took a matter of minutes, leaving five dead.

An ambulance officer called to the scene described what he saw: 'I went in and had a quick look. The scene was horrific, with bodies everywhere. In that confined space there was a smell from the gunfire and all the bleeding and whatever that you couldn't describe. It has an effect on you as an individual. I get flashbacks to it, I get visions of what was going on – the smell, the smell, the feeling of being there. For other ambulancemen it was worse: they were knee deep in it, dealing with the dead and dying.'

Less than two weeks later the SAS was back in action, laying an ambush for IRA members who attacked an RUC station in the County Tyrone town of Coalisland. The authorities allowed the attack on the heavily fortified station to go ahead, the IRA men commandeering a lorry and firing a heavy machine gun from the back of it. The security forces took no action at that point, but when the IRA unit drove into the car park of a church some distance away in order to abandon the lorry and disperse in getaway cars, the SAS opened fire. Locals said there was a call for the gang to surrender, followed by intense, prolonged gunfire. When it was all over, four IRA members lay dead with two others injured. The authorities celebrated the incident as a clean, clinical strike against the IRA.

Then in April came an IRA attack in London which had an extraordinary effect. Two bombs set off in the City of London, Britain's financial heartland, actually inflicted more financial damage than all the 10,000 bombs which had ever gone off in Northern Ireland. When the smoke and dust cleared it was found that the two bombs had caused more than £700 million of damage. The total paid out in compensation in Northern Ireland at that point was just over £600 million.

The device had been placed near the Baltic Exchange and the tall buildings around it created a canyon-like effect, preventing the blast from escaping and instead funnelling it into surrounding buildings. British newspapers carried full-page photographs of the devastation. The damage was so severe that the fact that the bomb had also killed three people, one of them a fifteen-year-old girl, was almost overlooked.

The spectacular destruction grabbed the attention of the world. Republican sources made no secret of the fact that they were both amazed and delighted at the extent of the damage and at the extraordinary bill for repairs. The idea of placing large bombs in the City, where so many expensive prestige buildings cluster in a tightly packed area, came late and largely by accident to them. Since 1988 they had carried out scores of attacks, but it took four years before they hit on the idea of bombing the City.

The scale of the Baltic Exchange damage opened a new avenue, the possibility of inflicting serious damage on the entire British economy. In the 1970s the IRA had naively held such a belief, but the idea faded as the government showed itself able to absorb, without great difficulty, the cost of dealing with terrorism and disorder. However, the fact that a single attack could cost Britain more than half a billion pounds lent a whole new dimension to the IRA campaign. The authorities were desperate to prevent any recurrence, and worried that if the IRA could strike again major financial institutions might relocate to other countries not subject to such dangers.

The Teebane attack claimed a political casualty in the form of Peter Brooke, in that he was judged to have made a *faux pas* on television on the night of the incident. Appearing on RTÉ's Friday night television programme *The Late Late Show*, he expressed his sympathy for the families of the dead but was later persuaded to sing one of his favourite songs, 'My Darling Clementine'. He later apologised in the Commons, saying his actions might have caused 'wholly justified offence' to the bereaved families. John Major turned down his resignation at the time but it was clear Brooke's days were numbered, and in April he moved on.

John Major's choice of successor was welcomed by Unionist politicians but caused dismay in Dublin. Sir Patrick Mayhew, as his name suggested, came from an Anglo-Irish background, but in his previous post as Attorney-General he had been involved in many acrimonious extradition disputes with Dublin. Within weeks of his arrival in Belfast Mayhew pushed ahead with a revival of the Brooke talks, with Sinn Féin again excluded because of its identification with the IRA. This session of talks would ultimately prove unsuccessful, but it did get beyond the procedural points which had defeated the Brooke discussions, and some serious debate took place.

In the talks the Unionist parties were primarily concerned to reduce the influence that Dublin had gained through the Anglo-Irish Agreement. They also wished to get rid of Articles 2 and 3 of the Irish constitution, which since 1937 had laid legal claim to Northern Ireland. Some Unionist politicians wanted a strong new devolved government re-established in Belfast, though others preferred to aim for closer links with Westminster, accompanied by a less powerful Belfast assembly. The first priority of the SDLP and the Irish government, on the other hand, was to protect the Anglo-Irish Agreement and if possible develop stronger north–south and Anglo-Irish links.

In pursuit of their conflicting goals the Unionist parties wanted to concentrate on discussing a new assembly while the SDLP and Dublin were more interested in dealing with north–south relations. A major stir was caused when Hume unveiled the SDLP's proposals, which advocated a direct role for both Dublin and Europe in running Northern Ireland. This controversial and innovative proposal dismayed Unionist politicians, some of whom had hoped the SDLP would settle for a Northern Ireland-centred arrangement with modest links to Dublin.

The talks sparked some interest when Molyneaux became the first Ulster Unionist leader to head a delegation to Dublin for talks with the Irish government, but in the end nothing emerged to bridge the gulf between the SDLP and the Unionist parties, and in November 1992 the exercise was wound up. The British government's approach continued to be that it would hope for an agreement among the constitutional parties with the purpose of isolating the republican and loyalist extremists. After the best efforts of Brooke and Mayhew, however, there seemed no real prospect of this coming about.

Political activity did not produce any significant progress and violence went remorselessly on. And, as always, there were innocent victims. One of the saddest incidents came in Warrington, near Liverpool, when two IRA bombs placed in litter bins in a shopping precinct killed two young children and injured 56 other people. Jonathan Ball was three years old, and an only child. Timothy Parry, aged twelve, had gone into the town to buy a pair of football shorts: in the explosion he suffered severe head injuries and died some days later. His father said, 'We produced a bloody good kid, he was a fine lad. He had his moments, he could be a cheeky, impudent pup, but a good kid. The IRA – I have no words for them at all.' The killings led to a wave of revulsion throughout Britain and especially in the Republic, where tens of thousands of people attended a Dublin peace rally.

The IRA, undeterred, within weeks staged another huge bombing in the City of London, repeating their Baltic Exchange attack of April 1992 by setting off a large bomb at Bishopsgate in the heart of the financial district. Again the damage was extraordinary, with estimates of the cost ranging as high as a billion pounds. Yet even as death and destruction continued at a high level, subterranean talks were going on. What became known as the peace process began to surface.

10.

Peace process
1993–94

Most of the 1990s would be dominated by what came to be known as the peace process, which was to change the face of Northern Ireland politics and Anglo-Irish relations. It was a highly controversial enterprise regarded with the utmost suspicion by many as it threaded its way along a long and tortuous course. One of its starting points was the 1985 Anglo-Irish Agreement, which led to a gradual but important rethink in republican ranks. On one reading, the agreement had redefined the whole Irish question: the IRA had traditionally regarded itself as being engaged in an anti-colonial, anti-imperialist freedom struggle, but suddenly the supposed imperialist power had made an important move which was difficult to portray in an imperialist light.

At the same time it became clear that Sinn Féin's vote was going down, the party chalking up 102,000 votes in 1983 but only 76,000 two years later. Sinn Féin had established a solid foothold in electoral politics, but it was a far cry from the heady days when it aspired to eclipse the SDLP and become the main voice of northern nationalism.

Hume – Adams

Even as the IRA escalated its violence in the late 1980s, Sinn Féin was exploring the potential for talking, sending feelers out to church and state and seeking contact with a wide range of opinion. The result was a web of talks over the years, most of which were held in strict secrecy. It was not until April 1993 that the lid was lifted on at least part of the process when, entirely by accident, Gerry Adams was spotted entering John Hume's home in Londonderry. Within hours political figures of various persuasions were issuing statements condemning Hume for consorting with what they called the mouthpiece of terrorists. The media clamoured for an explanation: no one accused Hume of supporting republican violence but both critics and supporters demanded to know what he was doing talking to Adams. The heat on Hume was all the fiercer because IRA violence was at a high level, the two Warrington boys having died just weeks earlier.

On the surface Hume appeared to have breached the general rule that mainstream politicians should not speak to those associated with violence. Yet although few knew it at the time, the Hume–Adams channel was just the tip of an iceberg, since for years many surreptitious contacts had taken place. It was not only Hume who had been in touch with the republicans but also the Catholic Church, the Irish government and, above all, the British government. London's line to the republicans stretched back not just for years but, intermittently, for decades. Almost all of this was however hidden from public view.

Sinn Féin had made approaches to many quarters over the years, often with the assistance of Father Alex Reid, a priest based in Clonard monastery off the Falls Road. As a result Adams had secretly met Catholic Cardinal Tomás Ó Fiaich and, on other occasions, representatives of the Irish government in talks authorised by Taoiseach Charles Haughey. To begin with, none of these produced visible results. 1988 had seen formal talks, whose existence were for once known to the public, between SDLP and Sinn Féin party delegations, with a series of meetings and exchanges of position papers. When the talks ended without agreement after some months most assumed this was the end of the matter. But Hume and Adams had privately agreed to keep in touch, a move which was the beginning of one of the most unusual relationships in Northern Ireland politics. During 1989 for instance they met four times, usually in rooms made available by Father Reid in the monastery.

The meetings did not inhibit Hume from publicly attacking the IRA. In one scathing denunciation he declared:

They are more Irish than the rest of us, they believe. They are the pure master race of Irish. They are the keepers of the holy grail of the nation. That deep-seated attitude, married to their method, has all the hallmarks of undiluted fascism. They have all the other hallmarks of the fascist – the scapegoat – the Brits are to blame for everything, even their own atrocities! They know better than the rest of us.

Hume and Adams, the two dominant figures in northern nationalism, are individuals who have already, in very different ways, left their mark on Irish history. They were direct rivals for the nationalist vote and indeed for the leadership of northern nationalism, their parties fighting many bitter battles. Yet through all the bruising conflicts they forged a personal relationship of some trust and, in time, a sense of pursuing a common purpose. Although they differed fundamentally in their analysis of the problem, and above all disagreed on how to resolve it, they actually had much in common in their backgrounds. Hume, like Adams, came from a working-class Catholic background. He was born in Derry in 1937, one of a family of seven living in a two-bedroomed house. His father fought with the British army in France in World War One and was later unemployed for many years.

He attended grammar school in Derry and then Maynooth College in the Republic, where for several years he trained as a priest. He changed direction and became a teacher before becoming involved in self-help community projects such as the Credit Union. Coming to public prominence on civil rights issues, he took the moderate line in the many arguments within the movement.

In common with Garret FitzGerald, he challenged the traditional nationalist assertion that the root of the problem was the British presence. The historic mission of nationalism, he argued, was to convince Unionism that its concerns could be accommodated in a new agreed Ireland. He built up an international reputation, accumulating considerable influence especially in the Republic and, as a European MP, on the continent. In particular he wielded great influence in Washington, where powerful Irish-American figures such as Senator Edward Kennedy looked to him for advice. By the early 1990s he was, in sum, the most influential nationalist politician in Northern Ireland.

His behind-the-scenes contacts with Adams interacted with events in the public domain. When Brooke made his 1990 statement that Britain had no selfish strategic or economic interest in Northern Ireland he did so at the private prompting of Hume, who had been arguing this point in his talks with Adams. Brooke's statement, while by no means regarded by republicans as conclusive, was nonetheless strong evidence in support of Hume's contention that Britain was essentially neutral. This thought would play an important part in the embryonic peace process.

It would emerge at a later date that the British government itself had for years had its own line of contact to republicans. In 1990 Brooke had given his approval to a proposal from John Deverell, the head of MI5 in Northern Ireland, to reopen contacts with the republicans. Deverell said he believed there was potential for progress, and Brooke gave him permission to explore. Brooke would later recall: 'We had a substantial debate about it. It was not negotiation. I was not sanctioning a whole series of things – it was the opportunity to carry on conversation. It was essentially an intelligence process.' This was the start of a long sequence of contacts between the government and the republicans.

A highly significant moment came in October 1991 when Hume wrote a draft declaration which he hoped could form the basis of an agreed position between the British and Irish governments. The idea was to demonstrate, with a joint declaration, that Britain was not standing in the way of Irish unity, in the eventual hope of persuading republicans to halt their attempt to unite Ireland by violence. The intention was to find common ground in everyone's ideological positions, and to reconcile what had always appeared irreconcilable. It was to prove the first of many such drafts which would, in December 1993, culminate in what became known as the Downing Street Declaration.

Hume's first draft included statements on self-determination, an assurance from Britain that it had no selfish interest in remaining in Ireland, and a heavy emphasis on the need for agreement. The document set the Northern Ireland problem firmly in an Anglo-Irish context, drawing on the Anglo-Irish Agreement and envisaging the two governments working ever more closely together. It also stressed the European dimension. While it did not explicitly demand an IRA ceasefire, it was obvious that it was intended to produce one. It was also implicit that if violence ended, Sinn Féin would be admitted to mainstream Irish political life. The crucial part of Hume's draft lay in its attempt to address the republican demand for Irish self-determination. This could not be achieved, he wrote, without the agreement of the people of Northern Ireland. This was a subtle concept, for in effect it combined the principles of self-determination and consent. It thus combined, at least in theory, what republicans sought with the Unionist demand that the majority opinion should prevail within Northern Ireland.

Hume took the document to both Haughey and Adams. In the subsequent dozen or more drafts, Hume, Dublin and the republicans tested out each other's positions, seeking both common ground and a formula which might bring John Major into the exercise. Haughey was cautious but Albert Reynolds, who succeeded him as Taoiseach and leader of Fianna Fáil in January 1992, was much more interested and pursued the idea with enthusiasm. Reynolds, a canny Longford businessman, had little direct experience of Northern Ireland matters but respected Hume's opinion and had an instinct that a peace process might be productive. The years that followed saw the further development of many secret contacts. Hume, Reynolds and the republicans exchanged documents and kept London informed while the republicans separately, unknown to Hume and Reynolds, also dealt directly with London. The web survived both political turbulence and numerous acts of IRA violence such as the City of London bombings.

It was obvious that John Major was taking many risks in keeping open the channels of contact. He had only a slender majority at Westminster, with an awkward squad of right-wing Tories ready to rebel at any moment, principally on important votes concerning Europe. He also had in his government ministers such as Lord Cranborne who were strongly committed to the Unionist cause. The parliamentary arithmetic meant nine Ulster Unionist MPs led by James Molyneaux could be of great value to Major, and might be vital to the survival of his government. But on the other hand Major was very much of the opinion that Northern Ireland warranted serious and sustained attention. This attitude was in itself unusual in that so many senior British politicians had throughout their careers attempted to devote as little time and energy as possible to the issue. Major was different, taking a decision in his first months in office to pay attention to the problem. He and Reynolds, whom he found 'easy to get on with, naturally cheery and loquacious', got into the habit of writing to each other and speaking frequently on the telephone, often calling each other at home. Major recalled in his memoirs, 'I liked Albert a lot, and I thought we could move things forward together.'

The back-channel

The secret British–republican link in these years, which came to be known as the back-channel, had three distinct phases. In the first, which began in 1990 and lasted for three years, London actively courted the republicans, sending nineteen messages while Sinn Féin replied only once. Occasional meetings took place, sometimes in Northern Ireland and sometimes in London. In the second phase, between February and November 1993, the pace quickened with an average of a message a week passing back and forward as the possibility of a formal meeting between republicans and the government was explored. The third short phase followed before the contacts effectively came to an end in November 1993.

The back-channel opened with an approach from the British government representative who had been in touch with the republicans in earlier periods. He explained he was due for retirement and said he wanted to meet Martin McGuinness to prepare the way for a new representative. This overture opened a line of communication which went from the government to 'the government representative' who spoke to a person known as 'the contact', who in turn was in touch with Sinn Féin.

In 1992 messages were passed back and forth on the Hume–Adams talks. The British also appear to have kept Sinn Féin informed of the progress of Mayhew's talks with the political parties, passing on a detailed internal government report and assessment on the discussions. This was followed, in December 1992 and January 1993, by meetings between the contact and the British representative, together with a series of telephone calls, sometimes on a daily basis. Sinn Féin was pointedly unenthusiastic until the government representative indicated a face-to-face meeting was possible. Many messages followed, the republicans now taking the exercise seriously and establishing a committee chaired by Adams to oversee the enterprise. In the event, however, the go-ahead never came from London. Instead, the republicans were told that ministers had changed their minds.

In the end, after dozens of messages and exchanges of documents and a number of face-to-face meetings, the two sides never got together for serious talks. Both laid out their positions in formal documents, but much of the back-channel concerned the arrangements for talks, and no substantive negotiations took place. The more meaningful negotiations throughout this period actually involved Adams, Hume and Dublin through the stream of draft declarations.

After all the years of moving at a snail's pace, the spring of 1993 ushered in a new phase of often frantic activity, with the public for the first time glimpsing a little of what had been going on. From then on, incident followed incident in a sometimes bewildering blur of events. Ahead lay moments of tremendous excitement, great controversy, much violence and on occasion near-despair.

The storm of protest which followed the disclosure of the April 1993 meeting between Hume and Adams did not deter the two men, and within weeks they issued the first of a series of statements saying they were involved in a search for agreement. However, the talks revelation put the still-secret joint declaration work under great strain. Reynolds would say later: 'When the news broke of the dialogue taking place between Adams and Hume, it just brought more tensions and pressure on the situation. I would have preferred to have dealt with the whole lot nice and quietly behind the scenes – you make more progress that way. But it burst into the open and I had no control over it. It didn't help.'

It was clear from an early stage that London regarded the joint declaration idea not so much as a potentially historic formula for peace but as an unwelcome hot potato. At the request of Reynolds, Major agreed that London would consider the declaration text but drew the distinction that his government would discuss it but would not negotiate on it. Mayhew as Northern Ireland Secretary was against the idea, wishing instead to persevere with his political talks. In a personal letter to Major, Reynolds wrote: 'There are risks, but peace is within our reach if we play our cards right. Peace, which could result from the present process, could transform the current climate and make that outcome not only possible but probable. I will therefore ask you in all sincerity to continue to give the process your full and enthusiastic backing.'

Eventually in the autumn of 1993 Hume, impatient at the pace of progress, went public, he and Adams announcing that they had made considerable progress and had agreed to forward a report to Dublin. They declared: 'We are convinced from our discussions that a process can be designed to lead to agreement among the divided people of this island which will provide a solid basis for peace.' This brought the already high level of public interest to an even more intense pitch, dominating news bulletins in Britain and Ireland. The statement produced acres of newsprint aimed at shedding light on how the north's two nationalist leaders, one identified with violence, the other with non-violence, could possibly be on the verge of agreement. The Hume–Adams statement gave the public another little glimpse of the secret world of talks and contacts. It was by then firmly established in the public mind that Hume and Adams had been in contact, but the bulk of the story remained hidden from view: the public, and the media, knew nothing of the years of talks between Adams and Hume, and of the British and Irish governmental contacts with Sinn Féin. They knew nothing of the succession of draft declarations, and were in complete ignorance of the fact that many of these had been passed to the British government.

Both London and Dublin were angry with Hume. They continued to work on the joint declaration process but both were anxious to keep it free from what they referred to as 'the fingerprints' of the Hume–Adams statement. Major despatched his cabinet secretary, Sir Robin Butler, to Dublin to tell Reynolds that the Hume–Adams initiative had become inextricably intertwined with the declaration work, and that this had effectively made the idea too hot to handle. The two governments should look to alternatives such as the Mayhew talks, Major suggested. The Reynolds–Butler meeting took place on 19 October, just four days before an act of violence in Belfast which started a cycle of killing that momentarily generated a sense of hopelessness. October 1993 was one of the most awful, yet most crucial, months in the troubles. It began in confusion mixed with hope, then plunged into violence and near despair, almost as dark as any period of the troubles. The death toll was the highest of any month since 1976.

IRA bombs and loyalist retaliation

An IRA bomb went off on the Shankill Road around lunchtime on a Saturday, at a time when the road was thronged with hundreds of shoppers. It was aimed at leaders of the paramilitary Ulster Defence Association who the IRA thought were meeting in offices above a fish shop. IRA members attempted to place the bomb in the shop, in a very risky operation which carried a high chance of causing civilian casualties. In the event the bombing did not go as planned, for as IRA member Thomas Begley was putting the device in place it detonated prematurely, killing him and nine Protestants. Four women and two children were among the dead but no UDA members were killed, for the upstairs office was empty at the time. The explosion demolished the old building. In the aftermath local men, police, firemen and ambulancemen tore at the rubble in a search for survivors, but the elderly building had collapsed like a house of cards, bringing heavy masonry crashing down on those inside.

A young police officer who arrived quickly at the scene said later: 'I was one of the first in. I remember an old man being recovered. His head was the first thing to appear from the rubble, and that was quite a frightening experience. I knew he was still alive because his eyes were blinking. An ambulanceman put an oxygen mask over his mouth but by the time he left the rubble he had died. After he was moved we continued to remove rubble from where we were standing, but unknown to anybody we were standing on other bodies. As the rubble was being removed – and it will stay with me until I die – I saw a young girl's foot. I knew it was a young girl's foot because her shoe size was about three or four. It poked through the rubble, and I wanted to stop digging then, because I knew I was going to see quite a horrendous sight; and in fact I did.' A paramedic later recounted: 'The scene was horrific. There was one lady lying in the road with head injuries and half her arm was blown off. She later died. But the worst part for me was when we unearthed the body of a young girl. I will never forget seeing that face staring up out of the rubble.'

The attack did not come out of the blue, for it was in effect the culmination of several months of increasingly desperate IRA attempts to assassinate leading loyalists. For months hardly a week passed without IRA gangs attempting to gun down or blow up those they believed to be associated with groups such as the UDA and UVF. Loyalist killings were running at a particularly high level and had developed a new feature. In addition to the standard pattern of loyalist attacks on random Catholic targets, loyalists had in addition begun to target members of Sinn Féin, together with members of their families and friends. In the five years leading up to the Shankill bombing, eighteen people with Sinn Féin connections were killed by Protestant extremists. Three of the dead were Sinn Féin councillors while another councillor lost a brother and a son in separate attacks. Republicans alleged collusion by the authorities in many of the killings, while the IRA retaliated by killing many alleged loyalist extremists. It was against this background of republican–loyalist violence that the Shankill attack took place.

The funeral of the dead bomber produced an electrifying moment when Adams was pictured carrying the coffin of Thomas Begley, an image reproduced on the front pages of most newspapers. The result was a huge outcry, with much questioning of how Adams could speak of peace while shouldering the coffin of a bomber who had caused so many deaths. From a republican point of view the bombing was one of the IRA's most disastrous mistakes since Enniskillen, in that at a stroke it killed nine civilians, lost one of its own members, and brought fierce international condemnation upon itself.

Reynolds later described a telephone call with Major who, he said, 'could hardly contain himself'. Reynolds recalled:

He said, 'What's this about? How do you expect me to continue with any process when I take up the papers this morning and in every paper on the front page is Gerry Adams carrying a coffin?' I said, 'Look, John, you have to understand that if the guy didn't carry the coffin he wouldn't be able to maintain his credibility with that organisation and bring people with him.'

Reynolds said of the British prime minister: 'Here you had a guy with goodwill keeping it high on his agenda, giving it more time than any prime minister had ever given to the Irish problem since Gladstone, and this was blowing up in his face. He was put in an extremely difficult and delicate position. I was really annoyed with it – to be honest I thought for some time that it would probably blow the whole thing sky high.'

At this point Northern Ireland descended into something close to sheer dread, for loyalist gunmen went on the rampage, killing six people in a series of shootings. They then attempted to match the Shankill death toll with a Saturday night attack on a bar in the quiet mainly Catholic village of Greysteel near Londonderry, a week after the Shankill bombing. Two gunmen opened fire on around 200 people in the bar, killing or fatally injuring eight people, seven of them Catholics.

A young man charged with the murders was televised on his way into court, yelling defiantly and laughing almost maniacally at relatives of the victims in a display of naked sectarian hatred. After his subsequent conviction, the man would for a time become a born-again Christian, but his performance added yet another night-marish dimension to the atmosphere of poison and fear. Twenty-three people had died in the space of a week; the local television news seemed to consist of nothing except more and more violence, the grieving bereaved, and threats of more to come. There was a seemingly endless succession of multiple funerals as the victims were buried.

Social functions and other gatherings were cancelled as people stayed indoors and took extra security precautions. In the evenings many parts of Belfast, particularly Catholic districts, were virtually deserted. A senior trade unionist gave a flavour of the atmosphere at the time:

> I do think they are actually taking us back to the early 1970s. I really don't come across anyone now who doesn't talk about how dreadful it is. Everybody is frankly scared to talk to people of the other community or even talk to people of their own community, in case anything they say might be overheard and give offence. You can see the fear everywhere. When I went to mass on Sunday attendance was down by a third, and there were armed RUC officers on guard duty in the car park. The priest said at the end of mass that police advice

was for us to leave quickly, not to congregate chatting, just to get into our cars and get going.

Although many at first assumed the peace process was over, it turned out that the killings had the opposite effect. When the first waves of shock and anger died down there was renewed determination in many quarters to keep the process going. Major was to suggest in his memoirs that the violence actually gave fresh impetus to a process which was about to expire: 'The process was on a knife-edge. I think it would have broken down had not the Shankill and Greysteel tragedies intervened.' A moving example of this at the human rather than political level came at the funeral of one of the victims of the Greysteel attack. Hume was approached by the daughter of one victim, who told him: 'Mr Hume, we've just buried my father. My family wants you to know that when we said the rosary around my daddy's coffin we prayed for you, for what you're trying to do to bring peace.' This caused Hume to break down in tears.

Overall, however, Hume was receiving more criticism than encouragement, to the point where it affected his health. He collapsed and spent several weeks in hospital. The violence was followed by more political shocks when Belfast journalist Eamonn Mallie revealed in November 1993 that, despite repeated public denials, the government had been in long-standing contact with republicans. The government admitted that there had been contact but said it had begun only in 1993, and that it had in essence been an investigation of a message from Martin McGuinness which had said: 'The conflict is over but we need your advice on how to bring it to a close.' It maintained that those meetings which had taken place had not been authorised by ministers.

London and Sinn Féin then each published their versions of their correspondence, which when examined were found to differ in important details. In particular McGuinness hotly denied that he had sent the 'conflict is over' message. Then came a development so embarrassing that it led to Mayhew offering his resignation to

Major, since a comparison of the two versions showed that vital parts had been altered by one or other of the parties. Someone was engaged in a major deception exercise, forging, omitting and doctoring documents. Each accused the other of fabrication.

When points of detail were raised with the NIO, the government at first did not respond for a full day and then announced that a number of 'errors' had come to light. Mayhew detailed twenty-two of these which, he said, had been caused by typographical and transcription errors. The changes he announced removed some of the glaring inconsistencies in the British version, but the manner in which the correction had to be made was seen as a blow to the government's credibility. Mayhew's resignation offer was refused. Later new information shed some light on how some at least of the contradictions could be reconciled. Former priest Denis Bradley, one of those involved in the contacts, admitted that he, not the IRA, was the author of the 'conflict is over' message, sent on his own initiative to break the logjam.

Major and Reynolds met at a summit in December 1993 which those present described as tense and bad-tempered. The various developments had created much bad blood between London and Dublin. Major took exception to what he later described as 'a series of Irish leaks, threats and distorted press briefing' for which he suspected Reynolds was responsible. Dublin thought Major's undeclared contacts with republicans amounted to double-dealing. Reynolds considered that he had properly informed Major of his own contacts with the republicans, and felt Major should have reciprocated instead of denying they existed. Reynolds said later: 'With a revelation like this naturally one would feel betrayed. If you're going along in good faith you expect all the cards on the table and you expect to know what's going on on both sides. I felt that I was let down, that I should have been told.'

The two prime ministers spent an hour without officials in a private meeting during which they aired their differences, emerging 'very pale and very tense'. Major was to recall this as 'the frankest and fiercest exchanges I had with any fellow leader in my six and a half years as prime minister'. A Dublin aide has recorded for history the memorable reply given by Reynolds when he was asked how it went. Reynolds, he reported, half-grinned and replied: 'It went all right – I chewed his bollocks off and he took a few lumps outa me.' Despite all the bad temper and rancour and difficulties, it was a key meeting with crucial results. Reynolds and Major retained their working relationship and, against all the odds, the drafting work went on.

The Downing Street Declaration

It finally came to fruition in the Downing Street Declaration of December 1993, which Major and Reynolds unveiled together. The document contained nothing that could be interpreted as a British declaration of intent to leave. Rather, it had as its heart a serpentine sentence which intertwined the concepts of self-determination and consent on which Hume and Adams had spent so much time. It read: 'The British government agree that it is for the people of the island of Ireland alone, by agreement between the two parts respectively, to exercise their right of self-determination on the basis of consent, freely and concurrently given, North and South, to bring about a united Ireland, if that is their wish.' It was in effect an ambitious attempt to construct a finely balanced double helix in which self-determination and consent were inseparable.

Many republicans had assumed that Major's desire not to offend the Ulster Unionist party, with its nine Commons votes, would prevent him from going so far. But Major had handled Unionist leader James Molyneaux carefully, ensuring that he did not damn the declaration out of hand. Major had thus achieved the feat of producing a document which kept mainstream Unionism on board while putting maximum pressure on the republicans.

The joint declaration contained references to many of the elements contained in the drafts worked on by Hume and Adams, but most of the points the republicans had wished to see were very much diluted. The republicans had wanted the British to 'join the ranks of the persuaders' of the value of a united Ireland, and had wanted Northern Ireland's future status to be decided by a single act of self-determination by the people of Ireland as a whole. They had also sought a timetable for a British withdrawal, but none of these made it into the declaration's final form. Yet although the document fell far short of what republicans had sought, Sinn Féin reacted not by rejecting it but by calling for clarification. Major replied by announcing that no clarification was necessary and a stalemate developed, with much of the euphoria which accompanied the declaration draining away as weeks and months passed.

February 1994 brought a major propaganda coup for the republicans when the Clinton administration dropped the long-standing ban on Adams entering the US. This was a crushing defeat for the British government, which for weeks had fought an intense diplomatic battle to keep Adams out of America. The transatlantic drama, involving major figures in Britain, Ireland and the US, went right to the Oval Office of the White House, and was settled just days before the visit took place, Clinton himself taking the final decision.

Major was so furious that for some days afterwards he refused to accept telephone calls from Clinton. He wanted Adams, Sinn Féin and the IRA isolated and ostracised, but Clinton had responded to the argument of the Irish government and Hume for the use of the carrot rather than the stick. They believed an American visit would give the republicans a glimpse of the new vistas of support which could be available to them, though only if they moved away from violence. In the event the impact of the short visit exceeded all the hopes of Adams and the fears of Major. The republican leader was given a celebrity reception, being fêted like a movie star throughout New York, appearing on the most prestigious television shows and meeting many of the most influential people.

The following month however brought a bizarre incident which represented an attempt by republicans to use a finely orchestrated blend of violence, politics and propaganda. Mortars similar to those used to attack Downing Street in 1991 were fired over a period of days on to runways at Heathrow, causing major security alerts. One of them hit the ground only forty yards from a stationary Jumbo jet and another landed on the roof of Terminal Four, but none of the devices exploded. For a time this appeared to have put paid to hopes that the IRA was slowly moving towards a ceasefire. The IRA campaign in the wake of the declaration had been running at a relatively low level, and this was a dramatic escalation. Most baffling of all, the IRA seemed to have thrown all caution to the wind by firing mortars which could have hit an aircraft, causing multiple civilian casualties.

Many of those who believed in the peace process were dumbfounded. It seemed as if the IRA response to the declaration was an indiscriminate attack on a major international airport, used daily not only by the British public but by travellers from all over the world. The effect of a mortar bomb exploding inside a crowded terminal, or hitting an airliner, was almost too terrible to contemplate. Yet when the full facts began to emerge the attacks took on a different aspect. Although the mortars contained Semtex plastic explosive, it turned out that a key component had been doctored so that they would not explode: the purpose had been to terrify but not to kill. The whole thing had been an extraordinarily elaborate hoax, designed to pressurise the British government without actually killing anyone.

The month of May brought a change of heart from the British government, which dropped its objections to clarifying the Downing Street Declaration and published a lengthy 'amplification'. But there was still no final response from the republicans, as everyone watched anxiously to see whether a ceasefire might be forthcoming.

As they waited there was yet more violence, this time from loyalists. On a June night UVF gunmen burst into a Catholic bar in the quiet County Down hamlet of Loughinisland and fired repeatedly into the backs of customers watching a soccer match on television. Within seconds customers were dead, dying or injured, with bodies piled on top of each other and blood running freely on the floor. Six

Catholics lay dead, one of them, aged eighty-seven, among the oldest victims of the troubles. The owner of the bar and seven regulars escaped the slaughter because they had just flown out to Romania on a charity mission to help rebuild an orphanage.

The scale of the carnage, together with the fact that Loughinisland had previously been sheltered from the violence, increased the impact of the attack on the little community. Shock, incomprehension and disbelief mixed with grief, while to the rest of the world it seemed as if the peace process and the Downing Street Declaration had come to nothing. The Loughinisland attack was to be the last of the large-scale multiple murders before the IRA and loyalist ceasefires. Nobody knew that at the time, however, and even if they had, it was little consolation to the families and friends of the innocents who died. Pessimism became almost universal when a large-scale Sinn Féin conference in June sent out a message which was interpreted as ruling out a ceasefire. In fact the IRA was heading towards a ceasefire, but in the run-up to it there was a last-minute wave of violence, in which a number of prominent loyalist figures were shot dead.

IRA *ceasefire*

On 31 August came the ceasefire announcement. Just after 11 a.m. excited journalists and newsreaders read out an IRA statement proclaiming that, as of midnight that night 'there will be a complete cessation of military operations'. Few people in Ireland have forgotten where they were when they heard the news that after twenty-five years of conflict and more than 3,000 deaths the IRA, one of the world's most formidable terrorist organisations, had finally decided to call a halt. There was jubilation in the nationalist community but among Unionists the reaction was more uncertain. The IRA had not said the cessation was permanent, and there was apprehension that the move could be a cynical tactical manoeuvre aimed at having London drop its political and security guard.

In republican areas too it was a moment of great uncertainty. Many wondered whether Sinn Féin had reached some secret deal with the British government, but word was quickly circulated that no such deal had been done. It was a huge step, undertaken unilaterally, and no one was sure what would happen next. One thing was clear: Northern Ireland had entered a new phase.

Decommissioning, Docklands & Drumcree
1994–96

Though it was clearly a momentous development, the cessation statement was received in many quarters with suspicion rather than celebration. Unionist politicians warned that it was a delusion and a trick rather than a genuine move, though most nationalists and republicans instinctively believed the conflict had drawn to an end. These differing views of the peace process were to bedevil it in the years ahead. Reynolds moved quickly to demonstrate his faith in Adams, meeting him and Hume within a week of the ceasefire for a historic public handshake aimed at consolidating the cessation.

As the weeks passed and the ceasefire held, another major development came in October when the loyalist paramilitary groups followed the IRA's lead. They not only declared a ceasefire but set a new tone by including an unexpected note of apology, offering 'the loved ones of all innocent victims over the past 25 years abject and true remorse'. The announcement carried all the more weight because it was made by Augustus 'Gusty' Spence, who had been jailed for life for the 1966 Malvern Street killing and had since become an icon of loyalist paramilitarism.

This change in tone reflected the existence of a new phenomenon within militant loyalism with the emergence, from that violent underworld, of a political element. Groups such as the UVF and UDA remained in being, but now they too went on ceasefire and sprouted new political wings. There had been previous such attempts, but they had been short-lived and unsuccessful. In particular the UVF now produced the Progressive Unionist party, with articulate spokesmen such as David Ervine and Billy Hutchinson.

They and most of the other new spokesmen were ex-prisoners who had learnt the hard way the cost of violence. Some like Hutchinson had served life sentences, spending a dozen years or more behind bars. A number had established discreet contacts with republicans whom they had met in jail, had come to know individual IRA members, and kept up contact with them after their release, often through community groups. The sight of the previously violent loyalists embracing the peace process with such enthusiasm gave the process a huge boost, for many had assumed the loyalist groups would continue to pose an active threat. Instead they became at many points a force for moderation, eager for dialogue and presenting a very different approach from that of mainstream Unionist politicians.

Paisley, however, declared that Protestants faced 'the worst crisis in Ulster's history since the setting up of the state' and denounced the process (which he would later lead). He asked his party faithful:

> Are we going to agree to a partnership with the IRA men of blood who have slain our loved ones, destroyed our country, burned our churches, tortured our people and now demand that we should become slaves in a country fit only for nuns' men and monks' women to live in? We cannot bow the knee to these traitors in Whitehall, nor to those offspring of the Vatican who walk the corrupted corridors of power.

Within the republican movement, meanwhile, it became clear that there was widespread though not universal approval of the IRA move. The initial reaction in the republican grassroots had been a mixture of competing feelings which included hope, fear, nervousness and uncertainty. It gradually became clear, however, that the predominant emotion was one of relief. Within the leadership of the IRA there were those who had doubts, but the generality of republicans welcomed the cessation.

Some of that sense of relief turned to irritation, and then by stages into a much more sour and dangerous anger, when it gradually became clear that the government had decided to play it long and resist the republican demand for early talks. Within weeks of the cessation, in fact, the British government had made a private assessment that the start of all-inclusive round-table negotiations was probably two years away. This approach was received with incredulity by nationalists who wished to move with all speed to enfold the republicans into the political system. The government, however, exuded scepticism and suspicion of republican motives, an attitude which was to prevail during the seventeen months which the cease-fire lasted.

Dublin pressed ahead with the approach of welcoming the republicans into politics, setting up a new body, the Forum for Peace and Reconciliation, in which they could publicly rub shoulders with mainstream nationalist politicians. Viewed from London, however, things looked very different. John Major had an undoubted personal commitment to working for peace but he had many reservations about republican motives. The Unionist community was uncertain and nervous about the future, and although many grassroots Protestants welcomed the ceasefire, most of their political representatives found it an unsettling experience. Unionist party leader James Molyneaux said of the cessation: 'It started destabilising the whole population in Northern Ireland. It was not an occasion for celebration, quite the opposite.' Major noted that Unionists were 'deeply troubled' by the ceasefire.

Within weeks of the announcement it became obvious that the 'cessation of military operations' did not mean that the IRA would be entirely inactive. The practice of carrying out 'punishments' of alleged wrongdoers in republican areas continued, and although the practice of shooting them in the legs was temporarily ended, scores of men and youths were savagely beaten. It also emerged in late 1994 that the IRA was still watching members of the security forces, and continued to size up potential targets for attack in both Northern Ireland and Britain. November 1994 brought a moment of crisis when a postal worker was shot dead during an IRA robbery in Newry, County Down. The ceasefire seemed in doubt, but the IRA leadership quickly issued a statement saying it had not sanctioned the robbery and had granted no one permission to use arms. Major noted in his memoirs that the killing 'turned out to be botched criminality rather than a deliberate ceasefire breach'.

Within weeks of the Newry killing came the sudden political fall of Albert Reynolds. Hailed as a hero of the peace process, he became embroiled in an unconnected political crisis and his government collapsed: rarely can such a political triumph have been followed so quickly by political oblivion.

The departure of Reynolds did not seem to endanger the process. The general nationalist view was that peace had come to stay, and that the process was robust enough to survive such domestic political turbulence. The new Fine Gael Taoiseach, John Bruton, had however been a frequent critic of the peace process and was never in tune with events to the extent that Reynolds had been. The republicans had looked to Reynolds to fight their corner with the British, commending him for in some ways acting as one of the elements of a broad nationalist front. Bruton, who had a deep distaste for Sinn Féin and the IRA, did not see this as his role.

As the months passed, day-to-day life in Northern Ireland steadily improved, with army patrols becoming less frequent and the RUC visibly relaxing. Police officers went on the streets without flak jackets and rifles, while armoured Land Rovers were increasingly replaced by saloon cars and even motor-cycle patrols. Many cross-border roads which had been closed for decades were reopened, while peaceline barriers were unlocked in various parts of Belfast.

An important development came in February 1995 with publication of what was known as the 'framework document'. This was a booklet largely drafted by Dublin diplomat Seán Ó hUiginn, and published jointly by the British and Irish governments, in which they set out a joint vision of the future. The framework document envisaged Northern Ireland remaining part of the United Kingdom, stressing the importance of Unionist consent. But it stipulated that the Irishness of nationalists should be formally expressed through progressively increased Dublin input, most tangibly through new cross-border institutions. Unionist politicians took strong exception to the document, refusing to accept it even as a basis for negotiations, while by contrast it was welcomed by nationalists. It was to form much of the basis for discussions in the years that followed.

The decommissioning problem

Negotiations were at first widely expected to start within months of the IRA ceasefire, but those who hoped for this were to be disappointed. Instead, the year that followed was dominated not by political negotiation but by protracted arguments about the IRA's armaments. The issue of what should be done with illegal weaponry once violence had been halted was obviously one of the most important issues in conflict resolution. During 1995, however, the peace process virtually stalled on the question of when arms decommissioning should take place. The issue had cropped up briefly in 1993 but it had not been emphasised. Now, in the wake of the IRA cessation, Major and Mayhew repeatedly called on the organisation to give up its weapons, journalists regularly pressing Adams on this point. Adams delivered what was to become a familiar republican response: 'I think the whole issue of decommissioning of weapons obviously has to be part of finding a political settlement, and there couldn't be a political settlement without that. But I don't think there's any point in anyone trying to leap ahead on any of these issues. Let's get a political settlement and of course let's get all of the guns out of Irish politics.' In his memoirs Major would accuse Sinn Féin of 'posturing and filibustering and avoiding genuine discussion'.

In March 1995, important adjustments were made to the positions of both governments. Mayhew, during a visit to Washington, laid down three new stipulations before Sinn Féin could be admitted to all-party talks. Republicans would have to demonstrate a willingness in principle to disarm, and then come to an understanding on the practicalities of decommissioning. There would also, he insisted, have to be 'the actual decommissioning of some arms as a tangible confidence-building measure' in advance of talks. The republican position was that the IRA had disengaged from armed conflict but had not been beaten and had not surrendered, and therefore did not contemplate any arms handover, regarding this as an act of capitulation. There was also a great deal of historical baggage. Irish insurgents had never in the past handed over their weapons in the wake of conflicts. The modern IRA had sprung from the vicious ghetto fighting of 1969, when the previous republican leadership was bitterly accused of leaving Catholic areas unarmed and undefended against loyalist incursions.

Dublin's initial reaction to what was known as Mayhew's 'Washington Three' speech illustrated that Bruton's approach was very different from that of Reynolds. The Reynolds technique was whenever possible to ease the republicans into politics and maintain pressure on the British to facilitate this. But Bruton, in responding to Mayhew's speech, took a line closer to the British stance. Rather than opposing the new precondition, he called for a gesture on decommissioning, thus helping to establish Mayhew's stance as a position agreed by the two governments.

It was not until May 1995, more than eight months after the cessation, that Sinn Féin representatives met British ministers. First Martin McGuinness met a junior minister in Belfast, then later that month Adams met Mayhew at a conference in Washington. By that stage Adams had already shaken hands with Bill Clinton, Nelson Mandela, Irish ministers and almost every major political figure in the Republic. Major did not meet Sinn Féin, though he had seen representatives of the parties linked to the loyalist paramilitary groups. The new loyalist parties remained enthusiastic about politics, and there were no real signs of strain on the loyalist cessation. The ceasefires had not however been underwritten by an agreed political settlement and this, coupled with traditional suspicions, meant a large element of uncertainty was always in the air. By mid-1995 the IRA ceasefire was showing signs of increasing strain, with

Adams and other Sinn Féin figures repeatedly warning that the peace process was in crisis.

Drumcree and the rise of David Trimble

Tensions increased palpably with the loyalist marching season. A major confrontation developed in July when the RUC attempted to reroute an Orange demonstration at Drumcree near Portadown in County Armagh away from a Catholic district. After days in which thousands of Orangemen congregated at Drumcree the march was eventually allowed through in what was seen as a triumph for militant loyalism. Paisley and the local Unionist MP, David Trimble, later celebrated the success by walking, hands joined aloft in triumph, through crowds of cheering supporters. Controversial marches were nothing new, but for the rest of the 1990s the Drumcree dispute was to recur on an annual basis, often leading to large-scale disturbances and violence.

September brought a highly significant development when James Molyneaux was ousted as leader of the Ulster Unionist party after sixteen years and replaced by Trimble, a former law lecturer who had been an MP for only five years. Most of the political spectrum was dismayed by his election in that he was regarded as the most hardline of the five candidates for the post. Trimble had come to the fore, following a long career in the junior ranks of politics, through his prominent support of the Orange Order at Drumcree. His election seemed to prove the point that the IRA ceasefire declared a year earlier had led to a hardening rather than a relaxation of Unionist attitudes. The Protestant show of determination at Drumcree, together with Trimble's election, showed that many Unionists viewed the peace process as a hazard rather than an opportunity.

Trimble's career had been mostly spent on the uncompromising wing of Unionism. His views seemed to mirror his temperament, in that while his manner was generally polite he had a reputation for occasional surges of temper. In his early days he had been a protégé of former Stormont minister William Craig, following him in his unexpected trajectory from militancy to moderation in the mid-1970s. Craig, it will be recalled, had staged Mosley-style rallies and had made speeches in which he spoke of the liquidation of Unionism's enemies. A few years later, however, he had unexpectedly advocated bringing the SDLP into the cabinet, an idea so radical and unacceptable to his colleagues that he lost the leadership of his Vanguard party and was expelled from mainstream Unionism. Trimble went with him.

In the years that followed, Trimble had reverted to a generally hardline position. In his memoirs Major described him as 'one of the mutineers' who thought Molyneaux's line was too soft. A government minister recalled his reaction to seeing Trimble described in a British newspaper as a moderate: 'I was having my breakfast when I read that,' he said. 'Nearly puked up my Frosties.' To the surprise of many, however, Trimble would turn out to be anything but a traditional hardliner.

Enter George Mitchell

In November 1995, following a lengthy and complex Anglo-Irish negotiation, the two governments finally reached agreement on a three-man international body to report on the decommissioning issue. Chaired by former US Senator George Mitchell, it included a Canadian general, John de Chastelain, and Harri Holkeri, a former prime minister of Finland. Mitchell was a major American political player, whose despatch to Belfast by Clinton was a signal of the sustained US interest in Northern Ireland. He had by turns been an army intelligence officer, a lawyer and a federal judge. A liberal Democrat, he spent fourteen years as a US senator. He was majority leader in the senate, where for six consecutive years his peers voted him the most respected member of that body, and he had turned down a nomination to the US Supreme Court. One journalist wrote of him: 'It was obvious from the word go that this was a mature and seasoned statesman, a major player with abilities far in excess of those normally seen in Northern Ireland. It was often embarrassing to watch the mismatch between his consummate skills and some of Belfast's political pygmies.'

November also brought the visit to Belfast of Bill Clinton, as the American president, proud of his contribution to the peace process, came to celebrate the reduction in violence. In Belfast and Londonderry he was given a rapturous reception, his visit turning into a huge communal celebration of peace as he delivered the message that the violence must be over for good. Within weeks of the visit and the festivities, however, came ominous signs that the IRA ceasefire was under increasing strain, as four alleged drug dealers and petty criminals were shot dead on the streets of Belfast. Responsibility for these and two earlier killings was claimed by a previously unknown group styling itself Direct Action Against Drugs, but few doubted the IRA was behind the shootings.

Overall however the death toll was the lowest for decades, with nine killings in 1995 compared to sixty-nine in the previous year. One of the nine deaths, that of former RUC Constable Jim Seymour, had a particular poignancy. He had been shot in 1973 and for twenty-two years lay in a hospital bed with a bullet in his head, apparently conscious but unable to move or speak. He was visited daily by his wife for those twenty-two years before he died at the age of fifty-five. This ordeal was a reminder of the lasting suffering inflicted during the troubles on a great many families.

1996: the IRA ceasefire ends

The next major development came in January 1996, when Senator Mitchell's international body delivered its report. It said that prior decommissioning would not happen and suggested that decommissioning should instead take place in parallel with political negotiations. Mitchell had become convinced that the demand for prior decommissioning was unworkable, not least because he had been briefed to that effect by both the RUC and the Gardaí. In his memoirs he recorded asking the RUC whether Adams could persuade the IRA to accept prior decommissioning. He was told, 'No, he couldn't do it even if he wanted to. He doesn't have that much control over them.' Mitchell already knew that parallel decommissioning would not find favour with Major for, as he revealed in his memoirs, Major had privately told him so. The American reported on their meeting: 'Major spoke directly to us. His words had a steely candour. If we recommended parallel decommissioning he would have to reject the report. He didn't want to, but he would have to.'

Reacting to the Mitchell report in the Commons, Major thanked the senator and his colleagues for their efforts, but said the road to talks lay either through prior decommissioning or by the holding of an election in Northern Ireland. Trimble was delighted at this new tack, since he had called for elections, but republicans and nationalists responded angrily. Dublin, Hume and the republicans wanted to get into talks as soon as possible, but it would clearly take months to organise and stage an election.

This was the state of the peace process when, on a Friday evening in February, after a confused series of warnings, a huge bomb concealed in a lorry exploded in London, not far from the giant Canary Wharf building in London's Docklands. The blast claimed two lives, causing immense damage and apparently ending the process. Most participants in the process were sent into shock by the explosion. The British and the Irish, the Unionists and the nationalists, the Americans and the rest of the world wondered whether it meant another generation condemned to live through violence.

The bomb galvanised political activity. During Reynolds's period of office the cessation had gone reasonably well from a republican point of view, and Sinn Féin was pleased with the framework document of February 1995. But from then on they claimed Major's approach was intended to maintain pressure on Adams and Sinn Féin, and not to pressurise Unionist politicians. The decommissioning impasse, the absence of all-party talks, and the lack of movement on issues such as prisoner releases, all combined to increase republican disillusion.

The British authorities at some points believed that the IRA ceasefire was secure and at others thought it under strain, with some republican elements in favour and some against. Yet London continued to resist the Dublin argument that the peace could be shored up by creating greater momentum on issues such as talks and prisoners. Those who were always sceptical of the ceasefire argued that the IRA was never serious, and that the resumption of violence proved that the government and the Unionist parties were right to react to it with the utmost caution. Those who believed in the cessation by contrast contended that it was faulty intelligence and analysis, married to excessive caution and delay, which helped bring about its breakdown.

The Canary Wharf bomb delivered the message that the gun and the bomb had not yet been removed from Irish politics. There was shock, dismay and near-despair not just in Britain and Ireland but in many parts of the world. Lives had been taken and immense damage caused to property and no one could be confident that the process would be rebuilt. There were further bombings, though it gradually became clear that the IRA was opting not for a return to a full-scale campaign of terrorism but was rather establishing a pattern of sporadic attacks in Britain. Northern Ireland was left largely untouched.

The end of May brought the poll Unionist politicians wanted and nationalists did not in the form of elections to a debating forum whose members were to provide delegations for inter-party talks. Sinn Féin opposed the exercise and boycotted the forum, but contested the election, and when the ballot boxes were opened it turned out that they were the main beneficiaries. The party vote surged to an unprecedented 15.5 per cent. The regular republican vote had turned out, but so too had many people who had never voted before, or who had refrained from supporting the party while IRA violence was at its height. The SDLP's vote dropped by a fraction, but John Hume and Gerry Adams both received massive personal endorsements. This was interpreted as a message from the republican and nationalist grassroots of overwhelming support for the peace process.

Yet what they got was not peace but more violence and disturbance. 1996 was punctuated by occasional bombing attacks, civil disturbances on a large scale, and important political developments. Political talks convened in Belfast in June without Sinn Féin. Adams, surrounded by the largest media posse ever seen in Belfast, led a delegation to the gates of the talks where the cameras recorded an official informing the Sinn Féin representatives that they would not be allowed in until a new ceasefire was called.

June brought a wave of IRA violence. In that single month an Irish policeman was shot dead in the Republic, a large bomb devastated much of Manchester's city centre and injured more than 200 people, and a mortar attack was staged on a British army base in Germany. The killing of the Irish detective Jerry McCabe, who was shot dead during a robbery, sent shock waves through the south. He was buried at a state funeral attended by the Irish president and the Taoiseach. The IRA at first denied responsibility but later admitted that 'individual volunteers' had been involved. The episode raised many questions about the state of play within the republican movement, centring on the IRA's evident lack of control of its members and its commitment to a renewed peace process.

Drumcree 1996

Next came what was known as Drumcree 1996. The Orange Order had been so proud of its success in pushing the 1995 march through that it had struck 'Siege of Drumcree' medals to commemorate the occasion. Unionist party members had been so pleased with Trimble's part in the exercise that they had elected him leader. When the occasion came round again in July 1996 there was much apprehension that another clash was on the cards, yet no one foresaw how grave a confrontation it would become. The Protestant marchers were determined to get through; the Catholic residents were equally determined that they should not. Academics Neil Jarman and Dominic Bryan summarised the clash of perspectives: 'Each parade which is challenged is a symbolic threat to Protestant security and the Unionist position, while each parade which passes through a nationalist area is a re-statement of the dominance of the Protestant community and the inferiority of nationalist rights.'

RUC Chief Constable Sir Hugh Annesley, in one of his last major decisions before retirement, again banned the parade from going along the Catholic Garvaghy Road. When Orangemen sought to get through they were halted by armoured Land Rovers, barbed wire and RUC officers in full riot gear. Rather than dispersing they stayed put around the grounds of a Drumcree church, announcing they would remain 'for as long as it takes'. Thousands of supporters joined them, including Trimble, and some loyalist protesters engaged in vitriolic abuse of the police. The protests were not confined to Drumcree, developing into one of the most destabilising episodes of the troubles. Loyalists staged hundreds of roadblocks and erected barricades over much of Northern Ireland, bringing life in whole areas to a standstill. Some towns were completely cut off, and there was widespread intimidation of police officers and their families. There was burning and looting in some areas of Belfast, widespread destruction of property, and more than a hundred people were injured. Near Drumcree itself a Catholic man was shot dead by loyalists.

The crisis came to a head on the morning of the Twelfth of July when it became evident that no negotiated settlement of the dispute was in sight. A number of loyalists appeared with a bulldozer fitted with makeshift armour, threatening to drive it through the police lines. Tens of thousands of Orangemen were poised to march in processions all over Northern Ireland, and there were not enough RUC members and troops to police them all. Faced with the prospect of widespread and uncontrolled disorder Annesley backed down, reversed his original decision, and let the marchers through. The logic of allowing the Orangemen along the Garvaghy Road meant it had to be cleared of its Catholic residents, many of whom had gathered to protest. Riot police cleared the road, with some rough-handling of residents captured in graphic detail by the television cameras. Nationalists in a number of districts responded with rioting, and in Londonderry a man was killed. The Orangemen got through and the immediate threat of unrestrained civil commotion was eased.

The cost was high. As one commentator put it: 'The underlying instability of the state was exposed, the very fabric of society ripped and damaged, and the most fundamental questions posed about the reformability of Northern Ireland. The episode left community relations in tatters and left a vast new reservoir of bitterness in its wake.' Sir Ronnie Flanagan, who was to succeed Annesley as head of the RUC, said of Drumcree 1996: 'Northern Ireland cannot withstand another summer like this one. The intensity of the violence which our officers withstood was of a scale that I hadn't seen over 25 years. The country stared into the face of great difficulty and crept right to the edge of the abyss.' Another senior policing figure went even further, saying privately: 'We were on the brink of all-out civil war. Letting the march through was bad but the alternative was a thousand times worse. We kid ourselves that we live in a democracy. We have the potential in this community to have a Bosnia-style situation.' A senior Presbyterian minister summed it up as 'Northern Ireland's Chernobyl, with almost a melt-down in community relations'.

Yet despite the intensified bitterness and the deepening chasm between the two communities, paramilitary groups on both sides did not revert to full-scale violence. Although fringe elements on each side staged arson and other attacks, the mainstream groups did not go back to uninhibited conflict.

The talks continue

The political talks went on, with George Mitchell moving from his role in decommissioning to chair proceedings which proved to be long-drawn-out, tedious and initially unproductive. Trimble took his party into the talks with more enthusiasm than his predecessor Molyneaux had ever shown, though his position within Unionism was not a secure one. In the forum election Protestant votes had been scattered around various Unionist parties so that while Trimble won 46 per cent of the vote, Paisley together with other hardline parties took 43 per cent. This competition was too close for comfort for any Unionist leader and was clearly not conducive to any thought of making substantial concessions in negotiations. Against such a background, it was hardly surprising that Trimble resisted suggestions that he should soften his party line on issues such as decommissioning. Paisley meanwhile – as yet unconverted – was still making life difficult for any Unionist leader who contemplated making an accommodation.

In early October the IRA carried out an ingenious and particularly cold-blooded attack on a prestige target, the army's Northern Ireland headquarters in Lisburn, County Antrim. The base was such an obvious target, and so heavily guarded, that it had long been assumed to be immune from republican assault. The IRA penetrated its defences, however, with three cars, two of them containing 800lb bombs. The bombs exploded, shattering the base's illusion of security and injuring thirty-one people. A soldier later died of his wounds. The devices were placed so as to inflict maximum casualties. The first went off without warning in a car park, while the second exploded fifteen minutes later a hundred yards away. It had been placed with singular callousness outside a nearby medical centre. The obvious intention was that the second device should blow up the injured and those bringing them for medical help.

The soldier killed was the first to die in Northern Ireland since August 1994. He died on the day John Major addressed the Conservative party's annual conference, and in his speech the prime minister attacked Adams in the most scathingly personal terms: 'For many months, Sinn Féin leaders have mouthed the word peace. Warrant Officer James Bradwell was 43, with a wife and with children, Mr Adams. He joined the army, prepared to lose his life defending the British nation. Soldiers do. But he was murdered in cold blood in the United Kingdom. I sent him there, Mr Adams, so save me any crocodile tears. Don't tell me this has nothing to do with you. I don't believe you, Mr Adams, I don't believe you.'

The 1996 death toll was twenty-two, an increase on the 1995 figure of nine. The IRA killed eight people, the INLA six and loyalists five. In private meanwhile Hume presented Major with a document known as 'Hume–Adams Mark 2' which was said to be a formula for a renewed ceasefire. There was little surprise when Major rebuffed the initiative. In doing so he described the 1994–96 ceasefire as fake and said he did not want another phoney cessation. Clearly there was to be no more engagement between London and the republicans in advance of the next British general election.

Breakthrough

1997–2000

1997

This year was to bring a continuation of violence but also, eventually, a restoration of the IRA ceasefire. Both republicans and loyalists remained active, an IRA sniper in south Armagh killing the last soldier to die in the 1990s, Bombardier Stephen Restorick. In the run-up to the Westminster general election in May, the IRA used small bombs and hoaxes to cause major disruption which included a last-minute abandonment of the Grand National steeplechase.

A number of killings carried out by loyalists during 1997 were regarded as particularly brutal. In one incident a Portadown Catholic, Robert Hamill, was beaten and kicked to death by a mob in the town centre, a killing which brought much criticism of a nearby RUC patrol for allegedly failing to intervene to help him. Three weeks later it was the turn of an RUC officer, Gregory Taylor, to be killed in a similar manner by loyalists. He had been in a County Antrim bar in a district where tensions were high because of a long-running Orange marching controversy in which police had halted a loyalist parade. Identified as a policeman, he was first jostled and abused in the bar and then, when he left in the early hours of the morning, attacked by loyalists who kicked and stamped on his head. In another widely condemned killing, Catholic teenager Bernadette Martin was shot in the head by a loyalist as she slept at the home of her Protestant boyfriend in a Protestant area of County Antrim.

The May general election transformed the peace process, with the departure of John Major and the arrival in Downing Street of Tony Blair. The statistics of the election, together with those from council elections in the same month, provided unmistakable evidence of a significant shift in the power balance between Unionism and nationalism. Nationalists were clearly on the move, making dramatic political advances in tandem with their social, economic and numerical growth. The changing statistics meant that, since Northern Ireland's history and politics had from the very start been based on the numbers game, its very fabric changed too. After the election, five of Northern Ireland's eighteen seats in the Westminster parliament were held by nationalists, with Martin McGuinness joining Gerry Adams as an MP. The combined SDLP–Sinn Féin vote, which in 1983 had totalled 240,000, rose to almost 320,000.

The striking increase in the nationalist vote meant Unionists lost control of four councils including, for the first time ever, Belfast. While Northern Ireland still had a clear Protestant majority Protestants were increasingly concentrated in the east and particularly in the towns around Belfast. In the city itself the Ulster Unionists and Sinn Féin, with thirteen councillors each, were the joint largest parties. On the nationalist side Sinn Féin was seen as reaping a rich harvest of new nationalist voters, in particular those who were apparently jolted into voting for the first time by the 1996 Drumcree disturbances. Sinn Féin was also believed to have received many votes from nationalists wishing to encourage the IRA towards another ceasefire.

Like everyone else, Blair was unsure whether there would be a second cessation. In a key speech he had declared:

> When the IRA ceasefire was called originally, we all took this as firm evidence that there was a real desire on the part of Sinn Féin to put the past behind it. When it ended, renewed violence did not just cause dismay, it caused fundamental doubts about the desire for peace. Is participation in the peace process a tactic in an otherwise unbroken armed conflict, or is it a genuine search for a new way forward? If it is the latter, then the door is open – but only if it is the latter.

His own election changed the political landscape, installing as it did a Labour leader whose large majority had given him great authority both inside and outside parliament. Within weeks he moved to break the deadlock, visiting Belfast to announce the re-opening of direct contacts with Sinn Féin. While this pleased republicans, Unionists drew comfort from his statement that 'none of us in this hall today, even the youngest, is likely to see Northern Ireland as anything but a part of the United Kingdom'.

His Northern Ireland Secretary, Mo Mowlam, was the first woman to hold the post. Where Mayhew was often described as patrician and remote, she quickly established a reputation for the common touch. In his memoirs George Mitchell summed her up: 'She is blunt and outspoken and she swears a lot. She is also intelligent, decisive, daring and unpretentious. The combination is irresistible. The people love her, though many politicians in Northern Ireland do not.' Most of her detractors were Unionist politicians who did not care for her informality and would later charge that she was too 'green'.

The new contacts between the government and Sinn Féin went well, raising hopes for a renewed ceasefire. Such hopes received a setback, however, with the IRA killing of two policemen on foot patrol in the County Armagh town of Lurgan. The fact that this attack took place only a few miles from Drumcree, just weeks before the now annual marching confrontation, led many to conclude that the IRA was bent on generating confrontation rather than stopping their campaign. Blair, though clearly shaken by the killings, persevered with the process and attempted to maintain its momentum. Crucially, London and Dublin together laid down that IRA decommissioning was not a precondition for Sinn Féin entry to talks. In what was seen as a calculated gamble by Blair and Mowlam it was announced that political talks would begin in earnest in September, and that Sinn Féin would be allowed in six weeks after a new IRA ceasefire. Part of the gamble lay in the possibility that, if Sinn Féin were allowed in, Trimble might lead his Ulster Unionists out. Paisley and other hardliners had already made it clear that if republicans entered the talks they would immediately leave.

Blair's gamble worked. Much bad feeling was generated among republicans and nationalists when the authorities pushed the Drumcree march through the Garvaghy Road. But even so the IRA announced a second cessation later in July, doing so this time in a low-key fashion. The general reaction too was low-key, for the Canary Wharf bombing had demonstrated that ceasefires could be broken as easily as they were called. A newspaper summed it up:

> Nobody in Northern Ireland was indifferent to the IRA cessation of violence, but nearly everyone pretended to be. Most people simply stayed home, lounged in the garden or visited the pub or the supermarket: no cheers went up, no champagne popped, no church bells rang. It was a most understated ceasefire.
>
> If few emotions were expressed it was not because they did not exist: rather it was that there were too many of them, and that they went too deep. There is hope for the future, relief and a deep desire for peace; but there is also bitterness, suspicion, fear and even rejection. The IRA is putting the same deal on the table again: soldiers and police and town centres and Canary Wharf are no longer at risk, but the organisation will not disband or hand over guns and will never say that the cessation is permanent. London and Dublin have accepted these terms; the Protestant and Unionist community is wondering whether it should too.

The spotlight thus fell on Trimble, who spent many weeks consulting widely on whether he should remain in the talks with republicans. It was clearly an agonising decision, and a critical one, but in the end his Ulster Unionist party decided to remain. John Major, looking back in his memoirs, would describe Trimble as a more flexible and adept leader than had been expected, though he also recalled clashes between Trimble and Mayhew when 'voices were raised and papers thrown down as David proved his macho credentials'. When Trimble led the way into the Stormont talks he took some other macho credentials with him, walking into the building flanked not just by his own party but also by members of the parties associated with loyalist paramilitary groups. Those who accompanied him included a number of loyalist ex-prisoners who had served life sentences for murder. Paisley and his associates left the negotiations at that point and did not return.

The talks moved painfully slowly, with Blair arriving at Stormont in October in an attempt to inject fresh impetus by meeting leaders of the parties, including Sinn Féin. His handshake with Adams was the first between a British prime minister and a republican leader since the 1920s.

At twenty-one, the death toll in 1997 was just one down from the previous year. The pattern of killings had reversed, with loyalists responsible for two-thirds of the deaths whereas republicans had killed roughly two-thirds of those who died in 1996. The end of the year brought turmoil, however, created once again by paramilitary violence.

Although the major republican and loyalist groups were on ceasefire a collection of minor paramilitary organisations were not, actively opposing the peace process and seeking to sabotage it. On the republican side such elements included the INLA, while on the loyalist side those still active included the Loyalist Volunteer Force (LVF), which was based mostly in Portadown and had broken away from the much larger UVF. The LVF's leader Billy Wright, King Rat, had become a larger-than-life public figure of considerable notoriety.

His prominence meant he was at great risk. As one paper had earlier put it: 'Figures like King Rat often remain active for a long time, but most in the end either wind up in jail or in an early grave. When their profile becomes so high, as King Rat's has, intense pressure goes on both the police and the IRA to deal with them. The question may be which one will get to him first.' As it turned out, the RUC got to him first and by the end of 1997 he was held in the Maze prison serving a sentence for intimidation. It was there that republicans caught up with him, and he was shot dead by an INLA prisoner using a smuggled weapon. The shooting, which took place two days after Christmas, ensured that 1998 would open not with peace but with a wave of retaliatory violence.

1998

A combination of violence and extraordinary political movement made 1998 one of the most remarkable years of the troubles. The shooting of Wright was followed by a stream of killings, particularly in Belfast, as loyalists took revenge by shooting Catholic civilians. When UDA prisoners in the Maze voted to withhold their support from the peace process, Mowlam took the unprecedented step of going into their H-block to meet them. Though controversial the move worked, and within hours of the meeting UDA prisoners renewed their support for the peace process. But on the outside the loyalist killings continued together with some republican attacks. Apart from the mainstream IRA, a group styling itself the Continuity IRA was also active. Consisting mainly of former IRA members who disapproved of the peace process, it was responsible for bombings which caused considerable damage to a number of towns.

As the killings continued one newspaper reported: 'People in Belfast now fall silent at television and radio news bulletins, waiting in dread to hear whether and where the gunmen have struck again, wondering how long the slaughter will go on at this appallingly metronomic rate. Hope remains alive for the peace process, but it takes a fresh pounding as news of each incident comes through.' The killings had immediate political implications for the talks, since the RUC said it believed that both the IRA and UDA had been involved in the killings. As a result the political representatives for each, Sinn Féin and the Ulster Democratic party, were for a time excluded from the negotiations. A particularly poignant incident took place in March in the quiet County Armagh village of Poyntzpass, which had until then largely escaped the worst effects of the troubles. When LVF gunmen machine-gunned a bar they killed a Protestant and a Catholic, Philip Allen and Damien Trainor, who had been best friends. But neither the violence nor the temporary expulsions, though disruptive, deflected the talks.

Unionists developed working relationships with the SDLP and Irish government, but no basis of trust was established between them and Sinn Féin. In fact the Unionists and Sinn Féin did not formally meet or speak during the negotiations, though they were often participants together in round-table talks. There were many uncertainties and difficult moments before, against the odds, it all seemed to come together. Tony Blair, Bertie Ahern, George Mitchell and the others gathered for a tense and often fraught all-night session which eventually produced, on 10 April, what came to be known as the Good Friday Agreement.

This historic agreement was a lengthy document, complex and subtle, which attempted nothing less than an ambitious rewriting of the 1920s settlement. The idea was to convince everyone that a level playing field was being provided as the new basis on which Northern Ireland politics and Anglo-Irish relations would be conducted in the future. The principles of powersharing and the Irish dimension, familiar from the 1973 Sunningdale Agreement, were very much in evidence. But this document went further, and was full of ingenious formulations which together provided a closely interlocking system designed to take account of all the political relationships within Northern Ireland, between north and south and between Britain and Ireland.

The accord addressed the republican preoccupation with self-determination but crucially it defined consent as requiring that the people of Northern Ireland would decide whether it stayed with Britain or joined a united Ireland. It provided for a rewriting of Articles 2 and 3 of the Irish constitution to remove what Unionists regarded as the objectionable claim to the territory of Northern Ireland. It provided for a new 108-member Belfast assembly, to which Westminster would devolve full power over areas such as education, health and agriculture, including the right to make new laws. London would retain responsibility for matters such as defence and law and order, though it promised to consider devolving security powers at a later stage.

The new devolved government was to consist of a First Minister, who it was clear would be a Unionist, and a Deputy First Minister who would be a nationalist. This was in effect a joint post requiring the two to agree on important decisions. Beneath them were to be up to ten departmental ministers. The ten ministries would be allocated in proportion to party strengths, on an agreed mathematical formula. A battery of safeguards was built into the assembly's rules to ensure that important decisions had to be taken on a cross-community basis, which meant they needed the support of both Unionist and nationalist members. A powerful committee system would shadow each government department, with committee chairs and membership again in proportion to party strengths.

The assembly was to be linked with London, Dublin, Scotland and Wales by a whole new constitutional architecture. A British–Irish council would be established, consisting of representatives of both governments and of the new devolved institutions in Northern Ireland, Scotland and Wales. There was to be a new British–Irish agreement and a north–south ministerial council, with associated implementation bodies, to develop cooperation on an all-Ireland basis. Major new commissions would review policing and emergency legislation. New bodies would safeguard human rights and equality while, most controversially, prisoners from subscribing paramilitary groups could expect release within two years. On the arms question the document said resolution of the decommissioning issue was an indispensable part of the process of negotiation, with all parties confirming their intention to use their influence to achieve the decommissioning of all paramilitary arms within two years.

There was a great deal more in the text and indeed between the lines of the 11,000-word document. Unionism and nationalism appeared to be given equal legitimacy and respect. Commentators such as Professor Brendan O'Leary argued that the subtlest part of the agreement was a 'tacit double protection' which meant that all the protections of rights afforded to nationalists would also be available to Unionists in a future united Ireland. There were very many loose ends, most ominously the fact that the decommissioning section was vague and open to different interpretations. But the deal was breathtaking both in its scope and in the fact that so many of the major political parties signed up to it. For many it seemed the stuff of history.

The republican community did not take long to give its general endorsement, but the agreement produced deep divisions within the Ulster Unionist party and, unsurprisingly, outright hostility from Paisley. Trimble secured his party's support, but some important party figures disapproved and did so vocally. Accepting the agreement was a huge step for Trimble, given that a large proportion of the Unionist community was clearly against making a deal with nationalists or republicans. Trimble kept many guessing as to whether he really wanted to head a government which included republicans, being at different times tough and conciliatory.

Mitchell, who saw him at close quarters, would write in his memoirs: 'Every day of the nearly two years of negotiations was for him a struggle to avoid being thrown off balance. Attacked daily by some Unionists for selling out the Union, criticised often by some nationalists for recalcitrance, he threaded his way through a minefield of problems, guided by his intelligence, his sure grasp of the political situation, and his determination to reach agreement.' At the same time, Trimble attracted criticism for not attempting to sell the accord to Unionists with sufficient enthusiasm. Blair, who spent much time in Northern Ireland in this period, was to prove a much more determined and effective salesman for the new deal.

The next step came with the holding of simultaneous referendums, north and south, on 22 May, to give approval to the Good Friday Agreement. Catholics were well over 90 per cent in favour, north and south, but there was much agonising within the Protestant community. In the end it split down the middle, with around half of Unionists voting Yes in the referendum and around half voting No. The final outcome was an overwhelming endorsement in the south and a 71 per cent Yes vote in the north. This was more than many of the agreement's supporters had dared hope for, and amounted to a solid vote for the accord. Yet at the same time the outcome contained an imbalance in that the 71 per cent was made up of virtually 100 per cent of nationalist voters but only half of Unionism. The stage was thus set for yet another chapter in the familiar running battle between Unionist moderates and hardliners. There was great continuity in this pattern. Edward Heath had years earlier said of Unionist opinion in the early 1970s that 'they split evenly between moderate reformers and hardline incorrigibles'. The story was almost exactly the same in 1998, a quarter of a century later.

Even with such divisions, however, the sense of a new era was in the air, many feeling that nothing would ever be the same again. The agreement and the referendum vote did not defeat traditional tribalism, but the 71 per cent vote represented, potentially at least, the emergence of a new majority in favour of making a deal. A newspaper summed up the possibilities of the agreement:

> It offers the chance to settle disagreements by argument instead of by force. It is not perfect; it will not simply dissolve away the ancient problems; it will face many hurdles and stiff challenges. But it has allowed all the main paramilitary groups, and nearly all the politicians, to subscribe to an agreement which is nobody's ideal but almost everyone's acceptable second choice. It doesn't mean the big paramilitary groupings disbanding and handing in their weaponry, for paramilitarism is a symptom of mistrust and that still abounds. But it does mean that the people of Ireland have spoken, and they have spoken of an end to violence. This is an enormous advance, for not too long ago the widely held assumption was that Northern Ireland was fated to be locked forever in endless war. That cheerless belief has now been replaced by the sense that the agreement amounts to the terms for an honourable peace.

Elections to the new Northern Ireland assembly in June produced a solid pro-agreement majority. There were strong showings for the

SDLP and Sinn Féin, but the vote again revealed a divided Ulster Unionist party. The party won the largest number of seats but its lowest-ever share of the vote, with Paisley and other anti-agreement elements only 3 per cent behind Trimble. When the assembly met, Trimble was elected as First Minister designate in readiness for the devolution of power, with Séamus Mallon of the SDLP elected Deputy First Minister designate.

When July arrived attention once again switched to the streets as Drumcree 1998 brought yet more confrontation. When the authorities banned the Garvaghy Road march, Orangemen created disruption across Northern Ireland. Orange roadblocks and protests were augmented by rioting youths, to the extent that one twenty-four-hour period brought 384 outbreaks of disorder, 115 attacks on the security forces, 19 injuries to police, with petrol bombs thrown on 96 occasions, 403 petrol bombs seized, 57 homes and businesses damaged, 27 vehicles hijacked and another 89 damaged. A newspaper reported:

> Those manning the roadblocks are not polite men in suits: often they are belligerent teenagers spoiling for a fight. Sometimes they are drunk. At times like these many of society's normal rules go by the board, as youths with cudgels become temporary rulers of their districts and its roads. Thus people on a routine car journey can suddenly come face to face with the prospect of anarchy and mob rule, of beery threats, of the loss of their vehicle or worse.

One of the many petrol-bombing incidents led to terrible tragedy, when in the early hours of the Twelfth of July three small boys died in a fire caused by a loyalist petrol bomb thrown into their house in the County Antrim town of Ballymoney. The Quinn children had a Catholic mother and a Protestant father. The protesters were chastened and the Drumcree disturbances quickly petered out. In the wake of the Ballymoney deaths tensions ebbed away and the sense of confrontation was replaced by a lull.

It did not last long, for August was to bring the Omagh bombing, when republican dissidents set off a car bomb in the County Tyrone town which killed twenty-nine people in what was regarded as possibly the worst single incident of the troubles. Its impact was all the greater since it came so unexpectedly, at a time when most presumed that violence was tailing off. The bomb was placed by a group styling itself 'the Real IRA', which was largely made up of former IRA members opposed to the peace process. The 500lb car bomb, placed in a crowded street on a busy Saturday shopping afternoon, produced devastation. An unclear telephone warning had caused police to direct many shoppers towards the device rather than away from it. The dead, all civilians, consisted of Protestants, Catholics and two Spanish visitors, and included young, old and middle-aged, fathers, mothers, sons, daughters and grandmothers. Unborn twins also died.

An eye-witness described how a burst water pipe sent a strong stream of water down the street: 'There were people, or actually pieces of people, bodies being washed in, which is something that you never forget. They were just basically piling up at the corner where the gully was. Bits and pieces of legs, arms, whatever, were floating down that street.' A woman told of carrying her injured daughter to one of the buses being used to ferry the dead and injured to hospital. She said: 'There were limbs hanging off, bodies being carried on doors, everything was chaotic. Then just as the bus was ready to leave, the door opened and someone handed a severed arm in. I think that was just too much for the driver. I think he cried all the way to the hospital.' The bus driver later said: 'It was like a scene from hell. I wasn't able to drive fast because people were screaming in pain. As we went over the ramps at the hospital I could hear the roars of pain.'

A volunteer nurse who turned up to help described the scene in the local hospital: 'Nothing could have prepared me for what I saw. People were lying on the floor with limbs missing and there was blood all over the place. People were crying for help and looking for something to kill the pain. Other people were crying out looking for relatives. You could not really be trained for what you had seen unless you were trained in Vietnam or somewhere like that.'

The incident generated a shock wave which reverberated around the world. Although at first there was speculation that the attack might spell the end of the peace process, it became evident within days that it had made most politicians more rather than less determined to go on. In the aftermath, the British and Irish governments hurried through tough new security measures, with Westminster and the Dáil recalled from summer recess to pass the necessary legislation. A fortnight after the explosion Clinton and Blair visited Omagh, meeting around 700 of the injured and relatives of the dead and injured.

September brought renewed political activity, with Trimble agreeing to his first ever direct contact with Adams. They met behind closed doors, the fact that they spoke but did not shake hands pointedly indicating that while new relationships were emerging they were accompanied by neither friendship nor trust. The hopes of the international community that a lasting settlement was on the way were symbolised by the conferring of the Nobel peace prize jointly on Hume and Trimble. Nationalists welcomed the move while Unionists regarded it more suspiciously, Trimble commenting that it was perhaps premature.

The twenty-nine fatalities caused by the Omagh bomb meant that the death toll rose steeply, to a total of fifty-seven in 1998 compared to twenty-one in the previous year.

1999

In 1999 the peace process stayed on track, but everything moved much more slowly than most of its supporters had hoped. Decommissioning remained an unresolved issue, with Unionists insisting on its centrality, while nationalists and republicans argued it had been given too high a priority.

The killings continued, though at a much-reduced rate. In south

Armagh republicans killed Eamon Collins, a one-time IRA member who later became one of the organisation's most vocal critics. Loyalists were also active, taking the life of solicitor Rosemary Nelson, who as a leading human rights lawyer had represented prominent republicans and Catholic residents of Portadown's Garvaghy Road. In addition to the violence there were reminders that the effects of killings carried out in previous times lasted for years. After much pressure the IRA admitted it was responsible for the deaths of most of 'the disappeared', a number of people who had vanished without trace, mostly in the 1970s. Gardaí in the Republic undertook major excavation work at a number of sites, uncovering some but not all of the bodies.

Various parts of the Good Friday Agreement were implemented, including the setting up of cross-border bodies and a new Human Rights Commission. Yet the devolution of power from Westminster to the assembly did not take place, being held up throughout the year by the decommissioning issue. Several intensive negotiating sessions attended by Blair and Ahern failed to make a breakthrough.

There was general relief, however, when confrontation was avoided at Drumcree 1999, the Orange Order opting for peaceful localised protest rather than widespread disruption. The summer brought renewed questioning of whether republicans were genuine about peace when the IRA was blamed for the killing of a west Belfast man, and for an attempt to smuggle in guns from America. These incidents gave rise to a formal government judgement in August by Mowlam on the state of the IRA cessation. She said she had 'come very close to judging that the IRA's ceasefire is no longer for real' but had concluded that it was not disintegrating or breaking down. She made a distinction however between breaches of the ceasefire and a full breakdown, declaring: 'I do not believe that there is a sufficient basis to conclude that the IRA ceasefire has broken down. Nor do I believe that it is disintegrating, or that these recent events represent a decision by the organisation to return to violence. The peace we have now is imperfect, but better than none.'

September brought George Mitchell back to Belfast at the request of Clinton, Blair and Ahern in an attempt to break the decommissioning deadlock. While Mitchell, Trimble and Adams were closeted for many weeks of tough talks, Mowlam was recalled to London by Blair, evidently against her will and possibly partly because Trimble and other Unionists made public complaints that she leaned towards the nationalists. Her replacement was Peter Mandelson, who as a close friend of Blair was expected to wield greater authority.

The Mitchell review produced movement which was initially regarded as a breakthrough. After ten weeks the parties emerged with what was assumed to be an understanding and then proceeded, after all the months of delay, to form an executive. After years of stipulating that he would not go into government with Sinn Féin without prior or simultaneous decommissioning, Trimble agreed to go ahead without any element of disarmament, though he made it clear he expected it to follow soon afterwards.

For the formation of the multi-party executive the Good Friday Agreement laid down a mathematical formula, known as the D'Hondt rules, which meant that Sinn Féin would occupy two of the ten executive seats. The big shock of the day came when Martin McGuinness, a particular Unionist hate-figure, became education minister. The other seats were taken by the Ulster Unionists, the SDLP and Paisley's Democratic Unionists. The DUP representatives became ministers but would not attend meetings of the executive. Power was transferred to this new devolved government at the beginning of December. Most of the executive parties gave every sign of enthusiasm as the new ministers, departments and assembly committees set to work.

The 1999 death toll was seven, the lowest figure since the outbreak of the troubles in the 1960s and a dramatic drop from the 1997 total of fifty-two. As the year closed, the drop in killings and the formation of the new cross-community government seemed to many to represent a double cause for celebration.

2000

As it turned out, the executive was to last only two and a half months before it was suspended in a welter of recrimination. In selling the idea of going into government to his party's ruling Ulster Unionist Council in November, Trimble had given his party an assurance that he would not stay in office as First Minister unless a decommissioning process began, giving a senior party official a postdated letter of resignation. It was an increasingly restless time for Unionism, since it was clear that Protestant support for the Good Friday Agreement was ebbing away. The revival of devolution had been a traditional Unionist aim, but when power was actually returned to Stormont many Unionists were transfixed and even shocked by the sight of Martin McGuinness taking responsibility for their children's education. As a result devolution was, initially at least, widely perceived by Unionists not as a triumph for themselves but as a victory for republicanism.

Unionists took further offence with the publication in January 2000 of the report into policing which had been commissioned as part of the Good Friday Agreement. The committee, chaired by former Hong Kong governor Chris Patten, produced a blueprint for a radically transformed police service with a new human rights ethos and many more Catholic members. Crucially, it recommended changing the name of Royal Ulster Constabulary to Police Service of Northern Ireland. The support of many Unionists for the RUC was so deep as to be proprietorial, and they and many police officers took this as an affront against the record of the RUC. The government nonetheless accepted the report's numerous recommendations.

It was against this background that a crisis developed during January as it became obvious that there was no immediate sign of IRA decommissioning. The organisation had appointed a representative to liaise with a Decommissioning Commission which had been set up under John de Chastelain, the Canadian general who had served as a member of George Mitchell's original committee on the weapons problem. But this liaison was a far cry from actual disarmament, and Trimble made it clear that he would resign as First Minister in the absence of actual decommissioning. His party's council was scheduled to meet on 12 February and he clearly hoped Mandelson would suspend the Good Friday institutions in advance of this.

An intensive flurry of political activity followed, with the Irish government seeking to extract from the republicans a commitment on arms. Republicans came up with a new form of words but it was judged to be insufficient to get through the Ulster Unionist party and Mandelson suspended the institutions, restoring direct rule from Westminster. The executive had lasted for just seventy-two days.

Suspension was traumatic for many but in particular for nationalists and republicans, many of whom had not really believed that Mandelson would suspend institutions which had taken years to put in place. Weeks of bitter exchanges followed until early May brought a breakthrough, the IRA offering to put its arms beyond use if the peace process remained on course and delivered on issues such as policing reform.

The IRA assurance that its guns would be 'completely and verifiably put beyond use' was hailed in most quarters as a highly significant development. It was coupled with IRA agreement to take the unprecedented step of allowing some of its arms dumps to be inspected by two international figures. These were Cyril Ramaphosa, former Secretary-General of the African National Congress, and former Finnish president Martti Ahtisaari. Although both the IRA statement and a joint Blair–Ahern statement spoke of putting arms completely and verifiably beyond use, neither spelt out precisely how this might be done.

While this was rejected by Paisley and other anti-agreement Unionists, the move was described as a historic opportunity by almost all other elements. An uncertain few weeks followed as Trimble referred the statement to his Ulster Unionist Council. In the event he won the vote by 459 votes to 403, a clear but hardly comfortable majority. Nonetheless the way was cleared for the return of devolution, which duly took place at the end of May. An inspection of some dumps was subsequently made by Ramaphosa and Ahtisaari in June.

The following month brought a difficult Drumcree, as the Orange Order in Portadown called on supporters to take to the streets all over Northern Ireland. Days of disruption and roadblocks followed, bringing many districts to a standstill. By the Twelfth of July, however, it became apparent that the Portadown Orangemen had overreached themselves. A large section of Protestant opinion did not approve of the disruption, taking particular exception to the refusal of Portadown Orange leader Harold Gracey to condemn violence. This, together with the prominence in protests of the west Belfast UDA's particularly militant commander, Johnny 'Mad Dog' Adair, alienated most Protestants. As a result support ebbed away and the protests fizzled out.

Adair was to the fore again in August when violent feuding broke out between the UDA and the UVF centring on the Shankill district of Belfast, resulting in the following months in well over a dozen deaths. Loyalists were responsible for 22 of the 29 deaths between January 2000 and July 2001, while the IRA was held responsible for the killings of a number of alleged drug dealers.

Other violence continued on the republican side with the Real IRA staging a series of bombing and mortar attacks. Although most of these were in Northern Ireland the incidents which generated most publicity took place in London. In one attack a missile fired from a rocket-launcher hit the headquarters of MI6 while in another a car bomb exploded outside BBC premises.

On the political front the Westminster general election of June 2001 was seen as a watershed. David Trimble suffered a major set-back, losing three of his party's nine seats, while Ian Paisley's DUP made gains. Sinn Féin too fared well, winning two seats and dealing a serious blow to the SDLP. In September John Hume announced his decision to step down as party leader. The results were seen as a setback for the more centrist parties and an advance for those on the extremes.

In July 2001 David Trimble carried out his pre-election threat to resign as First Minister in the absence of significant IRA movement on weapons decommissioning. This led to intensive rounds of negotiation with an IRA offer Trimble said did not go far enough followed by two six-week extensions to allow further talks.

All this took place against the background of a troubled summer, with many street clashes centring on the north Belfast area.

13.

Crises to cooperation
2001–2007

The years 2001 to 2007 were filled with unexpected events and a series of political and security crises. For most of the time the peace process was in question; for most of the time the Belfast assembly was suspended; for most of the time uncertainty reigned. Yet as this period closed Northern Ireland was to find itself with a new set of political leaders, with the actual or virtual departure of the big paramilitary battalions, and a whole new political dispensation.

The eventual breakthroughs of 2007 did not come about by accident. Rather, they were the product of years of sweat and tears, and indeed of blood: it was a long, winding and difficult road. In the grammar of politics slow but inexorable changes were taking place. David Trimble and his Ulster Unionists remained the largest Protestant party, but Ian Paisley and his Democratic Unionist party steadily and ominously closed the gap between them. Sinn Féin meanwhile overtook the SDLP to become the premier nationalist representatives. As had been the case for some time, the Unionist population remained deeply divided over the peace process, primarily because an integral part of it involved republicans at a high level in the devolved executive. While Sinn Féin argued that its electoral mandate gave it a right to a place in the administration, Trimble sought to step up the pressure on the IRA to decommission. His concerns were heightened when, in August 2001, three republicans were arrested in dubious circumstances in the South American country of Colombia, where they had been in territory controlled by guerrillas. They were accused of assisting the guerrillas. Although they maintained their innocence in the legal saga that followed, they were eventually given jail sentences before staging their escape to Ireland. This episode, along with several others, served to increase widespread suspicion that the IRA had not made the transition to purely political means. The constant political tussle led to endless negotiation, angry rhetoric and face-offs. During 2001 the assembly was twice suspended for twenty-four-hour periods, with Trimble threatening to resign. The IRA meanwhile made some moves on decommissioning, which by the end of that year he judged enough for him to continue in office as First Minister. But support for his party seemed to be draining away.

He was caught in a bind: on the one hand London, Dublin and nationalism in general pressed him to keep the administration going, while on the other his opponents, both in the DUP and within his own party, pushed him to leave government. The IRA maintained that it was holding fast to its 'complete cessation of military operations', but it grew increasingly obvious that it had its own definition of what exactly this meant. The practice of 'punishment' attacks on alleged wrongdoers in republican areas continued, and so did occasional killings. In 2000 and 2001 four alleged drug-dealers were shot dead, with the republicans either maintaining silence or denying responsibility. A republican opponent of the IRA was also killed. The Colombian incident suggested the IRA remained active internationally. Although the assembly continued to function, the political brinkmanship meant it had an unsettled air. Then two major crises in 2002 combined to put the executive out of business.

There was comparatively little surprise when Trimble declared that the uncovering of a republican spy-ring at Stormont was the last straw. It led to a suspension which was to last for over four years, during which the assembly and the devolved government were mothballed. The sight of police trooping into Stormont to search Sinn Féin offices left Trimble with little option, since the spy-ring drama followed another in March when at least three men broke into a sensitive police Special Branch office in Belfast and made off with documents and a notebook.

The office was in the heart of the heavily guarded complex at Castlereagh, one of the city's largest police installations, protected by armed officers and heavy gates and doors, many of them festooned with security cameras. Castlereagh was for much of the troubles the site of the RUC's primary interrogation centre, at which hundreds of republican and loyalist suspects were questioned for up to seven days. The object of many accusations of police ill-treatment, it had closed as an interrogation centre three years earlier. But the burgled office was a contact point for those wishing to contact the Special Branch, its documentation highly sensitive.

During the incident, which happened after ten o'clock on Sunday night, St Patrick's Day, three men entered and assaulted the detective constable on duty. Even on the most innocent explanation the break-in represented an extraordinary breach of security in which those responsible could have escaped with details of Special Branch informers or agents, placing lives in danger. The incident was so audacious that at first many attributed it to some kind of internecine struggle within the intelligence community, but it gradually became clear it was the work of the IRA. It pointed up the fact yet again that while the IRA had stopped attacking troops and police it nonetheless, in traditional republican parlance, 'reserved the right' to continue with a wide range of other illegality. Republican strategists may have concluded, because the executive had stayed in office though buffeted by several angry controversies, that they could get away with a great deal and that London, Dublin and the Ulster Unionists might fume but were prepared to put up with a fair amount of illegality rather than bring down the devolved government. If the republicans did believe this, they were wrong. The crisis of October 2002 led to almost five years of direct rule from Westminster. Police officers crowding up a Stormont staircase and carrying out computers and boxes of papers were filmed by a television crew. The coverage imparted the potent message that the authorities, or at least the police, had concluded that the way to deal with republicans was not politically, but with overpowering numbers of heavily armed police almost in riot gear. The incident created a political furore. Although the search was fairly perfunctory, it was clearly political dynamite for police to enter the offices of a party which was in government. Republicans reacted with much indignation as four people were arrested in swoops in north and west Belfast which involved 200 police officers. Official sources explained that they had uncovered a republican spy-ring which, they said, had provided the IRA with hundreds of confidential documents, some reportedly classified as top secret. Criminal charges followed, though they led eventually to an anti-climactic trial.

But one of those arrested was a republican figure who turned out to be one of the most fascinating characters thrown up by the troubles. This was Denis Donaldson, charged with possessing extremely sensitive government correspondence, covering a range of confidential and secret documents which included information on an army general, a police officer and senior loyalists. Although Donaldson had an IRA past, he was by this point well known as a middle-ranking political official, running Sinn Féin's Stormont offices with the title of head of administration. (A few years later he was to dramatically re-enter the saga of the peace process.) Republicans hotly denied the existence of any spy-ring, but to many observers the event served as strong, indeed sensational, evidence for the thesis that the republican movement contained unreconstructed elements who would readily resort to underhand methods. As such it immeasurably strengthened the hand of anti-Agreement Unionists. Many in Trimble's party viewed the raids as the clinching argument for those who maintained that republicans were not serious about leaving their paramilitary past behind. Chief Constable Hugh Orde later took the unusual step of publicly apologising for the manner of the raid, saying that while its form had been absolutely necessary in policing terms, he accepted that the style in which it was carried out had been over the top.

The political damage was spelt out by Tony Blair, who said: 'You cannot carry on in a situation where there is not simply the perception but the reality of a dual track, paramilitary and political at the same time. There's no way this is sustainable unless there's an absolutely clear commitment, unequivocally, to peaceful means. That's why there's a problem.' It emerged during this period that undercover agents were also still at work on the British side. Spying continued in both directions. The security services had taken intricate steps to carry out both human and technical surveillance on republican leaders, especially Adams and McGuinness. A car they used was discovered to have been fitted with an elaborate high-tech bugging device, while in 2008 one of their drivers fled the country amid suspicions that he had been working as a British agent. None of this, being generally regarded as par for the course for a government dealing with an entity such as the republican movement, carried anything like the political voltage generated by the Donaldson arrest.

By the time he was shot dead by unknown gunmen in a lonely Donegal cottage in 2006, the affair had already become an impenetrable maze. It had taken a second baffling turn when, within days of his release, after all charges had been withdrawn 'in the national interest', he appeared on the steps at Stormont flanked by Adams and McGuinness to deny that he had been a spy. But inside twenty-four hours he was revealed to have been an agent for the security services for over twenty years, and vanished from the public eye. Shortly before he was killed a reporter and photographer tracked him down. 'I just want to be left alone,' he said, denying that he was in hiding. An IRA statement said they had 'no involvement whatsoever' in his death.

With Trimble's resignation imminent in any case, the administration was suspended in October 2002. Opinions differed on how long it would last. 'Our party is evenly split,' a Trimble Unionist told one newspaper, 'between those who think we'll be back within a year and those who think we'll never be back.' A senior official said privately: 'At the moment there's so much bad blood around that I can't see it getting up again quickly. The general mood is pessimistic, worried.' In fact it would not be until spring of 2007 that the assembly was properly up and running again. Optimists took the view that suspension was a major setback, not fatal, and that advances made could be preserved. London, Dublin and various other elements, undeterred by all the obvious difficulties, maintained the pursuit of progress. The Stormont executive, it was said, was the centrepiece of the Good Friday Agreement, but by no means its only component. The Agreement also contained hugely significant constitutional clauses guaranteeing Northern Ireland's place in the UK so long as a majority wanted it, together with provisions on human rights, equality measures and policing. It also set out the Irish Republic's important part in the whole Anglo-Irish deal. London and Dublin made it clear they would do all they could to ensure that suspension would not damage the superstructure, even though one part had been dislodged. Thus the overall Agreement would survive, even though powersharing had temporarily gone.

The mainstream IRA was obviously still in existence yet the widespread assumption – which turned out to be correct – was that despite such republican misbehaviour the IRA was not going back to full-scale war. They might have indulged themselves in lawlessness but the IRA, and Sinn Féin, were highly enthusiastic about the executive.

David Trimble had meanwhile shared power with Sinn Féin, but the balance of power within his Ulster Unionists had shifted, apparently decisively, so that the anti-Agreement lobby was in the ascendancy. At the same time the party as a whole was fast losing ground to Ian Paisley, who was triumphantly claiming vindication for his consistent characterisation of republicans as incorrigible wrongdoers. The IRA went on to carry out major acts of decommissioning, culminating in a declaration that all its arms had been put beyond use and a statement that the IRA itself was leaving the stage. But its last phase of activity had attracted damaging controversy, first when a very large-scale bank robbery netted it millions of pounds. Second came a bar-room brawl which ended in the killing of a Catholic man by IRA members.

At this point, as for some years previously, it was loyalist guns which claimed most lives, mainly in feuding which saw the killings of a number of major UDA figures and convulsions in the loyalist paramilitary underworld. During the same period came startling revelations about the extent of intelligence penetration of both loyalist organisations and the IRA, as it emerged that important figures had been working as security force agents. Much of this came as a major shock to the general republican community, but it did not derail the peace process. On the political front highly significant developments changed the balance of power. For one thing, Sinn Féin displaced the SDLP as the primary voice of northern nationalism, a key event. This was a major shift in a political paradigm which had held for almost two decades. With John Hume as its leader the SDLP had bested the republicans in fifteen straight elections between 1982 and 1999, but his 2001 retirement as party leader came as confirmation that the pattern had altered, and Sinn Féin moved steadily and decisively ahead.

Some of the drop in the SDLP vote was probably due to the departure of Hume, who within nationalism was viewed as a towering figure both in conventional politics and as one of the architects of the peace process. There was also an evident feeling among some nationalist voters that Hume and the SDLP had accomplished their stated mission of helping sketch out a new political disposition, and that the time had come to support Sinn Féin as a younger and more vigorous party, better fitted to face the now dominant DUP. This in turn was fed by the emergence of Sinn Féin as a player in the Republic's politics, giving it a new significance in both parts of the island. Their southern vote was capped for a time, but it still strengthened the contrast between the fading SDLP and a party on the rise. An SDLP politician complained that Tony Blair had once supposedly told a party deputation, 'The problem with you is you don't have guns.' This alleged quotation certainly expressed the sense that the SDLP was stranded on the fringes of politics while the republican movement was assuming an ever more central position, both because it held arms and because it clearly spoke for a majority of nationalists.

In two elections in 2003 the parties were close together, but Sinn

Féin collected four Westminster seats while the SDLP won only three. A year later the republicans snatched the European seat which Hume had held for a quarter of a century. Each election brought further bad news for the SDLP and fresh advances for Sinn Féin, so that by the assembly elections of 2007 the constitutional nationalists took only 15 per cent of the vote while republicans amassed 26 per cent. All this meant that Northern Ireland's political parameters had fundamentally altered even by September 2004, when Blair and Ahern took the parties to Leeds Castle in Kent for an important round of talks. Sinn Féin were as usual central to the proceedings, viewed as keen to have devolution restored and in a position to bring about IRA decommissioning.

But on the Unionist side Paisley had now assumed central importance, the DUP having inflicted three successive electoral defeats on Trimble's party to become Northern Ireland's largest. Many assumed that the peace process would now be halted in its tracks, since Paisleyism for decades had been a synonym for refusal to tolerate compromise. But by this stage he and his party were emitting apparently deliberately mixed messages, combining the familiar hardline rhetoric with tantalising references to the possibility of making a deal. One striking instance of a softening in Paisley's traditional position had been his willingness to meet Ahern after years, indeed decades, of refusing to meet ministers from the Republic.

Blair and Ahern pressed on with trying to broker a Paisley–Sinn Féin deal. Some thought they were wasting their time. Others thought that Paisley's new pre-eminence, the party's now established ascendancy, and the lure of a position that could be depicted as that of Northern Ireland prime minister might change the habits of a lifetime. A further element of uncertainty arose from the fact that at this stage the then 78-year-old was evidently physically ailing, losing weight and tiring easily. The dip in health and ability was marked, but turned out to be temporary. In the ongoing manoeuvres Paisley and his party would not speak to Sinn Féin directly, though the two sides studied each other's position in minute detail, making their positions known via the governments. The DUP demanded full IRA decommissioning, to be verified by photo-graphic evidence, along with a complete end to IRA activity. A bad moment for the process came when Paisley, with a touch of biblical melodrama, called on the IRA to 'wear sackcloth and ashes'. Since Paisley had always been regarded as anti-republican, anti-nationalist and anti-Catholic, many took his remarks as confirmation that his goal was victory rather than accommodation. This caused republi-cans and others to wonder whether he might be intent not on arriv-ing at a real deal which would put the two sides in government together, but rather to divest the IRA of its weapons and then walk away. The IRA declared in reply that it would not submit to 'a process of humiliation'.

For all the alarms, Paisley convinced both governments that he was negotiating in earnest. As 2004 neared its end the engagement reached a climax, with high hopes that a deal was about to be clinched. But as so often in the peace process the outcome was pro-gress without a decisive breakthrough. In the end the unresolved sticking-point came down to camera-work, with the IRA refusing to agree to a photographer capturing how its weapons would be put beyond use. The organisation had appeared to be shaping up for a truly historic moment, with all its weaponry being put out of commission by the end of the year, in addition to assurances that paramilitary activity would end.

Yet the insistence on photographs was, republicans asserted, a concession too far. It was all too easy for them, as one observer put it, to imagine a picture of mangled IRA guns adorning the DUP election manifesto, or even the party's Christmas card. Previous acts of decommissioning had been carried out in the utmost secrecy, with witnesses being spirited away to secret locations. Republicans explained that the IRA would not agree to any act with connota-tions of humiliation or surrender. In this it was largely successful, in that few accused it of capitulation and no significant splits, apart from a few splinters, occurred in the republican movement. At the same time, however, the lack of pictorial evidence had limited the political impact within Unionism. Republican attitudes palpably hardened with Paisley's 'sackcloth and ashes' demand, though as the two prime ministers pointed out, the photography issue, though intractable, was practically the only sticking-point left. To some, as December 2004 began, a breakthrough therefore seemed tantalisingly close.

But the peace process had more surprises in store: two further major upsets piled on top of Castlereagh, the Stormont spy-ring, and other IRA activities. These caused much concern and severely strained relations between Sinn Féin and the Irish government in particular. The process struggled through: to some minds the controversies might even have helped it along by piling more pressure on republicans to demonstrate their sincerity.

On 20 December an armed gang stole £26.5 million from the Northern Bank in central Belfast. The IRA was widely believed to have been responsible for the raid, though both they and Sinn Féin denied it. But in early January Chief Constable Hugh Orde confirmed the PSNI believed that the IRA was responsible. Ahern, until then inclined to allow the IRA time to wind down, became infuriated with Sinn Féin when his own intelligence agencies told him that Adams and McGuinness must have known about the robbery in advance. 'Do they think we're eejits?' Ahern said, and made a point for some time of restricting their access to himself and his officials.

Unionists expressed anger, Paisley making clear his relief that he had not been ready before Christmas to sign up to a deal. Into this tension came the killing of Robert McCartney. A 33-year-old Catholic, he was beaten and stabbed late on the night of 30 January at a Belfast city-centre bar, near the republican districts of the Markets and his own home in nearby Short Strand. McCartney and a friend became involved in a non-political row and were set upon and dragged outside, allegedly by several men with IRA connections. A number of customers, including well-known republicans, had attended the Derry commemoration earlier in the day to mark the Bloody Sunday shootings. A clean-up operation successfully removed evidence from the bar and police struggled to find witnesses willing to go to court. A trial three years later acquitted three men.

The official republican response was uncertain and contradictory. Attempts to insist that McCartney's assailants should not be labelled as IRA were followed by an IRA offer to his family to shoot them. Sinn Féin suspended a number of their members, apparently for refusing to give evidence. But youths stoned police who searched the Markets in the immediate aftermath of the assault, and a Sinn Féin representative criticised the police operation. George W. Bush invited the partner of McCartney and his five sisters to the White House for St Patrick's Day celebrations, but withheld the invitation Sinn Féin had come to expect. The McCartney family left Short Strand, blaming intimidation. But the sisters, open about having sympathised with republicanism and supported the peace process until their brother's death, sustained for years their campaign to win convictions and at least initially won much international attention. Coming so soon after the Northern Bank robbery, the McCartney affair finally pushed the republican leadership to concentrate on putting the IRA out of action. It still proved to be a protracted business.

But in July 2005 a statement said the leadership of the IRA had ordered 'an end to the armed campaign', with all units ordered to 'dump arms'. These would be 'put beyond use', the operation to be verified by a Protestant and a Catholic cleric. In September Methodist minister Harold Good and Redemptorist priest Alex Reid confirmed that they had watched 'minute by minute' as the three independent international commissioners – two former senior army officers and a former ambassador – decommissioned 'huge amounts of explosives, arms and ammunition'. No detail of the methods used emerged, nor where and at how many sites it happened, and there were none of the photographs Paisley had demanded. Unionist and other scepticism persisted, but the move was generally taken to have pushed the situation on. (Republican and nationalist opinion noted acidly that the prolonged focus on IRA disarmament displaced comment on loyalist violence. Of the dozen deaths in 2004 and 2005 nine were the work of loyalists.)

It took yet another year and the choreography of a new agreement at St Andrews in Scotland, which included commitment to an assembly election the following spring, to bring the DUP leader into powersharing with Sinn Féin at Stormont, at the age of eighty. Loose ends remained, including the question of Sinn Féin support for the Police Service of Northern Ireland. But at St Andrews the DUP leader put his unique status, won as the foremost nay-sayer, behind making an agreement with nationalists and republicans. He had somersaulted without preparing his voters for the shift from 'smashing Sinn Féin' to sharing power with them. But he faced no critic of equal standing. By this point, after a lifetime spent tearing down other Unionist figures, especially those inclined towards any measure of compromise with nationalists, Paisley's party was firmly on top at last.

The DUP had trounced the once dominant Ulster Unionists in three successive elections while Sinn Féin had called a special party conference which mandated the leadership to give support to the PSNI when devolution of policing and justice was achieved. Paisley made his last move towards establishing the executive in two stages, mirroring republican gradualism. He promised that if Sinn Féin made good on their commitments to support policing and abandon violence, he would take office in May. The promise was made in public. A fortnight after the assembly election he and Adams announced the plan before television cameras at Stormont, at adjacent tables with colleagues alongside. The DUP had wanted the two to sit opposite each other, Sinn Féin that they should sit side by side. The diamond-shaped final arrangement, tables positioned with a corner between the two, made one of the most striking images in almost forty years of troubles when the cameras pulled back to maximum effect from the two faces. Paisley and Adams won numerous compliments for courage and imagination, Paisley in particular reaping praise as the octogenarian who had reversed lifelong negativity. 'The day Dr No said yes,' said one headline. One newspaper observed: 'Mr Paisley announced the timetable for devolution with a phrase no one has ever heard him use before: "Today we have agreed with Sinn Féin that this date will be Tuesday 8th May 2007."'

DUP European representative Jim Allister quit the party in protest but held on to his seat. Some internal DUP unhappiness persisted, and although for the next few years biting commentary from Allister nettled and inhibited the leadership, significant discontent failed to coalesce around him. Paisley duly took office as First Minister, with McGuinness the former IRA leader nominated by Adams to share the post as 'Deputy First'. As though confirming the end of one era and the start of another Blair announced his intention to resign as PM and Labour leader two days later. The following year was largely characterised by smiling public appearances of the joint Stormont figureheads. Jonathan Powell, Blair's hands-on manager of negotiations, ended his account of the dickering that produced DUP–Sinn Féin powersharing with the hope that there was now no reason why Northern Ireland should not remain at peace. His one caveat about the bedding-down process was that devolving police and justice could prove a hurdle. It did involve a prolonged stand-off but by that point, against most expectations, the parties appeared wedded to the new arrangements. The axis of the DUP and Sinn Féin, at first inconceivable and later envisaged as permanently fraught, proved so durable that the lesser parties in the executive, and others, took to complaining of it as a carve-up.

14.

DUP–Sinn Féin powersharing

Over time the idea that Northern Ireland was fated to perpetual uncertainty and the proposition that disagreement on some major issue was bound to endanger the institutions became less credible. Fears had been voiced that the intricate checks and balances of Stormont would mean repeated recourse to the courts to review decisions. In practice this rarely happened, in part because the legislature delivered few major decisions. The devolution of policing and justice took prolonged negotiation with repeated breakdowns and bursts of impatience. But there was no walking away. By the time that policing was finally devolved in April 2010 any crises that occurred proved soluble or at least capable of postponement. Critics blamed the sluggishness on the system of powersharing by which all the main parties were entitled to sit in the executive, with no incentive to go into opposition. Disapproval of the new arrangements focused on the tendency to put off decisions, and obscure the reasons for delay.

The major areas of dispute and obfuscation were on proposals to shrink council administration and reform of education, in particular the principle of academic selection for secondary schooling and the need to reduce the number of schools to reflect falling rolls. On rates and water charges, neither main party had the inclination to make changes.

Global attention for a time remained intrigued by the 'Chuckle Brothers', as they were slightly snidely described, the aged fundamentalist demagogue grinning hugely beside the equally amused former IRA leader. But amiability between Paisley and McGuinness did not mean that their parties came to like each other better. The benign relationship at the top failed to alter dynamics in the assembly. Despite his reputation, many liked to see Paisley fêted as a peacemaker in his old age, and the novelty carried him through his first year in his new office, which he patently relished.

The unlikely twosome travelled to the US together to look for investment and featured in constant photo opportunities at home. A period lean in legislative achievement focused less contentiously on the exotically paired figureheads. In segregated Northern Ireland, it could be argued that the mere appearance of amiability constituted a good example. OFMDFM (Office of the First Minister and Deputy First Minister) was a cumbersome acronym for an awkward construct, notoriously with a very large number of staff since many appointments were duplicated. Following prolonged failure to agree a 'victims commissioner', meant to coordinate aid and rehabilitation for the bereaved and injured, Paisley and McGuinness chose four commissioners. They were apparently intended between them to appeal to all four parties in the executive, each at the salary intended for a solo appointment.

For both the DUP and many republicans, the smiling became wearing. A good showing in a council by-election by Jim Allister's newly formed Traditional Unionist Voice crystallised fears in the DUP ranks of electoral reverses, and dislike of the Paisley turnaround and public partnership with McGuinness came to a head in 2008. After a half-century of almost unquestioned dominance, a certain rumbling in the ranks resulted in Paisley stepping down as moderator of his Free Presbyterian Church. Ian Paisley Junior became a lightning-rod for the disquiet, and after criticisms surrounding property dealings Ian Junior resigned as a junior minister, the son suffering for the alleged sins of the father. Resentfully, Paisley announced his intention to resign as First Minister and party leader, commenting: 'I felt that my son was very badly treated. I am not a fool, people who thought that they could get at me got at him. They thought they could damage me by the damage they sought to take out on him, but that did not move me.' (Ian Junior was later cleared of any wrongdoing by an official inquiry. He went on to win his father's Westminster seat.)

Long-time deputy Peter Robinson succeeded as party leader and First Minister, and although a very different personality from Paisley in time also related well to McGuinness. However, mistrust between the DUP and Sinn Féin over control of policing and justice hung over Stormont, with the other parties angry at being excluded from talks. After a five-month break in executive meetings, much criticised, the lead parties agreed that neither should nominate a justice minister, who would instead be elected on a cross-community vote. This meant the Alliance party won a department, despite lacking the assembly numbers of the Ulster Unionists and SDLP. The deal was not implemented for more than a year but shared determination to sustain the institutions between Robinson and McGuinness stood up well to tragedy in March 2009, when dissident republicans killed two soldiers, and days later the first PSNI officer.

It was widely seen as the most severe test of the new era. When the First and Deputy First Ministers stood on the steps of Stormont Castle either side of the Chief Constable to condemn the murders, McGuinness called the killers 'traitors to the island of Ireland'. But despite repeated interventions by Prime Minister Gordon Brown and Taoiseach Brian Cowen, both nearing the end of their terms in office, DUP ambivalence repeatedly postponed implementation of the policing deal.

Then in the early summer of 2009 *Daily Telegraph* revelations on Westminster expenses showed that Peter Robinson and his wife Iris, like many other MPs, but also holding positions as MLAs, and having employed various family members, had claimed large amounts. There was no question of illegality, but the couple were caught up in a wave of anti-politician resentment and reacted with ill-judged anger. Then, in January 2010, it emerged that Iris, always gaffe-prone and given to moralistic, supposedly bible-based denunciations of homosexuality and feminism, had attempted suicide after an affair with a young man, begun when he was nineteen. She resigned as councillor, MP and MLA and disappeared from public life. Robinson stood down for some months as First Minister in order to deal with family matters, with party colleague Arlene Foster standing in for him. But in the Westminster election of May 2010 he sensationally lost the East Belfast seat he had held for thirty-one years. Robinson survived the accumulation of personal crisis. Although shaken he faced no serious rival for the leadership, and the following year topped the poll in assembly elections for the same constituency.

McGuinness made no attempt to capitalise on Robinson's embarrassment and instead offered support. But then at about the same time as the Iris Robinson revelations began, Adams faced criticism for allegedly failing promptly to report alleged sexual abuse within his own wider family more than twenty years earlier. Despite the ensuing discomfort for Adams, and concern inside mainstream republicanism at the persistence of dissident violence, McGuinness and Adams retained their status and their electoral support.

The UVF and UDA declared they were winding up their organisations but stalled on decommissioning, eventually promising respectively to put guns 'beyond reach' and 'beyond use'. Over time their impact diminished, though there were occasional shootings.

By contrast, 2011 saw Sinn Féin achieve real weight for the first time at Dáil level, with Adams moving to take a seat just south of the border. The February election, called amidst economic storms and huge anger at a bank bail-out enacted by a Fianna Fáil-led government, more than trebled Sinn Féin's seats in the previous election. They challenged a shrunken Fianna Fáil as the principal opposition to a new Fine Gael–Labour coalition. Their new clout helped Adams and McGuinness weather the Sinn Féin boycott of the Queen's highly successful visit to Ireland in May. The DUP leader but no Sinn Féin member was present when the Queen with outgoing President Mary McAleese paid respects at the National War Memorial Gardens in Dublin to the 50,000 Irishmen killed during the First World War. The Queen also visited Croke

Park, the sports ground where almost a century earlier British soldiers fired at a crowd in the first Irish 'Bloody Sunday', and stood head bowed in silence at the Dublin Garden of Remembrance, dedicated to those who 'gave their lives in the cause of Irish freedom'.

Robinson also arrived with his wife – her first reappearance at a major public occasion – for a state dinner at which the Queen introduced her main speech of the four-day visit in Irish, and made what was hailed as graceful, regretful allusion to the wounds of British–Irish history – 'We can all see things which we would wish had been done differently or not at all' – in front of the south's establishment, David Cameron and politicians from Northern Ireland. There was warm admiration for the speech, the respectfulness and courtesy of the elderly royal couple, the beneficial effect on the image of an economically battered Ireland, and the contribution made to improved relations between the countries of the two women heads of state. Originally seen by many in the Republic as a northern interloper over-sympathetic to republicans, McAleese in particular reaped praise in the wake of the visit and, as she left office, for the efforts she and her husband had made to build links with northern Protestants and loyalist figures, her ability to relate to the Queen, and her willingness to commemorate Irishmen in British uniforms. Months later McGuinness unexpectedly stood in the election to succeed McAleese as Irish president. His campaign stirred sharp attacks on him for his IRA record, pushing him into statements of remorse and denial of having himself caused deaths. After a bruising campaign he came third, increasing the Sinn Féin vote.

The Queen's emollient gestures and words built on the speech made by David Cameron in June of the previous year, on publication of the Saville report into the 1972 Bloody Sunday incident, when British soldiers shot and killed fourteen civilians and wounded others at a civil rights march. Contrary to the rapidly produced Widgery report soon after the shootings, Saville (at a cost of £195 million), after twelve years of hearings, research and writing, found that the soldiers had fired first, that none of those killed had pre-sented a threat, and that army accounts of the incident had been falsified. Cameron's insistence that wrongdoing by agencies of the state must be admitted won praise for candour, and the warmth of his words about the bereaved softened grief and bitterness for some. Cameron told the Commons: 'What happened should never have happened. The families of those who died should not have had to live with the pain and the hurt of that day and with a lifetime of loss. Some members of our armed forces acted wrongly. The gov-ernment is ultimately responsible for the conduct of the armed forces and for that, on behalf of the government, indeed on behalf of our country, I am deeply sorry.'

The bottom line for his administration remained that Saville would be the last open-ended public inquiry into old killings involv-ing security forces or collusion with paramilitaries. The Historical Enquiries Team, set up by the PSNI in 2005 and led by detectives from English police forces, provided relatives with reports which brought some satisfaction but also sparked many demands for fur-ther investigation.

Opposition to the idea of a truth commission as held elsewhere came mainly from Britain and Unionists, on the grounds that it would suggest equivalence between paramilitaries and security forces, though with support for it coming from nationalists and also republicans. Few credited republican hints, including from Adams, that former IRA personnel might tell all to a commission. It was also clear that there would be no wholesale disclosure from the security authorities.

While official opposition to in-depth inquiries was explained by financial considerations, they could also be expected to unearth dis-turbing disclosures from the murky world of intelligence. This was already obvious from inquiries into a number of deaths, including the 1989 killing of solicitor Pat Finucane and a string of murders carried out by loyalist assassin Mark Haddock.

Sir John Stevens, later Commissioner of the Metropolitan Police, concluded intelligence practices had included 'the withholding of intelligence and evidence and the extreme of agents being involved in murder so that people have been killed or seriously injured'. Similar conclusions were reached by a former Canadian judge, Peter Cory, who found strong evidence that collusive acts were committed by the police, army and MI5. In 2011 David Cameron apologised to the Finucane family, formally admitting there had been 'state collusion' in the killing.

In 2007 an official report stated that UVF commander Mark Haddock was a long-time Special Branch informer whose handlers had for years protected him during a career in which he was involved in at least ten murders. While no one knew how many similar cases there were, the general belief was that there were enough of them to make the authorities anxious to draw a veil over the secret world.

Reconciliation remained at an early stage, with occasional sectarian clashes serving as reminders of unresolved prejudices. Some occasions made clear how far attitudes had changed, and what remained to be done. In January 2011 a former loyalist prisoner and paramilitary leader described his visit to the County Tyrone home of the grieving Harte family after Michaela, the daughter of football manager and GAA leader Mickey, was murdered on honeymoon in Mauritius. Winston Churchill Rea said he wanted to show sympathy to the Hartes and deliver cards from a Shankill Road soccer supporters' club. He later said that, after standing for hours outside in the queue of mourners, he had been greatly impressed by the largely GAA-organised occasion, having shared general Unionist dislike and ignorance of the GAA. McGuinness had told him he was glad he had made the journey and the county of Tyrone welcomed him. 'His approach to me spoke volumes,' said Rea. A year later Peter Robinson attended his first GAA match, sitting alongside McGuinness. In February 2012, when Ian Paisley was taken to hospital with heart problems, a joint statement from the two as First and Deputy First Ministers 'called on the community to give prayerful support to the Paisley family'. Events such as these attracted much interest, and many took great heart from them; but they did not really hit the headlines as absolutely astonishing developments. They tended to be viewed as just the latest in a long line of unprecedented moments which indicated how far the peace process had brought Northern Ireland, and how deeply the peace had bedded in.

15.

Perspectives

By 2012 it was firmly established that the troubles which had afflicted Northern Ireland for decades were in essence over. The new peace was not absolute, since rogue elements within loyalism and especially dissident republicanism remained sporadically active. Yet the universal judgement was that violence would never again approach the levels of the 1970s or even those of the 1990s. But the fact that so many sharp political divisions remain, that so many thorny issues persist, and that there had been so many deaths and injuries, mean that for a generation at least the effects of the troubles would not completely disappear.

It is obvious that they had their roots centuries earlier, stretching back at least to the plantations and the patterns established then. The Protestants of Northern Ireland have long been pilloried for their siege mentality, their resistance to change and for what their critics characterised as an unsavoury mixture of reactionary instincts and religious bigotry. The British encouraged them to move to Ireland essentially as a garrison community for Britain's own defensive purposes. Those settlers were bound to develop a siege mentality given that they experienced actual sieges, most famously Londonderry in 1688–9. Their differences with the Catholic Irish were continuously sharpened by the fact that the two sides competed for territory and power, setting patterns which endured through the generations.

It is easy enough to see how the Protestant mentality developed, as the new arrivals were given land and political power in a land where they were outnumbered by the naturally resentful Catholic

Irish. Centuries later their descendants received a second endowment in the form of the new state of Northern Ireland, which was conceived, designed and set up as a Unionist-controlled entity. The unwanted part of this for Unionists, the fly in the political ointment, came with the Catholic third of the population who considered themselves trapped in an artificial, unwelcoming and even hostile state. The two new parts of Ireland were both given a very high degree of independence. For Unionists it was a generous bequest, in that their British link was both guaranteed and in due course accompanied by substantial subsidies. At the same time they were allowed the freedom to govern very much as they chose. Westminster discreetly and gratefully withdrew – certainly psychologically – leaving Northern Ireland largely to its own devices. It was entirely natural that Unionists should have elevated, over all other considerations, the task of bolstering the fledgeling state's security and political defences. It was also hardly surprising, in the light of the lack of outside supervision, that they would resort to some questionable means. But the fact that the Union turned out to be safe brought little ease to many Protestants whose chronic insecurity scarcely diminished over the decades.

This constant unsettling anxiety led them in the first instance to exclude Catholics from virtually every important office in the land. The Unionist administration in the 1920s tightened up the system and was able to rebuff with ease any attempts to cry foul. Civil rights were not then in vogue, and the overwhelming numerical and political superiority of Unionism easily carried the day. Partly this was because critics, principally southern governments, put forward as their solution a united Ireland. Little or no thought was given by Dublin to the views and interests of Unionists who regarded themselves as British and saw absolutely no attraction in forsaking their nationality to join a southern state which they regarded as anti-British and dominated by the Catholic church. The system was long-lasting, even the Second World War failing to overturn the familiar rigid patterns.

One reason for its durability was the degree of disadvantage suffered by Catholics, which was less severe than that experienced by minorities in other countries. The Unionist state did not organise massacres of Catholics or their expulsion from its frontiers: it cannot be said to have engaged in active persecution or savage repression. Yet it was, as David Trimble acknowledged in 1999, a cold house for Catholics. If it was not tyranny, it was undoubtedly unfair. There was institutionalised inequality, with Protestants enjoying advantages in many aspects of life. The practice of treating Catholics differently from Protestants permeated all levels of politics and reached down to the necessities of life such as jobs, housing and policing.

Throughout the decades most Catholics believed they were treated as second-class citizens. Resentment rarely boiled over into active violent resistance, however, instead tending to take the form of a surly abstentionism and the often unspoken nursing of grudges. This was a demoralised community, undermined when their southern kith and kin in effect abandoned them at partition. Protests beyond the strictly rhetorical were uncommon: there simply seemed little or no point, so that attempted IRA campaigns ignominiously petered out.

When the 1960s arrived, bringing new times and new challenges, it became apparent that there were three types of Unionists. There were the moderates who agreed with Terence O'Neill that a new era had arrived and that modest reforms were in order. Opposed to these were the hardliners, who in clinging to tradition believed that almost any concession would set them on a slippery slope leading out of the UK. Some of these held this as a political maxim: others were simply straightforward bigots who were not just anti-accommodation but anti-Catholic. The third strand of Unionist opinion was made up of the sizeable number of waverers who oscillated between the two poles, sometimes favouring reform, sometimes retreating to the safety of the laager. Although their relative strengths were to vary from time to time, these three strands were visible all the way through the troubles.

They were evident in all the battles within Unionism. O'Neill was

pitted against Paisley, Craig and Faulkner; Chichester-Clark struggled against the first two, and then Faulkner was opposed by West,
Craig, Paisley, the UDA, UWC and the Orange Order. Although
Molyneaux, who led the Unionist party for sixteen years, was not a
reformer, he too had to contend with unruly elements. Later
Trimble found himself pitched against Paisley and others inside his
party. John Major once described the Unionist party as 'riven into
factions, with its leader's authority constantly under threat' – he
was referring to Molyneaux's later years but the description was
applicable to many other periods.

O'Neill had an instinct that some modernisation was called for,
but did not foresee the consequences of his new approach. He probably envisaged a Northern Ireland which would remain under
exclusively Unionist control, though with a relaxation of communal
divisions. But in the end he proved incapable of managing the tide
of change. His essential seigneurial decency was accompanied by
limited political skills and he went under, unable to balance civil
rights agitation and the urgings of Wilson and Callaghan with the
pressures from Unionist hardliners. At the same time the bright
young civil righters were running intellectual rings around most
Unionist politicians.

In the Wilson and Callaghan era the talk was of reform and concessions to nationalists. O'Neill, Chichester-Clark and Faulkner
each produced a number of measures, including one man – one
vote, but in the end none of these came close to satisfying nationalist opinion. With hindsight the reason is clear, since it is now evident
that no amount of piecemeal change would have sufficed.
Expectations among nationalists had risen so high, with the emergence of a university-educated middle class, that they would only
have been satisfied not by safeguards but by a substantial slice of
executive power.

A majority of civil rights supporters went on to support the
SDLP. Another section of nationalists supported republicanism, and
were prepared to support or at least tolerate violent methods. This
division of northern nationalists into two distinct elements, one

constitutional and one violent, followed a fault-line which went back into the distant past. For decades the SDLP were in the ascendant, but eventually the party was eclipsed by Sinn Féin. John Hume was one of the three dominant figures of the troubles, heading the party for twenty-two years before his resignation on health grounds in 2001. His stature within nationalism was illustrated by a major television poll in 2010 in which the Irish public voted him 'Ireland's greatest person', placing him ahead of other contemporary and historical figures. Pre-Hume, nationalists had tended to take the view that it was not worth putting their energies into interacting with the Stormont system, and that everything would some day be sorted out in a united Ireland. Hume pursued the theory, which came to seem obvious but at the time was a major departure, that it was honourable to engage in politics short of the nationalist ideal. Later he with others made another major psychological shift by aiming for a place in government inside Northern Ireland. Later still, as an architect of the 1985 Anglo-Irish Agreement, he helped set the Northern Ireland question in an international context, and particularly in a Belfast–London–Dublin triangle, with American and to a lesser extent European influences thrown in. In the late 1980s he was one of the first to discern the first stirrings of the peace process within militant republicanism. He was also the first to act on it, setting out on a hazardous path which would bring him much criticism but ultimate success and international acclaim including the Nobel prize for peace.

It was always unlikely that Unionist voters would approve of him, since they regarded everything he did as dangerous attacks on the Unionist position. Many Unionists clung to the idea of exclusion of nationalists, and all of Hume's steps were, in different ways, in the direction of inclusion and participation. He evolved through the inclusion of nationalists in government to establishing Dublin as a key element, then drawing in the international community and, finally and most controversially of all, the inclusion of militant republicans in politics and indeed in government. The irony is that as the settlement took shape, very much along the lines advocated by Hume for so long and amid such initial controversy, his serious health problems took him out of active politics. The SDLP went into decline, partly due to his departure and partly because many nationalists regarded his lifetime mission as accomplished.

A second key figure of the troubles was Gerry Adams whose Sinn Féin party replaced the SDLP as the primary voice of northern nationalism. Important to republicanism since the early 1970s, he became central both to his movement and to the peace process. For the first part of the troubles he was closely identified with the IRA and its violence, but in a second phase he came to be regarded as a figure who aimed to steer Sinn Féin and the IRA away from violent militarism and into a new brand of republican politics. When he first began to use the word 'peace' regularly, as he did in the early 1990s, many regarded this as sheer hypocrisy, since the IRA continued to kill. It took years, but gradually more and more influential figures came to believe he might be genuine. Eventually he and a group of senior republicans, including Martin McGuinness, oversaw the transformation of republicanism to the point where the IRA was displaced by Sinn Féin.

Before that happened the IRA killed many people, while few believed Adams's assertion that he was never an IRA member. The charge laid against him is that he helped lead an 'armed struggle' which went on for many years and cost many lives. The defence will be that he was pivotal in bringing the conflict to a close and creating a new settlement. History will judge whether the blame he deserves for keeping the war going should outweigh any credit due for helping bring it to a close. The arguments over that point will go on for generations but certainly what he did was in pragmatic terms appreciated in a number of quarters. Principally this could be seen among northern nationalists who put Sinn Féin, as the second largest party, into the highest levels of government. It could also be seen, less explicitly but nonetheless strongly, in the attitudes of London, Dublin and Washington, who viewed Sinn Féin as one of the most crucial components of the peace process.

Another dominant figure was Ian Paisley, who was in the thick of it for a full half-century. During most of that time he opposed all attempts at accommodation so strongly and effectively that he was the bane of British ministerial lives. James Callaghan accused him of 'using the language of war cast in a biblical mould'. Reginald Maudling wrote: 'He was one of the most difficult characters anyone could hope to deal with. I always found his influence dangerous.' William Whitelaw marvelled at his 'unrivalled skill at undermining the plans of others – he can effectively destroy and obstruct, but he has never seemed able to act constructively.' Roy Mason remembered him as 'an oafish bully, a wild rabblerouser, to many a poisonous bigot because of his No Popery rantings'. James Prior thought him 'basically a man who thrives on the violent scene. His aim is to stir the emotions of the Protestant people. His bigotry easily boils over into bombast.' In other words, few if any at Westminster found anything to commend in the Paisley record. The same went for nationalists and indeed the wider world in general, which regarded him as a symbol of bigotry and division. For most of his career he never defined politics as a process of winning friends and influencing people, and was unmoved by the mountains of criticism heaped upon him. What is incontestable is that for most of his long career he made no friends for the Unionist cause anywhere outside the bounds of Unionism, and caused much damage to Unionism's general image. The outside world might have recoiled from both his style and his substance but he held an undeniable appeal for a large proportion of Protestants, together with an inhibiting effect on those prepared to contemplate cross-community partnership. All that changed, of course, when he finally opted for his Road to Damascus-type conversion.

The troubles saw many difficult relationships. Britain's relations with Irish nationalists, both those in the SDLP and those in Dublin, went through many difficult patches. In the early days London kept Dublin at arm's length, though by the time of Sunningdale Heath had come to think of the Irish government as a partner in a joint venture. This sense disappeared however under the Labour administrations of the second half of the 1970s, as Harold Wilson's whimsical notions of somehow uniting Ireland were hurriedly abandoned in the face of loyalist opposition.

By contrast, Thatcher's reputation as a zealous guardian of British sovereignty was not borne out by her willingness to foster partnerships with first Haughey and later FitzGerald. It was the 1985 Anglo-Irish Agreement, which she signed, that set the pattern for closer London–Dublin relations in the years that followed. Dublin, after the initial panic of 1969 and the subsequent arms trial, quickly settled on the idea of forming an inter-governmental partnership with London, moving on to give the principle of containment and management of the northern problem precedence over other considerations.

One of the most problematic relationships was that between Britain and Unionism, since Unionist distrust of London was always present to a greater or lesser degree. Wilson pressurised the Stormont government, eventually took to threatening it and finally pretty much lost his temper with it. Heath gave Faulkner a chance, then surgically removed Stormont when he concluded a solely Unionist government was incapable of delivering stability. Heath and Whitelaw achieved a great deal in a short time by putting the Sunningdale agreement and powersharing executive in place, but it quickly collapsed as Wilson and Rees proved no match for the loyalist strike, with its potent mixture of industrial action and intimidation. After that Wilson, Callaghan and initially Thatcher took no steps which might result in open conflict between London and Unionists until, with the Anglo-Irish accord, she broke that mould.

What is striking, from a series of comments in various memoirs and elsewhere, is the nervousness and even fear displayed by British politicians about Unionism. The memory of the 1912 period, when the UVF imported guns and threatened the use of force, certainly lasted until 1949. In that year cabinet minutes noted: 'Unless the people of Northern Ireland felt reasonably assured of the support of the people of this country, there might be a revival of the Ulster Volunteers and of other bodies intending to meet any threat of

force by force; and this would bring nearer the danger of an outbreak of violence in Ireland.'

One of the London civil servants despatched to Belfast in 1969
reported back that force might have to be used to dismantle Catholic
barricades, but that such 'clobbering', as he called it, might be in the
long-term interests of Catholics. He wrote: 'It would be better than
the use of force against the Protestant extremists, however repulsive
their attitudes and behaviour, since they are the majority community and confrontation with them would fulfil Lord Craigavon's
prophecy that the eventual resolution of the Ulster problem would
come when the Protestants fought the British Army. And that, I
should think, HMG would wish to avoid at all costs.'

Maudling was to indicate that security moves against the IRA
were motivated not only by the menace from republicanism but by
the loyalist threat as well. He noted in his memoirs: 'I think if we
hadn't introduced internment there was the danger of the Protestant
backlash. What we were always worried about was if people did
not think the British government were doing all they could to deal
with violence, they might take the law into their own hands.' When
loyalists did take the law into their own hands, as their paramilitary
groups began their killing campaign in late 1971, the authorities at
first attempted to turn a Nelsonian blind eye.

In 1974 London shied away from direct confrontation with loyalists, conceding control of the streets, industry and commerce to the
UWC. More than two decades later John Major would write of a
Drumcree confrontation in which the Orange march was allowed
through after first being banned: 'This decision provoked a risk of
even greater violence, and had to be reversed.' This seems another
clear illustration of recurring British anxiety about a Protestant
capacity for disruption.

Part of the explanation for this was that London was aware of
the reality of Protestant numerical power. Even after the abolition
of Stormont in 1972 the institutions of the state, including its security apparatus, were predominantly Protestant. The security forces
were manifestly geared to containing disorder from the republican

side. Any British policy-maker had to recognise that if serious disorder came from the Unionist community there was, during the 1970s at least, no reliable instrument with which to contain it. This was most obviously demonstrated in the UWC strike, though by 1985 London did feel able to put forward an initiative which it knew would stir strong loyalist opposition.

London's problems with both republicans and loyalists tended to reinforce the standard British posture that they were dealing with two inherently unreasonable tribes and in effect holding the ring between them. This perspective allowed the average Englishman to exonerate himself from any element of responsibility for the conflict. This seems however too simplistic and too complacent a viewpoint. It is certainly true that the two traditions, Unionist and nationalist, were in conflict or at least competition with each other long before Britain brought the state of Northern Ireland into being. The settlement put in place in the 1920s lacked balance and was an almost guaranteed recipe for instability. While Unionists were throughout the troubles vilified for an unwillingness to share power, it seems obvious that any community allowed to wield virtually complete power would have great difficulty in coming to terms with the notion of relinquishing it. Part of any lack of reasonableness is traceable back to the system which London first set up and then neglected. It took half a century for the troubles to erupt, but the lethal energy with which they did is testimony to the lack of outside supervision. A critic of Britain could lay at London's door a litany of political and security misjudgements and mistakes in which internment and Bloody Sunday would figure prominently. The model of the troubles as a clash between two unreasonable warring tribes is thus a misleading or at least an incomplete picture.

The full story of the peace process during the 1990s doubtless remains to be told, with many secrets still to be unearthed. The republican route from guerrilla warfare to participation in government is an extraordinary tale, with an underground army gradually moving from violence into politics. One theory has it that the republicans simply realised that their campaign of violence was not working, and held out no hope of defeating the will of the British and that of Unionism. Another is that republicans shrewdly moved with the times, realising that a more political approach would pay richer dividends. This has certainly proved to be the case, with Gerry Adams attracting considerable status abroad, as well as a much-increased republican vote in Northern Ireland and mounting Sinn Féin support in the south. Adams and McGuinness eventually persuaded the world, much of which was originally highly sceptical, that they really were in the business of leading republicanism away from the centuries-old tradition of armed rebellion. They also finally succeeded, in the key year of 2007, in persuading Ian Paisley that they had made a genuine transition. It was in the spring of that year that an astonished world saw on television the unprecedented sight of Paisley and Adams appearing together to signal they had reached agreement on devolution. In May came a moment laden with even more significance when Paisley and Martin McGuinness, Protestant patriarch and iconic republican, stood shoulder to shoulder to pronounce that the war was over and that a new era of cooperation was coming into being. Blair and Ahern proudly looked on from the public gallery as, deploying a whole new rhetoric, Paisley spoke lyrically of 'a time when hate will no longer rule', while McGuinness spoke of peace and reconciliation. It was a moment which republicans had been moving towards over many years and with almost infinite caution. They took endless pains to avoid splits in their ranks, gradually allowing the idea to grow that the IRA and guns should be displaced by Sinn Féin and votes. It was the culmination of the peace process they helped begin.

But Paisley, who had been so vehemently against the process, had played his cards much closer to his chest and had not laid the groundwork so carefully, so that when it happened it came as a shock to many, causing some initial wobbles among his supporters. Different theories attempt to explain why he so abruptly dropped his lifelong opposition to partnership and reconciliation. Although Trimble's spell as First Minister did not last and ended in acrimony, it did set a precedent of opponents holding office together. In a sense he acted as a heatshield for Paisley's entry into government.

Blair, who spent many hours closeted in negotiations with Paisley, commented that he had 'heard the people telling him it was time for peace'. More specifically, he felt Paisley had been changed by his debilitating illness. 'He had a sense of impending mortality, political and personal, and wanted to leave behind something more profound and enduring than "No surrender",' Blair wrote in his memoirs. 'I felt this was a man looking into his own soul and feeling differently. He hadn't actually matured; but he had in some indefinable sense broadened.' Blair's aide Jonathan Powell concurred, writing that during the negotiations Paisley developed 'a bizarrely constructive intransigence – all negativism had switched to a driving desire to conclude the Northern Ireland question before he died'. Another theory put psephology before psychology. Paisley had never been comfortable about being a member of organisations not led by himself which helps explain why he went through his religious and political life outside the mainstream Protestant and Unionist institutions. He had his own church, his own party, even his own minor version of the Orange Order. But by 2007 he had decisively won the battle within Unionism. In elections over the decades his DUP had, with the single exception of European contests, traditionally finished second to the Ulster Unionists. But in 2003 he pulled ahead, coming first in the following five elections with margins of victory starting at 3 per cent but rising to an average of 15 per cent. His commanding position was emphasised by the fact that in 2005 the DUP won nine Westminster seats while the UUP slumped to just one, giving every appearance of a party in mortal decline. (The years that followed confirmed the UUP's continuing steep deterioration, with the DUP trouncing them in the next four elections.)

But although Paisley might dominate Unionism, he – and everyone else – was well aware that he was in no position to exercise control over republicans and nationalists. The days of one community dominating the other were long gone. For one thing the numbers game had altered decisively, the Catholic section of society expanding from the old level of one-third to well over 40 per cent. The 2010 Westminster election showed how close the differential had become, as the major Unionist parties took 44 per cent of the vote while the major nationalist groupings collected 42 per cent with, for instance, Sinn Féin twice topping the poll. There was no real sign of a nationalist majority being in sight, but the electoral and demographic landscapes were significantly changed. This was emphasised by the fact that London and Dublin had long accepted that no Belfast administration could function without the active participation of nationalists.

Society meanwhile had evolved considerably. Discrimination in voting and housing were things of the distant past while the employment scene too had been transformed. Anti-discrimination legislation, introduced in the 1970s and greatly toughened in the 1980s, proved highly effective in changing employment practices. Prominent cases in which plaintiffs won substantial awards, sometimes amounting to tens of thousands of pounds, forcefully made the point that companies with imbalances in their workforces risked financial penalties and attracting highly unwelcome publicity. Companies and indeed public bodies had to accept that the composition of workforces was officially closely monitored.

The much-expanded Catholic middle class increasingly made its presence felt at senior levels with, for example, a Catholic head of the civil service, and others taking many senior positions. In other fields too sectors which in the old days had been largely Protestant preserves became more representative. In the legal world two successive Lord Chief Justices were Catholic, as were increasing numbers of judges. Others took the posts of Attorney-General and Director of Public Prosecutions. Within academia Catholic representation rose steadily in the universities, among both staff and students.

In the security field employment patterns had always been religiously skewed by the fact that the police and locally recruited soldiers were largely Protestant, a fact which distorted employment patterns. But the figures changed as the military almost disappeared from active service and as policing patterns altered. By 2012, 30 per cent of police officers were Catholics, up from 8 per cent a decade earlier.

Thus it was that Paisley's political success offered him the prospect of high political office. Under the strict arithmetic laid down in the Good Friday Agreement the new template meant the post of First Minister was his for the asking. But many of his old battlecries such as 'Ulster is Protestant' were way out of date. The Catch-22 for him was that he would have to govern together with republicans – no sharing, no power. The huge challenge for him was this meant going into government with Sinn Féin; but if he did, he would have no extreme rival to launch anti-Agreement attacks in the way he himself had done so often in the past.

He went for it. In taking the position Paisley airily dismissed the often vicious battles of the past with two short sentences: 'That was yesterday. Today is today.' The figure who had been such a large part of the problem suddenly became a key part of the solution. Chatting with Blair, Ahern and the others after the ceremony in which he took up office, he said, in a remark which television microphones picked up, 'I wonder why people hate me when I'm such a nice man.' He chortled as he made the comment, apparently intending it as facetious. But it turned out to be a reflection of a new approach in which he suddenly, and slightly unnervingly, changed his entire political demeanour. The man often accused of coarsening political life established a new relationship with McGuinness which overnight elevated the tone of politics. The DUP–Sinn Féin partnership wobbled a little when, a year later, he stood down and Robinson succeeded him as First Minister. But the crisis over Robinson's wayward wife Iris, which at first seemed destabilising, actually strengthened the relationship due to the Sinn Féin support which helped sustain Robinson in office.

McGuinness and a grateful Robinson went on to develop a personal and political bond which saw them form what was virtually two-party government. The UUP and SDLP protested that they were not being treated with proper respect despite being executive colleagues, complaining that Sinn Féin and the DUP were working too closely together. This was a remarkable criticism of a type never before aired in Belfast where the more usual objection was that one element was trying to score points against the other. Democratic Unionist and republican politicians were given the leeway to disagree with each other, at times strongly, whether in the assembly, on the airwaves or in media pronouncements. But this letting off of steam was carefully regulated: nothing was to be uttered which might damage the system. Occasional truculence was allowed: damaging splits were not. A new civility in political life was accompanied by a new realpolitik. Sinn Féin and the DUP both protested, for example, when Westminster cut the amount of subsidy to the administration. But they knuckled down and, without public acrimony, deployed some of the new give and take and together agreed a budget. The lack of fireworks meant that for most people politics became only fitfully interesting and often downright boring: gone was the old sense that matters of life and death might hang on political decisions. Neither party was embarrassed by accusations that they had established a cosy consensus – 'I believe the people want us to work together,' Robinson declared.

This assertion was borne out by the assembly elections of 2011 which produced unmistakable votes of confidence in the institutions and in the DUP–Sinn Féin brand of powersharing. Both parties made gains, together winning 67 of the 108 assembly seats, enough to provide them with a solid lock on power. And although many voters complained the assembly system was inefficient and expensive, only one of the 108 members was opposed to its existence.

The new politics of Belfast was complemented by a huge improvement in Anglo-Irish relations, as illustrated by the Queen's visit to the Republic and other events such as David Cameron's apology for Bloody Sunday. Anglo-Irish relations were described as entering a golden age. London and Dublin, which until the 1960s had paid only minimal and fleeting attention to Northern Ireland matters, were together determined to protect the settlement. The breakthrough year of 2007 improved the atmosphere immensely, introducing a greater sense of stability than ever previously known. The sense also emerged that something close to a fair society had come into being. This came about gradually and mostly through highly effective anti-discrimination legislation. Occasional instances of religious discrimination still surfaced but these, once so common, became rarities. Historical and structural differences affected the Catholic working class disproportionately but, with republicans and nationalists at the highest levels of government, few attributed remaining differentials to active discrimination.

Yet although political and societal advances went beyond what most had ever thought possible, many difficult problems remained. While a partial transformation took place in policing, with many more Catholics and women recruited into the Police Service of Northern Ireland, the persistence of the dissident republican menace meant change sometimes came frustratingly slowly. By 2011 only a few specialised army units, such as bomb disposal teams, remained on duty. But the dissidents, and occasional flare-ups among loyalist paramilitary remnants, slowed down efforts to make policing more community-orientated.

Many issues remained unresolved. The question of marches, especially loyalist parades in or near Catholic districts, was largely but not completely put to rest. The question of how to deal with the legacy of the past, and how to bring some measure of closure to the thousands of families bereaved or otherwise affected, defied solution. No consensus on how to move forward has emerged, though debates on how to achieve this continued. Division remained an unfortunate fact of life, even though it far less frequently led to actual conflict. An integrated education movement was active for more than thirty years, motivated by parents determined to have their children taught alongside 'the other side', yet more than 90 per cent of children still attended single-religion schools. As might be expected, most of the children at mixed schools were sent there by liberal and progressive parents, whereas those who would benefit most from integration were from the toughest, most divided areas. Working-class children, in particular, could still go through primary and secondary education without ever meeting those of another religion. There were quite a few mixed marriages, some estimates putting the figure at around one in ten, but such couples stayed well below the radar, not advertising themselves and carefully choosing where to live.

While most of Belfast has the appearance of a modern city, in its backstreets were dozens of 'peacelines', walls dividing Catholic and Protestant communities, erected from the late 1960s onwards. In the west and north of the city, the most violent areas during the troubles, these monuments to mistrust and communal wariness continued to rigidly delineate the toughest neighbourhoods. Some, up to thirty feet high, were elaborate constructions of reinforced concrete, steel, heavy-duty mesh and razor-wire. Most of them were ugly although a few were prettified and artfully camouflaged with shrubs and climbing plants: these were sometimes sardonically referred to as 'designer peacelines'. Discussions began on how and when they might be demolished, but most believed this would be a long-term project, to be carried out only when those who lived in or near their shadow felt secure enough to contemplate their removal. While this recital of remaining problems may sound cheerless, the underlying sense was strong that, however slow and difficult progress may be, there is no realistic chance of a slide back to conflict. By 2012 Northern Ireland had got as close to peace as it had for decades. In 1972 almost 500 people died in a single year; in 2011 the toll was a single fatality. Troubles funerals, once regular, became rarities.

Northern Ireland, which began life amid violence and the threat of force, brought contentment to no one, apart perhaps from the British authorities, who from the 1920s on regarded it as something that could safely be ignored. Northern nationalists were dismayed by those arrangements, protesting that they amounted to an official denial of their Irish identity. To Unionists it brought power but no feeling of security, since the arrangement aggravated the most unfortunate features of their frontier mentality. For nationalists it infringed on their liberty; for Unionists it was a type of liberty but one that carried a price of eternal vigilance which allowed no political relaxation.

For most of the decades that followed there was a superficial peace, or at least lack of violence, but actually the system was storing up a world of trouble. The era of the recent troubles closed with the two national identities practically intact but, despite the social and political scars, with a fairer society with arguably (and hopefully) less hatred and resentment. The ultimate question of whether Northern Ireland will remain British, or become Irish, was still in the air and, since no one can predict the future, seems destined to remain for generations. That means there will always be a certain edge to political life. But the establishment of the new settlement seemed to point to a new sense that in the meantime politics could work, with the assembly providing a level playing field of a type which had never before existed. Many voters did not love it, but a substantial majority voted for it and seemed to value and appreciate it. It may not be the end of history, but it was certainly the end of a dreadful era. Northern Ireland does not have a celebratory culture, and the ending of the troubles did not generate euphoria: in fact initially it produced much suspicion. But eventually an underlying sense of relief became evident, along with a feeling that the opportunity existed for a new start. If there was a single central lesson drawn from the troubles, both by politicians and people, it was that cooperation was the key to creating a new and brighter era.

Chronology

1920
The Government of Ireland Act led to the creation of NI.

1921
The first NI parliament was elected with James Craig as the first prime minister.

A truce was agreed between the IRA and the British army. It was followed by negotiations leading to the Anglo-Irish treaty and the creation of the Irish Free State consisting of twenty-six counties of Ireland.

1949
The south became the Irish Republic.

The Ireland Act was passed by the British parliament: it regularised the new constitutional position and affirmed that the status of NI would only change with the agreement of the NI parliament.

1956
The IRA launched its 'border campaign'.

1962
February   The IRA border campaign officially ended.

1963
March   **Terence O'Neill became PM of NI.**

June   The Protestant *News Letter* praised Pope John XXIII.

September   Following reports of a Unionist party leadership crisis, Brian Faulkner denied trying to oust O'Neill.

1964
January   The Campaign for Social Justice was founded in Dungannon, County Tyrone.

August   Stormont recognised the Northern Committee of the Irish Congress of Trade Unions.

September   **The Divis Street riots broke out after police removed a tricolour from a republician office following protests by the Reverend Ian Paisley.**

October   **A British general election brought Labour to power.**

1965
January   **Taoiseach Seán Lemass met O'Neill at Stormont.**

February   **O'Neill visited Lemass in Dublin.**
            The Nationalist party assumed the role of official opposition.
            The Lockwood committee recommended Coleraine rather than Londonderry as the site for NI's second university.

Spring   The Campaign for Democracy in Ulster became active at Westminster.

1966
February   Paisley brought Edward Carson jnr to Belfast. Unionist party headquarters was petrol-bombed. Three Catholic schools were attacked.

March   The Ulster Protestant Volunteers, a loyalist group which supported Paisley, was formed.
The UVF issued a threat to the IRA.
In the British general election, Gerry Fitt was elected MP for West Belfast.

April   Easter Rising celebrations were held north and south. They were controversial and tense, but there were no serious disturbances. O'Neill later said the commemorations soured the whole situation and from that moment on life became very difficult. The *Protestant Telegraph* was launched by Paisley.

May   **77-year-old Protestant widow Matilda Gould was severely burned in a UVF fire-bomb attack on a Catholic-owned bar in Belfast. She died in June.**

June   Paisleyites and nationalists clashed in Cromac Square, Belfast, with prolonged rioting. Paisley and others were charged with unlawful assembly. **Catholic man John Patrick Scullion died two weeks after being shot by the UVF in the Falls district. Peter Ward was shot dead by the UVF, and two others injured, in the Malvern Street shootings. The UVF was banned.**

July   A nationalist workman threw a brick at the Queen's car during a royal visit to Belfast.
Paisley was imprisoned for unlawful assembly, his third conviction but first prison term.

September   **O'Neill flew back from England, declaring a conspiracy had been mounted against him in his absence. He won a party vote of confidence.**

November   Jack Lynch replaced Seán Lemass as Taoiseach.

1967
January/
February   **The Northern Ireland Civil Rights Association was formed.**

March   The Republican Clubs organisation was banned.

April   O'Neill dismissed agriculture minister Harry West over a Fermanagh land deal.

1968
April   All parades were banned for one month in Armagh to avoid clashes between republicans commemorating the Easter Rising and a threatened UPV counter-demonstration.
O'Neill's car was attacked by loyalist demonstrators in Belfast.

June   **Nationalist MP Austin Currie raised the Caledon housing issue after the local council allocated a house to teenage Protestant single girl. He staged a protest squat in the house, and was evicted by police.**

August   **The first civil rights march took place, from Coalisland to Dungannon in Tyrone, in protest at housing allocation. Hundreds of UPV members assembled to confront them.**

October   **A Londonderry civil rights march resulted in seventy-seven injured civilians as police batoned marchers.**

1968

The People's Democracy group was founded. The Nationalist party withdrew as official opposition.

Lynch met PM Harold Wilson, blaming partition for Northern Ireland's problems.

November **O'Neill and ministers Brian Faulkner and William Craig met Wilson and Home Secretary James Callaghan at Downing Street.**

O'Neill subsequently announced a five-point reform package which included an ombudsman, the end of the company vote in local elections, a review of the Special Powers Act, a new Londonderry Development Commission, and a points system for housing allocation.

A civil rights march was held in Armagh. Paisley supporters blocked the city centre.

December Paisley was summonsed for taking part in an illegal assembly.

O'Neill delivered his 'crossroads' speech.

O'Neill dismissed Craig from his cabinet.

Paisley greeted the historic gunrunning ship the *Clydevalley* on its return to NI.

1969

January **A PD march from Belfast to Londonderry was attacked by loyalists at Burntollet Bridge.**

RUC members broke doors and windows in the Bogside, Londonderry.

A PD march in Newry was followed by rioting and substantial damage.

O'Neill announced the Cameron commission, headed by a Scottish judge, to investigate the causes of the 1968 disturbances.

Faulkner resigned from O'Neill's cabinet, citing the decision to set up the Cameron commission.

Minister William Morgan also resigned.

Paisley was sentenced to three months' imprisonment in relation to the Armagh demonstration.

A Londonderry Commission was named to replace the Corporation.

February Paisley led 5,000 people from the Shankill to a rally in the Ulster Hall.

Twelve dissident MPs held a meeting in Portadown, calling for O'Neill's resignation.

O'Neill called a Stormont election which produced a poor result for him.

March It was announced that the RUC would carry arms on daytime duties in border areas.

Paisley and Ronald Bunting lost their appeals and were sent to jail.

Castlereagh electricity substation was wrecked by loyalist bombs. The IRA was wrongly blamed.

O'Neill announced the part-time mobilisation of 1,000 B Specials to guard public utilities.

April **A loyalist bomb damaged a water installation at Dunadry, County Antrim. The IRA was blamed.**

Bernadette Devlin won the Mid-Ulster Westminster by-election.

Rioting broke out in Londonderry after a banned demonstration.

More loyalist bombs damaged the Silent Valley water supply. The bombs cut off two-thirds of the water supply to Belfast.

A nationalist crowd stoned Hasting Street RUC station in Belfast. Civil rights demonstrators in Newry attacked the police station.

1969

       John Hume asked the civil rights movement to stay off the streets.
       James Chichester-Clark resigned from O'Neill's cabinet.
       The main Lough Neagh to Belfast water pipe was blown up by loyalists.
       An explosion in Annalong, County Down, caused by loyalists, again hit
       Belfast's water supply. Five hundred British troops were sent to NI.
       O'Neill resigned. Celebration bonfires were lit on the Shankill Road.
       A NI Boundary Commission was set up.

May   **Chichester-Clark defeated Faulkner to become prime minister.**
       An amnesty was announced for those convicted since October 1968. It
       resulted in the release of Paisley and the dropping of charges against a
       number of nationalist MPs.
       Chichester-Clark and colleagues met Wilson and Callaghan.
       **Wilson announced that the one man – one vote system would be used
       for 1971 NI local elections.**

July   A white paper on local government reorganisation recommended greatly
       reducing the number of local government bodies.
       Clashes during the Twelfth of July period led to serious rioting in various areas.

August   **Major clashes broke out between Bogside residents and the RUC after
       the Apprentice Boys march was stoned. Lynch sent 'field hospitals' to
       the border area. RUC stations were attacked in nationalist areas.
       In Londonderry the RUC used CS gas for the first time. There was
       rioting in Derry and later Belfast. Wilson and Callaghan met in
       Cornwall, and decided to provide troops if Chichester-Clark requested
       them. Callaghan later agreed to a request.**

14 August **The army arrived on the streets of Londonderry at 5 p.m. The army
       negotiated with the Bogside Defence Association and agreed to pull the
       RUC and B Specials back behind the army outside the Bogside.**

14/15   **Major clashes occurred in west and north Belfast. A number of people
August   were killed; 150 Catholic homes were burned and on the 15th barricades
       were strengthened in many areas.**

15 August **The army was deployed on the streets of Belfast.**

19 August Chichester-Clark was summoned to London where, at a stormy meeting, he
       was pressed for action on reform.
       The Hunt inquiry into policing was announced.
       Two senior British civil servants were appointed to the NI PM's office and
       the Ministry of Home Affairs. Callaghan arrived in NI, and was given a
       warm welcome in the Bogside.
       Chichester-Clark announced that a senior English judge, Lord Scarman,
       would chair an inquiry into the 1969 disturbances.

September The Cameron report on the 1968 disturbances was published.
       The army completed 'peacelines' in Belfast, barricades intended to separate
       some loyalist and nationalist areas.
       A Ministry for Community Relations was established.

October **The Hunt report on policing was published. It proposed disarming the
       RUC and abolition of the B Specials. English policeman Sir Arthur
       Young was appointed head of the RUC.
       In a night of loyalist rioting on the Shankill Road, a policeman and two
       civilians were killed.**

1969

A loyalist was fatally injured when his bomb exploded prematurely.

November A white paper recommended the creation of the Ulster Defence Regiment to replace the B Specials.

1970

January The UDR came into existence, becoming operational in April.
Sinn Féin split into Official and Provisional Sinn Féin. A corresponding IRA split had already taken place.

March Five Unionist MPs were expelled from the parliamentary party after refusing to support a motion of confidence in the government.

April Rioting in Ballymurphy, west Belfast, led to a major gun battle with the army. In a by-election Paisley won O'Neill's Bannside seat. O'Neill had resigned the seat to become Lord O'Neill.
The Alliance Party of Northern Ireland was formed. The B Specials formally ceased to exist.

May Lynch sacked ministers Charles Haughey and Neil Blaney from his cabinet amid allegations of illegal arms importation. Haughey and Blaney were arrested on arms conspiracy charges.

June Labour lost the Westminster general election.
Reginald Maudling became Home Secretary in Edward Heath's Conservative government.
Bernadette Devlin was jailed for her part in the August 1969 Londonderry rioting.
Serious rioting and clashes occurred in Belfast and Londonderry with five shot dead.

July A new act imposed mandatory six-month sentences for disorderly or riotous behaviour.
The army placed part of the Falls Road area of Belfast under curfew while it searched 5,000 homes for arms.
Irish foreign minister Patrick Hillery visited the Falls area unannounced, displeasing both Stormont and London.
All marches were banned for six months.
The army's shooting of an alleged petrol-bomber in Londonderry was followed by protests and five nights of rioting.

August The army began to use rubber bullets.
The SDLP was formed, with Gerry Fitt as leader.

September The one-hundredth explosion in NI took place in 1970.

October In Dublin, Haughey and others were acquitted on arms charges.

1971

January An independent commissioner was appointed to review local council boundaries.

February The IRA shot soldier Robert Curtis in north Belfast, the first serving soldier to die in the troubles. In a television address Chichester-Clark said: 'Northern Ireland is at war with the IRA Provisionals.'
Two RUC officers were shot dead in Belfast.
The RUC was issued with bulletproof vests.

March Maudling addressed Stormont, saying violence could not be tolerated.

1971

Three off-duty British soldiers were shot dead by the IRA at Ligoniel in north Belfast.

4,000 shipyard workers marched in Belfast demanding internment without trial. Chichester-Clark flew to London to demand support for tougher security measures. He was promised 1,300 extra troops.

Chichester-Clark resigned. Faulkner defeated Craig to become Unionist party leader and prime minister.

April   In the Commons Wilson said a bill existed for the imposition of direct rule from Westminster.

May   The new independent Housing Executive met for the first time.

June   Faulkner proposed the creation of three new parliamentary committees, some to be chaired by members of the opposition.

July   During prolonged rioting in Londonderry, a man and a youth were shot dead by the army in controversial circumstances.

Sinn Féin's Maire Drumm told a Bogside meeting: 'The only way you can avenge these deaths is by being organised . . . until you can chase that accursed army away. I would personally prefer to see all the British army going back dead. You should not just shout "Up the IRA", you should join the IRA.' She later received a six-month prison sentence for the speech.

The SDLP withdrew from Stormont citing the government's refusal to hold a public inquiry into the two Londonderry deaths.

August   Faulkner flew to London to press Heath for the introduction of internment.

Internment was introduced. Hundreds of people were arrested and there were major outbreaks of violence.

The SDLP announced a civil disobedience campaign, including a rent-and-rates strike.

Approximately 25 per cent of Catholic tenants took part in the strike. Many Catholic representatives withdrew from councils and public bodies over internment.

The Compton inquiry was established into the treatment of detainees in custody.

Heath held prolonged talks with Lynch at Chequers. Maudling in the Commons said 'a permanent, active and guaranteed place in the life and public affairs of NI shall be available both to the majority and minority community'. Internees were moved to Long Kesh.

Heath met Lynch and Faulkner at Chequers.

October   Five nationalist MPs staged a 48-hour hungerstrike in Downing Street in protest at internment.

A Catholic, G. B. Newe, was brought into government as a junior minister in Faulkner's office to advise on minority matters.

A nationalist alternative gathering, the Assembly of the Northern Irish People, was organised by the SDLP.

Paisley's Democratic Unionist party was launched at an Ulster Hall rally.

The Compton report said there had been ill-treatment of detainees but not brutality.

Wilson called for Irish unification after a fifteen-year transitional stage.

November   The Irish government referred the alleged ill-treatment of detainees to the European Commission on Human Rights.

1971

December   **A bomb left by the UVF at McGurk's Bar in north Belfast killed fifteen people.**
Unionist Senator Jack Barnhill was killed at his home by the Official IRA.
After a visit to NI, Home Secretary Maudling was criticised for speaking of an 'acceptable level of violence'.

1972

January   **On what became known as Bloody Sunday, thirteen men were shot dead in Londonderry by the army; another died later of his wounds.**

February   **The British embassy in Dublin was burned down by a protesting crowd.**
Faulkner met Heath at Downing Street.
William Craig launched the Ulster Vanguard movement.
Seven people were killed by a bomb planted by the Official IRA at Aldershot military barracks in England.
NI minister John Taylor was seriously injured in an Official IRA gun attack.

March   **The Abercorn Bar in Belfast city centre was bombed by the IRA, killing two people and injuring 130.**
A four-hour loyalist stoppage was called in protest at security policy.
Wilson met the IRA in Dublin and at a press conference said internment should end, security should be transferred to London, and IRA terms should be put on the agenda for talks.
Heath informed Faulkner he intended to remove security powers from Stormont.
Direct rule was introduced when Faulkner refused to give up security powers.
Craig's Vanguard movement held a large Belfast protest rally.
An IRA bomb in Belfast's Donegall Street killed seven people.
William Whitelaw, in the new post of Northern Ireland Secretary, arrived in Belfast.
The Stormont parliament was wound up, with a huge loyalist protest rally.

April   The Widgery report into Bloody Sunday was published, largely exonerating the army.

May   There were widespread protests after the Official IRA killed a local man who was in Londonderry on home leave from the army.
The Official IRA called off its campaign.
The SDLP called on those who had withdrawn from public life to return.

June   **The IRA called a ceasefire to allow for talks with the government.**
Whitelaw granted special category status to imprisoned republicans and loyalists.

July   **The IRA met Whitelaw in London for talks. These were unproductive and the IRA ceasefire ended a short time later.**
22 IRA bombs in Belfast killed eleven and injured scores on 21 July, Bloody Friday.
The army took control of no-go areas in Londonderry in Operation Motorman.
An IRA bomb attack killed eight people in the County Londonderry village of Claudy.

September   A conference of NI political parties was held in Darlington.

1972

October   **A government green paper on the future government of NI was published.**

December   **Loyalist bombs exploded in Dublin while the Dáil was debating anti-terrorist legislation, killing two people.**
Special category prisoners were moved to Long Kesh prison near Belfast where they joined internees.
The Diplock report on judicial procedure recommended an end to jury trial in troubles-related cases.

1973

January   **The UK and the Irish Republic joined the European Economic Community.**

February   **Two loyalists were interned, the first since internment began, sparking off a violent one-day loyalist strike.**
A general election in the south resulted in a Fine Gael–Labour coalition headed by Liam Cosgrave.

March   **A border poll asked voters if they wanted NI to remain within the UK: 591,820 said yes, 6,463 said no.** Most nationalists boycotted the poll.
An IRA gun-running boat, the *Claudia*, was captured; it contained arms from Libya.
A white paper was published, laying the groundwork for the assembly and the Sunningdale initiative.
The Unionist party's ruling council approved the white paper by 381 votes to 231, giving Faulkner the authority to negotiate.
Craig announced the creation of the Vanguard Unionist Progressive party.

May   Faulkner said he would not share power with those 'whose primary object is to break the link with Britain'.

June   SDLP senator and Belfast councillor Paddy Wilson and a woman were stabbed to death by UDA members.
Assembly elections were held.
An IRA bomb attack killed six people in Coleraine, County Londonderry.
The first meeting of the assembly took place amid rowdy scenes.

August   Former NI prime minister Lord Brookeborough died.
Faulkner and Heath were booed at the funeral.

October   **Interparty talks involving the UUP, SDLP and Alliance on the formation of an executive began at Stormont Castle.**
After a six-hour debate Faulkner won the support of the party's standing committee for sharing power with the SDLP by 132 votes to 105.

November   The UVF announced a ceasefire which lasted 43 days.
The UUP's ruling council agreed in principle to powersharing by 379 votes to 369.
Agreement was reached on the setting up of a powersharing executive to administer Northern Ireland.

December   Heath announced Whitelaw's replacement as NI Secretary by Francis Pym.
An assembly meeting degenerated into violence and was adjourned in 'grave disorder'.
The Sunningdale conference was held in England, clearing the way for the powersharing executive to be formed.

1974

January   **The powersharing executive took office.**
Faulkner was defeated by 457 votes to 374 in a vote by the UUP ruling
council on the Council of Ireland.
Faulkner resigned as UUP leader, to be replaced by hardliner Harry
West.
The Boland case, in which a former Irish government minister challenged
Sunningdale as conflicting with the Irish constitution, was heard in a Dublin
court. Faulkner flew to meet Cosgrave near Dublin to try to resolve
differences.
The first meeting of the assembly since Sunningdale resulted in violent
scenes during which five RUC men were injured.

February   Irish ministers met the Northern Ireland executive to discuss cross-border
links and harmonisation.
The British general election saw Heath replaced by a minority Labour
government under Wilson. In NI, anti-Sunningdale Unionist candidates
won eleven of the twelve seats with 51 per cent of the vote.

March   Merlyn Rees was named as new Northern Ireland Secretary.
The Assembly began to debate a motion calling for complete renegotiation
of the Sunningdale Agreement. The presiding officer allowed the debate to
run for almost two months.

May   Faulkner supporters began to organise a new party to be known as the
Unionist Party of Northern Ireland (UPNI).
The assembly voted by 44 votes to 28 in favour of the powersharing
executive. The vote triggered the Ulster Workers Council strike.
During the strike more than thirty people were killed by loyalist bombs
in Dublin and Monaghan. As the strike progressed Wilson made a
broadcast condemning 'people who spend their lives sponging on
Westminster', causing widespread Protestant resentment.
Faulkner and his colleagues resigned on 28 May.
The strike was called off following the collapse of the executive.

September Faulkner officially launched the UPNI.

October   In the British general election, ten of the twelve NI seats were retained by
anti-Sunningdale Unionists.
Five people were killed and 54 were injured when IRA bombs exploded
without warning in a pub in Guildford, Surrey.
Protesting republican prisoners burned down much of Long Kesh prison.

November A UDA delegation visited Libya.
Twenty-three republican prisoners escaped from Long Kesh. One prisoner
was killed during the escape and the others were recaptured.
Twenty-one were killed and 182 injured when IRA bombs exploded in
Birmingham bars.

December At Feakle, in County Clare, a group of Protestant churchmen met IRA leaders.
The IRA called a ceasefire until 2 January, and Rees permitted officials to
meet with Sinn Féin.

1975

January   The IRA announced an extension of its ceasefire.

February   **The IRA announced an indefinite ceasefire.**
Sinn Féin was allowed to set up 'incident centres' to monitor the ceasefire.

1975

March   The assembly was formally dissolved to allow for elections to a new
           constitutional convention.

May   In the convention elections, combined anti-Sunningdale Unionists had an
           overall majority. Faulkner's UPNI won only a handful of seats. The
           convention opened with the task of devising a system of government with
           the 'most widespread acceptance throughout the community'.

July   Three members of the Miami Showband were killed in an incident in which
           two UVF attackers also died.

August   Unionist talks with the SDLP broke down.

September Craig proposed the possibility of the SDLP entering government at the
           discretion of a Unionist prime minister, an idea known as 'voluntary coalition'.

October   The Vanguard party split over the voluntary coalition plan.
           **The convention voted by 42 votes to 31 in favour of a report advocating a
           return to Unionist majority rule.**

November   **The UVF was again banned after a day in which there were eleven
           deaths as a result of UVF attacks.**
           The Sinn Féin incident centres were closed.

December   Internment was ended, and the remaining detainees were released.

1976

January   **Six members of two Catholic families were killed by the UVF in County
           Armagh.**
           **Ten Protestant workers were shot dead at Kingsmills in County Armagh
           by the IRA. The SAS was deployed in south Armagh.**

February   Republican prisoner Frank Stagg died in England after a 62-day hungerstrike.

March   Those convicted of paramilitary offences were no longer eligible for special
           category status.
           The final convention meeting ended amid rowdy scenes, and the body was
           officially dissolved.

June–   The UUP was strongly criticised by other Unionists for holding talks with
September   the SDLP.

July   **The British ambassador to Ireland, Christopher Ewart-Biggs, was killed
           by the IRA in Dublin.**

August   The deaths of the three Maguire children led to the emergence of the 'Peace
           People'.
           Faulkner, by now Lord Faulkner, announced his retirement from political life.

September **Roy Mason replaced Rees as Northern Ireland Secretary.**
           **The first IRA man sent to the Maze (formerly Long Kesh) after the
           ending of special category status refused to wear prison uniform.**

October   Sinn Féin vice-president Maire Drumm was shot dead by loyalists while a
           patient in Belfast's Mater Hospital.

November   Peace People leaders Mairead Corrigan and Betty Williams were awarded
           the Nobel peace prize.

December   The Fair Employment Act was passed, making it an offence to discriminate
           in employment on religious or political grounds. It created the Fair
           Employment Agency.

1977

March   Faulkner died in a horse-riding accident.

In Dublin eight SAS men were fined after being detained on the southern side of the border.

Twenty-six men were sentenced to a total of 700 years in prison following a major UVF trial.

April   **Paisley and the UDA announced plans for a second loyalist workers' strike. It was opposed by the UUP and others.**

May   **The strike began on 2 May but was called off on 13 May.**

June   A general election in the south resulted in a Fianna Fáil government led by Jack Lynch.

July   Several people were killed in Belfast as a result of a feud between the Provisional IRA and the Official IRA.

August   The Queen visited Belfast as part of her jubilee celebrations.

US President Jimmy Carter expressed support for a NI government that would have widespread acceptance, offering economic aid in the event of such agreement.

September   The SDLP declared its support for 'an agreed Ireland'.

October   The Irish Independence Party was launched in opposition to the SDLP.

November   The SDLP conference rejected calls for a British withdrawal.

December   Five hotels were damaged by IRA bombs.

1978

January   The Fair Employment Agency reported that unemployment was higher among Catholics than among Protestants.

The European Court of Human Rights ruled that interrogation methods used on internees in 1971 did not constitute torture but did amount to 'inhuman and degrading treatment'.

February   **The IRA firebombing of La Mon Hotel outside Belfast killed twelve people.**

March   The Maze prison dispute escalated when republican inmates began spreading excrement around their cells.

April   Conservative spokesman Airey Neave said that powersharing was no longer practical politics.

James Callaghan announced that the number of NI MPs would be increased.

May   Belfast elected its first non-Unionist mayor, David Cook of the Alliance party.

July   The head of the Irish Catholic Church, Archbishop Tomás Ó Fiaich, visited the Maze prison and said it reminded him of a Calcutta slum.

August   The De Lorean car company announced plans to build luxury sports cars in south Belfast, with a £56 million government subsidy.

November   Widespread IRA bomb attacks caused serious damage. The deputy governor of the Maze prison was killed by the IRA.

1979

January   IRA bombs exploded across NI on the first day of the year.

February   Members of the loyalist Shankill Butchers gang were convicted and given long sentences for nineteen killings and other offences.

March   A leading police doctor said he had seen a large number of people who had been physically ill-treated in Castlereagh interrogation centre.

1979

    The IRA shot and killed the British ambassador to Holland, Sir Richard Sykes. Twenty-four IRA bombs exploded at different locations.
The Callaghan government was defeated in a Commons confidence vote, precipitating a general election.
Conservative NI spokesman Airey Neave was killed by an INLA bomb while leaving the Commons.

April   **Four RUC men were killed in an IRA bomb attack at Bessbrook, County Armagh.**

May   **The Conservatives won the general election, bringing Margaret Thatcher to power with former chief whip Humphrey Atkins as NI Secretary.**

August   **Two major IRA attacks on 27 August killed Lord Mountbatten and others in a boat off the Sligo coast, while 18 soldiers and a civilian died in an ambush near Warrenpoint in County Down.**

September   **Pope John Paul II visited Ireland**. Addressing himself to the IRA he appealed: 'On my knees I beg you to turn away from the paths of violence and return to the paths of peace.'

October   Atkins launched an initiative, inviting the parties to talks.

November   **Fitt resigned as SDLP leader, to be succeeded by Hume.**

December   Charles Haughey was elected leader of Fianna Fáil and became Taoiseach. **Four soldiers were killed by an IRA landmine in County Tyrone.**

1980

January   The Atkins conference opened with new Ulster Unionist party leader James Molyneaux boycotting the proceedings.

March   The Atkins conference was wound up.

May   **A meeting between Thatcher and Haughey in Downing Street appeared to improve Anglo-Irish relations.**

June   The European Commission of Human Rights rejected a case taken by a protesting Maze prisoner, but criticised British 'inflexibility'.
Dr Miriam Daly, a prominent republican activist, was shot dead at her home in west Belfast by loyalist gunmen.

August   Three people were killed and 18 injured in widespread violence on the anniversary of internment.

October   **Seven H-block prisoners began a hungerstrike to demand the return of special category status.**

December   **The H-block hungerstrike was called off with one IRA prisoner critically ill.**
A second Thatcher–Haughey summit in Dublin launched joint studies on possible areas of cooperation including economics and security.

1981

January   Bernadette McAliskey, née Devlin, and her husband were shot and seriously wounded by UDA gunmen at their County Tyrone home.
Two leading Unionists, Sir Norman Stronge and his son James, were killed by the IRA.

March   **A second H-block hungerstrike was begun in support of special category status for prisoners. IRA prison leader Bobby Sands was the first to refuse food.**

1981

Irish Foreign Minister Brian Lenihan said the Anglo-Irish talks could lead to Irish unity in ten years.

The death occurred of Frank Maguire, independent nationalist MP for Fermanagh–South Tyrone.

Paisley held major rallies in protest at Anglo-Irish talks.

April   **Sands won the Fermanagh–South Tyrone by-election.**

May   **Sands died on the sixty-sixth day of his hungerstrike. His funeral in Belfast was attended by tens of thousands.**
Three further hungerstrikers died, and five soldiers were killed by a bomb in Bessbrook, County Armagh.

June   **Two H-block prisoners were elected to the Dáil in a general election which brought to power a Fine Gael–Labour coalition headed by Garret FitzGerald.**

July   Two more hungerstrikers died.

August   Four more hungerstrikers died. Sinn Féin member Owen Carron won the Fermanagh–South Tyrone by-election caused by the death of Sands.

September   Paisley called for a 'third force' to be established on the lines of the B Specials. James Prior replaced Atkins as NI Secretary.

October   **The hungerstrike was called off.** Prior announced that all prisoners could wear their own clothes and made concessions on other prisons issues.

November   **The Anglo-Irish Intergovernmental Council was set up by the two governments.**
Unionist MP the Reverend Robert Bradford was killed by the IRA in south Belfast.
A loyalist 'day of action' was staged to protest at security policy, with rallies and work stoppages.

December   Paisley claimed a new third force had between 15,000 and 20,000 members.

1982

January   Prominent loyalist John McKeague was shot dead by the INLA.

February   A general election in the south returned Fianna Fáil and Charles Haughey to power.

March   Three soldiers were killed in west Belfast.

April   Prior proposed elections to an assembly which could have power devolved to it in stages.
Two people were killed, twelve were injured and £1 million worth of damage was caused by IRA bomb attacks in Belfast, Londonderry, and five towns.

May   **The De Lorean plant closed with the loss of hundreds of jobs.**

July   **IRA bomb attacks on military bands in London parks killed eleven soldiers.**

August   The SDLP decided to contest Northern Ireland assembly elections but not to take their seats.

October   Sinn Féin contested assembly elections on an abstentionist ticket, securing 10 per cent of the vote.
Three RUC officers were killed by an IRA bomb at Lurgan, County Armagh.
Three IRA members were shot dead by the RUC at Lurgan, County Armagh.

November   **The assembly met for first time, with no nationalists attending.**

1982

Lenny Murphy, leader of the UVF Shankill Butchers gang, was shot dead by the IRA.

The third southern general election to be held in fifteen months produced a Fine Gael–Labour coalition.

December **Seventeen people, including eleven soldiers, died in an INLA bombing in Ballykelly, County Londonderry.**

1983

January Judge William Doyle was shot dead by the IRA as he left a Catholic church in Belfast.

February The European Parliament's political committee voted for an inquiry on whether Europe could assist in tackling NI's economic and political problems. This was opposed by the British government and by Unionists.

March The Irish government announced the setting up of the New Ireland Forum.

April Fourteen defendants were jailed on the evidence of a UVF supergrass.

May A 1000lb IRA bomb exploded outside Andersonstown police station in Belfast.

The New Ireland Forum held its first meeting in Dublin.

June **In the British general election, Unionists won fifteen of the seventeen NI seats. Hume and Adams, who defeated Fitt in West Belfast, were elected to Westminster.**

July **Four UDR members were killed by an IRA landmine in County Tyrone.**

August After a 120-day trial of thirty-eight people implicated by IRA supergrass Christopher Black, twenty-two were jailed. Their sentences totalled more than 4,000 years.

September Thirty-eight IRA prisoners escaped from the Maze in a mass breakout. Nineteen were recaptured within days.

Thatcher and FitzGerald met at Chequers for the first meeting of the Anglo-Irish Intergovernmental Council.

Adams was elected president of Sinn Féin.

Three members of the congregation of Darkley Pentecostal church in south Armagh were shot dead in an INLA attack.

December **UUP assembly member Edgar Graham was shot dead by the IRA at Queen's University, Belfast.**

An Irish soldier and a Garda cadet were killed during the rescue of a supermarket executive kidnapped by the IRA.

Five people were killed and eighty were injured by an IRA bomb at Harrods department store in London.

1984

January Cardinal Ó Fiaich said that it was not morally wrong to join Sinn Féin. The Irish government said it could not identify with the cardinal's comments.

March **Adams was shot and wounded in Belfast by the UDA.**

INLA leader Dominic McGlinchey was extradited to NI from the Republic.

April The IRA shot dead the daughter of magistrate Tom Travers as she left mass with him in south Belfast.

May **The New Ireland Forum report was published.**

1984

June   DUP assembly member George Seawright lost the party whip after saying that Catholics and their priests should be 'incinerated'.
Three RUC members were acquitted of the murder of an unarmed IRA member.

July   In the Commons, Prior rejected the main recommendations of the New Ireland Forum report.

August   An Armagh coroner resigned after finding 'grave irregularities' in RUC files relating to the shooting of two INLA men by police in 1982.

September Douglas Hurd replaced Prior as Northern Ireland Secretary.
Seven tons of arms and ammunition intended for the IRA were recovered from the *Marita Ann* off the Irish coast, in the biggest arms seizure since the 1973 capture of the *Claudia*.

October   **An IRA bomb at the Conservative party conference hotel in Brighton killed five people.**
The European Commission of Human Rights ruled that the use of plastic bullets in riot situations was justified.

November At the end of a summit with the Irish government Thatcher ruled out the three main New Ireland Forum options in what became known as her 'Out, out, out' pronouncement.

December **Private Ian Thain was convicted of the murder of a civilian while on duty.**
35 defendants charged on the word of a republican supergrass were acquitted.
The Court of Appeal quashed the convictions of fourteen men jailed on the evidence of UVF supergrass Joseph Bennett.

1985

February The US government refused Adams a visa.
Hume met members of the IRA's army council but walked out within minutes when the IRA insisted on making a video recording of the occasion.
Three IRA members were shot dead by soldiers at Strabane, County Tyrone.
Nine RUC officers were killed in an IRA mortar attack in Newry, County Down.

May   **In the local government elections Sinn Féin won 59 council seats. This led to disruption of meetings by Unionists.**
Four RUC officers were killed by an IRA bomb at Killeen, County Armagh.

July   **Loyalist rioting over the rerouting of parades, especially in Portadown, led to loyalist attacks on police homes across Northern Ireland, forcing scores of RUC families to move house.**

August   Molyneaux and Paisley met Thatcher in Downing Street.

September Tom King replaced Hurd as NI Secretary.

November **Prime ministers Thatcher and FitzGerald signed the Anglo-Irish Agreement on 15 November, systematising cooperation with a permanent intergovernmental conference machinery and giving the Irish government a consultative role in NI affairs with a joint secretariat at Maryfield, outside Belfast.**
The new NI Secretary, Tom King, was assaulted by angry loyalists at Belfast's City Hall.
An estimated 100,000 Unionists gathered in Belfast city centre to voice their anger at the Anglo-Irish Agreement.

1985

December   **The first meeting was held of the Anglo-Irish Intergovernmental Conference.**
All fifteen Unionist MPs resigned in order to force by-elections.

1986

January   By-elections caused by the resignation of Unionist MPs gave the SDLP a second Westminster seat when Séamus Mallon was elected in Newry–Armagh.

February   The Irish government announced its intention to sign the European Convention on the Suppression of Terrorism.
Paisley and Molyneaux were invited to Downing Street. Although receptive to Thatcher's offer of further talks, they were heavily criticised by colleagues when they returned to Belfast.

March   **A Unionist day of action disrupted public services and halted most industry. There was rioting in some loyalist areas.**
Unionist leaders offered to talk to the government but only if the Anglo-Irish Agreement was suspended. This was ruled out by King.
Clashes took place between the RUC and loyalists in Portadown after a ban on an Apprentice Boys parade. Eleven Catholic homes in Lisburn, County Antrim, were petrol-bombed.

April   A loyalist was killed by a plastic bullet during renewed rioting in Portadown. Loyalist attacks on Catholic and RUC homes continued.
Unionist leaders announced a civil disobedience plan including non-payment of rates.
The UUP announced that it was ending its last links with the Conservative party.

May   The Chief Constable Sir John Hermon condemned the loyalist attacks on Catholic and RUC homes and accused politicians of consorting with paramilitary elements.
Belfast city council ended its adjournment protest against the Anglo-Irish Agreement.
King announced the dissolution of the NI assembly.

June   **In controversial circumstances John Stalker was removed from the inquiry into RUC 'shoot-to-kill' incidents. Suggestions of improprieties on his part were later dismissed and he was reinstated as Deputy Chief Constable of the Manchester police. The NI assembly was wound up. Twenty-two assembly members who refused to leave the chamber were physically removed by the RUC.**

July   Portadown Orangemen accepted a compromise route along Garvaghy Road. However, rioting and clashes with the RUC continued.
Hermon suspended two senior officers after investigations into the alleged 'shoot-to-kill' policy in 1982.

August   The IRA announced it was widening its list of 'legitimate targets'.
DUP deputy leader Peter Robinson was arrested and charged after crossing the border into County Monaghan with scores of other loyalists during a late-night protest demonstration.

September   UUP and DUP politicians attended the funeral of assassinated UVF member John Bingham.

November   **Sinn Féin decided to permit successful Sinn Féin candidates to take their seats in the Dáil. Ruairí Ó Brádaigh led a walkout.**

1986

Thatcher rejected the Irish call for Diplock trials to be heard by three judges. The UDA planted four bombs in Dublin.

Ulster Resistance was formed 'to take direct action as and when required' to defeat the Anglo-Irish Agreement. DUP leaders featured at early meetings.

A huge Anglo-Irish Agreement protest rally at Belfast City Hall ended with serious damage to nearby shops.

December King announced the repeal of the Flags and Emblems Act.

Paisley was expelled from the European Parliament after repeatedly interrupting a speech by Thatcher.

Lisburn Road RUC station in south Belfast was destroyed by an IRA bomb. Hundreds of homes and businesses were also damaged.

1987

January DUP politician David Calvert was shot and wounded by the INLA.

Robinson pleaded guilty in a Dublin court to unlawful assembly and paid £17,500 in fines. The UDA published a political manifesto called *Common Sense*, proposing devolved government with a form of powersharing. This was greeted by Unionist condemnation but some nationalist praise.

February The UDA planted incendiary bombs in the Republic. Unionist MPs delivered a petition with 400,000 signatures to Buckingham Palace. It called for a referendum in NI on the Anglo-Irish Agreement. Paisley and Molyneaux set up an inter-party task force to draft an alternative to the Anglo-Irish Agreement.

March Fianna Fáil led by Charles Haughey returned to power after a general election on 19 February.

President Reagan gave the first $50 million grant to an international economic regeneration fund set up alongside the Anglo-Irish Agreement.

April **Northern Ireland's second most senior judge, Lord Gibson, and his wife were killed by an IRA car bomb at Killeen, County Armagh.**

May Sinn Féin published a document entitled *Scenario for Peace*, demanding British withdrawal and an all-Ireland constitutional conference.

Paisley said that the DUP would have no part in any powersharing system, after rumours that the Unionist task force might be preparing to suggest it.

Eight IRA members were shot dead by the SAS as they launched an attack on an RUC station at Loughgall, County Armagh. A civilian was also killed.

June The Conservatives won a third general election victory. Eddie McGrady's defeat of Enoch Powell gave the SDLP three seats, while Adams retained West Belfast.

July Short Brothers closed a section of its plant in a dispute about removing loyalist flags and emblems.

September **Unionists ended a nineteen-month ban on meeting NIO ministers, meeting King for 'talks about talks'.**

November **The French authorities intercepted a large consignment of arms and explosives on its way to the IRA from Libya on board the *Eksund*. It later emerged that earlier large shipments had got through.**

An IRA bomb in Enniskillen killed eleven Protestants during a Remembrance Day ceremony.

Loyalist politician George Seawright was fatally injured by the IPLO.

1987

December   A new extradition bill was passed by the Dáil.

Senior UDA figure John McMichael, who had helped draft the *Common Sense* document, was killed by the IRA.

1988

January   **UDA members were arrested with a large haul of guns, revealing that loyalists had made a South African arms deal.**

Hume and Adams met at the request of a third person.

Attorney-General Sir Patrick Mayhew announced that there would be no prosecutions over the Stalker inquiry 'in the interests of national security'.

Molyneaux and Paisley met King to suggest administrative devolution with committees chaired according to party strengths.

The Birmingham Six lost their appeal against conviction.

February   A Sinn Féin conference approved further talks between Adams and Hume.

Private Thain, convicted of murder while on duty, was released from a life sentence after twenty-six months and returned to his regiment.

The FEA reported an increased Catholic share of public sector employment.

March   **Three IRA volunteers were shot dead by the SAS in Gibraltar.**

In Milltown cemetery, Belfast, UDA member Michael Stone attacked the funerals of the IRA members killed in Gibraltar. He killed three people and injured dozens of others.

Two plain clothes soldiers were attacked by a crowd and then shot dead at an IRA funeral in west Belfast.

Hume denied reports of tension within the SDLP over his talks with Adams.

Andy Tyrie was replaced as UDA leader.

April   At a republican Easter commemoration, McGuinness denied that talks with SDLP included the possibility of an IRA ceasefire.

Robinson, re-elected as DUP deputy leader, said there should be no talks with Sinn Féin even if the IRA ended its campaign.

King criticised the SDLP–Sinn Féin talks.

Adams said that as long as there was the possibility of common ground with the SDLP they were morally bound to seek it.

May   Three members of the RAF were killed in IRA attacks in Europe.

The IRA bombed an army base in Bielefeld, Germany.

A UVF gun attack on a Belfast bar killed three people.

Sinn Féin's Mitchel McLaughlin, a participant in the talks with SDLP, said it was time for all nationalists to agree on 'the Irish people's right to national self-determination'.

Further meetings took place between Sinn Féin and the SDLP.

Bishop Cahal Daly said SDLP–Sinn Féin dialogue was 'better than killing'.

Unionists said a precondition for talks would be an end to the SDLP–Sinn Féin dialogue.

June   The SDLP announced it would hold at least one further meeting with Sinn Féin.

A Conservative Association was launched in north Down.

UUP members brothers Chris and Michael McGimpsey took a case in the Irish courts arguing that the Anglo-Irish Agreement conflicted with Articles 2 and 3 of the Irish constitution.

An IRA bomb killed six soldiers at a Lisburn 'fun run'.

Sinn Féin's Pat Doherty said SDLP–Sinn Féin talks did not concern the IRA. There would be no ceasefire while British occupation continued, he said.

1988

July   SDLP MP Eddie McGrady said he hoped talks with Sinn Féin would either
           produce progress or be ended.
           It was announced that twenty RUC officers would be disciplined as a result
           of the Stalker–Sampson investigations.
           A Belfast city council meeting was abandoned after Unionist and Sinn Féin
           members came to blows.
           **Three members of the Hanna family were killed in an IRA border
           bombing intended for a judge.**
           Séamus Mallon said the future of the talks with Sinn Féin would depend on
           Sinn Féin's attitude to IRA violence.

August   A soldier was killed by an IRA bomb at Inglis barracks, London.
           Following another meeting with Adams, Hume rejected criticism of talks
           with Sinn Féin and called on republicans to abandon violence in favour of
           political methods.
           **Eight soldiers on a bus were killed by an IRA bomb at Ballygawley,
           County Tyrone. Thatcher ordered a security review.**
           Adams said IRA violence would continue until the British withdrew.
           Three IRA members were killed by the SAS in County Tyrone.

September **The end of the Sinn Féin–SDLP talks was announced. The SDLP said it
           regretted being unable to persuade the republicans to end their military
           campaign; Sinn Féin said it found the SDLP attitude 'perplexing'.**
           Sinn Féin said the SDLP had allowed the British to believe that an internal
           settlement was possible. The SDLP said the Irish had the right to self-
           determination but this could not be achieved by violence.
           Adams said talks with SDLP had been 'good for nationalist morale'.

October   Paisley was ejected from the European Parliament chamber after
           interrupting an address by the Pope. Leading UDA figure Jim Craig was
           killed by members of his own organisation.
           **Home Secretary Douglas Hurd announced a broadcasting ban on
           members and supporters of paramilitary organisations.**

November   An arms find in County Armagh was linked to Ulster Resistance.
           The DUP said it had severed all links with Ulster Resistance some time earlier.
           The European Court of Human Rights ruled against detention without
           charge for more than four days.

December   King said he would not meet Sinn Féin even if its elected representatives
           signed a non-violence oath.

1989

January   Hume said Unionists should sit down with Dublin and northern nationalists
           to make an agreement which would transcend the Anglo-Irish Agreement.
           At the Sinn Féin ard fheis Adams warned the IRA to be 'careful and careful
           again' to avoid civilian casualties.

February   Meetings in Duisburg, West Germany, involving four NI parties were
           publicised.
           Solicitor Pat Finucane was shot dead at his Belfast home by loyalist gunmen.
           Sinn Féin councillor John Davey was shot dead at his Magherafelt, County
           Londonderry, home by loyalists.
           An IRA campaign in Britain started with the planting of a bomb at Tern Hill
           military barracks.

1989

March   Adams said there was an urgent need for an unarmed political movement to secure self-determination.

Home Secretary Douglas Hurd warned that Britain was facing the threat of high-level IRA activity, adding that the IRA must be 'extirpated'.

April   The Anglo-Irish Intergovernmental Conference agreed to 'deepen and widen' its work.

Three alleged Ulster Resistance members were detained in Paris with a South African figure and an alleged arms dealer.

May   Sir John Hermon retired as Chief Constable of the RUC.

July   Fianna Fáil and Haughey were returned to power in a coalition with the Progressive Democrats.

Peter Brooke succeeded King as NI Secretary.

August   Adams praised 'the men and women of the IRA' at an internment rally in west Belfast.

A split was revealed in Noraid, the main republican support organisation in the USA, over Sinn Féin's political direction.

The UDA produced confidential security force files on alleged IRA suspects.

September   **An IRA bomb at Deal in Kent killed eleven military bandsmen.**

October   Adams told a Labour party fringe meeting that he supported the IRA's right to engage in armed struggle.

Twenty-eight UDR men were arrested in early morning swoops on the orders of the Stevens inquiry team.

The Guildford Four were released by the Court of Appeal.

Adams attacked Cahal Daly as an 'enthusiastic supporter of the RUC'.

November   **NI Secretary Peter Brooke said the IRA could not be militarily defeated and that the government would have to be imaginative and flexible in its response if there was a ceasefire, citing the example of Cyprus. Adams said Brooke had admitted the 'inevitability' of talks with Sinn Féin.**

Republican News said Sinn Féin would not consider talks with British as long as there was a precondition of an IRA ceasefire, dismissing Hume's claim of a debate within Sinn Féin as 'a figment of his imagination'.

The Conservative party accepted the affiliation of four NI Conservative Associations.

Cahal Daly said if the IRA ended its campaign 'a just settlement could be agreed much more quickly than the sceptics believe'.

Adams and McGuinness relaunched Sinn Féin's *Scenario for Peace* document, denying the existence of any debate in the republican movement about ceasefires. They called on Brooke to enter talks without demanding that the IRA campaign must end first.

Séamus Mallon praised Brooke for his remarks about the possibility of talks with Sinn Féin.

Cardinal Ó Fiaich urged the British to state that they would not stay 'for all time'.

Mitchel McLaughlin backed Ó Fiaich's remarks, saying they were a recognition that 'the question of Irish self-determination must be resolved'. Brooke called them 'wrong and unhelpful'.

December   Adams said the British should hold talks with Sinn Féin 'sooner rather than later'.

1989

> An IRA statement said the 1980s had ended with the British 'not only knowing in their hearts that they cannot defeat the freedom fighters of the IRA but being forced to admit it publicly'.

1990

January **Brooke launched a major political talks initiative.**
Unionists demanded the suspension of the Anglo-Irish Agreement and the Maryfield Secretariat as preconditions for talks.
Adams accused the SDLP of 'consistent and inexcusable failure on the national question over the last twenty years'.
The Bishop of Derry, Dr Edward Daly, called the IRA 'an evil sinister influence'.

February At the Sinn Féin ard fheis it was said that demands for an IRA ceasefire in advance of talks with Sinn Féin were unacceptable. Adams said that Brooke's remarks that the IRA could not be beaten meant talks with Sinn Féin were inevitable.
Brooke said there could be no talks while IRA violence continued.
McGuinness said Brooke was the first NI Secretary 'with some understanding of Irish history'. He urged him to spell out what he meant by 'imaginative steps' in the event of an IRA ceasefire. McGuinness said it made 'no sense whatsoever' for the British to demand as a precondition the ending of the IRA campaign.
Adams criticised Brooke for 'intransigence' in his response to McGuinness, saying republican resistance was inevitable so long as Britain remained in Ireland.

March The Dublin Supreme Court handed down the McGimpsey judgement on Articles 2 and 3. The most significant aspect of the ruling was that the Articles' claim to Northern Ireland was not merely an aspiration but a claim of legal right and thus a constitutional imperative.
Sinn Féin dismissed speculation about an IRA ceasefire.

April Adams said an unannounced IRA ceasefire was possible if Britain entered into talks with Sinn Féin about eventual disengagement from NI.
The NIO said: 'We do not negotiate with terrorists.'

June **Following the IRA killing of an ex-RUC reservist and his wife, Adams said Sinn Féin's relationship with the IRA was one of 'critical support'.**
The IRA planted bombs at a Territorial Army base in London, at the home of leading Tory Lord McAlpine, at an RAF base, and at the Carlton Club in the West End.

July The IRA planted a bomb at the London Stock Exchange.
Cahal Daly said Sinn Féin would have to be talked to at some stage but would have to repudiate violence.
Ian Gow MP was killed at his home in Sussex by an IRA booby-trap bomb.

August An IRA bomb was found in the garden of the Oxfordshire home of Sir Anthony Farrar-Hockley, a former army commander in NI.
Adams said the British had the power to bring the conflict to an end by entering into dialogue without preconditions.
Hume appealed to the IRA to end its campaign.

September An IRA bomb exploded at an army recruiting office in Derby.
The Governor of Gibraltar at the time of the 1988 SAS Gibraltar killings was seriously wounded by the IRA at his home at Milford in Staffordshire.

1990

An IRA bomb was found at an anti-terrorism conference in London. The IRA said Foreign Office minister William Waldegrave had been the target. In an interview with the *Independent* an IRA spokesman said the only debate within the republican movement was how to 'prosecute the war' adding, 'There will be no ceasefire, no truce, no cessation of violence short of British withdrawal.'

October   Brooke called the IRA 'a parasitic organisation' which fed off racketeering.

November   Mary Robinson was elected President of the Republic.
Brooke, in what became known as his 'no selfish interest speech', said Britain had 'no selfish strategic or economic interest' in the Union with NI.
Adams said that the onus was on those who believed there was an alternative to the IRA's armed struggle to prove it. He called for talks without preconditions and said Unionist politicians had no right to veto unification.
Hume said Brooke's speech showed that Britain was now neutral on partition and it was up to those who supported Irish unity to persuade those who were opposed.
Margaret Thatcher resigned as PM, to be replaced by John Major.

December   Cahal Daly, installed as the new Catholic primate, told a congregation that the IRA had no 'moral, rational or political' justification for its campaign. For the first time in fifteen years the IRA declared a three-day Christmas ceasefire.

1991

January   Sinn Féin chairman Tom Hartley said Sinn Féin would no longer speak for the IRA, adding, 'the IRA is capable of speaking for itself'.

February   Adams said speculation about an IRA ceasefire was unfounded. Brooke said there would be no place for Sinn Féin until it renounced violence.
Adams described as fictitious reports that he was preparing proposals for a ceasefire but said Sinn Féin was ready to take political risks and was prepared for give and take.
The IRA fired three mortars at Downing Street: one landed 15 feet from the back window of the prime minister's residence.
An IRA spokesman said: 'There is no talk or pressure from within the IRA to call a ceasefire, and no pressure from our comrades in Sinn Féin.'
One man was killed by an IRA bomb at Victoria rail station, London. Another bomb was planted at Paddington.
PM John Major said of the IRA: 'They really ought to know after all these years that we are not going to be pushed around by terrorist acts.'
An IRA bomb on a rail line into the City of London caused rush-hour disruption.

March   McGuinness said that he saw a window of opportunity in Dublin's opposition to an internal settlement and Brooke's 'no selfish interest' speech.
Brooke published his 'three strand' approach to talks and announced a suspension of Anglo-Irish Conference meetings.

April   Loyalist groups announced a ceasefire during a ten-week gap in Anglo-Irish meetings for the start of Brooke talks on 30 April.

June   At an IRA funeral, Adams said the Brooke talks were 'a non-starter' in the absence of Sinn Féin; he called on US President Bush to 'show more concern for the Irish situation'.

1991

Cahal Daly claimed that documents he had seen indicated there was a debate within the republican movement on the continuation of violence. Sinn Féin said there was no document calling for an end to the IRA campaign.

July   **The Brooke talks were wound up without agreement.**

August   **McGuinness said that Sinn Féin was ready to set aside criticism of Britain 'and risk everything' for 'a real peace agenda'.**

September   Adams said he was prepared to engage in 'open dialogue' and wanted to see an end to all acts of violence.

October   Brooke said there were signs that the leaders of the republican movement had begun to recognise that they could not combine the bullet and the ballot box.

November   Pat Doherty of Sinn Féin said the party 'does not support violence' but does 'support the IRA's right to exist'.
            Two IRA members were killed by their own bomb in England.

December   IRA firebombs exploded at Blackpool and Manchester.
            An IRA bomb on a rail line in London created widespread disruption.
            The IRA announced a three-day Christmas ceasefire. Adams called on the British and Irish governments to develop 'a real peace process'.

1992

January   Cahal Daly said that if the IRA called off its campaign there would be a responsibility on the British and Irish governments to 'find some means whereby the Sinn Féin tradition of republicanism can be fully represented at a conference table'.
            The IRA said it possessed 'the means and the will, not only to continue the struggle but to intensify it'. Subsequently an 800lb IRA bomb exploded in Bedford Street and a 500lb IRA bomb exploded in High Street, Belfast.
            McGuinness said Sinn Féin would 'make it as easy as possible' for the British government to get into talks with the party. Brooke said Sinn Féin could only become involved if there was a cessation of violence and not temporary ceasefires.
            A 5lb IRA bomb exploded in Whitehall Place, London.
            Eight Protestant workers were killed by an IRA bomb at Teebane, County Tyrone.
            Cahal Daly said Sinn Féin could expect no place in Irish politics while it was associated with the IRA. Adams said Teebane had been a 'horrific incident' and he denied any 'organic links' between Sinn Féin and the IRA.
            Haughey resigned and was succeeded as Taoiseach by Albert Reynolds.

February   An IRA spokesman said its campaign would cease only when it had secured a British declaration of intent to withdraw from NI.
            Loyalists killed five Catholics in a gun attack on a bookmaker's office on Belfast's Ormeau Road.
            The new Presbyterian moderator John Dunlop said there would have to be a proven, long-term commitment to peace before Sinn Féin could be allowed into talks.
            A Semtex bomb was defused near Downing Street after an IRA warning. Later in the month twenty-eight people were injured by an IRA bomb at London Bridge rail station, and another bomb was planted at the London office of the Crown Prosecution Service. Sinn Féin published *Towards a Lasting Peace in Ireland*. McGuinness said withdrawal had to come 'in consultation and cooperation' with Unionists.

1992

The chairman of the Ulster Bank, Sir George Quigley, said Ireland should become a one-island economy.

March   It was disclosed that senior Presbyterian ministers had met UDA leaders. Cahal Daly said there was no question of Catholic Church leaders talking to the IRA.

The IRA planted bombs at Tottenham, Wandsworth Common and Liverpool Street rail stations in London.

A 1,000lb IRA bomb devastated the centre of Lurgan, County Armagh.

A large bomb wrecked offices in Belfast city centre.

At the Fianna Fáil ard fheis Reynolds said that if Articles 2 and 3 were on the agenda for forthcoming renewed political talks so should the Government of Ireland Act.

Adams said a vote in the forthcoming British general election for Sinn Féin would be a vote for peace.

The IRA warned of a campaign in Britain: 'They haven't seen the half of it yet.'

Brooke confirmed that 'everything is on the table for talks'.

Launching Sinn Féin's election campaign Adams said the slogan of a ballot box in one hand, an Armalite in the other was outdated.

April   Presidential candidate Bill Clinton said he would lift the ban on Adams obtaining a visa to enter the US, and support the idea of a peace envoy if elected.

An IRA bomb attack on the Baltic Exchange area of the City of London killed three people and caused hundreds of millions of pounds' worth of damage. Another bomb damaged a flyover near Heathrow airport.

The Tories won the general election with a reduced majority. Adams lost his Westminster seat to the SDLP's Joe Hendron.

Sir Patrick Mayhew was appointed NI Secretary.

At an Easter commemoration Adams said if Major was 'prepared to grasp the nettle of his government's involvement in our country and sue for peace', republicans would assist him.

It emerged that Protestant churchmen had met Adams.

Political talks restarted at Stormont. A three-month gap in Anglo-Irish Conference meetings had been agreed.

May   More talks took place between Protestant churchmen and Sinn Féin representatives.

June   It was disclosed that Bishop Edward Daly had held two meetings in previous weeks with McGuinness and Mitchel McLaughlin. McGuinness called them 'useful and constructive'.

A policeman was killed by an IRA gunman as he carried out a routine vehicle check in Yorkshire, and a bomb was planted at the Royal Festival Hall. Later in the month, London Underground was briefly closed down by bomb hoaxes, and an IRA bomb in a hijacked taxi exploded in London's West End.

Sinn Féin's Jim Gibney said republicans accepted that British withdrawal would entail negotiations with all shades of opinion and would have to be preceded 'by a sustained period of peace'. In a later clarifying statement Gibney said a British declaration of a long-term intention to withdraw would mean conditions for peace could be speedily agreed.

July   A third meeting took place between Bishop Edward Daly and Sinn Féin representatives.

1992

Gibney said talks between Unionists and Dublin in the three-strand talks could be seen as 'historic landmarks'.

August   **Adams did not rule out a change in Sinn Féin's abstentionist attitude to a NI assembly.**
The UDA was proscribed after an increase in violence.
There were a number of arrests in London after the seizure of three vans, one carrying explosives.

September Mitchel McLaughlin said the republican movement 'cannot and should not ever try to coerce the Protestant people into a united Ireland'.
The IRA mounted a firebomb attack on the Hyde Park Hilton Hotel, London, and later in the month a 2,000lb IRA bomb wrecked the NI Forensic Science centre in Belfast, damaging 1,000 homes.
The DUP walked out of the political talks.
Former IRA Chief of Staff Seán MacStiofáin urged an IRA ceasefire.

October   Two IRA bombs exploded in central London. Further disruption was caused by IRA bombs at London Bridge and in the West End, at an underground station, at Southgate and outside Paddington Green police station, London. A man was killed by an IRA bomb in a bar in Covent Garden.
IRA bombs exploded at a hotel in Hammersmith and in the West End of London.
Five IRA bombs were found in London, one of them outside James Prior's flat, and another outside the Cabinet Office in Whitehall.

November **The political talks collapsed.**
A one-ton IRA van bomb outside Canary Wharf in London was defused.
A general election in the Republic led to a Fianna Fáil–Labour coalition.

December A 1,000lb IRA bomb in London's Tottenham Court Road was defused.
Further disruption was caused by two IRA bombs in Manchester city centre, and by a car bomb near a London tube station. Two bombs exploded in bins outside a north London shopping complex, and two IRA bombs were also found in Oxford Street.
In a speech at Coleraine Mayhew said he believed there were welcome signs of fresh thinking in some republican circles.
Adams in response to Mayhew said Sinn Féin's exclusion from the political process was 'undemocratic' and an 'obstacle to peace', adding that Britain should adopt a policy of ending partition.
The IRA announced a 72-hour Christmas ceasefire.
The UDA threatened the 'pan-nationalist front'.

1993
January   Mayhew called on the IRA to renounce violence and join in talks. Adams called Mayhew's speech propagandist and demanded immediate government talks with Sinn Féin.
Adams said there was now a new opportunity for peace in the wake of recent statements by Mayhew which he said might signal a change in the policy of not talking to Sinn Féin.
Cahal Daly predicted there could be peace 'by the end of the year'.

February The UDA attacked the homes of two Belfast SDLP councillors.
A gasworks was bombed at Warrington, and eighteen people were injured in an IRA explosion near Camden market in north London. Explosives were found near the home of Kenneth Clarke, the Home Secretary.

1993

March   **Two boys were killed in an IRA explosion in Warrington.**
A UDA attack killed four Catholics in Castlerock, County Londonderry.
Reynolds said he was ready to have peace talks with anyone. A spokesman
later said he meant only constitutional parties.
Hume called for an all-Ireland referendum on a blueprint for peace over the
heads of political leaders if necessary.

April   The IRA planted a bomb outside a Conservative club in central London.
After Adams was spotted entering Hume's home, it was revealed that talks
between the two had been going on in secret.
In newspaper articles Hume wrote: 'The IRA armed struggle [could be]
totally undermined by a simple declaration. The British government should
underline that the Irish people have the right to self-determination.'
**Reynolds said he was willing to talk to Sinn Féin if the IRA ended its
violence.**
Mayhew rejected joint sovereignty and stressed his desire to devolve wide
powers.
**In a joint statement Hume and Adams rejected any internal solution to
the conflict in the north. They also said they accepted that the Irish
people as a whole 'have the right to national self-determination' but
added, 'We both recognise that such a new agreement is only achievable
and viable if it can earn and enjoy the allegiance of the different
traditions on this island, by accommodating diversity and providing for
national reconciliation.' The statement was the trigger for a series of
media and political attacks on Hume, particularly in the Republic.
An IRA lorry bomb at Bishopsgate caused many millions of pounds'
worth of damage to the City of London financial district**. A journalist
was killed while trying to photograph the lorry.

May   Fine Gael leader John Bruton joined media and Unionist criticism of the
Hume–Adams talks.
Adams was refused a US visa.
Adams said the IRA demand for a British withdrawal was not aimed at
Protestants.
A 1,000lb IRA bomb exploded in central Belfast. The SDLP's Joe Hendron
said the Hume–Adams talks could not continue indefinitely if Adams did
not condemn IRA violence.
IRA bombs exploded in Portadown, County Armagh, in Magherafelt,
County Londonderry, and outside the Plaza hotel, Belfast. Hume said he
would have further talks with Adams despite IRA bombs.

June   **IRA bombs exploded at a gasometer at Gateshead in Tyneside,
destroying it, and at a petrol store depot in North Shields.
In a joint statement Hume and Adams said they had made progress
towards 'agreeing an overall strategy for lasting peace'.
President Mary Robinson visited west Belfast and shook hands with Adams.**
McGuinness said the initiation of a peace process 'requires a clear and
unambiguous indication from the British government that it accepts the
right of the Irish people to national self-determination'.

July   A security cordon was set up around the City of London to prevent IRA
attacks.

1993

A 1,500lb bomb exploded in the centre of Newtownards, County Down.
Republican News reported that the IRA had written to fifty heads of financial
institutions in the City of London warning of further attacks.
**Hume said he believed the IRA wanted to end its campaign and that
more talks with Adams were planned.**

August   The US ambassador to Dublin, Jean Kennedy-Smith, said a US peace envoy
was an 'option for the future'. Garret FitzGerald urged Hume to end talks
with Adams 'in the very near future' unless they yielded concrete results.
The IRA said that while it was ready for a 'meaningful peace process' it was
'equipped and utterly determined' to resist British policies.
The IRA planted a small bomb in the City of London.
It was revealed that former Irish diplomat Michael Lillis had held two
lengthy secret meetings with Adams in March.

September The IRA planted a 1,000lb bomb in the centre of Armagh.
A four-man US delegation arrived in Ireland for wide-ranging talks.
Hume said he didn't give 'two balls of roasted snow' what advice he was
given about talks with Adams.
Mallon said patience with continued IRA violence was 'finite'.
A meeting of the four SDLP MPs gave Hume their support.
The homes of Hendron and five SDLP councillors were firebombed by the
UDA.
**Hume and Adams announced they had reached agreement in their talks
and would submit their ideas in a report to Dublin for both governments
to consider.**
Unionist MP John Taylor said the Hume–Adams agreement could lead to
civil war.
Mayhew said it would be 'childish' for the British government not to look at
any report on Hume–Adams submitted by Dublin. There would have to be a
total cessation of violence for Sinn Féin to win a place at the conference
table.
The UDA threatened to step up attacks on the SDLP.
McGuinness said, 'The end of the process for us means a British withdrawal
from Ireland at some stage in the future.'
The IRA planted two 300lb and 500lb bombs in Belfast.
Mayhew said the only unit for self-determination was Northern Ireland.

October   Taylor called for a 'pan-Unionist front' to put pressure on the British
government.
Republican Sinn Féin President Ruairí Ó Brádaigh described the Hume–
Adams initiative as a 'proposed surrender'.
Major said the only message the IRA could send was that it had finished with
violence for good.
Mayhew demanded an unconditional end to IRA violence and ruled out the
notion of Britain 'persuading' Unionists to accept Irish unity. He said Sinn
Féin could only be involved in talks after IRA had ended violence and a
'sufficient period' had shown this was 'for real'.
Orange Order leader the Reverend Martin Smyth said that if there was
'convincing proof' the IRA had ended its campaign Sinn Féin could be
admitted to political talks.
IRA prisoners expressed support for the Hume–Adams talks.

1993

UUP leader James Molyneaux said that Sinn Féin would have to be 'quarantined' for five years after the IRA ended its campaign before being allowed to join talks.

Molyneaux met Major to express opposition to the Hume–Adams talks.

An IRA attempt to bomb UDA HQ on Belfast's Shankill Road killed nine Protestant civilians and an IRA bomber.

Adams was condemned for carrying the coffin of Thomas Begley, the IRA member killed in the Shankill explosion.

The IRA planted a bomb on a railway line in Berkshire.

Adams said that he would be able to persuade the IRA to end its campaign if the British responded positively to the Hume–Adams initiative.

Tánaiste Dick Spring stated six principles for progress on the north.

In a joint communiqué the British and Irish governments rejected the Hume–Adams initiative and renewed their support for the three-strand inter-party talks.

The UDA killed seven people in the Greysteel pub massacre, bringing to thirteen the number killed by loyalists since the Shankill bomb.

November   Citing the views of the Taoiseach in support, Major ruled out the Hume–Adams initiative. Speaking in the Commons, he told Hume it was 'not the right way to proceed'.

Paisley and Molyneaux held separate talks with Major. Molyneaux later said he was convinced Major was not going to be involved in any sort of secret deal on Hume–Adams.

A DUP blueprint for the government of NI was criticised for failing to acknowledge nationalist interests.

Mayhew said there had been no negotiations with Sinn Féin.

Major pledged that it would be for the people of NI alone to determine their constitutional future. He also said, 'We are ready to respond to a cessation of violence.'

McGuinness said he had been involved in 'protracted contact and dialogue' with the British government.

Hume and Adams issued a joint statement reaffirming their commitment to their peace initiative and saying they would explore ways of advancing it. Dublin government sources later described this as unhelpful.

A large haul of explosives and weaponry bound for the UVF was seized at Teeside docks.

The British government was presented with an Irish paper on the framework for peace.

Details were revealed of secret contacts between the British government and the IRA. These included a proposal for a two-week IRA ceasefire accompanied by delegate talks.

At a Stormont press conference Mayhew denied official contact and claimed that intermediaries 'in a chain of communication' had been activated because the IRA had sent a message that the 'conflict is over' and that they needed British advice on how to bring it to a close.

Mayhew claimed there was a difference between talking to the IRA and sending them documents.

Adams denied that such an IRA message was sent and claimed Major authorised the contacts.

The DUP called for Mayhew's resignation.

1993

Mayhew released the British government's version of the secret IRA–government contacts.

Paisley was suspended from the House of Commons after calling Mayhew a liar. At a press conference in Belfast Sinn Féin released some of their own documents and again denied Mayhew's claim that the IRA had sent a message of surrender.

December **Reynolds confirmed that 'the right to national self-determination based on consent freely given, north and south', was one element in the peace process being developed.**

Mayhew admitted to twenty-two errors in the version of the secret IRA–government talks which he had lodged in the Commons library.

Mayhew told the Commons that Britain 'would not join the ranks of the persuaders' for Irish unity.

Sinn Féin released a sheaf of documents detailing republican talks with British officials.

An IRA sniper killed a soldier in Keady, County Armagh. Subsequently 1,000 people attended a memorial service. Later in the month the IRA planted a bomb on a rail line near Woking, Surrey.

Reynolds said he was not seeking self-determination 'in Ireland as a whole collected in a single entity. There will be no change in Northern Ireland without a change of opinions there.'

The Combined Loyalist Military Command stated six principles which it said had to underpin any settlement.

Adams said: 'The Six Counties cannot have a right to self-determination. That is a matter for the Irish people as a whole to be exercised without impediment. However the shape of a future Ireland is a matter to be determined by all groups in Ireland obviously including the Unionists.'

The Downing Street Declaration was signed in London by Major and Reynolds. It included a commitment that the people of NI would decide its future and a demand that the IRA permanently renounce violence. Reynolds received a standing ovation in the Dáil.

Mayhew said any post-ceasefire talks with Sinn Féin would have to discuss the surrender of IRA arms.

Adams called for 'clarification' by Dublin of the Downing Street Declaration. The IRA planted two bombs on a Surrey rail line.

Major insisted that the Downing Street Declaration was not about undermining the Union or leading to joint authority.

Adams called for clarification via unconditional talks between the two governments and Sinn Féin.

US president Bill Clinton welcomed the Downing Street Declaration and said the question of an Adams visa was kept under review.

The IRA announced a three-day ceasefire.

McGuinness said: 'The political situation hasn't developed to a position where Sinn Féin can use its influence to end attacks on the British Crown forces'.

Douglas Hurd said the IRA could 'expect no quarter' if it rejected the Downing Street Declaration.

1994

January   IRA firebombs damaged eleven Belfast stores.

Mayhew said that troop withdrawals would happen after a ceasefire but the UK would not be a persuader for a particular constitutional outcome.

1994

Adams wrote to Major seeking clarification of the Downing Street Declaration.

Mayhew turned down the demand for clarification saying it would amount to negotiation.

Reynolds said he would continue to clarify the declaration for Sinn Féin.

The Reynolds government lifted the broadcasting ban on Sinn Féin.

Adams said he could not move until the British clarified the declaration.

Major told Hume the declaration spoke for itself.

Adams said he would not accept a ceasefire as a precondition for involvement in talks.

Clinton, against strong British advice, granted a visa to Adams.

Adams arrived in New York on a three-day visa to address a foreign relations conference.

February   US Vice-president Al Gore urged Adams to accept the Downing Street Declaration and reject violence. Adams addressed 1,500 people at the New York Plaza.

Reynolds said he had given enough clarification. Mayhew said if there was no IRA response in 'a very few weeks' the government would know what conclusions to draw.

Spring said there could be no minimalist internal solution and that everything must be on the table.

Mayhew ruled out a purely internal settlement. He said the British government would not be persuaders for Irish unity.

Major repeated Brooke's British neutrality formula on NI.

Former INLA leader Dominic McGlinchey was shot dead in a revenge killing.

March   **The IRA launched mortar attacks on Heathrow airport. None exploded.**

Adams said of the Heathrow mortars that every now and again there had to be something 'spectacular' to remind people of the conflict. Spring said the IRA's credit was running very low.

Adams said every side to the conflict had to accept democratic compromise.

The IRA called a three-day ceasefire. Adams said the ceasefire 'did not come easily'.

April   Cardinal Daly and Hume supported Sinn Féin's call for clarification.

Mayhew said ending the conflict did not require surrender.

The IRA killed an alleged drug dealer and attacked sixteen other people. In previous days a wave of IRA attacks had left three dead.

Reacting to the attacks Reynolds questioned the good faith of republicans.

Reynolds and Mayhew urged Sinn Féin to spell out what they wanted to be clarified.

May   Sinn Féin gave Reynolds a list of questions on the Downing Street Declaration to pass on to the British. The British government said Sinn Féin need not accept the declaration in full to participate in talks. The British government responded to Sinn Féin's demand for clarification by issuing a lengthy document.

June   **Spring said there would have to be a handover of IRA guns following a ceasefire.**

The crash of a Chinook helicopter on the Mull of Kintyre in Scotland killed twenty-five senior RUC officers, members of army intelligence and MI5 officers.

1994

Hume finished just behind Paisley in the European elections. Sinn Féin won 9.9 per cent of the vote.

The INLA attacked three loyalists on the Shankill Road, killing one and fatally injuring the two others.

Six Catholics were killed in a loyalist attack on a Loughinisland, County Down, pub.

Reynolds said that cross-border institutions with executive powers would be a *quid pro quo* for changes to Articles 2 and 3.

The government announced that forty IRA prisoners would be transferred from Britain to NI prisons.

July   Two tons of IRA explosives were found on a lorry at Heysham.

The CLMC said it would respond positively to an IRA ceasefire.

Mayhew called for the 'clear abandonment' of Articles 2 and 3.

The Libyan Foreign Minister said Libya would not supply the IRA with more weapons.

An IRA arms cache was found near Athboy, County Meath. It included twenty-four AK-47 rifles, a flamethrower, 30,000 rounds of ammunition, 300 magazines and detonators.

The IRA killed three loyalists and bombed three loyalist pubs in Belfast.

August   Adams confirmed a report that he had met the IRA leadership to discuss a ceasefire and was 'guardedly optimistic'.

A part-time soldier was shot dead by the IRA in his butcher's shop in Crossgar, County Down. He was the last security force fatality caused by the IRA before their ceasefire.

The Reverend Martin Smyth said a termination of IRA violence and the handover of weapons would mean that Unionists would have to 'learn to deal' with Sinn Féin.

An American delegation arrived for talks with Sinn Féin and other bodies.

Hume and Adams issued a joint statement affirming 'the right of the Irish people as a whole to national self-determination' by agreement.

The IRA called a 'complete cessation' of its campaign. Major called for evidence that it was permanent. Reynolds said the campaign was over 'for good' and that he would swiftly recognise Sinn Féin's mandate.

September   *Republican News* referred to the ceasefire as 'a suspension' of operations.

Reynolds, Hume and Adams met at Government Buildings in Dublin and shook hands publicly, afterwards saying they were 'totally and absolutely committed to peaceful and democratic methods'.

Major walked out of a Downing Street meeting with Paisley after the DUP leader refused to accept his word that there was no deal with Sinn Féin and the IRA.

Soldiers began to patrol without helmets.

The CLMC issued six conditions for a loyalist ceasefire including an assurance that the IRA ceasefire was permanent and that the constitutional position of NI was not in danger.

Taylor said he thought the IRA ceasefire was 'for real'.

A UVF bomb on the Belfast–Dublin train partially exploded in Connolly station, Dublin.

Major said the IRA had to say it had abandoned violence 'for good'.

The Clinton White House lifted its ban on contacts with Sinn Féin.

Major lifted the broadcasting ban on Sinn Féin and promised a referendum on the outcome of any negotiations. Ten border crossings were reopened.

1994

Reynolds promised referendums north and south.
Reynolds said achievement of Irish unity would take at least twenty years.
McGuinness expressed 'surprise and disappointment'.
Major ruled out an amnesty for paramilitary prisoners.
Major said exploratory talks with Sinn Féin could begin around Christmas if republicans indicated that they intended to give up violence for good.
Mayhew said IRA arms would feature in the discussion.
Adams was given a visa for a second trip to the US.
McGuinness said the word 'permanent' was not in the republican vocabulary.
The European Socialist Group in the European Parliament nominated Hume for the Nobel peace prize.

October
McGuinness told ex-prisoners that Sinn Féin would 'settle for nothing less than the objectives for which so many republicans and others have died'.
Reynolds called for an early army withdrawal to barracks, phased prisoner releases and an acceptable policing system in NI.
Mitchel McLaughlin said the Irish people would have the right to continue the conflict if the present conditions persisted.
Spring said Sinn Féin should be allowed to enter talks before the IRA handed in weapons and explosives.
The RUC patrolled in west Belfast unaccompanied by soldiers. Reynolds urged the British to speed up their response to the ceasefire.
Declaring the Union to be safe, the CLMC declared a loyalist ceasefire. They offered 'the loved ones of all innocent victims over the past 25 years abject and true remorse'.
Speaking in Belfast, Major said it was now his government's 'working assumption' that the IRA intended the ceasefire to be permanent. He lifted orders excluding Adams and McGuinness from Britain and announced the reopening of border roads.
Troops were withdrawn from street patrolling in Londonderry and County Tyrone towns. In Belfast, the RUC patrolled without flak jackets.
The Forum for Peace and Reconciliation set up by Reynolds opened in Dublin Castle. Its members included both constitutional nationalists and Sinn Féin.

November
The Clinton administration announced an aid package for NI.
Newry post office worker Frank Kerr was killed by the IRA during an armed robbery. The IRA said its 31 August ceasefire statement stood. Adams expressed 'shock and regret' while McGuinness described the incident as 'very wrong'. The release of nine IRA prisoners in the Republic was suspended. Reynolds resigned as Taoiseach and leader of Fianna Fáil. Bertie Ahern was elected as new leader of Fianna Fáil.

December
The British government announced that exploratory dialogue with Sinn Féin would begin on 7 December. Clinton appointed George Mitchell as his economic envoy to NI.
Adams said it was unlikely weapons would be decommissioned 'short of a political settlement'.
The first official meeting took place between British government officials and Sinn Féin.
Decommissioning of arms was identified as a major stumbling block. Acting Taoiseach Albert Reynolds said it was not 'a sensible precondition' to require the IRA to hand in weapons before multilateral talks.

1994

Major said 'huge progress' would have to be made towards the destruction of IRA arms before exploratory talks with Sinn Féin could become formal.

Fine Gael leader John Bruton was elected Taoiseach in a coalition involving Labour and Democratic Left. Delegations from the PUP and UDP met Stormont officials.

Bruton and Adams met and shook hands.

In what was seen as a policy reversal, Bruton said it was important not to get into a standoff over IRA arms.

A second meeting took place at Stormont between Sinn Féin and the NIO.

Sinn Féin said the question of IRA weapons was best addressed at all-party talks. After meeting Bruton at Downing Street, Major said 'substantial progress' was required on IRA weapons. Bruton cautioned against a one-item agenda.

Forty-six mortars were discovered by Gardaí outside Longford.

Nine postponed prison releases in the south went ahead.

Major said Sinn Féin promises on arms would not be enough: there had to be 'significant progress' before the British and other parties would join Sinn Féin at the talks table. McGuinness called this 'ludicrous'.

1995

January	It was announced that daytime army patrols in Belfast would end.
	The NIO announced the end of the ban on ministers meeting Sinn Féin, the UDP and PUP.
	The NIO announced that weapons decommissioning was not a precondition to Sinn Féin participation in talks.
February	The Irish government released another five IRA prisoners.
	A meeting between NIO officials and Sinn Féin at Stormont was called off after the party claimed the room was bugged.
	The document *Frameworks for the Future* was released by the two governments.
March	**Mayhew outlined conditions for Sinn Féin joining all-party talks, including 'actual decommissioning of some arms'.**
	The British government criticised Clinton's invitation to Adams to attend a St Patrick's Day reception.
	The UUP rejected the framework document.
	UDP representatives attended the Clinton St Patrick's Day reception and met officials of the US administration.
	The UUP's ruling council re-elected Molyneaux, but 15 per cent of votes cast went to a largely unknown 'stalking horse' candidate.
	Ancram met the UDP and PUP.
April	SDLP, UUP and DUP leaders met in preparation for a new round of inter-party talks.
May	**Mayhew met Adams in Washington during Clinton's economic conference.**
	Prince Charles paid a two-day visit to the Republic.
June	Sinn Féin pulled out of talks with the government.
	The RUC again rerouted an Orange march away from Belfast's lower Ormeau Road.

1995

July   Private Lee Clegg, imprisoned for shooting dead a teenage girl travelling in a stolen car, was released after serving four years of a life sentence.
Widespread rioting followed in many nationalist areas.
A confrontation developed when the RUC prevented Orangemen from marching along Portadown's Garvaghy Road. Trouble followed in other loyalist areas.
The RUC subsequently permitted the Orange march to go down the Garvaghy Road despite the protests of nationalist residents. Paisley and Trimble celebrated the success by walking together through crowds of cheering supporters.
A heavy RUC presence pushed an Orange march through the Ormeau Road.
Hume said the IRA would 'get rid' of its weapons if Sinn Féin were included in talks.
Mayhew and Ancram met Adams and McGuinness.

August   Reynolds said weapons decommissioning had not been a major British demand in the talks which led to the Downing Street Declaration.
Adams said republicans were ready to make 'critical compromises' to achieve peace.
The CLMC said it would not initiate a return to violence.
Molyneaux announced his resignation as UUP leader.

September Adams and Mayhew met but the stalemate over talks and weapons decommissioning remained unresolved.
Trimble was elected leader of the UUP, defeating Taylor, Ken Maginnis and others.
Mayhew met UDP and PUP representatives.

October   Trimble met Bruton in Dublin.
Mayhew told the Conservative party conference that the two governments were considering inviting an international commission to help resolve the decommissioning dispute.
At the UUP conference Trimble announced outline plans to end the Orange Order's block of delegates to the party council.

November Trimble met Clinton in Washington.
The NIO published a paper, *Building Blocks*. It proposed all-party preparatory talks and an international body to consider decommissioning.
New legislation came into effect restoring 50 per cent remission on sentences other than life sentences.
A referendum in the south narrowly confirmed the right to divorce.
The twin-track initiative launched preparatory talks as well as an International Body to examine decommissioning.
Clinton shook hands with Adams during a visit to Belfast in which the US president was greeted by large cheering crowds.

December The British and Irish governments sent separate talks invitations to the NI parties.
It was announced that Belfast's Crumlin Road prison was to close.
Robinson said that Sinn Féin could not be admitted to talks before the surrender of all weapons.
Direct Action Against Drugs, believed to be an IRA cover name, claimed the killing of an alleged drugs dealer in Belfast. It was one in a series of such shootings.

1996

January   The IRA killed a man in Lurgan using the DAAD cover name.

The NI Tourist Board reported that the number of tourist visitors in 1995 had been 68 per cent higher than in 1994.

British and Irish ministers met Sinn Féin leaders at Stormont.

The Mitchell Commission recommended that talks and weapons decommissioning should occur in parallel. In response Major announced plans for elections in NI. This was strongly criticised by the Irish government and the SDLP.

February   The Irish government proposed proximity talks in which the various delegations would meet ministers but not each other.

The IRA ceasefire ended after eighteen months with the bombing of London's Canary Wharf district, killing two men and causing enormous damage.

The Irish government suspended ministerial meetings with Sinn Féin and halted the release of IRA prisoners.

An IRA member died when a bomb he was carrying exploded prematurely on a London bus. Eight people were injured.

Hume and Adams met members of the IRA Army Council.

Major and Bruton announced that talks would start on 10 June to decide the format of the proposed elections. Sinn Féin would be excluded in the absence of a ceasefire.

March   The UUP and DUP said they would not attend talks which included Dick Spring.

The SDLP, Alliance and UDP met Mayhew and Spring for talks. Sinn Féin was barred from entering them.

The Irish and British governments disagreed on the election method for the proposed NI forum.

An IRA spokesman told *Republican News* there would be no decommissioning before a final settlement.

The NI Police Authority published its recommendations on changes to the RUC. There should be no change to the name, uniform, oath or centralised structure but the name 'RUC – Northern Ireland's police service' could be printed on letterheads, it suggested.

The Irish Forum for Peace and Reconciliation was adjourned pending a future ceasefire.

April   Loyalists rioted after the RUC blocked another Orange march on the Ormeau Road.

An IRA bomb failed to detonate under London's Hammersmith Bridge.

May   **Elections took place to the new NI Forum. An IRA statement said there would be no decommissioning in advance of an overall political settlement. The Irish and British governments announced details of multi-party talks.**

June   **Major and Bruton opened preliminary all-party talks at Stormont chaired by Mitchell but without Sinn Féin. The DUP at first refused to accept Mitchell as chairman.**

The NI Forum met for the first time in Belfast.

200 people were injured when a large IRA bomb exploded in Manchester.

Irish police found an IRA bomb factory in County Laois and arrested five men. The Irish government ended all contacts with Sinn Féin.

1996

Three mortar bombs were fired by the IRA at a British army base in Germany.

July **Orangemen were prevented from marching along Garvaghy Road at Drumcree, Portadown. A Catholic taxi driver was shot dead near Lurgan. Four days of loyalist roadblocks and disturbances ensued.**
The UUP, DUP and others withdrew from the talks in protest at the ban on the Drumcree march. Loyalist rioting and disruption were widespread.
The RUC reversed the Drumcree ban and forced the march down Garvaghy Road. Rioting followed in nationalist areas.
The RUC sealed off the lower Ormeau Road to allow an Orange march. Rioting intensified in nationalist areas.
The SDLP announced its intention to withdraw from the NI Forum.
Mayhew announced a review of marches in NI as disputes over parade routes escalated in many places.

August Ronnie Flanagan was named as the new RUC Chief Constable, succeeding Sir Hugh Annesley.

September A sixth INLA member was killed in the internal feud which had broken out in January.
The NI Forum resumed in the absence of the SDLP and Sinn Féin. Members voted to fly the Union flag while the Forum was in session.
Loyalists began picketing Catholic church services, particularly in County Antrim, in retaliation for nationalist protests against Orange parades.
An IRA man was killed and five men were arrested in police raids in London. Arms and explosives were found.

October An IRA bomb attack on army headquarters in Lisburn, County Antrim, fatally injured a soldier. It was the first IRA bomb in NI since 1994.

November The congregation at a Catholic church at Harryville, Ballymena, was attacked by loyalists.

December An RUC officer was shot and wounded by the IRA at the Royal Victoria Hospital, Belfast, as he protected DUP politician Nigel Dodds who was visiting his terminally ill son.

1997
January There was disruption in Belfast as a result of twenty bomb alerts.
The DUP attempted to have the loyalist parties excluded from the talks.
The IRA fired mortar bombs at an RUC patrol in Downpatrick.
The committee reviewing the marching issue recommended the creation of an independent parades commission.

February Ken Maginnis called on the government to apologise for the Bloody Sunday deaths.
Bombardier Stephen Restorick was killed by the IRA in south Armagh.
Mayhew ruled out either an apology for or inquiry into Bloody Sunday.

March Orange halls were firebombed in several places.

April Adams said a vote for Sinn Féin was a vote for peace.

May **The general election put Labour and Tony Blair in 10 Downing Street. It also returned Adams as MP for West Belfast and McGuinness as MP for Mid Ulster.**
Blair named Mo Mowlam as NI Secretary.

1997

Catholic Robert Hamill was beaten to death by loyalists in Portadown.
An RUC officer was shot dead in Belfast by the INLA.
Blair visited Northern Ireland and gave the go-ahead for exploratory contacts between government officials and Sinn Féin.

June
An RUC officer was beaten to death by a loyalist mob in Ballymoney, County Antrim.
Sinn Féin was barred from entering the resumed inter-party talks at Stormont. The Loyalist Volunteer Force and Continuity Army Council were banned.
A general election in the Republic led to the creation of a coalition between Fianna Fáil and the Progressive Democrats led by Bertie Ahern.
The Queen visited NI.
Two RUC officers were shot dead in Lurgan.
The governments tabled proposals for weapons decommissioning.

July
Adams announced that he had asked the IRA for a new ceasefire. A few days later the IRA announced another cessation.
Mowlam met Garvaghy Road residents and Orange leaders in advance of the annual confrontation over the Drumcree Orange parade.
The RUC decision to force the march down the Garvaghy Road led to days of rioting in nationalist areas across NI.
A teenage Catholic girl was shot dead at the home of her Protestant boyfriend in Aghalee, County Antrim.
The DUP withdrew from talks.
Ahern, Hume and Adams met in Dublin and reaffirmed a commitment to 'exclusively democratic and peaceful methods'.
A Northern Ireland select committee of the Commons was set up.

August
Mowlam met a Sinn Féin delegation.
Sinn Féin leaders were granted US visas for a fundraising trip.
Gardaí found an IRA bomb factory in County Cavan.
An Independent Commission on Decommissioning, headed by Canadian General John de Chastelain, was established to oversee the weapons issue.
Mowlam pronounced the IRA ceasefire sufficient to allow Sinn Féin to join talks.

September
Sinn Féin signed up to the Mitchell Principles of non-violence and entered all-party talks. The IRA later said it had 'problems' with the principles.
The UUP's ruling council left decisions on the talks to Trimble and his colleagues.
A bomb planted by the dissident republican Continuity IRA in Markethill, County Armagh, caused widespread damage.
The Ulster Unionists joined the talks, emphasising that they wanted to 'confront' Sinn Féin not negotiate with them. Party members walked into the talks accompanied by PUP and UDP delegations.
After some dispute the two governments agreed on the composition of the international decommissioning body to be chaired by de Chastelain.
The first in a series of DUP rallies was held in the Ulster Hall.

October
McGuinness said Sinn Féin was 'going to the negotiating table to smash the Union'.

1997

Substantive negotiations began at Stormont with the participation of eight parties and the two governments. Irish Foreign Minister Ray Burke resigned and was replaced by David Andrews.

Andrews said that he imagined a united Ireland in his lifetime 'won't be achievable'.

The Police Authority invited Sinn Féin to talks.

Adams and McGuinness met Blair for the first time at Stormont's Castle Buildings. Hours later the prime minister was mobbed by an angry crowd of loyalists at a shopping centre in east Belfast.

Mary McAleese was elected Irish president, the first to have been born in NI.

November   Flanagan said the IRA ceasefire was 'holding firm'. Security forces reduced patrolling, particularly by the army. Troops were withdrawn from west Belfast.

December   **Adams and McGuinness made their first visit to Downing Street.**
The Stormont talks were adjourned for Christmas, the parties having failed to reach agreement on an agenda.

UUP MP Jeffrey Donaldson said he was advising party leader Trimble to withdraw from the talks because of the 'concessions train'. Four UUP MPs wrote to Trimble expressing their concern over UUP participation.

LVF leader Billy 'King Rat' Wright was shot dead in the Maze prison by the INLA. In the resulting upsurge of violence seven Catholics and a Protestant were shot dead. The LVF was blamed for many of the killings, though there was suspicion of mainstream loyalist and IRA involvement.

1998

January   **Mowlam visited the Maze prison to persuade UDA inmates not to turn against the peace process.**
Sinn Féin formally rejected the two governments' new proposals for a settlement.

The IRA rejected the Anglo-Irish proposals, accusing the governments of giving in to Unionist demands. Ulster Unionists warned that if the government backtracked on the proposals they would withdraw from the talks.

Flanagan said he believed the UDA had been involved in recent killings, putting pressure on the PM to review the place of the UDA's political allies, the Ulster Democratic Party, in the Stormont talks.

A bomb planted by the Continuity IRA exploded outside a nightclub in Enniskillen, County Fermanagh.

The talks moved to London for a week. **The UDP was temporarily excluded because of UDA violence.**

Blair announced a new inquiry under Lord Saville into the Bloody Sunday deaths.

The LVF announced that it would continue to target 'known republicans'.

February   An alleged drugs dealer was shot dead outside a south Belfast restaurant. The IRA was believed responsible.

A UDA member was shot dead in Dunmurry, south Belfast, where another UDA man had been killed weeks earlier. Republicans were blamed for the shooting, and there were calls for Sinn Féin to be thrown out of the talks.

Adams insisted the IRA ceasefire was intact. He warned that the peace process would fail if Sinn Féin were expelled.

Sinn Féin was suspended from the talks because of Flanagan's assessment that the IRA had been involved in recent killings.

1998

A car bomb which damaged the village of Moira, County Down, was blamed on the Continuity IRA.

A Sinn Féin challenge to this expulsion in the Irish courts was unsuccessful.

A large car bomb caused widespread damage in Portadown.

March

Taylor said the 'general picture' of an agreement was coming together. A settlement in weeks was possible, Mowlam said.

A 600lb bomb was found in County Louth.

European Commission President Jacques Santer visited NI and promised European aid for peace efforts.

Two men were shot dead by the LVF in a bar in Poyntzpass, County Armagh.

Irish minister Liz O'Donnell said Articles 2 and 3 would be 'amended not dropped'.

Mowlam said: 'Agreement is within reach.'

Ahern said there was nothing to fear from change in the Irish constitution.

An LVF statement warned of more violence and specifically threatened 'collaborators'.

Sinn Féin called for a meeting with Blair before deciding to return to talks.

Mortar bombs were fired in Armagh.

Two men were charged with the Poyntzpass killings.

The SDLP met Blair in Downing Street. Hume said a deal must be done soon. Subsequently a joint government paper on British–Irish relations was released to the parties.

Blair met Adams at Downing Street in an attempt to get the peace process back on track. Blair said agreement was 'agonisingly close' and that he was 'stubbornly optimistic', but Paisley, speaking to the Chamber of Commerce, accused them of paying ransom to terrorism. He said the talks were 'dead in the water'. Clinton pledged a push for peace.

The UUP repeated its demand for the continued exclusion of Sinn Féin.

Mowlam said NI was 'on the brink of an historic opportunity', and there were widespread reports that Blair would take charge of the final stage of talks.

One of four men awaiting trial for the Poyntzpass killings was killed in the Maze prison by LVF prisoners.

Trimble and Adams attended a British embassy lunch in Washington.

Mowlam told a US media breakfast that she was unsure if Sinn Féin would settle. 'Do it now,' said Clinton.

There was Unionist anger when Sinn Féin announced that it would return to the talks.

A 1200lb bomb was found in Dundalk. Gardaí said it was intended for an attack in NI, probably by dissident republicans.

Adams said a deal was possible in three weeks and said he wanted Sinn Féin to be part of it.

Mitchell released a paper on north–south relations.

Talks resumed and Sinn Féin returned, Paisley demonstrating outside the gates.

After the talks resumed Mitchell set a deadline of 9 April for agreement, saying: 'The time for discussion is over. It is now time for decision.'

Ahern reassured Fianna Fáil backbenchers that constitutional change would only be as part of a balanced deal, and said there would be no deal without Sinn Féin.

1998

Mitchell said talks could succeed by 9 May.
An intense round of bilateral party meetings took place at Stormont.

April

Ahern said there were 'large disagreements' with London over the powers of cross-border bodies, adding, 'I don't think we can cloak that fact. I don't know whether we can surmount this.' The two governments and Trimble took part in intensive negotiations.
Mowlam said there would have to be reform of the RUC.
Gardaí found a huge fertiliser bomb in a car bound for Britain from a port near Dublin.
Ahern said: 'The Irish government will not be moving any further. David Trimble would need to understand that my compromises are completed. The Framework Document is what has to stand.'
Mitchell released a sixty-two-page draft document, asking the parties to observe complete secrecy over its contents.
An Adams newspaper article said history could be made but the deal would be 'transitional'. Paisley said the UUP was selling out, while Sinn Féin admitted there had been twelve protest resignations from its ranks.

7 April

The UUP rejected as 'too green' the draft from Mitchell, creating an air of crisis. The party said the Mitchell paper amounted to a 'Sinn Féin wish list'. Adams said it was time for Trimble to 'grow up and negotiate properly'. Within hours Blair announced he was flying to Belfast. On his arrival he said, 'I feel the hand of history upon our shoulders.'

8 April

Ahern arrived at Stormont for a series of meetings before returning to Dublin for his mother's funeral then flying back to Belfast. At Stormont he said: 'It requires everybody to move a little bit and we are all prepared to do that.' Meanwhile intense activity continued between the governments and parties.
Mowlam ended the day on an optimistic note, saying progress had been made 'on all fronts'.
The PUP's David Ervine described the Mitchell paper as 'unacceptable, unreasonable, unworkable'. His colleague Billy Hutchinson said, 'We are talking about people going back to war.'
Paisley arrived at Stormont in mid-afternoon and said: 'No matter what happens at these talks there is not going to be peace, there is going to be war.'
Four UUP MPs congratulated the party for rejecting the document, saying it 'cannot be amended to make it acceptable to the Unionist electorate'.

9 April

Blair spoke of an 'irresistible force' which he believed would overcome the 'immovable object' of conflict.
The midnight deadline passed with no deal.
Flanagan said: 'If there is a settlement it will undoubtedly have a very significant and positive effect' but added that it would not mean an immediate end to violence.
At 6 p.m. Trimble went to party headquarters to brief the party executive and received backing in a two-hour meeting.
At 8 p.m. PUP representative William Smith went to the Maze prison to brief loyalist prisoners.
Paisley repeated that Trimble would be 'finished' as a Unionist leader. He gave a stormy midnight press conference where he was heckled by PUP and UDP members who shouted, 'Your days are over, dinosaur.'
Clinton telephoned the participants at regular intervals through the night.

1998

10 April   There was an apparent breakthrough at about 2 a.m. as the UUP and the SDLP resolved differences. At 2.30 a.m. Clinton spoke to Adams. At 3 a.m. Taylor put the chances of an agreement being reached at 75 per cent. A Blair letter was provided to reassure UUP members on decommissioning. This had been requested by Trimble in the face of opposition from colleagues. Trimble reportedly told colleagues: 'I am doing it.' At 4.45 p.m. Trimble telephoned Blair and Mitchell to inform them.
Jeffrey Donaldson withdrew, leaving Stormont before the speeches.
Former UVF prisoner Gusty Spence said the parties were now 'exorcising the ghosts of history'.
Trimble said: 'The question now for Mr Adams is will he accept the consent principle and also to say whether his dirty, squalid little terrorist war is over.'
Mitchell announced the agreement to a plenary session of the party delegations and through television to the NI public: 'If you support this agreement, and if you also reject the merchants of death and the purveyors of hate, if you make it clear to your political leaders that you want them to make it work, then it will. The choice is yours. I am dying to leave, but I hate to go.'
Trimble said it was 'a great opportunity to start a healing process. I have risen from this table with the Union stronger than when I sat down.'
The Queen congratulated Blair by phone on the deal. A statement from Buckingham Palace on behalf of the Queen said: 'Naturally she shares everyone's delight at the outcome.' Paisley protested at the royal support for the agreement.
Robinson said it was 'a turbo-charged model of Sunningdale, the Anglo-Irish Agreement with a vengeance, a fully armed version of the Framework Document'.

11 April   Trimble received UUP executive backing by 55 votes to 23 after a four-hour meeting.

13 April   The Pope told an audience at his summer residence outside Rome: 'I wish to invite you to thank God for the positive results reached in recent days in Northern Ireland.'

16 April   Trimble said the Good Friday Agreement was 'as good as it gets'.

18 April   The UUP ruling council supported the agreement by 540 votes to 210.

24 April   The NI Forum met for the last time.

26 April   Ahern said the British government was 'effectively out of the equation' on the future of NI.

27 April   Former Hong Kong governor Chris Patten was named as chairman of the Independent Commission on Policing.

30 April   The IRA said it had no plans to decommission.

May   UUP MP William Thompson called on Trimble to resign.
A special Sinn Féin ard fheis voted overwhelmingly to support the agreement and allow members to take seats in the assembly. The presence of some members of the Balcombe Street gang, who had served long sentences for a 1970s bombing campaign in London, provoked a Unionist outcry.
The agreement was approved in referendums on both sides of the border. In NI 71.1 per cent voted in favour. In the Republic, 94.4 per cent backed the agreement, in addition voting to drop the state's

1998

constitutional claim to the north. An exit poll in NI suggested that 96 per cent of Catholics and 55 per cent of Protestants voted yes.

June   The IRA's leader in the Maze prison was quoted as saying that after arrangements outlined in the agreement came into effect, 'a voluntary decommissioning of weapons would be a natural development of the peace process'.

In elections to the new assembly, supporters of the deal won eighty seats and opponents won twenty-eight.

The Parades Commission announced that the Orange Order would not be allowed to march along Garvaghy Road, Portadown, in July.

July   **The assembly met for the first time. Trimble was elected First Minister designate and the SDLP's Séamus Mallon was elected Deputy First Minister designate.**

Ten Catholic churches across NI were attacked.

Days of rioting, roadblocks and disturbances followed the ban on the Orange march at Drumcree.

In a loyalist arson attack in Ballymoney, County Antrim, three young Catholic children were killed.

The legislation allowing for the early release of prisoners under the Good Friday Agreement came into force.

August   A Real IRA bomb damaged the centre of Banbridge, County Down.

The LVF announced a ceasefire. The organisation had not been included in the early release scheme.

A Real IRA car bomb in Omagh killed 29 people. It was the single deadliest attack of the troubles.

The Real IRA announced a ceasefire.

The INLA announced a ceasefire.

September Sinn Féin said it considered violence to be a thing of the past. McGuinness was nominated to talk to the arms decommissioning body.

Blair and Clinton travelled to Omagh to view the scene of the explosion and meet some of the relatives of the dead.

Clinton and Blair also met assembly members at Stormont.

Trimble promised to create a 'pluralist parliament for a pluralist people'.

Ahern suggested that a timetable should be established for the handover of weapons.

October   RUC officer Frank O'Reilly died as a result of injuries caused by a loyalist bomb blast in Portadown.

Trimble told the UUP conference that Sinn Féin could not join an executive without IRA decommissioning.

Hume told the SDLP conference that decommissioning was not a precondition for implementation of the Good Friday Agreement but that it was the will of the people that it should take place.

On RTÉ radio Ahern said there was irresistible movement towards Irish unity and that it would occur within twenty years.

December **Hume and Trimble received the Nobel peace prize in Oslo.**

Agreement was reached on the structure of the executive and of the cross-border bodies.

The LVF handed over some weapons for destruction.

1999

January — The UUP warned that an IRA failure to decommission would force a renegotiation of the Good Friday Agreement.

Catholic applications to the RUC were reported to have doubled since the 1994 ceasefires.

Plans were announced by the UUP for a committee to review the Orange Order's link with the party.

A member of the UUP assembly party lost the whip for opposing party policy in the assembly.

The RUC announced the closure of seven border army bases.

February — **The assembly voted to confirm the new government departments and cross-border bodies.**

March — The NI Human Rights Commission came into being. Blair called for IRA decommissioning to begin in order to clear the way for Sinn Féin to join the executive.

The Dublin and London governments signed treaties establishing the new north–south, British–Irish and intergovernmental arrangements. The 1985 Anglo-Irish Agreement was superseded by the new treaties.

Lurgan solicitor Rosemary Nelson was killed by a loyalist booby-trap bomb placed under her car.

The Chief Constable of Kent and the FBI were asked by the RUC to help in the investigation of the Nelson killing.

John Stevens, Deputy Commissioner of the Metropolitan Police, was asked by the RUC to investigate the 1989 killing of solicitor Pat Finucane.

Hume donated his £286,000 Nobel prize money to charitable organisations.

Prolonged talks took place at Hillsborough Castle on decommissioning and the formation of an executive.

April — The Hillsborough talks continued but remained at stalemate. The London and Dublin governments produced a declaration calling for a collective act of reconciliation and the putting beyond use of some weapons on a voluntary basis.

Trimble met the Pope in a ceremony with other Nobel prize winners.

It was reported that UUP party chairman Dennis Rogan faced expulsion from the Orange Order for attending the funeral mass of three Omagh victims.

May — An alleged drugs dealer was shot dead in a Newry bar. Suspicion fell on the IRA.

The Church of Ireland synod called on the Drumcree church vestry to withdraw the annual invitation to the Orange Order if it did not give assurance about their conduct.

The Drumcree rector made it clear that his church would not accept the synod recommendation.

The body of Eamon Molloy, one of the so-called 'disappeared', was found in County Louth. The body of the man, who had been missing since 1975, had been recovered by the IRA and left in a coffin in a cemetery.

June — A Protestant woman, Elizabeth O'Neill, was killed by a pipe bomb thrown into her house in Portadown by loyalists.

Another alleged drug dealer was shot dead by the IRA in County Down.

Trimble called on Blair to sack Mowlam for allegedly turning a blind eye to repeated IRA ceasefire violations.

A Blair plan to resolve the decommissioning stalemate was rejected by the UUP.

1999

The Parades Commission again rerouted the July Orange march away from Garvaghy Road.

Blair's deadline passed without agreement on decommissioning.

Another two of the bodies of the 'disappeared' were recovered.

July **Blair and Ahern set out a plan entitled *The Way Forward* under which devolution would begin on 15 July. Within days decommissioning would begin, to be completed by May 2000. Clinton urged all sides to accept the arrangement.**

The Parades Commission allowed the Orange Order to switch its main gathering to Belfast's Ormeau Park.

The UUP rejected Blair's urging that it should join a devolved government before the IRA started to give up guns. Mowlam called on the assembly to meet on 15 July to nominate an executive.

UUP members boycotted Stormont as the executive was nominated causing it to be declared invalid for lacking sufficient cross-community membership.

Mallon resigned as Deputy First Minister.

Adams said delays in setting up the executive made it almost impossible to meet a decommissioning deadline of May 2000.

Arrests were made in the US over alleged IRA transatlantic gun-running.

The IRA was blamed for the killing of west Belfast man Charles Bennett.

August **In a formal judgement Mowlam said she did not believe the IRA ceasefire was breaking down. She added however that the position of the IRA was deeply worrying, warning that she had 'come very close to judging the IRA's ceasefire is no longer for real'.**

September **Recalled by Blair and Ahern as a facilitator, Mitchell began a review of the peace process.**

Unionists reacted angrily to publication of the Patten report, which proposed far-reaching changes to policing and the RUC, including changing its name to the Police Service of Northern Ireland.

Michelle Williamson, whose parents died in the 1993 Shankill Road bomb, was granted the right to seek a judicial review of Mowlam's ceasefire decision.

October **Peter Mandelson replaced Mowlam as Northern Ireland Secretary.**

Adams called for UUP flexibility on the arms issue. UUP elements warned they would resist any move away from the party's 'no guns, no government' policy.

Former MI5 officer Michael Oatley described the demands for decommissioning as an 'excuse to avoid the pursuit of peace'.

November There were suggestions that Trimble was prepared to take the risk of accepting a deal with Sinn Féin.

Mitchell insisted parties 'now understand each other's concerns and requirements far better than before'.

The UUP and Sinn Féin both expressed a desire to set up an inclusive executive. Pressure mounted on Trimble from anti-Agreement Unionists.

The IRA said it was ready to discuss decommissioning and would appoint a representative to the de Chastelain decommissioning body.

Mitchell concluded his review saying that the basis existed for decommissioning and coalition government.

1999

Mandelson told the Commons that he would freeze the workings of the Good Friday Agreement if the IRA did not deliver on arms decommissioning.

It was announced that the RUC would be awarded the George Cross.

The UUP ruling council voted to accept a leadership compromise paving the way for the executive to operate. Trimble promised he would return to seek the support of the party council in February 2000. He revealed he had given a senior party official a post-dated letter of resignation as First Minister to come into effect in the event of inadequate movement on arms. The executive was formed, with Trimble at its head and Mallon as his deputy. Ten other ministers were appointed, two of them from Sinn Féin and two from the DUP. The DUP said they would function as ministers but would not attend executive meetings.

1 December **Devolution was restored at midnight.**

2 December **The Irish government formally amended Articles 2 and 3 of the Irish constitution laying claim to NI.**

The IRA appointed an interlocutor to the decommissioning body.

Adams displayed a security forces electronic bugging device which had been discovered attached to a car used by Sinn Féin leaders.

De Chastelain issued an upbeat report saying that recent events and meetings 'provide the basis for an assessment that decommissioning will occur'.

The RUC announced the planned closure of Castlereagh holding centre.

The Irish cabinet met members of the NI executive in the first meeting of the north–south ministerial council.

2000

January Loyalist Richard Jameson was shot dead in Portadown, apparently as part of a UVF–LVF feud.

De Chastelain met the two governments to deliver a report on progress on decommissioning. It was not immediately published, Blair reporting to the Commons that insufficient progress had been made.

Trimble made clear his intention to resign in the absence of progess on decommissioning in advance of his party council's meeting in February.

The governments continued to press Sinn Féin on decommissioning.

February **Mandelson announced the suspension of devolution and a return to direct rule.** This led to major controversy and recrimination from nationalists and republicans. Sinn Féin said a major advance on decommissioning had been outlined in a new IRA statement.

The government welcomed the new IRA statement as a significant development.

The Ulster Unionist Council endorsed Trimble's handling of the issue.

The IRA announced its withdrawal from arms talks, saying proposals on arms were now off the table.

Talks began on ways to resolve the crisis.

The bodies of two young men from the Portadown area were found at the nearby village of Tandragee. The killings were thought to be part of the loyalist feud in the area.

March **In Washington for St Patrick's Day, Trimble told a press conference that the executive might be formed again without prior IRA decommissioning if there were firm guarantees that decommissioning**

2000

would take place. There was widespread condemnation of his move
from critics in the Unionist party.

Martin Smyth announced his intention to challenge Trimble for the party
leadership at the next party council meeting.

**Trimble defeated Smyth by 57 per cent to 43 per cent. The council also
committed the party to refuse to re-enter the executive unless the
government abandoned its plan to drop the name of the RUC.**

April   Trimble again announced that a review would reconsider the question of
the Orange Order's seats on the party council.

Blair visited Belfast and Dublin.

May   Blair and Ahern spent two days at Hillsborough Castle meeting local parties.
The two governments then announced the target date of 22 May for a
return to devolution. They called on armed groups to make a commitment
to put weapons beyond use.

The IRA issued a statement saying that if the Good Friday Agreement were
fully implemented they would 'completely and verifiably put IRA weapons
beyond use'. They also agreed to a number of arms dumps being monitored
by international figures as a confidence-building measure.

Trimble said the IRA statement 'does appear to break new ground'.

Cyril Ramaphosa, former secretary-general of the African National
Congress of South Africa, and former Finnish president Martti Ahtisaari,
were named as monitors of IRA arms dumps.

The closure of selected security bases around Northern Ireland continued.

A man was shot dead in Belfast, apparently a victim of the continuing UVF–
LVF loyalist feud.

**On 27 May the Ulster Unionist Council approved rejoining the executive
on the basis of the IRA arms offer. The voting was 459 to 403, a 53–47 per
cent split.**

At midnight on 29 May devolution was restored.

The two DUP ministers resumed office but the party announced that if an
assembly vote did not bring down the executive they would resign their
executive offices, allowing other DUP members to take their places in rotation.

An alleged drugs dealer was shot dead in south Belfast, apparently by the IRA.

Tom Constantine, former head of the US Drug Enforcement Agency, was
appointed as oversight commissioner as part of the implementation of the
Patten report on policing.

June   Blair wrote to the wife of one of the Guildford Four personally apologising for
the imprisonment of the four for the Guildford and Woolwich pub bombings.

Flanagan said the IRA appeared to be involved in the May killing of an
alleged drugs dealer.

**A number of IRA arms dumps were inspected and secured by the
international monitors. Sinn Féin president Gerry Adams said of the
development: 'In 200 years there has not been an initiative like this.'
Blair described the move as a 'very substantial further step' towards a
permanent peace.**

Hooded and armed UDA members threatened an end to their ceasefire,
accusing nationalists of attacking Protestant homes in north and west
Belfast.

Around 2,000 troops were drafted into NI in preparation for possible loyalist
disturbances during the Orange marching season.

2000

A South African human rights lawyer, Brian Currin, was involved in efforts to mediate between Portadown's Catholic residents and the Orange Order.

July

The Northern Ireland Parades Commission banned the Drumcree march. The commission said a limited parade could take place within three to eight months, but only if the Order complied with a number of conditions. These included the opening of dialogue with Catholic residents and the avoidance of anything which might raise tensions.

The Order called for thousands of loyalists to take to the streets in protest against the ban. Nights of widespread loyalist violence followed. Dozens of roads were blocked by protests and barricades in many areas, with clashes between rioters and police. Harold Gracey, head of the Order in Portadown, refused to condemn the violence. He declared: 'I am not going to condemn violence because Gerry Adams never condemns it.' The Order's senior leaders refrained from endorsing his call and condemned the violence. Its Grand Master, Robert Saulters, said rioters were damaging the Order and should cease immediately.

In the days leading up to the Twelfth of July processions Portadown Orangemen announced plans to bring NI to a complete halt as part of the Drumcree protest.

Released UDA prisoner Johnny Adair appeared at Drumcree with supporters.

Archbishop Robin Eames, head of the Church of Ireland, said paramilitary involvement had 'removed any integrity which the Drumcree protest might have had'. He called on Portadown Orangemen to issue an immediate and unequivocal call for all violence to cease.

The Order succeeded in bringing much of NI to a standstill, paralysing economic life for short periods. Scores of roads were blocked and in some places there were violent clashes with the security forces.

The Orange Order's main Twelfth of July processions passed off peacefully, though they were preceded by a night which brought a killing, stabbings, and injuries to more than a score of RUC members. In the most serious incident a loyalist was shot dead by other loyalists in Larne, County Antrim.

It was announced that the Maze prison would be closed by the end of the year.

An arms consignment bound for dissident republicans was seized at the Croatian city of Split. A number of arrests were made.

The two DUP ministers on the executive resigned as part of the party's continued opposition to Sinn Féin involvement. Two other DUP members took up their executive posts.

The final prisoner releases were made under the Good Friday Agreement.

August

Sir Josias Cunningham, president of the Ulster Unionist party and an ally of its leader David Trimble, died in a road accident. He had been an important advocate of unity in the party.

In Londonderry an attempt by dissident republicans to stage a bombing in the run-up to a major loyalist parade in the city was foiled following a high-speed pursuit by police.

The RUC staged its last recruits passing-out parade before the force's planned transformation. The thirty-six new recruits were the last to join the RUC before it was overhauled by the recommendations of the Patten report.

A violent feud broke out between rival loyalist paramilitary groups, the UVF

2000

and UDA, centring on the Shankill area of Belfast. Following disturbances during a march on the Shankill Road two men were shot dead by the UVF and another was killed by the UDA.

In the weeks that followed houses and other premises were attacked in the Shankill and elsewhere. More than 160 families asked to be rehoused. Troops were drafted into the Shankill district, the first time in two years that they had appeared on Belfast streets.

Mandelson ordered the re-arrest and jailing of UDA leader Johnny Adair, who had been released early under the terms of the Good Friday Agreement. The NI Secretary commented: 'My priority is public safety and I cannot give freedom to an individual intent on abusing it. I am satisfied that this particular individual has breached the terms of his licence.'

Hume announced that he would give up his assembly seat in the near future.

September   Former NI Secretary Mowlam announced she would stand down from parliament at the next general election.

The inquests opened into the deaths of the twenty-nine people killed in the 1998 Omagh bombing.

Dissident republicans launched a rocket attack on the London headquarters of MI6.

DUP candidate, the Reverend William McCrea, won the previously safe UUP South Antrim Westminster seat in a by-election.

October   Real IRA member Joseph O'Connor was shot dead in Belfast. The IRA was believed to have been responsible.

Trimble's UUP critics forced another meeting of the party council to reconsider involvement in the NI executive.

There was a second inspection of IRA arms dumps by the international monitors.

The UUP's ruling council narrowly supported Trimble after he announced a plan to exclude Sinn Féin ministers from north–south ministerial meetings unless significant progress was made on decommissioning IRA arms.

Three more people were killed in the continuing loyalist feud.

November   A loyalist feud killing took place on 1 November, the fourth in four days.

December   Two sectarian killings took place in the first days of the month.

President Clinton, in the last weeks of his presidency, visited both parts of Ireland for the third time.

The loyalist feud was declared to be at an end by the UDA and UVF.

The two Sinn Féin ministers initiated a legal challenge to their exclusion from north–south meetings.

A Protestant civilian was killed, apparently by the UDA. The killing was not believed to have been as part of the feud.

General de Chastelain issued a pessimistic report on the decommissioning process.

Ronnie Hill, who had been in a coma since the IRA bombing of a Remembrance Day ceremony in Enniskillen in 1987, died.

2001

January   Blair visited Belfast in an attempt to make progress on disputed issues such as decommissioning, demilitarisation and policing.

2001

John Reid became Northern Ireland Secretary after the surprise resignation of Peter Mandelson.
A court ruled that Trimble had acted unlawfully in excluding the Sinn Féin ministers from north–south meetings. He lodged an appeal.

February Bishop Edward Daly gave evidence to the Saville inquiry into Bloody Sunday, now moving into its third year.

March A Real IRA car bomb exploded outside a BBC building in London.
Blair and Ahern met local party leaders at Hillsborough.

April A loyalist killing brought the feud death toll to sixteen in seventeen months.
Martin McGuinness confirmed he had been a leading member of the Derry IRA at the time of Bloody Sunday in 1972.

May **For the second time Trimble wrote a letter of resignation, to take effect on 1 July in the absence of progress on decommissioning. The IRA announced that it had established regular contacts with General de Chastelain.**

June **The UUP lost three of its nine Westminster seats in the Westminster general election while both the DUP and Sinn Féin made significant gains.**

July **Trimble's resignation as First Minister came into effect, triggering rounds of negotiation, in particular at Weston Park in Shropshire.**
Repeated rioting broke out in a number of areas, in particular Ardoyne and elsewhere in north Belfast.
Two youths were shot dead by loyalists.

August **A method of decommissioning suggested by the IRA was accepted by General de Chastelain. The move was rejected by Trimble, who said actual decommissioning was required. Reid suspended the Good Friday Agreement for a day to allow a six-week period for talks.**
Three Irish republicans were arrested in Colombia, leading to a major clamour for an explanation of their association with FARC guerrillas.

September Worldwide publicity was given to a loyalist protest in the Ardoyne area aimed at preventing Catholic schoolgirls from attending school.
John Hume announced his decision to stand down as SDLP leader on health grounds.
A second one-day suspension was announced to allow another six-week extension for talks. Trimble threatened to withdraw the UUP ministers from the executive.
Martin O'Hagan became the first journalist to be killed in the troubles when he was shot by loyalists.
NI Secretary Reid announced the second technical suspension of the assembly after its failure to reinstate a First Minister. He said that it was the last time this would be done.

October Reid declared that the UDA, UFF and LVF ceasefires were no longer recognised.
On 23 October the IRA announced that it had begun a process of putting arms beyond use. Within hours the IICD confirmed it had witnessed the disposal of arms in a 'significant act of decommissioning'.
On 24 October Trimble re-nominated UUP ministers to the NI executive, preventing its collapse.

November The RUC badge was removed from police stations of the new Police Service of Northern Ireland.

2001

On 3 November, in face of defections from his own party, pro-Agreement parties were able to re-elect Trimble First Minister by re-designating Alliance and Women's Coalition members as Unionists. Mark Durkan of the SDLP, who succeeded Hume as party leader, was elected Deputy First Minister. The election was followed by scuffles involving assembly members.

The long-running Holy Cross school confrontation was resolved.

The GAA voted to abolish Rule 21 which banned members of the security forces.

Flanagan announced that he would retire as Chief Constable within months.

December   SF's four MPs were provided with Westminster offices and allowances despite not taking the oath of allegiance or their seats.

Police Ombudsman Nuala O'Loan published a highly critical report on the police investigation of the Omagh bombing. The report was in turn strongly criticised by the Chief Constable.

William Stobie, the only person to stand trial in connection with the killing of lawyer Pat Finucane, was killed by loyalist associates.

Amid much criticism, particularly from American supporters, Adams visited Cuba and met Fidel Castro.

Twenty people died in troubles-related violence in 2001, all but five of them killed by loyalists.

2002

January   A man was convicted in the Dublin special criminal court of conspiracy to cause the 1998 Omagh explosion.

March   **Three unmasked men raided Special Branch headquarters inside Castlereagh police station complex in east Belfast and removed sensitive documents. Police said the IRA was responsible for the raid.**

April   **The IRA announced that a second batch of weapons had been put beyond use.**

May   Reid said that a ceasefire was not enough from the IRA, there also needed to be 'a sense that the war is over'.

Hugh Orde, a Metropolitan Police officer who had been a senior member of the Stevens inquiry into police collusion in Northern Ireland, was named as Chief Constable of the PSNI.

Serious sectarian clashes erupted in the Short Strand area of east Belfast.

June   SF exceeded expectations by winning five seats in the Dáil election.

August   A booby-trap bomb planted by the Real IRA at a Territorial Army base in Derry killed building worker David Caldwell.

September   Trimble announced that the UUP would withdraw from the executive in January if republicans did not demonstrate they had abandoned violence.

October   **Police raided SF offices at Stormont during an investigation into alleged IRA intelligence-gathering. In the aftermath, Reid announced the suspension of devolution and the reintroduction of direct rule. The IRA announced that it had broken off contact with the decommissioning body.**

Paul Murphy was appointed NI Secretary.

Ten people died in troubles-related violence in 2002, nine at the hands of loyalists.

2003

January   Shankill loyalist Johnny Adair was returned to prison by government order as an internal UDA feud continued to claim lives.

The UVF broke off contacts with the decommissioning body.

February   **John Gregg, a UDA brigadier, was one of two men shot dead in the loyalist feud. He had served a sentence for a gun attack on Gerry Adams in 1984.**

Adair's wife and more than twenty relatives and supporters fled to Scotland under police escort amid UDA threats.

March   The assembly election, scheduled for 1 May, was postponed.

IRA member Keith Rogers was killed in a shooting incident in south Armagh which was said to be part of a local republican dispute.

April   President Bush met Blair and Ahern in Northern Ireland. The three leaders called for 'a complete and irrevocable' break with paramilitarism.

The Stevens inquiry into security force collusion with loyalist paramilitaries concluded that collusion appeared to have reached very high levels.

May   The British government announced that the assembly election would be held in the autumn.

Blair criticised an IRA refusal to rule out all paramilitary activity. The IRA released a statement saying that it posed no threat to Unionists or the peace process and was committed to making conflict a thing of the past.

Freddie Scappaticci, a senior IRA figure, was exposed as a security force informer.

June   Trimble won a narrow vote in the UUP ruling council. Three UUP MPs resigned the party whip in protest at Trimble's leadership policies, plunging the party into crisis.

October   General de Chastelain confirmed that a third act of IRA decommissioning had been witnessed. It involved over 100 tonnes of weapons according to a senior Irish police officer.

Trimble rejected the IRA decommissioning acts as inadequate.

November   **Assembly elections left the DUP and SF in the dominant position in the Unionist and nationalist communities. The DUP won thirty seats, a gain of ten; SF won twenty-four, a gain of six; the UUP won twenty-seven, a loss of one; the SDLP won eighteen, a loss of six.**

December   Rebel UUP MP Jeffrey Donaldson resigned from the party along with assembly members Arlene Foster and Norah Beare. Within weeks they joined the DUP.

The death toll for the year was ten, seven at the hands of loyalists.

2004

February   A formal review of the working of the Good Friday Agreement began.

A number of republicans were held after an attempt to kidnap a dissident republican from a Belfast city centre bar. The incident was described by the NI Secretary as 'a serious breach'.

March   Trimble withdrew his team from the Good Friday review saying the failure by the government to exclude SF following the alleged false imprisonment of a dissident republican was 'quite appalling'. The review process stalled.

Trimble was re-elected leader of the UUP.

Blair and Ahern met the parties in Belfast.

2004

April   The government accepted the IMC recommendation that SF and the PUP be financially penalised as a result of continued paramilitary activity by the IRA and the UVF.

June   **The European election demonstrated the continued growth of the DUP and SF votes: Jim Nicholson held his seat for the UUP, Jim Allister replaced his party leader Ian Paisley who stood down, while SF took the seat previously held by the SDLP's retiring John Hume.**

July   The NIO confirmed that Blair and Ahern would host a new round of talks in late September, with preliminary talks to be held earlier.

August   Michael Green became the fourth victim of the UVF in a matter of months during a feud involving the UVF and the LVF.

September   **The parties met for talks chaired by Blair and Ahern at Leeds Castle. Three days of talks failed to produce an agreement but there was cautious optimism that progress could be made. The DUP continued to refuse face to face talks with SF. Paisley looked noticeably unwell.**

October   Jim Gray, a UDA leader in east Belfast, was shot dead by his former associates. For the first time Paisley led a DUP delegation for a formal meeting with a Taoiseach in Dublin.
The IMC stated that the IRA showed no signs of finally winding down its capability and that the UDA and UVF remained active. The IMC noted a 'disturbingly high' level of paramilitary violence.

November   On the thirtieth anniversary of the Birmingham pub bombings by the IRA which killed twenty-one people, Adams said: 'I certainly regret what happened and I make no bones about that.'
The British government restored recognition of the UDA ceasefire.
The two governments put proposals aimed at ending the deadlock to the DUP and SF.
President Bush telephoned Paisley and Adams to urge compromise.
The DUP demanded photographic proof of IRA decommissioning and Paisley called for the IRA to 'wear sackcloth and ashes' and show repentance for its actions. Adams described such comments as 'offensive'.
Adams held a first formal meeting with Chief Constable Orde.

December   Paisley met de Chastelain twice within days to discuss decommissioning.
On 8 December prime ministers Blair and Ahern visited Belfast to announce their proposals.
An IRA statement said that the organisation 'would not submit to a process of humiliation' but, in the event of an agreement, would end its activities and complete decommissioning. The IRA continued to reject DUP demands for photographic evidence.
On 20 December an armed gang stole £26.5 million from the Northern Bank in central Belfast. The IRA was widely believed to have been responsible. The IRA denied this, a denial supported by SF.
Four people were killed in troubles-related violence in 2004.

2005

January   **On 30 January a crisis arose with the killing of Robert McCartney, beaten and stabbed to death at a Belfast bar used by members of the IRA and SF. McCartney's partner and his sisters began a publicity campaign demanding justice, a campaign which attracted prolonged international attention.**

2005

The IRA and SF suspended and expelled a number of their members in the aftermath of the McCartney affair.

March   Robert McCartney's partner and sisters were received by President Bush at the White House on St Patrick's Day. Unlike in previous years, NI politicians were not invited to the celebrations.

April   Adams publicly called for the IRA to 'fully embrace and accept' democratic means as SF launched its Westminster election campaign.

May   **In the Westminster election the DUP won nine of NI's eighteen seats, defeating UUP leader David Trimble in Upper Bann. Trimble subsequently stepped down as leader to be replaced by Reg Empey. Sylvia Hermon survived as the one UUP MP. SF won five seats and the SDLP three.**
Peter Hain replaced Paul Murphy as NI Secretary.

July   **On 28 July the IRA announced the end of its military campaign. Adams described this as a 'courageous and confident initiative' while Blair said it was a 'step of unparalleled magnitude'.**

August   **The British government announced a two-year process of demilitarisation in NI, including the closure of army bases and the de-fortification of police stations.**
Unionists reacted angrily while nationalists generally approved. In particular Unionists objected to the planned disbandment of the Royal Irish Regiment.
Former NI Secretary Mo Mowlam died at the age of fifty-five after a fall at her home. She had been ill for some time.
Three republicans charged in Colombia with aiding the FARC, a Marxist revolutionary faction, reappeared in Ireland having fled after being released on bail.

September   Serious rioting broke out on Belfast's Springfield Road after the Parades Commission restricted an Orange parade. The Chief Constable said the Orange Order bore substantial responsibility for the rioting and attacks on police. The Orange Order described his remarks as 'inflammatory' and condemned police reaction as 'brutal and heavy-handed.'
The decommissioning body announced that the IRA had put all of its weapons beyond use in a final act witnessed by Father Alex Reid and Methodist minister the Reverend Harold Good.
Paisley said questions remained about IRA decommissioning in the absence of transparent evidence.

December   Three men accused of involvement in an alleged IRA spying incident at Stormont were acquitted of all charges. Their arrests had led to the collapse of the executive in 2002. The prosecution offered no evidence 'in the public interest'. One of the three, Denis Donaldson, SF head of administration at Stormont, appeared at a press conference with Adams and McGuinness to deny again the spying allegations. A week later Donaldson admitted having been a security force agent for more than twenty years. He was expelled from SF.
Eight people died in troubles-related violence in 2005.

2006

January   In response to widespread criticism the government dropped proposals to deal with paramilitary fugitives, the so-called 'on-the-runs'.

2006

April   **Denis Donaldson was found shot dead at a remote cottage in Donegal. The IRA denied responsibility.**
On 6 April Blair and Ahern arrived in NI to announce a plan for restoring devolution. Assembly members were given until 24 November to set up an executive. If not, the assembly would be closed and salaries and allowances would cease. They warned that the two governments would then work out their own arrangements to administer NI.

May   The assembly met on 15 May for the first time since October 2002 but progress was slow and deadlines slipped.

September   Paisley called for the IRA to disband.

October   **Three days of intensive multi-party talks took place at St Andrews in Scotland.**
A political roadmap was suggested by the two governments with a target date of 26 March 2007 for a new executive to be in operation. The parties were given until 10 November to respond to what the governments called the St Andrews Agreement. A meeting due to have been attended by Paisley and Adams was cancelled.

November   **7 March 2007 was announced as the election date for a new assembly. The existing assembly was to continue on a transitional basis.**
Proceedings at the transitional assembly were interrupted as loyalist killer Michael Stone attempted to force his way into Stormont. He was later convicted of the attempted murder of Adams and McGuinness.

December   Trimble announced that he would not defend his assembly seat having become a member of the House of Lords.
On 29 December SF agreed to call a special party conference on the issue of republican backing for the PSNI, the most contentious issue.
Three people died in troubles-related violence in 2005.

2007

January   **Blair returned early from a family holiday to help salvage talks which had stalled when SF appeared reluctant to go ahead with its policing meeting.**
PUP leader David Ervine died suddenly as the result of a heart attack.
The SF meeting overwhelmingly supported the leadership. The vote gave the executive the authority to declare its support for the PSNI and the criminal justice system.
A report by the Police Ombudsman's office concluded that a UVF gang in north Belfast which included RUC informers had killed at least ten people.

February   The government again denied reports that it was considering allowing the return of 'on-the-runs' to NI.
The last remaining British army watchtower in south Armagh was dismantled as part of the 'normalisation' plans.

March   **In assembly elections the DUP and SF consolidated their votes: the DUP won thirty-six of the 108 seats, a gain of six; SF won twenty-eight, a gain of four; the UUP won eighteen, a loss of nine; and the SDLP won sixteen, a loss of two.**
Unionist and republican candidates opposed to the powersharing administration failed to make a significant impression.
In Belfast one man, Joseph Jones, was beaten to death and another, Edward Burns, was shot dead in a feud between current or former members of the Continuity IRA. SF called on nationalists to help the PSNI investigation.

2007

The two prime ministers and secretary of state Hain repeatedly said the assembly would be dissolved, and direct rule restored, if no agreement on an executive had been reached by 26 March.

The governments agreed to let the deadline slip after the DUP agreed in principle to share power with SF, but asked for an extension of the deadline until May.

SF agreed to the delay but – along with the governments – insisted on visible evidence of DUP commitment.

The DUP executive agreed on sharing power with SF, and to the nomination of ministers.

After tense last-minute discussions Paisley, Adams and their party teams met face to face and agreed to form, by 8 May, an executive which would also include two UUP ministers and one SDLP minister.

In one of the most striking images in almost forty years of troubles, Paisley and Adams sat side by side for the public announcement of the agreement. Paisley said: 'We must not allow our justified loathing of the horrors and tragedies of the past to become a barrier to creating a better and more stable future.' Blair commented: 'Everything we have done over the last ten years has been a preparation for this moment.'

DUP MEP Jim Allister and a number of DUP local councillors resigned from the party in protest at its decision to share power with SF.

The last soldiers withdrew from a fortified base at Crossmaglen.

April   Trimble announced that he had joined the Conservative party.

May   **On 8 May direct rule by Westminster ended after almost five years. Paisley and McGuinness were sworn in as First and Deputy First Ministers at the head of a four-party executive.**

An off-duty policeman was injured by a car bomb in Castlederg, County Tyrone.

In the Irish general election Ahern was returned as Taoiseach. In a setback for SF their membership of the Dáil was reduced from five to four.

The UVF declared its renewed intention to wind down its activities, promising to put weapons 'beyond reach'. In a statement delivered by loyalist veteran Gusty Spence the organisation said the union with Britain was safe and accepted that the IRA's war was over.

SF took its seats on the Policing Board for the first time.

June   Brian McGlynn was shot dead in the Waterside area of Londonderry. The IMC subsequently blamed the INLA.

Gordon Brown replaced Tony Blair as prime minister. Shaun Woodward was appointed NI Secretary.

A Consultative Group on the Past, to consider ways of dealing with the legacy of the troubles, was established by the NI Secretary.

The NI Director of Public Prosecutions decided not to charge any member of the security forces in connection with the 1989 killing of solicitor Pat Finucane, citing insufficient evidence. The decision was criticised by the Finucane family.

November   Dissident republicans shot and wounded police constable Jim Doherty in Derry city.

A prominent County Armagh republican, Thomas 'Slab' Murphy, appeared in court in County Louth charged with tax evasion.

2007

The UDA announced that it was standing down the UFF, a cover name used for many of its killings. It also declared that UFF weapons would be put beyond use but not decommissioned.

December   Paisley and McGuinness led a delegation to the USA seeking investment in NI.

The SF education minister, Caitríona Ruane, announced the end of the 11-plus transfer test. There was widespread opposition to her proposals, particularly from Unionists.

Jim Allister, the former DUP MEP, formed a new anti-Agreement party to be known as the Traditional Unionist Voice.

A man facing murder charges connected with the Omagh bombing was acquitted. The judge's ruling was highly critical of the RUC investigation and the prosecution process.

Three people died in troubles-related violence in 2007.

2008

January   The Policing Board agreed to appoint a team of independent experts to re-examine evidence from the 1998 Omagh bombing.

The Consultative Group on the Past was involved in controversy after a suggestion that the British government might be asked to formally say it fought a war against the IRA. There was also anger amongst Unionists at the possibility of an amnesty.

Paisley and McGuinness visited Brussels to ask for continued EU financial backing for NI.

February   A former SF driver was taken into protective custody after reports he had acted as an informer.

Northern and southern ministers met in Dundalk to discuss cross-border cooperation.

The body of Andrew Burns was found in Donegal: the IMC concluded that dissidents were responsible.

The UUP retained a council seat in a Dromore by-election: the vote indicated a significant defection of DUP voters to the TUV.

Ian Paisley jnr resigned as a junior minister following questions over his links to a developer. He was later cleared of any wrongdoing.

McGuinness said he would have killed every British soldier in Derry in the aftermath of Bloody Sunday.

The DUP announced that the devolution of policing and justice powers would not take place in May as proposed, insisting that there was not 'adequate public confidence'.

March   Ian Paisley nominated Ian Paisley jnr to replace Jeffrey Donaldson on the policing board.

Paisley snr announced his intention to stand down as First Minister in May. He also announced that he would resign as DUP leader, a party he had created and led for almost forty years. He said he would continue as MP and MLA.

The Stormont committee considering the devolution of policing and justice said the May target for transferring the powers would not be met.

Adams told fellow republicans that the reunification of Ireland was 'no longer a far-off dream but a work in progress.'

April   Brian Cowen was elected as the new leader of Fianna Fáil.

2008

On the tenth anniversary of the Good Friday Agreement many of the individuals involved in the original negotiations attended a conference in Belfast to mark the occasion.

Peter Robinson was elected the new leader of the DUP.

NI Secretary Woodward announced that local elections in NI would be postponed for two years until 2010. It was announced that new boundaries would be proposed reducing the number of councils from twenty-six to eleven.

May   Bertie Ahern stood down as Taoiseach and was replaced by Brian Cowen. A three-day investment conference for US business leaders was held in Northern Ireland.

A booby-trap car bomb planted by dissident republicans seriously injured a Catholic PSNI officer in Castlederg, County Tyrone.

June   Adams met Gordon Brown in London in an attempt to resolve contentious issues, notably the devolution of policing and justice.

Robinson and McGuinness were elected First and Deputy First Ministers, and travelled to Downing Street for talks hosted by Brown.

The nine DUP MPs helped the Labour government win a crucial Commons vote to extend detention in the UK to forty-two days: the vote was won with a majority of nine.

President Bush made a brief visit to Stormont on his way back to Washington after a European tour.

Emmett Shiels was killed by dissident republicans in Londonderry.

A prolonged gap between executive meetings began in June as a result of DUP–SF disagreement on a series of issues notably the devolution of policing and justice.

July   NIO justice minister Paul Goggins made a formal apology in the Commons relating to the loyalist bombing of McGurk's bar in 1971 when fifteen people were killed. At the time and later it was suggested that the bomb was being handled in the bar. A report by the HET dismissed as 'irresponsible and inaccurate' army claims that the device was an IRA bomb being prepared. Talks continued between the UUP and the Conservative party on possible future links.

August   A ceremony to mark the tenth anniversary of the Omagh bombing in which twenty-nine people were killed was held in the town.

In a step closer to settling the long-running dispute on policing the DUP and SF announced that they had agreed on a single justice minister and that neither party would nominate members.

Gusty Spence said the organisation should fully decommission its weapons. Ian Paisley jnr suggested that the police should adopt a 'shoot on sight' policy towards dissident republicans.

September **An IMC report stated that the IRA's 'former terrorist capability has been lost . . . The Provisional IRA of the recent past is well beyond recall.'** Peter Robinson met UDA leaders to encourage them to renounce violence and decommission weapons.

October   The DUP stand-off continued to prevent meetings of the executive: the last meeting had been on 19 June. Gordon Brown urged the two parties to agree on a date for the devolution of policing and justice.

2008

The UUP and the Conservative party continued to hold talks on future links against a background of some resistance among UUP members, most notably the party's one MP, Lady Sylvia Hermon.

November   The only person accused of involvement in the Northern Bank robbery in December 2004 was acquitted on all charges.
The DUP and SF agreed to a resumption of executive meetings. The devolution of policing and justice would take place 'within months'. On 20 November the executive met for the first time in twenty weeks.

December   Conservative leader David Cameron addressed the UUP conference: 'Our party has taken the significant step of restoring Unionism's historic relationship with the Conservative party.'
Remains found in the Wicklow mountains were confirmed as those of Danny McIlhone, abducted and killed by the IRA in 1981.
Two people died in troubles-related violence in 2008.

2009

January   **It emerged that the report of the Consultative Group on the Past included a recommendation that each victim family be awarded £12,000.**
The British government moved to extend for twelve months the legislation on decommissioning for 'one last time' to provide an opportunity for remaining organisations to comply.

February   The Conservative party and the UUP announced that they would form an electoral alliance.
After many objections the NI Secretary ruled that the suggested £12,000 payment to victim families would not be sanctioned.
Jim McConnell was killed in Derry by dissident republicans.

March   **Soldiers Mark Quinsey and Patrick Azimkar were shot dead by the Real IRA in Antrim.**
Two days later PSNI officer Stephen Carroll was shot dead by the Continuity IRA in Armagh. McGuinness, who stood beside Robinson and Chief Constable Orde to condemn the killings, called those responsible 'traitors to the island of Ireland'.

April   McGuinness revealed that the PSNI had informed him of a threat from dissident republicans.

May   Kevin McDaid was killed in Coleraine by a loyalist mob.
Dissident republicans were blamed for an attack on the Londonderry home of senior SF member Mitchel McLaughlin.

June   SF candidate Bairbre de Brún topped the poll in the NI Euro election. Also elected were Diane Dodds (DUP) and Jim Nicholson (UCUNF). The former DUP MEP Jim Allister – now the TUV leader – won 66,197 votes, a major electoral embarrassment for the DUP.
The UVF and the UDA decommissioned weapons in a process supervised by the decommissioning body. The UVF was believed to have decommissioned the bulk of its weapons, the UDA partially.

July   Dissident republicans were blamed for an attack on the home of SF minister Conor Murphy.

September   Matt Baggott took over as the new PSNI Chief Constable.

2009

October — Tension continued to surround the details of devolution of policing and justice.

A PSNI officer's partner was injured when a bomb exploded under her car in east Belfast.

November — **The IMC reported that dissident republican activity in NI was at its highest level for nearly six years.**

One of NI's most senior judges was moved from his home following dissident republican threats.

December — Brown and Cowen repeated a call for the devolution of policing and justice powers 'at an early date'. McGuinness said that if no date was set there would be a 'full-blown crisis'.

McGuinness and Robinson clashed publicly over the devolution of policing and justice powers.

Peter Robinson's wife announced that she was retiring from political life.

Five people died in troubles-related violence in 2009.

2010

January — Cardinal Daly died on 31 December. Robinson as First Minister was widely criticised for failing to respond to his death for three days.

The UDA announced that weapons had been put 'verifiably beyond use', a process overseen by two witnesses with IICD oversight.

A BBC documentary revealed that Iris Robinson had attempted suicide in March 2009 when her affair with a teenager became known to the family. She announced her immediate retirement as councillor, MLA and MP. Mr Robinson announced that he was standing down temporarily as First Minister to deal with the family crisis and the issues surrounding it. There was widespread speculation about his ability to return to office. He was replaced temporarily by Arlene Foster.

Adams was widely criticised as accusations emerged concerning his handling of alleged sexual abuse within his wider family twenty years earlier.

A Catholic PSNI officer was seriously injured by a booby-trap car bomb at Randalstown. The victim was a GAA player and an Irish speaker.

The policing and justice stalemate continued with a summit held at Hillsborough. Brown and Cowen attended but left after three days without an agreement. A key sticking-point was the DUP's wish to link an overhaul of the Parades Commission with the devolution plan.

February — **Despite deep DUP splits an agreement was finally reached at Hillsborough: devolution was to take place on 12 April; there would be a working group on parades and another on issues logjammed at Stormont. Robinson resumed office as First Minister.**

The INLA announced the decommissioning of their weapons as did the Official IRA and the renegade south-east Antrim UDA. These organisations did this just before the decommissioning legislation expired and the IICD ceased to exist.

Margaret Ritchie was elected leader of the SDLP.

A car bomb exploded outside Newry court house.

The body of Kieran Doherty was found outside Derry. It was believed he was shot by the Real IRA.

2010

March   Paisley announced that he would stand down at the forthcoming
Westminster election. Lady Sylvia Hermon, the UUP MP for North Down,
resigned from the party and announced that she would stand as an
independent.

April   A British general election was announced for 6 May.
A car bomb planted by dissident republicans exploded outside Palace
Barracks, Holywood, where MI5 had a major base.
David Ford was confirmed as justice minister by the assembly.
A car bomb exploded outside a police station in Newtownhamilton, County
Armagh.
Chief Constable Baggott announced a delay to the scrapping of the PSNI
full-time reserve for at least nine months in face of the continued activity by
dissident republican groups.

May   In the 6 May general election SF topped the poll in NI but, while the DUP
vote held up well, Robinson sensationally lost the East Belfast seat he had
held for thirty-one years to Alliance candidate Naomi Long. Observers said
the Robinson vote had been affected by the adverse publicity on
Westminster expenses, the scandal involving his wife and a perception of
them as the 'Swish Family Robinson'. Robinson said he was determined to
remain DUP leader and First Minister.
The UUP fared badly and ended with no Westminster MPs. Lady Sylvia
Hermon retained her North Down seat as an independent. UUP leader Reg
Empey failed in his attempt to win a seat.
Owen Paterson was appointed NI Secretary.
Prime minister David Cameron visited NI on 20 May.
The HET confirmed an interim report that the Reavey family was entirely
innocent of involvement in the killing of ten Protestant workmen at
Kingsmills in 1976. Three Reavey brothers had been killed the day before by
loyalists.
DUP culture minister Nelson McCausland pressed the Ulster Museum to
give greater prominence to Ulster Scots, the Orange Order and creationism.
Loyalist Bobby Moffett was shot dead by two masked UVF gunmen in front
of shoppers on the Shankill Road.
A bomb exploded outside Strand Road police station in Derry city.
It was announced that Ian Paisley would become Lord Bannside.

June   Dawn Purvis resigned as leader of the PUP as a result of the killing of
Bobby Moffett.
**The Saville report into the 1972 Bloody Sunday killings was published.
Saville said that soldiers should not have been ordered into the Bogside
by their commander. It concluded that a soldier had fired the first shot,
that none of those killed presented a threat and that some of them had
been killed while fleeing or helping those already shot. The report said
that it was 'more likely than not' that McGuinness, then second in
command of the IRA in Derry, had been armed with a Thompson submachine gun.
On the day the report was released prime minister Cameron apologised
and gave his unequivocal backing to Saville's findings which he listed in
detail during a Commons statement widely praised for its generosity.**

2010

July   A proposal agreed by the DUP and SF for reshaping parades legislation was rejected by the Orange Order.

Three police officers were injured by gunfire during riots in Belfast's North Queen Street. Rioting was widespread across NI for four nights around the Twelfth of July and eighty police officers were injured.

Londonderry was named UK City of Culture for 2013, generating hopes that this would promote jobs and investment.

NI Secretary Paterson said that the government was ruling out the use of major inquiries as a way of dealing with the past.

Ian Paisley, installed in the Lords as Lord Bannside, said he would accept a SF First Minister: 'I have to accept the will of the people. Naturally as a Unionist I will continue to play my part to prevent [a SF majority] happening in the future.' And he added: 'Sinn Féin didn't become the majority party on my watch.'

The remains of Charles Armstrong, believed to have been kidnapped and killed by the IRA in 1981, were found in County Monaghan. He was the fifth of the sixteen so-called 'disappeared' to be found.

August   A bomb exploded outside Strand Road police station in Derry.

A primed bomb was found in the driveway of an army officer living in Bangor: it was believed to have fallen from his car.

A bomb exploded under the car of a PSNI civilian worker as he was driving near Cookstown. He escaped unhurt.

A bomb was found under the car of a Catholic policewoman in Kilkeel, County Down.

A Police Ombudsman's office report into the 1972 IRA bombings of the County Londonderry village of Claudy which killed nine people concluded that the victims were failed because police did not arrest Catholic priest Father Chesney despite intelligence that he was a senior IRA figure. Instead NI Secretary William Whitelaw met privately with Cardinal Conway and the priest was moved to Donegal. Cardinal Brady, under pressure to apologise to the victims' families, issued a statement saying that he 'was not convinced at all' that Father Chesney was involved in the Claudy bombing. McGuinness later said that he had visited Father Chesney in Donegal in 1980 just before he died.

September   In his political memoir Tony Blair described Adams and McGuinness as 'an extraordinary couple' and big political leaders. He admitted: 'Over time I came to like them both greatly, probably more than I should have, if truth be told.'

Tom Elliott, elected as leader of the UUP, said that he would not attend GAA matches or gay pride marches.

An inquiry concluded that the killing of loyalist Billy Wright in the Maze prison in 1997 was the result of prison incompetence not collusion.

President McAleese received the families of the Bloody Sunday victims at her Phoenix Park residence.

Home Secretary Theresa May said that the threat level for the UK from dissident republicans had been raised from moderate to substantial suggesting that an attack was a 'strong possibility'.

October   A bomb planted by dissident republicans on the Culmore Road in Derry damaged nearby businesses.

Human remains found in County Louth were those of Gerry Evans, one of the 'disappeared'. He was believed to have been abducted and killed by the IRA in 1979.

2010

Robinson labelled the separate systems of education in NI as a form of 'apartheid', a description rejected by McGuinness and the Catholic Church.

November   Gusty Spence, a founding figure of the modern UVF, called on the organisation to disband.

Margaret Ritchie became the first nationalist party leader to wear a poppy at Remembrance Day ceremonies.

Reg Empey was given a life peerage.

Gerry Adams announced that he would stand down as MP for West Belfast when an election was called in the south in order to stand for election to the Dáil in County Louth.

The British government agreed to contribute £7 billion to help the Irish Republic in its economic crisis. The government said it was in Britain's interest to do so.

SF candidate Pearse Doherty won a by-election in Donegal in a serious blow to the Fianna Fáil government whose majority was reduced to two.

December   A prison inspectors' report painted a damning picture of NI prisons. The cost of detaining a prisoner in NI was double that in the rest of the UK. The role of the Prison Officers Association in resisting change was singled out for criticism.

Bertie Ahern announced that he would stand down at the next election.

Two people died in troubles-related violence in 2010.

2011

January   **The murder of Michaela McAreavey, daughter of Tyrone GAA manager Mickey Harte, while on her honeymoon in Mauritius produced a remarkable outpouring of sympathy across community divisions. Robinson and McGuinness were joined by leading DUP politicians as well as President Mary McAleese, Chief Constable Baggott and two Church of Ireland bishops.**

A bomb planted by the Real IRA exploded outside the headquarters of the Londonderry City of Culture organisation. There were no injuries and only slight damage.

In Dublin the Irish Green party, junior partner in the coalition with Fianna Fáil, withdrew precipitating an early general election. As announced earlier, Adams immediately stood down as an MP to contest the election. Brian Cowen announced that he was standing down as Fianna Fáil leader. Micheál Martin was elected Fianna Fáil leader.

Security forces in Belfast disarmed two dissident anti-personnel devices intended for PSNI officers in north Belfast.

February   Robinson, then aged sixty-two, said in a BBC documentary that he had told his family 'that somewhere around the sixty to sixty-five age I would retire and put my hand to something else. By and large that's what I still intend to do.'

A Police Ombudsman's report concluded that RUC bias had misled the British government into believing that the IRA had been responsible for the bombing of McGurk's bar in 1971 which killed fifteen people.

An Irish general election resulted in a Fine Gael–Labour coalition government and a disastrous decline for Fianna Fáil. Adams topped the poll in County Louth and the party increased their number of TDs from four in 2007 to fourteen.

2011

March   A budget agreed by the DUP, SF and Alliance was pushed through despite
          opposition by the SDLP and the UUP.

          **The NI Secretary announced that 50/50 recruitment of Protestants and
          Catholics into the PSNI would cease from 28 March. Catholic
          membership of the force, which stood at 8 per cent in 1998, was now
          almost 30 per cent, Paterson saying this was the critical mass envisaged
          by Lord Patten.**

          Ian Paisley made his final appearance at Stormont.

          Two hundred families were moved overnight from their homes in the
          Oldpark area of north Belfast because of a bomb warning from dissident
          republicans.

April   **Catholic PSNI officer Ronan Kerr was killed by an under-car bomb as he
          got into his vehicle at his home in Omagh, three months after he
          graduated from police training college. McGuinness described the
          dissident republican campaign as 'futile'. Robinson attended the funeral
          mass 'to convey my respect for a brave young policeman'. The very large
          funeral was also attended by Taoiseach Enda Kenny, Adams and many
          other public figures. UDA leader Jackie McDonald also attended. The
          coffin, bearing the officer's PSNI cap and gloves, was carried by local
          GAA men and colleagues from the PSNI.**

          A Belfast Orange lodge initiated disciplinary proceedings against Unionist
          politician members who attended.

May   In the May assembly election the DUP and SF consolidated their positions as
          the decline of the SDLP and the UUP continued. Robinson and McGuinness
          resumed their roles as the First Ministers.

          **The Queen made what was hailed as a highly successful four-day visit to
          the Irish Republic. She went to a number of sites, such as Croke Park,
          which had previously been regarded as politically sensitive, and said her
          visit was a reminder of 'the importance of forbearance and conciliation,
          of being able to bow to the past but not be bound by it'.**

          There was angry condemnation by Unionists of the appointment of Mary
          McArdle as special adviser by culture minister Carál Ní Chuilín. McArdle
          had been convicted for her part in the 1984 IRA killing of Mary Travers,
          daughter of magistrate Tom Travers, as the family left mass in south Belfast.

          SF's 25-year-old Niall Ó Donnghaile was elected Lord Mayor of Belfast three
          weeks after being elected to the council.

June   Five years after it was established by the Irish government, the Smithwick
          tribunal into the circumstances of the IRA killing of two RUC officers in
          1989 held its first public session. It heard that the inquiry's legal team had
          met three former IRA members who were party to the killings.

          The PSNI blamed the UVF for rioting on successive nights at Short Strand in
          east Belfast.

          A new Derry footbridge – the Peace Bridge – across the river Foyle was
          officially opened to add a symbolic and practical link between the largely
          Catholic cityside and the largely Protestant Waterside.

          A dissident republican bomb-making operation was discovered as a result of
          Garda raids on farms in Louth and Kildare.

July   There were riots in east Belfast following an Orange parade. Police used
          plastic baton rounds and water cannon.

Chronology

2011

In advance of the Twelfth of July there was sporadic rioting in south Antrim, mainly triggered by the PSNI removal of loyalist flags. There was also rioting in north Belfast and in Londonderry after Orange parades.

August   There was fierce rioting involving nationalist youths in Derry after the annual Apprentice Boys parade.

September The Reverend David Latimer of Derry First Presbyterian church spoke at the SF ard fheis, and said he had formed a close working and personal relationship with McGuinness. The clergyman, who had spent four months as a chaplain to the British army in Afghanistan, was described as a 'traitor' by some Unionist politicians.
SF caused a stir by announcing that McGuinness would enter the Irish presidential election. In the course of campaigning McGuinness said he had been 'ashamed' of IRA bomb attacks such as that in Enniskillen in 1987. He described the attack as 'atrocious'.
In the space of three days two PSNI officers escaped uninjured when an explosive device was thrown at them in Newtownabbey; another officer escaped uninjured when a bomb exploded at his home in Claudy; and a viable explosive device was found at the home of a forensic medical officer.
The UUP leader said there would not be a revival of the UUP–Tory electoral alliance.
Gusty Spence died aged seventy-eight.

October   Four UDA leaders travelled to the USA to meet political, business and community leaders to lobby for loyalist communities.
Members of the Finucane family walked out of a Downing Street meeting, saying David Cameron had not offered them the full inquiry they had been led to expect. Instead a senior QC was appointed to review papers in the case.
McGuinness initially fared well in opinion polls during the presidential campaign but faced heavy criticism from much of the Irish media for his and the IRA's past. He was confronted by victims' families on a number of occasions.
Figures revealed that Catholics outnumbered Protestants in Northern Ireland's primary and secondary schools and universities.
The Orange order announced that no disciplinary action would be taken against the UUP leader for attending the funeral of PSNI officer Ronan Kerr.
Michael D. Higgins (Labour) was elected president of the Irish Republic.
McGuinness came third with 14 per cent, up from SF's 9.9 per cent in the February general election.

November Alasdair McDonnell was elected leader of the SDLP.
The PSNI proposed the closure of thirty-five police stations, a third of the total.
Ian Paisley announced that he would give up his position as senior minister at the Martyrs Memorial church at the end of 2011.
Unionist politicians protested angrily at the possibility that the crown would be removed as an emblem of the prison service. First Minister Robinson said he would resign and precipitate an assembly election if such a proposal emerged.
Taoiseach Enda Kenny met the Finucane family and said he would lobby for a full inquiry when in London and Washington.
At the DUP conference Robinson told delegates that the way forward was to build a shared society and reaffirmed his commitment to integrated education in some form.

The SF Lord Mayor of Belfast refused to award a Duke of Edinburgh certificate to an army cadet saying he did not wish to compromise his republican principles. He subsequently apologised in face of widespread criticism and loyalist demonstrations at the city hall.

December   It was reported that hundreds of former RUC officers who had retired on substantial pensions had been rehired by the PSNI.

Some of the Bloody Sunday families decided to continue with the annual January protest march.

A HET report on the 1975 attack on the Miami Showband concluded that one of the UVF gang was an RUC agent. The attack left three members of the band and two UVF members dead.

There were disputes in Belfast council over an Irish-language Christmas sign at the city hall and over the number of days the Union Jack would be displayed on the building.

The army defused a bomb near the PSNI station at Keady, County Armagh.

On 18 December Ian Paisley gave his final Martyrs Memorial Sunday sermon as senior minister.

The RUC Reserve went out of existence on the final day of the year.

One person died in troubles-related violence in 2011, the lowest figure since 1968.

2012
January   A bomb was discovered under a car being driven by a soldier visiting NI.

Two bombs exploded in Londonderry city causing considerable damage but no injuries.

A man was convicted of the 2009 killing of soldiers Quinsey and Azimkar. He was later sentenced to twenty-five years in prison. Another man was acquitted.

It was confirmed that Alliance leader David Ford would remain as justice minister but the second department headed by an Alliance member would be scrapped.

Robinson accompanied McGuinness to a GAA match in Armagh, the first GAA game attended by the DUP leader.

UUP leader Tom Elliott demoted colleague David McNarry after accusing him of revealing confidential details of UUP–DUP talks. The affair led to significant division in the party.

February   Ian Paisley spent a week in intensive care in the Ulster Hospital as a result of heart problems but later returned home.

Andrew Allen was shot dead in Buncrana, County Donegal, by a Derry-based dissident republican vigilante group. More than twenty men had been the victims of punishment shootings in the Derry area in the previous two years, with others forced to leave home.

Twelve of the thirteen men facing charges in the loyalist supergrass trial were acquitted on all charges. Only one man was convicted, on lesser charges.

SF MLA Mitchel McLaughlin said that the visit of the Queen had affected him 'tremendously'. He paid tribute to the generosity of spirit of the Queen and former Irish President, Mary McAleese. 'We have a bit of unlearning to do,' he added.

June   **The Queen made a two-day visit to NI and, at an event in Belfast's Lyric Theatre, met and shook hands with Martin McGuinness.**

Tables

TABLES 1–4 are updated versions of material first published in *Lost Lives* (Mainstream Publishing, Edinburgh, 1999).

TABLE 1 DEATHS BY YEAR

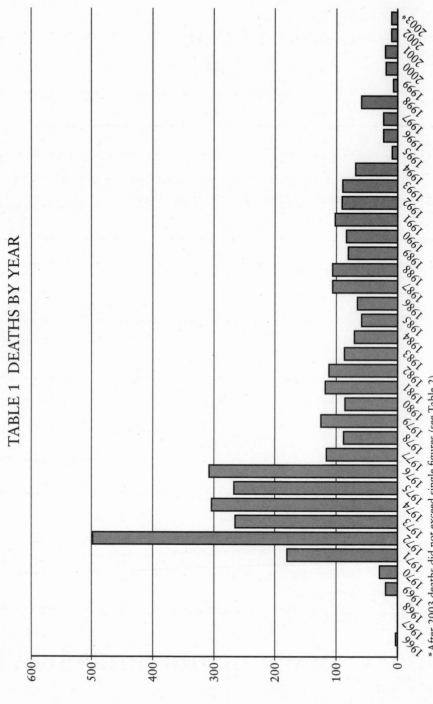

* After 2003 deaths did not exceed single figures (see Table 2)

TABLE 2 DEATHS BY YEAR AND STATUS

	All Civilians	Civilians in NI (Protestant)	Civilians in NI (Catholic)	RUC/PSNI	RUCR	UDR/RIR	ARMY	Paramilitaries Republican	Paramilitaries Loyalist	OTHER	TOTAL
1966	3	1	2	0	0	0	0	0	0	0	3
1967	0	0	0	0	0	0	0	0	0	0	0
1968	0	0	0	0	0	0	0	0	0	0	0
1969	14	6	8	1	0	0	1	2	1	0	19
1970	19	8	10	2	0	0	0	7	0	1	29
1971	94	27	65	11	0	0	44	23	0	0	180
1972	257	74	176	15	2	5	108	76	3	3	498
1973	136	48	82	9	4	26	59	36	11	0	265
1974	204	50	123	12	3	8	45	24	13	2	304
1975	173	62	101	7	4	7	15	31	7	2	267
1976	220	91	125	13	11	16	14	17	28	5	308
1977	55	20	33	8	6	14	15	8	12	3	116
1978	47	26	21	4	6	7	15	7	7	1	88
1979	43	16	21	9	5	10	37	9	1	2	125
1980	45	19	23	3	6	9	11	5	2	5	86
1981	53	18	33	13	8	13	10	17	3	5	118
1982	47	22	24	8	4	7	32	7	5	1	112
1983	38	17	18	9	9	10	5	8	2	2	87
1984	28	7	16	7	2	10	9	12	1	6	71
1985	23	6	17	15	8	4	2	5	0	2	59
1986	34	13	21	10	2	8	4	6	2	2	66
1987	43	27	16	9	7	8	3	26	7	0	106
1988	40	13	27	4	2	12	23	15	5	3	106
1989	38	14	22	7	2	2	24	3	3	5	81
1990	46	17	26	7	5	8	9	6	2	2	84
1991	61	18	41	5	1	8	5	14	8	1	102
1992	63	17	42	3	1	3	4	14	2	0	91
1993	69	21	45	3	3	2	6	4	2	1	90
1994	52	12	40	3	0	2	1	3	8	1	69
1995	8	1	7	0	0	0	0	0	1	0	9
1996	11	1	8	0	0	0	1	7	3	1	23
1997	15	6	9	3	1	0	1	1	2	0	23
1998	54	19	33	1	0	0	0	1	3	0	59
1999	6	1	5	0	0	0	0	1	3	0	7
2000	10	7	3	0	0	0	0	0	1	0	19
2001	16	7	9	0	0	0	0	1	8	0	20
2002	8	5	3	0	0	0	0	0	4	0	10
2003	4	1	3	0	0	0	0	1	2	0	10
2004	3	2	1	0	0	0	0	0	5	0	4
2005	8	6	2	0	0	0	0	0	1	0	8
2006	3	1	2	0	0	0	0	0	0	0	3
2007	1	0	1	0	0	0	0	2	0	0	3
2008	1	0	1	0	0	0	0	1	0	0	2
2009	2	0	2	1	0	0	2	0	0	0	5
2010	0	0	0	0	0	0	0	0	1	0	2
2011	0	0	0	1	0	0	0	0	0	0	1
2012*	1	0	1	0	0	0	0	0	0	0	1
TOTAL	**2096**	**727**	**1268**	**203**	**102**	**206**	**505**	**400**	**168**	**59**	**3739**

*Figures are correct up to June 2012.

TABLE 3 RESPONSIBILITY FOR DEATHS

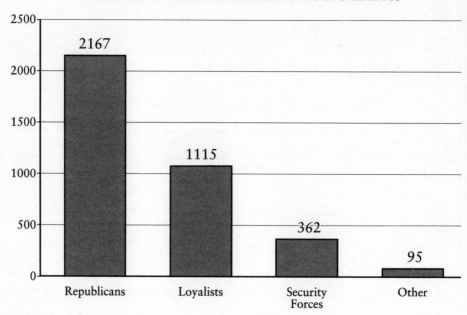

TABLE 4 RESPONSIBILITY FOR DEATHS

Year	IRA	INLA/IPLO	OIRA	Other Reps	UVF Red Hand	UDA/UFF	Other Loys.	ARMY	RUC/RUCR PSNI	UDR/RIR	OTHER	TOTAL
1966	0	0	0	0	3	0	0	0	0	0	0	3
1967	0	0	0	0	0	0	0	0	0	0	0	0
1968	0	0	0	0	0	0	0	0	0	0	0	0
1969	1	0	0	3	2	0	1	2	8	0	2	19
1970	16	0	10	4	0	1	0	5	0	0	3	29
1971	84	0	20	12	17	4	1	45	1	0	6	180
1972	231	0	4	28	35	71	15	79	6	1	12	498
1973	124	0	7	10	34	44	12	30	1	1	4	265
1974	130	0	9	13	79	41	11	15	2	0	6	304
1975	92	12	1	16	105	20	6	6	0	0	6	267
1976	139	5	4	18	71	49	6	14	2	0	3	308
1977	68	0	0	2	14	12	2	7	2	0	7	116
1978	60	0	1	2	8	2	0	12	0	0	4	88
1979	91	8	0	4	7	9	1	2	0	0	2	125
1980	45	8	0	5	4	9	1	7	2	0	5	86
1981	70	11	0	4	14	5	2	13	3	1	2	118
1982	52	32	1	1	7	1	0	4	7	1	0	112
1983	50	10	0	1	6	2	3	4	6	1	2	87
1984	44	4	0	1	2	2	2	8	3	0	1	71
1985	44	3	0	1	8	6	1	3	1	1	2	59
1986	37	2	0	2	7	12	3	4	2	1	3	66
1987	58	14	0	2	11	12	0	9	0	0	4	106
1988	66	3	0	2	13	6	0	10	1	0	2	106
1989	53	2	0	0	11	8	1	2	1	0	1	84
1990	50	2	0	1	24	16	1	11	0	0	3	102
1991	45	7	0	2	15	21	5	3	3	0	3	91
1992	34	6	0	1	16	31	1	5	3	1	-1	90
1993	36	2	0	1	25	12	1	0	0	0	3	69
1994	19	7	0	0	1	1	1	1	0	0	0	9
1995	7	0	0	0	5	0	0	1	0	0	3	23
1996	7	6	0	0	4	1	7	0	0	0	3	23
1997	3	2	0	0	0	4	0	1	1	0	3	59
1998	4	4	0	29	0	3	15	0	0	0	3	7
1999	4	0	0	0	6	6	3	0	0	0	0	19
2000	4	0	0	1	2	4	2	0	0	0	0	20
2001	2	0	0	3	1	6	9	0	0	0	0	10
2002	1	0	0	1	1	5	1	0	0	0	0	10
2003	0	0	0	3	2	1	0	0	0	0	0	4
2004	0	1	0	2	4	2	1	0	0	0	0	8
2005	0	0	0	1	0	1	0	0	0	0	0	3
2006	0	1	0	1	0	0	0	0	0	0	0	3
2007	0	0	0	1	0	0	1	0	0	0	0	2
2008	0	1	0	3	1	0	0	0	0	0	0	5
2009	0	0	0	1	0	0	1	0	0	0	0	2
2010	0	0	0	1	0	0	0	0	0	0	0	1
2011	0	0	0	1	0	0	0	0	0	0	0	1
2012*	0	0	0	1	0	0	0	0	0	0	0	1
TOTAL	**1771**	**154**	**57**	**185**	**572**	**431**	**112**	**302**	**52**	**8**	**95**	**3739**

*Figures are correct up to June 2012.

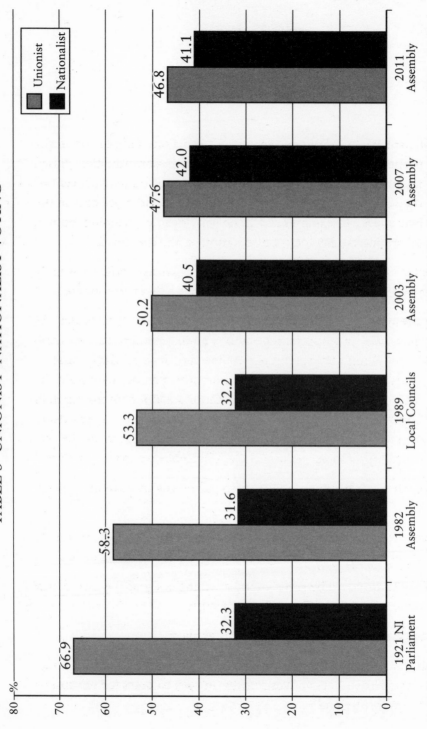

TABLE 5 UNIONIST–NATIONALIST VOTING

TABLE 5 totals the votes cast for Unionist and nationalist candidates in selected elections. It illustrates the narrowing of the gap between Unionist and nationalist votes over the years.

Glossary

Alliance Party – Founded in 1970, it was alone among the major parties in attracting support from both communities. Based mainly in the Greater Belfast area, it attracted up to 14 per cent of the vote in the 1970s though this fell to around 7 per cent in the late 1990s. It experienced a revival in 2010, winning both a Westminster seat and representation on the executive.

An Phoblacht / Republican News – Often known as *APRN*, the weekly newspaper is the official organ of the republican movement.

Apprentice Boys of Derry – One of the Protestant 'loyal orders'. Its main activity is organising various annual demonstrations commemorating the events surrounding the Siege of Derry in 1688. With around 10,000 members, some of its parades have been the subject of controversy. The organisation's major demonstration in Londonderry each August was often the occasion of increased tension. Many of the Apprentice Boys are also members of the two other 'loyal orders', the Royal Black Preceptory and Orange Order.

Ard Fheis – The term used by Irish parties for their annual conference.

Armalite – An American-made rifle favoured by the IRA, especially in the 1970s, because of its light weight and rapid rate of fire.

Army Council – The seven-member ruling body of the IRA, which determined the organisation's strategy.

B Specials – See Ulster Special Constabulary.

Campaign for Democracy in Ulster – A pressure group set up by Labour members at Westminster in 1965 to press for reforms in Northern Ireland.

Campaign for Social Justice – An early civil rights pressure group established in Dungannon in 1964.

Combined Loyalist Military Command – An umbrella group established in 1991 comprising the UDA, UVF and Red Hand Commando. The CLMC declared the loyalist ceasefire in October 1994.

Consultative Group on the Past – The body set up to recommend ways of dealing with the legacy of the troubles.

Continuity IRA (CIRA) – A breakaway republican group.

Dáil – More formally Dáil Éireann, the lower house of the Irish parliament.

Democratic Unionist party – Founded in 1971 in succession to the Protestant Unionist party, its long-time leader was the Reverend Ian Paisley, followed by Peter Robinson.

Diplock report – Produced in December 1972 by English judge Lord Diplock, it recommended that juries should be abolished in troubles-related trials. This gave rise to the term 'Diplock courts'.

E4A – A covert surveillance unit of the RUC which was involved in controversial shooting incidents in the early 1980s.

Fianna Fáil – Translated as 'Soldiers of Destiny', it was traditionally the largest of the Republic's political parties before being overtaken by Fine Gael. During the troubles it was led by Jack Lynch, Charles Haughey, Albert Reynolds, Bertie Ahern and Brian Cowen.

Fine Gael – Literally meaning 'Tribe of the Gael', it rose to become the largest political party in the Republic. In 1985 its leader and then Taoiseach Garret FitzGerald signed the Anglo-Irish Agreement with Margaret Thatcher.

Free Presbyterian Church – Church headed for decades by the Reverend Ian Paisley.

Garda Síochána – Usually known as the Garda, it is the police force of the Republic.

H-blocks – Cell blocks within the Maze prison, so named because of their shape. They were the focus of major republican protest campaigns, most notably the 1981 hungerstrike.

Historical Enquiries Team (HET) – The large-scale team set up by police as a 'cold cases' unit carrying out investigations into troubles killings. In each case a report was sent to the families.

Independent International Commission on Decommissioning (IICD) – The body established to monitor decommissioning by paramilitary groups.

Irish National Liberation Army – An extreme republican group, it was established in 1974 as a breakaway from the Official IRA. INLA members engaged in a number of republican feuds and three members died in the 1981 hungerstrike.

Irish Republican Socialist party – The small political wing of the INLA.

Long Kesh – The original name of the Maze prison until it was changed by the authorities in the mid-1970s. Republicans continued to use the term 'Long Kesh' throughout the troubles.

Loyal Orange Lodge – This is the basic unit of the Orange Order. The leader of a lodge has the title Worshipful Master. Lodges combine with others to form Districts which in turn form a County Grand Lodge. The leading body is the Grand Lodge of Ireland.

Loyalist Association of Workers – Set up in 1971 with close links to the UDA, it played a prominent role in harnessing loyalist industrial power for a short period in the 1970s. It was superseded by the Ulster Workers Council.

Loyalist Volunteer Force – A dissident faction of the UVF formed in the late 1990s, it was mainly made up of former mid-Ulster

UVF members opposed to the organisation's ceasefire. It carried out a number of sectarian killings, especially following the death of its leader, Billy Wright.

M-60 – The standard US army belt-fed general-purpose machine gun, several of which were acquired by the IRA in the 1980s and used in a number of attacks in which security force members were killed.

Northern Ireland Civil Rights Association – Established in 1967 and modelled on the tactics of the American civil rights movement, it launched a campaign centring on marches and demonstrations.

Northern Ireland Labour party – A socialist party founded in 1924 and with links to the British Labour party, it had its greatest success in the Stormont elections of 1958 and 1962, winning four seats in each. It later ceased to be a political force.

Northern Ireland Office – The department of the British government established in 1972 to administer Northern Ireland under direct rule from Westminster, through a Northern Ireland Secretary with a seat in the British cabinet.

Official IRA – A republican paramilitary group, it remained largely dormant after declaring a ceasefire in 1972. Decades later it said it had decommissioned its weaponry.

Óglaigh Na hÉireann – A breakaway republican group which used the name traditionally used by the IRA.

Orange Order – The largest of the 'loyal orders', it was founded in County Armagh in 1795, and by the time of the Home Rule controversies in the late nineteenth century had expanded into an important Protestant umbrella group. Throughout its existence its tradition of marching led to recurring controversy. Its extensive programme of marches culminates annually on 12 July in a commemoration of the victory of King William III at the Battle of the Boyne in 1690.

Peaceline – Originally large fences made from corrugated metal, most of these were erected in the late 1960s and early 1970s to provide a physical barrier between Catholic and Protestant districts. Many of the peacelines in north and west Belfast have been replaced by permanent structures. Several new walls were erected after 2000.

Plastic bullet – Officially described as a plastic baton round (PBR), it is a controversial riot-control weapon used extensively from 1973 on. The weapon resulted in sixteen deaths.

Police Service of Northern Ireland – A new body which replaced the Royal Ulster Constabulary in November 2001. It came into being in line with the widespread changes recommended by the Patten report which was commissioned at the time of the Good Friday Agreement.

Progressive Unionist party – The political wing of the UVF, it was a small political party strongest in working-class areas of Belfast. It went into decline after its most prominent spokesman, David Ervine, died in 2007.

Proportional representation – An electoral system designed to ensure that representation is closely related to votes cast in an election. In use for elections in the first years of Northern Ireland's history, it was abolished during the 1920s. It was reintroduced in the early years of the troubles and used for all elections other than for Westminster.

Provisional Irish Republican Army – Generally known simply as the IRA and by the security forces as PIRA, it was the largest of the republican paramilitary groups. Following a split with the Official IRA in 1969, its campaign of violence proceeded virtually unbroken for more than three decades. Known in Irish by republicans as Óglaigh na hÉireann, in 1994 it declared a ceasefire and in the twenty-first century announced that it was decommissioning its weapons and ceasing activity.

Real IRA (RIRA) – A breakaway republican group.

Royal Irish Regiment – A regiment of the British army established in 1992 when the UDR and Royal Irish Rangers were merged.

Royal Ulster Constabulary – The police force for Northern Ireland for eight decades, it came into being in 1921 and lasted until its replacement by the PSNI in 2001.

Royal Ulster Constabulary Reserve – Made up of both full-time and part-time members, it had an identical uniform to the RUC and functioned alongside regular officers.

Rubber bullet – A riot-control weapon, it was used extensively until its replacement by plastic bullets. According to official figures, 55,000 were fired between 1970 and 1974.

Sinn Féin – Essentially the political wing of the IRA, it claimed descent from a party established in the early years of the twentieth century. An all-Ireland political organisation headed by Gerry Adams, it eventually overtook the SDLP as the main nationalist party. For much of the troubles it was seen as subordinate to the IRA but in 2007 it became the predominant part of the republican movement when it went into government with other parties in Belfast, its chief negotiator Martin McGuinness becoming Deputy First Minister.

Social Democratic and Labour party – The main nationalist party in Northern Ireland for most of the troubles, it was established in 1970 with the aim of promoting a united Ireland by peaceful means. It was eclipsed by Sinn Féin. Its leader for most of the troubles was John Hume.

Special Air Service – A special forces unit of the British army officially known as 22 SAS Regiment, it was formally deployed in Northern Ireland in 1976.

Stormont – The building, completed in 1929, which housed the Northern Ireland parliament until its suspension in 1972. It became the seat of the assembly established after the 1998 Good

Friday Agreement. The term 'Stormont' is also used to refer to the Unionist government of the period 1921–72.

Supergrass – A person formerly active in a republican or loyalist group who agreed to give evidence against alleged former associates. The emergence of more than a dozen such figures in the early 1980s led to a series of large-scale trials in Belfast.

Taoiseach – The term, literally meaning 'chief', for the Irish prime minister.

TD – A member of the Dáil, the Irish parliament (in full, Teachta Dála).

Third Force – A loyalist militia, more often threatened than sighted, which was said to exist at various points during the troubles.

TUV – Traditional Unionist Voice, the party founded by ex-DUP Euro-MP Jim Allister to oppose the powersharing agreement.

Ulster Defence Association – The largest loyalist paramilitary organisation, the UDA was established in Belfast in 1971 and proscribed in 1992. In 2007 it announced its weapons were being put beyond use and promised it was giving up violence.

Ulster Defence Regiment – A regiment of the British army made up of full-time and part-time members recruited in Northern Ireland, it was raised in 1970 following the disbandment of the B Specials. In 1992 the UDR was amalgamated with the Royal Irish Rangers to form the Royal Irish Regiment.

Ulster Democratic party – The political wing of the UDA, its most prominent representatives were Gary McMichael and David Adams. It was wound up after failing to gain electoral success.

Ulster Freedom Fighters – A cover name first used by members of the UDA in 1973.

Ulster Protestant Volunteers – A loyalist group which supported Ian Paisley, its members often appeared at counter-demonstrations against the civil rights movement.

Ulster Special Constabulary – Established in 1920 by the new Unionist government, it was an armed auxiliary force under the command of the RUC. An exclusively Protestant force which attracted much nationalist criticism, it was abolished and replaced by the UDR.

Ulster Unionist Council – The 800-strong ruling body of the Ulster Unionist party.

Ulster Unionist party – The main Unionist party for most of Northern Ireland's history, it provided the government from 1921 until 1972, securing an overall majority in every election. David (later Lord) Trimble served as its leader for ten years from 1995. It was eventually eclipsed as the largest party by the DUP.

Ulster Volunteer Force – A loyalist paramilitary group which emerged in the mid-1960s, it carried out the first three killings of the troubles. Banned in June 1966, it was legalised in 1974 before again being declared illegal in 1975. It eventually declared a cease-fire though it did not completely abandon violence.

Ulster Workers Council – A loyalist grouping which helped organise the loyalist strike which brought down the powersharing executive in May 1974.

Unionist Party of Northern Ireland – A short-lived political party established by Brian Faulkner in 1974 to promote the aims of the powersharing tendency within Unionism.

United Ulster Unionist Council – An umbrella group of Unionist parties opposed to powersharing, it existed from 1974 until 1977.

United Unionist Action Council (UUAC) – An umbrella group of loyalist parties and other groups, it staged the 1977 loyalist strike.

Vanguard Unionist Progressive party – Established in 1973 by Unionist politician William Craig, it developed from the earlier Ulster Vanguard movement which emerged in early 1972. It was wound up in the late 1970s.

Bibliographical notes

Our bookshelves contain more than 500 books concerned with the troubles and Irish history generally, most of which contain bibliographies. Since this work is intended as a straightforward and accessible account of the troubles, we have opted for an informal note rather than a more formal bibliography.

We are indebted to Belfast's three most important reference sources, Belfast Central Library, in particular its newspaper archive, the Linen Hall Library and the Public Record Office of Northern Ireland, each of which is both invaluable and staffed by invaluable people. We also made use of material released by the National Archives in Dublin. The thirty-year rule means government papers after the late 1960s were not available, a minor exception being material released in the course of the Bloody Sunday inquiry. While there are official government reports by the dozen, the most valuable for our purposes were the Cameron and Scarman reports.

The history books we found most useful were those of Jonathan Bardon, Alvin Jackson and Patrick Buckland. John Whyte's work is a model of how to write with scrupulous fairness on the most controversial of subjects.

In terms of the troubles the most useful reference books were the Flackes & Elliott *Political Directory* and *Lost Lives*, to which both of us contributed, which records the circumstances of every death of the troubles. We drew too on the extensive files, documents, notes and records accumulated by David McKittrick in three decades of reporting on the troubles as a journalist. During this time he has had access to sources on all points of the political compass. David McVea also has records accumulated during three decades as a teacher of history and politics.

On specific aspects of the troubles, the most useful books were by Fionnuala O Connor, Brendan O'Leary & John McGarry, Robert Fisk, and Eamonn Mallie & Patrick Bishop. We also drew on work by Ed Moloney & Andy Pollak, Padraig O'Malley, Richard Rose, Bob Purdie, David Beresford, Peter Taylor, Paul Bew *et al.*, Henry Kelly, Steve Bruce, Eamonn McCann, and Arthur Aughey. We would particularly like to thank Eamonn Mallie for agreeing to our extensive use of the Mallie & McKittrick book *The Fight for Peace*.

A substantial amount of autobiographical material is available and was of great use to us. On the British side this includes books by Harold Wilson, Wilson's aides Joe Haines and Bernard Donoughue, James Callaghan, Edward Heath, former ambassador to Dublin Sir John Peck, Reginald Maudling, William Whitelaw, Merlyn Rees, Roy Mason, James Prior, Margaret Thatcher, Geoffrey Howe, John Major, Mo Mowlam, Tony Blair, and Blair's aides Jonathan Powell and Alastair Campbell.

There are also autobiographies by Terence O'Neill, Brian Faulkner, Paddy Devlin, Gerry Adams, Seán MacStiofáin, Basil McIvor, Garret FitzGerald, Albert Reynolds and Senator George Mitchell. In addition there are works on O'Neill, Faulkner, Adams, Wilson, Callaghan, John Hume, James Molyneaux, Thatcher, David Trimble, Peter Mandelson, Seán Lemass, FitzGerald and Charles Haughey.

We also drew on books by Albert Reynolds's aide Seán Duignan and Dick Spring's aide Fergus Finlay. The memoirs of civil servants such as Patrick Shea, Ken Bloomfield and Maurice Hayes were highly informative. Maurice Hayes in particular provided many pen portraits and descriptions which proved irresistible to us: our text is strewn and we hope enlivened with his wit and insights.

Index

Page numbers in *italics* refer to chronology entries.

Index

Index

Index

Index

Index

Index

Index

Author's Note

During frequent stays in Calcutta I was fortunate enough to meet some exceptional human beings. They have given me so much, and have had such an impact on my life, that I decided I wanted to tell a story about their lives, in a remarkable area of the world called the City of Joy.

This story concerns men, women and children who have been uprooted from their homes by implacable nature and hostile circumstances, and thrown into a city whose capacity for hospitality has been pushed beyond imagining. This is a story about how people learn, despite incredibly difficult odds, to survive, to share and to love.

My story about the City of Joy is based on three years of extensive research in Calcutta and various areas of Bengal. I was given access to personal diaries and correspondence, and the bulk of my research consisted of over two hundred lengthy interviews, conducted through interpreters in various languages including Hindi, Bengali and Urdu. These interviews, which I transcribed into English and French, are the basis for the dialogues and testimonies in this book.

The protagonists of the City of Joy wished to remain anonymous. Therefore, I have purposely changed the identities of some characters and certain situations. The story I tell here is, however, true to the confidences that the people of the City of Joy have shared with me, and to the spirit of this unusual place.

This book, though the fruit of extensive research, does not pretend to speak for the whole of India. I have enormous affection for India, and great admiration for its

intelligence, its achievements, its tenacity in overcoming difficulties. I know well its virtues, grandeurs and diversity. The reader should not extend to the country as a whole impressions he gathers here of one small corner of it – a small area of Calcutta called the City of Joy.

Dominique Lapierre

PART ONE
You Are the Light of the World

1

He had the appearance of a Mogul warrior: thick shock of curly hair, sideburns which met the drooping curve of his moustache, a strong, stocky torso, long muscular arms and slightly bowed legs. Yet thirty-two-year-old Hasari Pal was merely a peasant, one of the five hundred or so million inhabitants of India who were looking to the goddess Earth for their livelihood.

He had built his two-roomed hut with mud walls and a thatched roof; it was a short distance away from the village of Bankuli, West Bengal, a state in northeast India larger than Scotland and five times as populated as Greater London. His wife, Aloka, was a young woman with a clear complexion and the look of an angel. The wing of her nose was pierced with a gold ring and her ankles were ornamented with bangles that jangled as she walked. She had given him three children. The eldest, twelve-year-old Amrita, had inherited her father's almond eyes and her mother's peach skin. Ten-year-old Manooj and six-year-old Shambu were two sturdy boys with black tousled hair who would far rather chase lizards around the pond than guide the buffalo into the family rice field. In the peasant's home there lived also Hasari's father, Prodip, a gaunt man with a lined face, barred with a thin, grey moustache; his mother Nalini, a bent old woman as wrinkled as a walnut; his two younger brothers with their wives and children – in all, sixteen people.

Openings set very low in the framework of the hut maintained a certain degree of coolness in the torrid summer, and a little warmth during the chilly winter nights. Shaded by red-and-white bougainvillaeas, a

narrow veranda ran the length of the hut on two sides.

Seated beneath a sloping porch roof, Aloka was pedalling at a kind of wooden seesaw with a pestle fixed to its end, a machine which served to husk the rice. Tick-tack, tick-tack, as the pedal for the rice machine rose and fell, her daughter, Amrita, pushed new handfuls of grain under the pestle. The rice, removed from its husk, was picked up and sorted by the grandmother. As soon as she had a basketful she went to empty it at the *gola*, a small silo set on piles in the middle of the courtyard. Its loft was on two levels and served simultaneously as a granary and a dovecote.

All around the hut the golden rice plantations stretched as far as the eye could see, sprinkled with the dark green of mango orchards, the light green of palm tree clusters and the soft green of bamboo groves, set at far distances from each other. Like sparkling lacework reflecting the blue of the sky, irrigation canals stitched the landscape tightly into squares. Footbridges formed delicate arabesques over pools covered with lotuses, hyacinths and ducks. Children with sticks drove great shining buffalo across the small dikes, stirring up an ochre-coloured dust as they went. At the end of this stiflingly hot day, the reddening disc of Surya, the Sun god, was sinking beyond the horizon, and a welcome breeze was blowing in from the sea. From the vast, flat expanse of land resounded the joyous cry of a myriad birds swooping low over the rice tips in salute to the oncoming night. Bengal was indeed the celebrated jewel of troubadours and poets, a paradise where on moonlit nights the god Krishna came to play his flute with the *gopis*, his playmates, and to sweep his beloved wife, Radha, into his dance.

With the disappearance of the sun came 'the hour of the cow dust', the time when the cattle came back from their grazing, the men returned from the rice fields, and the chickens came home to roost. With his cotton

loincloth tucked up between his legs to make it easier
for him to walk, Hasari Pal whistled as he ambled
peaceably along, carrying his wooden plough over his
shoulder. As the night drew on, the doves redoubled
their circling and cooing. In the tamarinds a tribe of
mynahs, India's sparrows, struck up a deafening concert.
Two squirrels striped with the 'three finger-marks of
the god Rama' scampered about in the papaya. Herons
and egrets made hastily for their nests. A mangy dog
sniffed at the ground in search of a suitable place to spend
the night. Then, gradually, the high-pitched squeak of
the cicadas faded away. There was the last tick-tack of
the rice machine – then silence, a silence that was almost
immediately broken as the frogs started up their chorus.
And above that there rose the rhythmic croak of a buffalo
toad.

In less than five minutes, the tropical night had descended upon the land. As she did every evening, Hasari's wife, Aloka, blew into a conch shell to greet the
goddess of the night. One of her sisters-in-law rang a
small bell to chase away the evil spirits, especially those
who lived in the hundred-year-old banyan tree at the
end of the road. The cow was tied up in the shanty that
served as a stable. For a while a recalcitrant goat forced
everyone to scatter about, trying to catch it. Eventually,
however, order was restored and Hasari pulled a barbed
gate across the entrance to the courtyard, to keep out
jackals and foxes. Then his mother performed a ritual as
ancient as India itself – she filled the oil in the lamp which
burned before polychrome pictures of the tutelary gods:
Rama and his wife Sita, goddess of the fruits of the earth;
Lakshmi, the goddess of prosperity seated on a lotus
blossom; and Ganesh, the elephant-headed god of good
fortune. Two other pictures, discoloured by the years,
showed the childlike face of Krishna, greedily swallowing a bowl of butter, a popular representation of the
Cowherd god most dearly loved by the Hindu people;

and the Monkey god, Hanuman, a legendary hero of some of the most prodigious adventures of Indian mythology.

While the womenfolk cooked the meal outside over a clay oven, Hasari and his two brothers came and sat down beside their father under the veranda. The heady fragrance of a jasmine bush embalmed the night that was pinpricked with the elusive lights of dancing fireflies. In a sky studded with stars a thin crescent moon was shining. It was 'Shiva's moon', the new moon of the benefactor of the world, the thousand-eyed god of prosperity. The four men were sitting, deeply immersed in silent meditation, when Hasari noticed his father observe his sons one after another. Then he heard the old peasant murmur as if to himself, 'Coal doesn't change its colour when you wash it. What can't be cured must be endured.'

The old man couldn't remember how many generations of lotuses had bloomed and faded in the pond since he was born. 'My memory is like camphor. It evaporates with time,' he would say. 'There are so many things that I've forgotten. I am well advanced in years now and I do not know how many of the baskets of rice, filled by the gods of life at my birth, are left to me.' What Prodip Pal did remember, however, was that he had once been a prosperous peasant. He had owned as many as six granaries full of rice and eight acres of fertile land. He had been able to provide for the future of his sons and give his elder daughters generous dowries to procure them good husbands. For himself and his wife in their old age, he had kept the strip of land and the house he had inherited from his father. 'The pair of us should be able to live there in peace,' he had promised her, 'until the day when Yama, god of the dead, comes to claim us.'

The old man had been wrong in his expectations. That

plot of ground had been given to his father years ago by a *zamindar*, a large landowner, in recognition of his devotion. One day this benefactor's heir laid claim to the land. Prodip Pal refused to return it; the matter came before the courts. But the young *zamindar* had bought the judge and the peasant was obliged to abandon his land and his house. To pay the legal costs, he even had to sacrifice the dowry saved for his last daughter and the plots of his two youngest sons. 'That dishonest landowner had a heart harder than a jackal's,' he had remarked.

Fortunately his eldest son had been able to rescue the whole family under his own roof. Hasari was a good son. He did his utmost to convince his father that he was still the head of the family. The old man was indeed more familiar than anyone else with everyone's rights and duties, the local ways and customs and the boundaries of the rice fields and pastureland. He alone could maintain harmonious relations with the large landowners – a trump card of prime importance for the survival of a family of peasants. 'Fishes can't afford to live on bad terms with the crocodiles in the pool,' he often liked to say. Nevertheless, the fact remained that this man venerated by his children had lost everything. He was no longer under his own roof.

'And yet I couldn't complain,' he would concede. 'It was true that I was a ruined man but I still had my three sons. What a blessing those sons were!' Thanks to them he still enjoyed those things which, for an Indian peasant, constitute wealth: a small rice granary, a stack of straw, two cows and a buffalo, a piece of land, a little grain kept in reserve in earthenware jars in case of hard times, even a few rupees in a money box. And what of his sons' wives? They too had brought happiness into the household. They were all three as beautiful as Parvati*

* Wife of the god Shiva.

and would all three make worthy mothers for the Pandavas.* The Pals might well be poor, but they were happy. Tomorrow the lotuses would be moist with dew. The time for the harvest would come and with it the season of hope. And on the old *mowa* trunk, the orchids would proclaim the glory of God.

2

Yet further terrible trials lay in store for Prodip Pal and his family. Just like ten or twelve million other Bengali peasants during this second half of the twentieth century, they were to become the victims of that endemic phenomenon known to economists as the cycle of poverty – that unavoidable process of descending the social ladder by which the farmer becomes a sharecropper, then a peasant without land, then an agricultural labourer, then, eventually, is forced into exile. It was no use even dreaming of climbing a step in the opposite direction. Here everyone had to fight merely to defend his existing status, which was under constant threat. Improvement of that status was quite inconceivable, for poverty can only engender greater poverty. If it is true that coal does not change its colour when washed, it is equally true that poverty painted in even the most dazzling colours remains for ever poverty.

Their legal wrangles with the *zamindar* had left the Pals with only half an acre of good land, on which to produce about a thousand pounds of rice. That constituted barely a quarter of what was actually necessary to feed the family. To make up the deficit, Prodip Pal and his sons managed to sharecrop another plot of land.

* Five brothers, heroes of the great epic, the Mahabharata.

Although some owners demanded three quarters of the harvest in payment, Prodip was able to retain half of it. This arrangement was of vital importance. When they ran out of rice, they would survive on the fruits from the three coconut trees and on the vegetables from the high ground that required very little irrigation, such as the 'serpent gourds', a kind of cucumber that measured up to six feet in length, marrows and giant radishes. There were also the fruits from the jackfruit tree, some of which weighed nearly four pounds. The Pals were thus able to survive for two years. They even managed to buy two goats. And they regularly gave thanks to the gods, taking offerings to the little temple built at the foot of the most ancient banyan tree in the village.

During the third year, however, disaster struck once more. A parasite destroyed the entire field of rice in midgrowth. To overcome this catastrophe, the father set out on the path that led to the only brick house of the village. Its tiled roof dominated the other huts.

Nearly all the inhabitants of Bankuli had been compelled at some time or other to call on the *mahajan*, the jeweller-usurer, a potbellied man with a skull as smooth and shiny as a billiard ball. No matter how much distaste he provoked, the *mahajan* of Bankuli was, here as elsewhere in India, the key person in the village. He was its banker, its moneylender, its pawnbroker and, very often, its vampire. By mortgaging the family field, Hasari's father obtained the loan of four hundred pounds of rice on condition that he would return six hundred after the first harvest. It was a year of great deprivation for the Pals. But 'as the tortoise moves forward with difficulty to attain his objective', they succeeded in 'turning the page of the god of life'. Because of his debts and the inability to buy enough seed, the two following years were nothing short of a nightmare. One of Hasari's brothers had to give up his sharecropping and take a job as an agricultural labourer. By this time the cycle of

poverty had really begun to strangle the Pals. Bad weather added to their plight. One night in April, a storm brought down all the mangoes and coconuts. Consequently they had to sell the buffalo and Rani, one of the two cows, despite the fact that they were so useful during the working season. Rani obviously did not want to leave. She strained at her rope with all her might, uttering the most heart-rending bellows. No one could fail to read in her reaction a bad omen, a sign that Radha, beloved of the Cowherd god Krishna, was angry.

The departure of the animals deprived the Pal family of part of their precious daily milk and, above all, of the indispensable dung, which when mixed with chopped straw and fashioned into cakes was dried in the sun and used as fuel for cooking food. Every day Hasari's daughter and her cousins had to go out in search of replacement dung. Manna as precious as this, however, did not simply belong to anyone who cared to pick it up, and the villagers chased them away. And so they learned to be secretive and steal it. From dawn to dusk, Amrita's brothers scoured the countryside, with their elder cousins, in search of anything to eat or turn into cash. They picked fruits and wild berries. They collected dead wood and acacia twigs which Indians use to clean their teeth. They caught fish in the pools. They made garlands of wild flowers. And they took these meagre treasures to the market which was held three times a week, seven miles from their house.

Two further incidents were to aggravate the Pals' financial difficulties. Weakened by the lack of food, Hasari's youngest brother fell ill. One day he began to cough blood. For such poor people illness was more of a curse even than death. A doctor's fee and the cost of medicine could take several months' income. And so, to save his brother, Hasari resorted to the only remaining course of action: he broke open his baked clay money box and ran to the village priest begging him to intervene

with destiny, by celebrating a special *puja*, a ceremony of offering to the gods.

The boy regained sufficient strength to take part in the second event of that year which was to sink his family a little further into destitution: the marriage of his youngest sister. The girl's ageing father had at last found her a husband, and nothing was to prevent the wedding festivities from proceeding according to the traditional ritual. How many millions of Indian families, for generations, have been ruined by the marriages of their daughters? First there was the dowry, an ancestral custom officially abolished since Independence, but one that still prevailed in practice. The small farmer with whom Hasari's father had negotiated the marriage of his last daughter had demanded one bicycle, two cotton loincloths, a transistor, and half an ounce of gold, plus a few jewels for the young bride – all under the guise of a dowry. In total his requirements amounted to a good thousand rupees (about £60).

Custom required, furthermore, that the girl's father, alone, covered the cost of the ceremony, which meant finding another thousand rupees to feed the families and their guests, and buy presents for the officiating Brahmin. For these poor people it was a cruel bloodletting, but the marriage of a daughter is a sacred duty for a father. Once his daughter had left home, the old man would have completed his task on earth. Then at last he would be able to await in peace the visitation of Yama, god of the dead.

Prodip Pal went back to the usurer to ask for a new loan of two thousand rupees. As collateral, he took with him his family's only assets, his wife Nalini's last remaining jewels: a pendant with matching gold earrings and two silver bracelets. The old woman had received these ornaments on the occasion of her own marriage, according to that same custom of the dowry. If it was a cruel system, it was also a form of provision for the

future, in fact the only method of family savings in India. The sum loaned by the *mahajan* represented only half the actual value of the items, at a rate of interest that was astronomical: 5 per cent per month, 60 per cent for one year! The poor woman had little hope of seeing her jewels again – jewels that she had worn with such pride on feast days during the forty years of her life with Prodip Pal.

Next Prodip Pal asked his sons to cast their nets into the pool and fish for all the available carp and *ruyi*. Thanks to the celebrated harvest which preceded the war with China, Hasari, the eldest son, had been able to buy a few dozen fry to spawn in his water reserve. The fish had multiplied and grown so that now each one weighed several pounds. Kept until now as a provision against total famine, they would provide a surprise dish at the wedding banquet.

'Twilight is near,' the old man kept telling himself, 'but the sun still glows red. Our *chakra*, the wheel of our destiny, has not yet completed its turn.'

'It was very pale, alluvial earth,' Hasari Pal would recall. 'But it was our earth, Mother Earth, Bhu-devi the goddess Earth. I had never known earth that was any other colour and I loved it just as it was, without question. Don't we love our mother just as she is, whatever her complexion or faults? We love her. And if she suffers, we suffer with her.

'It was the month of May, the very heart of the Bengali summer. The air seemed to shimmer over the overheated countryside. Every day I gazed long and confidently at the sky. It was gradually assuming the tints and shades of peacock feathers. According to an announcement made by the Brahmin priest of the village, one more moon and the monsoon would be with us. The Brahmin was a very wise and knowledgeable man. He was also

very old and he knew all the villagers as if they were members of his own family, even though that was quite impossible because he was of high, noble birth, far above any caste we might belong to. On the first day of each new year our father and all the other family heads in the village used to go and consult him as to what the coming twelve months held in store as far as men, cattle and the harvests were concerned. Like a good many of his caste, our elderly Brahmin knew the laws of the seasons and the paths pursued by the heavenly bodies. He was the one who fixed the dates for the agricultural work and the family ceremonies. No one knew quite how he made his calculations but he studied the movement of the planets and prescribed which days were most auspicious for sowing seeds, for harvesting and for getting married. The wedding season was over for this year. Now was the time for the earth to be impregnated. The Brahmin had predicted a year of exceptional riches, a year blessed by the gods, a year such as only occurs once in ten years – or even longer; a year without drought or epidemics or cockchafers or locusts or any other calamity. He knew, our Brahmin priest.'

So the time to sow had come and each family went to make its *puja* to the gods. Hasari, with his father and his brothers, presented himself at the little altar at the foot of the banyan tree which stood at the entrance to the fields. 'Gauri, I offer you this grain,' his father recited, placing a grain of rice in front of the image of the wife of the god Shiva, protectress of peasants. 'Give us plenty of water and return it to us a hundredfold.' Three days later, sure enough, some beneficent storms came to soak the seedlings.

Hasari was certain that this year the gods were at one with the Bankuli peasants. His father had not hesitated to borrow from the bald-headed usurer an additional two hundred rupees against a proportion of the prospective harvest. Hasari had used twenty-five of these rupees to

hire a team of oxen to plough the field. About forty rupees went for seed; the rest had been spent to buy manure and pesticides. This would be one of the greatest harvests they had ever had and, since the premonsoon rains had fallen at the requisite time, the Pals could spare themselves the hiring of a water pump. Fortune was smiling indeed, for that would have cost them six rupees an hour, the equivalent of the price of four pounds of rice – a small fortune!

Every morning Hasari went with his father and brothers to squat at the edge of the field. For hours on end he stayed there, contemplating the growth of the soft, young green shoots. The beginning of the monsoon was predicted for Friday, June 12. Friday is not a very auspicious day in the Hindu calendar. It did not matter really: the monsoon was the monsoon and its arrival each year was the gift of the gods to the people of India.

3

Everyone – men, women, children, and even the animals – was anxiously staring at the sky. Usually a violent wind gets up a few days before the monsoon breaks. The sky darkens suddenly as clouds invade the earth, rolling one on top of the other like cottonwool and skimming across the surface of the fields at extraordinary speed. Then other enormous and seemingly golden-edged clouds succeed them and a few moments later a tremendous blast of wind explodes into a hurricane of sand. Finally, a further bank of black clouds, this time without their golden edges, plunges the sky and the land into darkness. An interminable roll of thunder shakes the air and the stage is set. Agni, the Fire god of the Vedas, protector of men and their hearths, hurls his

thunderbolts. The large, warm raindrops turn into cataracts. Children fling themselves stark naked into the downpour, shrieking for joy, men dance and women chant their thanksgiving prayers in the shelter of the verandas.

Water. Life. The sky is rendering the earth fruitful. This is rebirth, the triumph of the elements. In a few hours vegetation bursts forth from all directions, insects multiply, frogs come out in their multitudes, reptiles are found in profusion, and birds warble as they build their nests. Above all, the fields are covered, as if by magic, with a blanket of the most beautiful green that grows ever sturdier and ever taller. Dream and reality intermingle until after one or two weeks, in a sky at last more peaceful, appears the bow of Indra, king of all the gods, lord of the elements and of the firmament. To humble peasants this rainbow signifies that the gods have made their peace with mankind. The harvest will be good.

A good harvest would mean that this year the Pals' field, which measured only half an acre, might perhaps produce one thousand pounds of rice – enough to feed the entire family for more than three months. While they waited for the next harvest the men would have to hire out their services to the *zamindar*, a very risky employment, which provided at best four or five days of work per month, but most of the time only a few hours. Such labour then earned only three rupees (about 20 pence) a day plus a portion of puffed rice and six *bidis* – those very slim cigarettes made out of a pinch of tobacco rolled up in a *kendu* leaf.

Friday, June 12 came and went, however, without the slightest cloud. Throughout the days that followed, the sky remained steely white. Fortunately Hasari had taken the precaution of reserving the irrigation pump. Unable to afford this luxury, Ajit, the Pals' neighbour, had already begun to lament his lot. After a few weeks the young shoots in his small rice field began to turn yellow.

The village elders delved deep into their memories in an attempt to remember when the monsoon had ever in the past kept them waiting like this. One of them recalled that in the year Mahatma Gandhi died, it had not arrived until July 2. In the year of the war with China it hardly came at all, and at other times, such as the year when the prize bull died, it had poured down so hard around about June 15 that all the seedlings had been flooded out. That was no better.

Even the most optimistic began to worry. Was Bhagavan, the great god, angry? The Pals went with their neighbours to the village priest to ask him to celebrate a *puja* to induce the rain to come. In return for his services the Brahmin asked for two *dhotis* for himself, a sari for his wife, and twenty rupees (£1.20). Everyone went rushing to the *mahajan* to borrow more money. In old times a *puja* involved the sacrifice of an animal, a he-goat for example, but these days people hardly ever sacrificed animals any more. It was too expensive. The priest contented himself with lighting a wick impregnated with *ghee*, the ritual clarified butter, in front of the statue of Ganesh, the god who brings good fortune. Then he burned sticks of incense and intoned *mantras**
while the peasants listened respectfully.

Yet neither Ganesh nor any of the other gods heard their prayers and Hasari was compelled to hire the irrigation pump. For six hours the pulsating of its engine brought the lifeblood essential for their growth to the shoots in the Pals' field. During that time the shoots took on their beautiful emerald colour and grew four inches, which meant that they were now in urgent need of planting out. On the huge, cultivated plain beyond the green square of his field Hasari could see dozens of squares that were already quite yellow. Those peasants who had not been able to give their rice plants enough

---

* Sacred formulas in Sanskrit.

water were appraising the extent of the disaster. For them there would be no harvest. The spectre of famine was rising on the horizon.

Now no one scrutinized the sky any longer. The *mahajan's* radio announced that this year the monsoon would be very late arriving. It had not yet reached the Andaman Islands, which lay a long way out in the Bay of Bengal, almost off the coast of Burma. In any case the radio could no longer teach the Bankuli peasants anything. 'It could bring nothing but the evil eye,' reflected Hasari. 'So long as we hadn't seen the cuckoo jay, we knew there would be no rain for us.'

At the beginning of July a group of Bauls in ochre robes – wandering monks who sing the glory of the god Krishna – passed through the village. They stopped near the Gauri sanctuary under the banyan at the entrance to the fields and began to sing, punctuating their verses with the plucking of a single stringed lute, and with handbells and tiny cymbals. 'Bird of my heart, don't keep on roving,' they chanted. 'Don't you know that your wanderings cause us great suffering? Oh come to us, bird, and bring our water with you.'

All the Pals' attention was concentrated thenceforth on the pond that served as a communal water reserve. Its level was going down fast. The villagers speculated endlessly, trying to work out how long it would take the irrigation pumps to empty it, allowing for considerable evaporation in such torrid heat. The fateful moment came on July 23. That was the day they had to take out the fishes, which were floundering in the mud, and divide them among themselves. In such times of anguish, it was an occasion for unexpected rejoicing. To be able to eat fish was a real treat. Yet, in many a home, mothers renounced these treats with selfless foresight and dried the fish instead.

In the Pals' field the luminous emerald green soon changed first to grey green and then to a yellowish

colour. The rice drooped, then wilted and finally died – the very rice that they had nursed, caressed and loved. The rice they had suffered with, bowed their heads with and grown old with. 'I couldn't bring myself to abandon it,' Hasari was to confide. 'Totally overwhelmed by the magnitude of the calamity, I stood motionless at the edge of our field.' Before each strip of ground, other despairing peasants remained right through the night, their heads bowed in dejection. Perhaps they were thinking of the lament of the fakir, enraptured with God: 'There was a treasure in my field but today someone else holds its key and the treasure is no longer mine.'

It took Hasari the whole night to accept this tragic fact. At dawn he went home to sit under the veranda with his father and brothers. It was the old man, Prodip, who summed up their predicament: 'We shall not go back to the field again this season.' Moments later Hasari heard his mother lifting the lids of the storage jars lined up in the outhouse. The jars contained the rice that the Pals had set aside to await the next harvest. The poor woman began to evaluate how long the family could hold out on such meagre reserves. Hasari already knew the answer. 'If we rationed ourselves, allowing for a few handfuls of rice to be offered to the gods, we had only two months' food left.' His wife, sisters-in-law and children joined them. They all sensed that something was wrong but the old woman put the lids back on the jars and announced with apparent serenity: 'We have enough rice for a good four months. Afterwards, we'll have the vegetables.' Reassured, old and young went back to their chores. Only Hasari remained behind. He saw tears on his mother's cheeks. His father came and put an arm round his wife's shoulders. 'Mother of my sons,' he said, 'we shall both go without food for ourselves so that the rice lasts longer. The children must not suffer.' With a nod of her head she approved the idea.

Many of the villagers were already left with nothing. The first indication of this harsh reality was the disappearance from the village of the very poorest families – the Untouchables. They had realized that this year there would be not a single head of rice to be gleaned from the fields. No one actually said anything but people knew that the Untouchables had left for the great city of Calcutta, about sixty miles away. Next it was the turn of the fathers and the eldest sons, in homes where the earthenware jars were empty. Then whole families began to take to the road that led to the city.

Their neighbours' departure was a source of great grief to the Pals. The families had known each other for so long. Before leaving his house the ageing Ajit broke his clay pots and extinguished the oil lamp, the flame that burns constantly in every home; some of them had been alight for generations. With a hand that trembled slightly, he took down the pictures of the gods that had stood enthroned upon the small family altar and rolled them up in his knapsack. The gods wore great expansive smiles – smiles that seemed quite incongruous that morning. Prem, the eldest son, placed flowers and a few grains of rice outside the hole next to the doorway. This was the cobra's home. Prem recited a prayer to the snake, asking it to 'guard this house and keep it safe until we return'. Unfortunately, at that precise moment a black cat stalked past the hut. This did not augur well and so to thwart the evil spirits old Ajit had to draw them off on the wrong track. Thus he set off alone, heading north before gradually branching off to the south where he would rejoin his family. Before he left, the eldest son opened the parrot's cage. The parrot, at least, would be free. Instead of making straight for the sky, however, the bird seemed strangely at a loss. After some hesitation, it began to flutter from bush to bush behind its masters who were vanishing into the dust.

The summer passed almost without a single down-

pour and once again it was time for the winter sowing.
Without water, however, there would be no winter
sowing: no lentils, no sweet potatoes, no winter rice.
By this time Bhaga, the Pals' one remaining cow, was
nothing but skin and bone. It was a long time since they
had had any straw to give her, not to mention bran. She
was fed on the heart of the three banana trees which
provided a little shade for the hut. One morning Hasari
found her lying on her flank with her tongue hanging
out. It was then that he realized that all the livestock
was going to perish.

Cattle merchants closed in like vultures from the surrounding towns. They offered to buy any animals that
were still alive and went off with lorryloads of cows
picked up for fifty rupees (£3) and buffalo for scarcely a
hundred more. 'Don't upset yourselves,' they soothed
with feigned compassion. 'You can always buy your
cattle back next year.' What they omitted to say was that
their price then would be ten times as much. A few days
later it was the curriers' turn to come and take away the
carcasses of those animals with which the peasants had
not had the heart to part. Fifteen rupees was the price!
(Less than £1!) It was that or nothing.

November went by. The departure of the cattle had
cut off the peasants' only fuel supply. There was no
more dung with which to cook food and no more milk
either. Gone was the sound of children's laughter. Their
small stomachs swelled up like balloons and several of
them died, the victims of worms, diarrhoea and fever –
yet in reality victims of hunger.

At the beginning of January villagers heard that food
was being given out in the district capital, about twenty
miles away. At first no one wanted to go. 'We were
peasants, not beggars,' Hasari Pal was later to say. 'But
for the sake of the women and children we had to
resign ourselves to accepting charity.' Later government
officials went through the villages announcing a relief

operation called 'Work for Food'. Work sites were opened up in the area to deepen the canals, mend the roads, increase the size of the water reservoirs, raise the dikes, clear the undergrowth and dig holes for trees to be planted. 'We were given two pounds of rice for each day worked, a handout that was supposed to feed an entire family, and all the while the radio was saying that in the rest of the country the silos were full of grain.'

Towards January 20 a terrible piece of news began to spread: the well near the little altar to the god Gauri had run dry. Men went down to the bottom to sound it, only to find that, sure enough, the underground streams had dried up. The municipal authorities had to set up a rota system for the three other wells in the village that were still providing a little water. The water was rationed. At first there was a bucketful per family per day, then half a bucket. Eventually there was only one cup per person which had to be drunk on the spot at the mayor's house. Day and night long lines stretched out in front of the mayor's door. Eventually sentries armed with clubs had to be placed next to the only well that was not yet dry. A few miles to the north, wild elephants dying of thirst had surrounded a pool and were charging any person rash enough to come in search of water.

By now the fields were nothing but vast colourless expanses covered with a deep-cracked crust. The trees were in no better condition. Many of them were already dead and the bushes had long since been scorched.

The Pals' resistance was coming to an end. One day the old man gathered his family around him. From a knotted corner of his *dhoti* he took out five tightly rolled ten-rupee notes and two one-rupee coins and handed them to Hasari.

'You, my eldest son, take this money and go with your wife and children to Calcutta. In the big city you will find work. You will send us whatever you can. You are our only hope of not dying of starvation.'

Hasari stooped down and touched his father's feet. The small man laid his palm on his son's head, then on his shoulder, and gripped him tightly until Hasari stood up again. The women wept in silence.

Next morning, as the first rays of Surya, the Sun god, dawned pale on the horizon, Hasari and his family set off, without venturing to look back at those who watched them go. Hasari walked in front with Amrita, his daughter. His wife, Aloka, dressed in a green cotton sari, followed behind with their two sons, Manooj and Shambu. Over his shoulder Hasari carried a cloth knapsack in which his wife had packed a little linen and the sandals he had received from her parents as part of her dowry. It was the first time these peasants had left their village for so distant a destination. The two boys pranced for joy at the prospect of adventure. 'As for me, I was frightened,' Hasari was to admit, 'frightened of what lay in store for us.'

4

After a morning of walking, several hours in a swaying bus, and a night in a packed third-class train compartment, Hasari Pal and his family arrived at Howrah Station, one of Calcutta's two railway terminals. They were so stunned at the spectacle that confronted them that for several seconds they were unable to move. They were suddenly engulfed in a tide of people coming and going in all directions, of coolies bearing mountains of cases and packages, of vendors offering every conceivable sort of merchandise. Never before had they seen such riches: pyramids of oranges, sandals, combs, scissors, padlocks, glasses, bags; piles of shawls, saris, *dhotis*, newspapers, and of all kinds of food and drink. Wander-

ing monks called *Saddhus* mingled among the travellers and for a twenty-pice coin (about one pence) would lay hands on them or pour a few drops of holy water from the Ganges into their mouths. Shoe shiners, ear cleaners, cobblers, public writers and astrologers were all there, offering their services. Hasari and his family were dazed, dumbfounded, lost. Many of the other travellers around them seemed equally confused.

'What are we going to do?' the peasant asked himself. 'Where are we going to sleep tonight?'

For a while the Pals wandered about in the midst of the throng. They gazed curiously at a family who appeared to have made their home in a corner of the main hall. They were peasants from the State of Bihar, driven there like the Pals by the drought, and they understood a little Bengali. They had been living here now for several weeks. Beside their carefully tied bundles they had set out their cooking utensils and a *chula*, a small portable stove. They were quick to put the newcomers on their guard against the police who often raided the station to turn out anyone camping there. Hasari questioned them about the possibility of finding work, but they had found nothing themselves yet. To avoid dying of starvation they admitted to having been reduced to putting their children out on the streets to beg. The shame of it was written on their faces. Hasari explained that a young man from his village was working as a coolie in the market of the Bara Bazar and that he was going to try and make contact with him. The Biharis suggested that Hasari leave his wife and children with them while he went off to make inquiries. Comforted by the goodwill of these strangers, Hasari went to buy some *samosas*, triangular-shaped fritters filled with vegetables or minced meat, which he shared with his new friends, his wife and his children; they had eaten nothing since the previous day. Then he plunged resolutely into the flood of travellers emerging from the railway station.

The sight of this newly arrived peasant provoked an immediate tidal wave. A horde of pedlars surrounded Hasari with offers of ballpoint pens, sweetmeats, lottery tickets and a thousand other wares. Beggars assaulted him. Lepers clung to his shirt. Outside the station a cyclone of lorries, buses, taxis, handcarts, scooters, cycle rickshaws, horse carriages, motorbikes and bicycles swirled in a kind of collective madness. They crawled forward at a walking pace, amid a terrifying, chaotic racket. The honking of carrier tricycles, the tooting of horns, the throbbing of engines, buses' horns, cart bells, carriage bells, the clamouring of loudspeakers, it was like a competition to see who could make the most noise. 'It was worse than the thunder that heralds the first drops of the monsoon,' Hasari would say. 'I thought my head was going to burst.'

In the middle of all this commotion, he spotted an impassive policeman who was trying to direct the traffic. He fought his way over to him to inquire where the bazaar was in which his acquaintance was working. The policeman waved his club in the direction of an entanglement of metal girders which soared heavenward at the far end of the square. 'On the other side of the bridge!' he growled.

This bridge was the only link between the twin cities of Calcutta and Howrah. It stretched across the Hooghly River, a tributary of the Ganges, and was undoubtedly the most congested bridge in the world.

Over a million people and hundreds of thousands of vehicles crossed it every day in a hallucinating maelstrom. Hasari Pal was swept up at once in a stream of people who were pushing their way in different directions between two unbroken lines of vendors squatting on the ground behind displayed wares. In the six lanes of traffic, hundreds of vehicles were completely stuck in one gigantic bottleneck that stretched as far as the eye could see. Lorries roared in an attempt to overtake the

line of trams. Red double-decker buses were overloaded with people, who clung in clusters to their sides. Some of the buses leaned over at such extreme angles that they looked as if at any moment they would tip over altogether. There were handcarts too, crawling along beneath piles of crates, pipes and machinery and propelled by poor fellows whose muscles looked as if they were about to burst. Coolies, their faces distorted with the strain, trotted along with baskets and packages piled up on their heads. Others transported drums affixed to either end of a long pole lying on their shoulders. Herds of buffalo, cows and goats, driven along with sticks, attempted to wend their way through the labyrinth of vehicles. Often the panic-stricken animals escaped in all directions. 'How those poor beasts must be suffering,' Hasari commented to himself, recalling with nostalgia the tranquil beauty of his countryside.

On the other side of the bridge the traffic seemed even more congested. Suddenly Hasari noticed a small cart on two wheels, transporting two passengers. Between the shafts there was a man. 'Good God,' he thought, 'there are even human horses in Calcutta!' Hasari had just discovered his first rickshaw.

The nearer he drew to the bazaar, the more there were of these curious little vehicles lugging about people, or merchandise, or both. As his gaze followed their progress he began dreaming. 'Would I have the strength to earn a living for my family by pulling such a machine?'

The Bara Bazar was an area swarming with crowds, where the houses rose several floors high, so high in fact that Hasari was amazed that they managed to keep standing. The network of small streets, covered alleys and narrow passageways lined with hundreds of stalls, workshops and shops was like a beehive humming with activity. Entire streets were taken up with vendors selling ornaments and garlands of flowers. Squatting behind mountains of Bengal roses, jasmine, Indian pinks

and marigolds, children threaded buds and petals like
strings of pearls to make up garlands as thick as pythons.
Their pendants too were made out of flowers and inter-
laced with gold thread. Savouring the fragrance of these
flowers, Hasari bought for ten pice a handful of rose
petals to put on the *lingam* of Shiva, the benevolent and
terrible god of the Hindu religion, that he encountered
in a niche on a street corner. He paused for a moment
before the black, cylindrical stone that symbolized the
forces of life and asked the god who knew the where-
abouts of truth to help him to find the person he sought.

Further on Hasari passed through an arcade where
dozens of stalls sold nothing but perfume contained in a
multitude of vials and coloured bottles. Then he entered
a covered alleyway where, amid the glitter of gold and
small glassware, all he could see were jewellers. He could
hardly believe his eyes. There were hundreds of them,
lined up like prisoners behind the bars of the cages
containing their treasures. Women decked out in costly
saris pressed themselves against the bars; the merchants
seemed never to stop unlocking and locking the safes
behind them. They handled their minute scales with
surprising agility. Hasari also saw several poorer
women, wearing darned veils, jostling to get near the
grilles. Here, as in the villages, the jewellers were also
usurers.

Beyond this street of the *mahajans* lay the sari market.
Women lingered over sumptuous displays, particularly
in the shops that specialized in wedding attire, saris that
dripped with gold and spangles.

The sun that day was overpowering and the water
vendors, ringing their small bells, were doing good
business. Hasari gave five pice to one of them to quench
his thirst. Ever watchful, he scrutinized every coolie and
tradesman and questioned all the bearers, but only a
miracle could help him to find his friend in such a
seething mass. None the less he pursued his search until

nightfall. 'Working a ten-acre rice field was less tiring than that endless trek through the bazaar,' he would later recall. Exhausted, he bought five bananas and asked the way back to the great bridge.

His children swooped on the bananas like starving sparrows, and the whole family went to sleep on the railway station floor. Fortunately, the police did not raid the place that night.

Next morning Hasari took his elder son, Manooj, with him and together they explored another section of the Bara Bazar: first the metalworkers' and tinsmiths' corner, then the workshops where dozens of men and children with bare torsos spent their day rolling *bidis*, the thin Indian cigarettes. So dim was the light inside the rooms that the faces were hardly distinguishable. Hasari gave the name and description of his friend to anyone who was prepared to listen but it was like looking for a grain of rice in a bundle of straw. There were probably hundreds of coolies also called Prem Kumar and answering to his description. That second evening Hasari again took some bananas back with him. The Pals shared them with the neighbouring family who had nothing to eat.

After the third day of searching, with no more money to buy bananas, Hasari was reduced to an act of supreme humiliation for a proud peasant. Before making his way back to the railway station, he picked up all the peelings and scraps he could find. 'That evening my wife suggested that our daughter, Amrita, go to beg at the entrance to the station. Overwhelmed with shame and despair, she wept as she spoke. We were peasants, not beggars.' The Pals could not reconcile themselves to so abhorrent an idea. For one more day and night they waited but, as dawn broke on the following day, they sent their little girl and her two brothers to take up their positions where the rich travellers got out of their taxis and private cars.

Then, dejected, Hasari returned to the Bara Bazar. As he was passing a workshop where some coolies were loading iron bars onto a *telagarhi*, a long handcart, one of the coolies suddenly began to vomit blood. His companions laid him out on the ground. He was so pale that Hasari thought the man was dead. When the workshop owner came out, shouting because the *telagarhi* had not yet gone, Hasari rushed forward and offered to replace the ailing coolie. The man hesitated but his delivery could not wait any longer and he offered three rupees for the run, payable on arrival.

Without really realizing what was happening to him, Hasari braced himself with the others to shift the heavy load. Their employer had carefully avoided mentioning that their destination was a factory situated on the other side of the great bridge, well beyond the railway station. The coolies fought like beasts to pull the heavy load across, but to no avail. Halfway up the slope their vehicle came to a standstill. Hasari thought the blood vessels in his neck were going to burst. A policeman came and threatened the men with his stick because they were holding up traffic. 'Get out of the way!' he yelled, above the tooting horns. In response the oldest of the coolies bent down to put all his weight against one wheel and shouted to the others to drive them forward.

Exhausted but proud at the prospect of surprising his family with his first earnings, Hasari returned to the railway station late that evening. It was he, however, for whom the real surprise lay in store. His wife and children had disappeared. So too had the other family. After a long search he eventually found them on an embankment behind the bus terminal. 'The police chased us out,' explained Aloka, through her tears. 'They said if they ever saw us in the station again, they'd throw us into prison.'

The Pals had no idea where to go next. They crossed the great bridge and simply kept on walking. It was dark

but, despite the late hour, the streets were still full of
people. Bewildered by the throngs that milled about like
ants, jostling each other and shouting, they reached a
place in the very heart of the city. Pitiful in her poor
peasant sari, Aloka had taken her younger son in her
arms and held her daughter by the hand. Manooj, the
older boy, walked in front with his father. They were
so afraid of losing each other that they called out constantly to one another in the darkness. The pavement
was littered with sleeping people, wrapped from head
to toe in bits of *khadi* cloth. They looked like corpses.
As soon as they found an empty space, the Pals stopped
to rest a while. A family was camping nearby. The
mother was roasting *chapatis* on a portable stove. She
and her family came from Madras. Fortunately, they
spoke a few words of Hindi, a language Hasari could
vaguely understand. They too had left the countryside
for the mirage of Calcutta. They offered the Pals a hot
griddle cake and swept a corner of the pavement so that
the newcomers could settle themselves next to them.
The strangers' hospitality brought new warmth to the
peasant's heart. At least his family would be safe in their
company until he found work. That afternoon he had
learned a harsh lesson: 'Since men in this inhuman city
die on the job, I'll be damned if I can't manage one day
to replace one of these poor fellows.'

5

The city that Hasari had not hesitated to describe as
'inhuman' was in fact a mirage city, to which in the
course of one generation six million starving people had
come in the hope of feeding their families. In the 1960s,
Calcutta was still, despite its decline over the previous

half century, one of the most active and prosperous cities in Asia. Thanks to its harbour and its numerous industries, its metal foundries and chemical and pharmaceutical works, its flour mills and its linen, jute and cotton factories, Calcutta boasted the third highest average wages per inhabitant of any Indian city, immediately after Delhi and Bombay. One third of the imports and nearly half of India's exports passed along the waters of the Hooghly, the branch of the Ganges on the banks of which the city had been founded three centuries earlier. Here, 30 per cent of the entire country's bank transactions were undertaken and a third of its income tax was levied. Nicknamed the 'Ruhr of India', its hinterland produced twice as much coal as France and as much steel as the combines of North Korea. Calcutta drained into its factories and warehouses all the material resources of this vast territory: copper, manganese, chromium, asbestos, bauxite, graphite, and mica as well as precious timber from the Himalayas, tea from Assam and Darjeeling, and almost 50 per cent of the world's jute.

From this hinterland also converged each day on the city's bazaars and markets an uninterrupted flow of foodstuffs: cereals and sugar from Bengal, vegetables from Bihar, fruit from Kashmir, eggs and poultry from Bangladesh, meat from Andra, fish from Orissa, shellfish and honey from the Sundarbans, tobacco and betel from Patna, cheeses from Nepal. Vast quantities of other items and materials also fed one of the most diversified and lively trading centres in Asia. No fewer than two hundred and fifty different varieties of cloth were to be counted in the bazaars of Calcutta and more than five thousand colours and shades of saris. Before reaching this mecca of industry and commerce, these goods had often to cross vast areas that were extremely poor, areas where millions of small peasants like the Pals scratched a desperate living out of infertile patches of

land. How could those poor not dream, each time disaster struck, of taking the same road as those goods?

The metropolis was situated at the heart of one of the world's richest yet at the same time most ill-fated regions, an area of failing or devastating monsoons causing either drought or biblical floods. This was an area of cyclones and apocalyptic earthquakes, an area of political exoduses and religious wars such as no other country's climate or history has perhaps ever engendered. The earthquake that shook Bihar on January 15, 1937, caused hundreds of thousands of deaths and catapulted entire villages in the direction of Calcutta. Six years later a famine killed three and a half million people in Bengal alone and ousted millions of refugees. India's independence and the Partition in 1947 cast upon Calcutta some four million Muslims and Hindus fleeing from Bihar and East Pakistan. The conflict with China in 1962, and subsequently the war against Pakistan, washed up a further several hundred thousand refugees; and in the same year, 1965, a cyclone as forceful as ten three-megaton H-bombs capable of razing to the ground a city like New York, together with a dreadful drought in Bihar, once more sent to Calcutta entire communities.

Now, it was yet another drought that was driving thousands of starving peasants like the Pals to the city.

The arrival of these successive waves of destitute people had transformed Calcutta into an enormous concentration of humanity. In a few years the city was to condemn its ten million inhabitants to living on less than twelve square feet of space per person, while the four or five million of them who squeezed into its slums had sometimes to make do with barely three square feet each. Consequently Calcutta had become one of the biggest urban disasters in the world – a city consumed with decay in which thousands of houses and many new buildings, sometimes ten floors high or even higher, threatened at any moment to crack and collapse. With

their crumbling façades, tottering roofs and walls eaten up with tropical vegetation, some neighbourhoods looked as if they had just been bombed. A rash of posters, publicity and political slogans, and advertisement billboards painted on the walls, defied all efforts at renovation. In the absence of an adequate refuse collection service, eighteen hundred tons of refuse accumulated daily in the streets, attracting a host of flies, mosquitoes, rats, cockroaches and other creatures.

In summer the proliferation of filth brought with it the risk of epidemics. Not so very long ago it was still a common occurrence for people to die of cholera, hepatitis, encephalitis, typhoid and rabies. Articles and reports in the local press never ceased denouncing the city as a refuse dump poisoned with fumes, nauseating gases and discharges – a devastated landscape of broken roads, leaking sewers, burst water pipes and torn down telephone wires. In short, Calcutta was 'a dying city'.

And yet, thousands, hundreds of thousands, even millions of people swarmed night and day over its squares, its avenues and the narrowest of its alleyways. The smallest fragment of pavement was occupied, squatted upon, covered with salesmen and pedlars, with homeless families camping out, with piles of building materials or refuse, with stalls and a multitude of altars and small temples. The result of all this was an indescribable chaos on the roads, a record accident rate, nightmarish traffic jams. Furthermore, in the absence of public toilets, hundreds of thousands of the city's inhabitants were forced to attend to their bodily needs in the street.

In those years seven out of ten families had to survive on no more than one or two rupees a day, a sum that was not even sufficient to buy a pound of rice. Calcutta was indeed that 'inhuman city' where the Pals had just discovered people could die on the pavements surrounded by apparent indifference. It was also a powder flask of violence and anarchy, where the masses were to

turn one day to the saving myth of communism. To
hunger and communal conflicts must also be added one
of the world's most unbearable climates. Torrid for eight
months of the year, the heat melted the asphalt on the
roads and expanded the metal structure of the great
Howrah Bridge to such an extent that it measured four
feet more by day than by night. In many respects the
city resembled the goddess Kali whom many of its
inhabitants worshipped – Kali the Terrible, the image of
fear and death, depicted with a terrifying expression in
her eyes and a necklace of snakes and skulls around
her neck. Even slogans on the walls proclaimed the
disastrous state of this city. 'Here there is no more hope,'
said one of them. 'All that is left is anger.'

Yet on what a prestigious past this metropolis, now
judged inhuman by many of its inhabitants, could pride
itself! From the date of its foundation in 1690 by a
handful of British merchants until the departure of its
last British governor on August 15, 1947, Calcutta, more
than any other city in the world, had epitomized the
imperial dream of the white man's domination of the
globe. For nearly two and a half centuries it had been
the capital of the British Indian Empire. It was from here
that until 1912 its governor generals and its viceroys had
imposed their authority on a country with a population
greater than that of the United States of America today.
Calcutta's avenues had witnessed the passing of just as
many parading troops and as many high society ladies
in palanquins or barouches as the Champs-Elysées of
Paris or the London Mall. Even now, dilapidated by
decades of monsoons, its public buildings, its monuments, its business centre, its beautiful residences with
their balusters and colonnades still bore witness to that
heritage. At the far end of the avenue along which, in
1911, George V and Queen Mary had processed in a

gold-studded carriage between two rows of Highlanders
in Scottish kilts and white spats, there rose from the heart
of a thirty-acre park the imposing 137-room building in
which the Empire had lodged its viceroys. Raj Bhavan,
the royal palace, was a replica of Kedleston Hall, one
of the most beautiful country houses in England. The
viceroy, Lord Wellesley, had decorated its great marble
drawing room with busts of the twelve Caesars. Before
becoming, after Independence, the residence of the
Indian governor of Bengal, Raj Bhavan had hosted
festivities and celebrations of a sumptuousness beyond
the wildest imagination. On gala evenings, the representative of Her Most Gracious Majesty took his place
on a throne of purple velvet highlighted with gold,
surrounded by a whole retinue of aides-de-camp and
officers in dress uniform. Two beturbaned Indian servants gently wafted fans of scarlet silk to refresh him
while soldiers armed with silver-encrusted lances provided him with a guard of honour.

Many other no less glorious vestiges, often engulfed
by the chaos of construction and contemporary slums,
bore witness to the past majesty of this former jewel in
the crown: buildings, such as the stadium where on
January 2, 1804, the Calcutta team, led by the grandson
of the British Prime Minister, Robert Walpole, had
opened the batting against a team of old Etonians in the
first cricket match ever played in the Orient. Then there
was that proud, eight-hundred-acre enclave beside the
sacred waters of the Hooghly River, which harboured
one of the most impressive citadels ever constructed by
man. Built to protect the first three warehouses – one of
which, Kalikata, so called because it was situated near a
village dedicated to Kali, was to give its name to the city
– Fort William had served as a cradle for Calcutta
and for the British conquest of its enormous empire in
Asia.

Of all these symbols of former glory, however, none

was more striking than the huge set piece in white marble which rose from the far extremity of the Maidan park. Erected with funds given by the Indian people themselves to commemorate the sixty-three-year reign of the Empress who believed she embodied the vocation of the white man to look after the well-being of all people on earth, the Victoria Memorial conserved, at the very heart of the modern urban jungle, the most fabulous collection of treasures ever assembled within the confines of a colonial theme. All the mementos were there, piously preserved for the incredulous scrutiny of present generations: statues of the Empress at all the various stages of her splendour, together with all the royal envoys who succeeded each other here; a portrait of Kipling; sabres with pommels inlaid with gold and precious stones, worn by British generals during the battles which gave India to Britain; parchments confirming these conquests; manuscript messages from Victoria conveying her affection to her 'peoples beyond the seas'.

Despite the heat, the tropical diseases, the snakes, the jackals and even the tigers that sometimes, at night, prowled around the residences on Chowringhee Road, Calcutta had offered its creators a supremely easy and pleasurable life-style. For two and a half centuries, generations of British had begun their day with a drive in a horse-drawn carriage or a limousine under the shade of the banyan trees, magnolia bushes and palm clusters of the Maidan park. Every year, before Christmas, a glittering season of polo, horse racing and social receptions drew the entire élite of Asia to Calcutta. In the city's heyday, the primary occupation of its ladies had been to try on in their boudoirs the very latest outfits from Paris and London, made up by local dressmakers out of sumptuous fabrics and brocades woven in Madras or Benares. For nearly half a century the most sought-after rendezvous among these same privileged ladies was with Messieurs Malvaist and Siret, two famous French

hairstylists whom an astute financier had brought over from Paris.

It was because of its wealth of entertainment that the Calcutta of these times had earned the nickname of 'Paris of the East'. Not one of its parties began without a delightful serpentine excursion on the Hooghly, on one of those long gondolas propelled by forty or so boatmen in red-and-green turbans and white tunics girded with golden sashes. Alternatively there was always a promenade along the riverside pathways of the Garden of Eden, to which one viceroy, in love with Oriental architecture, had had a pagoda transported, plank by plank, from the lofty plateaux of Burma. At the end of every afternoon the garrison's brass band provided, on this spot overlooking the river, a concert of romantic music for the delectation of expatriates in crinolines, frock coats and top hats. Later in the evening, there were always a few rounds of whist or ombre in one of the innumerable clubs 'prohibited to dogs and Indians', which constituted the pride of British Calcutta. Then there was perhaps a dinner and dance under the ornamental ceilings of the luxurious ballrooms of the Chowringhee houses or on the teak dance floor of the London Tavern. Those with a predilection for dramatic art were spoiled for choice. Calcutta prided itself on being the artistic and intellectual capital of Asia. Every evening there was a Shakespeare performance at the New Play House and the latest London West End productions were staged in a host of other theatres. Geoffrey Moorhouse, a noted historian of Calcutta, tells us that at the beginning of the century one of the city's great society ladies, a Mrs Bristow, had even converted one of the reception rooms in her residence into an opera stage and hosted there the best tenors and divas from Europe.* The boards of the Old Empire

---

* *Calcutta*, by Geoffrey Moorhouse (Weidenfeld and Nicolson, London).

Theatre had borne the ballet shoes of the great Anna
Pavlova in an unforgettable recital that shortly preceded
her retirement. The Calcutta Symphony Orchestra gave
a concert every Sunday under the baton of its founder,
a Bengali merchant named Shosbree. Shortly after the
First World War, there flourished on Chowringhee Road
the most famous three-star restaurant in Asia. Firpo was
to remain, until the 1960s, the Maxim's of the Orient,
Calcutta's temple of gastronomic and social delectation.
Like having a reserved pew in St Paul's Cathedral, every
self-respecting family had a table reserved in Firpo's
large L-shaped dining room. The Italian restaurateur
received people like an Oriental potentate, or perhaps
even turned them away if their faces or attire did not
appeal to him. Enlivened by the musicians of Francisco
Casanovas, a Spanish nobleman who had switched to
the art of playing the clarinet, Firpo's dance floor had
formed the cradle of romance for the last generation of
white men in Asia.

Those who preferred the treasures of the rich Bengali
culture to Occidental delights were no less spoiled. Since
the eighteenth century, Calcutta had been the homeland
of philosophers, poets, storytellers and musicians. In the
person of Tagore, Calcutta had even given to India a
Nobel Prize for literature and in J. C. Bose a Nobel Prize
for science. It was also the home of Ramakrishna and
Vivekananda, two of the most venerated modern saints;
of Satyajit Ray, one of the most highly acclaimed figures
of world cinema; of Sri Aurobindo, one of the giants of
universal spirituality; of Satyen Bose, one of the great
scholars of the theory of relativity.

The vicissitudes of destiny had not completely obliter-
ated so prestigious a heritage. Calcutta was still India's
artistic and intellectual beacon and its culture continued
to be as alive and creative as ever. The hundreds of book
stalls in College Street were still laden with books –
original editions, pamphlets, great literary works, publi-

cations of every kind, in English as well as in the numerous Indian languages. Though the Bengalis now constituted barely half of the city's working population, there
was no doubt that Calcutta produced more writers than
Paris and Rome combined, more literary reviews than
London and New York, more cinemas than New Delhi,
and more publishers than all the rest of the country.
Every evening its theatres put on several theatrical productions, countless classical concerts and recitals at
which everyone, from a universally renowned sitarist
like Ravi Shankar to the humblest of flute or tabla
players, was united with the popular audiences before
whom they performed in the same love of music. Half of
India's theatre groups stemmed from here. The Bengalis
even claimed that one of their scholars had translated the
great French playwright Molière into their language,
long before the British had ever heard of him.

For Hasari Pal and the millions of exiles who crowded
into its slums, however, Calcutta represented neither
culture nor history. For them it meant only the faint
hope of finding some crumbs to allow them to survive
until the next day. In a metropolis of such magnitude
there were always a few crumbs to be gathered, whereas
in a village flooded with water or parched by drought,
even that possibility didn't exist any more.

6

After another day spent running about the Bara Bazar,
Hasari Pal returned one evening with a triumphant smile
that was altogether unexpected.

'May Bhagavan be blessed!' exclaimed Aloka when
she caught sight of her husband. 'Look, children, your
father seems pleased. He must have found the coolie

from our village. Or even better, perhaps he has found work. We're saved!'

Hasari had found neither his friend nor work. He was simply bringing his family two newspaper cones full of *muri*, rice roasted in hot sand that the poor eat as a last resort to stem their hunger. The dried grains were hard and had to be masticated for a long time, a process that prolonged the illusion of actually getting one's teeth into something.

Parents and children chewed for a while in silence. 'There you are. That's for you,' said Hasari, happily giving the remainder of his own share to his younger son who was looking at him with an expression of entreaty.

Aloka watched her husband's gesture with an aching heart. Among India's poor, food was always reserved in priority to those who could work and provide for the family's needs. Hasari had lost a lot of weight since their arrival in Calcutta. His bones were protruding. Two deep cracks had carved themselves beneath his moustache, his dark, shining hair had turned grey above his ears, a phenomenon that was rare in so young an Indian. 'Good God, how he has aged,' thought his young wife as she looked at him stretching out for the night on the bare asphalt of their piece of pavement. She thought of the first time she had seen him, so handsome, so sturdy under the ornamental canopy erected for their marriage in front of her family hut. He had come from his village, borne on a palanquin and escorted by his relatives and friends. The Brahmin priest had anointed his forehead with rice paste and small basil leaves. He had been wearing a brand-new white tunic and a very bright saffron-coloured turban. Aloka remembered her terror when her mother and aunts had left her alone with him after the ceremony. She was only fifteen and he was barely three years older. Their union had been arranged by their parents and they had never met before. He had

gazed at her insistently and asked her name. She recalled
too that he had added, 'You are a very beautiful girl and
I am wondering whether you will find me as appealing.'
She merely smiled in response because it was not decent
for a new bride to speak freely to her husband on their
wedding day. She had blushed then and, encouraged by
his gentleness, she in her turn had ventured a question:
did he know how to read and write? 'No,' he had replied
simply before adding with pride, 'but I know how to
do many other things.'

'That day the father of my children looked as strong
and solid as the trunk of the great banyan tree at the
entrance to our village,' reflected Aloka. And now he
seemed so fragile, curled up on his patch of pavement.
It was hard for her to appreciate that this was the same
man whose powerful arms had clasped her like a pair of
pliers on their wedding night. Although her eldest aunt
had given her some words of advice, she had been so
timid and ignorant then that she had struggled to escape
from his grasp. 'Don't be frightened,' he had said. 'I
am your husband and you will be the mother of my
children.'

Aloka was pondering on these memories in the darkness when an uproar broke out nearby. The neighbours,
those good people who had so generously welcomed the
distressed Pals, had just noticed that their daughter was
missing. She was a pretty girl of thirteen, sweet and
gentle, with a large plait down her back and green eyes.
Her name was Maya, which meant 'illusion'. Every
morning she used to go off to beg outside the entrance
to the big hotels on Chowringhee Road and Park Street,
where business men and rich tourists from all over the
world stayed. No one, however, had the right to hold
out his hand in such a gold mine of a district unless he
was directly controlled by the syndicate of racketeers.
Each evening Maya handed over her entire day's earnings
to the gang leader who, in return, paid her a daily wage

of five rupees (about 30 pence). Maya was lucky to have
been accepted at all because, in order to incite their
'clients' to greater generosity, the racketeers preferred to
exploit deformed or disabled youngsters, legless men on
planks with wheels, or mothers in rags with emaciated
babies in their arms. It was even said that children were
mutilated at birth to be sold to these torturers.

Young Maya was deeply pained by the obligation to
beg. On several occasions as she was about to leave
for 'work', she had thrown herself, sobbing, into her
mother's arms. Such scenes were frequent on the streets
of Calcutta where so many people were condemned to
suffer the very worst degradations in order simply to
survive. Yet, Maya had never shirked her task. She knew
that for her family the five rupees she brought back each
night meant the difference between life and death.

That evening she had not come home. As the hours
went by, her mother and father grew sick with worry.
They got up, sat down again, walked around in circles
uttering incomprehensible imprecations. In the three
months since they had found themselves stranded on
that pavement they had learned enough to know that
their anguish was justified. Just as elsewhere in the
world, abduction of children was a frequent crime in
Calcutta. The villains responsible generally went for
young girls between ten and fifteen, but small boys were
not entirely exempt. The children were usually sold to
a ring of pleasure house suppliers who dispatched them
to Madras, Bombay or New Delhi, or even exported
them to certain Arab capitals in the Persian Gulf countries. They were never seen or heard of again. The lucky
ones were locked in prostitution houses in Calcutta itself.

Shaken by their neighbours' distress, Aloka woke her
husband. Hasari immediately suggested to Maya's father
that they should go out and look for the girl. Accordingly, the two men plunged into the dark alleyways
packed with people sleeping in doorways and on the

pavements. Avoiding getting lost in such a labyrinth, where all the buildings looked alike, was no mean achievement for peasants used to finding their way in the familiar simplicity of their countryside.

After the two men had gone, Aloka sat down beside the neighbour's wife. The poor woman's cheeks, pock-marked from smallpox, were bathed in tears. She was holding a sleeping baby in the folds of her sari and two other small boys muffled in rags were asleep beside her. Nothing, it seemed, could disturb children's slumbers, not even, as here, the noisy exhausts of lorries or the harrowing grind of the trams passing right by their heads on the avenue, not even the cramps of a hungry stomach. During the time that these peasants had been living on their piece of pavement, they had marked out their territory as if they meant to remain there for ever. Their plot was a proper little campsite with one corner for sleeping and another corner for cooking, with a *chula* and a few utensils. It was winter and these shelterless people had no need to fear the torrential downpour of the monsoon. But when the December wind blew down from the Himalayas and swept through the avenues, it was as cold as death on the pavements. From every direction there rose the same haunting noises. The sound of coughing fits, of throats being cleared, the whistle of spitting. The worst for Aloka was to have to 'sleep on the bare ground. You woke up in the morning with limbs as painful as if they'd been beaten.' By some cruel stroke of irony, an advertisement on a hoarding seemed to flout them from the opposite pavement. It showed a maharajah sleeping snugly on a thick mattress. From his dreamland he inquired solicitously, 'Have you ever thought of a Simmons mattress as a present?'

Maya's father and Hasari Pal did not return for several hours and when they did it was without the little girl. Instantly something about her husband's behaviour surprised Aloka. The same man who had seemed so

exhausted before he left was now full of life. Maya's
father was in the same state. Without uttering a word,
they sat down on the pavement and began to laugh.
Aloka realized her husband had been drinking. 'I was
indignant,' she would remember. 'And my husband
must have sensed my anger because he slunk back to the
spot where he had been sleeping a few hours earlier like
a penitent dog. Our neighbour did the same and I could
tell by his wife's silence that the poor woman was
used to this kind of situation.' It was not really all that
surprising. Like all overpopulated cities, Calcutta was
packed with seedy drinking and gambling dens where
for a few pice the poor could procure some foul concoction in which to drown their sorrows for a while.

Aloka spent the night trying to console the neighbour's wife. The woman's grief tore at her heart all the
more acutely because she had just discovered that her
eldest son, a boy of fifteen, was in prison. He had been
going off every evening but coming back regularly each
morning with about ten rupees. He belonged to an
organized gang that looted railway cars. Two months
earlier the police had come and arrested him. Since then
the three younger children had never stopped moaning
that they were hungry. 'Poor woman! A daughter lost
God knows where, a drunken husband, a thief of a son
behind bars. What a dreadful fate!' Aloka lamented,
terrified at the thought that the same plight awaited her
own family if her husband did not soon find work.

The dawn had just broken, after a night of anxiety,
when young Maya reappeared. Her mother reared up
like a cobra. 'Maya,' she cried, clasping her child in her
arms, 'Maya, where have you been?'

The adolescent girl's face was shuttered, hostile. There
were traces of red on her lips and she smelled of perfume.
Freeing herself from her mother's grasp and gesturing to
her two small brothers, she handed her a ten-rupee note.

'Today they will not cry.'

7

Three hundred thousand people stranded in this mirage city lived like those two families in the streets. Others crowded into the jumble of planks and daub that were its three thousand slums.

A slum was not exactly a shantytown. It was more like a sort of poverty-stricken industrial suburb inhabited exclusively by refugees from rural areas. Everything in these slums combined to drive their inhabitants to abjection and despair: shortage of work and chronic unemployment, appallingly low wages, the inevitable child labour, the impossibility of saving, debts that could never be redeemed, the mortgaging of personal possessions and their ultimate loss sooner or later. They also had to contend with the total lack of any reserve food stocks and the necessity to buy in minute quantities – ten pice worth of salt, twenty pice worth of wood, one match, a spoonful of sugar – and the total absence of privacy, with ten or twelve people sharing a single room. Yet the miracle of these concentration camps was that the accumulation of disastrous elements was counterbalanced by other factors that allowed their inhabitants not merely to remain fully human but even to transcend their condition and become models of humanity.

In these slums people actually put love and mutual support into practice. They knew how to be tolerant of all creeds and castes, how to give respect to a stranger, how to show charity towards beggars, cripples, lepers and even the insane. Here the weak were helped, not trampled upon. Orphans were instantly adopted by their neighbours and old people were cared for and revered by their children.

Unlike the occupants of shantytowns in other parts of the world, in these slums the former peasants who took refuge there were not drop-outs. They had reconstructed the life of their villages in their urban exile. An adapted, perhaps distorted, life – but none the less so real that their poverty itself had become a form of culture. The poor of Calcutta were not uprooted. They shared in a communal world and respected its social and religious values, maintaining their ancestral traditions and beliefs. Ultimately – and this was of primary importance – they knew that if they were poor it was not their fault, but the fault of the cyclical or permanent maledictions that beset the places where they came from.

One of the principal and oldest of Calcutta's slums was situated in the suburbs, fifteen minutes' walk from the railway station where the Pal family first alighted. It was wedged between a railway embankment, the Calcutta–Delhi highway, and two factories. Either out of ignorance or defiance, the jute factory owner who, at the beginning of the century, had lodged his workers on this land which he had reclaimed from a fever-infested marsh, had christened the place Anand Nagar, 'City of Joy'. Since then the jute factory had closed its doors, but the original workers' estate had expanded to become a veritable city within a city. By now more than seventy thousand inhabitants had congregated on an expanse of ground hardly twice the size of a football stadium. That included some ten thousand families divided up geographically according to their various religious creeds. Sixty-three per cent of them were Muslims, 37 per cent Hindus, with here and there little islands of Sikhs, Jains, Christians and Buddhists.

With its compounds of low houses constructed around minute courtyards, its red-tiled roofs and its rectilinear alleyways, the City of Joy did indeed look more like an industrial suburb than a shantytown. Nevertheless it boasted a sad record – it had the densest concentration

of humanity on this planet, two hundred thousand people per square mile. It was a place where there was not even one tree per three thousand inhabitants, not a single flower, butterfly or bird, apart from vultures and crows – it was a place where children did not even know what a bush, a forest or a pond was, where the air was so laden with carbon dioxide and sulphur that pollution killed at least one member in every family; a place where men and beasts baked in a furnace for the eight months of summer until the monsoon transformed their alley-ways and shacks into lakes of mud and excrement; a place where leprosy, tuberculosis, dysentery and all the malnutrition diseases, until recently, reduced the average life expectancy to one of the lowest in the world; a place where over eight thousand cows and buffalo tied up to dung heaps provided milk infected with germs. Above all, however, the City of Joy was a place where the most extreme economic poverty ran rife. Nine out of ten of its inhabitants did not have a single rupee per day with which to buy half a pound of rice. Furthermore, like all other slums, the City of Joy was generally ignored by other citizens of Calcutta, except in case of crime or strike. Considered a dangerous neighbourhood with a terrible reputation, the haunt of Untouchables, pariahs, social rejects, it was a world apart, living apart from the world.

Stranded there in the course of successive migrations, those who occupied this slum belonged to all the races of the Indian subcontinent. Afghans of the Turkish-Iranian type, pure Indo-Aryans from Kashmir and the Punjab, Christian Bettiahs, negroid Oryans, Mongoloids from Nepal, Tibeto-Burmese from Assam, aborigines, Bengalis, Afghan moneylenders, *marwaris* from Raja-sthan, Sikhs proudly sporting their turbans, refugees from distant overpopulated Kerala – they were all there. So were several thousand Tamils from the south, who lived apart in wretched huts with dwarf pigs, their own

customs and their own language. Hindu sages were also to be seen there, installed in small ashrams built out of planks; groups of Bauls, those wandering Bengali mystic monks in ochre robes, for whom the City of Joy was a port of call; Muslim Sufis with goatees, dressed all in white; all kinds of fakirs decked out in the most unlikely clothes, or indeed sometimes without any clothes at all; a few Parsee fire worshippers; and Jains with masks over their mouths to prevent their taking any life by accidentally swallowing an insect. There were even a number of Chinese dentists. And the mosaic would not be quite complete without the mention of a small colony of eunuchs. Then there were the families of the local Mafia lords, who held a controlling hand over the slum's activities, be it real estate speculation on the cattle sheds, illicit distillation of alcohol, eviction for nonpayment of rent, summary trials, punishments meted out for the slightest verbal offence, the black market, smoking dens, prostitution, drugs, or the control of union and political activity.

A few Anglo–Indians, the descendants of children born of the union of casteless Indians and nonranking British soldiers, and a scattering of other ethnic groups completed the population of this Tower of Babel. Until recently only the white race of the Vikings and the Celts remained unrepresented in this ants' nest. One day, however, this gap was to be filled.

8

A few weeks after the arrival of the Pal family in Calcutta, it was the turn of a European to alight at the great glory hole of Howrah Station. With his thin moustache beneath a turned-up nose, his bare forehead, and relaxed

walk and manner, he looked very much like the American actor Jack Nicholson. He was dressed in jeans and an Indian shirt, with basketball shoes on his feet, and his luggage was confined to a cloth knapsack slung over his shoulder. Only a black metal cross dangling on his chest at the end of a piece of cord denoted his status. The thirty-two-year-old Pole, Stephan Kovalski, was a Catholic priest.

For him Calcutta was the culmination of a long journey that had begun in Krasnik, a little coal mining city in Polish Silesia, where he was born in 1933. The son and grandson of mining men, Stephan Kovalski had spent his early childhood in the gloomy environment of the pit into which his father used to descend each morning. He had just reached the age of five when his father took the whole family by train to join a group of cousins who had emigrated to the north of France; there, salaries offered to coal miners were six or seven times higher than they were in Poland. One evening in the summer of 1946, an ambulance had drawn up outside the entrance of the Kovalskis' mining home. Stephan had seen his father brought out of it. His head was wrapped up in bandages. It was the summer of the great strike which paralysed all the pits of the northern France coal basin. In the course of violent confrontations between the miners and the forces of law and order, Stephan Kovalski's father had suffered burns on his face and lost an eye. This traumatic experience had completely transformed this quiet and profoundly religious man. He rose up in rebellion against the suffering and the pain and took refuge in active, radical and desperate revolt. A former militant of Catholic Working Men's Action, he went over to join the ranks of the revolutionary Marxist League, an extreme left-wing organization. Recognizable at a distance because of the patch over his eye, he came to be nicknamed 'the Pirate'. He got himself mixed up in a number of serious incidents. There was

talk of industrial terrorism and he was arrested. A few days later, the mayor of the locality came to inform Stephan's mother, a generous, sweet-natured Polish woman, that her husband had hanged himself in his cell.

The young Stephan had been a helpless witness to his father's metamorphosis. This suicide was a terrible shock for the adolescent boy. Stephan stopped eating, to the extent that people feared for his life. He shut himself away in his room to meditate before a picture of the Sacred Shroud of Turin which his father had given him for his First Communion. The imprint of Christ's face after his removal from the Cross, together with a photograph of France's most famous female popular singer, Edith Piaf, and a few books including a life of Charles de Foucauld, an aristocrat and officer who had become a monk in the Sahara Desert, and a Polish translation of *The Keys of the Kingdom* by Cronin, were his only companions. One morning as he kissed his mother good-bye on leaving for school, he made an announcement, 'Mother, I'm going to be a missionary.'

Stephan Kovalski had been mulling over his decision for a long time. 'There were two factors that drove me to it,' he would recount years later. 'The need to get away after the death of my father but, above all, the desire to achieve by other means what he had attempted to accomplish by violence. At that time large numbers of new immigrants were working in the mines in the north of France: North Africans, Senegalese, Turks, Yugoslavs. My father, who never forgot he had been an immigrant himself, had enrolled them all in his revolutionary organization. It had become their family and he was something of a father to them. Some of them used to spend the evening at our house when they came out of the pit. There wasn't any television yet, so people talked – about everything, but especially about justice, solidarity, fraternity, about what they needed most. One day a Senegalese immigrant challenged my father:

"You're always saying you're close to us but do you really know anything about us? Why don't you go and live for a while in an African shantytown or in our poor countryside? Then you'd have a better idea of why we were forced to leave and come here to break up stones all day at the bottom of a mine." I had never forgotten what this man had said.'

The African's suggestion influenced the boy profoundly. Several years previously, during the cruel summer of 1940, Stephan had been devastated by the sight of the exodus of Belgian refugees, fleeing before the German armies on the road that ran along the back of the miners' estate. After school he had rushed off to take those wretched people something to drink. Later he witnessed the Nazi roundups of Jewish children. Together with his parents, he threw them bread and cheese from the family's own rations, underneath the barbed wire. All through the war these working-class people had shared their meagre resources with others. Stephan Kovalski's vocation to serve was born out of this very revolt against injustice, and out of the life of love and sharing in which he had grown up.

On leaving the mining community, he spent three years at a small seminary in Belgium. The religious instruction he received there seemed to him far removed from everyday exigencies, but deeper study of the Gospels reinforced his desire to identify himself with the plight of the poor. Each vacation period he went home to embrace his mother before hitchhiking on to the Paris area where he sought out a kind of bearded saint. At that time the Abbé Pierre, a French priest who was also a member of Parliament, with his old beret on his head and his rag and bone disciples at his side, provided help for the most needy with the proceeds from the sale of anything they could salvage, by clearing out the cellars and attics of the more privileged.

Later, at the Louvain seminary in Belgium, Kovalski

met the man who was to give a definitive direction to his journey. Padre Ignacio Fraile belonged to a Spanish order founded in the last century by a priest from the province of Asturias, now being considered for beatification by the Vatican. The Fraternity of San Vincente gathered together priests and consecrated laymen who took the vows of poverty, chastity, obedience and charity in order to 'seek out the poorest of the poor and the disinherited in the places where they are, to share their life, and to die with them'. Small communities of priests and brothers sprang up in the industrial suburbs of numerous cities in Europe, Latin America, Africa, Asia, everywhere in fact where people were suffering. There were several in France itself.

Stephan Kovalski was ordained a priest on August 15, 1960, on the Feast of the Virgin Mary. He was just twenty-seven years old. That very evening he caught a train to spend a few hours with his mother, who had been in hospital for three months, suffering from cardiac problems. Before embracing her son for the last time, she gave him a carefully wrapped box. Inside it, on a bed of cotton wool, he found a black metal cross engraved with two dates: that of his birth and that of his ordination. 'Never be parted from it, my boy,' she said to him, clasping her son's hand in her own. 'This cross will protect you wherever you go.'

Knowing that the most forsaken people were to be found not in Europe but in the Third World, Stephan Kovalski had studied Spanish during his last year at the seminary, in the hope of being sent to the shantytowns, or *favelas*, of South America. Instead, however, it was to India that his fraternity required him to go.

India! A subcontinent with exceptional potential wealth – yet where areas and social groups of overwhelming poverty survived. A land of intense spirituality and of savage racial, political and religious conflicts. A land of saints like Gandhi, Aurobindo, Ramakrishna

and Vivekananda, and of political leaders who were sometimes odiously corrupt. A land that manufactured rockets and satellites but where eight out of ten of its inhabitants had never travelled faster than their oxen could pull their carts. A land of incomparable beauty and variety, and of hideous prospects like the slums of Bombay or Calcutta. A land where the sublime often stood side by side with the very worst this world can offer, but where both elements were always more vibrant, more human and ultimately more alluring than anywhere else.

Impatient to leave, Stephan Kovalski applied for a resident's visa. His request marked the beginning of a prolonged purgatory. Month after month for five years the Indian authorities promised the delivery of the essential document. Unlike a temporary tourist visa, a resident's permit in fact required the approval of the Ministry of Foreign Affairs in New Delhi. The inclusion of his status as a priest on Stephan Kovalski's application had given rise to difficulties. For some time India had not been permitting foreign missionaries to enter its territory. The motives for this prohibition had never been officially defined but the massive number of conversions from Hinduism to Christianity had been unequivocally denounced.

While awaiting his visa, Stephan Kovalski made his home first in a shantytown of Algerians in the Saint-Michel district of Marseilles, then in a home for Senegalese immigrants in Saint-Denis, near Paris. True to his ideal of fraternity he shared in everything: the exhausting work that was remunerated with wages below the legal rates, the punishing mattresses of immigrants' hotels, the foul stews from barrack-room-style kitchens. He became successively a machine operator, fitter, turner, metal founder and storekeeper.

On August 15, 1965, the fifth anniversary of his ordination, Stephan Kovalski finally determined that the

waiting had gone on long enough. With the agreement of his superiors, he asked for a simple tourist visa. This time, in the space left for him to fill in his profession, he wrote 'skilled factory worker'. On the following day, his passport was returned to him complete with the precious visa duly stamped with the seal of the three lions of the Emperor Ashoka, chosen by the founders of modern India as the emblem of their republic. Despite the fact that the permit authorized him to stay in India for only three months, now at last the great adventure of Stephan Kovalski's life could begin. Once he was actually in Calcutta, his assigned destination, he would try and obtain a permanent resident's permit.

Bombay, the 'Gateway to India'! It was via this port on the west coast, which had for three centuries provided a first glimpse of the continent to hundreds of thousands of British soldiers and administrators, that Stephan Kovalski made his entrance into India. In order to familiarize himself with the country before reaching Calcutta at the other extremity of the huge peninsula, he chose to take the longest possible approach route. At Victoria Station, a prodigious caravanserai bristling with neo-Gothic bell towers, he climbed into a third-class compartment of a train leaving for Trivandrum and the south.

The train stopped at every station. As it did, all passengers got out to fulfil their bodily needs, to wash, to cook their food, in the middle of a teeming mass of vendors, bearers, cows, dogs and crows. 'I looked around me and did as the others did,' Stephan Kovalski was to relate in a letter to his mother. On purchasing an orange, however, he was to discover that he wasn't quite as the others were. He paid for the fruit with a one-rupee note but the vendor failed to give him any change. His request for it was met with an expression of fury and disdain: 'How could a *sahib** be so short of cash?' 'I peeled the

---

* A respectful name formally reserved for white foreigners.

orange and had broken off a quarter of it when a little girl planted herself in front of me, her big eyes black with kohl. Of course I gave her the fruit and she scampered off. I followed her. She had taken it to share with her brothers and sisters.' A moment later Stephan Kovalski had nothing but a smile to offer a young shoe-shine boy who was circling around him; but a smile does not fill an empty stomach. Kovalski foraged in his knapsack and offered the boy the banana he had promised himself he would eat out of anybody's sight. 'At that rate I was condemned to die of starvation very rapidly,' he would recall.

In addition to the congestion of the cars there was the sauna heat to contend with, the dust heavy with soot that burned the throat, and all the smells, exclamations, tears and laughter that made this railway journey a truly royal way to get to know a people. It was in the restaurant of one of the stations in the south that Kovalski experienced his first Indian meal. 'I began by watching the people around me,' he recounted. 'They were eating with the fingers of their right hands only. To make up small balls of rice and dip them into the sauce without the balls disintegrating and without burning your fingers to the bone involved a right set of gymnastics. As for your mouth, throat and stomach, they're set on fire by those murderous spices! I must have presented a somewhat comical spectacle, because all the clients of the restaurant cracked up. It wasn't every day that they could have a good laugh at a poor *sahib* who had undertaken to master his certificate of Indianization.'

Ten days later, after a short stopover in a shantytown near Madras, Stephan Kovalski arrived in Calcutta.

9

No amount of wretchedness, not even utter destitution on a piece of pavement in Calcutta, could alter the ritual of the world's cleanest people. With the very first grind of the tram on the rails of the avenue, Hasari Pal would get up to respond to 'the call of nature'. He went to the sewer which ran along open to the heavens on the opposite side of the avenue. It was a formality that was to become progressively shorter in duration for a man deprived of nourishment. He lifted up his cotton *longhi* and squatted down over the gutter, and on the edge of the pavement dozens of other men did likewise. No one took any notice of them. It was part of the life and the surrounding scenery. Aloka and the other women had done the same, even earlier, before the men awoke. Afterwards Hasari went to take his place in the line of men waiting at the fountain for their daily bath. This fountain was in reality a fire hydrant from which issued a brownish liquid pumped directly out of the Hooghly River. When his turn came Hasari would squat on his heels, pour a bowl of water over his head, and scrub himself vigorously from head to toe with 'poorman's' soap, a little ball made out of a mixture of clay and ashes. Neither the biting winter cold nor the pangs of an empty stomach would accelerate the completion of this ancestral ritual of purification, which young and old alike piously adhered to each morning.

Hasari then left with his two eldest children for the Bara Bazar. The market was always overflowing with so many goods that there was invariably some food, in a more or less rotten condition, to be gleaned from its refuse heaps. Hundreds of poor luckless families strayed

like this father and his children through the same labyrinth, hoping for the same miracle: the discovery of a
compatriot from their village, their district, their province, a relative, an acquaintance, the friend of a friend,
a member of their caste, their subcaste, a branch of their
subcaste; in short, someone who might be prepared to
take them under his protective wing and find them two
or three hours, perhaps a whole day, or even – miracle
of all miracles – several days of work. This ceaseless
quest was not quite as unrealistic as it might appear.
Every individual in India is always linked to the rest of
the social body by a network of incredibly diversified
ties, with the result that no one in this gigantic country
of seven hundred and fifty million inhabitants could ever
be completely abandoned – except, perhaps, for Hasari
Pal whom this 'inhuman city' seemed obstinately to
reject. That morning, the morning of the sixth day, he
left his children to forage among the refuse while he
went off once more to scour the bazaar in every possible
direction. He offered his services to dozens of traders and
transporters. Several times he even followed overloaded
carts in the faint hope that one of the coolies would
eventually keel over with exhaustion and he might take
his place. With his belly screaming with hunger, his head
empty and his heart heavy with despair, the former
peasant eventually collapsed against a wall. Through his
dizziness, he heard a voice. 'Would you like to earn a
few rupees?'

The small man with spectacles looked more like an
office employee than a trader from the bazaar. Hasari
stared at the stranger in astonishment and motioned that
he would. 'All you have to do is to follow me. I'll take
you somewhere where they'll take a little of your blood
and give you thirty rupees for it. That's fifteen for me
and fifteen for you.'

'Thirty rupees for my blood!' repeated Hasari, paralysed with amazement. 'Who's going to want to take

blood off a poor bum like me and on top of that give me thirty rupees?'

'Don't be a fool! Blood is blood!' replied the man with glasses. 'Whether it comes from a pandit or a pariah, from a *marwari* bursting at the seams with money or from a bum like you. It's all still blood.'

Struck by this logic, Hasari made an effort to get back on his feet and follow the stranger.

The man belonged to a profession practised extensively in a city where the slightest suggestion of profit inevitably attracted a swarm of parasitical intermediaries known as 'middlemen'. For every transaction or service provided there were one or more intermediaries who each took their cut. The individual with the glasses was a procurer. He tracked down donors for one of the numerous private blood banks that flourished in Calcutta. His technique was always the same. He went prowling around the entrances to the work sites, factories, markets, anywhere he knew he would find men without work, ready to agree to anything for the sake of a few rupees. The taboos of Islam forbade Muslims to give their blood. He was, therefore, interested only in Hindus.

For a man at the end of his resources, the sale of his blood represented a last chance of survival, and for astute and unscrupulous businessmen this meant the opportunity to make a fortune. The need for blood in the hospitals and clinics of an immense metropolis like Calcutta amounted to several tens of thousands of bottles a year. Since the four or five official blood banks of the State of Bengal were incapable of meeting such a demand, it was only to be expected that private entrepreneurs should try and take advantage of the market. All they had to do was wangle the complicity of a doctor, lay a request before the Health Department in his name, rent premises, acquire a refrigerator, a few syringes, pipettes and bottles, and engage a dispensary

assistant. The result was a roaring trade with an annual
turnover in excess of ten million rupees (£600,000).
Only the fierce competition to which these dispensaries,
private or otherwise, were subjected could, it seemed,
impede the flow of their profits. Hasari Pal had just put
his finger on one of the best organized rackets of a
city which, according to connoisseurs of such matters,
practised a multitude of rackets with a degree of art and
imagination that would turn Naples, Marseilles or New
York green with envy.

Hasari followed his bespectacled 'benefactor' through
the streets of the business quarter, then along
Chowringhee Road and at last into Park Street, the street
for luxury goods, restaurants and nightclubs. At the
upper end of the block and in the adjoining streets were
several blood dispensaries. That of No. 49 Randal Street
had been set up in what used to be a garage. Hardly had
Hasari and the procurer reached its door than they were
accosted by a man with an emaciated face and a mouth
reddened by a quid of betel. 'Are you coming for blood?'
the man asked in a low voice.

The procurer with the glasses acquiesced with that
inimitable waggling of the head that is so distinctively
Indian. 'In that case, follow me,' said the stranger with
a wink. 'I know another bank where they pay forty
rupees. Five for me, the rest for you two. Agreed?'

This man was another cog in the wheel and was
procuring for a rival blood bank two streets further on.
A notice bore the initials of its three owners. The CRC
was one of the oldest dispensaries in Calcutta. The ten
additional rupees it offered had nothing whatever to do
with generosity. It simply meant that it took ten liquid
ounces from its donors, instead of the usual eight. It is
true to say that it added to this remuneration a royal
bonus for a man with an empty stomach: a banana
and three glucose biscuits. Its boss was a well-known
haematologist, a Doctor Rana. He too was but another

cog in the wheel of the racket. As a director of one of
the state's official blood banks, he had no difficulty
in diverting donors and purchasers to his own private
dispensary. Nothing could be easier. All you had to do
was to tell the donors who turned up at the official blood
bank that the CRC paid better rates. As for the clients
who came to buy blood for an emergency or for a future
operation, the doctor simply had them informed that
bottles of the required blood group were provisionally
out of stock at the official bank but available at his CRC.

Yet such practices could pass for innocent commercial
games by comparison with the lack of medical precautions which cursed the majority of dispensaries. The
World Health Organization had stipulated a certain number of vital rules with regard to the analyses that must
be undertaken before any blood was taken for use in
transfusions. They were simple tests which cost little
and which made possible the detection of, among other
things, the hepatitis B virus or any venereal diseases.
Yet at the CRC, as at numerous other private blood
banks at that time, viruses seemed to be their very last
worry. All that really mattered was profit.

Hasari was invited to sit down on a stool. While
one male nurse knotted a rubber tourniquet around his
biceps, another stuck a needle into the vein in the hollow
of his elbow. Both of them watched the flow of red
liquid with a measure of fascination that grew as the
level in the bottle rose. Was it the sight of blood, the
idea that he was being 'emptied like the goatskin bottle
of a water vendor in the Bara Bazar', or the lack of food?
Hasari's strength began to fail him. His vision blurred
and he started to sweat thick beads of perspiration,
despite the fact that he was shivering with cold. The
voices of the attendants seemed to reach him from
another planet, through a strange clamouring of bells.
Through a halo, he could just make out the glasses of
his 'benefactor'. Next he felt the grip of two hands

holding him on his stool. Then everything went blank. He had passed out.

So banal was the incident that the attendants did not interrupt their work. Every day they saw men exhausted by deprivation faint as they sold their blood. If it had been up to them they would have pumped the inert bodies dry. They were paid by the bottle.

When Hasari opened his eyes again, a dreamlike vision appeared above him: one of the men in white overalls was offering him a banana.

'There you are, little girl. Get this fruit down you. That'll bring you back as Bhim!'* the attendant mocked him gently.

Then he took a receipt book out of his pocket and inquired, 'What's your name?' He scribbled out a few words, tore off the sheet, and directed Hasari in a per-emptory tone to 'Sign here'. Hasari made a cross and pocketed the forty rupees under the covetous gazes of the two vultures who had brought him there. The money would be divided up outside. What the peasant did not know was that he had put his signature to a receipt for forty-five rupees, and not forty. The attendants, too, were taking their commission.

Light-headed and reeling, lost in neighbourhoods that were unknown to him, Hasari would take hours to find the piece of pavement where his wife and children were waiting for him. Out of the seventeen and a half rupees that the procurers had left him, he decided to spend five on celebrating with his family the joy of actually having earned some money in the 'inhuman city'. He bought a pound of *barfi*, the delicious Bengali nougat richly wrapped in a thin silver film, and some *mansours*, yellow sweetmeats made out of chick-pea flour and sweetened milk. Further on he chose twenty or so paper cones full

---

* The strongest of the Pandavas, the five heroic brothers in the great epic tale of the Mahabharata.

of *muri*, the puffed rice that crunched between your
teeth, so that the neighbours on the pavement could
share in the celebration. Finally he could not resist the
desire to give himself a treat. He stopped in front of one
of the innumerable niches where vendors as impassive
as buddhas prepared their *pan*, those subtle quids made
out of a little finely chopped betel nut, a pinch of tobacco,
a suggestion of lime, chutney and cardamom, all rolled
up in a betel leaf skilfully folded and sealed with a clove.
Pan gave energy. Above all, it curbed the appetite.

When Aloka caught sight of her husband, a lump rose
in her throat. 'Dear God, he's been drinking again,' she
thought. Then, seeing him laden with parcels, she feared
that he had committed some felony. She ran to meet
him but the children had already preceded her. Like a
litter of lion cubs throwing themselves on the male
returning with a gazelle carcass, they were already
sharing out the nougat.

In the rush and tumble no one noticed the small red
mark that Hasari still bore in the fold of his arm.

10

It was here. He was sure it was. The exaltation that
suddenly seized Stephan Kovalski, the feeling of pleni-
tude at being at last 'with them', could not be designed
to deceive him. It was definitely here, in this grey, filthy,
poor, sad, stinking muddy place. In this wild turmoil of
men, women, children and animals. In this entanglement
of huts built of beaten earth, this jumble of alleyways full
of refuse and open drains, in this murderous pollution of
sulphur and fumes, in this uproar of voices, shouting,
weeping, tools, machinery and loudspeakers. Yes, it was
definitely to this slum at the far corner of the world that

his God had sent him. 'How rewarding it was to discover the absolute conviction that I had at last arrived where I was supposed to be,' he was later to say. 'My enthusiasm and yearning to share had been right to push me into embarking on an experience considered impossible for a Westerner. I was so deliriously happy, I could have walked barefoot over hot coals.'

A few days previously, as soon as he got off the train, Stephan Kovalski had paid a call on the bishop of Calcutta. The bishop lived in a beautiful colonial-style house surrounded by a vast garden in a residential area. He was an Anglo-Indian of about fifty, with a white cassock and a majestic manner. On his head he wore a purple skullcap, and on his finger an episcopal ring.

'I have come to live with the poor,' the Polish priest said to him simply.

'You'll have no difficulty in finding them,' sighed the prelate. 'Alas, the poor are everywhere here.'

He gave Stephan Kovalski a letter of recommendation to the parish priest of a working-class district on the other side of the river.

With its two white-painted towers, the church could be seen for some distance. It was an imposing building decorated with vividly coloured stained-glass windows, and inside was a rich supply of statues of the saints, collection boxes and fans suspended above the pews reserved for the faithful. Its name was like a challenge cast before the innumerable homeless people camping in the square and surrounding streets. It sprawled in luminous letters across the entire width of the façade: Our Lady of the Loving Heart.

The rector of the parish came from Goa – Father Alberto Cordeiro had very dark skin and carefully combed curly hair. With his rounded cheeks and his plumpish paunch beneath an immaculate cassock, he looked more like a monsignor of the Roman Curia than a priest of the poor. In the courtyard of the church was

parked his car, and several Christian servants assured him the soft comfortable existence which befitted a rector in charge of a parish.

The sudden advent of a foreign priest in jeans and basketball shoes somewhat disconcerted the ecclesiastic.

'Don't you wear a cassock?' he asked.

'It wasn't exactly the most comfortable attire to travel about your country, especially in the heat,' explained Stephan Kovalski.

'Ah,' sighed the rector. 'You Westerners can allow yourselves such flights of fancy. You will always be respected! Your skin is white! Whereas for us Indian priests a cassock is both a symbol and our protection. In a country that recognizes the sacred, it guarantees us a place apart.'

The Indian acquainted himself with the bishop's message.

'You really want to go and live in a slum?'

'That's why I'm here.'

Father Cordeiro appeared aghast. With a grave and preoccupied air, he began to pace up and down the room. 'But that's not what our mission as priests is about! Here the people only think of wearing you down. You give them the tip of your finger and instantly they take the whole of your arm. No, my dear fellow, you won't be doing them any service by going and sharing their existence. All you risk doing is encouraging their latent laziness and turning them into permanent dependants.'

He stopped walking and planted himself in front of Kovalski. 'And then, you won't be there indefinitely! When you go off home, it'll be here, in my house, that they'll come clamouring that the clergy aren't doing anything for them. But if we Indian priests were to take the plunge, they'd have no respect for us any more.'

The idea of going and living in the middle of a slum had evidently never occurred to the good Father

Cordeiro. Yet Kovalski would later realize that this reluctance to mix with the slum population did not necessarily spring from a lack of charity, but rather from a desire that was common enough among the local clergy, to keep a certain distance between themselves and the masses, and one that arose out of traditional Indian respect for social hierarchy.

Despite his very natural reservations, the rector proved to be most understanding. He entrusted Stephan Kovalski to one of his assistants, an Anglo-Indian Christian who undertook to find him a room in the large nearby slum of Anand Nagar, the 'City of Joy'.

It was five o'clock in the evening on the following day when the Pole and his guide presented themselves at the entrance to the slum. The red of the sinking sun was veiled in a shroud of greyish vapour. A smell of burning infused the city, as everywhere *chulas* were lit to cook the evening meal. In the narrow alleyways the air was laden with an acrid heaviness which burned the throat and lungs. One sound distinguished itself from all the others – the noise of coughing that racked innumerable chests.

Before arriving in Calcutta, Stephan Kovalski had spent a few days in a slum in the Madras area, built near a mine, in open countryside. It was a slum full of light and hope, for its occupants left it each morning to go to work outside and they knew that one day they would live in a proper industrial estate. At Anand Nagar the opposite was true: everyone gave the impression of having been there for ever, and of being likely to remain there for ever. It was an impression that was directly reinforced by the intense activity with which the slum vibrated. Could the people he discovered as he picked his way behind his Anglo-Indian guide conceivably be described as 'lazy'? 'Ants more likely,' he thought. Every

single one of them, from the most worn-out old man to children hardly yet able to walk, was busy with some task. Everywhere, on the doorstep to each hut, at the foot of every stall, in a succession of little workshops or minifactories, Kovalski discovered people industriously selling, trading, manufacturing, tinkering, repairing, sorting, cleaning, nailing, gluing, piercing, carrying, pulling, pushing. After walking only six hundred feet of exploration, he felt as if he were drunk.

Forty-nine Nizamudhin Lane – the address was painted across two planks nailed together which served as a door to a windowless hovel, scarcely more than one yard wide and twice as long. The floor was of beaten earth, and through the missing tiles of the roof one could see patches of sky. There was no furniture, no electricity, no running water. 'Exactly the room I need,' appreciated Kovalski, 'ideally suited to a life of poverty. With, as a bonus, the right environment.'

Outside the door ran an open drain overflowing with nauseating black slime. And just opposite rose a pile of refuse. On the left, a small platform planted over the drain sheltered a tiny tea shop under a bamboo roof. All the occupants of this area were Muslims except the old man running the tea shop who was a Hindu.

The owner of the room, a stout Bengali dressed in Western clothes, passed for one of the richest men in the slum. He owned a block of houses at the end of the alley, where the latrines and the well were. He had cups of tea with sweetened milk brought from the nearby tea shop.

'You're quite sure, Father, that this is where you want to live?' he asked, examining the visitor with incredulity.

'Quite sure,' said Stephan Kovalski. 'How much does the rent come to?'

'Twenty-five rupees a month (£1.50). Payable in advance.'

'Twenty-five rupees?' the Anglo-Indian exclaimed

indignantly. 'Twenty-five rupees for a miserable room without a window. That's highway robbery!'

'It'll do,' interrupted Stephan Kovalski, taking his money out of his pocket. 'Here's three months' rent.'

'I was so happy I would have given the moon for a lifetime lease of that hovel,' he recalled later. He was soon to discover how privileged he was: ten or twelve persons were living in huts like his.

The deal concluded, Father Cordeiro's envoy lost no time in presenting the newcomer to the few Christians of the City of Joy. None of them would believe that the *sahib* in jeans who appeared suddenly in front of their slum houses was an envoy from God. 'But as soon as they were convinced,' he would later recount, 'I might have mistaken myself for the Messiah!' In one of the compounds a young woman fell to her knees. 'Father, bless my child,' she said, holding out to him the baby she was clutching in her arms. 'And bless us all for we are not worthy that a priest should enter under our roof.' They all knelt down and Kovalski made the sign of the cross over their heads. Discovering that he was going to stay among them, they all wanted to organize his household. Some offered a bucket, others a mat, an oil lamp, a blanket. The poorer they were, the more eager they were to give. That night he returned home followed by an escort laden with gifts, 'just like one of the three kings from the Nativity'.

So began the first evening of his new Indian life, an evening that was to form one of the most intense memories of his existence. 'It was already dark. Night falls very early in the tropics. I lit an oil lamp lent to me by one family. They had even had the sensitivity to think of leaving me several matches. I unrolled the mat I had been given, then sat down on the ground with my back propped against the wall, and turned out my old knapsack bought, one day, in the Arab quarter of Marseilles. From it I took out my razor, my shaving brush,

toothbrush, the small medicine box given to me by friends at the factory when I left, a change of underpants and shirt and my Jerusalem Bible, in other words, all my worldly possessions. Between the pages of the Gospels was the picture that had never left my side during my years among the destitute and suffering. I unfolded it carefully and contemplated it for a long while.'

It was the photograph of the Sacred Shroud of Turin given to Stephan by his father years ago. The face of Christ imprinted on his shroud, the face of a man with downcast eyes and swollen cheeks, with punctured brow and a torn beard, that man who died upon the Cross was that evening for Stephan Kovalski the very incarnation of all the martyrs of the slum where he had just arrived. 'For me, a committed believer, each one of them wore that same face of Jesus Christ proclaiming to humanity from the heights of Golgotha all the pain but also all the hope of man rejected. That was the reason for my coming. I was there because of the cry of the crucified Christ: "I thirst", in order to give a voice to the hunger and thirst for justice of those who here mounted each day on the Cross, and who knew how to face that death which we in the West no longer know how to confront without despair. Nowhere else was that icon more in its rightful place than in that slum.'

Stephan Kovalski pinned up the picture with the aid of two matches stuck in the pisé wall. After a while he tried to pray, but his efforts were in vain. He was dazed. He needed some time to adjust to his new incarnation. As he was pondering, a little girl appeared on the threshold, barefoot and dressed in rags but with a flower in the end of her pigtail. She was carrying an aluminium bowl full of rice and vegetables. She set it down in front of Kovalski, joined her hands in the Indian gesture of greeting, bowed her head, smiled, and ran away. 'I gave thanks to God for this apparition and for this meal provided by brothers unknown to me. Then I ate, as

they do, with my fingers. In the depths of this hovel, I felt everything was assuming a very distinctive dimension. So it was that my fingers' contact with the rice made me understand that first night how much the food was not a dead thing, not something neutral, but rather a gift of life.'

Towards nine o'clock, as the noise of the streets died away, Kovalski began to be aware of the echoes of the life that was going on around him: conversations in the nearby rooms, arguments, tears, fits of coughing. Then the searing call of a muezzin surged out of a loudspeaker, followed immediately by the voices of women reciting verses of the Koran. A little later, the Muslims' prayer was succeeded by another litany. Coming from the tea shop opposite, it consisted of one simple syllable indefinitely repeated. '*Om* . . . *Om* . . . *Om* . . .' chanted the elderly Hindu who kept the shop. A mystic invocation which for thousands of years had assisted Hindus to enter into contact with God, this *Om* diffused an ineffable inner peace. Stephan Kovalski had heard it for the first time in the villages in the south and the vibrations of this simple syllable had seemed to him to be charged with such power, such profundity of prayer, that he had adopted it to open his own invocations to the Lord. Pronouncing the *Om* required no conscious effort. 'The *Om* came all by itself and prolonged itself, vibrating like a prayer in the heart,' he would say. 'That night, as I repeated the *Oms* that came from the other side of the street, I experienced the sensation not only of speaking to God but also of taking a step forward into the inner mystery of Hinduism, something which was very important in helping me to grasp the real reasons for my presence in that slum.'

Shortly after midnight silence enveloped the City of Joy. The prayer and the palavers were stilled, along with the coughs and the children's tears. Sleep had come to Anand Nagar. Numb with fatigue and emotion, Stephan

Kovalski too felt the need to close his eyes. Folding up his shirt and jeans to form a pillow, he stretched out on the narrow mat. He discovered then that his room was exactly as long as he was tall: six feet. After a last look at the Sacred Shroud of Christ, he blew out the lamp and closed his eyes with an inner felicity such as he had not experienced since the day of his ordination five years earlier.

It was then that a frenzied chorus struck up right above his head. Striking a match, he discovered a team of rats chasing one another about on the bamboo framework and rushing down the walls to the accompaniment of a cacophony of shrill cries. He leaped to his feet and, despite his desire not to wake his neighbours, set about chasing the intruders, hitting them with his shoe. But as fast as one group made off, others arrived through the holes in the roofing. The magnitude of the invasion forced him to give up. However disagreeable cohabitation of this sort might be, he realized that it was an inevitable part of his new life. With determined resignation he lay down again, but almost immediately he felt something stirring in his hair. Lighting the lamp once more, he shook his head and saw an enormous hairy centipede fall out of it. Fervent admirer of Mahatma Gandhi and his principles of nonviolence that he was, he nevertheless crushed it. Later he was to learn the identity of the creature: a scolopendra whose sting could be as venomous as a scorpion's. For the second time he lay down again and recited a chaplet of *Oms* in the hope of regaining some serenity. The City of Joy had further surprises in store, however, for the Pole's first night within its confines. Indian mosquitoes have as a distinguishing characteristic the fact that they are minute, make very little noise, and tease you endlessly before making up their minds to bite. The effect is a torture of anticipation which, if it were not Indian, would almost certainly be Chinese.

A few hours later, it was the sound of something resembling a bombardment that woke up Kovalski from a brief interval of sleep. On opening his door, he discovered a delivery van in the alleyway, unloading coal outside the shop of the man who sold fuel. He was just about to lie down again when he discerned in the darkness two small silhouettes creeping under the vehicle. The coal merchant, a man with wader's legs, had spotted the young sneak thieves too. He rained down such a shower of curses upon them that they scampered off. There was the sound of running, then a great splash and cries. Certain that one of the fugitives had just fallen in the large sewer that cut across the alleyway a little further down, Kovalski rushed to the rescue, but he had hardly taken three strides before a firm grasp arrested his progress.

Without even being able to recognize the face of the man who had grabbed him, he understood the message. 'I was being invited not to get mixed up with the private affairs of the City of Joy.'

11

The sale of blood enabled the five members of the Pal family to hold out for four days. During that period they fed themselves mainly on bananas. Found in abundance and sold cheaply, this fruit was a gift of providence for the poor of India. In Calcutta its nutritive and curative qualities had made it the object of a veritable cult. At the time of the great festivities in honour of the goddess Durga, patroness of the city, banana trees appeared on the altars, draped in white saris with red borders and venerated as the wife of Ganesh, god of good fortune.

The Pals also lived on what the two eldest children

gleaned from the Bara Bazar, while their father was out looking for work. The last few pice of the last rupee were devoted to the purchase of four cow dung cakes to use to boil up a last stew of scraps and peelings on the neighbours' *chula*. When, finally, there was nothing left, Hasari made a heroic decision. He would go back and sell some more of his blood.

From a physiological point of view, it was a mad idea; but then this 'inhuman city' was a city where madness prevailed. A medical report revealed that many men at the depths of despair did not hesitate to turn up at the doors of the blood banks every week. They did not generally live to old age: they would be found dead of anaemia in some street, or on a bed in Mother Teresa's home for the dying, snuffed out like the flame of a candle deprived of oxygen. The same report also revealed that in the case of one donor in four, the haemoglobin level of the blood was less than half the minimum acceptable level. How many dispensaries, however, were actually concerned with the haemoglobin content of the blood that they collected? In any case, as Hasari was to learn, there was a way of faking the requisite content.

That day the rates of the CRC blood bank were so alluring that crowds were waiting at the door. All the procurers for rival establishments had assembled there to attempt to divert some of the clientele towards their own employers. Hasari was immediately accosted by an individual with two gold front teeth. 'Forty rupees,' whispered the man with the air of a prostitute lowering her price. 'Thirty for you, ten for me.'

'Thirty rupees! That's almost double what I got last time,' thought Hasari, not yet knowing that in Calcutta the price of blood varied from day to day just like the rates for jute or mustard oil at the stock exchange in Dalhousie Square. The difference in fee stemmed in fact mainly from the capacity of the middlemen to assess the naïveté of their prey and hence to fleece them with

greater or less rapacity. With his very first glance, the
man with the gold teeth had registered the stigma on
Hasari's arm, which marked him as a professional.

The Paradise Blood Bank was aptly named. Painted
in pink and furnished with comfortable seats, it had been
set up in an outbuilding of one of the most modern and
expensive clinics in Calcutta, exclusively frequented by
rich *marwari* businessmen and their families. The nurse
in immaculate white overalls and cap, who was in charge
of admitting the donors, grimaced at the sight of the
candidate's pathetic appearance. She made him sit down
on a chair with a reclining back. Unlike the attendants
at the CRC, however, she did not plunge a needle into
his arm. Much to the amazement of the peasant, she
confined herself to pricking his index finger and making
a drop of blood fall onto a glass plate. As for the man
with the gold teeth, he realized all too well what was
happening. 'The bitch is sabotaging me,' he grumbled.

He had guessed correctly. An instant later the young
woman informed him politely that his client's blood did
not meet with the requirements of the dispensary. The
reason given would have precluded the majority of the
inhabitants of Calcutta's slums: inadequate haemoglobin
level.

The blow was a harsh one for Hasari.

'Don't you know anywhere else?' he pleaded with
the procurer as soon as they were back in the street. 'I
don't even have a coin to buy a banana for my children.'

The man laid a friendly arm around his shoulder. 'You
shouldn't fool around with things like that, friend. For
the moment, what you've got in your veins is water.
And if you don't watch out, your family'll soon be
seeing your ashes floating on the Hooghly.'

Hasari felt so hounded by poverty that this prospect
seemed inevitable anyway.

'This time we're done for,' he sighed. 'We shall all

die.' Hardened as he was by his extraordinary profession, the procurer was nevertheless moved by Hasari's distress. 'Don't cry, my friend. Come on, I'll give you a present.' He dragged the peasant over to the nearest chemist where he bought a bottle of tablets. The chemists of the Swiss laboratory that manufactured them had probably never foreseen the use the desperate people of the Third World would make of these tablets.

'There you are, friend,' said the procurer, handing Hasari a packet of ferrous sulphate tablets. 'Take three a day and come back here in a week's time. Remember, in seven days exactly. But just you mind!' he added, suddenly menacing. 'Don't you fail to turn up or that junk in your veins could well flow free of charge.' Then softening again, he concluded, 'I'll take you to a place where they'll think your blood's just fine, so fine that they'll want to drain it out to the very last drop.'

12

The events that marked the life of Stephan Kovalski the day after his first night in the City of Joy might well seem insignificant. Yet in a place where seventy thousand people live together in a state of promiscuity and deplorable conditions of hygiene, even the ordinary necessities of everyday living present particular problems. The performance of natural bodily functions was just one example. The envoy of the rector from the neighbouring parish had urged Kovalski to go to the latrines in a Hindu quarter which was also occupied by a number of Christians.

For a Hindu, the response to 'the call of nature' is an act that must be undertaken according to a very precise ritual. The place chosen must not be situated within the

proximity of a temple, a banyan tree, a riverbank, a pond, a well, or a crossroad frequented by people. The ground must not be light in colour or ploughed, but flat and open and, above all, set apart from all habitation. Before executing the act, a Hindu must remove his sandals – that is, if he has any – squat down as low as possible, and never get up in midperformance. He must take care, on pain of committing a grave offence, not to look at the sun, the moon, the stars, a fire, a Brahmin, or a religious image. He must observe silence and refrain from the sacrilege of turning around to examine his handiwork. Finally there are rules that prescribe the means by which he must go on to complete his ablutions with a mixture of earth and water.

The authors of these sacred instructions had obviously never envisaged that millions of people would one day be crammed into urban jungles, devoid of any open space set apart from places of habitation. For Hindus in the City of Joy, therefore, 'the call of nature' could only be attended to in public, over an open sewer in the alleyways, or in one of the rare cabins recently distributed by local town planners and christened 'latrines'.

What an adventure his first visit to one such public convenience was for Stephan Kovalski! At four o'clock in the morning, access to it was already obstructed by a line of several dozen people. The first had already been there for nearly two hours. The arrival of the *sahib* in jeans and basketball shoes provoked a lively upsurge of curiosity and amusement, and all the more so because, in his ignorance of the customs of the country, the Pole had already committed an unforgivable blunder: he had brought with him a few sheets of toilet paper. Was it conceivable that anyone should want to preserve in paper a defilement expelled from the body and then leave it for other people? Showing him a tinful of water he was holding in his hand, a young lad tried to make Stephan understand that he should wash himself, then clean the

bowl. Looking around him, Kovalski established that indeed everyone had brought a similar receptacle full of water. Some people even had several that they shuttled forward with their feet as the line gradually advanced. 'I understood that they were keeping places for others who were absent,' the priest later said.

A toothless old man came over to offer the Pole his pitcher. 'I took the object with a smile of gratitude, not realizing that I had just committed a second act of sacrilege that would unleash a further explosion of hilarity. I had grasped the receptacle with my left hand, which was reserved for impure contacts. Before reaching the public conveniences, I had to cross a veritable lake of excrement. This additional trial was by courtesy of the cesspool emptiers, who had been on strike for five months. The stench was so foul that I no longer knew which was the more unbearable: the smell or the sight. That people could actually remain good humoured in the middle of so much abjection seemed quite sublime to me. They laughed and joked – especially the children who somehow brought the freshness and gaiety of their games into that cesspool. I came back from that escapade as groggy as a boxer knocked out in the first round. Nowhere else had I ever been subjected to such an onslaught.'

On the way back, the Pole noticed a number of hostile gazes upon him. It was hardly surprising. The rumour had spread that the *sahib* was a Catholic priest. Right in the heart of the Muslim quarter this intrusion might well be interpreted as an act of provocation. 'God only knows how alone I felt that first morning!' he was to say. 'Not being able to breathe a single word of the languages spoken in the slum, it was like being deaf and dumb. And not being able to lay my hands on a little wine, I was deprived even of the comfort of being able to celebrate the Eucharist in the darkness of my den. Fortunately, there was still prayer!'

Prayer! For years Stephan Kovalski had begun each day with an hour's contemplation. Whether he was in a plane, a train or a roomful of immigrant workmen, he emptied himself, turned to God, gave himself up to him to receive his word, or simply to say to his Creator, 'Here I am, at your disposal.' He also liked to open the Gospels at random and pick out a sentence such as, 'Save me; or I perish', or 'Salvation is of the Lord', or 'In Thy presence is fullness of joy'. He would study every word and every syllable, turning them over in every possible direction. 'It's a spiritual exercise that helps me to achieve silence,' he would explain, 'to find emptiness in God. If God has time to listen to me, then inevitably he has time to love me.'

That day, however, Kovalski felt himself incapable of real silence, real emptiness. He had been bombarded with too many impressions since the previous evening. Somehow he could not manage to pray as he did on other mornings. 'Sitting in front of the picture of the Sacred Shroud, I began to recite *Oms* – aloud. Then I intercalated the name of Jesus. "*Om* . . . Jesus, *Om* . . . Jesus.*" For me it was a way of joining in the prayer of the slum people who were so close to God and lived with him constantly, while at the same time discovering a way of communicating with my revealed God whom they did not know. After a moment I was once more in his presence. I could speak to him.

'Lord, here I am. It's me, Stephan. Jesus, you know that I am but a poor man, so have mercy on me. You know that I haven't come here to earn favour. Nor have I come here for other people. I am here for you, to love you unconditionally. Jesus, my brother, Jesus, my saviour, I have arrived here in the depths of this slum with hands so empty that I cannot even celebrate the Eucharist in remembrance of your sacrifice. But then don't all these men with lowered eyes and swollen faces, don't all these innocent people martyred in this place of

suffering commemorate your sacrifice every day? Have mercy on them, Jesus of Anand Nagar.

'Jesus of the City of Joy, you who are eternally crucified, you who are the voice of the voiceless ones, you who suffer within each one of these people, you who endure their anguish, their distress and their sadness, but you who know how to express yourself through their hearts, their tears, their laughter, and their love. Jesus of Anand Nagar, you know that I am here simply to share – so that together they and I can show you that we love you – you and your Father, the Father of mercy, the Father who sent you, the Father who forgives. And to tell you, too, you who are the light and the salvation of the world, that here, in the City of Joy, we are living in darkness. So Jesus, our light, we need you, for without you we are lost.

'Jesus of Anand Nagar, let this slum deserve its name, let it be truly a City of Joy.'

13

'Holy mackerel! That fool can't even count up to seven!' stormed the procurer for the blood bank when he saw Hasari Pal walking resolutely in his direction. A full twenty-four hours had not yet passed since their fiasco of the previous day.

'Hullo, old friend!' Hasari called out to him cheerily. The peasant's cheerfulness took the man with the gold teeth by surprise.

'What's got into you, my friend? Have you won first prize in a lottery?'

'I think I've found a job, so I've come to give you back your tablets for turning blood red. Here, you can let someone else benefit from them.'

Fortune did indeed seem to be smiling at last on the Bengali peasant. Once more, he had gone to take up his stand near one of the numerous workshops on the outskirts of the Bara Bazar, one which made mechanical parts for railway carriages. It was the same place where he had once earned five rupees by standing in for the coolie who had passed out. This time two men were in the process of loading flat springs onto a handcart, when one of them tripped over a stone and dropped what he was carrying. The wretched man cried out with pain – the heavy metal part had crushed his foot as it fell. Hasari rushed to his rescue. Tearing a strip off his own cotton loincloth, he knotted it around the leg to stop the bleeding. In Calcutta, police assistance or an ambulance were rarely available in case of accident. All the owner of the workshop, a fat man in a buttoned vest, could do was to call a rickshaw. Obviously furious at the incident, he took several five-rupee notes out of his belt. He put one in the hand of the injured man and gave a second to the rickshaw puller. Seeing Hasari lifting the coolie into the carriage, he entrusted two more to him. 'Keep one for yourself. The other's to grease the palm of the attendant at the hospital entrance so he lets you in.' Then, turning to the puller waiting between the shafts of the carriage, he ordered harshly, 'All right, you bunch of lazy good-for-nothings, scram!'

Hasari Pal's hesitation in climbing into the carriage intrigued the man pulling it.

'Haven't you ever sat in a rickshaw before?'

'No,' acknowledged the peasant, perching himself timidly next to the coolie with the injured foot.

The human horse braced himself against the shafts and they set off with a jolt. The man's greying hair and wizened shoulders indicated that he was no longer young. But with rickshaw pullers, physical appearance bore little relationship to age. People grew old very rapidly pulling such machines.

'You don't look as if you're from around here?' the puller questioned Hasari after having picked up a little speed.

'No, I'm from Bankuli.'

'Bankuli!' repeated the rickshaw puller, slowing up sharply. 'But that's only twenty miles from my home! I'm from . . .'

Although he didn't actually catch the name of the village, lost as it was in the clamour of horns, Hasari would have liked to leap out and hug the man. At last he had found in this 'inhuman city' someone from his homeland. Still he made an effort to conceal his joy, for the sake of the coolie who was groaning more and more with every bump. The puller was now charging towards the hospital as fast as his bandy legs would carry him. At unpredictable intervals, however, his body would throw itself backwards in a desperate movement, trying to stop sharply in front of some bus or lorry cutting across his path.

Calcutta's general hospital was a city in itself, made up of a collection of somewhat dilapidated buildings, linked by endless corridors, with courtyards in which entire families were squatting. A plaque at the main entrance revealed that 'In 1878, in a laboratory seventy yards southeast of this door, Surgeon Major Ronald Ross of the Indian army discovered the manner in which malaria is transmitted by mosquitoes.' The rickshaw puller made directly for emergency admissions. He had often brought the sick and wounded to this hospital. Indeed, it was one of the special functions of rickshaws, to serve as ambulances in Calcutta.

'A whole string of people was waiting at the door in front of us and there was a lot of shouting and arguing going on,' Hasari would recount. 'There were women carrying babies so weak they didn't even cry any more. From time to time, we saw a stretcher go past with a corpse covered in flowers that bearers chanting prayers

were taking to a funeral pyre. When it came to our turn, I slipped the five-rupee note given to me by the workshop owner into the attendant's hand. The bribe paid off. Instead of sending us away with most of the other people, he told us to carry our friend into a room inside.'

The two men laid the coolie down on a stretcher still besmirched with the blood of the previous patient. A penetrating smell of disinfectant prevailed in the room, but what was undoubtedly most striking was the jumble of political inscriptions that adorned the walls. Every shade of opinion was mingled there in a kind of pictorial delirium: red flags, hammers and sickles, portraits of Indira Gandhi, and slogans. The astonishment of the Bengali peasant brought a smile to the lips of the rickshaw puller. 'Here, my friend, they remind you to vote for them, even when they're just about to carve you up.'

'I don't remember how long they kept our coolie in their operating room,' Hasari was to say. 'I kept asking myself what they could possibly be doing to him for all that time. Then an idea came to me. What if he were dead? Perhaps they'd killed him without meaning to and didn't dare let his corpse be brought out in case we demanded an explanation. But that was absurd because there were bodies coming out of the room next door all the time and it was impossible to tell whether they were dead or alive. They all looked as if they were asleep. In any case I had already realized that in this inhuman city poor fellows like us were not in the habit of asking for explanations. Otherwise, the rickshaw pullers, for example, would have smashed in the faces of all those bloody bus and lorry drivers.

'At last some employees came out carrying a shape curled up on a stretcher. A nurse was holding a bottle with a tube that went into the patient's arm. He was asleep. I took a closer look. It was our friend. He had a fat dressing on the end of his leg. It was only then that

I understood what they had done. Those bastards had cut his foot off!'

'There's no point in your waiting. He'll be asleep for several hours yet,' the nurse said. 'Come to pick him up in two days.'

The two men retrieved the rickshaw from the courtyard and left the hospital. For a moment they walked in silence. Hasari was visibly shocked.

'You're still green,' said the rickshaw puller. 'There's no point in getting worked up. You'll see plenty more like that.'

Hasari nodded. 'And yet I already feel as if I've had all I can take.'

'All you can take!' laughed his companion, jangling the bell on the shaft of his rickshaw. 'When you've had ten years of cruising about this slag heap, as I have, then you can say you think you've had all you can take!'

They had arrived at a crossroad where a policeman was directing traffic. The puller took a coin out of his shirt and put it in the policeman's hand as he passed. 'It's a custom here,' he explained with a grin. 'It saves you from all sorts of troubles. Especially when you don't have a licence to operate your rickshaw.' Then, sliding his palms along the shafts, he asked, 'How would you like to pull one of these machines?'

The question took Hasari by surprise. How could a bum like him ever have the chance to become a rickshaw puller? The idea seemed as ridiculous as if he had been asked if he would like to fly a plane.

'Any kind of job would suit me,' he replied, touched by the fact that the rickshaw puller was showing so much interest in him.

'Try it,' said his companion, pulling up sharply. He pointed to the shafts. 'Get between them and off you go! Jerk your back to get the wheels rolling.'

Hasari did as he was told. 'But if you think it's easy to get one of these jalopies moving, you've got another

think coming,' he was later to say. 'It takes the strength of a buffalo! And once it's moving, it's even worse. Once started, there's no stopping the thing. It runs all by itself, as if it has a life of its own. It's really a very strange sensation. To pull up suddenly in an emergency takes a special knack. With passengers on board, you might be pulling a good three hundred pounds.'

The rickshaw puller showed him some marks on the shafts, where the paint had worn off.

'Look here, son, the main thing is to find the point of equilibrium for the weight you're lugging about. You have to put your hands on exactly the place where the balance is established.'

Hasari simply could not get over the fact that someone could show so much patience and kindness towards him. 'This city isn't all that inhuman,' he thought as he handed the shafts of the rickshaw back to its owner. He mopped his forehead with a tail of his *longhi*. The effort had exhausted him.

'We should celebrate your initiation!' exclaimed the rickshaw puller. 'This is a big day for you. Let's go and have a glass of *bangla*!* I know a place behind Sealdah Railway Station that isn't too expensive.'

The rickshaw puller was somewhat astonished at his companion's lack of enthusiasm. Hasari pulled out the five-rupee note given to him by the workshop owner.

'My children and their mother haven't had anything to eat,' he said. 'I must take something back.'

'No problem! It's on me.'

They turned right and plunged into an area of low houses and narrow alleyways packed with people at the windows and in the streets. Music blared out from loudspeakers. Washing was drying on the edge of the roofs and green streamers dangled from the ends of bamboo poles. They went past a mosque, then a school

---

* Clandestinely distilled alcohol.

where under a porch roof a mullah was teaching a class
of little girls in trousers and tunics and veils over their
heads. This was a Muslim sector. Next they entered
into one of Calcutta's red-light districts. Women with
provocatively coloured skirts, low-cut bodices, and outrageously made-up faces were talking and laughing.
Hasari was struck dumb with astonishment. He had
never seen such creatures in his life before, for where he
came from the women wore only saris. 'Several of them
called out to me. There was one I found very attractive.
She must have been very rich because her arms were
covered in bracelets right up to her elbows. But my
companion went straight past her without stopping. He
was a serious-minded man.'

Numerous rickshaws cluttered the street. They were
all occupied by men who had come here in search of
amusement. A lot of poor fellows, coolies, workmen,
men without work, were wandering about on the pavements. Calcutta is a city of men, where hundreds of
thousands of refugees live without their families.

A woman grabbed Hasari by the wrist. 'Come with
me, baby,' she said, giving him a meaningful look. 'I'll
make you happy. For four rupees. That's all.' Hasari felt
himself blushing to the tips of his toes. The rickshaw
puller came to his rescue. 'Leave him alone!' he ordered
the girl, pointing one of his shafts at her stomach.
The prostitute replied with a torrent of invective that
attracted the attention of the entire street and made
the two friends roar with laughter. The puller took
advantage of the incident to give his companion a warning: 'If ever you're pulling a rickshaw and you happen
to get a girl like that for a fare, don't forget to make her
pay in advance. Otherwise watch it, she'll slip through
your fingers just like an eel.'

After the street with the girls, the two men crossed a
square, passed under an archway and entered an enclosed
area lined with old buildings with decaying façades and

balustrades, from which there hung an array of motley laundry. Buffalo, cows, dogs, chickens and pigs roamed about among children playing there with paper kites. Dots of every conceivable colour flew throughout the sky on the ends of pieces of string. In Calcutta kites were favourite toys, as if somehow those scraps of paper climbing high above the rooftops carried the children's ambition to escape their lot, all their need to flee their prison of mud, fumes, noise and poverty.

In a corner behind a palisade of planks, a man in a dirty vest sat beneath a tiled porch roof. He was the owner of the bar. The rickshaw puller directed Hasari to a bench at one end of the only table. The place reeked of alcohol. The owner clapped his hands. Instantly a hirsute little boy appeared with two glasses and a bottle that had neither label nor cork. It was full of a greyish liquid in which little white flakes were floating about. The rickshaw puller carefully counted out fourteen one-rupee notes, then folded them into a nice neat bundle and handed them to the proprietor. Having done so, he filled Hasari's glass. The peasant was struck by the acid smell given off by the concoction, but his companion seemed so delighted with it that he did not dare say anything. In silence, they clinked glasses and swallowed a mouthful.

It was then that Ram Chander – for that was the name of the rickshaw puller – began to speak.

'I had to leave my village after the death of my father. The poor man had never succeeded in wiping out the family debts that went back to his father and his grand-father. He had mortgaged our land to pay off the interest, but even that hadn't been enough, and when he died I had to borrow even more to give him a proper funeral. Two thousand rupees (£120)! First there were the four *dhotis* and no less than one hundred and twenty feet of

cotton for the *pujari* to get him to recite the prayers.
Then there were two hundred pounds of rice, as much
flour, quantities of oil, sugar, spices, and vegetables to
feed the guests. Finally, we had to have one hundred
pounds of wood for the pyre and baksheesh in cash for
those in charge of the cremation. I very quickly realized
that I would never be able to pay back all that money
by staying where I was, especially since, to procure the
loan, I had lost our only source of income by mortgaging
the next harvest.

'It was at that time, during the Festival of Durga, that
an old friend from my younger days came back to the
village. He was a rickshaw puller in Calcutta. "Come
with me," he said, "and I'll find you a cart to pull. You'll
earn ten to twelve rupees a day." So I decided to go with
him. I can still see my wife holding my son's hand in
the doorway of our hut and weeping. We had so often
spoken of my leaving and now the day had come. She
had prepared a knapsack for me with a *longhi* and a
change of shirt and a towel too. She had even made me
some *chapatis* and vegetable cutlets for the journey. To
my dying day I shall still see them in front of our hut.
Actually it was the memory of them that helped me to
survive, because it was only after four months that,
thanks to my childhood friend, I found work.

'In this damned city, the fight to forage out a job is
so hard that you could very well wait for years and die
twenty times of starvation in the meantime. And if you
haven't anyone to help you, then you've not a chance in
hell. Even at the very lowest level it's all a matter of
connections, and of cash too, of course. You've got to
be ready to pay out at every instant. This city is an
ogress. She creates people whose only aim is to strip you
of everything you have. How naïve I was when I arrived
here from the countryside! I was quite convinced that
my friend was going to lead me straight to the owner
of his rickshaw and ask him to take me on. The individual

in question is a Bihari who owns more than three hundred carriages, at least two hundred of which operate without a licence. He simply slips a percentage to the cops and that settles it. But as for the idea of getting myself employed right away, I soon got over that. The Bihari was never anywhere to be seen. No one even knew where he lived. He is a real boss. He couldn't give a damn whether it was you or Indira Gandhi who pulled his rickshaws, provided he got his dues every evening. He had a special employee to collect them and only through him could you get a rickshaw to pull. Now, don't imagine this man is any more approachable than his boss. You had to be introduced to him by someone he valued, someone who could tell him who you were, what caste you belonged to, what clan, what line of descendants. And you better salute him with your most respectful *namaskar*,* address him as a *sardarji*,† invoke the blessing of Shiva and all the gods upon his person and not forget the customary baksheesh, because, for a man like him, baksheesh is almost as important as the dues. You've got nothing, you're just a poor bum, you work your guts out to earn a few rupees and feed your family, but you have to spend your entire time getting out a coin for the cop at the crossroads because you have no legal right to operate in that street, another coin for another cop because you're transporting goods when you're only supposed to carry people, a note for the proprietor so he'll let you sleep in his cow shed, another for the man in the workshop to have him repair a spoke in your wheel, another for the former holder of the rickshaw who palmed his ramshackle vehicle off on you. It comes down to your being sucked dry all day long and then, if you don't watch out, you could well find yourself back without a rickshaw in any case, because

---

   * Hullo, greeting.
   † Chief/boss: term of respect.

the police have confiscated it or the person who hires it to you has fired you.

'As for me, I waited more than four months for the gods to decide to give me a break, and yet every morning I used to go and put a little rice, marigold buds, a banana or some other delicacy in front of the statue of Ganesh in the temple near the hut where I was staying. Three rickshaw pullers lived in the same hovel in the courtyard of a tumbledown old building behind Park Circus. They too had left their families behind in their villages. An old carpenter carved spokes and repaired cart wheels there. As they were all Hindus, they took their meals together. The old carpenter prepared the food. He cooked it over a *chula* which he fed with wood shavings from his work.

'It was there that my friend had given me shelter when I first arrived in Calcutta. Between two bamboo joists in the framework, he set up a plank for me to sleep on, just under the tiles of the roofing. In the pisé wall, a niche had been hollowed in which there presided a papier-mâché statuette of Ganesh with a pink elephant head. I remember thinking that with a god like that present under our roof it must surely all turn out okay for me in the end. I was right. One morning as I was coming back from the temple, I recognized the representative of the rickshaw owner on his bike. I had seen him several times before when he came to collect the dues, and my friend had spoken to him about me. He was quite a small man with shrewd eyes so piercing they might have been throwing out sparks. As soon as he put a foot on the ground, I launched myself at him.

'"*Namaskar sardarji!* To what honour do we owe the visit of a person of your importance? You, the son of the god Shiva!" He could not suppress a smile of satisfaction.

'"I've a fellow with a broken leg. Would you like to replace him? If you would, you can give me twenty-five

rupees immediately and you'll have to pay the disabled puller two rupees a day. That's on top of the regular six rupees' daily rental, of course."

'He warned me, just in passing, that the carriage did not have a licence to operate, which meant that in the event of my being caught by the police, I would be the one to have to pay the usual bribe. It was highway robbery. And yet I positively dissolved into expressions of thanks. "I shall be eternally grateful to you," I promised him. "From now on I shall be as the very youngest of your brothers."*

'The dream for which I had left my village had at last come true. I was going to earn a living for my family between the shafts of a rickshaw.'

14

At that time the City of Joy had only about ten wells and fountains for seventy thousand inhabitants. The nearest fountain to Stephan Kovalski's room was near a buffalo shed at the end of his alleyway. By the time he got to it, the neighbourhood was just waking up. Every dawn there was the same explosion of life. People who had spent the night, ten or twelve to a single rat-and-vermin-infested hovel, were born again with the day-light as if at the world's first dawning. Their daily resurrection began with a general process of purification. There, in alleyways awash with slime, beside the disease-ridden stream of a sewer, the occupants of the City of Joy banished the miasma of the night with all

---

* Given the power and authority with which the eldest son is endowed in the traditional Indian family, this is a special mark of respect and submission.

the ritual of a meticulous toilet. Without revealing so much as a patch of their nudity, the women managed to wash themselves all over, from their long hair to the soles of their feet, not forgetting their saris. After that, they would take the greatest care to oil, comb and braid their hair, before decorating it with a fresh flower picked from God only knew where. At every water point, men were showering themselves with tins. Young boys cleaned their teeth with acacia twigs coated with ashes, old men polished their tongues with strands of jute, mothers deloused their children before soaping their little naked bodies with a vigour undiminished even by the biting cold of winter mornings.

Stephan Kovalski continued on his way, observing everything about him. Before reaching the fountain, his eyes were suddenly attracted by the beauty of one young mother swathed in a red sari, sitting in the alleyway, her back firmly upright, with a baby placed on her outstretched legs. The infant was naked, with only an amulet on a thin cord around his waist. He was a chubby child who did not appear to be suffering from malnutrition. There was a strange flame in the way mother and child looked at each other, as if they were talking to each other with their eyes. Captivated, Kovalski put down his bucket. The young woman had just poured a few drops of mustard oil into her palms and was beginning to massage the little body in her lap. Skilful, intelligent, attentive, her hands moved up and down, actuated by a rhythm as discreet as it was inflexible. Working in turn like waves, they set out from the baby's flanks, crossed its chest and climbed back up to the opposite shoulder. At the end of the movement, her little finger slid under the child's neck. Then she pivoted him onto his side. Stretching out his arms, she massaged them delicately one after another, singing to him as she did so ancient songs about the loves of the god Krishna or some legend that stemmed from the depths of epic ages. Then

she took hold of his little hands and kneaded them with her thumb as if to stimulate the blood flow from the palms to their extremities. Thus his stomach, legs, heels, the soles of his feet, his head, the nape of his neck, his face, nostrils, back and buttocks were all successively caressed and vitalized by those supple, dancing fingers. The massage was concluded with a series of yogic exercises. The mother crossed her son's arms over his chest several times in succession to free his back, his rib cage, his breathing. Eventually it was the legs' turn to be raised, opened and closed over his stomach to induce the opening and complete relaxation of the pelvis. The child gurgled in sheer bliss.

'What I was witnessing was a real ritual,' Kovalski was to say, enthralled by so much love, beauty and intelligence. He could well imagine how much intangible sustenance the massage could bring to a little body threatened by so many vital deficiencies.

After this glimmer of light amid so much ugliness, the drudgery of collecting water seemed a very banal formality. Several dozen women and children were standing in a line and the fountain's output was so feeble that it took an age to fill a bucket. Still, what did it matter? Time didn't count in Anand Nagar and the fountain was a focal point of news. For Kovalski it was a marvellous observation ground. A little girl came up to him, gave him a big smile, and with great authority took charge of his bucket. Placing a finger on his wrist, she said to him in English: '*Daddah*,★ you must be in a great hurry.'

'Why do you think that?' asked Kovalski.

'Because you have a watch.'

When he got back to his house, the priest found several people outside his door. He recognized them as the

★ Big Brother.

occupants of the Christian compound to which, on his first evening, the envoy of the rector in charge of the neighbouring parish had taken him. The young woman who had asked him to bless her child was now offering him a *chapati* and a small bottle.

'*Namaskar*, Father,' she said warmly. 'My name is Margareta. My neighbours and I thought that you might not have anything with which to celebrate Mass. Here is some bread and wine.'

Stephan Kovalski surveyed his visitors, quite over-whelmed. 'They may not have anything to eat, but they've managed to get hold of bread and wine for the Eucharist.' He thought of the first Christians in Rome's catacombs.

'Thank you,' he said, concealing his emotion.

'We have set up a table in our courtyard,' added the young woman with a smile of complicity.

'Let's go,' said Kovalski, this time showing his joy.

These people belonged to the few families – there were about fifty of them – who together formed a tiny islet of Christians in the midst of the seventy thousand Muslims and Hindus in the City of Joy. Although they too were poor, they were slightly less destitute than the rest of the population. There were several reasons for this advantage. First and paradoxically, it was due to the fact that they were in such a minority: the smaller the number of people, the easier it is to provide aid for the least fortunate. Whereas the Hindu priests and Muslim mullahs in the area had to deal with more than three million faithful, the Catholic priest at the local church had less than a thousand parishioners. Secondly, to distinguish themselves from the majority of other sections of the community and improve their chances of securing white-collar work, many Christians made the effort to conquer that key instrument to social ascent – the English language. Finally, if they managed to elude the clutches of extreme poverty a little more successfully than most,

it was also because their religion did not teach them to
resign themselves to their fate. For Hindus, misfortune
was the result of the burden of acts carried out in previous
lives; this *karma* must be accepted in order that one might
be reborn under more auspicious circumstances. Exempt
from such taboos, Christians were free to haul themselves out of their lot as best they could. That is why
India is sprinkled with institutions and small groups of
élite that endow the Christian minority with a degree of
national influence which far outweighs the number
of its members. The same was also true in the City of
Joy.

The Christians in the slum came from the Bettiah
region, an agricultural area of Bihar, which until the
1940s had harboured one of the most important Christian
communities in northern India. The origins of that
community form an outstanding chapter in the great
saga of the world's religious migrations. It was initiated
towards the beginning of the eighteenth century when,
persecuted by a bloodthirsty sovereign, thirty-five Ne-
palese converts fled from their homeland together with
their chaplain, an Italian Capuchin. They found refuge
in a princely state where the Capuchin Father 'miracu-
lously' healed the wife of the local rajah. By way of
thanks the latter gave them land. This tradition of making Christians welcome was perpetuated by the rajahs
who succeeded him and so the small community pros-
pered and increased. A century later, it numbered two
thousand souls. With its whitewashed houses, its narrow
streets, its patios, its squares adorned with flowers, and
its large church; with its men in wide-brimmed hats and
its young girls in skirts and mantillas, the Christian
quarter of the town of Bettiah looked a little like a
Mediterranean village. One day a strange calamity was
to strike the area. The British called it blue gold; the
peasants called it indigo. The intensive monoculture of
the indigo plant to be used for dye was to provoke, in

1920, Gandhi's first great action. It was here, in the region of Bettiah, that the Mahatma began his campaign of nonviolent action for the liberation of India. Indigo was eventually supplanted in 1942 by a synthetic substitute. Blue gold did not, however, die without first taking its revenge: it had drained all the goodness out of the land and condemned thousands of peasants to exile.

The small number of families about to assist Kovalski's first Mass in Anand Nagar all came from those devastated lands. There were about twenty people in all, mainly women with babies in their arms and a few old men. Nearly all the heads of the families were absent, an indication that this compound was privileged, for others were full of men without work. In the congregation there was also an individual dressed in rags, whose wretched appearance was instantly forgotten because of his compelling, radiant expression. He was known as 'Gunga', the Mute. He was simpleminded and deaf and dumb, and nobody knew where he came from or how he had come to land in the City of Joy. One day Margareta had picked him up in an alleyway flooded out by the monsoon. He was on the point of drowning. Despite the fact that she was a widow and there were already eight people in her household, she had taken him in. One morning, he had vanished. For two years nobody had seen him. Then he had appeared again. He used to sleep on a few rags under the porch roof and seemed always quite content. One month ago, however, a neighbour had found him lying almost lifeless in an alleyway. Margareta had diagnosed cholera, loaded him onto a rickshaw, and taken him to the nearest hospital. With the help of a ten-rupee note, she had persuaded the duty nurse to find him a place on an emergency pallet. On the way home, she had visited the church of Our Lady of the Loving Heart and lit a candle. Three days later Gunga was back. When he saw Kovalski, he rushed up to him and stooped down to brush the dust from his

basketball shoes, then put his hands on his head as a mark of respect.

What the priest encountered on entering the Christian compound would remain for ever engraved upon his memory. 'They had covered a plank supported on two crates with a square of spotless cotton material and placed a candle at each corner. A bowl and cup served as paten and ciborium. A wooden crucifix and a garland of yellow marigolds completed the decoration of this improvised altar erected next to the well in the centre of the court-yard.'

For a while Stephan Kovalski stood and gathered his thoughts, meditating upon the miracle that he was about to accomplish against a backdrop of smoking *chulas*, pieces of rag drying on rooftops, and children in tatters chasing each other about in the gutters, amid all the uproar of horns, singing, shouting and life in general. With a piece of *chapati* – so like the unleavened bread Christ himself had broken at his last supper – he was about to 'create' the very Creator of this matter. In his hands a piece of bread was about to become God, the God who was at the origin of all things. To Kovalski this process was the most prodigious revolution that man might ever be called upon to bring about.

He had often celebrated Mass in a hut in a shantytown, in the communal living room of a house for immigrant workers, or in some corner of a factory workroom. But today, in the midst of these suffering, despised and broken people, he sensed all that would be unique about this offering, this sharing of bread.

'The will of God to share the plight of the most humble had always seemed an extraordinary phenomenon to me,' he was to say. 'As if taking upon himself the form of a man were not in itself enough to satiate his thirst for abasement, as if he wanted to draw closer still to the very poorest, the humblest, the most handicapped and rejected of this world. What an extraordinary source of

happiness it is to have the power to enable God to express through the Eucharist the infinite quality of his love.'

Kovalski was celebrating his Mass in a monasterylike silence when three pariah dogs, with tails cocked, scampered across the courtyard in hot pursuit of a rat that was almost as big as they were. The scene was so commonplace that no one paid any attention to it. A balloon seller passing during the reading of the Gospel did, on the other hand, attract a few glances. Flying at the tip of their bamboo canes, the colourful gold-beaters' skins stood out like stars against the expanse of grey sky. As the multicoloured clusters disappeared into the distance, Kovalski's voice rose resonantly above the assembled heads. The priest had carefully chosen the message of good news it conveyed. Looking with love upon the emaciated faces that confronted him, he repeated the words of Jesus Christ.

> Blessed are the poor in spirit, for theirs is the Kingdom of Heaven.
> Blessed are the sorrowful, for they shall find consolation.
> Blessed are those who hunger and thirst for what is right, for they shall be satisfied.

As he uttered these words, Stephan Kovalski felt a certain uneasiness. 'Do these people really need words?' he wondered. 'Aren't they already Christ, the vehicle, the Sacrament? Aren't they the poor of the Scriptures, Yahweh's poor, the ones in whom Jesus became incarnate when he said that where the poor were, there he was also?'

After a silence, he held out his arms as if to embrace the handful of suffering men and women. Wanting to imbue them with the Gospel message of that very first morning, he gazed intently at each of his new brothers and sisters. Then, letting Christ speak through his voice,

he proclaimed, 'Peace be with you for you are the light of the world.'

15

Stephan Kovalski's first wash in the slum began with yet another sacrilege. He had undressed down to his underpants, as he had seen the men on the way to the water pipe do. He had then gone out into the alleyway outside his room, duly armed with his bucket of water. He had squatted on his heels in that distinctive Indian position so difficult for a Westerner to maintain, tipped some water over his feet, and was in the process of vigorously scrubbing his toes when the elderly Hindu from the tea shop opposite called out to him in horror.

'Father, that's not how you're supposed to wash yourself. It's your head you should wash first, and your feet last, after you've cleaned everything else.'

The Pole was about to stammer some excuse when the little girl appeared who had brought him the plate of food the evening before. The vision of a half-naked *sahib* sprinkling himself with water amused her so much that she burst out laughing.

'Why are you washing yourself anyway, *Daddah*?' she asked. 'Your skin's already so white!'

A few moments later, Kovalski committed a fourth blunder by rolling up his bedding mat the wrong way. Instead of starting with the head end, he did the opposite. As his Muslim neighbour explained with a mime, it meant that on the following night he risked placing his head where his feet had been the night before. 'I knew that it would take time for me to grasp all the subtleties of slum life and not shock people any more,' the Polish priest acknowledged later. On the way back from the

fountain he had felt his neighbours' reserve even more distinctly. Women had rapidly pulled the veil of their saris over their faces. Children playing marbles had scurried away like rabbits. The vermin were the only ones who did not ostracize him. Like the rats, the centipedes and the mosquitoes of the night, the flies now danced sympathetic attendance on him. 'There were hundreds of them. Green ones, grey ones, big ones, tiny ones – they moved about in whole squadrons, ever ready to latch on to the slightest patch of skin. They had no reservations about getting into my ears, my nostrils, my eyes, right down my throat with each small ball of food. Nothing curbed their audacity. They didn't even deign to fly away when I pursued them. All they did was move on a few inches to inflict their torture on some more distant piece of me. I was completely at their mercy. In an attempt to escape their tortures, I tried to concentrate on happier memories, on my mother beating up the egg whites for a floating island, my favourite dessert, or on my father's face, as black as coal, when he came home at night from the mine.'

On that first morning, Stephan Kovalski sought help too from the picture of Christ. With his eyes fixed on the tortured face pinned to the wall, he chanted a litany of *Oms*. After a moment the invocation became completely unconscious, as he brought its rhythm into unison with the beating of his heart. This method of using his body rhythm to communicate with God freed him gradually from all exterior contingencies. The flies could attack him as they wished; he was no longer aware of them.

It was then that the smiling face of the parish priest's envoy appeared in the recess of the door. The man had come because he was concerned about how the Pole had survived his first hours in the slum. The account of his adventures at the latrines and his entanglements with rats and flies was a source of great consternation.

'Father Cordeiro has charged me to tell you that there

is a comfortable room for you at the presbytery,' he
insisted. 'That wouldn't prevent you from coming and
spending as much time here as you liked. I beg you to
accept it. This is no place for a priest.'

The Anglo–Indian shook his head sadly, then took out
of an imitation leather bag two large volumes that Father
Cordeiro had asked him to pass on to Kovalski. One
was a Bengali grammar; the other was an edition of
the Gospels in Hindi. The Pole received the gifts with
enthusiasm. He knew that they would be indispensable
in helping him to break down the wall of silence that
isolated him in his new existence.

Far from disheartening him, his inability to express
himself and understand had at first delighted Kovalski.
'For a foreigner like me arriving among such poor
people, it provided a unique opportunity to place myself
in the position of an inferior,' he was to explain. 'It was
I who needed others and not others who needed me' –
a consideration of fundamental importance for a man
who felt himself so privileged by comparison with those
around him that he wondered whether he would ever
really be integrated with them. 'Indeed, how could I
seriously believe it possible mentally and physically to
share the plight of those who lived in the slums, when
I enjoyed the health of a football player, didn't have a
family to feed, house and care for, and didn't have to
look for work or be obsessed with keeping my job;
when I knew that at any given moment I could leave.'
As he had hoped, the language handicap helped his first
contacts with people around him by giving them a sense
of importance, of superiority. How did one say 'water'
in Urdu? 'Tea' or 'bucket' in Hindi? By repeating the
words in their language the wrong way, by pronouncing
them incorrectly, he provoked their laughter and gradually won their sympathy until the day came when,
realizing that he wasn't just a passing visitor but one of
them, they gave him the most affectionate nickname in

their vocabulary, that of 'Daddah Stephan', Big Brother Stephan.

Hindi, the great *lingua franca* of modern India, now spoken by nearly a quarter of a billion people, was understood by the majority of the occupants of the City of Joy. It was one of twenty or thirty languages used in the slum; others were Bengali, Urdu, Tamil, Malayalam, Punjabi and numerous dialects. In the absence of a teacher, Kovalski began his learning process in a somewhat original fashion. Every morning after his hour of meditation, he gave himself a lesson in Hindi based on the Gospel texts that he knew better than the lines on his hand. He would sit down on his mat, his back straight up against the wall, his legs folded in the lotus position, his French version of the Jerusalem Bible on one thigh and on the other the fat volume of the Gospels in Hindi sent him by Father Cordeiro. The stylish, mysterious calligraphy of the work reminded him of Egyptian hieroglyphics. Like the illustrious French scholar Champollion who had deciphered these hieroglyphics, Kovalski realized that he had first to find a key. Patiently he searched for it, scrutinizing the verses of the Hindi text one by one, in the hope of discovering the name of a person or a place that had not been translated. After several days of looking, his eyes fell at last on a nine-letter word printed in Roman capitals. Instantly he identified the chapter from which it came and, with no difficulty at all, inscribed against each Hindi word the French equivalent. All he then had to do was pick out each letter one at a time to discover its transcription and reconstruct an alphabet. The key word seemed to him doubly symbolic. It was the name of a town in the image of the one where he was, a town where crowds of poor people had gathered to turn to God. It was also a symbol of an inextricable entanglement of people and things comparable to the slum of the City of Joy. The magic word was Capernaum.

16

All the cities of the former colonial world have banished them from their roads, as one of the most degrading aspects of man's exploitation of his fellow man. All, except Calcutta, where even today some hundred thousand slave horses harnessed to their rickshaws run up more miles per day than the thirty Boeings and Airbuses of Indian Airlines, India's domestic airline. Each day they transport more than one million passengers and no one, apart from a few visionary town planners, has thought of relegating these anachronistic carriages to a historical museum, for here human sweat provides the world's cheapest energy.

With their two large wheels with wooden spokes, their slender bodies and uncurved shafts, rickshaws look like the carriages of our grandmother's day. Invented in Japan at the end of the eighteenth century by a European missionary, their name derives from the Japanese expression *ji riki shaw* which means literally 'vehicle propelled by man'. The first rickshaws appeared in India around 1880, on the imperial avenues of Simla, the summer capital of the British Indian Empire. Some twenty years later a few of these vehicles arrived in Calcutta, imported by Chinese traders who used them to transport goods. In 1914 these same Chinese applied for permission to use them also to carry people. Faster than the palanquins of olden times and more manageable than hackney carriages, it was not long before rickshaws imposed their presence on the foremost port in Asia. The fashion was to reach numerous metropolises in Southeast Asia. For many former peasants among the millions of men who had sought refuge in Calcutta since Independence, their

shafts provided a providential means of earning a living. It is not known how many rickshaws now plough their way through the streets and alleys of the last city in the world to retain them. In 1939 the British limited their number to six thousand, and since no other licence to operate them has been issued since 1949, there are still officially fewer than ten thousand of them. Unofficial statistics suggest a figure five times larger, however, since four out of five operate illegally, with false plates. Each one of those fifty thousand rickshaws provides a living for two pullers, who take turns between the shafts from one sunrise to the next. The sweat of those hundred thousand drudges feeds as many families. It is, therefore, estimated that a total of over one million individuals look to the rickshaw for their daily bowl of rice. Economists have even calculated the financial implications of this unique activity in the catalogue of professions: £3 million, a quarter of the budget of the whole urban transport system of a city like Paris. A sizeable part of this amount – about £75,000 a year – represents the bribes paid by the pullers to the police and other authorities, to be able to exercise their trade in a city which has become so congested that more and more streets have been banned to them.

'There's nothing like a large glass of *bangla* for putting a tiger in your tank!' exclaimed Ram Chander, paraphrasing an old advertisement that had covered the walls of Calcutta. He steered his newfound friend outside.

'Hell, yes!' said Hasari Pal, 'it's like absorbing six *chapatis* in a row and a bowlful of fish curry.' He grimaced and rubbed his stomach. 'Except that this particular petrol rumbles a bit inside you.'

The fact that it 'rumbled' inside him was not surprising – the concoction the two companions had just imbibed was one of the most lethal mixtures ever brewed in stills

by man. It was called 'country liquor' and came from a village situated on the fringes of Calcutta's rubbish dump. There, throughout the year, all kinds of refuse, animal innards and cane juice were fermented for a month in large jars at the bottom of a putrid pool. The news pages in the daily papers never ceased recording the havoc worked by this poisonous alcohol which in India claimed as many victims every year as malaria. It had only one advantage and that was its price. Evading tax levies, it cost only seven rupees a bottle, four or five time less than a bottle of the most mediocre government-approved rum.

The two friends began walking together. Soon, however, Ram Chander was hailed by an elderly but very hefty woman, dressed in the white sari of a widow. Hasari helped her to climb into the rickshaw and Ram set off at a trot. As he watched the carriage pulling away, the peasant couldn't help remarking to himself how lucky his friend was. 'At least he can look other people in the eye. He has a job. He has his dignity. Whereas I'm just like the mangy dogs that roam about the streets. I don't exist.'

Before parting, the two men had arranged to meet the next day at the Park Circus esplanade, at the point where the tram lines crossed. Ram Chander had promised to try and introduce his friend to the rickshaw owner's representative. 'With a little bit of luck and a generous baksheesh, he might just find you an old heap to pull.' 'I should have refused to believe in anything quite so wonderful,' Hasari would say, 'but the *bangla* had given me wings. I felt like a paper kite.' The two men had also decided to go to the hospital to visit the injured coolie.

The peasant wandered about for a long time before finding his family. 'Everywhere there were uninterrupted rows of shops, stores, stalls and thousands of people on the pavements and in the roadways. It was as if one

half of the population spent its entire time selling things to the other half. There was an abundance of objects that I had never seen before, like instruments to peel vegetables with, or squeeze the juice out of fruits. There were piles of cooking utensils too, and tools and mechanical parts, sandals, shirts, belts, bags, combs, pens and dark glasses for the sun. In some places it was very difficult to move at all because of all the people and goods crammed into the roadway. On one street corner I bought several *alu-bhurta* from a pedlar. My children loved those potato fritters dusted with sugar, but with five rupees I couldn't buy many of them and perhaps I'd have done better to buy several portions of puffed rice for the whole family instead. But when your stomach and head are full of *bangla*, you're not responsible for your madness.'

Night had long fallen by the time Hasari at last recognized the avenue where he had set up camp. Before he actually reached his family's piece of pavement, he heard shouting and saw a mob. Fearing that something dreadful had happened to his wife or one of his children, he rushed to the scene, but it was the neighbour's wife who was howling. Her face was bleeding and there were the marks of blows on her shoulders and arms. Once again her husband had come home drunk. They had quarrelled and he had hit her with an iron bar. If the neighbours had not intervened he would have killed her. He had also beaten the two smallest children. Then he had picked up his ragged clothing and simply gone off, committing his family to the mercy of the devil. The poor woman found herself alone on the pavement with three young children and another on the way, not forgetting a son in prison and a prostitute daughter. 'Sometimes there are good reasons for cursing your *karma*,' thought Hasari.

By luck, that night, Hasari's two eldest children had managed to bring back some gourd and turnip scraps from their day's foraging in the rubbish of the Bara

Bazar. They were enormously proud of their achievement because so many people explored the refuse heaps
that good finds were few and far between. Their mother
borrowed the neighbouring woman's *chula* to cook a
soup which the Pals shared with her and her abandoned
children. They also shared the fritters. Nothing appeases
grief and fear more effectively than a good meal,
especially when you live on the pavement, with not
even a sheet of corrugated iron or canvas over your
head. That night the two families drew a little closer
together before they went to sleep. Only the poor may
need the help of the poor.

17

Every night at about eleven o'clock, it started up again.
First came the tears. Gradually they increased in intensity. The rhythm accelerated and developed into a series
of rattles which cascaded through the dividing wall. A
ten-year-old Muslim boy was dying of osteotuberculosis
in the hovel next door. His name was Sabia.

'Why this agony of an innocent in a place already
scarred by so much suffering?' protested an indignant
Kovalski.

During the first few evenings the priest had suc-
cumbed to cowardice. He had stopped up his ears with
cottonwool so as not to hear. 'I was like Job on the brink
of revolt,' he was to explain. 'In vain I scoured the
Scriptures by the light of my oil lamp. I could not find
a satisfactory explanation for the idea that God could let
such a thing happen. Who could ever venture to say to
a child like that, writhing in pain: "Blessed are the poor,
for theirs is the Kingdom of Heaven; blessed are the

sorrowful, for they shall find consolation; blessed are
those who thirst, for they shall be satisfied"? The prophet
Isaiah tried hard to justify the suffering of the innocent.
It was *our* suffering that the boy was enduring, Isaiah
affirmed, and he would help to save us from *our* sins.
The idea that the suffering of one human being could
help to save the world was certainly very alluring, but
how could I concede that the suffering of my little
neighbour was part of that redemptive process? Everything in me rebelled against the idea.'

It took several nights before Stephan Kovalski could
accept the experience of listening to Sabia's cries and
several more for him to listen to them not only with his
ears but also with his heart. He was torn between his
religious faith and his very human feelings of revolt.
Had he any right to be happy, to sing praises to God
while that intolerable torment was going on right next
to him? Every night when his young neighbour began
to groan again, he emptied himself and prayed. Then he
ceased to hear the tears, the cries, the noises; he ceased
to notice the rustle of the rats in the darkness; he no
longer smelled the stench of the blocked drain outside
his door. He entered into what he described as a state of
'weightlessness'.

'In the beginning my prayer was exclusively concerned with young Sabia's agony. I begged the Lord to
alleviate his suffering, to lessen his sacrifice. And if,
in his judgement, this trial was really useful for the
redemption of the sins of mankind, then I asked him,
the Father who had not hesitated to sacrifice his own
son, to let me assume a part of it, to let me suffer instead
of that child.' Night after night, his eyes turned in
the darkness towards the picture of the Sacred Shroud,
Stephan Kovalski prayed until the groans were still.
Tirelessly he prayed and pleaded: 'You who died on
the Cross to save mankind, help me to understand the
mystery of suffering. Help me to transcend it. Help me,

above all, to fight against its causes, against the lack of love, against hatred and against all the injustices that give rise to it.'

The illness of his young neighbour grew worse and the sounds of his agony increased. One morning the priest caught the bus to the nearest hospital.

'I need a syringe and a dose of morphine. It's very urgent,' he said to the attendant in charge of the hospital pharmacy, handing him thirty rupees.

'Since his illness was incurable and my prayer had proved abortive,' he would later say to justify himself, 'Sabia should at least be able to die in peace.'

Helped by her three daughters, aged eleven, eight and five, Sabia's mother spent her days squatting in the alleyway, making paper bags out of old newspapers. She was a widow and this activity represented the only income with which she could support her family. A hundred times a day she had to get up and clear everything out of the way to allow a cycle-car or cart to pass. Yet Stephan Kovalski had noticed that her smile never deserted her.

Hostile gazes beset him as soon as he stopped outside Sabia's hovel. Why did this infidel want to visit the little Muslim who was dying? Was he going to try to convert the boy to his religion? Tell him that Allah was not the true God? There were many in the area who mistrusted the priest. So many stories were told about the zeal of Christian missionaries, about their diabolical capacity to wheedle their way in anywhere. Wasn't it merely to reduce their vigilance that this particular one wore trousers and sneakers instead of a cassock? Nevertheless, Sabia's mother welcomed him with her remarkable smile. She sent her eldest daughter to fetch him a cup of tea from the old Hindu and invited the priest to come in. The smell of putrid flesh caused him to hesitate for a few seconds on the threshold. Then he plunged into the half-light.

The little Muslim boy was lying on a mattress of rags, his arms crossed, his skin pitted with sores, crawling with lice, his knees half bent back over his fleshless torso. Stephan Kovalski drew nearer to him and the boy opened his eyes. His gaze lit up with a spark of joy. Kovalski was totally overwhelmed. 'How could I believe my own eyes? How could so much serenity radiate from that little martyred frame?' His fingers tightened on the vial of morphine.

'Salaam, Sabia,' he murmured, smiling.

'Salaam, *Daddah*,' responded the child cheerfully. 'What have you got in your hand? Sweets?'

Startled, Stephan Kovalski dropped the vial which shattered as it fell. 'Sabia had no need of morphine. His features were imbued with a peace that quite disarmed me. Bruised, mutilated, crucified as he was, he remained undefeated. He had just given me the most precious gift of all: a secret reason never to despair, a light in the darkness.'

How many brothers and sisters of light like Sabia did Stephan Kovalski have in this haven of suffering? Hundreds, perhaps even thousands. Every morning after celebrating the Eucharist, he would visit some of them with the few reserves he had at his disposal: a little food, some medicine, or simply the comfort of his presence.

Nothing raised his spirits more than his visits to a blind Christian leper woman who lived next to the railway lines. Incredible as it might seem, this woman too, plunged as she was into unutterable stages of decay, radiated serenity. She would spend entire days in prayer, curled up in a corner of her hovel, without lighting or ventilation. Behind her, hanging from a nail in the mud wall, was a crucifix, and in a niche above the door nestled a statue of the Virgin blackened with soot. The leper woman was so thin that her shrivelled skin accentuated the angles of her bones. What age might she be? Certainly younger than she looked. Forty at the very most. As if

her blindness were not enough, leprosy had reduced her hands to stumps and eaten away her face. The widow of one of the municipality's lesser employees, she had lived in the slum for twenty years. No one knew how she had come to catch leprosy, but she was so consumed by the disease that it was too late to cure her. In another corner of the room her four grandchildren, aged between two and six, slept side by side on a piece of threadbare matting.

Around this Christian woman and her family had been woven one of those networks of mutual help and friendship that transformed the City of Joy into one of those privileged places to which Jesus of Nazareth referred when he called upon his disciples to 'gather in a suitable spot to await the last Judgement and the Resurrection'. Such help was all the more remarkable because the neighbours were all Hindus, a fact that would normally have prevented them from touching anyone suffering from leprosy, from entering that person's house or even, so it was sometimes said, from tainting their eyes with the sight of a leper. Yet, every day, those Hindus took turns bringing the Christian woman a dish of rice and vegetables, helping her wash, doing her housework, looking after her grandchildren. The slum, so inhuman in other respects, gave her something which no hospital could have provided. This broken woman suffered from no lack of love.

Some sixth sense always alerted her to Kovalski's arrival. As soon as she sensed him approaching, she would make an attempt to tidy herself. With what was left of her hands she would smooth down her hair, a touching gesture of coquetry amid such utter degradation. Next she would tidy up the area around her, groping to rearrange a tattered cushion for her visitor. Happy then, all she had to do was wait patiently, reciting her rosary. That morning the priest was going to fill her with joy.

'Good morning, Father!' she was quick to call out to him as soon as she heard his footsteps.

'Good morning, Grandma!' replied Kovalski, taking his shoes off in the doorway. 'You seem to be in good form today.'

He had never heard her complain or utter words of self-pity at her predicament, and on this occasion, again, he was struck by the sight of the joyous expression on her tortured face. She signalled him to sit down beside her and as soon as he was settled held out her arms in a gesture of maternal love. The blind leper woman caressed the priest's face as if to feel the life in it. 'I was utterly bewildered,' he was to say. 'It was as if she were giving me the very thing that she sought in me. There was more love in the soft touch of that rotten flesh than in all the world's embraces.'

'Father, I do so wish the good Lord would come and fetch me at last. Why won't you ask him to?'

'If the good Lord keeps you with us, Grandma, it's because he still needs you here.'

'Father, if I have to continue suffering, I'm ready to do so,' she said. 'Above all I'm ready to pray for other people, to help them endure their own suffering. Father, bring me their suffering.'

Stephan Kovalski told her about his visit to young Sabia. She listened with her sightless eyes fixed upon him.

'Tell him that I shall pray for him.'

The priest searched in his knapsack for the clean handkerchief in which he had carefully wrapped a piece of *chapati* consecrated during his morning Mass. The short silence intrigued the leper woman.

'What are you doing, Father?'

'Grandma, I've brought you Communion. Receive the body of Christ.'

She parted her lips and Kovalski placed the fragment of griddle cake on the tip of her tongue. 'Amen,' she

murmured after a moment, her face radiant with joy.
There was a long silence, broken only by the buzzing of
flies and the outbreak of an argument outside. The four
little sleeping bodies had not stirred.

When Stephan Kovalski rose to go, the leper woman
lifted up her rosary in a gesture of salutation and offering.

'Be sure to tell those who are suffering that I am
praying for them.'

That evening Stephan Kovalski was to jot down in
his diary: 'That woman knows that her suffering is not
useless and I affirm that God wants to use her suffering
to help others to endure theirs.' A few lines further on
he concluded: 'That is why my prayer for this poor
woman must not be one of sadness. Her suffering is
like that of Christ on the Cross; it is constructive and
redemptive. It is full of hope. Every time I leave the
hovel where my sister, the blind leper woman, lives, I
come away revitalized. So how can one despair in this
slum of Anand Nagar? In truth this place deserves its
name, City of Joy.'

18

He ruled over his fleet of carriages like a pimp over his
army of prostitutes. No one ever saw him, but everyone
– his pullers, his stewards and even the police – had for
the last fifty years accepted the power of Bipin Narendra,
the most influential rickshaw owner in Calcutta. Nobody knew just how many vehicles operated under his
ensign. Rumour had it that there were at least four
hundred, of which more than half functioned illegally
with no official plate. Yet if you had encountered Bipin
Narendra on the steps of the Kali Temple, you would

almost certainly have offered him alms. With his over-sized trousers, his broken-down sandals, his baggy shirt spattered with stains, and his crutch that supported a slightly wasted leg, he looked more like a beggar than a captain of industry. Only the omnipresent white forage cap planted on top of his bald skull elevated the poverty-stricken appearance of his personage. No one knew his age; even he knew it only approximately, to within two or three years. It was said that he must be in his nineties; he had never drunk a drop of alcohol, smoked a cigarette or eaten an ounce of meat in his life. Nor had he, of course, sweated between the shafts of those rickshaws which had killed hundreds of his pullers and made him a rich man.

His longest memory went back to the time when he had first left his native Bihar to come and earn his living in Calcutta. 'It was at the beginning of the Great War in Europe,' he used to recount. 'There were many soldiers in Calcutta and every day more and more of them boarded the waiting ships. There were parades in the Maidan and regimental bands played military music. Life was very entertaining – much more so than in the province where I was born. My parents were landless peasants, agricultural labourers, in fact. My father and brothers hired themselves out to the *zamindar* but there was only work for a few months in the year. That was no life.'

Bipin Narendra found his first job as an assistant to the driver of a bus that belonged to a Bihari from his village. His role consisted of opening the doors at every stop and getting the passengers on and off. Another man was employed as the conductor. It was he who collected the fares according to the distance involved. It was he, too, who rang the bell as a signal to move off. 'I envied him greatly because he pocketed a percentage on every ticket and, as it was usual for the conductor to split the proceeds with the driver, all the buses raced between

themselves to pick up passengers. Many say that the same system still applies today.'

After three years, the owner of the bus was able to buy a second vehicle and Bipin Narendra was given the job of conductor. He was quite unable to say how many thousands of miles he had covered in the huge metropolis. 'But the city was very different in those days. There weren't so many inhabitants and the streets were clean and well maintained. The British were very strict. You could earn money without resorting to subterfuge, by working honestly.'

Rickshaws had been a roaring success right from the day they had first appeared, because they provided a means of transport cheaper than any horse-drawn carriage or taxicab. One day in 1930 Bipin Narendra bought himself two of these machines. They cost two hundred rupees each, new, but he had managed to unearth some secondhand ones for only fifty rupees. He hired them out immediately to two Bihari expatriates from his village. Later he was to borrow sixteen hundred rupees from his boss and buy eight more brand-new Japanese rickshaws. That was the beginning of his fortune. After a few years, the man who from that time was only referred to as 'the Bihari' owned approximately thirty carriages. With the rent that he collected each day, he bought a plot of land in Ballygunge, in South Calcutta, and had a house built on it. Ballygunge was quite a poor area, occupied for the most part by Hindu and Muslim employees, where the price of land was not very expensive. In the meantime the Bihari had got married and thereafter, every time his wife became pregnant, he had one more room built onto his house. Now he was the owner of a four-storey mansion, the highest in the area, for his wife had given him nine children, three sons and six daughters.

The Bihari had been a hard worker. For nearly half a century he had got up every morning at five and set off on his bicycle to do the rounds of the rickshaw pullers,

to collect payment for the daily hiring. 'I could neither read nor write,' he was to say with pride, 'but I've always known how to add and I never missed out on a single rupee that was owed to me.' As each one of his sons reached working age, he gradually diversified his business affairs. He kept the eldest one with him to assist him in the management of his fleet of vehicles that now came to more than three hundred. The second son he put in charge of a bolt factory that supplied the railways. For the youngest he bought a bus which covered the route from Dalhousie Square to the suburb of Garia. To obtain the franchise for this particularly lucrative route, he had given a substantial bribe to a *babu* at the municipality. As for his daughters, he had married them all off, and married them well. A fortunate father indeed was the Bihari! The eldest was the wife of a lieutenant-colonel in the Army, the next in line that of a naval commander. He had married the two daughters next in line to tradesmen, the fifth to a *zamindar* in Bihar, and the youngest to an engineer in the highways department, a man who worked for the Bengal government. All in all, it was a superb accomplishment for the descendants of an illiterate peasant.

Yet in the evening of his life, the Bihari had lost much of his former enthusiasm. 'Business is not what it used to be,' he lamented. 'Nowadays you have to be furtive about earning money. Effort, success and good fortune have become crimes. Each successive government controlling our country has tried to liquidate the rich and appropriate the fruits of their labours, as if by making the rich poorer, the poor become richer! Here in Bengal, the Communists have instituted laws to restrict private ownership. They have decreed that no one individual has the right to own more than ten rickshaws. Ten rickshaws, can you imagine! As if I could support a family on ten rickshaws when I have constantly to pay out for maintenance, repairs, accidents, and baksheesh

for the police. So I had to look after my own interests. I did what all the large landowners did when they were prohibited from owning more than forty acres of land, I transferred the title of ownership for my carriages to the names of my nine children and twenty-two grand-children. And just for the record, I even put some rickshaws in the names of a dozen of my nephews. Officially my three hundred and forty-six vehicles belong to thirty-five different owners.'

In fact the one and only master of the entire fleet was the Bihari.

Few of his rickshaw pullers knew his face. Some of them did not even know his identity. During the last ten years, he had ceased to be seen around the area. 'Now I am nothing but an old man, doddering with the aid of a stick to meet the God of death, whom I await in peace and serenity,' he was to say. 'I have a clear conscience. I have always been kind and generous to those who pulled my rickshaws. Whenever one of them had difficulty paying his hiring fee, I would let him have one or two days' credit. Naturally I asked him for interest but I was reasonable. I asked for only twenty-five per cent per day. Similarly, if one of them was sick or the victim of an accident, it was I who advanced him the hospital fees for medicine or a doctor. Afterwards I increased the man's hiring fee to cover what I had paid out and the puller had several weeks in which to reim-burse me. Now, my factotum looks after all such mat-ters. Alas, nowadays the pullers don't have the same good outlook they used to have. They are forever asking for something. They'd like some magic wand to give them the ownership of their carriages. They have even formed a union for that goal. And they've taken strike action. The world is upside down! So now we owners too have had to organize ourselves. We, too, have created a syndicate, the All Bengal Rickshaw Owners Union. And we've taken on henchmen to assure our protection.

There was simply no alternative, with a government that spent its time turning workers against their bosses in the name of the so-called class struggle. Several big shots in high circles even wanted to ban rickshaws altogether, under the pretext that they were an insult to human dignity and that the pullers were exploited like workhorses. Rubbish! They can shoot their mouths off all they like about their so-called respect for the human being. Nothing is going to change the fact that there are over a million poor bastards without work in Calcutta, and that if you eliminate the livelihoods of a hundred thousand rickshaw pullers, you'll condemn eight or nine hundred thousand more people to starvation. It's a matter of common sense, but then politics and common sense aren't teats of the same cow! So you just have to get by as best you can.'

As long as his steward brought him the rent money each day after sunset, the Bihari would know that nothing had fundamentally changed. For this old man in the twilight of his life, there was still the joy of seeing his factotum's shirt bulging with bundles of bills. 'The wise men of our nation say that nirvana is the attainment of a state of supreme detachment. For me nirvana is to be able, at the age of ninety plus a few years, to count out each evening, one by one, the rupees earned by my three hundred and forty-six rickshaws on the asphalt of Calcutta.'

19

'When I was a child,' Stephan Kovalski recalled, 'I used to like to go for walks in the country and it amused me to chop the heads off flowers with a stick. Later, when I went to school, I used to like to pick a flower and put

it on my table. Then I told myself that flowers were beautiful right there where they grew, and so I stopped cutting them and admired them in their natural setting. It was the same with women. One day I told the Lord that I didn't want to pick any one single woman because I wanted to let them all bloom right there where they were.

'Saint John of the Cross once wrote, "Heaven is mine. Jesus is mine. Mary is mine. Everything is mine." As soon as you want to hold on to any one particular thing, everything else escapes you, whereas by detachment you can enjoy everything without actually possessing anything in particular. That's the key to voluntary celibacy, without which chastity would make no sense. It's a choice of love. Marriage, on the other hand, means giving yourself, body and soul, to one single human being. As far as the body and carnal love were concerned, that would not have been difficult, but it was impossible for me to give my soul to any one single person. I had already decided to give it to God and there was no one in this world with whom I could share that gift – not even my mother whom I adored. "Whoever has renounced a wife, children, a field, in my name will have them returned a hundredfold," said Christ; and he was right. I had never had a sister, yet there, in the City of Joy, I found plenty of them who brought me great joy. With them I shared a sense of communion and solidarity which was so essential in a slum where people have so much need of one another.

'Nevertheless, having said all that, how could I fail to dream sometimes of a certain human tenderness? How, amid so much misery, could I fail to succumb to desirable women, who were such beacons of grace and seduction in their multicoloured saris? In the ugliness of the slum, they were beauty itself. They were flowers. My problem was to adjust to their presence and remain lucid. Since I had decided not to seek a lasting love, with all its associ-

ated implications, I had no right to accept passing loves either. After all, I had responded once and for all to the appeal of the Lord of the Gospels and made mine his injunction to have no other household except the one that he would show me.

'I was not in a very comfortable position, particularly as my reputation for being a sort of Santa Claus often brought the women of the slum to me. An innuendo, a hand laid on mine, a flirtatious way of adjusting a sari, or a disturbing look sometimes led me to think their intentions might be suspect. But then perhaps I was mistaken, because in India links between men and women are frequently stamped with a certain ambiguity. Like the majority of other Indian women, still untouched by feminist liberation movements, the women in the City of Joy had no way other than seduction to attract masculine attention and assert their identity.

'I had hoped that my well-known status as a religious man would protect me from such manifestations of feeling, but I was wrong, and it wasn't really all that surprising. Wasn't there always, in every work of sacred Hindu literature, a scene in which the guru was tempted? And what about the erotic sculptures in the temples, where veritable orgies sprawled right across the bas-reliefs? I noticed that it was always during periods of relaxation that temptation hit me hardest, and not during intervals of intense trial. It was always during a phase when my relationship with God was in some way impoverished that I was at my most vulnerable. If you don't find your joy in God, you seek it elsewhere.

'I was particularly aware of this kind of danger in my relationship with Margareta, the young Christian widow who had brought me the bread and wine for my first Mass in the slum. It was not that she had ever made the slightest gesture or hint that was in any way compromising, but her body, moulded in a simple piece of muslin, exuded a sensuality, a fragrance, a magnetism, which I

found more difficult to resist than the attractions of other women. What was more, such a capacity for love, such an abandonment of herself emanated from her look, her smile, her voice and her bearing that this flower seemed ever open to me. Probably I was wrong. I suspected the surroundings of distorting my perception.'

One evening, at the end of one of those days that the fall of the barometer had made particularly trying, one of those days when your shirt sticks to your back and your mind is devoid of energy, Kovalski was trying to pray in front of the picture of the Sacred Shroud. In the moisture of the air, the little flame of his oil lamp made the face of Christ and his shadow dance in a ghostly ballet. He felt as if he were roaming about in a drifting vessel. In vain he struggled to concentrate his heart and soul on the Lord. He felt agonizingly deserted. It was then that he sensed her presence. He had not heard her enter but that was not very surprising. She moved about with the litheness of a cat. It was her scent that gave her away, the delicate fragrance of patchouli. He pretended not to notice her. He was praying aloud but soon the words became nothing but sounds. Her presence, her soft breathing in the darkness, the thought of the woman he could not see but whom he could smell, cast a spell over him in a way that was both marvellous and terrible. It was then as if the Lord abandoned him altogether. Suddenly from the other side of the wall came a moan, then a rattle, then uninterrupted groaning. The agony of Sabia, his little Muslim brother, had just begun again.

Those cries of anguish drove the Pole and the Indian woman instantly towards each other. Like two victims of a shipwreck clinging to the same buoy, they were two people in distress wanting to proclaim on the threshold of death their irresistible desire to live.

A kind of euphoria was flooding over Stephan when a knocking at the door wrested him from the grip of temptation. The Lord had rushed to his rescue.

'Big Brother Stephan!' called the mother of Sabia. 'Come quickly! Sabia is asking for you.'

20

Hasari Pal turned up at the Park Circus esplanade but Ram Chander, his friend the rickshaw puller, was not there. The peasant decided to wait. 'This man was my only hope,' he was to explain, 'my only assurance that somewhere in this infernal city a small lamp was burning for me also. I was prepared to wait until evening, all through the night if necessary – and all the next day too.'

Ram Chander arrived in the early afternoon. He was without his rickshaw and looked dejected.

'The bastards have pinched my rickshaw,' he growled. 'Last night, after I dropped off the old lady I took on when we parted, I was going home when a cop stopped me. It had just got dark. "Where's your lamp?" the son of a bitch asked me. I apologized, I told him I'd forgotten to take it with me that morning. But he didn't want to know. He suggested the usual arrangement.'

'The usual arrangement?' asked Hasari.

'Yes, of course! "Give me fifteen rupees," he says to me, "or I'll arrest you and take you to the police station." It didn't matter how much I protested that I didn't have that kind of money. He was totally unmoveable. He drove me off to the police station, beating me with his *lathi*.* There they confiscated my carriage and, to cap it all, they reported me officially and ordered me to appear at the police court tomorrow. They're going to saddle me with a fine of at least thirty rupees.'

Ram took a long puff on the cigarette he held wedged

---

* Club.

in the hollow of his hands. 'Let's go and get something
to eat,' he said. 'Even the worst troubles look better on
a full stomach.'

He led Hasari to a cheap restaurant in Durga Road
which was a regular haunt of his. It consisted of a small
low room with five marble-topped tables. The owner,
a fat Muslim, presided bare-chested over the cooking
pots. On the wall behind him hung a grimy engraving
of the Kaaba, the great black sacred stone of Mecca. On
each table stood a bowl of coarse salt and dried pepper,
and on the ceiling an antiquated fan showed ever-
increasing signs of fatigue with every turn of its blades.
There was a strong smell of frying. A young boy brought
them two plates of rice and a bowl of *dal* – boiled lentils.
The two friends poured the soup over the rice and stirred
the mixture with their fingers, then ate in silence. This
was a real feast for Hasari, his first proper meal since he
had arrived in Calcutta. By the time they had finished,
Ram Chander's optimism had been restored.

'There's enough wealth in this city to fill everyone's
stomach.' Hasari smoothed his moustache and looked
sceptical. 'It's true, I assure you,' continued the rickshaw
puller. 'You still think like a peasant. But soon you'll be
a real Calcutta *wallah** and know all the tricks!'

Ram Chander left three rupees on the table and they
set off for the hospital. They walked along a wide
avenue, which was a tram route, until they came to the
Sealdah Railway Station. Next to it was a market where
the rickshaw puller bought some mandarin oranges and
bananas for the injured coolie they were going to visit.

'Outside the hospital there were even more people
than on the previous day,' Hasari was to recount. 'Everyone was trying to get in. There was shouting and arguing
going on all around us. An ambulance with a red cross
narrowly missed running over some people who were

* An inhabitant of Calcutta.

crowding the emergency entrance where we had left our
friend the day before. I thought for a moment that the
angry crowd was going to tear the driver to pieces, but
he managed to extricate himself and open the door at
the back of the vehicle. Inside I could see several bodies
covered in blood. They looked as if they had been
burned, shreds of flesh were hanging off their legs. It
wasn't a pretty sight but we were in a hospital, after all,
not in a paddy field. In a corner of the courtyard was a
collection of rusty ambulances with broken windows
and flat tyres. Their red crosses were hardly visible. A
number of lepers had made their home in this junk yard.

'We wandered about the hospital corridors, trying to
find our friend. A nurse directed us to a room. I think
she must have been in charge because she was the only
one with a wide belt around her waist, an enormous
bunch of keys, and stripes on her shoulders. Also she
seemed to frighten everyone. To our left and right were
larger rooms where employees were writing, drinking
and chatting, surrounded by mountains of paper tied
together with little bits of string. Some of the papers
must have been there for a long time because they were
crumbling to dust – at least what the rats had left.
Talking of rats, we saw a number of them coming and
going. They must have a marvellous time in a place like
that. Ram informed me that they sometimes attacked
the sick and the injured. He cited the case of an old
woman who was paralysed, whose feet and hands were
gnawed away during the night.

'Ram slipped a five-rupee note to the male nurse in
charge of the ward for people who'd had operations. It
was a vast room with several windows and large green
fans on the ceiling. There were about fifty or so beds
squeezed up against each other. At most of the bed heads
hung a bottle from which a tube went into the patient.
Generally the liquid was clear like water but in some
instances it was red. That must have been blood from

some poor bum like me who had sold it to feed his
children. We went around between the beds, looking
for our friend. It wasn't very pleasant because there were
fellows there who weren't very nice to look at. There
was one poor old man imprisoned from head to toe in
a plaster cast. Nurses went from bed to bed pushing a
cart laden with bottles of every imaginable colour, with
cottonwool, dressings and instruments. Those women
must have their hearts in the right place to do that kind
of work. Some patients clung to their white saris; others
pushed them away with insults and threats.

'Our friend was lying on a *charpoy*, a frame strung
with light ropes, because there were no more iron beds
available. He looked pleased to see us. He told us that
his foot was very painful but, even as he said so, he must
have realized that it had been cut off because his eyes
filled with tears. Ram gave him the fruits. He smiled,
took a mandarin orange, and pointed to the next bed on
which lay a small body whose head, arms and legs were
swathed in bandages. The child had been burned in a
paraffin stove explosion and was groaning weakly. I
peeled the fruit the injured coolie had given me and
pressed a segment between the boy's lips. He opened his
mouth and, with great difficulty, swallowed. The poor
child, he was the same age as my Shambu.

'Our friend seemed to be in bad shape. His beard had
grown, which served to accentuate how ill he looked,
and his eyes appeared to have sunk into their sockets.
His expression was full of despair. Ram and I did our
best to comfort and reassure him that we wouldn't just
leave him in the lurch. He had no one to call his own
in Calcutta. We had become his only family. I'm not
speaking for Ram, but having a bum like me for family
was certainly no big deal.

'We stayed with him for quite a while. He must have
had a very high fever because his forehead was constantly
wet. Eventually a male nurse told us to leave. Our friend

took our hands in his and held on to them, but we had to go. We said a few more things to him to try and raise his spirits, and we promised to come back. Before leaving the room, I turned around for one last time. I saw his hand waving weakly, like a reed in the evening breeze.'

21

A Muslim family of seven – four children and three adults – occupied the hovel adjoining Stephan Kovalski's room. The head of the family was called Mehboub. He was a wiry, muscular little man in his thirties with a lively, determined expression beneath his shaggy eyebrows and a forehead half-concealed by a thick shock of curly hair. His wife, Selima, wore a little inlaid stone in her nostril. Despite the fact that she was several months pregnant, she was constantly on the go, sweeping, cleaning pots and pans, preparing meals, or doing the washing. Mehboub's mother, an old woman with short-cropped white hair who could hardly see, lived with them. For hours on end she would remain squatting in the alleyway murmuring snippets from the Koran. Nasir, the elder son aged ten, was employed in a small workshop. His two sisters went to the Koranic school. The youngest, who was three years old, scampered about the alleyway. The family was quite well off. For thirteen years Mehboub had worked as a day labourer in a naval yard in East Calcutta, forging propellers for boats. He earned about three hundred rupees a month (£20), a small fortune in a slum where thousands of families were unable to lay a hand on one rupee per person per day.

For several weeks Stephan Kovalski's relations with

his neighbours had been confined to the mere exchange
of a polite 'Salaam' each morning and evening. Evidently
these Muslims (and they were not the only ones) persisted in disapproving of the intrusion of a foreign Catholic priest into their neighbourhood. As always, it was
thanks to the children that relations gradually thawed.
A few attentions, indications of interest in their games,
was all it took to win them over.

A dramatic incident was to break the ice once and
for all. One evening Mehboub came home from work
looking totally dejected. The naval yard had just laid off
all its work force. It was a practice that had been current
since the introduction of a law obliging employers to pay
their workers on a monthly basis after several months of
regular work. With the exception of those whose
interests it served, no one wanted to see this law implemented. It was even said that government, management and the unions had actually joined forces against
it. The government, because the increase in the number
of workers paid on a monthly basis would fatally reinforce the strength of the unions; management, because
a labourer working on precarious terms was much more
readily exploited; the unions, because their membership
was composed of monthly workers eager to restrict
their advantages to their own minority. Furthermore, as
always in India, in addition to objective reasons there
were considerations of tradition, inherited from the past.
If all the day labourers became monthly workers, what
would become of the custom by which the eldest son of
a monthly worker was accorded the privilege of being
employed by the factory where his father worked? Thus
everyone conspired together to get around the law. To
avoid having to give employment contracts, people were
laid off periodically, then rehired. So it was that thousands of men lived under the shadow of not knowing
whether or not their jobs would be waiting for them on
the following day. After thirteen or fourteen years of

employment, when it was no longer possible to put off giving them a contract, they were laid off once and for all. This was what had just happened to Stephan Kovalski's neighbour.

This sturdy man, with the muscles of his legs, chest and shoulders strengthened by hard labour, began to waste away before Kovalski's very eyes, and in the space of a few weeks he shrivelled up like a dried fruit. His stomach racked with hunger, he walked miles each day around the industrial suburbs of Calcutta in search of any available means of earning a crust of bread. In the evening, worn out, he would enter the priest's room and sink down, without a word, in front of the picture of the Sacred Shroud of Christ. Sometimes he would remain there for an hour, seated in the lotus position before the face of the man he so resembled. 'Poor Mehboub,' Kovalski was to say. 'While you were praying in front of my icon, I was revolting against the Lord, just as I had done over little Sabia's agony. I found it so difficult to accept that he could allow such injustices to occur.'

The seven members of that family soon had to survive on the twenty rupees (£1.20) that Nasir, the elder boy, earned each month in the sweat shop where for twelve hours a day he dipped the clips for ballpoint pens into a chrome bath. Despite the fact that all day long he inhaled toxic vapours from the metal under electrolysis, Nasir was a sturdy lad, which in fact was not really surprising. In poor families the food was always kept for the one who was working. The others were left with the crumbs. Nasir supplemented his wages with the ten rupees that Kovalski gave him. Every morning at dawn he took a tin full of water and lined up for the priest at the latrines, then came running back to tell Stephan when his turn had come.

One evening, after meditating in front of the picture of Christ, Mehboub invited the priest to come into his

home. The room measured barely six feet by four. Two thirds of it was taken up by a low platform made out of planks which served as a table by day and a bed by night, when it was covered over with a patchwork of rags. The last born slept between his mother and his grandmother on the 'table bed', while Nasir and his two elder sisters slept underneath it. As for Mehboub, he stretched out on a mat outside, under the porch roof. The only other piece of furniture consisted of a metal trunk in which the clothes for the feast days of the Muslim calendar were religiously preserved, carefully wrapped in cinema posters taken from the walls of Calcutta. Like millions of other Indian women, Selima fed her *chula* with cakes of cow dung and cinders gleaned from the ballast of the railway track. Their hovel with no window, no water and no electricity was none the less meticulously clean, so much so that the floor of beaten earth was just like marble. No one would have dreamed of treading on it without first removing his shoes.

The more extreme the destitution, the warmer was the welcome. No sooner had Kovalski entered under their roof than his neighbours eagerly offered him tea, *jelebis** and other sweetmeats of which the Bengalis are so fond. In a matter of seconds they had used up their resources for several days, just to honour him in this way.

Naturally Stephan Kovalski wanted to help this family, but how could he do so without falling into the trap of becoming a foreign Santa Claus? A relatively minor incident provided him with a solution. One morning, as he was cooking rice on his paraffin stove, he burned his hand. He used his clumsiness as a pretext to ask his neighbour's wife if, in the future, she would prepare his meals. In payment for his board he offered her three rupees a day (20 pence), a princely sum by slum stan-

---

* Small syrupy fritters shaped like coils.

dards. For the Pole it was actually an opportunity to try out an experience on which he had set his heart. He insisted that the young woman prepare exactly the same food for him as she did for her family.

'How could I share faithfully the living conditions of my brothers in the City of Joy without knowing their most fundamental anguish,' he was to explain, 'the anguish that conditioned every instant of their lives: hunger – Hunger with a capital H – the hunger that for generations had gnawed away at millions of people in this country, to the point where the real gulf between the rich and the poor existed at the level of the stomach. There were the *dobelas* who ate twice a day, the *ek-belas* who ate only once, and the others who could not even be sure of one daily meal. As for me, I was a three-*bela*, the almost unique representative of a species of consumer unknown in the slums.'

The neighbour's wife looked with astonishment at the Pole.

'You, a *Father sahib*!' she protested. 'You, who people say are one of the richest men in your country, you want to eat the food of the poor? Stephan *Daddah*, it's not possible. You must be out of your mind!'

'Selima, little sister, how I wanted to beg your pardon!' Stephan Kovalski was later to say. 'How indeed could you understand even for one second, you who lived among the refuse, who never saw a bird or the foliage of a tree, you who sometimes had not even a scrap to offer your children, you who could feel another little innocent stirring inside you, a child who tomorrow would hang from your empty breasts screaming famine, yes, how could you understand how anyone could be mad enough to exchange a *karma* in paradise for this infernal slum and come to share your poverty?'

'I mean it, little sister,' confirmed Kovalski. 'From tomorrow onwards, you'll be the one to feed me, if you'll do me the kindness.'

Next day at noon, one of Selima's daughters brought
him a plate with his food for the day: a ladle of rice, a
little cabbage and turnip, some *dal* – the lentils which
often provided the poor of India with their only protein.
For the other *ek-belas* of the slum this would have been
a princely portion. With his European appetite, more
accustomed as it was to alimentary excesses than Indian
frugality, the Pole prepared to gulp his meal down in
two minutes. As he had feared, however, Selima had
remained true to Indian tradition which required that all
food should be inflamed with chilis and other incendiary
spices. He had no alternative but to absorb each mouthful
slowly and cautiously. Having one day protested in
front of an Indian doctor against this custom which,
he thought, took all the flavour away from the food,
Kovalski was to discover the real reason for this culinary
practice. Because it releases perspiration, stimulates
blood circulation and accelerates assimilation of food,
chili is first and foremost a means of duping the hunger
of millions of undernourished people. And it makes it
possible to swallow absolutely anything, even the most
rotten food!

Not having to undertake any strenuous physical activity, the Pole put up with his new diet quite valiantly
for the first two days. Whenever he felt the pangs of
hunger, he would go and drink a cup of sweet tea from
the old Hindu's shop across the way. On the third
day, however, things became different. Violent cramps
accompanied by dizziness and icy sweats began to gnaw
at his stomach. Hardly had he eaten his one meal than
he had to crawl on to his mat, brought down by the
pain. He tried to pray but his spirit seemed as empty as
his stomach. Throughout the next day and the days that
followed it, his hunger gave him no respite. He was
ashamed. So few people were lucky enough to have even
once a day a plateful of food like the one Selima cooked
for him. He noted his body's reactions. His pulse was

considerably faster, and so was his breathing. 'Am I
going to be able to hold out?' he worried, humiliated at
finding himself already reduced to a limp rag while
his companions in wretchedness managed to carry on,
pulling carts or carrying loads more fit for beasts of
burden, on far fewer calories. After a few days, however,
his troubles disappeared and the sensation of hunger
faded as if by magic. His body had adapted itself. Not
only did he no longer suffer, but he even experienced a
certain feeling of well-being.

It was then that he made a fatal mistake. A visitor
from France having brought him a tin of quenelles from
Lyons and a Camembert cheese, he went to offer these
delicacies from his former adopted homeland to the
neighbours who had so little. Mehboub would accept
them only on condition that his friend shared in the
treat. The result was disastrous. It awoke the Pole's
appetite in a way that was completely uncontrollable.
The nausea, cramps and attacks of sweating and dizziness
reappeared with increased vigour. Kovalski felt himself
becoming weaker daily. His muscles wasted visibly. His
arms, thighs, legs and pectorals were as if emptied of all
substance. He lost several pounds more. The slightest
task, even going to fill his bucket at the fountain, took
immeasurable effort. He had difficulty staying upright
for half an hour. He suffered from hallucinations.
Nightmares haunted his sleep. He even began to bless
the chorus of rats that woke him at the point when, in
his dreams, an endless procession of emaciated men was
bearing down upon him. He was physically living the
curse of hunger for himself. Physically and mentally,
Stephan Kovalski had joined the ranks of the majority
of the occupants of Anand Nagar – and thus he had
achieved his objective.

Yet he was no fool. He knew the exact range of
his experience, and its limitations. 'I was like those
volunteers in survival who know that they will be res-

cued after a certain amount of time. Whereas the real tragedy of the truly poor is despair. I knew that if my hunger exceeded bearable limits, I had only to make one gesture to eat as much as I wanted. I knew that if I were to be struck by the slightest ailment, thirty-six people would rush to my rescue.

'Mehboub and all the other occupants of the City of Joy were real castaways. To the cries of their empty stomachs was added the anguish of those who had no hope of rescue. And so their dignity seemed all the more admirable. Not a single complaint ever issued from the mouth of my neighbour. He allowed his turmoil to show only when his younger daughter cried with hunger. Then only did his fine face become stricken with pain. But he always reacted quickly. He would take hold of the little girl, sweep her up onto his knee, tell her a story, and sing her a song. Soon the child would begin to laugh. Forgetting her hunger, she would tear herself from her father's arms to go and play once more in the alleyway. There were times, however, when nothing would stop her tears. Then Mehboub would take his daughter in his arms and go into the neighbouring court-yard to beg a piece of *chapati*. A poor person would never close his door on him. That was the law of the slum.'

22

With his grey polo shirt, his beige linen trousers and his leather sandals, Musafir Prasad was quite unlike the other human horses. After twenty years of toiling between the shafts of a rickshaw, he had moved on to the side where the money was. At forty-eight, this onetime peasant immigrant from Bihar had become a boss. He was the

man who held the trust of Bipin Narendra, the old
rickshaw owner whom people referred to as 'the Bihari'.
Beneath his black wavy hair, shiny with mustard oil, his
brain functioned just like a computer. This man with
protruding ears and a nutcracker chin ran the empire of
three hundred and forty-six carriages and some seven
hundred human horses who pulled them; and he did so
without either pencil or paper – for the very good reason
that he could neither read nor write. Yet nothing escaped
the diabolical vigilance of this phenomenon who was
gifted with the quality of ubiquity. No matter whether
it was a hundred and ten degrees in the shade or the
monsoon was raging, he would cover several dozen
miles a day on his squeaking bike. Because of his slightly
bandy legs and the way he waddled as he pedalled, the
rickshaw pullers had nicknamed him 'the Wader'. And,
strange as it might seem, everyone in the streets of this
inhuman city liked the Wader.

'When the Old Man summoned me to hand it all
over,' he recounted, 'I thought God was bringing the
sky down on my head. For the twenty years I had been
working for him he had always confined me to the
subordinate tasks, such as repairing the rickshaws, talking to the police, accidents, odd jobs, and so on. But the
sacrosanct collection of the daily hiring fees was his task
and his alone. He never missed a single day, even when
he was up to his thighs in water. He was the only one
who knew all the ins and outs, for although the majority
of rickshaw pullers paid for the hire of their vehicle by
the day, there were others who settled their accounts on
a weekly or monthly basis. Some paid at a cheaper rate
than others because repairs were their responsibility, or
because their rickshaw was operating without a licence.
Since there were two men to each carriage, that made
about seven or eight hundred fellows to be managed.
An enormous task which only the Old Man's fat head,
it seemed, could control. But one day the Old Man

began to feel the burden of his years. "Listen to me, Musafir," he said to me. "You and I, we've known each other for many years. We are both Biharis and I trust you. You will be my representative. From now on you will collect the money and bring it back here each evening. For every rupee I will give you five pice." The Old Man was not someone with whom you discussed things. I prostrated myself, touched his feet, then raised my hands to my head. "You are the son of the god Shiva. You are my master," I replied, "and I shall be eternally grateful to you."

'Next day I got up at four because I wanted to go to the latrines and the fountain before the other people in my neighbourhood. The four companions with whom I lodged in a shack near the Old Man's big house were still asleep. They too worked for the Old Man as bus driver, mechanic, rickshaw puller and joiner. They too were Biharis, and they too had left their families behind in their villages to come and earn a living in Calcutta.

'At four-thirty, I straddled my bicycle and pedalled straight to the temple of Lakshmi, our goddess of prosperity, behind the Jagu Bazar. It was pitch dark and the Brahmin priest was still asleep behind his grille. I rang the bell and eventually he appeared, whereupon I gave him ten rupees and asked him to celebrate a *puja* just for me so that the day might begin under the best of auspices. I had taken with me a coneful of rice, some flowers and two bananas. The priest deposited my offerings on a tray and we entered the interior of the sanctuary. He lit several oil lamps, then recited *mantras* before the divinity. I repeated some prayers. The *puja* filled me with intense joy and the certainty that from that day onwards I was going to earn a lot of rupees. Solemnly I promised Lakshmi that the more money I had, the more offerings I would bring her.

'After the *puja*, I cycled off in the direction of Lowdon Street, near the Bellevue clinic nursing school, where

the Old Man had six rickshaws. Because of the early hour, all the pullers were still there. They were asleep on the canvas seats with their legs dangling in mid-air. Most of the pullers had nowhere else to live. Their vehicle was their home. Where they were two to a cart, there were quarrels which I was supposed to arbitrate. It wasn't easy to tell one that he could sleep in his old rattletrap, and not the other!

'Next I made for Theatre Road where the Old Man had a dozen carriages. Then I cut down Harrington Street, a pretty, residential road with fine mansions set in gardens and buildings where rich people and foreigners lived. Outside the gate to one of these houses there were always uniformed guards and an American flag. The Old Man had at least thirty rickshaws in that sector. Because it was a wealthy neighbourhood, it was also a problem area. There were always one or two characters who'd had their carriages pinched by the cops under some pretext or other. And the cops asked for a lot of baksheesh because they knew the men earned a better living there than elsewhere. You had only to look at the pavement outside the police station in Park Street, opposite Saint Xavier's College. It was permanently cluttered with a column of confiscated rickshaws slotted into each other and chained together. They stretched for more than a hundred yards. That first morning I had to go and bow and scrape and grease the brutes' palms with more than sixty rupees for the release of a number of carriages, a formality which invariably complicated my accounts because I had subsequently to make sure that the dues from the pullers concerned were raised for a prescribed number of days.

'After Harrington Street I set off as fast as I could for the rickshaw stand in front of the Mallik Bazar, on the corner of the great intersection of Park Street and Lower Circular Road where, of the thirty or forty carriages parked there, a good twenty were again the property of

the Old Man. Before this next call, however, I pulled up on the corner of New Park Street to drink a cup of tea – tea that was nice and hot and strong, with plenty of sugar, as only Ashu, a fat Punjabi installed on the pavement, knew how to make it. His was the best tea on the pavements of Calcutta. Ashu mixed the milk, sugar, and tea in his kettle with as much solemnity as a Brahmin carrying out *Arati*.* I envied him the way he spent his days, seated on his backside, lording it over his utensils, being appreciated and highly thought of by his customers.

'My pedalling took me next to the fish, meat and vegetable market on Park Circus, next to which a good fifty carriages were always parked. As I progressed through my rounds, the corner of my shirt into which I stuffed the notes swelled up to create a bulge at my waist. Sporting a fat belly in Calcutta was in itself a strange sensation but for the fat belly to be compiled of a cushion of bank notes belonged to the realms of make-believe. By this time many of the pullers were already carrying a fare or cruising the streets ringing the bells on their shafts to attract the attention of customers. That meant I had to scour half the city. At midday, however, I found myself outside the area's schools and colleges, where hundreds of rickshaws concentrated twice a day. Taking the children to school and back was, in fact, a speciality of the corporation and the only opportunity to earn a regular income, since each child usually had his regular puller. This arrangement was called a "contract" and by becoming the beneficiary of one or more daily contracts a puller could double or even triple the amount of the money order he sent each month to his family. It was also a fine guarantee of his standing with the clients. But how many fellows had that sort of luck?

* Ceremony of the offering of lights.

'I knew that to do my job properly, I needed a heart of stone like my boss. How else would I be able to claim the five- or six-rupee hiring fee from some poor sod whose carriage hadn't budged from the spot. I knew that some days many of them would have to go without food to pay me. Poor fellows! How are you supposed to pull two clients and all their parcels or two fat women from one of the rich neighbourhoods with nothing in your stomach? Every day pullers collapsed in the street. And each time some fellow couldn't get back on his feet, I had to look for a replacement. Thank God there was no shortage of candidates! But the Old Man had always gone to a great deal of trouble to choose the right pullers, to find out about their background. He had good reason for doing so. He didn't want to get mixed up with politics. Claims for this or that, blackmail, threats, strikes were a nightmare to him. "Musafir, I don't want any worms in my guava," he would say repeatedly, because rickshaw pullers now had their own unions and the government was trying to infiltrate them with phony pullers who would stir up action against the owners. Rickshaw pullers, people were saying, should be granted the ownership of their instruments of labour. Up till now it had never actually happened. I knew one or two who had become, as I had, their owner's representative. I even knew some who had managed to swap their shafts for the steering wheel of a taxi. But I didn't know of anyone who had managed to buy his own rickshaw – even an old jalopy with no operator's licence.

'The goddess Lakshmi, in her goodness, was not deaf to my prayers and my offerings. By the end of my first week I had a nice bundle of a hundred and fifty rupees to take to the *munshi** outside the post office in Park Street. My family in the village would be well and truly surprised. Their last postcard asking me for money had

* Public letter writer.

arrived only two days before. Their cards always said the same thing. Either they asked me for money or they informed me that my last money invoice had arrived safely and that they had been able to buy the paddy or whatever else for the family field. I had left behind in my home village my father, mother, wife, three sons, two daughters and three daughters-in-law plus their children. Altogether there were a good twenty mouths to feed off two poor acres. Without what I sent, famine would strike the dried mud hut in which, forty-eight winters previously, my mother had brought me into the world.

'At the post office in Park Street I had my regular *munshi*. His name was D'Souza and he was a Christian. He came from the other end of India, a place called Goa, below Bombay. The *munshi* always greeted me with a smile and some kindly words of welcome, for we were good friends. I had brought him business from my rickshaw pullers working in that area and he slipped me a commission on any transactions he undertook for them. It was in the usual run of things. There is nothing like money matters for cementing strong bonds between workers.

'That was what I was thinking about on the morning I saw Ram Chander, one of my pullers, rushing towards me with two ten-rupee notes in his hand. Ram was one of the few Bengalis who worked for the Old Man. The night before, he had had his carriage picked up by the cops for having no light. It was only a pretext for baksheesh in a city where the vast majority of lorries and cars operate without lights. Nevertheless, Ram Chander wasn't offering me twenty rupees to go and get his rickshaw out of the pound, but rather to take on the companion he had with him. "*Sardarji*, you are the most noble son of Ma-Kali,"* he exclaimed. "I'd like to

* The goddess mother Kali.

introduce a compatriot of mine to you. He comes from
my district. I and my family have known his clan and
his lineage for generations. He is a brave and honest
worker. For the love of Our Mother Kali, give him one
of your rickshaws to pull."

'I took the two notes he was holding out to me and
examined the man who seemed slightly reluctant to
come forward. Although he was very thin, his shoulders
and arms looked solid. I asked him to lift up his *longhi*
so that I could check the condition of his legs and
thighs too. The Old Man always used to do that before
employing a puller. He used to say that you shouldn't
entrust a rickshaw to a young goat. I weighed the pros
and cons before responding to the eager expectation of
the two Bengalis. "You're in luck. There's a man who
died last night near Bhowanipur market."'

23

The Muslim quarter of the City of Joy had burst into
celebration. During the last two days, in all the compounds, women had unpacked the festive clothes they
had so religiously preserved. The men had strung garlands of multicoloured streamers across the alleyways.
Electricians had installed loudspeakers and strings of
coloured light bulbs. On every street corner, confec-
tioners were heaping up mountains of sweetmeats on
their trays. Their poverty and anguish forgotten, the
fifty thousand Muslims in the slum were preparing to
celebrate one of the most important events in their
calendar, the birth of the prophet Muhammad.

Resounding strains of hymns and chants transformed
this stricken neighbourhood into a frenzied carnival.
Prostrate and facing in the direction of the distant, mysti-

cal Kaaba, thousands of the faithful filled the six mosques
for a night of uninterrupted prayer.

The barbers', tailors' and jewellers' shops were packed
with shoppers. The poor adorned themselves for the
occasion like princes. Hindu women came running to
assist their Muslim neighbours with the cooking of the
traditional feasts. Others, armed with combs, brushes,
flowers and ribbons, helped with the hairdos. Yet others
bought saffron, carmine and henna powder to embellish
their friends' faces, arms and feet with skilful motifs.
Children were the objects of a particularly subtle toilet.
With their eyes accentuated with great rings of kohl,
their skinny bodies draped in shiny silk tunics and muslin
veils, and their feet tucked into Turkish slippers, they
looked just as if they had stepped out of an illustration
of *A Thousand and One Nights*.

For all their noises, however, the popular rejoicing and
the loudspeakers could not drown the groans Kovalski
could hear. But the torture that Sabia, his little neighbour, was going through no longer repelled the priest.
Eventually he had conceded that it was indeed Jesus who
was suffering on the other side of the mud wall and that
his suffering was a prayer. One question, however,
continued to haunt him: Was the child's sacrifice really
indispensable?

> *Allah Akbar! God alone is great!*
> *Peace be with Muhammad his prophet!*
> *Allah Akbar!*
> *Peace be with Noah, Abraham, Moses, Zachariah,*
> *Jesus, and all the other prophets!*

The congregation took up in a chorus each verse as it
was called into the microphone by the blind mullah with
the goatee from the Jama Masjid, the City of Joy's
main mosque. With its cream façade pierced by latticed
windows and its four minarets tapered like candles, it

was the tallest and most colourful building in the slum. It rose from a square that formed the only uncluttered space in the ants' nest, beside a pool of stagnant water in which the occupants of the neighbourhood did their washing. A joyful crowd filled the square and all the surrounding streets. Above their heads fluttered a multitude of little green-and-white flags, red banners marked with the crescent of Islam, and banderoles decorated with verses from the Koran and the golden cupolas of the sacred mosques in Jerusalem, Medina and Mecca – magic symbols that illuminated with faith and dreams their decaying surroundings.

The blind mullah, a venerable patriarch in a white silk turban, walked at the head of the procession. Two religious figures dressed in grey *abayas* guided his way. Blaring from a cyclecar equipped with a loudspeaker, a litany of canticles taken up by thousands of voices gave the signal to move off. Every two minutes the mullah stopped, took over the microphone and chanted invocations that electrified the faithful. Soon the cortège extended for more than a mile, a prodigious stream of colour and voices flowing between the walls of the hovels and irrigating the pestilential labyrinth through which it passed with its vibrant faith and glittering finery. On this festive day Islam was infusing the slum with lights, noise and religious fervour.

From the doorway of his hovel, Kovalski looked on with amazement as the procession approached. How, he wondered, could so much beauty spring out of so wretched a place? The sight of the children was particularly compelling. The pinks, blues, golds and pastels of the girls' *shalwars* and *ghaghras*, and the boys' embroidered muslin *kurtas* and braided *topis*★ clothed the procession in an enchanting medley of colour. Kovalski

★ Trousers drawn in at the ankles; skirts; shirts without a collar; and toques, respectively.

recognized his neighbour, Mehboub, in the third row, holding the pole of a red-and-green standard decorated with a minaret. The feast day had metamorphosed the famished unemployed worker into a superb soldier of the prophet. Among the children paraded his elder son, Nasir, the one who lined up for the latrines on Kovalski's behalf, and also his two little daughters, together with Sabia's sisters, all dressed up and ornamented like princesses with sparkling glass bracelets, spangled sandals and multicoloured muslin veils. 'Thank you, Lord, for having given the down-trodden people of this slum so much strength to believe in you and love you,' the priest murmured softly to himself, overwhelmed by the crescendo of voices, proclaiming aloud the name of Allah.

It was at that point that he heard someone calling him. 'Big Brother Stephan, I would like you to bless my son before he is taken away. Sabia was very fond of you and you are truly a man of God.' Sabia had just died. He had died at the very moment the procession of the prophet was passing the hovel in Nizamudhin Lane that had sheltered his agony.

Even in her pain, Sabia's mother's dignity remained exemplary. At no time throughout her great trial had this woman's face betrayed the slightest despondency. Whether she was crouching in the street making her paper bags, wading through the mud with her bucket of water, or kneeling in prayer at her son's bedside, she had held her head high and managed to maintain the serenity of her smile and the beauty of a temple statue. 'I never met her without giving thanks to God for having lit such a flame of hope in this place of suffering,' Kovalski was to say. 'Because she never gave up. On the contrary, she fought like a lioness. In order to pay for the doctor's consultation and the expensive medicines, she took the last of her jewellery to the usurer – two bracelets, a pendant, a pair of earrings which had

survived other disasters. Often at night I heard her reciting verses from the Koran to ease her child's pain. Sometimes she would invite the neighbouring women in to pray with her at his bedside, just as the holy women of the Gospels prayed at the foot of the Cross. In her there was neither fatalism nor resignation. Nor did I ever hear her utter a single word of rebellion or complaint. That woman taught me a lesson in faith and love.'

Now, she cleared a way for him between the mourning women. The child was lying on a litter, swathed in a white shroud, with a garland of yellow marigolds placed upon his chest. His eyes were closed and every feature of his face had relaxed into an expression of peace. With his thumb Stephan Kovalski traced the sign of the Cross on the boy's forehead. 'Goodbye, my glorious little brother,' he whispered. A few moments later, borne by youths from the alleyway, Sabia left his hovel on his final journey to the Muslim cemetery at the far end of the slum. Immersed in prayer, Stephan Kovalski followed the small cortège. Because of the festivities, there were not many people along the route to mark the passing of an innocent child. In any case, death was so natural a part of everyday life in the City of Joy that no one paid particular attention to it.

PART TWO
Human Horses and Their Chariots of Fire

24

Hasari Pal stood and gazed at the rickshaw before him, as if it were Ganesh in person — Ganesh the elephant-headed god, benefactor of the poor who brought good fortune and removed obstacles. Instead of the rickshaw's shafts, Hasari could see a trunk; in the place of wheels large ears. Eventually he approached the vehicle with respect and rubbed the moonstone in his ring on the shafts, then touched his heart and his forehead with his hand.

'That carriage, lined up against the pavement, was a gift of the gods,' he was to say, 'an urban plough with which to make my sweat bear fruit and provide food for my children and for all my relatives waiting expectantly in the village. And yet it was just an old jalopy, completely run down and with no licence to operate. The paint was peeling off in strips, the straw stuffing was coming out of the holes in the seat, several hoops in the hood were broken, and the rubber tyres around the wheels were so worn that you could see the wood through them. Under the seat there was a locker designed to contain any essential accessories, a bottle of oil to grease the hubs every now and then, a wrench to tighten up the wheel bolts, a lamp to light at night, the linen screen that hooks onto the front of the hood when you're transporting Muslim women who wish to remain concealed from men's eyes, or to protect travellers during the monsoon downpours.

'If I mention these things, it's only because my friend, Ram Chander, had shown them to me in the locker of his rickshaw, the day we took the injured coolie to the

hospital. My locker was empty. Someone must have ransacked it when the previous puller dropped dead in the street. Ram had already warned me that if it was possible to steal the air we breathe, there'd be people in Calcutta prepared to do it.

'On the back of the carriage a metal plate bore a number and some inscriptions. I didn't know what the latter meant but I engraved the number on my mind like a talisman, like the magic formula that was going to open the gateway to a new *karma*. Overwhelmed with happiness, I had shown my friend and benefactor, Ram, the number 1 and the three 9s that were featured on the plate. It didn't matter that the number was a phony one, it was made up exclusively of figures that in our calendar augur well.

'Having admired it at length, I finally took my place between the shafts of the rickshaw, raised them respect-fully, and placed my fingers on the worn spot vacated only hours earlier by the hands of the poor fellow to whom the number 1999 had certainly not brought good fortune. I thrust my hips forward and heard the wheels creak. That creaking was like the reassuring sound of a millstone grinding the grains of rice from our land. How could I fail to believe in the benediction of the gods? What was more, that first day of my new life fell on a Friday, the best day in the week along with Monday, because that was when the most money was about. And it was the beginning of the month. From the fifteenth day onwards, people were apparently as tight as the trident of Shiva. Good old Ram had already revealed plenty of secrets and taught me the tricks of the trade. "There are all sorts of people," he'd said to me. "Good ones and bastards. There'll be those who make you run and others who'll tell you to take your time. Some will try and knock a few pice off the cost of the journey. But if you're lucky enough to pick up a foreigner, you can ask for more money." He had put me on my guard

against *gundas*★ who, like some prostitutes, specialize in giving you the slip without paying when you reach their destination. "You'd be well advised to lay in a stock of mustard oil to massage your limbs," he had also warned me, "because for the first few days your thighs, arms and back will be as painful as if every cop in Calcutta had busted his *lathi* on you."

'I found myself alone, alone with this extraordinary cart in the middle of an unknown city, teeming with people. It was terrifying. How would I ever find my way through the labyrinth of streets? Or manage to edge between the lorries, buses and cars that bore down upon me with a deafening roar, like waves from a tidal storm? I was panic-stricken.

'As Ram had advised me, I pulled my rickshaw to Park Circus to wait for my first client. Park Circus was a very busy junction where several bus routes and tram lines intersected. There were lots of little workshops and schools there, as well as a large market frequented by housewives from the rich neighbourhoods. A long string of rickshaws was permanently parked on this privileged junction. I can't say that the pullers waiting patiently there, sitting on their shafts, received me with shrieks of joy. There were so few crumbs to be gathered up in this inhuman city that the arrival of one more competitor was not exactly guaranteed to induce a state of joy. They were all Biharis. Most of them were very young, but the older ones had a really worn look about them. You could count their ribs beneath the threadbare cotton of their vests.

'The line shortened swiftly. Soon my turn would come. As it approached, I felt my heart pounding in my chest. Would I actually manage to pull this old heap? The prospect of plunging with it into the furious flood of traffic was already paralysing my arms and legs. To

★ Crooks.

give myself strength, I went and bought a glass of sugarcane juice for twenty-five pice, from the Bihari who passed bits of cane back and forth under his grinding wheel. He did a good business. There was a constant line in front of his grinder, for a glass of cane juice was often all that a fellow could manage to get down him all day. The poorest among us sometimes had to content themselves with buying a piece of cane and chewing on it to keep hunger at bay. That cost only ten pice (less than one penny). But drinking a whole glass was like putting a whole tank of petrol in your engine. I felt a blast of warmth descend from my stomach to my thighs. As for the old jalopy, I could gladly have pulled it to the highest peak of the Himalayas.

'The memory of the old, happy days, when I used to follow the slow progress of the buffalo through the rice field, went through my mind. Then, as if out of a dream, I heard a voice, "Rickshaw *wallah*!" I saw a young girl with two long braids down to her waist. She was wearing the white blouse and navy blue skirt of the girls from a nearby school. Clambering into my rickshaw, she asked me to take her home. Realizing that I hadn't the faintest idea where her street was, she gave me directions. I shall never forget those very first moments when I suddenly found myself in the middle of traffic. It was quite insane. I was like a man who had thrown himself into the water to get away from wild animals, only to find himself surrounded by a herd of crocodiles. The bus and lorry drivers led the dance. They seemed to derive a malignant satisfaction from terrorizing rickshaws, charging them like wild bulls amid the noise of their horns and engines. The wildest of all were the minibus drivers and the turbaned taxi drivers. I was so terrified that I moved forward at a walking pace, my eyes on the lookout to left and right. I concentrated on trying to keep the vehicle in balance, on finding the exact place to put my hands, in order to distribute the weight

most effectively. It was more easily said than done in the middle of bumpy thoroughfares, ditches, holes, ruts, the mouths of open drains, tram lines. You had to be a real acrobat! But Ganesh's trunk was watching over my rickshaw during that first run. It steered me through the obstacles and brought me to the girl's house safe and sound.

'"How much do I owe you?" inquired the girl as she stepped out of my carriage. I hadn't the faintest idea. "Give me whatever you think." She looked in her purse. "There's three rupees. That's more than the usual price, but I hope it brings you luck."

'I took the notes and put them next to my heart, thanking her effusively. I was deeply touched. I kept my hand on them for a while, as if to imprint myself with that first money earned in the role of a Calcutta rickshaw *wallah*. Feeling those notes between my fingers brought me a sudden surge of hope, the conviction that by working hard I could actually achieve what my family were expecting of me and become their feeding bird, the one who would distribute food to all the starving fledglings in our village hut.

'In the meantime it was to my wife and children that I wanted to present the money from that first journey. I rushed to the nearest vendor selling fritters and started to run for the pavement where we were camping, with a bag of fritters as my only passenger. My arrival instantly attracted a crowd. The news that a pavement dweller had actually become a rickshaw *wallah* had spread from one end of the street to the other, like the sound of a fire-cracker at Diwali.* It did not matter that my old heap was one of the most common vehicles to be found in Calcutta; kids crawled up its wheels to sit on the seat, men felt the weight of the shafts and women looked at

* The Hindu festival of light when Lakshmi, goddess of prosperity, is venerated.

me with admiration and envy. Arjuna going off in his chariot to the great war of our Mahabharata could not have made more of an impression. To all those poor people who, like us, had left their rice fields, I was a living proof that there was always grounds for hope.

'That reception spurred me on more effectively than a whole plateful of green chilis. I set off again and had barely covered a few yards before two enormous matrons hailed me to take them to the Hind Cinema in Ganesh Avenue. They must have weighed four hundred pounds between them and I thought my ramshackle carriage was going to give out at the first turn of the wheels. The hubs squeaked heartrending creaks, and the shafts shuddered in my palms like reeds on a stormy day. In vain I strained; I simply could not manage to find the right balance. I was like a buffalo harnessed to a house.

'My two passengers must have sensed my incompetence because one of them ordered me to stop. As soon as they had got out, they hailed another rickshaw. I don't know what chilis that puller had eaten that day but I watched him trot away with no more difficulty than if he had been carrying two statuettes of Durga to the Ganges.

'After such bitter humiliation, I felt a burning need to redeem myself. I was ready to pick up literally anyone, even free of charge, just to show what I was capable of.

'The opportunity presented itself on the corner of Park Street, a wide road in the city centre flanked by arcades. A young man and a girl coming out of a pastry shop with ice-cream cones in their hands signalled to me to pick them up. The boy asked me to put up the hood and fix up the linen screen that is used during the monsoon or to protect Muslim women from indiscreet eyes. Unfortunately, I didn't possess that accessory! All I could suggest was that they used my spare loincloth. The

young man helped the girl in and directed me to go around the block. I was intrigued but without any further question I fixed the material onto the hood and there we were, off on a journey with no destination. Hardly had I turned the corner than frantic jolts nearly made me lose my balance. Clinging onto the shafts to keep my course, I soon understood the reason for the jerking. My old jalopy was serving as a love nest.

'Calcutta, you are no longer a cursed city. Quite the opposite, let me bless you for having given me, a poor peasant exiled from Bengal, the opportunity to earn seventeen rupees on this first day. And let me bless you too, dear Ganesh, for having kept all snares and dangers from my carriage and harness, and for allowing me to complete seven runs without problem or accident. I decided to devote a part of my earnings to the purchase of one accessory that is the emblem of rickshaw pullers. The peasant's trade also has its noble tools, like the ploughshare and the sickle used to harvest the rice. These implements are fêted at the great *puja* of the god Viswakarma.*

'The instrument I was intent on buying was the bell that the rickshaw pullers carry, slipping their right index finger into its thin strap and thus using it to attract clients by jangling it against a rickshaw shaft. Bells come in all different shapes and sizes, and at a variety of prices. They range from the most ordinary grey scrap iron ones to superb copper bells that shine as brightly as the planet Brihaspati. Some of them give sounds like that of a crested crane fishing on the surface of a pond. Others are more like the call of a kingfisher pursuing a dragonfly. It was from a puller in Park Circus that for two rupees I bought my first bell. It had a fine leather strap which I fastened to my index finger next to my moonstone ring. With such jewels on my fingers, how could I fail

* The god of working tools.

to feel good energies welling up inside me? How could I not believe in the generosity of my *karma*?

'It would not take long for me to be disenchanted. Next morning when I awoke, my arms, legs, back, and the nape of my neck hurt so much that I had great difficulty in getting up on my feet. My friend Ram Chander had warned me – you don't turn into a human horse overnight, even if you are of good peasant stock. The prolonged effort involved in pulling, the brutal jolts, the exhausting acrobatics entailed in keeping the thing balanced, the violent and sometimes desperate stiffening of the whole body in order to stop in an emergency – it all gives you a brutal shock when you've hardly eaten for months and your body is already pretty worn out.

'In vain I followed Ram's advice to massage myself from head to toe in mustard oil, like the wrestlers on Howrah Bridge before a fight. I was quite incapable of taking up the shafts of my rickshaw. I could have wept. I entrusted the machine to the care of my wife and dragged myself off to the Park Circus stand. I was absolutely set on giving the five rupees for the day's rental to the owner's representative. I would have gone without food, I would have taken my moonstone to the *mahajan* just to pay off those five rupees. It was a matter of life and death; thousands of other starving peasants were waiting to get their hands on my rickshaw.

'At Park Circus I ran into Ram. He had just got his carriage back after his clash with the police the other evening. He thought it was a joke to see me shuffling along, bent over like an old man.

'"You haven't seen anything yet!" he jeered at me. "Before three months are up you'll be coughing red too."

'That's how I discovered that my friend, who always seemed so hearty and sure of himself, had an infection of the lungs.

'"Are you taking any medicine for it?"

'He looked at me in surprise.

'"You must be joking? You've seen for yourself the queues at the dispensary. You get there at dawn and by evening you're still there. You're better off treating yourself to a nice bit of *pan* every now and then."

'"*Pan?*"

'"Certainly. To camouflage the enemy. When you cough, you don't know whether it's blood or betel. That way you don't worry so much."

'Thereupon, Ram suggested that we go to visit our coolie friend in hospital. It was two days since we had been to see him. So much had happened during those two days! Taking pity on the state I was in, Ram offered to transport me in his rickshaw. It made quite an entertaining spectacle. The other pullers at the stand were hugely amused to see the pair of us going off like that. They didn't have that many opportunities for a laugh.

'It was a very strange sensation for me to find myself suddenly in the position of passenger! It was even more terrifying than being down in between the shafts. All those buses and lorries whose metal panels almost brushed your face! I was in the prime position to see everything, including the taxi bearing down on us like a stampeding elephant, which forced Ram into a pirouette at the very last second. And the heavily laden *telagarhi* emerging from the right that nothing, not even a wall, would have been able to stop. I admired the virtuosity with which Ram changed the position of his hands on the shaft so that the wheels took all the weight of the load. With his bell, you might have taken him for a Katakali dancing girl.

'The trek to the hospital was a long one. All the streets were blocked by processions with red banners, which completely obstructed the traffic. In Calcutta such processions seemed to be part of the general decor. I had already seen a number of them. Here the workers were

organized and kept parading all the time for their demands. That sort of thing didn't go on in the villages. Who were we supposed to go and demand anything from in the country? You can't march in protest against the sky because it hasn't yet sent the monsoon. Here there was a government to take your dissatisfaction to.

'We stopped in a bazaar to buy fruit. This time I was the one who paid for it with the money left from the previous day. I also bought a pineapple that I had the vendor peel and cut up into wedges. That way we'd be able to eat them with the coolie.

'The hospital was still overflowing with people. We went straight to the building where we had last seen our friend. Before we did so, Ram chained a wheel of his rickshaw to a streetlamp and took with him the contents of the locker. The same attendant was still watching over the patients who'd been operated on, and he let us in without any difficulty after we'd slipped two rupees into his pocket. There was still that appalling smell that seemed to grab you by the throat. We picked our way between the rows of beds to our friend's cot at the far end, near the window, next to the burned child whom I'd fed the orange. As I was having difficulty walking with my stiffness, Ram was quite a way in front of me when he called out, "He's not there any more!"

'Our friend's bed was occupied by an old Muslim with a goatee, whose body was covered with bandages. He couldn't tell us anything, nor could the attendant. I should say that we didn't even know the name of the injured coolie. Perhaps he had been moved elsewhere? Or perhaps they had simply discharged him to make room for someone else? We explored several wards. We even managed to get into the room adjacent to the one where they performed operations. Our friend was nowhere to be found.

'As we were coming out of the building we saw two male nurses carrying a body on a stretcher. We

recognized our friend. His eyes were open; his cheeks were sunken and grey with stubble. His lips were not closed. It was as if he were trying to say something to us. But for him it was all over. I couldn't help wondering whether there'd be more handcarts for him in his next incarnation, or whether he'd be a *sardarji* behind the wheel of a taxi.

'Ram questioned the nurses to find out where they were taking our friend. "He's an indigent," replied the older of the two. "He'll be thrown into the river."'

25

The death of young Sabia changed the attitude of Stephan Kovalski's neighbours. It dispelled their reticence. Even the most mistrustful now greeted the priest with 'Salaam, Father!' The children squabbled over who was to carry his bucket on the way to the fountain.

Then came another event that served to complete this transformation. A few doors away from his room lived a girl of fifteen who had become blind as a result of a virus infection. Her eyes were purulent and she suffered so much that she cursed the world and everything in it. Her name was Banno and she had long braids like a princess in a Mogul miniature. One day her mother came and stood before Stephan Kovalski, her hands joined together in a gesture of supplication.

'*Daktar*,* for the love of God, do something for my little girl,' she implored.

How could he cure an infection of that kind when all he had in the way of drugs were a few aspirin tablets, a little paregoric and a tube of some sort of pomade? All

---

* Doctor.

the same, Stephan Kovalski decided to apply a little of the pomade on the girl's eyes. Three days later the miracle had occurred; the infection had been stopped, and by the end of the week young Banno had recovered her sight. The news spread like wildfire. 'There's a white wizard in the neighbourhood.'

This exploit earned the Pole his final certificate of acceptance and a degree of notoriety which he could well have done without. Dozens of sick people and invalids wended their way to 49 Nizamudhin Lane. He was compelled to procure other medicines. His room became a haven of refuge for those in the very direst straits. It was never empty. One morning two bearers set down a bearded man whose shaggy hair was covered with ashes. He was attached to a chair. He had no legs and no fingers on his hands. He was a leper, yet his young face radiated a joy that was astonishing in one so disinherited.

'Big Brother, my name is Anouar,' he announced. 'You must look after me. As you can see, I'm very sick.'

His gaze alighted next on the picture of the Shroud of Christ.

'Who is that?' he asked, surprised.

'It's Jesus.'

The leper looked incredulous.

'Jesus? No, it can't be. He doesn't look as he usually does. Why does your Jesus have his eyes closed and look so sad?'

Stephan Kovalski knew that Indian iconography reproduced images of Christ in abundance, but those of a Christ with blue eyes, triumphant and brightly coloured, like the gods of the Hindu pantheon.

'He has suffered,' said the priest.

The Pole sensed that further explanation was necessary. One of Margareta's daughters translated his words into Bengali.

'His eyes are closed, so that he can see us better,' he went

on. 'And so that we, for our part, can look at him more readily. Perhaps if his eyes were open, we wouldn't dare to, because our eyes are not pure, nor are our hearts, and we carry a large share of the responsibility for his suffering. For if he is suffering it's because of me, you, all of us; because of our sins, because of the evil that we do. Still he loves us so much that he forgives us. He wants us to look at him. That's why he closes his eyes and those closed eyes invite me, too, to close my eyes to pray, to look at God inside me . . . and inside you too. And to love him. And to do as he does and forgive everyone and love everyone, especially those who suffer like him, they invite me to love you who are suffering like him.'

A little girl in rags who had remained hidden behind the leper's chair came forward and planted a kiss on the picture, caressing it with her small hand.

'*Ki koshto!* How he must suffer!' she murmured, after touching her forehead with three fingers.

The leper seemed to be deeply moved. His dark eyes were shining.

'He is in pain,' Stephan Kovalski went on, 'but he doesn't want us to weep for him, but rather for those who are suffering today, because he suffers in them, in the bodies and hearts of the lonely, the abandoned, the despised, as well as in the minds of the insane, the neurotic and the deranged. You see, that's why I love that picture. Because it reminds me of all that.'

The leper nodded his head thoughtfully. Then, raising his stump in the direction of the icon, he said, 'Stephan *Daddah*, your Jesus is much more beautiful than the one in all our pictures.'

'Yes, you are beautiful, Jesus of the City of Joy,' Kovalski was to write that evening in the notebook he used as a diary, 'as beautiful as the crippled leper you sent me today with his mutilated body, his sores and his smile.

It was you I saw in him, you who are the incarnation of all pain and anguish, you who experienced Gethsemane, who sweated blood, who knew what it was to be tempted by Satan, abandoned by the Father, brought down, discouraged, hungry, thirsty – and lonely.

'Jesus of Anand Nagar, I tried to care for that leper. Every day, I try to share in the plight of the poor. I bow my head with those who are crushed and oppressed like "grapes in a press and their juice has squirted onto my garments and my clothing has been stained". I am not guiltless, nor am I a saint. I am just a poor fellow, a sinner like all the rest. Sometimes I am crushed or despised like my brothers in the slum but with this certainty deep in my heart – that you love me. I also have another certainty – that no one can take away the joy that fills me, because you are truly present, here in the depths of this wretched slum.'

26

'With his pudgy fingers covered with rings, his shirt bursting open over his rolls of fat, and his hair shiny with perfumed oils, my first client of the day was frankly repulsive,' Hasari Pal recounted. 'And so arrogant on top of it. But I was too hard pressed to treat myself to the satisfaction of refusing to take him. He was a *marwari*.* No doubt he was used to rolling about in a taxi. He was in a hurry. "Faster!" he kept calling out and, in the absence of a whip, he bombarded my ribs with kicks that were particularly painful because he was wearing slippers with hard, pointed toes.

* A merchant, originally from the State of Marwar in Rajasthan, with a reputation for toughness in business.

'He hadn't actually told me where he wanted to go. When he got in, he had simply said, "Straight on and fast!" That *marwari* must have been used to speaking to horses, or slaves. "Turn right! Turn left! Faster!" He barked out his orders and I performed the appropriate acrobatics in between the buses and the lorries. Several times he ordered me to stop and then had me set off again immediately. Sharp stops like that, involving a jerk of the lower back and a pull in reverse to halt the full weight of movement, are horribly painful. It's as if all of a sudden your hamstrings are supporting the total weight of the rickshaw and the client. Setting off again was no less painful, but this time the pain came from the shoulders and forearms because it took a supreme effort to get the old machine rolling again. Poor old jalopy! With every stop and start its shafts shuddered as violently as my bones. I don't know whether it was because of the heat wave that had been scorching Calcutta for two or three days, but that day the bus and taxi drivers seemed to be afflicted with an extreme attack of nervous irritation. On the corner of one avenue a *sardarji* put his arm out of his window to grab the shaft of my rickshaw; he pushed it away with such violence that I lost my balance – a predicament that earned me a fresh outburst from my passenger and a whack from the policeman directing the traffic. A little further on, a group of kids hanging out of the doorway of a packed tram rained down a shower of kicks on my head. It was impossible to retaliate. These were humiliations that had to be swallowed in silence.'

Hasari's run finished that day outside the door of a restaurant in Park Street. Before putting down his shafts to allow his passenger to get out, he asked for five rupees. Staring at the puller as if the latter had just thrust a gun into his stomach to steal his wallet, the fat *marwari*, scarlet with fury, exclaimed, 'Five rupees! Five rupees for a journey with a lame horse!'

At this point, however, the incident took an unexpected turn. Alerted by the *marwari*'s protestations, a dozen rickshaw pullers who had been waiting outside a nearby restaurant came rushing over to form a circle around him. Frightened by their threatening air, the fat fellow calmed down and lost no time in foraging in his pocket. Without a word, he handed to Hasari a crisp, green five-rupee note. As the Bengali peasants say, 'When the dogs howl, the tiger sheaths its claws.'

This city was indeed a jungle, with laws and hierarchies like those in the forest. There were elephants, tigers, panthers, snakes and all kinds of other urban animals, and it was undoubtedly best to know which were which, if you didn't want to run into trouble. One day when Hasari was parked outside the Kit Kat, a nightclub on the corner of Park Street, a Sikh taxi driver signalled to him to clear out so that he could take his place. The puller pretended not to understand. The Sikh's turban stirred angrily behind the steering wheel. He trumpeted loudly with his horn, like an elephant preparing to stampede. Hasari really believed that he was going to charge his rickshaw, and so he seized his shafts to move off. He had made a mistake: he had failed to respect one of the laws of the Calcutta jungle, one that stipulates that a rickshaw must always give way to a taxi.

The most trying part of his existence as a human horse was not, however, the physical hardship; in his village there were jobs that were just as exhausting as pulling two obese *poussahs* from Park Street to the Bara Bazar. But those tasks were seasonal, interspaced with long periods of inactivity when a man could take a rest. The life of the rickshaw *wallah* was a form of slavery that spanned every day of the week and every week of the year.

'Sometimes I would have to take people to Howrah Station on the other side of the river. Over there there weren't any rickshaws drawn by men on foot, only cycle

rickshaws. I had never pedalled one of those machines but it seemed to me that there must be less effort involved. I mentioned this fact one day to Ram Chander but he merely placed the flats of his hands on his buttocks with an air of great long-suffering.

'"You poor fellow," he groaned, "you've no idea what it's like to spend ten or twelve hours on the saddle of a bike! To start with you get an arse full of sores. Then your balls get stuck up and after two or three years you can't screw any more. Your bike has made your prick as soft as cottonwool."

'Good old Ram, there was no one quite like him for making you realize that there was always someone worse off than you.'

27

'You'll see, my dear fellow, they'll gnaw you right down to the bone. They'll expect everything of you because of your white skin. Just think of it, a European in a necropolis like the City of Joy. Such a thing is completely unheard of!'

Stephan Kovalski couldn't help thinking of the words of the Indian rector from the parish of Our Lady of the Loving Heart as he handed out aspirin tablets to a woman who had brought him her child stricken with meningitis. The recovery of the young blind girl and his compassion for all the afflicted had been enough to guarantee the realization of Father Cordeiro's prediction. The 'Father' of 49 Nizamudhin Lane had become Santa Claus, a Santa Claus especially tailored for the needs of a slum, a man who was prepared to listen and could understand, onto whom the most neglected could project their dreams, in whom they found friendship and compassion.

Suddenly, he found himself credited with the smallest good thing that might occur, like the municipality's decision to dig ten new wells, or the exceptional mildness of the temperature at the beginning of that winter. The constant need to relate to a person is a characteristic trait of the Indian soul. No doubt it is due to the caste system and to the fact that within each social group there was always somebody in charge. Unless you knew this 'somebody', or had access to him, you had very little chance to obtain anything, whether it was from the civil administration, the police, or the hospitals. For the hundreds of despised and rejected occupants of his neighbourhood, Stephan Kovalski thus became the ultimate 'somebody', an almighty intercessor who could do absolutely anything because of his white skin, the cross of a man of God that he wore on his chest, and his wallet which, to poor people with nothing, must have seemed as fat as that of G. D. Birla, Calcutta's celebrated multimillionaire.

This kind of notoriety exasperated the Pole. He did not want to be Santa Claus, or Social Security, or Divine Providence. All he wanted to be was a poor man among the poor. 'My ambition was primarily to give them confidence in themselves, so that they would feel less abandoned and want to undertake actions to improve their own lot.'

A few weeks before the festival of Durga, his wish was to be fulfilled. One evening some of his neighbours, led by Margareta, walked into his room.

'Stephan, Big Brother,' declared the young Christian widow, 'we want to discuss with you how we can do something useful for the people here.'

Margareta performed the introductions. With her were a young Hindu couple, an Anglo-Indian Christian, a Muslim labourer and an Assamese girl in her twenties – six paupers who wanted to restore their own dignity and 'build something together'. The Hindu couple,

named the Ghoshs, were attractive, healthy and bright. Beneath her red cotton veil, decorated with a floral pattern, the young woman with her very smooth clear skin looked like a Renaissance madonna. The intensity of her gaze struck Kovalski immediately. 'That young woman was burning with an inner fire.' Her name was Shanta and she was the eldest daughter of a poverty-stricken peasant from Basanti, a large isolated borough in the Ganges delta. To provide for his eight children, her father used to go off with the local fishermen on regular expeditions to the flooded jungle of the Sundarbans. There they would collect wild honey. One day, however, her father did not return. He had been carried off by a man-eating tiger, of the kind that kill more than three hundred honey collectors a year in that part of the country. It was on the puddled clay floor of the little local primary school that Shanta had got to know the bearded fellow with the curly hair who was her husband. He was twenty-six-year-old Ashish (which means 'hope'), one of eleven children of a landless day labourer.

This couple's case was unique: they had married for love. Their defiance of all tradition had provoked such a scandal that they had been forced to flee from the village and seek refuge in Calcutta. After starving for nearly a year, Ashish had found a job as an instructor in one of Mother Teresa's training centres for handicapped children. As for Shanta, she was a teacher in a Howrah school. After the birth of their first child they had found their El Dorado: a room in a Hindu compound in Anand Nagar. Two regular incomes of two hundred rupees (£12) a month might seem a pittance, but in Anand Nagar it was a small fortune. The Ghoshs were privileged people, which made their readiness to serve others all the more remarkable.

The Anglo-Indian bore the extravagant name of Aristotle John. He was a small man with a sad face and the worried air typical of many members of a community

that has become particularly marginal in contemporary India. He worked on the railways. The fifty-two-year-old Muslim, Saladdin, had a short moustache and wore a little embroidered skullcap on his head. It was he who had been longest in the slum. Having escaped the massacres of Partition, for the last twenty years he had shared a hovel with three mullahs for whom he acted as cook and guide.

To build something together! In this 'gulag' where seventy thousand men fought each day for their survival, in this ants' nest which at times looked more like a death camp where hundreds of people died each year of tuberculosis, leprosy, dysentery, and all the diseases caused by malnutrition in this environment so polluted that thousands never reached the age of forty, there was everything to build. You needed a dispensary and a leprosy clinic, a home for rickety children, emergency milk rations for babies and pregnant women, drinking water fountains, more latrines and sewers. The urgent tasks were countless.

'I suggest we all make an individual survey,' said Kovalski, 'to find out what are the most immediate problems our brothers want to see given priority.' The results came in three days later. They were all identical. The most pressing desires of the inhabitants of the City of Joy were not the ones that the priest had anticipated. It was not their living conditions that people wanted to change. The sustenance they sought was not directed at their children's frail bodies, but at their minds. The six surveys revealed that the primary demand was for the creation of a night school so that children employed in the workshops, stores and tea shops in the alley could learn to read and write.

Kovalski gave Margareta the task of inviting the families concerned to find a hut which would serve as a classroom, and he offered to share in the remuneration of two teachers. 'I had achieved my main objective,' he

was to say, 'that of encouraging my brothers in Anand Nagar to take charge of themselves.'

That first step was the beginning of an enterprise based on solidarity and sharing that would one day completely revolutionize living conditions in the slum. At the very next meeting Kovalski suggested the creation of a team of volunteers to help accompany the sick to the Calcutta hospitals. To go by themselves for treatment in such caravanserais was often so nightmarish a prospect that most people didn't dare undertake the voyage.

Anyone could attend the meetings in the room at 49 Nizamudhin Lane. A new rumour soon spread: 'There are actually people willing to listen to the poor.' The idea was so revolutionary that the Pole christened his little team the Listening Committee for Mutual Aid. It was also a revelation: people discovered that there were others worse off than themselves. Kovalski made it a rule that each meeting should begin with the reading of a chapter from the Gospel. 'No reading could have been more appropriate to life in the slum,' he would say, 'no example could have been more apt than that of Christ relieving the burdens of his contemporaries. Hindus, Muslims, Christians, all men of goodwill could understand the link between the message of the Gospel and their lives of suffering, between the person of Christ and those who had taken it upon themselves to continue his work.'

No one seemed to feel this link with greater intensity than the young Assamese girl who had come that first evening to offer her services to Kovalski. With her braid hanging down her back, her slits for eyes and her pink cheeks, she looked like a little Chinese doll. Her name had all the resonance of a *mantra*. She was called Bandona, which means 'praise God'. Although she belonged to the Buddhist faith she had been instantly captivated by the Gospel message. By revealing that it was in the service of others that God is best found, the message

spoke to her impatience. 'Every time some unfortunate person explained his difficulties, her face was transformed into a mask of pain,' Kovalski was to comment. 'All suffering was her suffering.'

Yet this girl who was so hypersensitive to others was almost unhealthily modest when it came to anything that concerned her. In response to any personal question she would veil her face with the tip of her sari and lower her head. Kovalski's curiosity was aroused by this. One day when he was teasing her she replied curtly, 'Didn't your Jesus himself say that we are only here to carry out his Father's will and that our own identity does not matter? In which case, why are you so interested in me?'

Still the priest managed to glean a few bits of information that would enable him to understand how a girl from the lofty mountains of Assam had come to be washed up in the filth of a Calcutta slum. Her father was a small peasant of Assamese stock, who had settled in the region of Kalimpong, to the extreme north of Bengal, in the shadow of the first foothills of the Himalayan mountain range. Like all the other mountain people in that area, he worked a small terraced plot of agricultural land, painfully wrested from the hillside. It was enough to provide his wife and four children with a meagre living. One day, however, entrepreneurs from Calcutta set about exploiting the wood from the forests. They fixed a daily quota of trees to be chopped down. Years before, the region had already been radically changed by the development of the tea gardens. With the arrival of the lumbermen, the wooded jungles shrank. Peasants were compelled to venture even further afield to find the necessary wood to cook their food, and new land to cultivate. The number of bushfires increased and, since the vegetation no longer had time to recover before the monsoon cataracts came, erosion ravaged the soil. Deprived of their traditional grazing land, the cattle, too, became part of the destructive process. The growing

scarcity of natural products obliged families to increase the growth of crops needed for their own food. As firewood became progressively rarer, they had to use animal dung to cook their meals, thus depriving the land of its richest fertilizer. The yield dropped. Deterioration of the land became more rapid. Because of the deforestation, water was no longer retained, springs ran dry, reservoirs stood empty, the underground water dried up. Since this area was subject to one of the heaviest rainfalls in the world – up to thirty-three feet of water a year in Assam – with each monsoon the arable earth and humus was washed away to the plains, leaving only the bare rock. In a matter of years the whole region had become a desert. For those who lived there, there was no alternative but to leave, to leave for the city which had ruined them.

Bandona was four years old when her family set out for Calcutta. Thanks to a cousin who worked in a clothing shop, her family was lucky enough to find a room in Anand Nagar. Five years later her father died of tuberculosis. Her mother, a little woman who could not be daunted, had burned incense sticks before the blackened picture of the founder of the Buddhist sect of the Yellow Caps, and then, after a year, married again. Shortly afterwards, however, her husband had gone off to work in the south. Alone, she had brought up her four children by retrieving metal objects from the rubbish heaps and selling them to a scrap metal dealer.

At the age of twelve Bandona had started work, first in a cardboard factory and then in a workshop that turned out parts for trucks. From then on she became her family's only support, for her mother was struck down with tuberculosis. Bandona would go out at five in the morning and rarely get back before ten o'clock at night, after a two-hour bus ride and walking three miles. Often she would not come home at all: power cuts necessitated her sleeping at the foot of her machine so

she could make up the time lost when the electricity was restored. In Calcutta, tens of thousands of workers lived like that, chained to their machines because of load shedding and electricity failures. Bandona earned four rupees a day (25 pence), which only just enabled her to pay the rent for the family hovel and guarantee her mother and brothers a bowl of rice or two *chapatis* once a day. On Sundays and feast days, instead of resting or indulging in the usual distractions of her age group, she would prowl the slum looking for distressed people to help. That was how she came one evening to enter the home of Stephan Kovalski.

A number of donations from Europe made it possible for the priest to help her leave her workshop and work full-time in the service of the Listening Committee for Mutual Aid. No one had a better understanding of sharing and dialogue, of respect for other people's faiths and beliefs, than Bandona. She knew how to listen to the confessions of the dying, how to pray with the families of the dead, wash the corpses, accompany the deceased on the last journey to the cemetery or the funeral pyre. No one had ever taught her, yet she knew it all through intuition, friendship, love. Her extraordinary capacity to communicate enabled her to go into any compound, any hut, and sit down among people without encountering any prejudice of caste or religion, and this ability was all the more remarkable because she was not married. Normally it would be inconceivable that a young single woman would go anywhere at random, especially into a milieu outside her own caste. Married women never took a young girl into their confidence, even one belonging to their own caste, because tradition required that young girls know nothing about life so that they could come to their marriage innocent, on pain of being accused of immorality and thereupon rejected.

Two or three times a week, the young Assamese girl would accompany groups of sick and dying people to

the hospitals of Calcutta. Steering these unfortunates through terrifying traffic, then guiding them through corridors and packed waiting rooms, was quite a venture. In such institutions, a poor person without an escort would have only the remotest chance of actually reaching an examination room. Furthermore, even if given the opportunity, he would never have been able to explain what was wrong or understand the treatment he should follow because, nine times out of ten, he wouldn't speak the Bengali the doctor spoke, but only one of the twenty or thirty dialects of the enormous hinterland that exported its millions of poor to Calcutta. Demanding, storming the doors, forcing entry, Bandona fought like a wild beast to have her protégés treated like human beings and to see that the medicines prescribed were properly given to them, a benefit that rarely occurred. In a few weeks she was to become the pillar and heart of the Listening Committee for Mutual Aid. Her memory was the card index of all the miseries of the slum. Above all, however, it was the quality of her expression, her smile, her love that was to earn her a nickname. The poor soon called her *'Anand Nagar ka Swarga Dug'* – the 'Angel of the City of Joy'.

One evening, returning from one of her expeditions to a hospital, Bandona burst into Stephan Kovalski's room like a missile to inform him that a doctor had diagnosed a fatal skin disease on a pregnant woman from the slum. Only a serum made in England might possibly save her.

'Stephan, *Daddah*,' she pleaded, taking hold of the priest's hands, 'you must have that medicine sent over urgently. Otherwise that woman and her baby will die.'

The next day Kovalski rushed to the post office in Howrah to send a telegram to the head of his fraternity who could contact his connections in London. With a little bit of luck, the cure could arrive within a week. Sure enough, a week later Stephan Kovalski received, via

the excellent Indian postal service, a slip from customs asking him to come and pick up a parcel.

That was the beginning of an odyssey that he would not soon forget.

28

'He's going to die right here in the street,' Hasari thought with horror. His friend Ram Chander's chest had suddenly distended, desperately trying to take in air. His ribs stood out so that his skin looked as if it would burst, his face had suddenly turned yellow and his mouth was gaping open like that of a drowning man deprived of oxygen. A sudden fit of coughing made him shudder and shake, sounding like a piston in a water pump. He began to bring something up but as he had *pan* in his mouth, it was impossible to tell whether he was spitting out blood or betel juice. Hasari helped his friend onto the seat of his rickshaw and suggested that he take him home. Ram shook his head, and reassured his companion. 'It's only this damned cold,' he said. 'It'll pass.'

That year the Bengali winter was murderous. Winds from the Himalayas had brought the thermometer down to fourteen degrees, a temperature that was positively frigid for a population used to baking in an oven for eight months of the year. For the human horses it represented a particularly harsh trial. Condemned to switching from the sweatbath of a run to the cold of prolonged waiting, their undernourished bodies had little resistance. Many of them died.

'Ram was a brother to me in the jungle of Calcutta, where everyone preyed on somebody else,' Hasari Pal would later recount. 'It was he who had helped and supported me, he who had found me my rickshaw. Every time I saw his grey hair, I would speed up just to

park my carriage next to his. How many hours we spent, sitting side by side on the corner of Park Circus or Wellesley Street, or when it was hot, in front of the big market on Lower Circular Road which everyone called the "Air-Conditioned Market" because there were machines inside that blew out that marvellous substance which I used to think only the peaks of the Himalayas could provide – cool air. Ram's dream was one day to go back to his village and open a grocery shop. "Just to sit there all day in the same spot, without moving, without having to run around," he would say, chatting about his future paradise. And he would tell me about how he imagined his life, enthroned in his shop, all around him sacks overflowing with all kinds of *dal* and rice, and other sacks full of intoxicatingly aromatic spices, piles of vegetables, on the shelves all sorts of other items: bars of soap, incense sticks, biscuits, and sweetmeats. In short, he dreamed of a world of peace and prosperity, of which he would form the fixed centre, like those *lingam* of Shiva,* those symbols of fertility standing on their *yoni*† in the temples.'

Before this dream could be realized, however, Ram Chander had a promise to keep. He had to reimburse the *mahajan* in his village for the loan he had taken out to pay for his father's funeral rites. Otherwise the family field, which was serving as collateral, would be lost for ever. A few days before the payment term expired, he had managed to negotiate another loan with a usurer from a neighbouring village. For peasants, paying off one debt with the help of another loan, then paying off *that* loan with a third, and so on, was a common practice. When it came to the final reckoning they invariably lost their land.

Ram Chander's five years were due to expire in a few

---

* Stone in the form of a phallus, symbolizing the god Shiva.
† The female sexual organ.

weeks, just before the festival of Durga. Despite the deterioration of his health, Ram went on working. One morning Hasari ran into him outside the post office in Park Street. The robust fellow looked like a shadow of his former self. He had come to have the *munshi* fill in the form for his monthly money invoice. The sheer bulk of the package of notes he pulled out of his *longhi* amazed Hasari.

'I swear you've robbed the Bank of India!' Hasari exclaimed.

'No,' replied Ram with unusual gravity, 'but this month I've got to send them *everything*. Otherwise our field will be lost.'

Sending them everything meant that for the past month he had cut his own food down to starvation rations: two or three griddle cakes, a cup of tea or a glass of sugarcane juice a day.

'As soon as I saw the neighbour's boy running towards me, I understood,' Hasari was later to say. 'The news spread instantly around all the main rickshaw stations in the area and there were soon about thirty of us assembled in the little shed behind the Chittarajan Hospital where Ram Chander lived. He was lying on the plank that had served as his bed for the five years he had spent in Calcutta. His thick shock of grey hair was like a halo around his head. His eyes were half-open and his lips were shaped into one of his mischievous grins that were so familiar. He looked as if he were enjoying the joke he had just played on us. According to the carpenter-joiner who shared his lodgings, Ram had died in his sleep, which probably explained why he looked so peaceful. The night before, he had had several very violent fits of coughing. He had spat a great deal and even vomited blood. Then he had gone to sleep, and he never woke up again.

'Now we had to carry out the funeral rites. We held a discussion among the rickshaw pullers to establish whether we were going to carry him to the cremation *ghats* on foot or whether we should hire a Tempo. In Calcutta you can hire little three-wheeled carts for one hour, two hours, or however long you want, for thirty rupees an hour. In view of the distance to the Nimtallah ghat, we agreed to hire a Tempo, so I suggested we organize a collection. Some gave twenty rupees, others ten, others five. I searched in Ram's waist, in the place where I knew he hid his money, and found twenty-five rupees. His neighbours also wanted to join in the collection, for Ram was much loved in the neighbourhood. No one compared with him when it came to storytelling, and the children adored him. Someone brought cups of tea from the nearest tea stall and we all drank, standing around our friend. Whether it was because of his smile I don't know, but there was no sadness there. People chatted and came and went just as if he were alive and joining in the conversation. I went to the market next to Sealdah Station with three colleagues, to buy the items necessary to complete the funeral rites, beginning with the litter needed to transport the body to the *ghat*. We also bought incense sticks, a pot of *ghee*,* fifteen feet of white linen, and a long cord to tie the linen around the body; also garlands of white jasmine and a clay pot with which to pour water from the Ganges into the mouth and over the head of the deceased.

'We regarded ourselves as his family, so we performed his last toilet ourselves. It didn't take very long. Ram had died in his pants, *longhi* and working vest. We washed him and wrapped him in the shroud we had bought, so that only his face and the tips of his feet were visible. Then we lifted him onto the litter. Poor Ram! He really didn't weigh very much. No rickshaw puller

---

* Melted butter, purified five times.

is very heavy but he really broke all records for being a featherweight. He must have lost forty pounds since the winter. Recently he had been obliged to turn down passengers who were too fat. After all, you can't ask a goat to pull an elephant! Next we decorated the litter with the garlands of white jasmine and lit incense sticks at the four corners of it. One after another, we walked around the body in a final *namaskar* of farewell.

'Before leaving the shed, I gathered up his things. He didn't have much – a few cooking utensils, a change of *longhi*, a shirt and trousers for the festival of Durga, and an old umbrella. These were all his worldly possessions.

'Six of us climbed into the Tempo with Ram, and the others caught a bus to the cremation *ghat* by the river. It was just like the festival of Durga except that we were taking the body of our friend instead of a statue of the divinity to the sacred river. It took us over an hour to cross the city from east to west and we sang hymns throughout the journey. They were verses from the Gita, the sacred book of our religion. Every Hindu learns these verses when he is a child. They proclaim the glory of eternity.

'We met up with the others again at the *ghat*. There were always pyres burning there and several corpses were already waiting on litters. I made contact with the man in charge of cremations. He was an employee belonging to the *Dom* caste, who specialize in the cremation of the dead. They live with their families next to the funeral pyres. The man in charge asked me for a hundred and twenty rupees for wood. Wood for a cremation is very expensive. That's why indigents and people without families are thrown into the river without being burned. All together it would cost a hundred and fifty rupees to have the body of our friend vanish into smoke. When our turn came, I went down to the river to fill the clay pot with water and each one of us let a few drops fall onto Ram's lips. The Brahmin attendant

poured the *ghee* we had brought onto his forehead and recited the ritual *mantras*. Then we placed the body on the pyre. The employee covered it with more firewood until the body was completely imprisoned in a cage of sticks. The Brahmin poured more *ghee* over the faggots until we could see only a patch of white shroud.

'As the final moment drew nearer, I felt my throat tighten with emotion and tears well up in my eyes. No matter how hardened you were, it was a terrible thing to see your brother encased on a funeral pyre, ready for burning. Images flooded through my memory: our meeting outside the Bara Bazar warehouse when we took the injured coolie to the hospital, that first bottle of *bangla* we drank together afterwards, Sundays spent playing cards in the Park Circus restaurant, our visit to the rickshaw owner's representative to beg him to entrust a rickshaw to me. Yes, in this inhuman city, Ram had been a father to me and now, without him, I felt like an orphan. One of the other pullers must have noticed my grief because he came over to me, put a hand on my shoulder, and said, "Don't cry, Hasari. Everyone has to die some day." It wasn't perhaps the most comforting of remarks, but it did help me to get a grip on myself. I drew nearer to the pyre.

'Since Ram had no family in Calcutta, the Brahmin asked me to plunge the lighted torch into the pile of wood. As ritual required, I walked five times around the pyre, then thrust the torch into the place where the head was. Instantly the pyre flared up amid a shower of sparks. We were forced to draw back because of the heat. When the flames reached the body, I wished Ram a good journey. Above all, I wished that he might be reborn with a better *karma*, in the body of a *zamindar*, for example, or in that of a rickshaw owner!

'The cremation lasted several hours. When there was nothing left but a pile of ashes, one of the officials in charge of cremations sprinkled the ashes with water

from the Ganges, then put them in a baked clay pot.
And then we all went down to the river and scattered
the ashes on the current so that they would be borne
away to the eternity of the oceans. Then we all immersed
ourselves in the waters for a purifying bath and left the
ghats.

'There remained just one last rite for us to carry out.
Actually it was more a tradition than a rite. To conclude
that sad day we invaded one of the numerous dives that
were open day and night in the vicinity of the cremation
ghats and ordered up plenty of bottles of *bangla*. Then,
drunk out of our minds, we all went off for a meal
together, a real feast of curd, rice, *dal* and sweetmeats —
a rich man's feast in honour of a poor man's death.'

29

A crumbling old building, with a staircase that stank of
urine and filled with a confusion of silhouettes in *dhotis*
wandering about, the Calcutta customs office was a
classic shrine to bureaucracy. Brandishing like a talisman
the notice for his parcel of medicine, Stephan Kovalski
swept into the first office. Once inside, however, he
had no sooner taken a step before his commendable
enthusiasm deserted him. Seized by the spectacle before
him, he stopped in his tracks, transfixed. Before him
extended a battlefield of old tables and shelves, sagging
beneath mountains of dog-eared files, spewing out yel-
lowing paperwork tied vaguely together with bits of
string. There were piles of ledgers all of which appeared
to be chewed by rats and termites, and some of which
looked as if they dated back to the previous century.
The cracked cement of the floor was likewise strewn with
paper. From drawers that were coming apart bulged an

infinite variety of printed forms. On the wall Kovalski noticed a calendar for some year long past, which sported a dusty effigy of the goddess Durga slaying the demon-buffalo, the incarnation of evil.

A dozen *babus** in *dhotis* were seated in the middle of this chaos, beneath a battery of fans which throbbed out a veritable sirocco of moist air and sent the papers into a whirl of confusion. While some scrambled to catch documents as if they were chasing butterflies, others jabbed a single finger at antique typewriters, pausing after each letter to verify that they had actually managed to hit the right key. Others were talking on telephones that didn't appear to be connected to any line. Many of them seemed to be engrossed in activities that were not, strictly speaking, professional. Some were reading newspapers or sipping tea. Others were asleep, with their heads propped up on the papers that covered their desks, looking like Egyptian mummies on a bed of papyrus. Yet others, seated in their chairs in the hieratic position of yogis, looked as if they had attained the ultimate stages of nirvana.

On a pedestal near the entrance, three divinities from the Hindu pantheon, bound together by a tangle of cobwebs, watched over the enormous office, while a dust-covered portrait of Gandhi contemplated the chaos with supreme resignation. On the opposite wall, a yel-lowing poster proclaimed the glorious virtues of team-work.

The entry of a foreigner had not aroused the slightest bit of interest. Eventually Kovalski's eye fell on a little man with bare feet who happened to be passing with a teapot. The employee stabbed his chin in the direction of one of the officials who was typing with one finger. Stepping gingerly over stacks of files, the priest reached

---

* Originally a term of respect, now used to designate lesser officials in the civil service.

the man in question and handed him the slip he had received in the post. The *babu* in glasses examined the document at length, then, taking stock of his visitor, he inquired, 'Do you like your tea with or without milk?'

'With,' replied Kovalski, somewhat taken aback.

The man rang a bell several times, until a shadow emerged from among the pyramids of files.

He ordered tea. Then, fiddling with the document, he consulted his watch.

'It's nearly lunchtime, Mr Kovalski. Afterwards, it'll be a bit late to find your file before the offices close. Please, come back tomorrow morning.'

'But it's a question of a very urgent consignment of medicines,' protested the priest. 'For someone who could die.'

The official assumed a compassionate air. Then, pointing to the mountain of paperwork that surrounded him, he said, 'Wait for your tea. We'll do everything we can to find your parcel as quickly as possible.'

With these words, enunciated with the utmost affability, the *babu* got up and withdrew.

Next morning at precisely ten o'clock, the time when all the administrative offices in India open, Kovalski was back. A line of some thirty people preceded him. A few minutes before his turn came up he saw the same official with the glasses get up and leave, just as he had done on the previous day. It was lunchtime. Kovalski rushed after him. Still with the same courtesy, the *babu* merely pointed to his watch with a grave expression. He made his apologies: it was midday. In vain Kovalski pleaded with him; the man remained inflexible. The Pole decided to remain where he was and await the *babu*'s return. But on that particular afternoon the official did not reappear in his office.

As luck would have it, the next day was one of the two holiday Saturdays in the month. Kovalski had to wait until Monday. After three more hours of lining up

on the steps of the betel-stained staircase, he found himself once more before the *babu* with the glasses.

'Good morning, Father!' cried the latter amicably, before the inevitable, 'Do you like your tea with or without milk?'

This time Kovalski was full of hope. The *babu* began by popping into his mouth a wad of betel that he had just made up for himself. After several efforts at mastication, he got up and headed for a metal cabinet. Straining at the handle, he had to make a number of attempts at opening it before he actually succeeded. When the door finally did turn on its hinges, the cabinet expelled an avalanche of files, ledgers, notebooks and different documents, almost burying the unfortunate official altogether. Had there not been a human life at stake, Kovalski would have burst out laughing, but the urgency of the issue preserved his calm. He rushed to the victim's rescue, bent on extracting him forcibly from his ocean of papers and procuring the immediate surrender of the parcel of medicines. He was not quite familiar with the sometimes subtle ploys of local bureaucracy. In his haste, he tripped over a coconut that another *babu* had deposited on the floor next to his chair, to quench his thirst during the course of the morning. Fortunately there was no shortage of papers to soften the Pole's fall.

As it happened, the incident had a positive effect. The official with the glasses began to thumb through the pages of several ledgers that had spilled out of the cabinet. Kovalski watched him for a while, fascinated. The man was running his fingers down a confusion of boxes and columns in search of some cabalistic *mantra* scrawled in almost illegible ink. Suddenly he saw the *babu*'s finger stop on a particular page. He leaned forward and could hardly believe his eyes. In the midst of all this geological subsidence of paperwork and records, one single entry brought all the chaos back into touch with a living, palpable, indisputable reality. What he read was his

name. This bureaucracy was not quite as ineffective as even the Indians themselves claimed.

The discovery propelled the official in the direction of another section of the sea of papers that looked as if it might totally engulf him at any second. With all the dexterity of a pearl fisher, he fished out a yellow-covered file on which Kovalski deciphered his name for a second time. Victory! A few more moments of patience and Bandona's protégée could have her first injection of the life-saving serum. However, as if exhausted by the effort of his find, the *babu* straightened himself up, consulted his watch, and sighed, 'Father, we'll continue after lunch.'

That afternoon the *babu* looked more forbidding. 'The information on the ledger does not correspond to that on the slip you were sent,' he announced. 'It'll have to be verified in other ledgers.'

'Only the expression of sincere regret on the official's face prevented me from bursting into a rage,' Kovalski was to say.

The sixth and seventh days passed without their being able to find the correct ledger. On the eighth day, the *babu* claimed forty rupees from the priest to assign two additional employees to the search for the right refer-ences. Another whole week went by. Bureaucratic disas-ter was systematically swallowing up even the very best of intentions. Stephan Kovalski had given up all hope when, after six weeks, he received by post a further notice inviting him urgently to come and clear his parcel. By some miracle Bandona's protégée was still alive.

The *babu* received his visitor with all the transports of affection befitting an old friend. His joy at seeing Koval-ski again was very real. He asked for another thirty rupees for the purchase of revenue stamps and took charge of a pot of glue and a brush with four remaining bristles. Liberally he brushed the place reserved for the stamps, but in the meantime the stamps, caught up in

the whirlwind from the fans, fluttered away. Kovalski was compelled to produce another thirty rupees for three new stamps. Then he was invited to fill in a series of forms to establish how much duty he was to pay. Working this out, and also computing the amount owed for the various taxes, took nearly all day. The final sum was exorbitant: three hundred and sixty-five rupees, three or four times the declared value of the medicines. But then there was no price to be put on a human life.

'Even then my difficulties weren't altogether over,' the Pole would sigh. 'The customs office wasn't permitted to receive direct payment of the duty it prescribed. The duty money had to be cleared by the central bank which would then issue a receipt. This meant one more day wandering from counter to counter in that tentacular establishment.'

At last, clasping the precious receipt to his chest, Kovalski ran back to the customs office. By this time he had become such a familiar figure that everyone welcomed him with a cheery 'Good morning, Father!' His *babu*, however, displayed an unaccustomed reserve. He refrained from even examining the document and instead asked the priest to accompany him. Together they went down two floors and entered a storeroom where mountains of parcels and crates from all over the world were piled high on shelves. The *babu* asked one of the uniformed customs officers to go and fetch the package of medicines. Moments later, Stephan Kovalski at last confronted the precious dispatch, a box hardly bigger than two packs of cigarettes. 'It was like a mirage, a vision of life and hope, the promise of a miracle. The long wait, all that time spent in fruitless activity, all that desperate effort was at last going to result in the saving of a life.'

He held out his hand to take possession of the parcel.

'I'm sorry, Father,' apologized the uniformed customs official. 'But I can't let you have it.'

He pointed to a door behind him on which hung a sign with the words 'Goods incinerator'.

'The date for your medicines expired three days ago,' he explained, making for the door. 'We're obliged to destroy them. It's an international regulation.'

The *babu* who until now had remained silent, intervened swiftly, grabbing hold of the tail of the man's shirt.

'This Father is a holy man,' he protested. 'He works for the poor. He needs that medicine to save the life of an Indian woman. Even if the date has run out, you must give it to him.'

The uniformed customs officer surveyed Kovalski's patched shirt.

'You work for the poor?' he repeated respectfully. Kovalski nodded. Then he watched as the customs officer crossed out the word 'perished'.

'Father, don't say anything to anybody, and may God bless you.'

Despite the medicine, Bandona's protégée died four weeks later. She was twenty-eight years old, a widow, and she left four orphans. In an Indian slum, such a qualification didn't really apply to any children. When parents died, and God knows that happened often enough, they didn't leave orphans behind; other members of the family, an elder brother, an uncle, an aunt – or in the absence of any relatives, neighbours – would adopt them at once.

The young woman's death was very quickly forgotten. That was another characteristic of the slum. No matter what happened, life went on with an energy and vigour that was constantly renewed.

Scintillating serpents suddenly spattered the sky, as a burst of fireworks exploded over the slum. Diwali, the Hindu festival of light, was celebrated on the darkest night of the year and marked the official arrival of winter. In a country where all is myth and symbol, it represented the victory of light over darkness. Illuminations commemorated one of the greatest epic stories of the Ramayana legend, the return of the goddess Sita, brought back by her divine consort Rama, after her abduction to Ceylon by the demon Ravana. In Bengal, it is also thought that the souls of the departed begin their journey on this date in the year, and lamps are lit to light their way. It is also the festival of the goddess Lakshmi, who never enters a dark house, but only the houses that are brightly lit. And, since she is the goddess of wealth and beauty, she is venerated in the hope that she will bring happiness and prosperity. Finally, for many Bengalis this is also the festival of Kali, the sombre divinity who symbolizes the dark trials through which man must pass in order to attain the light. For the inhabitants of the City of Joy, Diwali is, above all, the hope at the end of the night.

Like other households in Hindu India, the hovels in the slum were the setting that night for frenzied card games. The festival perpetuated a custom born of another legend, that of the famous dice game in which the god Shiva wins back the fortune he has lost during a previous game against Parvati, his faithless wife. To achieve this victory the god enlisted help from his divine colleague Vishnu, who conveniently materialized as a pair of dice. Thus the festival of Diwali was also a form of homage to gambling.

Every Hindu gambled that night, be it at cards, dice or roulette. They played with ten-, five- or one-rupee notes, or even with just a few pice. When they had no money, they played with a banana, a handful of almonds, a few sweetmeats. It mattered not what they played with, just that they played. Even Kovalski could not escape the ritual. For, despite the fact that it was occupied by Muslims, even Nizamudhin Lane had its spark.

The old Hindu from the tea shop invited his foreign neighbour to join in a heated game of poker that went on until dawn. As in the legend, Shiva's devotee was allowed to win back the twenty rupees his opponent had taken from him, in the very last round.

It was as he was returning home that morning that Stephan Kovalski heard the news. Selima, the wife of his neighbour Mehboub, who was seven months pregnant, had disappeared.

The young Muslim woman had been discreetly approached by one of her neighbours three days earlier at the fountain. With her face pockmarked from smallpox, the portly Mumtaz Bibi was something of a mystery figure in this world where the lifestyle rendered everybody transparent. Although her husband was only a simple factory worker, she enjoyed a certain opulence. She lived in the alley's only brick house and it was not exactly a hovel. From her ceiling hung a rare and wondrous ornament: an electric light bulb. It was said, too, that a number of rooms in the surrounding compounds were her property, yet no one was able to specify precisely where her money came from. Malicious tongues had it that outside the neighbourhood Mumtaz exercised occult powers. The local Mafia godfather had been seen going into her house. There was talk of traffic in *bhang*, Indian marijuana, of the clandestine distillation of alcohol, of prostitution, and even of a network for buying up little girls for brothels in Delhi and Bombay.

No one, however, had ever managed to support such slander with any proof.

'Stop off at my house on the way back from the fountain,' she said to Selima. 'I have an interesting proposition for you.'

Despite her surprise, Selima did as she was asked. The poor woman had become little more than a shadow since her husband had lost his job. Her beautiful smooth face now looked haggard, and the small stone in her nostril had long since tumbled into the usurer's coffer. She, who had always carried herself with such dignity in her worn sari, now walked like an old woman. Only her belly remained unaffected, a belly that was swollen, taut, superb. She carried it with pride, for it was all she had. Two months later she would give birth to the tiny being that stirred inside her – her fifth child. Mumtaz Bibi had prepared a plateful of tidbits and two small cups of tea with milk. She motioned her visitor to sit down on the low platform she used as a bed.

'Are you set on keeping that child?' she asked, pointing at Selima's belly. 'If you'd agree to sell it to me, I could make you a good deal.'

'Sell you my child,' stammered Selima, flabbergasted.

'Not exactly your child,' the fat woman corrected her, 'only what you've got inside you at the moment. And for a good price: two thousand rupees (£120).'

The opulent dowager of Nizamudhin Lane was carrying on the very latest of Calcutta's clandestine professions: the sale of human embryos and foetuses. The mainsprings of the industry were a network of foreign buyers who scoured the Third World on behalf of international laboratories and institutes for genetic research. The majority of these buyers were Swiss or American. They used the embryos and foetuses either for scientific work or in the manufacture of rejuvenating products for a clientele of privileged people in specialized establishments in Europe and America. The demand had pro-

voked a fruitful trade for which Calcutta was one of the
central sources. One of the recognized providers of this
unusual merchandise was an ex-pharmacist named Sushil
Vohra. He obtained his supplies from several clinics
that specialized in abortions, and he looked after the
packaging of the consignments which left for Europe or
the USA, via Moscow on the Soviet airline, Aeroflot's,
regular flight.

The most sought-after foetuses were the most developed ones, but these were also the most difficult to
come by, a fact which accounted for the high sum offered
to Selima, compared with the less than two hundred
rupees paid for an embryo that was only two months
old. In fact, it was very rare indeed for a woman who
had reached her sixth or seventh month of pregnancy to
part with her child. Even in the poorest of families the
birth of children is always greeted with joy. They are
the only riches of those who have nothing.

Mumtaz assumed a maternal tone.

'Think good and hard about it, little one. You already
have four children. Your husband's out of work and
I've heard it said that your family doesn't eat every day.
This is not perhaps the time to add another mouth to
your household. Whereas, you know, with two thousand rupees you can fill plenty of plates with rice.'

Poor Selima knew that only too well. Finding a few
peelings and scraps to put on her family's plates was her
daily torture.

'What's my husband going to say when I come home
with two thousand rupees and nothing in my . . .?'

The dowager gave her a smile of complicity.

'That doesn't have to be a problem. I'll give the two
thousand rupees in small instalments. Your husband
won't think anything of it and you'll be able to buy
something to feed your family every day.'

The two women parted on these words, but just as
Selima was leaving, Mumtaz called her back.

'There's just one thing I'd forgotten,' she added. 'If you agree, you needn't have any fears about yourself. The operation is always carried out under the very best conditions. What's more, it only takes a few minutes. You'll only be away from home for three hours at the most.'

Strangely enough the idea of danger had not even crossed Mehboub's wife's mind; to a poor woman from the slums death was of no real concern.

All day and all night the wretched woman was haunted by that visit. Every movement she felt inside her seemed like a protest against the horrible exchange that had just been suggested to her. She could never agree to what amounted to murder, not even for two thousand rupees; but then there were other voices too that haunted Selima in the night, the familiar voices of her other children crying out with hunger. At dawn she made her decision.

It was all fixed for two days later. As soon as he got the news, the trafficker Sushil Vohra prepared a large jar of antiseptic fluid. A seven-month-old embryo was almost the same size and shape as a newborn baby. He took the container to a small clinic where the operation was to take place. The festival of light posed a few problems. The usual Hindu surgeons had all gone off to play cards or dice, but Sushil Vohra was not one to allow such obstacles to stop him. Undaunted, he sent for a Muslim surgeon.

The medical establishment into which Mumtaz directed Selima had few pretensions to the title of clinic. It was a kind of dispensary made up of a single room divided in two by a curtain. One half served as a reception and treatment area, the other as an operating room. The surgical equipment was of the most basic kind: a metal table, a fluorescent light, one bottle of alcohol and another of ether standing on a shelf. There was no sterilizer, no oxygen and no reserve supply of blood.

There weren't even any instruments. Each surgeon had to bring his own personal case.

Disturbed by the smell of ether that had impregnated the floor and walls, Selima sank down on a stool that constituted the only piece of furniture. The act that she was bracing herself to have performed seemed to her progressively more monstrous, yet she approached it with resignation. 'This evening my husband and children will be able to eat,' she kept telling herself. Between her blouse and her skin she could already feel the friction of the first notes Mumtaz had given her: thirty rupees, enough to buy almost twenty-five pounds of rice.

The surgeon called for the operation was a man in his fifties with a receding hairline and large hairy ears. He asked Selima to lie down on the table and examined her attentively. Behind him, the trafficker was growing impatient. The Aeroflot plane was due to take off in four hours. He would only just have time to take the jar to Dum Dum Airport. He had alerted his contact in New York. The transaction would earn him about £750 net.

'What are you waiting for, Doctor?'

The surgeon took out his instrument case, slipped on a gown, asked for some soap and a basin to wash his hands, then steeped a large piece of cottonwool in ether and placed it over Selima's nose and mouth. He toyed nervously with his moustache while the young woman lost consciousness, then took up his lancet. Twenty minutes later, mopping up with gauze compresses the blood flowing from the uterus, he placed the foetus with the placenta in the hands of the trafficker. The child would have been a boy.

It was after he had cut the umbilical cord that disaster struck. A reddish bubbling issued from Selima's womb, followed by black dots, and then a veritable torrent of blood spurted forth in a single gush. In a matter of seconds the floor of the room was covered in it. The surgeon tried to compress the lower abdomen with a

very tight bandage, but the red tide continued to escape. He undid the dressings and tried to feel out the position of the abdominal aorta. Applying his fist to the vessel, he pressed with all his might in an attempt to stem the haemorrhage. Without the assistance of a massive dose of coagulants, however, all his efforts were in vain. He tried to find her pulse, but Selima's wrist was already showing only the faintest and most irregular beat. At that point, he heard a door bang behind him and turned round. The trafficker had left with the jar. Mumtaz Bibi, the dowager, did likewise, having first swiftly recovered her thirty rupees from her victim's bodice. The surgeon spread the old sari over the dying woman. Then he took off his blouse soaked in blood and carefully folded it up. He arranged his instruments in their box and put everything into his canvas attaché case. And he too left.

Selima remained alone with the employee of the 'clinic'. Above the grinding of the fan the sounds of voices could be heard coming from outside. The cotton-wool impregnated with ether still concealed her face. The employee was a stunted little man with bushy eyebrows and a hooked nose, like an eagle's beak. To him the bloodless body on the table was worth more than all the Diwali card parties put together. He knew a useful address where they cut up unidentified corpses to obtain skeletons for export.

31

Fifty thousand bombs dropped on each of the fifty thousand rickshaws in Calcutta could not have caused more of an uproar. The rickshaw owners had just announced that they were increasing the daily rent paid by

the pullers. It was going up from five rupees to seven, starting the very next day.

For the pullers it was the worst blow inflicted by the rickshaw owners since the confrontations of 1948, when the owners had demanded that every vehicle should bring in two sets of fees, one for daytime and the other for night-time use. This claim had been the cause of their first strike, an eighteen-day *hartal**★** which had ended with victory for the human horses and with a major achievement on their part: the formation of a union. The person primarily responsible for this initiative was a former Bihari peasant with bushy grey hair, now aged fifty-four, a record age in a corporation where the average life expectancy was barely more than thirty. In some thirteen thousand days, Golam Rassoul had covered, between the shafts of his rickshaw, more than four times the distance between the earth and the moon. This survivor of more than a third of a century of monsoons, incidents and humiliations had realized that a powerful union was the only means by which the population of rickshaw *wallahs* could make its voice heard. Unlike the factory workers, however, the pullers worked individually and their limited ambitions made it extremely difficult to get them together for collective action.

Rassoul learned to read and write, compiled tracts, and contacted in the trade union movement an expert in mass meetings, a Communist member of the Bengal Parliament named Abdul Rahman. 'Lead a crusade,' he exhorted him, 'so that the Calcutta rickshaw pullers will stop being treated like animals!'

Thus was born the Rickshaw Workers Union, one of the most unusual unions in the world, an organization of human horses determined to raise their heads and group themselves together to defend their rights. Affiliated with the Communist Federation of Indian

★ Total stoppage of all activity; strike.

Trade Unions, the syndicate chose as its president Abdul Rahman, and as its general secretary its instigator, the grey-haired veteran rickshaw puller, Golam Rassoul. Two rooms on the fourth floor of the Trade Unions' dilapidated building became the new organization's headquarters. Every morning at six, before harnessing himself to his shafts outside Sealdah Station, Rassoul stood there to listen to the grievances of his comrades and to offer them the support of the union in their confrontations with the rickshaw proprietors or the police.

In the beginning the meetings attracted only very small numbers. Soon, however, pullers began to come from all over the city. In the afternoons, Rassoul would exchange his shafts for an object that was hardly part of a rickshaw puller's general equipment. Armed with a ballpoint pen, he would install himself behind the piles of dusty ledgers in the municipal department for 'hackneys and carriages', to oversee formalities for the renewal of rickshaw licences. The ceremony took place beneath cobwebs waving in the exhalations of an expiring fan, and overlooked by yellowing pictures of Kali, the bloodthirsty, four-armed goddess, dressed in a great floral robe. In theory the renewal cost twelve pice (a little less than one penny). The price had not changed since 1911. In practice, however, it was said that a puller would have to pay about thirty rupees in baksheesh to the police officials to procure the precious document. When their protector Rassoul was not there, the sum could well be three times greater.

Protector was the right word. In thirty years of union action, the indefatigable Rassoul had fought relentlessly. With protest meetings, hunger marches and strikes, he had inspired and organized the resistance of the human horses of Calcutta against the voracity of their employers and the interference of the police. He had fought against what he referred to as the arbitrariness of the municipal

authorities who were forever banning rickshaw pullers from new streets under the pretext of relieving the traffic congestion which grew worse every day. The urban disaster of Calcutta constituted a fatal threat to those trying to earn a living among its bottlenecks. Even the most acrobatic pullers found themselves caught like fishes in a net. To escape the net and avoid the forbidden streets, the men were obliged to embark on exhausting detours.

Now the exorbitant rise in rent was hitting them with a further blow. So it was that from street to street, from square to square, from the banks of the Hooghly to the skyscrapers of Chowringhee, from the slums of Howrah to the gracious portals of the residences on Wood Street, the city began to resound with a strange concert. Tap, tap, tap – the haunting sound of bells struck against the wood of rickshaw shafts. The time for anger had come.

'Some men have knives to defend themselves, or guns, or even worse weapons,' Hasari Pal would recount. 'All we had was a little bell of copper about the size of a betel nut. But that poor little bell, which made a sharpish sound when struck against the shafts or the base of a streetlamp, was mightier than any weapon. It was the voice of the rickshaws of Calcutta – our voice. And our voice must have made a real din that morning, to get the owners' representatives to rush and explain why their bosses had decided to raise the rent. Normally they gave us bad news without making any bones about it. Who has to provide slaves with explanations? But on this occasion, because of the uproar that was reverberating throughout the city, they must have realized we weren't going to swallow their decision like the dutiful little goats in the zoo at Alipore. The increase was far too high. Shouting as loudly as he could to make himself heard above the bells, Musafir, my owner's representative, challenged me publicly. "Do you know, Hasari, how much it costs nowadays to change the spoke in a

wheel?" "Or a new hood?" cried another factotum. "Or how much the baksheesh for the police comes to?" said a third.

'They were men in positions of confidence who had done their homework well. But we didn't give a damn about the cost of wheel spokes or baksheesh for the police. We hadn't been breaking our backs between the shafts of our rickshaws in order to weep for the owners' predicament. To a puller the only thing that really mattered was the bundle of rupees he took to the *munshi* each month to feed the family he had left behind in his village.

'A discussion started up, but as everyone was shouting at the same time, it was impossible to make yourself heard. The arrival of Golam Rassoul, the secretary of our union, put a stop to the noise. Despite his slight build – he looked like a sparrow that had fallen out of its nest – he had an enormous amount of authority. He confronted the line of representatives. "Go and tell your employers to give up their rent increase. Otherwise there won't be one single rickshaw left on the streets of Calcutta."

'Rassoul opened the cardboard box he had brought with him and handed out leaflets. None of us knew how to read or write, but we all guessed the contents. It was a call to strike. The representatives disappeared to report to their owners. They also had a syndicate.

'Pullers came running with their carts from every corner of the city. There were even cycle rickshaws from a long way away on the other side of the river, from Barrackpore and the distant suburbs. The cyclists were poor fellows just like us, except that they made more journeys in the course of a day.

'The Park Circus esplanade was soon so packed with people that the trams and buses couldn't get through. Police vans appeared to try and get the traffic moving again, but what could thirty police do against a crowd

like that? They dealt out a few random blows, then gave up. One union member unrolled a red banner affixed to two long bamboo poles. It bore the symbol of the hammer and sickle with the name of our union. Raised above our heads, it formed a victory arch.

'The noise of the bells increased with every minute, as new rickshaw *wallahs* appeared on the scene. It became quite deafening, just as if billions of cicadas were rubbing their wings together all at the same time. The owners must have heard that concert from their hiding places. Provided, of course, they hadn't all put cottonwool in their ears.

'The dejected look of the stewards when they came back was more eloquent than any words: their bosses were sticking to the increase they'd announced. Rassoul got up on a *telagarhi* with a loudspeaker. I couldn't help wondering how so powerful a voice could come out of so puny a chest. "Comrades!" he shouted. "The owners of your rickshaws want to increase their profits even more. Their voracity knows no limits. Yesterday they demanded the payment of two lots of rental, one for the day shift and the other for the night. Today they're increasing your fees by fifty per cent! Tomorrow, God knows what new demands they'll impose on you."

'Rassoul spoke for some time. His face disappeared behind his loudspeaker. He talked about our children and said that this increase would condemn them to starvation. He said that we had no way out of our position as slaves, that most of us had lost our land, and that if the hope of earning a living by pulling our rickshaws was taken away from us, there would be nothing left for us to do but die. He said that we had to get rid of this menace at all costs, that we were numerous and strong enough to impose our wishes and make the owners back off. And he ended up by asking us all to vote for an unlimited strike.

'"*Inkalabad zindabad!* Long live the revolution!" he

then proclaimed. "Rickshaw Workers Union *zinda-bad*!"

'We all took up the slogans in a chorus and repeated them several times. It made me think of my friend Ram Chander. How pleased he would have been to see all his companions gathered shoulder to shoulder in defence of their families' bowls of rice. He had so often fought alone. We were carried away, as if by the wind that blows before the monsoon. Long live the revolution! The revolution? Like all the others, I let the word roll off my tongue, but I didn't know exactly what it meant. All I wanted was to be able to take a few more rupees to the *munshi* each month and to be able to knock off a bottle of *bangla* with my friends now and then.

'Rassoul asked all those in favour of the strike to put up their hands. We looked at one another in silence. Who among us could face without apprehension a single day without the means of earning his living? Does a bird saw through the branch he's sitting on? The owners would be all right – they had their jars full of rice and *dal*. We could be reduced to skeletons before they lost a single roll off their paunches. And yet we had no real choice.

'A fellow next to me put up his hand. He was a Bihari; I knew him by sight. He was called "Scarface" because a blow from a policeman had smashed his cheek in. He coughed like Ram, but he didn't chew *pan*. When he spat there was no mistaking what the red stuff was. No doubt he'd said to himself that strike or no strike, it would make very little difference to him.

'Other hands went up. Then more. Finally, one by one, all the hands went up, including mine. It was odd to see all those hands in the air. Not one of them was closed in a fist. There was no hatred; rather, there was a kind of resignation. There was no use in Rassoul repeating that striking was our only weapon, you could sense that the pullers had put their hands up reluctantly.

How could you hold it against them? The rickshaw union wasn't the workers union at Dunlop or GKW or any other big factory. There, when the workers went out on strike, the union gave them funds. They could hold out for months.

'Rassoul took up his loudspeaker again to announce that the motion to strike had been carried unanimously. Then he called out, "Comrades, our revered president, Abdul Rahman, calls upon us all to meet at the Maidan esplanade this afternoon at three o'clock. United, we will make our anger felt. United, we'll break the owners." And he started up again with slogans about the revolution that we all repeated as a chorus. It was as if we were drunk. We shouted without thinking. We shouted because we were all poor men who had come together to shout together.

'The most tremendous thing about it was the feeling of revenge that suddenly came over us. The great city of Calcutta belonged to us, to us the pullers of men, the ones whom taxi, bus and lorry drivers insulted and despised, the ones whom the police tormented and beat, the ones whom passengers were always trying to cheat out of a few pice. We, the sweating, suffering slaves of the *sardarjis* and the owners, we the population of rickshaw *wallahs*, were suddenly the masters. Not a single vehicle could pass through the city centre any more, blocked as it was by thousands of rickshaws. It was like a flood, except that the monsoon had poured down empty carriages. I don't know how many of us there were – perhaps fifty thousand or more. Like the many arms of the Ganges, our various processions all converged on Chowringhee, along the Maidan, the great avenue that those gentlemen of the police force had closed to our old rattletraps three months previously, under the pretext that we took up too much room and caused traffic jams. Today they watched us pass with heads bowed beneath their white helmets, their guns in

their highly polished belts, and their *lathis* ready to batter the poor on the skull or the back.

'The union leaders had distributed red posters all along the route. They announced that we were the rickshaw pullers of Calcutta and that we were rejecting the new increase in rent. They also said that we'd had enough of police harassment and that we claimed the right to earn our rice like anybody else. Passers-by watched us with astonishment. Never before had they seen so many rickshaws at once. They were used to the city officials demonstrating or the railway employees or the tram conductors – in short, those who were fortunate enough to have a proper job and be well paid. That bums whom they regarded as beasts of burden, whom they never saw other than with their backs bent, should dare·to demonstrate too seemed to be quite beyond them.

'As we walked, we chanted slogans rounded off with three jangles of our bells. It made an impressive noise. On the corner of Lindsay Street, a coconut vendor cut the tops off his fruits and handed them out to us to keep us going. It was a shame that the procession forced us to go on walking because I would have very much liked to go and tell that fellow that he could get into my rickshaw and go wherever he wanted free of charge. It wasn't every day that we were offered something to drink in this city. Further on, in front of the arcades of the Grand Hotel, where I'd been to forage in the rubbish bins with my children, there were foreign tourists who couldn't get back to their cars because of our march. They seemed to find us interesting, because they were taking photographs. Some of them even came right into the middle of our procession to have their pictures taken with us. The rickshaw *wallahs* of Calcutta angry must be as exciting a sight as the white tigers in the zoo at Alipore. I don't know whether rickshaw people go on strike in other countries, but they could probably show

those pictures to their friends and relatives when they got home and tell them that there are some very strange experiences to be had in the streets of Calcutta.

'Our procession reached the rallying point on the edge of Chowringhee. As we joined up with one another, the march swelled to become a river wider than the Ganges. Our final destination was the Sahid Minar, the column on the Maidan that soars up so high, it seems to pierce the clouds. High up on the balcony you could see the police. Just think, all the thousands of rickshaws in Calcutta gathered together – that must have given the police a few headaches. At the base of the column was a platform decorated with red flags. It looked really splendid. As we arrived, union men invited us to leave our carts along the edge of the Maidan and go and sit in front of the platform. I couldn't help wondering how we were all going to find our own vehicles again among such a pileup of carriages.

'Golam Rassoul climbed onto the platform. For this occasion he had changed into a clean *dhoti* and *kurta*. For all his fine clothes, however, he still looked just as puny. There were several other people on the platform with him, but we didn't know who they were. After a moment Rassoul took hold of a microphone and called out something in Hindi. Nearly all the pullers got to their feet and yelled, "Abdul Rahman *zindabad!*" Rassoul repeated his words, this time in Bengali, which was how I learned of the arrival of the president of our union. He was a plump little man who looked like a *babu* from a political party. He can't have pulled many rickshaws, unless of course it was during some other life. He was surrounded by a dozen men who cleared his way through the people in front of him. They only just stopped short of sweeping the dust from under his feet. He waved his hand as he passed among them, and what he had on his finger was no mere moonstone, but several gold rings with enormous precious stones that glinted in the sun-

light. He climbed onto the platform and sat down with his entourage in the front row.

'Rassoul announced that he was going to present to us the representatives of the other unions who had come to bring us the support of their members. There were representatives from the jute mills, from Hindustan Motors, from the shipyards, and goodness knows where else. Each time the signal was given we sent up a torrent of "*Zindabads*" for each one, and each time we did so the crows dispersed in all directions. We had a warm feeling in the pits of our stomachs at the thought that there were people prepared to take an interest in poor fellows like us. Rassoul had us acclaim our president once more. Thrilled by the applause, the man with the rings got up to speak.

'He must have been very used to this kind of meeting, because his every movement seemed to be specially calculated. To start with there was his silence. For a full moment he stood and looked at us without saying anything, nodding his head slightly like a peasant content to contemplate the shoots in his rice field undulating far away to the horizon. Then he decided to speak, mixing sentences in Bengali and Hindi. I couldn't follow exactly what he was saying because he spoke mainly in Hindi, which most of the Bihari pullers could understand. But he spoke damn well, that *babu* Abdul. I managed to make out that he was telling us that the bosses were inflicting starvation on us, that they were making their futures out of our sweat and blood, and that all this would go on just as long as the capitalist government would not make up its mind to expropriate our carriages and give them to us, the people who actually had to pull them. It was really a very good idea and we applauded heartily. There were even men who shouted that we should demand expropriation immediately. That way there would never be any increase in rent.

'Abdul Rahman went on with his speech, talking

progressively faster and more loudly. You'd have thought he was reciting the Ramayana, for all the passion he put into his words. His finger pointed out imaginary owners and seemed to pierce them through with a knife. The effect was so spellbinding that some of my colleagues began to clap their hands, or shout, shaking their fists. The youngsters picking their way through the ranks to sell sweetmeats and tea, and even the fellows who were collecting the money, stopped to brandish their fists and shout along with the others. I don't know whether the owners and their factotums were watching this scene from afar and listening to our shouting, but if they were, they must have been making some very strange faces. If, at that moment, Abdul had asked us to go and set fire to their houses, I can well believe we would have followed him to a man. Instead, however, he took advantage of the assembly of poor fellows listening to him as if he were a guru straight out of Ganesh's trunk, to score political points and attack the government over the increase in police harassment and brutality. This was a chapter so close to our own hearts that a tremendous ovation interrupted his speech. Voices began to chant, "Everyone to the Writers' Building!"

'The Writers' Building is the enormous building in Dalhousie Square, in which the government offices are housed. Abdul Rahman raised his arms to try and still the shouting, but a wind of rage had suddenly blown up among his audience, like a tornado that announces a cyclone.

'Something strange happened next. One of the pullers emerged from the crowd and, pushing aside everyone who got in his way, ran to the platform, mounted the steps, and grabbed the microphone before Abdul or anyone else could intervene.

'"Comrades!" he cried. "What the *babu* is doing is lulling us off to sleep! He is trying to drown our anger in beautiful phrases! So that we remain lambs. So that

all the *sardarji* can go on devouring us without our protest!"

'We were in such a stupor that we got to our feet. That's when I recognized Scarface. The people on the platform hadn't dared to snatch the microphone from him. He spoke with difficulty because of his chest disease.

'"Comrades! It's by our actions that we should demonstrate our anger!" He raised his arm in the direction of Chowringhee. "We have no business standing here on this esplanade. Under the windows of the owners of our rickshaws is where we should be demonstrating. I know where one of them lives! Did you know that more than three hundred rickshaws belong to him alone – to Bipin Narendra, the man you call the Bihari? Comrades, it's to him and his associates that we should be demonstrating our strength. Let's go right now to Ballygunge!"

'Scarface was just catching his breath when a dozen men in khaki uniforms burst onto the platform. They surrounded him and dragged him to the foot of the steps, whereupon Abdul took the microphone again.

'"Provocation!" he cried. "That man is an agitator!"

'There were a few moments of confusion as Scarface was taken away. Several pullers rushed to his rescue but they were pushed brutally aside. It was not the evening appointed for the revolution.

'Abdul Rahman went on talking, then it was the turn of the representatives from other unions. You could sense that they were trying to warm us up a bit, but after the incident with Scarface our hearts were no longer in it. All we could see was the fact that all those speeches had prevented us from earning our living that day and that the next day would be the same. We were asking ourselves just how long we were going to be able to hold out with the strike. At the end of all the talking, the president of the syndicate took the microphone and

asked us to sing the workers' song with him. I knew
nothing about any such song but the older ones among
us, those who had been to meetings on the Maidan
before, knew it. Abdul Rahman and the people on the
platform struck up the song and thousands of voices on
the esplanade joined in. My friends told me that it was
the song of workers all over the world. It was called
"The Internationale".'

32

It had all begun with the simple matter of redistributing
the land. As soon as a leftist government had come to
power in Bengal, the Communist party had invited
those peasants who had no land to take possession of the
properties of the *zamindars* and to reorganize themselves
to farm them collectively. Aside from the murder of a
number of landowners who tried to resist, the process
was completed without much violence. It was then,
however, that the Naxalbari incidents broke out, and
immediately the question ceased to be that of a simple
confrontation between landowners and peasants and became one of the most serious political crises to threaten
India since Independence.

Naxalbari is a region at the heart of a narrow strip of
land formed by the north of Bengal between the borders
of Nepal and Bangladesh. Tibet and China are only a
hundred miles away. It is an area scattered with tea
plantations and jungles ideally suited to infiltration and
guerrilla activity. There is not one single town, only a
few villages and camps inhabited by peasants of tribal
origin who scratch a miserable subsistence from plots of
ground so poor that the planters did not want them.

A long tradition of Red activism fired these people,

who had already risen up against the authorities on several previous occasions. Nowhere was the new policy of land redistribution implemented with so much vigour – nor with so much violence. Urged on by Maoist students from Calcutta, possibly trained in Peking, the Naxalites murdered, waited in ambush, and attacked the forces of order. Soon the word 'Naxalite' had found its place beside those of Bolshevik and Red Guard in the lexicon of Indian Communism. Drawing their inspiration from the revolutionary teachings of Mao Zedong, the guerrillas mixed terrorism with popular warfare. In the village squares they lit bonfires to burn the title deeds and proof of debts before beheading, after the Chinese fashion, some of the moneylenders and the large landowners in front of enthusiastic crowds.

The contagion spread as far as Calcutta. Bomb attempts, assassinations, violent demonstrations, the sequestration of political leaders and factory owners increased. Not even the slums escaped. Molotov cocktails were thrown in the streets of the City of Joy, claiming a number of victims. The Naxalites had even gone so far as to desecrate the statue of Gandhi at the entrance to Park Street, by daubing it with tar. Completely overwhelmed, the government had found itself divided over what course of action to take. The Communists in power accused both Peking of seeking to destabilize the power of the left in Bengal, and the CIA of infiltrating the Naxalite commandos to pave the way for the return of conservative forces.

The accusations against the CIA were part of a traditional argument. Since the departure of the British, the American organization had become the habitual scapegoat whenever it was convenient to implicate foreigners in India's internal affairs. Such attacks would have been of no great consequence if they had not eventually resulted in a kind of psychosis of espionage, which meant that a certain number of foreign residents

were subjected to police interference. Stephan Kovalski was to be one of these victims.

The fact that he was a Polish Catholic priest was in itself suspect. To make matters worse, however, his circumstances were somewhat irregular. His tourist visa had expired ages ago and all efforts to obtain a permanent resident's visa had remained fruitless. Still, in India, bureaucracy can never be rushed. For as long as it had not officially rejected his request, Kovalski could hope that he would not be deported. What really ran the risk of weighing most heavily against him was the place where he lived. No official could seriously believe that a European would willingly and purely for his own satisfaction share in the misery and poverty of those who lived in the slums. His presence in the City of Joy must be for other motives.

So it was that one morning, at about eight o'clock, four inspectors in Western attire and belonging to the District Intelligence Branch of the Calcutta Police (DIB) showed up at the entrance to Nizamudhin Lane. The police intrusion provoked a lively reaction. Instantly the entire neighbourhood was alerted. Dozens of people came running to the scene. Some of them had armed themselves with sticks to prevent anyone taking away their 'Father'. The Polish priest himself would have been surprised to find out about the upheaval around his person. This morning hour was the time when he had his daily dialogue with his Lord. Seated in the lotus position, his eyes closed, his breath slowed to a minimum rate, he was praying before the picture of the Shroud of Christ.

'I didn't hear the police banging on my door,' Kovalski was to recount. 'How could I have heard them? That morning, as on every other, I was deaf to any noise, deaf in order to be alone with my God, in order to hear nothing but his voice in the very depths of myself, the voice of the Jesus of Anand Nagar.'

As custom dictated, the policeman who appeared to
be in charge took off his sandals before entering the
room. He was a chubby man and his teeth were reddened
with betel. From the pocket of his shirt protruded three
ballpoint pens.

'This is where you live?' he asked in an arrogant tone,
casting a look around.

'Yes, this is it.'

The picture of the Sacred Shroud attracted the policeman's attention. He closed in on it with a look of deep
suspicion.

'Who is that?'

'My Lord.'

'Your boss?'

'If you like,' agreed Stephan Kovalski with a smile.

The policeman was obviously in no mood for
pleasantries. He scrutinized the picture closely. Doubtless he had found a piece of evidence. He summoned
one of his subordinates and ordered him to take it off
the wall.

'Where are your personal effects?' he asked.

Stephan Kovalski indicated the small metal trunk that
a Christian family had lent him to protect his Gospels,
a few medicines and the small amount of linen he possessed.

The inspector examined each item, as he searched
methodically through the contents of the trunk. A horde
of beetles made off in all directions.

'Is this all?' he marvelled.

'That's all I have.'

The man's incredulous expression wrung a certain
pity from Stephan Kovalski, who found himself wanting
to apologize for having so few possessions.

'Do you have a radio?' he asked.

'No.'

The policeman looked up to inspect the framework
of the hovel and established that there was not even an

electric light bulb. He took out a notebook and began to draw a floor plan of the room. This took quite a while because none of his three ballpoint pens would work properly.

It was then that an unexpected diversion occurred. Alerted by some of the neighbours, Bandona burst into the room, fire in her eyes. She grabbed the inspector and pushed him towards the door. 'Get out of here!' cried the young Assamese girl. 'That is a poor man sent by God. God will punish you if you torment him.'

The policeman was so astonished that he raised not the slightest resistance. Outside the mob had grown – the street was full of people.

'She's right!' a voice cried. 'Leave our "Big Brother" alone.'

The policeman in charge appeared perplexed. Then turning to the priest, he joined his hands in front of his forehead and said courteously, 'I would be very grateful if you would accompany me to the general police head-quarters. I would like to furnish my superiors with the opportunity of a short conversation with you.'

Then addressing himself to Bandona and the assembled crowd, he added, 'Don't worry. I promise to return your "Big Brother" to you by the end of the morning.'

Kovalski waved goodbye to the friends who had come to his rescue and accompanied the inspectors to the police van parked at the entrance to the slum. Ten minutes later he got out in front of a dilapidated building not far from Howrah Hospital. Four flights up a dark staircase stained with red spittle of betel chewers led to a large room cluttered with worm-eaten cupboards full of piles of official papers protected from the circling fans by scraps of old metal. Apparently it was teatime because the inspectors in the room seemed far more preoccupied with emptying their cups and chatting than studying files concerned with state security. The entry of this *sahib*

in basketball shoes disrupted their various conversations.

'This is the Polish priest who lives in Anand Nagar,' announced the policeman with as much pride as if he had been bringing in the murderer of Mahatma Gandhi.

The one who seemed to be the senior officer, a small man with greying hair, dressed in an immaculate *dhoti*, invited Kovalski to sit down in front of him. After fetching Kovalski a cup of tea, he lit a cigarette and asked, 'Do you like it in our country?'

'Enormously.'

The police officer looked thoughtful. He had a strange way of smoking. He held his cigarette between his index and his middle finger and inhaled the smoke from the cavity formed by his thumb and bent index finger. He looked as if he were 'drinking' it.

'But don't you think that our country has more beautiful things to offer a foreign guest than its slums?'

'Certainly,' agreed Kovalski, 'but it all depends on what one is looking for.'

The chief inspector inhaled another puff. 'And what might you be looking for in a slum?' he asked.

Kovalski tried to explain. Listening to himself talk, he found himself so unconvincing that he was sure he was only increasing the suspicions of his interviewers. He was wrong. In India there is so much respect for compassion for others that his explanations aroused sympathy.

'But why aren't you married?' asked an inspector with a moustache.

'I *am* married,' the Pole said. Confronted with their sceptical expressions, he elaborated, 'I am married to God.'

The policeman who had searched his room proceeded to unfold the picture of the Sacred Shroud and put it on the grey-haired senior officer's desk.

'Sir, this is what we found in his place. He claims it's a picture of his "Lord".'

The chief inspector examined the picture carefully.

'It's Jesus Christ,' explained Kovalski. 'Just after his death on the Cross.'

The man nodded respectfully.

'And this is who you're married to?'

'I am his servant,' the priest replied, not wishing to complicate the discussion.

So great is the impact of the sacred in India that Stephan saw a light of sympathy on the faces surrounding him. This time he was sure he had dispelled their suspicions.

It was then that the chief inspector sat down in his chair again. His face had hardened.

'All the same I would like to know what your connections with the CIA are,' he said.

Kovalski was so stunned by the question that he was at a loss for words. 'I have no links at all with the CIA,' he eventually managed to articulate.

There was so little conviction in his voice that the senior officer persisted.

'And you are not in contact with anyone connected with the CIA?'

Kovalski shook his head.

'And yet the majority of foreigners who purport to be social workers are CIA agents,' added an assistant with a shiny skin. 'Why should you be an exception?'

Kovalski made a supreme effort to remain calm.

'I wouldn't know whether the majority of "social workers" are CIA agents,' he said steadily. 'But I read enough spy novels when I was young to be able to assure you that it would be very difficult for a poor fellow living twenty-four hours a day in a slum to be an effective agent. And your policing is quite efficient enough for you to know that the only visits I have are from people who live in the slums. So please be good enough not to waste your time and mine with such nonsense.'

The grey-haired senior officer had listened without

stirring. By now all his colleagues had formed a circle around him and the Pole.

'Shri Kovalski, forgive me for causing all this unpleasantness,' the chief inspector apologized, 'but I have my duty to perform. So tell me a little about your connections with the Naxalites.'

'The Naxalites?' repeated Kovalski, flabbergasted.

'The question isn't quite as absurd as you appear to think,' the chief inspector added curtly. Then, more gently, he went on, 'After all, don't your Jesus Christ and the Naxalites have a number of factors in common? Don't they claim to be rebelling against the same thing? Against the injustices that repress the poor and the weak, for example?'

'Yes, indeed,' agreed Kovalski. 'But with the important distinction that Jesus Christ conducts his rebellion with love; the Naxalites murder and kill.'

'So you're against the activities of the Naxalites?' intervened the assistant with the shiny skin.

'Resolutely. Even if at the beginning their cause was a just one.'

'Does that mean you're equally opposed to the Maoists?' inquired the senior officer.

'I'm opposed to anyone who wants to achieve happiness for some by cutting off other people's heads,' said Kovalski firmly.

At this point in the cross-examination there was a little light relief. The chief inspector lit up a fresh cigarette and the office boy refilled the teacups with boiling milk. Several of the policemen made themselves up a wad of betel which turned their teeth and gums an unattractive sanguineous colour. Then the questioning continued.

'If you're not a member of the CIA, nor of the Naxalite commandos, nor of the Maoist action groups,' recapitulated the chief inspector, 'then you must be a Jesuit?'

For a few seconds Kovalski was silent, torn between anger and the desire to burst out laughing.

'If you're now trying to get me to admit that I'm a missionary,' he said eventually, 'you're wasting your time again. I'm no more a missionary than a CIA agent.'

'But you know what the missionaries did in Nagaland,' insisted the chief inspector.

'No.'

'Come, come, Shri Kovalski, you really don't know that the missionaries joined forces with the separatist movements to spur the local people into rising up and reclaiming their autonomy?'

'I can assure you that the work of the vast majority of missionaries in this country – Jesuit or otherwise – has been an action to better the lot of the people,' replied Kovalski sharply, indignant at the turn taken by the interrogation. 'What's more, you know for a fact that when people here talk about the "missionary spirit", it is often to draw attention to the work of someone who has in truth devoted himself to others, who has given only love to his Indian brothers.'

There was silence and then, suddenly, the chief inspector stood up and offered his hands to his visitor, in a gesture marked with respect. His assistant with the shiny skin did likewise and so did the others, one after another. At last they had come to an understanding.

Before accompanying the Pole back, the chief inspector pointed to the picture of the Sacred Shroud spread out on his table.

'I am a Hindu,' he said. 'But I would like to ask your permission to keep this picture as a souvenir of our meeting.'

Stephan Kovalski could hardly believe his ears. That's fantastic, he thought. The chief of the police asking me for a picture of Christ! 'It was a present and I'm very attached to it,' replied the priest, 'but I could have a photographer make up a copy for you.'

The man seemed delighted at the idea. The chief

inspector then put down in front of Kovalski a sheet of paper bearing several administrative seals.

'In exchange, here is a document that will no doubt please you. This is your resident's permit. My country is proud to welcome authentic holy men like you.'

33

She is the triumphant goddess, the destroyer of the demons of evil and ignorance, wife of the god Shiva, daughter of the Himalayas, a queen of manifold incarnations, the feminine force of the gods, alternately the symbol of gentleness and of cruelty. The Puranas, the golden legends of Hinduism, devote thousands of verses to the legendary exploits she accomplishes under a score of names, guises and attributes.

In her tender guise, she is called Ouma, light and grace; Gauri, the goddess with the light skin; Parvati, queen of the mountains; or Jagan Mata, mother of the universe. In her destructive form she takes the names of Kali the Black one, Bhairavi the Terrible, Chandi the Furious, or Durga the Unattainable. It is under this latter name and in the guise of the divine conqueror of evil that she is specially worshipped in Bengal. Every child knows her fabulous story.

Hundreds of thousands of years ago a terrible demon ravaged the earth, throwing the seasons into confusion. He was the demon of evil, in other words, of ignorance, and the gods themselves could not get rid of him. Brahma, the Creator, had declared that only a son born to the god Shiva could conquer him, but Shiva's wife was dead and he, in his grief, could give no thought to bringing a son into the world. He lived the life of an ascetic, begging in the villages for his food, like so many

others seen in the India of today, with their long hair and their bodies covered with ashes.

Meanwhile the situation on earth grew worse and in the heavens the gods lamented the fact that Shiva could not consider marrying again. The gods themselves appealed to Kama, god of love and desire, to cause love to be born in the heart of Shiva. Kama set out, accompanied by his wife, Voluptuousness, and their friend, Spring. They came to the foot of the mountain where Shiva was meditating and, at a moment when the ascetic seemed to relax his concentration, Kama released from his floral bow the jasmine arrow that no one can resist. From that moment onward, Shiva began to think of Ouma, daughter of the Himalayas, in whose body his first wife had been reincarnated. After various trials, they were married and she took the name of Parvati, 'daughter of the mountain'.

Yet the demon of evil continued to lay waste to the earth and by the time a son of Shiva was available to tackle him, it might be too late. So it was that the gods united their diverse energies in a single breath of fire and concentrated it upon Parvati who was thereby transfigured. She became the great goddess, Durga, 'she whom nothing can reach'. In order to combat the demon in the ten directions of space, she had ten arms which the gods equipped with their own weapons. Her father, Himalaya, King of the Mountains, provided her with a lion as a mount, then the moon gave her a rounded face and death her long black hair. She was the colour of the dawn.

The demon then appeared in the form of a huge buffalo accompanied by the multitudes of his army. Battle commenced. Axes, arrows and javelins hurtled through space and the roaring lion on which the goddess was mounted pounced upon the army of demons like flames upon a forest. She herself, with her armoured hands, smote her enemies, their horses, elephants and

chariots so that they crashed into a heap of chaos. The furious bellowing of the giant buffalo made the world tremble; with his horns he uprooted the mountains and hurled them at the goddess, who pulverized them with her arrows. Thus the battle raged for three days. Several times Durga was on the point of defeat. At one point, on the evening of the third day, she interrupted her onslaught to raise to her lips a cup filled with the liquid of the gods. Then, with a terrible blow, she sank her trident into the monster's chest. Mortally wounded, the monster immediately tried to abandon his body. From his mouth there issued the figure of a hero, brandishing a scimitar. At once, however, the triumphant goddess decapitated him.

It was then that she turned completely black and became known as Kali, 'the Black one', as black as time which consumes everything. Then earth and heaven resounded with cheers of joy and songs of victory.

Once a year, at the end of the monsoon, the eight million Hindus in Calcutta commemorate this victory by celebrating a four-day festival, the splendour and fervour of which are probably without equal in the rest of the world. For four festive days the city becomes a city of light, joy and hope. Preparation for the festival begins several months beforehand, in the old quarter occupied by the potters' caste, where hundreds of artisans create a collection of the most magnificent statues ever consecrated to a deity or his saints. For one whole year the craftsmen compete between themselves to produce the most colossal and most sumptuous representation of the goddess Durga. Having constructed a framework out of braided straw, the potters coat their models with clay before sculpting them to produce the desired shape and expression. Finally they complete their handiwork by painting and clothing them. Ordered in advance by families, communities, neighbourhoods, factories or workshops, these thousands of Durgas are

all destined to take their place, on the first day of the
festival, under one of the thousand canopies, known as
pandals, erected in the streets, avenues and crossroads
of the city. The construction of these canopies, and
especially their decoration, is the subject of great rivalry.

Some weeks before the festival, Stephan Kovalski
received a visit from two gentlemen who introduced
themselves as representatives of the Neighbourhood
Committee for the Construction of Canopied Shrines in
Anand Nagar. Courteous in the extreme and far too
well-dressed to be actual occupants of the slum, the
visitors showed him a notebook full of subscriptions and
invited the priest to pay them the sum allocated to him,
namely, fifty rupees. In one morning alone, they had
already collected more than a thousand rupees by hus-
tling one after another the hovels in the alleyway, including those occupied by Muslims and Christians.

Kovalski was outraged that so much money should
be squandered on a festival, while so much poverty
prevailed. He was wrong. His rational Western reaction
failed to take into account the most essential point of all:
that these people lived in a state of osmosis with their
deities. And he forgot too the role these gods played in
everyday life. Any intervention of fortune, good or bad:
work, rain, hunger, a birth, a death – in fact *everything*
was ascribed to the gods. And that is why the country's
most important festivals never commemorate historic
anniversaries, not even the glorious day of Indian Independence, but always some religious event. No other
people honours its gods and its prophets as fervently as
does the population of Calcutta – despite the fact that
the heavens often seem to have completely abandoned
the city to its tragic destiny. Every day, or almost every
day, the slum and other areas of the city resounded with
the noise of some procession bearing witness to the
mystical marriage of a people and its creator.

The previous week, Kovalski had run into a brass

band on the corner of Chitpore Road. Blocking traffic, dancers performed their contortions, calling out the name of the prophet Hussain and swirling in the sunlight curved swords above their heads. It was Moharram, the great Muslim festival that marked the beginning of the Islamic holy year. In the slum, as elsewhere in the city, all the Shi'ite Muslims changed into their festival clothes. It was a municipal holiday, one of fourteen or fifteen such holidays in the calendar of this city that was a veritable mosaic of peoples and beliefs.

Two days previously, a thunderous burst of fireworks had woken the tenant of 49 Nizamudhin Lane with a start. The several Sikh families in the slum were celebrating the birth of the guru Nanak, the revered founder of their community, born in the Punjab at the other end of India. A procession of beturbaned men, armed with their traditional *kirpans*,* went through the slums to the triumphant sound of a brass band and made for the small local *gurdwara*.† Meanwhile, from every corner of the city, other processions, accompanied by carts richly decorated with garlands of flowers, made their way to other *gurdwaras*. Inside these sanctuaries priests took turns participating in an uninterrupted reading of the Granth, their sacred book. A huge blue-and-white tent had been erected on the grass of the Maidan for a colossal feast. One of the leaders of the Sikh community in Anand Nagar, Govind Singh, a likeable giant in a scarlet turban and a taxi driver by profession, had invited the Pole to be present at the celebrations. Hundreds of the faithful came to sit on the ground in long rows, with the women in tight trousers and Punjabi tunics on one side, and the men in their pointed turbans on the other. Generous people carrying cauldrons of rice and curried vegetables passed along the rows and ladled curry onto

* Small dagger/sword, one of the five attributes of the Sikhs.
† Sikh temple.

banana leaves placed before each guest. Little girls with dark eyes made up with kohl poured tea into small baked clay bowls which would be broken after use. All day long hundreds of loudspeakers proclaimed the joy of the Sikhs from one bank of the Hooghly to the other.

On the previous day the Bara Bazar, the huge market on the other side of the bridge, had been the scene of effervescent rejoicing. Followers of the Digambara Jains sect, a reformed branch of Hinduism born about the time of the Buddha, had been celebrating the return of their pilgrimage season, marked by the official end of the monsoon. Preceded by two life-sized horses made out of white cardboard and affixed to the chassis of a Jeep, the procession carved its way through lorries, handcarts, rickshaws, indeed vehicles of every kind, inextricably entangled with a seething multitude of pedestrians. In the middle of the cortège, on a flower-bedecked float pulled by men curiously dressed in the costumes of Elizabethan lackeys, the sect's pope sat enthroned, half-naked in a golden shrine, waving to the multitudes who acclaimed him with the clash of cymbals and drums.

Of all these celebrations, however, surely none bore witness to the presence of God in Calcutta with more intensity than the Hindu *pujas* in honour of the goddess Durga. Even though with the passing of the years the festival had changed somewhat to become more of a commercial fair, it still contributed to making this city a place of faith. Nowhere was this characteristic so clearly in evidence as in the slums, at the heart of those disinherited people for whom the experts of the Ford Foundation predicted no improvement in their condition before the year 2020. In the depths of their poverty, they had managed to preserve the heritage of their traditions, and none of these traditions was more visibly expressed than the taste for celebration.

Deep in their veins flowed a dedication to festivities

that for the space of a day or a week removed them from reality. Festivities for which people went into debt or without food in order to buy their families new clothes in honour of the gods. Festivities that were a more effective vehicle for religion than any catechism. Festivities that embraced the heart and the senses with the magic of song and the ritual of long and sumptuous liturgical ceremonies.

What did it matter, therefore, that swindlers made their cut out of the sweat and hunger of the poor? In the final reckoning it was the poor who were the richer. In Anand Nagar racketeers had no qualms about obliging rickshaw cyclists and *telagarhi* pullers to pay their bit towards the shrines, or stopping lorries and buses on the Great Trunk Road to fleece drivers and passengers. Even the leper quarter at the far end of the slum did not escape the fund-raising. No one knew exactly what percentage of the manna went straight into the pockets of the collectors, but what was left for the festival was enough to create magic.

As the day approached, a kind of vibration washed through the slums. Large bamboo frames shaped like Roman triumphal arches began to pop up everywhere. Artists dressed these structures in multicoloured materials. They decorated the supports and capitals with splendid patterns, in the form of mosaics or chequered squares, giving the drapes a geometry of exemplary refinement. The shrine destined to receive the statue of the goddess was itself a sumptuous floral creation, a veritable scaffold of roses, marigolds and jasmine that embalmed the surrounding stench. Most surprising of all was the improbable panoply of accessories that came with the decorations. No *pandal* was complete without an abundance of floodlights, garlands of bulbs, lamps, and even Victorian chandeliers. Small islands of light suddenly brought to the roofs and façades a supernatural halo. Discharged by loudspeakers, songs and music

poured out over the slum, day and night, endorsing the fact that everywhere in India celebrations are accompanied by excessive noise. This concert was the signal for a ritual of purification which, in the space of a few days, would completely transform a universe of squalor.

All Hindu families and a substantial number of Muslim and Christian households set about whitewashing their hovels inside and out – their verandas, the kerbstones of the wells, and their shop fronts. The pious old Hindu who kept the tea shop opposite Kovalski's hovel took advantage of the priest's absence to repaint the façade of his room in a beautiful white that filled the entrance with light. Then followed the people's special toilet. On this unique occasion in the year, thousands of poor people exchanged their worn clothes for the carefully preserved festival attire, or perhaps even bought for the occasion by going into debt with the neighbourhood usurer. All the Calcutta traders encouraged such purchases by offering special reductions in honour of the goddess. Like film stars, the Durgas passed through the hands of an army of dressers and makeup artists, who adorned them with sumptuous clothes and jewels, before they were turned out as food for the hungry gaze of their public. The installation of statues in their shrines was the occasion for a meticulous ritual undertaken under the watchful eye of the police.

On the appointed day, at six o'clock in the evening, the plaintive sound of conches and the haunting roll of thousands of *daks*,* which down through the centuries had beaten out the *pujas* to Durga, announced the official beginning of the festival. For four intoxicating days of kermis, the slum people, like millions of others in the city, would proceed with their families in a blaze of floodlights past the four *pandals* erected in the City

---

* Large double drum, hung horizontally round the neck.

of Joy. Hindus, Sikhs, Muslims, Buddhists, Christians were all brothers, united in a dream. The men wore woollen *sherwanis** over their trousers and their wives were dressed in green silk *kurtas*, with gold earrings which gave them the air of Oriental princesses. Mehboub's elder son, Nasir, who made ballpoint pens in a workshop, his sisters, and even the little one with his stomach swollen with worms, were also made up and attired like little princes, despite the fact that, tragically scarred by their mother's disappearance, the family had sunk into wretchedness. Next to Mehboub and his children, Kovalski recognized the old Hindu from the tea shop. His forehead was decorated with the three streaks of ashes of the worshippers of Shiva. Visibly moved by his *darshan*† with the deity, oblivious of the lights and the din of the loudspeakers, he was immersed, eyes closed, in a state of bliss. The sight of this holy man at prayer reminded Stephan Kovalski of the words of the prophet Isaiah, 'The prayer of the poor and the orphaned never rises to the Lord without response.'

On the fourth day at dusk, all the statues in the City of Joy were hoisted onto illuminated carts, draped in material and flowers, to be conducted solemnly in procession, accompanied by brass bands, bagpipes, drums and conches as far as the banks of the Hooghly. At the same time, all over the city, similar cortèges were heading for the same destination. Borne on lorries, handcarts, taxis, private cars, and even cycles and hand-pulled rickshaws, thousands of Durgas descended to the river, escorted by their devout owners. One of the rickshaws caught up in this tide bore the number 1999. At every stop along the way Hasari Pal turned around to gaze at the marvellous spectacle of the goddess he was transporting on the seat of his old carriage, a Durga almost as

* A long coat closed up to the neck.
† Visual encounter with a deity or great soul.

large as life, with ten arms and magnificent black hair crowned with a golden diadem, and with the eyes of a conqueror. 'Oh dear God,' he said to himself, 'even my rickshaw has become a shrine.'

That evening hundreds of thousands of the city's inhabitants squeezed themselves onto the banks of the river; it took Hasari hours to reach the water's edge. When at last he did manage it, the members of the family who owned the statue, who had followed it in a second rickshaw, garlanded the goddess with flowers and lowered her slowly and respectfully into the water. Hasari watched with emotion as she moved away, carried along by the current. Like all the other Durgas she was bearing away, to the immense expanse of the ocean, all the joys and the hardships of the people of Calcutta.

34

It was no easy venture! After the Hindi and Urdu he had so painfully deciphered by means of a comparative study of the Gospels, Stephan Kovalski had resolved to break through his linguistic isolation once and for all. Armed with a grammar book, every morning and evening he applied himself to conquering the Bengali language. By a stroke of good fortune, at the very beginning of the work there were a number of sentences translated from Bengali into English. Assuming that the names of towns and other proper nouns would be written the same way in both languages, he identified the corresponding words and broke them down to work out a Bengali alphabet for himself. In the chapter on pronunciation, diagrams showed the position of the tongue in relation to the palate, teeth and lips for each letter. Thus the O was

pronounced with the extremity of the lips slightly open but with the mouth closed. To make the *U* sound, you had to wedge the tongue against the upper teeth. It was so complicated that he had to go to the bazaar in Howrah to buy a mirror, a piece of equipment which greatly aroused the curiosity of his neighbours. Thus equipped, he was able gradually to master the gymnastics of the innumerable aspirated letters which made people appear permanently breathless when speaking the Bengali language. These efforts also provided him with the opportunity to make a discovery. 'The image that the glass threw back at me was far from cheering. My hairline had receded badly and my cheeks were hollow. They had taken on the grey tinge of the slum.'

His sad appearance was an indication that Kovalski's Indianization was well under way. One day his neighbours recognized that the process was almost complete. It was at the conclusion of a marriage ceremony. Some Hindu friends had just married their last daughter to the son of one of his neighbours. Kovalski knelt down in front of the father and mother to do what possibly no other foreigner had done before him. He wiped the dust from their sandals and raised his hands to his forehead. This gesture was a way of saying to them, 'Since my little sister has married my little brother, you are my parents. I have become a member of your family.'

That evening Kovalski went to the jeweller-usurer in the alleyway. He showed his metal cross with the two dates – the ones of his birth and his ordination – and asked him to engrave underneath them the word 'Premanand' he had chosen to be his Indian name. In Bengali, Premanand meant 'Blessed is he who is loved by God'. He asked the jeweller to leave a space next to the inscription, so that he could engrave, when the time came, the third most important date in his life. For that very day Kovalski had taken an extraordinary step, a step that was quite incomprehensible to Indians convinced that

nothing could change the condition given to them at birth, except death and another life.

He had been to an office in the Home Ministry to fill in the forms, asking the government of India for the honour of becoming officially one of the race of the poor in the City of Joy. He had applied for Indian citizenship.

Ashish and Shanta Ghosh, the young Hindu couple on the Committee for Mutual Aid, interrupted Kovalski one evening when he was engaged in one of his linguistic miming sessions in front of his mirror.

'Father, we've got some news for you,' said the boy, fretfully rubbing his beard. 'You'll be the first to know.'

Kovalski invited the visitors to sit down.

'We've decided to leave the slum soon and go back to our village.'

From beneath her red veil, Shanta watched for the priest's reaction.

'Dear God,' thought Kovalski, 'this is the greatest thing I've heard since I arrived in the City of Joy. If people actually start making their way back to their villages, we're saved!' He could not conceal his joy.

'What's made you . . . ?'

'For three years now we've been saving up pice after pice,' Shanta went on. 'And we've been able to buy two acres of good land near the village from a Hindu who was marrying off his daughter.'

'We're going to have a big pool dug out in the middle, to breed fish,' her husband explained.

'And the water will provide us with a second harvest in the dry season,' added Shanta.

Kovalski sensed that he was witnessing a kind of miracle, the miracle of which thousands of starving people compelled to take refuge in Calcutta dreamed.

'Shanta will go first with the children,' said Ashish. 'She will sow and pick the first crop of rice. I shall stay

here to earn a little more money. If the first harvest is adequate, I shall leave too.'

The young woman's beautiful dark eyes glowed like embers.

'But, above all,' she said, 'we want our return to bring something for the people of our village, something that will be like a breath . . .'

'Of fresh air,' said her husband. 'The Bengal earth could yield three harvests if it were properly irrigated. I shall try and form a cooperative.'

'And I shall start up a craft workshop for the women.'

His eyes half-closed, his mirror on his knees, Kovalski listened in wonder. 'May God bless you,' he said at last. 'For once light and hope will spring forth from a slum.'

35

The receptionist burst into the room without knocking.

'Monsieur le Consul, there is an Indian lady outside who insists that she wants to speak to you urgently. She says that in the slum where she lives a Polish missionary is dying of cholera. She says this missionary holds a French passport. This is why she has come to our consulate. He's refusing to allow himself to be taken to a clinic. He wants to be treated like all the others . . .'

Sixty-two-year-old Antoine Dumont, complete with his bow tie and rosette of the Légion d'honneur, was the representative of the French Republic in Calcutta. Ever since Louis XV's filibusters had come to these latitudes to tickle British supremacy and set up their warehouses, France had maintained a consulate in one of the old blocks in the neighbourhood of Park Street.

The diplomat scratched his moustache and stepped out into the corridor that served as a waiting room.

Thirty years of postings in Asia had accustomed him to putting up with many an annoyance occasioned by his compatriots or holders of French passports. Hippies, drug addicts, easy riders, deserters, tourists who'd been robbed: he had never begrudged any of them assistance and support. Nevertheless, this was undoubtedly the first time he had received an SOS concerning an ecclesiastic who was dying 'voluntarily' of cholera in the depths of an Indian slum.

The previous evening Shanta and Margareta had discovered Kovalski lifeless in his room. He was lying, completely drained, in the middle of his own vomit and excreta. It was just as if his insides had been eaten up by some invading parasite. His muscles had collapsed and his skin, stretched over his bones, looked more like parchment. He was conscious, but so weak that any effort to talk risked extinguishing the little life still burning in him.

The two Indian women had instantly diagnosed his illness: a lightning form of cholera which, oddly enough, showed a predilection for more robust constitutions.

Kovalski had felt the first symptoms of it during the previous night, when painful stomach cramps had sent him rushing to the latrines several times. Despite the heat, he had begun to shiver. Next he had felt a tingling sensation in the tips of his hands and feet, followed shortly afterwards by a general twitching of his muscles. His feet and legs turned a curious bluish colour. The skin of his hands dried up, before wrinkling and hardening. Although sweating profusely, he grew colder and colder. He felt the flesh of his face shrink over his cheekbones, then across his nose, his forehead, as far as his skull. It was more and more difficult for him to close his mouth and eyes. His body was racked with spasms. He began to vomit. His breathing became jerky and painful. He made an effort to drink but nothing, not even a few drops of water, would clear his throat which felt as if

paralysed. At about four or five in the morning, he could no longer feel his pulse. That was when he sank into a kind of torpor.

When he awoke, he wanted to get up to go back to the latrine, but he had not the strength to stand up, or even to kneel. He had to let himself go right there where he was. Soon he told himself he was going to die. The idea brought with it no fear. On the contrary, in his extreme weakness he experienced a kind of euphoria.

The two Indian women interrupted what he would later call 'a delicious sensation of tiptoeing towards nirvana'. Neither Shanta nor Margareta, however, felt disposed to let their 'Father' die without a fight. Margareta seized the bowl and sprinkled the sick man's face and torso to moisten his skin. Her first concern was to check dehydration, but the Indian woman knew that only an immediate infusion with plasma had any chance of stopping the disease. They must get the priest to an intensive care unit without delay.

'Hang on, Stephan *Daddah*,' she begged, as she moistened his face with a corner of her veil. 'We're going to take you to Bellevue.'

Every inhabitant of Calcutta, even the poorest of the poor, knew the name of the luxurious private clinic set among palm trees in the Park Street neighbourhood. There Bengal's medical élite operated on and nursed rich *marwaris*, senior government dignitaries and members of the colony of foreigners, in conditions of hygiene and comfort comparable to those of a Western establishment. Margareta knew that the Bellevue clinic would not refuse to take in her 'Father'. He was a *sahib*.

A grimace contorted Kovalski's face. He wanted to speak but had no strength to do so. The Indian woman bent over him. She realized then that he was refusing to leave his room. He wanted 'to be cared for like the poor here'. Stephan Kovalski had known dozens of men

struck down by cholera in the City of Joy. They stayed where they were. The toughest survived; the others died. During the monsoon the number of cases increased. Because of lack of space, medicines and doctors, the hospitals almost invariably turned them away. For him there was no question of being given privileged treatment.

Confronted by this unexpected resistance, the two women went to confer with their neighbours. It was decided that the rector of the church should be alerted. He was the only one, they thought, who might be able to persuade his fellow priest to allow himself to be transported to the Bellevue clinic. Father Cordeiro gave them a somewhat reserved reception and immediately dismissed any idea of his intervening personally with Kovalski.

'I can see only one solution,' he said. 'And that's to inform the Polish consul. Or better, the French consul, since Kovalski holds a French passport. After all, the person concerned is one of those for whom he's responsible. Only he can oblige that stubborn foreigner to let himself be cared for in the normal fashion. Or at least he can try.'

Margareta was designated as emissary. So effectively did she convince the diplomat of the urgent need for his intervention, that a grey Peugeot 504 decorated with a tricolour pennant pulled up at the entrance to Anand Nagar that very afternoon. The appearance of the car caused such a sensation that Antoine Dumont had difficulty squeezing his way through the crowd. Turning up his trouser bottoms, he ventured into the muddy alleyway. On two or three occasions, discomforted by the smells, he was compelled to stop and wipe his face and neck. Despite his long experience, he had never before penetrated into quite such a setting. 'This priest must be completely mad,' he repeated to himself, as he tried to avoid the puddles. On reaching the shrivelled

body in the depths of the hut, he volunteered with an enthusiasm that was slightly forced:

'Good day, Reverend! I bring you the respectful greetings of the French Republic. I am the French consul in Calcutta.'

Stephan Kovalski opened his eyes with difficulty.

'To what do I owe the honour?' he inquired feebly.

'Didn't you know that a consul's primary duty is to look after the citizens under his jurisdiction?'

'I'm very grateful to you, Monsieur le Consul, but I have no need of your concern. I have enough friends here.'

'It is precisely those friends who alerted me. Because your state of health requires . . .'

'Repatriation?' interrupted Kovalski, suddenly discovering a little energy. 'Is that what you came here to suggest to me? Repatriation for medical reasons? You really shouldn't have gone to so much trouble, Monsieur le Consul. I thank you for your kindness but beg you to save yourself unnecessary expense. The poor of the slums are not eligible for "repatriation".'

He let his head sink back and closed his eyes. The sharpness of his tone had not eluded the diplomat. 'This priest is a tough nut,' he thought to himself.

'At least agree to let yourself be cared for in a good clinic.' He sought after words that would convince. 'Think of all that your life can give your friends. And of the vacuum your death would undoubtedly leave behind you.'

'My life is in God's hands, Monsieur le Consul. It is for him to decide.'

'I'm quite sure that it is because he has decided that you should be cured that I find myself here,' argued the diplomat.

'Perhaps,' agreed Kovalski, touched by the logic of this argument.

'In that case, I beg you to allow your friends to transport you to . . .'

'To a hospital for everyone, Monsieur le Consul, not to a clinic for the rich.'

Dumont sensed that he was halfway there. A little patience and Kovalski would allow himself to be convinced altogether.

'The better the treatment you have, the sooner you'll be able to continue your activities.'

'My desire is not to continue my activities, Monsieur le Consul, but to be sure of being able to look at the people around me without shame.'

'I understand. But let me reassure you that not a single rupee will be taken from the poor to pay for your hospitalization. The consulate will cover any expenses.'

Kovalski sighed; the conversation had exhausted him.

'Thank you, Monsieur le Consul, but it isn't a question of money. For me it's a matter of respecting a commitment freely undertaken. This illness is providential. I implore you not to insist.'

A spasm shook the sick man. Antoine Dumont considered the inanimate body and wondered for a moment if he were dead. Then he noticed the irregular wheeze of the priest's breathing.

Outside in the alleyway, Ashish and Shanta, Bandona, Margareta, Aristotle John, Saladdin, old Surya, Mehboub, and numerous other neighbours were waiting anxiously. When the diplomat emerged, they all closed in.

'Well?' asked Margareta.

The consul adjusted his bow tie.

'Only half a victory! A clinic is out of the question, but he's agreed to go to "a hospital for everybody". That's his expression. I think we should respect his wishes.'

As soon as the diplomat had left, Margareta loaded Kovalski onto a rickshaw and took him to the City

Hospital, one of Bengal's capital's main medical centres. With its carefully manicured lawn, pool, fountain and bougainvillaea walk, the establishment offered rather fine surroundings. A red sign in the emergency wing pointed to a vast building, the doors and windows of which were nearly all broken. Margareta was tempted to ask the rickshaw puller to turn back. Even the most painful visions of the City of Joy had not prepared her for the shock of the sights that awaited her: bloodstained dressings strewn about the corridors, broken beds serving as rubbish bins, mattresses bursting open and crawling with bugs. Wherever you went you found yourself treading on some form of debris. Worst of all, however, were the people who haunted the place. The severely ill – suffering from encephalitis, coronary thrombosis, tetanus, typhoid, typhus, cholera, infected abscesses, people who had been injured, undergone amputations or been burned – were lying everywhere, often on the bare floor.

Margareta eventually managed to dig out a bamboo stretcher on which she installed the unconscious Kovalski. Since no one came to examine him, she slipped a note into the hand of a male nurse to procure a bottle of serum and a syringe which she, herself, inserted into the patient's arm. Then she asked for anti-cholera drugs. Like so many other establishments, however, the City Hospital was short of medicines. The press frequently denounced the pilfering that went on in hospitals which kept in business numerous little pharmacies outside its walls.

'I'm thirsty . . .'

Kovalski opened his eyes to the nightmare world of this 'hospital for everybody'. There was neither a jug nor water at the patient's bedside. From time to time a boy came around with a waterskin. He charged fifty pice a cup (3 pence). At the end of the corridor were the latrines. The door had been torn off and the drain was

blocked. Excrement had spilled over and spread into the corridor, much to the delight of the flies.

Hundreds of sick people jostled with each other daily outside the doors of establishments such as this, in the hope of receiving some form of treatment, of obtaining a place in a bed – or on the floor – in order at least to be able to eat for a few days. There was the same crush almost everywhere. In some maternity wings it was perfectly possible to find three mothers and their babies bedded down on a single mattress, a situation which sometimes caused the asphyxia of newborn babies. Regular press campaigns condemned the negligence, corruption and theft that paralysed certain hospitals.

In the hospital where Stephan Kovalski was, a costly 'cobalt bomb' had remained out of use for months because no one would take the responsibility for spending the six thousand eight hundred rupees necessary to have it repaired. Elsewhere a cardiac resuscitation unit was closed because of the lack of air-conditioning. In yet another hospital the two defibrillators and ten out of the twelve electrocardiograph machines had broken down, as had half the bedside monitors. Oxygen and gas cylinders for sterilization were lacking nearly everywhere. 'The only piece of equipment that seems to function properly, but then again, only when there are no power cuts, is the apparatus for electric shock treatment in Gobra Mental Hospital,' one newspaper reported. It had not been possible to open the new surgical wing at one large hospital simply because the Health Service had not yet approved the nomination of a lift attendant. The lack of technicians and plates nearly everywhere meant that most patients had to wait four months for an X-ray and weeks for any analysis. At a hospital near the Sealdah Station, eleven out of twelve ambulances were broken down or abandoned, with their roofs smashed in, their engines stolen, and their wheels stripped. In many operating units, the containers of forceps, scalpels, clips and

catgut were nearly empty, their contents having been stolen by staff members. The few instruments that actually remained were rarely sharp. The catgut was frequently of such poor quality that stitches burst. In many places reserve blood supplies were virtually nonexistent. In order to procure the precious liquid before an operation, patients or their families sometimes had to resort to those specialist racketeers with whom Hasari Pal had already been dealing. Such parasites found in the hospitals idyllic opportunities for self-enrichment. Some of them accosted the sick (especially poor people who had come up from the country) when they arrived, promised them immediate hospitalization or a medical examination in exchange for some money. Others passed themselves off as bona fide doctors, luring their victims into consulting rooms manned by nurses who were partners in complicity. They then asked the women to hand over their jewels in preparation for an X-ray and vanished.

In some hospitals the pilfering of food intended for patients had assumed such proportions that meals had to be transported in padlocked carts. In spite of these precautions, large quantities of food and milk were regularly diverted to the innumerable tea shops that had set themselves up in the vicinity of the hospitals. Sugar and eggs were systematically spirited away to be resold on the spot at prices twice as low as in the market. The newspapers revealed that such pilfering was not confined to food. Some establishments had no more doors or windows. At night, treatment had to be given by candlelight: all the electric light bulbs had disappeared.

As is often the case in India, however, the best fortunately mixed with the worst. In all these establishments there was also a network of people who bonded together to dispel isolation, anonymity, horror. A few mattresses away from Kovalski lay a poor fellow who, following an accident, had undergone one of the most delicate and

daring operations of modern surgery, a spinal fusion of
the rachis involving the grafting of the vertebral column.
Day by day, Kovalski followed his progress. In a
communal ward that was sordid in so many other aspects, that man was the object of admirable care and
attention. Each morning the nurses got him up and
helped him gradually regain the use of his legs. Every
time he did his rounds, the heavily overburdened surgeon would find the time to examine and to talk with
him, demonstrating as much solicitous concern as com-
petence. A few beds further on, a mother squatted on
the floor beside her baby's cradle. The child was suffering
from meningitis. No one would have thought of preventing the poor woman from remaining with her infant, and the people in charge of the food never went
past without offering her also a bowl of rice.

Highly surprised to discover that they had a *sahib* as a
companion in their hardship, several patients dragged
themselves over to ask Stephan to decipher the bits of
scrap paper used for prescriptions. This was an occasion
for Kovalski to marvel at the conscientiousness and
precision with which some of the overburdened doctors
prescribed their treatment for even the most anonymous
of their patients.

Nothing was ever totally rotten in this inhuman city.

The priest would no doubt have been most indignant at
what Margareta had done. She had just slipped twenty
rupees into the nurse's hand to get him a bed underneath
a fan. There was nothing unusual about this: patients
were constantly being turned out of their pallets to be
replaced by the purveyors of baksheesh.

Without the bottles of serum, medicines, and food
that the indomitable Indian woman brought him each
day, the Pole might well have died. She had organized
a collection in the slum and all the poor people had

contributed to the saving of their 'Big Brother'. Mehboub's children had gone along the railway lines picking up cinders. Surya, the old Hindu from the tea shop, had donated several bags of sweetmeats. The mother of Sabia, the child who had died of tuberculosis in the room next door, had cut out and stitched a shirt for *Daddah* Stephan. Even the lepers had given up the proceeds of several days' begging. Stephan Kovalski had failed: in his affliction he had not been able to be a poor man like his brothers of the slum.

36

Calcutta had never seen such a spectacle: thousands of rickshaws abandoned all over the city. The strike – the first great strike of the last human horses in the world – paralysed the town's most popular means of transport. 'But striking is a rich man's weapon,' Hasari acknowledged regretfully. 'Fine resolutions don't last long when your belly's gripped with the cramps of hunger and your head's as empty as a skin discarded by a cobra. Those brutes, the owners, knew that only too well. They knew we would crack. After only two days some of our comrades picked up their shafts again. Others followed. Soon we were all back on the road chasing after clients, even doing bargain-rate runs just to get something to eat right away. And we were forced to pay the new rent. It was very hard. But fortunately something always crops up in this city to stop you from crying too much over your lot.

'When I first made the acquaintance of my colleague Atul Gupta, I rubbed my eyes several times. I couldn't help wondering whether, instead of waiting for a client on the corner of Russell Street, I wasn't actually watching

a film, for Atul Gupta looked like a hero straight out
of a Hindu film. He was a handsome fellow, with a
well-groomed black moustache, carefully combed hair,
full cheeks, and the look of a conqueror. He was dressed
in a colourful shirt and proper *sahib*'s trousers, and –
what was even more incredible – he was wearing socks
and shoes, real shoes that enclosed the foot, not junk
plastic sandals. Yet there was something even more
surprising about him: he was sporting a gold watch on
his wrist. Can you imagine, a rickshaw puller wearing
a gold watch?

'I had seen films where heroes disguised themselves
as rickshaw *wallahs*, but that was in the movies. Gupta
was real. No one knew where he came from. It's true
that in Calcutta you lived alongside people about whom
you knew nothing, whereas in our village, everyone had
known each other for generations. Only one thing was
certain about Gupta: he must have been to school a
lot because he was more knowledgeable than all the
Brahmins in Calcutta put together. No one could recite
the Ramayana quite as he could. He was a real actor. He
would sit down anywhere and start to recite poetry.
Instantly a little group would form around him and in a
few seconds he would make us forget the cuts on our
feet, the cramps in our stomachs, the heat – everything.
He used to cast a spell over us. He had an amazing
way of personifying Rama, then Sita, then the terrible
Ravana, all in turn. We could have listened to him
for hours, days, nights, while he transported us over
the mountains, across the seas and the sky. Afterwards the rickshaw weighed less heavily. In a matter
of months Gupta became a hero among the pullers
of Calcutta. How had he come to finish up in the
skin of a poor fellow like me? The answer remained
a mystery.

'Some people claimed he was a spy, others that he was
a political agitator. He lived in a boarding-house in Free

School Street frequented by peculiar people, foreigners who went barefoot and wore necklaces and bangles around their ankles. Word had it that those people injected themselves with drugs and smoked, not *bidis* but the *bhang* that transports you to nirvana. In any case, Gupta himself didn't go barefoot and I never saw him with a cigarette between his lips. He worked as hard as any of us. At dawn he was always the first to arrive at the stand on Park Circus and he was still trotting around long after nightfall. It must be said that he didn't have years of working with an empty stomach behind him like the other pullers. His engine was still running nicely. But like the rest of us, he had no licence for his rattletrap. In Calcutta a good baksheesh would buy you the keys to paradise.

'In any case, licence or no licence, Gupta must have had some good days because women used to fight with one another to get into his rickshaw. No doubt they thought they were being pulled along by Manooj Kumar.* But then in our line of business it's better to be taken for the poorest of poor devils than to look like a film star. The more you stood out from the crowd, the more people kept tabs on you.'

One day when he was taking two young girls back to their house in Harrington Street, the handsome Atul Gupta was to experience the truth of these words for himself. A rubbish cart had broken down in the middle of the carriageway and the whole street was blocked. Gupta tried to bypass the obstruction by going onto the pavement, but a policeman intervened. There followed a violent altercation between Gupta and the policeman, who made no bones about hitting Gupta several times with his *lathi*. Furious, Gupta put down his shafts and hurled himself at the policeman. The two men rolled on the ground in a savage scrum. Eventually the policeman

* A famous Indian film star.

ran to get reinforcements and a crew of police rushed to capture the puller and seize his rickshaw.

When the police finally released him at noon the next day, Atul Gupta was just a mass of flesh and blood. They had beaten him all night and burned his chest with cigarettes. They had hung him from a hook, first by his arms, then by his feet, and whipped his body with a bamboo cane. It wasn't only because he had fought with one of their men that they punished him, but also because of his clean trousers, his shirt, his *sahib*'s shoes and his gold watch. A slave had no right to be different from all the other beasts of burden.

Not content with having beaten him, the police registered a complaint against Atul Gupta before the judges at the Bonsal Court, Calcutta's municipal court. On the day of the trial, the rickshaw pullers gave their comrade a proper guard of honour. Since he could hardly walk, they put him in one of their carriages decorated with flowers. 'He was just like a maharajah or a statue of Durga, our friend,' Hasari Pal was to recall, 'except that he had bandages on his arms and legs, and his eyes and face looked as if they had been painted with kohl, his features were so marked with bruises.'

The Bonsal Court was an old brick building on the other side of Dalhousie Square, in the centre of town. In the courtyard, at the foot of a great banyan tree, stood a small temple. The pullers helped Gupta get down in front of the altar decorated with portraits of Shiva, Kali and the Monkey god Hanuman because he was very religious and wanted to have a *darshan* with the deities before facing his judges. Hasari took hold of his hand to help him strike the clapper of the bell suspended above the altar. Gupta recited a few *mantras*, then placed a garland of flowers around the trident of Shiva.

On the pavement all along the railings, a crowd was squeezed in between a double row of vendors. The warm air intensified the smell of hot oil and frying. Further

away, in the entrance to the courtyard, people were lining up for public writers, who squatted behind type-writers. Inside the courtyard, others were having coco-nuts cut open or drinking tea or bottled drinks. There were even beggars on the steps up to the audience chambers. What was most striking of all, however, was the constant coming and going. People went in, came out, stopped to talk. Accused men went past chained to policemen. Legal men in black tailored jackets and striped trousers talked among themselves and to the prisoners' families.

Gupta and his friends went into a vestibule that smelled of mildew. Women were breast-feeding their babies on benches. Some people were in the middle of eating, others were asleep on the bare floor, wrapped up in a piece of *khadi*.

Someone informed Gupta that he must go and find himself a lawyer. At the end of a long dark corridor, there was a room full of them. They were seated behind small tables under fans that scattered their papers about. Gupta chose a middle-aged man who inspired confi-dence. He was wearing a shirt and tie under a black jacket as shiny as the surface of a pool in moonlight. The defending counsel led his client and escort to a staircase that stank of urine. At the turn of every landing, judges were dictating their opinions to clerks who typed them out with one finger.

The small troop at last arrived in a great chamber. A faded photograph of Gandhi decorated one wall. The back of the room was furnished with a pyramid of old metal trunks, which contained thousands of pieces of evidence used in the course of countless trials: knives, pistols, all kinds of weapons and stolen goods. In the middle of the chamber, benches were arranged in rows in front of a platform. On the platform were two tables and a cage linked to a tunnel of iron railings which ran right across the room. 'I had seen a tunnel like that once

before in a circus,' Hasari Pal was to recount. 'It was used to convey tigers and panthers into the ring.' Here it was used to bring prisoners before their judges. Atul Gupta did not have to use it because he was appearing before the court as a free man.

The room was soon completely full of rickshaw pullers drinking tea and smoking *bidis* as they awaited the arrival of the court. Gupta sat before the platform on a bench beside his counsel. Eventually two men in rather grimy *dhotis* made their entrance. They were carrying under their arms files bulging with papers, and they moved with an air of boredom. They were the clerks. One of them clapped his hands, ordering that the two great fans suspended from the ceiling be set in motion. The machines were so worn that their blades took a while to start up, like two vultures who, having just devoured a carcass, couldn't quite manage to take off.

A door opened at the back of the room and the judge entered. A very thin man with a sad expression behind his glasses, he was wearing a black robe trimmed with fur. Everyone stood up, even Gupta, who had great difficulty in remaining upright. The judge sat down in the ceremonial chair in the middle of the platform. The accused and his friends could hardly make out his face behind the volumes of the Indian penal code and the files that covered the table. He had hardly settled himself when a pigeon perched itself on one of his books and attended to its own particular needs. A clerk mounted the platform to wipe away the droppings with a corner of his *dhoti*. Several families of pigeons had built their nests in the heaps of files and the trunks at the back of the chamber.

A small figure, likewise dressed in a black robe, had entered behind the judge. He was so cross-eyed that it was impossible to tell whether he was looking to his right or left. He was the PP – the public prosecutor. Below, to the left of the platform, stood a police officer.

As Hasari Pal was to say, 'It was just as if they were getting ready to play a scene from the Ramayana with lots of characters.'

One of the clerks began to read out the charge accusing Atul Gupta of having assaulted the policeman in Harrington Street. The judge had taken off his glasses, closed his eyes and sunk back in his chair. All that could now be seen of him was his bald head, which gleamed above the heaps of files. When the clerk had finished, the judge's voice was heard asking Gupta's defence counsel what he had to say. Then Hasari saw the rickshaw puller place his hand on his lawyer's shoulder, to prevent him from standing up. Gupta wanted to conduct his own defence.

In the space of a few minutes he gave such a detailed account of the brutality to which he had been subjected that the entire room began to sniff and weep. The PP and counsel for the prosecution then intervened, but there was no real point. The judge too was sniffing behind his mounds of books and papers. Gupta was found not guilty and acquitted. Furthermore, the judge ordered that his rickshaw be restored to him.

The hearing had lasted less than ten minutes. 'The longest part of it was our applause,' Hasari was to say. 'We were proud and happy for our friend.'

News of Gupta's acquittal spread like wildfire among the city's rickshaw pullers. Scarface and Golam Rassoul, the pillars of the rickshaw pullers' union, suggested that an enormous demonstration be organized immediately outside the Writers' Building, the seat of the Bengal government, to protest against the police violence. Rassoul alerted the leaders of the *telagarhi wallahs*, the handcart pullers' union. They jumped at the chance: rickshaws and *telagarhis* were the scapegoats of the Calcutta police.

The procession set off from Park Circus in the early afternoon. Left-wing party leaders had provided

streamers, banners and red flags, so that it looked like a field of red marigolds on the move. In front, seated in a rickshaw decorated with flowers and red streamers, rode the hero of the day, pulled by men who took turns doing a hundred yards between the shafts. It was carriage number 1999 that had the honour of transporting him, the jalopy between the shafts of which Hasari Pal had sweated, suffered and hoped for four years.

Along the route hundreds of handcart pullers came to join the procession. Traffic was brought to a standstill and soon the paralysis stretched as far as the suburbs. This time the inhabitants watched the demonstrators pass without astonishment. Never before had a cortège marched past with so many flags and streamers. The Communists had sent their team, armed with loud-speakers. The leaders shouted and chanted slogans which the pullers repeated at the tops of their voices. It took more than three hours to reach Dalhousie Square. The police had barricaded the approaches to the government building with vans, lorries, and hundreds of men in khaki, armed with guns. The long red brick façade studded with statues was protected by more policemen.

The column had to stop at the barricade. A police officer in a flat cap stepped forward and asked the men at the head of the procession if they wished to convey a message to the Prime Minister's secretariat. Atul Gupta replied that the organizers of the demonstration demanded to be received by the Prime Minister in person. The officer said that he would pass on the request. The party leaders took advantage of the ensuing wait to give voice to fiery speeches against the police; they shouted revolutionary slogans.

After a few minutes the officer returned to announce that the Prime Minister agreed to receive a delegation of four rickshaw pullers. Rassoul and Gupta together with two other union members were authorized to cross the barrier. When they came back half an hour later, they

exuded an air of satisfaction, especially Gupta. He announced through a loudspeaker that the Prime Minister and the chief of police had given their assurance that there would be no recurrence of police brutality. Applause and cheers greeted the news. Gupta added that he had personally received a solemn promise that the policemen who had ill-treated him would be punished.

There was a fresh round of acclamations. Gupta, Rassoul and the two other delegates were then decorated with garlands of flowers. 'We felt as if something that was of great significance for us had just occurred,' Hasari Pal was to say. 'We could take leave of each other happily and in peace. Tomorrow would mark the beginning of better days.'

The procession broke up without incident. Rickshaw *wallahs* and *telagarhi wallahs* returned to their homes. Gupta climbed back into Hasari's rickshaw. They and a few friends went to a drinking place in Ganguli Street to celebrate their victory with some bottles of *bangla*. It was just as they were leaving the bar that Hasari heard a dull sound like that of a bursting bicycle tyre. Gupta uttered a cry, his head flopped onto his chest, then his whole body crumpled against the shafts. Hasari saw that he had a hole in his head, just above his ear, from which the blood had begun to flow. Gupta tried to say something, then his eyes turned completely white.

'Our enemies had avenged themselves. They had robbed us of our hero.'

37

A little colony had installed itself in the far reaches of the slum, in an area bounded by the railway tracks. From the outside nothing distinguished it from other quarters

in the slum. The same compounds in the form of a square around a courtyard were to be found there, with the same sort of laundry drying on the roofs and the same open drains. Yet this was a ghetto of a very particular kind. No other occupants of the slum ever ventured there, for it was in this place that the City of Joy's six hundred lepers lived, squeezed ten or twelve together in each room.

India numbers about five million lepers among its population. The horror and fear inspired by disfigured faces, hands and feet reduced to stumps, and wounds at times infested with vermin, condemned the lepers of Anand Nagar to total segregation. Although they were free to go about the slum, an unspoken code forbade them to enter the houses or compounds of the healthy. By having gone to Stephan Kovalski's room, the cripple Anouar had transgressed the rule, and the infraction could have cost him his life. There had already been several lynchings, although more out of fear of the evil eye than out of fear of contagion. Though they would give alms to lepers to improve their own *karma*, most Indians looked upon leprosy as a malediction of the gods.

In the heart of the leper colony, a hut made out of bamboo and dried mud provided shelter for a few mattresses. In this hovel lay a number of refugees from the pavements of Calcutta, who had come to the end of their Calvary. One of these was Anouar.

'That man too had a smile that was difficult to understand in the light of his suffering,' Stephan Kovalski was to say. 'He never uttered the slightest complaint. If ever I ran into him by chance in an alleyway, he would always greet me in a voice resonant with joy.

'"Well, Stephan *Daddah*, are you well today?"

'Coming from a human wreck grovelling in the mud, the question seemed so incongruous that I hesitated before replying. I had formed the habit of stooping down

to him and grasping the stump of his right hand with my hands. The first time I did it the gesture took him so much by surprise that he surveyed the people around him with an expression of triumph, as if to say, "You see, I'm a man just like you. The *Daddah* is shaking my hand."'

Stephan Kovalski knew that Anouar had reached the advanced stages of his illness and was going through utter torment. There was nothing more that could be done for him since the disease had reached his nerves. When the pain became too intolerable, he used to have himself carried to 49 Nizamudhin Lane where the priest gave him a shot of morphine. Kovalski had managed to procure some vials of it from the hospital in Howrah. He kept them for desperate cases.

The day after one of these injections Kovalski encountered Anouar in one of the alleyways. He looked unusually preoccupied.

'What's wrong with you, Anouar?' asked the Pole, concerned.

'Oh nothing, Stephan *Daddah*, I'm fine. But my neighbour, Saïd, is not too good. You ought to come and see him. He's so ill he can't eat or sleep.'

The cripple creeping along in the filth asked nothing for himself. Worried only about his neighbour, he was the living message of the Indian proverb, 'To hell with misery as long as we are miserable together.'

Stephan Kovalski promised to come that afternoon.

It was a journey into sheer horror. What the priest discovered was not so much a leper colony as a kind of ossuary. Were those skeletons consumed with gangrene, whose closed eyes were covered with white mushrooms, really human beings? Those breathing corpses whose cracked skin oozed out a yellowish liquid? Even so the sight was nothing by comparison with the stench. 'I had

never smelled anything like it. A mixture of decay, alcohol and incense. You needed to have Hope with a big H well anchored in the bottom of your heart to withstand it.' Squatting among the rubbish and excreta, children played marbles, with great shrieks of laughter. Kovalski had no difficulty in identifying Anouar's friend. Saïd was a man of barely forty, left with no hands and no feet. Leprosy had also eroded his nose and eaten away his eyebrows. Anouar performed the introductions. Saïd turned his blind face towards the priest and Kovalski thought he detected a smile on it.

'Stephan Big Brother, I'm fine,' he assured him. 'You shouldn't have taken the trouble to visit me.'

'It's not true,' corrected Anouar, shaking his mop of hair, 'you're in a lot of pain.'

Kovalski took hold of his arm and examined the stump. The wound was greenish in colour and maggots were crawling over the bone. Saïd too was beyond all treatment. Kovalski filled a syringe with morphine and looked for a vein beneath the hard, cracked skin. He could do nothing more.

Nearby, a woman was stretched out on a rough bed with a baby lying next to her. The child was a bouncing boy. An allergic reaction to her medicines had covered the mother's face with swellings and pustules. It was a common phenomenon and one that was so traumatic that many lepers refused any kind of treatment. The poor woman's body was concealed by a piece of cloth pulled up to her chin. Kovalski bent over and picked the child up in his arms. He was amazed at the force with which the boy's little hand gripped his finger.

'He's going to be a big fellow,' he promised the mother. The leper woman turned away. Kovalski thought he had hurt her.

'Here, you take him. He's yours and shouldn't be away from you.'

An interminable moment passed. The mother made

no move to take her son. She was crying. Eventually
she pushed back the sheet and held out her arms. She
had no fingers.

Kovalski placed the child carefully at her side. Then,
joining his hands in the Indian gesture of salutation, he
left without a word. Outside, a host of cripples, blind
men and limbless people awaited him. They had all come
running to receive a *darshan* from the 'Big Brother', who
had dared to enter their lair. 'They too were smiling,'
the priest was to say. 'And their smiles were neither
forced nor suppliant. They had the smiles of men, the
bearing of men, the dignity of men. Some of them
clapped their maimed hands to applaud me. Others
jostled with each other to get near to me, to escort me,
to touch me.'

Anouar led the visitor to a compound where four
lepers were playing cards, squatting on a mat. His arrival
interrupted them but he begged them to continue their
game. This proved to be an opportunity for him to
witness a juggling act worthy of the most celebrated
circus. The cards flew about between the palms of their
hands before tumbling to the ground in a ballet punctuated with laughter and exclamations.

In a neighbouring compound, beggar musicians performed a concert for him on flutes and drums. Everywhere he went in the leper colony, people came out of
their hovels. His visit was turning into a fête. 'Outside
the door to one shack, a grandfather who was almost
blind thrust in my direction a three-year-old boy he had
just adopted. The old man used to beg in front of
Howrah Station. One morning this child sought refuge
with him, like a dog lost without a collar. That same
old man who didn't have enough to feed himself every
day, and who would never be cured, had taken the
boy under his wing.' A little further on, Stephan was
awestruck by the sight of a small girl massaging, with
fingers that were still intact, the chubby body of her

little brother as he lay in her lap. Anouar led the way, propelling himself along on his plank on wheels, with a fervour that was redoubled by his pride at acting as guide for his 'Big Brother Stephan'.

'Stephan *Daddah*, come and sit over here,' he ordered, gesturing to a mat made out of jute sacks sewn together that a woman had just unrolled for him in one of the courtyards. Several lepers scrambled to settle themselves next to him. That was when he realized that he was being invited for a meal.

'I thought I had come to terms with everything about poverty, yet I felt revolted by the idea of sharing food with the most bruised of all my brothers,' Stephan was to admit. 'What a failure! What lack of love! What a long way I still had to go!' He hid his uneasiness as best he could and very soon the warmth of the lepers' hospitality dispelled it. Women brought metal bowls full of steaming rice and vegetable curry, and the meal began. Kovalski did his utmost to forget the fingerless hands battling with balls of rice and pieces of marrow. His hosts seemed overwhelmed with joy, wild with gratitude. Never before had a foreigner shared their food. 'Despite my heaving stomach, I wanted to show my friendship for them,' he would explain, 'show them that I wasn't afraid of them. If I wasn't frightened of them it was because I loved them. And if I loved them it was because the God with whom I lived and for whom I lived loved them also. These people needed more love than anyone else. They were pariahs among the pariahs.'

His generosity of heart did not, however, prevent Kovalski from feeling a certain indignation that men could allow themselves to be reduced to such a state of physical decline. He was well aware that leprosy was not a fatal disease. Provided it was treated in time, it was even quite easily cured and left no after-effects. It was that day, confronted by the horrible sight of so much mutilation, that he made his decision. He would set up

a leprosy dispensary in the City of Joy, a proper place with specialists who knew how to cure the disease.

Next day Stephan Kovalski climbed aboard the bus that went across the Hooghly. He was going to the south of Calcutta to lay his plans before the only person in the city who could help him to implement them.

38

Like a flower straining towards the sun, the sugarloaf-shaped dome of the temple of Kali surfaced from the imbroglio of alleyways, residences, hovels, stores and pilgrims' rest houses. This high place of militant Hinduism, built near a branch of the Ganges, on the banks of which the dead were burned, was the most frequented shrine in Calcutta. Day and night crowds of the faithful swarmed inside and around its grey walls. Rich families, their arms laden with offerings of fruit and food wrapped in gold paper; penitents dressed in white cotton, leading goats to the sacrifice; yogis in saffron robes, their hair tied up and knotted on the crowns of their heads, the sign of their sect painted in vermilion on their foreheads; troubadours singing canticles as plaintive as sighs; musicians, tradesmen, tourists; the motley throng milled about in an atmosphere of festivity.

This is also one of the most congested places in the overpopulated city. Hundreds of shops surround the temple with a string of multicoloured stalls. There is something of everything sold here: fruit, flowers, powders, imitation jewels, perfumes, devotional objects, gilded copper utensils, toys, and even fresh fish and caged birds. Above the antlike activity hovers the bluish mist of the funeral pyres and the smell of incense mingled with burning flesh. Numerous funeral cortèges wend

their way between the cows, the dogs, the children
playing in the street and the flock of faithful worshippers.
At the temple of Kali, the most vibrant life goes hand
in hand with death.

Around the corner from this sanctuary stands a long,
low structure with windows obstructed by plaster latticework. There is no door in the imposing sculpted
porchway. Anyone can enter at any time. A wooden
board announces in English and Bengali: 'Municipality
of Calcutta, Nirmal Hriday – the Place of the Pure
Heart – Home for Dying Destitutes.'

Stephan Kovalski had reached his destination. He
mounted the few steps and went into the building. An
indefinable smell which even disinfectants could not
obscure floated around. Once his eyes had grown accustomed to the dimness, he made out three rows of litters
with thin green mattresses, squeezed in tightly side by
side. Each one had a number painted in front of it.
Shadowy shapes moved silently between the rows. On
the beds lay fleshless bodies stretched out in various
postures of agony. In a second room, rows of similar
beds were provided for women.

What struck Kovalski immediately was the serenity
of the place. There was no horror here. No longer were
the wretched people who had come together in this place
tormented with anguish, solitude, destitution or neglect.
They had found love and peace.

The one hundred and ten occupants of the Place of
the Pure Heart owed that peace to the staunch little
woman in a white cotton sari with a blue border, whom
Stephan Kovalski spotted leaning over a dying man at
the far end of the room. India and the world were
beginning to recognize the name of this saint who for
some years now had been revolutionizing the practice
of charity. Newspapers and magazines had popularized
the nun who picked up abandoned children and dying
destitutes from the streets of Calcutta. Her work had

already spread beyond the frontiers of India, and nations had awarded her their highest distinctions. Her name was Mother Teresa and she had just turned fifty-four years of age when Stephan Kovalski walked in to meet her.

Despite her sturdiness, she looked older. Her face was already furrowed with deep wrinkles, her bent form bore witness to years of self-sacrifice and sleepless nights.

Agnes Bojaxhiu was born in Skopje, Yugoslavia, of Albanian parents. Her father was a prosperous merchant. She was attracted to the life of a missionary in India at a very early age. At eighteen, taking the name of Teresa in memory of the little Flower of Lisieux, she entered the Missionary Order of the Loreto Sisters and, on January 20, 1931, she stepped off a steamship onto the quay at Calcutta, then the largest city in the Empire after London. For sixteen years she taught geography to the daughters of well-to-do British and Bengali society in one of the most prestigious convents in Calcutta. One day in 1946, however, during a train journey to Darjeeling, a town on the slopes of the Himalayas, she heard a voice. God was asking her to leave the comfort of her convent, to go and live among the poorest of the poor in the vast city beyond. Having first obtained permission from the Pope, she changed into a plain white cotton sari and founded a new religious order whose vocation was to relieve the misery of the most neglected of men. In 1950, the order of the Missionaries of Charity was born, a congregation which thirty-five years later would have two hundred and eighty-five houses and several thousand charitable foundations throughout India and all the other continents, including countries behind the Iron Curtain. The home for the dying which Kovalski had just entered was born out of a particularly moving encounter experienced one evening by Mother Teresa.

It was in June 1952. The monsoon cataracts were beating down upon Calcutta with a noise that seemed to herald the destruction of the world. A white figure, stooping under the deluge, was skirting the walls of the Medical College Hospital. Suddenly she stumbled upon something stretched out on the ground. She stopped and discovered an old woman lying in the middle of a pool of water. The woman was hardly breathing. Her toes had been gnawed to the bone by rats. Mother Teresa scooped her into her arms and ran to the door of the hospital. She found the emergency entrance, went into a reception room, and deposited the dying woman on a stretcher. Instantly an attendant intervened.

'Take that woman away immediately!' he ordered. 'There's nothing we can do for her.'

Mother Teresa took the dying woman in her arms and set off again at a run. She knew another hospital, not far away. Suddenly, however, she heard a rattle. The body stiffened in her arms and she realized that it was too late.

Putting down her burden, she closed the poor creature's eyes and made the sign of the cross as she prayed beside her in the rain. 'In this city, even the dogs are treated better than human beings,' she sighed as she turned away.

The next day, she rushed to the municipal building and besieged its offices. The persistence of this European nun in a white cotton sari was a source of considerable astonishment. One of the mayor's deputies finally received her. 'It's a disgrace that people in this city are forced to die in the streets,' she declared. 'Give me a house where we can help the dying to appear before God in dignity and love.'

One week later the municipality placed at her disposal a former rest house for Hindu pilgrims, next to the great Kali temple. Mother Teresa was overjoyed. 'This is God's doing. The place is ideally situated. It is to the

precincts of this sacred spot that the destitute come to die, in the hope of being cremated on the temple pyres.' At first the intrusion of a nun dressed in a white sari and adorned with a crucifix, in a neighbourhood wholly consecrated to the worship of Kali, provoked curiosity. Gradually, however, orthodox Hindus became indignant. The word spread that Mother Teresa and her Sisters were there to convert the dying to Christianity. Incidents broke out. One day a shower of stones and bricks rained down upon an ambulance bringing the dying to the home. The Sisters were insulted and threatened. Eventually Mother Teresa dropped to her knees before the demonstrators.

'Kill me!' she cried in Bengali, her arms outstretched in a gesture of crucifixion. 'And I'll be in heaven all the sooner!'

Impressed, the rabble withdrew, but the harassment continued. Local delegations presented themselves at the town hall and the general police headquarters to demand that the 'foreign nun' be expelled. The chief of police promised to satisfy their demands but insisted upon first making his own inquiries. He made his way to the home for the dying and there found Mother Teresa kneeling at the bedside of a man who had just been picked up off the street, a skeletal figure lying there in a state of indescribable filth, with his legs swollen with purulent sores. 'Dear God,' he wondered, 'how ever can she put up with that?' Mother Teresa cleansed the horrible wounds, applied antibiotic dressings, and promised the unfortunate man that he would get better. Her face was bathed in an extraordinary serenity and the chief of police found himself strangely moved.

'Would you like me to show you around?' she asked him. 'No, Mother,' he excused himself. 'That won't be necessary.'

As he emerged from the building, the neighbourhood's young fanatics were waiting for him on the steps.

'I promised you that I would expel this foreign woman,' he told them. 'And I will do so on the day that you persuade your mothers and sisters to come here and do what she is doing.'

The battle was not won yet. During the days that followed, troublemakers continued to throw stones. One morning Mother Teresa noticed a gathering of people outside the Kali temple. As she drew near to them she saw a man stretched out on the ground with upturned eyes and a face apparently drained of blood. A triple cord denoted that he was a Brahmin, one of the priests from the temple. No one dared to touch him. They knew he was suffering from cholera.

She bent over, took the body of the Brahmin in her arms, and carried him to the home for the dying. Day and night she nursed him, and eventually he recovered. One day he was to exclaim, 'For thirty years I have worshipped a Kali of stone. But here is the real Kali, a Kali of flesh and blood.' Never again were stones thrown at the little Sisters in the white saris.

News of this incident spread throughout the whole city. Every day, ambulances and police vans brought the suffering to Mother Teresa. 'Nirmal Hriday is the jewel of Calcutta,' the nun was to remark one day. The jewel was granted the protection of the city itself. The mayor, journalists and many eminent people rushed to visit it. High-caste ladies came to offer their services and tend the dying with the Sisters. One of these was to become a great friend of Mother Teresa.

Amrita Roy, at thirty-five, was rich, beautiful and powerful. Her uncle, Dr B. C. Roy, a man with heart, was none other than the chief minister of Bengal, an associate who would smooth out many an obstacle in a city where every aspect of life was an ordeal: the climate, pollution, overpopulation and, above all, bureaucracy. Like Stephan Kovalski, Mother Teresa sometimes had to spend days in customs warehouses retrieving from

petty officials crates of medicines and boxes of powdered milk sent by friends around the world.

Taking in dying destitutes, however, was only a first step for Mother Teresa. The living too needed care, and among the most neglected of the living were the newborn babies that might be found one morning on a rubbish heap, in a gutter or in the doorway of a church.

One day 'the hand of God' directed Mother Teresa to the portals of a large unoccupied house on a road very near the place where her congregation had made its home. On February 15, 1953, 'Shishu Bhavan', the Children's Home, welcomed its first guest, a premature baby wrapped in a piece of newspaper, picked up from the pavement. He weighed less than three pounds and had not even the strength to suck at the bottle Mother Teresa gave him. He had to be fed with a nasal tube. The nun persisted and won her first victory in this new haven of love and compassion. Soon several dozen babies were bundled together in cots and playpens. Five or six more arrived every day. Her Sisters and good Father Van Exem, her confessor, were worried. How was she going to provide for so many people? Together with the occupants of the home for the dying, there were now several hundred mouths to feed.

Her response to this question was an all-illuminating smile. 'The Lord will provide!'

Sure enough, the Lord did provide. Gifts poured in. Rich families sent their chauffeurs with cars full of rice, vegetables, fish. One evening Mother Teresa encountered the man who had given her a room in his house in the very earliest days.

'It's wonderful,' she announced to him jubilantly, 'I've just obtained from the government a monthly grant of thirty-three rupees for a hundred of our children.'

'From the government!' repeated the man with compassion. 'I really feel sorry for you. Because you've no idea what a bureaucratic mess you'll be forced into.'

True to this prediction, six months had not gone by before a meeting was held in the government building. A dozen bureaucrats in *dhotis* examined the nun's account books. They asked questions, quibbled over details and criticized. Exasperated, Mother Teresa stood up. 'You think you can demand that I spend thirty-three rupees on the children you sponsor,' she exclaimed indignantly, 'when I can spend only seventeen on our other children who are by far the more numerous. How can I spend thirty-three rupees on some and seventeen on others? Who could do a thing like that? Thank you, gentlemen, but I will do without your money.' And she left the room.

In a city already overwhelmed by too high a birthrate, she declared war on abortion. She had her Sisters draw and put up posters announcing that she would take in every child that was sent to her. Under the cover of night, pregnant girls came to ask her for a place for their prospective babies.

The angel of mercy was constantly flying to the rescue of some new group of needy people. After the dying and the abandoned children, it was the turn of those most wretched of all creatures, the lepers. At Titagarh, a shantytown in an industrial suburb of Calcutta, she constructed, on land lent by the railway company, a building of rough bricks and corrugated iron, in which she harboured the worst cases, bringing them dressings each day, medicines and words of comfort. Soon hundreds of patients stormed the gate to this oasis of love.

Titagarh was only a beginning. Next she dispatched teams of Indian Sisters out into the city, their mission being to open seven more dispensaries. One of them set herself up in the slum where Mother Teresa had first tended the poor. Lepers flocked there in hordes. An employee at the town hall who lived in the vicinity protested against such unpleasant neighbours and threatened to alert the authorities. Eventually Mother

Teresa was compelled to give in. But, as always, she knew how to make the best of her defeat.

'What we need,' she announced to her Sisters, 'are mobile clinics.'

Several small white vans bearing the emblem of the Missionaries of Charity would one day patrol the enormous city to bring treatment to the most neglected areas.

It was one of these vehicles that Stephan Kovalski wanted to bring into Anand Nagar. Even better, he hoped two or three of Mother Teresa's Sisters would come to assist him in the running of the little leper clinic he planned to set up in the former Muslim school next to the buffalo sheds in the City of Joy. That was why he had come to see Mother Teresa.

He made his way between the rows of bodies and approached the kneeling figure. The nun was bathing the wounds of a man who was still young but who was so thin that he looked like one of the living dead discovered by the Allies in the Nazi concentration camps. All his flesh had melted away. Only his skin remained, stretched taut over his bones. The woman was speaking softly to him in Bengali.

'I shall never forget that man's expression,' Kovalski was to say. 'His suffering was transformed into surprise, then peace, the peace that comes from being loved.' Sensing a presence behind her, Mother Teresa stood up. She did not fail to notice the metal cross the visitor was wearing on his chest.

'Oh Father,' she excused herself humbly, 'what can I do for you?'

Stephan Kovalski felt awkward. He had just interrupted a conversation in which he identified something unique. The eyes of the dying man seemed to be imploring Mother Teresa to bend over him once more. It was deeply touching. The priest introduced himself.

'I think I've heard people talk about you!' she said warmly.

'Mother, I've come to ask for your help.'

'My help?' She pointed a large hand towards the ceiling. 'It's God's help you want to ask for, Father. I am nothing at all.'

At that point a young American in jeans came along carrying a bowl. Mother Teresa called him over and drew his attention to the dying man.

'Love him,' she ordered. 'Love him with all your might.' She handed the young man her tweezers and cloth and left him, steering Stephan Kovalski towards an empty area with a table and bench between the room for men and the one for women. On the wall was a board bearing a framed text of a Hindu poem which the priest read aloud.

> *If you have two pieces of bread,*
> *Give one to the poor,*
> *Sell the other,*
> *And buy hyacinths*
> *To feed your soul.*

The Pole outlined his plan for a leper clinic in the City of Joy.

'Very good, Father, very good,' commented Mother Teresa in her picturesque accent, a mixture of Slavonic and Bengali. 'You are doing God's work. All right, Father, I'll send you three Sisters who are used to caring for lepers.'

Her gaze strayed over the room full of prostrate bodies and she added, 'They give us so much more than we give them.'

A young Sister came over and spoke to her in a low voice. Her presence was needed elsewhere.

'Goodbye, Father,' she said. 'Come and say Mass for us one of these mornings.'

Stephan Kovalski was overwhelmed. 'Bless you, Calcutta, for in your wretchedness you have given birth to saints.'

39

The situation was growing steadily worse. Terrifying bottlenecks immobilized the flow of traffic more and more frequently. At certain times, advancing just one step was quite a feat. The roads in the city centre were frequently jammed with trams deprived of electricity, broken-down lorries with radiators steaming, double-decker buses with broken axles or even turned over on their sides. Hordes of yellow taxis with their paintwork in shreds forced forward to the clamour of horns. Buffalo carts and hand-pulled carriages creaking beneath enormous loads, and hosts of coolies carrying mountains of merchandise on their heads, tried to move across the engulfing tide. Everywhere swarms of pedestrians competed with rickshaws for a share of asphalt in streets disrupted by frequent burst water pipes or drains. Everything seemed to crack and crumble a little more with each passing day.

'There were clients, too, who pricked you in the stomach with the point of a knife and demanded the day's takings,' Hasari Pal was to recount. 'Drunkards who paid you with their fists, *gurdas* and prostitutes who vanished without settling up for the ride, elegant *memsahibs* who cheated you out of a few pice.'

One day Hasari asked the *munshi* to add to his money invoice a short message for his father in the space reserved for correspondence: 'We are well. I am earning my living as a rickshaw puller.' His chest swollen with pride at having been able to make this gesture for those

who expected everything of him, he hurried back to the pavement where he was camping with his wife and three children. He had an important piece of news to announce to them.

'Wife!' he called out as soon as he saw Aloka, crouched down, cleaning out the neighbouring woman's tin can. 'I've found us a place in a slum!'

A slum! For peasants used to a daily bath in a pool, the cleanliness of a hut and the healthy food of the countryside, the prospect of living in a slum, with no water, no drains, and sometimes no latrines, offered little to be joyful about. Still, anything was better than the pavement. There, at least, a few bits of cloth and sheet iron placed on four crates would furnish them with something resembling a lodging place, a precarious shelter to ward off the next winter and, a few months later, the excesses of the monsoon.

The shantytown, where Hasari had foraged out their thirty square feet of space, was situated right in the middle of the city on an extension of the great Chowringhee Road which skirted the Maidan park. Its foundation dated back to the time of the war with China, when thousands of refugees from the north descended upon Calcutta. One day a few families had stopped on the ground between two roads, put down their miserable bundles, set up a few stakes and stretched out some bits of cloth between them as a shield against the sun. Other families had joined this initial nucleus, and so the small encampment had become a shantytown, right in the heart of a residential area. No one raised any objections to it – neither the municipal authorities, nor the police, nor the owners of the land. The city was already pock-marked throughout with similar patches of misery, places where several hundred uprooted people lived, sometimes without so much as a drinking water point. Some of these little islands had existed for a whole generation. Not everyone, however, was quite so dis-

interested in the squatters. No sooner had a newcomer
installed himself on his square of mud or concrete than
someone set about fleecing him. That was one of the
stupefying things about the extortion business conducted
by the Mafia, with the cooperation of certain authorities.
It was a strictly indigenous 'Mafia' which had no reason
to envy its famous Italo-American model.

Even before he had moved in, Hasari received a visit
from a small, shady-looking man who claimed to represent the 'owner' of the colony – in other words, the
local godfather. Every time a handful of refugees stopped
somewhere to set up some kind of shanty, the Mafia
representative would turn up armed with a bona fide
demolition order issued by the city authorities. The
squatters then found themselves confronted with a
choice between paying regular rent or purchasing the
plot. For his thirty square feet Hasari Pal was forced to
pay out fifty rupees in 'key money' and a monthly rent
of twenty rupees payable in advance. The bloodsuckers
did not, however, confine their racket merely to collecting rents and other 'residential taxes'. Their control
extended, in fact, to all aspects of life in the slum. Being
the only local authority, the Mafia set itself up as the
'protector' of the population. In a way its claim was
true. The Mafia intervened whenever a conflict required
arbitration, or at election times by distributing a host of
favours in exchange for votes: ration cards, a lead off
the water pipes, the building of a temple, the admission
of a child into a government-run school.

Anyone who dared to question the legitimacy of this
underground power was punished without mercy.
Every now and then shanties caught fire. Sometimes a
whole neighbourhood went up in flames. At other times
a body was recovered, riddled with stab wounds. This
omnipresent dictatorship manifested itself in many and
various ways. Sometimes directly, as was the case in
Hasari's slum, where several Mafia representatives lived

right there. In other tenements planted in the vicinity of
a construction site, a distillery, a rubbish dump or a
quarry, the Mafia ruled via the manager or the owner
of the enterprise. These intermediaries exercised absolute
power over the inhabitants because the latter depended
on them for their daily bowl of rice. Elsewhere, it was
through committees and associations that it imposed its
law. These organizations were little more than cover-
ups. Whether they were religious in nature or represented a caste or a place of origin, they all provided
the Mafia and its political connections with the ideal
means by which to infiltrate the very depths of the slum
population. Thus it was no longer a simple matter of
rent and taxes. The Mafia meted out justice even within
the family unit. It fixed the level of fines, collected
donations for religious festivals, negotiated marriages,
divorces, adoptions, inheritances, dished out excom-
munications – in short it managed everyone's rites and
practices from birth to death inclusively: no Muslim
would ever find a place in a cemetery, no Hindu have
himself cremated, without paying a cut to the Mafia.

The Pals' departure from their pavement occurred
discreetly under cover of night. No sooner had they
piled their meagre possessions into the rickshaw and
turned the corner of the avenue, than a new refugee
family moved in to take their place.

40

The drama erupted just as Stephan Kovalski was coming
out of the latrines. He heard shouts and saw a mob of
children and adults charging towards him. At once a
deluge of stones and missiles rained down all around the
little public convenience, only narrowly missing the

priest. He leaped backwards only to discover the target of all the fury: a wretched woman in rags, with dishevelled hair and a face stained with blood and grime. Her eyes were full of hatred, her mouth was foaming and she was emitting animal sounds as she flailed her fleshless hands and arms about her. The more insults she uttered, the more the mob set upon her. It was as if all the latent violence in the slum was exploding at once: the City of Joy wanted to have a lynching! The Pole tried to rush to the rescue of the unfortunate woman but someone grabbed him by the shoulders and pushed him backwards. They were about to close in for the kill. Men were getting their knives out. Women urged them on with their clamouring. It was dreadful to see.

Suddenly, however, the priest saw a little grey-haired man brandishing a stick surface from the crowd. He recognized the old Hindu who kept the tea shop opposite him. Swinging his stick about, he rushed to the woman's side and, shielding her with his frail figure, turned on her aggressors.

'Leave this woman alone!' he shouted to them. 'God is visiting us.'

The rabble came to a halt, transfixed. The yelling stopped abruptly. All eyes were turned upon the frail figure of the elderly Hindu.

After a few seconds that seemed more like an eternity to Kovalski, he saw one of the assailants, armed with a knife, approach the old man. Having reached him, he prostrated himself, placed the weapon at his feet, and went through the motions of wiping the dust from his sandals and touching his forehead with it as a mark of respect. Then he stood up, turned on his heels and walked away. Others followed his example. In a few minutes the mob had disappeared.

The old Hindu went over to the mad woman who was looking at him like an animal run to earth. Slowly, delicately, with the tail of his shirt, he wiped the excreta

and blood from her face. Then he helped her up and, supporting her around the waist, led her away down the alleyway towards his tea shop.

It was quite some time before Kovalski came to know the history of that lover of justice and bearer of the luminous name of Surya, or Sun. Three years previously the hands that now handled bowls of tea and kettles had fashioned balls of clay thrown on a stone wheel. Between the fingers of the old Hindu in the course of their circuits those balls on the potter's wheel would be transformed into goblets, pots, cups, dishes, religious lamps, vases and even the gigantic six-foot-high vases used at weddings. Surya had been the potter for Biliguri, a large borough with about a thousand inhabitants, one hundred and twenty miles north of Calcutta. His ancestors had been village potters since time immemorial. The role of the potter formed as intimate a part of community life as that of the Brahmin priest or the moneylender. Every year, in every Hindu family, the pots were ceremonially broken; also they were broken every time there was a birth, as a mark of welcome to the new life, and every time there was a death, to allow the deceased to leave for the afterlife complete with his plates and dishes. They were also broken on the occasion of a marriage; in the bride's family because, by leaving, the young woman died to the eyes of her family, and in the groom's family because the arrival of the young wife meant the birth of a new household. Again, they were broken to mark numerous festivals because the gods wanted everything on earth to be new. In short, a potter was never in danger of being out of work.

Apart from Surya and his two sons who worked with him, there were only seven other artisans in the village. Their workshops all opened out on to the main square. There was a blacksmith, a carpenter, a basket maker

who also made traps and snares, and a jeweller who had his own design for what were called 'savings necklaces'. Whenever a family had saved up a little money, the women would rush to have one or two silver links added to their necklaces. There was also a weaver, a cobbler and a barber whose particular talents lay less in his skill in looking after his fellow villagers' hair than in ensuring the happiness of their offspring, for it was he who was the official matchmaker. Finally, on either side of Surya's workshop were two stores: that of the grocer and that of the confectioner. Without the latter's *mishtis*, sweetmeats that were sweeter than sugar, no religious or social ceremony could ever be properly observed.

Towards the end of the monsoon that year, there occurred in Biliguri one of those incidents that appear quite insignificant. Nobody, therefore, took much notice of it at the time. Ashok, the weaver's eldest son who worked in Calcutta, came back to the village with a present for his wife – a pail made out of plastic as red as hibiscus. Cut off as they were in the countryside, people had never seen a utensil like that before. The light supple material out of which it was made provoked general admiration. It was passed from hand to hand with wonder and envy. The first person to really understand the usefulness of this new object was the grocer. Less than three months later, his store was decorated with similar buckets in several different colours. Goblets, dishes and gourds subsequently arrived to further enrich his collection. Plastic had conquered a new market. At the same time it had mortally afflicted another craftsman in the village.

Surya watched his clientele rapidly diminish, and in less than a year he and his sons had foundered into destitution. The two boys and their families set out on the path to exile and the city. Surya himself tried to resist. Thanks to the solidarity of his caste, he found work about thirty miles away in a village not yet caught up in the plastic fever. The virus was on the rampage,

however, and soon all the villages in the area were contaminated.

Then the provincial government gave a manufacturer from Calcutta a grant so that he could construct a factory. One year later every potter in the region was ruined.

Surya had no recourse but to embark also upon the road to Calcutta. With him he took his wife, but the poor woman suffered from asthma and could not cope with the shock of urban pollution. She died after only a few months, on the corner of pavement where they had made their home.

After his wife's cremation on one of the pyres on the banks of the Hooghly, the potter wandered for some time beside the river, completely at a loss. About one mile from Howrah Bridge he noticed a man on the riverbank, filling a basket with clay. Surya started up a conversation with him. The man worked in a potters' workshop on the edge of the City of Joy, where they made the handleless cups used as teacups that were broken after use. Thanks to this miraculous encounter, the very next day Surya found himself squatting behind a wheel making hundreds of the small receptacles. The workshop supplied numerous tea shops scattered throughout the alleyways of the City of Joy.

One day the old Muslim who kept the tea shop in Nizamudhin Lane was found hanging from a piece of bamboo in the framework. He had committed suicide. Surya, who no longer felt physically able to do prolonged manual work, went to see the proprietor of the shop and obtained the concession for it. Ever since then he had been intoning his 'Oms' and heating his kettles of milky tea on a *chula* that filled the alleyway with smoke from one end of the day to the other. The old Hindu was such a good and holy man, however, that the residents of Nizamudhin Lane forgave him for the smoke.

Shortly after his arrival, Stephan Kovalski had re-

ceived a visit from his neighbour. The old man had
entered the priest's room with his hands pressed together
at the level of his heart. Despite the fact that the Hindu's
mouth was almost devoid of teeth, his smile warmed
the Pole's heart and he invited him to sit down. For a
while they remained there, surveying each other in
silence. 'In the West,' Kovalski was to note, 'people's
gazes barely brush over you. That man's eyes revealed
his entire soul.' After about ten minutes, the Hindu
stood up, joined his hands together, bowed his head and
left. He came back the next day and observed the same
respectful silence. On the third day, at the risk of shattering a delicate mystery, the priest inquired as to the
motive for his silence.

'Stephan *Daddah*,' he replied, 'you are a Great Soul
and in the presence of a Great Soul words are not
necessary.'

Thus it was that they became friends. In the midst of
the Muslim families that surrounded the Pole, the Hindu
became a kind of life raft to which Stephan could cling
whenever he lost his footing. Establishing a bond with
Hindus was indeed easier. For them God was everywhere: in a door, a fly, a piece of bamboo and in the
millions of incarnations of a pantheon of deities, in which
Surya considered Jesus Christ naturally had his place in
the same way as Buddha, Mahavira and even Muhammad. For them, these prophets were all avatars of the
Great God who transcended everything.

41

The city of Miami, Florida, lies approximately eight
thousand miles west of Calcutta. In reality, however,
the immensity of the gulf separating these two cities

would be better measured in light-years. Certainly, Miami possesses slums almost as poverty-stricken as those of Calcutta: its black ghetto and its miserable shantytowns built by refugees from Cuba and Haiti on its south-western fringes. During the 1970s, burglaries, armed robberies, muggings, rapes, a whole array of violent crimes engendered by drug addiction, a dismal poverty and a bleakness born of despair became such commonplace events in Miami that only the most outrageous among them inspired the city's headline writers. So great was the psychosis of fear gripping parts of the city that many residents preferred to move to safer suburbs or even emigrate to less troubled parts of the United States.

For all the poverty of its slums, no such psychosis of physical insecurity has ever overwhelmed the citizens of Calcutta. With the exception of the brief period of Naxalite terrorism, the people of Calcutta have never had to go out fearing for their physical safety or their property. Fewer violent crimes are committed each year in the vastly overpopulated capital of Bengal than are committed in downtown Miami alone. Fear is by and large a stranger to Calcutta's streets. A young girl can walk along Chowringhee Road or any of the city's other main thoroughfares in the middle of the night without the slightest fear of being attacked. An elderly woman can carry home a day's shopping down any of the main Calcutta streets without listening for a mugger's tread.

Side by side with its slums and its shantytowns, Miami, the city that proudly describes itself as the gateway to the American South, also harbours islands of wealth and luxury far beyond the wildest imagining of any inhabitant of Calcutta, even its most privileged residents whose feet have never ventured inside a slum. One such enclave was called King Estates. It was a vast marina nestling among elegant palm trees and clusters of jacaranda, a haven for multimillionaires and their

sumptuous villas. Most houses had swimming pools, tennis courts and private docks from which cabin cruisers and yachts, some almost the size of ocean liners, rode the bright blue sea. Several properties had heliports, others polo fields with stables to accommodate several dozen horses. A high iron grille sealed off this little island of privilege. Armed private guards, their patrol cars equipped with searchlights and sirens, prowled the enclave night and day. No one entered King Estates, even on foot, unless he or she possessed a magnetic pass whose code was changed weekly, or was personally inspected and cleared by one of the estate's guards.

It was a prison for the wealthy and one of its most distinguished inmates was a highly reputable Jewish surgeon called Arthur Loeb. His Mexican hacienda with its luminescent white walls, its patios, its fountains and its colonnaded cloisters, was among the estate's showpieces. Loeb was a giant of a man, his red hair barely flecked by grey, who was given over to four passions: police novels, deep-sea fishing, ornithology, and his luxurious one-hundred-and-forty-bed Bel Air Clinic where he treated diseases of the respiratory system with techniques that were at the cutting edge of medical science.

Married for twenty-nine years to Gloria Lazar, the blonde and gentle daughter of one of the pioneers of talking films, Loeb had two children: Gaby, twenty, a sparkling brunette studying architecture at the Miami College of Fine Arts, and Max, twenty-five, like his father a red-headed giant covered in freckles. Max was about to receive his diploma from the Tulane University Medical School in New Orleans. In two years, after he had completed his internship, he intended to specialize in thoracic surgery. He was a source of enormous pride and happiness to his father. Not only was he following in the elder Loeb's professional footsteps, his decision to specialize in chest surgery seemed to promise that the

direction of Loeb's Bel Air Clinic would one day pass
into his hands.

'Professor, I'm leaving the country.'

There was no mockery in the title 'professor'. His
children had given Arthur Loeb that affectionate nickname the day he had stepped onto the podium at Colum-
bia University to receive an honorary degree of Professor
of Medicine.

Arthur Loeb reined in his horse and turned to face his
son.

'What do you mean, you're leaving the country?'

'I'm going to India for a year.'

'To India? And what about your internship?'

'I've asked for a deferment.'

'A deferment?'

'Yes, Professor, a deferment,' repeated Max, trying
with difficulty to remain calm.

His father let out the reins. The horses set off at a slow
trot.

'And to what do we owe this surprise?' his father
asked after their horses had advanced several paces.

Max pretended not to notice the irritation lurking
behind the question.

'I need a change of air . . . and I want to be of service
to someone.'

'What do you mean "you want to be of service"?'

'Just that. To help people who need help.' Max knew
he couldn't go on beating around the bush much longer.
'I've been invited to fill in for someone in a dispensary,'
he said.

'Where in India? After all, India is a large place!'

'Calcutta, Professor.'

The word stunned Arthur Loeb so much that he
lost his stirrups. 'Calcutta! Of all places, Calcutta!' he
repeated, shaking his head.

Like many other Americans, Loeb felt very little sympathy for India. His dislike turned into downright revul-

sion when it came to Calcutta, a city synonymous for
him with misery, beggars and people dying on the city's
pavements. How many television programmes had he
seen, how many magazine articles had he read, in which
all the tragedies of Calcutta had been set before him in
lurid detail! Even more, however, than the spectre of
famine, over-population and poverty, it was the image
of one man in particular that provoked the surgeon's
special aversion to the world's largest democracy. It was
the face of a man with arrogance and hatred giving the
world lessons in morality from the rostrum of the United
Nations. Like so many Americans, Loeb recalled the
diatribes of Krishna Menon, India's envoy to the United
Nations in the 1950s, with an uncontrolled rage. A
dangerous visionary he had seemed, a kind of high priest
spitting out his venom all over the West in the name of
the values of the Third World, values which he claimed
were being strangled by the white man.

'Is that the best place you can find to exercise your
talents?' asked a bewildered Arthur Loeb. 'And do you
really think, you poor naïve creature, that your friends
are going to keep a place warm for you? By the time
you get back, they'll all have their diplomas and you'll
find yourself in with a new group who won't do you
any favours, believe me.'

Max made no reply.

'Does your mother know?'

'Yes.'

'And she approves?'

'Not exactly . . . but in the end, she seemed to understand.'

'And Sylvia?'

Sylvia Paine was Max's fiancée, a beautiful, tall blonde
girl of twenty-three, a healthy, athletic American girl.
Her parents owned the property next to the Loebs in
King Estates. Her father was the owner of the *Tribune*,
one of Miami's daily newspapers. She and Max had

known each other since they were children. They were
due to marry in June after his exams.

'Yes, Professor. She knows,' replied Max.

'And what does she think of the idea?'

'She suggested she come with me!'

Six weeks after their conversation, Max Loeb flew off
to Calcutta. Like the good sports they were, his parents
had given a farewell party in his honour. The invitation
cards stipulated that Max Loeb was going to spend a
sabbatical year of study and reflection in Asia. Asia was
a vast place and Max had agreed not to reveal his exact
destination to anyone, so as not to invite any disagreeable
comments from the small colony of multimillionaires of
King Estates. Naturally he spent his last evening in
America with his fiancée. He took her to dinner at
the Versailles, a fashionable French restaurant in Boca
Raton. There, he ordered a bottle of Bollinger, his
favourite champagne, and she proposed a toast to the
success of his mission and his earliest possible return.
Sylvia was wearing a very low-cut pink linen dress with
a simple string of pearls around her neck. Her hair,
caught up in a chignon and pinned with a shell comb,
revealed the nape of her neck and the superb bearing of
her head. Max could not take his eyes off her.

'You're so beautiful,' he said, 'how am I going to
manage without you?'

'Oh, you'll find plenty of beautiful Indian girls. People
say they are without equal in the world. They say they
even know how to prepare special drinks that make you
fall madly in love with them.'

Max thought of the slum Stephan Kovalski had described in his letter, but the idea of arousing Sylvia's
jealousy was not altogether unpleasant.

'I'll do my best to master their techniques so that I can
make you even happier,' he said with a wink.

He was joking. Max knew too well that beneath Sylvia's beautiful exterior there lay a private and modest nature. Poetry was her great passion. She knew thousands of verses by heart and could recite works of Longfellow, long extracts from Shelley, Keats, Byron, and even Baudelaire and Goethe. Although they had been lovers ever since their high school days (it had first happened on Max's father's cabin cruiser during an expedition to catch swordfish between Cuba and Key Largo), the course of their love had been more intellectual than physical. Apart from horse riding and tennis, they had really taken part in the usual pursuits of young people their age. 'We hardly ever went to parties,' Max would recount, 'and we detested dancing. Instead we preferred to spend hours lying on the sand beside the sea, discussing life, love and death. And Sylvia would recite to me the latest poems she had memorized since our last meeting.'

Sylvia had come to visit him in New Orleans on several occasions. Together they had explored the historical treasures of Louisiana. One night when a tropical storm confined them to a plantation on the banks of the Mississippi, they had made love in a bed in which Mademoiselle de Granville and the Marquis de Lafayette had slept. 'There was no doubting the fact that our marriage was written in the stars,' Max was to say. 'Despite the fact that Sylvia's family were Presbyterians and mine were practising Jews, we knew that no event could please our parents more.'

Then, suddenly, exactly seven months before the date fixed for the wedding, Max had decided to go off for a year. He had said nothing to his fiancée of the deeper reasons for his decision. There were some actions in a man's life, he thought, that did not call for explanation. Yet on that last evening, carried away by the euphoria of the champagne and the mild smell of a contraband Havana Montecristo cigar, he decided to admit the truth.

'Just in case anything should happen to me, I wanted everyone to know that I hadn't just gone off on a whim.' He told the story of how one day, in the university library, his gaze had fallen on the photograph of a child on the illustrated cover of a magazine published in Canada by a humanitarian organization. The child was a little Indian boy of five or six sitting in front of the crumbling wall of a house in Calcutta. A black shock of hair concealed his forehead and part of his eyes, but in between the locks of hair there shone two little flames – his eyes. What struck Max most of all was the boy's smile, a tranquil, luminous smile which dug two deep ditches around his mouth and revealed four shining teeth. He didn't appear to be starving but he was surely very poor because he was completely naked. In his arms he was clutching a baby, only a few days old and wrapped in pieces of rag.

'He was holding it with so much pride,' Max recalled for his fiancée, 'with so much gravity behind his smile and with such an obvious sense of his responsibilities, that for several minutes I was unable to take my eyes off him.

'The child was an inhabitant of the City of Joy and the baby in his arms was his little brother. The journalist who took the photograph wrote in his article about his visit to the slum and his encounter with a "white apostle who had come from the West to live among the world's most disinherited people". The white apostle in question was Stephan Kovalski. In answer to one of the journalist's questions, Stephan had expressed the wish that someone with advanced medical training, preferably a young doctor, should come to Anand Nagar for a year to work with him and help him to organize proper medical help in a place deprived of aid.

'I wrote to him,' concluded Max. 'And he replied that he would expect me as soon as possible. Apparently the winter is coming to an end there and soon it'll be the

scorching heat of the summer and the monsoon.'

Mention of the monsoon brought a quickening to the blue eyes of the American girl.

'The monsoon!' she echoed pensively. She was thinking of a poem by Paul Verlaine for which she had a special affection. '*Il pleut dans mon coeur,*' she recited in French, tenderly caressing Max's hand, '*comme il pleut sur la ville. Quelle est cette langueur qui pénètre mon coeur?*'★

42

The picture in its gold frame decorated with a garland of flowers was an expression of strength and beauty. On his elephant, caparisoned with carpets and encrusted with precious stones, the figure portrayed looked like a conquering maharajah. He was wearing a tunic embroidered with gold thread and studded with jewels. The only features that distinguished him from a man were his wings and his four arms brandishing an axe, a hammer, a bow and the arm of a set of scales.

His name was Viswakarma and he was not a man, nor indeed was he a prince, but rather a god belonging to the Hindu pantheon. One of the mightiest gods in Indian mythology, Viswakarma was the personification of creative power. The hymns of the Vedas, the sacred books of Hinduism, glorified him as 'the architect of the universe, the all-seeing god who fashioned the heavens and the earth, the creator, father, distributor of all the worlds, the one who gives the deities their names and who resides outside the realms of mortal comprehension'. According to the Mahabharata, the epic legend of Hinduism, Vi-

★ 'There is weeping in my heart, like the rain falling on the city. What is this languor that pierces my heart?'

swakarma was not only the supreme architect. He was also the artificer of the gods and the maker of their tools, lord of the arts and carpenter of the cosmos, constructor of the celestial chariots and creator of all adornments. It followed, therefore, that he was the protector of all the manual trades that enabled man to subsist, a fact that gave him a particular following among the labourers and artisans of India.

In the same way that Christians glorify 'the god of the universe, who gives bread, the fruit of man's labour', during the Offertory of the Mass, the Indians venerated Viswakarma, the source of labour and life. Each year after the September moon, in all the myriad workshops of the Calcutta slums, as in all the large modern factories of the suburbs, his triumphant effigy presided over man's places of work, richly decorated for a fervent two-day *puja*. It was a marvellous moment of communion between owners and workers, a wild rejoicing of rich and poor, united in the same adoration and the same prayer.

Like all the other slums, the City of Joy celebrated the festival of Viswakarma with special fervour for the god who provided their rice. After all, was it not true that the entanglement of huts that made up the slum harboured the most amazing ants' nest of workmen imaginable? Every day a hovel sighted behind an open door, the grinding of a machine, a pile of new objects outside a hut, would reveal to Stephan Kovalski the presence of some tiny new workshop or small factory. Here, he might discover half a dozen half-naked children engaged in cutting off sheets of tin to make pannikins; there, other urchins like Nasir, Mehboub's son, would be dipping objects into tanks exuding noxious vapours. Elsewhere, children made matches and Bengal firecrackers, gradually poisoning themselves as they handled phosphorus, zinc oxide, asbestos powder and gum arabic.

Almost opposite the Pole's hut, in the darkness of a

workshop, blackened figures laminated, soldered and adjusted pieces of scrap iron, amid the smell of burning oil and hot metal. Next door, in a kind of windowless shed, a dozen shadows made up *bidis*. They were nearly all victims of tuberculosis who no longer had the strength to manœuvre a press or pull a rickshaw. Provided they didn't stop for a single minute, they could roll up to thirteen hundred cigarettes a day. For a thousand *bidis*, they received eleven rupees, about 70 pence. A little further on, in a tiny room, Stephan Kovalski noticed one day an enormous ship's propeller next to a forge. The door was so narrow that the entrance of beaten earth had to be enlarged with a pickaxe to get the monster out. Eventually five men succeeded in shifting the propeller and levering it onto a *telagarhi*. The owner then harnessed three coolies to the cart and ordered them to proceed. Backs and hamstrings braced themselves in a desperate effort. The wheels turned, and the employer sighed with satisfaction. He would not need to take on a fourth coolie. But what would happen, Kovalski wondered, when the three unfortunates reached the bottom of the slope leading up to the Howrah Bridge?

How many years would it take him to discover all the places where men and children spent their lives making springs, lorry parts, spindles for weaving looms, bolts, aircraft tanks, and even turbine meshing to a sixth of a micromillimetre. With surprising dexterity, inventiveness and resourcefulness a whole work force was able to copy, repair, renovate any part and any machine. Here the slightest scrap of metal, the tiniest piece of debris was used again, transformed, adapted. 'Nothing was ever destroyed,' Kovalski was to say, 'because by some miracle everything was always born again.'

Amid the shadows, the dust and the clutter of their sweatshops, the workmen of Anand Nagar were the pride of the God who gives rice to man. Alas, they often gave him cause for remorse too.

Article 24 of the Indian constitution stipulates that 'no child must work in a factory or mine, nor be employed in any other dangerous place'. For reasons of profit and docility, however, a large proportion of the work force was extremely young. In fact, a child was almost always hired in preference to an adult. His little fingers were more adept and he was content with a pittance as a salary. Yet these pittances earned by children with so much pride meant so often the difference between their families' starvation and survival!

The workers in the slum were among the worst protected in the world. They were not eligible for any social security; they were often shamelessly exploited, working up to twelve or fourteen hours at a stretch in premises in which no zoo in the world would dare to keep its animals. Many of them ate and slept on the spot, without light or ventilation. For them there were no weekends or vacations. One day's absence and they could find themselves laid off. A misplaced remark, a claim, a dispute, being one hour late, could mean instant dismissal and without compensation. Only those who managed to acquire some form of qualification (as a turner, a laminator, expert press operator) had any real hope of keeping their jobs.

In the City of Joy alone there were thousands of them – perhaps fifteen or twenty thousand – and naturally several hundred thousand in Calcutta and millions throughout India. 'How was it that they had never used the weight of such numbers to change their lot?' Kovalski was one day to remark. 'That was a question that had always intrigued me and one to which I had never really found a satisfactory answer. Certainly, their rural origins had not prepared them for making collective demands. Their poverty was such that any kind of work, even in a sweatshop, was a blessing of a kind. When so many were unemployed, how could they protest against work that at least enabled them to take home to their families

the bowl of rice they needed each day? And when a family is reduced to the most extreme poverty because of a father's sickness or death, wasn't it understandable that one of the children should be prepared to work anywhere? No doubt morality would dictate otherwise, but who can talk about morality and what is right, when it all comes down to a question of survival?

'And what did the unions do to protect them? Along with three powerful central federations incorporating several million members, there are in India nearly sixteen thousand unions, of which seven thousand four hundred and fifty belong exclusively to Bengal. And there is no lack of strikes on their list of achievements. In Bengal alone more than ten million working days are lost each year. But in a slum like the City of Joy who would dare to instigate a strike? There are too many people waiting to step into your shoes.

'With all due deference to Viswakarma, the giver of rice, these people were the real damned of the world, the slaves of hunger. And yet with what ardour and faith they fêted their god each year and called down his blessing upon the machines and tools to which they were chained.'

Work had stopped in all the slum workshops since the previous evening. While all the workers hastened to clean, repaint and decorate their machines and their tools with foliage and garlands of flowers, their employers had gone to Howrah to purchase the traditional icons of the god with four arms, perched on his elephant, and the statues of him in painted clay, sculpted by potters from the *kumars*'* district. The size and splendour of the images depended on the magnitude of the business concern. In large factories, statues of Viswakarma were two or three times as large as life and were worth thousands of rupees.

* Potters.

In the space of one night all the dungeons of suffering had been transformed into places of worship, adorned with ornamented temporary altars bedecked with flowers. Next morning the entire slum resounded anew with the joyous din of the festival.

The slaves of the previous day now wore multi-coloured shirts and new *longhis*; their wives draped themselves in ceremonial saris, so carefully preserved throughout the year in the family coffers. Children were resplendent in the garb of little princes. The joyous saraband of the instruments and drums of a brass band replaced the thud of machines, around which the Brahmin priest now circled, ringing a bell with one hand and bearing the purificatory fire in the other, so that every instrument of labour might be blessed.

That day a number of workmen sought out Kovalski to ask him too to bless the means of their survival in the name of his god. 'Praise be to you, O God of the universe who gives bread to man, for your children in Anand Nagar love and believe in you,' the priest repeated in each workshop. 'And rejoice with them for this day of light in their lives of sorrow.'

After the blessings, the festivities began. The employers and foremen served the workmen and their families a banquet of curry, meat, vegetables, yoghurt, *puris** and *laddous*.† The *bangla* and *todi*‡ flowed freely. People drank, laughed, danced and, above all, they forgot. Viswakarma could smile from his thousand beds of flowers. He had united men through their labour.

The revelry went on into the middle of the night, in the beams of the floodlights. A populace deprived of television, cinema and virtually all other entertainments

---

* Puffed corn griddle cake fried in *ghee*.
† Small ball of curdled milk, sweetened, condensed and fried.
‡ Palm wine.

surrendered itself once more to the magic of festival. Workers and their families ran from workshop to workshop, pausing to marvel at the most beautiful statues and congratulate the creators, while loudspeakers poured popular tunes over the roofs, and fireworks illuminated the libations.

The next day, the workmen from each workshop loaded the statues onto a *telagarhi* or a rickshaw and accompanied them, to the sound of drums and cymbals, as far as the Banda *ghat* on the banks of the Hooghly. There they hoisted them onto boats and rowed out to the middle of the river. Then they threw the images overboard so that their clay bodies could dissolve in the sacred water, mother of the world. '*Viswakarma-ki jai!* Long live Viswakarma!' cried millions of voices at that special moment. Then each one returned to his machine and the curtain fell for another year upon the slaves of the Lord, the giver of rice.

43

'We called the festival of Viswakarma "the rickshaw *puja*",' Hasari Pal was to explain. 'Our factory, our workroom, our machines were all made up of two wheels, a chassis and two shafts. One wheel had only to break in a hole, or a lorry tear off a shaft, or a bus flatten the bodywork like a *chapati*, and it would be goodbye to Hasari! There would be no use going crying in the owner's *gamcha*.* All you could hope to get from him was a good beating. More than anyone else, we had a great need for the god's protection, not only for our carriages but also for ourselves. A nail in your foot, an

* A kind of large handkerchief.

accident, or the red fever that got Ram or Scarface, and you were done for.'

Like their pullers, the rickshaw owners were fervent worshippers of the god Viswakarma. Not for anything in the world would they have failed to take out insurance with him by organizing a *puja* in his honour that was as vibrant and generous as those held in all the other workplaces in Calcutta.

The celebrations were generally held in their homes. Only the old man, Bipin Narendra, known as the Bihari, persisted in concealing his address. 'Perhaps in case one day we got angry and decided to pay him a visit,' joked Hasari. So Bipin Narendra's eldest son rented a large house surrounded by gardens behind Park Circus and set up there a magnificent *pandal* decorated with garlands of flowers and hundreds of light bulbs fed by a generator rented for the occasion.

On the day before the festival, every puller set about giving his rickshaw a meticulous cleaning. Hasari had even bought the remains of a tin of black paint to camouflage the scratches on the woodwork. He carefully greased the hubs of the wheels with a few drops of mustard oil so that there would be no disagreeable noise to irritate the god's ears. Then he went to fetch his wife and children.

Aloka had prepared his festival clothes for him: a *longhi* with little maroon checks on it and a blue-and-white striped shirt. She herself was dressed in a ceremonial sari of red and gold, which they had brought with them from their village. It was her wedding sari and, despite the rats, the cockroaches, the humidity and the overflowing drains she had managed somehow to preserve its original freshness. The children too were splendidly dressed; they looked so clean and smart in fact that people came to admire them. The god could rest contented. The whole family might well live in a shanty made out of crates and bits of cloth but for

today at least the people who issued from that hovel were princes.

Aloka, her daughter and younger son climbed into the rickshaw. The old jalopy had never before transported such proud, elegant passengers. Together the three of them were like a bouquet of orchids. Manooj, the elder son, harnessed himself to the shafts because his father did not want to perspire in his beautiful shirt.

The house rented by the Bihari's son was not far away. One of the city's distinguishing features was that the rich people's quarters and the slums of the poor were close to one another.

Few rickshaw pullers had the good fortune to be able to celebrate the *puja* as a family. Most of them lived alone in Calcutta, having left their families in the villages. 'It was a shame for them,' Hasari said. 'There is nothing more enjoyable than celebrating a festival with the whole family together. It's as if the god becomes your uncle or cousin.'

The owner had done things well. His *pandal* was decorated just like a proper shrine. Interwoven red-and-white flowers and palm leaf trimmings formed a triumphal arch over the entrance. In the middle, on a carpet of marigolds and jasmine, was enthroned an enormous statue of Viswakarma, magnificently made up with rouge on his lips and kohl on his eyes.

'How imposing our god is! What power he exudes!' Hasari enthused. 'The statue's arms reached the tip of the tent, brandishing an axe and a hammer as if to force gifts from the heavens. His chest looked as if it could blow the winds of a storm, his biceps as if they could raise mountains, his feet stamp out all the wild beasts of creation. With such a god for protector how could the sorry-looking old carts fail to become celestial chariots? And the poor devils that pulled them winged horses?'

Hasari and his family prostrated themselves before the divinity. Aloka, who was very devout, had brought

offerings – a banana, a handful of rice, jasmine and marigold petals – which she placed at his feet. Her husband went to park his rickshaw next to the others in the garden. One of the owner's sons busied himself decorating it with garlands of flowers and foliage. 'What a pity he can't speak to thank you,' Hasari remarked. All those carts with their flower-covered shafts pointing like spears towards the heavens made a splendid spectacle. The former peasant barely recognized the shabby, creaking carriages that he and his colleagues pulled so breathlessly each day. 'It was just as if the stroke of a magic wand had given them a new incarnation.'

When all the rickshaws were in their places, there was a roll of drums, then a clash of cymbals. An elderly priest made his entry at this point, preceding a band of some fifty musicians in red jackets and trousers trimmed with gold. A young Brahmin whose bare torso was girded with a small cord began frenetically to bang the clapper of a bell to inform the god of their presence, then the priest passed slowly between the rows of carriages, sprinkling each one with a few drops of water from the Ganges and a little *ghee*. Every rickshaw *wallah*'s heart was constricted with emotion. For once it was not sweat or tears of pain that was flowing over their poor old carts, but the life-giving water of the god who would protect them and give their children food.

When the priest had blessed all the rickshaws, he returned to the deity to place upon his lips a little rice and *ghee* and to cense him with the burning *arati* the Brahmin carried in a little cup. One of the employer's sons then called out: '*Viswakarma-ki jai!* Long live Viswakarma!' The six hundred or so pullers present repeated the invocation three times. It was a sincere and triumphant roar that charmed the ears of the owner infinitely more than the hostile slogans shouted on the occasion of the recent strike.

'But why didn't we cry out at the same time, "Long live Viswakarma and long live the solidarity of rickshaw workers?"' wondered Hasari. 'And why not also, "Long live the revolution!" Wasn't Viswakarma god of the workers first and foremost, before he was god of the owners? Even if sometimes he did give us the impression that he had forgotten to oil the wheel of our *karma.*'

After the ceremony the Bihari's eldest son invited the pullers and their families to sit down on the grass. Pullers originating from the same regions grouped themselves together as did those who had come with their families. The Bihari's other sons then placed before each person a banana leaf on which they put several ladles of rice and mutton curry with some *chapatis*, pastries and a mandarin orange. It was a real banquet, one which stomachs contracted by deprivation could not absorb in its entirety. 'In any case,' Hasari was to say, 'what satisfied my stomach most was the sight of our bosses bending over to serve us. It was like seeing a family of tigers offering grass to a herd of antelopes.'

44

Someone was knocking at the door of 49 Nizamudhin Lane. It was Anouar. Stephan Kovalski helped the cripple over the threshold and settled him on the mat made out of rice straw that served as a bed. The leper looked embarrassed.

'Stephan, Big Brother, I have a big favour to ask of you,' he eventually said, joining his wasted palms together in a gesture of supplication.

'I am your brother. You can ask me anything.'

'Well, in that case, could you go and tell Puli that I would like to marry Meeta.'

'Meeta?' repeated Kovalski, surprised. 'But she's his wife!'

'Exactly, Stephan *Daddah*, that's why I would like it to be you who asks him. He'll listen to you. Everyone respects you.'

Puli was a lean little man of about fifty, with a very dark skin. Originally from the south, he had visited Calcutta one day and had never left. He must have contracted leprosy when he was young, during the long peregrinations of his nomadic life. At one time he had been an exhibitor of monkeys. Having changed to begging, for years he had haunted the steps of the Kali temple until a clash with the local gang leader of the begging racketeers forced him into exile on the steps of Howrah Railway Station on the other side of the river. His gifts as a comedian earned him an appreciable income. No traveller could resist the drollery of his mimicry or the horror of his wounds. He had been relatively spared by his illness and so he made up false dressings and painted them with red iodine. Puli lived in one of the most wretched compounds in the leper colony of Anand Nagar, together with his wife, Meeta, a sweet young woman of twenty-seven, and three lovely children aged from four years to six months.

Meeta was the youngest daughter of a refugee potter from East Pakistan. At the age of sixteen, when her parents were about to marry her to a potter of her caste, the girl discovered a small whitish patch on her right cheek that was insensitive to touch. After weeks of hesitation, she went to join the line for consultation at Howrah Hospital. The medical verdict was instantaneous. It was a patch of leprosy. As far as her parents were concerned, God had cursed their daughter. They banished her immediately from the family hut. Had they not done so, the whole family would have been in danger of being expelled. Reduced to begging around the station, Meeta was picked up by a Bengali who sold her

to a brothel in Calcutta. When the proprietor discovered that his new lodger was a leper, however, he beat her black and blue and threw her out. She was salvaged by some ragpickers, taken to Mother Teresa's home for the dying, and saved just in time. Afterwards she went back to begging near the station and it was there that the onetime exhibitor of monkeys found her. He immediately took her under his wing and, one year later, married her.

Anouar's request left Kovalski dumbfounded. He still did not fully appreciate to what extent the leper world was a universe apart, with its own distinctive laws. Leprosy, particularly in its advanced stages, exacerbates sexuality. This is why lepers have occasionally more than one wife and usually many children. Knowing that in any case they are cursed by God and excluded from the rest of the human race, lepers feel they have no taboos to respect. They are free. No representative of the law would ever come and poke his nose into their affairs. In Anand Nagar, these disfigured, crippled, fallen men did not go without women. The revenue they made from begging invariably enabled them to buy them. The last recourse of a very poor family who had not managed to marry off one of its daughters because of physical disgrace or some infirmity was often to sell her to a leper. One spouse was rarely, however, enough for the appetites of these disease-ridden men. Women, also, had sometimes more than one husband. Such polygamous transactions were set up by an intermediary and then solemnized with a ceremony that was as ostentatious and expensive as any other marriage.

'Big Brother Stephan,' insisted Anouar eagerly, 'I assure you that you won't have any difficulty convincing Puli. I've got enough to keep him happy.'

With these words, the leper thrust his stumps into the top of his loincloth and brought out a bundle of notes

tied up with a piece of string. 'Three hundred rupees isn't to be sneezed at!'

'Have you asked Meeta what she thinks?' inquired the priest with concern. This question was fundamental to him.

Anouar seemed surprised.

'Meeta will do as her husband orders,' he replied.

Naturally Kovalski refused. He was prepared to play virtually any other role in the service of his brothers, but not that of procurer. Anouar would have to address himself directly to his 'rival'.

After laborious negotiations, the transaction was finally concluded for five hundred rupees, two hundred more than the sum contained in the bundle Anouar carried at his waist. The cripple borrowed the difference (and more besides, to cover the cost of the marriage) from the colony's usurer, a fat Punjabi who had several beggars working for him.

In a community where each member believed himself to be unclean and condemned by God, religion had no role to play. No Brahmin or mullah ever came to celebrate a ceremony here. Hindus, Muslims and Christians lived together in relative indifference to the beliefs and rites of the religion of their origins. All the same, one or two odd customs such as the choice of an auspicious date for a wedding had been preserved. The colony even had its own astrologer, an old man with a white beard called Joga, who for forty years had exercised his profession as a fortune-teller on the esplanade of the Maidan. His work was not always easy, especially when, like Anouar and Meeta, the prospective marriage partners did not know their dates of birth. Old Joga contented himself with suggesting a month that was under the benign influence of the planet Venus and a day of the week that was not Tuesday, Saturday or Sunday, the three ill-omened days in the Indian weekly calendar.

*

The ghetto of the damned was in a state of full baccha-
nalian revelry. On the day appointed, dazzled by the
glare of the floodlights and bewildered by the bellowing
of a sound system gone wild, Stephan Kovalski entered
the neighbourhood of the cursed. Although in his heart
of hearts he disapproved of the nature of the alliance
about to be formed, he had not been able to bring himself
to turn down his friends' invitation. It was so rare, after
all, for anyone in good health to provide these pariahs
with the reassurance of their presence. Leper women
draped in bedizened muslin saris were waiting at the
door to adorn the bride and groom's guest of honour
with garlands of marigolds and jasmine and to place
upon his forehead the *tilak* of welcome, the patch of
scarlet powder symbolizing the third eye of knowledge.
That evening Kovalski would have plenty of need of
that additional eye to discover all the refinements of the
unwonted festivities of which he was to be the prince.
He had swapped his sneakers and his old black shirt for
gondola-shaped mules and a magnificent embroidered
white cotton *kurta*, gifts from the prospective husband
and wife to their partner in poverty.

The spectacle around him was beyond belief. In their
new shirts and coloured waistcoats, their cheeks clean-
shaven and their dressings immaculate, the lepers had
almost reassumed human form. Their gaiety was heart-
ening. The master of ceremonies was none other than
Puli, the bride's first husband. He had managed to dig
out from somewhere a morning coat and a top hat.

'Welcome to our gathering, Big Brother Stephan,' he
cried in his falsetto voice, clasping the priest to him.

His breath betrayed the fact that he had already paid
a few visits to the stock of *bangla* procured for the
reception. He steered his guest of honour in the direction
of the groom's hut. Kovalski hardly recognized the vile
shed. The lepers had repainted everything in honour of
Anouar's marriage. Garlands of flowers hung from the

bamboo framework and the beaten earth of the floor sparkled with a *rangoli* carpet. Expressions of popular joy on occasions of celebration and great solemnity, *rangolis* are marvellous geometric compositions outlined in rice flour and coloured powders and are designed to bring good fortune.

In the middle of the hut stood a solitary *charpoy*, it too decorated with garlands of flowers and covered with a superb Madras patchwork quilt made out of dozens of little striped squares. Seated on this regal bed was Anouar. Next to him was the throne on which he would soon have himself carried to the site of the ceremony. He received his best man with effusive tenderness. Then, quite abruptly, his expression became one of gravity.

'Stephan, Big Brother, have you got a bit of medicine for me?' he asked in a low voice. 'I'm in terrible pain this evening.'

Stephan Kovalski had learned from experience never to go visiting the lepers without taking a dose of morphine in the bottom of his pocket. That evening, however, he could not help but wonder what effect the powerful sedative might have on his friend during the ceremony and particularly afterwards when he found himself alone with his young bride. As a precaution he injected only half the vial. Hardly had he restored the syringe to his pocket than half a dozen married women garbed in long dresses of many colours, their hair adorned with diadems, and their necks and arms covered with costume jewellery, entered singing *bhajans*, religious hymns. Beneath all their makeup and finery their infirmities were forgotten. Despite the fact that Anouar was Muslim by origin, they had come to carry out one of the rites that was essential to all Hindu marriages, the *holud-nath*, the purification of the groom.

They took charge of Anouar's body and rubbed it with all kinds of unguents and yellow pastes which exuded a strong smell of musk and saffron. The scene

would have been comic, had not the object of all these attentions been a body that was half destroyed. Their anointing completed, the matrons went on to the groom's toilet, sprinkling him with water. Then they undertook to dress him. Anouar let himself be treated like a child. They slipped on a long *kurta*, a superb shirt in green silk with gold buttons. How could a man who dragged himself through the mud on a plank on wheels ever have dreamed of such a garment?

'That crippled leper all dressed up in so festive a setting suddenly brought a knot to my stomach,' the Pole was to admit.

In the absence of any religious authority, it fell to the master of ceremonies to direct the evening. No theologian of any religious creed would ever have found his way through the ritual imbroglio of the lepers of the City of Joy. Puli, however, was a star and, in any case, the marriage closely concerned him. There was nothing, therefore, that he left out, least of all the sacrosanct custom of which he would be the indirect beneficiary: the fiancé's sending of presents to his betrothed.

'Stephan, Big Brother, you are the best man, so you'll be the one to take the presents from Anouar to Meeta,' he announced. The invitation was accompanied by a wink which was to say, 'With you at least, I can be sure that nothing will disappear en route.'

Anouar proceeded to take out of his mattress a collection of small packages wrapped up in newspaper and secured with elastic bands. Each packet contained some article of finery or ornament. Apart from three real silver rings, the remainder were cheap trinkets from the bazaar, a toe ring, earrings, a stone for her nose, an amber necklace and a *matika*, the diadem worn by married women. In any event, the choice of these presents had been negotiated between Puli and Anouar. In addition to the jewels there were two saris, a few tubes of cosmetics and a box of cinnamon sweetmeats. Puli

deposited everything in a basket which he handed to Kovalski. Then he summoned the escort.

Eight lepers crowned with red cardboard shakos and dressed in yellow jackets and white trousers entered the hut. They were the musicians. Two of them held drumsticks between their consumed fingers, two others cymbals, and the two last dented trumpets. Puli raised his top hat and the small procession moved off amid the hubbub of a carnival. As majestic as King Belshazzar proceeding to Jerusalem, Stephan Kovalski stepped out with his basket of gifts balanced upon his head, taking care not to slip into a drain with his gondola-shaped mules.

Puli was so proud to be able to show off his guest of honour to the colony that he had the procession do a tour of the neighbourhood before entering Meeta's compound. The spectacle that awaited the Pole in this wretched hole of a colony where he had spent so many hours comforting the condemned of the slum was so extraordinary that he found himself wondering whether he was not in fact the victim of some hallucination. The entire courtyard was covered with muslin veils and strung with garlands of marigolds, roses and jasmine blossoms. Powered by an electricity generator especially hired for the occasion, dozens of light bulbs illuminated the courtyard with a clarity that it had never known before.

Kovalski surrendered his basket of offerings to one of the matrons standing guard at Meeta's door. Then, led by Puli and the band, who did their utmost to compete with the bellowing of the sound system, he returned to Anouar's hut. By this time it was almost midnight, that auspicious hour when in the heavens 'the day straddles the night'. The ceremony could commence.

There were no white mares caparisoned with gold and velvet to conduct the crippled man to the muslin-draped courtyard where his fiancée Meeta awaited him, her face

veiled with a square of red cotton. Nevertheless, his
chair, decorated with flowers and borne like a palanquin
by four other lepers, was equal to the most glorious of
mounts. Crowned with a golden turban and preceded
by the indescribable Puli, who greeted the crowd with
waves of his top hat, Anouar traversed the neighbourhood like a Mogul emperor processing to his coronation.
Behind him, Kovalski carried the piece of folded cloth
which in a moment would veil the face of the leper,
before he entered the courtyard appointed for the marriage. Amid all those noises, all that laughter, all the
smells, among the disfigured and the crippled, the Pole
experienced a 'fantastic lesson in hope' and marvelled
once more that 'so much life and joy could spring from
such abjection'.

Puli raised his hat and the music stopped. They had
reached the entrance to the courtyard and the bride-
groom's face had to be concealed. Two matrons took
the piece of cloth from Kovalski's hands and pinned it
to the dome of Anouar's turban. The groom's fine
bearded face disappeared from the gazes of the onlookers. Puli's top hat rose then above the surrounding
heads and the procession set off again to the sound of
trumpets and cymbals. 'In the kingdom of heaven their
faces will be the most beautiful of all,' reflected the priest
as his gaze encountered the range of distorted humanity
waiting all around the little courtyard.

In a cupful of oil placed in the centre of the *rangoli*
flooring burned a flame. This was the traditional sacrificial fire offered up to the gods, so they might bless the
union about to take place. The frail Meeta was seated on
a cushion, her head inclined forward, completely hidden
by her veil. She looked as if she was meditating. On her
hair shone the gilded diadem which Anouar had sent her
in his basket of presents. The smell of incense impregnated the air already heavy with smoke.

When the procession had made its way around the

courtyard three times, Puli made a sign to Kovalski for him to take his place to the left of the bride. Then he directed the bearers to place Anouar on her right. With his top hat planted firmly on his skull, his chest thrust out under a morning coat that was too large for him, he then began to officiate.

Dear Puli! No one could imitate a Brahmin the way he could. Assuming an attitude of inspiration, he began to pronounce in his rasping voice an interminable series of formulas. The assembly appeared to be spellbound by the monotonous chant, punctuated at regular intervals by the clash of cymbals. After this preamble he finally came to the main body of the ceremony. The *Panigrahan* was the essential rite of Brahmin marriage. Puli pulled a small violet cord out of his pocket and, taking the right palms of the bride and groom, tied them together, repeating their names aloud. Thus was celebrated the first physical contact of man and wife. While Puli recited further prayers, Kovalski gazed at those two mutilated limbs bound together, and what he saw made him think of a sentence he had read one day in a book by a French writer named Léon Bloy: 'We do not enter paradise either tomorrow or in ten years' time. We enter today if we are poor and crucified.'

Next came the most intense moment of the ceremony. The band and congregation fell silent as Puli invited the newlyweds officially to make each other's acquaintance. Slowly and timidly, with their free palms, they each removed the other's veil. The joyous bearded face appeared before Meeta's large eyes, slightly sad and blackened with kohl. Stephan Kovalski leaned forward to capture all the emotion of that moment, to try and guess too the thoughts of the young leper woman whose husband had sold her for five hundred rupees. Meeta's eyes were bright with tears.

An authentic Hindu wedding would have included a whole host of other rites, variable according to province

and caste. One of them, however, was universal. Without it no ceremony was complete. Puli invited the couple
to walk seven times around the sacrificial fire, their
palms still joined by the piece of cord. In his excitement
he had forgotten Anouar's infirmity. Again he had to
call for the bearers. The leper saw his big brother rise
from his cushion and approach him with open arms.

'Old friend, let me help you to accompany Meeta
round the flame,' said the priest with affection.

Kovalski picked up the fragile little body, and the
three of them walked slowly, seven times round the
cosmic fire. The residents of the courtyard and dozens
of neighbours who had scaled the roofs watched the
scene with emotion. When Kovalski had restored him
to his place, Anouar asked:

'What about you? When are you going to get married?'

Puli, who had overheard, burst out laughing. Waving
his hat about in something resembling a waltz, he inter-
jected, 'And I'll be the Brahmin again!'

They all laughed. Only poor Meeta seemed ill at ease
in her new role.

Now it was time for the feast. At a signal from
Puli, children brought piles of banana leaves which they
distributed to everyone present. Immediately women
came out of various houses, laden with steaming bowls
of rice, vegetables and fish. Little girls began to serve
the food. People talked, laughed, sang and cracked jokes.
To keep a child amused, an old leper without a nose
pretended to be wearing a mask. The fragrance of spices
filled the courtyard, as the banana leaves were gradually
filled. Even the neighbours on the roof tops were served.
The sound system made the tiles vibrate. Resplendent
on their cushions, the newlyweds and Kovalski received
the homage of the community, under the delighted eye
of Puli whose buffoonery increased by the minute. Every
now and then he would disappear only to reappear an
instant later in a state of even greater excitement. It did

not take Kovalski long to guess what he was up to.

Alcohol! The celebration was on the point of degener-
ating into a monumental drinking bout. Concealed up
to now at the back of the hovels, bottles of *bangla* began
now to circulate among the guests. The effect of the
drink was instantaneous and totally unexpected. Instead
of flattening such sick and undernourished constitutions,
the abrupt ingestion of alcohol electrified them. Those
lepers who still had limbs leaped to their feet and began
to dance. Stumps joined stumps in a frenzied farandole
that snaked its way about the courtyard to the laughter
and cheers of all the others present. Children ran about
after each other. Women, too, freed from their inhibitions by large glasses of *bangla*, hurled themselves into
dizzy circles and spun like tops about the courtyard.
They had so much energy! So much vitality! So much
zest for living! Once again Kovalski marvelled. Let no
one ever again say to him that lepers were just apathetic
people, a bundle of rags and tatters, a collection of
derelicts resigned to their lot. These men and women
were life itself, LIFE in capital letters, the life that
throbbed, the life that vibrated in them as it vibrated
everywhere else in this most blessed of cities, Calcutta.

It was then that something amazing happened. At a
signal from Puli's top hat, the dancing abruptly ceased,
the singing and shouting faded, then stopped completely. The garlands of lights went out all at once. After
one last hiccup, the generator came to a halt. Darkness
fell and a cloak of silence enveloped the assembly. There
was not a sound, not a word. Even the children were
quiet.

On his cushion of honour Stephan Kovalski held his
breath. Why this sudden obscurity? Why the stillness?
Bemused, he could just make out shadows slipping away
in the darkness and entering the different lodgings that
opened onto the courtyard. Others felt their way across
the roofs. Yet others melted into the blackness of the

ground. The newlyweds next to him had vanished. Straining his ears, he detected the faint sound of voices that sounded like groans. He even heard a number of quickly stifled cries. Then he understood.

The celebration was not over. It was still going on. It was reaching its climax in the ultimate ritual, a last act of homage to all-powerful Life. The lepers of the City of Joy were making love.

45

'It began with a feeling of utter fatigue and a strange aching in my bones, as if dozens of policemen had been beating me with their *lathis*,' Hasari Pal was to recount. 'I told myself that it was probably old age creeping up a bit early, as it did with many rickshaw pullers. In Calcutta even the leaves on the trees in the squares fell earlier than those in the countryside. Then I felt a strange warmth in my chest. Even when I was standing still, waiting for a fare, I felt the heat of it, bathing me in perspiration from head to toe. It seemed all the stranger for the fact that it was winter and, God knows, in Calcutta it can be as cold in winter as it's hot in summer. The fact that I never took off the old sweater given to me by a customer from Wood Street made no difference; I was still cold. Perhaps I'd caught the mosquito disease.* According to Chomotkar, a friend of mine who was a taxi driver, that illness gives you the same sort of shivers. He'd had it himself and had been cured with small white tablets. He brought me a whole load wrapped up in a piece of newspaper and told me to swallow two or three a day. We began the treatment with a bottle of *bangla*.

* Malaria.

Chomotkar claimed that *bangla* was a universal medicine, but I think he was wrong because I went on sweating like a pig. The heat in my chest began to burn so much that every breath was painful. Every time I took on a customer, even a lightweight like a schoolboy, I had to stop every two or three minutes to get my breath back. One day I was really frightened. It happened in Park Street. I had parked my rickshaw to go and buy some *bidis* under the arcades when suddenly, as I was going past Flury's pastry shop, I saw myself in the shop window. For a second I asked myself who the old man in front of the display of cakes might be, with his hollow, stubbled cheeks and his head of white hair. Suddenly I saw the image of my father on the morning he blessed me before I left for Calcutta. I shall never forget that sight.

'By the way she'd been looking at me for some time, I knew that my wife too was alarmed about my health. She had become particularly attentive to my every word and gesture. It was as if she was desperate for the slightest indication to reassure her, to prove to her that I was well. No doubt that was why she responded with such unusual enthusiasm whenever I expressed the desire to make love. The strange thing about it was that the more worn out with fatigue I felt, the more I desired my wife. It was as if all the vitality in my shattered body had taken refuge in my reproductive organ. What was more, it was not long before my wife announced that she was expecting a child. This news filled me with such joy that for several days I was oblivious of the fatigue, the cold and my sweating.

'Then afterwards things got very much worse. One day when I had just picked up a *marwari* with a pile of packages, I was forced to stop and put down my shafts. Something had wedged itself in my chest. I couldn't breathe any more. I collapsed onto my knees. The *marwari* was a kind man. Instead of abusing me and calling

another rickshaw, he tried to help me get my breath back by striking me sharply on the back. When he did so, I felt something hot gurgle into my mouth. I spat it out. The *marwari* surveyed the spittle and grimaced. Handing me a five-rupee note, he transferred his packages to another rickshaw. As he drew away he gave me a slight wave of his hand.

'I remained there for quite a while before getting up. But the act of spitting had brought me some relief. Little by little I got my breath back and found enough strength to move on. That wasn't the day the god was coming for me. My wife burst into sobs when I told her about the incident. Women are like animals. They sense the oncoming storm long before men do. She ordered me to go and see a quack immediately and buy some drugs. A quack was a street doctor. He would ask only one or two rupees whereas a real doctor who had completed his studies would expect five or ten times more. But before I went to find the quack, my wife suggested that we take offerings to the temple to ward off the ogress Suparnaka, who was responsible for so many sick people. On a plate she placed a banana, jasmine petals and the equivalent of a handful of rice and off we went to the temple, where I slipped the Brahmin the five-rupee note that the *marwari* had given me. He recited some *mantras*. We laid our offerings at the foot of the statue of Ganesh and lit several sticks of incense. When the elephant-headed god had disappeared behind a veil of smoke, we withdrew to leave him to crush the ogress with his trunk. Next day I had recovered enough strength to pick up the shafts of my rickshaw again.

'At that time a spell of icy cold had hit the north of the country. The tar on the Calcutta streets burned the bare soles of our feet just as acutely with the cold as it did with the heat during the worst dog days before the monsoon. The nights were terrible. It was no use our huddling together like dried fish in a packing case. The

cold bit into our skin and bones with teeth more pointed
than a crocodile's.

'The potions from the quack in Wellesley Street must
have contained some miraculous substance, because two
bottles were enough to appease the pain in my bones
and the heat in my chest within a matter of days. I was
quite convinced that soon I would be able to go back to
Flury's pastry shop and look at myself in the window
without fear. That was when I began to feel strange
scratchings at the base of my throat that provoked a
series of uncontrollable coughing fits. It was a dry,
painful cough which became progressively more violent
until it shook me like a coconut tree in a tornado,
then left me completely exhausted. It's true that such
coughing fits are a music as familiar to rickshaw pullers
as the ringing of their bells. All the same it was a
terrifying experience. It proved that the god had not
heard my prayer.'

46

With its handlebars bristling with headlights and horns,
its thick wheels painted green and red, its tank gleaming
like a streak of silver, and a seat covered with panther
skin, the motorcycle looked just like one of those flashy
machines you see in films. Strapped into leather trousers
with wide elephant thongs, topped with a silk shirt, its
rider drove through the muddy alleyways of the City of
Joy, spitting an exhaust inferno with obvious delight.
Everyone knew the strapping fellow in the dark glasses
who dispensed waves and smiles like a campaigning
politician. He was as familiar a character as the blind
mullah from the great mosque and the old Brahmin
from the little temple next to the railway lines. His name

was Ashoka, like the famous emperor in Indian history. He was the eldest son and first lieutenant of the local Mafia boss.

Despite a population of more than seventy thousand, the City of Joy had no mayor, no police force, no legal authority of any kind. As in the Pals' slum, this gap had however been promptly filled by the Mafia who reigned supreme over the City of Joy. It was they who directed affairs, extorted, arbitrated; no one disputed their power. There were several rival families among them but the most powerful godfather was a Hindu with thick-lensed glasses, who lived with his sons, his wives and his clan in a modern four-storey house built on the edge of the slum on the other side of the Grand Trunk Road, the main Calcutta–Delhi highway. He was about sixty and known as Kartik Baba, a name given to him by his father as a tribute to the son of Shiva, god of war.

Practically all the clandestine drinking dens in the slum were his property. Similarly, it was he who controlled the drug traffic and local prostitution. He could also pride himself on being one of the largest real estate owners in Anand Nagar. He had exercised great dexterity in choosing his tenants. Instead of refugee families, he preferred cows and buffalo. Most of the cattle sheds that harboured the approximately eight thousand five hundred head of cattle living in the slum belonged to him. This animal invasion, with its stench, its entourage of millions of flies and the river of liquid manure it discharged into the drains each day, went back to the days when for reasons of hygiene the municipality had banished the cattle sheds from the centre of Calcutta. There had been a great uproar about the creation of municipal dairies on the outskirts of the town but, as always, nothing had actually been done, and the animals had simply been rehoused in the City of Joy and other similar slums. The godfather had been one of the principal beneficiaries of this operation. It was more advan-

tageous to house a cow than a family of nine people. As he himself said, 'For the same rent and the same amount of space, there is no risk of the least complaint or demands of any kind.'

Everyone knew that the godfather had plenty of other sources of revenue at his disposal. In particular, he managed a network of fences who bought and resold goods stolen from the railways. The profits from this racket came to millions of rupees. Above all, however, he derived considerable benefit from a particularly odious form of exploitation. He exploited the lepers of Anand Nagar.

Not content merely to collect rent for their miserable shacks, he forced them to pay him a daily tax of one or two rupees in exchange for his 'protection' and a place to beg on the pavement at Howrah Station. Substantial political backing was necessary for the godfather actually to be able to implement such exactions with impunity. Rumour had it that he was a generous contributor to the coffers of the party in power, for whom he also acted as a diligent electoral agent. Ballot papers in the City of Joy, even those held between wasted stumps, formed part of his trafficking. Strangely, the residents were rather happy with this state of affairs and, since there existed no other uncontested body of authority in the slum, they even sought out frequent recourse to the godfather. Over the years he had thus become a redresser of wrongs, a kind of Robin Hood.

Of course, he rarely intervened personally. Instead he delegated that role to his eldest son Ashoka or to some other member of his family. Nevertheless, it was he who pulled the strings and he was never short of tricks to establish his authority. He would send his henchmen, for example, to provoke an incident in one of his drinking dens. Then he would dispatch Ashoka, or, in cases of extreme delicacy, would himself appear to restore peace and order and thereby show the community

exactly how good and how influential he was. Furthermore, when Ashoka or any of his other sons had got a
slum girl into trouble, he showed himself to be so
generous towards the parents that people hastened to
hush up the affair. In short he acted the role of a proper
nobleman.

The presence of the godfather's son's motorcycle outside Stephan Kovalski's door one morning caused a
sensation in Nizamudhin Lane. Rumours quickly ran:
'The godfather's picking a quarrel with Big Brother
Stephan. The godfather wants to turn the "Father" out
. . .' At first sight this anxiety appeared unjustified. After
prostrating himself before the priest with all the respect
he would accord the goddess Kali, the messenger of the
Mafia boss addressed Kovalski, 'Father, my father has
asked me to deliver an invitation to you.'

'An invitation?' marvelled the priest.

'Yes. He would like to discuss a small matter with
you. Something altogether insignificant . . .'

Kovalski knew that nothing was 'insignificant' to the
godfather. He judged it useless to stall.

'Fair enough,' he said, 'I'll follow you.'

Ashoka beat the air with his large, hairy hands.

'Not so fast! My father doesn't see people at just any
time of day! He'll be expecting you tomorrow at ten
o'clock. I'll come and get you.'

Crossing the City of Joy on the bulky and noisy
motorcycle of the heir to the throne, with all his sirens
going, Stephan Kovalski found the experience somewhat
comical. He could just imagine the parish priest's expression if he could only see him now. 'I don't know
how the Hindu and Mogul emperors received their
subjects,' he was to recount, 'but it would be very
hard for me to forget the princely fashion in which the
godfather of the City of Joy received me.'

His house was truly palatial. Outside the door were
three Ambassador cars complete with radio antennae

and protective screens at the windows, plus several
motorcycles like those the police use to escort ministers
and heads of state. The hall on the ground floor opened
onto a large room furnished with Oriental carpeting and
comfortable cushions. A small altar with a *lingam* of
Shiva, the images of numerous gods, and a little bell to
ring the *puja* adorned one corner of the room. Sticks of
burning incense exuded a heady fragrance.

The godfather was seated on a kind of throne sculpted
out of wood and encrusted with designs in mother-of-
pearl and ivory. He was wearing a white cap and a black
velvet waistcoat over a long white cotton shirt. Tinted
glasses with very thick lenses completely concealed his
eyes but his reactions could be discerned by the pucker-
ing of his bushy eyebrows. Ashoka motioned to the
visitor to sit on the cushion placed in front of his father.
Servants in turbans brought tea, bottles of iced lemon-
ade and a plate of Bengali pastries. The godfather
emptied one of the bottles, then began to tap the arm
of his chair with the fat topaz that adorned his index
finger.

'Welcome to this house, Father,' he said in a ceremonial and slightly hollow voice, 'and consider it your
own.' Without waiting for a reply, he cleared his throat
and dispatched a globule of spit into the copper urn
which glistened next to his right toe.

At this point Kovalski noticed that he was wearing
sandals with straps encrusted with precious stones.

'It is a very great honour to make your acquaintance,'
added his host. One of the servants returned with a tray
of cigars tied together in a bundle. The Mafia boss untied
the cord and offered a cigar to the priest, who declined
it. The godfather took his time lighting his own.

'You must be an altogether special person,' the godfather declared, exuding a puff of smoke, 'because it has
been reported to me that you have made an application
. . . I can't actually believe it . . . for Indian citizenship.'

'You are decidedly well informed,' Kovalski confirmed.

The godfather chuckled and settled himself comfortably in his chair.

'You must admit that it might seem somewhat surprising that someone should be tempted to exchange his affluent and privileged status of foreigner for that of a poor man in an Indian slum.'

'We probably don't have the same understanding of wealth, you and I.'

'At all events, I shall be proud to count someone like you among the ranks of my compatriots. And, if by any chance the response to your request is delayed, do let me know. I have connections. I shall try and intervene.'

'Thank you, but I put my trust in the Lord.'

The godfather made an effort to believe what he had just heard: was it possible that someone was refusing his support?

'Father,' he said after a growl, 'I have heard some strange rumours. It would seem that you intend to create a leper hospital in the slum. Is that right?'

'"Leper hospital" is a very grandiose expression. It's to be more a dispensary to treat the worst cases. I've asked Mother Teresa for the help of two or three of her Sisters.'

The godfather surveyed the priest sternly.

'You must know that no one can concern himself with the lepers in that slum without my authorization.'

'In that case, what's keeping you from helping them yourself? Your assistance would be most welcome.'

The godfather's eyebrows puckered above his thick glasses.

'The lepers in the City of Joy have been under my protection for twelve years, and that's probably the best thing that has ever happened to them. Without me the other inhabitants of this place would have thrown them out ages ago.' He leaned forward with a sudden air of complicity. 'My dear Father, have you asked yourself

how the people next door to your "dispensary" will react when your lepers start to show up?'

'I have faith in the compassion of my brothers,' Kovalski said.

'Compassion? You holy men are always talking about compassion! All you'll get by way of compassion is a riot. They'll set fire to your dispensary and lynch your lepers!'

The priest gritted his teeth, preferring not to reply. 'This scoundrel is probably right,' he thought.

The godfather relit his cigar and took a long draw on it, throwing his head back. 'I can see only one way for you to avoid all these trials and tribulations,' he said, throwing his head back again.

'Which is?'

'That you subscribe to a protection contract.'

'A protection contract?'

'It will cost you a mere three thousand rupees a month. Our rates are ordinarily much higher. But you are a man of God and, as I'm sure you realize, in India we are used to respecting what is sacred.'

Then, without waiting for any reply, he clapped his hands. His eldest son came hurrying in.

'The Father and I have come to an amicable agreement,' the godfather announced with evident satisfaction. 'The two of you can agree on the terms and conditions of the arrangement.'

The godfather was a nobleman. He did not concern himself with details.

That evening the founders of the Committee for Mutual Aid in the City of Joy assembled in Stephan Kovalski's room to discuss the godfather's ultimatum.

'The godfather's family is all-powerful,' declared Saladdin. 'Remember the last elections – the Molotov cocktails, the blows with iron bars . . . the people killed

and all those injured! Is it really worth the risk of setting it all off again, for the sake of a few crippled carcasses? We'll just have to agree to pay.'

'All the same, three thousand rupees for the right to take in and nurse a few lepers is exorbitant.' Margareta was indignant.

'Is it the sum that bothers you,' asked Kovalski, 'or the principle?'

She seemed surprised at the question.

'Why, the sum of course!'

'A typical answer,' thought Kovalski. 'Even here in the depths of the slum, extortion and corruption sticks to their skin like flies.' All the others shared Saladdin's view, all, that was, except Bandona, the young woman from Assam.

'May God damn this demon!' Bandona exclaimed. 'To give him one single rupee would be to betray the cause of all the poor.'

Her words had the effect of an electric shock on Kovalski.

'Bandona is right! We must take up the challenge, resist it, fight it. It's now or never that we can show the people here that they are no longer alone.'

Early the next morning, the bulbous, backfiring motorcycle belonging to the son of Kartik Baba came to a halt outside Kovalski's room. As his father had ordered, Ashoka had come to discuss the payment terms for the 'contract'. The meeting, however, lasted only a few seconds, just long enough for the priest to intimate his refusal to the young ruffian. This was the first defiance ever laid before the authority of the all-powerful head of the Mafia in the City of Joy.

One week later the little dispensary was ready to receive the first lepers. Bandona and a number of volunteers set out to bring back the six extreme cases Kovalski wanted to hospitalize first. He himself went at dawn to Mother Teresa's house to collect the three Sisters who

were to nurse the lepers. Hardly had they reached the square on which the mosque stood, however, when Bandona's group was intercepted by a commando of young thugs, armed with sticks and iron bars.

'No one's going any further!' shouted the leader, a pimply adolescent whose front teeth were missing.

The young Assamese girl tried to move forward but an avalanche of blows stopped her. At that same moment the priest arrived from the other end of the slum, accompanied by his three nuns. Seeing the commotion at the far end of the alley, he clenched his teeth. Then he heard a loud explosion and an outcry. A second gang had begun to use iron bars and pickaxes to ransack the old school that was to serve as the leper clinic. Terrified, the neighbourhood shopkeepers hastily barricaded their shop windows. On the Grand Trunk Road, the shrill grinding of dozens of metal shutters could be heard as traders rushed to lower them. When the destruction of the dispensary had been completed, a third gang appeared. They were carrying bottles and explosive devices in knapsacks strung over their shoulders. The street emptied in a flash. Even the dogs and the children, who were always swarming everywhere, took off. A series of detonations shook the entire neighbourhood, their echo resounding far beyond the boundaries of the City of Joy, as far as the railway station and beyond.

At Kovalski's side, Mother Teresa's Sisters began to recite the rosary aloud.

The priest led them into Margareta's compound, entrusted them to the protection of Gunga, the deaf mute, and ran in the direction of the explosions. A voice begged him to come back. He stopped and turned around only to find that Margareta was hurrying after him.

'Stephan, Big Brother,' she pleaded again. 'For the love of God, don't go any nearer! They'll kill you!'

At that moment they saw emerging from the road that skirted the slum a procession, with flags and banners

striped with slogans proclaiming in Hindi, Urdu and English: 'We don't want a leper hospital in Anand Nagar!'

A man with a megaphone marched at the head and chanted out other slogans that the horde behind him repeated. One of them said, 'No lepers here! Father *sahib* go home!'

These people didn't actually belong to the neighbourhood. There was nothing very surprising about that. Calcutta held the largest reserve of professional demonstrators in the world. Any political party or organization could rent a thousand of them, for five or six rupees per head per day. The same people who one morning shouted revolutionary slogans under the red flags of the Communists might well parade that evening or the next morning behind the banners of the Congress supporters. In a city that was a permanent boiling pot of tensions, any opportunity to let off steam was a good one. As soon as he spotted the emblem of Indira Gandhi's party on the banners demanding the expulsion of the lepers, the thirty-two-year-old local Communist party representative, a former foreman for Hindustan Motors, named Joga Banderkar, was also seized with the sudden impulse to demonstrate. Running as fast as his crippled leg would allow, he went to alert a few comrades. In less than an hour, the Communists in the slum had succeeded in assembling several hundred militants for a counter-demonstration. Thus the godfather's response to Stephan Kovalski's defiance was to result in a political confrontation.

There was nothing new about this sequence of events. Simple altercations between neighbours degenerated into scuffles between compounds, and those scuffles into battles waged between the residents of an entire neighbourhood, in which people were wounded and sometimes killed. On the day when he had saved the unfortunate mad woman from being lynched, old Surya

had explained the mechanics of such violence to Kovalski. 'You bow your head, you shut up, you put up with
everything indefinitely. You bottle up your grievances
against the owner of your hovel who is exploiting you,
the usurer who's bleeding you dry, the speculators who
push up the price of rice, the factory bosses who won't
give you a job, the neighbour's children who won't let
you sleep for coughing their lungs out all night, the
political parties who suck the life out of you and couldn't
give a damn, the Brahmins who take ten rupees from
you for a mere *mantra*. You take all the mud, the shit,
the stink, the heat, the insects, the rats, until one day,
wham! you're presented with an opportunity to shout,
ransack, kill. You don't know why but it's stronger than
you are, and you just pile on in there!'

Kovalski never ceased to be amazed and impressed by
the fact that in so harsh an environment, outbreaks of
violence were not more frequent. How many times had
he seen scuffles in the compounds dissolve unexpectedly
into a torrent of insults and invective, as if everyone
concerned wanted somehow to avoid the worst; for the
poor of Anand Nagar knew what the price of fights
really was. Recollections of the horror of Partition and
of Naxalite terrorism still haunted their memories.

Yet, that morning, nothing seemed to restrain the
fury of the men and women stampeding through the
slum. The two processions ran into each other on the
corner of the Grand Trunk Road. There was a savage
clash under a deluge of tiles, bricks and Molotov cocktails thrown from the roof tops. Stephan Kovalski saw
before him again the bleeding face of his father on that
evening in the summer of 1947, when police and striking
miners had fought around the pits. The confrontation
today was even more vicious. 'For the first time I read
on their faces something which I had believed was extinguished,' he was to explain. 'What I discovered there
was hatred. It twisted their mouths, inflamed their eyes,

drove them to perform monstrous acts, like throwing a bottle of explosives at a group of children trapped in the confusion, or setting fire to a coach full of passengers, or throwing themselves on some wretched old men incapable of escaping. There were plenty of women among the most heated fighters. I recognized some of them, although their contorted features rendered them almost unidentifiable. The slum had lost all reason. I realized then what would happen on the day the poor of Calcutta resolved to march upon the districts of the rich.'

All of a sudden there was a whistle, then a detonation followed by a blast of air so fierce that Kovalski and Margareta were thrown against each other. A bottle of petrol had exploded just behind them. Immediately they were enveloped in dense smoke. By the time the cloud had dispersed, they were in the thick of the throng. It was impossible to escape without risking being struck down on the spot. Fortunately the combatants seemed to be observing a pause in order to conduct a ritual as old as war itself – pillaging. Then it began to rain down bricks and bottles once more.

The ferocity reached a state of paroxysm. Dozens of wounded had fallen on all sides. Kovalski saw a child of four or five pick up one of the projectiles lying beside a drain. The device exploded, tearing off his hand. A few seconds later, he saw an iron bar flash above Margareta's head. He had just time enough to throw himself in front of her and deflect the blow. Already another assailant was bearing down on them with a cutlass. At the very instant he was about to strike, Kovalski saw a hand seize his attacker by the collar and hurl him backwards. Beyond the hand he recognized Mehboub, his Muslim neighbour who was himself armed with an iron bar. After his wife's death, the Muslim had entrusted his elderly mother and his children to the care of his elder son, Nasir, and then he had disappeared. Now here he was back again as a henchman for the godfather. His

forehead and nose were scarred with gashes and his moustache matted with blood; he looked more than ever like the picture of the Sacred Shroud before which he had so often composed himself. Meanwhile, all around them, blows rained down with redoubled savagery.

The most unrestrained fighters were the very young men. They seemed to be fighting one another for the sheer pleasure of it. It was terrifying. Kovalski saw one teenage boy plunge his knife into a woman's stomach. Then, he noticed the thickset silhouette and dark glasses of Ashoka, the godfather's eldest son. Until that moment neither Ashoka nor his father had appeared on the battlefield. Now Ashoka was issuing orders. The priest realized that something was going to happen.

He did not have to wait long to find out what. 'The carnage stopped as if at the wave of a magic wand,' he was to recount. 'The assailants put up their arms, turned on their heels and walked away. In a matter of minutes everything was almost back to normal. The groans of the wounded, the bricks and other bits of debris cluttering up the thoroughfare, and the acrid smell of smoke were the only signs that a battle had just taken place here. A reflex of reason had prevented the irreparable.'

The godfather was satisfied. He had inflicted the desired lesson and still kept control of his troops. Stephan Kovalski had been given due notice: no one in the City of Joy could defy the godfather with impunity.

47

'With all their speeches, their promises and their red flags, we were snared like pigeons in glue. No sooner had we elected them than all those left-wing *babus* turned their backs on us,' Hasari Pal was to recount, referring

to the elections that had brought the left to power in Bengal. 'They started off by voting a law that obliged the judges to order, not just the seizure of any rickshaws operating without official permission, but their actual destruction. These were the so-called defenders of the working class, the ones whose mouths were always full of 'rights' and 'justice', the ones who spent their time setting the poor against the rich, turning the exploited against their bosses, attacking the very means by which a hundred thousand of us were able to stop our wives and children from dying of starvation! To destroy the rickshaws of Calcutta was like burning the crops in the fields! And who would be the victims of such madness? The owners of the carts? Hell no! They didn't need the five or six rupees each old crate brought them per day to fill their bellies. Whereas for us, God knows, it meant death!'

As always, Hasari was after an explanation. The man they called Scarface had one. According to him, if the government *babus* wanted to burn all unlicensed carriages it was because those 'gentlemen' did not appreciate competition. He had discovered that several *babus* had their own rickshaws to exploit, for which they of course had arranged to obtain licences. As for Golam Rassoul, the union secretary who looked like a sparrow fallen from its nest, he had another explanation. Ever since he had been siding with the Communist *babus*, his head was packed with all sorts of theories that simple souls like Hasari often had difficulty in understanding. 'Because we had more opportunities to cultivate our calves than our brains,' Hasari was to admit.

Rassoul claimed that the people responsible for the persecutions were really the technocrats among the municipal officials. According to him, the *babus* in question begrudged the rickshaw pullers the fact that they worked on the fringes of the government system, in other words, they were not dependent on either the *babus* or the state.

'As if the state were in the habit of doing the rounds of the pavements and slums offering work to the starving unemployed,' Hasari was to retort. 'In any case,' Rassoul went on to explain, 'rickshaw pullers had no place in those technocrats' vision of tomorrow's Calcutta. The Calcutta of these visionaries would be one of machines, not human horses. Five thousand more taxis and buses would be better for everybody than the sweat of a hundred thousand poor bums.' In Rassoul's view, it was not all that difficult to understand why. 'Let us suppose,' he explained, 'that the government orders five thousand more taxis and buses to transport the one and a half million people who travel about in our old rattletraps each day. Well, you can imagine what an order like that would mean to the automobile manufacturers, the tyre makers, the garages and petrol companies, not to mention the pharmaceutical laboratories, because of all the lung disease the new pollution would provoke.'

For whatever reason, the newly elected *babus* decided to go after unlicensed rickshaws. The law was implemented and unauthorized carriages were confiscated. No puller dared to use the main avenues where there were policemen directing traffic. Other policemen began to check on them at the stands.

'Let me see your licence,' an officer would order the first puller in line.

'I haven't got a licence,' the puller would apologize, the poor fellow, taking a few rupees out of the folds of his *longhi*.

This time, however, the policeman would pretend not to see the notes. He was under strict orders: the time for baksheesh was simply over. Sometimes the puller did not even reply. He'd just shrug his shoulders with resignation. He was used to a rotten *karma*. The policeman would have the carriages slotted into one another and dragged to the nearest *thana*, the local police station. Soon, on the pavements outside all the *thanas* there were

long snaking lines of rickshaws stacked up against each
other, their wheels shackled with chains. Thus immobilized, the old carts presented a sad picture of desolation.
They were like the trees in an orchard uprooted by a
cyclone, like fishes caught in a net.

'What a calamity,' lamented Hasari with his companions. 'But as long as they were there, chained up
outside the *thanas*, there was still the hope that one day
they would be restored to those for whom they provided
a livelihood.' Even that hope was soon to be crushed,
however.

As the law prescribed, the judges ordered the destruction of the confiscated rickshaws. One evening they
were all loaded onto the yellow municipal rubbish carts
and taken to an unknown destination. Rassoul managed
to have the carts followed by a union spy and soon the
pullers discovered that their carriages had been collected
on the city's public dump, behind the tanners' quarter,
very probably to be burned.

Because they were so widely dispersed, it generally
took a fair amount of time to gather a significant number
of pullers together. But on this occasion, it took less
than one hour for them to form a formidable procession
on Lower Circular Road, with banners, posters and all
the usual trappings of that kind of demonstration. Led
by Rassoul, Scarface and all the union general staff, the
column set out on a march to the dump, shouting, 'Our
rickshaws are our rice!' As they advanced, other workers
joined them. In Calcutta demonstrating helped one to
forget an empty stomach. At every crossroad, policemen
stopped traffic to let them pass. In Calcutta that was the
norm. Those asserting their rights always took priority
over other citizens.

They marched like that for miles, through the outer-
most suburbs, until finally they reached a deserted area.
'And it was then,' Hasari was to say, 'that the shock
came. First there was a stench that burned your lungs

out, as if thousands of decaying carcasses were engulfing
you, as if heaven and earth were decomposing under
your nostrils. It took several minutes for us to get a grip
on our nausea and go on.' About a few hundred yards
ahead lay an enormous mound from which the smell
arose – the city's dumping ground. On a mattress of
rubbish as vast as the Maidan, dozens of lorries and
bulldozers moved about in a cloud of pestilential dust. A
myriad vultures and crows circled above the putrescence.
There were so many of them that the sky was as black
as a monsoon day. Most astounding of all, however, was
the number of ragpickers wriggling about like insects
among the refuse.

As they reached the rubbish platform, the pullers
noticed their carriages on the far side of the wretched,
stinking place. The rickshaws formed a long snake of
wheels and arches slotted into one another. 'How could
the god ever have allowed those purveyors of rice to
end up in a place like this?' wondered Hasari and his
comrades. It was totally incomprehensible. 'The god
must have been in the arms of some princess the day
the *babus* voted their law,' thought the former peasant.
'Either that or he just doesn't give a damn about us.'

What happened next was to remain for Hasari the
most terrible sight of his life. Behind the rickshaws and
below the level of the mound, three police vans were
concealed. When the procession spilled onto the dump,
the policemen rushed out of their vehicles to block its
way. They were not traffic policemen but specialized,
anti-riot policemen with helmets, guns and shields. They
had been given the order to drive back the demonstrators
and carry out the total destruction of all the rickshaws.

Rassoul armed himself with his loudspeaker and
shouted that the rickshaw *wallahs* had come to oppose
this destruction. In the meantime press photographers
had arrived. They looked somewhat out of place in these
surroundings, with their shoes and trousers, but the

dump was soon black with people. The ragpickers had stopped scrabbling among the rubbish and other people had come running from nearby villages. The policemen advanced, brandishing their guns, but not a single puller stirred. 'In view of the enormity of the crime about to take place, we were all prepared to fall under the guns of the police rather than back off,' Hasari would say. 'All these years had really hardened us and our last great strike had shown us that we could make our bosses tremble if only we remained united. We felt as solidly bound to one another as our shafts were to our carriages.'

It was then that the real drama began. A policeman struck a match and lit a torch which he then plunged into the body of a rickshaw, right in the middle of the line. The flames immediately set the hood and seat ablaze, then spread to the next vehicle. After one stunned second, the people in the foremost ranks of the procession hurled themselves at the barrage of policemen. They wanted to push the burning vehicles out of the way to save the others, but the policemen formed an insurmountable wall.

It was at precisely that moment that Hasari noticed Scarface. He had managed to hoist himself up onto a friend's shoulders. Letting out a shout, he reared up and, with a formidable thrust of his haunches, managed to leap over the policemen. He literally fell into the flames, and from there his comrades saw him launch himself onto the burning carriages to topple them into the ravine. It was a crazy thing to do. Even the policemen turned around in astonishment. A scream went up from the blazing mass. Hasari spotted an arm and a hand grasping one of the shafts, then smoke enveloped the scene and the smell of scorched flesh mingled with the stench of the whole surroundings. Silence fell over the dump. All that could be heard now was the crackling of the flames as they consumed the rickshaws. The *babus* had won.

When at last the fire had died down, Hasari asked one

of the refuse pickers for a tin. With it, he went and
collected Scarface's cinders from the embers. He and
his comrades would scatter them on the waters of the
Hooghly, the branch of the sacred river Ganges.

48

In winter, the same phenomenon occurred each evening.
No sooner had the women set fire to the cow dung cakes
to cook their dinner than the reddening disc of the sun
disappeared behind a greyish filter. Held there by the
layer of fresh air above, the wreaths of dense smoke
hovered stagnantly over the rooftops, imprisoning the
slum beneath a poisonous screen. Its inhabitants
coughed, spat and choked. On some evenings, visibility
was reduced to less than six feet. The smell of sulphur
overrode all others. People's skin and eyes burned. Yet
no one in the City of Joy would have dared to curse
the wintertime, that all too short a respite before the
summer's onslaught.

Summer, that year, struck like a bolt of lightning. In
a matter of seconds, night fell in the very middle of day.
Crazed with panic, the slum people rushed out of their
compounds and into the alleys. From the terrace where
he was sorting medicines, Stephan Kovalski saw an
atmospheric disturbance of a kind that was totally unknown to him. At first sight it could have passed for the
aurora borealis. What it in fact consisted of was a wall
of suspended particles of yellow sand bearing down
upon the slum with lightning speed. There was no time
to take shelter. The tornado had already reached them.

It devastated everything in its path, tearing off the
roofs of houses and tossing their occupants to the
ground. In their sheds the cows and buffalo bellowed

with terror. The slum was instantly covered with a shroud
of yellow dust. Then a succession of flashes lit the darkness, the signal for a cataclysm which this time bombarded
the slum with hailstones succeeded by a torrential downpour of rain. When finally the rain stopped and the sun
came out again, a cloud of burning vapour descended over
the slum. The thermometer rose from fifteen degrees to a
hundred and four degrees Fahrenheit. Stephan Kovalski
and the seventy thousand other inhabitants of the City of
Joy realized that the short winter truce was over. The
blazing inferno was with them once more. That March
17, summer had come to the city.

Summer! That season beloved of all temperate zones
inflicted upon the occupants of this part of the world
unimaginable suffering and, as always, it was the most
destitute people, the miserable slum dwellers, who were
most cruelly stricken by it. In the windowless hovels
crammed with up to fifteen people, in those tiny compounds scorched for twelve hours a day by the sun,
in the narrow alleys where never the slightest breath
disturbed the air, while extreme poverty and the absence
of electricity prevented the use of fans, the summer
months that preceded the arrival of the monsoon were
as atrocious a form of torture as hunger itself.

In the avenues of Calcutta people simply did not
move without the protection of an umbrella. Even the
policemen directing traffic were equipped with linen
shades attached to their crossbelts, so as to leave their
hands free. Other people sheltered themselves from the
sun beneath attaché cases, wads of newspaper, piles of
books, the tails of their saris or *dhotis* raised over their
heads. The furnace-like heat was accompanied by humidity that could sometimes reach 100 per cent. The least
movement, a few steps, going up a staircase, induced a
shower of perspiration. From ten o'clock in the morning
on, any physical effort became impossible. Men and
beasts found themselves petrified in the incandescence

of the unmoving air. Not a breath stirred. The reflection
off the walls of the buildings was so bright that anyone
imprudent enough to go out without dark glasses was
liable to a sensation of melted lead in his eyes. Venturing
barefoot onto the asphalt of the streets was even more
painful. The liquefied tar scorched strips of flesh from
the soles of the feet. Pulling a rickshaw on this fiery
carpet was an act of pure heroism – running, stopping,
setting off again with wheels that stuck fast in the burning tar. To try and protect his feet already ulcerated with
cracks and burns, Hasari Pal resolved to wear a pair of
sandals, an act which millions of barefooted Indians had
never accomplished. Thus for the first time in his life,
Hasari put on the beautiful pair of sandals received in
his wife's dowry on the occasion of his marriage. His
initiative was to prove disastrous. The sandals parted
company with his feet at the first patch of burning
asphalt, sucked off by the melting tar.

For six days the inhabitants of the City of Joy held
out; then the hecatomb began. With lungs charred by
the torrid air and bodies dried of all substance, those
who suffered from tuberculosis and asthma and a whole
host of babies began to die. The members of the Committee for Mutual Aid, with Stephan Kovalski, Margareta
and Bandona at their head, ran from one end of the slum
to the other to help the most desperate cases. 'Ran' was
not really the word, because they too were compelled
to move slowly for fear of falling unconscious after only
a few steps. Under the torment of such temperatures, a
body dehydrated in a matter of hours. 'The slightest
effort,' Kovalski was to recount, 'and all your pores
exuded a flood of sweat that drenched you from head to
toe. Then you experienced something like a shiver and
almost instantaneously your head began to swim. So
numerous were the victims of sunstroke and dehydration
that the alleys were soon strewn with helpless people
incapable of standing on their feet.'

Strangely enough, it was the Pole who, although used to a more temperate climate, seemed the best able to resist the rigours of such blazing heat. With his burning metal crucifix dancing about on his bare chest, his waist and thighs swathed in a cotton *longhi*, and his head covered with an old straw hat, he looked like a Devil's Island convict. On the tenth day, however, the temperature broke the record for the last quarter of a century. On the thermometer at the old Hindu's tea shop, the mercury touched a hundred and fourteen degrees Fahrenheit in the shade. Taking into account the humidity, it was the equivalent of a hundred and thirty degrees in the sun. 'The worst part about it was the perpetual dampness in which you were steeped,' Kovalski would comment. 'It soon caused a series of epidemics that decimated many families. On top of that, malaria, cholera and typhoid made their appearance again. But it was gastroenteritis that claimed the most victims. It was quite capable of killing a man in less than twenty-four hours.'

Yet this was only the beginning. Further trials lay in store for the Pole. Outbreaks of boils, carbuncles, whitlows and mycosis hit the slum. Thousands of people caught them. The blight reached many other parts of Calcutta, and certain professions like those of the rickshaw *wallahs* and the *telagarhi wallahs* who were used to walking barefoot through the muck were particularly vulnerable. Because of the lack of dressings and antibiotics, such skin diseases spread like wildfire. Next door to Kovalski, the bodies of Mehboub's children became open sores. Mehboub himself, having returned home, fell victim to a very painful crop of carbuncles, which the priest had to lance with a penknife. At the end of March the temperature rose again, and as it did so something quite extraordinary happened. The flies began to die. Next it was the mosquitoes' turn; their eggs perished before they hatched. All the centipedes, scor-

pions and spiders disappeared. The only vermin to survive in the City of Joy were the bugs. They came forth and multiplied as if they made it a point to fill the vacuum left by the others. Every evening Kovalski gave furious chase to them, yet still they flourished. Several of them had even taken refuge behind the picture of the Sacred Shroud. The frenzy with which he attacked and killed them gave the priest a measure of the lack of serenity to which he had been reduced. 'After all that time in India, the result was bitterly disappointing. Despite the litanies of *Oms* and the example of detachment that Surya, the old Hindu opposite, set me, I was still rebelling against the inhuman conditions inflicted upon my brothers here.'

One morning as he was shaving, the mirror cast back at him yet another shock. His cheeks were even more sunken and two deep furrows had appeared around his mouth and his moustache, accentuating the comical snub of his nose. His skin had assumed a waxlike hue. It was stretched over his bones like a piece of shiny old oilcloth.

The real martyrs of the heat, however, were the workers in the thousands of little workshops and rooms scattered throughout the City of Joy and other slums. Lumped together with their machines in huts without ventilation, they were like the crews of sinking submarines. The women's conditions were pitiful too. Trammelled in their saris and veils at the back of hovels transformed into ovens, the least household chore made them perspire all the sweat their bodies could muster.

Oddly, in a heat so suffocating that it prostrated even the most robust, it was inactivity that was most arduous. 'The heat seemed even more unbearable when you stopped moving,' Kovalski was to say. 'It came down on you like a leaden mantle, stifling you as it did so.' To stop themselves from suffocating, people tried to create a minute turbulence of air on their faces by waving a piece of cardboard or newspaper back and forth. 'The extraordinary thing was that they went on fanning them-

selves while they dozed, even while they slept.' The Pole
tried to do the same but as soon as sleep overtook him,
his hand would let go of the improvised fan. He realized
then that that kind of ability must be 'an adaptation of
the species, a reflex acquired in the course of generations
of combating the rigours of the climate'.

One night in April, Stephan Kovalski felt under his
armpits and on his stomach the beginnings of an itch
that within a few hours extended to every part of his
body. 'It felt as if millions of insects were gnawing away
at me.' The irritation became so intense that he could
not resist scratching himself. Soon his entire epidermis
was one big sore. Suffocating and drained of all strength,
he remained prostrate in his room. A slum is not, however, like one of those Western dormitory cities where a
man can disappear or die without his neighbour noticing.
Here, the slightest deviation from the norm aroused
curiosity.

The first person to be perturbed by the 'Father's'
failure to emerge was Nasir, Mehboub's elder son, who
lined up for him each morning at the latrines. He alerted
his father who ran to inform Bandona. In a matter
of minutes the whole neighbourhood knew that Big
Brother Stephan was sick. 'Only a place where men live
in such close contact with death could offer so many
examples of love and solidarity,' thought the priest on
seeing Surya, the old Hindu from across the way,
coming into his hut with a pot of tea and milk and a
plate of biscuits. A few moments later Sabia's mother
brought in a bowl of 'lady's fingers', green vegetables
that look like large beans. To give them a little more
flavour, she had garnished them with a piece of gourd
and some turnips, a real extravagance for a woman as
poor as she. Bandona arrived next. The young Assamese
girl diagnosed the ailment at a glance: it was indeed
insects that were biting Stephan Kovalski, but not the
bugs and other small creatures that generally infested the

hovels in the City of Joy. The Pole was being devoured by tiny parasites called 'acari', whose invasion beneath the epidermis produced a painful skin disease that was ravaging the slum.

'Stephan *Daddah*,' clucked Bandona with a smile, 'you've got scabies!'

At the end of April the thermometer rose several more degrees, and with this new assault a sound that usually formed part of the decor of the City of Joy was silenced. The only birds in the slum, the crows, ceased to caw. Some days later, their corpses were found on the roofs and in the compounds. A thin trace of blood trickled from their beaks. The heat had burst their lungs. The same fate was soon to befall other animals. First in their tens and then in their hundreds the rats began to die. In the hovel next to Kovalski's, Sabia's mother had stretched an old sari over the low ledge on which her youngest daughter who had chicken pox used to sleep. Finding a number of maggots on her child's forehead one day, the poor woman realized they must have dropped through a hole in the material. When she looked up at the framework, on a bamboo beam above her she saw a dead rat.

It was at this juncture that the municipal workers responsible for emptying the latrines and cleaning the manure from the cattle sheds chose to strike. In a few days the slum was submerged beneath a lake of excrement. Blocked by mountains of dung from the cattle sheds, the open drains overflowed, spilling out a blackish, stinking stream. Into the torrid, static air, there soon rose an intolerable stench, borne upward on the smoke of the *chulas*. To top it all, the month of May ended with a terrible premonsoon storm, during which the level of the drains and the latrines rose by almost two feet in one night. The corpses of dogs, rats, scorpions and thousands of cockroaches began to float around in the foul sludge. People even saw several goats and a buffalo drifting

through the alleyways with bellies inflated like balloons. The storm activated another unforeseen phenomenon: millions of flies hatched out. Naturally the floodwater invaded most of the hovels, transforming them into cesspools. Yet, in the very midst of the horror, there was always some kind of miracle to be found. The one which Stephan Kovalski experienced in the depths of his hut that Sunday in Pentecost took the form of 'a little girl in a white dress, with a red flower in her hair, who picked her way through all that dung, with the regal air of a queen'.

PART THREE
Calcutta My Love

49

A sharp deceleration thrust him backwards in his seat. The wing of the Boeing had just tipped towards the ground, unveiling a lush landscape of cultivated fields and coconut palms. After flying for two hours over the parched expanse of central India, it seemed to Max Loeb as if he were arriving in the middle of an oasis. Everywhere there was water: canals, shimmering pools, stretches of marshland covered with wild hyacinths and looking like floating gardens retained by narrow dikes. He thought of the Everglades of Florida and of the Mexican marshland borders of Xochimilco. The sombre shapes of a herd of buffalo emerged from out of the green. Then the aeroplane righted itself, revealing in one swoop the city.

It was an enormous city, devoid of either limits or horizon, traversed by a brownish coloured river on which the ships at anchor looked like petrified ducks; a city with contours rendered indistinct by the shroud of smoke that blanketed its entanglement of roofs. The glittering outline of a petrol tank, the silhouette of a crane on the riverbank, the metallic structure of a factory, pierced through the thick layer.

As the hostess announced that the aircraft was about to land in Calcutta, Max could just make out the Gothic bell tower of a cathedral, the stands of a racecourse and red double-decker buses moving along an avenue set in the middle of a park. Finally the Boeing drew level with the runway and landed.

As soon as the door was opened the furnace outside surged into the plane. 'I felt as if I was being hit by a blast from a giant hair dryer,' the American was to

recount. 'I recoiled under the shock and for a moment found myself struggling to get my breath back. When at last I did get out onto the gangway, I was blinded by the fierce reflection and had to hang on to a rail.'

A few moments later, in the confusion of the arrival terminal, Max spotted a garland of yellow flowers held aloft. It was Kovalski, brandishing the welcoming garland bought to greet the American visitor in traditional Indian style. The two men recognized each other instinctively. Their greetings were effusive but brief.

'I suggest I take you to the Grand,' said Kovalski, climbing into a taxi. 'That's the local luxury hotel. I've never actually set foot inside it but I imagine it's a more suitable place than the City of Joy for a first encounter with the realities of this dear city.'

The young American was perspiring more and more heavily. 'Unless, of course, you want to plunge straight in,' Kovalski added with a wink. 'And I really mean plunge. The sewer workers are on strike again. You realize that what you're coming into isn't exactly Florida!'

Max checked a grimace. He was just considering the proposed alternatives when his gaze fell on his companion's arm. 'What have you got there?' he asked, indicating the skin covered with scabs.

'I caught scabies.'

The young doctor grunted. No doubt Kovalski was right: it would make better sense to take a little time to acclimatize himself. To go straight from a millionaire's playground to the depths of hell might well do irreparable damage. Max was realistic enough to be wary of that sort of traumatic shock. How many hulking men from the Peace Corps had had trouble adjusting to real poverty! It would be wiser to adapt himself bit by bit, in the comfort of an air-conditioned room, and with the help of a few generous glasses of Scotch and some

mellow Montecristo cigars. After all, there was no real
rush.

After a moment, however, Máx turned abruptly to
his companion. 'I'd rather come with you to Anand
Nagar,' he announced.

An hour later, the new friends were facing each other
across a table, under the flickering light of one of the
slum's eating places. A fan, apparently on the point of
expiring, was stirring up a torrid atmosphere, heavy
with the smell of frying.

'Buffalo stew?' asked the American, daunted by the
look of the strange mixture one of the young serving
boys had placed in front of him.

'Not real "stew",' corrected the Pole, mopping greedily at his plate. 'Just the sauce. There isn't any meat in
it. But the bones, skin, marrow, and gelatine have been
so well simmered that it's full of protein. It's just like
eating a New York sirloin. And for thirty pice [about 2
pence] you can hardly expect them to serve duck and
olives, can you?'

Max made a face that spoke eloquently of his repug-
nance.

'I think you should realize that we were lucky to get
a table,' added Kovalski, eager to portray his slum in the
best possible light. 'This is actually the Maxim's of the
neighbourhood!'

The American stopped frowning but he continued to
examine his plate, the squalor of the decor and the
clientele. About twenty or so customers were engaged
in eating their meals amid the din of voices. They were
all factory workers without families, or employees from
the workshops, condemned to live near their machines
because of power cuts. The establishment belonged to a
fat, bald-headed Muslim called Nasser, who presided
over his steaming cauldron like a Buddha behind an
incense burner. Nasser was the leader of the local
Marxist–Communist party cell. No madness of the ther-

mometer could shift him from his observation post. He oversaw a dozen employees, who called the Pole 'Father', 'Uncle', or '*Daddah* Stephan'. Five of them were slum children, the eldest no more than eight years old. They worked from seven in the morning till midnight for their food and a monthly salary of ten rupees (60 pence). Barefooted, dressed in rags, they ran to fill buckets at the well, wash the tables, clean up, chase the flies away, serve the meals, sort out the customers. They were tireless and ever joyful little men. Three others in charge of cleaning the vegetables were mentally deficient. Nasser had picked them up when they were begging on the Great Trunk Road among lorries that only narrowly avoided flattening them. They lived on the restaurant's premises, sleeping on perches their employer rigged up for them out of planks suspended from the bamboo of the building framework. A blind man and a one-eyed man presided over the washing up. The blind man sported a small white goatee and sang verses from the Koran. Kovalski never went past the restaurant without going over to talk with him. 'Like Surya, the old Hindu in the tea shop, that man had the gift of recharging my batteries. He gave off good vibrations.'

How could anyone bring all these nuances to the attention of an American who had just landed from a different world? Kovalski knew from experience that the City of Joy was a place that had to be discovered in homeopathic doses – and which had, above all, to be deserved. It would be a long and difficult undertaking.

An exceptional event was to take place that first evening, however, which would accelerate the process and plunge Max Loeb into the very heart of his new surroundings. The Pole had given his companion a dessert to sample – a piece of *barfi*, the delicious Bengali nougat eaten in its thin sliver of silver paper – when a small man burst in, rushed over to Kovalski, threw himself at his feet, and spoke to him in Bengali, his hands joined

together in a gesture of supplication. There was an air of urgency and deep emotion about him, and Max Loeb noticed that several fingers were missing from both his hands.

'How much do you know about obstetrics?' asked Kovalski as he got to his feet.

The American shrugged his shoulders.

'Only what I learned at school . . . not much.'

'Come on! It's got to be better than nothing. It seems our friends here have been keeping a little welcoming surprise in store for you.'

The American's astonishment delighted the Pole. 'Yes, Doctor, they want to give you a brand-new baby!'

'And I'm supposed to help?'

'How did you guess?'

They hurried off behind the messenger, who was growing impatient in the street. Wading up to their calves through sludge, they moved cautiously forward. From time to time they stumbled on something soft – the carcass of a dog or a rat. Darkness falls early in the tropics and the night was as black as ink.

'Try not to fall into one of the main sewers,' observed Kovalski, alluding to the six-foot-deep gutters that ran through the slum.

'It'd be one good way of making me miss the Florida beaches!'

'Provided you came out alive! In this filth, you'd die in seconds because of the gas.'

For half an hour they picked their way along, past the astonished gazes of people who obviously wondered where these two *sahibs* might be going, through the muck, at such an hour.

'Duck your head!'

This warning saved the American from cracking his skull against a fat bamboo beam.

'You'll have to get used to bending down around here . . . Just bear in mind how good it is for your humility!'

Max bent his large body to enter a courtyard full of people; they were chattering noisily but the arrival of the two foreigners brought silence. With the fugacious light of a candle, the American made out noseless faces, the stumps of limbs moving about like marionettes. He realized that he was in the leper quarter.

The worst offender was the smell, an indefinable odour of rotten meat, of putrefying flesh. Like Stephan Kovalski on his first visit, Max could hardly believe his eyes. At the feet of those mutilated bodies, children were playing, splendid chubby children who looked as if they'd stepped straight out of an advertisement. A grey-haired old man led Kovalski and his companion towards a miserable room from which feeble groans were issuing. As they were about to cross the threshold, two very wrinkled old women tried to block their way, a flood of invective bursting from their betel-reddened mouths.

'Midwives,' explained the Pole, turning back to Max. 'Our arrival is an insult to them.'

The old man pushed the women unceremoniously out of the way and led the visitors inside. Someone brought a candle, whereupon Kovalski discovered a pale face with deep-sunken eyes that he recognized.

'Meeta!' he exclaimed, astonished.

The young wife of his crippled friend looked exhausted. She was bathed in a sea of blood. Only with difficulty did she open her eyes, but when she saw the turned-up nose and familiar forehead with its receding hairline above her, her mouth formed a faint smile.

'Stephan, Big Brother!' she sighed feebly.

Her withered hands reached out for him, as Max removed the rags that served as a compress.

'We'll have to hurry!' the American declared. 'If not, they've both had it!'

Between the thighs of the leper woman he had just discovered the tip of a small blood-covered skull. The baby was wedged halfway out of the uterus. Its mother

could not manage to push it out. Possibly it was dead already.

'Have you got anything to sustain her heart?' asked Max as he tried to find the young woman's pulse. Kovalski foraged in the bag that was his constant companion, in which he always carried a few emergency medicines, and took out a bottle.

'I've got some Coramine.'

Max grimaced. 'Nothing stronger? An intravenous cardiac stimulant?'

The question seemed so incongruous to the priest that, despite the circumstances, he could not help laughing.

'What do you think I am, a Miami drugstore?'

The American apologized with a slightly forced smile, and Kovalski asked for a cup of water into which he poured the medicine. Kneeling at the bedside of the young leper woman, he supported her head and helped her to drink slowly, involuntarily adding to her cup the droplets of sweat pouring off his own forehead. It was at least a hundred and ten degrees inside the hut.

'Tell her to start pushing again, as hard as possible,' Max ordered.

Kovalski translated this into Bengali and Meeta contracted her body, panting with the effort. Tears of pain rolled down her cheeks.

'No, not like that! She's got to push *down*. Tell her to take a deep breath first and then push hard as she breathes out. Hurry!'

Max was dripping with sweat. He mopped his face and neck. A rancid taste rose up in his throat. Was it the heat, the buffalo stew that wouldn't stay down, the stench, or the sight of all those mutilated bodies? He was gripped by an incoercible desire to vomit. Seeing him turn as white as a sheet, Kovalski emptied the remainder of the bottle of Coramine into the cup from which the leper woman had just been drinking.

'Get this down quickly!'

Max started at the sight of the receptacle.

'Are you out of your mind?'

'You've got no choice. They're all looking at you. If you show your revulsion, they might turn nasty. You never know with lepers.'

Seeing Max turn more livid in colour, however, he said, 'There's nothing to worry about. You can't catch her sort of leprosy. It's not contagious.'

Max raised the cup to his lips, closed his eyes, and drank the contents down in a gulp. A little girl with black eyes made up with kohl came and fanned him with a piece of cardboard. He felt better. Bending over to examine the woman in labour more closely, he could see that the child was coming out the wrong way. It wasn't the upper part of the head that was emerging but the nape of the neck. Max knew that there was only one way of extricating the baby: he would have to turn it.

'Do you think the baby's still alive?' Kovalski asked.

'How can I tell without a stethoscope?'

The young doctor put his ear to the leper woman's stomach. He straightened up with an expression of disappointment.

'No heartbeat. But that doesn't mean much. He's turned the wrong way. For God's sake, tell her to push harder!'

The Coramine was taking effect; the leper woman's contractions were coming with increased vigour. Max knew that he must take advantage of every thrust. There could be no doubt about it; this was his last chance.

'Go around the other side,' he said to Kovalski. 'While I try to turn the baby, you massage her stomach from top to bottom to help the downward motion.'

As soon as Kovalski had stepped over the body, the doctor slid his hand in behind the baby's neck. Meeta groaned at the movement of his fingers.

'Tell her to breathe deeply and to push evenly, without jerking.'

All the leper woman's muscles tightened. Her head thrown back, her mouth contorted, she made a desperate effort.

What happened next might well seem improbable. The American's hand had just reached the baby's shoulder when two balls of fur brushed against his head and rebounded on the stomach of the mother. In the framework of the hovel, some of the rats had survived the heat wave. They were as large as cats. In his surprise, Max withdrew his hand. Was it his abrupt movement or the shock of the creatures' landing? One thing was certain: the baby's body righted itself.

'Push, push, push!' cried Max. Ten seconds later, a bundle of flesh enveloped in mucus and blood passed into his hands. He lifted it up like a trophy.

It was a magnificent boy weighing at least six pounds. He saw the baby's lungs inflate and his mouth open to let out a cry that unleashed an amazing echo of joy in the courtyard of the compound. One of the midwives severed the cord with a sharp blow and tied it off with a piece of jute. The other brought a basin to begin the ablutions.

The American's heart missed a beat at the colour of the infant's clothing. 'These people must be tougher than steel,' he thought to himself. Since no Brahmin would agree to enter into a leper compound, the honour of undertaking the first rite that follows the birth of a child fell to Stephan Kovalski. Suddenly he felt someone touching his feet and, looking down, found Anouar who had just arrived on his piece of wood on wheels. Having wiped the dust off Kovalski's sneakers, the crippled man then raised his stumps to his forehead as a mark of respect. He looked overjoyed.

'Stephan, Big Brother, you've given me a son! A son!' Paralysed with anxiety, Meeta's husband had kept out of the way until this triumphal moment. Now he brought a bowlful of grains of rice. Wedging it between his stumps,

he raised it up as an offering to the priest. 'There,' he said, 'put the rice next to my boy, that the gods may grant him a long and prosperous life.' Then he took an oil lamp from one of the midwives. According to ritual, its wick must burn without interruption until the following day. If it went out, the newborn baby would not live.

In his first letter to his fiancée, Max Loeb would report of the demonstrations of enthusiasm that followed. 'All the lepers were overwhelmed with joy. It was impossible to restrain them. Withered hands flung themselves round my neck. Pitted faces embraced me. Cripples brandished their crutches and clapped them together like drumsticks. "*Daddah*, Big Brother, God bless you!" the people cried. Even the midwives joined in the celebration. Children brought biscuits and sweetmeats which we had to eat on pain of breaching the rules of hospitality. I was suffocating, nauseous. The smell of decay was even more unbearable in the courtyard than inside the hovel. Yet Stephan, my companion, seemed completely at home. He grasped the fingerless hands held out to him, while I confined myself to joining mine together in this beautiful gesture of greeting that I had seen people use at the airport. The cries of that newborn baby filled the night – my first night in Calcutta.'

50

'There aren't just tigers and snakes in the jungle of Calcutta,' mused Hasari Pal. 'You also meet lambs and doves there, even among taxi drivers.' The latter were generally real villains who had no sympathy whatsoever for human horses. Riding along like rajahs in their

black-and-yellow motor palanquins, they never missed an opportunity to assert their superiority.

One day in a traffic jam, one of these 'rajahs' had nudged Hasari and his carriage into a gutter. It was then that the miracle occurred. The driver, a small, bald man with a scar around his neck, actually stopped to apologize. This was no *sardarji* from the Punjab, with a rolled beard, a turban and a dagger, but a Bengali like Hasari, originally from Bandel, a little place on the banks of the Ganges, some twenty miles from the Pals' village. He hastened to help Hasari extricate his rickshaw from the gutter and even suggested sharing a bottle of *bangla* with him. Next day he turned up during a torrential downpour. Abandoning their respective vehicles, the two men took refuge in a dive at the back of Park Street.

The taxi driver was called Manik Roy. He had started out as a bus driver, until one night a gang of *dacoits*, thieves who worked the highways, stopped him on the road. Having made his passengers get out and having relieved them of their possessions, the robbers then proceeded to slit their throats. By what miracle Manik had been found still alive, the following day, he could not say, but as a reminder of that horrific night he still bore an impressive scar on his neck. This was how he had come to be nicknamed Chomotkar which means, literally, 'Son of Miracle'.

In Hasari's eyes that man was indeed the 'son of miracle', but for quite another reason. Instead of gripping the shafts of a rickshaw, his hands caressed a steering wheel; instead of treading asphalt and holes, his feet travelled deftly between three small rubber pedals; instead of straining and sweating, he earned his children's rice seated calmly on the seat of a chariot more noble than Arjuna's. A taxi! What rickshaw puller had not dreamed that one day the four arms of the god Viswakarma would gently touch his rattling cart and transform

it into one of those black-and-yellow vehicles that
streaked through the avenues of Calcutta.

One day Son of Miracle invited Hasari for a ride in
his taxi. He could not have offered him a finer gift. 'It
was like going off to Sri Lanka with the army of
monkeys,' Hasari was to say, 'or inviting me to take my
seat in the chariot of Arjuna, king of the Pandavas.'
What a treat it was to settle himself on a seat so well
upholstered that the back sank in at the slightest pressure
of his body; to discover before his eyes all kinds of dials
and pointers that provided information about the state
of health of the engine and other parts. Son of Miracle
put a key into a slot and instantly there was a joyful
backfire beneath the bonnet. Then he depressed one of
the pedals with his foot and manœuvred a lever under
the steering wheel. 'It was fantastic,' Hasari would say.
'Those simple actions were enough to set the taxi in
motion. It was fantastic to think that all you had to do
to get it going and then give it more and more speed
was to press the toe of your foot on a tiny little pedal.'
Dumbfounded, Hasari watched his companion. 'Could
I, too, manage those actions?' he wondered. 'Had Son
of Miracle already been a taxi driver in a previous incarnation? Or had he only learned to drive a car in his
present existence?' The driver noticed his companion's
perplexity.

'A taxi is much easier to drive than your carriage,' he
affirmed. 'Look, one simple touch of this pedal and you
stop dead.' The vehicle came to such an abrupt halt that
Hasari was flung against the windscreen. Son of Miracle
burst out laughing.

The rickshaw puller had discovered another world, a
world that called on mechanical slaves not muscles, a
world in which there was no such thing as fatigue
and where you could talk, smoke and laugh while you
worked. Son of Miracle knew all the high spots, the
luxury restaurants, nightclubs and hotels in the Park

Street area. He was in business with a whole network
of hotel procurers who kept the best fares for him.
These middlemen were themselves in partnership with
doormen and waiters. The system worked like a dream.

Son of Miracle picked up the day's first two clients in
front of the Park Hotel. They were foreigners. They
asked to be driven to the airport. 'Then something
happened that gave me quite a shock,' Hasari was to
recount. 'Before moving off, my friend got out of his
taxi, went around and tipped up a sort of small, metal
flag on a box affixed to the left of the car windscreen. On
this box I discovered a sight that seemed so extraordinary
that I couldn't take my eyes off it. As we went along,
every five or six seconds a new number wrote itself up
on the box. I could virtually see the rupees tumbling
into my companion's pocket! Only the god Viswakarma
could have invented such a machine, a machine that
manufactured rupees and made its owner richer by the
instant. It was incredible. We rickshaw *wallahs* never
saw money falling into our pockets like that. Each of
our journeys had a corresponding fare that was fixed in
advance. You could talk it over and ask a little more or
accept a little less but the idea that all you had to do was
press on a pedal and rupees would rain down on you
like wild roses on a windy day was as inconceivable as
that of bank notes growing in a paddy field.' When Son
of Miracle stopped his taxi outside the airport, the meter
was showing a sum that seemed so astronomical to
Hasari that he began to wonder whether it really represented rupees at all; but it did. That one journey paid
a full thirty-five rupees, almost as much as Hasari earned
in half a week. On the way back, Son of Miracle stopped
off at a large garage on Dwarka Nath Road.

'When you've saved up enough rupees,' he announced, 'this is where you'll come for your nirvana.'

The passport to this nirvana was a small booklet with
a red cover and two pages containing stamps, an identity

photograph and a fingerprint. Son of Miracle was right: this slip of cardboard was the brightest jewel of which a rickshaw puller could dream, the key that would enable him to rise above his *karma* and open the door to a new incarnation. This document was a West Bengal motor vehicle driver's licence, and the garage was the most important driving school in Calcutta, the Grewal motor training school. Inside, a spacious yard harboured lorries, buses and instruction cars, and a kind of class-room with benches under a covered area. On the walls, pictures depicted the various parts of a car, traffic signs found on the streets and highways, and sketches of every possible accident. There was also a vast coloured map of Calcutta including a whole list of routes for the information of prospective taxi drivers. There were so many things to attract his attention that Hasari didn't know where to look first. What humble rickshaw puller could ever hope one day to cross the threshold of this dream school? To follow a course of instruction and pass the test involved an impossible expense, almost six hundred rupees, more than four months' worth of money invoices to his family back home in the village.

Yet, as he climbed back into the taxi, Hasari Pal felt as if that dream was suddenly tattooed upon his flesh. 'I shall try to get my full strength back to work even harder. I shall reduce my food to save even more, but one day, I swear on the heads of my sons Manooj and Shambu, I shall pack my rickshaw bell away in the box with our festival clothes and I shall hand back my shafts and my old crate to Musafir and install myself and my beautiful red booklet behind the steering wheel in a black-and-yellow taxi. Then I shall listen with pride to the rupees raining down in the meter like the fat rain-drops of a monsoon storm.'

51

'It's not exactly the Miami Hilton,' Kovalski apologized, 'but just keep telling yourself that people here live twelve to fifteen in rooms twice as small as this.'

Max grimaced as he inspected the lodgings the Pole had found for him in the very heart of the City of Joy. Yet by comparison with many others, it was indeed a princely lodging, complete with a brand new *charpoy*, a cupboard, a table, two stools, a bucket, a jug, and on the wall a calendar with the face of a fine, chubby baby. The room even boasted a window opening onto the alleyway. Another of its advantages derived from the fact that the floor had been raised about one foot and was thus, in theory at least, protected from the monsoon floods and from the currently overflowing drains.

'And the john?' asked the American, anxiously.

'The latrines are at the end of the alleyway,' Kovalski replied apologetically. 'But it's better not to use them too often at the moment.'

Max's perplexed expression amused Kovalski. With a straight face he added, 'And the best way not to have to go too often is to eat nothing but rice. That way your intestines are bound up with concrete.'

The arrival of Bandona interrupted their joking. Max was charmed by the Oriental beauty of the young Assamese girl. In her bright red sari she looked like a princess in a miniature painting.

'Welcome to Anand Nagar, Doctor,' she said shyly, offering the American a bouquet of jasmine.

Max breathed in the very strong scent exuded by the flowers and for a second he forgot his surroundings, the noise, and the smoke from the *chulas* that was stinging

his eyes. He was transported thousands of miles away. The perfume was identical to that of the tuberose bushes, which in springtime swathed the terrace of his house in Florida. 'How strange it was,' he would recall, 'to smell that fragrance in the middle of so much shit.'

It took the young woman only a few minutes to make the American's room more welcoming. Moving about as noiselessly as a cat, she unrolled a mat on the strings of the *charpoy*, lit several oil lamps, set alight some incense sticks and put the flowers in a copper pot on the table. This done, she looked up at the ceiling.

'And you up there, I'm ordering you to let the doctor sleep. He's come from the other end of the world and he's *very* tired.'

That was how Max discovered that he was, in fact, to share his room. He would have rather done it with this pretty Oriental girl, or with some goddess of the *Kama Sutra*, than with the furry creatures he had already encountered in the leper woman's house. Suddenly a kind of croaking made itself heard. Bandona laid a hand on Max's arm with an expression of joy that crinkled her almond eyes.

'Listen, Doctor,' she urged, straining her ears. 'It's the *tchik-tchiki*. He's greeting you.'

Max looked up at the roof and saw a green lizard looking down at him.

'That's the best omen you could have,' announced the young woman. 'You will live for a thousand years!'

Since the Mafia boss's Molotov cocktails had reduced to ashes the building in which Kovalski had hoped to nurse the lepers and set up an operating room for other inhabitants of the slum, it fell to the American's room to become during daytime the City of Joy's first dispensary. From seven in the morning till ten at night and sometimes even later, this single room was to become recep-

tion room, waiting room, consulting room, nursing ward and operating theatre all combined, a room full of suffering and of hope for several hundred of the seventy thousand slum dwellers. 'The setup was primitive in the extreme,' Max was to say. 'My table and bed were used for both examining and treating. There was no sterilizer and my instruments were reduced to three or four tweezers and scalpels contained in my student's case. God, this was far away from our Bel Air Clinic in Miami!' The stock of bandages, gauze and cotton was on the other hand rather well supplied. Kovalski had even passed on to Max a gift from one of his Belgian lady admirers: several boxes of sterilized compresses for the treatment of burns. The priest had spent three agonizing days discussing with the customs officials before obtaining their release without paying four hundred rupees in duty and the baksheesh solicited. It was medicines that they lacked most. All the American had at his disposal was contained in a small metallic trunk: a small quantity of sulphone for the lepers, Ryfomicine for tuberculosis patients, quinine for malaria, a small stock of ointments for skin diseases, and a few vitamins for those children who were suffering most acutely from malnutrition. Finally there were about ten antibiotic tablets for cases of virulent infection. 'There was nothing to brag about,' Max would recount, 'but as Kovalski kept telling anyone prepared to listen, love would make up for it all.'

The Indian word-of-mouth telephone was a supremely efficient news system. No sooner had the dispensary opened, than the entire slum knew of its existence. In the alleys, compounds and workshops people talked of nothing else but of the 'rich Big Brother' who had come from America to alleviate the misery of the poor. The City of Joy had received the visit of a 'great sorcerer', a 'big *daktar*', a 'worker of miracles', who was going to cure the inhabitants of all their ailments. Kovalski allocated Bandona to assist Max in his

task. It would take someone as shrewd as the young Assamese girl to identify those who were really sick from those who were pretending, and to sift out the urgent and most extreme cases, the chronically ill and the incurable.

A tidal wave! Dozens of mothers rushed to the dispensary with children covered in boils, abscesses, anthrax, alopecia, scabies, sick from every possible disease caused by the heat wave and the viruses which ran rampant about the City of Joy. At least two out of every three children were affected by gastroenteritis and parasites. What a training ground it was for a young doctor, with the additional premium of dealing with many diseases that were virtually unknown in the West! Without the aid of Bandona, Max would never even have been able to identify them.

'You see those chalky traces on the pupils, Big Brother Max,' she would say, showing him the eyes of some small child. 'That's a sign of xerophthalmia. In one or two years this kid will be blind. They don't know that where you come from.'

Max Loeb was out of his depth, drowned, submerged. Nothing he had learned at school had prepared him for this confrontation with the physiological poverty of the Third World at its very worst. Manifestations such as eyes that were extremely yellow, chronic weight loss, painfully swollen ganglions in the throat corresponded with nothing he knew or recognized. Yet these were the symptoms of the most widespread disease in India, the one that caused by far the highest mortality: tuberculosis. The National Institute for Tuberculosis affirmed that some two hundred and sixty million Indians were exposed to it.*

During the first week, the American examined and treated as best he could 479 sick people. 'They arrived in

---

* *India Today*, November 30, 1982.

an interminable, pathetic procession,' he was to recount. 'Sometimes there was a touch of folklore about it. Most of the children were naked with a thin cord about their loins, holding a small bell at the level of their navel. It made examining them by auscultation more practical, but made treatment less easy because their little bodies slipped through your fingers like eels. Many of the women were tattooed, some of them from head to toe. They turned up decked out with all their wealth: a single bangle made out of coloured glass or real jewels in some delicate setting, earrings, a semi-precious stone pinned to a nostril, gold or silver ornaments on their wrists, fingers, ankles and occasionally their toes. Sometimes they wore necklets ornamented with religious symbols: for Muslims a miniature Koran or a crescent; for Hindus a Shiva's trident; for Sikhs a small silver sword; for Christians a cross or a medallion. As for the animists, they wore all kinds of other gris-gris and amulets.

'The ochre and bright red dye with which the women and young girls plastered their hands and feet, together with the stains from the red betel chewed not only by men but also by many women to stifle their hunger, didn't make my diagnoses any easier. How was I supposed to distinguish changes in skin colour or inflammation of the mucous membranes in the mouth or throat under all that dye? Some patients tried to make up for it by helping me a bit too much – like one wizened old man who obligingly coughed up a great clot of blood into his hand and showed it to me with supreme satisfaction. Oh, the millions of bacilli that were swimming about in that palm! From my very first day, I strove to apply a few rudimentary principles of asepsis and hygiene. It was by no means easy. I didn't even have a washbasin to disinfect my hands between each patient. And here, germs, sickness and death were so much a part of everyday life! I saw one woman wipe the running

ulcer suppurating on her leg with a corner of her sari. Another spread the ointment I had just applied so delicately to her wound with the flat of her hand.

'Fortunately, there were comic interludes too, like the time when a jet of urine from one infant hit me straight in the face. His mother tried to dry me quickly by rubbing my eyes, mouth and cheeks energetically with the tip of her veil. Then there was the hilarious character who turned up with a prescription that was several years old, on which Bandona read that, as he was suffering from a general cancer in its terminal stages, he should take six aspirin tablets a day. Or this other man who arrived, bearing with as much solemnity as if he were transporting a sacred picture of the god Shiva, an X-ray of his lungs that was at least twenty years old.

'But it was the tragic cases that were most prevalent. One day I was brought a little girl whose body was atrociously burned all over. A locomotive had released its steam when she was picking up remnants of coal along the railway line. On another occasion, a young Hindu girl showed me a light patch on her pretty face. The mere prick of a needle in the centre of the patch was enough for Bandona to be able to diagnose an illness hardly studied in the American medical faculties: leprosy. Again there was the young father of a family who was suffering from acute syphilis. I had to explain to him, via my young Assamese assistant, the dangers of contagion involved for his wife and children. Or the mother who brought me a lifeless bundle of flesh to which diphtheria had reduced her baby. Not to mention all those who came because a miracle effected by the "great white *daktar*" was their only hope: people with cancer, severe heart conditions, madmen, blind men, the mute, the paralysed, the deformed.

'Most unbearable of all, and something I thought I would never get used to, was the sight of those rickety babies with their inflated stomachs, tiny monstrosities

placed on my table by their supplicant mothers. At a year or eighteen months they weighed not so much as nine pounds. They were suffering so acutely from deficiency that their fontanels hadn't closed. Deprived of calcium, the bone structure of their heads had been deformed and their dolichocephalic features gave them all the look of Egyptian mummies. With this degree of malnutrition, the majority of their brains' grey cells had probably been destroyed. Even if I did manage to pull them through, they would most probably be idiots according to medical classification.'

Max was subsequently to learn that all those little victims represented only a sad sample of an affliction that was striking the country as a whole. A great Indian scientific authority on the subject, the director of the Nutrition Foundation of India, asserts that India is producing today more and more 'subhumans' because of inadequate nourishment.* According to this expert, the health of generations to come will find itself in jeopardy. A hundred and forty million Indians at least, that is nearly half the population of the United States, are likely to suffer from malnutrition. Of the twenty-three million children born each year, only three million, according to this same authority, have a chance of reaching adulthood in good health. Four million are condemned to die before the age of eight or to become unproductive citizens because of mental and physical defects. Because of nutritional deficiencies, 55 per cent of all children under the age of five will manifest psychic and neurological problems occasioning behavioural disorders, while several million adults suffer from goitres, causing similar disorders.

On the second day, a young Muslim woman in a black tunic and veil placed a baby wrapped in a piece of

* Dr C. Gopalan, 'The Nutrition Factor', *Indian Express*, January 9, 1983.

rag on Max's table. Fixing on the doctor a wild look, she unfastened her tunic, bared her chest and cupped her two breasts in her hands.

'They're dry!' she exclaimed. 'Dry! Dry!'

Then her gaze fell upon the calendar hanging on the wall. At the sight of the chubby baby displayed on the piece of cardboard she let out a shriek. 'Nestlé makes your children healthy', the slogan on it read. The young mother hurled herself at the calendar and tore it to shreds. At that moment another woman burst in. Pushing aside the young Muslim mother, she rushed at the American and thrust her baby into his arms.

'Take him!' she wailed. 'Take him away to your country! Save him!'

It was an inconceivable action that translated the enormity of the despair these mothers felt. 'For nowhere else,' Kovalski would say, 'had I seen women adore their children in quite the way that they did here, where they deprived themselves, sacrificed themselves, gave their life's blood that their infants might live. No, it was not possible: so much love could not be lost.'

As for Max Loeb, he was sure that for the rest of his life he would see 'those flames of distress burning in the eyes of the mothers of the City of Joy, as they witnessed impotently their children's agony'. That evening Calcutta provided him with yet another unforgettable memory. 'CALCUTTA DOCTORS BRING A TEST-TUBE BABY INTO THE WORLD' announced with a huge headline a local newspaper.

52

'They say the cobra always strikes twice,' Hasari Pal was to recount. 'In other words, no disaster occurs on its own. I already had the red fever in my lungs. And now

it was another blow. Early one morning, I was awoken by the noise of an engine and the grinding of caterpillar tracks. "I'll bet those bastards have come," I said to my wife as I got up.'

Adjusting his *longhi*, he rushed outside. Already the whole slum was in an uproar. For several days there had been rumours about eviction. The 'bastards' had indeed arrived: a bulldozer and two vans bursting with policemen armed with *lathis* and tear-gas cylinders. A black Ambassador car arrived to join them, out of which stepped two *babus* in *dhotis*, wearing waistcoats over their shirts. They conferred with the police officer in charge and then, after a moment, advanced upon the group of slum dwellers.

The elder of the two, who was holding some papers in his hand, was the first to speak. 'The municipality has directed us to carry out the destruction of your settlement,' he announced.

'For what reason?' asked a voice.

The *babu* appeared disconcerted. He was not accustomed to the poor asking questions.

'Because your settlement is impeding construction work on the future subway line.'

The inhabitants looked at one another, flabbergasted.

'What is this "subway"?' Hasari asked his neighbour Arun, who claimed to have travelled as far away as Afghanistan.

Arun was compelled to admit that he did not know. The *babu* consulted his watch and began to speak again.

'You have two hours to get your things together and leave. After that . . .'

Without going to the trouble of providing more expansive explanations, he gestured towards the bulldozer. The official had spoken without raising his voice, as if he had come to communicate the most banal information. Hasari observed his neighbours' responses. They said not a word, and the silence was so surprising

that even the *babus* appeared embarrassed by it. Without a doubt, they had anticipated protestations, threats, some kind of reaction. 'But no. They had come to chuck us out just as you would turn out rats and cockroaches, and we – we said nothing,' Hasari would recall. 'True enough: no one could really miss the slum. All the same, in the scale of disasters, that heap of shacks was a better bargain than the pavement. Here at least people had a piece of canvas and some scraps of cardboard over their heads.'

In fact the lack of reaction was due to quite another reason. 'We simply had no more resources,' Hasari would add. 'This city had finally broken our capacity to react and in this rotten tenement we had no one to come to our defence – no union, no political leader. As for those thugs of the Mafia who had managed so well to extract rent from us, they were nowhere to be seen. And why not admit it also: we had all been hit by so many blows that one blow more or less didn't really matter. That vicious wheel of *karma* never lost its grip.'

The two *babus* joined their hands in farewell and got back into their car, leaving the occupants alone to face the police and the bulldozer. It was then that something totally astonishing happened. Hasari saw his neighbour Arun grab the bamboo beams that supported the roof of his shack and run at the forces of law and order. With this signal something snapped; the initial stupor lifted, everyone felt a sense of rage wash over them. One by one, the shanties collapsed as a deluge of building materials hit the police. Several policemen fell to the ground, whereupon the fury of the assailants redoubled. They fell on the policemen, beating them with planks, bricks and tiles. Women and children cheered the men on. Hasari saw someone take a nail and puncture the eyes of an injured policeman. He saw one of his neighbours sprinkle another with a bottle of paraffin and set fire to him. Some of the police tried to shoot at the mob before

retreating to their vans, but other occupants of the slum ran after them with bottles of petrol; the police vans caught fire. Then someone threw a bottle at the bulldozer and it exploded. A cloud of blackish smoke enveloped the battlefield. When the fighting finally stopped, people paused to survey the extent of the disaster. Several badly burned policemen lay huddled in the middle of a chaos that defied description.

As for the slum itself, it was as if a cyclone had reduced it to dust. There was no need now for a bulldozer; the anger of the poor had done the job, and work on the subway could begin as planned.

Hasari, his wife and children prepared for a hasty escape before the police returned in full force. They had lost virtually everything. Hardly had they reached the first junction when the shriek of whistles and sirens filled the sky. Like hundreds of other fugitives in search of a patch of pavement, Hasari and his family could do nothing now but hope for the mercy of the gods. 'But that day the gods of Calcutta had run out of ears.'

All morning they wandered through the city before they eventually ended up near the portal of a church, on the pavement in Lower Circular Road. There, a makeshift settlement of several families belonging to an Adivasi tribe lived. The Adivasis, who came from the north of India, were the country's aborigines, and their plight was a particularly wretched one. The site in question had the advantage of being near to a fountain. Above all, however, it was close to Park Circus, where Hasari went to pick up his rickshaw each morning. The puller with whom he shared his vehicle was a young Muslim with fuzzy hair who came from Bihar. His name was Ramatullah, and around his neck there hung a miniature Koran on a small chain. He worked from four until midnight and sometimes even later if he could find

passengers. In order to save as much money as possible
for his family, he slept on his carriage, his head and legs
dangling over either side of the shafts. It was not very
comfortable, but at least while he was doing that, no
one could steal the rickshaw.

Ramatullah was a marvellous companion. Ever since
he had seen Hasari coughing and spitting blood, he had
made frequent gestures of friendship. If Hasari did not
turn up in the morning at the usual time, he would run
all the way to Harrington Street to collect the two
children his friend was supposed to take to school every
day, because he knew that to lose a 'contract' like that,
so sought after by the other pullers, would have been a
catastrophe. In the afternoons he would come a little
earlier to save Hasari the fatigue of a last run, and each
time he did so, he gave the sick man the money he had
earned in his place.

By the frightened look with which Ramatullah greeted
him that morning, Hasari understood he must have had
a really dejected expression. He told Ramatullah about
the battle in the slum and the eviction of its residents;
but nothing, it seemed, would divert the compassionate
eyes of the Muslim from his friend's face.

'You ought to go and see a doctor at once,' Ramatullah
said. 'You're as green as an underripe lemon. Go on, get
in the rickshaw. Today, you are the first *marwari* of the
morning!'

'A featherweight *marwari*! You're in luck,' observed
Hasari, settling himself on the seat.

Ten minutes later, the Muslim steered his Hindu friend
into the cramped shop of a specialist in Ayurvedic medicine in Free School Street. Two other patients were
already waiting on a bench. The doctor, a fat, bald man
in an impeccable white *dhoti*, was seated at the rear of
the room in an armchair. It was as if a *zamindar* or a
rajah were giving an audience. On shelves that ran
around the room, all the pharmacopoeia of India's Ayur-

vedic medicine, a range of jars and bottles full of herbs and powders, was on display. After each consultation the doctor would get up, select several jars, and go and sit at a table behind a set of scales similar to those used by jewellers, where, after weighing each ingredient with meticulous care, he made up mixtures.

When it came to Hasari's turn, the physician considered him with a sceptical air and scratched his bald head. All he asked Hasari was how old he was. Then he took down at least ten jars from his shelves. It took him a long time to work out his different preparations. In addition to various pills and tablets, he also concocted a potion to restore Hasari's strength. In payment he asked for twenty rupees. This price was considerably more expensive than a pavement quack's would have been, but Ramatullah assured his companion that there could be nothing better than the drugs of this man of science when it came to getting rid of the red fever. He knew two friends who had been cured by him. 'I pretended to believe him but, in the bottom of my heart, I knew there was no cure for the red fever. The fact that it had taken a diehard like Ram Chander was proof enough.'

On his way back to Park Circus, Hasari heard the squeak of tyres beside him. It was Son of Miracle who had been driving past in his taxi. He had a wild expression on his face, as if he had just downed three bottles of *bangla*. 'When you can hardly stand up and your morale is really rock bottom, suddenly meeting up with a familiar face smiling at you is as comforting as seeing Surya's ball of fire appear after a week of the monsoon,' Hasari was to say.

'Just the person I was looking for!' his friend called out. 'I've got great news for you, but first you'll have to buy me a drink.'

Son of Miracle swept Hasari and Ramatullah into an alley behind Free School Street where he knew a clandestine drinking den. There he ordered up two

bottles of *bangla*. After his first glass his eyes began to sparkle.

'One of my neighbours is leaving my slum and going back to his village,' Son of Miracle said at last. 'So his room will be free. It's a solidly built room, with a real roof, walls and a door. I thought of you right away . . .'

'I didn't even hear the rest,' Hasari would remember. 'My vision suddenly blurred and rickshaw bells began to jangle furiously in my head. Then I saw the blurred shape of a man burning like a torch and I felt my skull knock against something hard. I don't know how long it lasted, but when I opened my eyes, I was stretched out on the ground and above me I saw the crimson faces of Son of Miracle and Ramatullah. Their heavy hands were slapping me as hard as they could to bring me back to life.'

53

Of all the animals and insects with which Max Loeb had to share his new lodgings, he found none more repugnant than the cockroaches. There were hundreds, thousands of them – creatures that managed to resist all insecticides and devoured absolutely everything, including plastic. By day they remained more or less inactive, but as soon as night fell they came out in full force, moving about at breathtaking speed, zigzagging in all directions. They had no respect for any part of your body, not even your face. Hardiest of all were the black beetles. They had a more elongated shape and a smaller girth than the fat brown cockroaches. Their only enemies were the giant hairy spiders that clung like octopuses to the most substantial pieces of bamboo in the framework.

On the second evening Max was able to witness a

performance that was to become one of his main sources of evening entertainment. By the light of his lamp he spotted a lizard as it launched itself onto a beam in hot pursuit of a beetle. On the brink of capture, the insect made a fatal mistake and took refuge under a spider's stomach. Max then saw the spider seize the intruder with its legs and sink the two hooks with which its abdomen was armed into the beetle's body. In a few minutes it had emptied the beetle like an egg. Executions of this kind were frequent. Every morning Max had to shake his pyjamas to rid himself of the empty carcasses of beetles that had fallen on him in the course of the night.

Shortly after his arrival, Max Loeb was to be the victim of an incident that would enable him to get to know his neighbours far better than if he had spent a whole year with them. One evening he was sprawled out on his string bed reading, when he noticed a small creature, slightly bigger than a grasshopper, moving swiftly down the pisé wall next to him. He hardly had time to leap to his feet before the little beast had sunk its sting into his ankle. Max let out a shriek, more of fear than of real pain, and crushed the aggressor with his sandal. It was a scorpion. He immediately put a tourniquet around his thigh to prevent the poison spreading, but the precaution had hardly any effect. Overwhelmed by violent nausea, icy sweats, shivering and hallucinations, he collapsed onto his bed.

'I can't remember anything about the hours that followed,' he would recount. 'All I can recall is the sensation of a damp cloth on my forehead and the vision of Bandona's almond eyes above me. The young Assamese girl was smiling at me and her smile was very reassuring. There was a crowd in my room and it was broad daylight. People were busy all around me. Some were massaging my legs, children were fanning me with pieces of cardboard, others were making me sniff balls

of cottonwool impregnated with a strange smell that was nauseatingly pungent. Others brought me cups of potions, and yet others were advising goodness knows what.'

The incident provided an opportunity for the entire neighbourhood to get together and talk, to comment and demonstrate its friendship. What surprised the young American most, however, was that no one seemed to take the matter very seriously. Here a scorpion sting was something quite banal. Someone explained to Max that he had been stung seven times. Another man exposed his thigh, repeating 'Cobra! Cobra!' in a way that suggested that a scorpion sting was nothing. Yet those small creatures killed between ten and twenty slum people every year, particularly children.

'How did you get to know about it?' Max asked Bandona.

'Big Brother Max, when your neighbours didn't see you go out to attend to "the call of nature", they wondered whether you were sick. When they didn't see you at the fountain, they thought you must be dead, so they came to get me. You can't hide anything here – not even the colour of your soul.'

54

To say that Stephan Kovalski received the news with transports of joy would be an exaggeration, but he was convinced that it was a sign from God, confirming the meaning of his mission at a time of distress. It came at an instant in his life when this man who had shared everything and accepted everything had begun to feel his strength deserting him. To add to the excessive heat, the strike of municipal workers who cleaned the latrines

had transformed the City of Joy into a cesspool more difficult than ever to tolerate. At night, desperate for sleep in the oppressive humidity, Kovalski dreamed of the vast wheat plains of his native Poland or of the deserted beaches of Brittany. He dreamed of space, of rural fragrances, forests, flower beds and animals in the wild. When he first arrived in the slum he had plugged up his ears in order not to hear the cries of suffering. Now he found himself yearning to veil his face in order that he might no longer see or feel anything. In short, he was in the depths of a depression, and even the presence of Max Loeb did not alleviate it. It was at this point that Ashish and Shanta came to tell him the news.

'Stephan, Big Brother, we've found you a room in our compound,' announced Shanta in a trembling voice. 'No one wants to live in it because the previous owner hanged himself from the framework. People call it the "hanged man's room". But it's right next door to ours.'

Kovalski was being offered a room in one of those little courtyards where something like a hundred people lived together, were born and died together, ate and starved together, coughed, spat, urinated, defecated and wept together, where they loved each other, insulted each other, helped and hated each other, where they suffered together and hoped together. For a long time now Kovalski had been wanting to leave the relative anonymity of his alleyway to go and live in a compound, to devote himself even more completely to others. Now, Ashish and Shanta had arranged everything. As ritual required, they presented their protégé to the senior man in the compound, a former sailor and a Hindu who had been stranded in Calcutta on a drinking bout during shore leave. Krishna Jado had lived in Anand Nagar for twenty-seven years. His extreme thinness, his wheezing breath and husky voice betrayed the fact that he had tuberculosis. The head man in his turn introduced the Pole to the other tenants, who welcomed him warmly.

As Shanta commented, 'A Father *sahib* landing in a compound, it was like Santa Claus coming to you.'

Eleven families, nearly eighty people, lived in a rectangle, about thirty-five feet long and nine feet wide. They were all Hindus. That was the rule: people of different religions avoided cohabiting in the same compound, where the slightest difference in custom could assume major proportions. How could it be conceivable for a Muslim family to grill a piece of beef on their *chula* immediately next door to the devotee of a religion that declared the cow sacred? The reverse was true for pork. In a society where religious practices were endowed with such importance, it was better to forestall any potential conflicts. Every hour of every day was the opportunity for some form of festival or celebration. Hindus, Sikhs, Muslims and Christians seemed to compete with each other in their imagination and fervour. Aside from the major religious festivals, the births and the marriages, all kinds of other commemorative celebrations kept the compounds in a perpetual state of excitement. One day it might be a girl's first period that was being celebrated; the next, all the girls who were due to be married might be paying tribute to the *lingam* of the god Shiva, to ask him for a husband as good as he. At some other time a prospective mother would be celebrating the first month of her pregnancy, or then again a huge *puja* might be made, complete with Brahmin, musicians and banquet, to glorify the moment when a baby received his first mouthful of rice from the hands of his father.

The ceremony that was in full swing when Stephan Kovalski arrived at his new dwelling was no less astonishing. Assembled behind the well, some fifteen women were singing canticles at the top of their voices. Metal dishes placed before them overflowed with offerings: mounds of rice grains, bananas, flower petals, incense sticks. Noticing the surprise of his new tenant, the head

man explained: 'They are imploring Sitola to save little Onima.'

The child had caught chicken pox and Sitola is the goddess of such diseases. All the occupants of the compound joined in the *puja*. They had embarked on a three-day fast. After, no one would eat either eggs or meat – insofar as they ate them anyway – or any other food that wasn't boiled, until the child was better. None of the women would wash or hang out her linen on pain of annoying the deity. Thus there was no *bara khana** to celebrate Stephan Kovalski's arrival, but the warmth of his reception compensated for the absence of the traditional celebratory meal. All the other residents of the compound waited for the new arrival with garlands of flowers. Shanta and the neighbouring women had decorated the threshold and floor of his room with *rangoli*, the magnificent geometric compositions designed to bring good fortune. In the middle of them, Kovalski read a message of welcome from his brothers in the City of Joy. It was a sentence quoted from the great Bengali poet, Rabindranath Tagore, 'You are invited to the festival of this world and your life is blessed.' He made his entrance escorted by many of the neighbours from his former home. Old Surya, little Sabia's mother, the coal man from across the way, Nasir, Mehboub's elder son, most of the adults and children from the alleyway where he had spent the last hard years were there, weeping freely. Although distances in the slum were only small, their Big Brother Stephan might just as well have been leaving for another planet. It was perhaps Sabia's mother who gave the most articulate expression to the grief they all felt: 'Before you go away, give us your blessing, Big Brother Stephan. In a way, from now on we shall all be orphans.'

The priest raised his hand and slowly made the sign

---

* Banquet.

of the cross over their heads, repeating softly in an undertone the words of the Beatitudes, 'Blessed are you, for you are the children of my Father, you are the light of the world.'

Then he made his way to the 'hanged man's room' to put down his knapsack and his rolled mat made out of rice straw.

'Is that all you own?' asked one woman, surprised.

He intimated that this was the case. Immediately one of his neighbours appeared with a stool, another brought him some cooking utensils, a third wanted to give him his *charpoy* but this Kovalski declined. He wanted to continue living as one of the poorest of the poor. From this point of view his new lodgings were the perfect answer to his wishes. During the fifteen months that no one had lived there, a colony of rats had settled in. Small ones, fat ones, enormous males with tails one foot long, baby rats that emitted strident cries – there were dozens of them. They infested the framework, ran down the walls, ferreted in all the corners. Their droppings covered the floor. Nothing seemed to daunt them. By some miracle, they had survived the heat and the latest storm appeared only to have decupled their energy. In the 'hanged man's room', they were the masters. The new resident's first move was to claim from them a piece of the wall, by hanging up his picture of the Sacred Shroud, and also a piece of floor space on which to sit in his meditation position and thank the Lord for having granted him this new opportunity for love and for sharing.

Love and sharing! These few square feet of communal courtyard were an ideal place for the realization of a programme of that kind. Here people lived in a state of complete openness. The slightest emotion, deed or word was immediately seized, interpreted and made the subject for comment. Such a promiscuous environment forced you to take special precautions. You had to learn

to wash while holding the corner of your *longhi* between your teeth to conceal your nudity. You had to clean the bowl of the latrines in a particular fashion and walk without letting your gaze stray onto a woman engaged in urinating in the gutter. The shock really hit him that evening. Driven out of his room by the rats, Kovalski sought refuge under the little veranda outside his door, only to stumble across the several bodies that were already occupying it. During those blisteringly hot nights nearly everyone slept outside. Fortunately a low brick wall erected at the entrance to the compound protected it from the drains that overflowed into the alley. Kovalski created a space for himself between two sleepers. 'There was so little room that I had to lie down head to foot alongside my neighbours, like sardines in a can.'

He was to retain two memorable impressions of that first night. Neither of them related to his neighbours' snores, the cavalcade of beetles and bats across his face, the bouts of coughing and spitting to which the tuberculosis sufferers around him were subject, the barking of the pariah dogs at the rats, the vociferations of drunks trampling over sleeping bodies, the metallic clatter of buckets being brought back from the fountain by the womenfolk. The first indelible impression of that night was the crying of infants prey to nightmares. Their cries, intercut with snippets of sentences, made it possible to understand the terrifying visions that haunted the slumbers of those little Indian children. There was a strong preoccupation with tigers, spirits and *bhuts*, or ghosts. 'That was the first time I had heard a tiger actually referred to by its name,' Kovalski was to say. 'In India people always called it "the big cat", "the great wild beast", "the great feline", but never "the tiger", for fear of attracting the attention of its spirit and thereby

making it appear. It was a taboo that had been brought originally from the countryside where tigers still devoured more than three hundred people a year in Bengal alone. The threat of them haunted many a child. What mother in the City of Joy had not said to her offspring at some time or other, "If you're not good, I'll call the big cat."'

The second striking memory was of a 'vociferous cock-a-doodle-doo from a cockerel sounding in my ears at four-thirty in the morning, when I had only just got to sleep.' Kovalski had not noticed the bird tied to a post of the veranda when he lay down the night before. It belonged to the occupants of the room next door. They were the only tenants he had not yet met, because apparently their activities frequently took them out of the compound. They had returned only late that night. Kovalski sat up and saw 'five women sleeping head to foot, swathed in veils and multicoloured saris'. Remarking to himself that he had never seen such tall Indian women before, when he heard them speak, he was so surprised at their low gruff voices he thought perhaps he was dreaming. Finally he understood. His neighbours were eunuchs.

55

Max Loeb had just taken a cigar out of his box of Montecristo No. 3s and was about to light it when he heard something bombarding the roof of his room. It was the tenth night after his arrival. He had experienced tropical tornadoes before but never before had he witnessed quite such a downpour of rain. A fresh premonsoon storm had just hit Calcutta.

Max poured himself a double Scotch and waited. He

did not have to wait long. The disaster began with a cataract between two tiles, then the rain began to penetrate from all sides. In seconds the room was transformed into a lake, the level of which rose with menacing rapidity. In the hovels nearby families were fighting to save their few possessions. People were shouting, calling to each other. At the first drops the American had piled onto his bed the canteen of medicines, his case of instruments, his personal effects, and the three boxes of milk powder that Kovalski had brought him to save babies suffering from the fourth and fifth degrees of malnutrition. At the very top of the pyramid he placed what he called his 'survival kit': three bottles of whisky and three boxes of cigars. The deluge was at its worst when Max heard a faint knocking at his door. Paddling up to his ankles, he went to open it and discovered in the beam of his torch 'the reassuring vision of a young girl dripping with rainwater. She was holding a large black umbrella her father was sending me.' A few moments later the unemployed fellow from the hovel next door arrived with his arms loaded with bricks to raise the level of the low wall at the entrance and the *daktar*'s bed and table. Solidarity in a slum was no empty word.

After about an hour the downpour eased up a little. The marvellous dream of taking refuge 'in the luxury of a suite with a private bathroom in the Grand Hotel' had just crossed Max's mind when his door was shattered to pieces. Three figures burst in. Immediately two hands grabbed his shoulders and pushed him up against the wall. Max felt the point of a knife pricking him in the stomach. 'A holdup,' he thought. 'That's all I needed.'

'Milk!' snarled the big fellow with the broken nose who was threatening him with his knife. 'Milk, quick!'

Max was determined not to play Buffalo Bill in the depths of this slum. He pointed to the three cartons of milk.

'Help yourself!'

Each thief grabbed a box and they ran off. As he went out of the door, the man with the broken nose turned around and announced in English, 'Thank you! We'll be back!'

It had all happened so quickly that the American found himself wondering whether he had been dreaming. He made an attempt to put the planks from the door back in position but as he did a horrible smell brought him to a halt. Something wet touched his calf. He heard a gurgling sound and realized then that, swollen by the rain, the pestilential waters from the drains in the alley were in the process of overflowing into his room.

A night of horror thus began. There were no more matches, no torch, not a glass to be had. Everything had been submerged in the floodwater. What malevolent creature, Max wondered, had bitten him the day he had responded to Stephan Kovalski's appeal? He thought of Sylvia's velvety skin, of her breasts that tasted of peaches, of the touching childlike air she had about her when she recited her poems. He looked at his watch. It was afternoon in Miami. The jasmine would be sweet-scented on the veranda and people would be listening to the lapping of the water against the boats on the canal.

At dawn, Bandona appeared in the frame of the broken door. It was difficult to read the expression on her face in the dim light of the morning after the flood, but the young Assamese seemed very upset. Her small almond eyes were set, her features rigid.

'Max, Big Brother, come quickly. My mother is feeling very bad. She's bringing up blood.'

A few moments later they were both wading up to the middle of their thighs in slime. Bandona proceeded with caution, sounding the ground beneath with a stick because some of the open sewers actually cut across the alley. Every now and then she would stop to avoid the corpse of a dog or a rat, or to prevent Max from being splashed by the reckless flounderings of children who

were laughing and swimming about in the putrid flood-water. The surprising thing about it was that nowhere in this nightmare had life come to a halt. At one crossroad they encountered a comical little man in a turban, perched on the seat of a carrier tricycle. A dozen children, up to their chests and sometimes even their shoulders in water, were milling around him. The carrier tricycle was equipped with a cogwheel which rotated against a set of numbers. 'Roll up, roll up, a grand lottery prize for ten pice!'

'A grand lottery prize in this filth?' marvelled Max. And why not? Two biscuits and a piece of candy were a maharajah's reward for youngsters with empty stomachs.

Contrary to expectations, Bandona's mother was up on her feet. She was a small woman with a bun, all wizened like an elderly Chinese country woman. She was chatting and joking with the neighbouring women who had squeezed themselves into her very clean and meticulous room. On the wall, behind the low ledge that served as a bed for her and her five children, there were two pictures of Buddhist wise men, their heads covered with yellow bonnets, and a photograph of the Dalai Lama. In front of these icons burned the flame of an oil lamp.

'*Daktar*, you shouldn't have gone to this trouble!' she protested. 'I'm very well. The great God doesn't want me yet.'

She ordered the American to sit down, and she served him tea and sweetmeats. Reassured, Bandona recovered her smile.

'All the same, I'd like to examine you,' insisted Max.

'It's not worth the trouble. I tell you again, *Daktar*, I am very well.'

'Mother, the doctor has come especially from America,' Bandona intervened.

The word 'America' had a magical effect. But there

was no question of having all the people leave the room. In a slum anything and everything is undertaken in public, even a medical examination.

Half an hour later Max laid his stethoscope down.

'Bandona, your mother is as sound as a rock,' he affirmed in a comforting tone.

It was then that tragedy struck. The old woman was trying to stand up to pour some water into the teapot when a sudden fit of coughing took her breath away. She collapsed. A flow of blood issued from her mouth. Max rushed to help Bandona lift her onto the bed. As Bandona mopped up the blood, Max could tell by the movement of her lips that she was praying. The aged Assamese woman surveyed all the people around her. There was not a trace of fear in her expression, only total serenity. Max prepared a syringe containing a cardiac stimulant but he had no time to inject the needle. The old Assamese woman stiffened abruptly. She let out a sigh and it was all over.

A howl rang out through the room. It was Bandona. She was clasping her mother in her arms and sobbing. For a few minutes there was the heartrending sound of weeping, wailing and lamentation. Women tore their faces with their nails, men beat their skulls with their fists. Distraught children imitated their parents. Other manifestations of grief rose from the compound and the neighbouring alley. Then, just as suddenly as she had broken down, Bandona stood up again, dusted off her sari and rearranged her braids. Dry-eyed and solemn-faced she took control of the situation.

'What I witnessed next was a riot of orders and injunctions,' the American was to recount. 'In the space of ten minutes that young woman had organized and arranged everything. She sent her brothers off to the four corners of Bengal on a mission to alert relatives, she dispatched neighbours and friends to the bazaar to buy what was necessary for the funeral: a bier – white according to

Buddhist tradition – vermilion powder for the ritual decoration of the corpse, candles, incense, *ghee*, cotton *khadi*, and bunches of jasmine, marigolds and lilies. To cover the cost of all this she had her two gold bracelets and her pendant taken to the Afghan usurer at the end of the alley to obtain a loan of a thousand rupees. To welcome, feed and thank the dozens of relatives and friends who would come for the occasion, she arranged to buy a hundred pounds of rice, as much flour for *chapatis*, vegetables, sugar, spices and oil. Finally she had a hundred rupees taken to the bonze at the pagoda in Howrah for him to come and recite Buddhist *slokas* and perform the appropriate religious rites.'

Three hours later everything was ready. Swathed in white cotton, Bandona's mother reclined on a litter embalmed with jasmine. Her feet and hands, duly streaked with vermilion, were visible, as was her face, from which death had wiped away nearly every wrinkle. She looked like an Egyptian mummy. All around her, dozens of incense sticks gave off the sweet scent of rosewood. Things proceeded very quickly. The bonze in his saffron robe pronounced prayers, striking a pair of cymbals as he did so. Then he anointed the deceased's forehead with *ghee* and camphor, and he sprinkled grains of rice over her body to facilitate the transmigration of her soul. Then four men belonging to the family took hold of the stretcher. When Bandona saw her mother leaving the hovel where they had both lived and struggled for so many years, she could no longer conceal her grief. Immediately the other women began to wail, sob and moan once more. Already, however, the litter was receding into the flooded alleyway.

Only the men accompanied the deceased to the funeral pyre. They sang canticles with a syncopated rhythm to Ram, God, for in the absence of a specifically Buddhist

place of cremation, Bandona's mother was going to
be burned according to Hindu ritual. It took the little
procession an hour to wend its way to the funeral *ghats*
on the banks of the Hooghly. The bearers set the litter
down under a banyan tree while Bandona's eldest
brother went to negotiate the hiring of a pyre and the
services of a priest. When his mother was placed on one
of the piles of wood, the Brahmin poured a few drops
of Ganges water between her lips. Her eldest son then
walked five times around her remains before plunging
in a flaming torch. As the flames engulfed the pyre, there
rose the sound of voices singing.

Knowing that a body takes four hours to be consumed,
Max slipped discreetly away to go and bring a little
comfort to Bandona. Just before he got back to her
hovel, however, he suddenly felt the ground give way
beneath his feet. A blackish stream rushed into his
mouth; then his nostrils, ears and eyes were submerged
beneath the gurgling filth. He struggled against it but
the more he floundered, the more he was sucked down
towards the bottom of the cesspool. Two or three times
in the course of his existence, his life had been saved by
virtue of his prowess as a swimmer. This time, in this
unholy slime, he was paralysed: the density and consist-
ency of the liquid made his attempts to surface ineffective. He realized then that he was going to drown.

It is said that at such an instant you see your life pass
before you in a flash. In this eddy of putrefaction, he
had only time to glimpse a strange vision: 'that of my
mother carrying an enormous birthday cake out onto
the terrace of our house in Florida'. It was at that moment
that he lost consciousness.

What followed was told to Max Loeb by others. The
body of a *sahib* swirling about in the sewers of the City
of Joy could not pass unnoticed for long. Some people
had seen him disappear. They had rushed over and,
without hesitation, had plunged in after him, had re-

trieved his inanimate form and taken him to Bandona's house.

For the second time that day, the young Assamese woman took charge of the operation. She got everyone moving. Kovalski, Margareta, and the others came running. She even succeeded in inducing a doctor to come from Howrah. Artificial respiration, cardiac massage, injections, the washing out of his stomach – everything possible was done to try and bring Max back to life. After three hours of relentless efforts, Max finally opened his eyes to be greeted by 'a whole collection of marvellous faces, who seemed to be pleased at my awakening! In particular there were two almond eyes gazing at me fondly, eyes that were still red from having cried much that day.'

56

'You could do with a good clean up,' Kovalski announced the next day to the survivor of the sewers of Anand Nagar. 'What would you say to a little chlorophyll bath? I know a magnificent place.'

Max looked hesitant. 'To be honest with you, I'd prefer a bubble bath in a five-star luxury hotel.'

Kovalski raised his arms to the heavens.

'That's really banal! Whereas the place I want to take you to . . .'

An hour later a bus dropped the two *sahibs* outside the entrance to an oasis that seemed improbable so close to the most prodigious urban concentration on earth. It was a tropical garden, several dozen acres in size, with thousands of trees of every variety in Asia. The universe of lush vegetation they entered more than warranted their surprise. There were huge banyan trees ensnared

by interwoven creepers; many hundred-year-old cedars with trunks as thick as towers; clusters of mahogany and teak trees; pyramid-shaped ashok trees; gigantic magnolias with beautiful leaves like the glazed tiles of Chinese pagodas. 'The garden of Eden had just sprung up before my eyes, still stinging as they were from the filth and fumes of the City of Joy,' Max Loeb was to say. Even more extraordinary were the number and variety of birds that populated the park. There were bright yellow orioles; splendid woodpeckers as large as pigeons, with golden backs and conical beaks; majestic black kites with forked tails, circling in the sky before swooping down on their prey. There were proud sandpipers with long incurved beaks roosting in migrating flocks perched on tall stilts. Flying from one clump of bamboo to the next were magpies, russet wagtails and large parakeets with yellow plumage. Suddenly a kingfisher with bright violet-red feathers and a large red beak came and landed in front of the two visitors. They stopped to avoid frightening him, but he was so tame that he moved to another piece of bamboo to be even nearer to them.

'What a release it is to watch a bird in the wild!' enthused Kovalski. 'A creature in his natural state, his free state. He takes no notice of you. He just hops from one branch to another, catches an insect, calls out. He shows off his plumage.'

'He does what birds are supposed to do,' Max said.

'That's exactly what's so great about it; he isn't even looking at us.'

'If he were looking at us, everything might become contrived.'

'Absolutely. He's truly a free spirit. As in the kind of environment where we live we never meet truly free spirits. People are always in the grip of some problem or other. And as you're there to help, you're obliged to ask yourself questions about them, to try and understand

their predicaments, study their antecedents, and so on.'

Max thought of the arduous day he had just been through. 'It's true. The least encounter in a slum is an occasion of tension.'

Kovalski pointed to the bird.

'Except when it comes to the children,' he said. 'Only a child is a creature devoid of tension. When I look into the eyes of a child of the City of Joy, I see God. A child doesn't assume an attitude, doesn't seek to play a role, doesn't change to suit events, he is open. Like that bird; a bird that lives out his bird's life to perfection.'

Max and Kovalski had sat down on the grass. To both of them it was as if they were millions of miles away from Anand Nagar.

'I think it is here that I drew the strength to hold out over these last years,' admitted the Pole in a confidential mood. 'Here and in praying. Every time I felt too depressed, I jumped on a bus and came here. A dragonfly fluttering on a bush, the cooing of a brown woodpecker, a flower closing as evening approaches – those are the things that have been my lifebuoys in this experience.'

There was a long silence. Then suddenly the Pole asked, 'You're a Jew, aren't you?'

Seeing Max's surprise, Kovalski apologized. 'It's a typically Indian reflex to ask that question. Here a man is determined by his religion. Religion conditions everything else.'

'Yes,' Max said, 'I am a Jew.'

Kovalski's face lit up.

'You're privileged. Judaism is one of the world's most beautiful religions.'

'That hasn't always been the view of all Christians,' Max observed calmly.

'Alas no, but what millenary heroism that has inspired in you! What unshakeable faith! What dignity in suffering! What tenacity in listening to the one God! Haven't you inscribed the *Shema Israel* on the doors of

your homes? What a lesson that is to the rest of humanity! For us Christians in particular.'

Kovalski laid a hand on the American's shoulder. 'Spiritually, you know, we Christians are Jews,' he went on. 'Abraham is the father of us all. Moses is our guide. The Red Sea is part of my culture – no, of my life. Like the tablets of the Law, the desert, the Ark of the Covenant. The prophets are our consciences. David is our psalmist. Judaism brought us Yahweh, the God who is all-powerful, transcendent, universal. Judaism teaches us to love our neighbour as we love God! What a wonderful commandment that is. Eight centuries before Christ, you realize, Judaism introduced to the world the extraordinary notion of a one, universal God, a notion that could only be the fruit of revelation. Even Hinduism, despite all its intuitive, mystical power, has never been able to envisage a personal God. It was the exclusive privilege of Israel to have revealed that vision to the world and never to have strayed from it. That's really fantastic. Just think, Max, the same luminous moment of humanity that saw the birth of Buddha, Lao-tzu, Confucius, Mahavira, also witnessed a Jewish prophet called Isaiah proclaiming the primacy of Love over Law.'

Love! It was in India that both the Jew and the Christian had discovered the real meaning of the word. Two of their brothers from the City of Joy were to remind them of it that very evening on their return. 'A blind man of about thirty was squatting at the end of the main street in front of a small boy struck down with polio,' Max would recount. 'He was speaking to the boy as he gently massaged first the youngster's needle-thin calves, then his deformed knees and thighs. The boy held on to the man's neck with a look overcome with gratitude. His blind companion was laughing. He was still so young, yet he exuded a serenity and goodness that was almost supernatural. After a few minutes he stood up and took the boy delicately by the shoulders to get him

on his feet. The latter made an effort to support himself
on his legs. The blind man spoke a few words and the
lad put one foot in front of him into the murky water
that swamped the street. Again the blind man pushed
him gently forward and the child moved his other leg.
He had taken a step. Reassured, he took a second. After
a few minutes they both were making their way down
the middle of the alley, the little boy acting as guide for
his brother in darkness and the latter propelling the
young polio victim forward. So remarkable was the
sight of those two castaways that even the children
playing marbles on the kerbstones stood up to watch as
they passed.'

57

With her gaudy bracelets and necklaces, brightly
coloured saris, dark eyes circled with eyeliner, eyebrows
pencilled in, and her pretty mouth reddened with betel
juice, twenty-year-old Kalima was the pin-up of the
compound. Even Kovalski was disturbed by a presence
that spread sensuality and gaiety into the dark hole in
which he now found himself. Above all, he admired the
wide blue ribbon and the jasmine flower with which this
creature ornamented her thick waist-length black hair.
Such refinement in the midst of so much ugliness delighted the Pole. The only problem was that Kalima was
not a woman, but a eunuch.

Kovalski had seen the proof of this while he was
washing on his second morning. The 'young woman'
had let his veil fall for a fraction of a second and the
priest had caught sight of his penis, or at least what was
left of it. Kalima was not a man dressed in woman's
attire. He was indeed an authentic representative of the

secret and mysterious caste of the *Hijras*, which had communities scattered throughout India. He had been castrated.

A few days later an impromptu celebration was to give Kovalski the opportunity to discover what functions this picturesque person and his companions served in the slum. Night had just fallen when the cries of a newborn baby suddenly filled the compound. Homaï, the wife of the one-eyed Hindu who lived on the other side of the courtyard, had just brought a son into the world. At once his grandmother in a white widow's veil rushed across with the other women of the family to the eunuch's room to invite him urgently to come and bless the child. Kalima and his friends hastily put on their makeup, changed into their festival saris and adorned themselves with their baubles. Kalima also fastened several strings of bells around his ankles while his companions smeared their *dholaks*, the small drums from which they were never separated, with red powder. Thus arrayed, the five eunuchs emerged jangling their instruments and singing in their gruff voices, 'A newborn baby has appeared on the earth. We have come to bless it. *Hirola! Hirola!*'

The eldest of the little troupe, a eunuch with fuzzy hair and prominent cheekbones, was called Boulboul – the Nightingale. Dressed in a bright red skirt and bodice, with a gold ring through his nose and gilded earrings in his ears, he led the ceremony, swaying his hips as he did so. He was the guru of the group, its master, its 'mother'. His disciples, with Kalima at their head, followed, skipping and singing. 'Sister, bring me your child,' called out Boulboul, 'for we wish to share in your joy. *Hirola! Hirola!*' The grandmother in the white widow's veil hastened to go and fetch the baby, then offered it to Kalima. The eunuch took the little body gently in his arms and began to dance, hopping from one foot to another, to the sound of bells, turning and swaying to

the jerky rhythm of the drums. With his gruff voice he intoned:

> *Long live the newborn child!*
> *We bless you,*
> *That you may live for a long time,*
> *That you may always have good health,*
> *That you may earn lots of money.*

The singing had attracted the inhabitants of the neighbouring compounds. The courtyard had filled. Clusters of children had even scaled the roofs. No one appeared to be daunted by the crushing temperature. This was an occasion for celebration. While Kalima and his companions went on dancing, the guru Boulboul went off to collect the fee for his troupe. Eunuchs charged a good deal for their services and no one dared to haggle for fear of incurring their maledictions.

'Our newborn baby is as strong as Shiva,' the dancers next proclaimed, 'and we beg the all-powerful god to transfer the sins of all his past lives to us.' In a way this appeal was the eunuchs' credo, the justification of their role in society. Mystical India had sanctified the most underprivileged of its pariahs by granting them the role of scapegoat.

The guru returned with a bowl of rice sprinkled with pieces of ginger. With the tip of his index finger he dabbed up the red powder from one of the drums and marked the baby's forehead with it. This symbolic gesture transferred onto his person, onto his companions and onto all the *Hijra* caste the past sins of the newborn child. For eunuchs, the red powder, which is the emblem of marriage among Hindu wives, represents their ritual union with their drums. Next the guru scattered a few grains of rice onto the instrument, then threw one whole handful at the door of the infant's home to bless the mother, and then another over the child. After that,

raising the bowl above his head, he began to spin around on the spot.

Accompanied by the others striking their drums and clapping their hands in time, he sang, 'We shall bathe in the sacred rivers to wash away all the sins of the newborn child.' Then, before the admiring eyes of the onlookers, Kalima began to dance, cradling the infant in his arms. His fine features and the femininity of his movements perfected the illusion. Pathetic in the realism of his performance, the eunuch smiled maternally at the little bundle of flesh which was making his entry into the world of the City of Joy. The ceremony concluded with a display of mime. Kalima restored the baby to his grandmother and fixed a cushion under his sari. Personifying a woman in the final stages of pregnancy, he began to dance around in a circle. Then he aped the first pains of childbirth. Uttering cries that grew ever more heartrending, he fell to the ground while the other eunuchs patted him on the shoulders and back as if to help him give birth. When finally he was completely exhausted, his guru fetched the newborn baby and deposited him in his arms, whereupon Kovalski saw Kalima's face light up with happiness. He saw his lips addressing the child words of love. Then his bust and his arms began to move in a rocking motion. The eunuch was tenderly cradling the new addition to the compound.

58

'Good God,' thought Max Loeb suddenly, 'there is such a thing as paradise!'

A servant in a white turban and tunic, with the hotel coat of arms emblazoned on his breast, had just come into his room. He was bearing on a silver tray a double

whisky, a bottle of soda and a bowlful of cashew nuts. The American had been unable to resist the temptation to recharge his batteries. The chlorophyll bath in the tropical garden had not been enough. He had taken refuge in an air-conditioned suite in Calcutta's luxury hotel, the Grand. A foaming Niagara of perfumed froth was already tumbling into the bathtub of his marble bathroom. The nightmare of the City of Joy had receded to another planet. He slipped a ten-rupee note into the servant's hand. Just as he was leaving, however, the servant swung around in a half circle. He was a very wrinkled little man with a grey beard.

'Would you like a girl, *sahib*? A very pretty young girl?'

Startled, Max put down his glass of whisky.

'Very pretty and sweet-natured,' elaborated the servant with a wink. The American swallowed another mouthful of alcohol. 'Unless you'd prefer two girls together,' urged the Indian, 'young girls but very, very skilful. The entire range of the *Kama Sutra*, *sahib*.

Max thought of the erotic sculptures in the temples of Khajurao which he had admired in a photograph album. He remembered, too, his fiancée's words during their last dinner together. 'They're lovers without equal, those Indian girls,' Sylvia had said. The Indian plucked up his courage. He knew his clientele all too well. As soon as they arrived in Asia, Europeans and Americans turned into devils. No temptation seemed spicy enough for them. 'Perhaps you'd prefer a boy, *sahib*? A fine looking young boy, sweet and . . .' The servant made an obscene gesture and matched it with another wink. Max nibbled at a cashew nut. The servant remained undaunted by the American's silence. With the same air of complicity, this time he suggested 'two young boys', then after a few moments, he volunteered 'two young boys and two girls together', then a eunuch, and finally a transvestite. 'Very clean, *sahib*, very safe.'

Max could just imagine the face Kovalski would make when he described this scene to him. He got up to turn off the tap in the bathroom. When he returned the servant was still there. His catalogue of pleasures was not yet exhausted.

'If sex doesn't tempt you, perhaps you'd like to smoke a little grass?' he suggested. 'I could get you the best in the country. It comes straight from Bhutan.' Next he added, 'Unless of course you prefer a really good pipe' – a gleam came into his watery eyes – 'our opium comes from China, *sahib*.' Quite undeterred by the lack of enthusiasm inspired by his merchandise, the servant then ventured to suggest 'a nice syringe full of coke', along with various other locally manufactured drugs, like *bhang*, the local hashish. Quite obviously, however, the honourable foreigner wasn't buying.

Not wanting to leave the room a complete failure, the man in the turban finally suggested that most banal of all transactions that resounds like a litany in the ears of every tourist in this world. 'Would you like to change some dollars, *sahib*? For you I can manage a special rate: eleven rupees to the dollar.'

Max emptied his glass. 'I'd rather you brought me another double whisky,' he ordered as he stood up.

The servant surveyed him with a look of sadness and pity.

'You don't appreciate the good things of this life, *sahib*.'

Of course Max Loeb appreciated the 'good things' in life. Especially after weeks of doing penance in the cesspool of the City of Joy. After downing his second double whisky, he asked the beturbaned servant to send him one of those *Kama Sutra* princesses he had been offered. This first experience with one of the descendants of the sacred prostitutes who had once inspired the temple sculptors did not, however, develop at all in the way he had expected. Brought to his door by the owner

of the establishment into which she had been sold, the
girl, a tiny thing outrageously made-up, looked so terrified that Max did not dare even to caress her long dark
oily hair. Instead he decided to put on a feast for her.
He called room service and had them bring up a lavish
assortment of ice cream, pastries and cakes. The young
prostitute's eyelashes began to flutter like the wings of
a moth around a lamp. Never before had she seen such
marvels. To her it was quite obvious: this client was
none other than the Lord Shiva in person.

'We gorged ourselves to bursting point,' Max was to
tell Kovalski, 'like two school kids who wanted to
believe in Santa Claus.'

Several evenings later Max's taxi passed through a grand
portal guarded by two armed sentries, and along a drive
lined with jasmine bushes which infused the night with
a penetrating tropical scent. 'I've got to be dreaming,'
he told himself when he caught sight of the colonnades
of a vast Georgian residence at the end of the driveway.
On either side of the steps and along the roof of the
terrace burned a garland of oil lamps. 'It's Tara,' he
thought in amazement, the Tara of *Gone with the Wind*,
on a night given up to festivity. The magnificent structure really did seem to have emerged from a dream.

Built at the beginning of the last century by a British
magnate in the jute industry, it was one of the residences
that had earned Calcutta its nickname, 'the City of
Palaces'. Besieged on all sides by slums and overpopulated neighbourhoods, today it was an anachronism. Yet
some of the attractions of this vestige of a vanished era
still remained – not least of them the lady of the house,
the statuesque and charming Manubaï Chatterjee, a
thirty-five-year-old widow and a great lover of modern
painting, Indian music and horse riding. Gracious and
slender like a poor peasant woman – so many of India's

women put on weight as soon as they become rich, often losing all grace and natural beauty – Manubaï was active in a number of cultural organizations and charitable works. It was in her capacity as president of the Indo-American Friendship Society that she was giving this evening's party. Tomorrow the United States would celebrate the bicentennial anniversary of its Declaration of Independence.

It took Max a moment to acclimatize himself. Even after an evening feast with a prostitute and a few nights between the expensive sheets of a five-star hotel, he was so impregnated with the reality of the City of Joy that it had become like a second skin to him. Was it true that only a few minutes' taxi ride away from this oasis there were newborn babies with stomachs blown up, mothers with tragic eyes, exhausted men, death ever present in the form of a bier borne on four sets of shoulders, workshops like convict prisons, the noise of weeping, cries, quarrels?

On the lawn of the floodlit grounds several hundred guests thronged. The entire business community from Dalhousie Square was there: everyone who was anyone in industry, people in the import and export business, fat *marwaris* in embroidered *kurtas* and their wives no less fat in sumptuous saris encrusted with gold, representatives of the Bengali intelligentsia – the great film-maker Satyajit Ray who had made *Pather Panchali*, a film the whole world hailed as a masterpiece; the famous painter Nirode Najundar, whom international critics had called the Picasso of India; the celebrated composer and performer of sitar music Ravi Shankar, whose concerts in Europe and America had accustomed the ears of Western music lovers to the subtle sonority of the Indian lyre.

Barefoot servants in white tunics with red velvet cummerbunds and turbans were offering the guests trays laden with glasses of whisky, Golconde wine and fruit juices; others presented silver platters overflowing with

cocktail snacks. At the far end of the lawn, Manubaï had had a vast, vividly coloured *shamiana* erected to provide cover for a buffet table laden with the finest dishes the rich Bengali cuisine could offer. To the left of the tent, musicians in braided uniforms played themes from Gilbert and Sullivan operettas and American swing music. 'It was all deliciously nostalgic,' Max would later recount. 'At any moment I expected to see the viceroy and vicereine of India arrive in a white Rolls-Royce escorted by Bengal Lancers.'

Draped in a sari of colours suited to the occasion – blue and red scattered with a dusting of little golden stars – Manubaï was moving from one group to another. Like the two or three hundred other guests, Max was dazzled by the grace and beauty of this Indian lady who received people like a sovereign. Yet what a difficult path had been hers before she reached the point where she could create this illusion! Although nowadays widows no longer throw themselves into the flames of their deceased husband's funeral pyre, a widow's position in Indian society is still far from enviable. How many battles Manubaï had had to fight after the death of her husband who had been the owner of Calcutta's leading house of commerce, simply in order to remain in her princely mansion and continue to enjoy there a decent revenue. The flames of the funeral pyre had hardly died away before her in-laws had given her notice of her expulsion. For two years, anonymous telephone calls had called her a money grabber and a whore. Insults and threats – she had borne them all, treating her enemies with silence and contempt, devoting herself to the education of her two children, travelling, furthering the careers of young artists, supporting charity organizations. She had just bequeathed her emerald-coloured eyes to the first eye bank in Bengal, an institution which she herself had founded to help some of the victims of blindness that were so numerous in that part of the world.

Suddenly Max felt an arm slip through his.

'You must be Dr Loeb?'

'That's right,' he said, slightly disturbed by the young woman's odorous perfume.

'I've heard all about you. It seems you're a truly remarkable fellow. You live in the slums and you've set up a dispensary to care for the sick . . . Am I wrong?'

Max felt himself blush. The faces of Saladdin, Bandona, Margareta, of all his Indian companions from the City of Joy passed before his eyes. If there were really remarkable people anywhere, they were the ones – people who never even had a chance to spend a night in a luxury hotel to forget the horror of their life's surroundings, people for whom there were never receptions or compliments.

'I only wanted to spend some time doing something useful,' he replied.

'You're too modest!' Manubaï protested. She took his hand in her long fingers and steered him forward. 'Come,' she said, 'I'm going to introduce you to one of our most learned men, our future Nobel Prize for medicine.'

Forty-six-year-old Professor G. P. Talwar was a lively, smiling man. He had done part of his studies at the Pasteur Institute in Paris. Head of the biology department of the Institute for Medical Sciences in New Delhi, the shrine of Indian medical research, he had been working for several years on a revolutionary vaccine capable of altering the shape of India's future. He was about to invent the world's first contraceptive vaccine. A single prick of a needle would be enough to make a woman sterile for a year. Max thought of the hundreds of little bundles of flesh deposited on his table by desperate mothers. There was no doubt about it. He had just met one of humanity's benefactors. Already, however, Manubaï was leading him over to another of her protégés.

With his curly fair hair and jovial face, the Englishman James Stevens looked more like an advertisement for toilet soap than a disciple of Mother Teresa. Yet this thirty-two-year-old man dressed like an Indian in a full shirt and white cotton trousers was, like Stephan Kovalski and doubtless other unknown people, a kind of anonymous Mother Teresa. He had dedicated his life to the poor, in this case Calcutta's most underprivileged and neglected people, the children of lepers. Nothing would have predestined this prosperous haberdasher for his mission in India, had it not been for the fact that one day his taste for travel had led him to Calcutta. This visit had moved him so profoundly that it transformed his life. Back in England, he had liquidated all his assets, then returned to India where he married an Indian girl. Using his own funds to rent a large house with a garden in the suburbs, he started to comb the slums in an old van, gathering up sick and starving children. By the end of the year his home harboured about a hundred little inmates. He gave it the symbolic Indian name of *Udayan*, meaning 'Resurrection', and into it he sank all his savings. Fortunately, generous people like Manubaï helped. Stevens would not for all the world have missed one of her parties. For this connoisseur of good whisky and sherry they were exotic escapades onto some other planet.

Max Loeb's own escapade would that night end in a place of which he would never have ventured to dream: the canopied bed of Calcutta's first hostess. How did this come about? He had enjoyed too many whiskies and too much Golconde wine to be able to recall exactly. He remembered only that when, towards midnight, he had joined his hands together in front of his heart to take leave of Manubaï, she had rejected his gesture.

'Max, stay a little longer. The night is deliciously cool.' Her emerald green eyes seemed to implore him.

Two hours later, after the last guest had gone, she had

led him to her bedroom, a huge room that took up almost all of the first floor of her house. The parquet flooring shone like a mirror. Furniture made out of tropical woods exuded a delicious smell of camphor, and at the far end of the room stood a bed with posts of twisted teak supporting a velvet canopy, from which tumbled the delicate laciness of a mosquito net. The walls were hung with brightly coloured floral wallpaper. On one of them was displayed a collection of old yellowing prints depicting views of the colonial Calcutta of yesteryear and scenes from life in Bengal. The opposite wall was entirely bare except for a huge portrait of a man with a stern face. It was not a painting but a photograph, and the face it featured occupied the room just as intensely as if the man had been alive.

Max remembered that Manubaï had turned on a record player, and suddenly the voice, the poignant, grainy voice of Louis Armstrong, accompanied by the stirring sonority of his trumpet, had invaded the room. Neglecting the Indian woman for one instant, Max fell back happily onto the couch in front of the bed. A barefoot servant brought whisky and bottles of soda. Manubaï settled herself beside him and they kissed. Max recalled that at a certain moment the sounds of birds had come in through the window, mingling their trilling with the brilliance of the trumpet. It was fantastic.

The young woman had extinguished all the lights except for a large Chinese lamp. It bathed the room in a voluptuous half-light, and the portrait of her husband was as if erased from the wall.

What followed would become for Max a succession of confused and exciting images. Having danced a few steps, the Indian woman and the American had drifted gently towards the soft cushions and silken sheets of the four-poster bed. They had shut themselves away together behind the invisible wall of the mosquito net. Stretched out side by side they had waited for the voice

of the unforgettable black musician to die away. Then they surrendered themselves to pleasure.

It was broad daylight when the sound of knocking at the door made Max leave Manubaï's arms and go to open it.

'Sahib, there's someone wanting to see you. He says it's urgent.'

Max slipped on his clothes and went downstairs behind the servant.

'Stephan! What the hell are you doing here?'

'I suspected that after your party, you'd want a lie in,' replied the Pole, laughing, 'so I came to dig you out.' Then, more seriously, he added, 'The leper bus is due. We need you, Max. There'll be some amputations to be done.'

'The leper bus' was the nickname Kovalski had given to the ambulance that Mother Teresa sent him every Wednesday, with three of her Sisters. Having been unable to open his small leper clinic in the slum, this was the only means he had been able to find of caring for the worst cases. To avoid any further confrontation with the godfather and his hoodlums, he parked the ambulance on the pavement of the avenue leading to the railway station, well outside the boundaries of the City of Joy.

Those Sisters of Mother Teresa were real driving forces. The eldest of the three, a tall girl with very clear skin, beautiful and distinguished in her white sari with a blue border, was not yet twenty-five. Her name was Gabrielle. An Indian from Mauritius, she spoke the picturesque, lilting French of the islands. Swallowing her Rs, she had nicknamed Kovalski 'Dotteu Stef'. 'Dotteu Stef, here', 'Dotteu Stef, there' – Sister Gabrielle's calls made Kovalski laugh. 'They were like orchids scattered over putrefaction.' Yet the Wednesday sessions were harsh trials indeed.

That morning, as always, there was a massive rush as soon as the red-and-white bodywork of the small van 'donated to Mother Teresa by her co-workers in Japan' appeared on the avenue. Lepers came from the City of Joy and from the nearby pavements where they had spent the night. Clinging to their crutches, to their crates on wheels, dragging themselves along on planks, they swarmed around the three folding tables the Sisters set up right there on the pavement. One table was used for the distribution of medicines, another for injections, and a third for dressing wounds and for amputations. Gently but firmly, Sister Gabrielle tried to sort the mass of cripples into some kind of orderly line. By the time Max and Kovalski arrived, the line stretched back more than a hundred feet.

The stench! Max saw some passers-by hurry off, their noses buried in their handkerchiefs. On the whole, however, the spectacle was a big attraction. Dozens of people congregated around the two *sahibs* and the three Sisters, to watch. Soon the avenue was completely blocked. 'I felt like a magician at a fair,' the American would say, still caught up in the euphoria of his night of pleasure; but his euphoria was to be short-lived.

The scene was straight out of Dante's *Inferno*. Hardly had a leper placed his stump on the table when a swarm of maggots would come crawling out of it. Bits of flesh fell away from limbs that were completely rotten. Bones crumbled like worm-eaten pieces of wood. Armed with a pair of forceps and a metal saw, Max cut, trimmed, pared. It was butcher's work. Amid a sticky swirl of flies and sudden squalls of dust, in the overpowering heat, he shed streams of his own sweat over the wounds. Sister Gabrielle acted as anaesthetist. She had nothing to relieve the pain of certain amputations – no morphine, no curare or *bhang*. She had only her love. Max would never forget the vision of that Indian girl 'taking a leper

in her arms and pressing him to her as she hummed him a lullaby while I cut off his leg'.

Yet, as was so often the case, in the midst of the worst trials there were scenes that were unbelievably funny. Max would always remember 'the compassionate face of a helmeted policeman, furiously inhaling the smoke of two sticks of incense that he had stuck right into his nostrils, as he watched the amputations'. Taking advantage of the large audience, several lepers began to give a performance of somersaults and clownish antics which was greeted with laughter and the dropping of small coins. Other lepers preferred to attract attention with outbursts of anger. Brandishing their crutches at the Sisters, they demanded medicine, food, shoes, clothing. Sister Gabrielle and 'Dotteu Stef' constantly had to calm their onslaughts. It is sometimes harder to give than to receive, as Kovalski had often found it to be.

Max had been operating for three hours when two lepers deposited on his table a bearded crippled man whose hair was covered with ashes. Kovalski instantly recognized his old friend.

'Max, it's Anouar!' he shouted to the American. 'Anouar whose wife gave birth the evening you arrived.'

'I thought I knew the face from somewhere. And it couldn't have been from Miami!'

Despite the tragedy of the situation, they broke into laughter. Almost instantaneously, however, Kovalski's gaiety dissolved. Poor Anouar seemed in the worst of states. His eyes were closed. He was perspiring. He was speaking incoherently. His fleshless torso swelled almost imperceptibly with his uneven breathing. Max had great difficulty in finding his pulse.

'Gangrene,' said Kovalski, examining the dirty, malodorous dressing which enveloped his forearm. 'It's got to be gangrene.' Helped by Sister Gabrielle, they carefully undid the bandaging. Anouar seemed to be insensible. When they got down to the bare flesh Max

felt his legs 'sink suddenly into a sea of cottonwool'. Anouar's rotten arm, the crowd of faces before him, the penetrating whistle of passing buses, Kovalski's voice, all suddenly toppled over into a maelstrom of colours and sounds. Then, all at once, everything went blank. There was a dull sound on the pavement. Max Loeb had collapsed in a faint. Letting go of the leper's arm, Sister Gabrielle and Kovalski grabbed hold of him and laid him in the ambulance. The priest saw Gabrielle's hand flash through overheated air and crash down onto Max's cheek.

'Wake up, *Dotteu! Réveille-toi!*' she cried as she redoubled the smacks delivered to his face. Finally the American opened his eyes. He was amazed to find the faces bending over him. Memories of his night welled into his mind.

'Where am I?' he asked.

'On a pavement in Calcutta in the middle of cutting off leprous arms and legs,' Kovalski replied sharply, somewhat annoyed by the incident.

He was immediately angry with himself for this reply.

'It's nothing, old friend. Just a little tiredness because of the heat.'

A moment later Max took up his forceps and his butcher's saw once more. This time he had to cut off a whole arm up to the shoulder – Anouar's arm, rotten with gangrene. No doubt there was nothing else to do; the man had been stricken for so long. In the absence of antibiotics, the infection must already have run through his whole system. Kovalski and Gabrielle laid the poor fellow on his side. A murmur of voices came from the onlookers as Max's pair of forceps rose above the prostrate man. Max himself had the impression of cutting into a sponge, so putrefied were the skin, muscles and nerves. The severing of a blood vessel induced a spurt of blackish blood which Sister Gabrielle mopped up with a compress. When he reached the bone just

below the shoulder joint, Max changed instruments. Everyone could hear the grinding of the teeth as they bit into the wall of the humerus. After a few strokes of the saw, Max felt his legs 'sinking into cottonwool' again. He clenched his fingers on the handle and pressed with all his might. To avoid thinking, feeling, seeing, he talked to himself. 'Sylvia, Sylvia, I love you,' he repeated as his hands accelerated mechanically back and forth. Like a tree, felled by a final stroke of an axe, the limb came away from the body. Neither Kovalski nor Sister Gabrielle had time to catch it before it fell onto the ground. Max put down the saw to wipe his forehead and the nape of his neck. It was then that he witnessed a scene that was to haunt him for the rest of his life: 'a mangy dog carrying off in its mouth a human arm'.

59

He was the object of such veneration that peasants placed offerings of milk and bananas outside his hole. His entry into a hut was considered a divine blessing. Hindu Scriptures were full of fables and stories about him. Temples had been constructed in his honour and all over India, at the beginning of each month of February, the great festival dedicated to him gathered together millions of worshippers. Despite the fact that he claimed more victims per year than cholera, no devout person would ever have committed the sacrilege of raising a hand against him, for the cobra snake was one of the thirty-three million gods in the Hindu pantheon.

Poor Kovalski! His entire compound in the City of Joy would long remember the shriek of terror he let out when he went into his room one evening. Rearing up

on shining coils with its tongue vibrating and its fangs
exposed, a flat-headed cobra was waiting for him beneath
the picture of the Sacred Shroud. Neighbours came
rushing to the scene. The Pole had already seized hold
of a brick with the intention of crushing the creature,
when Shanta Ghosh, his pretty neighbour whose father
had been devoured by a tiger, stayed his arm: 'Big
Brother Stephan, don't kill him, whatever you do, don't
kill him!' Alerted by these cries, more people came
running with hurricane lamps. 'We could have been in
the middle of a scene from the Ramayana,' Stephan
Kovalski was later to say, 'the one where the army of
monkeys hurl themselves into the lair of the demon
Ravana.' In the end Ashish, Shanta's husband, with the
help of two other men managed to capture the reptile in
the folds of a blanket. Someone brought a basket and
put the snake in it. A short while afterwards calm once
more prevailed in the compound.

Kovalski had understood the message. 'That cobra
was not put in my room as a token of welcome,' he said
to himself. 'Someone here does not wish me well.' But
who? That night he could not close his eyes. One detail
in particular had not escaped his notice. Whereas all the
other residents had come rushing to his rescue, the door
to the adjoining room occupied by the eunuchs had
remained closed. This fact was all the more strange
because during those sultry nights everyone fled the
furnace of their rooms to sleep in the courtyard. The
priest extracted the lesson from his adventure without
bitterness. Despite the demonstrations of affection his
life of sharing and compassion among his disinherited
brothers had afforded him, he knew that for some he
remained a white-skinned *sahib* and a priest – a foreigner
and a missionary. Until now the relative anonymity of
an alley had protected him. But in the restricted world
of a compound, things were very different. In this
concentration camp atmosphere, anything that did not

conform with the group became a foreign body with all the dangers of rejection that that implied.

At daybreak, when the Pole returned from the latrines, a squat little man with short-cropped, curly white hair, a jet black complexion and a slightly flat nose entered his room. Kovalski recognized the occupant of a hovel on the other side of the well.

'Father, we too were eligible for the cobra's strike,' he declared with a wink. 'Your cobra was for your white skin and the cross you wear on your chest. Ours was for our curly hair and because we came from the forests.'

'And also because you're a Christian,' added the priest, indicating the medal of the Virgin Mary hanging around the Indian's neck.

Kovalski had adopted the Indian habit of first defining a man by his religion.

'Yes, because of that too,' admitted the man with a smile. 'But primarily because we're from the forests,' he insisted.

The forests! The mere mention of the word in the depths of this leafless, flowerless slum amid all the noise and acrid smoke of the *chulas* conjured up before Kovalski's eyes a whole sequence of magical images: images of freedom, of life that was primitive but wholesome, of happiness and stability achieved at a price but none the less real.

'Are you an Adivasi?' he inquired.

The visitor nodded his head. Kovalski thought of all the accounts he had read of the aborigine people. They had been the first to settle in India. When? No one really knew. Ten, twenty thousand years ago. Nowadays there remained some forty million aborigines, divided up into several hundred tribes, dispersed over the entire subcontinent. This man was one of them. Why had he left his forest to come and live in this slum? Why had he exchanged his jungle for this one? It was some weeks before Kovalski was able to reconstruct the path fifty-

eight-year-old Boudhou Koujour, his Adivasi neighbour, had trod.

'The drums had been beating all night,' Boudhou would
recount. 'It was festival time. In every village in the
forest, beneath the ancient banyans, the giant tamarinds
and the lofty mango trees our women and girls were
dancing side by side in long rows. How beautiful our
womenfolk were with their tattoos, their shining skin,
their supple bodies and their rhythmically swaying hips!
From time to time a group of men with turbans and
bare chests, carrying bows and arrows and wearing
bells around their ankles and peacock feathers on their
foreheads, would leap into the moonlit circle of dancing
women and break into a frenzied dance. The women
had begun to chant wildly. It was no longer possible to
think of tomorrow or of anything else. Your heart
pounded to the rhythm of the drums. Problems and
difficulties ceased to exist. All that mattered was life, the
life that was joy, impulse, spontaneity. The effect was
intoxicating. The supple bodies stooped, rose again,
dipped, uncoiled, stretched. Our ancestors were with us
and the spirits too. The tribe was dancing. The drums
were beating, responding to each other, now softly, now
more loudly, blending into the night.'

That festive night, the aborigines of Baikhuntpur, a
jungle valley on the borders of the States of Bihar and
Madhya Pradesh, renewed their thousand-year-old rites.
At dawn next day, however, a surprise awaited them.
Towards six in the morning, two hundred henchmen
sent by the area landowners descended like a cloud of
vultures. After setting fire to all the huts, they demanded
payment of outstanding farm rent and all interest on
loans. They arrested the men with the help of the police,
sequestrated the cattle, raped the women and seized all
the inhabitants' goods. This raid brought to a climax

several centuries of confrontation between the people living in the forest and the large landowners who wanted to take possession of their fields and crops. The ancient law, inscribed upon the memory of humanity, which determined that whoever clears the jungle becomes its owner should have been enough to safeguard the aborigines against such covetousness. At one time nomads, then semi-settled, in the course of a few centuries the aborigines had become small-scale peasants. Their agriculture was strictly at a subsistence level, intended to feed their families. Products that grew wild in the forest were there to supplement their diet. Boudhou told the priest how he and his children used to climb trees to shake the berries off the branches, how they used to scratch the ground to unearth certain roots, how they knew how to peel off a particular bark, skin certain tubers, extract bone marrow, locate edible mushrooms, pick succulent lichen, draw off sap from leaves and trees, gather buds, collect wild honey. He spoke, too, of how they used to set snares, traps, nooses and bait for small game, and automatic traps equipped with clubs or arrows for bears and other larger animals. How they caught various insects, worms, ants' eggs and giant snails. Each family gave the community anything they caught that was surplus to their needs to be passed on to widows, orphans and sick people. 'It was a hard life but we were free and happy.'

One day, however, the drums were reduced to silence. He and his family and the other households in the valley were compelled to move on. First they went to Patna, the capital of Bihar, then to Lucknow, the great Muslim city, but nowhere could they find work. Thus it was that, like so many others, they had taken the road to Calcutta. Put off by the close confinement of the slums, at first they had installed themselves on the outskirts of the city with other aborigines. They had worked hard at baking bricks and they had lived like dogs. Then one

day a room fell vacant in the City of Joy. On that day India suffered a fresh defeat: a man who had been Man par excellence, primitive Man, free Man, was integrated into a slum.

Some evenings later Kovalski arrived home to discover that tragedy had struck the compound. At first all seemed quiet. Even the laughter of the children and the shouting of the drunks were stilled. A few steps further on he heard the sound of groaning. In the half-light he could just make out figures squatting outside the eunuchs' door. Under the veranda there was a *charpoy* on which he could see a shape enveloped in a white sheet. Several small oil lamps were burning around about it and in the brightness of their flames he noticed two feet. 'Someone in the compound has died,' he told himself. Beside the *charpoy* he recognized Kalima's dark tresses with their distinctive blue ribbon and white flower. The young dancer was sobbing. The priest slipped into his room and prayed as he waited on his knees before the picture of the Sacred Shroud. A moment passed and then he heard feet treading softly behind him. It was his neighbour Ashish.

'Stephan, Big Brother, there's been a fight,' he explained in a low voice. 'Boudhou, the Christian Adivasi, has killed Bela, one of the eunuchs. It was an accident but the poor thing is well and truly dead. It was because of your cobra.'

'My cobra?' stammered Kovalski, abashed.

'For several days the Adivasi had been conducting a secret inquiry to find out who put the cobra in your room,' Ashish went on. 'He had found out that a snake charmer had given a performance to celebrate a marriage in a compound not far from here. The eunuchs were all engaged to dance at the same wedding. The Adivasi managed to find the snake charmer, who admitted that

one of the *Hijras* had insisted he sell him a cobra. The
Hijra had offered him two hundred rupees, a truly fantastic price for a small creature like that. The *Hijra* explained
that he wanted to perform a sacrifice so eventually the
snake charmer agreed and that's how the cobra came to
be in your room. By having it kill you, Bela no doubt
wanted to expiate some obscure sin. Who knows? There
are those who say that by killing you, he hoped to
appropriate your sex for a future incarnation.'

Kovalski wanted to speak but his voice was strangled
in his throat. He could hardly breathe. The Indian's
words eddied in his head like bubbles. Ashish recounted
how that evening the Adivasi had turned up at the
eunuch's hovel to punish him. He had only wanted to
teach him a lesson, but Bela had gone demented. He had
seized a knife to defend himself. An effeminate eunuch,
even of substantial build, was no match for a forest
dweller used to hunting bear with a spear. In the ensuing
set-to the *Hijra* was impaled on his own knife. No one
had had time to intervene. In a compound, the tensions
are so great that, like a thunderbolt, death can strike at
any moment.

Kovalski was shattered. He could hear the sound of
the eunuchs' sobbing through the open door. Soon the
sobbing stopped. He heard footsteps and voices and
realized that his neighbours were preparing to carry their
companion to the cremation pyre on the banks of the
Hooghly. He knew how expeditiously funeral ceremonies were conducted in India because of the heat. What
he did not know, however, was that tradition would
not allow eunuchs to bury or burn their dead other than
at night, out of sight of 'normal' people. What was
more, India denied in death what it granted its eunuchs
in life: the status of women. Before swathing their 'sister'
in his shroud, Bela's companions had been obliged to
dress him in a *longhi* and a man's shortsleeved shirt, and
Boulboul, the sad-faced guru, had cut off his long braids.

Ashish had just left when Kovalski heard a scratching at the casing of his door. Turning around, he saw
Kalima's necklaces and bangles gleaming in the darkness.

'Big Brother Stephan, we would like to ask you to do
us the honour of taking our sister to her funeral pyre,'
declared the young eunuch in the very deep voice which
never ceased to come as a surprise.

As he delivered his request, his companions were
addressing three other men in the compound. Once
again the appeal was rooted in respect for tradition; in
India women do not have the right to accompany a
funeral cortège. Deprived of the comfort of this last
homage, the *Hijras* gave their 'sister' a poignant farewell.
As Kovalski, Ashish and the two other bearers took hold
of the funeral litter, the guru Boulboul fell to his knees,
uttering a succession of *mantras*. Crazed with grief, Kalima and the other eunuchs tore at their faces with their
nails and gave voice to the most heartrending wailing.
Then the four *Hijras* bared their feet and began to beat
the corpse with their sandals 'to prevent our sister from
being reincarnated as a eunuch in her next life'.

60

There was no longer any doubt in Kovalski's mind:
the eunuchs' attitude towards him had changed. The
carrying out of the funeral rites had created a bond
between them. Since he had borne to the funeral pyre
the corpse of the *Hijra* who had tried to kill him by
putting a cobra in his room, the four other eunuchs in
the neighbouring room had stepped up their tokens of
friendship. Often, as he came home in the evening, he
would now find some trace of their passing: a wick for

his oil lamp, a dish of delicacies, the wall on which he hung his picture of the Sacred Shroud freshly white-washed. These gestures both touched and embarrassed him. 'I certainly had got used to all forms of cohabitation. Nevertheless, the presence of this strange family on the other side of the wall made me uneasy. And yet of all the neglected, despised, rejected people in the slums, weren't they those who should be pitied most? Ah, what a long way I still had to go before attaining that true spirit of charity and acceptance.'

Ultimately, it was Kalima who dispelled Kovalski's prejudices. Every morning after his ablutions, the young dancer came to chat with the man whom in his deep voice he called 'my Big Brother Stephan'. Although the language of the *Hijras* was a secret tongue known only to them, Kalima knew enough Hindi to make himself understood, and of all the destinies that had come together in this wretched place, his was assuredly one of the most curious.

Kalima was the son of a rich Muslim merchant in Hyderabad, a city in the centre of India. When he was a child, his genital organs were only slightly developed, yet there was no doubt about the fact that he was a boy. Very soon, however, his femininity revealed itself. At an age when his classmates were battling it out on the cricket or hockey field, he devoted himself to learning dancing and music. Instead of Boy Scout uniforms and sportswear, he preferred *shalwars* with their baggy trousers and the long tunics young Muslim girls wear. He liked to put on perfume and makeup. To curb what they considered evil inclinations, his parents had married him off at the age of fourteen to the daughter of a rich jeweller. Kalima had tried to fulfil his conjugal duty, but the result had been so disastrous that his wife had run back to her parents on the morning after their wedding.

One day, among the crowd of worshippers who had come on pilgrimage to the tomb of a local Muslim saint,

an old *Hijra* with short hair and a gaunt face had spotted the youth and followed him back to his home. Less than a week later, Kalima left his family for ever and went off with the eunuch. He confided a few details of the strange ritual of his adoption ceremony to Kovalski. His 'god-mother', or rather his guru, was called Sultana. Like the majority of *Hijras*, Sultana had no breasts and so she had pressed a piece of cotton soaked in milk onto her chest and obliged her godchild to suck it. This was a condition of acceptance into his new family. Kalima then received one hundred and one rupees, silver and brass utensils, clothes, saris, petticoats, glass bracelets and *chotis* – threads of black cotton which, once knotted in the hair, would become, like the triple braid of the Brahmin, the hallmarks of his new caste. After his adoption, Kalima was subjected to a grand initiation ceremony, to which all the members of the community and the leaders of the other *Hijra* castes in the area were invited. His 'godmother' and the other gurus dressed the new disciple in a skirt and blouse previously blessed in a sanctuary. Kalima then dressed his 'godmother' in the same way and kissed his feet and those of all the other gurus present, who in return gave him their blessing.

It was after this ceremony of ritual transvestism that Kalima received his female name. All the gurus were consulted as to the choice. Kovalski was surprised that they had christened the boy with the name of the most bloodthirsty goddess in the Hindu pantheon. With his fine features and his carefully plucked eyebrows, Kalima had nothing demonic about him. It was true that his rugged voice gave him away but, because of his delicate bone structure, the proud bearing of his head and his flowing walk, he could easily pass for a woman.

Kalima's initiation was not yet complete. The worst was yet to come, for a real *Hijra* must not be confused with a transvestite. Transvestites belonged to another caste, a pariah caste even lower on the social ladder. In

the muddy alleyways of the City of Joy, Kovalski had often come across these tragic individuals disguised as women, outrageously over-made-up, fitted out with false breasts – ridiculous actors who sang, danced and wriggled their rumps at the head of wedding marches and religious processions, pathetic, obscene clowns, employed to make others laugh at their own expense and to transform the most sacred rites into grotesque parodies. Those men, however, managed to carry out their profession without sacrificing their masculinity. Some of them had several wives and whole streams of children. The deception was part of the game.

The *Hijras'* position in society was entirely different. They must be neither men nor women. Mothers, who called them to take upon their shoulders the sins committed by their newborn babies in previous lives, had the right to verify this fact. And damned be those guilty of deception!

The ceremony took place in the middle of the first winter. Castrations were always carried out in winter in order to reduce the risk of infection and allow the wound to heal more rapidly. The risks were by no means negligible. No statistics really revealed how many *Hijras* died each year from the aftermath of emasculation. Still, the Indian press never missed the opportunity to denounce dramas like that of a Delhi hairdresser, aged about thirty, who died after his emasculation carried out by eunuchs who had persuaded him to join their group. At one time the operation was performed in particularly atrocious conditions. *Hijras* took away their victim's masculinity with a horsehair which was tightened progressively each day until the genital organs were severed completely.

One day Kalima was taken by Sultana, his godmother-guru, to an isolated village where a small community of eunuchs lived. The community's astrologer selected an auspicious night for the operation. The

Hijras called such nights when castrations were carried out 'black nights'. Sultana made his young disciple drink several glasses of *todi*, an alcoholic drink made from palm tree juice in which some powder of *bhang*, a narcotic with analgesic properties, had been dissolved. While Kalima lost consciousness his guru lit a great fire. A priest recited *mantras* and poured a bowlful of *ghee* into the flames. Tradition required that the flames flare up if the castration was to take place. This night the flames leaped into the sky like fireworks. This signified that Nandni-na and Beehra-na, goddesses of the *Hijras*, would accept the new recruit. The officiant could now tie a thread around the young man's penis and testicles and draw the knot progressively tighter to anaesthetize the organs. Then, with a slash of a razor blade, he sliced straight through.

A scream rent the night air. The agonizing pain had woken Kalima. Immediately a saraband of drums struck up and all the eunuchs began to dance and sing round the flames, while a soloist intoned a canticle intended to chase away all maleficent powers and evil spirits. The other *Hijras* punctuated each phrase with a resounding *Hanji!* Yes!

> *A new Hijra has been born!*
> *Hanji!*
> *A sari without a woman!*
> *Hanji!*
> *A cart without wheels!*
> *Hanji!*
> *A stone without fruit!*
> *Hanji!*
> *A man without a penis!*
> *Hanji!*
> *A woman without a vagina!*
> *Hanji!*

Sultana himself applied the first dressing to his disciple's wound. It consisted of a kind of plaster made of ashes, herbs and oil mixed together. The recipe dated back to the days of the Mogul conquest, a time when the eunuch caste had experienced a veritable Golden Age. That was the era when, all over India, poor parents sold their children to traders who emasculated them. One nobleman at the court of one of the Mogul emperors possessed twelve hundred eunuchs. In those days some *Hijras* raised themselves to elevated positions, not merely as guardians of the harem, court dancers or musicians, but even as confidants of kings, provincial governors and army generals.

Once Kalima had recovered from his mutilation, Sultana entrusted him to the care of professional musicians and other gurus, who taught him the traditional songs and dances. They also taught him how to mime a mother cuddling her child or breast-feeding a baby, to act the part of a young bride or a woman expecting a child or in labour. Soon he was awarded the title of '*Bai*' or 'dancer and courtesan', and then began a period of travelling for the young eunuch. *Hijras* travel a great deal from one end of India to another to visit their 'relatives'. Kalima's guru had a 'sister' in New Delhi, 'aunts' at Nagpur and 'cousins' in Benares. Links between eunuchs and their 'relatives' are much stronger than any of those they might maintain with their real parents. It was in Benares, on the banks of the Ganges, that tragedy suddenly struck. At dawn one day as he was on his way to the *ghats* to dip himself in the waters of the sacred river and worship the sun, Kalima saw his 'godmother' collapse in the street. The *Hijra* was dead, struck down by a heart attack.

Fortunately for Kalima, it was the time of the year for pilgrimages and there were many *Hijras* in the holy city. Almost immediately a guru volunteered to take him as his disciple. He had prominent cheekbones and a doleful

expression. He came from Calcutta, his name was Boulboul, and he was Stephan Kovalski's neighbour.

61

To sleep! sleep for fifteen, twenty hours at a stretch! On
concrete, with rats, centipedes, scorpions, *anywhere*, but
just sleep! Since his arrival in the compound, Stephan
Kovalski's dream was turning into an obsession. His
nights had been reduced to three or four hours of relative
silence punctuated by outbreaks of coughing and spitting. As early as four-thirty the musical squalling of a
transistor sounded the reveille. Garuda, the eunuchs'
cockerel, then preened himself to let off his volley of
cock-a-doodle-doos. Other such birds answered him
from every corner of the slum, and from all around the
veranda there burst forth a concert of tears and cries
from children whose stomachs were empty. Shadows
armed with tins full of water rose in haste to go in
search of a latrine or some gutter spared by the cesspool
emptiers' strike. Little girls were already lighting the
chulas, scouring the pots and pans from the previous
evening, putting the mats away, bringing buckets of
water from the fountain, making up cow dung cakes,
or delousing their elder sisters' hair. They were the first
to set to work.

Every morning at about five o'clock, Kovalski saw
little Padmini, the youngest daughter of the Adivasi
who had killed the *Hijra* over the cobra, set off for
somewhere. He wondered where so tiny a girl might go
at such an early hour. One morning he followed her.
After padding across the slum behind her, he saw her
scale the railway embankment. It was the time, dawn,
when the passenger trains arrived in Calcutta from the

various towns in the Ganges valley. As soon as Kovalski
heard the sound of the first train, he saw the child take
a stick from under her patched blouse. The tip of it had
been split so that she could fix a one-rupee note to it.
As the locomotive slowly passed her, she held out the
stick. A blackened hand grabbed the note. Then Kovalski
saw the driver go into the tender and throw out a
few pieces of coal. Padmini scrambled to pick up the
miraculous manna and ran off with it in her skirt. Her
father would keep half of it, religiously breaking it up
into small pieces for use on the family *chula*. The other
half would be resold. This trade was only one of innumerable tricks invented by the underprivileged people
of the City of Joy in order simply to survive.

Yet, despite his lack of sleep, Kovalski did not miss
his alley. The compound was a matchless observation
ground for one who felt himself, as he did, married to
the poor. What a hive of activity the place was from
daybreak till night. There was no end to the comings
and goings: at every moment there seemed to be some
bell ringing, a gong, a whistle, or a voice announcing
the arrival of a vendor of this or that, a Brahmin priest
who had come to sell a few drops of Ganges water, or
an entertainer of some kind. The most popular visitor
was the exhibitor of bears, especially among the children.
As soon as his drum was heard, the entire courtyard
would come running. Nor was there any lack of enthusiasm for the monkey, goat, mongoose, rat, parrot or
scorpion trainers, or the viper and cobra charmers. The
same was true of the chroniclers, puppet shows, poets,
storytellers, troubadours, fakirs, mimers, strongmen,
dwarfs, conjurers, illusionists, contortionists, acrobats,
wrestlers, madmen, saints . . . indeed all the Zampanos
and Barnums that hunger for entertainment and celebration had invented to enable the slum people to escape
the sadness of their lot.

The compound was first and foremost the children's

domain. 'Marvellous children of the City of Joy,' Kovalski would say. 'Little innocent beings nourished on
poverty, in whom the life force never ceased to flourish.
Their freedom from care, their zest for life, their magical
smiles and dark faces set off by luminous gazes coloured
the entire world in which they lived with beauty. If the
adults here managed to retain some spark of hope, was it
not because of them, because of their dazzling freshness,
because of the earnestness of their games? Without them
the slums would have been nothing but prisons. It was
they who managed to turn these places of distress into
places of joy.'

Kovalski counted seventy-two children in those few
square feet of space so rarely penetrated by the sun's
rays. It was in the rough-and-ready school of life that
they learned their lessons, discovering how to fight their
own battles as early as the age of three. Even before that
age there were never any intermediaries between them
and their world. They did everything directly with their
own little hands: eating with the right hand; sweeping,
cleaning, going to the latrines with the left. A stone or
a piece of wood served as their first toy. Right from
the start this direct link with objects encouraged their
relationship with all things and nurtured their creative
instincts. With their hands as their only tools, their
communion with nature was immediate and deep-rooted
and would influence their entire lives. So too would their
games, games that were concrete and simple. No Lego
sets or electric or automatic playthings for them. The
children of the compound invented their own toys. The
piece of string that Padmini, the little girl who went
to fetch the coal from the railway embankment each
morning, attached to her left foot with a stone on the
other end of it made a perfect skipping rope. The skipping left her hands free for the simultaneous composition
of a dance or piece of mimicry. Kovalski was enchanted
by her display: the child's postures were those of the

temple divinities. All the genius of Indian dance was contained in that frail poverty-stricken body in the depths of the compound. For the boys, a simple piece of plank became a Ben Hur chariot on which the older enthusiasts pulled the smallest ones about. A few pebbles and fruit pits provided marbles for heated games played from one end of the courtyard to the other and even right into Kovalski's room. One day Mallika Ghosh, the little girl next door who always came running to him with a bowl of milky tea, made a doll out of rags. But realizing all of a sudden that there were quite enough real babies in the compound for them to play at being mothers, she and her friends decided to turn their doll into an object of worship. The rag doll became Lakshmi, goddess of prosperity, to whom the poor of the slums pledge a very special veneration.

Hopscotch, spinning tops, yo-yos, hoops . . . the energy, the fervour, the ingenuity, the zest for play displayed by those small beings with their distended stomachs, never ceased to amaze Kovalski. One day the neighbouring woman's little boy ran between the priest's legs in hot pursuit of a hoop. Kovalski caught hold of the toddler's arm and asked him to teach him how to operate his toy. The toy in question was a simple scrap iron wheel propelled along by a stick with a hook. After three attempts, the Pole gave up to a deluge of laughter. Mastery of the Indian hoop requires a long apprenticeship and it takes the dexterity of an acrobat to keep it balanced among so many people and obstacles.

The toy par excellence, however, the game to crown all games, and the one that unleashed as much enthusiasm among the parents as it did among the children, the one that aroused most competition, rivalry and conflict, the one that carried with it all the dreams of freedom and escape harboured by these immured people, was a toy made out of a simple wooden framework and paper and string. Here the kite was more than just a game. It was

the reflection of a.civilization, of the joy of being borne
along, guided, mastered by the forces of nature. It was
an art form, a religion, a philosophy. The shredded
remains of the hundreds of kites that dangled from
the electric cables across the slum were the decorative
emblems of the people of the City of Joy.

The tiniest children tried their hands with bits of
packing paper. By the age of six or seven they were
already seeking to perfect their aircraft. By that time,
they were quite capable of turning a piece of *khadi*, an
end of a shirt, or a rag into a real airship. They decorated
them with geometric designs and asked their 'big brother
Stephan' to write their names in calligraphy on the
wings. The most sophisticated devices, complete with
tail and drift, were the work of the oldest boys. Sometimes the pieces of string that secured them were coated
with paste and powdered glass to sever the strings of
rival kites.

One evening, a premonsoon squall precipitated the
launching of one of these aircraft. The whole compound
was caught up in a fever. 'It was like being at Cape
Canaveral on the brink of a space launching,' Kovalski
was to say. Twelve-year-old Jaï, one of the sons of the
onetime sailor from Kerala, climbed onto the roof and
ran across the tiles to launch his cloth bird into an
ascending gust of air. Buffeted by the squall, the kite
took off, each upward lurch encouraged by a burst of
cheers. 'It was as if every mouth were blowing heavenward to help it climb more quickly.' The boy leaped
from one roof to another to steer his creation, restrain
it, and direct it towards a stronger current.

Dozens of youngsters from the slum had broken their
bones performing these kinds of acrobatics. 'Up, up,
up!' yelled the people. Jaï had manœuvred it so well that
the great white bug with the two pink ribbons trailing
behind its tail rose above the electric cables. There was
a tremendous burst of applause. Gaiety had taken over.

The eunuchs banged frantically on their drums. Even Kovalski felt himself carried away by the general exultation. It was then that a second kite appeared in the air. The adjoining Muslim compound was offering a challenge. From then on the business became far too serious to be left in the hands of the children. Jaï's father and Ashish Ghosh, the young therapist who was preparing to leave the slum to go back to his village, sprang onto the roof. They took charge of the aircraft's string. The rival was to be shot down and captured, no matter what the price. Men from the other compound also hoisted themselves up onto the tiles. A savage duel ensued, punctuated by the enthusiastic yells of the onlookers. The game had become a battle. For long minutes the result remained undecided. Each team manœuvred to try and hook the other's string. A sudden reversal of the wind direction, instantly exploited by the team from Kovalski's compound, enabled them to block the ascent of the Muslim kite and push it onto the electric cables. Pandemonium broke out. In their fury, the Muslims hurled themselves at the two Hindus. Tiles began to fly in all directions and the saraband of drums was redoubled. More men clambered onto the rooftops and from below in the compounds the women urged the combatants on. The two flying machines collided, became entangled with one another, and eventually tumbled like dead leaves onto the electric cables. All the same, down below on the rooftops the fierce confrontation did not stop. Bodies rolled down into the courtyard and the bamboo frameworks shattered, scattering panic-stricken rats.

Powerless to intervene, Kovalski took refuge in his room. Through the open doorway, he could see young Jaï, little Padmini and other adolescents looking incredulously at 'the grown-ups who had stolen their children's game and were fighting each other like wild beasts'.

62

'Keep our leaving a secret?' exclaimed Ashish Ghosh. 'In an ants' nest where all spend their time spying on everyone else? Impossible!'

Son of Miracle wagged his head. The taxi driver knew very well that his young neighbour was right. A slum was a cooking pot in which people simmered together from one end of the year to the other. Every activity, even the most intimate, like making love or talking in your sleep, was accomplished here with the full knowledge of everybody else. Nevertheless, the taxi driver would have preferred that the word that accommodation was about to become vacant be kept a secret until he had had time to negotiate its reallocation to Hasari Pal with the landlord. He might just as well have tried to prevent the day from dawning!

The impending departure of the Ghoshs soon became the sole topic of general conversation. It was not so much the imminent vacation of a room that provoked so much interest, as the news of the departure itself. After a few years in the slum, everyone's dream, the dream of returning home to the village, became so much a mirage that it seemed insane for anyone to even attempt it. That a couple should decide to give up two salaries to go and plant rice was inconceivable. Strangely, too, the reactions back in the Ghoshs' village were equally negative. 'When the goddess, Lakshmi, has put oil in your lamp, it's a crime to extinguish the flame and go elsewhere,' the boy's parents repeated angrily, threatening to prevent him from returning by force.

All the same, aspiring successors to the hovel crowded around the Ghoshs' door in such large numbers that the

landlord himself turned up unexpectedly. He was a corpulent Bengali with hair that shone like a statue of Vishnu coated with *ghee*. Even the foulest hovel in the City of Joy had a legitimate owner. Some of them even had four, one for each wall. Many of these landlords owned several houses, and sometimes a whole compound.

'The fact that the fat Bengali has appeared in person does not bode well at all,' thought Son of Miracle and, sure enough, it was not long before his worst fears were realized. The owner blithely informed him that he was going to double the rent for the next tenant. Instead of thirty rupees a month, the room would cost sixty. (£3.50), an outrageous price for a rabbit hutch with no electricity and no windows, and certainly quite incompatible with the miserable means available to a rickshaw puller stricken with the red fever. Hasari's beautiful dream had just been shattered.

Yet the taxi driver would not admit defeat. 'My nickname was Son of Miracle and, bent on living up to my name, I decided to put up a fight to get that dwelling for Hasari,' he was to recount. 'So I said to my wife, "Prepare a dish of rice with a banana and a little jasmine, and we'll go and see the Brahmin about making a *puja*."' The Brahmin was an extremely thin little man. He lived with his family in the enclosure of a small temple, in one of the poorest parts of the slum, between the railway tracks and the boarded shacks of a community of people originally from Tamil Nadu. Son of Miracle paid him two rupees. The Brahmin put a *tilak* on the visitors' foreheads and likewise on the foreheads of Shiva and Nandi, the bull of abundance, enthroned beside the deity in its little shrine. Then he took his ceremonial tray, incense sticks, a pot of *ghee*, a small bell, a five-branched candlestick with little cups in which there burned small flames known as *panchaprodip*, and a pitcher containing Ganges water. He recited *mantras*, rang the bell, and

proceeded to the ceremony of fire, walking with his candlestick around the statues. He put particular emphasis on the bull, for it is to Nandi that Hindus attribute the power to grant any desire.

After his *puja* to the gods of the heavens, Son of Miracle decided to address himself to the gods of the earth.

'We must get the godfather to help,' he announced to Ashish Ghosh. 'He's the only one who could cut down that pirate's demands.'

'Do you really think the godfather would put himself out over so trivial a matter?' asked Ashish.

'Of course he will! In fact it's exactly the kind of intervention that he likes. After all, doesn't he call himself the "defender of the little ones", the "protector of widows and orphans", the "guru of the poor"?'

Accordingly, Son of Miracle requested an audience. Two days later an envoy from the godfather came to fetch him, whereupon he underwent the same ritual as had Kovalski. The taxi driver was ushered first into a kind of anteroom where bodyguards were playing cards and dominoes and smoking cigarettes. Then the godfather's eldest son appeared to conduct the visitor into the vast reception room. Son of Miracle stared, wide-eyed with wonder. The godfather was in truth a nobleman. He sat enthroned like the great Mogul at the far end of the room on his armchair encrusted with precious stones, but his dark glasses and the heavy folds of his jowls gave him the air of an ageing toad. Without a word, he projected his chin in the direction of the taxi driver to indicate that he was ready to listen.

Son of Miracle presented his request forcefully. After three minutes the godfather raised his fat, hairy hand covered with rings. He had understood. Any further explanation would be superfluous. He signalled to his son to approach the throne and whispered in his ear the price of his intervention. 'Irrespective of the fact that

the godfather was the protector of the poor and the oppressed, he was like a race horse: he didn't run without his oats,' the taxi driver was to say. 'Much to my surprise, however, this time it wasn't a question of money. Instead, he gave me to understand through his son that in exchange for his intervention with the overdemanding owner, he intended to set up a drinking dive in the compound. Not bad, eh? And there was no question of raising the slightest objection. You don't refuse hospitality to someone who's giving you a roof over your head.'

One of the most notable events that could ever occur in the life of a slum – a family's departure and return to its village – passed off completely unnoticed. Having given up the idea of leaving separately, the Ghoshs and their three children piled their things into a rickshaw and left the compound one morning at dawn. There was no farewell banquet or celebration, only a few emotional displays from neighbours who had lived and suffered with them in the same prison for years. The young people of the compound had, however, prepared a going-away present for them. It was Padmini, the little girl who collected coal from the locomotive, who actually presented it to Mallika, the Ghoshs' eldest daughter. The gift was the rag doll which some weeks earlier they had metamorphosed into Lakshmi, goddess of prosperity, now coated with *ghee* and garlanded with rose petals.

Kovalski accompanied the departing family to the station. After a two-hour train journey as far as the small town of Canning, then three hours on a steamboat on the River Matla, a branch of the Ganges delta, followed by an hour's bus journey and two hours across the dikes on foot, they would be home again at last – after six years in exile! They were living proof that the tide of

exodus could turn, that the tragedy of Calcutta was not ineluctable, that it need not be for ever. That was how Kovalski wished to look upon their departure. Yet his grief at losing his brother and sister was immense. Since that distant evening when Margareta had first shown them into his room in Nizamudhin Lane, a profound affection had grown up between him and these two bright young people who were ever ready, day or night, to fly to the rescue of anyone in distress and constantly prepared to devote themselves to the most neglected. On the point of putting his family in the train, Ashish paused and faced the priest.

'Big Brother Stephan,' he said in a voice taut with emotion, 'as you know we are Hindus, but it would please us if you would give us the blessing of your Jesus before we go.'

Much moved, Kovalski raised his hand above the five heads clustered together in the midst of the throng and slowly made the sign of the cross.

'May the blessing and the peace of Christ be with you,' he murmured, 'for you are the light of the world.'

It was only when the train had pulled away and the faces at the window had vanished into the scalding air at the end of the platform that Kovalski became aware that he was crying.

How the fat Bengali landlord knew the exact date of the Ghoshs' departure was something of a mystery. At about six o'clock on that very same morning, however, he burst into the compound accompanied by half a dozen thugs. In Calcutta anyone could recruit a small army to keep his personal affairs in order. It cost less to engage a man than to hire a bullock to pull a cart. The landlord came armed with an enormous padlock to secure the door of the vacant hovel.

Just as the battle of Hastinapur brought lustre to the

Mahabharata epic, so the battle which now ensued was to become a striking page in the history of the City of Joy. On this occasion, however, the adversaries were not mythological warriors disputing the glorious capital of a kingdom but vulgar good-for-nothings, ready to tear each other's guts out for the possession of a miserable rat hole in the heart of a slum. The godfather had sent his son, Ashoka, at the head of a commando unit armed with clubs. Pushing the owner and his guards aside, they took up their position in front of the Ghoshs' former home. Fighting broke out. Kovalski saw someone brandish a knife and slice off one of the combatant's ears. The occupants of the compound were seized with panic. Women fled, screaming. Others barricaded themselves in with their children. Terrified, the eunuch's cockerel emitted cock-a-doodle-doos that brought out the entire neighbourhood. The tiles from the roofs began to fly, followed by *chulas*, buckets and bricks. Wounded people crawled away, groaning. It was like a scene out of a play, except that here people were really fighting, and with unparalleled ferocity.

It was at this point that the godfather made his appearance. Dressed in an immaculate white *dhoti* with gilded sandals on his feet and an ivory-handled cane in his hand, he looked more than ever like a Grand Mogul between the two bodyguards who fanned him. 'It's the emperor Akbar coming to appease the anger of his subjects,' thought Kovalski. Instantly the fighting stopped. No one, not even the *gundas* engaged at the docks, would have dared to dispute the authority of the lord of the City of Joy. Reassured, the residents returned to their homes in time to witness an extraordinary scene. The godfather advanced towards the fat Bengali landlord, entrusted his cane to one of his guards, raised both his hands to the level of his face and joined them in a gesture of salutation. Then, taking back his cane, he pointed the tip of it at the large black padlock the proprietor was

gripping. With a barely perceptible movement of the head, he invited one of his guards to take possession of it. Not a word was spoken and the Bengali put up not the least resistance. On the contrary, he bade the godfather a respectful farewell and withdrew with what was left of his escort, whereupon the godfather did a tour of the compound to savour his triumph and caress the cheeks of a number of children in their mothers' arms.

Son of Miracle was exultant. He had lived up to his name. True, the victory had been expensive – he had had to hand out quite a lot of money to the neighbours to induce them to accept the idea of the drinking den, the price of the godfather's intervention – but the result was well worth the sacrifice. Hasari would at last be able to escape the degradation of the pavement and settle with his family in a compound near Son of Miracle's own: a four-star compound where the slum houses were built out of mud and bricks, and topped with proper roofs. Even better, it had the bonus of an authentic white-skinned holy man and no fewer than four authentic eunuchs as immediate neighbours. The godfather had lost no time in making sure this outstanding event would be celebrated in the proper fashion. The bottles of *bangla* and *todi* for his new clandestine drinking den were already awaiting the revellers.

63

There was no doubt in Max Loeb's mind: the incredible vision was an effect of the heat. 'I'm delirious,' he thought to himself. He put down his scalpel and rubbed his eyes but the vision was still there, planted in the murky water in the middle of the alleyway.

'Dad!' he finally yelled, dashing out of his room.

The tall figure with the russet hair was indeed Arthur Loeb, although with his trousers rolled up to his knees, the surgeon looked more like a fisherman after shrimps. For a moment father and son stood facing each other, unable to utter a word, until finally Arthur held out his arms and Max rushed into them. The sight of the two *sahibs* embracing each other provoked much hilarity among the crowd that thronged the door of the dispensary.

'Is that your hospital?' asked Arthur Loeb at last, pointing to the mud-walled room.

Max nodded his head and they laughed together, but Arthur Loeb's features became suddenly set. His gaze had just encountered all the pitted faces, the skeletal babies in their mothers' arms, the protruding chests of tuberculosis sufferers coughing and spitting as they waited for their consultation.

'It's a real gathering of the lame, the sick and the dying here,' he stammered, stricken by what he saw.

'I'm sorry this is all I can offer you by way of a reception committee,' apologized Max. 'If you'd warned me in advance, you'd have qualified for a band with dancing girls, transvestites, eunuchs, garlands of flowers, welcoming *tilak*, and all the trimmings! India is a lavish land!'

'Welcoming *tilak*?'

'That's the red dot they put on your forehead. It's known as the third eye and it enables you to see the truth beyond appearances.'

'For the moment what I can see is staggering enough,' Arthur admitted. 'Surely there must be a place less alarming in this city to celebrate our reunion.'

'What would you say to a Punjabi dinner? I think it's the best cuisine in India. And the best restaurant is right in your hotel. I take it you are staying at the Grand Hotel?'

Arthur nodded.

'Eight o'clock at the Tandoori restaurant of the Grand then!'

Max pointed to the line of sick and crippled people who were beginning to grow impatient. 'And tomorrow, you can come and give me a hand! Respiratory illnesses are your speciality, aren't they? Well, you are going to have fun!'

As soon as they could afford it, Calcutta residents would get their own back on themselves from the excesses of the heat and go to the other extremes. To defy the madness of the temperature, one city industrialist had even gone so far as to install an ice-skating rink in his garden. Like all up-to-date places equipped with air-conditioning, the restaurant Max had chosen was like an icebox. Fortunately the beturbàned head waiter had dug out a magnum of Dom Perignon which quickly warmed the two frozen table companions and whetted their appetites. Max knew all the Punjabi dishes. He had first discovered them in this very place, in the company of Manubaï Chatterjee, the beautiful Indian woman who had supervised his gastronomical initiation.

Arthur raised his glass. 'Here's to your speedy return home, Max!'

'First let's drink to your discovery of Calcutta!' suggested Arthur's son, clinking glasses with his father.

They drank several mouthfuls.

'What a shock that was this afternoon, damn it,' said Arthur.

'And yet you didn't really see anything tragic.'

The surgeon looked incredulous.

'Do you mean to say there's worse?'

'I know it must be hard to imagine when you've come straight from a paradise like Miami,' said Max, thinking of his father's luxurious clinic. 'In fact, no one can really have any idea of the living conditions of the millions of people here without actually sharing them like the Polish

priest I told you about in my letters. And like me, to a lesser extent.'

Arthur listened with a mixture of respect and astonishment. Images of his son as a child and as an adolescent flooded into his mind. Nearly all of them related to one salient feature of his character: a morbid fear of dirt. Throughout his life, Max had changed his underwear and clothes several times a day. At high school, among his friends, his mania for washing had earned him the nickname of 'Supersuds'. Later at medical school, his obsessive fear of insects and all forms of vermin had occasioned some memorable practical jokes, like his finding a colony of cockroaches between his sheets or a whole family of tarantulas in his dissection kit. Arthur Loeb couldn't get over it. The gods of the City of Joy had metamorphosed his son. He wanted to understand.

'Didn't you want to run away when you first landed in this cesspool?' he asked.

'Sure I did,' replied Max without hesitation. 'Especially as Kovalski, sadist that he is, had kept a hellish surprise in store for my arrival: one of his leper friends in labour. You should have seen my face! But that wasn't the worst of it.'

Max told his father of the infernal heat, of the hundreds of living dead who invaded his room in the hope of some impossible miracle, of the cesspool emptiers' strike that had transformed the slum into a sea of excrement, of the tropical storms, the flood, the holdup in the middle of the night, the scorpion sting and his tumble into the sewer.

'From my very first week onwards the City of Joy offered me its complete catalogue of charms,' he concluded. 'So, it was bound to happen. I cracked up. I jumped in a taxi and cleared out. I took refuge here and indulged myself. But after three days I felt a kind of nostalgia and I went back.'

The waiters brought several aromatic dishes laden with a mountain of orange-coloured pieces of chicken and mutton.

His father grimaced.

'Don't worry. That colour is typical of dishes from the Punjab,' explained Max, delighted to be able to show off his knowledge. 'To begin with, the pieces of meat are macerated in yoghurt steeped in all kinds of spices. Then they're coated with a kind of chili paste. That's what gives them their colour. After that they're baked in a *tandoor*, that's a special clay oven. Have a taste, they're marvellous.'

Arthur Loeb took a bite, but almost immediately Max saw his father's cheeks turn crimson. He heard him stammer a few words. The poor man was asking for some champagne to put out the fire in his mouth. Max quickly filled his glass and ordered some *nan*, the delicious oven-baked wheaten bread that was ideal for soothing burning palates. Arthur chewed his way through several pieces in silence. Suddenly, after five minutes had passed, he looked up again.

'Supposing I were to buy your City of Joy?'

Max nearly swallowed his chicken bone.

'You mean the slum?'

'Precisely. I could raze it to the ground, rebuild it anew with running water, provide the whole lot with drains, electricity, even television. And give the residents their homes as a present. What do you say to that, my boy?'

Max emptied his glass slowly and thoughtfully.

'Dad, it's a brilliant idea,' he said at last. 'The only trouble is that we're in Calcutta, not in South Miami or in the Bronx. I'm afraid a project like that would be difficult to implement over here.'

'If you're willing to pay the price, you can implement anything,' replied Arthur, slightly irritated.

'I'm sure you're right. It's just that, over here, money

isn't enough. All kinds of other considerations come into play.'

'Such as?'

'First of all no foreigner is allowed to purchase real estate. It's an old Indian law. Even the British at the height of their power had to submit to it.'

Arthur swept away the objection with a wave of his hand.

'I'll use Indian front men. They can buy the slum for me and the end result will be the same. After all, it's the end result that matters, isn't it?'

Either as a consequence of the spicy cooking or of the traumatic memory of his first visit to Anand Nagar, the surgeon was very excited. 'An achievement like that would have a more direct impact than all the nebulous programmes of aid to underdeveloped countries discussed in the United Nations,' he finished up by saying.

'No doubt,' acknowledged Max with a smile. He could just imagine the expressions on the faces of the government *babus* when they learned that an American *sahib* wanted to buy up one of Calcutta's slums. There remained, however, a more serious objection. Since immersing himself in the poverty of the Third World, Max had been induced to revise a fair number of his bright theories on how the problems of the poor should be solved. 'When I first arrived in the slum,' he told his father, 'one of the first thoughts Kovalski shared with me came from a Brazilian archbishop struggling shoulder to shoulder with the poor out in the country and the *favelas*. According to him, our help serves only to make people more dependent *unless it is supported with actions designed to wipe out the actual roots of poverty.*'

'Does that mean that it's no use taking them out of their hovels full of crap and setting them up in new housing?'

Max nodded his head sadly.

'I've even come to learn the validity of a strange reality

here,' he said. 'In a slum an exploiter is better than a
Santa Claus . . .' Confronted by his father's stupe-
fied expression, he went on to explain, 'An exploiter
forces you to react, whereas a Santa Claus immobilizes
you.'

'It took me several days to understand exactly what Max
meant,' Arthur Loeb was later to admit. 'Every morning
I climbed into a taxi and went to join him in his slum.
Hundreds of people had been lining up outside the door
of his dispensary since dawn or even since the night
before. Bandona, the delightful Assamese girl, cleared a
corner of the room for me. It was she who sorted out
the patients. With an infallible eye she directed the most
serious cases to me, generally patients in the terminal
stages of tuberculosis. In all my career I had never seen
such ruined systems. How those spectres ever found the
strength to take even the few steps to my small table, I
do not know. As far as I was concerned, they were
already dead. But I was wrong. Those walking dead
were really *alive*. They jostled each other, argued and
joked. In the City of Joy the life force always seemed to
prevail over death.'

Above all, these daily plunges into the very heart of
the poverty and suffering of an Indian slum would enable
Dr Loeb to understand better what form effective help
should take. 'I had been prepared to give tens of thousands of dollars to buy a whole slum and build it anew,'
he was to say, 'when in fact the urgent need was for
a ration of milk to be distributed to rickety babies
whose fontanels were still open, for people who ran a high
risk of epidemics to be vaccinated, for thousands of
tuberculosis sufferers to be rescued from fatal pollution.
That experience shared with my son and Bandona made
me appreciate a fundamental truth. It's at grass roots
level that gestures of solidarity are really noticed and

appreciated. A simple smile can have as much value as all the dollars in the world.'

A simple smile! Every Wednesday morning, Max hired a minibus at his own expense. Into it he piled ten or so rickety children, youngsters suffering from paralysis, from polio, from physical and mental handicaps. Some of the mothers, together with Bandona and Margareta, accompanied the young doctor and his pitiful little troop. On one Wednesday morning the bus contained an extra passenger, Max's father. The vehicle crossed the large metal bridge over the Hooghly and, with great blasts of its horn, tackled the madness of the traffic jams. No. 50 Circus Avenue was a decrepit old two-storey building. A simple painted sign at the entrance announced: Estrid Dane Clinic, 1st Floor. Could this vast, dusty and badly lit room, furnished only with two large tables, really be a clinic? wondered the American professor as he allowed his bewildered gaze to roam over the austere decor. The scene he was about to witness, however, was to give him one of the greatest medical thrills of his life.

Once all the children were in their places, the mistress of the establishment appeared. She was an elderly lady with bare feet, small in build, and almost insignificant in appearance. She was wearing the white sari and very short hair of a Hindu widow. One detail struck the American instantly: her smile, a luminous smile that encompassed the whole of her wrinkled face, her bright eyes and her delicate mouth reddened with betel juice. Hers was a smile of communion, life, hope. 'That smile alone,' Arthur Loeb was to say, 'lit up the wretched refuse dump we were in with a supernatural brilliance and consolation. It was pure charisma.'

At the age of eighty-two, Estrid Dane was one of the glories of Indian medical science. Yet she was neither doctor nor healer nor bonesetter. For forty years in the clinic she had opened in London, her long, slender hands,

her gentle voice, and angelic smile had cured more
physical ailments than many a specialist institution. The
greatest professors sent her their hopeless cases. The
press and television reported on her activities. 'The old
Indian lady with the miraculous hands', as she was called,
was known throughout almost all of England. In the
twilight of her life, Estrid Dane had decided to return
to her homeland and dedicate her final years to her
fellow countrymen. She had settled in this run-down old
building in Circus Avenue and it was here that, each
morning, with the help of a few young students whom
she was training in her technique, she performed her
miracles anew.

Margareta and Bandona deposited the inert body of a
small, emaciated boy of five or six on the first table. His
arms, legs, eyes, head, everything about him was devoid
of life. Arthur Loeb could not help thinking of 'a little
corpse that had kept its freshness'. His name was Subash.
He was a polio victim. On the previous day his mother
had brought him to Max. 'Take him,' she had implored
with an expression that was heartrending. 'I can't do
anything for him.' Max had examined the child, then
returned him to his mother's arms. 'Bring him back
tomorrow. We'll take him to Estrid Dane.'

'The old Indian lady's hands were placed gently on
the child's thorax and fleshless thighs,' Arthur Loeb
would recount, 'and her eyes, her mouth, the dimples
of her cheeks, all wrinkled as they were, broke into a
fresh smile. To me it was as if that smile struck the
patient like a laser beam. His eyes shone, his little teeth
appeared between his lips. His lifeless face lit up a shade.
Incredible as it seemed, he too was smiling.' Then
Estrid's hands began their awe-inspiring ballet. Slowly
and methodically the Indian woman probed Subash's
muscles, his tendons, his bones, to try and distinguish
the dead areas from those where there might still be a
spark of life. 'You sensed that this woman was searching

with her brain and her heart as much as with her hands,'
the American was to continue, 'that she was constantly
asking herself questions. Why was such and such a
muscle wasted? Because of the breakdown of its link
with the nervous system or because of undernourish-
ment? Why had this particular area lost all sensation? In
brief, what were the possible causes of each lesion? Her
hands stopped continually to seek out the fingers of one
of her students and guide them to a deformity or a
sensitive area. Then she would give a long explanation
in Bengali to which all the girls listened with religious
respect. The truly magical part of her treatment came
only after the stocktaking. Throughout the entire half
hour that followed, Estrid Dane's palms, firm and tender
by turns, kneaded the body of the little polio victim,
forcing him to react, rekindling in him the flame apparently extinguished. It was absolutely spellbinding. Each
movement seemed to say to him, "Wake up, Subash,
move your arms, your legs, your feet. Live, Subash!"'

Squatting in the shadows behind the Indian woman,
Subash's mother kept watch on the slightest movement
near her child. Like all the other onlookers, the two
Americans held their breath. There was not a sound to
be heard but the friction of Estrid's hands on the cracked
skin of her small patient.

No miracle really occurred. No one saw the paralysed
boy suddenly get up and rush into his mother's arms.
None the less what did happen remained for the Drs
Loeb, father and son, a demonstration of what they did
not hesitate to describe as 'exceptional medical prowess'.
'Suddenly,' the professor was to recall, 'a series of vibrations seemed to shake the child's body. His right arm
came to life first, then his left. The head that had seemed
for so long to be soldered to his chest by his chin in a
prone position gave a slight movement. Timidly,
weakly, the life was being breathed back into that mum-
mified body. It was obvious that the fingers of the old

Indian woman in the widow's sari had somehow set the
engine moving again. They had reawoken the nervous
system, compelled it to send its impulses through that
little living corpse. This was only a first result and the
road to complete recovery was, I knew, a long one.
Nevertheless that terrible city of Calcutta had taught me
the most beautiful lesson in hope of my life.'

64

'They look like a herd of goats being led to the slaughter-
house,' thought Stephan Kovalski watching the family
entering the compound. 'With his cotton loincloth
tucked up between legs that were as thin as matchsticks,'
the priest was to recount, 'the father walked in with a
basket on his head containing the family possessions: a
chula, a few cooking utensils, a bucket, a pitcher, a little
linen, and their festival clothes wrapped up in newspaper
secured with strands of jute. He was a frail man with a
large drooping moustache, a thick mop of salt-and-
pepper hair, and a face that was unshaven and furrowed
with wrinkles. A certain suppleness about his bearing
suggested that he was younger than he looked. Behind
him, with lowered eyes and her veil pulled down over
her forehead, trotted a woman with a light complexion
dressed in an orange sari. She was holding on her hip
the family's last born child, a bony little boy with close-
cropped hair. A young girl with her head uncovered and
two long braids followed with two boys in vests, aged
fourteen and ten. Their heads were bowed and indeed
they looked as timorous as a herd of goats being led to
the slaughter.'

Son of Miracle was waiting for Hasari and his family
at the entrance to the hard-won trophy that was to be

their new home. He had had the floor decorated with a *rangoli* covering. The residents of the compound immediately formed a circle around the somewhat dazed newcomers and the taxi driver began the introductions. He had bought several bottles of *bangla* from the godfather's clandestine supply, and glasses circulated from hand to hand. The head of the compound pronounced a few words of welcome and clinked glasses with Hasari, who could not get over the warmth of the reception. 'After all those years of suffering it was as if the great god Bhagavan had suddenly opened the gates of paradise.'

Stephan Kovalski was by no means the last to join in this little celebration. Along with the eunuchs, the Pals would now be his nearest neighbours, and his stomach had survived so many onslaughts that now it could certainly put up with a few mouthfuls of alcoholic poison, even in the blazing heat. Not everyone, however, had the same powers of endurance. Kovalski saw Hasari's pupils dilate suddenly and turn a strange whitish colour. Before anyone had time to react, the rickshaw puller staggered and fell to the ground. His body was shaken by a series of convulsions, his throat and cheeks distended as if he were about to vomit. Kovalski fell on his knees and raised the sick man's head.

'Spit it out. Spit all that poison out,' he urged him. In response to these words he saw the lips half open beneath the bushy moustache. 'Spit, old brother, spit,' he repeated. The Pole heard a gurgling in the depths of Hasari's throat and saw a stream of reddish froth appear from between the corners of his mouth. The residents of the compound realized then that it wasn't the *bangla* from their welcoming festivities that was making their new neighbour vomit. He too had the red fever.

That evening, as the sun's disc was vanishing beyond the mantle of smoke that imprisoned the slum, the sound of a horn tore the priest away from his meditation before the picture of the Sacred Shroud. The sound was as

familiar to him as the cawing of the hooded crows. As soon as he regained consciousness, Hasari had decided to honour his new hovel with a *puja*. He had placed incense sticks in the hinges of the door and in the four corners of the room. Then, as thousands of millions of Indians had done each evening since the dawn of humanity, he had blown into a conch to draw down upon himself and his kinsfolk 'the beneficent spirits of the night'. Kovalski prayed with a particular fervour that this cry might be heard. 'But for some time now the gods of the slum had seemed to be suffering from a cruel deafness.'

Although he would much rather have shared his sleeping spot with a couple of eunuchs than with a diseased consumptive, Big Brother Stephan did not hesitate: he invited Hasari and his eldest son to share the bit of veranda outside his room. There were too many Pals to lie down outside their own hovel, and the stifling heat of the premonsoon weeks made sleep inside the slum houses impossible. Kovalski would never forget the first night he spent lying beside his new neighbour, not only because of the sound Hasari's lungs made with each breath – like the noises coming from a blacksmith's forge – but primarily because of the confidences he was to hear. Hardly had the priest lain down on the floor when Hasari turned to him.

'Don't go to sleep yet, Big Brother,' he entreated. 'I need to talk to you.'

Many times Kovalski had heard appeals of that kind, sometimes from complete strangers.

'I'm listening, brother,' he said warmly.

Hasari appeared to hesitate.

'I know that my *chakra* will soon cease to turn for this life,' he declared.

Kovalski knew well the meaning of those words. Hasari was expressing foreknowledge of his impending end. The Pole protested, but only as a matter of form.

After the crisis of the afternoon, he knew, alas, that neither Max nor anybody else could save the unfortunate man. 'I am not afraid of death,' continued the rickshaw puller. 'I've had such a tough time since I left my village that I am almost sure . . .' again he hesitated, 'almost sure that today my *karma* is less heavy and will have me born again into a better incarnation.'

Kovalski had often discerned this hope in the confidences of the people he had helped to die in the slum. It had a calming effect on them. Tonight, however, it was of other things that his new neighbour wanted to talk. 'Big Brother,' he went on, propping himself up on his elbows, 'I do not want to die before I've . . .' He choked, shaken by a fit of coughing. Kovalski thumped him on the back. All around them there rose the snores of sleeping people. In the distance they could hear the sound of shouting and the blaring of a loudspeaker; somewhere there was a celebration going on. Long minutes passed, during which the Pole wondered what sudden concern could be preoccupying his neighbour at so late an hour. He did not have to wait long for an answer. 'Big Brother, I cannot die before I've found a husband for my daughter.'

For an Indian father there was no more powerful obsession than that of marrying off his daughter. Amrita, the rickshaw puller's daughter, was only sixteen years old but if the cruel years on the pavement and in the shantytown had not tarnished her freshness, the gravity of her expression bespoke the fact that she had long since ceased to be a child. The role of a girl in Indian society is a thankless one. No domestic task, no drudgery is considered too much for her. Up before everyone else and last to go to bed, she leads the life of a slave. A mother before ever having children of her own, Amrita had brought up her brothers. It was she who had guided their first steps, foraged for their food in the hotel refuse, sewn together the rags that served as their clothes,

massaged their fleshless limbs, organized their games, deloused their heads. Right from her earliest years, her mother had unflaggingly prepared her for the one big event of her life, the one which for a day would transform a child of poverty into the subject of all the conversation in the small world of the poor who surrounded her: her marriage. All her education was directed towards that end. The shanty of cardboard and planks in their first slum, the pavement squats, had been for her places of apprenticeship. It was there that the skills of a model mother and perfect wife had been passed on to her. Like all Indian parents, the Pals were aware that one day they would be judged on the manner in which their daughter conducted herself in her husband's house and, as her role could only ever be one of submission, Amrita had been trained from the very first to renounce all personal inclinations and relinquish all play in order to serve her parents and brothers, something that she had always done with a smile. Ever since she was a small child she had accepted the Indian idea of marriage, a conception that meant that Hasari would one day say to Kovalski, 'My daughter does not belong to me. She has only been lent to me by God until she marries. She belongs to the boy who will be her husband.'

Indian custom generally requires that a girl should be married well before puberty, hence the occurrence of the child 'marriages' that seem so barbaric to Westerners. In such cases it is only a question of a ceremony. The real marriage takes place only after the girl's first period. Then the father of the 'bride' goes to the father of the 'groom' and informs him that his daughter is now capable of bearing a child. A more definitive ceremony is subsequently arranged and it is then that the young girl leaves her parents' home to go and live with the boy to whom she has been 'married' for years.

The daughter of a poor rickshaw puller not being a particularly desirable match, Amrita's first period had

come before she was 'married', almost on the eve of her
eleventh birthday. As tradition would have it, the little
girl had then abandoned the skirt and top of a child and
put on an adult's sari, but there had been no celebration
on the piece of pavement occupied by the Pals. Her
mother had simply wrapped up in a sheet of newspaper
the piece of rag that had absorbed the first blood. When
Amrita came to marry, she and her entire family would
take the piece of linen to the Ganges and immerse it in
the sacred waters so that the young wife might be blessed
with fertility. In order to make this glorious occasion
come without further delay, Amrita's father had first to
resolve a problem, a very crucial one indeed.

As his father before him had done for his sisters and
as millions of other Indian fathers had done for their
daughters, Hasari had to get together a dowry. Indira
Gandhi might well have forbidden this ancestral custom
but that did not prevent its continuing in modern India
in a way that was even more tyrannical. 'I can't give my
daughter to a man who is paralysed or blind or a leper!'
the rickshaw puller was to lament to Kovalski. Only
such disinherited people would agree to take a girl in
marriage without a dowry. The poor man never stopped
doing all kinds of calculations but they all came back to
the same fateful figure. Five thousand rupees was the
sum he had to collect before the very humblest of boys
would accept his daughter. Five thousand rupees! That
meant two whole years of running about between the
shafts of his rickshaw or a lifetime of being indebted to
the slum's *mahajan*. But what lifetime and how much
running about? 'When you cough red,' he was to go on
to say, 'you watch the sun rise each morning and wonder
whether you'll see it set.'

Kovalski entrusted his new neighbour to Max, who
put him on a powerful treatment based on antibiotics
and vitamins. The effect on a virgin metabolism, totally
unaccustomed to medicines, was spectacular. The at-

tacks of coughing became less frequent and he recovered enough strength to start pulling his carriage again in the humid heat of the weeks that preceded the monsoon. The imminent arrival of the annual deluge enhanced his prospects of increased income since rickshaws were the only vehicles that could get about the flooded streets of Calcutta. Still, even that would not be enough to guarantee the indispensable five thousand rupees.

It was then that fortune intervened in the form of a new encounter with one of the vulture-like procurers that prowled the streets in search of business. The meeting took place outside the agency for the SAS airline company on the corner of Park Street where the exhausted puller had just set down two ladies and their heavy suitcases. Struck by an attack of coughing that shook him like a reed in a tornado, Hasari was so unwell that two other pullers rushed to help him lie down on the seat of his carriage. Suddenly a face pockmarked from smallpox appeared above Hasari's. The eyes were full of sympathy.

'Well now, my friend,' volunteered the stranger. 'You don't look too well!'

This friendly remark comforted Hasari. There were not many people who treated you like a 'friend' in this inhuman city. He wiped his bloodied mouth with a corner of his vest.

'It must really be a tough job to have to pull one of those carriages when you're coughing your head off!' continued the stranger.

Hasari nodded. 'You're not kidding!'

'What would you say if I were to offer you as much money as you earn in two months sweating between your shafts, without your having to do anything,' the stranger then inquired.

'As much money as . . .' stammered Hasari at a loss for words. 'Oh, I would say that you were the god Hanuman in person.' Then suddenly he remembered the

middleman who had accosted him one day in the Bara Bazar: 'If it's my blood you're after, you're on the wrong track,' he announced sadly. 'Even the vultures wouldn't want anything to do with my blood. It's rotten.'

'It's not your blood I'm after. It's your bones.'

'My bones?'

The puller's expression of horror brought a smile to the procurer's face.

'That's it,' he explained calmly. 'You come with me to my boss. He'll buy your bones for five hundred rupees. When you kick the bucket he'll collect your body and take your skeleton.'

This man was one of the links in a singular trade that made India the prime exporter of human bones in the world. Each year, some twenty thousand whole skeletons and tens of thousands of different carefully packed bones departed from India's airports and seaports, destined for medical schools in the United States, Europe, Japan and Australia. This extremely lucrative business brought in just over a million pounds a year. Its centre was Calcutta. The principal exporters – eight in number – all had a house of their own and their names featured in the register of the local customs headquarters. They went under the names of Fashiono & Co., Hilton & Co., Krishnaraj Stores, R. B. & Co., M. B. & Co., Vista & Co., Sourab and Reknas Ltd., and finally Mitra & Co. Precise administrative regulations governed the exercise of this trade. A special manual entitled the *Export Policy Book* specified in particular that 'the export of skeletons and human bones is authorized upon the furnishing of a certificate of origin from the corpse signed by a police officer of at least substantive superintendent rank'. The same document stipulated that the bones could not be exported except for the purposes of study or medical research. It did, however, provide for the fact that exportation could be effected 'for other reasons, upon examination of individual cases'.

The fact that Calcutta was the centre of this strange activity had nothing to do with the mortality rate in its slums. This commerce owed its prosperity to the presence in the city of a community of several hundred immigrants from Bihar who belonged to an extremely low caste, that of the *Doms*. *Doms* are destined from birth to take care of the dead. Often they are also looked upon as footpads, pillagers of corpses. They usually live near the funeral pyres of the Hooghly and near cemeteries or hospital morgues and they do not mix with other residents. It was they who provided the exporters with most of the remains necessary for their activities. They came by their macabre merchandise in a variety of ways: primarily by picking up the bones and corpses cast up on the bank of the Hooghly, for tradition determined that many bodies – those of certain *Saddhus*, lepers, or children less than a year old, for example – should be committed to the river rather than cremated. At the entrance to the cremation area they would also intercept families who were too poor to buy wood for a pyre or pay for the services of a priest. The *Doms* would offer to undertake the funeral rites themselves for a more advantageous price. Such poor people were completely ignorant of the fact that their relative's remains would be cut up in a nearby hut, that his bones would be sold to an exporter, and that one day his skull, his spinal column, perhaps even his complete skeleton would be exhibited for the edification of American, Japanese or Australian medical students. Hospital mortuaries provided another reliable source of bones. In the Momimpur morgue alone, more than two and a half thousand unclaimed bodies fell into the hands of the *Doms* each year. When demand was exceptionally great, they would even go and compete with the jackals for the bones of the dead buried in the Christian and Muslim cemeteries. In short, there was never any real danger of running out of merchandise. Yet the ingenuity of the traffickers had just

conceived of a fresh means of supply. The idea of buying
a man while he was still walking about, in much the same
way that you might purchase an animal for slaughter, in
order to secure the right to dispose of his bones when
he died, was as diabolical as it was ingenious. It made it
possible to accumulate unlimited stock for there was
certainly no shortage of poor or moribund people in
Calcutta.

'Five hundred rupees!' The sum tumbled about in
Hasari's head like the balls in a lottery barrel. The procurer had not been mistaken. He knew how to spot his
prey at a glance. The streets were full of poor devils
coughing their lungs up, but not all of them were in a
position to provide the necessary guarantees. For the
purchase of a man to represent a profit-making venture,
he must have a family, an employer, friends, in other
words an identity and an address. How else could his
body be retrieved after his death?

'Well, friend, do you agree?'

Hasari looked up into the pockmarked face awaiting
his response. He remained silent but the man showed
no sign of impatience. He was used to this. 'Even a
fellow with his back against the wall doesn't just sell his
body like a piece of *khadi*.'

'Five hundred rupees, no less! What do you say to that?'
In the company of Ramatullah, the puller who shared
his rickshaw, Hasari was still marvelling at the astonishing offer he had just been made. He had asked the
procurer for time to think it over until the next day.
Ramatullah was a Muslim. Persuaded that when he died,
Allah would come to drag him straight into paradise by
the hair, any idea of bodily mutilation after death was
repugnant to him. The mullahs of his religion even
forbade the donation of organs to science, and the few
Indian eye banks had not one single Muslim on their

files. Nevertheless the sum was so considerable that he could not fail to be dazzled by it.

'Hasari, you've got to do it,' he eventually advised. 'Your great God will forgive you. He knows you've got to get your daughter married.'

The former peasant was equally anxious not to offend the gods. The Hindu faith required that, for the soul to 'transmigrate' into another form after death, the body should first be destroyed and reduced to ashes by the fire that purifies all. 'What will become of my soul if my bones and my flesh are cut up by those butchers instead of being burned in the flames of a funeral pyre?' lamented the rickshaw puller. He resolved to confide in Kovalski. In principle the priest's attitude fell into line with that of the Muslim Ramatullah. The Christian idea of resurrection implied the existence of an intact body coming to life again in all its vigour and beauty to take its place alongside its Creator in its original state of wholeness. Years of living in the poverty of a slum, however, had led Kovalski to accept occasional compromises between the ideals of faith and the imperatives of survival.

'I think you should take this opportunity to further the completion of your mission here below,' he declared reluctantly, drawing the rickshaw puller's attention to his daughter who was busy delousing her little brother at the other end of the compound.

As a two-storey building eaten away by the humidity, next door to a kind of warehouse, there was nothing to distinguish the appointments of 'Mitra & Co.' from those of hundreds of other small-scale enterprises scattered throughout the city, except that this company bore no notice to indicate the nature of its undertakings. The procurer with the pockmarked skin knocked several times at the door of the warehouse and soon a face appeared in the half-open door. The procurer indicated Hasari.

'I'm bringing a client,' he announced.

The door opened wide and the porter motioned to the two men to enter. The smell that hit them was a suffocating stench of the kind that tears at your throat, overpowers and flattens you. Hasari had never smelled anything like it. For a moment he wavered in his resolve, but his companion pushed him forward. It was then that he saw the source of the stench. He had just entered a place such as only the imaginations of Dante or Dürer could have conceived, an unbelievable catacomb for the next world in which dozens of skeletons of all different sizes were ranged upright along the walls like a parade of phantoms, where rows of tables and shelves were covered with human remains. There were thousands of bones from every part of the body: hundreds of skulls, spinal columns, thoraxes, hands and feet, sacra, coccyges, whole pelvises, and even hyoids – those little U-shaped bones in the neck. Perhaps most astonishing of all, however, was the supermarketlike display of this macabre bazaar. Every skeleton, indeed every bone, bore a label on which the price was marked in US dollars. An adult skeleton for demonstration purposes, with movable bones and metal articulation, was worth between $230 and $350, according to its size and the quality of workmanship. For a mere $100 or $120, you could acquire a child's skeleton without articulation, a complete thorax for $40, a skull for $6. The very same 'items' could cost ten times more, however, if they had been subject to special preparation.

Mitra & Co. maintained a whole team of specialist bone extractors, painters and sculptors. These craftsmen worked in a poorly lit room at the end of the gallery. Crouched among their mountains of human remains, they looked like the survivors of some prehistoric cataclysm, scraping, decorticating, assembling and decorating their funereal objects with precise gestures. Sometimes real works of art emerged from their hands,

like the collection of articulated skulls with jaws that could be dismantled and moveable teeth, ordered by the dental faculty of a large American university in the Midwest. Of all the precious merchandise exported from India, doubtless none was packaged with more care. Each item was first protected by a small cotton pad, then wrapped in a carefully stitched piece of linen before being placed in a special cardboard box and then in a packing case covered with labels marked 'Very Fragile. Handle with Care'. 'Dear God,' thought Hasari, flabbergasted by what he saw. 'Those poor chaps' bones were never given such celebrity treatment when they were alive.'

Not all the merchandise delivered up by the *Doms* was necessarily destined for such dignified use. Thousands of skulls, tibias, collarbones, femurs and other pieces that had been gnawed by jackals or had spent too long in the water ended up more prosaically between the teeth of a crushing mill and then in a boiling pot where they were turned into glue. It was from precisely that subsidiary process that the stench arose.

In a cabin at the far end of the gallery, they found the man who negotiated the purchase of 'living' skeletons. In his white overalls he presided over a dusty table heaped with files, paperwork, registers and folders, threatened every fifteen seconds by the motion of a rotating fan. Actually, not a single paper ever flew away, thanks to an entire collection of paperweights made out of the skulls of newborn babies and decorated with red and black tantric symbols. Mitra & Co. also exported thousands of skulls to Nepal, Tibet and even China, to be used for devotional purposes. Other countries imported them to make them into votive cups or ashtrays.

The toothless employee examined the rickshaw puller attentively. The latter's prominent collarbone, his lean thorax, and vertebrae protruding like a catfish's spine reassured him. There was no doubt about it: the merchandise was bona fide. It would not be unduly long

before what was left of this poor fellow enriched the stocks of Mitra & Co. He gave the procurer a satisfied wink. All he had to do now was draw up a formal purchase agreement and inform the *Doms* who lived closest to the slum where Hasari resided so that they knew where to recover the corpse when the time came.

These various formalities took three days, at the end of which Hasari was entitled to a first payment of one hundred and fifty rupees. Like all the other companies engaged in the same trade, Mitra & Co. were reluctant to invest their money on too long-term a basis. Hasari was, therefore, informed that the sum outstanding would be paid as soon as his state of health showed further deteriorating signs.

65

Some rudimentary scenery on trestles was enough. It was as if all the greyness, all the mud, the stench, the flies, the mosquitoes, the cockroaches, the rats, the hunger, the anguish, the sickness and the death had faded away. The time for dreams had come once more. With their eyes starting out of their heads and their emaciated bodies racked with laughter or with tears, the imprisoned people of the City of Joy were rediscovering the thousand enchantments and dramatic episodes of the ancient folk story that had moulded them. The Ramayana epic was to India what the Golden Legend, the Chanson de Roland and the Bible had been to the crowds assembled on Europe's cathedral steps. For three months the troupe of actors and strolling musicians had installed itself and its carts bulging with drapes and costumes in between the two large buffalo sheds at the very heart of the slum.

News of their arrival had spread from one compound to the next like the announcement of a kindly monsoon. Thousands of people flocked to the site. Children who had never seen such a thing as a tree, a bird, or a hind came to delight in the cardboard forest where the handsome prince Rama and his divine Sita would experience the joy of love before being torn from each other's arms. Hours before the presentation of the first tableau, the little esplanade in front of the stage was already covered with a sea of brown heads and motley veils. All the nearby roofs accommodated clusters of spectators. The audience trembled in anticipation of the curtain rising, impatient to let themselves be borne away from their squalid existence for a few hours by their heroes, eager to find in the song's twenty-five thousand verses fresh reasons for continuing to live and to hope.

Written, so tradition has it, by a sage at the dictation of the gods two and a half thousand years ago, the Ramayana opens with a marvellous love story. The handsome young Rama, the only one of all the princes to be able to bend the bow of the god Shiva, receives as his reward the princess Sita. Her father wishes to give his throne to the young couple but, succumbing in his weakness to one of his favourite ladies, he exiles them instead to the wild forests of central India. There they are attacked by demon brigands whose leader, the terrible Ravana, harbours a lustful passion for Sita. Tricking her husband into leaving her alone, the demon succeeds in seizing the princess and lifting her onto his winged chariot drawn by flying, carnivorous donkeys. He transports her to his fabulous island of Lanka – none other than Ceylon – where he shuts her up in his quarters, seeking in vain to seduce her.

In order to win back his wife, Rama forms an alliance with the king of the monkeys who places at the prince's disposal his principal general, Hanuman, and the whole army of monkeys aided by bands of squirrels. With one

single prodigious leap across the sea, the monkey general reaches Ceylon, finds the captive princess, reassures her, and after a thousand heroic and comic reversals reports back to Rama. With the help of the monkey army, the latter manages to sling a bridge across the sea and invade the island. A furious battle is then waged against the demons. Eventually Rama personally defeats the odious Ravana and good thus triumphs over evil. The freed Sita appears, overwhelmed with joy.

Complications, however, set in, for Rama sadly pushes her away. 'What man could take back and cherish a woman who has lived in another's house?' he exclaims. The faultless Sita, wounded to the quick, then has a funeral pyre erected and casts herself into the flames. Virtue, however, cannot perish in the fire: the flames spare her, testifying to her innocence, and all ends with a grand finale. The bewildered Rama takes back his wife and returns with her in triumph to his capital, where he is at last crowned amid unforgettable rejoicing.

The ragamuffins of the City of Joy knew every tableau, every scene, every twist and turn of this flowing epic. They followed each move made by the actors, the mimes, the clowns and the acrobats. They laughed, cried, suffered and rejoiced with them. Over their rags they felt the weight of the performers' costumes, on their cheeks they felt the thickness of their makeup. Many of them even knew whole passages from the text word for word. In India it is quite possible for a person to be 'illiterate' and still know thousands of verses of epic poetry by heart. Old Surya from the tea shop, the children of Mehboub and Selima, Kovalski's former neighbours, the coal man from Nizamudhin Lane, Margareta and her offspring, the lovely Kalima and the other eunuchs, the former sailor from Kerala and his aborigine neighbours, Bandona and her Assamese brothers and sisters, the godfather and his thugs, hundreds of Hindus, Christians and even Muslims packed themselves in side

by side, night after night, before the magic stage. Among the most assiduous spectators was Hasari Pal. 'That broken man went every night,' Kovalski was to say, 'to draw new strength from his encounter with the exemplary tenacity of Rama, the courage of the monkey general, and the virtue of Sita.'

To the rickshaw puller 'those heroes were like tree trunks in the middle of raging floodwaters, lifebuoys that you could cling to!' He could remember how when he was a small child, carried on his mother's hip as she walked the narrow dikes across the rice fields, she used to sing softly to him the verses of the mythical adventures of the monkey general. Later, whenever bards and story-tellers passed through the village, his family would gather along with all the others in the square, to listen for nights on end to the extravagant recitations, always so rich in resonance, which had nourished the beliefs of India since time immemorial and given a religious dimension to its everyday life. There was not one infant on that vast peninsula who did not fall asleep to the sound of his elder sister intoning a few episodes from that great poem, not one children's game that did not derive its inspiration from the confrontations between good and evil, not a single schoolbook that did not extol the exploits of the heroes, not a marriage ceremony that did not cite Sita as an example of the virtues of fidelity. Each year, several grand festivals commemorated the victory of Rama and the benevolence of the Monkey god. Each evening in Calcutta, thousands of dockers, coolies, rickshaw pullers, labourers and starving people would assemble around the storytellers on the embank-ment of the Hooghly. Squatting for hours, their eyes half-closed, these people, whom happiness seemed to have somehow overlooked, exchanged the harshness of their reality for a few grains of fantasy.

Above the multitudes squeezed around the trestled boards, there often rose the slightly balding pate of

Stephan Kovalski. Despite his difficulties in grasping the subtleties of the language and the little free time he had, he greatly loved to watch the performances. 'It was the perfect way to get to know the memory of a people,' he would say. 'The Ramayana is a living encyclopedia. There, in my slum, I suddenly went back in time. The perfumes, gifts, weapons, court life, music, the habits of wild elephants, the forests of India soon held no secrets from me. But above all, that great popular epic was an ideal means to meet with the mentality of my brothers and enter more completely into my new skin. Espousing their mentality meant no longer thinking of the Red Sea when you talk of a dry passage across the waters, but rather of the straits of Ceylon. It meant no longer citing one of our miracles as evidence of a supernatural event, but rather the exploit of the monkey general Hanuman who transported the Himalayas in his hand just so that the captive Sita could smell a flower. It meant wishing a woman about to give birth that she will be the mother of one of the five Pandavas. Entry into the mentality of a people involves using its imagery, its myths and its beliefs. That applied to the Muslims too. What smiles I brought to their faces when I mentioned the name of the emperor Akbar, when I referred to Muhammad, or compared a little girl to the princess Nur Jahan or to some other Mogul queen, or when I deciphered an Urdu text on a calendar hanging at the back of one of their hovels.'

66

His name was Nissar. He was twelve years old and he was a Muslim. The whole compound agreed: that boy was an archangel. His luminous face, the keenness of his

gaze, his natural authority made him a being apart. The
harelip that revealed his dazzling teeth and the small
monkey with the sad eyes that never left his shoulders
further accentuated how different he was. 'Nissar was a
diamond with a thousand facets, a firework, a glittering
light in the world,' Kovalski was to comment. Yet the
skinny little boy with short hair was not the son of any
of the families in the compound. He had been found one
evening half-dead on a pavement in Dalhousie Square
and picked up by Boudhou Koujour, the aborigine who
killed the eunuch with the cobra. Driven away from his
village in Bihar by parents who could no longer feed
him, Nissar had travelled on the roofs of trains to get to
the mirage city. After wandering around for a few days,
feeding himself on scraps, he found in an alleyway of
the Bara Bazar the object that was to become both a
means of earning a living and his talisman: a patched old
jute sack. Like thousands of other starving youngsters,
Nissar became a ragpicker. Every evening he went to
deposit his pitiful findings in the den of a ragpicker
wholesaler and received in exchange a few small coins,
sometimes one or two rupees. One day a secondhand
dealer gave him a monkey. Christened Hanuman, the
animal slept with him on the pavements and they became
inseparable companions. On monsoon nights, Nissar
would shelter them both as best he could under the
awning of a shop or in the arcades on Chowringhee
Avenue. His great love was the cinema. As soon as he
had earned a few pice, he would rush off with his
monkey to one of the caravanserais, purveyors of dreams
to the poor of the slums. His favourite actor was a certain
Dilip Kumar, who always took the parts of princes and
maharajahs draped in brocade tunics, jewels, and in the
company of beautiful courtesans.

The integration of this young abandoned Muslim into
the little Hindu world of the compound posed very few
problems. His two years of drifting on the asphalt of the

great city had endowed him with a special kind of aura. This fact was in itself remarkable for the living conditions of the other youngsters in the compound were hardly less harsh. As soon as they could walk, they were expected to do their bit, just like adults, towards their collective survival. They were spared no task, not even the drudgery of fetching water which, because of the weight of the buckets, often caused irreparable damage to their fragile, undernourished bone structure. Two or three out of fifty were lucky enough to go to school. (The evening classes subsidized by Kovalski did not yet involve anyone in this compound.) By the time they were seven or eight they were nearly all working. Some of them were salesmen or assistants in a grocer's store, a cobbler's workshop, or a *pan* or *bidi* shop. Others toiled from dawn to dusk in one of the eating houses in the main street. Others knew the slavery of the small factories found in such profusion in the slums. The two sons of the former sailor from Kerala earned their food, and the twenty rupees a month which enabled their parents to buy just sixteen pounds of rice, by making chains for ships for ten hours at a stretch in one of the innumerable sweatshops.

Before Nissar arrived, three boys from the compound had already been working as ragpickers. It had not, however, proved to be a very profitable occupation. In a slum nothing is ever thrown away. Anything that can be salvaged – the smallest bit of coal, the remains of a cow dung cake, a shred of shirt, a broken bottle end, a coconut shell – can become the object of covetousness.

'You won't find anything here but small fry. To bring back a good catch you have to go where the real fish are,' the young Nissar announced one evening to the three little Hindu ragpickers.

Hasari had overheard the remark. 'That kid must know where there's gold to be struck,' he told himself. Obsessed as he was with the idea of finding the money

for his daughter's dowry, the idea of a secret source of wealth excited him. 'Whatever happens he's got to take Shambu with him,' he confided to Kovalski, pointing to his second son who was flying a kite up on the roof. Hasari never stopped computing figures: 'Suppose I add the five hundred rupees for my bones to the eight hundred I can expect to earn wading about with my rickshaw in the monsoon slush. If, on top of that, Shambu brings back two or three hundred rupees from ragpicking with the young Muslim, that makes . . . that makes (since he had had the red fever Hasari's reckoning had slowed down) . . . that makes it close to two thousand rupees! Just think, Big Brother Stephan! All I'd have to do then would be to pay a little visit to the *mahajan* with the earrings belonging to the mother of my children and that'd be it!' Hasari could already see the Brahmin binding his daughter's hand to that of her husband.

A gold mine! The rickshaw puller had not been dreaming. It was indeed for an El Dorado, a land of milk and honey, that the Muslim boy with the harelip set off each morning with his monkey. Yet in that same place, on a bed of rubbish, the police had one day set fire to all unlicensed rickshaws. The name under which it appeared in the municipal records and plans did not instantly evoke the idea of wealth, but in a city where even a poster taken off a wall or a bent nail was of some value, the Calcutta dumping ground might well seem like a promised land to the thousands of human ants that scrabbled about on it. Young Nissar was among their number and henceforth the three other little ragpickers from the compound would accompany him together with Shambu Pal whom he had agreed to take with him.

'Get your son up tomorrow at the first crow of the eunuchs' cockerel,' Nissar ordered the rickshaw puller. 'We leave at dawn.'

★

Nissar led his comrades to the mouth of the great
Howrah Bridge. Pointing to one of the overloaded
buses, he directed Shambu to cling onto the spare wheel.
The others climbed onto the rear bumper. Every day
tens of thousands of people made use of Calcutta's public
transport in this way without paying. They were not
the only defrauders. The real champions of this system
were some of the conductors themselves who, it was
said, pocketed part of the takings by selling passengers
false tickets. In the hellish traffic, a journey undertaken
balancing on the bumpers or the spare tyre, or clinging
onto the clusters of humanity that hung from the windows, was a dangerous acrobatic feat. Nearly every
week there was some mention in the papers of the death
of an illicit passenger squashed between the metalwork,
crushed by the wheels of a lorry, or electrocuted by a
tram.

'Off, fellows!'

Nissar's order rang out through the already scorching
early morning air. The five children let themselves drop
onto the asphalt. The bus had just emerged from the last
suburb to the east of the city and the road now ran across
a vast, flat expanse of marshy land. Shambu rubbed his
eyes still heavy with sleep. A mile and a half away to
the east, the sky was black with clouds of vultures.

'Is it over there?' he asked.

Nissar waggled his head. With his old jute sack slung
over one shoulder and his monkey on the other looking
for nits in his hair, he took the head of the group. He
was happy in his role as a ragpicker. Ragpickers were
free and each day brought with it new hope of some
outstanding discovery. They walked for half a mile until
suddenly, just as his father had done on the evening the
rickshaws were burned, Shambu experienced the shock
of the stench rising from the dump; but the nostrils of a
child reared on the pavements of Calcutta are less sensitive than those of a peasant used to the aromas of the

countryside. Shambu followed Nissar and the others without faltering. Apart from the vultures and the cows that grazed on the refuse, large numbers of men, women and children were already at work on the huge mound. Nissar stopped his party three hundred yards short of the approach ramp used by the rubbish lorries.

'We're going to have to be quick,' he announced in a voice that his harelip turned into a whistle. 'It's the hotels and hospitals day. Mustn't miss out on their goods.'

Sure enough, once a week the municipal rubbish lorries brought the refuse from the establishments mentioned. Their arrival was always greeted with a frantic onslaught. It was only to be expected. Real treasure often lay concealed in their loads, the kind that represented top value on the dumping ground exchange: flasks, bandages, syringes, remnants of coal, scraps of food.

'You, Shambu,' ordered the young Muslim, pointing to a kind of low burrow, 'park yourself in that hole. As soon as you see a bit of red rag in the window of a lorry, give a whistle to let me know. That means it's coming from a hospital or a hotel.' Nissar took a five-rupee note out of his belt. Showing it to his companions, he went on, 'I'll run over to the lorry waving this note. The driver will slow down to grab it. That's when we all have to jump onto the back. The driver will make for a distant corner of the dump and ditch all his load as quickly as possible. We'll really have to look quickly before the others get there.'

The young Muslim with the harelip had spoken with all the calmness and authority of a commando leader. They all rushed to their respective positions to await the first lorry. Most of the other ragpickers already foraging about in the mound lived in the small number of hovels that stood nearby. The ragpickers were mostly women and children, for the local men were otherwise occupied, macerating the guts of animals and vegetable scraps in watertight jars, which they then submerged at the bot-

tom of foul reservoirs of green, stagnant water. They subsequently distilled these concoctions and the juice extracted was put into bottles and delivered to the clandestine gambling dens of Calcutta and the drinking places in the slums. 'That puts the life back into a man!' Hasari used to say, remembering his libations with Ram Chander and Son of Miracle. Yet the forbidden alcohol, the famous *bangla*, had killed more Indians than had any number of natural disasters.

The first yellow lorry arrived, then another, then a third. None of them, however, was carrying the red signal. Nobody moved. Hasari's son felt as if his pupils were about to burst. He had never seen such a spectacle. Just above him in the searing early morning light, an extraordinary ballet was unfolding. A host of barefoot women and children were scouring the hill of refuse with baskets in one hand and spikes in the other. The arrival of each vehicle unleashed a frenzied seething of activity as everyone scrambled after it. A suffocating cloud of sulphur dust enveloped each unloading. Even more mind-boggling was the flurried searching that went on around the bulldozers there to level out the mountains of refuse. Children slipped without hesitation under the monsters to be the first to explore the manna turned over by their steel scoops. How many had perished, suffocated by their solid bulk or crushed by their caterpillar tracks? Shambu felt a cold sweat break out on his back. 'Would I be capable of such courage?' he wondered. Just then a fourth lorry appeared, but still there was no red rag at the window. Above him, the ballet continued. To protect themselves against the sun and the dust, the women and girls had covered their heads and faces with old but colourful pieces of cloth which made them look like harem princesses. As for the boys, with their felt hats, their caps full of holes and their worn-out shoes that were far too big for them, they all looked like Charlie Chaplin in his early films.

Each had his speciality. The women tended to look for bits of coal and wood. The children preferred things made out of leather, plastic or glass as well as bones, shellfish and papers. They all picked up anything edible with equal enthusiasm: rotten fruit, peelings, crusts of bread. This kind of picking was the most difficult and often the most dangerous. Shambu saw a vulture bear down like a torpedo on a small boy to snatch the piece of meat he had just found. Vultures were not the only creatures to compete with men for grazing ground. Pigs, cows, goats, pariah dogs and, at night, even hyenas and jackals had chosen to make their homes on the dump, as had millions of other small creatures and insects. The flies were the most aggressive. Greenish in colour, they buzzed about in their myriads, clinging to men and beasts, even to their eyes, mouths, or the inside of their noses and ears. Those flies were completely at home among all that decaying matter and they made quite certain that everyone knew it.

The most surprising factor about this nightmare was that all the ingredients of normal life had been established here. Among the heaps of stinking rubbish, Shambu could see ice cream salesmen on their decorated carrier tricycles, water vendors laden with large goatskin bottles, fritter makers squatting under sunshades behind their smoking braziers, *bangla* retailers surrounded by bottles set out like bowling pins. So that mothers could forage more effectively among the refuse, there were even babysitters to look after their children, usually very young girls seated under old black umbrellas with holes in them, with several fly-covered babies in their laps.

The dumpsite was also a busy trading centre, a bazaar, a money market. A whole tribe of secondhand salesmen and scrap merchants had grafted themselves onto that of the ragpickers. Each one had his speciality. Using archaic scales, traders in vests and *longhis* would buy by the

weight anything the foragers had unearthed. Every evening wholesalers would come with lorries to harvest the various treasures which, once cleaned and sorted, would be resold to factories for recycling.

Shambu felt his heart begin to pound. He had just seen the tip-off signal in the window of a lorry. Stuffing his fingers into his mouth, he whistled in the manner agreed. Instantly he saw Nissar, straddled by his monkey, loom up in the cloud of dust and jump onto the running board to hand over his five-rupee note. The driver put on his brakes. This was the signal. With the agility of lizards, the five little ragpickers from the City of Joy climbed aboard the lorry full of refuse.

'All of you, flat on your bellies!' Nissar ordered.

The lorry accelerated to climb the access slope to the dump. Half-submerged in the filthy cargo the five ragpickers were well out of sight of any onlookers. 'That rubbish was sticky and burned you at the same time,' Shambu was to recount, 'but worst of all, I felt as if thousands of creepy-crawlies were coming out of it and jumping onto me. The enormous cockroaches were the most frightening. They ran over my legs, my arms, my neck.'

Instead of heading for the bulldozers, the driver veered off in the opposite direction. This was part of the 'deal'. Nissar and his band would have ten minutes in which to forage alone. It all went off like a holdup in the films. The lorry pulled up sharply. The five boys leaped down and the rubbish lorry unloaded its avalanche of refuse. They scrabbled, located, sorted and stowed their booty away as fast as they could. With bottles, stray bits of cooking utensils and crockery, broken tools, pieces of tile, old tubes of toothpaste, run-down batteries, empty tins, plastic soles, scraps of clothing and papers, their bags were filled in a trice.

'Let's hurry, fellows! Here come the others.'

Nissar knew only too well that they had to scram

from there before the furious crowd of other ragpickers fell upon them. Caught up in the fever of the search, Shambu sank his spike into the stinking mass for one last time and let out a cry. 'I had just seen something glinting among all that shit. I thought it was a coin and struck out frenziedly to free it. What I brought out on the end of my hook was a bracelet, and on the end of the bracelet was a watch.'

'At first an expression of total stupefaction came over Hasari Pal's face,' Kovalski was to say. 'Then he took the object in his hands and lifted it up with so much emotion and respect that we thought he wanted to offer it to some deity. All he actually wanted to do was put it to his ear.' The voices in the compound fell silent. For several seconds Hasari remained like that, immobile, incapable of uttering a word, as if transfigured by the jewel that ticked in unison with the beating of his heart.

It was at this point that something very strange occurred. Propelled by some mysterious force, an eddy of scorching air suddenly surged off the rooftops to shower the compound with the sound of broken tiles. Immediately thereafter a series of thunderbolts rolled across the sky. Hasari and all the other residents looked up at the heavens. Above the smoke of the *chulas* appeared great waves of black clouds. The rickshaw puller felt tears obscure his vision. 'That's it,' he thought. 'The monsoon has come. I am saved. I shall be able to die in peace. Thanks to this watch and to the downpour that is about to fall, thanks to the five hundred rupees for my bones, my daughter will have a good husband.'

67

'The city had changed our eyes,' Hasari was to recount. 'In the village we would scrutinize the sky for days on end, waiting for the first clouds to come bearing water. We would dance and sing and implore the goddess Lakshmi to make our fields fertile with a beneficent downpour. But in Calcutta there was nothing to make fertile. Neither the streets, nor the pavements, the houses, buses, nor trucks could be rendered fruitful by the water that makes the rice grow in our countryside. That doesn't mean that here we did not yearn for the monsoon; we yearned for it because of the appalling heat that reduced you to a state where you could have stopped in the street and just lain down and died. Sometimes there wasn't any need to stop to wait for death. Instead it would take you by surprise in midaction, when you were taking a schoolboy to school or a *marwari* to the cinema. You just collapsed suddenly. Sometimes your own carriage would run over you before tipping over onto a bus or the pavement. That was known as the "stroke of Surya", the stroke of the Sun god.

'All that night and throughout the next day big, black clouds rolled across the sky, plunging the city into almost total darkness. The clouds mingled with the fumes and the dust. Soon, above the rooftops, there appeared a kind of blackish mantle. It was as if Sani, the planet that augurs ill, wanted to punish us with asphyxiation. People were suffocating. They fought in the streets over nothing. The policemen's sticks began to twitch without your even knowing why. I was having more and more difficulty breathing. Even the crows and the rats scavenging among the piles of rubbish in Wood Street had

a peculiar look about them. The children never stopped crying. Dogs barked ceaselessly. I found myself wondering whether, rather than the monsoon, this might not be the end of the world that was approaching.

'Lots of people begged me to take them to the hospital. They wanted someone to help them breathe. But I knew that in the hospitals they wouldn't even help people to die. At the entrance to Lower Circular Road, I picked up an old woman groaning on the pavement. She was all dried out. Her skin was like cardboard. I bought a coconut and made her drink the tepid, slightly sweet milk from it. Then I took her to the hospital where, such a long time ago, our coolie friend had died.

'After three days had gone by, a violent wind blew up, a tornado of sand and dust such as we had already had during the premonsoon storms. In a matter of minutes the whole city was covered in a sheet of yellow sand. Apparently that sand comes from the Himalayan Mountains and from the plateaux on the Chinese side. It was terrifying. Sand and dust permeated everything. People's eyes and mouths were full of it. I don't know whether it was because of those gusts of wind or because of the red fever, but all of a sudden I felt quite unable to lift the shafts of my old cart. I was reduced to nothing by some force from the beyond. I lay down on the canvas seat with my legs in the air, trying to get my breath back. My head was buzzing, my eyes hurt and my stomach was knotted with cramps. How long did I lie there like that? In the absence of the sun, hidden as it was by black clouds, I completely lost all track of time.'

The nightmare lasted for several days. In the City of Joy the drought began to dry up the wells and fountains. The number of victims of dehydration multiplied and Max exhausted his small supply of serum in the space of a few hours. On the sixth day, towards noon, the thermometer rose to one hundred and seventeen degrees Fahrenheit. The wind had dropped and the slum stifled

beneath a blanket of fire. Yet still no drop of water fell. Persuaded that this year the monsoon would not come, many of the residents lay down in their hovels to wait for the wheel of their *karma* to put an end to their torment.

The next day, a few short squalls restored a little hope. Towards midday, however, despite all the offerings placed on the altars to the gods, the thermometer went wild again. Its excesses were a harsh test of strength for Max, Bandona and all the other members of the Committee for Mutual Aid. An SOS could summon them at any moment to the bedside of the latest heat victim.

Returning from one of these visits, Max had just got back to his room, exhausted, when he felt a damp, perfumed cloth on his sweating face. Bandona was gently mopping his brow. He grasped her hand and raised it to his lips. The unexpected contact with her skin, so fresh and so alive, in those sordid surroundings that smelled of ether and alcohol, threw him completely. The patients crowding at the door were dumbfounded. This kind of public demonstration of affection was quite uncommon in India.

He let go of the young woman's hand but kept the piece of linen, delighting in its perfume. The scent reminded him of something. He sought in his mind and suddenly the vision of Manubaï Chatterjee came to him. Hers was an unwonted, unreal image in this stricken slum. Despite the furnacelike heat, he shivered. The beautiful, rich Indian woman had brought so much enrichment to his life since that memorable night not so long ago, when for a while he had forgotten his slum on the pillows of her muslin-draped four-poster bed. The very incarnation of the India of tales, myths and spells, Manubaï had reminded him that luxury too was part of creation, that even in Calcutta it was possible to live surrounded by floral gardens, to eat and drink to

repletion, and to rejoice in the pleasures of existence. Indifferent to what people might say about her, she had thrown several dinners in his honour in her sumptuous dining room decorated with paintings of tropical birds. She had taken him to diplomatic evenings, to receptions on the verdant lawns of the Tollygunge Golf Club, to bridge parties at Government House. Caressing her body vibrant with sensual fragrances, listening to the exhilarating sound of her laughter, had given him a taste of the pleasure and refinements of an India of thousand-year-old enchantments.

Yet it was from another woman that he had drawn the will and the strength to pursue his task among the poor of the City of Joy. Bandona had no house, no servants and no four-poster bed. She had never known anything but sweatshops, hovels, mud and hunger, but her illuminating smile, her availability to others, her magical ability to bring relief and comfort were worth any amount of riches. In a world where tortured people every day besieged the door of his dispensary, bringing him their wounds, their illness and their misery, in the face of all that suffering, naked despair and death, it was this angel of mercy who had given Max the courage to stand firm. How could the shared experience of so much horror and the giving of so much love have failed to create an exceptional bond between them?

In this concentration camp where never a wink could pass unnoticed, it was quite inconceivable that such a bond should be outwardly manifested. Kovalski had warned Max: a slum was a pot boiling in a constant state of ferment. Any event that was the slightest bit out of the ordinary risked blowing the lid off and causing an explosion. Unlike Manubaï Chatterjee who, by virtue of her social position, could cast off her chains and defy the existing order, Bandona had not the least hope of ever being incarnated as Radha, the divine love of Krishna, the Herdsman god and flautist.. She was a prisoner of the

rites and taboos that governed relationships between men and women in India. Like all the other young girls in her position, her destiny was to be given as a virgin to a husband, whom others – her father, an uncle or a grandmother – would choose for her. Emotional and physical attraction would play no part in her union. She would see her husband for the first time at the ceremony. As for her wedding night, like all the future couplings of her married life, it would be primarily a ritual intended to conceive a male heir.

The circumstances of this ritual never failed to take Kovalski by surprise. 'Suddenly I would hear a strange stirring among the people sleeping around me. Then in the darkness, I would make out people getting up discreetly. There would be the sound of doors, then stifled cries. The couples of the compound were making love. I knew then that it was *purnima*, the full moon.'

At midday, three days after the episode with the perfumed handkerchief, when a further rise of the thermometer was subjecting the hovels of the City of Joy to a white heat, Bandona came into Max's room. She was holding an offering so rare in a slum that it was reserved for the gods.

'Doctor, Big Brother,' she said kindly as she laid a bouquet of jasmine on the table, 'don't be afraid. You're not alone. I am here to share it all with you.'

Max took the flowers and sniffed at them. So intoxicating was the perfume they exuded that it was to him as if the decay, the stench, the blazing heat, the rat-infested framework, the mud of the walls, and the cockroaches were all borne away in a dream. All that remained of that damnable cesspool was the bouquet of happiness and the young girl in a bright pink sari, as motionless and meditative as a madonna in a cathedral.

'Thank you, sweet Bandona,' he murmured at last, before borrowing Kovalski's favourite compliment. 'You are a light of the world.'

Max could not remember clearly the events that followed. The heat and fatigue had distorted his faculties.
'I think,' he was later to tell Kovalski, 'that I went over
to her and pressed her to me in an irrepressible need to
possess that light. Bandona did not repulse me. On the
contrary, with an embrace full of infinite tenderness, she
offered me her love.'

It was then that they heard a strange pattering noise
on the roof. Max thought people were bombarding the
tiles of his room with pebbles. Then he heard shouting
in the neighbouring buildings, immediately followed by
a great commotion on all sides. A mighty thunderclap
shook the walls and roofing of the little room. Max saw
a troop of crazed rats emerge from the framework.
Almost immediately all the tiles began to vibrate with a
dull, powerful, regular sound. Bandona gently pulled
away from Max's chest and looked up at the roof.
Her small, almond eyes were brimming with tears of
joy.

'Max, Big Brother, do you hear? The monsoon has
arrived.'

68

'It must have been late afternoon when I saw the first
drop of water fall,' Hasari was to recount. 'It was enormous, but as soon as it hit the asphalt, the heat caused
it to evaporate instantaneously.' To the former peasant,
banished for ever from his land by drought, every year
that first drop of water was like 'manna from the heavens
and proof that the gods could still weep for the plight
of mankind on this earth'. He thought of the singing
and shrieks of joy that would be erupting in his village
at that very moment. He imagined his father and his

brothers squatting on the small dike at the edge of the rice field and gazing with wonder upon the young shoots, endowed with new vigour by dew from the heavens. 'Will I ever see them again?' he sighed.

That first downpour of the monsoon was exceptionally violent. The water was battering the ground with the sound of drums beaten by a million fingers. Swiftly, Hasari put up the hood of his rickshaw, then gave himself up to the sheer joy of being soaked by the flood. 'After a moment a breath of air blew through the warm shower, bringing with it a touch of coolness,' he would say. 'It was as if the portals of some giant icehouse had opened onto the city to release a little coolness into the overheated air stirred up by the tornado. By this time the beating of the water obscured all other sounds. All you could hear was the noise of the sky emptying itself. Instead of seeking shelter, people had rushed out into the rain. Children, completely naked, danced and laughed and performed somersaults. Women let themselves be drenched and their saris clung to their bodies like the thin bark of bamboo canes.

'At the rickshaw stand on Park Circus and elsewhere, the pullers had begun to sing. Other workers joined them from the neighbouring streets and took part in the thanksgiving. It was as if the whole city had gone down to the river to bathe and purify itself, the only difference being that the river was falling from the heavens instead of flowing over the ground. Even the old palm trees in the Harrington Street gardens trembled with joy. Trees that had looked like dusty old men were now all shiny with vitality, freshness and youth.

'The euphoria lasted for several hours. While this communal bathing went on, we all felt like brothers. Coolies and *sadarjis*, rickshaw *wallahs*, *babus*, *marwaris* from the Bara Bazar, Biharis, Bengalis, Hindus, Muslims, Sikhs, Jains – all the different people of this great city were taking part in the same grateful *puja* by letting

ourselves be soaked in the same life-giving deluge.

'The rain stopped suddenly to reveal the most extra-ordinary sight: in the sunlight the entire city began to steam like a gigantic boiling washtub. Then the down-pour began again.'

In the slum Max could hardly believe his eyes. 'A whole race of people who only a second earlier had seemed half-dead had just been resurrected in a fantastic explosion of happiness, exuberance and life,' he would remember. 'The men had torn off their shirts, women rushed out fully clothed, singing. Swarms of naked children were running about in all directions under the magical shower and shrieking for joy. It was a real festival, the carrying out of some ancestral ritual.' At the end of his alleyway, he noticed a tall figure with white skin. Amid all the general levity, Kovalski was dancing unrestrainedly in a circle with the other residents of the City of Joy. On his streaming chest his metal cross jumped about as if to beat out the time. 'He looked like the god Neptune under the waters of some celestial spring!'

69

For three days the deluge continued, a deluge such as Bengal had not known for several years. From one compound to the next and throughout the alleyways of the City of Joy there soon rang out the word that had haunted the memory of India for as long as the monsoon had existed. *'Barha!'* 'Flood!' The jubilation of the initial moments was succeeded by a frantic hunt for umbrellas, bits of canvas, cardboard or plastic, for anything that might serve to patch up the roofs and hold back the water invading the slum houses. There followed a search

for containers and any utensils that could be used for bailing.

The water, however, always came back. It welled from out of the ground, for the slum was built on marshland. Finally, people went after bricks and any other materials they could use to raise the *charpoys* in the hovels, the only refuge on which the castaways could shelter their children and their few possessions. The situation grew rapidly worse and soon the dreaded noise was heard. The lapping of the water rose above the general commotion. Voices assumed a distinctive resonance because the sheet of water made them echo. One evening Max made out a feeble cry coming from the room next door. Intrigued, he went to investigate. The little girl who had brought him the umbrella during the premonsoon cataracts had slipped into the blackish floodwater and was in the process of drowning. He grabbed her by the hair and carried her back to his room.

His room by now was more a pestilential bog. Awash with the downpour, the latrines, the sewers and the drainage channels from the cattle sheds were overflowing, and their vile tide had just spilled over the small protective wall outside his door. To save the cartons of milk and the medicine chest, Bandona had suspended a sheet from the four corners of the framework to form an improvised hammock which looked like the sail of Medusa's raft in Delacroix's painting. Elsewhere umbrellas had come to the rescue. The trick was to hang them upside down under the gutters in the roof and empty them as soon as they were full.

Hunger soon added itself to the discomfort caused by the overflowing excrement, the stench and the humidity. Their cow dung cakes reduced to sponges, the women could no longer cook food. Striking a match had become a real survival feat. 'Look here, Big Brother,' Kalima explained to Kovalski, 'you rub the match vigorously under your armpit to warm the sulphur and then you

strike it!' Sure enough, the miracle occurred: in the middle of the deluge a small flame emerged from between the eunuch's fingers. Kovalski tried to repeat the performance, but the armpit of a Polish Catholic priest, it would appear, does not secrete the same fluids as that of a *Hijra* from the India of the fakirs: the attempt ended in failure.

Kovalski set out in search of Margareta, Saladdin, Bandona and other members of the Committee for Mutual Aid, groping his way through the darkness and wading up to his waist in the foul flood. Help had to be organized urgently. The rain was still falling. The water level was rising. The situation was becoming desperate.

The rest of Calcutta was experiencing a similar nightmare. In the lower districts to the east, around Topsia, Kasba and Tiljala, thousands of residents had been compelled to flee or take refuge on the rooftops. The entire city was plunged into darkness: the cataracts had drowned the transformers and the electric power cables. No trains could reach the stations any more. The traffic on the roads had come to a standstill and supplies had begun to run out. One pound of potatoes was already worth the astronomical sum of five rupees (30 pence), eggs cost over a rupee each.

Much to the delight of the rickshaw pullers, there was no longer any other form of urban transport. Hasari, who had been counting on these catastrophic days to make up his daughter's dowry, was ecstatic. 'What a joy it was to survey the spectacle of disaster presented by the proud red double-decker buses of Calcutta, the blue-and-white trams, the *sardarji* Sikhs' arrogant yellow taxis, and the privately owned Ambassador cars with their uniformed drivers. With their engines flooded, their chassis up to the doors in mud, abandoned by their passengers, deserted by their crews, they looked like

wreckage from the boats on the banks of the Hooghly.
What a glorious opportunity we had been given at last
to avenge the brutality we had taken from drivers and
all the humiliating haggling the clients had inflicted on
us. For once we could ask for the fares our efforts
warranted. Our carts with high wheels and our legs were
the only vehicles that could get about the flooded streets.
To my dying day I shall hear the desperate appeals of
people wanting me to carry them in my rickshaw. All
of a sudden I had ceased to be a despised, insulted animal,
whose sides people pummelled with their feet to make
me go faster, and from whom people lopped ten or
twenty pice off the agreed price once they reached their
destination. Now people fought with each other, offered
two, three, or even four times the usual price just to be
able to sit on the drenched seat of the only boats still
afloat on the sea of Calcutta.'

The shortest of trips made the former peasant a small
fortune – almost an entire day's earnings before the
monsoon. Yet how much suffering it cost him! Obscured by the floods, every obstacle became a trap. The
bits of old iron on which his bare feet risked impaling
themselves at any moment were just one example.
'Wading up to your thighs through the slime, stumbling
over the corpses of rats and dogs was a joke,' Hasari
would say though, 'by comparison with the torture the
rain inflicted on our carcasses. Sweating in those cataracts
without ever being able to dry yourself off doesn't do
wonders for your system. It was no use wringing out
my *dhoti* and vest after each fare, and rubbing my hands
and feet down; I was constantly bathed in moisture.
Steeped in the infected water, many of my colleagues
contracted skin diseases. Some of their feet looked like
the lumps of old meat you see in butchers' stalls. They
were covered with ulcerations and wounds. But the real
danger lay in the bouts of intermittent heat and cold –
especially in my case. Many of my colleagues left their

lungs somewhere in the monsoon. They called it pneumonia or something like that. That's when you caught a raging fever, then shivered with cold and ended life without even coughing. Ramatullah, the Muslim friend with whom I shared my rickshaw, claimed that it was much more pleasant than the red fever because it was all over with very quickly and you didn't have to spew your lungs out.'

When Hasari showed his friend Son of Miracle the proceeds from his first two days in the monsoon, the taxi driver, condemned to unemployment by the flood, let out a hoot of admiration. 'Hasari, as far as you're concerned, that's not water pouring out of the sky, it's gold nuggets!'

The rickshaw puller's joy was to be short-lived. The next day when he arrived at the Park Circus stand to pick up his rickshaw, he found his colleagues gathered around an old cart. He recognized his carriage and looked for Ramatullah among the group, but in vain. It was only then that one of the pullers, one of the oldest on the rank, said to him, 'Your pal is dead, Hasari. He fell down a manhole. That's the third fellow to drown since yesterday. Apparently some *babu*'s given the order to take off all the drain covers to make it easier for the water to flow away.'

Kovalski was passing in front of his former room in Nizamudhin Lane when he felt a small hand brush against him. He grabbed hold of it only to find that it was inert. He tugged at the little body floating on the surface of the water and hoisted it onto the platform of the tea shop belonging to Surya, the old Hindu. He called out, paddled over to Mehboub's house and tried his onetime neighbour's door, then knocked at Sabia's mother's hovel. There was nobody around. The alleyway looked like a film set deserted by its extras. All he

could hear was the beating of the rain, the lapping of the water, and the piercing cries of the rats as they fled from their lairs. From time to time one of them would drop into the water with a splash. Testing the ground with every step to avoid falling into the deep drains that cut across the alley, Kovalski covered several hundred feet. Suddenly a voice rose from the cesspool, his voice, a deep, powerful voice which soared upwards through the pouring rain to the opaque vault of a sky streaked with lightning. 'Nearer my God to thee, nearer my God to thee . . .' sang the priest at the top of his lungs as had the shipwrecked passengers of the *Titanic* on the night their liner sank beneath the waves.

The Indians belonging to the Committee for Mutual Aid were waiting in Max's room. Everyone was up to his knees in water. The atmosphere was gloomy.

'Big Brother Stephan, panic has broken out,' announced the old man Saladdin who was used to the slums being flooded. 'Everywhere people are running away. At least five hundred occupants have already taken refuge in the great mosque.'

The Jama Masjid was the only building with several storeys.

'And this is only the beginning,' said Margareta whose soaked sari was clinging to her skin. 'Apparently the Ganges is overflowing its banks.'

'That's enough bad news!' interrupted the Anglo-Indian Aristotle John. 'We're not here to whine but to decide how we can help.'

'Aristotle John is right!' said Kovalski, whose sneakers full of water were sending up a steady flow of bubbles.

A silence ensued. Each one was conscious of the enormity of the task. Max was the first to speak.

'We ought to vaccinate people quickly – against cholera, typhoid . . . There's a risk of epidemics . . .'

'How many doses have you got?' asked Kovalski, pointing to the medicine chest in the hammock.

'Pathetically few. We'll have to try and get some from the hospitals.'

The young doctor's naïvety made the assembly smile. 'This American is incorrigible,' reflected Kovalski. 'After all these months in Calcutta, he still thinks as if he's in Miami.'

'Shouldn't we start by organizing emergency provisions for the refugees?' suggested Saladdin. 'Thousands of people are going to find themselves without food and water.'

'Definitely!' said Kovalski.

It was at this point that Bandona's voice was heard. 'Big Brother Stephan, our first priority must go to the old and infirm who have stayed in their homes,' she said gently but firmly. 'Many of them will drown if someone doesn't go and find them.'

When it came to need, no one knew the order of priorities better than the young Assamese girl. On this occasion, however, she was wrong. Her appeal had suddenly reminded Kovalski of something even more urgent.

'The lepers!' he exclaimed. 'The lepers! You three go for the sick and the elderly,' he directed Bandona, Max and Saladdin. 'I'll go with Aristotle John and Margareta to the lepers. We'll all meet at the Jama Masjid!'

The Jama Masjid, the great Friday mosque! That night the rectangular building with four modest minarets at its corners was like a lighthouse in a storm. Hundreds of escapees clutched at the Arabian latticework of its windows, jostling each other and calling out. Others were still arriving. Fathers, sometimes with three or even four children perched on their shoulders, mothers carrying pitiful bundles on their heads and frequently babies in their arms, waded through the filthy water to try and get near the only door. Inside, the spectacle was another scene out of Dante's *Inferno*. Children, frightened by the darkness, screamed with terror.

Women shouted, bickered and wept. Everyone was trying to reach the galleries on the first floor because the flood water had already invaded the ground level and was rising rapidly. Suddenly, however, a torrent was released from the roof and submerged the galleries. Some young men managed to break down the doors leading onto the terrace and set up a barricade. The atmosphere became more and more suffocating and some of the refugees fainted. Babies suffering from dysentery emptied their bowels. The first dead were evacuated, passed from arm to arm over the heads of the crowd. It was not long before the rumours spread: eroded by the water, hundreds of hovels were in the process of collapsing all over the slum.

The little leper colony situated below the level of the railway lines was completely submerged. In order to cover the last few feet, Margareta had to hoist herself onto Kovalski's back, an acrobatic feat that was somewhat delicate in a sari. Not a single inhabitant had left. The parents had put their children up on the roofs and the relatively able-bodied lepers had piled *charpoys* one on top of another to protect the sick and the infirm. Kovalski discovered Anouar perched on one of these improvised pyramids, half-immersed in water. The crippled man had survived his amputation. He was smiling.

'Anouar, old friend, I've been looking for you,' said the priest breathlessly.

'Looking for me? But why? This isn't the first time the monsoon has made our feet wet!'

Again Kovalski was amazed at the leper's stoical, almost cheery attitude. 'These lights of the world really deserve their place next to the Father,' he thought. 'They have been to the very extremes of suffering.'

'The rain is still falling. You could all be drowned.' Even as he spoke, the priest became aware of the meaninglessness of his words. How could he hope to evacuate

these poor people when he himself and his companions had several times nearly disappeared into the eddies of dark water that engulfed the whole area. He must get reinforcements. Reinforcements? The idea seemed somewhat comical in a night of general panic. It was then that he saw before him the image of a man with small cruel eyes behind thick-lensed glasses, a man with protruding ears and the fat jowls of a pleasure seeker. He called out to Margareta and Aristotle John.

'I'm heading for the godfather,' he shouted to them. 'He's the only one who can help us to get everyone out of here.'

With its four storeys of solid masonry, its flights of steps built out of brick, and its stone balconies, the godfather's house emerged like a fortress out of the floodwater. Lit up by a powerful generator, its numerous rooms illuminated the waves that beat against its walls with an unusual clarity. 'It's the doges' palace!' Kovalski remarked to himself, not without a certain admiration. Nothing, not even this deluge, could modify the behaviour of the doge of the City of Joy. Insensible to what was going on outside, to the cries and appeals of residents fleeing their collapsing hovels, he remained as impassive as ever, enthroned in his chair encrusted with precious stones. Even the abrupt entrance of a figure dripping in putrid slime, led by his son, unleashed not the faintest shadow of surprise on his toadlike face.

'Good evening, Father,' he said in his hissing voice and fixed his old adversary with a stare. 'What kindly breeze brings you here in weather like this?'

He clapped his hands and a beturbaned servant brought tea and soft drinks on an engraved copper tray.

'The lepers,' said Kovalski.

'Them again?' marvelled the godfather, and his forehead puckered. 'It would seem that it's always to the lepers that I owe the honour of an encounter with you. What is it this time?'

'They will probably all drown if they're not evacuated urgently. We need men and a boat immediately.'

Whether out of the fear of losing an appreciable source of income or out of an unexpected upsurge of human solidarity, Kovalski could not say, but the City of Joy's Mafia boss reacted in a manner that was quite spectacular. He stood up and clapped his hands, whereupon Ashoka, the little thug with the big motorcycle, came rushing back. An initial private conference was held, then other members of the family appeared. Less than ten minutes later, a boat set out with Kovalski and a team of *mafiosi* on board. As the first strokes of the oars bore the vessel away into shadows reverberating with the sound of shouting and other noises, Kovalski heard again the hissing voice of the godfather. Turning back, he saw the squat little man framed in a lighted window. He would never forget the words of the Mafia boss, ringing out across the swirling water.

'Ashoka,' he shouted to his son at the top of his lungs. 'Bring all the lepers back here. Tonight, our house is open to the wretched ones.'

Max Loeb's bulky, wet body collapsed onto the pile of milk cartons. Exhausted by the hardest night of his life, he was back in his room in the first light of dawn. The downpour was now being succeeded by lighter rain that was warm and less violent, and the rise of the water seemed to have relented a little. All through the night he had accompanied Bandona on her rescue operations, carrying his medicine chest at arm's length above the floodwater. The head and heart of the little Assamese girl contained a complete list of all the most distressed cases in the slum. With the help of a team of young men who had placed themselves spontaneously at their disposal, they had waded from one hovel to the next to rescue blind and paralysed people, bedridden patients

with tuberculosis, beggars, and even a deaf and dumb madwoman with her newborn baby. Only once had they arrived too late. When they entered the shack occupied by the old blind leper woman to whom Kovalski took Communion every week, they found her wasted body already afloat in her widow's shroud. Her rosary was twined about her wrist and her mutilated face looked unaccountably serene.

'Her torment is over now,' murmured Bandona as she helped Max to hoist the body onto the low ledge. 'The God she used to call upon has heard her at last. He has taken her to be with him.'

The simplicity of this explanation in the midst of such a nightmare moved the American deeply. 'It was that night that I realized that I could never be quite the same again,' he was to write a few days later to Sylvia, his fiancée in Miami.

The arrival of the first boatload of lepers at the godfather's house was the occasion for deeds that even a heart as full of love as Kovalski's would not have imagined. He saw Ashoka take Anouar in his arms and carry him carefully to the *charpoy* in his room. He saw the women of the house strip off their beautiful muslin veils to rub down naked children shivering with cold, for the temperature had suddenly dropped ten degrees. He saw the godfather's wife, a plump matron with arms jingling with bracelets, bring in a cooking pot full of rice and steaming pieces of meat. Above all, he saw a sight that would obliterate for ever the horrifying spectacle of Molotov cocktails exploding outside his small leper clinic: the godfather himself reaching out his gold-ringed fingers to receive the çastaways, helping them to disembark, drying their mutilated limbs, serving them tea, and offering them dishes of sweetmeats and pastries.

'In that catastrophic flood,' Kovalski was to comment, 'all the people of the City of Joy had become brothers. Muslim families took Hindus into their homes, young

people nearly drowned carrying the elderly on their shoulders, rickshaw pullers transported the sick free of charge in vehicles that were three-quarters submerged, owners of eating houses did not hesitate to risk their lives to get provisions to the refugees shut up in the mosque.'

In the midst of disaster God was not forgotten. Stopping off at his room, now invaded by more than three feet of water, Kovalski discovered two candles burning in front of his picture of the Sacred Shroud. Before escaping with the other residents of the compound, Kalima, the eunuch, had lit them 'to greet the deity of Big Brother Stephan and ask him to make the rain stop'.

All the same, the God of the Christians, the Bhagavan of the Hindus, and Allah the merciful appeared to be deaf to all entreaty. The torment of the flood victims of Calcutta was to go on for days. As Max had feared, cholera and typhoid began to break out. There were no medicines and no chance of evacuation. People died. Corpses that could not be incinerated or buried were simply abandoned in the flooded streets. In the space of only a few hours Max stumbled upon three bodies drifting about in the current. Paradoxically, with all that liquid around, there was not a drop of drinking water left. The inhabitants hung up rags and umbrellas to try and collect a little rain, but some had to drink directly from the infected strait of water that engulfed them. The food situation was just as tragic, despite the fact that teams of rescue volunteers were working miracles. Saladdin had managed to dig out a boat and two large pots. Paddling as hard as his strength would permit, the old man did the rounds of the eating houses to fill up his receptacles with rice and wheat flour and to take this precious cargo to the people marooned in the mosque.

The strangest thing about this cataclysm was that life still went on as before. On the corner of a submerged alleyway, Max remained rooted to the spot, confronted

by a scene that would never leave him: that of a group of children up to their shoulders in water, laughing and splashing in front of a tiny platform on which an old man was selling little plastic cars and dolls, oblivious of the rain.

For eight days and eight nights the anger of the heavens remained unrelenting. Then gradually it did begin to wane, but it took more than a month for the tide to retreat altogether. Slowly Calcutta began to hope again. A few buses ventured out into the collapsed avenues. More than four hundred miles of streets had been destroyed or damaged. Half a million citizens had lost everything. Thousands of houses and buildings, either decayed or still under construction, had crumbled away. Whole neighbourhoods were without electricity or telephones. Hundreds of water mains had burst.

It was in the slums, however, that the full horror of the disaster was most readily apparent. When the water subsided, the City of Joy was nothing but a polluted marsh. A glutinous, stinking mud covered everything, interspersed with the decaying carcasses of dogs, cats, rats, lizards and even humans. Millions of flies soon hatched out of the putrefaction and made straight for any survivors. Epidemics broke out in various quarters. To try and contain them, Bandona and Aristotle John distributed tons of disinfectant provided by the municipality. Alas, the operation caused heavy losses among the volunteers. Max had to amputate several hands and feet burned to the bone by corrosive substances.

By the time Kovalski, concealed behind a two-week beard and covered with dirt and vermin, finally regained his compound, all the other occupants had already returned. They were all busy clearing away traces of the inundation. Kalima and his eunuch companions from the room next door were quick to come and greet him.

'Welcome back, Big Brother Stephan,' said Kalima warmly. 'We've been waiting for you.'

What was his emotion when Kovalski discovered that in his absence the eunuchs had washed, scrubbed and completely repainted his hovel! Before the picture of the Sacred Shroud, a pattern of *rangoli*, the attractive auspicious motifs traced on the ground in coloured powder, paid homage to his God. Before resting, the priest gave thanks for so much love shown in the depths of this wretched slum. He was deep in meditation when a bearded figure burst in. Hasari had lost so much weight that the priest hardly recognized him.

'Now I can die,' announced the former peasant, brandishing a bundle of bank notes in his triumph. 'Look how much I've earned. I'm going to find a husband for my daughter.'

70

His entire wealth lay heaped together on a small copper tray: a conch, a little bell, a pitcher full of Ganges water, a pot of *ghee* and the *panchaprodip*, the five-branched candlestick used in the ceremony of the offering of fire. Forty-three-year-old Hari Giri, a puny little man with pale skin and an enormous wart on his forehead, was the neighbourhood *pujari*, the Hindu priest. He lived in a humble dwelling near the huts occupied by the Madrasis, the most poverty-stricken inhabitants of the slum. In front of his dwelling stood the small temple dedicated to Sitola, goddess of smallpox. With her scarlet head and black eyes, her silver diadem and necklace of cobras and lions, she looked even more terrifying than Kali the Terrible, patron goddess of Calcutta. It was primarily, however, for his devotion to another divinity that the Brahmin was renowned among the residents of the slum. Daughter of the elephant-headed god Ganesh, Santoshi

Mata was the goddess with the power to grant a husband to every young Indian girl. The cult devoted to her provided the *pujari* with a not inconsiderable source of revenue. Of all the ceremonies in Hinduism, that of marriage is in fact the most profitable for a Brahmin, so much so that Hari Giri had studied astrology in order to set himself up as a professional matchmaker. Hasari's anxiety could not leave him entirely untouched. One evening he paid the rickshaw puller a visit to ask him the time and date of his daughter's birth. 'I shall be back soon with some good news for you,' he assured him.

A few days later he did indeed return.

'Your daughter's horoscope and caste are in perfect harmony with those of a boy with whom I am acquainted,' he announced triumphantly to Hasari and his wife. 'The family concerned are *kumars*.* They have two potteries in the neighbouring slum and are highly respectable people.' Then, addressing himself exclusively to Hasari, he added, 'The boy's father would like to meet you very soon.'

Profoundly moved, Hasari prostrated himself on the ground to wipe the Brahmin's bare feet, then raise his hands to his forehead. No self-respecting *pujari* would be satisfied with this kind of gratitude, however. Holding out his hand, he claimed an advance on his fee. This visit was to mark the beginning of a tragicomedy with many a twist of plot, of which Kovalski was to become, by force of circumstances, one of the principal protagonists. Although it is customary for the long and detailed negotiations that precede a marriage to be conducted in public in the middle of the courtyard, the parties concerned often prefer a more discreet place when it comes to the discussion of financial matters.

'My room was always at everyone's disposal,' the priest was to say. Thus it was there, in front of the

* Potters by birth.

Sacred Shroud, that the two parties met. As to the 'parties' concerned, that certainly did not mean either young Amrita or her prospective husband, who would not meet until the evening of their nuptials. Rather, it meant the father of the prospective boy, a surly man of medium build with hair matted with mustard oil, Hasari, the Brahmin with the wart on his forehead, and Kovalski. After a long exchange of greetings and social niceties, the primary issues were broached.

'My son is an exceptional boy,' declared the father unhesitatingly. 'And I want his wife to be no less so.'

Naturally everyone correctly understood the exact meaning of this line of approach. He was not referring to moral qualities or even to physical ones, but to the price that must be paid for so 'exceptional' a son. 'This character's after the moon,' Hasari remarked to himself. He turned to Big Brother Stephan, seeking reassurance. He had insisted upon Kovalski agreeing to be present at the debate. 'In front of the *sahib*, they won't dare to exaggerate,' he told himself. For once, however, the former peasant had made a psychological error. Contrary to Hasari's expectations, the *sahib*'s presence was to become a source of security for the opposite camp: 'If the girl's father can't pay, the *sahib* will just have to pay instead.'

'My daughter is just as exceptional as your son,' retorted Hasari, not wishing to be outdone.

'If she is such a jewel, you will no doubt have anticipated giving her a generous dowry,' said the father of the boy.

'I have anticipated doing my duty,' assured Hasari.

'Well, let's see then,' said the father, lighting up a *bidi*.

An Indian girl's dowry is made up of two parts. One part consists of her trousseau and personal jewels that remain in principle her property. The other part is made up of the gifts she will take to her new family. Hasari's reckoning was intended to take in both. The whole list

was not very long, but each item represented so many trips through the waters of the monsoon, such deprivation, so many sacrifices, that the rickshaw puller felt each concession he was giving away meant a little of his own flesh and blood. The list included two cotton saris, two bodices, a shawl, various household utensils, and a few imitation jewels and ornaments. As for the presents for the groom's family, they were made up of two *dhotis*, as many vests, and a *punjabi*, the long tunic that buttons up to the neck and goes down to the knees. It was true that it was a poor man's dowry but it represented some two thousand rupees, a fabulous sum for a poverty-stricken rickshaw *wallah*.

The boy's father's eyebrows wrinkled. After a silence, he inquired, 'Is that all?'

Hasari shook his head sadly, but he was far too proud to try and play upon the pity of his interlocutor.

'My daughter's qualities will make up for what is lacking.'

'Maybe,' growled the boy's father, 'but it does seem to me that one or two toe rings would not be entirely superfluous. And also a nose brooch and a gold *matthika*.* As for the gifts for my family . . .'

The Brahmin interrupted to declare, 'Before continuing with your bartering, I would appreciate it if you could come to an agreement on the price of my services.'

'I had thought two *dhotis* for you and a sari for your wife,' replied Hasari.

'Two *dhotis* and a sari!' guffawed the *pujari*, beside himself. 'You must be joking!'

Kovalski saw great beads of sweat break out on his friend's forehead. 'Dear Lord,' he thought, 'they're going to fleece him down to the very last hair.'

Kalima and some of the other neighbours were glued to the opening to the little room, trying not to miss any

* An ornament worn on the forehead.

of the palavering and keeping the rest of the compound informed.

The discussion went on for a good two hours without achieving anything; they all maintained their positions. Marriage negotiations were traditionally very long-winded affairs.

The second meeting took place three days later in the same place. As was customary, Hasari had prepared small gifts for the father of the boy and for the *pujari*. Nothing very much: a *gamcha* each. Nevertheless those three days of waiting seemed to have sapped the rickshaw puller's strength. He was having more and more difficulty in breathing. His coughing fits, provisionally suppressed by Max's emergency treatment, had started up again. Haunted by the fear of dying before he had fulfilled his duty, he was ready to concede to any demands. He might never be able to implement them. This time it was the *pujari* who opened fire, but his claims were so excessive that for once the two fathers were in agreement. They rejected them.

'In that case, I shall withdraw,' threatened the Brahmin.

'That's too bad. We shall just have to find another *pujari*,' responded Hasari.

The Brahmin burst out laughing.

'The horoscopes are in my possession! No one will ever agree to take my place!'

His reply provoked general hilarity in the compound. Women exchanged comments on the proceedings. 'This *pujari* is a true son of a bitch,' announced one of the matrons. 'What's more he's sly! I'll bet he's in cahoots with the boy's father!' another replied. Inside the room, they had reached an impasse. Suffering from a surge of fever, Hasari had begun to shake. 'If you muck up my daughter's marriage, I'll skin you alive,' he stormed inwardly, his bloodshot eyes fixed upon the Brahmin. The *pujari* went through the motions of getting up to

leave, but Hasari caught hold of his wrist. 'Stay!' he begged.

'Only if you pay me a hundred rupees right away.'

The two helpless fathers exchanged glances. After a few seconds' hesitation they each rummaged in the waistbands of their *longhis*.

'There you are!' said Hasari tartly, tossing a bundle into the hand of the man with the wart.

The latter instantly became all sweetness and light. The negotiations could recommence. No king's or millionaire's marriage could have been the subject of keener discussion than this proposed union of two raga-muffins in a slum. It took no fewer than eight sessions to settle the question of the dowry. Crises of weeping alternated with threats; ruptures with reconciliations. There was always some new requirement. One day the boy's father claimed, on top of everything else, a bicycle; next day he wanted a transistor radio, an ounce of gold, an additional *dhoti*. Six days before the wedding, a misunderstanding threatened to end everything. The groom's family swore that they were supposed to receive twelve saris and not six, as Hasari claimed. Having run out of arguments, one of the young man's uncles came rushing to Kovalski.

'*Sahib*, all you have to do is provide the six missing saris. After all, you're rich! They say you're even the richest man in your country!'

This marathon completely exhausted the poor rick-shaw puller. One morning when he had just collected his carriage he felt the ground dissolve beneath his feet.

'I felt as if with every step I was sinking into a drainage hole,' he was to tell Kovalski. 'I saw the cars, lorries and horses revolving around me as if they were attached to a merry-go-round at a fair. I heard the screech of sirens, then everything went blank, a great dark blank.' Hasari let go of his shafts. He had fainted.

When he next opened his eyes, he recognized the thin

face of Musafir, the representative of the owner of his rickshaw, looming over him. Musafir had been doing his rounds, collecting the rent, when he noticed the abandoned rickshaw.

'Hey there, fellow, have you drunk a bit too much *bangla*?' he asked in a friendly way, patting the puller's cheeks.

Hasari indicated his chest.

'No, I think it's my motor that's giving out.'

'Your motor?' inquired the man anxiously, suddenly on the alert. 'Hasari, if your motor's really giving out, you're going to have to hand in your machine. You know how adamant the old man is about things like that. He's always saying, "I want buffalo between my shafts, not baby goats."'

Hasari nodded. There was neither sadness nor revolt in his expression, only resignation. He knew too well the laws of the city. A man whose motor failed him was a dead man. He had already ceased to exist. He thought of the poor coolie he had transported to the hospital during the first days of his exile. He thought of Ram Chander and of all those whom he had seen die in the arms of their rickshaws, their strength sapped, consumed, annihilated by the climate, by hunger and by their superhuman effort. He looked with tenderness upon the two great wheels and the black bodywork of his old cart, the punctured canvas seat, the hoop and material of the little hood, in the shelter of which so many young people had loved each other and so many of the city's inhabitants had braved the excesses of the monsoon. Above all, he looked at those two instruments of torture between which he had suffered so much. How many thousands of miles had his ulcerated feet traversed on the molten asphalt of this mirage city? He did not know. He knew only that every step had been an act of will to induce the *chakra* of his destiny to complete just one more turn, an instinctive gesture aimed at survival

and escape from the curse of his condition. Now, that *chakra* was going to stop once and for all.

He looked up at the owner's representative astride his bicycle. 'Take your rickshaw back,' he said. 'It will make someone happy.'

He got to his feet again and for one last time he pulled rickshaw No. 1999 back to the stand on Park Circus. While he was saying goodbye to his friends, Hasari saw the representative call out to one of the young men waiting on the edge of the pavement. They were all refugees, part of the last exodus that had emptied the Bengal and Bihar countryside, ravaged by a fresh drought. All of them longed for the opportunity to take a turn at harnessing themselves to a rickshaw. Hasari went over to the one the representative had chosen and smiled at him. Then he took the small copper bell from his finger.

'Take this little bell, son,' he said, jangling it against a shaft. 'It will be your talisman to keep you safe from danger.'

Before going home, Hasari made a detour to call on the skeleton salesman and claim the second part of the proceeds from the sale of his bones. The cashier examined the visitor with care and, judging that his state of decline was well under way, he agreed to a further payment.

It took three more days of heated arguing before everyone agreed upon the size of the dowry. As tradition required, this agreement was sealed with a special ceremony in the Pals' compound, with all the other residents as witnesses. Coconuts, incense and a whole carpet of banana leaves were laid on the ground to enable the *pujari* to carry out the various rites and pronounce the *mantras* for the occasion. Hasari was invited to announce that he was giving his daughter away in marriage and to enumerate the list of goods that would constitute her dowry. Much to Kovalski's fury, this formality

immediately provoked a further cascade of incidents. The groom's family demanded to see the goods in question. A real showdown ensued. 'I might have been in the middle of the Bara Bazar,' Kovalski was to recount. 'They demanded proof of the cost of such and such a jewel, they protested that the wedding sari wasn't beautiful enough, they thought the transistor radio was pathetic. Each recrimination took away a little more of the small amount of breath left in Hasari's chest.' On the eve of the wedding, a new drama erupted. The groom's father, uncles and a whole group of his friends came bursting in to check the preparations for the celebrations.

'There will be at least a hundred of us,' declared the father. 'And we want to be sure there'll be enough to eat.'

Kovalski saw Hasari start.

'A hundred,' he protested. 'But we agreed that there wouldn't be more than fifty of you.'

There followed an argument, to the amusement of the entire compound. The visitors dissected the menu, demanding that a vegetable was added here, a fruit or a sweetmeat there. With his back to the wall, Hasari tried to front it out.

'All right, if you reduce the number of guests by twenty,' he eventually conceded.

'Twenty? Never! By ten at the very most!'

'Fifteen.'

'Twelve and not one more.'

'All right, twelve,' sighed Hasari, to put an end to the matter. But his agony was not yet over.

'What about the musicians?' One of the groom's uncles was concerned. 'How many will there be?'

'Six.'

'Only six? But that's pathetic! A boy like my nephew warrants at least ten musicians!'

'It's the best orchestra in the slum,' protested Hasari. 'They've even played at the godfather's house!'

'Best or not, you'll have to add at least two more musicians,' retorted the uncle.

It was then that a further demand was made. For some mysterious reason, connected, it seems, with subtle astrological calculations, Indian weddings nearly always take place in the middle of the night. Anouar, the leper, and Meeta had got married at midnight. Amrita's horoscope and that of her future husband determined the same hour. So the *pujari* had decided, after reading the celestial cards.

'Where's the generator?' asked the groom's father. 'It's dark at midnight and a wedding without lots of lights is not a proper wedding.'

Hasari remained dumbfounded. His own sweat had glued his back to the wall. His mouth opened in response to a desire to vomit and, with his breath painful and wheezing, he felt the ground once more dissolve beneath his feet. Faces, walls, sounds all swam together in a haze. Clasping the post of the veranda, he groaned. 'I'm not going to make it. I know I won't make it. They're going to do me out of Amrita's marriage.' Yet the groom's father's requirement was justified.

For the millions of slum people condemned because of the lack of electricity to live in perpetual obscurity, there could be no celebration without illuminations. An orgy of light, like the one provided on the evening of Anouar's wedding, was a way of defying misfortune. Hasari shook his head sadly, showing them his empty palms. This man who felt his end so very close at hand had had no reservations about incurring debts for generations to come in order to execute his final duty. He had taken the two rings and the small pendant that had formed part of his wife's dowry, plus the watch his son Shambu had found among the refuse, to the usurer. He had killed himself working. He had sold his bones. He had exceeded the possible. Yet now he must submit to the supreme humiliation. .

'If you persist in your demands,' he said, pausing after each word to regain his breath, 'there is only one solution: we shall have to cancel the wedding. I have no more money.'

So it was that less than fourteen hours before the ceremony, they had reached an impasse of the kind that might mean total breakdown. For the first time Hasari appeared resigned. 'The man who had struggled so hard had the look of one who was already elsewhere,' the Pole was to say. Bluff or no, the other camp maintained the same attitude. 'Surely to God,' Kovalski said to himself, 'they're not going to let the whole thing cave in over a little matter of lighting.' Alarmed, he decided to intervene.

'I know a compound not very far away where they have electricity,' he said. 'A cable could easily be led off it to here. With four or five lamps, there would be plenty of light.'

For the rest of his life Kovalski would carry with him the sight of the gratitude in his friend's face.

The contest was still not won, however. Less than seven hours before the ceremony, a new crisis erupted. But this time the person responsible was the rickshaw puller himself. Recollecting suddenly that the standing of a wedding was assessed as much on the munificence of the nuptial procession as on the opulence of the festivities, he inquired of the groom's father as to the manner in which he intended to have his son arrive at the domicile of his future wife. Even in this slum of mud and pestilence, such a journey was usually undertaken on a horse caparisoned with gold and velvet.

'In a rickshaw,' replied the father. Kovalski thought Hasari was going to suffocate.

'In a rickshaw?' he hiccuped. 'You did say "in a rickshaw"?' The groom's father nodded his head.

Hasari gave him a withering look. 'My daughter will never marry a man who comes to her wedding in a

rickshaw, as if she were a common poor man's daughter,' he thundered. 'I demand a taxi. A taxi and a procession. Otherwise I shall take my daughter back.'

Providence was once more to call upon Son of Miracle. Informed of the latest point of difference between the two families, the taxi driver was quick to offer his car to transport the cortège. His generosity moved the former peasant in a very special way. After all, it had been in that same car that he had once experienced the greatest revelation of his life. It was as he sat in that vehicle that he had watched the rupees on the meter 'fall like the monsoon rain'. 'That taxi will bring luck to my daughter and her household,' he said to himself, his cheerfulness and confidence restored.

A few hours later, Hasari would at last witness the marvellous sight towards which all his arduous efforts had been directed. 'Look, Big Brother Stephan. How beautiful my daughter is,' he murmured ecstatically. Swathed in a scarlet sari sprinkled with golden stars, her head bowed, her face concealed behind a muslin veil, her naked feet painted red, her toes, her ankles and wrists sparkling with the jewels that were her dowry, Amrita, led by her mother and the women of the compound, was going to take her place on the rice straw mat placed in the centre of the courtyard, just in front of the little brazier in which the sacred and eternal flame burned. In sheer happiness, his lips parted in a smile that rose from the very depths of his soul, Hasari rejoiced in the most beautiful spectacle of his life, a magical scene that wiped out so many nightmare images at a single stroke: Amrita crying of cold and hunger on the winter nights spent on their piece of pavement, foraging with her little hands through the refuse from the Grand Hotel, begging under the Chowringhee arcades . . . This was a moment of triumph, of apotheosis, of final revenge on a rotten *karma*.

A brass band burst into sound, accompanied by sing-

ing and shouting. Preceded by a troupe of transvestite dancers, outrageously made-up with rouge and kohl, the procession made its grandiose entry into the courtyard filled with the smoke of the *chulas*. 'It was as if a prince out of *A Thousand and One Nights* had just dropped out of the sky,' Kovalski was to say. 'With his cardboard diadem encrusted with bits of coloured glass, the groom looked like one of the maharajahs you see in engravings, surrounded by his courtiers.'

Like Anouar, before taking up his position the boy had to submit to the ritual of *parda*, the imposition of a veil, so that the eyes of his betrothed would not be able to see his face before the moment prescribed by the liturgy. Then the *pujari* motioned to him to go and sit beside Amrita. So began the interminable and picturesque ritual of a Hindu wedding ceremony, punctuated with *mantras* in Sanskrit, the language of sages and men of letters, which of course no one in this slum could understand, not even the Brahmin who recited them.

The congregation had not failed to notice that the best man's place to the right of the bride had remained vacant. Hasari had offered this place, the first in the hierarchy of precedence, to his brother in poverty, the Big Brother from the hovel next door, the man of God who, together with Son of Miracle, had been his providence, his friend, his confidant. Kovalski, however, had not been able to occupy the place. At the very moment the groom and his procession made their entrance, a series of convulsions had brutally shaken Hasari's chest. The priest had rushed to carry the poor man into his room. The eyes and mouth that only a moment previously had been exultant with joy had closed again in an expression of intense pain. When the convulsions stopped, his body remained stiff and motionless. Then, as if under the influence of an electrical impulse, his chest and all his muscles contracted anew. His lips parted. They were

completely blue, a clear indication of respiratory difficulties.

Kovalski straddled the body and, putting all his weight on the thorax, started to massage it vigorously from bottom to top. The rickshaw puller had been reduced to skin and bone to such an extent that it was like getting hold of a skeleton. The sternum and ribs creaked under the pressure of his fingers. Soaking his beautiful white best man's *punjabi* with perspiration, the Pole worked away with all his might and, miracle of all miracles, a very feeble, almost imperceptible breath soon quivered through the fleshless form. Kovalski realized that he had succeeded in restarting the motor. To consolidate this victory, he gave his brother the most beautiful demonstration of affection he could. Bending right over him, he put his lips to Hasari's mouth and began to blow rhythmic puffs of air into lungs consumed with the red fever.

Kovalski was to write of the events that followed in a letter to the superior of his fraternity. 'Hasari opened his eyes. They were swimming with tears and I realized he must be in pain. I tried to give him a drink but the water trickled over his lips without his being able to swallow it. He was breathing very faintly. At one point he seemed to be straining to listen. He appeared to be able to hear the noises coming from the courtyard, the voices and the music of the festivities. He smiled weakly at the joyous commotion. Hearing the wedding going on had such a curative effect that he wanted to speak. I put my ear closer to his mouth and heard, "Big Brother, Big Brother," then some words that I could not make out.

'A few moments later he took hold of my hand and squeezed it. I was amazed at the strength with which he clasped my fingers. The hand that had grasped the shafts of his rickshaw for so many years was still like a vice. He looked at me then with eyes that were full of suppli-

cation. "Big Brother, Big Brother," he repeated, then murmured some words in Bengali. That time I understood that he was referring to his wife and sons, that he was asking me to take care of them. I tried to reassure him. I knew that the end was near and he must have been thinking the same thing because with several movements of his hand he conveyed to me that he wanted to leave the compound without anybody noticing. No doubt he was afraid that his death would disrupt the celebrations. I had foreseen such an eventuality and asked Son of Miracle to have Hasari transferred to his compound as soon as possible.

'Towards three o'clock in the morning, with the help of Kalima and Hasari's son Shambu, the little ragpicker, we were able discreetly to move the rickshaw puller. The revellers noticed nothing. The godfather had sent along an extra supply of *bangla* and many of the guests were already drunk. Hasari must have been conscious that he was leaving his home because he joined his hands across his chest in a gesture of *namaskar* as if to bid everyone farewell.

'After that, it all happened very quickly. At about five in the morning, Hasari was shaken by a violent attack. Then his lips parted and a jet of foaming blood spurted out. Shortly afterwards his chest caved in with a rattle. It was all over. I closed his eyes and recited the prayer for the dead.'

Less than an hour later a series of heavy blows shook the door to the room where Son of Miracle and Kovalski were watching over the mortal remains of their friend, now enveloped in a white *khadi* shroud and adorned with a garland of marigolds. The taxi driver went to open it. In the shadows he could just make out two very dark-skinned faces.

'We're the *Doms*,' announced the elder of the two. 'The deceased was under contract. We've come to collect his body.'

71

'Brothers, sisters, listen!' Stephan Kovalski raised a finger in the direction of the ringing bells and closed his eyes to absorb fully the crystalline notes that came cascading across the fume-laden sky. 'Christ our Saviour is born' announced the peal from the illuminated church of Our Lady of the Loving Heart. It was midnight on Christmas Eve.

At that instant, from one end of the immense metropolis to the other, other chimes sounded out the same news. Despite the fact that Christians represented a small minority in Calcutta, the birth of Jesus was celebrated with as much devotion and display as that of Krishna, Muhammad, Buddha, the guru Nanak of the Sikhs, or Mahavira, saint of the Jains. Christmas was one of approximately twenty official religious festivals marked with a general holiday in a city where such a miscellany of faiths and such devotion to God prevailed.

Filled with decorations, in the darkness the church looked more like a maharajah's palace on a coronation night. In the courtyard, only a few feet away from the pavements where thousands of homeless people slept huddled in the bitter cold, a monumental crib with life-size models reconstructed the birth of the Messiah in the straw of a Bethlehem stable. A colourful crowd, the women in magnificent saris, their heads covered with embroidered veils, the men and children dressed like princes, filled the vast nave adorned with banners and garlands. The splendid bouquets of tuberoses, roses and marigolds that decorated the altar and choir had been brought by a Christian woman from the City of Joy in gratitude for the miraculous healing of her hus-

band, who had recovered from cholera. All around the pillars, before the innumerable plaques recording the names of the British men and women who had been buried in this church since its construction two centuries earlier, wreaths of foliage and flowers formed a triumphal arch.

Suddenly a burst of firecrackers shook the night. To the accompaniment of the organ, the congregation joined in singing a hymn celebrating the advent of the holy infant. The rector, Alberto Cordeiro, looking more opulent than ever in his immaculate alb and his red silk vestments, made his entrance. Escorted by his deacons and a double row of choirboys, he processed through the nave and ceremoniously approached the altar. 'So much pomp among so much poverty,' marvelled Max Loeb who attended midnight Mass for the first time in his life. The Jewish doctor did not know that the good priest had once tried to dissuade Kovalski from going to live among the poor of the City of Joy, for fear that he might 'become a slave to them and lose their respect'.

Similar services were beginning in churches elsewhere in Calcutta. All around St Thomas, the smart parish in the Park Street area, dozens of private cars, taxis and rickshaws were unloading worshippers. Park Street and the neighbouring streets glittered with garlands and luminous stars. The night was resonant with Christmas carols. On the pavements children sold little Santa Clauses they had made and decorated in their slum workshops. Others offered cardboard fir trees glistening with snow, or cribs. All the shops were open, their windows full of presents, bottles of wine, alcohol and beer, baskets bursting with fruits, confectionery and special preserves. Wealthy Indian ladies escorted by their servants did last-minute shopping for the midnight supper. Whole families besieged Flury's, the celebrated ice cream and pastry shop. Others swept into Peter Kat, Tandoor, or into the restaurants at the Moulin Rouge,

the Park Hotel or the Grand Hotel. This last was declared to be fully booked. Its dinner, with entertainment and souvenirs, cost three hundred rupees for two, almost the price for which Hasari Pal had sold his bones.

Deep in the alleyways of the City of Joy, Christmas was no less lively. Garlands of lights and streamers had been strung up wherever there were Christian homes. Loudspeakers spread the sound of carols and hymns. Each family had decorated its home. Taking advantage of Kovalski's absence, Margareta had put a new coat of paint on the walls of his room, drawn a *rangoli* pattern on the floor, placed a small crib under the picture of the Sacred Shroud, opened up the Gospels at the page of the nativity, and lit candles and sticks of incense. From the framework she had hung garlands of marigolds and roses that formed a kind of canopy above the little oratory.

For all the Christians of the City of Joy, however, it was the enormous luminous star poised on the end of a bamboo cane above Kovalski's hovel that was the most beautiful symbol of that magical night. The Hindu Ajit and the Muslim Saladdin had had the idea of hoisting the emblem into the sky over the City of Joy, as if to say to the despairing people of the slum: 'Be not afraid. You are not alone. On this night when the God of the Christians was born, there is already a saviour among us.'

That night the 'saviour' in question had remained, with the agreement of the parish priest, among his brothers. With his head and shoulders wrapped in a shawl because of the biting cold, Kovalski was celebrating the mystery of the Eucharist for some fifty worshippers who had assembled in Margareta's compound. How many years had gone by since his first Mass, celebrated on that same piece of plank supported on two crates? Five, six, seven? How could anyone measure the passing of time in this world without past or future? In this

world where the life of so many hinged upon surviving the present minute? Listening to the carols that filled the night, he thought, 'This concentration camp is a monastery.' The thought had often come to him and, on this Christmas night, one conviction impressed itself upon him more forcefully than ever: nowhere was the message of a God who was made man to save humanity more alive than in this slum. The City of Joy and Bethlehem were one and the same place. Before uplifting to the heavens the fragment of unleavened bread that took the place of the host, the priest felt the need to speak a few words.

'It is easy for any man to recognize and glorify the riches of the world,' he said, seeking out faces in the shadows. 'But only a poor man can know the riches of poverty. Only a poor man can know the riches of suffering . . .'

Hardly had he spoken these words when a strange phenomenon occurred. First there was a sudden gust of wind, then a mass of hot air swept into the compound, tearing down the garlands and streamers, extinguishing the luminous stars and bringing the tiles off the rooftops. Almost immediately after that, a formidable thunderclap rent the night. Kovalski could not help wondering if the monsoon was on its way back. After a few seconds, however, all was calm once more.

'And it is because the poor are the only ones to be able to know such riches that they are able to stand up against the wretchedness of the world, against injustice, against the suffering of the innocent,' he said. 'If Christ chose to be born among the poor, it is because he wanted the poor to teach the world the good news of his message, the good news of his love for mankind.

'Brothers and sisters of the City of Joy, it is you who today are the bearers of that flame of hope. Your Big Brother can promise you that the day will come when the tiger shall lie down with the young child, and the

cobra will sleep with the dove, and all the peoples of all the nations will be as brothers and sisters.'

Kovalski was to relate how as he spoke these words he saw again a photograph of Martin Luther King, Jr, meditating in front of a Christmas crib. In the caption to this photograph, King told how before that crib he had had a vision of an enormous banquet on the hillsides of Virginia, where slaves and the sons of slaves sat down with their masters to share in a meal of peace and love. That evening Kovalski felt himself impelled by the same dream. One day, he was quite certain, the rich and the poor, slaves and their masters, executioners and their victims, would all be able to sit down at the same table.

The priest picked up the morsel of griddle cake and raised it to the heavens. What he then saw above the rooftops seemed so extraordinary to him that he could not take his eyes off it. Sheaves of lightning were streaking the sky, lighting up an enormous mass of black cloud scudding past at great speed. A fresh cannonade of thunder immediately rolled across the night, followed this time by a burst of wind so forceful that, in the depths of their compound, Kovalski and his congregation felt as if they were being literally sucked up into it. A few moments later the clouds shed a deluge of lukewarm water. It was then that Kovalski heard the voice of Aristotle John shouting above the uproar, 'A cyclone, it's a cyclone!'

On the other side of the city, in an old colonial mansion with balusters in the residential district of Alipore, a man was listening to the rising howl of the tornado. His interest was of a professional nature: T. S. Ranjit Singh, a thirty-eight-year-old Sikh originally from Amritsar in the Punjab, was on duty that Christmas night at the meteorological centre for the region of Calcutta. Situated among hundred-year-old banyan trees beneath which

Rabindranath Tagore had composed some of his poems, the centre's antennae received and collated weather bulletins from all the stations planted along the shores of the Bay of Bengal, in the Andaman Islands, and even as far away as Rangoon in Burma. Similarly, twice a day the station laboratory picked up photographs of the Indian subcontinent and the seas that bordered on it, taken from the upper stratosphere by the American satellite *NOAA7* and by its Soviet counterpart *Meteor*. The Arabian Sea to the west and the Bay of Bengal to the east had always been areas with a predilection for giving birth to the savage hurricanes known to meteorologists as cyclones. Caused by harsh variations in temperature and atmospheric pressure between sea level and higher altitudes, the whirlwinds unleashed forces comparable to those of hydrogen bombs of several megatons. From time to time they ravaged the shores of India, causing thousands, sometimes tens of thousands, of deaths, destroying and submerging in one fell swoop regions as vast as the whole of England. India's entire memory had been traumatized by the nightmare of its cyclones.

On the night in question, however, Ranjit Singh had no particular reason to be alarmed. Not all tropical depressions became cyclonic whirlwinds, particularly when they occurred as late in the season as this. The photograph transmitted by the American satellite at seven in the evening was even somewhat reassuring. The Sikh examined it attentively. The diffused zone of stratocumulus it showed had little chance of becoming dangerous. Situated more than eight hundred miles south of Calcutta, it was tracking northeast, in other words, in the direction of Burma. The last readings from the weather stations, transmitted by teleprinter, had come in barely an hour ago. It was true that they indicated areas of low pressure all over the region but the wind speed everywhere was less than thirty miles an hour. Reassured, the Sikh decided to spend his Christmas

Eve as pleasantly as possible. Opening his attaché case, he took out the two tin boxes his wife had prepared. They contained a real midnight feast: fish curry with cubes of white cheese in a sauce, little balls of vegetables, and baked *nan*. He also took out a small bottle of rum he had brought back from an inspection in Sikkim and filled a glass. Oblivious of the squalls that were banging at the shutters, he swallowed a first mouthful with relish. Then he began his meal. When he had finished eating, he poured himself a fresh glass of rum, got up, and appeased his conscience by casting an eye over the teleprinter roll in the adjoining room. With some satisfaction he confirmed the absence of any message and went back to his seat. 'There we go,' he remarked to himself as he savoured his drink. 'Yet another uneventful night.'

At two in the morning, he awoke with a start to the rattle of the teleprinter. The Vishakhapatnam station to the north of Madras was announcing gusts of winds of one hundred and twenty knots, a little more than one hundred and thirty miles per hour. Shortly afterwards the station on the Nicobar Islands confirmed this information. The mild depression of the previous day had transformed itself into a major cyclone. The anger of the god Indra was raging across the Bay of Bengal.

One hour later, an SOS from an Indonesian cargo boat caught up in the storm confirmed that danger was imminent. Its position, latitude 17° 25' north, and longitude 91° 10' east, indicated that the cyclone was located about three hundred and fifty miles away from the coast of Bengal. It had changed direction sharply and was heading towards Calcutta.

The Sikh lost not a second. Instantly he informed his superior, the chief engineer, H. P. Gupta, who was sound asleep with his family in his government flat situated in a wing of the building. Then he called the local station for All India Radio, the national broadcasting network, and the cabinet office of the Minister for

Internal Affairs in order that the people living in the delta area might be immediately informed of the imminence of a 'cyclonic wind of very severe intensity'. Next he turned to a radiotelephone positioned on a console behind his table. The apparatus relayed his HQ directly to an ultra-modern piece of equipment on top of the highest building in Calcutta. From beneath its fibreglass dome the parabolic antenna for the radar of the Indian meteorological department could locate a cyclone over four hundred miles away, trace its course, determine the dimension of its 'eye', and calculate the volume of torrential rain it was liable to dump on hitting its target. That night, however, the radar was switched off and the great sky-blue room, decorated with photographs of all the cyclones that had ravaged Bengal in the course of the previous ten years, was deserted. The next tour of observation was not due to begin until seven on Christmas morning.

72

Ashish Ghosh, the young peasant who had been daring enough to return to his village after six years of exile in the City of Joy, had not gone to bed that night. Together with his wife and their three children he had struggled against the onslaughts of the wind and pouring rain which were gradually demolishing his mud and thatch hut. His village, Harbangha, consisted of an assembly of small dwellings in the middle of infertile rice fields, inhabited for the most part by refugees from what had once been East Pakistan and was now Bangladesh. It was one of the world's poorest regions, a marshy area without roads, traversed by rivers, creeks, canals and estuaries; an inhospitable expanse of land constantly

beset by some calamity, by floods, for example, or tornadoes, tropical storms, droughts, the collapsing banks, the bursting dikes, the invasion of salt water. This was unproductive ground which did not yield even an annual harvest of fifteen hundred pounds of rice per acre for its two million peasants. Life was even harder for the one million inhabitants who possessed not even a paddy field. Risking their own lives, the fishermen tried to keep their families from perishing in a region that was enormously rich in fish, but where lack of equipment put the chance of a catch in the lap of the gods. Half a million dayworkers offered their labour for hire but only at harvest and tilling time did they actually find any work. For the rest of the year they cut down wood and gathered wild honey in the enormous virgin forests of the Sundarbans, an area as large as England but almost as impenetrable as the Amazon, infested with snakes, crocodiles and man-eating tigers that each year devoured three or four hundred people among them.

Ashish Ghosh had brought back with him from the City of Joy one of the primary symbols of economic ascent for a poor refugee, a transistor radio. At about six in the morning he switched it on. The static caused by atmospheric disturbance impaired his reception. Nevertheless, through the crackling, he could make out a voice relentlessly repeating the same message. He jammed the appliance to his ear and instantly understood. A few minutes later the Ghoshs were fleeing into the downpour, leaving behind them the fruits of their six years of exile, deprivation, saving and suffering in the inferno of their slum: their house with its store of seeds and fertilizer, their field, the large pool so arduously dug out, where the first carp had just been born, their two bullocks bellowing in their thorny enclosure, the three goats and Mina, their beautiful cow with her swollen udders and her horns curved like those of the wild sheep of the Himalayas. Ashish turned around to

look back at it all through the tornado. Squeezing the
arm of his sobbing wife, he promised, 'We'll be back.'
It was then that with eyes lashed by the pouring rain he
saw his hut borne aloft 'like a flycatcher's nest carried
away by a monsoon squall'.

The image of a large whitish snail pierced in the centre
by a black hole suddenly appeared on the green-tinted
screen. At the top, on the left, the digital chronometer
announced the time in orange letters. It was seven
thirty-six. The Calcutta radar had just detected the monster. Its position – latitude 19° north, longitude 89° 45'
east – its breadth – three hundred and five miles – and
the dimension of its eye – twenty-two miles – confirmed
the alarm messages being issued by all the weather
stations in the region. They were evidently dealing with
a major whirlwind, with what the Indian meteorologists
refer to in their jargon as a 'severest cyclonic storm'.
Half an hour later a detail was to further reinforce their
concern. Although the eye of the cyclone, the black hole
in the middle, remained perfectly visible, a series of
milky spirals had begun to form around the cavity,
gradually obscuring it behind a whitish veil. This was
evidence that the whirlwind was in the process of becoming swollen with millions of tons of water.

Without losing a second, Haresh Khanna, the frail
little technician who had just taken up his post in charge
of the radar that Christmas morning, picked up his
radiotelephone to alert the meteorological centre. Originally from Bombay, the other great Indian metropolis
frequently visited by cyclones, Khanna had followed
the progress of whirlwinds on his screen on dozens of
occasions. Never yet, however, had he seen the eye
cover itself with this milky veil. After transmitting his
observations, he climbed to the building's terrace. From
up there it was possible to embrace the whole city at a

glance. Holding his old umbrella firmly over his head, Khanna could distinguish through the sheets of rain the metallic latticework of the Howrah Bridge with, just behind it, the rooftops of the City of Joy and, to the left, the imposing pink mass of the railway station, then the brown waters of the river with its hundreds of barges, the green expanse of the Maidan, the long brick façade of the Writers' Building, and finally the entanglement of thousands of terraces and rooftops that formed the gigantic metropolis which All India Radio was slowly wresting from its holiday slumbers.

Fortunately the monster was still far, very far away, over the sea. The wind and rain that had been lashing Calcutta since the previous night were only precursory signals, the prodromes of the cataclysm.

Fisherman Subash Naskar, twenty-six, owed his life to an extraordinary reflex action. Instead of trying to take shelter from the wall of water about to engulf his village, he turned around, plunged into the huge tidal wave, and let himself be carried inland. He would never be fully aware of what really happened, but the next thing he knew he was six miles away, clinging to the window of a temple. All around him lay disaster: he was the only survivor. It was a little after ten in the morning. The monstrous spinning top had just struck the land.

It was sheer hell, a hell of wind, water and fire. It had begun with a blinding light like a colossal ball of fire that streaked across the horizon and lit up the landscape. Caused by the accumulation of electricity up among the clouds, this extremely rare phenomenon scorched the tops of all the trees within an area one hundred and twenty miles wide and thirty deep. Then, siphoning up the relatively shallow sea along the coast, the whirling column impelled the resulting freak wall of water for-

ward. Under the combined effect of the wind and the tidal wave, houses, huts and trees were pulverized, pounded, mangled; fishing boats were sucked up and ejected miles away; buses and railway carriages were picked up and tossed about like bundles of straw; tens of thousands of people and animals were borne away and drowned; thousands of square miles were submerged under a magma of salt water, sand, mud, debris and corpses. In the space of a few seconds, an area as large as Guatemala with a population of three million inhabitants had been expunged from the map.

Caught in midflight by the raging torrent, like thousands of others, Ashish Ghosh and his family owed their safety only to the proximity of a small mosque perched on a hill. 'My wife and children hung on to me,' he was to recount, 'and I managed to drag them all as far as the building. It was already packed with survivors. All the same I was able to clamber onto a window ledge and glue myself to some bars, still clinging to my family. We remained there, suspended above the flood, all through that day and the following night. By the next morning there were only about twenty of us still alive.' At one point Ashish saw in the distance a family of six people, clinging as best they could to a tree trunk, but it was not long before an eddy engulfed the fragile skiff together with all its castaways.

Terror reigned for ten hours before the whirlwind veered away and headed out to sea. Two days later Ashish and his family, and the first escapees, reached the approach to the small town of Canning, thirty miles further inland. Haggard and hungry, clinging to each other for support, they walked like sleepwalkers, without looking right or left. For miles they had struggled through a landscape of devastation and ruin, stumbling everywhere over corpses. The nurse who ran the little local dispensary would never forget the pitiful sight of 'that column of survivors silhouetted against the dark

line of the sky. Even at a distance you could sense their dreadful distress,' she would say. 'Some were carrying small bundles or a few utensils. They were propping up the injured, shuffling along with their children clutched in their arms. All of a sudden I caught the smell of death. Those people had seen their parents, wives and husbands drown before their very eyes. They had seen their children carried away by the floods, their houses collapse, their land disappear.'

For three days Calcutta remained ignorant of the magnitude of the disaster. The whirlwind had destroyed telephone lines, radio transmitters, roads and seaborne transport. Anxious not to find themselves accused of lack of foresight or negligence, the authorities deliberately prolonged this state of ignorance. The first announcements minimized the seriousness of the tragedy. It had been an ordinary tornado, so it was claimed, of the kind that occurred every year anywhere along the Indian coast! And just in case anyone was tempted to take a look for himself, the area was cordoned off by police and border guards.

What a shock it was, therefore, when the first accounts of the escapees began to filter through! The press went wild. It talked of ten or twenty thousand dead, of fifty thousand head of cattle drowned, of two hundred thousand houses razed to the ground, of a million acres rendered barren by seawater, of fifteen hundred miles of dikes demolished or damaged, of three or four thousand wells made for ever unusable. It also revealed that at least two million people were in danger of dying of hunger, thirst and cold because of the lack of an immediate organized relief effort.

All world catastrophes have had their petty disputes and wranglings over relief and aid. But here a desperate poverty made the need for aid more urgent than any-

where else. Yet it took another three days for the Calcutta and New Delhi authorities to agree on the first rescue operations, three days of which certain individuals were quick to take advantage. The people in question wore the ochre robes of monks belonging to the mission of Ramakrishna, the Bengali saint who in the last century preached mutual aid and love between Hindus and other communities. As soon as the cataclysm was announced, they rushed from Madras, Delhi, and even Bombay. The policemen cordoning off the area let them pass: barefoot angels of charity must not be intercepted. Going about in pairs, they mingled with the survivors and offered to take in as many orphans as they could. So much generosity did not fail to touch the hearts. Children abruptly deprived of their parents by the disaster were quickly rounded up. 'Those men were generosity itself,' one thirty-five-year-old widow was to testify. 'One of them said to me, "Whatever you do, don't worry about your little girl. She will be quite safe. We shall find her work and in two months' time we shall bring her back to see you together with her four or five hundred rupees in wages. In the meantime, here are a hundred rupees in advance." I knelt down and kissed the feet of my benefactor and gave him my daughter.' Like so many other victims of the tragedy, that poor woman would never see her child again. She did not know that these purported monks were pimps.

The genuine solidarity of the inhabitants of Calcutta, however, would compensate a thousandfold for such impostors. Max would never forget 'the explosion of generosity' the catastrophe engendered throughout the city, and especially among the poor of the slums. People rushed in thousands to the headquarters of the various health organizations, to the clubs, the mosques, and even to the door of his dispensary, to offer a blanket, clothing, a candle, a small bag of rice, a little oil, some sugar, a bottle of paraffin, some cow dung cakes, or matches. 'A

country capable of so much solidarity is an example to the world,' thought the young American doctor on seeing all those poor people spontaneously giving the little they had to their brothers in misfortune. Dozens of organizations, most of them unknown, were galvanized into action, hiring motorized tricycles, taxis, and even handcarts to convey the first relief to the survivors. Together these organizations formed a prodigious Indian mosaic, representing as they did churches, sects, confraternities, unions, castes, sports teams, schools and factories. Kovalski, Max, Bandona, Saladdin, Aristotle John, Margareta and the whole team of Indian volunteers from the City of Joy's Committee for Mutual Aid were naturally in the front line of this humanitarian mission. Even Gunga, the deaf mute, was there. They had filled up a whole truck with medicines, milk powder, rice, blankets and tents. Their load also included two inflatable rafts and two outboard motors, the personal and combined gifts of the godfather and Arthur Loeb, Max's father. The only thing that prevented them from leaving was a slip of paper: the road permit from the authorities. All week Kovalski and Max dashed from office to office, trying to extract the precious magic document. Contrary to what might have been expected, their status as *sahibs*, far from facilitating proceedings, aroused the suspicion of many officials. Kovalski knew all too well that the bugbear of the CIA was always suspected of lurking behind a foreigner. Despairing of his cause, the Pole decided to resort to a lie. 'We're working with Mother Teresa,' he announced to the man in charge of delivering the permits.

'Mother Teresa?' the *babu* repeated respectfully, drawing himself up behind his ocean of paperwork. 'The Saint of Calcutta?'

Kovalski nodded.

'In that case you and your lorry can leave immediately,' declared the man, initialling the pass with a stroke

of his pen. 'I am a Hindu, but we Indians all respect saints.'

The delta road was a journey to the far reaches of hell. A mere ten miles away from the city, the way was already immersed in a sea of mud. The wreckage of overturned lorries was everywhere. 'It was like looking at a naval cemetery,' Kovalski was to recall. Wearing a turban of a scarlet that contrasted sharply with the lividity of his complexion, the driver manœuvred as if engaged in a slalom competition. He cursed, braked and sweated. With water up to its bonnet, the heavy vehicle was constantly skidding. Soon the first columns of survivors came in sight. 'There were thousands of them, tens of thousands of them,' Max was to write to his fiancée. 'They were up to their chests in water, carrying their children on their heads. Some had taken refuge on ledges where for six days they had been waiting for help. Dying of hunger and thirst, they cried out, throwing themselves into the water and wading towards our lorry. About twenty of them managed to clamber onto it. To make them listen to reason, Kovalski and Saladdin shouted that we were doctors and were carrying only medicines, and by some miracle they let us pass. A little further on another miracle occurred. Among the hordes encircling us, Kovalski recognized a regular customer from the little restaurant he frequented in the City of Joy. He was a militant Communist sent by the party to organize the refugees. He allowed us to continue. Aristotle John and Saladdin walked ahead to guide the lorry. Soon, however, the engine hiccuped, coughed, and stopped once and for all – flooded out.

'We put the rafts in the water and piled our cargo into them. A new night had fallen. There was not a single light for hundreds of square miles around us, but a myriad fireflies lit up a spectral landscape of shredded trees, gutted huts, and bushes draped with detritus carried there by the whirlwind. Here and there, torn down

electric wires had already electrocuted several ferrymen. Suddenly we heard shouting and the roll of drums in the night. Hundreds of escapees who had taken refuge among the ruins of a village perched on a little mound were waiting anxiously in the darkness for help. I shall never forget the triumphal welcome they gave us. Before even showing any interest in what we had brought, Muslim mullahs led us to the little mosque that had survived the catastrophe. In the very midst of disaster, we had first to give thanks to Allah!'

That night, the young doctor was to be particularly struck by one detail as he first set foot on the ground: the bellies of all the children who came running towards him, clapping their hands, singing and dancing. They were huge, protruding, inflated bellies, empty bellies full of worms. As for Kovalski, he was to be seized by the vision of a 'woman holding herself erect among all the wreckage, her baby in her arms. She did not beg or moan but stood as dignified and motionless as a statue, with all the poverty of the world inscribed on her expression. Poised beyond time, or rather at the very heart of time, a time that is an eternity to those in distress, that mother with her child was the Bengal Mother, a symbol of that Christmas of misfortune.'

Poor Kovalski! There he was, the man who thought he had seen everything, shared in everything, and understood everything about the suffering of the innocent, condemned to take a further step towards the heart of the mystery. Why had the God of love, the God of justice allowed these people, who were among the world's most disinherited, to be so cruelly afflicted? How, he asked himself, will the incense of our temples ever be able to efface the smell of the death of all these innocents?

The smell of death! Despite the generous premiums offered in return for the destruction of the corpses, the professional grave-diggers sent by the authorities had fled after only two days. How could Hindus be dis-

tinguished from Muslims in such a charnel house? How could some be burned and others buried without mistakes arising? Teams of convicts from a penitentiary sent to take their place exhibited no more enthusiasm for the task. Soldiers had to be sent in as a last resort. They were duly equipped with flamethrowers. The entire delta was thus transformed into one gigantic barbecue, the stench of which could be smelled as far away as Calcutta.

There remained only the living to be dealt with. For four weeks Kovalski, Max and their Indian companions kept combing several miles of one isolated sector. Going from one group of survivors to the next, they vaccinated them with compressed-air Dermo-jets, treated fifteen thousand sick people, vermifuged twenty thousand children, distributed some twenty-five thousand food rations. It was a drop of water in the ocean of need, the Pole would admit, but a drop of water that would be missed if it were not there, he added, citing Mother Teresa's famous remark. On the morning the committee's team packed its bags to return to the City of Joy, the survivors in the area gave their benefactors a small celebration. People who no longer had anything, poverty-stricken people stripped even of hope itself because the sea had rendered their fields unfertile, managed somehow to dance and sing and express their gratitude and joy. Overwhelmed, Kovalski thought of the words of Tagore: 'Misfortune is great, but man is even greater than misfortune.' As the celebration drew to a close, a little girl dressed in rags, with a water lily in her hair, approached the priest to offer him a gift on behalf of all the villagers. They were Muslims but they had made up a little Crucifix out of shells with the figure of Christ on it. Accompanying the gift, there was a piece of paper on which an uncertain hand had inscribed a message in capital letters. As he read the words aloud, Kovalski thought he could hear the voice of the Gospels.

'Blessings on you, brothers! Brothers, you came to

our aid when we had lost everything, when the light of hope had been extinguished in our hearts. You fed the hungry, clothed the naked, cared for those who were suffering. Thanks to you we have rediscovered our taste for life.

'Brothers, from now on you will be our closest relatives. Your leaving fills us with sadness. We express our eternal gratitude to you and pray God that he will grant you a long life.

                    The survivors of the cyclone'

One morning, some weeks after this catastrophe, the City of Joy and all the other districts of Calcutta seethed with an unaccustomed excitement. Woken with a start by the explosion of firecrackers and the sound of shouting, Max hurried out of his room. Outside he found his neighbours singing, shouting, congratulating one another, dancing and clapping their hands. Children chased one another with shrieks of joy. Exultant in their happiness, people were offering one another sweetmeats and cups of tea. Youngsters were exploding fireworks over the roofs. Since no festival had been forecast for that day, the American could not help wondering what the reason was for this sudden outburst of morning enthusiasm. Then he saw Bandona racing towards him with a garland of flowers in her hands. He had never seen the young Assamese girl so cheerful. Her small almond eyes sparkled with joy. 'These scourged, humiliated, starved, broken people are truly indestructible,' he thought with amazement. 'Their zest for life, their capacity for hope, their will to survive enables them to triumph over all the maledictions of their *karma*.'

'Max, Big Brother, have you heard the news?' the Angel of the City of Joy called out breathlessly. 'We've won! Now we're as strong as the people in your country, as strong as the Russians, the Chinese, the British . . .

We shall be able to irrigate our fields, to harvest our rice several times a year, and to put lighting in our villages and slums. We shall all be able to eat to our heart's content. There will be no more poor people. Our great Durga Indira Gandhi has just made an announcement on the radio: this morning we exploded our first atomic bomb!'

Epilogue

The living conditions of the inhabitants of the City of Joy have improved conspicuously since the events recorded in this book. A young French teacher went one day to visit the slum. On her return to her home city, she talked to her students with so much emotion about what she had seen that they helped her to found an organization whose members would undertake each year to send a sum of money to the Committee of Mutual Aid in the slum. The organization was soon to include three hundred people. An article subsequently appeared in the French magazine *La Vie*, which would multiply the number of members by ten. One year later, a second article again doubled the membership. Donations now provided by some seven thousand members of the organization made it possible to set up in the slum a proper medical-social infrastructure. Dr Sen, a Bengali doctor with a generous heart, who had been treating the poor free of charge for thirty years, was to become the committee's president. Later two young French people, in love with India, went to live out there to bring new strength and impetus to the team. Dispensaries, homes for rickety children, maternity clinics, soup kitchens for the old and the needy, training centres for adolescents, and workshops to teach adults skills were gradually set up by the residents themselves with the help of funds sent out from Europe. Campaigns were launched to detect and vaccinate against tuberculosis. This action extended beyond the walls of the City of Joy: rural development programmes also introduced irrigation, dug wells and set up dispensaries in several impoverished and deprived areas of Bengal. It was naturally to the

handful of Indians who had assembled one evening in Kovalski's room to 'think about the possibility of helping others' that people appealed to create and run all these centres. Today it is Bandona, Saladdin, Ajit, Margareta, Aristotle John, and some two hundred and fifty Indian social workers, nurses and instructors, helped by local doctors and a few foreign volunteers, who form the mainsprings of this network of mutual help, aid, care and education.

For their part, the Bengal government and the Calcutta municipality have not been sparing in their efforts. With the help of funds lent by the World Bank, a vast rehabilitation programme was launched in the slums. The alleyways of the City of Joy were paved over, some of them were raised, new latrines were dug, piped wells were sunk, electric cables were extended. These benefits were to have unforeseen consequences. The fact that rickshaws and taxis could now gain access to the interior of the slum encouraged employees, small business men and traders to seek premises in the City of Joy. Indeed, situated only ten minutes' walk away from the great Howrah Railway Station and so close to the centre of Calcutta, the slum constituted a much more convenient location than the new residential suburbs constructed fifteen to twenty miles out of the city. Rents suddenly shot up, and the number of jewellery-usurers multiplied tenfold in less than two years, a sign of certain economic change. Unscrupulous entrepreneurs became caught up in unbridled speculation. Three- or four-storey apartment buildings began to crop up and many of the poor had to leave.

The first victims of this new situation were the lepers. The change of government in Bengal deprived the godfather of the support he had hitherto enjoyed. A new Mafia installed itself in the City of Joy and it decreed the expulsion of the lepers. They left in small groups, without protest or violence. Kovalski succeeded in re-

housing Anouar, his wife and children, and the majority
of his friends in one of Mother Teresa's homes. To
compensate for the lepers' eviction, the eight thousand
buffalo in the cattle sheds were allowed to remain. They
still form part of the population of the City of Joy.

Three weeks after the cyclone, Ashish and Shanta Ghosh
returned with their children to their devastated village
on the edge of the Sundarban forest. With a courage and
application strengthened by their hard apprenticeship in
the slum, they rebuilt their hut, cleaned up their fields,
and returned to their life as peasants. Their experience
of sharing spurred them into taking an even closer
interest in their neighbours' lot. Shanta started up several
craft workshops for the women of the village while her
husband founded an agricultural cooperative which was
markedly to improve the resources of the people living
in that particularly destitute area.

Sadly, the example of this family was to remain almost
unique. Rare indeed were the occupants of the City of
Joy who have to this day managed to escape their hovels
and return to the countryside. Recent developments
have, however, introduced certain elements of fresh
hope. A distinct decline has been recorded in the number
of poor peasants fleeing to Calcutta, a fact that may be
explained in terms of a marked improvement in the yield
provided by Bengali agriculture. Today, in more than
half the province, two annual rice harvests are produced,
and approximately a quarter of the territory even manages three. This transformation has enabled hundreds of
thousands of landless peasants to find work where they
live nearly all the year round. Furthermore, whereas
twenty years ago Calcutta represented the only hope
of finding work in the whole of northeast India, the
establishment of new industrial centres in Orissa, Bihar
and other provinces in that area has created new labour

sites that have considerably reduced emigration to Calcutta. Thus, provided there are no further major catastrophes, it is possible to hope for a stabilization of the population of Calcutta, and perhaps even for the beginning of a future reflux of the slum dwellers to the countryside of their origin.

Max Loeb went back to America. Speaking of his experiences, he declared that except perhaps for a trip to the moon, a stay in an Indian slum was the most extraordinary adventure a man of the end of the late twentieth century could live through. Other young doctors, male and female, have continued to come from all over the world to give several months of their lives to the residents of the City of Joy. As for Max, his stay has transformed his perception of life and his relationships with others. He continues to keep in close contact with Kovalski. Together with Sylvia, now his wife, he has founded an organization to send medicines and medical equipment to the Committee for Mutual Aid. Above all, however, Max returns regularly to visit his friends in Anand Nagar. Again and again he likes to say, 'The smiles of my brothers in the City of Joy are lights that will never be extinguished in me.'

One day, Aloka, Hasari Pal's widow, brought Stephan Kovalski a brown envelope covered with official stamps.

'Big Brother Stephan, a registered letter arrived for you this morning,' she announced.

Kovalski saw instantly that it came from the Home Ministry. With a pounding heart, he opened it. 'Dear God,' he shuddered, 'I'll bet the government is kicking me out.' Anxiously he scanned the type, until suddenly his eyes fell on words that he had to reread several times before he grasped their meaning. 'The Government of

India hereby grants the said Stephan Kovalski the certificate of . . .' The letter went on to declare that after
he had pledged his loyalty at the time appointed and
according to the regulations prescribed by the law, he
would be entitled to all the privileges, prerogatives and
rights and would be subject to all the obligations, duties
and responsibilities of an Indian citizen.

'An Indian citizen,' stammered the Pole. To him it
was as if all at once the heart of the slum were beating
in his chest. Seized with vertigo, he leaned against the
pillar of the veranda and closed his eyes. When he opened
them again, he took hold of the cross he wore around
his neck and gazed at the two dates his mother had
had inscribed upon it, that of his birth and that of his
ordination. His vision dimmed by tears of happiness, he
considered then the little blank space in front of the
Indian name he had had engraved several years previously. This was the name that, on the day of his
citizenship, would replace that of Stephan Kovalski. In
Hindi, as in Bengali, 'Premanand' meant 'Blessed is he
who is loved by God'. It summed up perfectly the
meaning of his relationship with the humble, the poor,
and the broken individuals that were the people of the
City of Joy. Next to the patronym which henceforth
would be his, he would this very day add the date of his
final entry into that great family of his Indian brothers,
for this was the third most important day in his life.

Acknowledgements

First and foremost, I would like to express my
enormous gratitude to my wife, Dominique. She shared
every moment of my extensive research in the City of
Joy and she was my irreplaceable collaborator in the
preparation of this book.

I would also like to acknowledge my great thanks to
Colette Modiano, Paul and Manuela Andreota, and
Gérard Beckers, who spent many hours correcting my
manuscript and helping me with their encouragement
and their extensive knowledge of India.

I also want to thank my friends in India, who with
such generosity facilitated my research and made my
numerous stays in India so enjoyable and fruitful. It
would take several pages to name them all individually,
but I would like to mention in particular Amit, Ajit and
Meeta Banerjee and Mehboub Ali, Pierre Ceyrac,
Tapan Chatterjee, Ravi Dubey, Behram Dumasia,
Pierre Fallon, Christine Fernandès, Georges and
Annette Frémont, Gaston Grandjean, Adi Katgara,
Ashwini and Renu Kumar, François Laborde, Anouar
Malik, Harish Malik, Sunil Mukherjee, Aman Nath,
Jean Neveu, Camellia Panjabi, Nalini Purohit, Emma-
nuel and Marie-Dominique Romatet, James and Lallita
Stevens, Baby Thadani, Amrita and Malti Varma, and
Francis Wacziarg.

A book that was especially informative about the past
of Calcutta was *Calcutta* by Geoffrey Moorhouse.

I also wish to acknowledge my gratitude to those
who sustained me with their encouragement and their
affection during the long and difficult task of
researching and writing this book, in particular, my

daughter Alexandra, Jacques Acher, Gilbert and Annette Etienne, Jean and David Frydman, Louis and Alice Grandjean, Jacques and Jeannine Lafont, Adélaïde Oréfice, Marie-Jeanne Montant and Tania Sciama.

Without the enthusiasm and faith of my friend and literary agent, Morton Janklow, and of my publishers, I would never have been able to write this book. My warmest gratitude goes to Robert Laffont and his assistants in Paris; Tom Guinzburg, Henry Reath, Sam Vaughan, Kate Medina, and Larry Kirshbaum and their associates in New York; Mario Lacruz in Barcelona; Giancarlo Bonacina and Carlo Sartori in Milan; Peter Gutmann in Munich; Antoine Akveld in Amsterdam; Anthony Cheetham, Mark Booth, Susan Lamb and Louise Weir in London; Harkin Chatlani and Melroy Dickson in Bombay; and, finally, to my friend, collaborator, and translator Kathryn Spink, herself the author of many remarkable books, one of which on Mother Teresa is entitled *The Miracle of Love*.

Finally, I would like to express my gratitude to all the friends in India who gave me so much of their time as I collected the material for this book, but who wish to remain anonymous.

Afterword

My love story with
the City of Joy

That very first monsoon morning when I walked into
it, I knew that this wretched inhuman slum of Calcutta
called the City of Joy was one of the most extraordinary
places on our planet. When I left it two years later with
some twenty pads full of notes and hundreds of hours of
tape, I knew I had the material for the greatest book of
my career, an epic of heroism, love, and faith; a
glorious tribute to man's capacity to beat adversity and
survive every possible tragedy. During this long,
difficult, and sometimes painful research, I had to share
all sorts of situations. I learned how people could live
with rats, scorpions, and insects, survive on a few
spoons of rice and one or two bananas a day, queue up
for hours for the latrines, wash with less than a pint of
water, light a match in the monsoon, or share their
living quarters with a group of eunuchs. Before being
adopted by the inhabitants of the slum, I had to learn
their customs, experience their fears and plights, share
their struggles and hopes. This certainly was one of the
most extraordinary experiences for a writer. It changed
my life. Living with the heroic inhabitants of the City of
Joy completely transformed my sense of priorities and
my assessment of the true values of life. After this
confrontation with the real issues of existence – hunger,
disease, total absence of medical facilities, lack of work,
etc. – I no longer fight for things like a parking space
when I return to Europe or America. Sharing for all

these months the lives of a population who might have as little as the equivalent of twenty-five US cents per day to survive on also taught me the real value of things. Now I instinctively turn the electricity off when I leave a room, use my bar of soap to the very end, avoid throwing into the garbage can what can be saved or used again. These unique experiences also taught me the beauty of sharing with others. For two years nothing was asked of me but always given. The generosity of my friends in the City of Joy showed me the true meaning of the beautiful Indian proverb that says 'All that is not given is lost.'

It took me one full year to write the epic of the City of Joy. I wrote the book in my home in the South of France, in the beautiful and privileged privacy of Provence's pine woods and vineyards. To remind me constantly of the anthill of Calcutta, its noises, its smells, its colors, every day before I began writing I first looked at a few of the two thousand photographs I had taken and ran some of the tapes of the local life I had recorded.

The final version of *The City of Joy* was first published in France, then in Spain, Italy, Holland, Germany, England, and the United States of America. Everywhere the success was immediate, enormous, and for me totally unexpected in its dimensions. The book has now sold more than six million copies in thirty-one languages and editions, including five editions in Braille.

Although I was convinced I had written a most inspiring epic, I was really surprised that this story of a Calcutta slum would shoot up so fast to the top of all bestseller lists. But even more surprising was the mail that began to pour into my Paris apartment. Thousands of readers began to send me letters from all over the world. Every one of these letters was a homage of

gratitude for having written *The City of Joy*. Many of them really touched me to the bottom of my heart and even drew tears from my wife and I (see excerpts of some of these letters further). In almost each of the envelopes was a check, sometimes a small package with a piece of jewelry, a gold ingot, or a stack of stock exchange shares. One letter contained a small anonymous message saying: 'The book *The City of Joy* is so beautiful that we are happy to send the enclosed items. Please sell them. They will be more useful in the City of Joy than around our fingers.' Taped to the sheet of paper were two wedding rings.

One day, as I was leaving my Paris apartment to rush to Charles de Gaulle airport to fly to New York, the door bell rang. Behind the door was an old lady with a travel bag. 'I have just arrived by train from Toulouse,' she said. 'I have come here to write my will in favor of your heroes of the City of Joy.' The story of these heroes has touched so many hearts that school kids have organized collections in their classes, or produced plays and shows on their behalf. Hundreds of readers have offered to adopt a child from the City of Joy, or to devote their next vacation to going there to help.

On my side, I have offered half of all my royalties to the heroes of my book or to humanitarian institutions struggling in Calcutta and its vicinity to improve the life of the poorest of the poor. Since the book was first published in 1985, almost two million dollars have been sent from my royalties and from donations of readers to create, support, and develop a whole series of top priority projects. These projects include refuge centers for leper and polio children, dispensaries, schools, rehabilitation workshops, education programs, sanitary actions, etc. (See list in APPENDIX I). To process and channel the funds, I have founded an association called 'ACTION AID FOR LEPERS' CHILDREN OF

CALCUTTA' which now has several thousand members.

I am fanatically concerned that every cent given from my royalties or received from readers goes directly to the destitutes who need help. Those who assist my wife (who is also named Dominique) and I are all volunteers. Among them are her five sisters, a couple of ladies from our local parish, and a retired general manager. We are using one room of our Paris apartment as our association headquarters and we personally pay for the electricity and telephone. We have no overheads.

I have organized our fund transfers to India in such a way as to make sure every dollar we send is going to the right person for the right purpose. This is very important and sometimes quite difficult to achieve. But because we are a small organization – and we want to remain small for obvious reasons – we can trace every one of our payments to a precise action in the field. If we have succeeded so well in meeting this objective, we largely owe it to the exceptional people working in the local Indian institutions that we support. All of them are true unknown Mother Teresas. They are the most humble, dedicated, and efficient apostles of love and solidarity I have ever met. May I pay tribute to Agnes, Ali, François, Gaston, James, Kamruddin, Sabitri, Sunil, Wohab and all their associates. They are the arms, the legs and the spirit of our modest action on the battlefront against poverty.

Among the many other projects that I hope the royalties of *The City of Joy* and the donations of new readers will be able to finance in the future, one is particularly dear to my heart. This project concerns an irrigation program affecting nineteen villages in Bengal where more than one hundred thousand people live. Thanks to this effort they will become two meals a day people. Their land, which gives one harvest or, in the

case of drought, no harvest at all, will yield two and even three crops. This is attacking poverty at its roots. People will no longer have to leave their parched fields in case of a climatic catastrophe to pile up in slums like the City of Joy. And perhaps one day, if projects of this sort multiply, the inhabitants of the City of Joy will be able to leave their inferno to return to the beauty of their countryside. I promise that the donations received, as well as my royalties, will continue working relentlessly toward meeting that wonderful goal.

One afternoon in December 1987, the mayor of the city of Calcutta, Mr. K. K. Basu, and his whole Municipal Council, offered my wife and I a splendid reception at the City Hall to express Calcutta's gratitude for 'the way I had told the world about the virtues of courage, vitality, and hope of its population.' On this occasion we were made citizens of honor of the metropolis and we were decorated with its gold medal of honor.

But the most surprising and significant award I was to receive on that memorable day was an impressive document which showed the impact my book had had on the administrators of the city. The development project of the Municipal Corporation was called 'Calcutta – "City of Joy": Designs for Tomorrow.' Among the very first actions that this document outlined to change living conditions in the city and make it a real 'City of Joy' was the daily distribution to the three million residents of the slums of ten litres of drinking water.

The City of Joy becomes a film

Late in 1985, the great British director Roland Joffé and
the Canadian producer Jake Eberts came to see me in
Paris to express their interest in bringing my book to the
screen. Joffé had directed two of my favorite films, *The
Killing Fields* and *Mission*, and Eberts had been involved
in the production of *Gandhi*, a magnificent cinematic
tribute to the father of modern India, partly inspired by
Freedom at Midnight, the book I had co-authored with
Larry Collins about the struggle of India for its
independence. Joffé was exactly the man to give an epic
dimension to the story I had put together with words.
He assigned the writing of the script to Mark Medoff,
the brilliant and compassionate author of *Children of a
Lesser God*.

One evening in October 1989, as I was lying in a
hospital bed in Toulouse recovering from an operation
which was to cure me of cancer, I received a phone call
from Calcutta. Joffé wanted to know if I would be upset
if they changed Kovalski, the Polish priest in the book,
into a woman, in order to avoid an all male cast. I
agreed instantly. For me what counted was that the film
would translate the spirit of the book to the screen, not
the sex of its characters!

The shooting of *The City of Joy* began on February 9,
1991, exactly where the story takes place, that is, in the
heart of the Calcutta anthill. Patrick Swayze, the
American star of *Dirty Dancing* and *Ghost* is the
American doctor Max Loeb of the book. Two of India's
greatest actors, Om Puri and Shabana Azmi, personify
Hasari Pal, the rickshaw-puller, and his wife, Aloka. A
two million dollar replica of the slum was built to serve
as a movie set near Calcutta's harbor.

But many scenes were shot in the streets, causing
some inconveniences to the population, soon to be
exploited by a handful of politicians and professional

agitators more eager to have their names printed in the newspapers than to improve their fellow citizens' living conditions. Copies of the script found their way to scandal magazines which hastened to publish the scenes involving lepers or Mafia activities to fuel a controversy that India was being exploited by Hollywood.

Filming was interrupted on several occasions and makeshift bombs thrown on the set. Printed film reels were held up for days in the torrid and humid warehouses of Indian Customs. Co-producer Iain Smith had to appear in Court every other day for some reason or other. But Joffé, his actors, and his crew proved stronger than all adversities. Inspired themselves by the virtues of courage and resilience of the characters they were portraying, they managed to overcome all obstacles. Their film is a triumphant and unforgettable homage to the human spirit. For me, it is a memorable and superb translation on screen of the epic of hope and faith I once set out to write on paper.

In March 1991, as Roland Joffé was filming *The City of Joy* in Calcutta, I was invited with my wife to a small ceremony in the slum where it all began, organized by a group of its residents. As we walked into the area, I was surprised to discover a huge banner hanging across one of its main alleys. 'DOMINIQUE LAPIERRE – WELCOME HOME – THE CITY OF JOY', it said. From the waiting crowd ran a young girl with a bouquet of flowers. I recognized my old friend Padmini, the heroic little Bengali girl who used to get up every morning at four to go to the railway embankment to pick up burning pieces of coal fallen from the locomotives. A miserable treasure, the sale of which helped her family survive day after day. Padmini was beaming. 'Take these flowers, Dominique *dada* (Big Brother),' she said. 'Because, thanks to you, we are no longer alone in our City of Joy.'

BEYOND LOVE

A new epic on the anonymous heroes of this world

My experiences in the City of Joy certainly changed my perspectives as a writer. I learned there that the heroes of my future books would never be Saddam Hussein, Noriega nor the underworld ganglords. My future heroes would be those who, like Kovalski, Hasari Pal, Max Loeb or Mother Teresa, prove every day that if 'adversity is big,' as the Indian poet Tagore once wrote, 'man can be bigger than adversity.'

One day in late 1985, as I was visiting New York City, I read in a newspaper that Mother Teresa had arrived in the heart of Manhattan with a group of her Indian sisters to open a home for destitute patients suffering from a new plague that the Western world was apparently not prepared to confront. This plague was AIDS. For me, who had seen Mother Teresa and her sisters fighting in Calcutta's dying homes and leper colonies to alleviate the sufferings of the slum destitutes, this piece of news was a real surprise. It was as if the miserable Third World was coming to the rescue of the affluent West. I took a taxi and rushed to the address of this home in Greenwich Village. Mother Teresa had called it 'The Gift of Love.'

The first thing I saw hanging on a wall of the hall was a poster on which Mother Teresa had inscribed a few lines summing up her philosophy on life. Those lines said:

> *Life is an opportunity, benefit from it.*
> *Life is a beauty, admire it.*
> *Life is bliss, taste it.*
> *Life is a dream, realize it.*
> *Life is a challenge, meet it.*

Life is a duty, complete it.
Life is a game, play it.
Life is costly, care for it.
Life is wealth, keep it.
Life is love, enjoy it.
Life is mystery, know it.
Life is a promise, fulfill it.
Life is sorrow, overcome it.
Life is a song, sing it.
Life is a struggle, accept it.
Life is a tragedy, confront it.
Life is an adventure, dare it.
Life is luck, make it.
Life is too precious, do not destroy it.
Life is life, fight for it!

MOTHER TERESA

In 'The Gift of Love' I was soon to meet some remarkable people. One was sister Ananda, a young Indian woman who had been a leper herself in Benares where her father was burning the dead on the banks of the Ganges river. Another was a young American doctor confronted with the tragic effects of a disease he was incapable of curing. Another was a young patient who had been an archeologist in Israel. These three people and their dramatic ordeal propelled me on the road to a three-year investigation through the research laboratories and hospitals of America and Europe to reconstruct in minute details the adventure of the most fantastic scientific and medical challenge of the end of this millennium.

My new book *Beyond Love* is the epic story of the doctors and scientists, sisters and patients, heroes and dreamers fighting the greatest plague of our time. It is the story of people from all over the world whose courage, dedication, and heroism is beyond ordinary human love.

Beyond Love was first published in France, Italy, and Spain where it sold more than one million copies and became an instant Number One bestseller. But more important, it triggered a new avalanche of mail to my Paris flat. (Excerpts of letters in APPENDIX I.) For this book told of a new epic of courage, a new epic of man's capacity to be bigger than adversity. Like *The City of Joy*, *Beyond Love* is now published in some thirty languages and editions and will soon be made into a major motion picture directed by Arthur Penn, the prestigious American director of such classics as *Bonnie and Clyde* and *Little Big Man*.

As a result of this book, I am frequently invited by colleges, schools, charitable institutions, and support organizations to give lectures about my experiences researching *Beyond Love* and the message of this new work. My only condition for attending these functions is that all profits derived from the sales of tickets or donations be equally divided between a local organization supporting AIDS patients and my leper children in Calcutta. During 1990 and 1991, I have given over thirty lectures in Europe, India, and North America.

DOMINIQUE LAPIERRE

Appendix I

WORK CARRIED OUT FOR THE DISINHERITED OF CALCUTTA WITH THE ROYALTIES OF *THE CITY OF JOY* AND DONATIONS FROM READERS

1. The complete and continuous support of 200 leper children living in the *Udayan* 'Resurrection' home; the construction of a 4th unit to take in 50 more children; the purchase of a plot of land to extend the farming development intended to make the home more self-supporting from the point of view of food.

2. The complete and continuous support of 125 physically handicapped youngsters from the Mohitnagar and Maria Basti homes.

3. The construction and fitting out of the Backwabari home for children with motor-neurone disease, suffering from extremely severe handicaps.

4. The expansion and equipping of the Ekprantanagar home, in a poverty-stricken Calcutta slum, which provides shelter for 140 children of seasonal workers who labour in the brick furnaces. The provision of drinking water on tap has visibly transformed the living conditions in this home.

5. Equipping a school close to this home to educate, in addition to the 140 boarders, 350 very poor children from the neighbouring slum.

6. The reconstruction of 100 huts for families who lost everything in November 1988 when a cyclone hit the Ganges delta.

7. The creation of two medical units in villages of the Ganges Delta making possible not only medical care and treatment of tuberculosis, but also preventive measures, detection and education (eye camps to perform cataract operations, wide-scale vaccination, family planning campaigns).

8. The total maintenance of the Bhangar dispensary (nearly 100,000 consultations a year). The installation of radiology equipment in the main dispensary and the creation of a mobile unit for radiological detection, vaccinations, care and nutritional aid.

9. The provision of drinking water and latrines in several villages in the Ganges Delta.

10. The creation and total support of a school and two medical centres in two particulary disinherited slums in Calcutta's great suburban area.

11. The construction and total maintenance of a home in Palsunda for abandoned children between the ages 6 and 9.

12. The gift of 10 water pumps running on solar energy to ten very poor villages in the States of Bihar, Haryana, Rajasthan and Orissa, to enable the residents to produce their food even in the height of the dry season.

13. The running of a rehabilitation workshop for lepers in Orissa.

14. The sending of medicines and the provision of 70,000 high protein meals for the leper children at the *Udayan* 'Resurrection' home.

15. Various works undertaken for the disinherited and the lepers in the State of Mysore, for abandoned children in Bombay, along with the residents of a village in Guinea (Africa), and seriously ill abandoned children in a hospital in Lublin (Poland).

All these tasks are long term undertakings which must be maintained at all costs. This depends on us all. I would be grateful if the readers of this book would spread the word in order that together we may continue to keep the flame of life, love, and sharing in these islands of light and hope burning.

HOW YOU CAN HELP US

– By sending a donation to our association 'Action Aid for Lepers' Children of Calcutta' 26, avenue Kléber, 75116 Paris, France.

If you can, please avoid sending any check below 20 dollars, because bank charges on checks below this amount are unreasonable. We acknowledge all the donations with an official receipt. Please allow four or five weeks to receive this receipt.

– We also now have a representative in the USA: Marie Allizon – 7419 Lisle Avenue, Falls Church, VA 22043.

– You can help us enormously by photostating this message and sending it to all your friends and relatives. Little streams make big rivers and every drop is vital. And please share with those around you this beautiful Indian proverb which is the motto of our action:

'All That is Not Given is Lost.'

ABOUT VOLUNTEERS WHO WANT TO HELP IN CALCUTTA AND ABOUT ADOPTIONS

Many readers of *The City of Joy* have offered to go to Calcutta to help. This is most generous but I am afraid not very realistic. Firstly because Indian authorities only give a three-month tourist visa to foreign visitors. This is much too short a period for anyone to achieve anything really useful. Secondly because only very specialized help could really be useful. Unless you are a doctor or an experienced paramedic in the fields of leprosy, tropical diseases, malnutrition, bone tuberculosis, polio, or rehabilitation of the physically handicapped, I think your generous will to help could be more of a burden for the locals in charge than anything else. Moreover, you have to realize that living and working conditions on our various projects located outside of Calcutta are extremely hard for unaccustomed foreigners.

As for adoptions, they are usually very difficult. I suggest you contact Mother Teresa directly.

Many readers wish to know the address of Mother Teresa and James Stevens. Here they are:

Mother Teresa: MISSIONARIES OF CHARITY
54/A, A.J.C. Road, Calcutta 700 016, India

Rev. James Stevens: UDAYAN
Post Box n° 10264, Calcutta 700 019, India

WHAT THE PRESS SAID ABOUT
THE CITY OF JOY

– '*The City of Joy* will make any one a little richer for having read it.'

Washington Post

– 'This book is imprinted on my mind forever.'

New York Times

– 'Let's not hesitate to shout it: this book is a masterpiece.'

Le Monde (Paris)

– 'More than a book, a story of love.'

La Stampa (Rome)

– 'A fantastic lesson in hope.'

ABC (Madrid)

– 'An epic in fraternity and courage.'

The Times (London)

– 'When you close this book, you are no longer quite the same: your heart is burning with love.'

Die Welt (Hamburg)

WHAT THE READERS OF *THE CITY OF JOY* WROTE TO THE AUTHOR

– '*The City of Joy* is an inspiration to the world.'

Pope John Paul II

– 'I was given *The City of Joy* for Christmas. It is one of the greatest books I have ever read. I couldn't put it down. Reading it so moved me that I had a feeling of: I must do something!.. I thought you might like to know that your great gift of telling the story of *The City of Joy* will spread ripples that will bring benefits to the lives of others.'

Karen Eberhardt, Sebastopol, California

– 'Thank you for the most important book I have ever read.'

Eleanor Northrop, St. Paul, MN, USA

– 'This marvellous book has changed my life. I have decided to give up smoking and devote the money thereby saved to more useful causes.'

Rina Anoussi, travel agent, New York City

– 'I am a young invalid in a wheelchair. I want to thank Dominique Lapierre for this book of courage and hope which changed my life.'

Bernard Kieken, Grenoble, France

– '*The City of Joy* has been a sort of detonator which has revealed me in full light the victory of love over evil and suffering.'

Corinne Simonetta, lawyer, Paris, France

– '*City of Joy* is deeply moving – an extraordinary monument to the human spirit. I am most grateful for the actual gift of the book so well as the author's gift of the spirit.'

Bettie Noyce, Berkeley, California

– 'Thank you for writing *The City of Joy* and allowing one, in a small way, to share in an unforgettable experience.'

Sarah Vanderburch, Seattle, Washington

– '*The City of Joy* is truly inspiring and very uplifting.'

Jenny Popatia, Houston, Texas

– 'I was deeply moved and enlightened by your book *City of Joy.*'

Edward Stermer, Iowa City

– 'Thank you for your most beautiful gift to the world – *City of Joy.*'

Marilyn Zinner, San Francisco, California

THE CHRISTOPHER AWARD

Among other distinctions, *The City of Joy* received in 1986 the Christopher Award. This very prestigious American distinction honors each year a book that illustrates the Christopher philosophy:

'It is better to light a candle than curse the darkness.'

Appendix II

WHAT THE PRESS SAID ABOUT *BEYOND LOVE*

– 'A gripping adventure story that succeeds by its skillful manipulation of plot, suspense and character.'
The International Herald Tribune

– 'A remarkable testimony of human solidarity.'
The Independent on Sunday (London)

– 'A grandiose book with a rightful apocalyptic pitch.'
New York Times

– 'Tragic, moving and courageous it is; depressing it is not, despite the subject matter. This is the story of people who refuse to let the disease defeat them, who refuse to judge, to condemn. This is the only book to read about AIDS.'

The Times (London)

– 'The engrossing account of the fantastic battle against AIDS.'

New York Daily News

– 'A breathtaking book writtten with beating drums.'
Le Figaro (Paris)

– 'A book of epic proportions.'

Gay Times (London)

– 'An epic poem. A hallucinating voyage full of hope and faith.' .

Corriere della Sera (Milan)

– 'Brilliantly told.'

The Mail on Sunday (London)

– 'A fantastic gallery of portraits of the knights of today's medical research.'

El Pais (Madrid)

– 'An extraordinary book.'

Paris Match (Paris)

WHAT THE READERS OF *BEYOND LOVE* WROTE TO THE AUTHOR

– '*Beyond Love* is a remarkable testimony of human solidarity'

Pope John Paul II

– 'This book is a very rare work of scientific discipline and sensibility.'

André Lwoff, winner of the Nobel Prize in Medicine

– '*Beyond Love* beautifully captures the soul of the scientists'

Dr Samuel Broder, Director of the US National Cancer Institute

– 'There are not enough superlatives to say how much this book has submerged me with interest'

Eloïse Thérèse, Mount St-Mary's College, Los Angeles

– '*Beyond Love* may have changed my life. I am twenty years old and I wanted to go into computer science. This book helped me discover a universe I was not familiar with: the universe of medical researchers. My goal is now to go into medical research. Thank you.'

Sandra Chanderlot, Faculty of Sciences, Paris

– '*Beyond Love* is a superb hymn to fraternity, a modern allegoric epic where the knights of science and the barefooted parias are galloping side by side, a breathtaking fresco, a crusade of love and faith, a police thriller whose crime is a plague. Please be thanked for this great book.'

                              Jean Neveu, Kampala, Ouganda

– '*Beyond Love* is a magnificent lesson of faith in man, the proof that love can overcome absurdity.'

                              Bernadette Moro, Madrid, Spain

Dominique Lapierre is also the co-author, with Larry Collins, of classic world bestsellers such as *Is Paris Burning?* (which was made into a major motion picture in 1966), ... *Or I'll Dress You in Mourning, O Jerusalem, Freedom at Midnight, The Fifth Horseman.*

QUEENS GATE SCHOOL
133 QUEENS GATE
LONDON SW7 5LE
TEL 071-589 3587

QUEENS GATE SC
133 QUEENS GATE
LONDON SW7 5LE
TEL 071-589 358

Contents

Half of the royalties on this book are donated to the people
of the City of Joy

The author and his wife have founded *Action Aid for Lepers'
Children of Calcutta*, whose headquaters are at 26, avenue
Kléber, 75116 Paris, France. Donations received by the
association, which has over 5,000 members throughout Europe
and the United States, go towards supporting a home for
250 children of Lepers in Calcutta.

First published by Arrow 1986

9 10

© Dominique Lapierre 1985
English translation © Pressinter, SA 1985

Afterword copyright © 1991 by Pressinter, SA

This book is sold subject to the condition that it shall not,
by way of trade or otherwise, be lent, resold, hired out,
or otherwise circulated without the publisher's prior consent
in any form of binding or cover other than that in which it is
published and without a similar condition including this
condition being imposed on the subsequent purchaser

Originally published in French as *La Cité de la Joie* by
Editions Robert Laffont.

First published in Great Britain by Century 1986

This Arrow edition 1992

Arrow Books Limited
Random House, 20 Vauxhall Bridge Road, London SW1V 2SA

Random House Australia (Pty) Limited
16 Dalmore Drive, Scoresby, Victoria 3179, Australia

Random House New Zealand Limited
18 Poland Road, Glenfield
Auckland 10, New Zealand

Random House South Africa (Pty) Limited
PO Box 2263, Rosebank 2121, South Africa

RANDOM HOUSE UK Limited Reg. No. 954009

A CIP catalogue record for this book
is available from the British Library

Papers used by Random House UK Limited
are natural, recyclable products made from wood grown in
sustainable forests. The manufacturing processes conform to
the environmental regulations of the country of origin

ISBN 0 09 914091 8

Printed and bound in Norway by
AIT Trondheim AS

DOMINIQUE LAPIERRE

The City of Joy

Translated from the French
by Kathryn Spink

All that is not given is lost
Indian proverb

QUEENS GATE SCHOOL
133 QUEENS GATE
LONDON SW7 5LE
TEL 071-589 3587

ARROW

To Tâtou, Gaston,
Pierre, François, James,
and to 'the lights of the world'
of the City of Joy

ersten Jahren nach unserer Geburt – im Handumdrehen werden wir vom Baby zum Erwachsenen. Danach sehen wir, zumindest äußerlich, für den Rest unserer Tage mehr oder minder gleich aus, werden durch das Zutun unserer Gene und der Schwerkraft einfach schlaffere und weniger ansehnlichere Versionen unseres jüngeren Selbst.

Und was das Emotionale und Intellektuelle betrifft … Da muss ich einfach darauf vertrauen, dass der langsame Verfall unserer äußeren Verpackung durch den einen oder anderen Pluspunkt aufgewogen wird. Was sich hier in Pandora nur bestätigt. Auf dem Weg in den Flur muss ich über den Alex lachen, der ich damals war, im Gegensatz zu dem, der ich heute bin. Und winde mich zugleich innerlich bei dem Gedanken an mein früheres Ich – dreizehn Jahre alt und, wie ich rückblickend sagen muss, ein egozentrischer und nervtötender Wichtigtuer, wie er im Buche steht.

Ich öffne die Tür zur »Besenkammer«, wie ich das Zimmer damals in dem langen, heißen Sommer liebevoll nannte, als ich es bewohnte. Im Licht der Deckenlampe ist es tatsächlich so klein, wie ich es in Erinnerung habe – wenn überhaupt, kommt es mir jetzt noch kleiner vor. Ich trete in meiner vollen Größe von eins fünfundachtzig hinein und frage mich, ob ich, wenn ich jetzt die Tür schließen und mich hinlegen würde, meine Füße zum winzigen Fenster hinausstrecken müsste wie Alice in ihrem Wunderland.

Ich blicke an den Regalen zu beiden Seiten dieses Schlauchs empor. Die vielen Bücher, die ich in langen Stunden alphabetisch geordnet habe, stehen immer noch dort. Aus einem Impuls heraus nehme ich eines zur Hand – einen Band von Rudyard Kipling – und blättere zu dem berühmten Gedicht »Wenn«, die klugen Worte eines Vaters an seinen Sohn. Beim

Lesen steigen mir Tränen in die Augen, wenn ich an den Dreizehnjährigen denke, der ich damals war: ein Junge auf der verzweifelten Suche nach einem Vater. Und als ich ihn dann fand, begriff ich, dass ich bereits einen hatte.

Ich stelle Kipling wieder an seinen Platz, und mein Blick fällt auf das kleine Buch, das daneben steht. Das Tagebuch, das meine Mutter mir zu Weihnachten, ein paar Monate vor meinem ersten Besuch in Pandora, geschenkt hatte. Sieben Monate lang hatte ich es jeden Tag gewissenhaft geführt – in einem, so wie ich mich selbst kenne, zweifellos ziemlich aufgeblasenen Ton. Wie alle Teenager hielt ich meine Überlegungen und Gefühle für einzigartig und bahnbrechend, meine Gedanken für derart überragend, dass kein Mensch sie vor mir gedacht haben konnte.

Traurig schüttele ich den Kopf und seufze wie ein alter Mann über meine Naivität. Als wir nach jenem langen Sommer in Pandora nach England zurückgefahren waren, hatte ich das Tagebuch hiergelassen. Und jetzt, zehn Jahre später, liegt es in meinen mittlerweile großen Männerhänden. Eine Erinnerung an meine letzten Monate als Kind, bevor das Leben mich zwang, mich in der Welt der Erwachsenen einzurichten.

Mit dem Tagebuch in der Hand gehe ich nach oben. Dort, auf dem dämmrigen, stickigen Flur, bin ich mir unschlüssig, in welchem Zimmer ich mich während meines Aufenthalts hier heimisch fühlen möchte. Ich hole tief Luft und gehe den Flur entlang zu *ihrem* Zimmer, nehme allen Mut zusammen und öffne die Tür. Vielleicht bilde ich es mir nur ein – und nach zehn Jahren Abwesenheit muss es wohl Einbildung sein –, aber ich bin überzeugt, den Duft des Parfüms zu erschnuppern, das sie damals trug …

Mit Nachdruck ziehe ich die Tür ins Schloss. Noch fühle ich

mich nicht in der Lage, die Büchse der Pandora zu öffnen mit all den Erinnerungen, die aus jedem Zimmer entweichen würden. Da gehe ich lieber nach unten. Draußen herrscht mittlerweile finstere Nacht. Ich schaue auf die Uhr und rechne die zwei Stunden Zeitunterschied dazu: Es muss kurz vor neun sein, und mir knurrt der Magen vor Hunger.

Ich lade den Wagen aus, verstaue die Lebensmittel, die ich im Dorfladen gekauft habe, in der Speisekammer und gehe mit etwas Brot, Feta und einem sehr warmen Bier auf die Terrasse. Dort sitze ich dann in der Stille, die nur hin und wieder vom schläfrigen Zirpen einer Zikade unterbrochen wird, trinke mein Bier und frage mich, ob es wirklich eine gute Idee war, zwei Tage vor den anderen herzukommen. Schließlich bin ich ein Meister der Nabelschau und betreibe die Kunst derart überzeugend, dass mir kürzlich angeboten wurde, mich darin professionell zu betätigen. Zumindest dieser Gedanke bringt mich zum Lachen.

Um mich abzulenken, schlage ich mein Tagebuch auf und lese die Widmung auf der Innenseite.

Für meinen Schatz Alex – Frohe Weihnachten! Versuch, es regelmäßig zu führen. Es könnte interessant zu lesen sein, wenn du älter bist. Alles Liebe, Mum.

»Tja, Mum, hoffen wir mal, dass du recht hast.« Ich lächle matt und blättere durch die Seiten hochtrabender Prosa, bis ich zu Anfang Juli komme. Und im Licht der einen funzeligen Birne, die in der Pergola über mir hängt, beginne ich zu lesen.

Juli 2006

Ankunft

Alex' Tagebuch

10. Juli 2006

Mein Gesicht ist vollkommen rund. Man könnte es mit einem Zirkel ziehen, und ich wette, dass die Kreislinie nur an sehr wenigen Stellen von den Konturen meines Gesichts abweichen würde. Ich kann es nicht leiden.

Im Inneren dieses Kreises habe ich zwei Apfelbäckchen. Als ich kleiner war, haben die Erwachsenen immer daran herumgezupft. Sie nahmen die Haut zwischen die Finger und zwickten mich. Kein Gedanke daran, dass meine Wangen keine Äpfel sind. Äpfel sind unbelebt. Sie sind hart und schmerzunempfindlich. Und wenn sie verletzt werden, dann nur äußerlich.

Meine Augen allerdings sind ganz schön. Sie ändern die Farbe. Meine Mutter sagt immer, wenn ich innerlich lebendig und voll Tatendrang bin, leuchten sie grün. Wenn ich unter Stress stehe, haben sie die Farbe der Nordsee. Ehrlich gesagt finde ich, dass sie ziemlich oft grau sind, aber sie sind relativ groß und haben die Form eines Pfirsichkerns, und meine Augenbrauen, die dunkler sind als meine Haare – mädchenblonde Schnittlauchlocken –, geben einen netten Rahmen für sie ab.

Im Moment starre ich in den Spiegel. Mir ist nach Heulen zumute – wenn ich mir nicht gerade ins Gesicht sehe, kann ich in meiner Phantasie jeder beliebige Mensch sein. Hier in der winzigen Bordtoilette bildet das grelle Licht einen Heiligenschein um meinen Kopf. Flugzeugspiegel sind die allerschlimmsten, in ihnen sieht man aus wie ein zweitausend Jahre alter Toter, der gerade exhumiert wurde.

Dann sehe ich unter meinem T-Shirt das Fleisch über meiner Shorts hervorquellen. Eine Handvoll davon forme ich zu einer gelungenen Miniversion der Wüste Gobi. Ich lasse Dünen entstehen mit kleinen Senken dazwischen, in denen wie in einer Oase Palmen wachsen könnten.

Dann wasche ich mir gründlich die Hände.

Meine Hände gefallen mir eigentlich ganz gut, sie haben sich noch nicht dem Trend zur Fettsackigkeit angeschlossen, dem mein restlicher Körper im Moment folgt. Meine Mutter sagt, das sei Babyspeck, der Hormonknopf »in die Breite gehen« habe eben aufs erste Antippen reagiert, während der Knopf »in die Höhe schießen« bislang den Dienst versage. Der Streik ist offenbar von längerer Dauer.

Im Übrigen habe ich bislang herzlich wenig fette Babys gesehen. Von der ganzen Aufregung, rumzukrabbeln und die Welt zu erkunden, sind die meisten ziemlich dünn.

Vielleicht fehlt mir ein bisschen Aufregung.

Das Gute ist: Beim Fliegen hat man das Gefühl, schwerelos zu sein, selbst wenn man fett ist. Und hier im Flieger sitzen Hunderte von Leuten, die viel fetter sind als ich, wie ich gesehen habe. Wenn ich die Wüste Gobi bin, dann ist mein Sitznachbar die Sahara. Sobald seine Unterarme sich auf der Armlehne breitmachen, übertreten seine Haut, seine Muskeln und sein Fett wie ein wabernder Virus die Grenzen meiner persönlichen Distanzzone. Das nervt mich wirklich. Ich sorge dafür, dass mein Körper in dem mir zustehenden Platz bleibt, selbst wenn ich nach der Landung grausam verspannt sein werde.

Wenn ich im Flugzeug sitze, denke ich aus irgendeinem Grund ans Sterben. Aber um ehrlich zu sein, denke ich eigentlich immer ans Sterben, egal, wo ich bin. Vielleicht ist es beim Totsein ein bisschen wie mit der Schwerelosigkeit hier in dieser Metallröhre. Auf unserem letzten Flug hat mich meine kleine Schwester gefragt, ob sie tot sei, weil jemand ihr gesagt hatte, Opa sitze irgendwo hier oben auf einer Wolke. Und als wir an einer vorbeiflogen, dachte sie, wir wären jetzt bei ihm.

Warum erzählen Erwachsene Kindern solchen Blödsinn? Das sorgt nur für Probleme. Ich meinerseits habe das alles sowieso nie geglaubt.

Meine Mutter hat schon vor Jahren aufgehört, mir solchen Mist aufzutischen.

Meine Mutter liebt mich, das weiß ich, auch wenn ich in den letzten Monaten zum Fettsack mutiert bin. Und sie hat mir versichert, dass ich mich eines Tages werde bücken müssen, um mich in einem wasserfleckigen Spiegel wie diesem zu sehen. Angeblich werden in unserer Familie alle Männer sehr groß. Aber das ist auch kein richtiger Trost. Ich habe gelesen, dass Gene oft eine Generation überspringen, und Pechvogel, der ich bin, werde ich nach Hunderten von Jahren der erste fette Zwerg der Beaumonts sein.

Außerdem lässt sie bei ihrer Prognose die andere DNA außer Acht, die zu meiner Entstehung beigetragen hat ...

Dieses Gespräch werde ich in den kommenden Ferien führen, koste es, was es wolle, und ganz egal, wie oft Mum versuchen wird, sich um das Thema zu drücken. Ich mag mich nicht mehr mit einem Phantom als Vater abspeisen lassen.

Ich muss es wissen.

Alle behaupten, dass ich nach ihr gerate. Aber was sollen sie auch sonst sagen? Sie können mich ja schlecht mit einer nicht näher identifizierten Samenzelle vergleichen.

Außerdem könnte der Umstand, dass ich nicht weiß, wer mein Vater ist, meinen bereits existierenden Größenwahn noch beflügeln. Was gar nicht gut ist, allemal nicht für ein Kind wie mich, sofern ich überhaupt noch ein Kind bin. Oder jemals war, was ich persönlich bezweifle.

Jetzt, in diesem Moment, in dem mein Körper über Mitteleuropa hinwegrast, kann mein Vater jeder sein, den ich mir zum Vater wünsche. Zum Beispiel, wenn wir kurz davor sind abzustürzen und der Kapitän hat nur einen einzigen zusätzlichen Fallschirm – wenn ich mich ihm als seinen Sohn vorstelle, dann muss er doch *mir* den Schirm geben, oder?

Andererseits ist es vielleicht besser, wenn ich es nicht weiß. Meine Stammzellen könnten von irgendwoher aus dem Fernen Osten kommen, und dann müsste ich Mandarin lernen, um mich mit meinem Vater zu unterhalten. Und Mandarin zu lernen ist verdammt schwer.

Manchmal wünsche ich mir, Mum würde mehr wie andere Mütter aussehen. Ich meine, sie ist nicht Kate Moss oder so, sie ist nämlich schon ziemlich alt. Aber es ist megapeinlich, wenn meine Mitschüler und meine Lehrer und alle Männer, die zu uns ins Haus kommen, sie auf diese ganz bestimmte Art anschauen. Jeder liebt sie, weil sie warmherzig ist und witzig und gleichzeitig kochen und tanzen kann. Und manchmal kommt mir der Anteil, den ich von ihr bekomme, nicht groß genug vor, und ich wünschte, ich müsste sie nicht mit so vielen anderen teilen.

Weil sie mir die Wichtigste ist.

Als sie mich bekam, war sie nicht verheiratet. Hundert Jahre zuvor wäre ich in einem Armenhaus zur Welt gekommen, und wir wären vermutlich ein paar Monate später beide an Tuberkulose gestorben. Dann würden wir jetzt nebeneinander in einem Armengrab liegen, und unsere Skelette wären bis in alle Ewigkeiten vereint.

Ich überlege mir oft, ob diese lebende Erinnerung an ihre Verruchtheit – sprich: ich – ihr nicht unangenehm ist. Ist das der Grund, weswegen sie mich aufs Internat schickt?

Verruchtheit, sage ich lautlos zum Spiegel. Das ist ja fast onomatopoetisch. Ich habe ein Faible für Wörter. Ich sammle sie wie meine Mitschüler, je nach Reifegrad, Fußballkarten oder Mädchen. Es gefällt mir, sie hervorzukramen und in einen Satz einzufügen, um einen Gedanken so präzise wie nur möglich auszudrücken. Vielleicht werde ich später einmal beruflich mit ihnen spielen. Seien wir ehrlich, für Manchester United werde ich angesichts meiner gegenwärtigen Statur nie auflaufen.

Jetzt hämmert jemand an die Tür. Ich habe die Zeit vergessen, wie immer. Ich schaue auf die Uhr und stelle fest, dass ich seit über zwanzig Minuten hier drin bin. Jetzt muss ich mich einer Horde wütender Passagiere stellen, die alle dringend pinkeln müssen.

Ein letzter Blick in den Spiegel, ein letzter Blick auf den Fettsack. Dann schaue ich zu Boden, atme tief durch und trete als Brad Pitt hinaus.

Kapitel 1

»Ich weiß nicht genau, wo wir sind. Wir müssen mal kurz anhalten.«

»Verdammt, Mum! Es ist stockdunkel, und wir hängen über einem Abgrund! Hier gibt es nichts, wo wir mal kurz anhalten können.«

»Immer mit der Ruhe, mein Schatz. Ich finde schon eine Stelle, wo ich gefahrlos ranfahren kann.«

»Gefahrlos? Dass ich nicht lache! Hätte ich das gewusst, hätte ich meine Steigeisen und meinen Eispickel mitgebracht.«

»Da oben ist eine Parkbucht.« Ruckelnd steuerte Helena den ungewohnten Leihwagen um die Serpentine und brachte ihn in der Bucht zum Stehen. Nach einem Blick auf ihren Sohn, der sich die Augen zugehalten hatte, legte sie ihm beschwichtigend eine Hand aufs Knie. »Jetzt kannst du wieder schauen.« Sie äugte durchs Fenster in das Tal, das tief unter ihnen lag, und auf die entlang der Küste funkelnden Lichter. »Es ist wunderschön«, murmelte sie.

»Nein, Mum, es ist nicht ›wunderschön‹. ›Wunderschön‹ wird es erst sein, wenn wir nicht mehr irgendwo in einem fremden Land im Outback herumirren, keine drei Meter von einem Steilhang entfernt, der, wenn wir abstürzen, unseren sicheren Tod bedeutet. Haben sie hier noch nie was von Leitplanken gehört?«

Ohne auf ihn zu achten, tastete Helena nach dem Schalter

für die Innenbeleuchtung. »Schatz, gib mir doch mal die Karte.« Alex reichte sie ihr, und Helena starrte mit suchendem Blick darauf.

»Mum, sie steht auf dem Kopf«, sagte Alex.

»Schon gut.« Sie drehte die Karte um. »Immy schläft noch?«

Alex schaute nach hinten zu seiner fünfjährigen Schwester, die quer über dem Rücksitz lag und fest ihr Plüschlämmchen an sich gekuschelt hielt. »Ja, und das ist auch gut so. Sonst würde diese Fahrt sie für den Rest ihres Lebens traumatisieren. Wenn sie sehen würde, wo wir gerade sind, würde man sie nie wieder in eine Achterbahn bekommen.«

»Gut, jetzt weiß ich, wo ich mich verfahren habe. Wir müssen wieder den Berg runter …«

»Den Steilabhang«, präzisierte Alex.

»… beim Schild nach Kathikas links abbiegen und der Straße folgen. Hier.« Helena reichte Alex die Karte zurück und legte den Gang ein, den sie für den Rückwärtsgang hielt. Der Wagen machte einen Satz nach vorn.

»Mum! Um Gottes willen!«

»Entschuldigung.« Helena wendete unbeholfen und lenkte den Wagen wieder auf die Straße.

»Ich habe gedacht, du wüsstest, wo das Haus ist«, brummte Alex.

»Mein Schatz, als ich das letzte Mal hier war, war ich gerade zwei Jahre älter als du. Im Klartext, das ist fast vierundzwanzig Jahre her. Aber wenn wir im Dorf sind, erkenne ich es bestimmt wieder.«

»Wenn wir das Dorf jemals erreichen.«

»Jetzt sei doch nicht so miesepetrig!« Erleichtert sah Helena den Wegweiser nach Kathikas vor sich auftauchen und bog ab. »Es lohnt sich, du wirst schon sehen.«

»Nicht mal ein Strand ist in der Nähe. Außerdem kann ich Oliven nicht leiden. Und die Chandlers erst recht nicht. Rupert ist ein Arschlo…«

»Alex, jetzt reicht's! Wenn du nichts Positives zu sagen hast, dann halt bitte den Mund und lass mich fahren.«

Während Helena aufs Gaspedal trat, damit der Citroën den steilen Anstieg bewältigte, verfiel Alex in mürrisches Schweigen. Helena bedauerte, dass das Flugzeug Verspätung gehabt hatte und sie erst kurz nach Sonnenuntergang in Paphos gelandet waren. Bis sie durch den Zoll waren und ihren Leihwagen übergeben bekommen hatten, war es Nacht gewesen. Dabei hatte sie sich so auf diese Fahrt in die Berge gefreut und darauf, an diesen ganz besonderen Ort ihrer Kindheit zurückzukehren und ihn durch die Augen ihrer eigenen Kinder neu zu entdecken.

Aber andererseits, dachte sie, entsprach das Leben im Grunde nur selten den Erwartungen, vor allem nicht, wenn es um kostbare Erinnerungen ging. Und ihr war klar, dass sie den Sommer, den sie als Fünfzehnjährige hier im Haus ihres Patenonkels verbracht hatte, im Rückblick verklärte.

Aber so lächerlich es war, sie wäre schrecklich enttäuscht, wenn Pandora sich als weniger perfekt erweisen sollte als in ihrer Vorstellung. Ihr Kopf sagte ihr, dass es unmöglich so sein konnte wie damals und dass das Wiedersehen mit dem Haus einem Wiedersehen mit der ersten großen Liebe nach vierundzwanzig Jahren gleichen würde: in der Erinnerung von jugendlicher Kraft und Schönheit, in der Realität aber mit grauen Schläfen und dem körperlichen Verfall preisgegeben.

Und sie wusste auch, dass auch *das* denkbar war …

Würde er noch hier sein?

Helena hielt das Lenkrad fest umklammert und verbannte den Gedanken aus ihrem Kopf.

Pandora, das Haus, war ihr damals weitläufig wie ein herrschaftlicher Landsitz vorgekommen, aber in Wirklichkeit musste es kleiner sein. Die antiken Möbel, die Angus, ihr Patenonkel, zu seiner Zeit als oberster Befehlshaber der letzten noch auf Zypern stationierten Soldaten der britischen Armee aus England importiert hatte, waren ihr erlesen, elegant und unantastbar erschienen. Die graublauen Damastsofas im abgedunkelten Salon, dessen Fensterläden immer geschlossen blieben, damit die Sonne die Möbel nicht ausbleichen konnte, der antike Schreibtisch im Büro, an dem Angus jeden Morgen gesessen und mit einem schlanken Miniaturschwert seine Post geöffnet hatte, der ausladende Mahagoniesstisch, dessen glänzend glatte Oberfläche sie immer an eine Eisbahn denken ließ ... das alles stand ihr fast übermächtig vor Augen.

Seit Angus vor drei Jahren aus gesundheitlichen Gründen nach England zurückgekehrt war, stand Pandora leer. So fest er auch beteuert hatte, die medizinische Versorgung auf Zypern sei ebenso gut wie der englische National Health Service, wenn nicht gar besser, hatte er zu guter Letzt doch notgedrungen, wenn auch widerwillig eingeräumt, dass es nicht besonders praktisch war, in einem abgelegenen Bergdorf zu leben, wenn man keine zwei gesunden Beine mehr hatte und regelmäßig eine beschwerliche Fahrt ins Krankenhaus auf sich nehmen musste.

Am Ende hatte er kapituliert, war nach England gezogen und vor einem halben Jahr an Lungenentzündung und Kummer gestorben. Es war ohnehin unwahrscheinlich gewesen, dass sich ein geschwächter Körper, der die überwiegende Anzahl seiner achtundsiebzig Jahre in einem subtropischen Klima verbracht hatte, an die immerwährende Feuchtigkeit und das Grau eines schottischen Vororts gewöhnen würde.

Seinen gesamten Besitz hatte er seinem Patenkind Helena vermacht, einschließlich Pandora.

Sie hatte geweint, als sie von seinem Tod erfahren hatte, und schuldbewusste Tränen vergossen wegen ihrer ständigen guten Vorsätze, ihn häufiger im Pflegeheim zu besuchen, wofür sie dann doch nie die Zeit gefunden hatte.

Der scheppernde Klingelton ihres Handys aus den Tiefen ihrer Handtasche riss sie aus ihren Gedanken.

»Schatz, gehst du ran?«, bat sie Alex. »Das ist wahrscheinlich Dad, der hören will, ob wir schon angekommen sind.«

Alex wühlte sich wie praktisch immer vergeblich durch die Handtasche seiner Mutter und fand das Handy erst, nachdem es bereits verstummt war. Er sah aufs Display. »Ja, das war wirklich Dad. Soll ich ihn zurückrufen?«

»Nein. Wir rufen ihn an, wenn wir da sind.«

»Falls wir hinfinden.«

»Natürlich finden wir hin. Langsam kenne ich mich wieder aus. Jetzt dauert es keine zehn Minuten mehr.«

»Gab es Haris Taverne schon, als du hier warst?«, fragte Alex, als sie an einem grell erleuchteten Restaurant mit einer funkelnden Neonpalme im Vorgarten vorbeifuhren. Im Inneren waren Spielautomaten und weiße Plastikstühle zu erkennen.

»Nein. Wir sind auf einer neuen Umgehungsstraße, auf der es viel Durchgangsverkehr und jede Menge Laufkundschaft gibt. Zu meiner Zeit war die Straße zum Dorf hinauf noch nicht einmal geteert.«

»Da gab's Sky TV. Können wir abends mal hingehen?«, fragte er hoffnungsvoll.

»Mal sehen.« Zu Helenas Urlaubsvorstellungen gehörten eher laue Abende auf der wunderschönen Terrasse mit Blick auf die Olivenhaine, dazu ein Glas des hiesigen Weins und frisch vom Baum gepflückte Feigen, aber weder Fernseher noch Neonpalmen.

»Mum, wie primitiv ist das Haus eigentlich? Ich meine, gibt's überhaupt Strom?«

»Natürlich gibt es Strom, du Dummchen.« Helena hoffte nur, dass Angelina, die Frau im Ort, die die Schlüssel zum Haus hatte, ihn auch angestellt hatte. »Schau, jetzt biegen wir ins Dorf ab. In ein paar Minuten sind wir da.«

»Vielleicht könnte ich ja mit dem Rad zu der Kneipe fahren«, sagte Alex skeptisch. »Wenn ich irgendwo ein Rad auftreiben kann.«

»Ich bin damals praktisch jeden Tag vom Haus ins Dorf geradelt.«

»War das ein Hochrad?«

»Sehr witzig. Es war ein altmodisches Hollandrad mit drei Gängen und vorn einem Korb.« Bei der Erinnerung musste Helena lächeln. »Ich habe immer Brot aus der Bäckerei geholt.«

»Wie das Fahrrad, auf dem die Hexe im *Zauberer von Oz* sitzt, wenn sie bei Dorothy am Fenster vorbeifährt?«

»Genau so eins. Und jetzt sei still, ich muss mich konzentrieren. Wegen der neuen Umgehung kommen wir vom anderen Ende in den Ort, ich muss mich erst orientieren.«

Vor sich sah Helena bereits die Lichter des Dorfs funkeln. Als dann die Straße schmaler wurde und der Kies unter den Reifen knirschte, drosselte sie das Tempo. Die ersten Häuser aus dem hiesigen gelbweißen Stein tauchten auf, um die Straße schließlich in einer geschlossenen Reihe zu säumen.

»Schau, da vor uns ist die Kirche.« Helena deutete auf das Bauwerk, das einst das Herz der kleinen Gemeinde Kathikas gebildet hatte. Im Vorbeifahren sah sie ein paar Jugendliche, die um die Bank vor der Kirche herumlungerten. Ihre Aufmerksamkeit galt den beiden schwarzäugigen Mädchen, die dort saßen. »Das ist das Zentrum des Dorfs.«

»Na, hier tobt ja der Bär.«

»Angeblich haben in den letzten Jahren zwei sehr gute Tavernen aufgemacht. Und schau, da ist der Laden. Der ist ja größer geworden! Dort bekommst du alles, was dein Herz begehrt.«

»Dann spring ich mal rein und hol die neueste CD von den *All-American Rejects*, ja?«

»Alex, jetzt reicht's wirklich!« Allmählich verlor Helena die Geduld. »Ich weiß, dass du nicht herkommen wolltest, aber du hast Pandora noch nicht mal gesehen. Gib dem Haus wenigstens eine Chance, um meinetwillen, wenn schon nicht um deinetwillen!«

»Sorry, Mum. Ja. Tut mir leid.«

»Früher war das Dorf richtig hübsch, und was ich so sehe, hat es sich nicht allzu sehr verändert«, sagte Helena erleichtert. »Morgen schauen wir uns mal um.«

»Wir fahren ja schon wieder zum Dorf hinaus«, bemerkte Alex nervös.

»Ja. In der Dunkelheit kannst du es zwar nicht sehen, aber rechts und links sind lauter Weinfelder. Früher, zur Zeit der Pharaonen, wurde der hiesige Wein bis nach Ägypten exportiert, so gut war er. So, und hier biegen wir ab, ich bin mir ziemlich sicher. Halt dich gut fest, die Straße ist holprig.«

Als sich der Feldweg zwischen Weinstöcken hindurch bergab schlängelte, schaltete Helena in den ersten Gang zurück und blendete das Licht auf, um den tückischsten Schlaglöchern ausweichen zu können.

»Und hier bist du jeden Tag hochgeradelt?«, fragte Alex erstaunt. »Irre! Es wundert mich, dass du nicht in den Weinstöcken gelandet bist.«

»Manchmal bin ich das auch, aber im Lauf der Zeit kennt man die schlimmsten Stellen.« Es hatte etwas Beruhigendes, dass die Schlaglöcher noch genauso tief waren wie in ihrer Erinnerung. Helena hatte eine Teerstraße befürchtet.

»Mummy, sind wir gleich da?«, fragte ein verschlafenes Stimmchen vom Rücksitz. »Es rumpelt so.«

»Ja, mein Schatz, wir sind gleich da. Keine zehn Sekunden mehr.«

Wir sind gleich da ...

Sie bogen auf einen noch schmaleren Weg, an dessen Ende die wuchtige Silhouette von Pandora auszumachen war. Ängstliche Beklommenheit mischte sich in Helenas Vorfreude. Sie steuerte den Wagen durch die rostigen Eisentore, die bereits damals Tag und Nacht offen gestanden hatten und sich mittlerweile sicher nicht mehr in den Angeln bewegen ließen.

Helena blieb stehen und stellte den Motor ab.

»Da sind wir.«

Keine Reaktion von ihren beiden Kindern. Mit einem Blick nach hinten stellte sie fest, dass Immy wieder eingeschlafen war. Alex neben ihr starrte unverwandt in die Nacht hinaus.

»Lassen wir Immy schlafen, bis wir den Schlüssel gefunden haben«, schlug Helena vor und öffnete die Fahrertür. Ein Schwall warmer Nachtluft flutete ins Auto. Helena stieg aus und atmete den unvergesslichen Geruch von Oliven, Trauben und Staub ein – kein Vergleich zu Teerstraßen und Neonpalmen. Der Geruch war wirklich der mächtigste Wahrnehmungssinn des Menschen, dachte sie. Er konnte einen bestimmten Moment oder eine bestimmte Atmosphäre mit untrüglicher Präzision heraufbeschwören.

Sie verkniff sich die Frage, was Alex von dem Haus dachte. Schließlich gab es noch nichts zu denken. Außerdem würde sie es nicht ertragen, etwas Abschätziges zu hören. Sie standen im Stockdunkeln hinter dem Haus, das durch die mit Läden verschlossenen Fenster wie eine abweisende Kaserne wirkte.

»Mum, es ist schrecklich finster.«

»Ich mache die Scheinwerfer wieder an. Angelina sagte, sie würde die Hintertür offen lassen.« Im Licht der Scheinwerfer ging Helena über den Kies zur Tür, dicht gefolgt von Alex. Der Messingknauf ließ sich mühelos drehen, sie stieß die Tür auf, tastete nach dem Lichtschalter und hielt kurz die Luft an, ehe sie ihn betätigte. Unvermittelt erfüllte Licht den rückwärtigen Flur.

»Gott sei Dank«, sagte sie leise, öffnete eine weitere Tür und machte wieder Licht. »Das ist die Küche.«

»Das sehe ich.« Alex ging durch den großen, stickigen Raum, in dem ein ausladendes Spülbecken, ein uralter Herd, ein großer Holztisch und vor einer Wand eine gewaltige Anrichte standen. »Nicht gerade luxuriös.«

»Angus hat so gut wie keinen Fuß in die Küche gesetzt. Für den Haushalt und alles, was damit zusammenhing, war seine Haushälterin zuständig. Ich glaube nicht, dass er je in seinem Leben auch nur einmal am Herd stand. Die Küche war ausschließlich zum Arbeiten da und nicht zum Wohnen und Wohlfühlen, wie wir es heute kennen.«

»Wo hat er dann gegessen?«

»Draußen auf der Terrasse natürlich. Das tut hier jeder.« Helena drehte den Wasserhahn auf. Zögernd begann er zu tröpfeln, dann schoss ein ganzer Schwall heraus.

»Einen Kühlschrank gibt's hier wohl nicht«, meinte Alex.

»Der steht in der Speisekammer. Angus hat so oft Gäste gehabt, und die Fahrt nach Paphos war so weit, dass er in die Speisekammer zusätzlich ein Kühlsystem einbauen ließ. Und bevor du fragst, nein, eine Tiefkühltruhe gab es damals nicht. Die

Tür ist gleich links. Schau doch mal, ob der Kühlschrank noch da ist, ja? Angelina sagte, sie würde uns Milch und Brot hinstellen.«

»Mach ich.«

Helena schlenderte weiter, machte im Vorbeigehen überall Licht und gelangte zu dem großen Eingangsbereich im vorderen Teil des Hauses. Der Steinfußboden mit seinem ausgetretenen Schachbrettmuster hallte unter ihren Füßen. Sie schaute die Treppe empor. Das solide Geländer war kunstvoll aus Eichenholz gefertigt, das Angus eigens aus England hatte importieren lassen. Hinter ihr stand eine Standuhr Wache, tickte aber nicht mehr.

Hier ist die Zeit stehen geblieben, sinnierte sie und öffnete die Tür zum Salon.

Die Sofas mit dem graublauen Damastbezug waren mit Tüchern abgedeckt. Sie zog eines fort und ließ sich in das daunenweiche Polster sinken. Der Stoff war zwar noch makellos, fühlte sich aber ein wenig spröde an, als hätte er seine Festigkeit in all den Jahren, in denen niemand auf den Sofas gesessen hatte, etwas eingebüßt. Helena stand wieder auf und ging zu einer der beiden Terrassentüren, öffnete die Holzläden, drehte am steifen Griff und trat ins Freie.

Ein paar Sekunden später fand Alex sie dort auf die Balustrade der Terrasse gestützt stehen. »Der Kühlschrank pfeift auf dem letzten Loch«, sagte er, »aber es gibt Milch, Eier und Brot. Und hiervon haben wir auf jeden Fall mehr als genug.« Er zeigte ihr eine riesige rosarote Salami. Helena schwieg. Er stellte sich neben sie. »Schöner Blick«, sagte er.

»Es ist atemberaubend, findest du nicht?« Sie freute sich, dass es ihm gefiel, und lächelte.

»Sind die winzigen Lichter da unten die Küste?«

»Ja. Morgen früh wirst du das Meer sehen. Und die Olivenhaine und die Weinberge, die sich von hier bis ins Tal hinunterziehen und beiderseits der Berge.«

Alex schaute nach unten, dann nach rechts und links. »Das Haus liegt, ähm, ziemlich abgeschieden, oder? Ich kann nirgends ein anderes sehen.«

»Ich hatte schon befürchtet, sie könnten hier alles zugebaut haben wie unten an der Küste.« Sie drehte sich zu ihm. »Komm mal her, mein Schatz.« Sie schloss ihn in die Arme. »Ich freue mich, dass wir hier sind.«

»Schön. Es freut mich, dass du dich freust. Hättest du etwas dagegen, wenn wir jetzt Immy holen? Ich habe Angst, sie könnte aufwachen und Angst bekommen und dann weglaufen. Außerdem bin ich am Verhungern.«

»Lass uns doch noch schnell oben ein Zimmer suchen, in das wir sie gleich legen können. Und dann kannst du mir vielleicht helfen, sie nach oben zu tragen.«

Helena ging mit Alex über die Terrasse zurück. Unter der mit Wein überwachsenen Pergola, die willkommenen Schutz vor der Mittagssonne bot, blieb sie kurz stehen. Der lange gusseiserne Tisch, an dem die weiße Farbe schon abblätterte und der großteils unter vertrocknetem Weinlaub verschwand, wirkte verlassen.

»Hier haben wir immer zu Mittag und zu Abend gegessen. Und dafür mussten wir uns alle immer richtig anziehen. Bei Angus kam es nicht infrage, mit Badeanzug oder nasser Badehose am Esstisch zu sitzen, ganz egal, wie heiß es war«, erzählte sie.

»Das verlangst du aber nicht von uns, Mum, oder?«

Helena fuhr ihrem Sohn durch das dichte blonde Haar und gab ihm einen Kuss auf den Scheitel. »Ich werde von Glück reden können, wenn ihr euch überhaupt an den Tisch setzt, ganz egal, was ihr anhabt. Wie sich die Zeiten doch ändern«, sagte sie mit einem Seufzen und nahm ihn an der Hand. »Komm, gehen wir nach oben und schauen uns dort um.«

Es war fast Mitternacht, als Helena schließlich auf dem kleinen Balkon vor Angus' Schlafzimmer saß, in dessen ausladenden Mahagonibett Immy jetzt tief und fest schlummerte. Helena hatte beschlossen, erst am kommenden Tag, wenn sie entdeckt hatte, wo die Bettwäsche aufbewahrt wurde, einen der beiden angrenzenden Räume für sie herzurichten. Alex lag in einem anderen Zimmer auf der bloßen Matratze. Zum Schutz vor Mücken hatte er alle Fensterläden geschlossen, auch wenn im Zimmer dadurch eine Atmosphäre wie in der Sauna herrschte. An diesem Abend wehte nicht das leiseste Lüftchen.

Mit einem Griff holte Helena ihr Handy und eine zerdrückte Zigarettenschachtel aus der Handtasche, legte beides auf den Schoß und betrachtete es. Zuerst die Zigarette, beschloss sie. Der Zauber sollte noch nicht gebrochen werden. Sicherlich würde ihr Mann William nicht mit Absicht etwas sagen, was sie schlagartig in die Wirklichkeit zurückholte, aber die Wahrscheinlichkeit war dennoch groß. Und es wäre nicht mal seine Schuld, schließlich war es nur vernünftig, wenn er ihr erzählte, dass der Handwerker gekommen sei, um den Geschirrspüler zu reparieren, und sie fragte, wo sie die schweren Plastiksäcke aufbewahre, weil er morgen früh den Abfall für die Müllabfuhr vor die Tür stellen müsse. Er würde davon ausgehen, dass sie sich freute zu hören, wie umsichtig er den Haushalt führte.

Und sie würde sich ja auch freuen. Nur noch nicht in diesem Moment …

Helena zündete die Zigarette an, inhalierte und fragte sich, weshalb Rauchen in einer lauen mediterranen Nacht etwas derart Sinnliches hatte. Ihren allerersten Zug hatte sie nur wenige Schritte von hier entfernt gemacht. Schuldbewusst hatte sie sich damals dem Reiz des Verbotenen hingegeben. Jetzt, vierundzwanzig Jahre später, hatte sie genauso ein schlechtes Gewissen und wünschte, sie könnte sich das Rauchen endgültig abgewöhnen. Damals war sie zu jung gewesen, um zu rauchen, jetzt, mit fast vierzig, war sie zu alt dafür. Bei dem Gedanken musste sie lächeln: Ihre Jugend hatte in den Jahren zwischen ihrem letzten Besuch und ihrer ersten Zigarette in diesem Haus und dem heutigen Abend stattgefunden.

Damals hatte sie so viele Träume gehabt, ihr Leben als erwachsene Frau hatte noch vor ihr gelegen. Wen würde sie lieben? Wo würde sie leben? Wie weit würde sie mit ihrer Begabung kommen? Würde sie glücklich werden …?

Mittlerweile waren die meisten dieser Fragen beantwortet.

»Bitte, lasst den Urlaub so perfekt wie möglich werden«, beschwor sie im Flüsterton das Haus, den Mond und die Sterne. In den letzten Wochen hatte sie ein merkwürdig ungutes Gefühl gehabt, als stünde etwas Unheilvolles bevor, und das hatte sie einfach nicht abschütteln können. Vielleicht hatte es damit zu tun, dass der Meilenstein-Geburtstag mit Riesenschritten näher rückte – oder vielleicht auch nur damit, dass sie wieder hierherkommen würde …

Schon spürte sie, wie die magische Stimmung Pandoras sich um sie legte, als würde das Haus all ihre Schutzschichten entfernen und ihre Seele enthüllen. Genau wie beim letzten Mal.

Sie drückte die halb gerauchte Zigarette aus und warf sie in die Nacht hinaus, griff nach dem Handy und wählte ihre Nummer in England. William hob beim zweiten Läuten ab. »Guten Abend, mein Schatz, ich bin's«, sagte sie.

»Ihr seid also gut angekommen?«, fragte er, und allein der Klang seiner Stimme beruhigte Helena.

»Ja. Wie sieht es zu Hause aus?«

»Gut, sehr gut.«

»Und wie geht's dem dreijährigen Jungterroristen?«, fragte sie lächelnd.

»Irgendwann hat Fred sich Gott sei Dank beruhigt. Er ist sauer, dass ihr ihn mit seinem alten Vater allein zurückgelassen habt.«

»Er fehlt mir. In gewisser Hinsicht.« Helena lachte leise. »Aber ohne ihn wird es einfacher sein, das Haus in Schuss zu bringen, bevor ihr kommt.«

»Ist es bewohnbar?«

»Ich glaube schon, aber morgen früh sehe ich mehr. Die Küche ist ziemlich einfach.«

»Apropos Küche, heute ist der Mann wegen des Geschirrspülers gekommen.«

»Ach ja?«

»Ja. Er hat ihn repariert, obwohl wir zu dem Preis ebenso gut einen neuen hätten kaufen können.«

»Oje.« Helena unterdrückte ein Lächeln. »Die Müllsäcke sind links von der Spüle in der zweiten Schublade von oben.«

»Nach denen wollte ich dich auch fragen. Du weißt ja, morgen kommt die Müllabfuhr. Rufst du morgen früh an?«

»Mach ich. Ein Kuss für Fred und für dich. Tschüs, mein Schatz.«

»Tschüs. Schlaf gut.«

Helena blieb noch eine Weile sitzen und sah zum wunderschönen Nachthimmel hinauf, an dem Tausende von Sterne funkelten. Es kam ihr vor, als würden sie hier viel heller leuchten als zu Hause. Allmählich wich das Adrenalin einem Gefühl von Erschöpfung. Leise ging sie ins Zimmer und legte sich neben Immy aufs Bett. Und zum ersten Mal seit Wochen schlief sie sofort ein.

Alex' Tagebuch

11. Juli 2006

Ich höre sie. Sie schwirrt in der Dunkelheit um mich herum und wetzt die Zähne, um sich auf ihre Mahlzeit zu stürzen.

Sprich, auf mich.

Haben Mücken Zähne? Müssen sie wohl, wie sollten sie sonst durch die Haut dringen? Aber wenn es mir tatsächlich einmal gelingt, einen von diesen elendigen Quälgeistern an der Wand zu zerquetschen, knirscht es nicht. Eigentlich hört man gar nichts. Auf jeden Fall geht kein Zahn kaputt – und wie sich das anhört, weiß ich, seit ich mit vier vom Klettergerüst gefallen bin und mir den oberen Schneidezahn abgebrochen habe.

Manchmal sind sie dermaßen unverschämt, dass sie einem ins Ohr sirren und einen darauf aufmerksam machen, dass sie gleich über einen herfallen. Da liegt man dann, fuchtelt mit den Armen durch die Gegend, und sie tanzen unsichtbar um einen herum und lachen sich vermutlich schlapp über ihr hilfloses Opfer.

Ich hole Bee aus meinem Rucksack und drücke ihn an mich. Das stört ihn nicht, er braucht ja keine Luft zu holen. Nur damit das klar ist, Bee ist, obwohl er so heißt, keine Biene, sondern ein Plüschhase und genauso alt wie ich. Er heißt Bee, weil B für Bunny steht. So nannte ich ihn als kleines Kind – laut Mum war das ei-

39

nes der ersten Wörter, das ich sagen konnte –, und dabei ist es geblieben.

Sie hat auch gesagt, dass jemand »ganz Besonderes« ihn mir ein paar Tage nach meiner Geburt geschenkt hat. Wahrscheinlich meint sie damit meinen Vater. So traurig und lächerlich es ist, dass ich mit meinen dreizehn Jahren immer noch mit einem uralten Plüschhasen im Bett liege – das ist mir egal. Er, also Bee, ist mein Glücksbringer, mein Rettungsanker und mein Freund. Ihm erzähle ich alles.

Ich habe mir schon öfter vorgestellt, wie es wäre, die Milliarden von geliebten Kuscheltieren zusammenzubringen und zu befragen. Die würden bestimmt alle sehr viel mehr über das Kind Bescheid wissen, bei dem sie geschlafen haben, als die Eltern. Einfach, weil sie zuhören, ohne ständig dazwischenzuquatschen.

Ich bedecke meine angreifbarsten Körperstellen so gut es geht mit diversen Kleidungsstücken, allen voran meine fetten Backen, an denen sich eine Mücke mit einem Mahl den Bauch für den Rest ihrer Tage vollschlagen kann.

Irgendwann schlafe ich ein. Zumindest denke ich, dass ich schlafe. Oder vielmehr hoffe ich, dass ich träume. Ich bin nämlich in einem Höllenfeuer, Flammen umzüngeln mich, die Hitze brennt mir das Fleisch von den Knochen.

Als ich aufwache, ist es immer noch dunkel, dann stelle ich fest, dass ich keine Luft bekomme, und merke, dass eine Unterhose auf meinem Gesicht liegt, was erklärt, weshalb es dunkel ist und ich keine Luft bekomme. Ich nehme sie weg, atme tief ein und sehe Lichtstreifen durch die Läden sickern.

Es ist Morgen. Ich bin von oben bis unten in Schweiß

gebadet, aber wenn mich das widerliche Mückenscheusal nicht erwischt hat, dann hat es sich gelohnt.

Ich schäle meine feuchte Haut von der Matratze und die klatschnassen Kleidungsstücke von meinem Leib. Über der Kommode hängt ein kleiner, halb blinder Spiegel. Zu dem wanke ich, um mein Gesicht zu betrachten. Und sehe auf der rechten Backe einen riesigen roten Stich prangen.

Beim Fluchen verwende ich Wörter, die meine Mutter gar nicht gutheißen würde, und frage mich, wie es dem Mistvieh gelungen ist, sich unter die Unterhose vorzu-arbeiten. Ich hatte vergessen, dass Mücken zu einer Eli-teeinheit gehören, die sich auf die Kunst der Infiltration versteht.

Abgesehen von dem Stich ist mein restliches Gesicht so rot wie die röteste Seite eines Cox Orange. Ich öffne die Läden, trete auf den kleinen Balkon hinaus und blin-zele wie ein Maulwurf. Die Morgensonne brennt wie das Höllenfeuer aus meinem Traum.

Als meine Augen in der Lage sind, etwas wahrzuneh-men, stelle ich fest, dass der Blick tatsächlich gigantisch ist. Meine Mutter hat also recht. Das Haus liegt sehr hoch oben, wir kleben regelrecht am Berg, die gelb-braune und olivgrüne Landschaft unter mir ist ausgedörrt, genauso wie ich. In weiter, weiter Ferne glitzert das blaue Meer in der Sonne. Dann schaue ich direkt nach unten und be-obachte die kleine Gestalt auf der Terrasse.

Meine Mutter benutzt das Geländer als *barre*. Als sie die obere Hälfte ihres Körpers wie eine Schlangenfrau nach hinten faltet, fällt ihr goldenes Haar wie eine Kaska-de herab. Unter dem Trikot kann ich ihre Rippen zählen. Diese Ballettübungen macht sie jeden Morgen, sogar an

41

Weihnachten und auch wenn sie erst sehr spät ins Bett gegangen ist und ein paar Gläser Wein getrunken hat. Sollte sie die Übungen irgendwann einmal nicht machen, weiß ich, dass etwas ganz und gar nicht in Ordnung ist. Andere Kinder bekommen zum Frühstück Coco-Pops und Toast von Eltern, die aufrecht auf ihren zwei Beinen stehen. Ich bekomme den Kopf meiner Mutter zwischen ihren Beinen zu sehen, wenn sie mich bittet, den Wasserkessel aufzusetzen.

Einmal wollte sie mich dazu bringen, mit ihr Ballett zu machen. Aber das gehört zu den Dingen, in denen wir uns wirklich grundlegend unterscheiden.

Plötzlich habe ich unglaublich und unerträglich Durst. Und mir ist schwindelig. Die Welt dreht sich, ich taumele ins Zimmer, falle aufs Bett und schließe die Augen.

Vielleicht habe ich Malaria. Vielleicht macht die Mücke mir den Garaus, und ich habe nur noch wenige Stunden zu leben.

Was immer es ist, ich brauche Wasser und meine Mutter.

KAPITEL 2

»Dehydrierung. Zu wenig Flüssigkeit. Das ist alles. Rühren Sie dieses Pulver in ein Glas Wasser und heute Abend noch einmal ein Tütchen. Und reichlich trinken, junger Mann.«

»Sind Sie sicher, dass es nicht Malaria ist, Herr Doktor?« Misstrauisch beäugte Alex den kleinen Zyprioten. »Sie dürfen es mir ruhig sagen, ich kann das schon verkraften.«

»Natürlich ist es keine Malaria, Alex«, fuhr Helena auf. Sie wandte sich zum Arzt, der gerade seine Tasche schloss. »Danke, dass Sie so schnell gekommen sind. Bitte entschuldigen Sie die Störung.« Sie begleitete ihn zum Zimmer hinaus und die Treppe hinunter in die Küche. »Ich dachte, er deliriert. Ich habe es wirklich mit der Angst zu tun bekommen.«

»Natürlich, das ist verständlich. Es ist auch kein Problem. Ich habe Colonel McCladden jahrelang behandelt. Sein Tod … das ist sehr traurig.« Mit einem Achselzucken reichte er Helena seine Visitenkarte. »Für den Fall, dass Sie mich wieder brauchen. Allerdings wäre es besser, wenn Sie mich in der Praxis aufsuchen, ich fürchte, ich muss Ihnen den Hausbesuch in Rechnung stellen.«

»Oje, ich glaube, ich habe nicht genügend Bargeld im Haus. Ich wollte heute Nachmittag im Dorf zur Bank gehen«, antwortete Helena peinlich berührt.

»Kein Problem, die Praxis ist nur ein paar Häuser weiter. Bringen Sie das Geld einfach vorbei.«

»Danke, Herr Doktor, das mache ich.«

Helena folgte ihm zur hinteren Haustür hinaus. Nach ein paar Schritten drehte er sich um und ließ den Blick über das Haus schweifen. »Pandora«, sagte er bedächtig. »Sie kennen den Mythos, nicht wahr?«

»Ja.«

»Es ist ein wunderschönes Haus, aber wie in der Legende mit der Büchse, nach der es benannt ist, war es für viele Jahre verschlossen. Sind Sie diejenige, die es wieder öffnen wird?«, fragte er lächelnd und zeigte dabei zwei Reihen weißer, gerader Zähne.

»Hoffentlich nicht so, dass alle Übel der Welt daraus entweichen können«, sagte Helena verhalten. »Das Haus gehört ja jetzt mir, Angus war mein Patenonkel. Er hat es mir hinterlassen.«

»Ich verstehe. Werden Sie es genauso ins Herz schließen wie er?«

»Das habe ich schon lange. Ich war als Teenager einmal hier und habe es nie vergessen.«

»Dann wissen Sie sicher auch, dass es das älteste Haus hier in der Gegend ist. Manche Leute sagen, dass an dieser Stelle schon vor Tausenden von Jahren ein Haus gestanden hat und dass Aphrodite und Adonis einmal eine Nacht hier verbracht und den Wein gekostet haben. Im Dorf gibt es viele Gerüchte …«

»Über das Haus?«

»Ja.« Er sah ihr ins Gesicht. »Sie erinnern mich sehr an eine andere Dame, der ich einmal vor vielen Jahren hier in Pandora begegnet bin.«

»Wirklich?«

»Sie war bei Colonel McCladden zu Besuch, und ich wurde gerufen, um sie zu behandeln. Sie war sehr schön, genau wie Sie«, sagte er mit einem Lächeln. »Nun, sorgen Sie dafür, dass der Junge reichlich Flüssigkeit trinkt. *Adio*, Madame.«

»Das mache ich. Auf Wiedersehen und danke.«

Helena sah ihm nach, wie er in einer weißen Staubwolke davonfuhr. Dann blickte sie an Pandora hinauf, und trotz der sengenden Hitze lief ihr ein Schauer über den Rücken, und das mittlerweile bekannte Gefühl von drohendem Unheil stieg wieder in ihr auf. Sie zwang sich, sich auf die anstehenden Aufgaben zu konzentrieren. Als Erstes wollte sie sich den Pool ansehen. Mit raschen Schritten ging sie ums Haus und überquerte die Terrasse, wobei sie bemerkte, dass in den vermoosten leeren Steintöpfen ein paar bunte Blumen fehlten. Sie machte sich gedanklich eine Notiz. Der Pool, zu dem man von der Terrasse über ein paar bröckelnde Stufen hinabgelangte, sah erstaunlich gut erhalten aus, aber natürlich musste er erst von einer dicken Schmutzschicht befreit werden, ehe man ihn mit Wasser füllen konnte.

Helena machte kehrt, und mit einem Blick nach oben fiel ihr auf, wie anders Pandora sich von hier unten ausmachte. Wenn man sich dem Haupteingang näherte, wirkte das Haus schmucklos und streng, aber von vorn sah es ausgesprochen einladend aus. Dazu trug natürlich auch die Terrasse mit der Pergola bei, zudem hatte jedes Zimmer im ersten Stock einen kleinen schmiedeeisernen Balkon, sodass das Haus fast an eine italienische Villa denken ließ. Helena fragte sich, warum ihr das damals nicht aufgefallen war, aber dann wurde ihr klar, dass sie erst nach ihrem Besuch hier eine Weile in Italien gelebt hatte und deswegen den Vergleich damals gar nicht hatte anstellen können.

Sie ging nach oben ins Schlafzimmer und fand Immy in ihrem schönsten pinkfarbenen Festtagskleid vor dem Spiegel stehen. Unwillkürlich musste sie lächeln, als ihre Tochter bewundernd ihren kleinen Körper hin und her drehte und ihr flachsblondes Haar fliegen ließ, während sie ihr Spiegelbild aus großen, unschuldig blauen Augen betrachtete.

»Ich dachte, wir hatten uns geeinigt, dass du deine Sachen auspackst, mein Schatz.«

»Aber das hab ich doch gemacht, Mummy.« Mit einem ungehaltenen Seufzen riss Immy sich von ihrem Spiegelbild los und deutete auf die über den gesamten Boden verstreut liegenden Kleider, zum Beweis, dass sie nicht mehr im Koffer waren.

»Ich meinte, in die Schubladen auspacken, nicht auf den Boden. Und zieh das Kleid aus, das kannst du jetzt nicht tragen.«

»Warum nicht?« Immy zog einen Flunsch. »Das ist mein Lieblingskleid.«

»Ich weiß, aber es ist für Festtage und nicht für Tage, an denen man durch ein heißes und staubiges altes Haus läuft.«

Immy verfolgte, wie ihre Mutter die Kleidungsstücke in einem Haufen aufs Bett warf und sich daranmachte, sie zu verräumen. »Außerdem riechen die Schubladen komisch.«

»Sie riechen nur etwas abgestanden«, erklärte Helena. »Wir lassen sie ein Weilchen auslüften, dann verschwindet der Geruch von selbst.«

»Was machen wir heute? Gibt es hier im Fernsehen den Disney Channel?«

»Ich …« Es war fast Mittag, der Vormittag war mit der panischen Suche nach einem Arzt vergangen, der sich um ihren scheinbar delirierenden Sohn kümmern konnte. Helena ließ sich aufs Bett fallen und wünschte sich plötzlich ebenfalls, es gäbe hier den Disney Channel. »Wir haben heute viel vor, mein Schatz, und nein, hier gibt es nicht einmal einen Fernseher.«

»Können wir einen kaufen?«

»Nein, das können wir nicht«, antwortete Helena gereizt, bereute ihren unwirschen Tonfall aber sofort. Sowohl gestern auf der Reise als auch heute Vormittag war Immy so brav gewesen und hatte sich die ganze Zeit still mit sich selbst beschäftigt. Sie nahm ihre Tochter in den Arm und drückte sie an sich.

»Mummy muss sich um ein paar Sachen kümmern, und dann erkunden wir das Haus, ja?«

»Ja, aber vielleicht habe ich Hunger. Ich habe kein Frühstück bekommen.«

»Das stimmt. Dann müssen wir wohl bald einkaufen gehen. Ich schaue nur nach Alex, dann brechen wir auf.«

»Ich weiß was, Mummy!« Immys Gesicht hellte sich auf, sie hüpfte von Helenas Schoß und wühlte in ihrem kleinen Rucksack. »Ich male für Alex eine ›Gute-Besserung-Karte!‹«

»Das ist eine wunderbare Idee, mein Schatz«, pflichtete sie ihr bei, als Immy freudestrahlend Papier und bunte Filzstifte zückte.

»Oder …« Nachdenklich steckte sich Immy den Stift in den Mund. »Wenn er nicht wieder gesund wird – vielleicht sollte ich lieber ein paar Blumen pflücken für sein Grab?«

»Das kannst du auch, aber ich verspreche dir, er wird nicht sterben, also finde ich die Idee mit der Karte eigentlich besser.«

»Ach, als ich heute Morgen bei ihm war, hat er das aber gesagt.«

»Nein, er wird nicht sterben. Mal die Karte, und ich bin gleich wieder da.«

Helena verließ den Raum und ging zu Alex ins Zimmer. Manchmal wünschte sie sich, ihr Sohn würde sich zu einem ganz normalen Jugendlichen entwickeln, der eine Vorliebe für Hoodies, Fußball und Mädchen hatte und sich abends in Shopping-Zentren herumtrieb, wo er im Kreis seiner Kumpel alte Damen mit üblen Scherzen erschreckte. Stattdessen hatte er einen überragenden IQ, was theoretisch gut klang, praktisch aber mehr Probleme aufwarf, als sein Überfliegergehirn jemals würde lösen können, und zudem erinnerte sein Verhalten eher an einen alten Mann als an einen Teenager.

»Wie geht's dir?« Vorsichtig lugte sie zur Tür herein. Alex lag in seiner Boxershorts auf dem Bett, einen Arm über die Stirn gelegt.

»Umph«, bekam sie zur Antwort.

Sie setzte sich auf die Bettkante. Der uralte Ventilator, den sie aus Angus' Schlafzimmer herübergetragen hatte, damit er eine kühlende Brise auf die glühende Stirn ihres Sohnes blies, ächzte und ratterte.

»Kein guter Start, was?«

»Nee.« Alex hatte die Augen immer noch geschlossen. »Tut mir leid, Mum.«

»Ich fahre mit Immy ins Dorf, um ein bisschen einzukaufen und den Arzt zu bezahlen. Versprichst du mir, dass du literweise Wasser trinkst?«

»Ja.«

»Kann ich dir etwas mitbringen?«

»Einen Mückenschutz.«

»Also wirklich, mein Schatz, die zypriotischen Mücken tun dir nichts.«

»Ich kann sie nicht leiden, ganz egal, welche Nationalität sie haben.«

»Also gut, ich besorge dir was. Und wenn es dir morgen besser geht, fahren wir nach Paphos. Ich muss einiges anschaffen, unter anderem Ventilatoren für alle Zimmer, Bettwäsche, Handtücher, eine neue Gefrierkombination und einen Fernseher mit DVD-Spieler.«

Alex öffnete die Augen. »Echt? Ich dachte, Fernsehen wäre hier tabu?«

»Ich glaube, ein DVD-Spieler ist für Immy und Fred gerade noch vertretbar, vor allem an heißen Nachmittagen.«

»Wow. Klingt nach Fortschritt.«

»Gut.« Helena sah zu ihrem Sohn und lächelte. »Bleib heute im Bett, denn geht es dir morgen hoffentlich wieder so gut, dass wir unseren Ausflug machen können.«

»Bestimmt. Ist ja nur Dehydrierung.«

»Ja, mein Schatz.« Sie gab ihm einen Kuss auf die Stirn. »Versuch zu schlafen.«

»Mach ich. Und tut mir leid wegen der Malaria.«

»Schon in Ordnung. Bis später.« Auf dem Weg nach unten hörte Helena in der Küche ihr Handy klingeln. Im Laufschritt erreichte sie es gerade noch rechtzeitig.

»Ja, hallo?«

»Bist du das, Helena? Hier ist Jules. Wie geht es dir?«

»Gut, doch, uns geht's gut.«

»Schön. Wie ist das Haus?«

»Wunderschön. Genau wie in meiner Erinnerung.«

»Vor vierundzwanzig Jahren? Du meine Güte! Ich hoffe, sie haben seitdem mal das Bad renoviert!«

»Das haben sie nicht.« Als Helena Jules' Befürchtungen bestätigte, konnte sie ein gewisses Frohlocken nicht unterdrücken. »Ein bisschen Farbe und neue Toilettensitze wären durchaus angebracht, aber ich glaube, es ist so weit einwandfrei, zumindest bautechnisch.«

»Das ist ja immerhin etwas. Gut zu hören, dass uns das Dach nicht im Schlaf auf den Kopf fällt.«

»Die Küche müsste auch renoviert werden«, ergänzte Helena. »Ich glaube, wir werden mehr den Grill als den Backofen in der Küche benutzen. Um ehrlich zu sein, ist es vielleicht nicht ganz das, woran du gewöhnt bist.«

»Wir werden schon zurechtkommen. Und natürlich bringe ich eigene Bettwäsche mit, du weißt ja, das mache ich immer. Wenn du sonst etwas brauchst, gib Bescheid.«

»Danke, Jules. Wie geht's den Kindern?«

»Ach, Rupes und Viola geht es ganz gut, aber ich war jetzt wochenlang eingespannt mit Preisverleihungen und Festversammlungen. Sacha hatte natürlich jedes Mal eine Ausrede parat, um nicht mitzukommen.«

»Ach.« Helena wusste, dass Jules solche Anlässe insgeheim liebte. »Und wie geht es Sacha?«, erkundigte sie sich höflich.

»Er arbeitet Tag und Nacht, trinkt viel zu viel … du kennst ihn doch. Ich habe ihn in den letzten Wochen kaum zu Gesicht bekommen. Guter Gott, Helena, ich muss los. Heute Abend kommen Freunde zum Essen, ich muss noch alles vorbereiten.«

»Dann sehen wir uns in ein paar Tagen.«

»Exakt. Lass dir Zeit mit dem Braunwerden, hörst du? Sonst kann ich dich nie mehr einholen. Hier schüttet es. *Ciao*, meine Liebe.«

»*Ciao*«, murmelte Helena unglücklich ins Handy und ließ sich auf einen Stuhl fallen. »O mein Gott.« Sie wünschte sich sehnlich, sie hätte sich nicht von Jules erweichen lassen, sie mitsamt ihrer Familie zwei Wochen hier aufzunehmen. Sie hatte jede nur denkbare Ausrede angeführt, aber Jules hatte sich über alles hinweggesetzt. Und so würden in einer Woche die vier Mitglieder der Familie Chandler – Jules, ihre zwei Kinder und ihr Mann Sacha – in Pandora einfallen.

Helena wusste aber auch, dass sie ihr Grauen vor dem Besuch für sich behalten musste. Sacha war Williams bester und ältester Freund, und Viola, die Tochter, war sein Patenkind. Ihr blieb also nichts anderes übrig, als gute Miene zum bösen Spiel zu machen.

Wie soll ich das nur schaffen …? Helena fächelte sich in der drückenden Hitze Luft zu, betrachtete die schäbige Küche mit Jules' kritischem Blick und wusste, dass sie ihre abfälligen Kommentare nicht ertragen würde. Sie band sich die Haare zu einem Knoten und freute sich über die kühle Luft am Nacken.

Ich schaffe das schon, sagte sie sich. *Ich muss …*

»Fahren wir jetzt?« Immy war hinter sie geschlichen. »Ich hab Hunger. Kriege ich im Lokal Pommes mit Ketchup?« Sie schlang ihre Arme um die Taille ihrer Mutter.

»Ja, wir fahren jetzt.« Helena stand auf und brachte ein mattes Lächeln zustande. »Und ja, die kriegst du.«

Auf der Fahrt durch die ausgedehnten Weinfelder Richtung Dorf brannte die Mittagssonne durch die Scheiben. Immy saß verbotenerweise auf dem Beifahrersitz, und als sie sich aufrecht hinkniete, um zum Fenster hinauszusehen, schlackerte der Sicherheitsgurt wie ein Modeaccessoire um ihren schmächtigen Körper.

»Mummy, können wir ein paar Trauben pflücken?«

»Ja, das ist eine gute Idee! Obwohl sie ein bisschen anders schmecken als normale Weintrauben.« Helena brachte den Wagen zum Stehen, und sie stiegen aus.

»Hier, schau.« Sie bückte sich und umfasste eine schwere Traube kräftig lilaroter Früchte, die unter dem Weinlaub verborgen war, riss sie ab und reichte Immy ein paar einzelne Trauben.

»Kann man die wirklich essen, Mummy?«, fragte Immy skeptisch. »Weißt du, die sind ja nicht vom Supermarkt.«

»Sie sind nicht besonders süß, weil sie noch nicht ganz reif sind, aber versuch mal eine!«, sagte Helena aufmunternd und steckte ihrer Tochter eine in den Mund.

Immy biss mit ihren kleinen weißen Zähnen durch die dicke Haut. »Schmeckt ganz gut. Sollen wir Alex ein paar mitbringen? Kranke bekommen doch immer Weintrauben.«

»Gute Idee. Wir pflücken zwei ganze Trauben.« Helena begann, eine zweite Traube abzubrechen, hatte aber das eindeutige Gefühl, beobachtet zu werden, und richtete sich auf. Als sie den Mann sah, erstarrte sie. Keine zwanzig Meter entfernt, inmitten der Reben, stand er und schaute sie unverwandt an.

Zum Schutz vor dem grellen Sonnenlicht schirmte sie die Augen ab und hatte die irrationale Hoffnung, die Gestalt dort wäre eine Halluzination, denn es konnte doch gar nicht … es war doch unmöglich …

Aber da war er, genau so, wie sie ihn in Erinnerung hatte, und er stand an praktisch genau derselben Stelle, an der sie ihn vor vierundzwanzig Jahren das erste Mal gesehen hatte.

»Mummy, wer ist der Mann? Warum guckt der uns so an? Tut er das, weil wir Trauben gestohlen haben? Kommen wir jetzt ins Gefängnis? *Mummy?!*«

Helena stand immer noch wie versteinert da, ihr Kopf versuchte das Unmögliche, das ihre Augen dem Gehirn übermittelten, zu entschlüsseln. Immy zerrte an ihrem Arm. »Jetzt komm schon, Mummy, schnell, bevor er die Polizei holt!«

Widerstrebend riss sich Helena von dem Anblick los und ließ sich von ihrer Tochter zum Wagen führen, die zum Beifahrersitz rannte und sich erwartungsvoll neben sie setzte.

»Jetzt fahr!«, befahl Immy.

»Ja, ich fahre ja schon.« Automatisch drehte Helena den Schlüssel im Zündschloss, der Wagen sprang an.

»Wer war der Mann?«, fragte Immy, als sie wieder über den Feldweg holperten. »Kennst du ihn?«

»Nein … Nein, ich kenne ihn nicht.«

»Ach, du hast aber ausgesehen, als kennst du ihn. Er war so groß und schön wie ein Prinz. Und die Sonne hat ihm eine Krone gemacht.«

»Ja.« Helena richtete ihre ganze Aufmerksamkeit darauf, den Wagen sicher durch die Weinfelder zu manövrieren.

»Wie er wohl heißt?«

Alexis …

»Ich weiß es nicht«, flüsterte sie.

»Mummy?«

»Ja?«

»Jetzt haben wir die Trauben für Alex liegen lassen.«

Im Dorf hatte sich erstaunlich wenig verändert, im Gegensatz zu dem hässlichen Legoland, das sich mittlerweile im kunterbunten Durcheinander die Küste entlangzog. Die schmale, staubige Hauptstraße lag verwaist da; in der sengenden Mittagshitze zogen sich die Einwohner in die Kühle ihrer Steinhäuser zurück. Helena bemerkte zwei Bars, die es damals noch nicht gegeben hatte, aber davon abgesehen sah alles mehr oder minder aus wie früher.

Nachdem sie Geld geholt hatte, ging sie mit Immy in den hübschen Innenhof von Persephones Taverne. Dort setzten sie sich in den Schatten eines Olivenbaums. Immy war hingerissen von der Schar magerer Kätzchen, die kläglich miauend um ihre Beine strich.

»Ach, Mummy, können wir nicht eine mit nach Hause nehmen? Bitte, bitte«, bettelte Immy und steckte einer kleinen Katze ihr letztes Pommes zu.

»Nein, mein Schatz, das geht nicht. Sie leben hier mit ihrer eigenen Mummy«, sagte Helena mit Nachdruck. Ihre Hand zitterte unmerklich, als sie das Glas mit dem jungen hiesigen

Wein zum Mund hob. Er schmeckte noch genauso wie in ihrer Erinnerung, etwas scharf, aber süß. Sie fühlte sich, als wäre sie durch den Spiegel in die Vergangenheit gefallen …

»Mummy! Krieg ich jetzt ein Eis oder nicht?«

»Entschuldige, mein Schatz, ich war in Gedanken. Natürlich bekommst du ein Eis.«

»Meinst du, dass es hier Phish Food von Ben und Jerry's gibt?«

»Das bezweifle ich. Wahrscheinlich hast du die Wahl zwischen Vanille, Erdbeere und Schoko, aber lass uns doch fragen.«

Immy rief den jungen Kellner an den Tisch, das Eis wurde erörtert und bestellt, ebenso wie ein zypriotischer Kaffee für Helena, mittelsüß, um das Glas Wein zu verdünnen.

Zwanzig Minuten später verließen sie die Taverne und schlenderten über die staubige Straße Richtung Wagen.

»Schau mal, Mummy, da drüben auf der Bank sitzen lauter Nonnen.« Immy deutete zur Kirche. »Denen muss doch furchtbar heiß sein in den Kleidern.«

»Das sind keine Nonnen, Immy, das sind die alten Frauen aus dem Dorf. Sie tragen Schwarz, weil ihre Ehemänner tot sind. Sie heißen Witwen«, erklärte Helena.

»Und sie tragen Schwarz?«

»Ja.«

»Kein Rosa? Nie?«

»Nein.«

Immy schaute entsetzt. »Aber ich muss das doch nicht machen, wenn mein Mann stirbt, oder?«

»Nein, mein Schatz. Aber hier auf Zypern ist das so Tradition.«

»Dann werde ich nie hierherziehen«, beschied Immy und hüpfte zum Auto.

Nach einem Besuch in der Arztpraxis, wo Helena am Empfang die Rechnung für den Hausbesuch beglich, suchten sie den einzigen Dorfladen auf, wo es nach wie vor alles zu kaufen gab, was man brauchte. Außerdem hatte er mittlerweile einen DVD-Verleih eingerichtet, worüber Alex sich freuen würde. Mit dem Kofferraum voll Einkäufe kehrten Helena und Immy schließlich nach Pandora zurück. Alex erschien in der hinteren Tür.

»Hallo, Mum.«

»Hallo, mein Schatz, geht's dir besser? Kannst du mir vielleicht mit den Einkaufstaschen zur Hand gehen?«

Alex half Helena, die Taschen in die Küche zu tragen.

»Mein Gott, ist das heiß.« Helena wischte sich über die Stirn. »Ich brauche dringend einen Schluck Wasser.«

Alex schenkte ihr aus dem Krug, der im Kühlschrank stand, ein Glas ein und reichte es ihr. »Da.«

»Danke.« Mit wenigen Zügen trank Helena es leer.

»Ich gehe wieder rauf und lege mich hin. Mir ist immer noch ein bisschen schwummerig«, sagte Alex.

»Gut. Kommst du später zum Essen runter?«

»Ja.« Auf halbem Weg zur Tür blieb er stehen und drehte sich noch einmal um. »Ach, übrigens, da ist jemand gekommen, der dich sehen will.«

»Ach ja? Warum hast du mir das denn nicht gleich gesagt?«

»Er sitzt draußen auf der Terrasse. Ich habe ihm gesagt, ich wüsste nicht, wann du wiederkommst, aber *er* wollte unbedingt warten.«

Mit Mühe gelang es Helena, sich ungerührt zu geben. »Wer ist denn dieser *er*?«

»Woher soll ich das wissen?« Alex zuckte mit den Achseln. »Aber er kennt dich offenbar.«

»Ach ja?«

»Ja. Ich glaube, er hat gesagt, er heißt Alexis.«

Alex' Tagebuch

12. Juli 2006

Ich stehe bei mir im Zimmer am Fenster und linse um die Läden herum, damit sie mich von der Terrasse aus nicht sehen können.

Ich habe den Mann im Blick, der meine Mutter besuchen gekommen ist. Im Moment marschiert er nervös auf und ab, die Hände hat er in die Taschen gesteckt. Er ist groß und hat eine gute Figur, und er ist sehr gebräunt. Außerdem hat er dichtes schwarzes Haar, an den Schläfen sind erst ein paar weiße Strähnen zu sehen, er ist also eindeutig kein alter Mann. Wahrscheinlich ist er nur ein bisschen älter als meine Mum. Und jünger als mein Stiefvater.

Als er kam, habe ich ihn mir genau angesehen und festgestellt, dass er blaue Augen hat, sehr blaue Augen. Vielleicht ist er also kein Einheimischer. Außer natürlich, er trägt farbige Kontaktlinsen, was ich allerdings bezweifle. Fasst man die einzelnen optischen Komponenten dieses Mannes zusammen, kommt man nicht umhin, ihn als gut aussehend zu bezeichnen.

Ich sehe meine Mutter auf die Terrasse schweben. Sie geht so anmutig, als würden ihre Füße den Boden gar nicht berühren. Das kommt daher, weil sie die obere Körperhälfte nicht bewegt, nur die Beine. Einen guten Meter vor ihm bleibt sie mit locker herabhängenden Armen stehen. Ihr Gesicht kann ich nicht sehen, aber seines – das sich zu einem Ausdruck reiner Freude in lauter kleine Falten verzieht.

Jetzt schlägt mein Herz ganz schnell, und ich weiß, das kommt nicht mehr von der Dehydrierung. Und auch nicht von Malaria. Das ist die blanke Panik.

Keiner von ihnen sagt ein Wort. Eine gefühlte Ewigkeit stehen sie so da, als würden sie einander mit Blicken aufsaugen. Auf jeden Fall sieht *er* so aus, als würde er Mum am liebsten auf der Stelle aufsaugen. Dann streckt er die Hände aus, tritt zu ihr und bleibt vor ihr stehen. Er nimmt ihre zarten Hände in seine Pranken und küsst sie ehrfürchtig, als wären sie heilig.

Das geht gar nicht. Ich will es nicht sehen, aber ich kann einfach nicht wegschauen.

Endlich hat dieses Lippen-auf-Hand-Getue ein Ende, er nimmt meine Mutter in seine muskulösen Arme und drückt sie an sich. Sie ist so zart und blass und blond im Vergleich zu seiner schwarzen Kraft, dass sie mich an eine Porzellanpuppe erinnert, die von einem großen braunen Bären zerquetscht wird. Sie hat den Kopf in einem komischen Winkel zurückgeworfen, so fest drückt er sie an seine Brust. Außerdem hält er ihren Hals in seiner Armbeuge, und ich hoffe bloß, dass er ihr nicht den Kopf abreißt, wie das einmal mit Immys Porzellanpuppe passiert ist.

Gerade als mir die Luft ausgeht, weil ich sie schon so lange anhalte, lässt er sie los, und ich atme schnappend ein. Gott sei Dank nichts mit Lippen-auf-Lippen. Das wäre einfach voll daneben.

Aber es ist noch nicht vorbei.

Offenbar ist es ihm ein Anliegen, ständig irgendeinen

Teil ihrer Anatomie zu berühren, also nimmt er wieder ihre Hand. Und führt sie zu der mit Wein überwucherten Pergola, sodass ich sie nicht mehr sehen kann.

Verdammt! Langsam gehe ich zum Bett zurück und lasse mich darauf fallen.

Wer zum Teufel ist er? Und was hat er mit *ihr* zu tun?

Sobald ich ihn da auf der Terrasse gesehen habe, war mir klar, dass er nichts Gutes bedeutet. Er hat gewirkt, als würde das Haus ihm gehören. Soll ich Dad anrufen? Den Dad, der nicht mein Dad ist? Aber mehr Vater als ihn habe ich nicht, habe ich noch nie gehabt. Ich habe doch gewusst, dass er irgendwann mal nützlich werden würde.

Er würde sich bestimmt nicht freuen zu hören, dass seine Frau auf der Terrasse von einem großen braunen zypriotischen Bären zerquetscht wird, oder? Ich schalte mein Handy ein. Was soll ich sagen?

»Dad, du musst sofort kommen! Mum steht unter der Pergola und ist in Todesgefahr!«

Verdammt, das geht einfach nicht. Er hält mich sowieso für seltsam. Mir ist klar, dass ihm nichts anderes übrig bleibt, als mich zu tolerieren, weil er Mum liebt und sie ohne mich nicht zu haben war. Leider bin ich bei den meisten Ballspielen eine ziemliche Niete, auch wenn ich mich voll ins Zeug lege. Als ich kleiner war, hat er versucht, sie mir beizubringen, aber ich hatte immer das Gefühl, ihn zu enttäuschen, weil ich's nie in die Jugendmannschaft geschafft habe. Und wenn er zum Zuschauen kam, habe ich's vor lauter Nervosität völlig vermasselt. Hätte ich ein gutes Ballgefühl, wäre unser Verhältnis ein ganzes Stück besser, aber zumindest liebt er Mum und beschützt sie vor den vielen anderen, die sie haben wollen.

Wie der jetzt unter der Pergola.

Was für eine Ironie, oder? Da habe ich mich so gefreut, sie ein paar Tage für mich zu haben, ohne Dad, der mir immer das Gefühl gibt, ich wäre im Weg, und keine vierundzwanzig Stunden später wünsche ich mir, er wäre hier.

Vielleicht sollte ich ihm doch eine SMS schreiben. Ich schaue auf mein Handy, mein Guthaben beträgt gerade mal achtzehn Pence. Die reichen nicht. Und selbst wenn, was könnte er schon machen?

Außer mir ist niemand hier. Immy noch, aber die zählt nicht.

Tja … mir bleibt wohl keine Wahl: Da muss ich ran.

Ich werde in die Schlacht ziehen, um die Ehre meiner Mutter zu retten.

KAPITEL 3

»Du ... du hast dich gar nicht verändert.«

»Doch, Alexis, natürlich habe ich mich verändert. Ich bin vierundzwanzig Jahre älter geworden.«

»Helena, du bist schön, genau wie damals.«

Sie spürte, dass eine Röte ihre ohnehin erhitzten Wangen überzog. »Woher wusstest du, dass ich hier bin?«

»Ich habe im Dorf ein Gerücht gehört. Mittags hat mich dann Dimitrios angerufen und gesagt, dass er auf dem Weg von Pandora ins Dorf eine Dame und ein Kind mit goldenen Haaren gesehen habe. Da wusste ich, das konntest nur du sein.«

»Wer ist Dimitrios?«

»Mein Sohn, Helena.«

»Aber natürlich! Natürlich!« Helena lachte vor Erleichterung. »Immy und ich haben unterwegs angehalten, um ein paar Trauben zu pflücken, und da habe ich ihn gesehen, er hat mich angestarrt. Ich dachte, das wärst du ... wie dumm von mir ... Er sieht aus wie du.«

»Du meinst, er sieht aus wie ich früher.«

»Ja. Ja, genau.«

Eine Weile schwiegen sie.

»Und wie geht es dir, Helena?«, fragte er schließlich. »Wie ist es dir in all den Jahren ergangen?«

»Es war ... gut. Ja, doch, gut.«

»Und du bist verheiratet?«

»Ja.«

»Von deinen Kindern weiß ich bereits, ich habe deinen Sohn gesehen und von deiner Tochter gehört.«

»Ich habe drei, aber der Kleine, Fred, ist noch zu Hause in England bei seinem Vater. Sie kommen in ein paar Tagen nach. Und du?«

»Ich war verheiratet mit Maria, der Tochter des alten Bürgermeisters hier in Kathikas. Sie hat mir zwei Söhne geschenkt, aber als Michel, der Jüngere, acht war, ist sie bei einem Autounfall ums Leben gekommen. Jetzt leben wir drei Männer zusammen, ernten unsere Trauben und keltern unseren Wein wie schon mein Vater, mein Großvater und mein Urgroßvater vor uns.«

»Das tut mir sehr leid, Alexis. Das muss schrecklich für dich gewesen sein.« Helena hörte selbst, wie banal ihre Worte klangen, aber etwas anderes fiel ihr nicht ein.

»Gott gibt und Gott nimmt, und zumindest meine Jungs haben es heil überstanden. Und Dimitrios, den du im Weingarten gesehen hast, wird bald heiraten, das heißt, das Erbe wird an die nächste Generation weitergegeben.«

»Ja. Ich … Hier hat sich wirklich wenig verändert.«

Alexis sah sie skeptisch an. »Doch, Helena, hier auf Zypern hat sich sehr vieles verändert, wie überall. Das nennt man Fortschritt. Manches ist gut, anderes ist weniger gut. Ein paar Wenige werden sehr reich und wollen immer noch mehr, wie überall. Aber hier in Kathikas leben wir, zumindest im Augenblick noch, in einer wahren Oase. Allerdings strecken die Bauunternehmen schon ihre habgierigen Finger nach unserem fruchtbaren Land aus. Versucht haben sie es bereits.«

»Das kann ich mir nur allzu gut vorstellen. Es ist einfach perfekt hier.«

»Ja. Und du darfst nicht glauben, dass jeder bei uns im Dorf der Versuchung widerstehen wird, vor allem die Jungen nicht. Sie möchten schnelle Autos und Satellitenschüsseln und den amerikanischen Lebensstandard, den sie im Fernsehen sehen. Wieso auch nicht? Wir wollten auch mehr, Helena. Also sollten wir Schritt halten und aufhören, wie unsere eigenen Eltern zu klingen.« Er lachte leise.

»Alexis, wir sind so alt und gesetzt wie unsere Eltern damals.«

»Dann lass uns die Kinder sein, die wir damals waren, nur für einen Moment.« Er griff nach ihrer Hand, und in der Sekunde trat Alex auf die Terrasse.

Helena zog ihre Hand fort, aber sie wusste, dass ihr Sohn die Berührung gesehen hatte.

»Wo ist Immy?«, fragte er barsch.

»In der Küche, vermute ich. Alex, du hast Alexis schon kennengelernt.«

»Wir tragen den gleichen Namen. Er bedeutet so viel wie ›Beschützer‹ oder ›der die Fremden abwehrt‹«, sagte Alexis freundlich.

»Ich weiß. Mum, ich hoffe bloß, dass Immy in der Zwischenzeit nicht weggelaufen ist. Du kennst sie doch.«

»Sicher nicht. Magst du sie nicht holen und mit ihr auf die Terrasse kommen, damit sie Alexis kennenlernen kann? Und bitte setz den Wasserkessel auf. Ich brauche dringend eine Tasse Tee«, fügte Helena hinzu und ließ sich auf einen Stuhl fallen. Plötzlich fühlte sie sich vollkommen ausgelaugt.

Alex warf ihr einen finsteren Blick zu und ging ins Haus zurück.

»Ein gut aussehender Junge«, sagte Alexis. »Gut gebaut.«

Helena seufzte. »Er ist ... Auf jeden Fall ist er außergewöhnlich. Und brillant und nervig und schwierig und ... aber ich liebe ihn sehr«, sagte sie mit einem müden Lächeln. »Vielleicht erzähle ich dir eines Tages mehr von ihm.«

»Vielleicht erzählen wir uns eines Tages mehr von vielem«, erwiderte Alexis leise.

»Da ist sie.« Alex führte eine tränenüberströmte Immy auf die Terrasse. »Sie ist in der Küche von einer riesigen gestreiften Hornisse gejagt worden. Deren Stachel bestimmt tödlich sein kann.«

»Ach, mein Schatz, warum hast du nicht nach mir gerufen?« Helena breitete die Arme aus, und Immy lief zu ihr.

»Das habe ich ja, aber du bist nicht gekommen. Alex hat mich gerettet. Ein bisschen.«

»Helena, sie sieht dir so ähnlich. Sie ist … wie sagt man? Ach, deine Doppelgängerin, genau.« Alexis lächelte.

»Ich nenne sie Mini-Mum. Verstehen Sie das, Alexis?«, sagte Alex brüsk. »Nein, wahrscheinlich nicht. Auch egal.«

»Alexis, möchtest du eine Tasse Tee? Ich gehe rein und mache eine Kanne«, ging Helena entschieden dazwischen.

»Ja, gern. Warum nicht die englische Tradition befolgen und bei heißem Wetter etwas Heißes trinken?«

»Es ist allgemein bekannt, dass eine heiße Tasse Tee eine kühlende Wirkung hat. Deswegen trinken sie ihn in Indien ja auch«, sagte Alex belehrend.

»Und es hatte nichts damit zu tun, dass sie alle auf Teeplantagen lebten«, sagte Helena und sah tadelnd zu ihrem Sohn. »Immy, magst du mir helfen? Ich bin gleich wieder da.«

Alex setzte sich auf den Stuhl, auf dem seine Mutter gesessen hatte, verschränkte die Arme vor der Brust und funkelte Alexis an. »Und woher kennen Sie meine Mutter?«

»Wir haben uns vor vielen Jahren kennengelernt, als sie das letzte Mal hier war, zu Besuch bei Colonel McCladden.«

»Sie meinen bei Angus, ihrem Patenonkel? Und Sie haben sie seitdem nicht gesehen?«

»Doch, schon«, antwortete Alexis mit einem Lächeln, »aber das ist eine andere Geschichte. Und, Alex, wie gefällt es dir hier?«

»Dazu kann ich noch nichts sagen. Als wir angekommen sind, war es dunkel, und ich habe den ganzen Tag mit Verdacht auf Malaria im Bett gelegen. Es ist sehr heiß, und überall gibt es Mücken und Hornissen. Die kann ich nicht leiden.«

»Und das Haus?«

»Das ist cool. Und ich meine nicht kühl, weil es irre heiß ist, aber ich mag Geschichte, und davon gibt's hier reichlich«, musste Alex einräumen.

»Die ganze Gegend ist historisch sehr interessant. Wenn du dich für Geschichte interessierst, kennst du ja vielleicht die griechischen Sagen. Laut ihnen wurde Aphrodite in Paphos geboren und hat ihr Leben mit Adonis hier auf der Insel verbracht. Du kannst sein Bad sehen, es liegt nicht weit von hier entfernt.«

»Hoffentlich hat er den Stöpsel rausgezogen, sonst ist das Wasser mittlerweile ziemlich abgestanden«, brummelte Alex.

»Es gibt dort wunderschöne Wasserfälle, inmitten von Bergen«, fuhr Alexis fort. »Man kann von hoch oben ins Wasser springen, das ist sehr klar und sauber und in der Hitze ausgesprochen erfrischend. Wenn du magst, kann ich es dir zeigen.«

»Danke, aber Extremsport ist nicht mein Ding. Und« – Alex beäugte ihn skeptisch –, »was machen Sie hier so?«

»Meine Familie baut hier seit vielen Jahrhunderten Wein an. Wir machen Wein. Davon können wir als Familie gut leben. Und in letzter Zeit exportieren wir immer mehr ins Ausland. Ach, hier kommt ja deine Mutter.«

Helena stellte das Tablett auf den Tisch. »Ich habe Immy

oben ins Bett gelegt, sie ist völlig erschöpft von der Hitze und der Hornisse. Alex, möchtest du eine Tasse Tee?«

»Ja.« Er erhob sich. »Setz dich, Mum, ich schenke ein. Ich habe gerade von Adonis' Bidet gehört.«

»Du meinst die Wasserfälle? Ach, die sind wunderschön, Alexis, nicht wahr?« Helena warf ihm ein Lächeln zu, als hingen sie einer gemeinsamen Erinnerung nach.

»Wenn Dad kommt, fährt er ja vielleicht mal mit uns hin«, sagte Alex laut. »Übrigens, wann kommt er denn?«

»Am Freitag, wie du nur allzu gut weißt. Alexis, Milch?«

»Nein danke, Helena.«

»Aber vielleicht kommt er ja auch früher, Mum, oder? Ich meine, vielleicht will Dad uns ja überraschen und steht im nächsten Moment in der Tür.«

»Das bezweifle ich, Alex, er hat viel zu tun.«

»Aber du merkst doch genau, wie du ihm fehlst. Er ruft dich ständig an. Es würde mich überhaupt nicht wundern, wenn er doch früher kommt.«

Als Helena ihrem Sohn die Tasse Tee reichte, warf sie ihm mit gerunzelter Stirn einen Blick zu. »Das hoffe ich wirklich nicht. Ich möchte das Haus vorher gern etwas mehr in Schuss bringen.«

»Brauchst du dabei in irgendeiner Weise Hilfe, Helena?«, fragte Alexis. »Es hat ja doch eine ganze Weile leer gestanden.«

»Um ehrlich zu sein – wenn du jemanden kennst, der den Pool herrichten könnte, das wäre großartig. Er muss gründlich gereinigt und dann aufgefüllt werden.«

»Welchen Pool?« Unvermittelt lebte Alex auf.

»Wenn du dort« – Helena deutete in die Richtung – »durch die kleine Pforte und die Stufen hinuntergehst, kommst du zu einem wunderschönen kleinen Pool. Leider sieht es aus, als wären alle Oliven ins Becken gefallen, und wahrscheinlich müssen ein paar kaputte Fliesen ersetzt werden.«

»Dann soll Georgios sich das mal anschauen«, sagte Alexis. »Er ist der Cousin meiner Frau, ein Maurer.«

»Sie sind verheiratet?«, fragte Alex erfreut.

»Leider nicht mehr. Ich bin verwitwet. Meine Frau ist vor vielen Jahren gestorben. Aber jetzt rufe ich Georgios an.« Er wählte auf seinem Handy eine Nummer und unterhielt sich kurz und angeregt auf Griechisch, dann legte er es lächelnd wieder auf den Tisch. »Er schaut heute Abend vorbei, und vielleicht ist der Pool fertig, bis dein Mann kommt.«

»Das wäre großartig«, sagte Helena dankbar. »Und vielleicht kannst du mir auch sagen, wo ich in Paphos eine neue Kühlkombination kaufen kann, einen Herd, eine Mikrowelle – im Grunde eine ganze Küchenausstattung. Nächste Woche kommen Scharen von Menschen. Aber ich weiß nicht, vielleicht können sie gar nicht so schnell liefern.«

»Du brauchst dir die Sachen nicht bringen zu lassen. Ich habe einen Transporter, um meinen Wein zu den Hotels und Restaurants hier in der Gegend zu liefern. Ich kann dich hinfahren, und dann nehmen wir die Sachen gleich selbst mit.«

»Bist du sicher, dass das geht?«

»Aber natürlich, Helena. Es wäre mir ein Vergnügen.«

»Und kennst du im Dorf vielleicht auch jemanden, der mir mit dem Haushalt und beim Kochen helfen könnte?«

»Natürlich. Angelina, die die Schlüssel für dich hinterlegt hat. Sie hat im letzten Jahr, das der Colonel hier in Pandora verbrachte, für ihn gearbeitet. Sie hat bestimmt Zeit, und sie liebt Kinder. Ich werde mit ihr sprechen und ihr sagen, dass sie bei dir vorbeischauen soll.«

»Danke, Alexis, du bist wirklich unsere Rettung«, sagte Helena glücklich und trank einen Schluck Tee. »Dann kann ich sie auch fragen, ob sie ab und zu auf die Kinder aufpassen würde, damit wir abends einmal weggehen können.«

»Mum, ich kann das machen«, schlug Alex vor.

»Ja, mein Schatz, ich weiß, danke.«

»Und in welchem Zustand ist das Haus?«, fragte Alexis.

»In meinen Augen sieht alles gut aus«, meinte Helena mit einem Achselzucken, »aber ich bin keine Fachfrau.«

»Dann soll Georgios sich das auch ansehen, wenn er schon hier ist. Die Wasserrohre und die Stromleitungen ... darum hat sich seit Jahren niemand gekümmert, und wir wollen doch nicht, dass etwas passiert.«

»Ich weiß.« Helena seufzte. »Das Haus ist wirklich eine Büchse der Pandora. Ich wage es kaum, sie zu öffnen.«

Alexis drehte sich zu Alex. »Du kennst die Legende des Hauses?«

»Nein«, brummte er mürrisch.

»Es ist eine schöne Legende. Es heißt, dass jeder, der zum ersten Mal nach Pandora kommt, sich während seines Aufenthalts hier verliebt.«

»Wirklich?« Alex hob fragend die Augenbrauen. »Gilt das auch für Fünfjährige? Vorhin ist mir aufgefallen, dass Immy ihr Schmuselämmchen reichlich verträumt angesehen hat.«

»Alex, sei nicht so frech!« Jetzt riss Helena der Geduldsfaden.

»Ach, er ist ein Junge und hat Angst vor der Liebe«, sagte Alexis mit einem nachsichtigen Lächeln. »Aber wenn es so weit ist, wird er sie mit offenen Armen begrüßen, so wie wir alle. Und jetzt muss ich gehen.« Er stand auf, und Helena folgte seinem Beispiel.

»Es war wunderbar, dich zu sehen, Helena«, sagte er und küsste sie innig auf beide Wangen.

»Ganz meinerseits, Alexis.«

»Dann hole ich dich morgen früh um halb neun ab, und wir fahren nach Paphos, ja? *Kalispera*, Alex, pass gut auf deine Mutter auf.«

»Das tue ich immer«, brummte Alex.

»Auf Wiedersehen.« Alexis nickte ihm noch einmal zu und ging dann über die Terrasse davon.

»Also wirklich, Alex.« Helena seufzte verärgert. »Musstest du wirklich so unfreundlich zu ihm sein?«

»Das war ich doch gar nicht.«

»Doch, das warst du, und das weißt du auch. Warum magst du ihn nicht?«

»Woher weißt du, dass ich ihn nicht mag?«

»Jetzt komm, Alex, du hast keinen Hehl daraus gemacht und dich unmöglich benommen.«

»Es tut mir leid, aber ich traue ihm einfach nicht. Und jetzt möchte ich mir mal den Pool ansehen, wenn's recht ist.«

»Nur zu.«

Helena sah ihrem Sohn nach, der über die Terrasse auf die Pforte zuging. Sie war froh, dass er sie eine Weile allein ließ … dass beide sie eine Weile allein ließen, diese zwei Männer, die den gleichen Namen trugen und immer einen Platz in ihrem Herz haben würden. Allmählich ließ der Schock nach, Alexis so unvermittelt zu sehen, und sie überlegte sich, dass er damals kaum mehr als ein Junge gewesen war, nur ein paar Jahre älter als ihr Sohn jetzt. Mittlerweile war er ein Mann in den besten Jahren, aber im Grunde war er noch genauso wie damals.

Nachdenklich rieb Helena sich die Nase. Die erste Liebe vergaß man nie … Und alle glaubten, ihre Erfahrung wäre einmalig und unvergleichlich in ihrer Macht, ihrer Leidenschaft und ihrem Zauber. Natürlich hatte sie jenen ersten Sommer mit Alexis hier in Pandora vierundzwanzig Jahre lang in ihrem Gedächtnis bewahrt wie einen Schmetterling, der für alle Ewigkeiten in Bernstein gefangen ist.

Sie waren so jung gewesen … Sie fast sechzehn, er neunzehn. Und noch immer wusste er nichts von den Folgen ihrer Beziehung und von ihrem, Helenas, weiterem Leben. Und dass diese Liebe ihr Leben verändert hatte.

Plötzlich packte sie die Angst, und wieder fragte sie sich, ob es wirklich eine gute Idee gewesen war, nach Pandora zu kommen. Vielleicht war es das Schlimmste, was sie überhaupt hatte machen können? In ein paar Tagen würde William hier sein, und er hatte noch nie von Alexis gehört. Aber was hätte es denn für einen Sinn gehabt, ihm von jemandem zu erzählen, der kaum mehr als ein Schatten aus ihrer Vergangenheit war?

Aber jetzt war Alexis kein Schatten mehr, sondern ein realer Mann aus Fleisch und Blut. Helena konnte nicht mehr länger verdrängen, dass ihre Vergangenheit und ihre Gegenwart in Kürze aufeinanderprallen würden.

Helenas Handy klingelte in dem Moment, als sie Alex und Immy das Abendessen vorsetzte.

»Alex, gehst du bitte ran?«, bat sie, als sie das schwer beladene Tablett auf den Terrassentisch stellte.

»Hallo, Dad«, sagte er. »Ja, uns geht's gut. Abgesehen davon, dass Mum mich und Immy jetzt gleich zwingen wird, pürierte Ziegenhoden in Fischdreck zu essen, oder so sieht es zumindest aus. Ich rate dir, lass dir die Pizza schmecken, solange du noch kannst. Ja, ich gebe dir Mum. Tschüs.«

Helena hob die Augenbrauen und seufzte entnervt, als Alex ihr das Handy reichte. »Hallo, mein Schatz, alles in Ordnung? Nein, ich will sie nicht vergiften. Sie dürfen Feta, Hummus und Taramosalata probieren. Wie geht's Fred?« Helena klemmte sich das Handy zwischen Schulter und Kinn und stellte das Geschirr und die Speisen vom Tablett auf den Tisch. »Gut. Jetzt reiche ich dir Immy, und wir telefonieren später. Ja, Ciao. Hier ist Daddy.« Helena drückte Immy das Telefon in die Hand.

»Hallo, Daddy … ja, mir geht's gut. Alex ist heute Morgen fast gestorben und Mummy und ich haben in einem Feld einen Prinzen gesehen als wir Trauben gepflückt haben aber die Polizei hätte uns verhaften können also haben wir sie alle liegen lassen aber auf dem Rückweg haben wir sie doch geholt und der Daddy von dem Prinz hat uns besucht und hat Tee bei uns getrunken und war richtig nett und ich habe zum Mittagessen Ketchup und Pommes bekommen und hier ist es sehr heiß und …« Immy holte Luft und schwieg. »Ja, ich hab dich auch lieb, und du fehlst mir auch ein bisschen. Okay, Daddy, bis bald.« Sie schmatzte mehrere feuchte Küsse in die Leitung und drückte fachkundig die rechte Taste, um das Gespräch zu beenden. Sie schaute auf ihren Teller. »Alex hat recht, das sieht eklig aus.«

Innerlich verdrehte Helena die Augen über Immys Gespräch mit ihrem Vater. Sie legte ihrer Tochter zwei Scheiben Pittabrot auf den Teller und gab etwas Hummus darauf. »Probier mal«, sagte sie aufmunternd.

»Kann ich bitte Ketchup dazu bekommen, Mummy?«

»Nein, das kannst du nicht.« Helena steckte ein Stückchen Brot mit Hummus in Immys Mund und wartete, bis die Geschmacksnerven ihrer Tochter in Aktion traten und sie schließlich zufrieden nickte. »Gut, ich wusste doch, dass dir das schmecken würde.«

»Aus was ist der Pamps denn?«, fragte Immy.

»Kichererbsen.«

»Du meinst Erbsen, die kichern?«

»Sei nicht so dumm, Immy«, sagte Alex kopfschüttelnd. Er hatte immer noch keinen Bissen angerührt. »Das hat mit Kichern nichts zu tun, das geht auf den lateinischen Namen ›cicer‹ zurück. Tut mir leid, Mum.« Er hob entwaffnend die Hände. »Ich habe immer noch keinen Appetit.«

»In Ordnung«, sagte Helena. Sie war nicht in der Stimmung für einen Machtkampf. »Ist das mit dem Pool nicht großartig? Bis Daddy kommt, sollte er aufgefüllt sein. Und jetzt probier mal vom Taramosalata, Immy. Und in Paphos kaufen wir morgen ein paar Sonnenliegen und …«

»I-gitt!« Ungeniert spuckte Immy den Bissen auf den Teller zurück.

»Immy!«

»'tschuldigung, aber das ist abscheußlich!«

»Abscheulich, Immy, aber bitte mach mich nicht nach«, sagte Alex streng und tat sein Bestes, ein Lachen zu unterdrücken. »Du bist erst fünf.«

»Genau. Außerdem schimpfen Prinzessinnen nicht über das Essen. Stimmt's, Alex?« Auch Helena konnte sich ein Lächeln nur mit Mühe verkneifen. »Und jetzt, Immy – solange ich Daddy zurückrufe, bringt Alex dich ins Bett, ja? Dann komme ich und erzähle dir eine von deinen Lieblingsgeschichten.«

»Ja, die, wo du in Wien Ballett getanzt hast und ein Prinz dich zu einem Ball in seinen Palast eingeladen hat.«

»Versprochen«, sagte Helena. »Und jetzt ab mit dir.«

Während ihre beiden Kinder im Haus verschwanden, rief sie William an.

»Guten Abend, mein Schatz«, sagte er. »Und? War das Abendessen ein Erfolg?«

»Das überlasse ich deiner Phantasie.«

»Das ist vielleicht auch besser so. Wie war dein Tag?«

»Ereignisreich.«

»So klang es. Wer ist der Prinz, von dem Immy erzählt hat?«

»Ach, nur der Sohn eines alten Freundes.«

»Ah so.« Eine Pause. »Helena, mein Schatz«, sagte William langsam, »ich möchte dich etwas fragen.«

»Ja?«

»Ich … also, ich weiß nicht genau, wie ich es dir sagen soll, aber … es geht um Chloë.«

»Etwas nicht in Ordnung mit ihr?«

»Nein, gar nicht, offenbar geht es ihr sehr gut. Das sagt zumindest ihre Hausmutter im Internat. Allerdings habe ich heute von ihrer Mutter einen Brief bekommen.«

»Einen Brief? Von Cecile? Du meine Güte!«, sagte Helena überrascht. »Sie hat sich tatsächlich die Mühe gemacht, dir zu schreiben? Das grenzt bei deiner Ex ja fast an ein Wunder, oder?«

»Doch. Aber die Sache ist …«

»Ja?«

»Sie möchte, dass Chloë ein paar Wochen zu uns nach Zypern kommt.«

Alex' Tagebuch

12. Juli, Fortsetzung

Dieser Urlaub wird, um mit meiner kleinen Schwester zu sprechen, mit jeder Minute abscheußlicher.

Mücken, Hitze, ein uraltes Haus inmitten verdorrter Felder, wo kein Mensch je etwas von Breitband gehört hat und ein Traubenpresser ständig meine Mutter an sich pressen möchte. Ganz zu schweigen davon, dass nächste Woche Jules, Sacha, Viola und Rupes – ihr gehirntoter Neandertaler-Sohn – kommen.

Am liebsten würde ich eine Kampagne zugunsten aller Kinder starten, deren Eltern beste Freunde sind, um auf das Leid der Kinder aufmerksam zu machen. Nur weil die älteren Herrschaften in ihrer Jugend Süßigkeiten und Geheimnisse ausgetauscht und diese später durch Alkohol und noch später durch Gespräche über Töpfchen-Training ersetzt haben, heißt das nicht, dass die Nachkommen dieser besten Freunde ähnliche Gefühle füreinander hegen.

Mir schwant immer das Übelste, wenn ich die Worte höre: »Alex, mein Schatz, die Chandlers kommen zu Besuch. Du wirst doch nett zu Rupes sein, ja?«

»Ja, liebste Mutter, ich will's versuchen.« Aber wenn Rupes mir dann bei einem »freundschaftlichen« Rugbyspiel zufällig mit Absicht in die Eier tritt, oder wenn er wie ein Irrer schreiend zu seiner Mum läuft und mich beschuldigt, ich hätte seine Playstation kaputt gemacht, obwohl sie ihm doch auf den Boden gefallen ist und ich nur draufgetreten bin, weil ich sie übersehen habe – dann ist das mit dem Nettsein eine ganz schöne Zumutung.

Rupes ist ungefähr so alt wie ich, was es noch schlimmer macht, und wir sind wie die Faust und das Auge. Er ist alles, was mein Stiefvater William sich von mir wünschen würde: super bei Ballspielen, immer für einen Witz zu haben, beliebt … und klammheimlich hintenrum ein richtiges Ekelpaket. Außerdem ist er dumm wie Brot, hält Homer für den Star der Simpsons und glaubt, dass er deswegen als Philosoph bekannt ist.

Viele Gemeinsamkeiten gibt es zwischen Rupes und mir nicht. Er hat eine kleine Schwester, Viola, mit roten Haaren, Sommersprossen, Hasenzähnen und derart blasser Haut, dass sie wie ein kleines Gespenst mit dem Hintergrund verschmilzt. Mum hat mir mal erzählt, dass sie adoptiert ist. Ich an der Stelle der Chandlers hätte ja versucht, ein Kind zu finden, das zumindest halbwegs meinem Genmaterial entspricht, aber vielleicht war damals nichts anderes als Viola im Angebot. Und angesichts von Rupes' maßlosem Ego und so schüchtern, wie sie ist, kenne ich sie ehrlich gesagt eigentlich gar nicht.

Um dem Ganzen die Krone aufzusetzen, hat mir meine Mum eben erzählt, dass jetzt auch noch meine Stiefschwester Chloë kommt. Ich erinnere mich nur vage an sie, weil ich sie seit sechs Jahren nicht mehr gesehen habe. Die Teufelin, wie sie bei uns zu Hause liebevoll genannt wird, also die Ex meines Stiefvaters, hat Chloë verboten, ihren Vater zu sehen, als Mum mit Immy schwanger war.

Armer Dad. Er hat alles versucht, um sie besuchen zu dürfen, wirklich alles. Aber die Teufelin hat Chloë einer Gehirnwäsche unterzogen, sodass sie ihren Vater für den Leibhaftigen hielt, weil er ihr kein Eis für ein Pfund kaufen wollte – ehrlich gesagt lehnt er das auch bei uns heute noch strikt ab –, und schließlich musste er klein beigeben. Nach endlosen, finanziell ruinösen Prozessen um Besuchsrechte, die er alle verlor, meinte sogar die Sozialarbeiterin, dass es besser sei, nicht weiter Einspruch zu erheben, weil die Teufelin ihrer Tochter die Hölle heißmacht, sobald sie ihren Vater auch nur erwähnt, und das würde sie, also Chloë, psychisch zu stark belasten. Also hat er ihr zuliebe eingelenkt. Aber ich weiß, dass sie ihm fehlt, auch wenn er selten von ihr spricht. Zum Geburtstag und zu Weihnachten schreibt er ihr immer eine Karte, und jeden Monat darf er einen Scheck ausstellen für das sündteure Internat, das sie besucht.

Tja … warum also taucht sie urplötzlich wieder auf?

Nach Mums Aussage, weil die Teufelin einen Freund hat. Der arme Typ. Sie ist eine absolute Schreckschraube. Ich gebe freimütig zu, dass sie mich in Angst und Schrecken versetzt hat, als ich sie das eine Mal sah. Sie ist nämlich ernsthaft und ultimativ verrückt und sieht vermutlich in Schwarz richtig klasse aus. Sie muss das Gebräu, das sie ihrem armen Kerl eingeflößt hat, mit irgendwas versetzt haben, weil er diesen Sommer tatsächlich mit ihr nach Südfrankreich fahren will. Und offenbar möchte er Zeit mit ihr allein verbringen.

Wie auch immer, das Ende vom Lied ist, dass Chloë bei uns geparkt wird.

Meine Mutter sah eindeutig nervös aus, als sie mir das gerade erzählte, aber sie hat sich wacker geschlagen und gesagt, dass es doch schön sein wird für Dad, nachdem er seine Tochter so viele Jahre nicht gesehen hat. Das Schlimmste war aber, dass Mum meinte, es werde ein bisschen eng werden, weil Chloë ein eigenes Zimmer brauche. Und »man« müsse zusammenrücken.

Ich hab den Wink mit dem Zaunpfahl sehr wohl verstanden.

Aber, sorry, ich werde nicht, unter keinen Umständen und um keinen Preis, im selben Zimmer wie Rupes schlafen. Notfalls schlafe ich im Bad oder draußen oder sonst wo, aber nicht mit ihm in einem Zimmer. Wenn's sein muss, kann ich mich tagsüber mit endlosen Eingriffen in meine Privatsphäre abfinden, solange ich nachts meine Ruhe habe.

Das heißt, liebste Mutter, da beißt du auf Granit.

Sie sagte auch, wir müssten Chloë das Gefühl geben, dass sie bei uns willkommen und Teil unserer Familie ist. Unserer Nicht-Kernfamilie.

Das nenne ich dysfunktional, oder wie? Jemand sollte eine Studie über uns machen. Vielleicht sollte ich das gleich selbst übernehmen.

Ich liege auf dem Bett, schaue zur Decke hoch, nachdem ich mich mit dem zypriotischen Mückenspray, das Mum mir im Dorf besorgt hat – und das vermutlich so viele verbotene Pestizide enthält, dass ich sowieso dran sterbe –, beinahe erstickt habe, und überlege mir, wie viele Blutlinien es in unserer Familie eigentlich gibt.

Das Problem ist …

Ich wünschte, ich würde meine Blutlinien alle kennen.

KAPITEL 4

Als Helena am nächsten Morgen aufwachte, fühlte sie sich wie gerädert. Sie hatte kaum geschlafen, so viele Gedanken waren ihr durch den Kopf gegangen, bis sie im Morgengrauen schließlich doch noch eingeschlafen war. Die Fahrt nach Paphos zum Einkaufen würde eine willkommene Ablenkung sein.

Wie vereinbart holte Alexis sie um halb neun mit seinem Transporter ab, und alle vier kletterten auf die breite Vorderbank. Immy war begeistert, ganz vorn zu thronen, während Alex mürrisch zum Fenster hinausschaute und kein Wort sagte. Helena hatte ihm angeboten, in Pandora zu bleiben und Georgios mit dem Pool zu helfen, aber er hatte darauf bestanden mitzukommen. Sie kannte auch den Grund: Sie stand unter Bewachung.

»Wow, Mummy, das ist ja wie auf einer kreiseligen Rutsche!«, rief Immy, als sie über die Serpentinen zur Küste hinabkurvten.

»Helena, du wirst Paphos nicht wiedererkennen«, sagte Alexis. »Die Stadt ist schon lange kein stilles Fischerdorf mehr.«

Als sie den Stadtrand erreichten, war Helena entsetzt über die hässlichen Betonbauten mit den grellen Neontafeln, die sich schier endlos die Straße entlangzogen. Gigantische Plakatwände warben für alles, von Luxuswagen über Timeshare-Apartments bis hin zu Nachtclubs.

»Schau, Mummy, da ist ein McDonald's! Können wir da einen Cheeseburger und Pommes essen gehen?«, bettelte Immy.

»Es ist traurig, nicht wahr?«, sagte Alexis leise mit einem Blick zu Helena.

»Schrecklich«, pflichtete sie bei. Im selben Moment fiel ihr Auge auf eine auf Englisch getrimmte Bar mit einem schrillen Transparent vor der Tür, auf dem mit der Übertragung von Fußballspielen und einem All-you-can-eat-Sonntagsbraten geworben wurde.

Sie parkten vor einem beeindruckenden Großmarkt für Haushaltswaren, und da erkannte Helena, wie recht Alexis hatte: Paphos hatte sich in ein Shopping-Paradies verwandelt, auf das jede englische Stadt stolz sein würde.

»Diese verdammte Globalisierung, einfach grauenvoll!«, sagte sie kopfschüttelnd beim Aussteigen.

Wenige Minuten später standen sie im Laden. Bei einem Stapel mit Spitzendecken blieb Helena stehen, nahm eine in die Hand und suchte nach dem Etikett. »China«, sagte sie zu Alexis. »Als ich das letzte Mal hier war, haben die Frauen die Spitze selbst geklöppelt und auf dem Markt verkauft. Und man hat ihnen dafür den Preis geboten, den man zu zahlen bereit war.«

»Du findest es schade, dass wir nicht mehr so ›rückständig‹ sind. Aber alles, was wir jetzt machen, haben wir von euch britischen Besatzern gelernt«, gab Alexis mit einem süffisanten Lächeln zurück.

Ein paar Stunden später, nach einem kurzen Besuch bei McDonald's als Friedensangebot an Immy, fuhren sie nach Pandora zurück, beladen mit Haushaltsgeräten und anderen Einkäufen. Helena hatte ein kleines Vermögen ausgegeben und dafür einen Teil des Geldes aus Angus' Erbschaft verwendet. Sie hoffte, ihr Patenonkel würde es gutheißen, dass sie es für Pandora ausgab. Das Haus konnte eindeutig eine Generalüberholung vertragen.

Alex, der den ganzen Tag kaum ein Wort gesprochen hatte, half Alexis und Georgios weiterhin schweigend, den Transporter auszuladen und die Kartons auf die Schubkarre zu wuchten, die Alexis morgens im Haus abgestellt hatte.

Während Helena Tagesdecken über Betten breitete, fleckige Lampenschirme aus orangefarbenem Glas gegen neue aus cremefarbener Seide austauschte und duftige Voilegardinen aufhängte, musste sie widerwillig einräumen, dass die Globalisierung doch gewisse Vorzüge hatte.

»Der Gefrierschrank läuft, der neue Herd steht an seinem Platz, den alten bringe ich zum Verschrotten, und die Geschirrspülmaschine und die Waschmaschine warten darauf, dass der Klempner sie morgen anschließt.« Unvermittelt war Alexis in der Tür von Helenas Zimmer getreten und sah ihr zu, wie sie das alte Holzbett mit frischer weißer Wäsche bezog. Er blickte sich im Raum um und lächelte. »Ach, die Hand einer Frau … sie ist durch nichts zu ersetzen.«

»Es ist ein Anfang.«

»Vielleicht sogar der Anfang einer neuen Ära für Pandora?«, fragte er leise.

»Glaubst du, dass Angus etwas dagegen hätte?«

»Eine Familie ist genau das, was dieses Haus braucht. Hätte es immer schon gebraucht.«

Helenas Blick wanderte über die geweißelten Wände des Raums. »Ich würde dieses Zimmer gern streichen, dann würde es etwas freundlicher wirken«, sagte sie.

»Dann mach das doch – meine Söhne können morgen beginnen. Sie haben das im Handumdrehen erledigt«, schlug Alexis vor.

»Ach, Alexis, das ist wirklich nett von dir, aber sie haben doch bestimmt Besseres zu tun.«

»Du vergisst, dass ich ihr Chef bin. Sie tun das, was ich ihnen sage.« Er grinste.

»Die Zeit vergeht wie im Flug«, sagte Helena. »Mein Mann kommt am Freitag, er bringt Fred mit.«

»Ach ja?« Nach kurzem Überlegen sagte Alexis: »Also, du wählst die Farbe, und wir machen die Arbeit.«

»Zum kläglichen Dank für deine ganze Hilfe öffne ich jetzt die Flasche Wein, die du mitgebracht hast.«

»Helena, du siehst blass aus. Bist du müde?« Zögernd legte Alexis ihr eine Hand auf die Schulter. »Du bist eine englische Rose, du verträgst die Hitze nicht. Du hast sie noch nie vertragen.«

»Mir fehlt nichts, Alexis, wirklich nicht.« Helena entzog sich seiner Berührung und lief die Treppe hinunter.

Später, nachdem Alexis und Georgios sich verabschiedet hatten und während Alex den DVD-Spieler aufstellte, unterstützt von Immy, die ihren Bruder aufgeregt umtänzelte, legte Helena sich schuldbewusst in ihre neue Hängematte, die Alexis zwischen zwei Olivenbäume im Garten neben der Terrasse aufgespannt hatte.

Eine wunderbare Brise ließ die Blätter leise rauschen und wehte ihr Haarsträhnen in die Stirn. Die Zikaden stimmten sich bereits auf ihr Konzert zur Dämmerung ein, die Sonne brannte nicht mehr vom Himmel, sondern tauchte alles in ein sanftes Licht.

Helena dachte an die bevorstehende Ankunft ihrer unbekannten Stieftochter. William hatte am Abend zuvor ausgesprochen nervös geklungen; ihm war unverkennbar klar, um welch großen Gefallen er seine Frau und die Kinder damit bat. Helena machte sich ebenfalls Sorgen. Alex war das anerkannte Kuckuckskind der Familie – gab es wirklich Platz für ein zweites?

Sie fragte sich, wie er wohl auf Chloë reagieren würde, ganz zu schweigen von den beiden Kleinen, die ihre Halbschwester noch überhaupt nicht kannten. Aber wie konnte sie William die Chance verwehren, kostbare Zeit mit seiner Tochter zu verbringen – auch wenn Chloë das Familiengefüge durch ihre Anwesenheit höchstwahrscheinlich gewaltig aus dem Gleichgewicht bringen würde?

Und Chloë selbst? Wie würde es ihr ergehen, sich in eine Familie einfügen zu müssen, die zu hassen ihr jahrelang eingeimpft worden war? Helena wusste, dass Chloë das eigentliche Opfer der Situation war: ein Kind, das vom Strudel eines erbitterten Scheidungsprozesses erfasst und von einer verlassenen Frau als Waffe missbraucht worden war. Auch wenn Cecile beteuerte, ihre Tochter nur vor den angeblich gefährlichen Klauen ihres Vaters zu beschützen, hatte Chloë durch einen Akt übelster emotionaler Erpressung zweifellos seelische Wunden davongetragen, weil ihr verwehrt worden war, beim Heranwachsen eine normale Beziehung zu ihrem Vater aufzubauen.

Mittlerweile war sie knapp fünfzehn, was für jedes Mädchen ein schwieriges Alter war, zumal für eines, das man gezwungen hatte, die Liebe zu seinem Vater zugunsten einer Mutter zu leugnen, die nichts anderes duldete. Helena wusste auch, dass sie ihr Herz öffnen musste, um darin auch für Chloë einen Platz zu finden.

»Mum, tut mir leid, aber das geht definitiv nicht. Das kommt überhaupt nicht infrage. Nein, nein und nochmals nein!«

»Aber, mein Schatz, das Zimmer ist doch so groß! Da ist reichlich Platz für euch beide. Und du verbringst ja sowieso keine Zeit dort, außer zum Schlafen.«

Alex saß mit verschränkten Armen da, und Helena meinte

regelrecht sehen zu können, wie ihm der Rauch aus den Ohren stieg. »Mum, darum geht's nicht, und das weißt du auch. Ganz genau weißt du das.«

»Alex, ich sehe wirklich keine andere Möglichkeit.«

»Ich schlafe bei Immy oder Fred oder bei beiden. Wahlweise lasse ich mich lieber auf einer Liege draußen auf der Terrasse von Mücken tot stechen, bevor ich im selben Zimmer schlafe wie *er*. Er stinkt.«

»Das stimmt, Mummy. Er pupst die ganze Zeit«, warf Immy wenig hilfreich ein.

»Nur zu deiner Info, Immy, das tust du auch, aber darum geht's nicht«, fuhr Alex fort. »Abgesehen davon, dass er tatsächlich stinkt, kann ich ihn nicht leiden. Er ist ein Penner.«

»So ein Unsinn!«, fuhr Helena auf.

»Kein Obdachlosenpenner, Mum, sondern ein Penner, sprich, ein absolutes Arsch…«

»Schluss, Alex, jetzt reicht's! Ob es dir passt oder nicht, eine andere Möglichkeit gibt es nicht. Ich muss Chloë ein eigenes Zimmer geben. Sie ist ein Teenager, und sie kennt keinen von uns außer Dad und …«

»Warum schläft sie dann nicht bei ihm?«

»Himmelherrgott, Alex, spar dir deine dummen Witze.« Helena erhob sich und machte sich daran, die Teller vom Abendessen zusammenzustellen. »Ich bemühe mich nach Kräften, es allen so weit wie möglich recht zu machen, und hatte gehofft, ich könnte auf deine Hilfe zählen. Vielen Dank.« Sie trug das Geschirr in die Küche und stellte es mit lautem Geklapper ins Spülbecken. Um sich etwas abzureagieren, schlug sie mit der Faust auf die Ablage.

»Hier, Mummy.« Immy erschien mit einem Teelöffel in der Hand. »Ich helf dir abräumen.«

»Danke, mein Schatz«, sagte Helena matt. »Kannst du Alex bitten, den Rest reinzutragen?«

»Nee. Der ist weg.«

»Weg wohin?«

»Weiß nicht, hat er nicht gesagt.«

Eine Stunde später brachte Helena Immy zu Bett und gönnte sich danach ein ausgedehntes Bad in Angus' uralter, wunderbar tiefer Wanne. Zum Abtrocknen verwendete sie eines der neuen flauschigen Handtücher, die sie am Vormittag in Paphos gekauft hatte, schlüpfte in ihren Morgenmantel und ging wieder nach unten, um sich auf die Terrasse zu setzen. Gerade wollte sie sich heimlich eine Zigarette anzünden, als Alex aus der Nacht auftauchte.

»Hallo. Ich wollte mich nur entschuldigen«, sagte er und ließ sich schwer auf einen Stuhl fallen. »Ich will wirklich keine Schwierigkeiten machen, aber ich tue alles, um nicht in einem Zimmer mit Rupes zu schlafen. Es …« Er fuhr sich durchs Haar. »Ich kann das einfach nicht.«

»Also gut.« Helena gab sich geschlagen. »Lass mich darüber nachdenken. Wir werden schon eine Lösung finden.«

»Danke, Mum. Ich gehe dann mal und genieße meine Privatsphäre, solange ich noch eine habe. Bleib nicht zu lange auf.«

»Der Pool sollte morgen Nachmittag voll sein. Das ist doch gut, oder?«

»Schon.« Alex nickte halbherzig. »Und? Wird Mr. Hansdampf, der seiner geliebten Helena jeden Wunsch von den Augen abliest, morgen wiederkommen?«

»Alex, hör auf!« Helena spürte, wie sie wider Willen rot wurde. »Ich bin nicht seine geliebte Helena, und abgesehen davon weiß ich wirklich nicht, was ich ohne ihn getan hätte.«

»Natürlich bist du seine geliebte Helena, Mum. Der steht

total auf dich, und das weißt du auch«, widersprach Alex nüchtern. »Mir wird echt übel, wenn ich sehe, wie er dich anstarrt. Wenn Dad da ist, sollte er sich besser in Acht nehmen. Ich glaube kaum, dass Dad das so toll findet, wenn Mr. Hansdampf sich die ganze Zeit hier rumtreibt.«

»Alex, es reicht. Alexis ist nur ein alter Freund.«

»Mehr nicht?«

»Nein, mehr nicht.«

»Und du hast ihn seit deinem letzten Besuch hier nicht mehr gesehen?«

»Nein.«

»Also, mir hat er gesagt, dass er dich seitdem sehr wohl gesehen hat, das heißt, einer von euch lügt.«

»Und jetzt reicht es endgültig! Ich lasse mich doch von meinem dreizehnjährigen Sohn nicht ins Kreuzverhör nehmen. Was in der Vergangenheit war, bleibt auch dort. Jetzt ist jetzt, und jetzt bin ich glücklich mit deinem Stiefvater verheiratet. Als freundlicher Mensch hilft Alexis mir, Pandora – ein Haus, dem er sich übrigens auch verbunden fühlt – wieder mit Leben zu füllen. Schluss, aus, Ende. In Ordnung?«

Alex zuckte mit den Achseln. »Okay. Aber sag nicht, ich hätte dich nicht gewarnt. Ich mag ihn nicht.«

»Das hast du mehr als deutlich gemacht, Alex. Ich warne dich, ich werde nicht mehr dulden, dass du unhöflich zu ihm bist. Hast du mich verstanden?«

»Ja, Mum. Gute Nacht«, brummte Alex und wandte sich zum Gehen. Dann hielt er inne und sah nachdenklich zu ihr.

»Mum?«

»Ja?«

»Was hat das mit dem gleichen Namen auf sich?«

»Wie bitte?«

»Ich meine … Es ist reiner Zufall, dass wir den gleichen Vornamen haben, oder? Ich und … Alexis?«

»Natürlich ist das reiner Zufall, mein Schatz. Mir gefiel der Name, als ich ihn damals kennenlernte, er gefiel mir, als du geboren wurdest, und er gefällt mir heute immer noch.«

»Und weiter nichts?«, bohrte Alex nach.

»Warum in Gottes Namen sollte mehr dabei sein? Es gibt Tausende von Männern, die ›Alex‹ heißen.«

»Na ja, okay, es ist bloß … nichts. Gute Nacht, Mum.«

»Gute Nacht, mein Schatz.«

Sobald sie wusste, dass Alex endgültig nach oben verschwunden war, ging sie in die Küche. Sie machte sich eine Tasse Tee, kehrte auf die Terrasse zurück und betrachtete den sternenübersäten Himmel. Vielleicht würde der ihr helfen, das ganze Kuddelmuddel ihrer Gefühle ein bisschen zu ordnen.

Sie wusste, dass der Moment mit jedem Tag näher rückte – der Moment, den sie seit Alex' Geburt fürchtete.

Eigentlich war es ein Wunder, dass Alex sie bis jetzt noch nie direkt gefragt hatte. Schließlich war ihm schon recht früh klar geworden, dass nicht nur die Mutter, sondern auch der Vater einen Anteil an der Entstehung eines Kindes hatte. Seit sie William geheiratet hatte – da war Alex drei gewesen –, hatte er diese Rolle übernommen. Sie hatten Alex beide ermutigt, ihn »Dad« zu nennen, und auch sonst hatte er die gegebene Situation akzeptiert, ohne weitere Fragen zu stellen.

Vielleicht, dachte Helena, wollte ein Teil von Alex es gar nicht wissen für den Fall, dass die Antwort zu schrecklich war. Und das war sie ja auch. Natürlich könnte sie lügen und sagen, sein Vater sei gestorben, überlegte sie sich und trank einen Schluck Tee. Sie könnte einen Namen erfinden, eine Vergangenheit … eine Zeit, in der sie einen wunderbaren Mann geliebt hatte und sie Alex gezeugt hatten, weil sie ihn sich so sehr wünschten …

Mit einem schweren Seufzen ließ Helena den Kopf in die Hände sinken. Die Egoistin in ihr wünschte, der Mann wäre tatsächlich tot, dabei war er nur allzu lebendig … und gegenwärtig.

Intellektuell war ihr Sohn reif genug, um die Wahrheit zu verkraften, das war Helena klar, doch emotional würde sie ihn vermutlich überfordern. Vor allem in diesen schwierigen Jahren, an der Schwelle vom Kind zum Erwachsenen.

Alex wirklich gerecht zu werden war noch nie einfach gewesen. Allein schon an seiner ungezügelten Wissbegierde und der ausgesprochen klugen und erwachsenen Art, wie er Informationen aufnahm, hatte sie schon sehr früh bemerkt, dass er ein ungewöhnliches Kind war. Er konnte wie ein altgedienter Politiker argumentieren und manipulieren, um im nächsten Moment zu seinem biologischen Alter zurückzukehren und wieder ein Kind zu sein. Helena erinnerte sich genau, dass die Vorstellung des Todes ihn gequält hatte, nachdem er das Konzept einmal verstanden hatte, der Gedanke, dass er nicht immer »hier« sein würde. Darüber hatte er sich als Vierjähriger in den Schlaf geweint.

»Aber keiner von uns ist immer hier«, flüsterte Helena traurig in den Nachthimmel, an dem Millionen Sterne funkelten. Sie haben alles gesehen, dachte sie, aber sie behalten ihre Weisheit für sich.

William sagte immer, sie würde Alex zu sehr verwöhnen und auf jede seiner wunderlichen Marotten eingehen, und vielleicht stimmte das ja auch. Sie war die Einzige, die seine Verletzlichkeit erkannte und die wusste, wie schwer er an dem Gefühl trug, »anders« und damit ausgeschlossen zu sein. Schon an der Grundschule hatte man ihr vorgeschlagen, den damals achtjährigen Alex testen zu lassen, weil er seinen Klassenkameraden an Intelligenz haushoch überlegen war. Widerwillig hatte sie sich darauf eingelassen, denn im Grunde hatte sie sich dagegen gewehrt, ihm bereits in dem Alter einen Stempel zu verpassen. Bei den Tests hatte er sich als »hochbegabt« mit einem überragenden IQ erwiesen.

Trotzdem hatte Helena ihn nicht von der örtlichen Schule genommen, sie wollte, dass seine Kindheit so normal wie möglich verlief. Im vergangenen Jahr dann hatte der Direktor angeregt, Alex solle sich um ein Stipendium für einen Platz am angesehensten Internat in England bewerben.

»Mrs. Cooke, ich glaube wirklich, wir würden Alex keinen Gefallen tun, wenn wir ihn nicht ermutigen, sich zumindest zu bewerben. Wir tun hier unser Bestes, aber er will gefordert werden, und die Gesellschaft von Jungen mit ähnlich überragender Intelligenz würde ihm zweifellos besser bekommen.«

Sie hatte sich mit William besprochen, der dem Rektor zugestimmt hatte, doch Helena, die selbst auf ein Internat geschickt worden war, zeigte sich nicht überzeugt.

»Es ist ja nicht gesagt, dass Alex das Stipendium wirklich bekommt. Wenn nicht, können wir es uns beim besten Willen nicht leisten, ihm die Schule zu bezahlen«, hatte William argumentiert. »Soll er es doch versuchen und sich bewerben. Dann sehen wir weiter.«

Dann hatte Alex das Stipendium tatsächlich bekommen, und angesichts der allgemeinen großen Freude hätte Helena es kleinlich gefunden, sich nicht auch zu freuen. Schließlich war es eine gewaltige Leistung und eine große Anerkennung. Und eine unglaubliche Chance für ihn.

Als sie Alex fragte, ob er sich freue, zuckte er mit den Achseln und wendete den Blick ab, sodass sie seine Reaktion nicht deuten konnte.

»Mum, wenn du dich freust, dann freue ich mich auch. Dad freut sich auf jeden Fall.«

Womit sie genauso klug war wie zuvor.

William war ebenso begeistert wie stolz gewesen, obwohl Helena sich fragte – und wegen des frevelhaften Gedankens innerlich Abbitte leistete –, ob seine Freude nicht auch damit zusammenhing, dass Alex dann aus dem Haus sein würde.

Ihr war überaus bewusst, dass William Alex akzeptiert hatte, weil er sich in sie, Helena, verliebt hatte und Alex nun einmal zu ihr gehörte. Die Frage, ob er Alex wirklich gewollt hatte, stellte sich gar nicht, denn er hatte keine Wahl gehabt. Das war die schlichte Wahrheit, sosehr man auch versuchen mochte, sie schönzureden. Und Alex hatte das natürlich sofort erfasst.

Und ihr Sohn wusste auch ihre Gefühle zu deuten – vielleicht besser als jeder andere Mensch. Manchmal kam es ihr vor, als würde sein Blick durch sie hindurch zu ihrem Innersten vordringen, egal, wie sehr sie ihre Gefühle zu verbergen versuchte.

Helena nahm die eine erlaubte Zigarette des Tages aus der Packung und zündete sie an.

Sie konnte noch so oft beteuern, Alexis' Motive seien völlig selbstlos, Alex *wusste*, dass es nicht stimmte.

Er *wusste*, dass sie ihm nicht die ganze Wahrheit erzählte.

Sein Wissen trog ihn nicht.

Keine vierundzwanzig Stunden später hatten Alexis' Söhne Dimitrios und Michel das große Schlafzimmer in zartem Taubengrau gestrichen.

Als die beiden morgens in Alexis' Lieferwagen in Pandora

vorgefahren waren, hatte Helena sie vor dem Haus empfangen und wieder einmal mit Verblüffung festgestellt, wie unterschiedlich sich die Gene niederschlagen konnten. Zwar hatten beide jungen Männer dunkles, leicht gewelltes Haar, einen olivfarbenen Teint und eine athletische Statur, doch während Dimitrios Alexis' warme Augen und zuvorkommende Art geerbt hatte, war Michel, der Jüngere, der Inbegriff eines griechischen Gottes. Alle Facetten seines Äußeren spielten auf eine derart nuancierte Art zusammen, dass er noch besser aussah als sein Vater.

Während sich die beiden Brüder mit Pinseln und Farbrollern ans Werk machten, tat Helena ihr Bestes, dem männlichen Ambiente Pandoras mithilfe ihrer Neuerwerbungen vom Vortag eine weibliche Note zu geben. Immy half ihr, im Garten Blumen und Olivenzweige zu pflücken und in große Steinkrüge zu arrangieren, die sie als Vasen zweckentfremdeten. Durch die Fenster, die in allen Räumen weit offen standen, brannte die Sonne herein und vertrieb den muffigen Geruch eines leer stehenden Hauses. Pandora erwachte wieder zum Leben.

Am frühen Vormittag war eine attraktive junge Frau mit tiefschwarzem Haar in die Küche gekommen, die sich zu Helenas Erstaunen als Angelina entpuppt hatte, Angus' ehemalige Haushälterin – Helena hatte sich eher einen mürrischen alten Hausdrachen vorgestellt. Mit blitzenden Augen und unter großem Körpereinsatz schrubbte Angelina Böden, saugte Staub und scherzte dabei lachend mit Alexis' Söhnen.

»Mum, in einer Stunde kann man im Pool schwimmen«, verkündete Alex. Er hatte Helena im Salon angetroffen, wo sie gerade den Staub aus den Kissen der Damastsofas klopfte. »Georgios ist gerade dabei, ihn zu füllen.«

»Großartig! Dann weihen wir ihn mit einer Runde Schwimmen ein.«

»Das Wasser wird kalt sein, weil die Sonne es noch nicht aufgewärmt hat, aber erfrischend«, sagte er zuversichtlich.

»Genau das Richtige nach der anstrengenden Arbeit.«

»Ja. Bis jetzt war das noch kein richtiger Urlaub, stimmt's? Ich habe eher das Gefühl, als wären wir gerade in ein neues Haus gezogen.«

»In gewisser Hinsicht stimmt das ja auch«, meinte Helena. »Aber es lohnt sich, findest du nicht? Ich möchte so gern, dass Dad sich hier wohlfühlt.«

»Es wird ihm hier sicher gefallen.« Unvermittelt umarmte Alex sie. »Ich bin ganz aufgeregt wegen des Pools.«

»Schön«, sagte Helena. Sie war erleichtert, dass sich Alex' düstere Stimmung vom Vortag verzogen hatte.

»Ab sofort werde ich jeden Morgen vor dem Frühstück schwimmen, um fitter zu werden«, verkündete er. »Bis später.«

»Gute Idee, mein Schatz.«

»Madam, Tasse Tee?« Angelina trug ein schweres Tablett durch den Salon auf die Terrasse, dicht gefolgt von Immy.

»Sehr gern, danke. Und Angelina, bitte nennen Sie mich Helena.«

»Hockay, Helena, ich versuche«, erwiderte sie in ihrem gebrochenen Englisch.

»Mummy, wir haben im neuen Herd Kekse gebacken, um ihn auszuprobieren.« Immy streckte ihr einen Teller entgegen, den sie achtsam mit beiden Händen hielt. »Davon muss jeder einen essen, weil die lecker sind!«

»Das glaube ich sofort.« Helena freute sich, dass Immy so schnell Vertrauen zu Angelina gefasst hatte. Angesichts der Horden, die in den kommenden Tagen über das Haus und sie hereinbrechen würden, war sie für jede Hilfe dankbar. Sie folgte den beiden auf die Terrasse und ließ sich unter der Pergola auf einen Stuhl fallen. »Danke, Immy.« Sie biss in einen Keks. »Mmm, die sind wirklich lecker.«

»Also, Angelina hat mir geholfen, aber eigentlich habe ich sie gemacht, stimmt's?«

»Natürlich, Immy«, bestätigte Angelina und streichelte ihr zärtlich die Wange.

Eine Stunde später versammelten sich alle zum Einweihungsbad am Pool, wo sich Helena, Immy und Alex fest an den Händen fassten und mit einem lauten Schrei ins Wasser sprangen.

Zehn Minuten später überließ Helena den Pool den plantschenden Kindern und legte sich am Beckenrand in die Spätnachmittagssonne, um ihre Gänsehaut zu wärmen.

»Guten Abend, Helena.«

Ein Schatten fiel auf sie, sie schaute auf.

»Guten Abend, Alexis.«

»Wie ich sehe, ist bei euch alles in bester Ordnung, ja?« Er hockte sich neben sie, und plötzlich kam sie sich in ihrem spärlichen Bikini ziemlich nackt vor. Sie setzte sich auf und zog die Knie an die Brust.

»Nur dank dir und deiner Familie. Ich bin euch wirklich so dankbar, Alexis.«

»Das ist nichts weiter als meine Pflicht. Schließlich war Pandora über zweihundert Jahre lang im Besitz meiner Familie, bevor dein Patenonkel meinen Vater überredete, das Haus ihm zu überlassen.«

»Es ist trotzdem sehr freundlich von dir, mir zu helfen.«

»Ach! Bitte sei nicht so förmlich und britisch zu mir! Du klingst, als würden wir uns kaum kennen.«

»Das tun wir ja auch nicht ... nicht mehr«, fügte Helena nach einer kurzen Pause hinzu.

»Dann müssen wir uns wieder besser kennenlernen. Kommst du heute Abend zum Essen zu mir?«

»Ich … Alexis, ich kann Immy und Alex nicht allein lassen.«

»Ich habe mit Angelina gesprochen, sie bleibt gern zum Kinderhüten hier.«

»Du hast *was* gemacht?«, fuhr Helena auf. »Vielleicht wäre es besser gewesen, vorher mit mir darüber zu sprechen.«

»Ja«, räumte Alexis sofort zerknirscht ein. »Ich hätte dich vorher fragen sollen. Bitte entschuldige, Helena.«

»Ich habe sowieso keine Zeit, es gibt hier viel zu viel zu tun. Morgen kommen William und Fred.«

»Mummy! Mir ist kalt! Ich brauche ein Handtuch, ich will raus.«

»Bin schon da, mein Schatz.« Helena stand auf und wandte sich zum Gehen, doch Alexis hielt sie am Arm fest.

»Lass uns wenigstens bald miteinander reden und uns erzählen, was in den vergangenen Jahren passiert ist.«

Sie sah zu ihm und setzte zu einer Antwort an, doch dann schüttelte sie nur wortlos den Kopf und entzog sich seinem Griff.

Alex' Tagebuch

13. Juli 2006

Ich treibe im eiskalten Pool auf dem Rücken und kann keine irdischen Geräusche wahrnehmen, weil meine Ohren unter Wasser sind. Von meinem Wasserbett schaue ich nach oben und sehe über mir die dunkle gewölbte Kuppel, die die Halbkugel von Erde und Himmel darstellt. Sie ist wie eine Höhle, deren Decke vor lauter noch ungeborenen Diamanten funkelt. Ich lausche den glucksenden Geräuschen in meinen Ohren, schließe die Augen und stelle mir vor, ich wäre wieder im Schoß meiner Mutter. Abgesehen davon, dass aus keinem Zapfhahn Pommes oder Schokolade oder Kohle fließt oder was immer die Mutter einem über die Nabelschnur zum Essen weitergibt.

Diese Sache mit der Entstehung von Leben ist wirklich ein Wunder.

Heute Abend geht es mir besser, ich habe nämlich einen neuen Schoß – äh, ich meine, ein neues Schloss, wobei auch das eine Übertreibung ist. Aber es ist ein Zimmer für mich allein. Also gut, Platz habe ich nur in Embryonalhaltung – sobald ich die Arme ausstrecke, berühre ich beiderseits die Mahagoniregale, auf denen Hunderte von ledergebundenen Büchern stehen –, aber das ist egal. Das Zimmer gehört mir und mir allein, und das Wichtigste ist: Es ist eine Rupes-freie Zone.

Mal abgesehen davon habe ich reichlich Lesestoff, der

für die ganzen Ferien vorhalten wird, denn meine neuen vier Wände sind das, was meine Mutter angesichts der Abmessungen des Raums etwas hochtrabend »die Bibliothek« nennt. Letztlich ist es kaum mehr als eine Besenkammer (die es hundertpro auch mal war), und zwar direkt neben dem Salon. Aus medizinischen Gründen darf ich allerdings niemanden zu mir hereinbitten, weil voraussichtlich nicht genügend Sauerstoff vorhanden ist, um zwei Lungen zu versorgen. Außerdem müsste diese Person auf mir liegen, Platz zu stehen gibt es nämlich nicht.

Mum meinte, ich könne ruhig ein paar Bücher auf höhere Regale umschichten, damit ich wenigstens meine Sachen irgendwo unterbringen kann.

Davon abgesehen bietet das Zimmer den Luxus einer abschließbaren Tür sowie eines kleinen Fensters hoch oben in der Wand. Der gruselige Mr. Hansdampf hat es irgendwie geschafft, zum Schlafen ein Feldbett für mich hineinzubugsieren.

Ich schwimme zum Beckenrand, klettere hinaus und schüttele das Wasser ab, dann lege ich mir ein Handtuch um die Schultern, das allerdings von den vorherigen Benutzern nasser ist als ich. So lasse ich mich auf eine Liege fallen und von der immer noch irre heißen Nachtluft trocknen. Ich hoffe bloß, ich bin nicht der Grund dafür, dass meine Mutter heute Abend die Flügel so hängen lässt.

Seit Mr. Hansdampf vor gut zwei Stunden gegangen ist, hat sie kaum ein Wort mit mir gesprochen. Allerdings war sie Immy gegenüber ähnlich wortkarg, das heißt, vielleicht sind wir beide aus unbekannten Gründen in Ungnade gefallen.

Ich hoffe ... also, ich hoffe, es hat nichts damit zu tun,

dass Dad morgen kommt. Dass er ihr Liebesdingens mit Mr. Hansdampf stört. Eigentlich glaube ich das nicht, ich bin mir sicher, dass sie Dad liebt, aber ich weiß auch, dass Frauen schwer zu verstehen sind. Wer bringt ihnen eigentlich bei, dermaßen unberechenbar zu sein?

Immy checkt diese Frauenmasche allmählich auch schon. Zuerst bringt sie mich mit irgendwelchen Tricks dazu, so ein dröges Immy-Spiel zu spielen, bei dem sie unweigerlich eine Prinzessin oder eine Fee ist und rosa Tüll über ihre Jeans trägt, während ich alles vom Schwarzen Peter bis zum perversen Gartenzwerg bin. Und plötzlich, ohne jede Vorwarnung, stampft sie mit dem Füßchen auf, sagt, dass sie keine Lust mehr hat, und geht schmollend davon.

Glaubt sie echt, das würde mich stören?

Ich knie mich auf die Liege und äuge durch die Oliven, die rund um den Pool wachsen. Wenn ich den Hals recke, sehe ich Mum auf der Terrasse sitzen. Sie trägt einen weißen Kaftan, das Mondlicht färbt ihr blondes Haar weiß und lässt die leichte Bräune, die sie in den letzten Tagen bekommen hat, verblassen.

Wie eine Alabasterstatue sieht sie aus.

Oder ein Gespenst.

Und wenn ich sie so sehe, weiß ich, dass sie gerade in der Vergangenheit ist, in einem anderen Leben.

Kapitel 5

Fred hatte schließlich seiner Müdigkeit nachgegeben, jetzt lag sein Kopf schwer auf Williams Schoß, aber seine klebrigen kleinen Finger hielten sein neues Flugzeug noch fest umklammert. William bemühte sich, die schlimmsten Schokoladereste um den Mund seines Sohnes mit etwas Spucke zu entfernen. Nach der Landung würde er mit Fred als Erstes die Herrentoilette aufsuchen und ihm eine Vollwaschung verpassen müssen, bevor Helena ihn sah. Irgendwie übte die Haut seines Sohnes eine magnetische Anziehung auf Schmutz aus.

Dankbar für ein paar Minuten Ruhe schloss William die Augen. Dieser Flug mit Fred war eine lehrreiche Erfahrung für ihn. Normalerweise war er der Geschäftsmann im Anzug, der mühsam seinen Ärger beherrschte, wenn ein kleines Monster brüllend die Füße in seine Rückenlehne rammte oder quengelnd das Gesicht zwischen die Vordersitze steckte, während ein überfordertes Elternteil das Kind zu beruhigen versuchte.

Dank des Adrenalinüberschusses, den Fred ihm beschert hatte, konnte er nicht schlafen, also dachte er über seine Ankunft in Helenas Welt nach. Er war in den vergangenen Tagen zu sehr damit beschäftigt gewesen, in seinem Architekturbüro alles geordnet zu hinterlassen, um sich weiter Gedanken darüber zu machen.

Pandora ... Dem versonnenen Ausdruck auf dem Gesicht seiner Frau, wann immer sie von dem Haus sprach, hatte er entnommen, was es ihr bedeutete. Und William wusste, dass er sie nicht enttäuschen und nichts Negatives sagen durfte. Selbst wenn das Haus und der Ort ziemlich durchschnittlich waren und Zypern die wüstenartige Ansammlung von Steilabhängen, als die er sich die Insel vorstellte – er hatte sich fest vorgenommen, sich das nicht anmerken zu lassen.

In den letzten Tagen hatte Helena eindeutig geistesabwesend, wenn nicht gar abweisend geklungen. Vielleicht war es für sie selbst eine Enttäuschung gewesen, in die Realität einer zur Perfektion verklärten Erinnerung zurückzukehren. Aber er war sich nicht sicher. Was seine Frau betraf, gab es für ihn keine Gewissheiten.

Auch wenn ihr zehnter Hochzeitstag bevorstand, hatte William nach wie vor das Gefühl, sie nicht ganz fassen zu können. Selbst wenn er sie nackt in den Armen hielt, wenn sie sich so nahe waren, wie zwei Menschen sich körperlich nur nah sein konnten, hatte sie eine bestimmte Aura, eine gewisse Distanziertheit, war ein Teil von ihr einfach nicht anwesend.

Dabei war sie alles andere als kalt, im Gegenteil, eine warmherzigere und liebevollere Frau konnte man sich kaum vorstellen. Und ihre Kinder vergötterten sie. *Er* vergötterte sie. William fragte sich, ob womöglich ihre Schönheit Zurückhaltung und Ehrfurcht hervorrief. Im Lauf der Jahre hatte er immer wieder die Reaktionen anderer Menschen, Männer wie Frauen, auf sie beobachtet. Niemand rechnete damit, körperlicher Vollkommenheit zu begegnen: Jeder arrangierte sich mit seinen Mängeln, weil er sie an seinen Mitmenschen wiedererkannte. Doch mit ihrem goldenen Haar, der blassen, makellosen Haut und der perfekt proportionierten Figur kam Helena dem Ideal von Weiblichkeit verdächtig nahe. Die Tatsache, dass sie zudem Mutter war, steigerte nur ihren Reiz, war sie doch keine unberührbare Eisprinzessin, sondern ein Mensch aus Fleisch und Blut. Wie oft hatte er das Gefühl, dass er ein bloßer Sterblicher war und sie eine Göttin – dabei tat oder sagte sie nichts, was dieses Gefühl beförderte. Trotzdem empfand er hin und wieder große Unsicherheit, und er konnte nicht glauben, dass diese wunderbare Frau ausgerechnet ihn erwählt haben sollte.

Dann tröstete er sich mit dem Gedanken, dass er ihr das gab, was sie brauchte, dass er das Yin zu ihrem Yang war. Sie waren ausgesprochen unterschiedlich – sie künstlerisch, ätherisch und verträumt, er bodenständig, solide und verstandesbetont – und entstammten zwei völlig verschiedenen Welten, und dennoch waren die vergangenen zehn Jahre die glücklichsten seines Lebens gewesen. Und er hoffte, dass auch sie glücklich gewesen war.

Doch seitdem der Brief vom Anwalt ihres Patenonkels eingetroffen war, in dem es hieß, sie habe in einem gottverlassenen Nest irgendwo auf Zypern ein uraltes Haus geerbt, war sie noch verschlossener geworden. Und in den vergangenen Wochen hatte er eindeutig den Eindruck bekommen, dass Helena sich zunehmend von ihm entfernte. Andererseits gab es nichts, das dieses Gefühl erhärtet hätte. Eigentlich war Helena genauso gewesen wie immer: Sie hatte den Haushalt geführt, hatte sich um die Kinder gekümmert und war für ihn und die zahllosen anderen Menschen da gewesen, die sich magisch von ihrer Wärme und Herzlichkeit angezogen fühlten.

Auch wenn William kein Mensch war, der zur Innenschau neigte – als das Flugzeug in Paphos zur Landung ansetzte, konnte er seine Beklommenheit nur mit Mühe beiseiteschieben.

»Immy, das ist echt affig. Wenn du das hochhältst, weigere ich mich, neben dir zu stehen.«

»Alex, sei nicht so gemein. Immy hat den ganzen Vormittag daran gesessen. Es ist zauberhaft, mein Schatz«, sagte Helena zu ihrer Tochter. »Und Daddy wird sich auch drüber freuen.«

Immys Unterlippe zitterte. Hinter sich zog sie ein Papierbanner mit der Aufschrift »WILKOMEN IN ZÜPERN DADDY UND FRED« in die Ankunftshalle. »Alex, ich hasse dich. Du bist der stinkigste Bruder überhaupt.«

»Aber nicht so stinkig wie Fred«, widersprach Alex, während er und Immy sich zu Helena in die Menschentraube rund um die Türen des Ankunftsbereichs stellten.

»Solange wir warten, kann ich ja zum Autoverleih gehen, der ist gleich dort drüben, und den jetzigen Wagen gegen einen Minivan tauschen«, sagte Helena. Sie fühlte sich etwas überfordert. »Ihr zwei bleibt hier stehen und wartet auf Dad und Fred. Ihre Maschine ist vor zwanzig Minuten gelandet, sie sollten bald kommen. Und Alex, bitte behalt Immy im Auge«, fügte sie hinzu, ehe sie in der Menge verschwand.

»Ooooh, ich freue mich ja so!«, quietschte Immy und wedelte begeistert ihr Banner durch die Luft. »Da schau, da sind sie ja ... DADDYYYYY!«

William erschien in der Tür, vor sich her schob er einen mit Koffern beladenen Gepäckwagen, und obenauf thronte Fred. Immy rannte zu ihm und warf sich ihm in die Arme.

»Grüß dich, Immy, mein Schatz«, brachte William hervor, halb erstickt von den Küssen seiner Tochter. Durch ihre langen blonden Haare hindurch warf er Alex ein Lächeln zu. »Grüß dich. Und wie geht's dir?«

»Gut, Dad, danke.« Alex übernahm den Gepäckwagen und bückte sich etwas, um Fred ins Gesicht zu sehen. »Hallo, Kleiner. Schlag ein!«

»Hallo, Alex.« Fred drosch seine kleine Handfläche mit Kraft

99

gegen Alex' weit größere und zeigte ihm dann sein Flugzeug. »Dad hat mir was geschenkt.«

»Echt? Wow, dann musst du ja richtig brav gewesen sein.« Alex nahm Fred auf den Arm.

»Nee, war ich gar nicht.«

»Im Flugzeug? Hat dir das Flugzeug gefallen?«

»Ja-a.« Fred nickte und rieb sich seine sommersprossige Nase. »Wo ist Mummy?«

»Ja, wo ist Mummy?« William, der neben ihnen stand, ließ den Blick suchend über die Menge schweifen.

»Da drüben beim Autoverleih.« Alex sah Helena auf die Familie zukommen und winkte.

Fred wand sich aus seinen Armen und stürmte zu seiner Mutter.

Wie immer, wenn William seine Frau längere Zeit nicht gesehen hatte, beobachtete er sie zuerst eine Weile, und jedes Mal bezauberte sie ihn aufs Neue. Heute trug sie ein blaues T-Shirt und eine abgeschnittene blaue Jeans, hatte sich das lange Haar nachlässig zum Pferdeschwanz gebunden und sah aus wie ein Teenager.

Mit Fred auf dem Arm kam sie auf ihn zu.

»Hallo, mein Schatz.« Er legte ihr einen Arm um die Schultern und gab ihr einen Kuss.

»Grüß dich.« Sie lächelte ihn an. »Guten Flug gehabt?«

»Ereignisreich war er«, sagte er seufzend. »Aber wir haben es heil überstanden, Fred, stimmt's?«

»Ja-a. Mummy, fahren wir jetzt nach Ziper?«, fragte Fred.

»Wir sind doch auf Zypern, mein Schatz. Aber wir können nach Hause fahren.«

»Aber ich bin doch gerade erst hergekommen!« Fred sah verständnislos drein.

»Ich meine unser Haus hier auf Zypern. Der Wagen steht dort draußen.« Helena deutete auf einen der Ausgänge.

»Dann gehen wir mal«, sagte William.

»Helena, es ist wunderschön, wirklich wunderschön.« Eineinhalb Stunden später stand William oben auf dem Balkon und ließ den Ausblick auf sich wirken.

»Gefällt es dir?«

»Ja, sehr. Und das Haus … in den wenigen Tagen, die du hier bist, hast du Wunder gewirkt. Alles sieht so frisch und freundlich aus.« Er trat in das gemeinsame Zimmer und schnupperte. »Riecht das nicht nach Farbe?«

»Doch.«

»Erzähl mir nicht, du hättest obendrein noch Zeit gehabt, ein Zimmer zu streichen!«

»Nein. Das hat jemand anderes für mich gemacht.«

»Ich bin beeindruckt«, sagte William. »In England brauche ich Wochen, um jemanden zu finden, der ein Wasserrohr repariert – keine Chance, ein Haus binnen ein paar Tagen streichen zu lassen. Es sieht hinreißend aus. Und gar nicht so, wie ich es mir vorgestellt hatte.«

»Wie hattest du es dir denn vorgestellt?«

»Ich weiß nicht. Schlicht … mediterran, glaube ich. Karg, eher spartanisch. Aber dieses Haus könnte man in jedes beliebige englische Dorf stellen, ohne dass es fehl am Platz wirken würde. Es sieht aus wie ein altes Pfarrhaus und gar nicht wie eine Villa auf Zypern. Es hat Charakter.«

»Es ist sehr alt.«

»Und dieser wunderschöne Stuck.« Mit dem geschulten Auge des Architekten sah William sich im Raum um. »Hohe Decken.« Er fuhr mit der Hand über die polierte Oberfläche der Mahagonikommode. »Und ich vermute, dass die Möbel zum Teil auch sehr wertvoll sind.«

»Angus wollte sich hier ein kleines Stück England erschaffen«, erklärte Helena. »Er ließ alles herschiffen, einschließlich der großen Standuhr unten im Flur.«

»Und jetzt gehört alles dir.«

»Uns«, verbesserte Helena ihn lächelnd.

»Und es ist vermutlich ziemlich viel wert.«

»Ich könnte es nie verkaufen«, sagte sie verhalten.

»Nein, aber es schadet ja trotzdem nicht zu wissen, wie viel es wert ist. Vielleicht solltest du es schätzen lassen.«

»Vielleicht.« Helena versuchte geflissentlich zu überhören, wie ihr Mann Pandora und Geld in einem Atemzug nannte. »Komm, Schatz, ich zeige dir den Garten.«

Am späten Nachmittag gingen sie im Pool schwimmen, wo sich schon die Kinder tummelten. Danach schlug Helena ein frühes Abendessen in Persephones Taverne vor. »Ich zeige dir das Dorf«, sagte sie zu William, als er den Wagen über den holprigen Feldweg manövrierte. »Und die Kinder können zur Abwechslung Chicken-Nuggets und Pommes bekommen.«

Nachdem sie die eine Straße des Dorfs hinauf- und hinabgeschlendert waren und William beteuert hatte, er wolle irgendwann die hübsche orthodoxe Kirche von innen besichtigen, gingen sie zu Persephones Taverne.

»Hier ist es ja sehr gemütlich«, sagte William, als sie sich setzten. Er hob Fred, der vor Übermüdung völlig überdreht und kaum zu bändigen war, auf den Schoß.

»Dad, kann ich die Kerze ausblasen?«, fragte er.

»Nein, lass das lieber. Schau, hier ist dein Auto.« Helena ließ ein Spielzeugmobil quer über den Tisch zu ihrem Sohn rollen.

»Hier hat sich seit meinem Besuch damals kaum etwas verändert, und das Essen ist wirklich gut.«

»Wir müssen aber nicht wieder die kichernden Erbsen essen, Mummy, oder?«, quengelte Immy.

»Nein, aber Daddy und ich nehmen die Meze. Davon solltest du wirklich mal probieren«, sagte Helena, als der Wein gebracht wurde und sie die Bestellung aufgab. »Ach, William, ich habe eine Haushälterin gefunden, die auch gern auf die Kinder aufpasst. Ja, Fred, dein Essen kommt gleich. Hier, Immy, iss schon mal ein Stück Brot gegen den ärgsten Hunger.« Routiniert führte Helena drei Unterhaltungen gleichzeitig.

»Ich glaube, die können wir gut brauchen«, meinte William müde und wandte sich an Alex. »Und was sagst du zu Pandora? Gefällt es dir?«

»Der Pool ist toll«, sagte Alex und nickte.

»Und das Haus?«

»Ja, auch ganz okay.«

»Hast du gehört, England hat das Test Match gegen Westindien gewonnen.«

»Nein, hier gibt's kein Fernsehen.«

William gab sich geschlagen. Wenn Alex sich maulfaul gab, ließ man ihn am besten in Ruhe.

Zum Glück wurde bald das Essen aufgetragen, und die Kinder fielen darüber her.

»Die Meze sind phantastisch«, sagte William. »Möchtest du auch davon probieren, Fred?«

Fred gab einen undefinierbaren Laut von sich, schüttelte heftig den Kopf und hielt sich die Hand vor den Mund.

»Ich hoffe nur, dass er sich nicht den Rest der Ferien von Chicken-Nuggets und Pommes ernährt, Schatz«, sagte William streng.

»Und wenn, wird er auch nicht daran sterben, oder?«, gab Helena zurück und steckte ihrem kleinen Sohn eine weitere Gabel in den Mund.

»Die Iren haben jahrelang nur von Kartoffeln gelebt«, sagte Alex.

»Und sind zu Tausenden gestorben«, antwortete William.

»Das war während der Hungersnot, als die Kartoffelpflanzen alle eingingen und die Menschen verhungert sind. Und die halbe Weltbevölkerung ernährt sich von Reis«, fuhr Alex unbeirrt fort. »Letztlich vor allem Kohlenhydrate mit ein paar Ballaststoffen.«

»Mummy, ich muss mal, und Alex soll mitgehen«, unterbrach Immy das Gespräch.

»Ich Glückspilz«, murmelte Alex. »Also, dann komm.«

»Ich auch! Ich auch!« Fred kletterte vom Stuhl und trabte seinem Bruder und seiner Schwester hinterher.

Am Tisch breitete sich Ruhe aus. William schenkte ihnen beiden Wein nach. »Und mit Alex lief alles gut?«, fragte er.

»Ja, es ging gut. Oder zumindest so gut wie immer mit ihm.« Helena warf William ein schiefes Lächeln zu. »Du kennst ihn doch.«

»Natürlich. Und wie ist es, nach all den Jahren wieder hier zu sein?«

»Wundervoll, doch, wirklich wundervoll. Ich …«

»Mummy! Guck mal, wer da ist! Dein Freund!« Unvermittelt tauchte Immy bereits wieder hinter Helena auf. »Ich hab ihm gesagt, er muss kommen und meinen Daddy kennenlernen.«

Helena drehte sich um und sah in Alexis' dunkelblaue Augen.

»Guten Abend, Helena«, sagte er unverkennbar befangen. »Es tut mir leid, dich mit deiner Familie zu stören, aber deine Tochter hat darauf bestanden.«

»Aber du störst doch nicht, Alexis. Das ist mein Mann William.«

Alexis entwand seine Hand Immys eisernem Griff und streckte sie über den Tisch. »Freut mich, Sie kennenzulernen, William.«

»Ganz meinerseits. Alexis, wenn ich mich nicht täusche?«

»Ja.«

Daraufhin setzte Stille ein. Verzweifelt ging Helena im Kopf hundert Sätze durch, um das Schweigen zu brechen, doch keiner erschien ihr auch nur im Entferntesten passend.

»Daddy, weißt du, Alexis ist mit uns in seinem großen Auto nach Paphos gefahren«, kam Immy ihr zu Hilfe. »Er war mit uns einkaufen und hat Mummy geholfen, das Haus für dich und Fred herzurichten.«

»Wirklich? In dem Fall muss ich mich für Ihre Hilfe bedanken, Alexis«, sagte William bemüht.

»Kein Problem. Gefällt es Ihnen in Pandora?«, fragte er.

»Das Haus ist wunderschön, und die Lage ist traumhaft.«

»Bevor Angus es gekauft hat, hat es Alexis' Familie gehört, und Alexis gehören auch die Weinfelder rundum.« Helena hatte schließlich ihre Sprache wiedergefunden.

»Sie sind Winzer?«, fragte William.

»Ja.« Alexis deutete auf den Krug, der auf dem Tisch stand. »Den Wein trinken Sie gerade.«

»Er ist gut, wirklich sehr gut. Kann ich Ihnen ein Glas anbieten?«

»Nein danke, William, ich muss zu meinem Gast zurückkehren. Ein Weinhändler aus Syrien, und ich hoffe, dass er von mir kauft.«

»Dann besuchen Sie uns doch in Pandora, dann trinken wir zusammen ein Glas«, schlug William vor.

»Danke, sehr gern. Schön, Sie kennenzulernen, William. *Kalispera*, Helena, *Kalispera*, Immy.« Mit einem Nicken ging er davon.

Alex hatte Alexis am Tisch stehen sehen, als er mit Fred die Toilette verließ, und gewartet, bis er gegangen war. »Was hat denn der hier gemacht, Mum?«, fragte er, als er und Fred sich wieder setzten.

Sein abschätziger Tonfall sagte William alles, was er zu wissen brauchte.

Sobald sie wieder in Pandora waren, brachte Helena die beiden Kleinen ins Bett und ließ sich dann ein Bad einlaufen. Sie hatte in der vergangenen Nacht nicht geschlafen, vielleicht aus Anspannung wegen Williams und Freds Ankunft, und war am Ende ihrer Kräfte.

»Der DVD-Spieler im Salon ist angeschlossen.« Alex schlenderte, ohne zu klopfen, ins Schlafzimmer, eine Gewohnheit, die William regelmäßig verärgerte, wie Helena wusste.

»Schön«, sagte sie. »Ich lege mich gleich in die Badewanne. Gehst du jetzt ins Bett?«

»Ja. Zumindest habe ich in meiner Bibliothek ein paar Bücher zur Auswahl. Gute Nacht, Mum.«

»Gute Nacht, mein Schatz.«

»Gute Nacht, Alex.« William betrat das Schlafzimmer, als Alex gerade ging.

»Gute Nacht, Dad.«

William drückte die Tür fest hinter ihm ins Schloss und folgte Helena ins Bad. Als sie in die Wanne stieg, setzte er sich auf den Rand. »Ruhe«, sagte er lächelnd, fuhr sich durch das dunkle Haar und gähnte. »Ich glaube, heute Nacht werde ich gut schlafen.«

»Fünf Stunden mit Fred im Flugzeug kosten einen in der Tat den letzten Nerv«, bestätigte Helena. »Er ist mitten in der Geschichte eingeschlafen. Ich hoffe nur, dass er morgen früh etwas länger schläft, sonst ist er den Rest des Tages unausstehlich.«

»Die Chancen stehen nicht schlecht«, sagte William und seufzte. »Und woher kennst du Alexis?«

»Ich habe ihn bei meinem Besuch damals kennengelernt.«

»Ein gut aussehender Mann.«

»Ja, wahrscheinlich schon.«

»Damals muss er der reinste Herzensbrecher gewesen sein.« In seiner Stimme lag ein fragender Unterton.

Helena seifte sich angelegentlich ein.

»Jetzt komm schon.« Mit dezenten Fragen würde er hier nicht weiterkommen. »War damals etwas zwischen euch?«

»Kannst du mir bitte das Handtuch geben?«

»Hier.« William reichte es ihr. Wieder einmal staunte er, dass weder die Schwangerschaften noch das Alter Spuren auf dem Körper seiner Frau hinterlassen hatten. Wie sie so dastand und ihr das Wasser über die Haut rann, ließ sie ihn an eine Nymphe denken. Ihre kleinen Brüste waren noch straff, der Bauch flach. Sie dabei zu beobachten, wie sie aus der Wanne stieg und sich in das Handtuch hüllte, erregte ihn. »Also? Du hast meine Frage noch nicht beantwortet.«

»Während ich hier war, hatten wir einen Urlaubsflirt, mehr nicht.«

»Und du hast ihn seitdem nicht gesehen?«

»Nein.«

»Also war es ... unschuldig?«

»William«, sagte Helena seufzend, »das war vor vierundzwanzig Jahren. Was damals war, ist doch unwichtig, oder nicht?«

»Ist er verheiratet?«

»Ja, aber seine Frau ist gestorben.«

»Das heißt, er ist Witwer.«

»Ja.« Helena frottierte sich das Haar und griff dann nach dem Morgenmantel.

»Wusstest du, dass er hier sein würde?«

»Ich hatte keine Ahnung. Ich habe seit vierundzwanzig Jahren nichts von ihm gehört.«

»Du hast recht, das ist lange her.«

»Ja, das stimmt. Und jetzt – möchtest du nicht in die Wanne steigen, solange das Wasser noch warm ist? Ich mache währenddessen unten alles zu. Und apropos unten, ich würde morgen früh gern nach Paphos fahren und ein paar Pflanzen für die wunderschönen Gefäße auf der Terrasse und das kleine Beet neben dem Pool besorgen. Angelina ist hier, sie könnte ein paar Stunden auf die Kleinen aufpassen. Magst du mitkommen?«

»Natürlich.«

»Schön. Dann bis gleich.«

Während William sich auszog und in die Wanne stieg, machte er sich Vorhaltungen, dass er so in Helena gedrungen war. Das war ihr gegenüber ungerecht – und paranoid. Wie sie sagte: Was immer vor fast fünfundzwanzig Jahren passiert war, tat heute nichts mehr zur Sache. Aber so, wie Alexis seine Frau in der Taverne angesehen hatte … Intuitiv wusste William, dass es der Blick eines verliebten Mannes war.

Alex' Tagebuch

14. Juli 2006

Zu Dad: »Grüß dich, Schatz.«

Zu Immy oder Fred: »Schatz, nnnnein!«

Zu mir: »Ach, mein Schatz!«

Jetzt sind wir also wieder im Land der Schätze: Wir sind die Familie Schatz, und meine Mutter ist Frau Schatz. Wieso hat sie sich eigentlich die Mühe gemacht, uns allen eigene Namen zu geben, wenn sowieso einer für alle herhalten muss?

Schwierig wird das vor allem, wenn sie aus der Küche ein kollektives »Schatz!« ruft und wir alle aus sämtlichen Teilen des Hauses herbeiströmen, bis sie entschieden hat, welchen Schatz sie in diesem Moment gerade braucht. Im Großen und Ganzen finde ich sie als Mutter großartig, aber mit dieser Schatz-Suche macht sie mich wahnsinnig. Das muss ein Überbleibsel aus ihrer Zeit als Ballerina sein, solche Sachen sagen Theaterleute ja gern.

Wir sind eine Familie von fünf Leuten beziehungsweise von sechs, wenn demnächst diese Chloë kommt, also recht groß nach heutigen Maßstäben. Innerhalb dieser Familie sollte doch bestimmt jeder seine Individualität bewahren dürfen. Und was wäre identitätsstiftender als ein Name?

Seit Neuestem kopiert Fred sie damit. Ich mache mir schon Sorgen, dass er in der Schule mal richtig Ärger bekommt, wenn er den Schläger der Klasse »Schatz« nennt.

Andererseits, solange sie Mr. Hansdampf nicht auch noch in ihre »Schatz«-Liste aufnimmt, kann ich zähneknirschend damit leben.

Früher einmal war ich natürlich Schatz Nummer eins. Ich war der Erste, vor allen anderen.

Ehrlich gesagt finde ich es manchmal schwierig, sie teilen zu müssen. Sie ist wie ein weicher, runder Käse, und als ich klein war, hatte ich den ganzen Laib für mich. Dann hat sie Dad kennengelernt, und ein gewaltiges Stück wurde abgeschnitten, obwohl wahrscheinlich immer noch die Hälfte für mich übrig blieb. Dann kam Immy daher, die ein großes Stück abbekam, und schließlich Fred, der auch eins kriegte. Und garantiert schneidet sie für Chloë wieder eine Scheibe ab, das heißt, mein Stück wird ständig kleiner.

Als Immy heute in die Arme ihres Vaters gelaufen ist, hat es mir wirklich einen Stich gegeben, dass ich keinen habe. Keinen Vater, meine ich. William gibt sein Bestes, aber mal ganz ehrlich, im Fall einer Feuersbrunst würde er seine richtigen Kinder zuerst retten, darauf verwette ich meine gesamte Sammlung von Tim-und-Struppi-Devotionalien. Wodurch sich mein Käsestück theoretisch noch mal halbiert, weil Dad und Immy und Fred ja immer noch ein Stück von deren jeweiligem Käselaib abkriegen.

Dad schien sich wirklich zu freuen, als ich den Zuschlag für das Stipendium bekam. Er hat eine Flasche Champagner aufgemacht, und ich durfte auch ein Glas trinken. Vielleicht hat er darauf angestoßen, dass ich demnächst die meiste Zeit nicht zu Hause sein werde und er sich nicht mehr mit mir abfinden muss.

Wieso steigere ich mich eigentlich in letzter Zeit derart in diese Vater-Geschichte hinein? Mehr noch als sonst.

Vielleicht, weil mir meine Mutter bis jetzt immer genügt hat. Ich brauchte niemand anderen.

Aber in letzter Zeit habe ich das Gefühl, dass sie uns klammheimlich davonschlüpft – und ich kenne sie gut.

Sie ist nicht sie selbst.

Und ich auch nicht.

KAPITEL 6

Den frühen Vormittag verbrachten William und Helena in dem kleinen Gartencenter, das Helena am Stadtrand von Paphos entdeckt hatte.

Dieser Tage unternahmen sie nur selten etwas zu zweit, ohne die Kinder, und so banal der Einkauf im Grunde war, genoss es Helena, Hand in Hand mit William durch die sonnenbeschienenen Pflanzenreihen zu schlendern und verschiedene leuchtende Geranien, dazu mehrere Oleandersträucher und Lavendelbüsche auszusuchen, von denen sie wusste, dass sie die Hitze aushalten würden. An einem Stand vor dem Gartencenter wurden Obst und Gemüse aus der Umgebung feilgeboten, und so kauften sie noch Unmengen prall reifer Tomaten, Melonen, Pflaumen und süß duftender Kräuter, ehe sie alles im Kofferraum verstauten und nach Pandora zurückfuhren.

»Sadie ist dran. Sie will mit dir sprechen.« William kam in die Küche, wo Helena gerade das Mittagessen vorbereitete, und reichte ihr das Handy.

»Danke. Hallo, Schatz, wie geht's?« Helena klemmte sich das Handy nach altbewährter Manier zwischen Kinn und Schulter und wusch weiter den Salat. »Ach nein, wirklich? … So ein Mistkerl! Wie geht's dir? Nein, ich bin mir sicher … Ja, es ist wunderschön hier. Gestern sind William und Fred angekommen, und wir wollen den Nachmittag zusammen am Pool verbringen und die Ruhe genießen, bevor die Chandlers einfallen. Einen Moment, Sadie.« Sie drehte sich zu William und deutete auf das mit Tellern und Besteck beladene Tablett. »Kannst du das hinaustragen und den Kindern sagen, dass sie aus dem Wasser kommen und sich abtrocknen sollen, weil es gleich Mittagessen gibt?«

William verließ die Küche mitsamt dem Tablett, und Helena kehrte zu ihrem Telefonat mit Sadie zurück. »Natürlich lernst du jemand anderen kennen. Ich fand ja sowieso nie, dass er wirklich der Richtige für dich ist ... Was? Also, wenn du das wirklich willst, obwohl ich nicht weiß, wo du schlafen kannst. Wir platzen sowieso schon aus allen Nähten ... Also gut.« Helena seufzte. »Kopf hoch! Sag Bescheid, wann du ankommst, und ich hole dich vom Flughafen ab. Ciao, Schatz.«

William war in die Küche zurückgekehrt. »Die Kinder sind aus dem Wasser. Kann ich noch etwas nach draußen tragen?«

Helena gab die Salatblätter in eine Schüssel, die schon halb mit Tomaten- und Gurkenscheiben gefüllt war, wendete alles mit den Händen und reichte es William.

»Und, wie geht es Sadie?«, erkundigte er sich.

»Ganz schlecht. Mark hat sich von ihr getrennt.«

»Ah ja.«

»Ich weiß, dass du ihn nicht besonders leiden konntest und ich, ehrlich gesagt, auch nicht, aber Sadie hat ihn geliebt.«

»Das habe ich den stundenlangen Anrufen entnommen, in denen sie dir sein Loblied gesungen hat.«

»Ja, aber Sadie ist meine beste Freundin, und ich muss für sie da sein. Die Sache ist ...«

»... sie möchte ein paar Tage herkommen, um ihr gebrochenes Herz zu kurieren und sich an der Schulter ihrer besten Freundin auszuweinen«, schloss William.

»Mehr oder minder«, sagte Helena.

»Wann kommt sie?«

»Sie ruft jetzt bei der Fluglinie an und versucht, ein Ticket zu buchen.«

»Das heißt, sehr bald.«

»Wahrscheinlich. Es tut mir leid, mein Schatz, aber sie klang schrecklich.«

»Sie kommt schon drüber hinweg, wie sonst auch immer«, brummte er leise.

Helena holte eine Aufschnittplatte aus dem Kühlschrank und warf dabei einen Blick zu William. »Es mag ja wie eine Zumutung klingen, aber bitte vergiss nicht, dass Sadie und ich fast wie Schwestern sind. Wir kennen uns seit der Grundschule, und ich liebe sie, so einfach ist das. Da kann und will ich nicht Nein sagen.«

»Ich weiß.« William seufzte resigniert. »Und ich mag Sadie wirklich gern. Ich mache mir bloß Sorgen, dass dieser sogenannte Urlaub in Schwerarbeit ausartet und das Haus zu einem kostenlosen Hotel umfunktioniert wird, in dem ich und vor allem du für den reibungslosen Ablauf sorgen.«

»Das ist der Sinn und Zweck von Pandora – dass viele Menschen hier sind. Das war damals auch schon so.«

»Ja, und ich wette, es gab eine Heerschar dienstbarer Geister, die sich aufopfernd um die Bedürfnisse der Gäste gekümmert haben«, gab William zurück. »Ich möchte einfach nicht, dass du so viel arbeitest. Du siehst doch jetzt schon erschöpft aus.«

»Ich frage Angelina, ob sie mir mehr zur Hand gehen kann, vor allem in der Küche. Sie hat früher für Angus gekocht, und der war ausgesprochen heikel, das heißt, sie kocht bestimmt sehr gut.«

»Also gut«, sagte William. Er wusste, dass Helena ohnehin

nicht umzustimmen war. »Kommst du auch nach draußen?« Er nahm sie an der Hand, und sie folgte ihm ins helle Sonnenlicht auf die Terrasse.

Die drei Kinder hatten sich bereits unter der Pergola am Tisch versammelt, mehr oder minder bekleidet, außer Fred, der völlig nackt war.

»Mum, es tut mir leid, aber ich habe keine Lust, die ganzen Ferien damit zu verbringen, am Pool auf Fred und Immy aufzupassen«, maulte Alex und ließ sich auf einen Stuhl fallen. »Immy will bloß die ganze Zeit reinspringen, und ich kann sie nicht allein lassen für den Fall, dass sie sich wehtut oder untergeht, und das ist einfach … langweilig.«

»Alex, ich weiß. Nach dem Mittagessen löse ich dich ab, ja?«, sagte Helena und gab jedem Salat auf. »Stellt euch vor, Tante Sadie kommt uns eine Weile besuchen.«

»Noch ein Stück weniger«, murmelte Alex fast unhörbar.

»Wie bitte, Alex?«, fragte William.

»Nichts. Kannst du mir das Pittabrot geben, Immy?«

»Das heißt, dass wir uns noch mal etwas mit den Zimmern überlegen müssen«, sagte Helena. »Wir könnten die Abstellkammer leer räumen, in der lauter Sachen von Angus stehen. Sadie könnte dort schlafen. Der Raum ist relativ groß, aber das bedeutet mindestens einen halben Tag Arbeit.«

»Und du bräuchtest einen Müllcontainer. Demnach zu urteilen, was ich auf den ersten Blick gesehen habe, war Angus ein Sammler«, meinte William.

»Aber stell dir bloß vor, was du dort alles finden könntest«, sagte Alex begeistert. »Ich helfe dir. Mir macht es Spaß, mich durch altes Gerümpel zu wühlen.«

»Wie unschwer an deinem Zimmer zu Hause zu erkennen ist«, warf William ein.

Helena ignorierte den Kommentar. »Danke, Alex«, sagte sie. »Wir könnten uns gleich heute Nachmittag dranmachen.«

»Daddy, wann fährst du mit uns zum Wasserpark?«, fragte Immy.

»Bald, Immy, aber ich glaube, im Augenblick reicht der Wasserpark, den wir hier haben.«

»Aber hier gibt's keine Rutschen und so Sachen.«

»Immy, iss deinen Schinken und spiel nicht damit. Daddy ist gerade erst angekommen. Hör auf, ihn zu drängeln«, schaltete Helena sich ein.

»Es sei denn, du möchtest, dass ich heute Nachmittag mit ihnen in den Wasserpark fahre, damit sie dich in Ruhe lassen, während ihr die Kammer ausräumt?«, schlug William vor. »Und vergiss nicht, morgen kommt Chloë, ich muss sie vom Flughafen abholen. Und übermorgen kommen dann die Chandlers.«

»Jaaa, Daddy! Heute! Heute!« Fred stimmte in Immys Jubel ein und trommelte mit seinem Löffel auf den Teller.

»Schluss!«, sagte William streng. »Wenn ihr versprecht, eure Teller leer zu essen, dann fahren wir später, wenn die Sonne ein bisschen tiefer steht.«

»Mit dem Müllcontainer könntest du recht haben«, überlegte Helena. »Aber wo in aller Welt soll ich einen beschaffen?«

»Krieg ich einen Orangensaft, Mummy? Ich hab Durst«, sagte Fred.

»Fred, ich hole dir ein Glas.« William erhob sich und sagte mit einem gequälten Lächeln zu Helena: »Da kann dir sicher dein Freund Alexis helfen. Warum rufst du ihn nicht an?«

Helena und Alex blieben in der Tür zur Abstellkammer stehen, aber nur, weil kein Platz war, um weiter vorzudringen.

»O Gott, Mum, wo fangen wir bloß an?« Als Alex die Möbel

und die schier zahllosen braunen Kartons betrachtete, die sich bis an die Decke stapelten, bedauerte er es beinahe, nicht mit den anderen zum Wasserpark gefahren zu sein.

»Hol den Stuhl aus Immys Zimmer, den benutzen wir als Leiter und stellen die Kartons in den Flur. Dann können wir den Raum wenigstens betreten.«

»In Ordnung.«

Alex stieg auf den Stuhl und reichte Helena den obersten Karton.

Als sie ihn öffnete, stieg er wieder vom Stuhl herunter und sah ihr zu.

»Irre! Das sind ja lauter alte Fotos. Schau dir das an! Ist das Angus?«

Helena betrachtete den gut aussehenden Mann mit blonden Haaren, der in voller militärischer Aufmachung abgelichtet war. Sie nickte. »Ja. Und da ... da steht er auf der Terrasse, hier in Pandora, mit ein paar Leuten, die ich nicht kenne, und ... du meine Güte, die Frau neben ihm ist ja meine Mutter!«

»Deine Mum war sehr hübsch. Sie sah genauso aus wie du«, sagte Alex.

»Oder ich wie sie. Und ja, sie war sehr hübsch.« Helena lächelte. »Bevor sie meinen Vater heiratete, war sie Schauspielerin, eine ziemlich erfolgreiche sogar. Sie trat in London im Theater in mehreren Stücken auf und galt als richtige Schönheit.«

»Und das hat sie alles aufgegeben, um deinen Dad zu heiraten?«

»Ja. Obwohl sie bei der Hochzeit weit über dreißig war. Und mich bekam sie erst mit vierzig.«

»War das damals nicht sehr ungewöhnlich, so spät noch ein Kind zu bekommen?«

»Doch, sehr.« Helena warf ihrem Sohn ein Lächeln zu. »Ich

glaube, ich war ein Versehen. Deine Oma war überhaupt kein mütterlicher Typ.«

»Habe ich sie gekannt?«, fragte Alex.

»Nein. Sie starb noch vor deiner Geburt. Ich war dreiundzwanzig, ich tanzte damals in Italien.«

»Fehlt sie dir, jetzt, wo sie tot ist?«

»Um ehrlich zu sein, Alex, eigentlich nicht. Mit zehn wurde ich auf ein Internat geschickt, und davor hatte ich ein Kindermädchen. Im Grunde hatte ich immer eher das Gefühl, im Weg zu sein.«

»Ach, Mum, das ist ja schrecklich.« Alex tätschelte ihr mitfühlend die Hand.

»So schrecklich war das gar nicht.« Helena zuckte mit den Schultern. »Ich kannte nichts anderes. Mein Vater war wesentlich älter als meine Mutter, fast sechzig, als ich geboren wurde. Er war sehr wohlhabend, er hatte eine Farm in Kenia und verschwand immer wieder monatelang, um auf die Jagd zu gehen. Meine Eltern waren das, was man heute Jetset nennen würde, ständig unterwegs, und wenn sie zu Hause waren, haben sie Feste veranstaltet … ein kleines Mädchen hat da nur gestört.«

»Ich habe Opa auch nie kennengelernt, oder?«

»Nein. Er starb, als ich vierzehn war.«

»Wenn er so reich war, hast du dann nicht viel geerbt, als er gestorben ist?«

»Nein. Meine Mutter war seine zweite Frau. Er hatte aus erster Ehe zwei Söhne, die haben alles geerbt. Außerdem konnte meine Mum überhaupt nicht mit Geld umgehen, bei ihrem Tod war kaum etwas übrig geblieben.«

»Klingt nicht gerade nach einer tollen Kindheit.«

»Ach, sie war einfach anders. Auf jeden Fall habe ich sehr früh gelernt, Verantwortung für mich selbst zu übernehmen.«

Wie immer, wenn sie über ihre Kindheit sprach, wurde Helena zunehmend unbehaglich zumute. »Und sie hat in mir den Wunsch geweckt, später eine richtige Familie zu haben. Aber komm, stellen wir den Karton zur Seite. Wenn wir in jeden einzelnen hineinschauen, werden wir nie fertig.«

»Also gut.«

In den nächsten zwei Stunden räumten sie Angus' ganze Vergangenheit ans Licht. Alex entdeckte eine Truhe mit seinen alten Uniformen und folgte seiner Mutter mit einer khakifarbenen Schirmmütze auf dem Kopf und einem Paradeschwert in die Küche.

»Ausgesprochen fesch, mein Schatz.« Helena schenkte ihnen beiden Wasser ein und leerte ihr Glas auf einen Zug. »Das ist wirklich keine Arbeit für einen brüllend heißen Nachmittag, aber wir haben schon mehr als die Hälfte.«

»Ja, aber was sollen wir mit dem ganzen Zeug machen? Ich meine, du kannst das doch nicht alles einfach wegwerfen, oder?« Alex fuhr mit dem schweren Schwert durch die Luft.

»Das Schwert könnten wir doch irgendwo hier im Haus an die Wand hängen, und die Kartons mit Fotos und anderen Erinnerungsstücken stellen wir in den Schuppen, bis ich Zeit habe, sie mir anzusehen. Und der Rest ... Ich glaube, wir brauchen wirklich einen Container. Wahrscheinlich sollte ich Daddys Rat folgen und Alexis anrufen. Vielleicht weiß er ja, wo ich einen besorgen kann.«

Schweigend verfolgte Alex, wie Helena eine Nummer wählte und für das Gespräch auf die Terrasse ging. Kurz darauf kam sie zurück und nickte erfreut. »Sehr schön. Er hat gesagt, er kommt mit seinem Transporter, lädt alles auf und fährt es für mich zur Müllhalde. Wir brauchen also gar keinen Container. Komm, lass uns weitermachen, Alexis will um fünf hier sein.«

Als William vor Pandora vorfuhr, entdeckte er Alexis, der gerade einen großen Karton in den Schuppen trug. Vor dem Haus parkte ein Transporter, der beladen war mit beschädigten Möbelstücken, ausrangierten Lampenschirmen und mottenzerfressenen Teppichen. William ließ Fred und Immy auf dem Rücksitz weiterschlafen, öffnete weit die Türen, damit die Abendbrise hereinwehte, und machte sich auf die Suche nach Helena.

»Hallo, mein Schatz.« Sie stand oben in der Tür der leeren Kammer, einen Besen in der Hand und einen triumphierenden Ausdruck auf dem staubigen Gesicht. »Ist das nicht großartig? Die Kammer ist viel größer, als ich dachte. Ich glaube, da passt spielend ein Doppelbett rein. Alexis sagt, bei ihm steht eines, das er uns leihen kann.«

»Ah. Schön.«

»Es muss natürlich gestrichen werden, aber der Blick auf die Berge ist herrlich. Der Boden ist nicht gefliest, es sind nur Holzdielen, aber die können wir später einlassen.«

»Großartig«, sagte William. »Dein Freund hilft dir also wieder.«

»Ja, er ist vor einer Stunde mit seinem Wagen gekommen. Die Kartons, die ich sichten will, hat er im Schuppen verstaut, und die restlichen Sachen will er zum Müll fahren.«

William nickte. »Er hat dir sicher sehr geholfen, aber du hättest auch mich bitten können, die Kartons in den Schuppen zu tragen.«

»William, du warst nicht hier, und Alexis hat sich anerboten, mir zu helfen. Mehr nicht.«

Ohne etwas zu erwidern, machte William kehrt und ging den Flur entlang zur Treppe.

»Du bist doch nicht sauer, oder?«, rief sie ihm nach.

»Nein.« William verschwand die Treppe hinunter außer Sicht.

Frustriert schlug Helena mit der Hand auf den Türrahmen. »Himmel noch mal, du hast doch selbst vorgeschlagen, dass ich ihn anrufen soll!«, fluchte sie leise vor sich hin, bevor sie ihm nach unten folgte. Alexis stand in der Küche.

»Fertig. Ich fahre jetzt zur Müllkippe.«

»Möchtest du nicht auf ein Glas Wein bleiben?«

»Nein danke. Wir sehen uns bald.«

»Ja. Und hab noch mal vielen herzlichen Dank.«

Alexis nickte lächelnd und ging zur hinteren Tür hinaus.

Nachdem Helena zwei müde, übellaunige Kinder aus dem Wagen geholt, ihnen zu essen gegeben und sie im Salon auf das Sofa gesetzt hatte, damit sie sich eine DVD ansehen konnten, schenkte sie sich ein Glas Wein ein und ging auf die Terrasse. Sie hörte Alex im Pool planschen, sah William an der Brüstung lehnen und ließ sich unter der Pergola nieder. Sie hatte keine Lust, sich bemerkbar zu machen. Schließlich kam William zu ihr und setzte sich neben sie.

»Es tut mir leid, Helena, das war kindisch von mir. Es kommt mir einfach komisch vor, dass ein anderer Mann die Dinge erledigt, für die normalerweise ich zuständig bin. Ich habe das Gefühl, ich würde hier in deine Welt eindringen und gehöre eigentlich gar nicht her.«

»Mein Schatz, du bist doch noch keinen Tag hier, du musst dich erst noch eingewöhnen.«

»Nein, es ist etwas anderes«, sagte er mit einem Seufzen. »Pandora ist dein Reich, dein Haus, es ist dein Leben aus einer anderen Zeit. Ob das nun stimmt oder nicht, so kommt es mir auf jeden Fall vor.«

»Gefällt es dir hier nicht?«

»Es ist wunderschön, aber ...« William schüttelte den Kopf. »Ich brauche etwas zu trinken. Bin gleich wieder da.« Er verschwand im Haus und kehrte mit einer Flasche und einem Glas in der Hand zurück.

»Kann ich dir nachschenken?«

Helena nickte, und er füllte ihr Glas nach.

»Der Wein ist wirklich sehr trinkbar. Dein Freund weiß eindeutig, was er macht.«

»Er heißt Alexis, William, und ja, er weiß, was er macht, schließlich hat er das von klein auf gelernt.«

»Also … Wahrscheinlich sollten wir ihn zum Dank einen Abend zum Essen einladen.«

»Das ist wirklich nicht nötig.«

»Doch, das ist es schon. Um ehrlich zu sein« – er trank noch einen Schluck –, »wahrscheinlich bin ich nervös wegen morgen.«

»Du meinst, wegen Chloës Ankunft?«

»Ja. Meine Tochter, die ich nicht mehr kenne und der eingetrichtert wurde, dass ich ein Schuft bin … Ich habe keine Ahnung, wie sie sein wird, aber es war garantiert nicht ihre Idee, zu uns zu kommen. Sie findet es bestimmt nicht so toll, abgeschoben zu werden, damit ihre Mutter sich ohne sie in Frankreich amüsieren kann. Sie könnte ausgesprochen schwierig sein, Helena, und« – William trank wieder einen Schluck –, »ich könnte es ihr nicht einmal verdenken.«

»Mein Schatz, wir schaffen das schon. Außerdem werden jede Menge Leute hier sein, die eventuelle Spannungen etwas abfedern werden.«

»Und davon wird es reichlich geben, ganz sicher.«

»Das schaffen wir schon«, wiederholte Helena und drückte ihm fest die Hand. »Das haben wir doch immer.«

»Ja, aber …« William seufzte. »Ich hatte gehofft, wir würden mehr als nur alles schaffen. Ich hatte gehofft, wir könnten uns in diesem Sommer ein paar schöne Wochen machen.«

»Und ich weiß nicht, warum das nicht klappen sollte. Die Besetzung unserer Gästeliste klingt auf jeden Fall interessant.«

»Apropos, hast du schon von Sadie gehört?«

»Ja, sie kommt mit derselben Maschine wie die Chandlers. Ich wollte bei ihnen nachfragen, ob sie sie nicht vom Flughafen mitnehmen können.«

»Guter Gott!« William grinste gequält. »Die berüchtigte Jules und ihr geprügelter Gatte, ganz zu schweigen von Rupes und Viola, eine suizidgefährdete Sadie … und eine Tochter, die ich kaum kenne.«

»So betrachtet klingt es wirklich grauenhaft«, stimmte Helena ihm zu. »Vielleicht sollten wir kneifen und sofort nach Hause fliegen.«

»Du hast recht, ich sehe alles zu schwarz. Entschuldige. Übrigens, hast du Immy und Fred schon von Chloës Ankunft erzählt?«, fragte William.

»Nein. Mit Alex habe ich darüber gesprochen, aber ich dachte, du würdest es den beiden Kleinen lieber selbst sagen.«

»In Ordnung, dann sollte ich das wohl mal machen. Hast du einen Vorschlag, wie ich es ihnen beibringen soll?«

»Beiläufig, würde ich meinen, als wäre nichts weiter dabei. Und vergiss nicht, Blut ist dicker als Wasser. Chloë ist ihre Halbschwester, fünfzig Prozent ihrer Gene sind dieselben.«

»Stimmt. Es sind bloß die anderen fünfzig Prozent, die mir Sorgen bereiten. Was, wenn sie ihrer Mutter ähnlich ist?«

»Dann möge Gott uns beistehen. Wie wär's, wenn wir es Immy und Fred gemeinsam sagen?«

»Das wäre schön.« William nickte erleichtert. »Danke, Helena.«

Wie Helena erwartet hatte, waren die beiden Kleinen wenig beeindruckt von der bevorstehenden Ankunft ihrer unbekannten Schwester.

»Daddy, ist die nett?«, fragte Immy und kuschelte sich in seinen Schoß. »Wie sieht sie denn aus?«

»Früher hieß es immer, Chloë sehe aus wie ich.«

»Also hat sie kurze braune Haare und große Ohren? Scheußlich!«

»Danke, Schätzchen.« William küsste seine Tochter auf den Kopf. »Sie ist viel hübscher als ich, das verspreche ich dir.«

»Wird Klo jetzt immer bei uns wohnen?«, fragte Fred von unter dem Tisch, wo er mit einem seiner Lastwagen spielte.

»Sie heißt Chloë, Fred«, verbesserte Helena ihn, »und nein, sie bleibt nur bei uns, solange wir auf Zypern sind.«

»Wohnt sie sonst allein?«

»Nein, sie lebt bei ihrer Mummy«, antwortete William.

»Tut sie nicht, weil ich hab sie bei uns nie gesehen.«

»Mein Schatz, sie hat eine andere Mummy als du«, sagte Helena, auch wenn sie wusste, dass es sinnlos war, einem Dreijährigen die Zusammenhänge zu erläutern. »Wie auch immer, Zeit fürs Bett.«

Der übliche Proteststurm erhob sich, aber schließlich lagen beide nebeneinander unter der Decke. Helena gab ihnen einen Kuss auf die leicht verschwitzte Stirn.

»Gute Nacht, und ab ins Traumland mit euch.« Sie zog die Tür hinter sich ins Schloss und stieß auf dem Flur fast mit Alex zusammen, der gerade mit seinem Rucksack nach unten in sein neues Schlafquartier ging.

»Mum, alles in Ordnung?«

»Ja. Und bei dir?«

»Auch.«

»Du weißt, du hättest erst morgen ausziehen müssen, Dad holt Chloë um vier ab. Vormittags wäre immer noch reichlich Zeit, um das Bett frisch zu beziehen und Ordnung zu schaffen.«

»Ich will es aber so.« Er ging die ersten Stufen hinunter.

»In Ordnung. Ich habe dir vorhin einen Ventilator reingestellt, damit du nicht wieder einen Hitzschlag bekommst.«

»Danke.« Alex hielt inne und sah zu ihr. »Willst du die Kartons draußen im Schuppen alle anschauen?«

»Ja, wenn ich Zeit habe, aber bestimmt nicht in den nächsten Tagen.«

»Darf ich?«

»Solange du nichts wegwirfst.«

»Natürlich nicht. Du kennst mich doch, Mum, ich mag alles, was mit Geschichte zu tun hat. Vor allem mit meiner eigenen«, sagte er mit Nachdruck.

»Aber, Alex« – Helena ging auf seine letzte Bemerkung gar nicht ein –, »das meiste wird dir gar nichts sagen. Vergiss nicht, Angus war nicht mit mir verwandt, er war mein Patenonkel.«

»Aber trotzdem, vielleicht finde ich ja das eine oder andere über ihn heraus. Das wäre doch interessant, oder nicht?«

»Ja, natürlich.« Helena wusste genau, worauf ihr Sohn anspielte. Er suchte nach Hinweisen, aber sie wusste, dass er in Angus' Kartons keine finden würde. »Nur zu, aber ich möchte nicht, dass du dich den ganzen Tag in deinem Zimmer verbarrikadierst. Wir bekommen Besuch, ich werde deine Hilfe brauchen.«

»Natürlich, Mum. Gute Nacht«, sagte er und ging weiter die Treppe hinab zu seinem neuen Schlafzimmer.

»Gute Nacht«, erwiderte sie.

Alex' Tagebuch

Ich sitze in meinem winzigen Kabuff auf dem Bett. Der Ventilator, den mir meine Mutter gegeben hat, steht so nah bei mir, dass er mich binnen einer Minute trocken föhnt. Vor mir habe ich einen Karton, den ich gerade aus dem Schuppen hereingeschleppt habe. Er ist randvoll mit Briefen und Fotos, die vielleicht einen Bezug zu mir und meiner Vergangenheit haben. Vielleicht aber auch nicht.

Meine Mutter ist nicht dumm. Sie weiß, wonach ich suche. Sie weiß genau, dass ich dringend wissen will …

Wer ich bin.

Sie macht nicht den Eindruck, als befürchte sie, dass diese Kartons einen Schlüssel zum großen Geheimnis bergen könnten, also wird in Angus' Sachen vermutlich nichts von Interesse auftauchen.

Ich frage mich wirklich, was hinter dieser Heimlichtuerei mit ihrer Vergangenheit steckt. Sie spricht so gut wie nie über ihre Eltern oder wo und wie sie aufgewachsen ist. Heute war sie für ihre Verhältnisse diesbezüglich ausgesprochen redselig.

Da ist mir klar geworden, dass die meisten jungen Menschen eine Oma und einen Opa haben, die sie kennen oder an die sie sich zumindest gut erinnern können. Das Einzige, was ich mit Sicherheit weiß, ist, dass meine Mutter Helena Elisa Beaumont heißt und ich in Wien geboren wurde (das konnte sie mir nicht verheimlichen, das steht auf meiner Geburtsurkunde) und bis zum Alter von drei Jahren dort lebte, als sie Dad kennenlernte und wir wieder nach England zogen. Angeblich war ich als Kleinkind zweisprachig. Heute schaffe ich es gerade noch, auf Deutsch korrekt bis zehn zu zählen.

Ich liege da, die Hände unter dem Kopf verschränkt, und starre zur rissigen vergilbten Decke hinauf. Und ich denke an meinen Freund Jake – ich verwende den Begriff recht großzügig, er bedeutet lediglich, dass wir uns manchmal unterhalten und er weniger dumm ist als der Rest der Klasse –, dessen Mutter gemütlich und füllig ist und bieder aussieht wie die meisten Mums von Söhnen im Teenageralter. Sie arbeitet Teilzeit als Sekretärin in einer Arztpraxis und setzt mir, wann immer ich zum Teetrinken bei ihnen bin, einen richtig guten selbst gebackenen Kuchen vor, und alles an ihr ist …

… normal.

Auf dem Sideboard wird ihr ganzes Leben fotografisch präsentiert, daneben die frisch gebackenen Scones. Jake weiß alles über seine Großeltern, und er weiß auch, wer sein Vater ist, schließlich sieht er ihn jeden Tag. Das einzige Geheimnis, das er entschlüsseln muss, besteht darin, wie er seine Mutter überreden soll, ihm zehn Pfund zu leihen, damit er sich das neueste Playstation-Spiel kaufen kann.

Warum sind also meine Mutter und meine Vergangenheit ein solches Rätsel?

Ich atme tief durch, mir ist klar, dass ich mich wieder in diese Sache hineinsteigere. Obwohl das für jemanden wie mich – ein »begabtes« Kind – angeblich normal ist. Ich kann Statistiken nicht leiden und bemühe mich, ihnen nicht zu entsprechen, aber manchmal ist es schwierig. Um mich abzulenken, setze ich mich wieder auf und ziehe einzelne vergilbte Schwarz-Weiß-Fotos aus dem Karton. Darauf sind unbekannte Menschen zu sehen, die mittlerweile bestimmt tot sind. Einige Bilder tragen auf der Rückseite ein Datum, andere nicht.

Als jüngerer Mann sah Angus wirklich gut aus, vor allem in Uniform. Erstaunlich, dass er nie geheiratet hat. Außer natürlich, er war schwul. Er sieht zwar nicht so aus, aber wer weiß? Ich habe mir oft überlegt, woher man weiß, dass man schwul ist. Ich mag ja schräg sein, aber ich bin eindeutig nicht andersrum.

Endlich bin ich auf dem Boden des Kartons angelangt. Ich habe mich durch Berge von Fotos und Unterlagen bezüglich der Verschiffung von Whisky aus Southampton und Einfuhrzoll auf dieses Gemälde und jenes Möbelstück durchgearbeitet. Dann stoße ich auf ein dickes braunes Kuvert, das an »Colonel McCladden« in Pandora adressiert ist, und greife hinein.

Und ziehe einen Stoß dünnster blauer Luftpostkuverts heraus. Ich schaue hinein und sehe, dass der darin liegende Brief noch intakt ist. Oben steht ein Datum, 12. Dezember, aber weder Jahr noch Anschrift.

Ich lese die erste Zeile:

Meine über alles Geliebte.

Man braucht nicht Sherlock Holmes zu sein, um zu erahnen, dass es sich hierbei um einen Liebesbrief handelt. Die Schrift ist wunderschön, mit Tinte geschrieben und so flüssig und geschwungen, wie man damals eben schrieb.

Ich überfliege den Inhalt. Er ist eine Eloge auf eine Unbekannte, die durchgängig nur »meine über alles Geliebte« heißt. Und dazu lauter Sätze wie »*Ohne dich ziehen sich die Tage endlos dahin, ich verzehre mich danach, dich wieder in meinen Armen zu halten*«.

Nicht ganz mein Ding, dieses ganze romantische Zeug. Ich bin eher für Thriller zu haben. Oder für Freud.

Am ärgerlichsten ist allerdings, dass am Ende des Briefes keine Unterschrift steht, nur ein Schnörkel, der nicht zu entziffern ist und jeder von vielleicht zwölf Buchstaben sein könnte.

Ich stecke den Brief in den Umschlag zurück und öffne zwei weitere. Sie lesen sich ähnlich und geben ebenso wenig Aufschluss über das Jahr und die Identität.

Dann schaue ich noch mal in den braunen Umschlag, ob er auch wirklich leer ist, und finde noch einen gefalteten Zettel.

»*Ich gehe sicherlich recht in der Annahme, dass diese Briefe Ihnen gehören. Hiermit schicke ich sie dem Absender zurück.*«

Mehr nicht.

Das heißt, der Verfasser der Zeilen war eindeutig Angus. Was eine Frage beantworten und bestätigen würde, dass er eindeutig nicht schwul war.

Ich gähne. Heute Abend bin ich müde, schließlich habe ich den halben Tag in der Hitze Kartons durch die Gegend geschleppt. Morgen früh gebe ich die Briefe meiner Mutter. Die sind eindeutig mehr ihr Ding als meins.

Ich schalte das Licht aus und lege mich wieder hin, hole Bee von unter dem Kissen hervor und stecke ihn mir in die Armbeuge. Die Brise vom Ventilator streicht mir übers Gesicht, das ist sehr angenehm. Ich frage mich, wie ein Mann wie Angus Truppen befehligen und Menschen erschießen und gleichzeitig solche Briefe schreiben konnte.

Dieses ganze Liebesdingens ist mir ein Rätsel, aber ich vermute, irgendwann werde ich schon noch herausfinden, was es damit auf sich hat.

Irgendwann.

KAPITEL 7

Wo zum Teufel war sie bloß? Nervös fuhr William sich durch die Haare. Das Flugzeug war vor über einer Stunde gelandet. Kurz danach waren die Passagiere aus dem Ankunftsbereich geströmt, jetzt herrschte gespenstische Ruhe.

Er rief Helena auf dem Handy an, aber sie ging nicht ran. Er hatte sie mit den Kindern bei einer örtlichen Autovermietung in Paphos abgesetzt, da sie zu dem Schluss gekommen waren, dass sie zwei Autos brauchten. Am Abend zuvor hatte Helena gemeint, sie würde mit den Kindern anschließend vielleicht an einen Strand fahren. William hinterließ ihr eine Nachricht, sie möge ihn dringend zurückrufen, ließ noch einmal den Blick durch die Ankunftshalle schweifen und marschierte dann zum Informationsschalter.

»Guten Tag, können Sie bitte überprüfen, ob meine Tochter in dem 13.10-Uhr-Flug von Gatwick saß? Ich soll sie abholen, aber sie ist noch nicht aufgetaucht.«

Die Frau nickte. »Name?«

»Chloë Cooke, mit einem e am Ende.«

Die Frau gab etwas in den Computer ein, scrollte nach unten und schaute schließlich zu William. »Nein, Sir. In der Maschine war niemand mit diesem Namen.«

»Verdammt«, murmelte William lautlos. »Könnten Sie vielleicht nachsehen, ob sie heute mit einem anderen Flug aus England angekommen ist?«

»Ich kann's versuchen, aber das waren heute bislang zehn, auch von kleineren Regionalflughäfen.«

»War auch ein Flug von Stansted dabei?«, fragte William aus einer Ahnung heraus.

»Ja, der ist eine halbe Stunde vor dem Gatwick-Flug gelandet.«

»Gut, könnten Sie da bitte mal nachsehen?«

Wieder tippte die Frau etwas, und schließlich nickte sie. »Ja, auf dem Flug von Stansted war eine Miss C. Cooke.«

»Danke.«

Als William sich vom Schalter entfernte, stieg Erleichterung gepaart mit Zorn in ihm auf. Seine Exfrau hatte offenbar umgebucht, ohne ihn zu informieren. Eigentlich hätte er damit rechnen sollen, dachte er wütend. Doch er unterdrückte seinen Ärger und machte sich auf die Suche.

Zwanzig Minuten später war er drauf und dran, die Flughafenpolizei zu kontaktieren und die Entführung einer Minderjährigen zu melden, als er neben der Ankunftshalle auf eine kleine Bar stieß.

Dort war niemand zu sehen außer einem jungen Mädchen und einem dunkelhaarigen Mann, die rauchend auf Barhockern saßen. Aus der Ferne bemerkte William, dass das Mädchen lange, glänzende kastanienbraune Haare und eine sehr schlanke Figur hatte. Sie trug einen Minirock, dazu ein enges T-Shirt und hatte die endlos langen Beine übereinandergeschlagen. An ihren Füßen steckten flache Pumps, die sie immer wieder von der Ferse gleiten ließ. Beim Näherkommen erkannte er das Mädchen als Chloë – eine Chloë, die sich in den vergangenen Jahren vom Kind in eine bildschöne junge Frau verwandelt hatte.

William entging der Reiz seiner Tochter ebenso wenig wie dem Mann, der ihr gegenübersaß und dessen Hand leicht auf ihrem bloßen Oberschenkel ruhte. William steuerte rasch auf sie zu und erkannte dabei, dass der Mann älter war, als er aus der Ferne gewirkt hatte. Er unterdrückte den Drang, sich sofort auf ihn zu stürzen, und blieb stattdessen einen guten Meter vor den beiden stehen.

»Guten Tag, Chloë.«

Sie drehte sich zu ihm und verzog den Mund zu einem feinen Lächeln. »Hi, Daddy. Wie geht's?«

Unverfroren zog sie noch einmal an ihrer Zigarette und drückte sie aus, als William auf sie zukam und ihr förmlich einen Kuss auf die Wange gab.

Wie einer fremden Person, aber die war sie ja auch.

»Darf ich dir Christoff vorstellen? Er hat mir beim Warten Gesellschaft geleistet.« Chloë richtete ihre riesigen rehbraunen Augen wieder auf ihren Verehrer. »Er hat mir von den ganzen coolen Bars und Clubs hier in der Gegend erzählt.«

»Sehr schön. Aber jetzt lass uns gehen.«

»Gut.« Elegant glitt Chloë vom Hocker. »Christoff, deine Handynummer habe ich ja. Ich rufe dich an, und dann kannst du mir Paphos zeigen.«

Der junge Mann nickte wortlos und hob kurz die Hand, als Chloë William zur Bar hinaus folgte.

»Wo ist dein Koffer?«, fragte er mit einem Blick auf die kleine Reisetasche in ihrer Hand.

»Ich habe keinen«, antwortete sie lässig. »Mehr als ein paar Bikinis und Sarongs brauche ich hier sowieso nicht. Es ist cool, ohne großes Gepäck zu reisen.«

»Tut mir leid, dass ich nicht rechtzeitig hier war, um dich abzuholen. Deine Mum hat mir natürlich den falschen Flug mitgeteilt«, sagte er, als er mit ihr ins helle Sonnenlicht hinaus- und auf den Wagen zuging.

»Wir dachten, wir würden in London sein, aber dann waren wir doch im Cottage in Blakeney, und Mum hat festgestellt, dass ich von Stansted aus fliegen kann. Sie hat versucht, dich anzurufen, konnte dich aber nicht erreichen.«

William wusste genau, dass er das Handy nicht aus dem Auge gelassen hatte, in Alarmbereitschaft für die kurzfristigen Änderungen, die mit allen Terminabsprachen mit seiner Ex-frau einhergingen. Aber er schluckte seinen Ärger hinunter. In den kommenden Wochen würde er das um des lieben Friedens willen noch sehr viel häufiger tun müssen, wie er sehr wohl wusste.

»Ich habe den ganzen Flughafen nach dir abgesucht, es war reiner Zufall, dass ich die Bar entdeckt habe. Eigentlich darf man sie erst mit achtzehn betreten, Chloë, das stand an der Tür.«

»Aber du hast mich ja schließlich doch gefunden. Ist das dein Auto?«

»Ja.« William öffnete die Tür.

»Wow, ein Minivan.«

»Ja, wir sind ein großer Haufen. Steig ein.«

Chloë warf ihre Tasche auf den Rücksitz, fuhr sich mit beiden Händen durchs Haar, um es von ihrem langen, schlanken Hals zu heben, und gähnte. »Ich bin völlig kaputt. Ich musste heute Morgen um halb vier aufstehen. Der Flug war um sieben.«

»Hat Mum dich zum Flughafen gebracht?«

»Um Himmels willen, nein. Du weißt doch, wie sie am frühen Morgen ist. Sie hat mir ein Taxi bestellt.« Sie drehte sich zu William und lächelte. »Ich bin jetzt ein großes Mädchen, Daddy.«

»Du bist vierzehn, Chloë. Es dauert noch zwei Jahre, bis dir offiziell das Rauchen erlaubt ist, wenn ich das mal anmerken darf.« William ließ den Wagen an und fuhr zur Parklücke hinaus.

»Nächsten Monat werde ich fünfzehn, also entspann dich, Daddy. Außerdem rauche ich nur ab und zu, ich bin nicht süchtig oder so.«

»Na, dann ist ja alles gut«, sagte William, auch wenn er wusste, dass die Ironie an seiner Tochter abperlen würde. »Wie sieht's aus mit der Schule?«

»Ach, also weißt du, die Schule … Ich kann's nicht erwarten abzugehen.«

»Und was zu tun?« William war schmerzlich bewusst, dass ein Vater normalerweise die Antwort auf diese Frage kennen müsste. Dieser Gedanke bedrückte ihn noch mehr.

»Weiß ich noch nicht. Vielleicht ein bisschen reisen und dann modeln.«

»Ah ja.«

»Eine Agentur hat mich schon kontaktiert, aber Mum sagt, dass ich erst die mittlere Reife machen muss.«

»Da hat sie recht, das solltest du wirklich.«

»Heutzutage fangen Mädchen schon mit zwölf zu modeln an. Bis ich sechzehn bin, bin ich viel zu alt.« Chloë seufzte.

William lachte. »Das glaube ich kaum, Chloë.«

»Na, es wird euch beiden noch leidtun, dass ihr mir die Chance verbaut habt, viel Geld zu verdienen und berühmt zu werden.«

»Deine Mum hat dir von Immy und Fred erzählt, oder nicht?« William zog es vor, das Thema zu wechseln.

»Du meinst, meine kleinen Geschwister? Klar.«

»Wie geht's dir bei der Vorstellung, sie jetzt zu sehen?«

»Cool. Ich meine, das ist doch nichts Ungewöhnliches, oder?

Meine beste Freundin Gaia ist die Tochter von einem Rockstar – Mike irgendwer –, der war zu deiner Zeit offenbar ein richtiger Star. Sie hat dermaßen viele Stief- und Halbgeschwister, dass sie den Überblick verloren hat. Ihr Dad ist über sechzig, und seine Freundin ist wieder schwanger.«

»Es freut mich, dass dir die Situation ganz normal vorkommt, Chloë. Das ist gut.«

»Klar. Wie Gaia sagt, zu Weihnachten ist es besonders toll, wenn die Eltern geschieden sind und wieder geheiratet haben, weil sie einen dann alle mit Geschenken zu bestechen versuchen.«

»Das ist eine … eine ungewöhnliche Sicht der Dinge.« William schluckte. »Helena freut sich darauf, dich wiederzusehen.«

»Ah ja?«

»Ja, und Alex auch, ihr Sohn. Erinnerst du dich an ihn?«

»Eigentlich nicht.«

»Ich warne dich vor, Alex ist ungewöhnlich. Er gilt als hochbegabt, das heißt, manchmal kommt er ein bisschen seltsam rüber. Aber das ist er eigentlich gar nicht, er ist nur intelligenter, als man es von jemandem in seinem Alter erwartet.«

»Du meinst, er ist ein Nerd?«

»Nein, er ist einfach …« – William bemühte sich, die richtigen Worte zu finden, um seinen Stiefsohn zu beschreiben –, »er ist einfach anders. Die Chandlers kommen auch, das sind alte Freunde der Familie, und Sadie, Helenas beste Freundin. Das Haus ist also voll. Es wird sicher sehr lustig.«

Von Chloë kam keine Antwort. William warf einen Blick zu ihr hinüber und stellte fest, dass sie eingeschlafen war.

Als er vor Pandora vorfuhr, war das Haus verwaist. Sanft weckte er Chloë.

»Wir sind da.«

Chloë öffnete die Augen und streckte sich. Dann sah sie zu ihrem Vater. »Wie spät ist es?«

»Zehn nach vier. Komm, ich zeige dir den Ausblick.«

»Okay.« Chloë stieg aus und folgte William ums Haus zur Terrasse.

»Cool«, sagte sie und nickte zustimmend.

»Es freut mich, dass es dir gefällt. Helena hat das Haus von ihrem Patenonkel geerbt, das heißt, innen muss noch einiges renoviert werden«, erzählte William, als Chloë durch die Terrassentür in den Salon trat.

»Ich finde es genau richtig so, wie es ist. Wie ein Haus in einem Agatha-Christie-Film«, meinte Chloë. »Gibt's einen Pool?«

»Ja, durch die Pforte links auf der Terrasse.«

»Cool. Dann geh ich mal schwimmen.« Chloë zog ihr T-Shirt und den Rock aus, darunter kam ein winziger Bikini zum Vorschein. So schlenderte sie wieder nach draußen.

William sah ihr nach, wie sie über die Terrasse davonging, und ließ sich schwer auf einen Stuhl unter der Pergola fallen.

Entweder war Chloë eine erstklassige Schauspielerin, oder seine Befürchtungen, was ihre Einstellung ihm gegenüber betraf, waren völlig unbegründet. Die ganze vergangene Woche hatte er sich den Kopf zerbrochen, was er ihr entgegenhalten sollte, falls sie ihm vorwarf, er habe sie im Stich gelassen und würde sie nicht lieben, und sich für die emotionalen Tretminen gewappnet, die ihre Mutter zweifelsohne gelegt hatte.

Sie war, um ihre eigenen Worte zu verwenden, »cool«. So cool, dass William sich fragte, ob ihre Gleichgültigkeit nicht vielleicht ebenso verletzend war wie die Ablehnung, die er erwartet hatte. Es schien ihr einfach überhaupt nichts auszumachen, dass sie ihn fast sechs Jahre nicht gesehen hatte.

Aber konnte eine Vierzehnjährige wirklich derart selbst-

bewusst sein? Oder war das alles nur Fassade, eine Schutz-
schicht, um das verängstigte kleine Mädchen, das dahinter-
steckte, zu verbergen? William war sich seiner Ahnungslosig-
keit, was die weibliche Psyche betraf, nur allzu bewusst. Er
würde Helena fragen müssen.

Zehn Minuten später fuhr sie mit dem neuen Leihwagen
vor, aus dem sich seine Familie geräuschvoll über die Terrasse
und ihn verteilte.

»Hi, Daddy.« Immy warf sich ihm in die Arme. »Ich hab eine
große Sandburg gebaut, und dann hat Fred sie kaputt gemacht.
Ich hasse ihn.«

»Ich schieß dich tot!!« Fred kam mit einer gezückten Wasserpistole auf die Terrasse gelaufen.

Schreiend vergrub Immy ihr Gesicht an Williams Schulter.
»Schick ihn weg!«

»Leg das hin, Fred. Du machst Immy Angst.«

»Tu ich nicht. Am Strand hat sie mich totgeschossen.« Zur
Unterstreichung seiner Aussage nickte er heftig. »Wo ist Klo?«

»Chloë, Fred.« Helena hängte gerade die nassen Handtücher
über die Brüstung. »Ja, wo ist sie?«

»Im Pool«, antwortete William und setzte Immy ab.

»Und wie ist sie drauf?«, fragte Helena leise.

»Bestens, alles bestens. Du wirst feststellen, dass sie ein ganzes Stück größer geworden ist, seit wir sie das letzte Mal gesehen haben. In jeder Hinsicht«, fügte William hinzu und verzog
vielsagend das Gesicht.

Helena sah Alex am Rand der Terrasse stehen, wie er vorzu-
geben versuchte, er würde nicht durch die Oliven zum Pool hi-
nunterblicken. »Sollen wir alle zu ihr gehen und sie begrüßen?«

»Nicht nötig, ich bin schon da.«

Chloë kam auf die Terrasse, Wassertropfen glitzerten auf ihrer straffen Haut. »Hallo.« Sie ging auf Helena zu und küsste sie auf beide Wangen. »Dein Haus gefällt mir sehr.«

»Danke«, sagte Helena und lächelte.

»Und das sind meine kleinen Geschwister? Wollt ihr mir nicht Hallo sagen?«, fragte sie aufmunternd.

Wortlos starrten Immy und Fred das exotische Wesen mit den langen Beinen an und blieben stocksteif stehen.

»Ach, sind die süß! Immy ist dir ja wie aus dem Gesicht geschnitten, Helena, und Fred sieht genauso aus wie Daddy.« Sie näherte sich den beiden und ging in die Hocke. »Hallo, ich bin Chloë, eure große böse Stiefschwester.«

»Daddy hat gesagt, du würdest aussehen wie er, aber du hast keine großen Ohren und außerdem schöne lange Haare«, sagte Immy schüchtern.

Lächelnd warf Chloë einen Blick zu William. »Na, dann ist das ja geklärt.« Sie reichte Immy eine Hand. »Magst du mir dein schönes Haus zeigen?«

»Ja. Mummy und ich haben Blumen in dein Zimmer gestellt«, sagte Immy und nahm Chloës Hand.

»Vielleicht habe ich auch ein paar Bonbons in meiner Tasche.« Als Immy sie zum Haus führte, warf sie einen Blick zu Fred zurück.

»Darf ich mit?« Fred lief auf seinen kurzen Beinchen zu Chloë und Immy.

»Chloë, du schläfst direkt neben mir.« Immys hohe Stimme war bis auf die Terrasse zu hören.

»Ich auch«, sagte Fred. »Wo sind die Bonbons, Klo?«

Helena warf einen Blick zu William und lächelte. »Das war nicht allzu schlimm, oder? Mein Gott, sie ist wirklich sehr hübsch.«

»Ja, das stimmt. Außerdem kommt sie mir für eine Vierzehn-jährige viel zu reif vor.«

»Vergiss nicht, Schatz, sie ist fast fünfzehn. Außerdem werden Mädchen schneller erwachsen als Jungs. Hast du Lust, mir etwas Kaltes zu trinken zu holen? Ich bin am Verdursten.«

»Aber natürlich, gnädige Frau. Ich möchte auch was trinken.« Mit einem Nicken ging William davon.

Helena drehte sich um und sah Alex hinter sich stehen. »Ist alles in Ordnung? Du siehst aus, als wärst du einem Gespenst begegnet.«

Alex öffnete den Mund, brachte aber kein Wort hervor, und so zuckte er stattdessen mit den Schultern.

»Alex, du hast Chloë gar nicht begrüßt.«

»Nein«, krächzte er.

»Warum gehst du nicht mit den anderen nach oben?«

Er schüttelte den Kopf. »Ich lege mich ein bisschen hin. Ich glaube, ich kriege eine Migräne.«

»Zu viel Sonne, vermute ich mal, mein Schatz. Ruh dich aus, und ich rufe dich, wenn das Abendessen fertig ist«, schlug Helena vor. »Angelina hat im Ofen etwas für uns stehen lassen, das köstlich riecht.«

Mit einem Brummen verschwand Alex im Haus.

»Hat er was?«, fragte William, der Alex begegnete, als er mit zwei Gläsern eisgekühlter Limonade herauskam. Helena war die Einzige, die die Stimmungen ihres Sohnes zu deuten wusste.

»Ich glaube nicht.«

William setzte sich, und Helena trat hinter ihn und massier-te ihm die Schultern. »Ach, ich habe deine Nachricht erst auf dem Rückweg vom Strand bekommen. Hat es am Flughafen dann doch geklappt?«

»Cecile hat Chloës Flug umgebucht und mir nicht Bescheid

gesagt, das war der Grund. Ich habe sie schließlich in einer Bar gefunden, wo sie mit einem schmierigen Zyprioten, den sie irgendwo aufgegabelt hat, und einer Zigarette in der Hand dasaß.«

»Oje.« Seufzend ließ Helena sich auf den Stuhl neben ihm fallen und trank von ihrer Limonade. »Aber jetzt ist sie ja hier. Und sie schien eben überhaupt nicht verunsichert. Sie war doch geradezu die Coolness in Person.«

»Kann das wirklich echt sein, oder tut sie nur so?« William schüttelte den Kopf. »Ich kann es einfach nicht sagen.«

»Na ja, das Gute ist, dass sie eindeutig kinderlieb ist. Immy und Fred sind ja ganz hingerissen von ihr. Und ich habe wirklich nicht den Eindruck, dass sie dich verabscheut oder auch nur ablehnt«, sagte Helena.

»Wenn das wirklich der Fall ist, dann wäre das angesichts der Umstände höchst erstaunlich.«

»Schatz, die meisten Kinder lieben ihre Eltern bedingungslos, unabhängig davon, was sie tun – oder nicht tun. Chloë ist eindeutig nicht auf den Kopf gefallen. Wenn ihre Mutter schlecht über dich geredet hat, dann hat sie das sicher durchschaut.«

»Das hoffe ich. Zumindest habe ich in den nächsten Wochen Zeit, wieder eine Beziehung zu ihr aufzubauen, nur für den Fall, dass ich sie erst mit einundzwanzig wieder zu Gesicht bekomme«, antwortete William trübsinnig.

»Chloë wird langsam erwachsen. Sie wird zunehmend selbst entscheiden, was sie will, gleichgültig, was ihre Mutter tut oder sagt, und dazu kann durchaus auch gehören, dich zu sehen, wenn *sie* Lust dazu hat und nicht, wenn ihre Mutter sie aus dem Weg haben will.«

»Hoffen wir mal. Jetzt muss ich mich irgendwie an ein Kind

gewöhnen, das ich kaum kenne. Das Problem ist, sie ist kein Kind mehr, und ich habe keine Ahnung, was ihre Mutter ihr erlaubt und welche Grenzen sie ihr setzt. Was, wenn sie sich mit diesem Typen treffen möchte, den sie am Flughafen kennengelernt hat? Das haben sie offenbar vereinbart. Ich möchte ja nicht wie der strenge Vater rüberkommen, nachdem ich sie so lange nicht gesehen habe, aber andererseits ist sie erst vierzehn.«

»Das kann ich verstehen. Aber Kathikas ist nicht gerade die heißeste Partymeile Europas, oder?« Helena warf ihm ein beruhigendes Lächeln zu. »Ich bezweifle, dass hier allzu viele Gefahren für sie lauern.«

»Männer sind eine einzige Gefahr für Chloë«, sagte William mit einem Seufzen. »Die Jungs hier im Ort werden sie umschwärmen wie Bienen den Honigtopf. Die Vorstellung, dass so ein Kerl meine Tochter mit seinen schmierigen Pfoten begrabscht ...« Er schauderte.

»Die normale Reaktion eines Vaters«, sagte Helena und lachte. »Weil du nur zu gut weißt, wie du in dem Alter warst.« Sie stand auf. »Wie wär's, wenn du nach oben gehst und die Kleinen in die Badewanne packst, während ich mich um das Abendessen kümmere? Chloë muss am Verhungern sein, und ich fände es schön, wenn wir alle gemeinsam essen.«

»In Ordnung.« William erhob sich müde. »Ich bin schon unterwegs.«

»Kommt Alex gar nicht?«, fragte Chloë, als Helena die glühend heiße Auflaufform auf den Tisch stellte.

»Nein. Er hat gesagt, er hat Migräne. Die bekommt er regelmäßig, der Arme.«

»Das ist schade, er hat mich noch nicht mal begrüßt«, meinte Chloë und balancierte gekonnt Immy und Fred auf ihrem schmalen Schoß. »Als ich ankam, hat er mich einfach nur an-gestarrt und keinen Ton gesagt.«

»Morgen ist er wieder auf dem Damm, er muss sich nur richtig ausschlafen. Das riecht ja köstlich.« Helena entfernte die schützenden Wachspapierschichten über dem Gericht und ver-teilte es auf die Teller. »Angelina sagte, das heißt *kleftiko*, lang-sam gegartes Lamm.«

»Lamm wie mein Lämmchen?«, fragte Immy. »Nein, das esse ich nicht.« Sie schüttelte den Kopf und verschränkte die Arme vor der Brust. »Das ist vielleicht die Mummy oder der Daddy von meinem Lämmchen.«

»Immy, jetzt stell dich nicht so an. Du weißt genau, dass Lämmchen ein Stofftier ist, kein echtes. Jetzt setz dich auf dei-nen Stuhl und iss schön brav, wie es sich für ein großes Mäd-chen gehört«, sagte William streng.

Immys Unterlippe zitterte, als sie von Chloës Schoß kletter-te. »Lämmchen ist schon echt, Daddy.«

»Natürlich ist es echt, Herzchen.« Chloë streichelte Immy den Kopf und half ihrer Schwester, sich auf den Stuhl neben sie zu setzen. »Daddy ist gemein.«

»Genau, Daddy ist gemein«, pflichtete Immy entschieden bei.

»Daddy, schenkst du mir auch ein Glas ein?«, bat Chloë, als William die Weinflasche öffnete.

William warf einen fragenden Blick zu Helena.

»Darfst du zu Hause Wein trinken?«, fragte Helena.

»Na klar, Mum ist doch Französin.«

»Also gut, ein kleines Glas«, meinte William.

»Jetzt mach dir nicht ins Hemd, Daddy. Beim Schulabschluss-ball hab ich beim Bacardi-Breezer-Trinken gewonnen.«

»Besser als jeder Preis in Erdkunde«, sagte William so leise, dass niemand es hören konnte. »Dann lasst uns mal essen.«

Nach einem relativ friedlichen Abendessen bestanden die beiden Kleinen darauf, dass Chloë mit ihnen nach oben ging und etwas vorlas.

»Und danach gehe ich zu Alex und begrüße ihn kurz, und dann haue ich mich ins Bett«, sagte Chloë. Sie wurde schon an beiden Händen vom Tisch fortgezogen. »Gute Nacht allerseits.«

»Gute Nacht, Chloë.« Helena machte sich daran, die schmutzigen Teller auf das Tablett zu stapeln. »William, sie ist ja reizend, und sie kommt so gut mit den Kleinen klar. Es ist großartig, noch jemanden zu haben, der mit anpackt.«

William gähnte. »Das stimmt. Lassen wir den Rest doch bis morgen früh stehen. Ich muss mich auch ›hinhauen‹. Wann kommen denn Sadie und die Chandlers?«

»Erst am Nachmittag, wir haben also reichlich Zeit.«

»Vielleicht können wir sogar eine Stunde am Pool liegen. Bisweilen kann man ja Glück haben, Helena, oder nicht? ... Helena?«

Sie lenkte ihre Aufmerksamkeit wieder auf ihren Mann. »Entschuldige, was hast du gesagt?«

»Nichts Wichtiges. Ist alles in Ordnung?«

Sie zeigte ihm das herzlichste Lächeln, das sie in dem Moment zustande brachte. »Ja, mein Schatz, alles in bester Ordnung.«

Alex' Tagebuch

Ich nehme alles zurück, was ich in meinem letzten Eintrag geschrieben habe.

Alles. Jedes einzelne Wort, jeden Gedanken, jede Tat.

Das »irgendwann« erwies sich nämlich als HEUTE: 16. Juli um etwa sechzehn Uhr dreiundzwanzig.

Der Moment, in dem ich mich verliebte.

Mistkacke! Ich fühle mich krank. Am ganzen Körper. Mein Herz, das in den vergangenen dreizehn Jahren anständig seine Arbeit geleistet und das Blut zuverlässig durch meine Adern gepumpt hat, hat einen schweren Schaden davongetragen. Es hat etwas in sich eindringen lassen. Und dieses »Etwas« ist so was von perfide. Ich spüre, wie es anschwillt und wächst und mit seinen Tentakeln durch meinen Körper tastet, mich lähmt, mich schwitzen und frieren und die Kontrolle verlieren lässt – über mich.

Nur wenige Stunden nach diesem »Herzenswandel« wird mir klar, dass dieses zentrale Organ nicht mehr im Einklang mit meinem Körper agiert, etwa damit, wie schnell oder langsam ich gehe. Es reagiert heftig und pumpt wie wild, obwohl ich still daliege, und das nur, weil ich an sie denke: an diese Chloë.

Vergiss Aphrodite, vergiss Mona Lisa (der sowieso ein ernsthaftes Problem mit ihrer Stirnglatze ins Haus steht), vergiss Kate Moss. Meine Liebste ist hinreißender, bezaubernder und atemberaubender als sie alle zusammen.

Jetzt geht das wieder los – mein Herz pumpt das Blut wie wild durch meinen Körper, als hätte ich gerade einen Marathon gewonnen oder schwerverletzt einen Haiangriff überstanden.

Das passiert, sobald ich an sie denke.

Wobei alle möglichen anderen Sachen auch passieren, aber auf die gehe ich jetzt nicht näher ein.

Jetzt weiß ich wenigstens genau, dass ich nicht schwul bin. Und auch nicht mit einem Ödipuskomplex behaftet.

Ich bin liebesKRANK. Ich brauche ein ärztliches Attest, das mich vom Leben entschuldigt, bis ich das überwunden habe.

Aber schafft man das überhaupt? Kann man das überwinden? Nach allem, was ich so höre, kriegen manche das nie hin. Vielleicht geht das jetzt den Rest meines Lebens so weiter.

Ich meine, Himmel, ich habe noch nicht mal den Mund aufgemacht, um mit ihr zu sprechen. Was zum Teil daran liegt, dass meine Lippen den Dienst verweigern, sobald ich sie sehe. Undenkbar, in ihrer Gegenwart zu essen und gleichzeitig zu versuchen, etwas zu sagen. Das wäre die totale Überforderung. Sieht ganz danach aus, als müsste ich mich in diesen Ferien auf eine Nulldiät einstellen. Es sei denn, ich verlege mich auf Mitternachtsgelage.

Wie soll ich das schaffen, sie jeden Tag zu sehen und ihre butterweiche Haut direkt neben mir zu haben, ohne sie berühren zu dürfen?

Außerdem sind wir verwandt, wenn auch nicht blutsverwandt, es könnte also schlimmer sein. Wenn ich's mir recht überlege, wäre es eigentlich ziemlich cool, den Jungs zu sagen: »He, ich habe mich in meine Schwester verliebt«, und zu sehen, wie sie reagieren.

Als ich sie heute anstarrte und das mit dem Herzen losging, habe ich erkannt, dass sie tatsächlich wie Dad aussieht. Und da habe ich mir überlegt, wie erstaunlich die Sache mit den Genen ist und welche Wandlung sie von ihm (Mann, von durchschnittlichem Aussehen, alt, aber zumindest behaart) zu ihr (dem Inbegriff der Frau) durchlaufen haben. Sie ist einfach vollkommen.

Ich ziehe das T-Shirt und die Boxershorts aus, aber die Socken an. Vergangene Nacht haben mich die Mücken wie verrückt in die Knöchel gestochen, aber heute Nacht erwischen sie mich nicht. Dann suche ich nach der Packung mit der 10 den-Strumpfhose, die ich mir heute im Supermarkt gekauft habe, in der Nähe des Strands, zu dem wir mit Mum gefahren sind. Die Kassiererin hat mir zwar einen komischen Blick zugeworfen, aber das war mir egal.

Ich mache die Packung auf und dehne die Strumpfhose probehalber, begeistert über meine Eingebung. Das Ding, das Zwickel heißt, ziehe ich mir über den Kopf und das Gesicht und sinke triumphierend ins Kissen. Ich kann problemlos atmen, weil sie hauchdünn sind, das heißt, den Mistviechern habe ich endgültig die Petersilie verhagelt.

Während ich unter dem Bett nach dem Umschlag mit den Briefen suche, schiebe ich mir die Strumpfhose wieder aus dem Gesicht. Heute Morgen habe ich Mum die Briefe nicht gegeben, weil sie ständig beschäftigt war. Und nachdem sich meine Einstellung in den vergangenen vierundzwanzig Stunden derart radikal verändert hat, lese ich sie jetzt womöglich mit völlig anderen Augen.

Ich ziehe einen x-beliebigen heraus, stelle meinen iPod an und lege mich wieder hin, um mir die Zeit mit jemandem zu vertreiben, dessen Herz offenbar genauso schnell schlug wie meines, seit ich Chloë erblickte.

Zur Musik von Coldplay, die ich eigentlich selten höre, die meiner neuen Stimmung aber mehr entsprechen als Sum 41, schließe ich die Augen und stelle mir vor, sie stünde vor mir.

Als ich die Augen wieder aufmache, merke ich, dass ich sie mir nicht nur vorgestellt habe – sie steht direkt vor mir!

Scheiße!!

Ihre Lippen bewegen sich, aber wegen des iPods kann ich nicht verstehen, was sie sagt. Ich schalte es aus, dann merke ich zu meinem absoluten Horror, dass ich splitterfasernackt bin, außer an den Füßen. Ich fahre hoch und ziehe eilig das Laken über mich.

»Hi, Alex, ich bin Chloë. Ich wollte einfach mal Hallo sagen.« Sie lächelt mich lässig an.

Jetzt komm schon, Blödmann, krieg endlich den Mund auf! Zur Ermutigung fahre ich mir mit der Zunge über die Lippen und bringe ein ersticktes »Miii« zustande.

Sie schaut mich etwas merkwürdig an, ich habe keine Ahnung, weshalb.

»Geht's dir mittlerweile besser? Kein Kopfweh mehr?«

Ich nicke, und dann nicke ich einfach immer weiter.

»Ich wollte einfach danke sagen, dass ich dein Zimmer haben darf. Das hat Immy mir erzählt. Bist du sicher, dass du hier schlafen kannst? Größer als 'ne Besenkammer ist es ja nicht.«

»Doch. Doch.« Ich nicke immer noch, wie bei einem Tick, der sich nicht abstellen lässt.

»Okay, na dann, vielleicht reden wir morgen weiter.«

»Okay. Supi.«

O Scheiße! Ich kann mit der Nickerei einfach nicht mehr aufhören! So was von grottenpeinlich.

»Na, dann gute Nacht.«

»Nacht.«

Gerade will sie die Tür schließen, als sie innehält und fragt: »Hast du Ohrenschmerzen oder so?«

Das Nicken hört auf, jetzt schüttele ich den Kopf.

»Bloß Kopfweh?«

Wieder Genicke.

»Ah so.«

Jetzt nickt sie auch und will wieder gehen, aber dann sagt sie:

»Ich frage mich bloß …«

»Was?«

»Ob du dir deswegen eine Strumpfhose über den Kopf gezogen hast. Gute Nacht, Alex.«

KAPITEL 8

Am nächsten Tag wachte Helena bereits in der Morgendämmerung auf. Trotz ihrer Beklommenheit versuchte sie verzweifelt, wieder einzuschlafen, denn sie wusste, dass ihr ein langer Tag bevorstand. Doch die Gedanken, die ihr ungebeten durch den Kopf gingen, verlangten nach handfester Ablenkung. Schließlich gab sie sich geschlagen, stand auf, schlüpfte in ihre Trainingskleidung und trat auf die Terrasse.

Langsam, fast bedächtig ging die Sonne auf, während Helena zum Aufwärmen am Geländer ein paar *pliés* machte. Dabei überlegte sie sich, wie unpassend es wäre, ein Zimmer in den Farben des Sonnenaufgangs zu streichen, aber wie großartig die gleichen Farbtöne am Himmel miteinander harmonierten. Sie beugte sich vor, ihre Fingerspitzen fuhren über die Steinplatten der Terrasse, dann richtete sie sich auf und beugte sich nach hinten, sodass ihr Arm einen grazilen Bogen über ihrem Kopf beschrieb. Beim Tanzen kamen ihre Gedanken durch die körperliche Betätigung zur Ruhe, sie konnte klarer denken.

An diesem Morgen wusste sie allerdings nicht, wo sie beginnen sollte.

Was sollte sie denn denken?

Vor einigen Monaten hatte die Vorstellung sie beglückt, mit ihrer Familie nach Pandora zu fahren. Doch seitdem war sie durch die Umstände in den hochgradig nervösen Zustand geraten, in dem sie sich jetzt befand. Und im Moment wäre ihr nichts lieber, als die Flucht zu ergreifen – vor der Vergangenheit und der Gegenwart sowie den Auswirkungen beider auf ihre Zukunft.

Sie wünschte sich nichts sehnlicher, als das Geheimnis zu lüften, sich alles von der Seele zu reden. William und Alex nach all den Jahren die Wahrheit zu sagen, um sich endlich von der Last, die sie tagaus, tagein zu erdrücken drohte, zu befreien – aber das war unmöglich.

Damit würde sie alles zerstören.

Also würde sie genauso weitermachen wie bisher. Und allein mit dem Geheimnis leben.

Sie vollführte eine *arabesque* und fragte sich düster, wie lange ihr Körper wohl noch zu derartigen fließenden Bewegungen fähig sein würde. Als junge Frau hatte alles dafür gesprochen, dass sich ihr Traum von einer Laufbahn als Ballerina erfüllen würde: ein starker, aber gleichzeitig anmutiger und geschmeidiger Körper, der sie nur sehr selten im Stich ließ, ein musikalisches Gespür, dank dessen sie die Noten intuitiv interpretieren konnte, und dazu eine noch ungewöhnlichere Fähigkeit, die sie vor allen anderen auszeichnete, nämlich ihre beträchtliche schauspielerische Begabung.

Im Royal Ballet war sie schnell aufgestiegen, sie selbst war in ganz Europa als vielversprechendes Talent gehandelt worden. Das Ballett der Mailänder Scala hatte sie engagiert, mit vierundzwanzig war sie dann mit ihrem Tanzpartner Fabio als erste Solotänzerin zum angesehenen Wiener Staatsballett gegangen.

Und dann …

Und dann …

Helena seufzte.

Dann hatte sie sich verliebt. Und nichts war mehr wie zuvor.

»Ist alles in Ordnung, Helena? Du siehst müde aus. Konntest du nicht mehr schlafen?«

Eine halbe Stunde später stand William hinter ihr in der Küche und betrachtete sie nachdenklich.

»Mir sind die ganzen Dinge durch den Kopf gegangen, die noch anstehen, bevor die Chandlers und Sadie kommen, und da dachte ich, dass ich genauso gut aufstehen und alles erledigen kann. Bevor es zu heiß wird, würde ich auch gern die Blumen einpflanzen, die wir im Gartencenter gekauft haben. Dazu bin ich noch nicht gekommen, und wenn sie noch länger in den kleinen Töpfen bleiben, habe ich Angst, dass sie vertrocknen.« Helena holte die Frühstücksflocken aus dem Schrank und stellte einen Stapel Schüsseln auf das Tablett, um es auf die Terrasse zu tragen.

»Liebling, ich habe wirklich ein schlechtes Gewissen. Ich halse dir nicht nur Chloë auf, sondern auch noch Jules samt Anhang.«

»Das stimmt nicht ganz, Jules hat sich selbst eingeladen«, stellte Helena richtig.

»Ich weiß doch genau, dass sie anstrengend sein kann, aber Sacha macht das Leben im Moment sehr zu schaffen. Geschäftlich läuft es für ihn gerade nicht besonders gut.«

»Ach ja?«

»Nein. Hör, mein Schatz, ich verspreche dir, dass ich dir so viel wie möglich abnehme. Ich dachte, dass Angelina heute kommt?«

»Sie kommt auch. Ich werde sie bitten, das Abendessen zu machen und die Badezimmer zu putzen. Du weißt doch, wie heikel Jules ist.«

William ging zu ihr und massierte ihr die Schultern. »Ach, Helena, du bist wirklich sehr verspannt. Bitte vergiss nicht, dass die Wochen hier als Urlaub gedacht sind.«

»Das vergesse ich nicht. Aber dadurch, dass heute so viele Leute ankommen, gibt es einfach viel zu tun.«

»Ich weiß, aber wir sind auch viele. Du musst uns einfach sagen, was wir machen sollen.«

»Ja«, antwortete sie mit einem matten Lächeln. »Also, ich gehe jetzt nach oben und suche Handtücher heraus. Kannst du das Frühstück für Immy und Fred vorbereiten? Obwohl ich weiß, dass Fred schon den Süßigkeitenschrank entdeckt hat, ich habe die Fährte von Bonbonpapier gesehen.«

William nickte. »Ja, natürlich. Und wenn du möchtest, unternehme ich etwas mit ihnen, dann sind sie dir nicht im Weg. Wir gehen auf Entdeckungsfahrt. Ich würde sowieso gern ein bisschen die Umgebung erkunden.«

»Danke, Schatz, das wäre mir eine große Hilfe.«

»Helena?«

»Ja?« Sie blieb in der Tür stehen.

William sah zu seiner Frau, dann seufzte er achselzuckend. »Ach, nichts.«

Mit einem Nicken verschwand sie nach oben.

Um vier Uhr nachmittags war das Haus bereit für die Gäste. Helena hatte es sogar geschafft, noch rasch die Geranien in die Töpfe auf der Terrasse zu pflanzen, und angefangen, das überwucherte Beet beim Pool zu jäten, wo der Lavendel stehen sollte. Die Arme schmerzten ihr vor Erschöpfung, als sie den Teekessel anstellte, und während das Wasser heiß wurde, machte sie sich auf die Suche nach Alex. Am Morgen hatte er verlauten lassen, dass er immer noch Migräne habe, und hatte sein Zimmer den ganzen Tag nicht verlassen. Sie klopfte an seiner Tür und öffnete sie leise für den Fall, dass er schlief. Doch er lag auf dem Bett und las.

»Hallo, mein Schatz. Wie geht es dir?«

»Geht so.«

»Solltest du wirklich lesen, wenn du Kopfweh hast?«, fragte Helena. »Und warum machst du das Fenster nicht auf? Hier ist es wirklich stickig.«

»Nein!«

»Du brauchst nicht zu schreien, ich habe nur einen Vorschlag gemacht.«

»Ja, 'tschuldigung, Mum.«

»Und wenn es wegen der Mücken ist, dann ist das wirklich lächerlich. Sie kommen erst in der Abenddämmerung raus.«

»Das weiß ich.«

»Was macht dein Kopf?«

»Sieben von zehn, das heißt, etwas besser.«

»Warum setzt du dich dann nicht auf eine Tasse Tee zu mir auf die Terrasse?«

Alex warf ihr einen ängstlichen Blick zu. »Wo ist Chloë?«

»Unten am Pool.«

»Nein danke, ich bleibe lieber hier.«

Helena seufzte. »Ist irgendwas nicht in Ordnung?«

»Nein, wieso?«

»Weil du seit Chloës Ankunft etwas seltsam bist, deswegen. Sie hat doch nichts gesagt, das dich verletzt hat, oder?«

»Nein, Mum, echt jetzt! Ich habe Kopfweh, das ist alles. Bitte!«

»Ist ja schon gut, Alex, ich will dir nur helfen.«

»Verdammt, Mum, du bist heute stressig.«

»Das stimmt nicht!«

»Doch! Was ist los?«

»Nichts. Wenn die Chandlers kommen, erwarte ich dich im Empfangskomitee.«

Alex nickte widerstrebend. »Okay, bis später.« Und damit vertiefte er sich wieder in sein Buch.

Mit einer Tasse Tee in der Hand ging Helena auf die Terrasse und versuchte, sich etwas zu sammeln. Wenn sie durch die Oliven blickte, konnte sie Chloë mit Kopfhörern im Ohr am Pool liegen sehen. Sie war wirklich unglaublich schön. Ihren langen Beinen nach zu schließen hatte sie die Größe ihres Vaters geerbt, doch im Aussehen, mit ihrem zarten Knochenbau und den glänzenden, glatten Haaren schlug sie eher nach ihrer Mutter. Cecile, Williams Exfrau, war Französin und besaß sowohl die Eleganz als auch die Arroganz, die offenbar unweigerlich mit einer französischen Herkunft einhergingen.

Unleugbar fühlte sich William zu schwierigen Frauen hingezogen. Zwar wirkte er eher nüchtern und hatte eindeutig ein Bedürfnis nach klaren Strukturen, ebenso jedoch besaß er ein Auge für Schönheit und einen Hang zum Kreativen. Und selbst wenn er es gern leugnete, fand er Mittelmäßigkeit ebenso schwer zu ertragen wie sie.

Wenn William nur wüsste, auf welch große Schwierigkeit er sich unwissentlich eingelassen hatte, dachte Helena wehmütig. Aber er wusste es nicht und würde es, mit ein wenig Glück, auch nie erfahren.

Das Knirschen von Kies auf der Auffahrt kündete von der Ankunft der Chandlers. Helena atmete tief durch und ging über die Terrasse, um sie zu begrüßen.

»O Gott, ist das heiß hier!« Jules Chandler schwang die Beine unter dem Lenkrad hervor. Sie war groß und kräftig gebaut und auf eine maskuline Art recht attraktiv. »Helena, meine Liebe, wie geht's, wie steht's?« Jules packte sie am Hals in einer Art Klammergriff, was wohl eine Umarmung sein sollte.

»Alles bestens. Willkommen, Jules.« Helena lächelte zu ihr

empor und kam sich neben ihr wie immer schmächtig und zerbrechlich vor.

»Danke. Kinder, raus mit euch«, bellte sie in Richtung Rücksitz. »Grauenhafter Flug, lauter Leute mit geschorenem Schädel und Turnschuhen. Und an den Männern hing mehr Schmuck als an den Frauen.« Jules fuhr sich durch das dichte hellbraune Haar, das sie immer kurz trug, damit sie nach ihrem frühmorgendlichen Ausritt ohne großen Aufwand duschen konnte.

»Hallo, meine Süße, wie geht es dir?« Sadies Arme, die sie als Nächstes umfingen, waren weit zarter.

»Mir geht's gut, Sadie. Und dafür, dass du Liebeskummer hast, siehst du blendend aus.«

»Danke.« Sie zog Helena zu sich. »Ich habe mir letzte Woche eine Botox-Session gegönnt, als Abschiedsgeschenk von dem Scheißkerl«, flüsterte sie ihr ins Ohr.

»Die hat wirklich Wunder bewirkt.« Helena empfand Sadies Gegenwart als großen Trost.

»Hi, Tante Helena.« Die neuerdings tiefe Stimme von Rupert, Jules' Sohn, überraschte sie, ebenso wie seine Größe und sein durchtrainierter Körper. Er sah aus wie der archetypische Sportler.

»Du meine Güte, Rupes, du bist aber gewachsen«, sagte sie, als er seinen weißblonden Schopf zu ihr beugte, um ihr einen Kuss zu geben.

»Ich bin jetzt dreizehn, Tante Helena, da muss ich doch wachsen.«

Mein Sohn auch, dachte sie. *Aber der ist körperlich noch ein Kind, während du schon erwachsen aussiehst.*

»Hi, Tante Helena.« Zwei dünne, weiße, mit Sommersprossen übersäte Arme schlangen sich um ihren Hals.

»Viola, mein Schatz.« Helena drückte sie an sich. »Ich glaube, du bist auch gewachsen!«

»Nein, bin ich nicht. Ich bin noch genauso klein wie früher, und sie nennen mich in der Schule auch immer noch Rotfuchs, aber was soll ich machen?« Viola zog ihre sommersprossige Nase kraus und lächelte, sodass ihre vorstehenden Schneidezähne zum Vorschein kamen.

»Wir wissen genau, dass du rotblond bist, und wenn du älter bist, werden alle ganz neidisch sein, weil du nie teure helle Strähnchen brauchen wirst.«

»Ach, das sagst du immer, Tante Helena.« Viola kicherte verlegen.

»Ich sage es, weil es die Wahrheit ist, oder etwa nicht, Sadie?«

»Absolut«, sagte Sadie mit Nachdruck. »Was würde ich nicht dafür geben, wenn ich deine Haarfarbe hätte, Süße.«

»Viola, wo ist denn Daddy?«, fragte Helena und schaute verwirrt ins Wageninnere.

Jules schnaubte und klang dabei fast wie eines der Pferde, die bei ihr im Stall standen. »Gute Frage. Auf jeden Fall nicht hier, wie man sieht.«

»Wo ist er dann?«, fragte Helena.

»Im Moment? Wahrscheinlich in irgendeiner Kneipe in London, wo er am Tresen rumhängt.«

»Du meinst, er ist gar nicht mitgekommen?«

»Nein. Irgendetwas ist bei der Arbeit dazwischengekommen, und er hat in letzter Minute abgesagt. Das ist so verdammt typisch für ihn.«

»Kommt er denn überhaupt noch?«

»Angeblich morgen, aber darauf würde ich mich nicht verlassen. Bei Daddy verlassen wir uns auf überhaupt nichts mehr, Kinder, stimmt's?«

»Mummy, sei nicht so gemein! Es ist nicht Daddys Schuld, dass er so viel arbeiten muss.« Viola liebte ihren Vater abgöttisch und nahm ihn immer in Schutz.

Jules hob die Augenbrauen und sah zu Helena. »Na, du kannst sicher verstehen, dass ich ernsthaft angefressen bin.«

»Ja.« Helena nickte schwach.

»Und wo ist der anbetungswürdige William?«, fragte Sadie.

»Mit seinen anbetungswürdigen Kindern auf Entdeckungstour«, antwortete Helena.

»Du hast ihn wirklich gut erzogen. Ich muss Sacha schon zwingen, auch nur zur Schulfeier mitzukommen«, sagte Jules verächtlich. Sie holte gerade ihr Gepäck aus dem Kofferraum. »Ich bin gleich bei euch«, rief sie, als die anderen Helena ums Haus zur Terrasse folgten.

Dort stand Chloë, die mittlerweile aus dem Pool gekommen war und sich einen winzigen Sarong um die Hüften gebunden hatte. Ihre Haut färbte sich bereits goldbraun. »Hi, alle zusammen. Ich bin Chloë.«

»Das weiß ich«, sagte Sadie und küsste sie auf beide Wangen. »Ich habe dich einmal gesehen, da warst du ungefähr sechs, aber du wirst dich nicht an mich erinnern.«

»Nein«, stimmte Chloë zu. »Ist es nicht cool hier?«

»Es ist wunderschön«, sagte Sadie und sah sich bewundernd um.

»Und ich bin Rupert, Jules' und Sachas Sohn. Hi, Chloë.«

Chloë musterte ihn beifällig. »Hallo. Hast du schon den Pool gesehen?«

»Nein.«

»Soll ich ihn dir zeigen?«

»Klar. Ich würde gern mal reinspringen.«

»Dann komm mit.«

Als die beiden Richtung Pool abzogen, schaute Sadie zu Helena und hob spöttisch die Augenbrauen. In dem Moment schleppte Jules einen ihrer voluminösen Koffer auf die Terrasse. »Also, wo bringe ich den unter?«

Nachdem Helena ihr ihr Zimmer gezeigt hatte und Viola den Raum, in dem sie und Rupes schlafen würden, verschwand sie, ehe Jules sich über irgendetwas beschweren konnte, und ging den Flur entlang weiter zu Sadies Zimmer. Ihre Freundin kniete auf dem Bett und schaute zum Fenster hinaus.

»Der Blick ist großartig.« Mit einem Lächeln wandte sie sich zu Helena. »Ich wünschte, ich hätte auch einen Patenonkel, der das Zeitliche segnet und mir ein solches Haus vermacht.«

»Ich weiß, ich habe wirklich Glück. Komm, gehen wir nach unten, setzen uns auf die Terrasse und trinken etwas.« Helena senkte die Stimme. »Ich vermute, angesichts der Größe ihres Koffers wird es bei Jules noch eine Weile dauern.«

»Es würde mich nicht wundern, wenn sie ihre eigene Tapete und den Kleister dazu mitgebracht hat, um das Zimmer noch vor dem Abendessen zu renovieren.« Sadie verzog spöttisch das Gesicht. »Am Flughafen hat sie darauf bestanden, meinen Pass zu nehmen«, fuhr sie fort, als sie gemeinsam nach unten gingen. »Ich kam mir vor wie ihr drittes Kind.«

»Ich weiß, sie möchte alles unter Kontrolle haben. Tee? Oder etwas Stärkeres?«, fragte Helena, als sie in die Küche gingen.

»Da jeden Moment die blaue Stunde beginnt, eindeutig etwas Stärkeres.«

Mit einem Glas Wein in der Hand gingen sie auf die Terrasse und setzten sich unter die Pergola. »Ach Gott, bin ich froh wegzukommen. Hab tausend Dank, dass du mich in meiner Not hier aufnimmst. Es ist traumhaft.« Sadie stieß mit Helena an und trank einen Schluck. »Wo ist eigentlich Alex?«

»In seinem Zimmer, er hat Migräne.«

»Oje. Und wie geht es ihm sonst?«

»Wie immer.« Helena zuckte mit den Schultern.

»Und wie findet er die Vorstellung, aufs Internat zu kommen?«

»Darüber spricht er nicht. Mein Gott, Sadie, ich hoffe wirklich, dass ich die richtige Entscheidung getroffen habe.«

»Wie kannst du nur daran zweifeln, Süße? Er hat ein akademisches Stipendium für eine der besten Schulen in ganz England bekommen!«

»Alex mag ja ein geistiger Einstein sein, aber emotional und körperlich ist er noch sehr jung. Als ich Rupes eben gesehen habe, der gerade einmal vier Monate älter ist, habe ich einen richtigen Schreck bekommen. Du weißt doch, wie schwer sich Alex tut, mit Gleichaltrigen zu kommunizieren. Wenn sie dann noch einen Kopf größer sind als er, wird das kaum helfen. Ich mache mir große Sorgen, dass sie ihn schikanieren.«

»Bei Mobbing wird in Schulen heute nicht lange gefackelt. Außerdem mag er für sein Alter ja klein sein, Helena, aber er weiß sich ganz gut zu wehren. Unterschätz ihn nicht.«

»Ich will auch nicht, dass er so ein arrogantes Oberschichtsgör wird.«

»Du meinst wie Rupes?«, fragte Sadie mit einem vielsagenden Lächeln.

»Genau. Abgesehen davon wird er mir entsetzlich fehlen«, gestand sie.

»Ich weiß, ihr seid euch wirklich sehr nah, aber ist das nicht ein Grund mehr, ihn aufs Internat zu schicken? Er sollte von Mamas Rockzipfel wegkommen, zu seinem eigenen Wohl.«

»Das sagt William natürlich auch immer. Und wahrscheinlich habt ihr recht. Aber genug von mir, wie geht es dir?«

Sadie trank hastig einen Schluck Wein. »Ich überlege mir, ein Seminar zu besuchen, um mich nicht ständig in kaputte, bindungsunfähige Typen zu verlieben. Wirklich, Helena, ich weiß nicht, wie ich es immer schaffe.«

Helena betrachtete Sadies alabasterweiße Haut, das rabenschwarze Haar und die langen, schmalen Finger, mit denen sie den Stiel ihres Weinglases hielt. Sie war weniger schön als vielmehr exotisch, und auch wenn sie auf die vierzig zuging, konnte sie sich mit ihrer schlanken Figur noch wie ein junges Mädchen kleiden. An diesem Tag trug sie ein einfaches Baumwollkleid und dazu Flipflops und sah höchstens wie dreißig aus.

»Das weiß ich auch nicht, Sadie, aber in jemand Langweiligen würdest du dich doch nie verlieben, oder? Du hast ein Faible für das Außergewöhnliche.«

»Ich weiß, ich weiß.« Sadie seufzte. »Eine unglückliche Seele zieht mich magisch an. Je kaputter die Typen sind, desto stärker ist mein Wunsch, ihnen zu helfen. Dann kommen sie wieder auf die Beine, fühlen sich stark und verschwinden mit einer anderen!«

»Hat dein Letzter das auch gemacht?«

»Der ist zu seiner Ex zurückgegangen, eben derjenigen, die ihn ursprünglich hatte sitzen lassen, weil er ihrer Ansicht nach emotional zurückgeblieben war. Ha!« Sadie verzog den Mund und lachte. »Vielleicht wäre das ein gutes Geschäftsmodell! Eine Art Erziehungslager für junge Hunde: Überlass mir deinen Kerl für zwölf Wochen, ich bringe ihn auf Vordermann, trimme ihn auf Gehorsam und schicke ihn stubenrein zu dir zurück, und sobald du nach ihm pfeifst, kommt er angelaufen. Wie klingt das?«

»Gute Idee. Bloß würdest du die süßesten kleinen Hunde für dich behalten wollen«, antwortete Helena lächelnd.

»Stimmt. Außerdem habe ich beschlossen, dass ich für die nächste Zukunft solo bleiben will. Und da ich, wie du weißt, immer genau einen Tag im Voraus absehen kann, besteht zumindest heute Abend keine Gefahr! Wie geht es William, meinem Lieblingsmann?«

»Gut, wie immer.«

»Er liebt dich, hat Geld und ist großartig mit den Kindern, am Grill und im Bett.« Sadie trank einen Schluck Wein. »Wenn du ihn je abservierst, bekomme ich ihn, versprochen?«

»Versprochen.«

»Aber im Ernst, Helena, die Sache mit der Männersuche wird langsam dringend. Meine biologische Uhr tickt nicht nur, sie braucht mittlerweile einen erstklassigen Uhrmacher, der sie repariert.«

»Das stimmt doch nicht, Sadie. Heutzutage bekommen Frauen auch mit über vierzig noch Kinder«, sagte Helena.

»Vielleicht sind Kinder im großen Plan des Lebens einfach nicht für mich vorgesehen«, meinte Sadie seufzend. »Dann muss ich mich damit abfinden, Hunderte Patenkinder und kein einziges eigenes zu haben.«

»Immy sagt, dass du ihre Lieblingspatentante bist, also musst du irgendetwas schon richtig machen.«

»Ja, ich habe ein Händchen dafür, Geldscheine in Kuverts zu stecken, das stimmt. Trotzdem danke«, sagte Sadie.

»Hallo, Mum. Hallo, Sadie.«

Alex war unbemerkt auf die Terrasse geschlichen.

»Alex, Süßer, wie geht's?« Sadie breitete die Arme aus, um ihn zu begrüßen, und pflichtschuldig ging er zu ihr und ließ sich umarmen. »Wie geht's meinem Wunderknaben?«

»Geht so«, brummelte Alex, richtete sich auf und sah sich ängstlich auf der Terrasse um.

»Die anderen sind am Pool. Warum gehst du nicht auch runter und schwimmst eine Runde?«, schlug Helena vor. »Ein bisschen Bewegung würde dir bestimmt guttun.«

»Es geht schon wieder, Mum, danke.« Unbeholfen stand er vor ihnen da.

»Mein Schatz, würdest du dann aus dem Kühlschrank die Flasche Weißwein holen?«, bat Helena. »Ich glaube, Sadie würde gern noch einen Schluck trinken.«

»Das würde Sadie sehr gern«, kam es von Sadie.

Als Alex im Haus verschwand, sagte Helena seufzend: »Es macht die Sache nicht besser, dass er Rupes nicht leiden kann. Vielleicht ist das der Grund, weshalb er sich den ganzen Tag in seinem Zimmer versteckt hat.«

»Ich fürchte, da bin ich ganz seiner Meinung«, flüsterte Sadie. »Rupes ist ein arroganter Schnösel.«

»Ah, da seid ihr ja.« Jules erschien auf der Terrasse, angetan mit einem leuchtend gelben Sarong. Chloë hätte er phantastisch gestanden, aber Jules sah damit wie eine verwelkte Sonnenblume aus. Sie ließ sich auf einen Stuhl fallen. »Alles ausgepackt. Gibt's irgendwo ein Glas Wein für mich?«

»Alex, mein Schatz, sei doch so lieb und hole für Jules noch ein Glas, ja?«

Alex, der gerade mit der Flasche durch die Tür trat, schnitt eine Grimasse, verschwand aber wieder im Haus.

»Du meine Güte, der hat ja ziemlich zugenommen, seit ich ihn das letzte Mal gesehen habe. Womit in aller Welt hast du ihn denn gemästet, Helena?«, fragte Jules laut.

»Das ist Babyspeck, weiter nichts. Der verschwindet, sobald er anfängt zu wachsen«, erwiderte Helena ruhig und hoffte, dass ihr Sohn Jules' Bemerkung nicht gehört hatte.

»Das bleibt zu hoffen. Heutzutage sieht man immer mehr

fettleibige Kinder. Wenn er noch dicker wird, musst du ihn auf Diät setzen.«

Sadie entging Helenas Unbehagen nicht, woraufhin sie schnell das Thema wechselte. »Ist das Haus nicht ein Traum, Jules?«

»Es muss natürlich umfassend saniert werden, und neue Badezimmer braucht es auch, aber die Lage ist sehr schön. Danke«, sagte Jules zu Alex, der ihr gerade ein Glas reichte. »Wie geht's in der Schule?«

»Die habe ich abgeschlossen.«

»Das weiß ich«, antwortete Jules scharf. »Ich meine, freust du dich auf die neue?«

»Nein.«

»Und warum nicht? Rupes kann es gar nicht erwarten. Du weißt ja, er hat das Sportstipendium für Oundle bekommen.«

»Ich will nicht von zu Hause weg, deswegen«, sagte Alex leise.

»Ach, daran gewöhnst du dich schnell. Rupes fand es klasse auf dem Internat. Er war Schulsprecher und hat bei der Schulfeier endlos Sportpreise abgeräumt.« Mit mütterlichem Stolz in den Augen sah Jules im selben Moment Rupes mit Chloë vom Pool heraufkommen.

»Hallo, Alex, wie geht's?« Rupes versetzte Alex einen kräftigen Schlag auf den Rücken.

»Gut, danke.« Er nickte.

»Chloë und ich wollen später ins Dorf und sehen, was da so abgeht, stimmt's?« Rupes schaute lächelnd zu Chloë und legte ihr beschützend eine Hand auf die Schulter.

»Nein danke, ich habe Kopfweh. Bis später.« Abrupt machte Alex kehrt und verschwand im Haus.

Jules sah ihm stirnrunzelnd nach. »Fehlt ihm was?«

»Nein, gar nichts«, sagte Helena.

»Na, er war ja schon immer ein komischer Kauz. Rupes, vergiss nicht, ihm wegen des Internats gut zuzureden, er hat ziemlich Angst davor, der Arme.«

»Ja, das machen wir, Chloë, stimmt's? Keine Bange, Helena, den kriegen wir schon hin«, sagte Rupes herablassend.

Helena hätte sich am liebsten in ihr Weinglas übergeben. »Ich glaube, ich habe einen Wagen gehört!«, rief sie erleichtert und sprang auf, um William und die beiden Kleinen zu begrüßen.

Alex' Tagebuch

Weh mir, ach weh mir!

Ich habe gerade gezählt, wie viele Tage dieser Kotzbrocken noch hier ist, dann habe ich ausgerechnet, wie viele Stunden das sind, und in einer Million zweihundertneuntausendsechshundert Sekunden ab jetzt ist er …

WEG.

Zwei Wochen, zwei volle, ganze Wochen, in denen Rupes Chloë herumkommandiert, ihre makellose Haut betatscht und Witze reißt, die nicht im Geringsten witzig sind, aber sie lacht trotzdem.

Sie kann ihn doch unmöglich gut finden, oder? Diesen geistigen Dünnbrettbohrer? Und ich dachte, elegante, intelligente Frauen mögen Männer mit grauen Zellen und keine bräsigen, arroganten Muskelpakete.

Das Abendessen war die reinste Hölle. Rupes sorgte dafür, dass er neben ihr saß, und hatte immer noch seine Ray Ban auf die Stirn geschoben wie ein Haarreifen, obwohl es stockfinster war. Er hält sich für soooo cool, wie Chloë mit erschreckender Regelmäßigkeit sagt.

Und wie er lacht! Ein würgendes Geräusch, als hätte er sich an einer Erdnuss verschluckt und würde versuchen, sie wieder hochzuwürgen. Dabei zittert sein Adamsapfel ganz widerlich, und er wird knallrot, als hätte er zu viel Port getrunken.

Bin ich neidisch, weil er einen Adamsapfel hat?

Weil er zwei Meter größer ist als ich?

Weil Chloë offenbar auf ihn steht?

Ja! Ja! Ja!

Ich dresche aufs Kissen, dann gucke ich darunter und stelle fest, dass ich Bee ins Gesicht geboxt habe. Ich küsse die Füllung, wo mal seine Nase war, und entschuldige mich bei ihm. Ich halte seine kleinen grauen Pfoten in meinen kleinen braunen Pfoten.

»Du bist der einzige Freund, den ich habe«, sage ich feierlich. Er gibt wie immer keine Antwort. Schließlich ist er eine leblose Masse aus altem Stoff und Baumwolle.

Früher einmal habe ich wirklich geglaubt, dass er echt ist. Bin ich verrückt? Das habe ich mich schon oft gefragt. Aber was ist denn normal im Sinn von nicht verrückt? Ein blonder Brutalo, der sich darauf versteht, Mädchen anzubaggern? In dem Fall bin ich lieber ich …

Glaube ich zumindest.

Ich weiß, höfliche Konversation ist nicht meine Stärke, und nicht kommunizieren zu können ist eindeutig ein Nachteil. Vielleicht sollte ich in eines dieser Klöster gehen, in denen die Mönche immer schweigen. Das wäre genau das Richtige für mich.

Abgesehen davon, dass ich nicht an Gott glaube und kein Kleid tragen will.

Ich vermute, dass Dads Meinung von Rupes auch nicht die beste ist. Das ist immerhin etwas. Beim Abendessen hat er ihn ein paarmal verbessert, weil er Unsinn geredet hat, und hat ihm mangelnde Geografiekenntnisse vorgeworfen. »Nein, Rupes, Vilnius ist nicht in Lettland, das ist die Hauptstadt von Litauen.« Dafür hätte ich meinen alten

167

Herrn küssen mögen. Obwohl ich, ehrlich gesagt, erstaunt bin, dass Rupes überhaupt weiß, dass Vilnius eine Stadt ist und kein überbezahlter Fußballstar.

Er ist ja nur vier Monate älter als ich, aber offenbar hält er sich schon für ein vollwertiges Mitglied der Erwachsenengesellschaft und glaubt, man würde sich interessieren für das, was er sagt. Das kommt von seiner schaurigen Mutter. Sie hängt ihm an den Lippen und beachtet die arme Viola überhaupt nicht, die sich als richtig lieb erweist. Sie ist fast elf, also gerade einmal zwei Jahre jünger als ich, obwohl sie viel jünger wirkt, eher wie Immy und Fred.

Ich mag kleine Kinder, immer schon. Es gefällt mir, dass sie aus heiterem Himmel absurde Fragen stellen. Ein bisschen wie ich, nur habe ich mittlerweile gelernt, sie mir eher zu denken als laut auszusprechen.

Und Viola ist klug. Beim Abendessen hat sie mir gestanden, dass sie Pferde nicht besonders mag. Was grausam ist, weil ihre Mutter sie zwingt, sich jeden Tag in den Sattel zu schwingen und an Wettbewerben teilzunehmen und ihnen die Mähne zu kämmen und die Fesseln zu striegeln, was immer »striegeln« überhaupt heißt.

Jules erinnert mich an ein Pferd. Sie hat große Zähne und eine große Nase, und am liebsten würde ich ihr eine Trense in den Mund stecken, damit sie selbigen hält.

Allerdings bringt mich das alles einer Lösung meines Problems nicht näher: Wie sage ich Chloë, dass ich sie liebe?

Heute Abend hat sie mit mir gesprochen. Sie hat mich gefragt: »Alles in Ordnung bei dir, Alex?« Ich wäre beinahe dahingeschmolzen, so wunderbar war das. Sie sagte es mit so viel Gefühl, sehr konzentriert, die Betonung lag auf »Alex«. Was doch etwas heißen muss.

Ich konnte natürlich nichts erwidern wegen dieser Sache, dass meine Lippen in ihrer Gegenwart jegliche Mitarbeit verweigern, aber ich glaube, ich habe ansprechend genickt. Aber wenn ich ihr gegenüber den Mund nicht aufbringe, wie soll ich ihr dann erklären, dass sie das wunderbarste Mädchen der Welt ist?

In dem Moment fällt mein Blick auf den braunen Umschlag mit den Liebesbriefen, der auf meinem Bett liegt. Und dann auf Keats *Gesammelte Gedichte* auf dem Regal über mir.

Und ich weiß die Lösung.

KAPITEL 9

»Süße, da nähert sich gerade der Traum von einem Mann.« Sadie kam zu Helena und William in die Küche, wo sie am nächsten Morgen das Frühstück vorbereiteten.

»Das kann nur Alexis sein«, brummte William.

»Wer ist das?«

»Helenas alter Freund.«

»Den hast du mir ja verschwiegen, Süße«, sagte Sadie. »Und? Ist er von hier? Ist er noch zu haben?«

»Ja. Und ja. Er wohnt im Dorf, ein paar Kilometer von hier, und er ist Witwer.«

»Das klingt ja verheißungsvoll! Soll ich mit ihm auf die Terrasse gehen? Ihm einen Kaffee anbieten? Eine Ganzkörpermassage?«

»Warum nicht?«, antwortete Helena mit einem Achselzucken.

»Na dann! Ich schminke mir nur kurz ein bisschen die Lippen. Bin gleich wieder da.«

»Sadie ist unverbesserlich«, sagte William mit einem Lächeln. »Aber ich mag sie. Mehr als eine gewisse andere Frau, die gegenwärtig unter diesem Dach weilt.«

»Jules ist bisweilen etwas … überbordend. Aber das meint sie im Grunde gar nicht so.«

»Helena, du bist einfach zu nett. Jules ist eine Xanthippe, wie sie im Buche steht. Und es tut mir leid, dass ich sie uns zwei

Wochen aufgehalst habe. Sie hat einfach ein unglaubliches Gespür dafür, grundsätzlich das Falsche zu sagen. Wie Sacha das jeden Tag aushält, ist mir schleierhaft. Vielleicht ist sie brillant, was erotische Dienstleistungen angeht, und widmet sich intensiv der Schweifpflege. Genug Übung sollte sie ja haben.« William atmete hörbar ein. »Gestern Abend hat sie mich zu Tode gelangweilt mit ihren Martigalen und Trensen.«

»Als ich heute Morgen in die Küche kam, hat sie mir gesagt, dass sie die Speisekammer umgeräumt und alles in den Kühlschrank beziehungsweise den Gefrierschrank gestellt hat und dass es gesundheitsgefährdend sei, alles draußen stehen zu lassen«, erzählte Helena. »Ich habe versucht, ihr Angus' Kühlsystem zu erklären, aber sie hat erwidert, sie wolle weder sich noch ihre Kinder der Gefahr von E. Coli oder Salmonellen aussetzen.«

»Ich bin froh, dass du das so gleichmütig hinnehmen kannst. Ich habe jetzt schon meine liebe Not mit ihr. Wenigstens ist sie heute den ganzen Tag unterwegs und hat Viola und ihren Rüpel von Sohn mitgenommen. Der sah ziemlich angefressen aus, zusammen mit seiner Schwester zu einer alten Ruine geschleppt zu werden. Wahrscheinlich hatte er gehofft, den ganzen Tag um Chloë herumzuscharwenzeln. Also« – William drehte sich zu ihr –, »wozu hast du heute Lust?«

»Ich dachte, wir könnten mit den Kindern zu den Adonis-Bädern fahren. Die liegen versteckt in den Bergen, und die Wasserfälle sind wirklich großartig. Man kann von den Felsen in den Tümpel darunter springen.«

»Gut, dann ist ein Familienausflug angesagt. Das heißt, wenn wir Immy und Fred vom DVD-Spieler fortreißen können. Sie sitzen heute Morgen schon wieder vor dem Fernseher.«

»Wenigstens streiten sie sich nicht, und es ist draußen ziemlich heiß.« Helena blickte gedankenverloren zum Küchenfenster hinaus.

»Komm, gehen wir doch mit dem Kaffee auf die Terrasse und sehen nach, ob sich Sadie schon über Alexis hermacht.« Helena folgte William nach draußen.

Alexis saß mit einer angeregt plaudernden Sadie am Tisch und lächelte erleichtert, als William und Helena dazukamen.

»*Kalimera*, Helena. Wie geht es dir?«

»Gut, danke.« Sie nickte.

»Alexis hat mir gerade erzählt, er sei Weinbauer«, berichtete Sadie, als William das Tablett mit dem Kaffee absetzte. »Ich habe ihm gesagt, dass ich die perfekte Endverbraucherin bin. Kaffee, Alexis?«

»Danke, nein, ich kann nicht bleiben. Helena, ich bin gekommen, um dir das zu geben.« Alexis deutete auf ein Holzkästchen, das auf dem Tisch stand. »Das habe ich in der Schublade einer kaputten Kommode gefunden, als ich sie auf den Müll bringen wollte. Ich fand es zu hübsch, um es wegzuwerfen.«

»Es ist ziemlich erlesen.« William studierte das kleine Kästchen. »Es ist aus Rosenholz, und das sind kunstvolle Perlmuttintarsien«, fügte er hinzu und fuhr mit den Fingerspitzen darüber. »Der Farbe des Holzes nach zu urteilen würde ich sagen, dass es ziemlich alt ist. Vielleicht ist es ein Schmuckkästchen.«

»Vielleicht sind in der Polsterung noch ein paar Smaragde versteckt?«, fragte Sadie scherzhaft, als William das Kästchen öffnete. Sie beugte sich weit vor, um über den grünen Filz auf dem Innendeckel zu streichen. »Aber ich kann nichts spüren.«

»Danke, dass du es aufbewahrt hast, Alexis. Es ist wirklich wunderschön. Ich werde es auf meine Kommode stellen«, sagte Helena.

»Aber natürlich – das ist die Büchse der Pandora!« Sadie lächelte. »Süße, pass auf, du weißt doch, wie die Geschichte ausgeht.«

»Ja«, antwortete Helena, »deswegen solltet ihr sie besser schnell wieder schließen, bevor alle Übel der Welt entweichen.«

»Ich bin auch gekommen, um euch alle zu fragen, ob ihr freundlicherweise zu der Verlobungsfeier kommen würdet, die ich am nächsten Freitag für Dimitrios, meinen Ältesten, veranstalte. Es wäre uns eine Ehre, wenn ihr dabei sein könntet«, sagte Alexis.

»Das ist sehr nett, aber wir sind wirklich sehr viele Leute«, antwortete William. Helena fragte sich sofort, ob er nicht nach einer Ausflucht suchte.

»Das ist kein Problem. Es ist eine große Feier, und alle sind willkommen. Ihr wisst doch, wir Zyprioten feiern gern.«

»Das klingt gut, wir kommen gern, Alexis. Danke«, sagte Helena mit einem trotzigen Blick Richtung William.

»Und möchten Sie heute Abend nicht zu uns zum Essen kommen?«, fragte Sadie. »Uns fehlt ein Mann, und der arme William braucht Verstärkung, um all der Frauen Herr zu werden, stimmt's nicht, mein Lieber?«

»Ja«, sagte William tonlos, der wusste, dass er soeben den Kürzeren gezogen hatte.

»Danke, sehr gern. Dann sehen wir uns heute Abend.« Alexis nickte und erhob sich. »Auf Wiedersehen.«

»Wenn wir einen Ausflug unternehmen wollen, sollte ich allmählich die Kinder zusammentrommeln. Chloë und Alex sind noch nicht mal aufgestanden.« William wollte gerade die Terrasse verlassen, als Helena sich erschreckt die Hand vor den Mund schlug.

»O mein Gott, mir ist gerade eingefallen, dass die Verlobungsfeier am Tag unseres zehnjährigen Hochzeitstags ist!«

William sah zu ihr. »Wir müssen ja nicht hingehen.«

»Aber wir haben doch gerade zugesagt.«

»Du meinst, du hast gerade für uns alle zugesagt«, korrigierte er sie.

»Es tut mir leid, Schatz. Aber würde es nicht ausgesprochen unhöflich wirken, die Zusage zurückzuziehen? Zumal nach allem, was Alexis und seine Söhne für uns getan haben? Und wer weiß, vielleicht wird es sogar richtig schön sein, zur Abwechslung einen Abend auf ein großes Fest zu gehen und nicht die Massen hier bekochen zu müssen.«

»Wenn du meinst«, sagte William brüsk und ging ins Haus.

Sadie sah ihm nach und sagte dann leise: »Und jetzt erzähl mir von Alexis. Da war doch früher mal was zwischen euch.«

»Wie um alles in der Welt kommst du denn da drauf?«

»Wegen der Blicke, die er dir zuwirft. Das sieht ein Blinder, und William bemerkt es auch. Jetzt komm schon, Helena, erzähl mal.«

»Wirklich, Sadie, das war nur eine Liebelei unter Teenagern in dem Sommer, als ich hier bei meinem Patenonkel war.«

»War da keine Liebe im Spiel?«

»Er war mein erster Freund. Natürlich hat er eine besondere Bedeutung für mich gehabt. Das geht doch jedem so.«

»Er hat immer noch eine Schwäche für dich, auch nach all diesen Jahren.« Sadies Blick wurde verträumt. »Wie unglaublich romantisch.«

»Abgesehen von der Tatsache, dass ich glücklich mit einem anderen Mann verheiratet bin.« Helena fuhr mit den Fingern die Perlmuttintarsien auf dem Kästchen nach. »Und dass ich drei Kinder habe.«

»Sei ehrlich: Empfindest du noch etwas für ihn? Irgendwie habe ich den Eindruck, dass du mir etwas verheimlichst.«

»Ich mag ihn, und ich denke auch gern an die Wochen zurück, die wir miteinander verbracht haben, aber mehr nicht, Sadie, nein.«

»Wirklich nicht? Ich meine, ist es wirklich reiner Zufall, dass dein Erstgeborener so heißt wie deine erste Liebe?«

»Sadie, jetzt hör auf! Mir gefiel der Name einfach, mehr nicht.«

»Und du schwörst, dass du ihn seitdem nie mehr gesehen hast?«

»Bitte, Sadie, du bist wie ein Hund, der sich an seinem Knochen festgebissen hat. Können wir es einfach gut sein lassen?«, bat Helena.

»Natürlich, meine Süße, entschuldige.«

Helena stand auf. »Ich sollte wohl mal besser William helfen, die Kinder einzusammeln. Möchtest du zu den Adonis-Bädern mitkommen, oder verbringst du lieber den Tag hier faul am Pool?«

»Ich bleibe hier und bereite mich auf das Abendessen mit dem hiesigen Adonis vor, danke«, sagte Sadie mit einem Augenzwinkern. »Bis später.«

Die Fahrt durch die Berge zu den Wasserfällen war genauso steinig und schwierig, wie Helena sie in Erinnerung hatte. Die Straße war schmal, voll tiefer Schlaglöcher und mit vielen steilen Steigungen und Gefällen.

»Gott sei Dank ist das nicht unser Wagen«, sagte William, der das Auto geschickt über die Holperbahn manövrierte. »Die Reifen möchte ich hinterher nicht sehen, ganz zu schweigen von den Stoßdämpfern.«

»Mummy, das ist ja wie in der Achterbahn!«, rief Immy aufgeregt, die sich unbeeindruckt auf dem Rücksitz herumschleudern ließ. Alex saß mit weißem Gesicht neben ihr, umklammerte mit beiden Händen den Rand des Sitzes und starrte unverwandt geradeaus, während Chloë auf dem hintersten Sitz die Augen geschlossen hatte und auf ihrem iPod Musik hörte und Fred unglaublicherweise an sie gekuschelt schlief.

»Bist du damals die Strecke gefahren?«, fragte William.

»Nein«, sagte Helena und lachte. »Du wirst es nicht glauben – ich war Sozius auf einem Moped!«

»Erstaunlich, dass du das überlebt hast. Und wer ist gefahren?«

Nach kurzem Zögern sagte sie: »Alexis.«

Williams Griff um das Lenkrad verstärkte sich. »Vielleicht wirst du später so freundlich sein und mir erzählen, was genau zwischen euch gelaufen ist«, sagte er und senkte die Stimme. »Er ist ja eindeutig der Ansicht, dass zwischen euch noch nicht alles vorbei ist. Und ich finde es nicht gerade erhebend, so unverhohlen Hörner aufgesetzt zu bekommen!«

»William, bitte! Nicht vor den Kindern!«, wisperte Helena verzweifelt.

»Ich bin einfach nur sehr frustriert, Helena. Du musst zugeben, dass du dich seit meiner Ankunft seltsam benimmst. Wenn du mich nicht hier haben willst und ich dir im Weg bin, dann sag's einfach, dann verschwinde ich, okay? Also, Kinder, es sieht aus, als wären wir da.«

William bremste abrupt, der Wagen blieb mit einem Ruck stehen. Sie waren tief in einem Tal, ringsumher ragten majestätisch die Berge auf. Helena stieg aus und half Immy und Fred aus ihren Sitzen. Sie schluckte schwer, damit die beiden nicht bemerkten, dass sie den Tränen nahe war.

William war bereits zum Eingang marschiert, und sie kannte ihn gut genug, um ihm nicht nachzurufen. Sie war an seine gelegentlichen Wutausbrüche gewöhnt, normalerweise aber verrauchte sein Zorn schnell, und dann entschuldigte er sich zerknirscht. Außerdem war ihr nach dem Gespräch mit Sadie klar, weshalb William so empfindlich reagierte: Er fühlte sich bedroht, und sie wusste, dass sie ihn beruhigen musste.

»Haben alle ein Handtuch? Gut, dann los.«

Helena nahm Fred an der Hand, Immy hielt sich bei Chloë fest, Alex bildete die Nachhut.

William hatte bereits die Eintrittskarten gekauft. Er nahm Fred auf den Arm und drückte ihn an sich. »Na, Kerlchen, bist du bereit, in richtig kaltes Wasser zu springen?«

»Au ja, Dad.«

Sie klatschten sich ab und gingen Richtung Wasserfall.

Nach einer abenteuerlichen Rutschpartie über die Felsen stand Helena bis zur Taille im klaren, eiskalten Wasser, um sie herum paddelten die beiden Kleinen. William und Alex stiegen gerade auf einen Felsen, um hineinzuspringen. Chloë saß in der Sonne am Rand des Teichs und zog die bewundernden Blicke der männlichen Besucher auf sich.

»Schau mal, ich springe!« Alex winkte ihr von der rutschigen Felskante sieben Meter über dem Wasser zu und landete mit einem lauten Platschen im Teich.

»Yeah, Alex!« Als er wieder auftauchte, klatschte Chloë begeistert in die Hände. »Das war so cool!«

»Jetzt steige ich auf den Felsen darüber«, rief er und schwamm bereits wieder zum Rand.

Helena schaute nach oben und sah, wie hoch das war. »Pass bitte auf, Alex«, rief sie. In dem Moment machte William sich bereit, vom unteren Felsen zu springen. Für seine fünfundvierzig Jahre wirkte er überaus jugendlich, ging ihr durch den Kopf. Noch zeigte sich kein einziges graues Haar in seinem dunklen Schopf, er war schlank und geschmeidig, seine Haut leicht gebräunt.

»Jaaa, Daddy!«, rief Immy aufgeregt. William winkte ihnen zu und sprang zum Jubelgeschrei seiner Kinder in die Tiefe.

»Ich auch, Mummy«, bettelte Fred und paddelte Richtung Beckenrand. Helena zog ihn an sich. »Wenn du größer bist, mein Schatz.«

»Will aber jetzt!«

William schwamm zu seinem Sohn und schwang ihn in die Luft. »Willst du reinspringen?«

»Ja!«

»Und – jetzt!« Er hob Fred hoch über seinen Kopf und ließ ihn fallen. Die Schwimmflügel verhinderten, dass er unterging, und er juchzte vor Vergnügen.

»Schau mal, Helena, Alex springt jetzt von dem richtig hohen Felsen«, rief Chloë. »Wird ihm auch nichts passieren?«

»Ich hoffe nicht«, sagte sie, doch da war Alex bereits gesprungen. Als er auftauchte, kreischte Chloë und klatschte wieder in die Hände.

»Rupes hat gesagt, dass Alex ein Feigling und ein Nerd ist, aber ich möchte ihn mal von dort oben springen sehen«, sagte sie leise zu Helena.

»Das ist Alex beides nicht, in vieler Hinsicht ist er unglaublich mutig«, sagte Helena, als ihr Sohn etwas außer Atem, aber übers ganze Gesicht strahlend auf sie zuschwamm.

»Mum, hast du mich gesehen?«, fragte Alex.

»Ja. Du warst großartig, mein Schatz.«

»Du warst echt toll. Ich weiß ja nicht« – Chloë biss sich auf die Unterlippe und sah hinreißend verletzlich aus –, »wenn ich es vom unteren Felsen versuchen würde, würdest du mir beim Springen die Hand halten, Alex?«

»Klar. Dann komm.«

Helena bemerkte, mit welchem Stolz ihr Sohn Chloë zu den Felsen führte, und mit einem Schlag wurde ihr klar, weshalb er sich in den vergangenen Tagen so merkwürdig verhalten hatte: Er war in Chloë verknallt.

Mit einem gewaltigen Platschen landeten die beiden gemeinsam im Wasser, und die Menge, die sie beobachtet hatte, jubelte Beifall.

Zwanzig Minuten später hatte Immy genug. »Mummy! Meine Haare sind nass, und mir ist kalt, und ich hab Durst. Ich will raus«, quengelte sie.

»Bleibst du bei Fred?«, sagte Helena zu William, als sie ihre Tochter aus dem Felsentümpel hob. »Ich hole uns etwas zu trinken, und wir treffen uns auf der Terrasse.«

Sie holte aus dem Wagen ein paar Getränkedosen und setzte sich mit Immy im Schatten eines Olivenbaums auf eine Bank. Einen Moment schloss sie die Augen und dachte an die Zeit vor vielen Jahren zurück, als Alexis mit ihr hier gewesen war. Damals war der Wasserfall noch keine Sehenswürdigkeit, sondern einfach ein schöner Ort, den praktisch nur die Einheimischen aus der Umgebung kannten. Auch sie waren damals gemeinsam von den Felsen gesprungen und im tiefen, klaren Wasser geschwommen.

Und hier, am Rand des einsamen Felsbeckens, an diesem von Legenden umrankten Ort, war Helena vom Mädchen zur Frau geworden.

»Mummy?! Hörst du mir zu?!«

»Natürlich, mein Schatz.« Helena riss sich aus ihren Gedanken.

»Ich habe gesagt, ich habe Hunger und brauche eine Tüte Chips.«

»Bald gibt es Mittagessen, so lange musst du noch warten. Schau, hier kommen die anderen ja schon.«

»Ich zeig's dir, wenn du willst«, sagte Alex gerade zu Chloë. »Es ist ein irres Buch, und Angus hat eine Erstausgabe davon.«

»Das würde ich echt gern sehen.«

»Cool. Wenn wir zu Hause sind, zeige ich's dir.«

»Cool.«

An diesem Tag war Alex wie ausgewechselt, dachte Helena. Seine schönen Augen funkelten, und sein Gesicht war angeregt und glücklich, während er sich mit seiner Stiefschwester unterhielt und sie immer wieder bewundernd ansah.

»Wow, schau dir das an!« Kichernd blieb Chloë vor einer Statue von Adonis und Aphrodite stehen, die sich nackt umarmten. »Ziemlich gut gebaut, der Knabe!« Dann las sie die Worte vor, die auf Englisch in eine Steintafel neben der Statue gemeißelt waren:

»Adonis und Aphrodite, der Gott und die Göttin der Liebe und der Schönheit. Der Legende nach lebten sie hier gemeinsam mit ihren vielen Kindern. Damen, die unfruchtbar sind und den Wunsch haben, schwanger zu werden, sollten Adonis' Fortsatz berühren, worob sie viele Kinder bekommen werden.«

»Chloë, untersteh dich«, sagte William, der mit Fred an der Hand dazukam. »Und du, Alex, pass auf, dass deine Mum ihm nicht zu nahe kommt. Das ist das Letzte, was wir brauchen, Schatz, stimmt's?«

Helena schluckte schwer und nickte.

»Stimmt.«

Alex' Tagebuch

Heute bin ich geflogen!

Aber nicht mit dem Flugzeug, sondern nur mit meinen rudernden Armen. Ich flog durch die Luft, während meine Angebetete mich ansah und klatschte und jubelte, als ich, platsch!, im Wasser landete.

Egal, dass mein Bauch jetzt ganz rot ist, da, wo mein Speck dem Wasser eine Reibungsfläche bot, oder dass ich mir den Knöchel verrenkt habe, weil ich auf den glitschigen Felsen ausgerutscht bin. Oder dass ich einen riesigen blauen Fleck von weiß der Teufel woher im Gesicht habe; vielleicht war es ihr Ellbogen, der Kontakt mit meiner Wange aufnahm, als wir Händchen haltend ins Wasser sprangen.

Angesichts der Freude auf ihrem Gesicht verliert Schmerz jede Bedeutung. Ich bin ihr Held. Ich bin ihr Beschützer. Sie findet mich COOOOOL.

Sie mag mich!

Ein Vorteil war natürlich, dass diese dämliche Lippenlähmung im Eier-schrumpfenden Eiswasser von Adonis' Bidet von selbst verschwand. Vielleicht hat das Wasser ja wirklich Zauberkraft – wie auch immer, als sie etwas zu mir sagte, konnte ich zum ersten Mal tatsächlich etwas erwidern.

Also haben wir uns unterhalten, und wie sich herausstellte, liest sie gern. Wenn sie nicht Model werden kann, möchte sie als Mode-Journalistin arbeiten, und sie kennt immer die neuesten Ausgaben von *Vogue* und *Marie-Claire*.

In den nächsten Minuten wird sie meine Besenkammer betreten, um sich das Exemplar von Thomas Hardys *Am grünen Rand der Welt* anzusehen, das ich auf den überfüllten Regalen von Angus' Bibliothek entdeckt habe. Sie sagt, sie würde es gerade für die Abschlussprüfung lesen. Oder vielmehr, richtig weit ist sie mit der Lektüre offenbar nicht gekommen, aber der Film mit Alan Bates und Julie Christie hat ihr gut gefallen, und sie fand Terence Stamp als Captain Troy klasse. (Ich persönlich finde Alan Bates als Gabriel Oak ja besser, aber über Geschmack lässt sich nicht streiten.) Am liebsten würde ich ihr das Buch ja schenken, aber das fände meine Mutter vielleicht nicht so gut, es ist eine alte Ausgabe und vermutlich sehr wertvoll.

Und … mittlerweile sollte sie mein Gedicht entdeckt haben.

Während sie nach dem Heimkommen vom Wasserfall duschte, bin ich nach oben gesaust und habe es in ihr Zimmer gelegt.

Wahrscheinlich liest sie es jetzt, in diesem Moment.

Ich habe es natürlich nicht unterschrieben, aber sie wird erraten, von wem es ist. Ich habe aus den Liebesbriefen paraphrasiert, die ich in Angus' Fotokiste gefunden hatte, und ein paar Metaphern von Keats entlehnt. Ich zumindest fand das Ergebnis ziemlich gut.

Außerdem tröste ich mich mit dem Gedanken, dass Größe nicht alles ist. Man denke nur an den Formeleins-Zwerg und seine Riesenfrau. Oder an die winzigen Jockeys, die allesamt Supermodels zur Freundin haben.

Wenn man jemanden liebt, kommt es nicht darauf an, wie groß oder klein er ist.

Abgesehen davon steckt in mir noch einiges an Wachstumspotenzial, und auf meinem Sparkonto liegt etwas Geld, von dem ich mir, bis der Schub einsetzt, ein paar Turnschuhe mit richtig hohen Absätzen kaufen kann. Wahrscheinlich hilft es, reich wie Krösus zu sein, aber Geld ist auch nicht alles, ebenso wenig wie Größe. Außerdem habe ich auch auf dem Gebiet noch einiges an Wachstumspotenzial.

Wie sich herausstellt, ist ihre Schule nicht so weit weg von der, die ich ab September besuche. Vielleicht können wir uns am Sonntag zum Tee treffen, nachdem wir uns unter der Woche täglich Briefe geschrieben haben, in denen wir uns immerwährende Liebe schwören …

Plötzlich sieht alles gar nicht mehr so düster aus.

Und vielleicht werden diese Ferien doch kein so großer Albtraum, wie ich es mir heute Morgen noch dachte.

Hilfe! Da klopft jemand an meine Besenkammertür. Das muss sie sein. Ich hole tief Luft und hinke hinüber, um zu öffnen.

Kapitel 10

»Hi, Alex. Ich wollte mir das Buch ansehen, von dem du mir erzählt hast. Und ich habe Rupes mitgebracht.«

Mit einem Lächeln nahm Chloë Rupes' Hand und führte ihn in das winzige Zimmer.

»Äh, na, okay.« Alex zog das Buch aus dem Regal und reichte es Chloë.

»Wow, wie schön! Findest du nicht, Rupes?« Chloë strich vorsichtig über den brüchigen Ledereinband.

»Kann schon sein. Bücher sind nicht so mein Ding.«

»Wirklich?« Chloë sah ihn erstaunt an. »Ich dachte, du hast es mit … Lyrik?«

Rupes zuckte mit den Schultern. »Ich bin eher für Sport zu haben.«

Chloë kicherte. »Sei nicht so zurückhaltend, Rupes. Es ist doch gut, wenn ein Mann eine empfindsame Seite hat, und dass du die hast, kannst du nicht leugnen.«

Rupes sah verwirrt drein. »Äh, na ja, wahrscheinlich schon.« Er warf einen Blick auf Alex' Bett und griff sich den zerlumpten Hasen, der auf dem Kissen lag. »Was haben wir denn da?«

»Entschuldige, könntest du ihn bitte zurücklegen? Ich mag es nicht, wenn andere Menschen ihn anfassen«, sagte Alex scharf.

»Junge, den solltest du besser loswerden, bevor du aufs Internat gehst.« Rupes warf Chloë einen verschwörerischen Blick zu und schnalzte in gespielter Empörung mit der Zunge, während er den Hasen an den Ohren baumeln ließ. »Die anderen Jungs werden dir wegen dem das Leben zur Hölle machen. Stimmt's nicht, Chloë?«

Alex entriss Rupes seinen Hasen und drückte ihn an die Brust. »Um ehrlich zu sein, Rupes, ist mir das scheißegal, aber trotzdem danke für die Warnung.«

»Viele Mädchen in meinem Schlafsaal haben noch einen Teddy oder so«, sagte Chloë freundlich.

»Genau. Das sind Mädchen. Wie ich höre, bist du heute von einem hohen Felsen gesprungen, Alex. Hast du dir dabei den blauen Fleck geholt?«

Alex zuckte mit den Achseln und schwieg.

»Demnächst werde ich für uns im Pool einen Wettbewerb veranstalten, dann kannst du uns allen ja deine Schwimmkünste vorführen. Bist du dabei, Alex?«

»Sehen wir mal.«

»Okay, bis später. Kommst du mit, Chloë?«

»Ja. Danke, dass du uns das Buch gezeigt hast, Alex.« Sie warf ihm ein Lächeln zu. »Wir sehen uns beim Essen.«

»Du siehst heute Abend wirklich sehr hübsch aus, Sadie.« William kam auf die Terrasse, wo Sadie allein saß und einen Wodka trank.

»Danke, sehr freundlich von dir. Man tut sein Bestes«, sagte sie und lächelte.

»Darf ich dir Gesellschaft leisten? Helena duscht gerade.«

»Aber natürlich. Ich freue mich doch, wenn ich ein paar Minuten exklusiv mit einem meiner Lieblingsmänner verbringen darf«, sagte sie. »Schau dir nur den Sonnenuntergang an. Großartig.«

»Ja, unglaublich. Überhaupt ist es hier viel schöner, als ich es mir vorgestellt hatte, vor allem das Haus.«

»Es hat sehr viel Atmosphäre, und Helena hat wirklich wahre Wunder vollbracht. Es fühlt sich wie ein richtiges Zuhause an.«

»Wenn ich schon allein mit dir hier sitze, möchte ich dich fragen, welchen Eindruck Helena auf dich im Moment macht.«

»Sie sieht müde aus, aber das kommt vermutlich daher, weil sie ständig im Einsatz ist, damit sich alle in Pandora wohlfühlen.«

»Und in den vergangenen Wochen?«

»Um ehrlich zu sein, habe ich sie kaum gesehen, William. In der Arbeit war es sehr hektisch, dazu das Durcheinander in meinem Privatleben – warum? Glaubst du, dass etwas nicht in Ordnung ist?«

»Ich weiß es nicht. Helena versteht sich ja darauf, ihre Gedanken für sich zu behalten. Solange wir auch schon verheiratet sind – sie stellt mich in gewisser Hinsicht immer noch vor ein Rätsel. Vor allem, was ihre Vergangenheit betrifft.«

»Das ist aber doch sicher auch ein Teil ihres Charmes, oder nicht?«, fragte Sadie. »Ich kenne keine Frau, die weniger neurotisch ist als Helena. Es mag ja sein, dass sie innerlich klein und bedürftig ist, aber das würde sie niemals zeigen.«

»Genau. Sie hat sich immer im Griff.« William trank einen Schluck Wein. »Aber wie kann man nur so lange mit jemandem zusammenleben und immer noch das Gefühl haben, den Menschen nicht richtig zu kennen? So ergeht es mir im Moment mit Helena. Hat sie jemals mit dir über diesen Alexis gesprochen?«

»Du meinst den Alexis, der jeden Moment hier auftaucht und den ich nach allen Regeln der Kunst zu verführen gedenke?« Sadie lachte vergnügt. »Sie sagte, sie hätten damals, als sie vor all den Jahren in Pandora war, eine Liebelei gehabt, aber recht viel mehr war das meiner Ansicht nach nicht.«

»Wirklich nicht?«, fragte William zweifelnd. »Ich weiß, dass du es mir nicht sagen würdest, Sadie, selbst wenn sie dir in allen Details davon berichtet hätte.«

»Stimmt, keine Silbe käme mir über die Lippen. Aber in diesem Fall kann ich dir bei meiner Pfadfinderinnenehre schwören, dass es nichts zu erzählen gibt.«

»Ich merke nur, dass sie noch distanzierter ist als sonst, und …« Seufzend schüttelte er den Kopf. »Ich habe einfach das Gefühl, dass etwas nicht ganz stimmt.«

»Hallo, ihr Mitcamper!« Unvermittelt erschien Jules auf der Terrasse. »Das Wasser ist eiskalt. Kannst du den Verwalter beauftragen, sich bis morgen früh darum zu kümmern?«

»Das sollte doch in dieser Hitze kein Problem sein, oder?«, meinte Sadie.

»Nein, aber es ist doch offensichtlich, dass die ganzen Sanitäreinrichtungen dringend überholt werden müssen. Bei meiner Toilette geht die Spülung nicht richtig.«

»Das Haus ist sehr alt, Jules, da kann nicht alles einwandfrei funktionieren«, antwortete William ruhig.

»Und es wird ein Vermögen kosten, es zu reparieren, von der Instandhaltung ganz zu schweigen. Helena erwartet doch hoffentlich nicht, dass du dafür aufkommst?«

»Helena verfügt über einige finanzielle Mittel. Durch Angus' Erbschaft ist sie in der Lage, alle Kosten selbst zu decken. Übrigens« – William wechselte das Thema –, »hast du heute von Sacha gehört? Hat er gesagt, wann er kommen will?«

»Ich habe mein Handy nicht angeschaltet. Ich bin im Urlaub, auch wenn er das nicht ist«, antwortete Jules barsch.

»Ich bin mir sicher, dass er lieber hier wäre, Jules, aber vielleicht ist der Druck auf ihn einfach zu groß. Im Finanzgewerbe läuft es nicht mehr so glatt wie früher. Und es war wirklich sehr mutig von Sacha, sich nach eurer Rückkehr aus Singapur selbständig zu machen.«

»*Kalispera*. Guten Abend in die Runde.« Mit einem Timing, das ebenso perfekt war wie sein gestärktes weißes Hemd und die braunen Chinos, erschien Alexis auf der Terrasse und stellte zwei Flaschen Wein und einen großen Strauß weißer Rosen auf den Tisch. »Sadie. William« – er lächelte sie nacheinander an –, »und darf ich mich vorstellen?« Er reichte Jules die Hand, und ihre frostige Miene taute schlagartig auf. »Alexis Lisle.«

»Jules Chandler. Sind Sie Zypriote oder Engländer?«

»Ich bin Zypriote, aber meine Familie geht auf einen Engländer zurück, der im achtzehnten Jahrhundert nach Zypern kam und eine meiner Vorfahrinnen heiratete. Wir tragen immer noch seinen Nachnamen.«

»Alexis, etwas zu trinken?« William reichte ihm ein Glas Wein.

»Danke. Und *cheers*, wie ihr Engländer sagt.«

Alle hoben das Glas, und in dem Moment kam Helena hinzu. Sie sah hinreißend aus in ihrem schlichten weißen Sommerkleid. »Guten Abend, Alexis«, begrüßte sie ihn, gab ihm aber keinen Kuss. Vielmehr wandte sie sich an William. »Schatz, würdest du nach oben gehen und den Kleinen gute Nacht sagen?«

»Natürlich. Soll ich sonst noch etwas machen, wenn ich schon im Haus bin?«

»Nein, aber sag den Älteren bitte, dass das Essen in einer Viertelstunde auf dem Tisch steht.« Als er an ihr vorbeiging, strich sie ihn leicht am Arm.

»Könntest du vielleicht auch Viola sagen, dass sie ins Bett gehen soll? Sie sitzt vor dem Fernseher und sieht eine DVD. Sag ihr, dass sie bis acht lesen darf und dann Licht aus«, sagte Jules.

William nickte und verschwand im Haus.

»Alexis, kommen Sie, setzen Sie sich zu mir.« Sadie klopfte auf den Stuhl, auf dem William gesessen hatte. »Ich würde gern mehr über Ihre Kellerei erfahren!«

Mit halbem Ohr hörte Helena zu, als Alexis die Arbeit auf dem Weingut erklärte. Auf der anderen Seite redete Jules auf sie ein und beschwerte sich über die schlechten Wasserleitungen, aber sie achtete gar nicht darauf.

»Ja«, sagte sie geistesabwesend und hoffte, das Richtige geantwortet zu haben.

»Du willst die Bäder also nicht renovieren?«

»Um ehrlich zu sein, habe ich mir noch keine Gedanken darüber gemacht. Entschuldige, Jules, ich muss nach dem Essen sehen.« Helena stand auf und floh in die Küche. Sie rührte den Schweinefleisch-Schmortopf um, den Angelina im Ofen hatte stehen lassen, probierte den Reis, der auf dem Herd köchelte, und goss ihn ab.

Von hinten schlang sich ein Arm um ihre Taille. »Unsere Kleinen sind im Bett, und ich habe auch Viola nach oben gebracht. Armes kleines Ding – konnte ihre Mutter sich nicht mal die Mühe machen, ihr gute Nacht zu sagen? Manchmal frage ich mich wirklich, warum sie sie überhaupt adoptiert haben«, sagte William leise. »Wer in der Familie das Lieblingskind ist, ist wohl kein Geheimnis.«

»Jules ist manchmal ein bisschen schroff mit ihr, aber Sacha liebt seine Tochter über alles«, sagte Helena beschwichtigend.

»Ich weiß wirklich nicht, wie du so nett über Jules reden kannst, wo sie mit ihrem Verhalten alle anderen auf die Palme bringt. Wie auch immer, ich finde Viola hinreißend, und da sie mein Patenkind ist, möchte ich, dass sie hier so glücklich wie möglich ist.«

»Da bin ich ganz deiner Meinung. Ich werde versuchen, mich möglichst viel um sie zu kümmern. Sie ist eine verlorene kleine Seele«, sagte Helena nachdenklich und kippte die letzten Reiskörner in die große Servierschüssel. »Etwas liebevolle Zuwendung würde ihr sehr guttun.«

Mit sanftem Druck drehte William Helena zu sich und gab ihr einen Kuss auf die Stirn. »Es tut mir leid wegen vorhin.«

»Das ist schon in Ordnung, es ist ja auch meine Schuld. Ich habe mit Sadie gesprochen, und ich verstehe ja, dass es … schwierig ist für dich.«

William strich ihr eine Strähne aus den Augen. »Ja, das stimmt. Und wirklich, Schatz, es würde mir helfen, wenn du mir erzähltest, was genau zwischen euch vorgefallen ist.«

»Das werde ich, versprochen. Aber nicht jetzt«, sagte Helena und drehte sich wieder zum Herd. »Wie auch immer, Sadie lässt ihn nicht mehr aus den Klauen, also brauchst du dir keine Sorgen zu machen.«

»Stört dich das?«

»Aber natürlich nicht!«, fuhr Helena auf. »Ich …«

»Hallo, Daddy. Wie geht's?« Chloë schlenderte in die Küche, einen türkisfarbenen Sarong als Kleidersatz um den Körper geschlungen.

»Gut«, sagte William seufzend. »Und bei dir?«

»Alles cool. Ist es in Ordnung, wenn Rupes und ich nach dem Essen ins Dorf laufen? Wir wollen uns ein paar Bars ansehen.«

»Solange du keinen Alkohol trinkst und vor Mitternacht wieder hier bist, sollte das in Ordnung sein«, sagte er resignierend.

»Danke, Daddy. Mmmm, irgendetwas riecht hier sehr gut.«
Chloë spähte in den gusseisernen Topf, den Helena gerade aus
dem Ofen holte. »Übrigens, wer ist denn dieser schnuckelige
Edeltyp da draußen auf der Terrasse?«

»Er heißt Alexis. Er ist … ein Nachbar«, erklärte Helena.

»Sieht für einen alten Knacker gar nicht mal so schlecht aus.
Sadie schmeißt sich jedenfalls ganz schön ran«, sagte Chloë lachend. »Bis gleich.«

»Warte mal eben.« William reichte ihr eine zugedeckte
Schüssel. »Mach dich nützlich und trag bitte den Reis nach
draußen.«

»Chloë, hast du Alex gesehen?«, fragte Helena, als sie den
beiden nach draußen folgte und den Topf auf den Tisch stellte.

»Ich glaube, er ist in seinem Zimmer. Soll ich ihn holen?«,
erbot Chloë sich.

»Ja, bitte.«

»Keine Ursache.«

»William, ist das Ihre Tochter?«, frage Alexis und sah Chloë
nach, die ins Haus ging.

»Ja.«

»Sie ist sehr hübsch. Sie müssen ein stolzer Vater sein.«

»Das bin ich auch. Aber wie alle Väter mache ich mir Sorgen, dass sie allzu schnell erwachsen werden will. Noch etwas
Wein, Alexis?«

Ein paar Minuten später kam Alex mit Chloë auf die Terrasse
gehinkt. Seine Miene war düster.

»Magst du dich neben Sadie setzen, mein Schatz?«, schlug
Helena vor.

»Gern.«

»Dein Vater hat erzählt, dass du heute vom Adonis-Wasserfall
gesprungen bist, Alex«, sagte Alexis, als er sich setzte.

»Stimmt.«

»Das war mutig von dir, vor allem von dem hohen Felsen.«

»Nicht mal ich wollte von dort springen«, sagte William und reichte Teller mit dampfendem Reis und Eintopf um den Tisch.

»Wir sollten auch mal dorthin fahren«, unterbrach Jules. »In der Schule war Rupes im Kunstspringen der Beste.«

»Es ist nicht ratsam, von ganz oben zu springen, auch wenn das Wasser tief ist. Unten sind Felsen. Wenn man mit den Füßen auftrifft, ist das in Ordnung, aber nicht mit dem Kopf – das ist nicht gut«, meinte Alexis warnend.

»Ich bedauere, dass ich nicht mitgefahren bin. Es klingt wunderschön. Alexis, würden Sie einmal mit mir dorthin fahren?«, bat Sadie.

Einen Moment sah er zu Helena, dann senkte er den Blick. »Natürlich. Und alle anderen, die mitkommen möchten.«

»Ich auf jeden Fall.« Rupes trat auf die Terrasse, umweht von einer Wolke Aftershave. Er setzte sich neben Chloë. »Das sieht gut aus, Tante Helena, danke«, sagte er, als ein Teller vor ihn gestellt wurde.

»Ich glaube, es ist Zeit, dass du die ›Tante‹ weglässt, jetzt, wo du dreizehn und offiziell ein Teenager bist. Bitte, fangt doch alle an«, sagte Helena und setzte sich endlich selbst.

»Ich möchte auf das Wohl der Gastgeberin anstoßen, die Pandora mit so großem Einsatz für uns alle so schön hergerichtet hat. Auf Helena.« William hob das Glas.

»Auf Helena«, stimmten alle ein.

Nach dem Essen schnappten sich Rupes und Chloë ihre Handys und eine Taschenlampe und machten sich auf den Weg ins Dorf. Alex humpelte in sein Zimmer zurück, Sadie wiederum bestand darauf, die Küche aufzuräumen, und nötigte Jules, ihr dabei zu helfen.

Woraufhin Helena, William und Alexis zu dritt auf der Terrasse zurückblieben.

»Alexis, einen Brandy?«

»Gern, danke.«

William reichte ihm ein Glas. »Erzählen Sie doch – wie schätzen Sie die Konkurrenz der Weine aus der Neuen Welt ein? Dem Angebot im Supermarkt nach zu urteilen sind sie hier recht beliebt.«

Abwesend hörte Helena zu, als sich die beiden Männer über Geschäfte unterhielten. William zeigte sich von seiner besten Seite, von seinem Ärger war nichts mehr zu merken. Sie waren beide umgängliche Menschen, dachte Helena, und es gab keinen Grund, weshalb sie nicht gut miteinander auskommen sollten. Solange keiner von ihnen je die Wahrheit erfuhr …

Eine Stunde später verabschiedete Alexis sich. Jules war bereits zu Bett gegangen, jetzt lehnte Sadie sich zurück und gähnte.

»Alexis hat mir vorhin von seiner Frau erzählt und wie schwer es für seine Jungen war, als sie starb. Da war sie erst vierunddreißig, die Arme. Aber das Schöne ist – obwohl das Leben ihm so übel mitgespielt hat, macht er weder einen deprimierten noch verbitterten Eindruck. Er ist ein durch und durch netter, anständiger Mensch, und das gibt mir meinen Glauben an das männliche Geschlecht zumindest zum Teil zurück. Gut, ihr Lieben, ich bin reif fürs Bett. Die viele Sonne ist anstrengend. Gute Nacht.«

»Sie hat recht, Alexis ist wirklich ein netter Mensch«, sagte William nachdenklich, nachdem Sadie gegangen war. »Aber ich kann mir die beiden trotzdem nicht als Paar vorstellen.«

»Das kann man nie wissen. Unverhofft kommt oft.«

»Sicher. Aber Alexis ist eindeutig nicht bereit, die Vergangenheit loszulassen. Nicht die mit seiner Frau, wohlgemerkt, sondern die mit dir.« William sah auf die Uhr. »Wo bleiben denn nur Chloë und Rupes? Es ist fast ein Uhr.«

»Ich bin mir sicher, Rupes passt auf, dass ihr niemand zu sehr auf die Pelle rückt.« Erleichtert ging Helena auf den Themenwechsel ein.

»Ehrlich gesagt, mache ich mir viel größere Sorgen, dass er selbst ihr zu sehr auf die Pelle rückt«, antwortete William grimmig. In dem Moment schreckte ein Motorengeräusch auf dem Feldweg sie auf. »Guter Gott, sie werden doch wohl nicht wegen Alkoholkonsums von Minderjährigen festgenommen worden sein? Vielleicht hätten wir sie doch nicht allein ins Dorf gehen lassen dürfen.« William sprang auf und marschierte zur Auffahrt, Helena folgte ihm dicht auf den Fersen.

Beim Näherkommen erkannten sie, dass es sich um ein Taxi handelte. Schließlich blieb es stehen, die hintere Tür wurde geöffnet, und jemand mit einer Reisetasche in der Hand hievte sich schwerfällig von der Rückbank.

»Danke.«

Der Neuankömmling ließ die Tür mit einem Knall zufallen und kam auf William und Helena zu.

»Hallo, Leute, ich hab's geschafft.«

»Sacha! Warum hast du uns nicht Bescheid gegeben, dass du kommst? Wir hätten dich doch vom Flughafen abgeholt. Schön, dich zu sehen, Kumpel!« Im bewährten Ritual männlicher Begrüßung umfassten sie sich an den Unterarmen und versetzten sich gegenseitig einen Schlag auf den Rücken.

»Ich habe Jules auf die Mailbox gesprochen und sie gebeten, mich abzuholen, aber offenbar hat sie die Nachricht nicht bekommen. Also habe ich mir ein Taxi geschnappt. Guten Abend, Helena. Wie geht es dir?«

Als er ihr einen Kuss auf die Wange gab, wäre Helena fast zurückgewichen, so stark roch er nach Alkohol.

»Komm auf die Terrasse, wir machen dir einen Kaffee. Du hast sicher einen langen Tag hinter dir.«

Als sie in das gedämpfte Terrassenlicht traten und Sacha sich auf einen Stuhl plumpsen ließ, bemerkte William sein fahles Gesicht. Tiefe Falten hatten sich in seine Stirn und um die Nase gegraben. Seine sonst störrische, aber gepflegte rotbraune Mähne war fettig und an den Schläfen stark ergraut.

»Mir wäre ein Brandy lieber als ein Kaffee«, sagte Sacha und deutete auf die Flasche.

William schenkte ihm ein halbes Glas ein.

»Jetzt komm schon, Will, mach's voll«, drängte Sacha.

Mit einem Blick zu Helena schenkte William widerstrebend mehr Brandy nach.

»Soll ich Jules sagen, dass du da bist?«, fragte Helena.

»Bloß nicht«, sagte Sacha und kippte einen großen Schluck hinunter. »Mit Verlaub, schlafende Hunde soll man nicht wecken.« Er lachte rau über seinen geschmacklosen Scherz.

»Ich gehe jetzt ins Bett, es ist schon spät.« Helena erhob sich. Ihr war wirklich nicht danach, weiter bei den beiden zu sitzen. Ohnehin würde es ein Gespräch unter Männern werden. »Gute Nacht.«

»Nacht, Helena«, murmelte Sacha.

»Ich komme bald nach, Liebling«, sagte William, und im selben Moment piepste sein Handy, um ihn auf eine ankommende SMS aufmerksam zu machen.

Sind gleich da. Alles cool C u R x

Er verzog das Gesicht. »Das war von meiner Tochter, um mir zu sagen, dass sie und dein Sohn sich gerade auf den Heimweg gemacht haben, zwei Stunden später als vereinbart.«

»Ach, natürlich! Chloë ist ja hier.« Sacha hatte das Glas bereits geleert und griff nach der Flasche, um sich selbst nachzuschenken. »Wie geht es ihr?«

»Ein typischer Teenager, sie kann es gar nicht erwarten, erwachsen zu werden. Du kannst dir vorstellen, dass ich, in Anbetracht ihrer Mutter, das Schlimmste befürchtet hatte, dabei ist sie hinreißend. Wenn ich tatsächlich bei ihrer Erziehung ein Wort mitzureden gehabt hätte, wäre ich sehr stolz.«

»Komm, du warst während der prägenden Jahre bei ihr, und es ist nicht deine Schuld, dass die blöde Kuh, die du geheiratet hast, völlig neben der Spur ist.«

»Chloë ist selbst mit fünfzig Prozent meiner Gene hinreißend. Das findet dein Sohn offenbar auch.« Er hörte das leichte Lallen in der Stimme seines Freundes und versuchte, dessen düstere Stimmung etwas aufzuheitern.

»Das glaube ich sofort. Verfluchte Frauen, stimmt's nicht? Sind doch alle gleich. Wickeln uns arme, nichtsahnende Männer mit ihrem Charme um den Finger. Und wenn sie uns dann am Haken haben, verbringen sie den Rest ihres Lebens damit, an uns herumzunörgeln. Schau dir doch Jules an. Auf der Liste ihrer Lieblingspersonen stehe ich vermutlich irgendwo zwischen Hitler und dem Leibhaftigen.«

»Das meinst du nicht im Ernst, Sacha.«

»O doch«, widersprach er mit Nachdruck und lachte freudlos. »Ehrlich gesagt ist das das Einzige, was mich bei Laune hält: Jules' Gesicht, wenn sie es erfährt.«

»Wenn sie was erfährt?«

Sacha sah zu William, die Verzweiflung stand ihm ins Gesicht geschrieben. Dann schüttelte er den Kopf und lachte bitter.

»Wahrscheinlich ist es sinnlos, es noch länger geheim halten zu wollen.«

»Wovon, um Himmels willen, redest du da?«

Sacha kippte noch einen großen Schluck Brandy hinunter. »Tja, also: Ich habe das Haus mit zwei Hypotheken belastet und zahlreiche Privatdarlehen aufgenommen, um flüssig zu bleiben. Aber jetzt, Will, ist es aus und vorbei. Mein Geschäft ist bankrott. Und als Folge davon haben meine Familie und ich alles verloren.«

Alex' Tagebuch

Es ist nach ein Uhr nachts, und ich liege hier und traue mich kaum zu atmen, um die Schritte nicht zu überhören.

Ich muss wissen, ob Chloë heil nach Hause gekommen ist.

Vorhin hörte ich ein Auto und dachte, das wären sie. Aber dann hörte ich eine Stimme – Sacha ist angekommen. Und dann ... Ich bin mir nicht sicher, aber wenig später dachte ich, ich würde einen Mann weinen hören. Vielleicht sehen sie sich im Salon ja eine DVD an oder so, schließlich kann ich mir weder bei Dad noch bei Sacha vorstellen, dass sie sich voreinander die Augen ausheulen. So etwas machen Männer nicht.

Unsere Tränendrüsen sind vom Moment der Zeugung an darauf programmiert, nur im Geheimen in Aktion zu treten. Mit Ausnahme zweier besonderer Anlässe: Geburten und Beerdigungen.

Und selbst dann ist es etwas prekär, denn nach allem, was ich so mitbekommen habe, muss ein Mann für die Frau in seinem Leben »da« sein. Sie darf Rotz und Wasser heulen, und alle Welt würdigt ihre Mitfreude (Geburt) oder ihr Mitgefühl (Tod). Aber sobald wir Männer öffentlich auch nur eine Träne vergießen, werden wir als Heulsuse abgestempelt.

Einmal kam ich ins Krankenhaus, ich war vom Fahrrad

gestürzt und hatte mir Teer in die Kniescheibe gerammt. Die Tränen sind einfach so aus meinen Augen gelaufen, so verdammt weh hat das getan! Aber habe ich von Schwester Brutalo auch nur ein Wort des Mitleids gehört, als sie die winzigen, grausam schmerzhaften Körnchen einzeln mit der Pinzette herauszupfte?

Einen Teufel habe ich gehört! Obwohl ich auf der Straße einen Hautfetzen zurückgelassen hatte, der der nächsten Kröte eine Ganzkörperhauttransplantation ermöglicht hätte, befahl Schwester Brutalo mir, »ein großer Junge« zu sein.

Na, na, du bist doch schon ein großer Junge, der weint doch nicht …

Kein Wunder, dass Frauen Männer kritisieren dafür, dass sie nicht »in Kontakt« mit ihren Gefühlen sind. Wie sollen wir denn, wenn wir unseren Gefühlen keinen Brief schreiben dürfen, geschweige denn, sie anrufen oder – das ultimative Verbrechen – sie tatsächlich zulassen, indem wir unseren Tränendrüsen gestatten, ihrer Aufgabe nachzukommen?

Aber wer erzieht denn das Gros der Jungen, die diese Welt bevölkern?

GENAU!!!

Die Frauen!!

Ich unterbreche meine philosophischen Betrachtungen und frage mich, ob ich nicht gerade eine gigantische, weltumspannende Verschwörung aufgedeckt habe. Wird mein Name eines Tages im selben Atemzug genannt werden wie Aristoteles? Hippokrates? Homer Simpson?

Die Frage ist doch: Was genau wollen Frauen von uns?

Was immer es ist, weiter kann ich nicht darüber grübeln, denn auf dem Gang höre ich vertraute Stimmen.

Sie ist zu Hause. Gott sei Dank! Jetzt kann ich entspannt einschlafen im Wissen, dass Chloë ein paar Meter über mir wohlbehalten im Bett liegt.

Ich höre das Trippeln ihrer Füße, als sie in ihr Zimmer geht und tut, was immer Mädchen eben tun, bevor sie sich ins Bett legen. Ohne Genaueres zu wissen, klingt es, als wäre sie auf Patrouillengang. Aber wahrscheinlich zieht sie sich nur aus, hängt die Kleider in den Schrank, sucht nach dem Nachthemd, bürstet sich die Haare, fischt unter dem Bett nach der Zeitschrift, die ihr gestern Nacht aus der Hand gefallen ist, und so weiter und so weiter.

Ich schalte das Licht aus, sage ihr, dass ich sie liebe, und bereite mich darauf vor einzuschlafen. Als ich gerade am Wegdämmern bin, klopft es an meiner Tür.

Dann geht sie auf, ohne dass ich etwas gesagt hätte.

»Alex, bist du wach?«

»Jetzt schon.«

Was will *der* denn von mir?

Als Rupes hereinkommt, setze ich mich auf.

»Hi.«

»Hi.«

Rupes zwängt seinen Muskelberg in den engen Zwischenraum zwischen Bett und Tür und zieht sie hinter sich ins Schloss. Ein beängstigendes Vorgehen.

»Ich will dich was fragen.«

»Ja? Was denn?«

»Hast du Chloë ein Gedicht geschrieben und ihr heute Vormittag ins Zimmer gelegt?«

Ich bin entsetzt, dass er das weiß. »Äh … vielleicht.«

»Dacht ich's mir doch. Es hat ihr gefallen.«

»Wirklich?« Meine Laune hebt sich. Hat sie Rupes als

ihren Postillon d'amour geschickt, weil sie zu schüchtern ist, selbst zu mir zu kommen?

»Ja. Die Sache ist, sie glaubt, es ist von mir.«

Was?!

Wie kann sie nur? Rupes ist zu dumm, um einen Kinderreim korrekt abzuschreiben, ganz zu schweigen davon, Verse zu schmieden, die einem Wordsworth persönlich alle Ehre gemacht hätten.

»Ja«, sagt er grinsend, wie er da hoch über mir aufragt. »Sie ist heute Abend ausgesprochen nett zu mir gewesen. Das ganze Gesülze hat offenbar funktioniert. Da habe ich mir überlegt, ob du und ich nicht handelseinig werden können?«

Ich sitze schweigend in der Dunkelheit.

»Also, ich bezahle dich, und du schreibst mir noch ein paar Briefe. Sagen wir, einen Fünfer pro Stück?«

Jetzt schweige ich nicht mehr aus Absicht, sondern weil es mir die Sprache verschlagen hat.

»Sehen wir es doch realistisch, Mann, du wirst nie bei ihr landen. Du bist ihr kleiner Stiefbruder. Das wäre, das wäre ja ... inzestisch.«

»›Inzestuös‹, meinst du wohl.« Seine nonexistente Sprachbeherrschung öffnet mir die Lippen. »Das wär's aber nicht. Wir sind nicht blutsverwandt, deswegen spricht nichts dagegen, wenn wir ... wollen.«

»Leider ist sie aber scharf auf mich, nicht auf dich. Also, ja oder nein?«

»Das würde ich nie, unter keinen Umständen, jemals in Erwägung ziehen. Vergiss es, Rupes. Nein.«

»Sicher?«

»Sicher.«

Ich höre ihn durch die Lücke zwischen seinen großen Schneidezähnen zischend Luft holen. »Dein Pech, wenn du einem Kumpel nicht aushelfen willst, vor allem, wenn du was dafür bekommen hättest. Na, du wirst deine Meinung schon noch ändern. Nacht.«

Als er das Zimmer verlässt, lasse ich mich wieder flach auf den Rücken fallen, und der Wirbelsturm der Gefühle, der in mir tobt, raubt mir den Atem.

Nein! Nein! Nein!

Meine arme, süße Chloë. Man hat dir eine Gehirnwäsche verpasst, du bist hypnotisiert worden ... der Verstand ist dir abhanden gekommen! Ich werde dich beschützen, ich werde dich retten, denn du weißt nicht, was du tust.

Ich weiß, jetzt ist offener Krieg ausgebrochen, und ich liege wach und plane meinen Feldzug.

Eine ganze Weile später träume ich, dass meine Tür aufgeht und Hände unter meiner Achsel herumtasten und etwas wegziehen.

In meinem Traum bin ich zu müde, um aufzuwachen und diesen Jemand daran zu hindern.

KAPITEL 11

»Eine Tasse Tee für dich.«

William stellte den Becher auf Helenas Nachttisch, setzte sich auf die Bettkante und ließ sie langsam aufwachen.

»Wie spät ist es denn?«, fragte sie verschlafen.

»Kurz nach sieben.«

»Du bist aber früh auf. Und du bist erst weit nach drei ins Bett gekommen.«

William seufzte. »Es geht Sacha wirklich schlecht. Tut mir leid, dich zu wecken, aber ich dachte, wir sollten uns unterhalten, bevor die anderen aufstehen.«

»Was ist denn passiert?« Helena setzte sich auf und griff nach dem Tee.

»Seine Firma steht vor dem Bankrott.«

»O mein Gott, William«, sagte sie erschrocken. »Aber vielleicht kann er ja eine neue gründen, oder er lässt sich wieder irgendwo anstellen.«

»Leider ist es wohl ein ganzes Stück schlimmer. Was ich dir jetzt sage, muss unter uns bleiben.«

»Natürlich.«

»Sacha hat etwas getan, das nachvollziehbar, aber wahnsinnig ist. Als seine Firma dringend Geld brauchte, um nicht unterzugehen, hat er das Haus mit einer Hypothek belastet und dann persönliche Darlehen aufgenommen, um die Belastungen zu bezahlen.«

Helena stöhnte. »Das kann nicht wahr sein.«

»Leider doch«, widersprach William. »Ich will nicht ins Detail gehen, aber das Fazit ist, sobald das Unternehmen Insolvenz anmeldet, verliert er alles. Einschließlich dem Haus. Er hat auch alle Aktien verkauft, das heißt, die Chandlers sind blank, wie er mir sagte, wenn auch im volltrunkenen Zustand.«

»Aber die Banken werden ihm doch bestimmt nicht das Dach über dem Kopf wegnehmen? Jules gehört doch rechtlich auch die Hälfte, oder nicht?«

»Nein, ihr gehört nichts. Sacha erzählte mir gestern, dass das Haus eine Art Stammsitz ist, es ist seit knapp zweihundert Jahren im Besitz der Familie und das Einzige, was seine Eltern ihm bei ihrem Tod hinterlassen haben. Aber es ist wirklich ein Vermögen wert. Wie auch immer, deswegen wurde Jules nie als Mitbesitzerin eingetragen. Von den immensen Hypotheken abgesehen wird das Haus beim Verkauf viel Geld für die Schuldentilgung bringen, ganz zu schweigen vom ganzen Hausrat. Deswegen wird er von der Bank enteignet werden.«

»O mein Gott, William.« Helena war entsetzt. »Kannst du ihm irgendwie helfen?«

»Er braucht einen richtigen Insolvenzverwalter, aber er hat seinen Laptop mitgebracht, ich kann also zumindest alles in Ruhe mit ihm durchgehen. Aber nach dem, was er mir gestern Abend sagte, hat er alle Möglichkeiten abgeklopft und glaubt, dass es keine Rettung mehr gibt.«

»Er war gestern Abend sehr betrunken. Vielleicht ist es nicht so schlimm, wie er glaubt.« Nachdenklich nippte Helena an ihrem Tee.

»Ich glaube schon, dass es so schlimm ist. Er will mir die Zahlen heute Vormittag zeigen. Aber von seiner Situation einmal abgesehen – ich wollte mit dir darüber reden, welche Auswirkungen das auf unseren Urlaub hier haben wird.«

Mit einem müden Seufzen lehnte Helena sich zurück. »Kannst du dir vorstellen, wie Jules darauf reagieren wird?«

»Ja, und die Vorstellung gefällt mir gar nicht. Man möchte ja hoffen, dass sie in dieser Stunde der Not zu ihrem Mann hält, gleichgültig, was er getan hat und welche Folgen es für sie haben wird, aber irgendwie glaube ich nicht daran. Und du?«

»Ich habe keine Ahnung, wie sie reagieren wird. Vermutet sie schon etwas?«

»Offenbar nicht. So schwierig Jules manchmal ist – zu hören, dass man über Nacht alles verloren hat, ist ein übler Schlag.«

»Was ist mit den Kindern?«

»Sacha sagt, dass sie ihre Privatschulen vergessen können. Nicht, dass es Rupes schaden wird, wenn er mal kleinere Brötchen backen muss. Es besteht eine kleine Chance, dass er ein Stipendium auf Darlehensbasis bekommt, weil sie ihm ja bereits das Sportstipendium zuerkannt haben. Sacha ist überzeugt, dass Jules ihn verlassen wird. Seien wir ehrlich, viel Grund zu bleiben hat sie nicht.«

»In guten wie in schlechten Zeiten, so heißt es doch? Immerhin sind sie seit achtzehn Jahren verheiratet.«

»Ja, aber mittlerweile sind sie doch eigentlich nur noch der Kinder wegen zusammen und weil sie keine Alternative haben, aber doch nicht aus Liebe.«

»Du meine Güte«, sagte Helena schaudernd. »Also, was sollen wir anderen heute machen? Wenn Sacha Jules von der Sache erzählt, wäre es besser, wenn niemand im Weg ist. Bloß sollte ich vorher alles wegräumen, was an Zerbrechlichem herumsteht«, fügte sie trocken hinzu.

»Keine Sorge, heute erzählt er ihr nichts. Ich werde zuerst mit ihm die Zahlen durchgehen, aber ich vermute, dass er sofort nach London zurückfliegen muss, um Insolvenz anzumelden.«

»Hoffen wir, dass es in letzter Minute doch noch einen Ausweg gibt.«

»Nach allem, was ich weiß, müsste schon ein Wunder geschehen. Was Pandora betrifft, sollten wir einfach weitermachen wie bisher. Ich wollte nur, dass du weißt, was vor sich geht. Vielleicht kannst du Jules davon abhalten, zu viele gehässige Bemerkungen zu machen, weil ihr Mann sich an seinem ersten Urlaubstag mit mir und seinem Laptop im Büro verschanzt.« William griff nach ihrer Hand. »Liebling, es tut mir leid, dich mit all dem zu belasten.«

»Du kannst ja wohl kaum etwas dafür.« Sie lächelte matt. »So ist das Leben nun mal, willkommen in der Wirklichkeit.«

»Mummy! Da steckst du! Komm und schau mir beim Reinspringen zu. Biiiitte!«

»Ich komme, mein Schatz, ich bin schon da.« Helena hatte sich gerade hinsetzen wollen, um in Ruhe Kaffee zu trinken, aber jetzt ging sie zum Pool hinunter, wo Immy in einem pinkfarbenen Badeanzug ungeduldig am Beckenrand stand.

»Schaust du auch zu?«

»Ganz gebannt«, bestätigte Helena.

»Ich springe!« Immy hielt sich die Nase zu und sprang. Helena applaudierte überschwänglich.

»Sehr schön, mein Schatz!«

»Können wir zu den Felsen fahren, damit ich so reinspringen kann wie Alex und Daddy? Ich kann es doch gut genug, oder?«

»Natürlich, aber für ein kleines Mädchen ist das ein bisschen gefährlich.« Helena setzte sich an den Beckenrand und ließ die Füße im kühlen Wasser baumeln. Chloë lag in ihrer Aufgabe als Bademeisterin auf ihrer Luftmatratze, von der Fred sie kichernd zu schubsen versuchte.

»Hi, Tante Helena.« Unvermittelt stand Viola neben ihr.

»Hallo, mein Schatz. Alles in Ordnung?«

Viola zuckte mit den Schultern »Geht schon.«

Ihr sommersprossiges Gesicht war blass und sah angespannt aus. Helena nahm ihre Hand. »Magst du mir davon erzählen?«

»Ja.« Viola setzte sich neben sie. »Weißt du, dass Daddy hier ist?«

»Ja.«

»Ich habe ihn heute Morgen im Salon auf dem Sofa gesehen, als ich mir eine DVD anschauen wollte.«

»Wahrscheinlich wollte er Mummy gestern Nacht nicht wecken, weil es so spät war«, erklärte Helena.

»Das ist es nicht. Zu Hause schläft er immer im Gästezimmer. Aber als er aufgewacht ist, sah er so schrecklich aus. Seine Augen waren ganz rot, und er hat irgendwie … zermatscht ausgesehen. Und als ich ihm einen Guten-Morgen-Kuss geben wollte, hat er mich angebrüllt und gesagt, ich soll verschwinden.« Viola seufzte. »Glaubst du, dass ich etwas ausgefressen habe?«

»Natürlich nicht, mein Schatz.« Helena legte einen Arm um Violas magere Schultern und drückte das Mädchen an sich. »Manchmal haben wir Erwachsene Probleme, die nichts mit unseren Kindern zu tun haben. Das ist wie bei dir, wenn eine Lehrerin dich schimpft oder eine deiner Freundinnen etwas sagt, das dich kränkt. Aber das hat nichts mit Mum und Dad zu tun.«

»Nein, aber ich schrei sie nicht an, bloß weil es mir schlecht geht.«

»Das stimmt«, meinte Helena. »Aber ich verspreche dir, keiner der beiden ist sauer auf dich. Daddy hat nur ein paar Probleme bei der Arbeit, das ist alles.«

»Also, wenn er es mir erzählen würde, könnte ich ihm vielleicht helfen, so wie er mir hilft, wenn sie mich wieder wegen meiner roten Haare aufziehen.«

»Ich glaube, was Daddy jetzt am meisten hilft, ist zu wissen, dass du ihn lieb hast.«

»Aber natürlich habe ich ihn lieb, ganz fest sogar.«

»Weißt du was – hast du Lust, mit uns allen zum Baden an einen schönen Strand zu fahren? Dort können wir schwimmen und etwas zu Mittag essen. Was hältst du davon?«

»Ja, Tante Helena, das wäre schön«, sagte Viola und lächelte matt.

»Ich bin auch dafür!«, rief Chloë aus dem Pool. »Ich würde schrecklich gern im Meer schwimmen.«

»Ich auch!«, stimmte Immy ein.

Eine Stunde später saßen alle Kinder im Wagen. Sogar Alex hatte eingewilligt mitzukommen, nachdem er gehört hatte, dass Rupes mit seiner Mutter unterwegs war. Offenbar sollte er ihr helfen, neue Kissen zu kaufen, da sie Helenas für zu dünn befand.

»Können wir nicht warten, bis sie wieder da sind, Helena?«, bat Chloë. »Rupes würde bestimmt auch gern mitkommen.«

»Wenn wir nicht gleich fahren, wird es zu spät«, log Helena. Sie wollte unbedingt fort sein, ehe Mutter und Sohn zurückkamen.

»Wartet auf mich!« Sadie kam aus dem Haus gelaufen, gerade als Helena den Minivan rückwärts zur Einfahrt hinausfuhr. »Ich möchte auch mit.«

»Spring rein.« Helena lächelte, als ihre Freundin sich neben sie setzte.

»Ich gehe mit euch auf Tauchstation. Die Atmosphäre in dem Haus ist ja so geladen, als würde bald ein Gewitter losbrechen.«

»Eine kluge Entscheidung«, sagte Helena.

»Was in aller Welt ist denn da los?« Sadie senkte die Stimme, damit Viola sie nicht hören konnte, obwohl das Geschrei und Gelächter aus dem Fonds jedes Gespräch übertönten. »Sacha hat sich mit William im Büro verbarrikadiert, Jules hat ihn wegen nicht näher benannten Fehlverhaltens demonstrativ ignoriert und ist dann mit einem mürrischen Rupes im Schlepptau abgerauscht.«

»Das erzähle ich dir später, aber es ist nichts Gutes.«

»Das zumindest habe ich mitbekommen. Ach je, es ist wirklich ein Jammer, dass das, was immer es ist, ausgerechnet hier in Pandora passieren muss. Wir dürfen uns davon nicht den Urlaub verderben lassen.«

»Nein, es ist nicht schön, aber es sollte nicht lange dauern. Sacha wird wohl sehr bald nach England zurückfliegen müssen«, flüsterte Helena.

»Wird Jules ihn begleiten?«

»Das, meine Liebe, ist die große Preisfrage.«

Der Lara Beach lag im Nationalpark und war als Gebiet von außergewöhnlicher Schönheit ausgewiesen: felsig, zerklüftet und noch so, wie die Natur diesen Küstenstrich geschaffen hatte, denn jede Erschließung war untersagt worden. Nach einer holprigen Fahrt über einen Feldweg parkte Helena den Wagen auf einer leicht erhöhten Landzunge oberhalb eines sichelförmigen Strands. Das klare Wasser glitzerte in der Mittagssonne.

Alle stürmten hinaus, beladen mit Eimern und Spaten, Handtüchern und Decken, und liefen den Pfad zum grellweißen Sand hinab.

Nachdem sie die drei Jüngeren mit Lichtschutzfaktor 50 eingecremt, mit Schwimmflügeln ausgestattet und ihnen Mützen aufgesetzt hatten, ließen Sadie und Helena sich im Sand nieder und sahen ihnen beim Herumplanschen im seichten Wasser zu.

»Ist es nicht großartig, wie Immy und Fred Chloë ins Herz geschlossen haben? Und umgekehrt. Sie ist sehr lieb zu ihnen, und die beiden sind ganz vernarrt in sie. Sieh sie dir nur an – sogar Alex wirkt heute glücklich«, sagte Sadie. »Sie haben sich wirklich zu einer richtigen Familie zusammengefunden.«

»Unsere bunt zusammengewürfelte Kinderschar?«, fragte Helena und lächelte spöttisch. »Ja, in der Hinsicht hätte es nicht besser laufen können. William und ich hatten uns große Sorgen gemacht, wie es mit Chloë werden würde. Aber vielleicht liegt es ja doch in den Genen, wie und wer wir sind und wie wir auf bestimmte Situationen reagieren. Chloë hat eindeutig ein freundliches, liebevolles Naturell. Und offenbar hegt sie wirklich keinen Groll gegen William oder gegen mich.«

»Nicht, dass sie Grund dafür hätte, aber ich weiß, was du meinst. Pass auf, Helena, vielleicht gefällt es ihr in eurer Familie so gut, dass sie gar nicht zu ihrer Mutter zurück möchte. Wie kämst du damit klar?« Mit einem Grinsen stand Sadie auf. »Also, ich gehe zu den Kindern ins Wasser und schwimme eine Runde. Du auch?«

»Gleich. Teste mal, wie das Wasser ist, ich komme nach.«

Kreischend wegen der Kälte stürzte Sadie sich in die Fluten. Helena hob ihr Gesicht in die Sonne und dachte über die Chandlers nach. Sie fragte sich, ob das Leben einen auf die eine oder andere Weise unweigerlich dafür büßen ließ, wenn man einen Pakt mit dem Teufel schloss und eine Beziehung mit einem Verrat begann. Wenn das stimmte, dann stand ihr die Buße noch bevor …

»He, Mum, das Wasser ist toll. Kommst du nicht rein?« Alex

schüttelte sich wie ein Hund und ließ sich neben sie auf die Decke fallen.

»Doch, gleich.«

»Ach, übrigens«, sagte Alex, während er mit den Füßen Muster in den Sand zog, »ich bin noch gar nicht dazu gekommen, dir davon zu erzählen, weil du immer so viel zu tun hast, aber ich habe in einem der Kartons ein paar alte Briefe gefunden. Ich bin mir nicht sicher, aber ich vermute, dass Angus sie geschrieben hat, und zwar an eine geheimnisvolle Frau.«

»Wirklich? Das ist ja spannend, die musst du mir zeigen. Gibt es gar keinen Hinweis, wer sie sein könnte?«

»Nein. Die meisten habe ich schon gelesen, aber er nennt sie nie beim Namen. Weißt du, ob Angus je eine … eine Freundin hatte?«

»Auf jeden Fall nicht zu der Zeit, als ich bei ihm war. Ich habe ihn immer für einen eingefleischten Junggesellen gehalten, aber wer weiß, was er in jüngeren Jahren getrieben hat? Ich freue mich darauf, sie zu lesen, mein Schatz, wenn ich einmal mehr als eine Minute Zeit habe.«

»Ein richtiger Urlaub ist das für dich ja nicht, Mum, oder? Seit wir hier sind, bist du ständig am Arbeiten.«

»Das ist meine Rolle, und es macht mir Spaß.« Sie zuckte gleichmütig mit den Schultern. »Und wie gefällt es dir hier?«

»Teils, teils. Mir ist es lieber, wenn wir, die Familie, unter uns sind. Ich weiß, du magst es nicht, wenn ich das sage, aber Rupes ist wirklich ein Arsch…«

»Und du brauchst es auch nicht zu wiederholen, Alex. Wie findest du Chloë? Gestern hatte es den Anschein, als würdet ihr euch richtig gut verstehen.«

Alex zögerte, räusperte sich und senkte den Kopf, damit seine Mutter nicht sah, wie rot er wurde. »Ich finde sie klasse.«

»Gut. Das finde ich auch.«

»Und Viola ist auch nett. Sie ist ein richtig liebes Mädchen geworden, aber sie tut mir ganz schön leid. Jules nimmt sie irgendwie überhaupt nicht wahr. Übrigens, Mum, war Angelina heute Morgen bei mir im Zimmer, um das Bett zu machen?«, fragte er.

»Vermutlich. Weshalb?«

»Als ich meine Badesachen geholt habe, habe ich Bee nicht gefunden. Ich schaue noch mal nach, wenn wir zurück sind, aber vielleicht dachte sie ja, dass er Immy oder Fred gehört, und hat ihn zu ihnen ins Zimmer gelegt.«

»Das ist möglich. Aber weit kann er nicht gekommen sein. Und da du mit Vorliebe Dinge suchst, die direkt vor deiner Nase sind, liegt er beim Heimkommen vermutlich auf deinem Kopfkissen und starrt dich erwartungsvoll an. Ich gehe jetzt schwimmen, kommst du mit?«

Helena stand auf, reichte ihrem Sohn die Hand, und gemeinsam liefen sie in die Wellen.

Später ließen sie sich in der rustikalen Taverne mit Blick auf die Bucht köstlichen gegrillten Fisch schmecken.

»Müde, Mummy.« Nach dem Essen kuschelte sich Fred, dem am ganzen Körper Sand klebte, auf ihren Schoß und steckte den Daumen in den Mund.

»Das kommt vom Herumspringen in den Wellen.« Helena strich ihm über das glatte braune Haar, das so sehr dem seines Vaters glich.

»Wir gehen wieder ins Wasser«, sagte Alex, als er und Chloë aufstanden. »Viola, magst du mitkommen?«

»Ja, gern.«

Alex streckte die Hand nach ihr aus, und Viola ergriff sie, woraufhin Immy aufsprang und Chloës Hand nahm.

»Viola hat ja richtig Zutrauen zu Alex gefasst«, bemerkte Sadie, als sie ihnen nachsah.

»Er war den Kleinen gegenüber immer schon sehr fürsorglich«, sagte Helena und leerte ihr Weinglas. »Manchmal etwas zu sehr. Zu Hause kommt er oft zu mir in die Küche und verlangt zu wissen, wo genau Immy und Fred gerade sind, sie könnten ja irgendwo verloren gegangen sein. Das gehört zu seinem übertriebenen erwachsenen Verantwortungsgefühl. So hat mir das jedenfalls der Psychiater erklärt, der ihn untersuchte.«

»Helena« – Sadie zögerte und warf dann einen Blick zu ihrer Freundin –, »hat er dich je nach seinem Vater gefragt?«

»Nein. Auf jeden Fall nicht direkt.«

»Das wundert mich, vor allem angesichts seiner geistigen Reife. Gedanken macht er sich bestimmt darüber«, meinte Sadie. »Pass auf, ich glaube, die Frage kommt eher früher als später.«

»Vielleicht will er es ja gar nicht wissen«, erwiderte Helena und schaute auf Fred, der zufrieden in ihren Armen schlief.

»Weiß William, wer es ist?«

»Nein.«

»Hat er dich gefragt?«

»Ja, bald nachdem wir uns kennengelernt hatten. Ich habe ihm gesagt, dass es jemand sei, den ich in Wien kannte und den ich lieber vergessen würde, und dass das Kapitel für mich abgeschlossen sei. Das hat er respektiert, bis heute«, antwortete sie etwas brüsk. »Das geht niemanden etwas an außer mich.«

»Und Alex.«

»Sadie, das weiß ich. Ich lass das auf mich zukommen.«

»Schätzchen, ich mag dich wirklich sehr gern, aber ich habe nie verstanden, weshalb du die Identität seines Vaters hütest wie ein Staatsgeheimnis und nicht einmal *mir* erzählt hast, wer es ist. So schlimm kann es doch nicht sein, wer immer es ist.«

»Doch, glaub mir, es ist noch viel schlimmer. Sadie, tut mir leid, aber darüber will ich nicht reden. Wirklich, ich habe meine Gründe.«

»Also gut«, sagte Sadie achselzuckend. »Ich weiß, wie wenig du von dir preisgeben magst, aber als deine beste Freundin warne ich dich, der Jüngste Tag naht. Und um deines Sohnes willen wirst du dich damit befassen müssen. So, und jetzt gehe ich noch mal schwimmen.«

Mit dem schlafenden Fred auf dem Schoß konnte Helena nicht aufstehen, und so sah sie Sadie nur nach, wie sie sich zu den anderen im Wasser gesellte. Ihre bohrenden Fragen waren Helena unangenehm, aber sie konnte die Beweggründe ihrer Freundin nachvollziehen. Und sie wusste, dass sie recht hatte.

Alex' Tagebuch

19. Juli, Fortsetzung

Ich wusste doch, es war zu schön, um wahr zu sein.

Ein phantastischer Tagesausflug mit meiner Angebeteten, ich komme nach Hause, und das Schlimmste erwartet mich. Das Allerschlimmste.

Meine Mutter meinte, Bee würde auf dem Kissen liegen und mich erwartungsvoll anstarren. Zum Teil hatte sie recht. Er starrte mich tatsächlich erwartungsvoll an. Sehr erwartungsvoll sogar.

Allerdings nicht der leibhaftige Bee – oder der schon ziemlich zerfledderte Bee, um genau zu sein –, sondern sein Bildnis: ein Schwarz-Weiß-Foto von ihm. Mit verbundenen Augen (offenbar eine Socke) hing er an den Ohren von einem Olivenbaum, Freds Wasserpistole am Bauch.

Darunter eine Nachricht:

Tu, was ich sage, oder das Karnickel ist hin. b.w.

Ich drehe das Bild um, da steht noch was:

Wenn du jemandem davon erzählst, siehst du ihn nie wieder.

Ein Teil von mir würde Rupes am liebsten gratulieren, weil er sich eine derart schlaue Erpressung hat einfallen lassen. Das hätte ich ihm nie zugetraut. Ein anderer Teil von mir möchte ihm die Augen auskratzen, möchte schreien und toben und heulen wie ein Werwolf, bis er mir meinen kostbarsten Besitz zurückgibt.

Ich habe es also mit einer Geiselnahme zu tun. Ich muss

Ruhe bewahren, muss rational denken und die Optionen erwägen, die mir offenstehen.

Option 1:

Ich kann schnurstracks zu meiner Mutter laufen und ihr das Foto zeigen. Sie wird wütend auf Rupes sein und verlangen, dass er mir den Hasen zurückgibt.

Ergebnis: In der Nachricht steht, dass ich Bee nie wiedersehe, wenn ich jemandem davon erzähle. Rupes ist ein gnadenloser Gegner, er wird seine Drohung höchstwahrscheinlich wahr machen und Bee beseitigen, bevor er ihn mir zurückgeben kann.

Nur ein kleiner Scherz, Tante Helena, ein bisschen foppen, aber leider habe ich den Hasen offenbar verlegt. Er ist spurlos verschwunden. Tut mir ja echt leid, aber es ist doch wirklich nur ein alter Stoffhase.

Örk. Bei der Vorstellung wird mir ganz schlecht. Dieses Vorgehen würde meine Mutter zweifellos doch noch davon überzeugen, dass Rupes ein mieser Wichser ist, aber ich bezweifle, dass ich dadurch meinen armen kleinen Freund wieder in die Arme schließen könnte.

Außerdem würde ich dann wie das Muttersöhnchen dastehen, für das Rupes mich sowieso schon hält. Da ich noch weitere zehn Tage in seiner Gesellschaft verbringen muss, möchte ich mir die ganzen mentalen und körperlichen Arten der Folter gar nicht ausmalen, die er sich einfallen lassen könnte.

Nicht nur das Leben meines kleinen Freundes, auch mein eigenes könnte auf dem Spiel stehen.

Ups, Tante Helena, das tut mir echt leid. Ich stand auf der Terrasse direkt neben Alex, als er sich einfach ein Stück zu weit über die Brüstung gebeugt hat. Ich habe wirklich noch versucht, ihn festzuhalten, bevor er fünfhundert Meter in den Tod gestürzt ist, aber ich war einfach eine Sekunde zu spät.

Mir läuft es kalt über den Rücken. Werde ich jetzt auch noch paranoid? Rupes mag ja ein Schläger und ein Ekel sein, aber ein Mörder?

Möglich ist das durchaus. Also …

Option 2:

Ich willige in seine Forderung ein.

Ergebnis: Bee ist in Sicherheit, ich bin in Sicherheit, und Rupes darf mit Chloë knutschen.

Vielleicht ist Drittgenanntes schlimmer als meine und Bees Doppelhinrichtung. Zu sagen, dass das Schwert des Damokles über mir schwebt, ist eine absolute Untertreibung.

Jetzt komm, Alex, streng mal deine grauen Zellen an! Das ist doch wirklich der Moment, in dem dein überragendes, Drehmoment-getuntes und mit Spoilern aufgemotztes Gehirn gefragt ist! Diese nervige »Gabe« – »Ach, Alex' Intelligenz ist überragend und abnormal, hebt ihn von allen anderen ab, er ist ein Nerd, ein Streber, ein Ehrgeizling« –, mit der Gott mich gestraft hat.

Nur damit es einmal gesagt sei: Das bin ich alles nicht. Mit Zahlen kann ich nichts anfangen, und Einsteins Relativitätstheorie ist ein serbokroatisches Dorf für mich. Als Serbokroatien noch existierte, was es nicht mehr tut, außer vermutlich in geheimen Höhlen in der Region, die früher einmal Jugoslawien war. Aber nicht mehr ist.

Und schließlich, nachdem ich zwei etwas angeschmolzene Crunchie-Riegel gegessen habe, die ich für Notfälle in meinem Rucksack aufbewahre, nimmt in meinem Überfliegergehirn ein Plan Gestalt an.

Ich weiß, körperlich kann ich Rupes den Ruchlosen nicht bezwingen. Der macht mich mit zwei Fingern platt und hängt mich neben meinem armen kleinen Freund auf. Obwohl dann vermutlich der Ast abbrechen würde.

Aber ich kann einen gemeinen Brief schreiben. In mindestens zwei verschiedenen Sprachen.

Kapitel 12

Nachdem Helena nach Hause gekommen war und Immy und Fred in der Küche bei Angelina und ihren köstlichen frisch gebackenen süßen Brötchen gelassen hatte, machte sie sich auf die Suche nach William. Er war oben im Bad und hatte gerade geduscht. »Wie sieht es aus mit Sacha?«

»Er ist vor rund einer Stunde mit dem Taxi zum Flughafen gefahren, um nach London zurückzufliegen. Morgen früh geht er gleich ins Büro, um Konkurs anzumelden.«

»Was hat Jules gesagt?«

»Ich habe sie nicht gesehen. Laut Angelina war sie gegen Mittag kurz hier und ist dann mit Rupes wieder weggefahren.«

»Wird Sacha sie anrufen?«

»Das hat er schon. Oder vielmehr, er hat ihr auf dem Handy eine Nachricht hinterlassen, dass es Probleme gibt und er wieder nach Hause fliegen muss. Offenbar hat sie ihr Handy immer noch nicht angestellt, zumindest nicht für ihren Mann.« Seufzend trocknete er sich weiter ab. »Sacha geht es gar nicht gut.«

»Das glaube ich sofort. Wie lange wird er wegbleiben?«

»Er will mich morgen Abend anrufen, um mir Bescheid zu geben, wie's aussieht.«

»Aber eigentlich muss er doch so bald wie möglich mit Jules unter vier Augen reden, oder nicht?«

»Der Ansicht bin ich auch, aber was sollen wir machen? Und er hat ja heute Vormittag wirklich versucht, mit ihr zu sprechen, aber sie sagte, sie habe keine Zeit, und ist mit Rupes im Wagen davongebraust.«

»Oje.« Helena seufzte. »Das heißt also, wir müssen so tun, als wäre alles bestens, obwohl wir wissen, dass sie demnächst obdachlos und ohne einen Penny dastehen.«

»Den Anschein hat es, ja.«

»Und was wird Jules sagen, wenn sie herausfindet, dass wir es wussten und sie nicht? Schließlich ist es ihr doch immer so wichtig, alles im Griff zu haben.« Helena drehte die Dusche an und stellte sich unter das lauwarme Rinnsal, das aus der Leitung floss.

William knöpfte sich das Hemd zu. »Wir können nur hoffen, dass er sie morgen anruft, sobald er Konkurs angemeldet und die ganze Prozedur in Gang gesetzt hat. Dann werden sie und die Kinder nach Hause fliegen müssen. Übrigens, Alexis war vorhin da. Er fragte, ob es in Ordnung sei, wenn er kurz mit seiner Großmutter nach Pandora komme. Offenbar ist sie sehr alt und gebrechlich, hat aber wohl früher mal hier gearbeitet.«

»Das stimmt«, sagte Helena, während sie sich einseifte. »Sie war Angus' erste Haushälterin und schon in Pandora, als er es kaufte. Und sie war bei meinem Besuch damals immer noch hier. Angus hat mir einmal erzählt, dass sie und Alexis' Großvater sich bei der Lese auf einem Weinfeld kennengelernt haben.«

»Ich habe sie für sieben Uhr zu einem Glas Wein eingeladen. Ich wollte nicht ablehnen.«

»Danke. Sie kam mir damals schon uralt vor, weiß Gott, wie betagt sie mittlerweile sein muss. Wenn ich so zurückdenke …«, Helena schauderte fast ein wenig bei der Erinnerung daran, »sie ist ein bisschen … merkwürdig. Jetzt sollte ich mich aber beeilen.«

Chloë hatte sich anerboten, die Kleinen zu baden, und als

Helena nach unten kam, kuschelten sie zu dritt auf dem Sofa und sahen sich *Schneewittchen* an.

Helena gab ihrem sauberen, duftenden kleinen Sohn einen Kuss auf die nassen Haare.

»Alles in Ordnung, mein Schatz?«

Fred machte sich gar nicht die Mühe, das Milchfläschchen aus dem Mund zu nehmen, sondern schob es sich einfach wie ein versierter Raucher in den Mundwinkel. »Will *Power Wangers* und keinen Mädchenkram.«

»Morgen darfst du entscheiden, was wir sehen, das haben wir so vereinbart«, sagte Chloë streng.

»Nicht fair.« Und nachdem er diesen Einwand vorgebracht hatte, zwirbelte er sich eine Haarsträhne um den Finger und nuckelte zufrieden weiter.

»Danke, Chloë«, sagte Helena aufrichtig.

»Kein Problem. Ich liebe Disney-Filme. Danach bringe ich die beiden ins Bett.«

»Dann bis später beim Essen.« Helena ging auf die Terrasse, wo Jules am Tisch saß, einen Stapel Hochglanzbroschüren vor sich.

»Und das hier hat den phantastischsten Blick«, sagte sie gerade zu Sadie. »Ich glaube, fast noch schöner als hier. Viertausend Quadratmeter Land, vier Schlafzimmer und einen fabelhaften Zwanzig-Meter-Pool.«

William war hinter Helena getreten, in der Hand ein Tablett mit Gläsern und Wein, und warf ihr einen skeptischen Blick zu. »Möchte jemand ein Glas?«, fragte er und stellte das Tablett auf den Tisch.

»Aber ja«, sagte Jules, als hätte sie nur auf das Angebot gewartet. »Hallo, Helena, Viola sagt, ihr hättet einen schönen Tag am Strand verbracht. Danke, dass ihr sie mitgenommen habt.«

»Der Tag war wirklich schön. Und bei dir?«

Jules grinste. »Ich war auf Haussuche.«

»Ach ja?« Helena gelang es, eisern weiterzulächeln, als William ihr ein Glas reichte.

»Na ja, ich habe vom Erbe meiner Mutter noch etwas Geld, damit kann ich doch hier etwas kaufen, oder nicht? Quasi als Anzahlung, und dann soll Sacha bei einem der Broker, mit denen er sich ständig herumtreibt, eine Hypothek aufnehmen und den Rest bezahlen. Alle unsere Freunde haben im Süden ein Haus gekauft, nur Sacha hat sich immer geweigert. Er sagt, die Instandhaltung sei zu aufwendig. Und deswegen sind wir jahrein, jahraus auf Freunde angewiesen, deren Häuser meistens nicht ganz das Wahre sind. Außerdem mag ich es im Grunde gar nicht, irgendwo zu Gast zu sein.«

Darauf fiel niemandem eine Erwiderung ein, weshalb Jules unbekümmert fortfuhr: »Und deswegen ist es jetzt an der Zeit, dass ich Nägel mit Köpfen mache. Jetzt wird ein Haus gekauft. Prost!«

»Prost!« Die anderen stießen mit ihr an und tranken zur inneren Stärkung einen kräftigen Schluck.

»Der Immobilienmarkt hier floriert, und der Hauskauf läuft relativ ähnlich ab wie in England, vor allem, seit Zypern der EU beigetreten ist und die Gesetze angepasst wurden. Das hat mir heute Nachmittag ein reizender junger Mann erklärt. Wenn man nicht da ist, kümmern sie sich um die Immobilie und vermieten sie auch. Das heißt, man hat ein jährliches Einkommen, dazu die Wertsteigerung – das muss doch eine gute Investition sein, William, meinst du nicht?«

»Ich kenne den Markt hier nicht, Jules. Ich müsste mich erst damit beschäftigen, bevor ich dir eine Antwort geben könnte.«

Jules legte einen Finger an die Nase. »Glaubt mir, bei solchen Sachen habe ich einen guten Riecher. Vergesst nicht, vor

Rupes' Geburt war ich eine erfolgreiche Immobilienmaklerin. Ganz zu schweigen davon, dass unsere Familie endlich bekommt, was sie braucht – ein eigenes Haus in der Wärme, in das wir *unsere* Freunde einladen können.«

»Hast du schon mit Sacha darüber gesprochen?«, brachte William mühsam hervor.

»Nein«, antwortete Jules leichthin. »Ich habe beschlossen, in diesem Urlaub nicht mehr mit Sacha zu rechnen. Wenn er wiederkommen sollte, gibt es für ihn vielleicht etwas zu staunen. Wer weiß?« Sie lachte laut. »Wie auch immer, jetzt hoffe ich, dass ich schön heiß duschen kann. Viola ist mit Rupes im Pool. Ihr habt ein Auge auf sie, ja?«

Nachdem Jules verschwunden war, saßen William, Helena und Sadie benommen am Tisch.

»Sie ist wirklich ganz schön fies«, sagte Sadie nach einer ganzen Weile leise.

»Ich bin mir sicher, dass sie nicht die Hälfte von dem meint, was sie sagt.« Helena erhob sich. »Ich schaue nach dem Abendessen. Unterhaltet euch nur weiter.«

»Sacha ist einer der reizendsten Männer, die ich kenne«, fuhr Sadie fort. »Was in aller Welt hat er an Jules gefunden? Du müsstest das doch wissen, William, du bist sein ältester Freund.«

»Ich muss dir recht geben, Sadie. Auf ein hübsches Gesicht ist er immer schon geflogen, auch an der Uni«, sagte er nachdenklich. »In Oxford war er ständig von einer Schar hinreißender blonder Frauen umgeben. Dann hat er die Uni verlassen, und ungefähr ein Jahr später hat er Jules kennengelernt. Zu der Zeit hat sie bereits als Maklerin gearbeitet. Sie war das Gegenteil seiner früheren Freundinnen: vernünftig, intelligent, mit beiden Beinen fest auf dem Boden.«

»Wenn er jemanden wollte, der ihn an der Hand nimmt und

auf den rechten Weg bringt, hat er eindeutig die richtige Entscheidung getroffen«, meinte Sadie.

»Ich glaube, genau das wollte er. Und in jüngeren Jahren war sie wirklich nett und attraktiv«, erzählte William weiter. »Und sie war schrecklich verliebt in Sacha, sie hätte alles für ihn getan. Als er Oxford verließ und Künstler werden wollte, aber seine Eltern ihm keinen Penny mehr gaben, hat sie ihn finanziert.«

»Irgendetwas muss entsetzlich schiefgelaufen sein, dass sie so verbittert geworden ist«, sagte Sadie.

»Wenn ich mich recht erinnere, fing das ganze Unglück an, als Jules mit Rupes schwanger war und nicht mehr Vollzeit arbeiten konnte. Da musste Sacha eine richtige Arbeit annehmen. Aber ehrlich gesagt hätte er nie ins Finanzgeschäft gehen dürfen. Er konnte ja sein eigenes Geld nicht zusammenhalten, ganz zu schweigen von dem anderer Leute. Sie haben ihm den Job nur gegeben, weil er so charmant war und Verbindungen in die höchsten Kreise hatte.«

»Das ist sicher der Grund, weshalb Jules ihn sich ausgesucht hat. Sie ist sehr auf den sozialen Aufstieg bedacht«, bemerkte Sadie süffisant.

»Das stimmt. Sie hatte hochfliegende Ziele für ihr gemeinsames Leben«, sagte William und nickte. »Und sie war begeistert, als ihm die Stelle in Singapur angeboten wurde. Leider herrscht im Londoner Bankenviertel mittlerweile ein mörderischer Konkurrenzkampf, das Einzige, das zählt, ist Leistung. Die alten Zeiten, als es auf Verbindungen und Seilschaften ankam, sind passé, zum Glück, wie man sagen muss. Jeder steht oder fällt mit seinen Fähigkeiten, und Sacha ist sehr tief gefallen.«

»Meine Güte, was für ein Unglück«, sagte Sadie und drehte sich um, als sich Schritte näherten. »Schau, wer da kommt.«

»*Jia sas.* Ich hoffe, ich störe nicht.«

Hinter ihnen stand Alexis, auf dessen Arm sich eine winzige, verhutzelte Frau stützte, tief gebeugt vom Alter und von der Arthritis und traditionell ganz in Schwarz gekleidet. Helena, die in dem Moment aus der Küche kam, trat auf sie zu und begrüßte sie.

»Christina – es ist wirklich sehr lange her.« Sie küsste die alte Dame auf beide Wangen.

Christina sah zu ihr hoch und legte eine klauenartige Hand um ihre, dabei brummelte sie etwas auf Griechisch. Ihre Stimme war dünn und rau, als bereite das bloße Sprechen ihr Mühe. Ihre Augen wanderten zum Haus, und sie lächelte, wobei sie zwei lückenhafte Reihen schwarzer Zähne entblößte. Dann hob sie zitternd die Hand und flüsterte Alexis etwas zu.

»Sie fragt, ob du etwas dagegen hättest, mit ihr ins Haus zu gehen, Helena«, übersetzte er.

»Natürlich nicht. William, könntest du bitte kurz nachsehen, ob Chloë die Kleinen schon ins Bett gebracht hat?« Helena wollte vermeiden, dass Immy und Fred die alte Dame so kurz vorm Schlafengehen sahen, zumal diese mehr als nur eine flüchtige Ähnlichkeit mit der Hexe aus dem Film hatte, den sie gerade gesehen hatten.

»Natürlich.« William, der sofort verstand, worum es Helena ging, verschwand im Haus.

»Ich hole Viola aus dem Wasser«, sagte Sadie und stand auf. »Sie muss mittlerweile völlig aufgeweicht sein.«

Alexis und Helena stützten Christina auf ihrem langsamen Weg über die Terrasse zum Salon.

»Wie krank ist sie denn?«, fragte Helena leise.

»Sie sagt, dass sie keine Lust mehr zu leben hat und dass ihre Zeit auf Erden um ist. Also wird sie bald sterben«, antwortete Alexis ruhig.

Sie gingen in den Salon, aus dem die Kinder mittlerweile verschwunden waren. Helena deutete auf einen Ohrensessel. »Ich glaube, das ist der bequemste Platz für sie.«

Sie und Alexis halfen Christina, sich im Sessel niederzulassen, und setzten sich rechts und links von ihr. Die Augen der alten Dame schossen durch den Raum, und Helena sah die Wachheit in ihnen, die den gebrechlichen Körper der alten Frau Lügen strafte.

Ihr Blick blieb auf Helena ruhen, und sie starrte ihre Gastgeberin unverwandt an, bis diese zur Seite sah. Dann sprach sie auf Griechisch schnell auf Alexis ein.

»Sie sagt, dass du sehr schön bist«, dolmetschte er, »und dass du sie sehr an eine Frau erinnerst, die früher häufig hier zu Gast war.«

»Ach, wirklich?«, sagte Helena. »Das hat mir jemand anderes vor ein paar Tagen auch schon gesagt. Wer war diese Frau? Kannst du sie fragen?«

Abwehrend hob Alexis eine Hand und richtete seine ganze Aufmerksamkeit auf das, was seine Großmutter gerade sagte.

»Sie sagt, dass hier ein Geheimnis verwahrt wird und …« Alexis brach ab und schaute auf seine Hände.

»Und was?«, fragte Helena.

»Dass du es hütest«, sagte er betreten.

Helenas Herz schlug heftig gegen ihre Rippen. »Jeder hat Geheimnisse, Alexis«, erwiderte sie leise, doch er hörte ihr gar nicht zu, sondern starrte auf seine Großmutter, und je länger sie sprach, desto besorgter wurde sein Blick. Dann sagte er etwas zu ihr, doch sie redete unentwegt weiter, so heftig er den Kopf auch schüttelte. Plötzlich schien alle Energie der alten Dame verbraucht, sie sank schweigend in den Sessel zurück und schloss die Augen.

Mit einem blütenweißen Taschentuch fuhr Alexis sich über die Stirn. »Ich entschuldige mich, Helena. Sie ist eine alte Frau, ich hätte sie nicht herbringen dürfen.« Und zu Christina sagte er liebevoll: »Komm, jetzt gehen wir nach Hause.«

»Bitte, Alexis, erzähl mir doch, was sie gesagt hat.«

»Nichts, gar nichts. Das Gefasel einer alten Frau«, beruhigte Alexis sie, während er Christina zur Terrassentür führte, wobei er sie halb tragen musste. »Achte nicht darauf. Es tut mir leid, dass ich deinen Abend gestört habe. *Antio*, Helena.«

Helena sah ihnen nach und musste plötzlich Halt suchend den Türrahmen umklammern. Ihr war, als würde sie gleich ohnmächtig werden, sie bekam keine Luft, ihr war übel …

»Mein Liebling, alles in Ordnung?« Ein starker Arm packte sie um die Taille.

»Ja, ich …«

»Komm und setz dich. Ich bringe dir ein Glas Wasser.«

William führte sie zum Sofa und eilte dann in die Küche. Helena rang um Fassung. Angus hatte schon damals gesagt, dass Christina verrückt sei. Als hervorragende Haushälterin hatte er sich mit ihren Marotten abgefunden, und auch deswegen, weil sie kein Englisch sprach und deshalb keinen Klatsch weitertragen konnte.

William kehrte mit einem Glas Wasser zurück und nahm ihre Hand. »Die ist ja eiskalt, Helena.« Er fasste prüfend an ihre Stirn. »Bist du krank?«

»Nein, nein … Gleich geht es mir wieder besser.« Helena trank einen Schluck Wasser.

»Was hat sie denn gesagt, das dich derart aus der Fassung gebracht hat?«

»Eigentlich gar nichts. Ich glaube, ich bin einfach …«

»Erschöpft.«

»Ja. In ein paar Minuten ist alles wieder gut. Es geht mir ja jetzt schon besser, wirklich.« Sie stand auf. Doch die Beine gaben unter ihr nach, sie griff nach Williams Arm.

»So, jetzt reicht's. Ich bringe dich nach oben, und du legst dich ins Bett. Und ich will keine Widerrede hören.«

Als wäre sie leicht wie eine Feder, hob er sie in die Arme und ging mit ihr zur Treppe.

»Aber was ist mit dem Abendessen? Ich muss doch nach der Moussaka …«

»Ich sagte, keine Widerrede. Und für den Fall, dass du es noch nicht weißt, ich bin durchaus in der Lage, ein Essen auf den Tisch zu stellen. Und ich habe eine ganze Schar williger Helfer, die mir verdammt noch mal zur Hand gehen können.« Sacht legte William sie aufs Bett. »Bitte glaub mir, mein Schatz, wenigstens dieses eine Mal. Pandora kann ein paar Stunden ohne dich auskommen. Du brauchst Ruhe.«

»Danke, Schatz.« Sie fühlte sich immer noch entsetzlich schwach und matt.

»Helena, du bist wirklich sehr blass. Bist du sicher, dass dir nichts fehlt?«

»Ja. Ich bin bloß müde, das ist alles.«

»Weißt du«, sagte er und küsste sie zärtlich auf die Stirn, »wenn es etwas gibt, was immer es ist – ich kann damit umgehen. Bitte glaub mir das.«

»Morgen geht es mir bestimmt besser. Aber bitte sag den Kindern nichts, ja? Du weißt doch, wie panisch Alex wird, wenn ich nicht hundertprozentig auf dem Damm bin.«

»Ich sage ihnen, dass du früh ins Bett gehen wolltest. Das ist nämlich durchaus erlaubt.« Mit einem Lächeln stand er auf. »Und jetzt versuch zu schlafen.«

»Das mache ich.«

Langsam verließ William den Raum und ging zur Treppe. Sosehr Helena es auch leugnen mochte, die alte Frau hatte etwas gesagt, das sie verstörte. Er wünschte sich nur, dass sie sich ihm endlich anvertrauen würde.

Und dass sie Geheimnisse hütete, war nicht zu leugnen – allein schon die Identität von Alex' Vater. Und angesichts von Helenas innerer Anspannung und Alexis' ständigen Besuchen in Pandora brauchte man keinen Doktortitel, um zwei und zwei zusammenzuzählen …

Das würde bedeuten, dass seine Frau gelogen hatte, denn sie hatte geschworen, dass sie ihn seit ihrem Aufenthalt hier vor vierundzwanzig Jahren nie mehr gesehen hatte.

Hier, in Pandora, prallte Helenas Vergangenheit mit ihrer Gegenwart aufeinander – und auch mit seiner. Sicher hatte er dann doch das Recht, das zu erfahren?

Im Moment würde er sie in Ruhe lassen, doch während William nachdenklich die Stufen hinunterging, schwor er sich, Pandora nicht eher zu verlassen, bis er die Wahrheit kannte.

Alex' Tagebuch

Tja.

Das war ein richtig toller Abend.

Dantes Inferno ohne die ganze Aufregung des Infernos. Alle saßen am Tisch mit einer Miene, als würden gleich ihre Genitalien auf dem Grill landen. Also gut, wir haben Dads Chicken Wings gegessen (er hatte vergessen, die Moussaka aus dem Ofen zu nehmen, die zu einem Kohleklumpen verbrannt war, und musste auf die eine Zubereitungsart zurückgreifen, die ihm zu Gebote steht), aber so schlecht waren sie gar nicht, nur etwas angekokelt.

Es passiert nicht häufig, dass ich mir wie der Partylöwe vorkomme, aber heute Abend war das der Fall, was wohl Bände spricht über die Stimmung am Tisch. Ich könnte sagen, dass es Jules' Schuld war, weil sie ständig über ihren abwesenden Mann herzog und ihn als Trottel beschimpfte, was Viola unglücklich machte, oder Rupes' Schuld mit seinem Schmollen, weil Chloë mit einem Typen losgezogen ist, den sie am Flughafen kennengelernt hat. Oder Sadies Schuld, der wieder mal ihr Ex zu schaffen machte, sodass sie die ganzen schmutzigen Details vor uns ausbreitete. Oder Dads, der, als er das verkokelte Mahl aufgab, ein Gesicht wie Gevatter Tod machte.

Ich könnte jeden dieser Gründe zur Erklärung der bleiernen Schwere anführen, die über uns hing wie die

Rauchschwaden vom Grillen, doch sie entsprächen alle nicht der Wahrheit.

Es war, weil Mum nicht da war.

Sie ist der leibhaftige Superkleber. Unsichtbar hält sie den ganzen Laden hier zusammen.

Das merkt man aber erst, wenn sie nicht da ist und alles auseinanderbröselt.

Vorher hatte ich nach ihr gesehen. Ich war zu ihr gegangen, sobald Dad sagte, sie habe »sich hingelegt«.

»Sich hinlegen« ist ein herablassender Euphemismus, den Erwachsene ihren Kindern gegenüber verwenden, die das kommentarlos zu akzeptieren haben.

Mütter werden nicht »müde«. Das fällt nicht in ihren Aufgabenbereich. Sie rackern, bis sie kaputt ins Bett fallen, und das bitte erst nach dem Abwasch.

Meiner Erfahrung nach bedeutet »sich hinlegen« also nicht, dass meine Mutter müde ist. Vielmehr kann das alles heißen, von zu viel Gin Tonic bis hin zu Krebs im Endstadium.

Ich habe sie genau beobachtet und als ich sie umarmte auch ihren Atem gerochen – an den Nachwehen eines Gelages litt sie eindeutig nicht. Und was Krebs im Endstadium betrifft, so ist das vermutlich eine Möglichkeit, aber da ich heute mit ihr am Meer war und sie geschwommen ist und mit uns herumgealbert hat und fit wie ein Turnschuh aussah, müsste das Endstadium mit schier affenartiger Geschwindigkeit über sie hereingebrochen sein.

Vielleicht war sie unter ihrer Sonnenbräune etwas blass – obwohl ich mich immer gefragt habe, wie in aller Welt man Blässe erkennen soll, wenn jemand gebräunt ist? Eine lächerliche, überflüssige Floskel, genau wie »Probieren geht über studieren«. Was denn probieren? Und wenn man es probiert, und dann ist es Arsen, bleibt einem keine Zeit mehr, irgendetwas zu studieren.

Ich schweife ab. Mein Instinkt sagt mir, dass meine Mutter nicht in Kürze das Zeitliche segnen wird, also muss ich den Schluss ziehen, dass es etwas mit dieser seltsamen Nonne zu tun hat, die mit Mr. Hansdampf herkam und etwas sagte, das sie verstört hat.

Der Mann ist ein einziges Ärgernis. Ich wünschte, er würde uns endlich in Ruhe lassen, aber nein, bei der kleinsten Gelegenheit steht er schon wieder auf der Matte. An Dads Stelle würde ich mittlerweile ziemlich fuchtig werden. Denn was er will, ist klar.

Aber das ist nicht zu haben.

KAPITEL 13

Um Mitternacht hatte Helena kapituliert und eine halbe Schlaftablette genommen. In ihrem Kulturbeutel steckten zwei für Notfälle, und das seit drei Jahren, als der Arzt ihr kurz nach Freds Geburt das Mittel verschrieben hatte.

Und vergangene Nacht war wirklich ein Notfall gewesen. Sie hatte oben gelegen und gehört, wie ihre Familie unten auf der Terrasse aß, und war sich wie ein gefangenes Tier vorgekommen. Gefangen in ihren eigenen Gedanken, die ihr unerbittlich durch den Kopf kreisten.

Als sie William die Treppe heraufkommen hörte, hatte sie die Tablette genommen und dann getan, als wäre sie nicht mehr wach. Und schließlich war sie tatsächlich in seligen Schlaf gefallen.

Beim Aufwachen flutete helles Morgenlicht ins Zimmer und nicht wie sonst die graue Morgendämmerung. Angesichts ihrer Freude darüber verstand sie, wie schnell man süchtig werden konnte. Sie streckte sich und spürte, dass ihre Muskeln bei diesem Schnellstart nur mühsam mithalten konnten. Sie sah auf die Uhr: halb zehn. So lange hatte sie seit Jahren nicht mehr geschlafen.

Auf dem Nachttisch stand eine Tasse Tee, und daran lehnte ein Zettel.

Schatz,
hoffentlich geht es dir etwas besser. Ich schaffe alle aus dem Haus,

damit du ein bisschen Ruhe hast. Mach das Beste draus, und KEINE
HAUSARBEIT! Bis später, W.

Lächelnd faltete sie den Zettel zusammen, doch im selben Moment fiel ihr ein, was die alte Frau am vergangenen Abend zu ihr gesagt hatte. »O mein Gott«, flüsterte sie und ließ sich wieder ins Kissen sinken.

Die Stille war ohrenbetäubend. Keine Schreie, kein Kichern, kein gedämpfter Disney-Soundtrack trieb durchs Haus. Durstig griff sie nach dem Tee und nahm einen Schluck. Er war nur noch lauwarm.

William machte ihr jeden Morgen eine Tasse Tee. Auch wenn er den Wäschetrockner ebenso wenig bedienen konnte wie die Steuerung eines Raumschiffs und im Fernsehen Cricket sah und nebenbei auf die Kinder aufpasste anstatt umgekehrt, zeigte er ihr auf hundert Arten seine Fürsorge.

Weil er sie liebte. Vor zehn Jahren war er in ihr Leben getreten und hatte sie gerettet. Bei dem Gedanken wurde Helena ganz elend zumute. Wenn er die Wahrheit erführe, würde er ihr nie verzeihen. Und sie würde ihn und die wunderbare Familie, die sie gemeinsam gegründet hatten, verlieren.

Im Lauf der Jahre hatte es immer wieder Phasen gegeben, in denen Helena monatelang nicht daran gedacht hatte. Aber am vergangenen Abend hatte sie das Gefühl gehabt, als würde die alte Christina in ihre Seele blicken und erkennen, was dort lag. Als würde das Verborgene langsam an die Oberfläche steigen. Helena biss sich auf die Unterlippe, Tränen brannten ihr in den Augen.

Was sollte sie tun? Was *konnte* sie tun?

»Als Allererstes aufstehen«, sagte sie sich. Sie spürte, dass sich Selbstmitleid in ihr breitmachen wollte, und das konnte sie nicht leiden. Ihre Familie brauchte sie, sie musste sich zusammenreißen.

Sie beschloss, ihre üblichen halbstündigen Gymnastikübungen durch zwanzig Bahnen im Pool zu ersetzen, die sie nicht nur erfrischen, sondern vielleicht auch die Nachwirkungen der Schlaftablette vertreiben würden. Also zog sie sich den Bikini an und ging nach unten. Angelina beseitigte in der Küche gerade die Spuren des vergangenen Abends.

»Es tut mir leid, hier herrscht das reine Chaos.«

»Nein, dafür ich werde bezahlt«, sagte Angelina und lächelte. »Das ist meine Arbeit. Ihr Mann sagt, Sie müssen sich heute ausruhen. Ich bin Boss, hockay?«, fügte sie hinzu.

»Danke.«

Helena ging zum Pool, und beim Schwimmen erwachten langsam ihre Lebensgeister. Die gleichmäßigen Bewegungen beruhigten sie. Hinterher ging sie nach oben, duschte und bemerkte dann den Umschlag mit den alten Briefen, den Alex ihr am Vorabend auf den Nachttisch gelegt hatte.

Damit kehrte sie zum Pool zurück, ließ sich auf einer Liege nieder und zog einen Brief heraus.

20. April

Meine über alles Geliebte,
ich sitze auf der Terrasse, blicke über den Olivenhain hinaus und denke daran, wie du das letzte Mal hier bei mir warst. Zwar ist seitdem keine Woche vergangen, doch mir erscheint es wie eine Ewigkeit.

Ich weiß nicht, wann ich dich wiedersehen werde, und das macht unsere Trennung umso schrecklicher.

Ich habe ernsthaft in Erwägung gezogen, nach England zurückzukehren, aber bekäme ich dich dann wirklich häufiger zu sehen? Ich weiß, dass dein Leben dich oft in die Welt hinausführt, und hier füllt zumindest meine Arbeit die Leere zwischen deinen Besuchen.

Abgesehen davon missbehagt mir die Vorstellung, im grauen London zu leben und in einem Büro der Admiralität Unterlagen über den Schreibtisch zu schieben. Hier hilft mir die strahlende Sonne, die finsteren Momente zu überwinden, wenn ich mir eingestehen muss, dass das, was ich über alles liebe, nie das Meine sein kann.

Mein Liebling, du weißt, ich würde alles darum geben, um mit dir zusammen zu sein. Ich habe Geld. Wir könnten an einen Ort gehen, wo uns niemand kennt, und ein neues Leben beginnen.

Natürlich weiß und verstehe ich, dass es triftige Gründe gibt, weshalb du nicht hier in meinen Armen bist, aber bisweilen frage ich mich doch, ob du mich wirklich so liebst, wie ich dich liebe. Sonst …

Verzeih, aber gelegentlich werde ich vom Kummer überwältigt, dann folgen die dunkelsten Stunden. Ohne dich kommt mir das Leben vor wie ein langer, schleppender Gang nach Golgatha. Meine Geliebte, verzeih meine Trauer. Wie gern würde ich von dem Glück schreiben, das unser wäre, wäre nur das Leben ein anderes.

Ich warte mit gewohnter Ungeduld auf deinen nächsten Brief.

Und schenke dir mit diesen Zeilen mein Herz, das voller Liebe ist.

A.

Während Helena den Brief zusammenfaltete und wieder in das Kuvert steckte, spürte sie den Klumpen, der wie ein Apfelstückchen in ihrer Kehle festsaß. Sie konnte kaum glauben, dass ihr Patenonkel, der immer einen so nüchternen und beherrschten Eindruck auf sie gemacht hatte, einen derart leidenschaftlichen Brief schreiben konnte. Aus irgendeinem Grund rührte es sie, dass selbst er dem fundamentalsten und unbezähmbarsten Gefühl erlegen war: der Liebe.

»Wer war sie?«, fragte sie sich laut. Dann drehte sie sich auf den Bauch und sah zum Haus.

Pandora wusste es.

Zwei Stunden später ging Helena ins Haus, wo Angelina einen Salat mit Ziegenkäse für sie vorbereitet und auf den Tisch gestellt hatte. Mit einem Glas Wasser dazu ging sie auf die Terrasse hinaus. Eine durchschlafene Nacht und der seltene Luxus eines stillen Vormittags hatten ihre innere Unruhe etwas gemildert, auch wenn sie einer Lösung ihres Problems um keinen Deut näher gekommen war.

Außerdem hatte sie es tröstlich gefunden, die übrigen Briefe von Angus zu lesen und nach Hinweisen auf die unbekannte Geliebte zu suchen. Das Leben eines jeden Menschen barg einen dunklen Fleck, gleichgültig, wie er sich der Außenwelt darstellte, und der Zufall stiftete bei jedermann irgendwann einmal Chaos. Das Gefühl, dem Schicksal hilflos wie ein Blatt im Wind ausgeliefert zu sein, das sie in ihrer Jugend so oft befallen hatte, war vermutlich weit allgemeiner verbreitet, als sie glaubte. Angus' Briefe führten ihr vor Augen, dass er trotz seiner einflussreichen Position, in der er für Hunderte von Männern und bisweilen auch ihr Leben verantwortlich gewesen war, sein Schicksal ebenso wenig in der Hand gehabt hatte wie sie, Helena.

Unabhängig von der Identität dieser Frau – die wohl verheiratet gewesen war, wie Helena vermutete – war es traurig, dass Angus seine letzten Jahre allein verbracht hatte. Außerdem waren die Briefe, der knappen beiliegenden Nachricht nach zu urteilen, ja an ihn zurückgeschickt worden. Vielleicht, ging ihr durch den Kopf, vom Ehemann dieser Unbekannten …

Helena fragte sich, ob es nicht doch ein Fehler gewesen war herzukommen. Bei ihrem letzten Besuch hatte Pandora ihr Leben verändert und eine Abfolge von Ereignissen in Gang gesetzt, die ihr ganzes weiteres Schicksal bestimmten und die sie schließlich dahin geführt hatten, wo sie jetzt war. Ein Gefühl überkam sie, als würden sich unsichtbare Schlangen zu einem Kreis um sie schließen, aus dem es kein Entrinnen gab.

»Ich hätte es ihm vor Jahren sagen müssen«, flüsterte sie. Wieder stiegen ihr Tränen in die Augen. »Ich hätte auf seine Liebe vertrauen sollen.«

Eine Weile später schlenderte sie zur Hängematte am Pool hinunter, legte sich hinein, döste ein wenig und genoss die himmlische Ruhe. Als sie Schritte hörte, öffnete sie die Augen und sah Alexis über die Terrasse auf sich zukommen.

Sie rollte sich aus der Hängematte und ging ihm entgegen.

»Guten Tag.«

»Guten Tag, Helena.«

»Ich wollte mir gerade eine Tasse Tee machen. Möchtest du auch eine?«, fragte sie und ging an ihm vorbei die Treppe hinauf.

»Wo sind alle?«

»Ich weiß es nicht, aber auf jeden Fall nicht hier«, erklärte sie, als sie gemeinsam über die Terrasse zum Haus gingen. »William war der Ansicht, dass ich mich erholen muss, also macht er mit dem Rest der Familie einen Ausflug.« Helena schaute auf ihre Uhr. »Es ist fast vier, sie werden sicher bald zurückkommen.«

Während Helena den Kessel aufsetzte, sagte Alexis: »Dein Mann ist ein guter Mann.«

»Ich weiß.«

»Helena, ich bin gekommen, um mich für meine Großmutter zu entschuldigen. Sie ist verrückt, ihre Worte haben nichts zu bedeuten.«

»Das mag sein, aber sie hat trotzdem recht.« Helena drehte sich zu ihm und seufzte resigniert, dann lächelte sie matt. »Alexis, es gibt zu viele Geheimnisse. Wahrscheinlich ist die Zeit gekommen, dass ich einen Anfang mache und dir die Wahrheit sage.« Sie füllte das kochende Wasser in die Teekanne und rührte um. »Komm, setzen wir uns auf die Terrasse. Ich muss dir etwas erzählen.«

Entgeistert sah er sie an, er hielt die Tasse noch auf halbem Weg zwischen Tisch und Mund.

»Helena, warum hast du mir das nicht gesagt? Du weißt doch, ich wäre für dich da gewesen.«

»Du hättest nichts tun können, Alexis.«

»Ich hätte dich geheiratet.«

»Alexis, die Wahrheit ist, dass ich erst im September des Jahres sechzehn wurde. Du hättest sogar wegen der Beziehung mit einer Minderjährigen angezeigt werden können. Und das wäre meine Schuld gewesen, weil ich dich angelogen und mich für älter ausgegeben hatte, als ich war. Weißt du nicht mehr, ich sagte dir, ich sei siebzehn. Alexis, es tut mir sehr leid.«

»Helena, ob du mir dein wahres Alter gesagt hättest oder nicht, ich hätte dich so oder so geliebt. Dass du jünger warst, macht alles nur noch schlimmer, und zwar für dich, nicht für mich.«

»Der Sommer hier hat auf jeden Fall mein weiteres Leben bestimmt. Ist es nicht erstaunlich, wie sehr jede unserer Entscheidungen die nächste beeinflusst?«, fragte Helena nachdenklich. »Das Leben ist wie eine Reihe von Dominosteinen, wenn der erste umgestoßen wird, fallen die anderen nacheinander wie von selbst. Manche behaupten, man könnte sich von seiner Vergangenheit lösen, aber das stimmt nicht. Sie ist Teil der Person, die man ist und die man in Zukunft sein wird.«

»Du sagst, dass der Sommer dein weiteres Leben bestimmt hat. Aber meines auch. Denn keine Frau konnte es je mit dir aufnehmen, Helena«, gestand er bekümmert. »Aber jetzt weiß ich wenigstens, weshalb ich nie mehr von dir gehört habe, nachdem du vor all den Jahren nach England zurückgereist warst. Ich dachte …« Seine Stimme war belegt, die Gefühle drohten ihn zu überwältigen. »Ich dachte, du würdest mich nicht mehr lieben.«

»Natürlich habe ich dich geliebt!« Helena rang die Hände. »Ich dachte, ich würde sterben, als ich den Kontakt zu dir so abrupt abbrach. Aber ich wollte dich nicht in die Enge treiben, ich wollte dir den Schmerz nicht zumuten, diese Entscheidung treffen zu müssen. Ich hatte dir gesagt, ich sei dafür zuständig, aber das war ich nicht, ich hatte ja von nichts eine Ahnung! Ich war so naiv. Ich … es war unsagbar schrecklich, ich …«

»Hättest du es mir gesagt, dann wäre ich für dich da gewesen, das weißt du doch. Aber du hast es mir nicht gesagt, also kann ich jetzt nur noch mit deinem Schmerz mitfühlen und über die Folgen traurig sein«, sagte Alexis einfühlsam.

»Wenigstens hast du später geheiratet und zwei großartige Söhne bekommen.«

»Ja. Meine Frau war ein guter Mensch, und ich danke dem lieben Gott jeden Tag für die Söhne, die sie mir geschenkt hat. Aber es war natürlich ein Kompromiss. Ich konnte für sie nie die gleichen Gefühle aufbringen wie für dich.«

»Aber das Leben ist ein einziger Kompromiss, Alexis. Genau das lernen wir doch erst im Lauf der Jahre.« Sie zuckte mit den Achseln. »Und jetzt sind wir beide reifer geworden.«

»Du siehst keinen Tag älter aus als damals.«

»Das ist lieb von dir, aber es stimmt nicht.«

»Hast du William davon erzählt?«, fragte er.

»Nein. Ich habe mich immer zu sehr geschämt.«

»Nachdem du es jetzt mir gesagt hast, solltest du es ihm vielleicht auch sagen. Er ist dein Mann, und ich sehe doch, dass er dich liebt. Er wird es bestimmt verstehen.«

»Alexis, es gibt viele Dinge, die ich William nie erzählt habe, viele Geheimnisse, die ich für mich behalte, um uns alle zu schützen.« Trotz der Hitze fröstelte Helena.

»Du kannst mir alles erzählen, ich würde deswegen nie schlecht von dir denken. Weil die Liebe, die damals war … sie ist heute noch da.«

Helena blickte zu ihm und sah die Tränen in seinen Augen. Hilflos schüttelte sie den Kopf. »Nein, Alexis, ich bin nicht mehr das unschuldige junge Mädchen von damals. Ich habe ein Netz aus Lügen gewoben, das uns alle umfasst. Ich habe mit sechzehn unser Kind getötet. Du kannst dir gar nicht vorstellen, wie oft ich mir seitdem gewünscht habe, ich hätte mich damals einfach dem Schicksal gefügt und wäre hergekommen, hätte hier gelebt und dich geheiratet. Das werde ich mir nie verzeihen, wirklich nie.«

»Helena, ach Helena …« Alexis stand auf und zog sie tröstend in die Arme. »Bitte, du darfst dir keine Vorwürfe machen. Du warst so jung, und du hast dich entschieden, die schwere Last allein zu tragen. Das ist traurig, aber solche Dinge passieren nun mal. Du bist nicht die einzige Frau, die diese furchtbare Entscheidung gefällt hat.«

»Was kümmern mich andere Frauen! Wann immer ich meine Kinder ansehe, denke ich an das, das fehlt. Ich sehe den leeren Stuhl …«

Helena weinte an seiner Schulter, während er ihr übers Haar strich und auf Griechisch Zärtlichkeiten flüsterte.

»Mummy! Mummy! Wir sind wieder da! Geht es dir besser?

Daddy hat gesagt, wenn es dir besser geht, fahren wir heute Abend ins Dorf und bekommen Pommes und Ketchup! Es geht dir doch besser, oder? Hallo, Alexis.«

Helena löste sich aus Alexis' Umarmung, drehte sich langsam um und sah William hinter Immy stehen.

»Hallo, Schatz«, sagte er kühl.

»Ooooh, Mummy, du siehst ja nicht besser aus. Deine Augen sind ganz rot und klein. Daddy, ich glaube nicht, dass es Mummy besser geht, aber ein paar Pommes würden ihr bestimmt helfen«, plapperte Immy unbeeindruckt von der angespannten Atmosphäre weiter.

»Ich lasse euch allein. Auf Wiedersehen, Helena. Auf Wiedersehen, William.« Alexis ging über die Terrasse, vorbei an William, der ihn demonstrativ ignorierte.

»Einen ruhigen Nachmittag gehabt?« Seine Stimme troff vor Sarkasmus.

»Ja, danke. Wo wart ihr denn?«, fragte sie und rang verzweifelt um Fassung.

»Am Strand.«

»An welchem denn?«

»Coral Bay. Ich gehe jetzt zum Pool, um eine Runde zu schwimmen.« Er wandte sich ab.

»Ja, ich kümmere mich um die Kinder, und … William?«

»Ja?«

»Danke, dass du mir Zeit für mich gegeben hast.«

»Wie ich sehe, hast du sie gut zu nutzen verstanden.«

»William?« Sie trat auf ihn zu. »Können wir reden?«

Abwehrend hob er die Hand. »Nicht jetzt, Helena. Bitte. Ja?«

Als Helena ihm nachsah, wie er die Treppe zum Pool hinunter verschwand, wurde ihr unendlich schwer ums Herz.

Alex' Tagebuch

Uff!

Was ist in den vergangenen vierundzwanzig Stunden in diesem Haus bloß passiert? Ich wünschte, jemand würde mich mal aufklären, was vor sich geht. Irgendetwas ist hier nicht ganz koscher.

Heute Abend war Dad an der Reihe, ein Gesicht zu machen, als hätte er im Lokal keine Pommes, sondern eine Schlange verschluckt, die seitdem an seinen Eingeweiden herumfrisst und Gift durch seine Adern jagt. Ich weiß nicht, wie das mit Mums Kranksein war, aber Dad sieht wirklich schlecht aus.

Mum machte wacker einen auf »alles ist bestens, Kinder, ist es nicht schön hier?«, worauf vermutlich alle hereinfielen, nur ich nicht.

Und obwohl ich mich riesig freue, weil Rupes die beleidigte Leberwurst spielt, nachdem sich Chloë in allen schillernden Details über ihre Fummelei mit dem Flughafentypen gestern Abend ausließ (auch wenn mich das ebenfalls an den Rand des Selbstmords treibt), ist definitiv nicht zu leugnen, dass irgendetwas in diesem Haus ernsthaft aus dem Ruder gelaufen ist.

Dad ging dermaßen in seinem Unglück auf, dass er nicht einmal Einspruch erhob, als Chloë sagte, sie werde sich heute Abend wieder mit dem Flughafentypen treffen. Oder als Fred sich und den Tisch mit Schokoladeneis beschmierte und einen Wutanfall bekam, als ihm weitere Malaktionen verboten wurden.

Außerdem hat Dad sehr viel mehr getrunken als sonst. Und Mum auch, wenn ich so drüber nachdenke. Normalerweise trinkt sie kaum, aber heute Abend gleich drei Gläser. Und dann stand Dad auf und sagte, er wolle Fred und Immy heimfahren und ins Bett bringen, und ging wortlos davon. Und ließ Mum, Sadie, Schreckens-Jules, Beleidigte Leberwurst und die süße kleine Viola zurück.

Apropos, Viola ist wirklich nett. Für eine Zehneinhalbjährige ist sie erstaunlich belesen, auch wenn es bei ihren Lieblingsbüchern offenbar viel um Tangas und Knutschen geht. Aber ich hoffe, sie überzeugt zu haben, ihre Lektüre auf *Jane Eyre* auszudehnen, von dem in der Bibliothek meiner Besenkammer eine sehr schöne Ausgabe steht. Ich glaube, das Buch passt zu ihr. Sie ist ja auch ein verlorenes Seelchen.

Aber ich schweife ab. Bald nachdem Dad gegangen war, wurde das Gespräch noch angespannter. Jules redete nonstop von dem Haus, das sie kaufen will, ohne je den Umstand zu erwähnen, dass sie einen Ehemann hat und dieser gegenwärtig auf Tauchstation ist.

Ich konnte Sacha eigentlich immer schon gut leiden. Auch wenn er Alkoholiker ist und eine mehr als nur flüchtige Ähnlichkeit mit Oscar Wilde hat (und allem, was daraus folgt), und obwohl jeder in seiner und meiner Familie (außer Viola) seufzend die Augenbrauen hebt, wenn sie von ihm sprechen, als wäre er ein ungezogenes Kind, dem man alles nachsieht – trotz all dem ist er eindeutig intelligent. Und unter dem Nadelstreifenanzug ein Exzentriker, der es gar nicht erwarten kann, endlich mal ordentlich auf den Putz zu hauen.

Möge Gott zu verhindern wissen, dass mir Finanzen zum Schicksal bestimmt sind. So schnell könnte niemand gucken, wie ich die Bank of England gesprengt hätte.

Aber zurück zu heute. Wir waren kaum vom Strand zurück, ich habe gerade die nassen Handtücher aus dem Kofferraum geholt, als Mr. Hansdampf mit säuerlicher Miene an mir vorbeirauschte.

Offenbar hat er Mum besucht, während wir beim Baden waren.

Im hintersten Winkel meines Gehirns regt sich ein grauenhafter Verdacht, aber ich weigere mich, ihn zur Kenntnis zu nehmen. Dann wäre er real, und das darf einfach nicht sein.

Unmöglich.

Stattdessen verwende ich meine nicht unbeträchtliche Intelligenz auf mein ureigenes Problem: die erfolgreiche Rettung meines Hasen.

Der Brief ist fertig. Ich weiß, ich gehe damit ein Risiko ein, aber wie bei allen Unternehmungen dieser Art gilt das Motto: Wer nicht wagt, der nicht gewinnt.

Ich lese mir den Brief noch mal vor und gestatte mir, bei den besonders klugen Stellen zu lachen. Colette gepaart mit Schweinchen Schlau gepaart mit Alex dem Großen.

Das alles auf Französisch.

Ohne dass Rupes es gemerkt hat, habe ich seine Sprachkenntnisse abgefragt. Er kann nicht einmal bis *cinq* zählen, ohne sich zu verhaspeln. Im Gegensatz zu Chloë, die ja eine halbe Französin ist.

Sie wird das verstehen.

Ich habe einen Zettel unter seine Tür gesteckt mit der Nachricht, dass der Brief zur Übergabe bereit ist, und zwar morgen früh um acht am Pool. Ich weiß, dass bei Geiselnahmen vor allem die Übergabe grausam scheitern kann, also habe ich ihm mitgeteilt, er soll den Hasen vor sich auf den Boden legen, damit ich ihn sehen kann, und erst dann händige ich ihm den Brief aus.

Er wird ihn lesen, und die französischen Wörter werden ihm nichts sagen, also wird er zufrieden sein.

Nur für den Fall der Fälle verstecke ich Immy zwischen den Bäumen und trage ihr auf, Zeter und Mordio zu schreien, sobald mein Gegner eine falsche Bewegung macht. Etwa, wenn er den Brief an sich nimmt und dann auf hinterlistige Art den Hasen zurückerobert.

Sie zu bestechen hat mich ein Vermögen an Süßigkeiten gekostet, aber was soll's, solange es funktioniert? Dann wird mein bester und ältester Freund für die Dauer von Rupes' Aufenthalt sein Dasein in der Hundehütte fristen müssen, die ich hinten im Gartenhaus entdeckt habe.

Ich ziehe mir den Zwickel über den Kopf und schalte das Licht aus. Dann mache ich die Augen zu, aber ich kann einfach nicht einschlafen. Wenn ich an meinen morgigen Rettungseinsatz denke, rast mir das Adrenalin durch die Adern, aber auch wenn ich an etwas anderes denke.

Ist es möglich? O Gott, bitte nicht. Ich würde sogar – schluck – Bee opfern, damit es nicht so ist.

Mum kann doch nicht *ihn* lieben.

Das ... das kann einfach nicht sein.

»Da bist du also. Ich habe überall nach dir gesucht.«

Helena drehte sich um, als Sadie den Kopf zum Büro hereinsteckte. »Entschuldige. Ich schaue gerade, ob ich nicht in Angus' Schreibtisch etwas über diese geheimnisvolle Frau finde, die er offenbar geliebt hat und von der ich dir gestern Abend erzählt habe.«

»Und? Bist du fündig geworden?«

»Nein, aber es gibt eine verschlossene Schublade, und den Schlüssel dazu kann ich nicht finden.«

»Dann wirst du sie vermutlich aufbrechen müssen. Der Schlüssel könnte überall sein. Du musst herausfinden, wer sie war, Helena, die Geschichte ist so romantisch.«

»Ich möchte an dem Schreibtisch ungern etwas kaputt machen, er ist so wunderschön.« Helena strich über den glatten grünen Lederbelag auf der Schreibfläche.

»Abgesehen davon, dass ich dich fragen wollte, wie es dir geht, wollte ich dir auch sagen, dass heute Morgen am Pool etwas höchst Merkwürdiges vor sich gegangen ist.« Sadie setzte sich auf die Schreibtischkante. »Vorhin habe ich zum Fenster hinausgeschaut und gesehen, wie Rupes und Alex sich an gegenüberliegenden Seiten des Pools aufstellten. Es sah aus wie ein Duell im Morgengrauen«, berichtete Sadie und lachte. »Dann habe ich ein lautes Platschen und jede Menge Geschrei gehört, und danach herrschte Stille.«

»O mein Gott! Hast du sie seitdem wiedergesehen?«, fragte Helena ängstlich.

»Ja. Rupes marschierte gerade zu seinem Zimmer, als ich die Treppe hinunterging, und dann sah ich Alex in seine Besenkammer verschwinden. Er sah aus, als wäre er in voller Montur in den Pool gesprungen.«

»Wirklich? Ich hoffe sehr, dass Rupes ihn nicht schikaniert, aber offensichtlich ist die Sache ja glimpflich ausgegangen.«

»Das stimmt.«

»Dann sehe ich mal nach Alex.« Helena erhob sich. »Ich bin seit sieben hier und habe gar nichts gehört, weil dieser Raum nach hinten hinausgeht.«

»Versteckst du dich?«, fragte Sadie. Helena hatte bereits die Tür erreicht.

»Was meinst du damit?«

»Du weißt genau, was ich meine. Sonst schmeißt du morgens hier den Laden und versteckst dich nicht still und leise im Büro. Habt ihr, du und William, euch gestritten?«

»Nein. Warum?«

»Gestern Abend hat er kaum ein Wort mit dir gesprochen. Dabei ist er normalerweise so … aufmerksam.« Sadie verschränkte die Arme. »Wegen irgendetwas ist er sauer.«

»Also, ich habe keine Ahnung, was das sein könnte.«

»Und du … es tut mir leid, meine Süße, aber du siehst schrecklich aus.«

»Danke.«

»Du machst ständig ein finsteres Gesicht, Helena. Warum willst du mir nicht sagen, was los ist? Vergiss nicht, ich bin deine beste Freundin. Ich halte zu dir.«

»Es ist alles bestens, wirklich. Es ist nur … in den letzten Tagen ging's mir nicht so gut, das ist alles.«

»Gut, wie du willst.« Sadie seufzte. »Aber die Atmosphäre im Haus ist zum Schneiden.«

»Wirklich? Das tut mir leid, Sadie. Offenbar bin ich eine schlechte Gastgeberin.«

»Unsinn! Du bist großartig, und das weißt du auch, also steigere dich jetzt nicht in Schuldgefühle hinein. Darum geht es nicht. Es hat doch nichts mit Alexis zu tun, oder?«

»Warum fragst du?« Helena hatte immer noch den Türgriff in der Hand.

»Gestern am Strand war William bester Laune, dann kamen wir nach Hause, und er ging gleich zu dir auf die Terrasse. Und keine halbe Minute später sehe ich Alexis verschwinden. Offenbar war er hier, während wir beim Baden waren.«

»Das war er auch«, sagte Helena mit einem resignierten Seufzen.

»Was deinem Mann bestimmt nicht besonders gefallen hat.«

»Nein. Aber ich kann ihn nicht davon überzeugen, dass zwischen Alexis und mir nichts läuft, wenn er felsenfest anderer Meinung ist. Wie auch immer, jetzt muss ich nach Alex sehen.« Und damit verließ Helena den Raum.

Wenig später folgte Sadie ihr und ging in die Küche, wo William gerade Toast machte. »Guten Morgen«, begrüßte sie ihn. »Noch ein perfekter Tag im Paradies. Gut geschlafen?«

»Sehr gut, danke. Kaffee?«

»Gern. Übrigens, wie ist der Dresscode für die Feier heute Abend?«

»Welche Feier denn?«, fragte William.

»Das Verlobungsfest von Alexis' Sohn. Weißt du nicht mehr? Er hat uns doch alle eingeladen. Vielleicht wird es richtig schön.«

Einige Sekunden herrschte betretenes Schweigen, dann sagte William: »Das hatte ich in der Tat vergessen … und auch, dass heute unser zehnter Hochzeitstag ist. Angesichts der Umstände ist es wahrscheinlich am besten, wenn ihr anderen geht, und ich bleibe hier und passe auf die Kinder auf. Es würde viel zu spät für sie werden, und sie würden sich nur danebenbenehmen«, fügte er verdrossen hinzu.

»Ich glaube, Helena hat Angelina schon gebeten, die Kinder zu übernehmen«, meinte Sadie, als er ihr einen Becher Kaffee reichte. »Und natürlich musst du mitkommen. Heute ist für euch zwei ein ganz besonderer Abend.«

In dem Moment kam Helena in die Küche. »Worum habe ich Angelina gebeten?«

»Auf die Kleinen aufzupassen, wenn wir auf das Verlobungsfest von Alexis' Sohn gehen«, wiederholte Sadie. »Und übrigens, alles Gute zum Hochzeitstag euch beiden«, sagte sie aufmunternd.

»Ach ja, danke, Sadie.« Helena warf kurz einen Blick zu William, der ihr den Rücken zukehrte.

»Ich trinke meinen Kaffee auf der Terrasse, Sadie, kommst du mit?«, sagte er und stand auf.

Als Helena allein in der Küche zurückblieb, sank sie auf einen Stuhl und legte den Kopf in die Hände. Seit gestern Nachmittag übersah William sie geflissentlich. Als sie am vergangenen Abend nach Hause gekommen waren, hatte er bereits im Bett gelegen und vorgeblich geschlafen. Und gerade hatte er ihr trotz Sadies Worte nicht zum Hochzeitstag gratuliert und auch nicht die Karte erwähnt, die sie ihm auf den Nachttisch gelegt hatte. Ausgerechnet an diesem Tag.

Am liebsten hätte Helena ihre Kinder gepackt und die paradiesische Zuflucht verlassen, die sich zunehmend als Hölle auf Erden entpuppte.

Mit einem Blick gen Himmel flehte sie um einen Ausweg. Aber es wollte sich ihr keiner zeigen.

Da Jules, Rupes, Sadie und Chloë sich am Pool sonnten und William in ein Buch vertieft war, ergriff Helena die Flucht. Sie packte ihre drei Kinder und Viola in den Wagen und fuhr nach Latchi. Sadie hatte recht – dem äußeren Anschein zum Trotz war die Stimmung in Pandora bis zum Zerreißen angespannt.

Alex war selbst für seine Verhältnisse ausgesprochen mürrisch, die ganze Fahrt zur Küste saß er schweigend neben ihr.

»Deine Augen sind ganz rot, mein Schatz. Bist du sicher, dass dir nichts fehlt?«, fragte sie.

»Mir fehlt nichts.«

»Vermutlich das Chlor vom Pool heute Morgen. Gibt es zwischen dir und Rupes irgendwelche Schwierigkeiten?«

»Nein, Mum, das habe ich dir schon gesagt.«

»Also gut, wenn du meinst.« Helena war zu erschöpft, um sich auf eine längere Diskussion einzulassen.

»Das meine ich.«

»Wie auch immer, Latchi wird dir gefallen«, fuhr sie mit gespielter Munterkeit fort. »Der Ort ist sehr hübsch, und rund um den Hafen gibt es viele Souvenirläden. Da kannst du dein Feriengeld für die übliche Auswahl regionaler Qualitätserzeugnisse ausgeben.«

»Ein Euphemismus für den Mist, den ich immer kaufe, meinst du?« Alex verzog das Gesicht. »Garantiert verzaubert.«

»Jetzt komm schon, Alex, das war ein Witz. Du kannst dein Geld ausgeben, wofür du magst.«

»Schon gut.« Er wandte sich ab und sah zum Fenster hinaus. »Was ist?«

»Ich könnte dich dasselbe fragen«, antwortete er.

»Mir geht's gut, aber danke der Nachfrage.«

»Wer's glaubt, wird selig«, brummte er. »Mir geht's so gut wie dir.«

»Okay«, sagte Helena und seufzte. »Jetzt sind wir quitt, aber vergiss nicht, in dieser Partie bin ich die Erwachsene und du das Kind. Wenn du ein Problem hast, bitte versprich mir, dass du zu mir kommst.«

»Okay.«

»Gut. Und jetzt suchen wir einen Parkplatz.«

Helena saß am Strand und sah den Kindern beim Plantschen im Meer zu. Es tat gut, eine Weile die beklemmende Atmosphäre von Pandora hinter sich lassen zu können, wo sie das Gefühl hatte, ihr Leben könne von einer Sekunde auf die andere umschlagen. Also tat sie das, was sie in solchen Momenten ihres Lebens immer tat: dankbar sein für das, was sie hatte.

Vor ihr spielten drei glückliche, gesunde Kinder. Im allerschlimmsten Fall blieb ihr immer noch Pandora. Sie hatte also ein Dach über dem Kopf, und von Angus' Erbschaft würde sie mehrere Monate ihren Lebensunterhalt bestreiten können. Vielleicht würde sie Pandora verkaufen, wieder nach England ziehen und Ballettunterricht geben müssen – das hatte sie sich in letzter Zeit ohnehin schon überlegt. Das Wesentliche war, es würde für ihre Kinder und auch für sie weitergehen. Schließlich hatte sie es schon einmal geschafft, sie würde es wieder schaffen. Aber sie hoffte von ganzem Herzen, dass es nicht dazu kommen würde.

»Daddyyy, schau! Schau, was Mummy mir geschenkt hat!«

Fred drückte ein Spielzeugauto auf Williams ölig glänzenden, sonnengebräunten Bauch.

»Wow! Noch ein Auto! Du bist aber ein Glückspilz, was?«
Lächelnd fuhr er seinem Sohn durchs Haar.

»Und ich habe ein Stickerheft bekommen«, fuhr Immy dazwischen und klebte William eine glitzernde pinkfarbene Fee auf die Stirn. »Die ist für dich, Daddy.«

»Danke, Immy.«

Immy wirbelte zur anderen Seite des Pools, um die anderen Sonnenbadenden ebenfalls mit ihrer Großzügigkeit zu bedenken.

Nachdem auch Chloë von Immy hochgeschreckt und beschenkt worden war, schlenderte sie zu ihrem Vater und ließ sich auf dem Fußende seiner Liege nieder.

»Daddy?«

»Chloë?«

»Also, dieses Fest heute Abend …«

»Ja?«

»Muss ich mit?«

»Ja. Wir sind alle eingeladen, und ich möchte, dass du mitkommst.«

»Okay. Kann ich dann Christoff mitbringen?«

»Das ist der Mann, den du am Flughafen kennengelernt hast?«

»Ja. Er will heute Abend wieder mit mir ausgehen, also dachte ich, er könnte sich an uns ranhängen.«

»Nein, er kann sich nicht an uns ›ranhängen‹. Er ist nicht eingeladen, und das ist eine Familienfeier.«

»Ach, Dad, ich sage ihm, er soll nicht zu viel essen.«

»Nein. Und das ist mein letztes Wort.«

Chloë seufzte schwer und zuckte dann mit den Schultern. »Na gut.« Und damit ging sie in Richtung Haus davon.

Als Helena vom Duschen zurückkam, klopfte es an ihre Zimmertür.

»Herein.«

»Ich bin's.«

Es war Jules, deren Nase sich schälte.

»Hallo.« Helena lächelte matt und schlüpfte in ihren Morgenmantel, während Jules sich aufs Bett setzte.

»Helena, ich dachte mir, vielleicht hast du Lust, dir morgen mit mir das Haus anzusehen, das ich kaufen möchte? Ich habe William schon gefragt, aber ehrlich gesagt schien er nicht besonders interessiert.«

Nach kurzem Zögern sagte Helena: »Natürlich komme ich mit.«

»Danke.« Jules nickte erleichtert. »Ich würde gern eine zweite Meinung hören, bevor ich den Vertrag unterschreibe und die Anzahlung leiste.«

»Wann ist die fällig?«

»Irgendwann nächste Woche.«

»Du meine Güte, das geht ja schnell. Wirst du Sacha davon erzählen, bevor du unterschreibst?«, fragte sie vorsichtig.

»*Wem?*«

»Du hast also nichts von ihm gehört?«

»Doch, habe ich schon, er hat mir zweimal auf die Mailbox gesprochen. Aber ich glaube, es ist an der Zeit, dass ich einige Entscheidungen ohne ihn treffe, findest du nicht?«

»Jules, das geht mich nichts an.«

»Nein.« Jules betrachtete ihre Nägel. »Das weiß ich.« Dann sah sie zu Helena und setzte ein munteres Lächeln auf. »Also, wenn ich es wirklich kaufe, sind wir praktisch Nachbarn. Das Haus ist gleich auf der anderen Seite des Dorfes. Das wäre doch schön, oder?«

»Ja, natürlich wäre das schön. Übrigens, du hast doch das Fest heute Abend nicht vergessen, oder?«, fragte Helena, um das Thema zu wechseln.

»William hat mich daran erinnert. Ich freue mich schon darauf. Eine gute Gelegenheit für mich, ein paar Einheimische kennenzulernen.« Jules stand auf und sah sich im Schlafzimmer um. »Ich wette, du kannst es gar nicht erwarten, das Haus auf Vordermann zu bringen. Die grauen Wände hier sind ja entsetzlich trist. Bis später.«

Um halb sieben traf man sich auf der Terrasse, um auf den Abend anzustoßen. Sadie hatte allen im Haus erzählt, dass es Helenas und Williams zehnter Hochzeitstag war, und hatte Angelina gebeten, eine Flasche Sekt und die Canapés zu servieren, die sie zuvor gemacht hatte.

»Chloë, ist das eine Bauchbinde, die du dir da um die Hüften geschlungen hast?« Entgeistert starrte William auf den winzigen Lederrock, der kaum das Gesäß seiner Tochter bedeckte.

»Ach, Dad, sei nicht so prüde. Tagsüber laufen wir hier alle fast nackt rum, warum dann nicht auch abends?« Sie ließ ihr langes glänzendes Haar herumschwingen und schlenderte zu Rupes, der ein knallpinkfarbenes Hemd trug. Die Farbe hob seine ohnehin roten Wangen noch hervor.

»Mum, du siehst hübsch aus«, sagte Alex, der in dem Moment auf die Terrasse kam. »Und übrigens, herzlichen Glückwunsch zum Hochzeitstag.«

»Danke, mein Schatz«, sagte Helena glücklich.

»Dad, findest du nicht, dass sie hübsch aussieht?«, fragte Alex mit Nachdruck.

William drehte sich um und betrachtete das kornblumenblaue Seidenkleid, das seine Frau trug. Das mochte er besonders gern, es passte zur Farbe ihrer Augen. Traurigkeit überwältigte ihn, als er feststellte, dass sie mit den sonnengebleichten Haaren, die ihr offen ums Gesicht hingen, und der leicht gebräunten Haut schöner aussah als je zuvor. Und keinen Tag älter als an dem Tag vor zehn Jahren, an dem er sie geheiratet hatte.

»Doch«, sagte er. Und wandte sich ab.

Eine Stunde später, als sich alle gerade auf die diversen Autos verteilten, um zu Alexis' Haus aufzubrechen, kam ein Taxi langsam den Berg hinuntergefahren.

»Man sehe und staune – die Rückkehr des verlorenen Sohnes«, sagte Jules. Sie trug ein goldglitzerndes Oberteil mit passendem Kopfband, das sie auf griechische Art über die Stirn gebunden hatte.

»Das ist ja Daddy!«, rief Viola überglücklich und lief dem Wagen entgegen.

»Hallo, meine Süße.« Sacha war noch kaum aus dem Auto gestiegen, da warf seine Tochter sich schon in seine Arme. Er drückte sie fest an sich.

»Du hast uns gefehlt, Daddy.«

»Ihr habt mir auch gefehlt.« Er betrachtete die versammelte Runde. »Ich muss ja sagen, das ist ein schöner Empfang! Ihr seht alle sehr schick aus. Geht ihr aus?«

»Wir gehen zu einer Party, Daddy«, erklärte Viola.

»Ich verstehe!«, sagte Sacha und nickte. »Darf ich mitkommen?«

»Natürlich darfst du – oder, Mummy?«

»Eine tolle Sause hast du dir doch nie entgehen lassen, oder, Schatz? Wahrscheinlich hast du den Alkohol bis nach London gerochen«, antwortete Jules sarkastisch.

»Warum bleibt ihr beiden nicht hier? Wir fahren mit den Kindern vor, dann habt ihr Zeit, euch zu begrüßen, und ihr kommt später nach«, schlug William vor in der Hoffnung, Sacha und Jules würden endlich unter vier Augen miteinander reden.

»*Er* kann nachkommen, wann er will, *ich* fahre jetzt. Jetzt kommt, sonst verspäten wir uns noch. Bis später, *Schatz*.« Jules machte aus ihrem Abscheu keinen Hehl. Energisch schob sie ihre Kinder in den Wagen.

Sacha zuckte hilflos mit den Schultern, als seine Frau die Fahrertür mit einem Knall zuzog.

»Neuer Plan«, sagte William zu Helena. »Ich bleibe mit Sacha hier, damit er sich duschen und umziehen kann, dann kommen wir nach. Du fährst voraus.«

»Weißt du denn, wohin du fahren musst?«, fragte sie.

»Ungefähr. Ich finde es schon.« William lenkte seine Aufmerksamkeit auf Sacha. »Jetzt komm, Kumpel, lass uns erst einmal kurz miteinander reden.«

Alex' Tagebuch

Es passiert selten, dass ich wirklich wütend bin.

So sauer, dass die Wut mir ein Loch ins Herz brennt und Flammen in meiner Seele lodern.

Jetzt kann ich nachvollziehen, dass man in einem hochemotionalen Moment jemanden umbringen kann.

So ging es mir heute Morgen am Pool.

Ich hätte von vornherein wissen müssen, dass es nicht gutgehen würde.

Meine treulose Verbündete Immy legte einen gigantomanischen Wutanfall hin, weil sie als Spionin nicht ihr Lieblingskleid anziehen durfte.

Ein überdimensionaler Kobold in einer ausladenden pinkfarbenen Tüllwolke mit glitzernden Flipflops und einer gelben sternförmigen Sonnenbrille wäre inmitten der Olivenbäume womöglich etwas auffällig gewesen. Und hätte meinen Plan sabotiert.

Ich wette, James Bond hatte mit Moneypenny nie solchen Ärger. Wie auch immer, ich musste auf Immy verzichten und mich allein meinem Schicksal stellen.

Rupes erschien zur vereinbarten Zeit. Er trug seine scheußliche Ray Ban und machte einen auf cool.

»Hast du den Brief?«, fragte er von der anderen Seite des Pools.

Breitbeinig und mit verschränkten Armen stand er da,

als würde er zusammen mit seinem Rugby-Team für die Kamera posieren.

Angst machte er mir damit keine. Zumindest keine große.

»Hast du den Hasen?«, fragte ich zurück.

»Ja. Lass den Brief sehen.«

»Lass den Hasen sehen.«

Rupes drehte sich um und fischte von unter der Matratze einer Sonnenliege eine Plastiktüte. Verdammt! Offenbar hatte er Bee vorher dort deponiert, und ich hätte ihn mir einfach holen können. Dann wäre dieses ganze Palaver überflüssig gewesen. Der Kopf meines geliebten Bees ragte aus dem Beutel. Ich nickte. Zeigte Rupes den Briefumschlag.

»Auf Französisch, wie vereinbart.«

»Lies vor.«

»Klar.«

Ich räusperte mich.

»Ma chère Chloë. Prendre vers le bas la lune!«

»Auf Englisch, du Vollidiot!«

»Entschuldige. ›Vergiss die Sterne! Am Firmament ist ein neues Licht erglüht! Du leuchtest wie ein neugeborener Engel, frisch und jung vor den betagten Planeten. Deine Augen sind wie Sma…‹«

»Okay, reicht.« Rupes sah aus, als würde er sich gleich übergeben. »Gib ihn mir.«

»Ich will den Hasen im selben Moment. Wir gehen aufeinander zu, und dann findet die Übergabe statt.«

Achselzuckend ging Rupes um den Pool. Wir begegneten uns am tiefen Ende.

Er schwitzte heftig. Ich war ultracool. »Hier.« Ich

streckte die Hand mit dem Brief aus und die andere, um die Hasentüte zu nehmen.

Er streckte die Hände zu mir aus. Er packte den Brief, ich packte die Henkel des Beutels.

Dann, blitzschnell, entriss er ihn mir wieder und warf ihn in den Pool.

Es platschte gewaltig, und mir blieb vor Schreck der Mund offen stehen, denn der Beutel schwamm nicht. Er sank. Ich musste zusehen, wie mein heiß geliebter Bee langsam aus meinem Blickfeld abtauchte.

»Danke.« Rupes wedelte mit dem Kuvert und lachte wie ein Irrer. »Jetzt kannst du zeigen, was für ein toller Taucher du bist, und die alten Stofffetzen retten. Schade, dass Chloë nicht hier ist, um dich anzufeuern!«

»Du Schwein!«, brüllte ich und öffnete den Reißverschluss meiner Shorts, um ins Wasser zu springen. Dann fiel mir ein, dass ich keine Unterhose anhatte, und schloss ihn wieder.

»Komm schon, lass mal sehen, was du kannst!«, höhnte Rupes, und ich sprang. Schwere Bermudas, die Taschen voll mit den Fundstücken der letzten Tage, zogen mich nach unten.

Ich holte tief Luft und ging auf Tauchgang, das Chlor verätzte mir fast die Augäpfel (unter Wasser schwimme ich nie ohne Taucherbrille, weil ich hinterher eine verblüffende Ähnlichkeit mit dem Teufel habe) und fischte im Trüben nach Bee.

Weit konnte er ja wohl nicht sein. Er wog doch so gut wie nichts, warum war er untergegangen? Ich tauchte auf, um Luft zu holen, alles war unscharf. Rupes stand da und lachte sich tot. Nur leider nicht wortwörtlich.

Noch so eine idiotische Redewendung, aber das war jetzt nicht der geeignete Moment für linguistische Betrachtungen.

Ich holte wieder Luft und schwamm nach unten, meine Lunge platzte schier vor Wut und Panik und Sauerstoffmangel. Und dort, am Boden des zwei Meter zwanzig tiefen Beckenendes, lag Bee.

Ich tauchte wieder auf und wünschte, ich könnte meine Bermudas auszuziehen, aber ich wusste, dass ich die höhnischen Bemerkungen über die zwergenhafte Größe meiner Weichteile nicht ertragen würde. Also tauchte ich wieder ab, bekam den Rand des Beutels zu fassen und zog. Und zog noch fester.

Er bewegte sich nicht. Ich drohte zu ertrinken. Also schwamm ich wieder nach oben, mir war schon ganz schwarz vor Augen. Ich schnappte nach Luft, schwamm an den Beckenrand und hielt mich fest, um tief durchzuatmen. Der Gedanke, dass Bee dort unten ertrank und das Chlor die spärlichen Überreste seines abgenutzten Fells auflöste, spornte mich an. Ich holte noch mal tief Luft, tauchte wieder nach unten, packte das Ohr meines kleinen Freundes und zog mit aller Kraft daran. Und gelobt sei Gott, er bewegte sich. Die Sekunden, in denen ich mit meinem Körpergewicht, meiner Bermudas und einem gefühlt zwei Tonnen schweren Kohlesack wieder an die Oberfläche schwamm, werden als die qualvollsten meines bisherigen Lebens in die Geschichte eingehen.

Ich hätte ertrinken können.

Mein schlimmster Feind und mein bester Freund hätten mich das Leben kosten können. Als meine Hand aus dem Wasser auftauchte und nach dem Beckenrand tastete, um mich die letzten dreißig Zentimeter hochzuziehen, sah ich Rupes immer noch lachen.

»Ich erfülle nur den Auftrag meiner lieben Frau Mama und bereite dich aufs Internat vor. Bis später, Alex.«

Und mit einem Winken zog er breit grinsend ab.

Die Beine, mit denen ich mich und meinen Hasen die Leiter hinaufhievte, zitterten wie Wackelpudding, dann brach ich auf dem Beckenrand zusammen.

Ich betrachtete das jämmerliche klatschnasse Fellhäufchen neben mir. Und sah, dass ein großer Stein an seine Pfoten gebunden war. Das Ohr, an dem ich ihn in Sicherheit gezogen hatte, hing jetzt an einem einzigen Faden.

Ich weiß nicht, wie ich den heutigen Tag überlebt habe. Meine Wut und mein Gefühl von Beschämung sind grenzenlos. Ich habe mir überlegt fortzulaufen, mich in das nächste Flugzeug nach Marrakesch zu setzen und mich dort als Schlangenbeschwörer zu verdingen, wenn ich nur meine Schlangenphobie überwinden könnte. Außerdem würde ich damit meine Mutter strafen, und das wäre nicht fair.

Stattdessen muss ich zu dieser Party gehen und es ertragen, dass mein Feind auch dort sein wird. Mein einziger Trost ist, dass er in seinem Hemd aussieht wie ein großes rosafarbenes Schwein und dass Chloë ihn mittlerweile vollkommen ignoriert. Ich werde die Zeit nutzen, um einen Plan zu schmieden, und meine Rache wird fürchterlich sein.

KAPITEL 15

Das Verlobungsfest fand im großen Hof der alten, vom Wein völlig überwucherten Kellerei statt, die an einem der höchsten Punkte des Dorfs stand und den Blick auf ein tiefes Tal freigab. Über dem Hof hingen Lichterketten, die sich durch die Äste der silbrigen Olivenbäume wanden, dazu brannten Dutzende von Laternen.

Eine Schar munterer einheimischer Frauen stand hinter einer Reihe von langen Klapptischen und verteilte Teller, auf denen sich köstlich duftende Speisen häuften: gefüllte Weinblätter, Schwein und Lamm vom Spieß, Spinattaschen, gegrillter Fisch und dazu Berge von Reis und Salat.

Als die Gäste aus Pandora eintrafen, war das Fest bereits in vollem Gang. In einer Ecke spielte eine dreiköpfige zypriotische Band, die aber meist vom Geplauder der zweihundert Gäste übertönt wurde. Wein wurde aus einem riesigen Eichenfass direkt in die Gläser ausgeschenkt.

»Ein Paradies für Säufer«, sagte Jules süffisant und nahm sich ein Glas Weißwein. »Das würde Sacha gefallen«, fügte sie hinzu und ging davon, um sich unter die Einheimischen zu mischen.

»Mum, darf ich auch ein Glas Wein trinken?«, fragte Alex, als er bemerkte, dass sowohl Chloë als auch Rupes eines in der Hand hielten.

»Ja, ein kleines«, willigte Helena ein. Sie trank einen Schluck aus ihrem Glas und kam sich sehr allein vor. Wann war sie das letzte Mal ohne William auf einem Fest gewesen? Es war so lange her, dass sie sich nicht erinnern konnte. Der Umstand schmerzte sie umso mehr, als er und sie heute Abend eigentlich ihren eigenen Hochzeitstag feiern sollten.

»Schau, Alex, da drüben ist ein Feuerschlucker.« Viola, die von Jules sich selbst überlassen worden war, kam zu ihm und deutete in eine Ecke des Hofs. »Können wir näher hingehen?«

»Warum nicht?«

Sie zwängten sich durch die Menge der festlich gekleideten Menschen und gingen zu dem Feuerschlucker.

»Meinst du, dass mit Daddy was nicht in Ordnung ist?« Viola musste sich auf die Zehenspitzen stellen, um ihm ins Ohr zu flüstern.

»Das weiß ich nicht, Viola, aber ich glaube nicht.«

»Ich schon. Ich glaube, dass ihm was fehlt.«

Alex griff nach ihrer Hand und drückte sie fest. »Viola, Eltern sind komisch. Versuch, dir keine Sorgen zu machen. Was immer es ist, es wird sich bestimmt wieder einrenken. Meiner Erfahrung nach wird in den allermeisten Fällen alles wieder gut.«

»William ist nicht dein richtiger Dad, oder?«

»Nein.«

»Weißt du, dass mein Dad auch nicht mein richtiger ist? Und meine Mum auch nicht?«

»Ja, das weiß ich.«

»Aber ich hab ihn lieb, so, wie er ist. Weißt du, er ist immer für mich da. Es ist doch eigentlich egal, oder?«

»Was?«

»Ob man ihre Gene hat oder nicht. Ich glaube nicht, dass mein richtiger Vater so nett und so gut zu mir sein könnte wie der, den ich habe. Hast du William auch lieb? Ich mag ihn richtig gern.«

»Ich … ja, schon.«

»Ich find's toll, dass er mein Patenonkel ist. Alex?«

»Ja?«

»Meinst du, dass sie uns genauso lieb haben, als wenn wir ihre eigenen Kinder wären?«, fragte sie zögernd.

»Natürlich, Viola. Wahrscheinlich sogar noch mehr. Immerhin haben sie dich eigens ausgewählt.« Unbeholfen umarmte er sie und deutete dann auf den Feuerschlucker. »Schau, wie hoch er den Feuerstab in die Luft wirft.«

»Wow«, sagte sie staunend, und ihre Miene wirkte ganz verzaubert.

»Da seid ihr ja.« Helena trat hinter sie.

Eine Kellnerin trug ein Tablett mit Weingläsern vorbei, und Helena trank ihres leer und nahm ein neues.

»Mum, pass auf! Du weißt doch, dass du nicht mehr als zwei trinken darfst, sonst wirst du beschwipst.«

»Alex, du bist nicht meine Anstandsdame, und heute ist ein besonderer Abend«, fuhr Helena ihn an.

»'tschuldigung! Komm, Viola, gehen wir noch weiter nach vorn, da kannst du mehr sehen.«

Wieder sich selbst überlassen ließ sich Helena durch die vielen Menschen treiben und hörte sie angeregt miteinander plaudern. Sie war überzeugt, dass so gut wie alle miteinander verwandt waren, wenn nicht direkt, dann doch entfernt durch die vielen Hochzeiten untereinander im Ort. Vor den Musikern versammelten sich die ersten Gäste, um das Tanzbein zu schwingen, und in ihrer Mitte standen Dimitrios und seine Verlobte Kassie, die vor Glück um die Wette strahlten.

Helena überlegte sich, dass das Leben diese beiden Menschen vermutlich nie in die Ferne verschlagen würde, und wahrscheinlich würden sie eine neue Generation tatkräftiger

Jungen in die Welt setzen, die eines Tages die Weinkellerei weiterführen würden. Sie würden sich an ihrem Glück erfreuen, an ihren Kindern und an der engen Gemeinschaft, in der sie lebten.

Unvermittelt stieg Neid in Helena auf. Und eine große Traurigkeit.

»Wie geht es dir an diesem Abend, Helena?«

Die Stimme unmittelbar hinter ihr schreckte sie auf, sie drehte sich um und sah Alexis vor sich.

»Guten Abend.« Sie riss sich zusammen, sie wollte den anderen mit ihrem melancholischen Selbstmitleid nicht die Stimmung verderben. »Es ist ein wunderbares Fest, danke für die Einladung.«

»Es ist mir eine Freude und meinem Sohn auch. Ich möchte nur sicherstellen, dass ihr euch alle amüsiert.«

»Das tun wir.« Dann zögerte sie kurz. Eigentlich wollte sie das Thema nicht wieder ansprechen, aber irgendetwas drängte sie dazu. »Alexis, bitte entschuldige meinen gestrigen Gefühlsausbruch.«

Er lächelte wehmütig. »Die Entschuldigung ist überflüssig. Ich wünschte nur, du hättest es mir schon vor Jahren gesagt. Aber was geschehen ist, ist geschehen. Wichtig ist, dass wir aus dem Vergangenen lernen und uns weiterentwickeln. Apropos, wo ist William? Ich habe ihn heute Abend noch gar nicht gesehen.«

»Er kommt später mit Jules' Mann.«

»Ich verstehe.« Alexis seufzte. »Ich fürchte, er ist nicht glücklich, dass er mich mit seiner Frau in den Armen gesehen hat.«

»Das stimmt. Und zufälligerweise ist heute unser zehnter Hochzeitstag.«

»Dann, Helena, solltest du ihm die Umstände erklären. William sollte die Wahrheit kennen. Es wird ihm helfen, dich zu verstehen. Und mich.«

Wenn es nur so einfach wäre, dachte Helena. In dem Moment stieg Jubel auf unter den Zuschauern, die Dimitrios und seiner Verlobten beim Tanzen zusahen.

Alexis blickte hinüber und lächelte. »Wären das nur wir, die wir unser Leben gemeinsam beginnen. Aber« – er zuckte mit den Schultern –, »das sollte nicht so sein. Und jetzt habe ich mich damit abgefunden, dass es auch nie mehr so sein wird. Es ist mir wichtig, dass du das weißt. Du gehörst einem anderen, und ich weiß, dass er dich sehr liebt. Wirklich, Helena, ich möchte mich bei dir und auch bei William entschuldigen. Mein Verhalten war unverzeihlich. Ich wollte einfach nicht wahrhaben, dass du nicht mehr die Meine bist … aber das muss ich hinnehmen. Komm, jetzt möchte ich dir einige Menschen aus deiner Vergangenheit vorstellen.«

Er reichte ihr die Hand, und nach kurzem Zögern ergriff sie sie. »Ja. Danke, Alexis.«

Seine Freunde – damals, als sie sie das letzte Mal gesehen hatte, allesamt Jungen – waren jetzt Väter mit zur Fülligkeit neigenden Ehefrauen. Sie drückten Helena an sich, begrüßten sie herzlich, sagten ihr, wie schön sie noch immer sei, und erkundigten sich nach ihrer Familie und nach Pandora. Helena freute sich über ihre Aufmerksamkeit, aber innerlich gingen ihr Alexis' kluge Worte durch den Kopf, und sie fragte sich, ob William wirklich kommen oder ob sie den Abend ihres zehnten Hochzeitstags ohne ihn verbringen würde.

Verdient hätte sie es ihrer Meinung nach.

Mittlerweile machten sich die Gäste, die die Tanzfläche bevölkerten, bereit, den traditionellen zypriotischen Tanz aufzuführen, der seit Jahrhunderten von Generation zu Generation weitergegeben wurde. Helena sah Jules und Sadie in der Menge, sie hatten die Arme über den Kopf erhoben und versuchten, den Schritten ihrer Partner zu folgen.

»Papa! Papa! Du musst den *Zorba* für uns tanzen.« Der schwitzende Dimitrios versetzte seinem Vater einen Klaps auf den Rücken.

»Ja, Alexis! Tanz für uns! Tanz!«, stimmte die Menge ein.

»Und, Helena, du musst mit ihm tanzen, wie ihr damals hier getanzt habt!«, rief Isaák, ein alter Freund von Alexis.

»Ja, zeig doch mal, was du kannst. Das ist doch das, was du früher angeblich gemacht hast!«, rief Jules aus der Menge. Zahlreiche Hände schoben Helena zu Alexis; er stand in der Mitte eines großen Kreises von Menschen, die sich alle an den Schultern umfassten.

»Erinnerst du dich?« Er lächelte ermutigend. »Mein achtzehnter Geburtstag, genau hier.«

»Wie könnte ich das je vergessen?«, erwiderte sie leise.

»Fangen wir an?«

Er schnalzte mit den Fingern zum Zeichen, dass sie bereit waren, und der Bouzouki-Spieler schlug die bedächtigen ersten Takte.

Als sich der Kreis um sie zu bewegen begann, machten auch Helena und Alexis die ersten präzisen, knappen Schritte. Sie tanzten getrennt, aber doch gemeinsam, und auch wenn Helena den *Zorba* seit praktisch einem Vierteljahrhundert nicht mehr getanzt hatte, war er ihr noch genauso vertraut wie damals. Sie folgte allein der Musik und ihrem Körper. Sie war keine knapp vierzigjährige Ehefrau und Mutter mehr, sondern eine lebenslustige Fünfzehnjährige, die auf einem sonnenbeschienenen Weinfeld mit dem Jungen tanzte, den sie liebte.

Die Schritte, die so einfach waren, wenn die Musik langsam spielte, wurden zunehmend komplizierter, je mehr sich das Tempo steigerte. Immer schneller drehte sich Helena um Alexis, bis irgendwann die Tänzer, die sie beide umkreisten, mit den Füßen aufzustampfen und sie anzufeuern begannen. Alexis zog Helena in seine Arme, hob sie hoch über den Kopf und wirbelte sie schneller und immer schneller durch die Luft, vereint in einem wilden Strudel der Leidenschaft.

Selbstvergessen breitete Helena die Arme aus und warf den Kopf in den Nacken, sie vertraute Alexis grenzenlos. Um sich her verschwamm alles zu einem bunten Blitzen, Beifall und Gejohle hallten ihr in den Ohren.

Sie tanzte! Sie kam sich lebendig vor, berauscht, wunderbar …

Die Musik wurde langsamer, Alexis ließ sie sacht zu Boden gleiten, dabei streifte ihr Körper seinen. Er küsste ihr die Hände und drehte sie von sich fort, damit sie einen tiefen Knicks machen und er sich verbeugen konnten.

Immer lauter wurden die Rufe nach einer Zugabe, bis Alexis schließlich um Ruhe bat. »Danke, danke.« Er wischte sich mit einem Taschentuch den Schweiß von der Stirn. »Das ist zu viel für einen alten Mann.« Widerspruch wurde laut, doch Alexis hob wieder beschwichtigend die Hände. »Heute sind wir hier, um die Verlobung meines Sohnes mit seiner wunderschönen Braut zu feiern.«

Und während Alexis seinen Sohn und seine zukünftige Schwiegertochter zu sich bat, tauchte Helena in der Menschenmenge unter.

»Tante Helena, du warst wirklich toll.« Viola griff nach ihrer Hand, Bewunderung stand in ihren Augen.

»Wow, Liebes, das war phantastisch!«, sagte Sadie. Eine kleine Gruppe hatte sich um Helena geschart.

»Ich wusste gar nicht, dass du so tanzen kannst«, sagte Rupes lässig.

»Ich auch nicht«, sagte eine Stimme hinter ihr. Schnell drehte sie sich um.

»William, wo bist du denn die ganze Zeit gewesen?«

»Ich habe mich um Sacha gekümmert. Aber wie es aussieht, hast du dich auch ohne mich bestens amüsiert.«

»Ja, das Fest ist sehr schön«, sagte sie trotzig. »Und jetzt brauche ich ein Glas Wasser.«

»Kann ich dir eins holen?«, erbot er sich.

»Nein danke, das mache ich selbst.«

William folgte ihr. »Was zum Teufel geht hier vor sich?«

»Nichts! Ich habe getanzt, weiter nichts.«

»Guter Gott, Helena, du bist meine Frau!«

»Ja, das bin ich. Und was habe ich falsch gemacht?«

»Ich bin doch nicht dumm, Helena! Das hat doch jeder gesehen, der Augen im Kopf hat.«

»Was?«

»Himmelherrgott, muss ich das wirklich noch eigens sagen? Ich habe dir geglaubt, und ich habe dir vertraut, immer und immer wieder, ich habe die Tatsache ignoriert, dass er angeschossen kommt, sobald ich aus dem Haus bin.« William griff sich ein Glas Wein vom Tisch und trank einen Schluck, aber als er die zwei Bedienungen bemerkte, die ihn neugierig beobachteten, zog er Helena in eine stille Ecke.

»Der vollkommene, allzeit anwesende, immer hilfsbereite Alexis! Mr. Hansdampf, wie dein Sohn ihn nennt! Sogar gestern noch bin ich mit den Kindern weggefahren, weil ich dachte, du brauchst etwas Ruhe und Zeit für dich – und dann komme ich zurück, und wen sehe ich da mit dir in den Armen auf der Terrasse stehen? *Ihn!*«

»Er war nur gekommen, um nach mir zu sehen«, antwortete Helena leise.

»Das glaube ich sofort. Und dann komme ich heute Abend hierher und sehe euch beide tanzen … als würdet ihr zusammengehören! Sag mir die Wahrheit, Helena, dieses eine Mal im Leben! Du liebst ihn immer noch, stimmt's? Verdammt noch mal, sag's mir einfach!« Er packte sie an den Schultern. »Sag's mir!«

»Hör auf, William, bitte! Nicht hier, nicht jetzt … Wir unterhalten uns später darüber, das verspreche ich dir.«

Er warf ihr einen Blick zu, dann seufzte er resigniert, nahm die Hände von ihren Schultern und schüttelte den Kopf. »Aber eines sage ich dir gleich: Ich will nicht mit jemandem zusammenleben, der nicht mit mir zusammen sein will. Herzlichen Glückwunsch zum Hochzeitstag, Helena.«

Damit machte er auf dem Absatz kehrt und verschwand in der Menge.

Tränen stiegen Helena in die Augen, als sie zum Weinfass ging und ihr Glas nachfüllte. Gerade wollte sie einen Schluck davon trinken, als jemand sie unbeholfen von hinten umarmte und sie den ganzen Wein verschüttete.

»Guten Abend, meine Schöne.«

»Sacha, du bist wirklich gekommen«, sagte sie beklommen.

»In der Tat.« Schwungvoll führte er die Flasche Brandy, die er in der Hand hielt, an die Lippen.

Auch wenn Helena mehr als üblich getrunken hatte, war sie nüchtern genug, um zu erkennen, dass er eindeutig sternhagelvoll war. »Du siehst schrecklich aus.«

»Wahrscheinlich.« Er schwankte leicht. »Aber ehrlich gesagt geht es mir gerade prächtig. Du musst nämlich wissen, mein Engel, dass ich allen Grund zum Feiern habe.«

»Wirklich?«

»O ja.«

»Warum?« Sie wusste nicht, ob sie die Antwort wirklich hören wollte.

»Weil ich in ein paar Minuten frei bin! Und du weißt, was das heißt, liebste, süßeste Helena, oder nicht?«

»Nein, Sacha, ich habe keine Ahnung.«

»Es heißt … ach, du weißt genau, was das heißt. Aber jetzt muss ich meine wunderbare Gattin suchen gehen und ihr die frohe Botschaft verkünden.«

Torkelnd verneigte er sich und ging davon. Alexis hatte gerade seine Ansprache beendet, und Helena sah, wie Sacha sich in die Mitte des Kreises vordrängte und zu Alexis stellte. Sie sah sich suchend nach William um, konnte ihn aber nirgends entdecken.

»Meine Damen und Herren! Verzeihen Sie, dass ich so dazwischenplatze«, sagte Sacha. »Ich bin Sacha Chandler, und ich möchte mich den Glückwünschen des Herrn neben mir anschließen. Sir, wie heißen Sie?«

»Ich bin Alexis.«

»Alexis. Ein famoser Name.« Sacha versetzte Alexis einen kräftigen Schlag auf die Schulter. »Sind Sie verheiratet?«

»Ich war verheiratet, ja.«

»Oje. Ist die Ehe den Bach runtergegangen? Ein Besuch beim Scheidungsanwalt?«

»Nein, meine Frau ist gestorben«, sagte Alexis leise und sah zu Boden.

Die Menge war verstummt, alle hielten die Luft an. Unvermittelt trat William neben Sacha und fasste ihn an die Schulter.

»Komm, Kumpel, Zeit, nach Hause zu gehen.«

»Nach Hause? Ich bin doch gerade erst gekommen!«, rief

Sacha und schüttelte Williams Hand ab. »Außerdem habe ich selbst eine Ankündigung zu machen. Wo ist meine wunderbare Frau Julia?«

»Ich bin hier.« Jules stand ganz hinten in der Menge.

»Also, ich muss dir was sagen.« Sacha nahm einen weiteren Schluck aus seiner Brandyflasche. »Und ich muss es dir *jetzt* sagen, sonst habe ich nie mehr den Mut. Also, hör mir gut zu: Meine Firma ist nicht bloß liquidiert worden, sie ist dem Erdboden gleichgemacht. Ich besitze keinen Penny mehr. Und ein Haus auch nicht, weil ich es doppelt und dreifach mit Hypotheken belastet habe, also wird die Bank es sich im Handumdrehen unter den Nagel reißen. Mein Engel, wir sind bettelarm und brotlos obendrein und besitzen nichts als die Kleider, die wir am Leib tragen. Keine schicken Schulen mehr für die Kids. Sie gehen demnächst auf die staatliche Schule, und deine Klepper werden beim Chinesen ums Eck im Kochtopf landen.«

Er lachte rau und prostete seinem ebenso entsetzten wie gebannten Publikum mit seiner Flasche zu. »Also, meine Damen und Herren, das wär's! Eine Doppelfeier! Der Beginn einer Ehe, das Ende einer anderen. Prost.« Er hob die Flasche an die Lippen.

In der Menge wurde gewispert, wer kein Englisch sprach, bat die Nebenstehenden um eine Übersetzung. William war es endlich gelungen, Sacha am Arm zu packen und wegzuziehen.

Wie gelähmt hatte Helena Sachas betrunkene Ansprache verfolgt, doch nun drängte sie sich zu William vor. In der Dramatik dieses Moments mussten sie ihr früheres Gespräch erst einmal vergessen. »Guter Gott, und was jetzt?«, flüsterte sie verzweifelt.

Beide schauten zu Sacha, der sich Halt suchend an William klammerte.

»Geh und rede mit Jules«, sagte er. »Frag sie, was sie vorhat.«

Helena suchte überall, aber Jules und Rupes schienen wie vom Erdboden verschluckt. Viola fand sie schließlich haltlos an Alex' Brust schluchzen.

»Was machen wir jetzt, Mum?«, fragte er beklommen über Violas tizianrote Locken hinweg.

»Ich fahre uns alle so bald wie möglich nach Hause. Lass mich nur alle einsammeln. Geh du mit Viola schon mal zum Wagen, er ist offen.«

»Okay. Mach schnell«, drängte er.

»Ich beeile mich.«

Helena hastete davon und fand William und Alexis schließlich mit Sacha in ihrer Mitte auf einem Mäuerchen sitzen.

»Jules und Rupes sind verschwunden, aber ich möchte Viola, Chloë und Alex nach Hause bringen.«

»Ich habe vorgeschlagen, dass William und Sacha die Nacht hier verbringen«, sagte Alexis. »Das ist vielleicht besser, bis sich die ganze Aufregung etwas gelegt hat.«

Helena warf einen fragenden Blick zu William, der nickte.

»Leute, ich muss kotzen, tut mir leid«, keuchte Sacha und erbrach sich.

»Helena, fahr zu den Kindern nach Hause, hier kannst du sowieso nichts ausrichten«, sagte William und suchte nach einem Taschentuch, um Sacha den Mund abzuwischen. Alexis war aufgesprungen, um ein Glas Wasser zu holen. »Gib Bescheid, wenn Jules auftaucht. Ich bleibe hier und passe auf, dass mein alter Freund nicht an seinem eigenen Erbrochenen erstickt.«

»Bist du sicher, dass es für dich in Ordnung ist hierzubleiben?«, fragte sie und hoffte, William würde an ihrem Blick erkennen, wie sehr sie in dieser Situation mit ihm fühlte.

»Alexis und ich haben uns gerade kurz unterhalten, er hat

mehrere Gästezimmer. Ich möchte nicht, dass die Kinder Sacha in diesem Zustand sehen. Keines der Kinder. Das ist nicht fair ihnen gegenüber. Abgesehen davon, dass Jules ausrasten könnte. Sie hätte auch allen Grund dazu«, fügte er seufzend hinzu.

»Also gut.« Helena suchte seinen Blick, aber seine Miene war nicht zu deuten. »Melde dich zwischendurch.«

»Das mache ich«, sagte er und wendete sich wieder Sacha zu.

Alex Tagebuch

Ähemm.

Also, tja. Und so weiter. Was soll ich sagen? Ich bin … sprachlos. Oder wortlos. Oder wie auch immer.

Im Gegensatz zu manch anderen, die heute Abend eher … nun ja, dramatische Ansprachen hielten.

Es war ein folgenschwerer Moment. Nicht ganz auf Churchills Niveau, aber ich muss Sacha trotzdem meine Hochachtung aussprechen. Er war vollkommen knülle und hat sich trotzdem kein einziges Mal verhaspelt.

Wie war das mit den ruhigen, entspannten Ferien?

Es ist ungefähr ein Uhr nachts, und ich habe mich in meinem Bunker verbarrikadiert. Die griechische Tragödie, die am heutigen Abend geboten wurde, und zwar dem versammelten schockstarren und atemlosen Dorf, hat auch Folgen für mich:

Jetzt habe ich Schuldgefühle. Entsetzliche Schuldgefühle.

Es heißt ja, man soll sich gut überlegen, was man sich wünscht, weil es einem nicht gefallen könnte, wenn der Wunsch in Erfüllung geht. Und es gefällt mir in der Tat nicht.

Als ich meinen durchnässten Hasen heute Vormittag an den Füßen an einen Bindfaden aufhängte, den ich mit Müh und Not vor mein kleines Fenster gespannt hatte, damit

er – der Hase, nicht der Bindfaden – einen Luftzug abbe-
kommt (ich wollte ihn nicht draußen befestigen, dort hätte
er gleich wieder verschwinden können), bat ich Gott, eine
gerechte Strafe über Rupes zu verhängen, weil mir keine
einfiel, die grausam genug war. Später wäre mir schon eine
eingefallen, aber mein Gehirn hatte vor lauter Chlor und
Zorn seine übliche Leistungsfähigkeit eingebüßt.

Und ehe ich mich versehe, wartet der da oben mit dem
großen Coup auf: Rupes hat kein Zuhause und keinen
Penny mehr. Keinen Penis mehr fände ich zwar besser,
aber ich will nicht kleinlich sein.

Und das Allerbeste ist, höchstwahrscheinlich wird er
auf irgendeine Gesamtschule in einem Problemviertel gehen müssen. Wenn es ein solches Viertel in diesem Kaff, in
dem sie wohnen, überhaupt gibt. Aber da die Chandlers
mehr oder minder bankrott sind, werden sie wahrscheinlich selbst in ein Problemviertel ziehen müssen.

Und dort wird Rupes von einer Hoodies- und Messer-
bewehrten Schlägertruppe überfallen werden, die ihm das
Internat gründlich austreibt und etliches andere dazu.

Ach, welch Entzücken!

Aber da fällt mir gerade ein, dass er die Sache womöglich selbst in die Hand nimmt, sich zum Bandenanführer
aufschwingt und das Los seiner Familie als Drogendealer
aufbessert. Dann besteht er darauf, dass seine Gang die
Turnschuhe und Hoodies gegen Brogues von Lobb und
Mäntel von Aquascutum eintauscht. Aber dann, halte ich
im Stillen dagegen, wird er früher oder später doch gefasst
werden, denn er wird seiner eigenen Arroganz zum Opfer
fallen und im Knast landen, wo er mit Vergewaltigern und
Kinderschändern die Zelle teilt.

Doch so überwältigt ich war, dass mein Gebet erhört wurde – und so prompt –, nach einem Blick auf Violas Gesicht kam ich mir vor wie ein Schwein. Ein absolutes Schwein.

Es ist also ein Pyrrhussieg, wie derlei Siege es meist sind.

Jules und Rupes sind wie ein heimliches Liebespaar in die Nacht verschwunden und ließen die kleine Viola zurück, die sich die Augen auf meinen Klamotten ausheulte.

Als wir zu Hause waren, brachte Mum, die seit ihrem Dirty Dance mit Mr. Hansdampf – kotz! – erheblich nüchterner geworden war, Viola ins Bett und trug mir und Chloë auf, ebenfalls schlafen zu gehen.

Wir setzten uns noch eine Weile auf den Fuß der Treppe und unterhielten uns leise, bevor wir uns eine gute Nacht wünschten. Chloë fand das Ganze eher saukomisch, allerdings hatte sie, glaube ich, noch mehr getrunken als Mum. Diese Gewohnheit wird ein Ende finden müssen, wenn wir erst einmal verlobt sind. Sie wollte mir vor allem von dem traumhaften Michel vorschwärmen, dem jüngeren Sohn von Mr. Hansdampf, und wie süß der ist … eine weitere Gewohnheit, die es zu unterbinden gilt.

Sie war ziemlich angefressen, weil Mum darauf bestand, dass sie mit uns nach Hause kommt, offenbar hatte Michel ihr angeboten, sie später auf seinem Moped heimzufahren. Und auch, weil Sadie ihrerseits geblieben ist. Sie hat einen etwa Zehnjährigen aufgegabelt, und der hat ihr ebenfalls angeboten, sie später auf seinem Moped heimzufahren.

Ich weiß, dass sie Mums beste Freundin ist und dass sie witzig ist, aber muss man sich nicht irgendwann einmal eingestehen, dass es jetzt reicht? Dass man zu alt ist?

Zum Beispiel mit fünfundzwanzig?

Sadies Minirock konnte es, was fehlende Länge betrifft, mit Chloës durchaus aufnehmen, und ich finde wirklich, dass jemand, sprich: Mum, ihr ernsthaft ins Gewissen reden sollte, sich etwas mehr ihrem Alter gemäß zu kleiden. Am besten nach Art einer Nonne und auf keinen Fall und niemals kniefrei.

Teenager-Spätlese, sagt man da freundlich.

Ich habe mir einmal *Die Reifeprüfung* angesehen. Den Film habe ich nicht verstanden, echt nicht.

Ich schlüpfe aus Shorts und T-Shirt und falle ins Bett, nur um mich in einer Wasserlache wiederzufinden.

Verdammt!

Ich schaue hoch und sehe Bee, der nach wie vor den Langzeitrekord im Kopfüberhängen für Hasen brechen will, und stelle fest, dass er den ganzen Tag auf mein Kissen und das Bett getropft hat. Ich stehe auf und nehme ihn ab. Er ist relativ trocken. Kein Wunder, das ganze Wasser ist jetzt in meinem Bett.

Es gelingt mir, mich um hundertachtzig Grad zu drehen, damit ich bloß in den Füßen eine Lungenentzündung bekomme und nicht in der Brust.

Ich schließe die Augen und versuche zu schlafen, aber das Adrenalin rast durch meinen Körper, und mein Herz will meinen Körper glauben machen, er habe gerade einen Zehn-Kilometer-Lauf bergauf absolviert. Und das bei Temperaturen von sechzig Grad plus. Ich kann sein Schlagen nicht genügend beruhigen, um mich zu entspannen und einzuschlafen. Und ich weiß auch, warum.

Von Rupes und seiner komischen Familie abgesehen steht bei meiner auch nicht alles zum Besten.

Der Tanz. Er und *sie* …

Die Konsequenzen sind schlicht und ergreifend grauenvoll. Meine Mutter – die tragende Säule unserer Familie, unser aller Stütze – hat sich von Dad entfernt. Und das heißt auch, dass sie sich von *uns* entfernen könnte.

Die Tatsache, dass ich einen Stiefvater habe, dass wir uns notgedrungen tolerieren müssen, dass er kein Eis um mehr als ein Pfund kauft und mich für einen komischen Vogel hält, weil mir Plato lieber ist als Pelé, ist nicht gerade ideal.

Aber heute Abend ist mir klar geworden, dass er gar nicht so schlecht ist. Um ehrlich zu sein, ist er eigentlich ein ganz guter Kerl. Er ist … solide, im Gegensatz zu anderen Alternativen, die ich nennen könnte. Die sind keine … *er* ist keine … Alternative.

Ein zaghaftes Klopfen an meiner Tür.

»Alex? Bist du wach?«

Es ist Viola. Mist. »Äh, nein, eigentlich nicht.«

»Schon gut.«

Dann höre ich sie auf ihren Füßchen davontapsen. Und kriege wieder ein so schlechtes Gewissen, dass ich mich in eine aufrechte Position quäle und die Tür aufmache. »Aber jetzt bin ich wach«, sage ich zu der schemenhaften Gestalt in dem weißen Nachthemd. »Ist alles in Ordnung?«

Sie schüttelt den Kopf. »Vorhin habe ich Mummy mit Rupes nach Hause kommen hören, aber sie hat sich in ihr Zimmer eingesperrt und gesagt, ich soll sie in Ruhe lassen«, flüstert sie unglücklich.

Ich strecke die Hand nach ihr aus. »Möchtest du ein bisschen zu mir in meine Besenkammer kommen?«

»Ja, bitte.« Sie nimmt meine Hand und huscht in mein Zimmer.

KAPITEL 16

Um halb sechs wurde William wach, helle Sonne fiel in den Raum, die Läden vor den Fenstern waren nicht geschlossen. Erst allmählich wurde ihm bewusst, dass er nicht in seinem Bett im Cedar House im englischen Hampshire lag und auch nicht in Pandora, sondern in einem der Gästezimmer von Alexis Lisles elegantem Wohnhaus, das neben der Weinkellerei stand.

Langsam drangen die Erinnerungen an den vergangenen Abend durch seine Benommenheit. Er stöhnte leise.

Was für ein heilloses Durcheinander!

Er streckte sich ausgiebig, um richtig wach zu werden, stand aus dem schmalen Bett auf und schaute auf die Gestalt, die im zweiten Bett lag. Nachdem er sich vergewissert hatte, dass Sacha fest schlief und sein Atem tief und regelmäßig ging, und da er bezweifelte, wieder einschlafen zu können, zog er sich an und schlich nach unten in den kühlen gefliesten Eingangsflur.

Im Haus war alles still, und so trat er vor die Tür und ging die lange Auffahrt hinunter, überquerte die ungepflasterte Straße und wanderte weiter durch die Weinfelder, die jenseits davon begannen.

Während er durch das weiche, diesige Morgenlicht spazierte, ließ er die Ereignisse des vergangenen Abends Revue passieren. Abgesehen von Sachas alkoholisierter Offenbarung hatte er selbst sich vermutlich auch nicht ganz korrekt verhalten.

Helena …

Die Eifersucht war wie ein Buschfeuer in ihm aufgelodert, als er beim Fest ankam und sie mit solcher Hingabe in Alexis' Armen tanzen sah. Und nachdem ihn seit Tagen die Ungewissheit über das Verhältnis der beiden zueinander gepeinigt hatte, war seine Wut einfach explodiert.

Die Tatsache schließlich, dass sie an dem Abend eigentlich ihren zehnten Hochzeitstag hätten feiern sollen, hatte alles noch schlimmer gemacht.

William pflückte sich von einem Weinstock eine Handvoll Trauben und war überrascht, wie süß die Früchte schmeckten. Allerdings war ihm klar, dass sie seinen Durst an diesem Morgen nicht stillen würden. Die Sonne brannte immer heißer herab, er musste unbedingt Wasser trinken. Also machte er sich auf den Rückweg und grübelte weiter über Helenas emotionale Verschlossenheit ihm gegenüber.

Warum hatte er das Gefühl, dass sie sich immer bedeckt hielt? Dass irgendetwas sie daran hinderte, wirklich die Seine zu sein?

Hatte es mit Alexis zu tun?

Es gab nur eine Möglichkeit, das herauszufinden. Er musste mit dem Mann selbst sprechen.

Als er ins Haus zurückkehrte, hörte er aus einem Raum am anderen Ende des Flurs Geräusche dringen. Er ging darauf zu, öffnete vorsichtig die Tür und blickte in eine große, von der Sonne durchflutete Küche, wo Alexis bereits Kaffee kochte.

»Wie geht es dir, William? Hast du gut geschlafen?« Alexis drehte sich zu ihm und lächelte freundlich.

»Ja, wenn auch nur für ein paar Stunden, danke. Alexis, ich muss mich wirklich bei dir entschuldigen, dass wir dir derartige Schwierigkeiten bereiten. Und wegen der sehr unschönen Szene gestern Abend.«

»Solche Dinge passieren nun mal, William. Ich habe vorhin nach Sacha gesehen, er schläft immer noch wie ein Toter.«

»Der Schlaf wird ihm guttun. Ich bezweifle, dass er in den letzten Monaten viel davon bekommen hat.«

»Kaffee?«

»Gern, und einen Schluck Wasser bitte, Alexis.«

Alexis schenkte ihnen beiden ein Glas Wasser und Kaffee aus der Kanne ein, die auf dem Herd stand, und stellte alles auf den Tisch. »Bitte, mein Freund, nimm Platz.«

Die beiden setzten sich einander gegenüber und tranken zunächst wortlos den heißen, belebenden Kaffee.

Schließlich brach William das Schweigen. »Alexis, entschuldige, angesichts des Vorfalls gestern Abend ist es nicht die richtige Zeit für dieses Gespräch, aber ich muss dich etwas fragen. Ich weiß nicht, wie ich es sonst erfahren könnte. Was genau steckt hinter der Beziehung zwischen dir und Helena?«

Alexis schwieg wieder eine Weile, dann nickte er bedächtig. »Es ist gut, dass du mich das fragst. Und dass wir unerwartet die Gelegenheit zu diesem Gespräch unter vier Augen haben. Ich hatte auch schon auf einen passenden Moment gewartet. Nun ...« Er seufzte. »Ich glaube, es ist kein Geheimnis, dass Helena und ich früher, als wir jung waren, eine Sommerromanze hatten. Nach ihrer Abreise habe ich sie nur noch ein einziges Mal wiedergesehen.«

»Sie hat mir aber gesagt, dass sie dich seit dem Sommer nie mehr gesehen hat.«

»Sie sagt die Wahrheit. Ich sah sie noch einmal, als sie mit dem Ballett der Scala im Amphitheater in Limassol aufgetreten ist. Sie wusste nicht, dass ich dort war.«

»Ach so«, murmelte William.

»Und ich gebe zu, als ich hörte, dass sie nach all den Jahren nach Pandora zurückkommen würde … Ich kann nicht leugnen, dass ich mich insgeheim fragte, ob unsere früheren Gefühle füreinander wiederaufleben würden. Aber, William, ich weiß, dass es zwischen uns nie mehr geben kann als alte Erinnerungen und Freundschaft. Und das ist die Wahrheit. Es ist offensichtlich, dass sie dich liebt, und das hat sie mir auch gesagt. Bitte verzeih mir, William. Du darfst nicht an ihrer Liebe zu dir zweifeln. Und wenn ich dir Anlass zu Zweifeln gegeben habe, dann entschuldige ich mich aus ganzem Herzen dafür. Nichts davon ist Helenas Schuld, das schwöre ich.«

»Danke.« Eine Woge der Erleichterung erfasste William. Es fiel ihm schwer weiterzusprechen. »Aber ich habe trotzdem den Eindruck, dass mehr dahintersteckt, als sie mir sagt. Stimmt das, Alexis?«

»Das, mein Freund« – Alexis warf ihm einen Blick zu –, »musst du deine Frau fragen.«

Helena schaute auf die Uhr und stellte erschrocken fest, dass es schon nach neun Uhr war. Sie fragte sich, warum die beiden Kleinen nicht zu ihr ins Bett gekommen waren wie sonst, wenn sie länger schlief und William noch nicht auf war. Sie griff nach ihrem Morgenmantel, der an der Tür hing, und ging nach unten in die Küche.

»Hallo, Mummy! Du bist nicht auf gewesen, also habe ich Fred und mir Frühstück gemacht«, verkündete Immy stolz.

Helena sah auf die Verwüstung und hob eine halb gegessene Tafel Blockschokolade und ein umgekipptes Glas mit Oliven vom Boden auf. Über Tisch und Boden waren Mehl und Zucker verschüttet, die bald Heerscharen von Ameisen anlocken würden.

»Hallo, Mummy«, ertönte eine Stimme von unter dem Tisch.

Helena hob das Tischtuch an und wusste mit einem Blick auf Freds Gesicht, wohin die zweite Hälfte der Schokolade verschwunden war.

»Guten Morgen, Fred«, sagte sie matt. Ohne mindestens eine Tasse Kaffee konnte sie nicht einmal daran denken, mit dem Aufräumen zu beginnen. Sie setzte den Kessel auf.

»Kann Immy mir jeden Tag Frühstück machen, Mummy? Das kann sie wirklich gut, viel besser als du«, krähte Fred fröhlich.

»Das glaube ich sofort. Warum seid ihr denn nicht zu mir ins Bett gekommen und habt mich geweckt? Das macht ihr doch sonst immer«, sagte sie.

»Das haben wir ja versucht, Mummy, aber du bist nicht wach geworden. Du musst richtig müde gewesen sein. Hier, was zu trinken für dich.« Mit einem Lächeln reichte Immy ihrer Mutter einen Plastikbecher mit einer übel riechenden, schleimig grünen Flüssigkeit. »Das hab ich gemacht. Schmeck mal. Da sind lauter gute Sachen drin.«

»Ich ... ich probiere es später.« Der Geruch ließ Helena würgen. Sie hatte mit den Nachwehen des gestrigen Abends zu kämpfen, und zwar nicht nur, was ihren Alkoholkonsum betraf, sondern auch in emotionaler Hinsicht. »Danke, Immy«, brachte sie hervor und stellte den Becher ab.

»Wo ist Daddy?«, fragte Fred aus seinem Versteck.

»Er ist mit Onkel Sacha weggefahren, sie haben ... etwas zu erledigen. Er kommt später wieder.« Helena beschloss, auf Kaffee zu verzichten, schenkte sich stattdessen aus dem Kühlschrank ein großes Glas Wasser ein und trank in großen Zügen. In dem Moment kam Angelina zur Tür herein.

»Guten Morgen, ihr Kleinen.« Sie schaute unter den Tisch zu Fred und gab Immy einen Kuss. »Schöner Abend gestern, Helena?«

»Ja, danke.«

»Meine Freunde sagen, es war schönes Fest. Und Sie tanzen wunderschön mit Mr. Alexis.« Angelinas dunkle Augen funkelten vor Freude.

»Mummy, hast du getanzt?«, fragte Immy staunend.

»Ja, Immy, alle haben getanzt. Angelina, vielleicht könnten Sie mit den beiden zum Pool gehen und sie beim Planschen beaufsichtigen? Würde euch das gefallen, ihr zwei?«

Wie der Blitz kam Fred unter dem Tisch hervorgeschossen. »Au ja!«

»Ich gehe, aber zuerst« – Angelina stemmte die Hände in die Hüften und schaute Immy und Fred streng an –, »wer hat in meine saubere Küche so große Unordnung gemacht?«

»Wir! Wir!«, krähte Fred und hüpfte aufgeregt auf und ab, während Immy schuldbewusst dreinschaute.

»Dann räumen wir erst auf und dann schwimmen. Hockay?«

»Hockay«, stimmten die beiden zu.

Dankbar ergriff Helena die Chance, die Küche zu verlassen und zu duschen.

»Guten Morgen, Tante Helena. Ich habe schon nach dir gesucht.« Als Helena die Treppe hinaufging, wurde sie oben bereits von Viola erwartet.

»Wie geht es dir, mein Schatz?«, fragte sie.

Viola sah zu Helena hinunter und zuckte unglücklich mit den Schultern. »War das alles ein schlimmer Traum?«

»Ach, Viola, es tut mir so leid, aber wir wissen beide, dass es mehr war als das. Möchtest du zu mir ins Zimmer kommen? Dann können wir uns ein bisschen unterhalten.«

»Ja.« Viola folgte Helena ins Schlafzimmer und auf den kleinen Balkon hinaus. »Mummys Tür ist noch zugesperrt, ich hab's gerade wieder versucht.«

»Vielleicht schläft sie noch, aber wenn du sie sehen möchtest, können wir sie bestimmt wecken.«

»Nein, sie sagt nur lauter hässliche Sachen über Daddy. Es ist bestimmt nicht alles sein Fehler, aber sie gibt ihm trotzdem an allem die Schuld.«

»Viola, mein Schatz.« Das Mädchen tat Helena so schrecklich leid. »Du musst versuchen zu verstehen, dass sie genauso durcheinander und entsetzt ist wie du.«

»Glaubst du, dass sie sich jetzt scheiden lassen? Alex sagte, dass das möglich ist.«

»Ich weiß wirklich nicht, was passieren wird. Auf jeden Fall werden sie sich erst einmal unterhalten müssen.«

»Aber sie reden doch nie miteinander! Daddy versucht es zwar, aber Mummy schreit ihn immer nur an. Sie hört ihm nicht zu, nie. Und was wird aus mir, Tante Helena?«

»Mein Schatz, deine Mum und deinen Daddy hast du doch trotzdem noch und Rupes auch. Aber vielleicht werdet ihr umziehen müssen, und dann kommst du auf eine andere Schule, das ist alles.«

»Das ist mir egal, ich kann meine Schule sowieso nicht leiden. Aber wenn Daddy und Mummy sich scheiden lassen, dann will ich bei Daddy bleiben!« Viola vergrub das Gesicht in den Händen. »Ich hab ihn trotzdem lieb, auch wenn Mummy ihn nicht mehr mag.«

»Das weiß ich, mein Schatz, und er hat dich auch lieb.«

»Wenn ich nicht bei Daddy leben kann, darf ich dann bei euch wohnen? Du bist so nett und Alex auch. Und ich helfe auch mit Immy und Fred, das verspreche ich«, schlug Viola verzweifelt vor.

»Es würde uns sehr gut gefallen, wenn du bei uns leben würdest, aber ich glaube, deine Mum wäre damit nicht einverstanden.«

»Das ist ihr doch egal. Für sie gibt es nur ihren Liebling Rupes. Sollen doch die beiden heiraten, wenn sie sich schon so sehr lieben.« Viola stieß ein unglückliches Lachen aus.

»Ach, Viola, das darfst du nicht sagen. Mummy liebt dich sehr.«

»Das stimmt nicht, Tante Helena. Ich weiß überhaupt nicht, warum sie mich adoptiert hat.«

»Weil sie dich geliebt hat. Und immer noch liebt.« Helena fiel es schwer, die richtigen Worte des Trosts zu finden.

»Außerdem« – Violas Gesicht wurde finster – »lügt sie.«

»Wieso sagst du das?«

»Mummy hat Geld, von dem sie Daddy nie erzählt hat.«

»Woher weißt du das?«

»Einmal habe ich in ihrer Handtasche einen Kontoauszug von ihr gesehen, gleich nach Omas Tod. Am Ende der Ziffer waren ein paar Nullen.«

»Wirklich?« Helena fiel ein, dass Jules neulich von Geld gesprochen hatte, das ihre Mutter ihr hinterlassen habe. »Aber das ist doch eine gute Nachricht, oder? Vielleicht ist ja doch alles nicht so schlimm.«

»Aber vielleicht will sie es nicht mit Daddy teilen. Was gemein ist, weil er sein ganzes Geld mit uns teilt. Meinst du, ich soll es ihm sagen?«

»Erst einmal nicht.«

»Also gut.« Unglücklich wischte sich Viola die Nase. »Meinst du, er kommt heute, damit ich ihn sehen kann?«

»Das weiß ich nicht. Ich glaube, das hängt von deinen Eltern ab.«

»Aber was ist mit mir?«

»Ach, mein Schatz.« Zärtlich hob Helena das Mädchen auf ihren Schoß. »Es tut mir wirklich so leid, aber im Moment bist du hier bei uns gut aufgehoben, und ich bin überzeugt, dass deine Eltern sich aussprechen und eine gute Regelung finden. Das ist für sie beide auch ein großer Schock.«

»Aber, Tante Helena, ich möchte Daddy sehen. Er braucht jemand, der ihm einen Kuss gibt.«

»Das weiß ich, und ich bin überzeugt, dass du ihm den auch bald geben kannst. So, und jetzt – was meinst du, wollen wir deinen Badeanzug holen, und dann gehen du und ich zu Immy und Fred an den Pool?«

»Okay«, sagte Viola resigniert, entwand sich Helenas Umarmung und trottete mit hängenden Schultern aus dem Zimmer.

Um elf Uhr ging es Helena bereits wesentlich besser. Das Schwimmen und die Munterkeit ihrer Kinder hatten sie wieder in Schwung gebracht, obwohl sie in Gedanken immer wieder in der Weinkellerei war und sich fragte, was wohl zwischen William, Alexis und Sacha vor sich ging.

Irgendwann tauchte Alex am Pool auf, später auch Chloë, und die beiden ließen sich für die Jüngeren ein paar Spiele einfallen. Erleichtert bemerkte Helena, dass Viola in das Lachen und Kreischen der anderen einstimmte, als Alex sie alle um das Becken jagte.

»Helena.« Mit einem Lächeln trat Angelina zu ihr. »Heute Vormittag ich putze das Haus, aber wenn ich bin fertig, kann ich mit den Kleinen ins Dorf, hockay? Meine Eltern möchten sie gern kennenlernen. Wir trinken gemeinsam Tee. Und Alexis ... ich meine, Alex und Chloë und Viola mit den schönen Haaren auch, wenn sie möchten.«

»Sie kommen bestimmt gern mit, Angelina, aber bitte, machen Sie sich nicht so viel Mühe.«

»Ist keine Mühe! Wir lieben Kinder, das wissen Sie. Vielleicht, später, ich habe auch Kinder, aber bis dahin ich adoptiere Ihre.«

»Das dürfen Sie gern«, sagte Helena dankbar.

Als sie zum Haus hinaufging, um sich den nassen Bikini auszuziehen, fand sie Rupes allein auf der Terrasse sitzen.

»Hallo, Rupes«, sagte sie vorsichtig.

»Hi.«

»Wie geht es dir?«

Er zuckte lustlos mit den Achseln.

»Hast du deine Mutter heute Vormittag schon gesehen?«

Er nickte.

»Wie geht es ihr?«

»Wie soll es ihr schon gehen?«

Helena setzte sich neben ihn. »Nicht besonders gut, vermute ich.«

»Sie schämt sich zu sehr, um das Zimmer zu verlassen. Sie sagt, sie will im Moment niemanden sehen.«

»Das kann ich verstehen. Würde es etwas nützen, wenn ich mit ihr rede? Ihr erkläre, dass deswegen niemand schlecht von ihr denkt? Dass das alles nicht ihre Schuld ist? Wir wollen euch allen nur helfen.«

»Ich weiß nicht, ob das etwas nützen würde.« Wieder zuckte Rupes mit den Achseln. »Es geht um ihren Stolz.«

»Natürlich.« Helena legte ihm eine Hand auf den Arm. »Das findet sich schon alles, glaub mir. Das tut es immer.«

»Nichts findet sich.« Rupes schüttelte ihre Hand ab. »Dad hat unser Leben kaputt gemacht. So einfach ist das.« Er stand auf und verschwand über die Terrasse ums Haus und außer Sicht. Helena wusste, warum. Sie sollte ihn nicht weinen sehen.

Sie ging weiter in die Küche und bemerkte, dass ihr Handy blinkte.

Eine SMS von William.

Hi. Sacha geht's nicht gut. Melde mich später.

Helena sah auf das Display, dann merkte sie, was fehlte: der Kuss am Ende.

Nach dem Mittagessen packte Angelina die Kinder ins Auto und fuhr mit ihnen ins Dorf. Rupes war noch nicht von seinem Spaziergang zurückgekehrt, und Sadie war auch noch nicht nach Pandora zurückgekommen. Helena gab sich einen Ruck, ging nach oben und klopfte leise an die Tür zu Jules' Zimmer.

»Ich bin's. Helena. Darf ich reinkommen?«

Keine Antwort.

»Jules, ich kann gut verstehen, dass du niemanden sehen willst, aber kann ich dir nicht wenigstens etwas zu trinken bringen? Tee? Kaffee? Einen dreifachen Wodka?«

Gerade wollte Helena wieder gehen, als Jules sagte: »Ach, was soll's! Warum nicht? Wenn du einen vierfachen Wodka draus machst. Die Tür ist auf.«

Helena betrat den Raum. Jules saß mit untergeschlagenen Beinen mitten auf dem Bett, sie trug noch das goldene Oberteil vom Vorabend. Überall waren Kleidungsstücke verstreut, der gewaltige Koffer lag halb gefüllt auf dem Boden.

»Willst du abreisen?«, fragte Helena.

Jules machte eine hilflose Geste. »Das wollte ich zuerst und habe angefangen zu packen, aber dann ist mir eingefallen ...«, sie unterdrückte ein Schluchzen, »dass ich nichts habe, wohin ich fahren kann.«

»Ach, Jules.« Helena setzte sich neben sie und legte einen Arm um ihre Schultern. »Es tut mir alles so schrecklich leid.«

»Wie konnte er es nur so weit kommen lassen, ohne mir etwas davon zu sagen?«, rief sie. »Ich bin doch kein Ungeheuer,

Helena, oder? Ich meine, so abweisend? Immer wieder habe ich ihn gebeten, mit mir über seine Arbeit zu sprechen, aber er macht einfach dicht und schenkt sich noch ein Glas Wein ein.«

»Natürlich bist du kein Ungeheuer, und ich bin sicher, dass Sacha dir nicht absichtlich alles verschwiegen hat. Vermutlich ist im Lauf der Zeit eins zum anderen gekommen, bis er sich dachte, bei all den Lügen käme es auf eine mehr oder weniger auch nicht mehr an.« Helena seufzte. »Es war sehr dumm von ihm, dir nichts zu sagen, und an der ganzen Misere hast du wirklich keine Schuld. Das darfst du nie vergessen.«

»Das sage ich mir ja auch ständig, aber wann immer ich daran denke, wie er da vorn stand und volltrunken vor den vielen Leuten unsere dreckige Wäsche ausbreitete, habe ich mir überlegt, was sie sich gedacht haben müssen: eine Frau, deren Mann sich in der Stunde der Not nicht an sie wenden kann. Dabei habe ich mich so bemüht, eine gute Ehefrau zu sein, Helena, wirklich. Und bei Gott, das war nicht immer einfach.« Sie warf einen kurzen Blick zu ihr. »Wie du weißt, ist Sacha kein William.«

»Ja, da gebe ich dir recht. Hör mal, die Kinder sind mit Angelina im Dorf, niemand ist im Haus. Warum machst du dich nicht ein bisschen frisch und kommst nach unten, wir setzen uns auf die Terrasse und essen etwas?«

Jules nickte. »Ja, danke, Helena.«

Zehn Minuten später saß Jules am Terrassentisch, verschlang eines der Hähnchen-Sandwichs, die Helena schnell gemacht hatte, und trank ein großes Glas Wein.

»Ehrlich gesagt, mir fehlen buchstäblich die Worte. Ich weiß wirklich nicht, was ich denken oder sagen soll. Vermutlich muss ich Sachas Ansage ernst nehmen und davon ausgehen, dass alles weg ist.«

»Ihr müsst euch wirklich zusammensetzen und euch aussprechen, damit du über alles Bescheid weißt.«

»Eines weiß ich jetzt schon: Sollte der Idiot mir unter die Augen kommen, würde er gleich keine Zähne mehr haben, um auch nur ein Wort zu sagen! Nein« – Jules schüttelte den Kopf –, »im Moment kann ich seinen Anblick wirklich nicht ertragen. Und falls er anruft, sag ihm bitte, dass er mir vorläufig aus dem Weg gehen soll.«

»Falls es dich tröstet, ich bezweifle, dass es ihm besser geht als dir.«

»Von mir braucht er sich nie wieder auch nur einen Funken Mitleid zu erhoffen. Als wäre nicht alles schon schlimm genug – musste er wirklich obendrein nicht nur mich, sondern auch die Kinder in aller Öffentlichkeit bloßstellen? Das verstehe ich wirklich nicht, Helena. Welcher Teufel hat ihn da bloß geritten?«

»Verzweiflung gepaart mit Alkohol, würde ich sagen.«

»Ach, ich weiß, dass er ein Alkoholproblem hat, schon seit Jahren. Aber ich habe aufgehört, etwas zu sagen, weil er mich dann immer als Nörglerin hinstellt«, sagte Jules und trank hastig einen großen Schluck Wein. »Was hätte ich denn tun sollen? Bis er selbst erkennt, dass er ein Problem hat, ist ihm nicht zu helfen. Und mir mit meiner Zukunft im Moment auch nicht.«

»Ich kann gut nachvollziehen, dass es dir gerade so vorkommt, Jules, aber es gibt immer eine Lösung.«

»Entschuldige, Helena, ich weiß, du willst nur helfen, aber ich will im Moment keine aufmunternden Plattitüden hören. Er hat mich nie geliebt, das ist die bittere Wahrheit, und Gott allein weiß, weshalb er mich überhaupt geheiratet hat.«

»Bitte, Jules, sag das nicht! Natürlich liebt er dich.«

»Nein. Er liebt mich nicht und hat es auch nie. Punkt. Das

war mir immer schon klar. Das Problem ist, ich habe ihm jahrelang alles, aber wirklich alles nachgesehen, nur damit wir zusammenbleiben, und habe mich mit den Brosamen Zuneigung zufriedengegeben, die er mir hingeworfen hat.«

»Ich bin mir sicher …«

»Spar dir deine Worte«, fuhr Jules auf. »Ich weiß, ich bin darüber verbittert geworden, aber wenn du wüsstest, was ich im Lauf der Jahre alles ignoriert habe, du würdest es nicht glauben …« Jules wandte sich ab und unterdrückte wieder ein Schluchzen. »Wirklich, ich habe alles versucht, ich habe ihn bei seinen künstlerischen Ambitionen unterstützt, ich habe ein Kind bekommen – und sogar das kleine Mädchen adoptiert, das er so gern haben wollte, als ich kein zweites Mal schwanger geworden bin –, habe ihm ein behagliches Zuhause geschaffen und abends ein warmes Essen auf den Tisch gestellt. Ich habe sogar die ganze Wäschepalette von *Agent Provocateur* durchprobiert, aber es hat alles nichts genützt. Man kann nichts erzwingen, was nicht da ist … nie da war.«

Helena schwieg. In diesem Moment ging es nur darum zuzuhören.

»Ich glaube, Sacha hat nach jemandem gesucht, der sein Leben ins Lot bringt«, fuhr Jules fort. »Ich war immer ein pragmatischer Mensch, und er war ein Träumer und lebte im Wolkenkuckucksheim. Wahrscheinlich habe ich ihn auf den Boden der Tatsachen geholt und seinem Leben eine gewisse Struktur gegeben. Verantwortung zu übernehmen war nie seine Stärke, wie du wohl weißt.« Jules seufzte. »Aber weißt du, was mich wirklich rasend macht?«

»Was?«

»Dass alle Mitleid mit *ihm* haben! ›Der arme Sacha, der mit dieser Schreckschraube verheiratet ist!‹ Und sag nicht, dass du und William nicht genauso denkt, Helena, das weiß ich doch. Das tut ihr alle!« Jules schlug mit der Faust derart fest auf den Tisch, dass die Weinflasche umgefallen wäre, hätte Helena sie nicht im letzten Moment aufgefangen. »Und ich wette, sogar jetzt gilt das ganze Mitgefühl ihm, nicht mir. Und selbst Viola, meine eigene Tochter, nimmt ihn mir gegenüber in Schutz. Ich weiß, viele werden sich freuen und sagen, dass ich jetzt meine gerechte Strafe bekomme.«

»Jules, ich glaube nicht, dass das stimmt.«

»Ach, Helena, jetzt komm schon!«, herrschte Jules sie an. »Du und William findet euch doch nur um seinetwillen mit mir ab! So dumm und blind bin ich auch nicht, und ich habe es satt! Satt!«

Sie schenkte sich nach. »Mein Gott, ich wünschte wirklich, ich wäre wie du«, sagte sie dann.

»Warum um Himmels willen möchtest du sein wie ich?«

»Weil die ganze Welt dich anbetet, Helena. Du schwebst in deinem goldenen Licht einher, die Menschen fühlen sich zu dir hingezogen, sie baden sich in deinem Glanz, und wenn sie in deiner Nähe waren, haben sie das Gefühl, als wäre etwas von deinem Zauber auf sie übergegangen. Aber im Gegensatz zu dir habe ich keinen natürlichen Charme. Ich bin unbeholfen, sozial ungeschickt, schüchtern, wenn du's unbedingt wissen willst, und deswegen kommt das, was ich tue oder sage, meistens falsch bei den Leuten an. Aber bei dir – ich bin sicher, selbst wenn du etwas falsch gemacht hast, dann weißt du genau, wie du es wieder geradebiegen kannst.«

»Ich sage dir, Jules, das stimmt nicht. Ich habe ein paarmal entsetzliche Fehler gemacht!«, sagte Helena aufgewühlt.

»Haben wir das nicht alle …?« Jules schaute beiseite und trank wieder einen kräftigen Schluck Wein. »Und vielleicht …

aber wirklich nur vielleicht, hätte mir gar nichts Besseres passieren können«, flüsterte sie. »Vielleicht ist ein Neuanfang genau das, was ich brauche. Mein Gott, Helena, ich möchte doch nur jemanden, der mich liebt. Mehr nicht. Wie auch immer, ich weiß, dass ich mich mit Sacha zusammensetzen und wir alles besprechen müssen, aber nicht jetzt. Erst wenn ich meine Gedanken etwas geordnet habe. Im Moment weiß ich nur eines, nämlich, dass unsere Ehe am Ende ist. Schluss, aus, vorbei. Und bitte widersprich mir nicht, sonst schreie ich.«

»Ich sag nichts, versprochen.«

»Und keine Sorge, sehr viel länger bleibe ich nicht hier. Meine Familie hat euch allen den Urlaub schon gründlich genug vermiest. Gib mir nur zwei Tage Zeit, um mir zu überlegen, was ich jetzt tun soll, ja?«

»Wirklich, Jules, lass dir Zeit. Du kannst bleiben, solange du magst.«

»Weißt du was, Helena? Du bist wirklich ein lieber Mensch, trotz allem …« Jules seufzte. »Also, ich gehe jetzt nach oben und versuche zu schlafen. Der Wein hat seinen Zweck erfüllt. Vergangene Nacht habe ich kein Auge zugetan.«

»Ich bin da, wenn die Kinder zurückkommen, also mach dir deretwegen keine Gedanken.«

»Danke. Und ganz egal, was in der Vergangenheit passiert ist, du bist mir eine gute Freundin gewesen. Das weiß ich wirklich zu schätzen.« Jules drückte Helenas Hand so fest, dass sie fast zusammengezuckt wäre.

Mit schwerem Herzen sah Helena ihr nach, wie sie über die Terrasse und ins Haus ging.

Und fragte sich, wer von ihnen beiden unglücklicher war.

Alex' Tagebuch

Entschuldigung, aber …

Das muss ich jetzt einfach so sagen, ich verkneife es mir schon so lange, aber jetzt kann ich nicht mehr. Also:

Der Nachmittag war ein Heidenspaß! Eine Großfamilie fremder Zyprioten, die uns widerlichen Kuchen, ungenießbare Kekse und einen Kaffee servierten, der zur Geschmacksverstärkung mit Sandkörnchen versetzt war.

Sie sprachen mit uns – und nicht zu knapp –, es gab bloß ein klitzekleines Problem …

Ich verstand nur Bahnhof, und das nicht mal auf Griechisch.

Ha! Jetzt habe ich's gesagt.

Ich sag's aber kein zweites Mal.

Als die Knallparty dann in vollem Gang war, ist Chloë verschwunden. Sie sagte, sie müsse kurz was besorgen. Ich bat, sie begleiten zu dürfen, aber sie sagte, sie müsse »etwas für Mädels« kaufen, und das ist für mich natürlich tabu.

Die ganze geheimnisvolle Welt der Mädchen ist unbekanntes Terrain für mich. In meiner alten Schule standen die weiblichen Mitglieder unserer Klasse immer stundenlang in einer Ecke zusammen und haben sich über »Sachen« unterhalten. Und sobald ich oder ein anderes männliches Wesen in ihre Nähe kam, haben sie gekichert und getuschelt und uns gesagt, wir sollen Leine ziehen.

Es ist wirklich ein Jammer, wenn sich mit dem Beginn der Pubertät die große Kluft zwischen Männern und Frauen auftut. Bis ich elf war, gehörte ein Mädchen namens Ellie zu den Menschen, mit denen ich am besten befreundet war. Wir haben uns über den Schulhof gejagt und unser Pausenbrot und unsere Geheimnisse geteilt. Sie hat mir gestanden, in wen sie verknallt war, und ich habe ihr gestanden, dass ich in niemanden verknallt war. In der sechsten Klasse herrschte nicht gerade ein Überangebot an Scarlett Johanssons und Lindsay Lohans.

Allgemein heißt es ja, dass Charakter wichtiger sei als Schönheit. Das ist ungefähr so, als würde man sagen, man hätte sich das scheußliche Sofa nur gekauft, weil es bequem ist. Man muss es sich ja trotzdem die nächsten dreißig Jahre, die man darauf sitzen will, anschauen und sich schämen, wenn Freunde vorbeikommen und glauben, man hätte einen schlechten Geschmack.

Ich würde mich jederzeit und immer für die elegante, unbequeme Alternative entscheiden.

Vielleicht bin ich ja oberflächlich, aber Chloë ist die metaphorische Chaiselongue der Damenwelt. Sie ist grazil, hat einen exquisit geschnitzten Rücken, kunstvoll gedrechselte Beine und ist so schmal, dass man bisweilen herunterfallen würde, wenn man darauf einschliefe. Aber sie wäre immer ein Objekt von großer Schönheit und würde in hundert Jahren bei Sotheby's Tausende von Pfund erbringen.

Wahrscheinlich ist sie ein bisschen wie meine Mutter. Die beiden sind nicht blutsverwandt, aber bestimmte Eigenschaften sind ihnen trotzdem gemein.

Und um unser aller willen hoffe ich doch sehr, dass Treue dazugehört.

Um auf meine Freundin Ellie zurückzukommen, klammheimlich hatte ich immer den Verdacht, dass sie in *mich* verknallt war. Das waren die glückseligen Tage, als ich noch keine Leiter brauchte, um meinen Mitschülerinnen in die Augen zu blicken.

Man könnte sogar sagen, dass ich der Klassenschwarm war. Auf dem Fest nach der Schulaufführung von *Oliver* – bei der ich »Where is Love« derart bewegend interpretierte, dass unser mürrischer Direx angeblich zu Tränen gerührt war – haben sie sich hinter dem Kunstbau regelrecht geprügelt, um mit mir zu knutschen. Ich musste sie bitten, sich ordentlich in einer Schlange anzustellen.

Damals wurde mir klar, dass Ruhm ein unwiderstehliches Aphrodisiakum ist.

Das war kurz vor der achten Klasse, als die Mädchen in die Höhe schossen und zu merkwürdigen, geheimnistuerischen Wesen von einem anderen Stern mutierten. Als sich BH-Größen und Lipgloss und – igitt! – dieses monatliche Dingens, das unvorstellbar ekelhaft klingt, zu einer Welt vereinten, die sich dem Verständnis meiner Geschlechtsgenossen entzieht. Es kam mir vor, als würden wir anhand unserer Hormone aus dem bunten Durcheinander, in dem wir gelebt hatten, ausgefiltert und in zwei Gruppen unterteilt werden, zwischen denen nie wieder Einklang herrschen kann.

Hier ist es fast Mitternacht.

Dad und Sacha sind immer noch »unterwegs« und kommen erst, wenn Mum jeden scharfen und spitzen Gegenstand im Haus versteckt hat, damit Jules ihren Mann nicht umbringen kann. Am Abend packte sie Rupes und Viola ins Auto und fuhr mit ihnen zum Essen ins Dorf, und Sadie ist immer noch verschwunden, obwohl sie Mum mit einer SMS in grausig schillernden Details von ihrem »Vögelfest« berichtet hat.

(Mum sollte mittlerweile wissen, dass ich, wenn sie ihr Handy herumliegen lässt, ihre Nachrichten lese. Sie hat noch nicht gecheckt, wie man eine Zugangssperre einrichtet, und ich werde es ihr bestimmt nicht zeigen.)

Eigentlich war es richtig schön, abends nur mit Mum und den Kleinen zu essen, ohne jemand anderen. Vorher war ich in Mums Zimmer geschlichen, um zu überprüfen, ob auch keine gepackten Koffer herumstehen. Gepackt von wem auch immer. Das heißt, Dad ist nicht weg. Noch nicht. Und abends beim Essen klang Mum auch nicht so, als wollte sie ihn verlassen.

Noch nicht.

Viel mehr Sorgen machte sie sich um Chloë, die ihr simste, sie sei bei Michel und werde »später« heimkommen. Dahin war sie bei der Kaffeeparty heute Nachmittag also verschwunden! Oje. Aber ich weiß, ich muss die Zähne zusammenbeißen; bis wir heiraten, muss Chloë ihre Freiheit genießen dürfen, auch wenn es mich manchmal hart ankommt. Und besonders hart kommt es mich an zu wissen, dass sie mit dem Sohn von Mr. Hansdampf zusammen ist …

Wobei, auf dem Heimweg von der Kaffeeparty bettelte Viola, dass Angelina bei Mr. Hansdampf vorbeifuhr, damit sie hineinlaufen und ihrem Daddy einen Kuss geben konnte. (Das nenne ich Ironie, ein bankrotter Säufer, der sich in einer Weinkellerei versteckt!) Und mich erkor sie zu ihrem Begleiter.

Als wir aus dem Auto stiegen, kam Mr. Hansdampf mit

einem strahlenden Lächeln aus dem Fassraum und sagte Viola, Sacha sei mit William unterwegs, aber er werde ihm ausrichten, dass sie vorbeigekommen sei. Und zum Trost zeigte er uns in der Scheune die kleinen Katzen.

Und als sich Viola hingerissen neben die Kätzchen hockte und eines auf den Schoß nahm, flüsterte er mir zu: »Das muss sehr schwer für sie sein. Es ist gut, dass sie dich hat.«

»Ich weiß nicht, ob Viola das auch so sieht«, sagte ich leise.

»Alex, unterschätz dich nicht. Du bist ein freundlicher und rücksichtsvoller junger Mann.«

Dann gingen wir, aber vorher sagte Mr. Hansdampf noch, Viola könne jederzeit, wann immer sie wolle, kommen und sich die Kätzchen ansehen.

Es war wirklich nett, ein Kompliment zu bekommen. Das hat mich etwas durcheinandergebracht. Und dann gibt es noch die gute Nachricht, dass Dad und er sich noch nicht gegenseitig umgebracht haben, obwohl sie unter einem Dach wohnen. Es sei denn natürlich, Mr. Hansdampf hat gelogen und Dad und Sacha liegen irgendwo zwischen den Weinstöcken verscharrt.

Es klopft. Ich stehe auf, um die Tür aufzumachen.

»Alex, bist du wach?«

Es ist Mum. »Ja.«

Sie drückt auf die Klinke, aber die Tür ist natürlich zugesperrt, um unliebsamen Eindringlingen den Zugang zu verwehren.

Aber Mum sollte ich wohl reinlassen.

»Ich mache mir Sorgen wegen Chloë. Sie ist noch nicht zu Hause«, sagte Helena. Sie hatte den Kopf zu Alex' Zimmer hineingesteckt.

»Mum, sie kommt immer spät zurück.«

»Ich weiß, aber solange Dad nicht da ist, bin ich für sie verantwortlich, und ich habe keine Ahnung, wo sie ist. Sie geht auch nicht an ihr Handy. Du hast nicht zufällig von ihr gehört, oder?«

»Nein, tut mir leid. Sie ist doch irgendwo mit Alexis' Sohn unterwegs, oder?«

»Ja, aber ich kann erst ins Bett gehen, wenn sie zu Hause ist, und ich bin müde.«

»Wie wär's, wenn du Alexis anrufst und ihn fragst, ob er weiß, wohin sie gegangen sind?«

»Es ist fast ein Uhr, und er ist heute Abend, nach dem gestrigen Fest, bestimmt früh ins Bett gegangen. Es wäre nicht nett, ihn zu wecken. Nein«, sagte Helena und seufzte, »dann werde ich einfach auf sie warten müssen. Entschuldige, dass ich dich gestört habe, Alex. Schlaf gut.« Sie warf ihrem Sohn ein müdes Lächeln zu, schloss die Tür und ging zurück in die Küche.

Dort machte sie sich eine Tasse Pfefferminztee und setzte sich hinaus, um auf Chloë zu warten. Sie versuchte, nicht daran zu denken, worüber die drei Männer in der Weinkellerei wohl gerade sprachen …

Helena schreckte hoch, als ein Moped die Kiesauffahrt heraufkam. Sie sah auf die Uhr. Es war halb drei, sie musste wohl eingedöst sein. Gut zehn Minuten später hörte sie Chloë über die Terrasse schleichen.

»Guten Abend, Chloë, oder vielleicht sollte ich eher guten Morgen sagen.«

Beim Klang von Helenas Stimme fuhr Chloë zusammen.

»Wow! Du bist ja noch auf«, flüsterte sie.

»Ich habe auf dich gewartet. Komm in die Küche und trink eine Tasse Tee mit mir.«

Das war kein Vorschlag, sondern ein Befehl. Zerknirscht folgte Chloë Helena ins Haus. »Kann ich einfach nur ein Glas Wasser haben?«, bat sie, als sie sich an den Tisch setzte. »Hältst du mir jetzt eine Strafpredigt?«

»Ja und nein.« Helena schenkte ihnen beiden ein Glas Wasser ein und verzichtete auf den Tee. »Aber solange dein Vater nicht hier ist, bin ich die verantwortliche Erziehungsberechtigte. Und ich habe mir Sorgen um dich gemacht.«

»Helena, das tut mir wirklich leid. Kommt Dad denn bald zurück?« Geschickt versuchte Chloë, das Thema zu wechseln.

»Wir telefonieren morgen wieder, dann wird er mir sagen, was Sacha vorhat. Jules ist oben und weigert sich, ihn zu sehen.«

»Das wundert mich nicht. Das war doch gestern Abend oberpeinlich, oder nicht?«

»Toll war es nicht, da bin ich deiner Meinung. Was sagte denn Michel dazu?«, fragte Helena, um wieder zum eigentlichen Thema zurückzukehren.

»Dass es seit Jahren die beste Show war, die im Dorf geboten wurde, und kostenlos dazu. Es gab heute kein anderes Thema.«

»Du bist heute Abend also im Dorf gewesen?«

»Ja. Wir waren in der neuen Bar an der Ecke, gegenüber der Bank.«

»Ich weiß, dass du getrunken hast, Chloë, das rieche ich an deinem Atem.«

»Helena, heute trinkt jeder mit vierzehn. Und es waren bloß zwei Gläser Wein. Der Abend war richtig klasse. Michel hat mich seinen Freunden vorgestellt. Die sind cool, auch wenn ihr Englisch zu wünschen übrig lässt.«

»Bis um zwei Uhr? Die Bar macht doch sicher um elf Uhr zu.«

»Hinterher ist Michel noch mit mir auf dem Moped rumgefahren.« Chloë wurde rot.

»Chloë, mein Schatz, Michel ist achtzehn, du bist vierzehn. Ist er nicht ein bisschen zu alt für dich?«

»Nächsten Monat werde ich fünfzehn, vergiss das nicht. Das ist nichts. Dad ist fast sechs Jahre älter als du. Wo ist da der Unterschied?«

»In deinem Alter spielt das sehr wohl eine Rolle, Chloë. Er ist erwachsen, und du bist noch ein Kind. Rechtlich, wenn schon sonst nicht.«

»Jungs in meinem Alter langweilen mich«, sagte Chloë herablassend. »Rupes zum Beispiel. Richtig dumm ist er. Er hat mir auf Französisch einen Liebesbrief geschrieben, der war voll daneben! Er hat mich sein ›süßes, liebes Schwein‹ genannt – da hat er wohl *ma cocotte* mit *mon cochon* verwechselt. Und dann hat er noch geschrieben, dass ich Augen wie ›kleine glühende Kohlestückchen‹ habe. Außerdem«, fügte sie verträumt hinzu, »ist Michel der coolste Typ, den ich kenne. Er ist ganz anders als die Jungs, mit denen ich mich sonst abgebe.«

»Wirklich?«

»Ja. Er ist sanft, außerdem ist er sehr klug und unterhält sich mit mir wie mit einer Erwachsenen. Und seinem Akzent könnte ich den ganzen Tag zuhören.« Chloë schauderte fast vor

Wonne. »Weißt du, normalerweise bin ich diejenige, die sagt, wo's langgeht. Ich weiß, dass Jungs mit mir ausgehen wollen, aber mir war keiner von ihnen wirklich wichtig, wenn du weißt, was ich meine.«

Das wusste Helena nur zu gut. »Möchte er dich wiedersehen?«

»Er sagt, er leiht sich morgen von seinem Vater den Wagen und zeigt mir Aphrodites Geburtsort, und dann will er mich zum Mittagessen einladen.«

»Chloë, ich will dir keine Predigt halten und möchte mich auch nicht zu deiner Mutter aufschwingen …«

»Dann tu's nicht, Helena.«

»Gut. Aber *bitte* pass auf.«

»Das mache ich, ich bin nicht dumm. Und zu deiner Information, ich bin noch eine, wenn du weißt, was ich meine. Das sind die meisten meiner Freundinnen nicht mehr.«

»Dann sorg dafür, dass es so bleibt. Und wenn nicht, dann bitte, komm zu mir und wir … wir organisieren etwas.«

»Danke, Helena. Du bist echt cool.«

»Chloë, glaub mir, ich finde es nicht gut, aber es ist immer besser, auf Nummer sicher zu gehen. Und bitte, vergiss nicht, es wird nie mehr als eine Urlaubsromanze sein.«

»Warum nicht? Michel hat mir heute Abend erzählt, dass er gern in England arbeiten möchte, wenn er mit der Uni in Limassol fertig ist.«

»Das kann ich mir gut vorstellen. Aber dieses Gespräch führt jetzt zu nichts, ihr habt euch erst gestern Abend kennengelernt, und …«

»Aber es kommt mir vor, als würde ich ihn schon seit Ewigkeiten kennen.«

»Das kann ich verstehen. Aber wenn ihr euch wirklich regelmäßig sehen wollt, dann müssen wir uns auf ein paar Regeln verständigen, in Ordnung?«

»Okay«, meinte Chloë achselzuckend. »Aber darf ich bitte morgen mit ihm wegfahren?«

»Darüber muss ich erst mit deinem Dad sprechen. Und wenn Michel so erwachsen ist, wie du sagst, wird er verstehen, dass wir wissen müssen, wo du bist. Du bist noch minderjährig.«

»Okay.«

»Eine der Regeln ist, dass du um Mitternacht zu Hause bist, damit wir unbesorgt ins Bett gehen können. Und genau dahin gehe ich jetzt.«

»Weißt du was, wenn ich morgen den ganzen Tag unterwegs bin, stehe ich früh auf und mache den Kleinen Frühstück, dann kannst du ausschlafen. Wie wär's damit?«

»Abgemacht. Das muss Liebe sein«, sagte Helena und lächelte.

»Danke. Bis morgen.«

Ein paar Minuten später lag Helena im Bett, zu müde, um einzuschlafen. Es erschien ihr erst wie gestern, dass auch sie in den frühen Morgenstunden nach Pandora heimgeschlichen war, nur um von Angus abgepasst zu werden, der ihr eine Standpauke hielt. Er hatte die ganze Zeit in seinem Büro gesessen und auf sie gewartet.

Jetzt hatte sie gerade eine moderne Fassung des gleichen Gesprächs mit ihrer Stieftochter geführt, und diesmal ging es um den Sohn des Mannes, den sie damals geliebt hat.

Wie Chloë gesagt hatte, die Zeiten hatten sich geändert, es gab Freiheiten, die Alexis und ihr verwehrt gewesen waren. Grenzen waren in so vieler Hinsicht gefallen – es gab weniger gesellschaftliche Schranken, das Reisen war viel einfacher geworden, und bei den Kommunikationsmitteln hatte eine wahre Revolution stattgefunden.

Vielleicht, wenn Chloë und Michel es wirklich wollten, hätten sie eine gemeinsame Zukunft.

Wenn es tatsächlich zu einer Verbindung ihrer Kinder käme, wurde Helena mit einem bitteren Lächeln bewusst, wären sie und Alexis tatsächlich miteinander verwandt.

Nur nicht so, wie sie es sich einmal vorgestellt hatten.

Am nächsten Tag war Helena gerade dabei, Angelina beim Wechseln der Bettwäsche zu helfen, als Alex ihr ihr Handy brachte.

»Dad für dich«, sagte er.

»Danke, Alex.« Sie hielt es ans Ohr. »Hallo, mein Schatz, was ist passiert? Ich habe mir Sorgen gemacht.«

Alex war im Schlafzimmer geblieben, also ging sie auf den Balkon hinaus.

»Hallo«, antwortete William. »Ich wollte nur hören, ob Sacha bei dir ist.«

»Nein. Ich dachte, er wäre bei dir.«

»Mist!« William klang aufgebracht. »Als er heute Morgen aufstand, wirkte er ruhiger und klang auch etwas vernünftiger. Alexis und ich haben ihm ein Frühstück vorgesetzt und mit ihm gesprochen. Ich habe ihm gesagt, dass er so bald wie möglich nach England fliegen und sich mit den Banken auseinandersetzen soll. Danach wollte er eine Weile herumfahren, um allein zu sein, also habe ich ihm das Auto geliehen und ihm das Versprechen abgenommen, dass er in zwei Stunden wieder da ist. Jetzt ist es fast zwei Uhr, und er ist immer noch nicht zurück. Ich dachte, er könnte vielleicht nach Pandora gefahren sein, um mit Jules zu sprechen, die verrückterweise vorhin hier auftauchte, um sich bei Alexis wegen des Vorfalls neulich Abend zu entschuldigen.«

»Nein, Sacha ist nicht hier. Wann ist er weggefahren?«

»Gegen zehn, das heißt, vor fast vier Stunden, und er geht nicht ans Handy. Ich hätte ihm nie das Auto geben dürfen. Was, wenn er wieder getrunken und einen Unfall gebaut hat?«

»Als er weggefahren ist, war er also nüchtern?«

»Ja, aber das heißt gar nichts.« William seufzte.

»Was sagt Jules dazu, dass ihr Mann verschwunden ist?«

»Sie ist mit Alexis irgendwohin gefahren, er wollte ihr etwas zeigen. Sie sagte, es sei ihr piepegal, wo er jetzt steckt. Übrigens, wie geht's den Kindern?«

»Denen geht's allen gut. Vielleicht weißt du schon, dass Chloë heute den ganzen Tag mit Michel unterwegs ist, Alexis' Sohn. Das habe ich dir gesimst. Er hat sie vormittags abgeholt und versprochen, auf sie aufzupassen.«

»Ja, ich habe ihn vorhin wegfahren sehen.« Es entstand eine kurze Pause. »Ich bleibe noch eine Weile und warte auf Sacha, aber wenn er nicht kommt, kann ich genauso gut nach Hause fahren.«

»In Ordnung.«

»Tschüs, Helena, bis später.«

Sie atmete tief durch. Das anstehende Gespräch, sobald William wieder hier war, würde nicht angenehm werden, das war ihr klar. Als sie vom Balkon ins Zimmer zurückging, stand Alex immer noch da.

»Alles in Ordnung?«, fragte er.

»Ja. Dad kommt später nach Hause.«

»Gut. Wie geht's Sacha?«

»Momentan ist er verschwunden, aber er wird bestimmt wieder auftauchen.« Helena ging zu Alex und nahm ihn in den

Arm. »Es tut mir leid, die letzten Tage waren wirklich ziemlich schwierig. Und danke, dass du dich so lieb um Viola kümmerst.«

»Mal ehrlich, Mum, ist zwischen dir und Dad alles in Ordnung?«

»Aber natürlich. Weshalb fragst du?«

»Ich habe euch bei dem Fest gesehen. Er war doch sauer, weil du mit Mr. Han…, mit Alexis getanzt hast, oder nicht?«

Es war sinnlos zu lügen. »Doch. Aber alle hatten zu viel getrunken, und alles ist etwas aus dem Ruder gelaufen.«

»Ja, das stimmt. Mum?«

»Ja?«

»Kannst du mir versprechen … kannst du schwören, dass du nicht mit Alexis durchbrennst?«

Helena nahm seine sonnengebräunten Apfelbäckchen zwischen die Hände und lächelte ihn an. »Das schwöre ich dir, mein Schatz. Er ist ein alter Freund, mehr nicht.«

»Stimmt das wirklich?«

»Ja, ganz bestimmt. Ich liebe William, und ich liebe unsere Familie. Ihr seid mein Ein und Alles, bitte glaub mir das.«

»Ach.« Vor Erleichterung sackten Alex' Schultern nach unten. »Gut. Und …«

»Ja?«

Kurz herrschte Stille, während Alex sich offenbar für etwas wappnete. »Ich … ich muss dich noch etwas fragen.«

»Nur zu.«

»Und ich möchte dir vorher sagen, ich werde nicht sauer sein, aber ich muss es einfach wissen. Die Sache ist … ist er, ist Alexis mein …«

»Helena! Bist du hier oben? Ach, da bist du ja!« Jules stürzte ins Zimmer, sie war ganz aufgeregt, ihre Augen strahlten. »Stell dir mal vor!«

Alex warf Helena einen entnervten Blick zu und verschwand.

»Jules, was ist passiert?«

»Ich bin zu Alexis gefahren, und er hat mich auf ein Glas Wein eingeladen. Ich wollte mich bei ihm wegen der Party entschuldigen, und er war unglaublich nett, er meinte, dass die meisten Gäste kein Englisch verstehen und alle sowieso viel zu beschwipst waren, um Genaueres mitzubekommen«, sprudelte Jules hervor. »Du kannst dir ja vorstellen, wie sehr mich das erleichtert hat. Und das führte dazu, dass ich ihm beim Mittagessen die ganze lange Geschichte erzählt habe.«

»Das hat dir gutgetan, oder? Auf jeden Fall siehst du sehr viel besser aus.«

»Aber ja. Ich meine, das meiste wusste er wahrscheinlich sowieso schon von William, aber er war so verständnisvoll und mitfühlend. Dann fragte er mich nach meinen Plänen, und ich sagte, ich wüsste nicht, was ich jetzt machen soll, weil mein Haus in England ja verkauft wird, aber dass ich dir auch nicht länger zur Last fallen will und …« Jules holte kurz Luft. »Dann sagte er, er hätte hier ein Haus, in dem wir wohnen könnten, bis ich mir überlegt habe, wie es weitergeht. Ist das nicht nett von ihm?«

»Unglaublich!«

»Natürlich habe ich ihm angeboten, dafür zu bezahlen, eine kleine Miete zumindest – du weißt ja, ich habe ein bisschen Geld von meiner Mutter geerbt –, aber davon wollte er nichts hören. Er sagte, dass es sowieso leer stehe, und dann hat er es mir gezeigt, und ehrlich gesagt habe ich etwas ähnlich Heruntergekommenes wie Pandora erwartet, aber stell dir vor, es ist nagelneu! Er hat es letztes Jahr gebaut, für sich, um dort einzuziehen, wenn sein Sohn das große Haus für sich und seine

Familie braucht. Und Helena, es ist traumhaft! Ganz in der Nähe der Kellerei, ein kleiner Fußpfad führt hinunter, wunderschön möbliert und mit einem riesengroßen Pool. Alexis sagt, er habe den Baugrund eigens ausgesucht, weil man von dort den schönsten Blick aufs Dorf hat. Und er sagte, ich könne dort wohnen, solange ich möchte, und dazu so viel Wein, wie ich trinken könne. Also« – erschöpft ließ Jules sich auf Helenas frisch bezogenes Bett fallen –, »was sagst du dazu?«

»Es klingt, als wäre der Retter in der Not erschienen, um dir wieder auf die Beine zu helfen«, sagte Helena so herzlich, wie es ihr möglich war. »Ich freue mich für dich, Jules. Du weißt, du darfst gern hierbleiben, aber ich kann verstehen, dass du eine Weile deine eigenen vier Wände haben möchtest.«

»Der Mann ist ein richtiger altmodischer Gentleman. Zum Dank werde ich ihn zum Essen einladen, er wohnt ja sowieso keine zweihundert Meter entfernt.«

Helena fiel auf, dass Jules strahlte wie ein junges Mädchen. Über Nacht waren die Jahre von ihr abgefallen. Offenbar schenkte Alexis ihr die Aufmerksamkeit, nach der sie sich so sehnte.

»Also.« Jules stand auf. »Du siehst kaputt aus, Helena. Ich gehe jetzt mit den Kindern zum Pool, damit du ein bisschen Ruhe hast. In Ordnung?«

»In Ordnung.«

In einer für Jules ungewohnten Geste der Zuneigung schloss sie Helena in die Arme. »Vielen Dank für alles.«

Als Jules mit den Kindern zum Pool verschwand, legte Helena sich in ihre Hängematte. Sie musste ihre Gedanken ordnen, ehe William zurückkam.

Gerade döste sie ein, als sie Schritte im trockenen Laub hörte.

»Hallo, meine Schöne.«

Sie spürte einen zarten Kuss auf der Stirn, schlug die Augen auf und sah Sacha.

»Was machst du denn hier?« Helena richtete sich kerzengerade auf. »William macht sich wahnsinnige Sorgen um dich.«

»Ich brauchte einfach ein bisschen Zeit für mich. Ich wollte nachdenken. Wo sind Jules und die Kinder?«

»Unten am Pool.«

»Ah ja.« Sacha nickte. »Ich bin gekommen, um mich von ihnen zu verabschieden. Ich fliege heute nach Hause.«

»Ja.«

»Wie du dir denken kannst, gibt es in England einiges zu regeln. In meinem Kopf und auch sonst.«

»Das glaube ich. Viola ist sehr unglücklich.«

»Ja, und sie hat auch jedes Recht dazu. Weißt du, ich wollte dir nur sagen, solange ich noch die Chance dazu habe, dass es mir leidtut wegen ... allem.«

»Danke.« Helena stand aus der Hängematte auf. »Du solltest zu deiner Frau gehen. Warte noch fünf Minuten, bis ich die Kinder aus dem Wasser geholt und ins Haus gebracht habe, bevor sie dich sehen. Du musst allein mit Jules reden.«

»Ich weiß.« Er legte ihr eine Hand auf den Arm. »Aber lass mich vorher noch sagen, dass ich weiß, wie sehr ich mein Leben verkorkst habe. Ich war egoistisch. Ich habe viele Menschen verletzt und ausgenutzt, einschließlich dich und Will. Und die Schuld liegt allein bei mir. Ich kann meine Vergangenheit nicht ändern, aber jetzt möchte ich versuchen, das wiedergutzumachen.«

»Wenigstens bei deinen Kindern, wenn schon sonst nicht.« Helena stand ihm mit verschränkten Armen gegenüber.

»Ja. Ich ... Helena, bevor ich gehe, möchte ich dich noch etwas fragen. Ich ... Helena, bitte!«

Aber sie ging bereits davon.

Keine halbe Stunde später kam Jules ins Haus und fand Helena in der Küche. Sie hatte Viola und den beiden Kleinen gerade selbst gemachte Limonade und kleine Kuchen vorgesetzt, die Angelina zuvor gebacken hatte.

»Alles in Ordnung?«, fragte Helena vorsichtig.

»Ja. Viola? Daddy ist unten am Pool«, sagte Jules. »Möchtest du zu ihm gehen?«

Violas Gesicht hellte sich auf. »O ja! Darf ich aufstehen, Tante Helena?«

»Aber natürlich.«

»Wir auch?«, fielen Immy und Fred einstimmig ein.

»Nein«, antwortete Helena fest, während Viola zur Tür hinauslief.

»Jetzt bin ich aber froh, dass das vorbei ist«, sagte Jules brüsk, sobald Viola verschwunden war. »Ich habe ihm gesagt, dass ich die Scheidung einreiche.«

»Bist du dir wirklich sicher, Jules? Wäre es nicht besser abzuwarten, bis sich alles wieder ein bisschen beruhigt hat?«

»Nein, das wäre es nicht. Hast du etwas dagegen, wenn ich mir ein Glas Wein einschenke? Es ist nach sechs.«

»Natürlich nicht.«

»Er hat gesagt, dass er in alle meine Forderungen einwilligt. Zumindest wirkte er ausnahmsweise einmal nüchtern.« Jules lachte kurz auf und schenkte sich Wein ins Glas. »Im Gegensatz zu seiner Fast-Ex.«

»Er hat mir gesagt, dass er nach England zurückfliegt.«

»Ja, das stimmt. Und ich habe ihm gesagt, dass ich mit den Kindern den Rest des Sommers hierbleibe. Soll doch er alles mit dem Haus regeln und mit den Gerichtsvollziehern darüber streiten, was wir behalten dürfen. Die Pferde sollten einiges wert sein, und sie zumindest gehören mir. Ich habe ihm gesagt, dass er sie verkaufen soll, und zwar zum besten Preis, den er bekommen kann.«

»Gute Idee.« Unvermittelt empfand Helena regelrecht Bewunderung für Jules.

»Rupes weigert sich, seinen Vater zu sehen. Er ist wütend auf ihn. Oundle war sein Traum. Morgen rufe ich als Allererstes den Schatzmeister der Schule an und frage, ob er uns irgendwie entgegenkommen kann.«

»Einen Versuch ist es sicherlich wert.«

»Ja. Auf jeden Fall sollte die Scheidung nicht allzu lange dauern, es gibt ja schließlich so gut wie nichts mehr zwischen uns aufzuteilen. Mit dem Geld meiner Mutter kann ich mich und die Kinder erst einmal über Wasser halten. Ich glaube, was wir jetzt brauchen, ist ein Neuanfang. Ich muss mir überlegen, wie es weitergeht, immerhin beginne ich ein ganz neues Kapitel in meinem Leben. Viola wird todunglücklich sein, wenn Sacha ihr sagt, dass wir uns scheiden lassen, aber«, fügte Jules hinzu und nickte bedächtig, »langfristig ist es das Beste.«

Alex' Tagebuch

23. Juli 2006

Wenn ich dann in *die* Schule komme, hoffe ich bloß, dass sie von mir nicht den üblichen Aufsatz über »Meine langweiligen Ferien« verlangen. Den könnte ich nämlich nicht schreiben. Weil meine nicht langweilig waren. Sie würden denken, ich hätte das alles frei erfunden. Ich würde mir etwas zusammenphantasieren. Was mir, um ehrlich zu sein, schon ein paarmal unterstellt wurde.

Ein kurzes Update über die Bewohner und Nichtbewohner von Pandora:

Sacha kam und ging wieder.

Dad kam, fuhr mit Sacha zum Flughafen und kam wieder.

Jules fuhr weg und kam wieder.

Chloë kam.

Michel kam mit ihr und ging wieder.

Dad fährt gleich wieder.

Mum fährt mit ihm.

Sadie ist weder gekommen noch gegangen.

Und ich auch nicht.

Heute Abend passt Jules auf uns Kinder auf, damit Mum und Dad zusammen essen gehen können. Eine Nachholfeier zum zehnten Hochzeitstag nach dem Fiasko neulich. Das ist ein gutes Zeichen.

Immerhin ist Chloë heute Abend zu Hause. Der mit

dem Mädchennamen hat sie vor einer Stunde nach Hause gebracht, rechtzeitig zum Abendessen.

Dieser »Michelle« sieht verdammt gut aus, das muss ich leider zugeben. Als er heute mit uns auf der Terrasse saß und Chloë ganz schüchtern tat und unter dem Tisch seine Hand hielt, habe ich ihn genau in Augenschein genommen. Er ist groß und schlank und hat einen dunklen Teint und die blauen Augen seines Vaters. Er sieht mir gar nicht ähnlich, und ich wäre wahrlich überrascht, wenn er sich tatsächlich als mein Halbbruder erweisen sollte.

Nicht, dass bei dieser genetischen Lotterie Aussehen irgendetwas besagt. Wie oft sieht man auf der Straße richtig hübsche Kinder neben einem Elternteil einhergehen, das eher wie ein Mitglied der Addams Family aussieht.

Heute Nachmittag war ich so dicht dran.

Ich hatte mir ein Herz gefasst, um die Worte wirklich über die Lippen zu bringen. Ich hatte meine Mutter in die Enge getrieben, und ich glaube, sie hätte es mir gesagt. Und dann platzte diese blöde Kuh Jules ins Zimmer, und der Moment war vorbei.

Aber keine Sorge, liebste Mutter, es wird sich schon noch eine Gelegenheit ergeben. Bevor ich nach Hause fahre, will ich wissen, wer genau ich bin.

Neulich kam mir ein wirklich schrecklicher Gedanke: Was, wenn meine Mutter es tatsächlich nicht weiß?

Wenn ich – die grauenhafteste Vorstellung überhaupt – das Ergebnis eines betrunkenen One-Night-Stands bin?

Der Gedanke entsetzt mich, aber die Frage drängt sich doch auf, weshalb das Geheimnis der einen Hälfte meiner Gene besser gehütet wird als das Ende des letzten Harry-Potter-Bands.

So schlimm kann es doch nicht sein, oder?

Aber wahrscheinlich geht nur wieder mal meine Phantasie mit mir durch. Dass ich von dieser Frage so besessen bin, ist relativ neu. Und heute ist es mir zum ersten Mal fast gelungen, sie direkt zu fragen. Vielleicht müsste ich mich nur einmal in aller Ruhe mit ihr hinsetzen, ein Vier-Augen-Gespräch zwischen Mutter und Sohn, und sie fragen.

Genau.

Abgesehen davon bin ich heute Abend sehr glücklich. Um nicht zu sagen, ekstatisch. Morgen früh zieht mein Todfeind aus. Ich brauche mich nicht mehr in meine Besenkammer zu sperren und morgens auf die erste Schwade von stinkendem Aftershave zu warten, die durch mein Schlüsselloch hereintreibt und mich an seine Erpresserexistenz erinnert. Der Hase ist endlich trocken, und das Bad hat ihm, rein optisch, ausgesprochen gutgetan. Ich hatte ganz vergessen, dass er früher einmal weiß war.

Jules hat heute Abend Mr. Hansdampfs Loblied gesungen. Vielleicht besteht ja die Möglichkeit, dass er sich – wenn es ihr gelingt, mehr als zwei oder drei Sekunden den Mund zu halten, er sich die Augen verbindet und sie sich eine Tüte über den Kopf zieht – in sie vergucken könnte.

Also gut, jetzt geht wirklich die Phantasie mit mir durch.

Zumindest hat Mum mir geschworen, dass sie nicht mit ihm durchbrennen will, und das muss ich ihr jetzt einfach glauben. Ich hoffe, sie sagt Dad heute Abend dasselbe.

Und wenn sich diese Sache mit »Michelle« nicht als eine weitere Kurzzeitlaune von Chloë herausstellt, werde ich Mittel und Wege finden müssen, ihr Einhalt zu gebieten. Aber im Moment habe ich nichts dagegen, dem Ganzen freien Lauf zu lassen.

Das heißt, heute Abend ist alles etwas ruhiger. Das einzige Haar in der Suppe ist die arme Viola, die wie ein trauriges kleines Gespenst durchs Haus geistert. Irgendwie hängt sie sich an mich – was mich nicht wundert, wenn ihre Mum ständig »Kopf hoch« zu ihr sagt, nachdem Sacha ihr ein paar Stunden zuvor mitgeteilt hat, dass er und Jules sich scheiden lassen.

Chloë war auch sehr lieb zu ihr und ist mit ihr zu einem Mädelsgespräch in ihrem Zimmer verschwunden. Schließlich ist sie auch ein Scheidungskind. Hinterher kam Viola zu mir, zuerst dachte ich, es wäre Chloë wegen des atemberaubenden Dufts ihres Parfüms, der durchs ganze Haus zieht. Um sie aufzumuntern, hat Chloë ihr ein Fläschchen davon geschenkt und dazu ein Armband.

Heute Abend hat Viola mir gesagt, dass es ihr besser geht, wenn sie bei mir ist. Das hat mich gefreut. Ich habe mein Bestes getan, sie in den Arm zu nehmen und sie weinen zu lassen – so viel, dass ich fast schon befürchtete, mein Bett würde wieder nass werden, nachdem es doch gerade erst richtig ausgetrocknet ist.

Ich habe ihr noch ein Buch aus der Bibliothek gegeben, die ich mittlerweile alphabetisch nach Autorennamen geordnet habe, und zwar Dickens' *Nicholas Nickleby*. Da erfährt Viola zumindest, dass das Leben für manche Menschen noch viel schlimmer ist als für sie. Obwohl ihres, zugegebenermaßen, im Moment wirklich kein Zuckerschlecken ist.

Mit etwas weniger Glück könnte meines auch so aussehen.

Ich kann nur beten, dass das Essen heute Abend ein Erfolg wird.

KAPITEL 18

»Gute Nacht, mein Schatz. Bis morgen früh.« Helena drückte Fred einen Kuss auf die Stirn und ging weiter zu Immys Bett.

»Wo gehst du hin?« Ihre Tochter betrachtete sie skeptisch. »Du hast ja Lippenstift dran.«

»Daddy und ich gehen aus.«

»Darf ich mitkommen?«

»Nein, Daddy und ich gehen allein weg. Chloë ist hier und Alex und Jules.«

»Ich kann Jules nicht leiden. Sie stinkt«, sagte Fred.

»Jetzt Ruhe, ihr beiden, schlaft gut.« Helena ging zur Tür und schaltete das Licht aus. »Träumt süß.« Als sie ihre Handtasche aus dem Schlafzimmer holte, hörte sie das Handy darin klingen.

Ausnahmsweise gelang es ihr, es zu finden, ehe der Anrufer auflegte.

»Hallo?«

»Helena! *Mia cara!* Wie geht es dir?!«

Es war eine Stimme aus der Vergangenheit, aber sie hätte sie überall wiedererkannt.

»Fabio!«, sagte sie aufgeregt. »Mein Gott, wie schön, von dir zu hören!«

»Eine Überraschung, ja?«

»Eine kleine, doch. Es muss doch, ich weiß nicht … über zehn Jahre sein.«

»Mindestens, denke ich.«

»Wo bist du gewesen? Wie ist es dir ergangen? Woher hast du meine Handynummer?«

»Das ist eine lange Geschichte, *cara*, und du weißt, es wird mir eine Freude sein, sie dir zu erzählen.«

Helena hörte William unten nach ihr rufen. »Fabio, ich würde zu gern den ganzen Abend mit dir plaudern, aber wir wollen gerade essen gehen. Kann ich dich zurückrufen? Wo bist du? Noch in New York?«

»Nein, ich bin mittlerweile wieder in Mailand, aber ich gehe mit dem Ballett von La Scala immer wieder auf Tournee. Und wo bist du? In England?«

»Nein, im Augenblick nicht. Ich bin auf Zypern. Mein Patenonkel ist gestorben und hat mir sein Haus hier vermacht, und da verbringe ich mit meiner Familie gerade den Sommer.«

»Aber in drei Wochen komme ich doch nach Limassol! Weißt du noch, wie wir an einem heißen Sommerabend dort in dem wunderschönen Amphitheater getanzt haben? Das müssen jetzt fünfzehn Jahre her sein.«

»Wie könnte ich das je vergessen?« Bei der Erinnerung glänzten Helenas Augen. »Unser Haus ist gar nicht so weit von Limassol entfernt, und ich würde dich schrecklich gern sehen, Fabio.«

»Und ich dich, *mia cara*. Es war zu lange.«

»Das stimmt.«

»Dann schaue ich mal, ob ich früher als geplant nach Zypern fliegen kann, und dann nehme ich ein oder zwei Tage deine Gastfreundschaft in Anspruch.«

»Großartig. Ist das Handy die beste Möglichkeit, dich zu erreichen?«

»Ja, auf dem kannst du mich Tag und Nacht erreichen. So,

meine Helena, morgen unterhalten wir uns weiter und arrangieren alles. *Buona notte.*«

»*Buona notte*, Fabio.«

Helena blieb einen Moment auf dem Bett sitzen, das Handy in der Hand, und dachte zurück.

»Mum, wer war das?«

Alex stand in der Tür. »Mein Schatz, das war mein alter Tanzpartner, von dem ich seit mindestens zehn Jahren nichts mehr gehört habe. Es freut mich sehr, dass er sich gemeldet hat.« Lächelnd gab sie Alex einen Kuss auf den Kopf. »Jetzt muss ich aber gehen, Dad wartet unten schon auf mich.«

Als Helena sich neben William auf den Beifahrersitz setzte, machte die Nähe zu ihm sie regelrecht nervös – ebenso wie die Tatsache, dass sie wirklich mal wieder allein waren.

»Also, wohin fahren wir? Wenn du nichts dagegen hast, würde ich lieber nicht in Persephones Taverne gehen«, sagte er.

»Wir können nach Peyia fahren, der Ort ist ganz nett, ein paar Kilometer Richtung Küste. Nicht so hübsch wie Kathikas, aber ich erinnere mich an eine kleine Taverne gleich am Ortseingang. Angus war einmal dort mit mir essen. Der Blick ist phantastisch.«

»Das klingt gut. Dann lass uns doch nach Peyia fahren, und dort können wir uns dann erkundigen.«

Nachdem sie sich ein paarmal verfahren hatten, kamen sie schließlich nach Peyia, wo sich Touristen und Einheimische auf den Straßen tummelten. Vor einem kleinen Geschäft hielt William an und fragte dort nach dem Restaurant, von dem Helena gesprochen hatte.

»Glück gehabt, der Inhaber wusste genau, welches Lokal du meinst. Er hat mir sogar den Weg aufgezeichnet«, sagte William, als er sich wieder in den Wagen setzte, und wedelte mit einem Blatt Papier.

Schließlich hatten sie die Taverne erreicht und stiegen eine lange Treppe hinauf, an deren Ende sie auf eine weit geschwungene Steinterrasse traten. Die von Kerzenlicht erhellten Tische waren von einer Pergola überdacht, über die sich üppig wuchernder Wein rankte. Das Lokal war gut besucht, aber sie fanden an der niedrigen Mauer, die die Terrasse begrenzte, noch einen freien Tisch, von dem sie einen atemberaubenden Blick auf den Sonnenuntergang und die Küste hatten.

»Na, das ist ja mal eine nette Abwechslung«, sagte William, nachdem er eine Karaffe roten Hauswein bestellt hatte. »Guten Abend, Helena, ich heiße William. Wie schön, dich wiederzusehen.« Er reichte ihr über den Tisch hinweg die Hand, die sie förmlich schüttelte.

»Du hast recht, es ist wirklich lange her, dass wir allein an einem Tisch saßen.«

»Aus dem einen und anderen Grund ist der Urlaub nicht ganz so geworden, wie wir ihn uns vorgestellt haben, oder?«

»Das ist wahr.«

»Dann hoffen wir mal, dass jetzt, wo Sacha wieder nach England geflogen ist und Jules mit den Kindern morgen in Alexis' Villa zieht, alles etwas ruhiger wird. Weißt du schon, was du möchtest?«

»Ich nehme das Hühnchen-Souvlaki.« Helena hatte nicht den geringsten Appetit.

»Und ich den Fisch.« William bat den Kellner an den Tisch und bestellte. Dann hob er das Weinglas. »Prost. Und nachträglich herzlichen Glückwunsch zum Hochzeitstag, mein Schatz.«

»Danke. Dir auch«, antwortete sie angespannt.

»Im Auto hast du erzählt, dass der viel gerühmte Fabio nach Zypern kommt«, sagte William. »Offenbar führen alle Wege

Helenas, ob Vergangenheit, Gegenwart oder Zukunft, nach Pandora.«

»Das ist jetzt wirklich Zufall. Die Balletttruppe der Scala gibt eine Woche lang im Amphitheater von Limassol Vorstellungen. Als ich noch dabei war, sind wir hier auch schon aufgetreten.«

»Ich wünschte, ich hätte dich tanzen sehen können.«

»Das tust du doch jeden Morgen.«

»Und neulich Abend«, ergänzte er mit einem wehmütigen Lächeln. »Ich meine, auf einer richtigen Bühne und du auf Zehenspitzen und mit einem Tüllröckchen um die Mitte.«

»Du meinst mit einem Tutu.«

»Genau.« William trank einen Schluck Wein, dann sagte er: »Wie ist es dir in den letzten Tagen ergangen?«

»Gut. Es gab einfach viel zu tun mit den vielen Menschen im Haus.«

»Das meinte ich nicht.«

»Nein.« Helena spielte angelegentlich mit einem Stück Brot und wechselte rasch das Thema. »Ist es nicht erstaunlich, dass Sadie immer noch nicht zurückgekommen ist? Sie ist nach wie vor bei dem Typen, den sie auf dem Fest kennengelernt hat. Er ist fünfundzwanzig und offenbar Schreiner und hat den tollsten Körper, den sie je gesehen hat.«

»Wie schön für sie, mein Schatz, aber wirklich, wir müssen über uns reden.« William wollte sich nicht beirren lassen. »Alexis und ich haben uns unterhalten. Er hat sich in aller Form bei mir entschuldigt und gesagt, dass er sich dir und mir gegenüber nicht korrekt verhalten habe. Ehrlich gesagt ist es nicht besonders schön, mit ansehen zu müssen, wie ein anderer Mann die eigene Frau begehrt, aber ich habe seine Entschuldigung angenommen. Und ich muss zugeben, er ist ein anständiger Kerl. Er war sehr nett zu Sacha und hat ihm eine Reihe vernünftiger Ratschläge gegeben. Wie auch immer, damit ist also seine Seite der Sache geklärt. Und wie ist es bei dir, Helena? Sehnst du dich nach Alexis, so, wie er sich nach eigener Aussage nach dir gesehnt hat?«

»Nein, William, das schwöre ich dir. Als ich ihn wiedersah, habe ich natürlich an die Zeit damals zurückgedacht, aber mehr nicht, bitte glaub mir. Auch wenn ich dich nicht überzeugen kann«, fügte sie mit einem Seufzen hinzu, »aber es ist die Wahrheit.«

»Aber ich glaube dir doch. Wo wären wir denn sonst? Wir wissen doch beide, dass Vertrauen in einer Ehe das Wichtigste ist. Um ehrlich zu sein, habe ich manchmal das Gefühl, dass genau das auf dich nicht zutrifft. Ich meine, dass du mir nie deine persönlichsten Gedanken anvertraust.«

»Ja«, sagte Helena und nickte. »Verzeih mir, William, aber das fällt mir einfach schwer.«

»Alexis hat mir auch gesagt, dass es etwas gibt, das du mir erzählen solltest.«

»Ach ja?« Helena schluckte schwer, in ihrem Kopf begann es zu hämmern.

»Ja. Anders gesagt, er meinte, du solltest mir etwas erzählen, um deiner selbst willen.« William griff nach ihrer Hand. »Also, mein Schatz, was ist es? Was war damals?«

»Ich …« Unvermittelt traten ihr Tränen in die Augen. »Ich kann nicht.«

»Doch, das kannst du.« In dem Moment trug der Kellner das Essen auf, und Helena hatte einen Moment Zeit, sich zu fassen.

Als der Kellner gegangen war, griff William wieder nach ihrer Hand und fuhr fort: »Mein Liebling, in den letzten Tagen hatte ich Zeit, über alles nachzudenken, und man muss kein Genie sein, um zu erraten, was passiert ist. Ich mache es dir einfacher – warst du schwanger von Alexis?«

»Ja.« Helena war entsetzlich übel, aber jetzt war das Wort – war die Wahrheit – ausgesprochen, und sie konnte es nicht mehr zurücknehmen.

»Und was ist aus dem Kind geworden?«

»Ich … ich habe es abtreiben lassen.«

»Wusste Alexis Bescheid?«

»Nein. Ich habe erst in England festgestellt, dass ich schwanger war.«

»Hast du es ihm gesagt?«

»Damals nicht, nein. Das habe ich ihm erst neulich gesagt, an dem Tag, als du mit den Kindern allein zum Strand gefahren bist.«

»Mein Gott, kein Wunder, dass ihr beide so befangen aussaht, als wir nach Hause kamen. Ich wusste doch, dass etwas vorgefallen war, aber ich wusste nicht, was, also habe ich das Schlimmste befürchtet. Jetzt, wo ich es weiß, finde ich es vollkommen verständlich, dass er dich getröstet hat. Das hätte ich auch getan, wenn du mir genug vertraut hättest, um es mir zu sagen.« In Williams Blick lag ein gewisser Unmut, aber auch Mitgefühl. »Und was hast du dann gemacht?«

»Ich wusste, dass ich das Kind nicht behalten kann. Ich war damals schon am Internat der Royal Ballet School und musste bis zu den Herbstferien warten, um etwas zu unternehmen. Ich habe in den Gelben Seiten eine Klinik herausgesucht und einen Termin vereinbart. An dem Tag habe ich meiner Mutter gesagt, ich hätte eine schreckliche Magenverstimmung. Den Rest der Woche habe ich dann im Bett verbracht und mich erholt.«

»Du hast das Ganze also allein durchgestanden?«

»William, ich konnte es doch niemandem sagen. Ich war gerade sechzehn geworden, ich hatte panische Angst.«

»Und du hast dir nie überlegt, Alexis zu informieren? Du hättest es ihm doch auf jeden Fall schreiben können, oder nicht? Er hat dich eindeutig geliebt, obwohl mir schleierhaft ist, wieso er dir als Fünfzehnjähriger eine erwachsene Beziehung aufgezwungen hat. Dafür könnte ich ihm den Hals umdrehen.«

»Er wusste nicht, dass ich noch so jung war, William. Ich hatte ihm gesagt, dass ich fast siebzehn bin. Ich habe ihn angelogen, weil ich wusste, dass er mich sonst nicht anfassen würde.«

»Und du wolltest angefasst werden.« Gequält verzog William das Gesicht. »Entschuldige, Helena, aber ich finde dieses Gespräch ziemlich schwierig.«

»Deswegen habe ich es dir ja nie gesagt«, flüsterte sie.

»Ist das der Grund, weshalb du vor der Abfahrt nach Pandora so angespannt warst? Wegen der Vorstellung, dass Alexis noch hier sein und die Wahrheit herauskommen könnte?«

»Zum Teil ja«, räumte sie ein. »Aber ich dachte nicht, dass es dir auffallen würde.«

»Natürlich ist es mir aufgefallen. Es ist uns allen aufgefallen. Wir haben uns Sorgen um dich gemacht.«

»Wirklich? Das tut mir leid. Ich …« Helena schüttelte den Kopf und versuchte, die Tränen zu unterdrücken, die zu vergießen sie kein Recht hatte. »Ich wusste einfach nicht, was ich tun soll.«

»Ich persönlich bin der Ansicht, dass die Wahrheit – so schmerzlich sie sein mag – immer das Beste ist. Wie auch immer, mein Liebling, jetzt weiß ich wenigstens, was war, und es tut mir so leid, dass du das alles allein durchstehen musstest, noch dazu in diesem Alter.«

»Bitte entschuldige dich nicht, William. Ich kann mir meine Entscheidung nach wie vor nicht verzeihen und bin nie richtig über die Sache hinweggekommen.«

»Das solltest du aber versuchen, Helena. Wir alle machen das, was wir in einer bestimmten Situation für das Beste halten, und selbst dir muss rückblickend klar sein, dass du dich völlig richtig entschieden hast«, fügte William sanft hinzu. »Es sei denn natürlich, du möchtest eigentlich hierher zurückkommen und Alexis heiraten.«

»Es war eine Jugendliebe für einen Sommer … Ich … Wir kamen aus zwei verschiedenen Welten, und wir waren noch so jung. Ich habe den Kontakt zu ihm völlig abgebrochen. Ich hielt es für besser, wenn er nie davon erfährt.«

»Und du hast das all die Jahre für dich behalten und mit niemandem darüber gesprochen?«

»Ja.«

»Und du hast danach keinen Kontakt zu Alexis mehr gehabt?«

»Ich sagte doch … ich konnte einfach nicht.« Wieder stiegen ihr Tränen in die Augen. »Du kannst dir gar nicht vorstellen, wie sehr ich mich geschämt habe – mich immer noch schäme.«

»Wir können nur hoffen, dass du jetzt, nachdem du mir davon erzählt hast, darüber hinwegkommst und dir klar wird, dass du keine andere Möglichkeit hattest. Liebling, du tust mir so unendlich leid. Du warst ja noch so jung – kaum älter als Chloë heute, wenn ich es recht bedenke. Ein erschreckender Gedanke. Und vermutlich warst du nicht einmal so welterfahren wie sie heute. Es ist wirklich schade, dass du deiner Mutter nichts davon erzählen konntest.«

»Um Himmels willen!« Helena warf ihm einen entsetzten Blick zu. »Wahrscheinlich hätte sie mich vor die Tür gesetzt. Sie war sehr altmodisch und auf Anstand bedacht. Wahrscheinlich eher wie eine Großmutter.«

»Vielleicht ist das der Grund, weshalb es dir so schwerfällt, anderen Menschen zu vertrauen – weil du nicht offen mit deiner Mutter reden konntest. Ganz zu schweigen davon, ihnen persönliche Gedanken anzuvertrauen. Bitte, mein Schatz« – William nahm Helenas Hand –, »glaub mir, dass ich für dich da bin. Das bin ich wirklich.«

»Das weiß ich. Es tut mir unendlich leid.«

»Und jetzt noch eine Frage, wenn wir schon gerade reinen Tisch machen.«

»Ja?«

»Bist du sicher, dass du mir nicht sagen willst, wer Alex' Vater ist? Nachdem ich überzeugt war, dass es Alexis ist – und das glaubt Alex zweifellos auch –, bin ich jetzt so klug wie zuvor.«

»William, bitte! Ich habe dir schon mal gesagt, dass es irgendein Mann war, mit dem ich eine Nacht verbracht habe«, sagte Helena. Vor Anspannung zogen sich tiefe Falten über ihre Stirn.

»Ich weiß. Aber so, wie ich dich kenne – und zumal nach dem, was du mir gerade gesagt hast –, kann ich das nicht ganz glauben. Es passt nicht zu dir, nur eine Nacht mit jemandem zu verbringen. Es sei denn, du warst damals eine völlig andere Person.«

»Du meinst, ein Flittchen?« Sie seufzte. »Nach der Offenbarung heute Abend glaubst du das doch sowieso.«

»Aber weshalb denn? Du warst neunundzwanzig, als wir geheiratet haben – natürlich hast du vor mir andere Männer gekannt. Ich war ja auch kein Unschuldsknabe, also bitte glaub nicht, ich würde dich in irgendeiner Weise verurteilen. Es ist nur so, dass ich jetzt seit zehn Jahren mit dir verheiratet bin und einfach gern die Wahrheit wissen würde, mehr nicht.«

»Können wir es dabei belassen, William? Ich habe dir gesagt, was du wissen wolltest, und …« Sie konnte die Tränen der Frustration und der Erschöpfung nicht mehr zurückhalten.

»Ja, es reicht«, sagte er verständnisvoll. Ihre Verzweiflung rührte ihn. »Danke, dass du mir von der Schwangerschaft erzählt hast. Das Schlimmste ist jetzt vorbei.«

Wenn dem nur so wäre, dachte Helena bekümmert.

Auf der Heimfahrt hielt William über den Schaltknüppel hinweg ihre Hand wie damals, als sie sich gerade erst kennengelernt hatten. Die Anspannung war von ihm gewichen, er sah gelöst aus. In der Auffahrt stellte er den Motor ab und drehte sich zu Helena.

»Ich liebe dich, Helena, bitte glaub mir das. Was immer du vor mir getan hast, ist nicht wichtig. Du bist eine wunderbare Ehefrau und Mutter und ein großartiger Mensch, also bitte hör auf, dich zu grämen. Bitte.« Zärtlich küsste er sie auf die Lippen und streichelte ihr übers Haar. »Und jetzt möchte ich mit dir ins Bett, sofort und auf der Stelle. Komm, wir schleichen durch die Küchentür ins Haus, damit uns niemand abfängt.«

Händchen haltend gingen sie zur rückwärtigen Eingangstür, die William so leise wie möglich öffnete, dann schlichen sie auf Zehenspitzen durch den dunklen Flur und die Treppe hinauf.

Später lag Helena in Williams Armen und genoss den Luftzug, den der Ventilator über ihre bloße Haut blies. William war wie immer danach sofort eingeschlafen. In der Anspannung der vergangenen Wochen hatte sie vergessen, wie tröstlich es sein konnte, sich zu lieben. Sie empfand große innere Ruhe und war froh, dass sie es ihm gesagt hatte, auch wenn es noch vieles andere gab, das er nicht wusste.

Einen kurzen Moment fragte sie sich, ob der Rest ihrer Geschichte nicht ein Geheimnis bleiben könnte. Ob sie das alles nicht endlich loslassen und immer so bleiben könnte wie jetzt, geborgen in Williams Armen. Und nicht auf den Moment wartete, wenn er die Wahrheit erfuhr. Und sie verließ.

Helena schloss die Augen. Jetzt war er hier, bei ihr, und sie waren sich wieder nah. Dafür musste sie dankbar sein. Mit diesem Gefühl schlief sie ein.

»Mummy, bist du wach?« Immys seidiges Haar kitzelte sie an der Nase.

»Nein, ich schlafe tief und fest.« Sie wusste, dass Immy sie genau beobachtete.

»Oh, du redest aber, dann musst du wach sein.«

Fred knuffte sie in den Arm, und sie fuhr zusammen. »Au! Lass das!«

»Ich wecke dich«, erklärte er. »Ich will Milch.«

»Guten Morgen, mein Liebling.« William schlängelte eine Hand an Immy vorbei, um Helena an der Schulter zu streicheln. »Ich gehe nach unten und mache Tee.« Er stand auf und griff nach seiner Boxershorts. »Kommt, ihr beiden«, sagte er zu Fred und Immy. »Ihr könnt mir helfen.«

»Daddy, warum habt du und Mummy nichts an?«, fragte Immy, die ihm folgte.

»Letzte Nacht war es sehr heiß«, hörte Helena ihn sagen, als die drei den Raum verließen.

»Also, Daddy, ich finde, deine Unterhose solltest du im Bett trotzdem anlassen.«

»Ich auch«, sagte Fred.

Helena musste lächeln. Sie fühlte sich erfrischt, als wäre ein Unwetter über sie hinweggefegt und hätte eine sanfte, klare Luft mit sich gebracht.

»Vielleicht können wir jetzt endlich richtig Urlaub machen«, murmelte sie.

August

Abschied

Alex' Tagebuch

Die letzten Wochen waren genau so, wie ein Familienurlaub sein sollte.

Keine griechischen Tragödien mehr, keine Hasenschlächter, Traubenpresser, Scheidungen oder Betrunkene.

Und nach der ganzen Aufregung und Anspannung war es richtig nett.

Obwohl ich das Wort eigentlich nicht leiden kann. »Nett« heißt ein hübsches Haus in einer Vorortsiedlung, in Partnerlook-Anoraks gekleidete Paare, die zusammen wandern gehen, einen wohlerzogenen Hund und einen Nissan Micra in der Garage haben. Mittelschichtsdurchschnittlichkeit. So wie das Gros der westlichen Welt.

Aber natürlich hält sich niemand für durchschnittlich. Andernfalls würden die Leute sich ja reihenweise erschießen. Wir alle streben doch nach Individualität. Wir sind keine Ameisen, die mich mit ihren geballten Kolonien und ihrer erstklassigen Organisation immer wieder erstaunen, wenn sie einen Angriff auf ein Stück Schokolade durchführen, das Fred auf den Küchenfußboden gefallen ist.

Sie erinnern mich an die Nazis, die Russische Revolutionspartei oder die Millionentruppe des Großen Vorsitzenden Mao: straff organisiert, durchtrainiert und gehirntot.

Ich würde ja wirklich gern den Anführer der Ameisen kennenlernen. Wahrscheinlich ist er – wie alle psychopathischen Diktatoren – klein und hässlich und hat eine Vorliebe für Gesichtsbehaarung.

Vielleicht, wenn ich mir einen Schnurrbart wachsen ließe, könnten sich da ganz neue Karriereaussichten ergeben …

Allerdings ist nichts im Leben perfekt, denn Michel und Chloë sind immer noch zusammen. Besser gesagt, sind sie selten nicht zusammen. Leider ist er ein netter Typ, ich kann ihn wirklich gut leiden, so als Mann: Er ist zurückhaltend und intelligent und freundlich.

Er himmelt sie an, und sie himmelt ihn an. Das einzig Gute ist, dass Chloë demnächst zu ihrer Mutter nach Frankreich fahren muss, um den Rest der Ferien mit ihr zu verbringen. Sie wird mir natürlich grausam fehlen, aber wenigstens ist sie dann in Sicherheit. Und wenn wir uns das nächste Mal sehen, dann in heimatlichen Gefilden. Oder vielmehr schulischen.

Und das ist auch so ein Haar – oder Haarbüschel – in der Suppe: Beim Ankommen hier lag noch der ganze Sommer vor mir, bis diese Schule ein Thema wurde. Und jetzt ist es plötzlich August, es ist nicht mehr Ferienanfang, sondern der Anfang vom Ferienende.

Vor ein paar Tagen hörte ich meine Mutter beim Etikettenservice telefonisch meine Namensschildchen bestellen. »Alexander R. Beaumont.«

Ich weigere mich preiszugeben, wofür das »R« steht. Nur so viel: Es ist untragbar grauenhaft. Genau wie die Schuluniform, in die der Name genäht werden wird. Ich habe auch darauf verzichtet, in diesem Tagebuch den Namen der Schule zu erwähnen, auf die ich gehen werde. Nur so viel: Zum Frühstück besteht Krawattenzwang, und Generationen von britischen Königen haben sie besucht.

Ich habe ein Stipendium erworben. Seien wir ehrlich, wegen meines Abstammungsnachweises hätten sie mich nicht genommen in Anbetracht dessen, dass ich nur die Herkunft des Eis kenne, nicht aber die des Spermas, das mich gezeugt hat.

Ob sie wohl wissen, dass ich unehelich bin?

Einerseits ist das ein Beweis dafür, dass sich die Zeiten geändert haben. Andererseits, nach allem, was ich über die Geschichte unserer königlichen Familie gelesen habe, werde ich mich mit meinem unbekannten Genpool in bester Gesellschaft befinden.

Was mir wirklich Angst macht, ist, dass meine Klassenkameraden außer meinem Namen nichts über mich wissen. Ich werde mich vor einer Schar Wildfremder beweisen müssen, mit denen ich die nächsten fünf Jahre auf Gedeih und Verderb zusammenleben muss. Der eine, einzige Mensch, der mich versteht, wird meilenweit weg sein. Mein heimisches Zimmer wird wochenlang verwaist sein.

Wenn ich weggehe, möchte Fred meine Goldfische haben und Immy meinen tragbaren DVD-Spieler. Wie zwei kleine Geier fallen sie über meine Habseligkeiten her, noch bevor ich aus dem Haus bin. Zu gern würde ich mir einreden, dass ich ihnen fehle, dabei werden sie sich sehr bald an meine Abwesenheit gewöhnen. Einer weniger, der sich um den Familientisch schart – das fällt kaum auf. Und um meinen nächsten scharen sich Hunderte.

Und was, wenn sie alle wie Rupes sind? Dann bin ich spätestens zu den Herbstferien tot.

Wenn ich daran denke, dass meine neue Schule in weniger als einem Monat anfängt, schiebe ich ernsthaft Panik. Ich meine, ich komme aus einer Mittelschichtsfamilie, ich war noch nie auf Moorhuhnjagd und denke bei »Polo« in erster Linie an ein Auto. Die Schule, auf die ich gegangen bin, war derart unterfinanziert, dass sie uns einmal die Woche mit dem Bus ins nächste kommunale Schwimmbad gefahren haben.

Angeblich sollte die Entscheidung bei mir liegen, ob ich die Schule besuche oder nicht. Aber als mir das Stipendium zugesprochen wurde, vergaßen sie einfach, mich zu fragen, ob ich das überhaupt wollte, und nahmen mein Einverständnis als gegeben hin.

Ein Vorteil ist, dass wenigstens Chloë in der Nähe sein wird. Ihre und meine Schule veranstalten offenbar gemeinsame »Tanzvergnügen«. Verdammt, da sollte ich vielleicht besser Walzer und American Smooth lernen angesichts dessen, dass ich im Moment bestenfalls Kniebeugen zu Gnarls Barkleys »Crazy« hinkriege.

Obwohl es mir das Herz bricht, wenn ich sie und »Michelle« zusammen sehe – der Gedanke, dass sie in England ganz in meiner Nähe sein wird, klebt es wieder zusammen. Und wie es so schön heißt: aus den Augen, aus dem Sinn. Das sowie der Umstand, dass Chloë eindeutig von meinem Stipendium beeindruckt ist, geben mir den einzigen Trost, der sich mir momentan in meiner krawattenbewehrten einsamen Zukunft bietet …

Ich liege auf dem Bett in meiner Besenkammer – obwohl oben natürlich ein ganzes Zimmer leer steht. Aber als meine Mutter fragte, ob ich nicht wieder umziehen wolle, lehnte ich ab. Seltsam, dass ich hier unten bleiben will, aber hier fühle ich mich wohl. Und der Lesestoff geht mir auch nicht aus.

Heute Abend entscheide ich mich für Keats-Gedichte und lese »An Fanny«. Die Worte sind wunderschön, und es ist ja eine Binsenweisheit, dass sich auch im Kummer gleich und gleich gern gesellt. Es geht mir einfach besser zu wissen, dass jemand anderes vor mir bereits ähnliche Gefühle empfand wie ich.

»*Gib deine Seele – gib dein ganzes All,*
Halt nichts zurück, nichts – nichts! Ich würde sterben.«

Dann höre ich leise Schritte zweier Paar Füße im Gang – ein männliches und ein weibliches –, und eine Träne stiehlt sich mir in den Augenwinkel.

Die Pein unerwiderter Liebe kenne ich nur allzu gut.

Kapitel 19

Helena beugte sich vor, ihr linkes Bein vollführte eine *arabesque*. Diese Position behielt sie einige Sekunden bei, dann tanzte sie in raschen Pirouetten über die Terrasse und ließ sich schwitzend auf einen Stuhl fallen.

Um halb neun brannte die Sonne bereits vom Himmel. Als der Juli allmählich in den August übergegangen war, waren die Temperaturen spürbar gestiegen, und die Bewohner von Pandora hatten sich zunehmend entspannt der Hitze hingegeben. Selbst die Kleinen waren vergleichsweise träge, die unerbittliche Sonne dämpfte ihren sonst unbezähmbaren Bewegungsdrang. Mittlerweile schliefen sie morgens bis nach neun Uhr, und der ganze Haushalt hatte sich ihrer Entschleunigung angepasst.

Genau so hatte Helena sich die Wochen in Pandora vorgestellt: Die Tage verbrachte man am Pool oder am Strand, unterbrochen vom Mittagessen und einem Mittagsschlaf für alle. William hatte endlich auch gedanklich Jackett und Krawatte abgelegt, verbrachte seine ganze Zeit mit der Familie und wurde zunehmend entspannter. Seit sie ihm von dem verlorenen Kind erzählt hatte, waren sie sich noch nähergekommen, sowohl körperlich als auch emotional. Helena wurde sich bewusst, dass sie noch nie derart zufrieden gewesen war und sich noch nie derart geliebt gefühlt hatte wie in den vergangenen Tagen. Nachdem Pandora anfangs nichts als Chaos gestiftet hatte, wob sie jetzt um alle ihren magischen Bann.

Die langen warmen Abende verbrachten sie auf der Terrasse, entweder im Familienkreis oder mit dem einen oder anderen Besucher. Michel, Chloës Freund, war mittlerweile ein ständiger Hausgast. Sowohl Helena als auch William waren zu dem Schluss gekommen, dass es besser war, ihn in die Familie zu integrieren und Chloë auf diese Art im Auge zu behalten. Wie Helena erklärt hatte, war der Reiz des Verbotenen im Verbund mit elterlichen Vorschriften nicht zu unterschätzen.

William schien es nicht zu stören, dass seine Tochter vom Sohn des Mannes umworben wurde, der früher einmal unter sehr ähnlichen Umständen in seine Frau verliebt gewesen war – oder wenn, dann ließ er es sich nicht anmerken.

Eines Abends war Alexis zum Essen gekommen, dieses Mal auf Williams Einladung hin. Die anfänglichen Spannungen zwischen ihnen waren verschwunden, und Helena hatte den Eindruck, dass die beiden Männer eine aufrichtige, wenn auch verhaltene Sympathie füreinander hegten. An manchen Abenden hatten sie auch Besuch von Sadie und Andreas bekommen, ihrem unwiderstehlichen Schreinerburschen. Obwohl ein Gespräch mit Andreas aufgrund seiner extrem beschränkten Englischkenntnisse nahezu unmöglich war, wirkten die beiden sehr glücklich. Wie Sadie sagte, kommunizierten sie auf der Ebene, auf die es ankam. Selbst Helena musste zugeben, dass »Adonis«, wie die beiden Frauen ihn im Scherz nannten, hinreißend aussah.

»Ich lebe für den Moment, und die Rechnung bezahle ich später«, hatte Sadie achselzuckend gesagt, als Helena sie fragte, welche Zukunft sie für die Beziehung sehe. »Und selbst wenn ich es wüsste, könnte ich es ihm nicht verständlich machen«, hatte sie lachend hinzugefügt. »Das kommt mir im Moment sehr entgegen.«

Jules wiederum hatte sie kaum gesehen, seit sie mit ihren Kindern in Alexis' Villa gezogen war. Aber laut Viola, die auf dem Fahrrad, das Helena ihr geliehen hatte, regelmäßig vorbeischaute, ging es ihr ganz gut. Helena nahm sich vor, Jules später anzurufen. Zwar wollte sie nicht, dass Jules sich ausgeschlossen fühlte, aber sie hatte auch keine Lust, irgendetwas heraufzubeschwören, was den gegenwärtigen Frieden in Pandora stören könnte.

Als sie nach ihren Übungen wieder zu Atem gekommen war, schlenderte sie über die Terrasse, blieb aber immer wieder stehen, um die Blumen zu bewundern, die sie in die verwitterten Steingefäße gepflanzt hatte. Während sie verblühte Blüten abzupfte und dabei prüfte, ob die Erde noch feucht war, stellte sie wieder einmal zufrieden fest, dass alles prächtig gedieh. Rosafarbene und weiße Geranien, doppelt so groß wie diejenigen, die sie zu Hause in Hampshire gepflanzt hatte, wetteiferten mit duftenden Gardenien und feurig roten Hibiskusblüten um Aufmerksamkeit.

Am Ende der Terrasse angekommen, stützte sie sich auf die Balustrade und betrachtete den Garten, der zu den Olivenhainen hin abfiel. Mithilfe Anatoles, eines Verwandten Angelinas aus dem Dorf, hatte sie die Beete mit Oleander, Lavendel und Nachtschatten bepflanzt, die die Hitze mit etwas Glück aushalten und jedes Jahr wiederkommen würden. Während sie staunend den Blick auf sich wirken ließ, flatterte ein Schmetterling vorbei, ein gelber Tupfer vor dem leuchtend blauen Himmel. Nur der gedämpfte Chor der Zikaden erfüllte die morgendliche Stille.

Helena überquerte die Terrasse und ging in die Küche. Im Rückblick musste sie William recht geben: Die Wochen vor diesem Urlaub waren ausgesprochen anstrengend gewesen. Allein schon, dass sie vor der Ankunft nicht gewusst hatte, was sie bei einer eventuellen Begegnung mit Alexis empfinden würde und was sie ihm sagen sollte, weshalb sie damals, nach dem gemeinsamen Sommer, spurlos aus Pandora verschwunden war. Jetzt musste sie glauben, dass der Sturm vorübergezogen war und zwar einige Spinnweben fortgerissen, das Gefüge im Großen und Ganzen aber unbeschadet gelassen hatte.

Und das restliche Durcheinander ihres Lebens, das das Schicksal und ihre eigene Unklugheit ihr beschert hatten ... Wer wusste schon davon?

Sie würde jeden Tag so nehmen, wie er kam. Und der heutige war wunderschön.

»Guten Morgen, mein Schatz.« William kam in die Küche und küsste sie auf die bloße Schulter, als sie den Wasserkessel füllte. »Und was steht heute auf dem Plan?«

»Nichts allzu Anspruchsvolles. Ich muss Angelina bitten, das Gästezimmer für Fabio herzurichten, er kommt in zwei Tagen.«

»Du freust dich bestimmt sehr auf ihn, aber ich muss zugeben, es war wunderschön nur mit uns beiden.« Er schlang die Arme um ihre Taille und küsste sie auf den Nacken.

»Ja, das stimmt, aber du hast recht: Ich bin aufgeregt wie ein kleines Kind.« Helena löste sich aus seiner Umarmung und holte die Müslischüsseln. »Vergiss nicht, dass du Chloë für ein paar Stunden von Michel wegreißen willst, um vor ihrer Abfahrt noch einmal mit ihr essen zu gehen. Du solltest die Gelegenheit nutzen, dich noch einmal mit ihr in aller Ruhe zu unterhalten.«

»Ich werde mich bemühen, aber sie zu überzeugen, mit ihrem uralten Vater in ein Lokal zu gehen und währenddessen auf den jugendlichen Charme Michels zu verzichten, wird nicht leicht werden.«

»Ach, und dann wollte ich dich die ganze Zeit schon bitten,

einen Blick auf die Schublade in Angus' Schreibtisch zu werfen. Ich möchte das Schloss ungern aufbrechen, aber ich möchte trotzdem wissen, was drin liegt.«

»Jetzt lass mich erst mal mit den Kindern im Pool schwimmen, und dann schaue ich sie mir an.«

Helena sah auf ihre Uhr. »Es ist fast zehn! Ich hätte ja nie geglaubt, dass ich das einmal zu dir sagen würde, aber kannst du bitte Immy und Fred wecken gehen? Sonst kriegen wir sie abends nicht vor Mitternacht ins Bett.«

Summend bereitete Helena in der Küche weiter das Frühstück vor, während William nach oben ging. Als sie zufällig zum Fenster hinaussah, bot sich ihr ein höchst erstaunlicher Anblick: Rupes kam gefährlich wackelnd auf Violas kleinem Fahrrad den Berg hinabgefahren.

Neben der hinteren Tür bremste er abrupt und ging zur Haustür.

»Komm rein, die Tür ist offen!«, rief Helena.

Mit hochrotem Kopf und schweißnassem T-Shirt betrat Rupes die Küche.

»Guten Morgen, Rupes. Du bist ja völlig verschwitzt. Möchtest du ein Glas Wasser?«

»Ja, gern, Helena. Es ist wirklich irre heiß. Ich werde froh sein, wenn wir wieder zu Hause sind. In der Villa ist die Klimaanlage kaputt, ich kann nicht schlafen.«

»In der Zeitung hieß es gestern, dieser Sommer sei hier auf Zypern der heißeste seit fast hundert Jahren.« Helena schenkte Rupes ein großes Glas Wasser aus dem Kühlschrank ein und reichte es ihm. »Wie geht's deiner Mum?«

»Ganz gut.« Rupes leerte das Glas mit drei Zügen. »Auf jeden Fall besser als vorher. Andererseits, recht viel schlimmer als vor ein paar Wochen könnte es ihr auch nicht gehen, oder?«

»Nein. Wie auch immer, schön, dich zu sehen.«

»Ich bin gekommen, um etwas auszurichten. Zwei Sachen: Mum möchte euch heute Abend alle zum Essen einladen, wenn ihr nicht schon etwas anderes vorhabt.«

»Ach, das ist aber nett. Ich wollte sie nachher anrufen und ihr dasselbe vorschlagen. Ich muss Angelina fragen, ob sie auf die Kleinen aufpassen kann, für sie würde es zu spät werden, aber wir anderen kommen gern.«

»Und außerdem … äh … ist Alex hier?«

»Irgendwo ist er sicher. Soll ich ihn holen?«

»Das wäre nett.«

Helena ging in den Flur. »Alex? Schatz, da möchte jemand mit dir sprechen.«

»Ich komme«, ertönte eine verschlafene Stimme.

»Er kommt gleich. Ich fürchte, wir sind alle richtige Langschläfer geworden«, sagte Helena entschuldigend. »Wie geht es Viola? Sie hat gestern gar nicht bei uns vorbeigeschaut.«

»Es geht schon. Unser Vater fehlt ihr, außerdem macht ihr die Hitze zu schaffen.«

»Das glaube ich sofort, mit ihrer hellen Haut.« Helena zermarterte sich den Kopf, worüber sie sich mit Rupes noch unterhalten konnte, und war erleichtert, als Alex dazukam. Beim Anblick seines Besuchers machte er ein langes Gesicht.

»Hallo, Rupes«, brummte er.

»Hallo, Alex.«

»Um was geht es?«

»Also, na ja, die Sache ist die …«

»Dann lasse ich euch mal allein, ja?«, warf Helena ein. Offensichtlich war sie bei diesem Gespräch nicht erwünscht. »Bis heute Abend, Rupes. So um acht?«

»Ja, genau.«

Nachdem Helena die Küche verlassen hatte, räusperte Rupes sich. »Also, du ... du weißt, was ... was in unserer Familie passiert ist?«

»Ja.«

»Das Problem ist, meine Eltern können es sich jetzt nicht leisten, mich nach Oundle zu schicken, nicht einmal mit meinem Sportstipendium. Das deckt nur zwanzig Prozent der Gebühren, verstehst du?«

»Ich verstehe«, sagte Alex trocken.

»Mum hat sich mit dem Schatzmeister in Verbindung gesetzt und ihm die Lage erklärt, und er meinte, sie könnten eventuell erwägen, mir ein Vollstipendium zu geben, natürlich vermögensabhängig. Schließlich wollen sie mich für das Rugby-Team immer noch haben. In ein paar Wochen bin ich in der Bewerberrunde für das englische Unter-Achtzehn-Team.«

»Das ist doch gut, oder?«

»Ja, schon.«

»Aber?«

»Na ja ... meine Noten waren bei der Aufnahmeprüfung nicht so toll. Ehrlich gesagt hatte ich mich nicht besonders darauf vorbereitet, weil ich ja wusste, dass sie mich als Sportler wollen. Aber eine ihrer Voraussetzungen für das Vollstipendium ist, dass ich in einer Woche ihre eigene akademische Aufnahmeprüfung mache.«

»Ah«, sagte Alex. »Ich verstehe.«

»Die Sache ist die, wenn ich durchfalle, komme ich auf irgendein staatliches Gymnasium.« Rupes ließ den Kopf hängen.

»Okay, ich verstehe. Aber was habe ich damit zu schaffen?«

»Ja, was denn schon?« Aufgebracht wedelte Rupes mit den Händen durch die Luft. »Wir wissen doch alle, dass du ein Gehirn so groß wie Russland hast.«

»Russland ist zwar weit kleiner, als es früher einmal war, aber trotzdem danke.«

»Alex.« Rupes legte die Hände flach auf den Tisch. »Ich muss diese Prüfung bestehen, aber ich bin schlecht in Englisch, noch schlechter in Französisch und gerade Durchschnitt, was Mathe und die ganzen naturwissenschaftlichen Fächer angeht. Ich brauche Nachhilfe in den Sprachen. Kannst du …« Er räusperte sich wieder. »Kannst du mir helfen?«

Alex pfiff durch die Zähne. »Verdammt, Rupes, du fragst mich, ob ich dir Nachhilfe gebe?«

»Genau so ist es. Mum hat sich Prüfungsunterlagen schicken lassen. Kannst du sie mit mir durchgehen?«

Alex stützte das Kinn auf die Hand und seufzte. »Rupes, um ehrlich zu sein, weiß ich nicht, ob ich der Richtige dafür bin. Ich habe noch nie jemanden unterrichtet.«

»Jemand anderen als dich habe ich nicht. Wenn du willst, bezahle ich dich auch. Ich habe ein paar Pfund auf der hohen Kante, auch wenn meine Eltern nichts haben. Ehrlich gesagt würde ich alles tun. Du bist meine einzige Hoffnung.«

»Ich kann nicht garantieren, dass du bestehst. Letztlich steht und fällt es mit dir.«

»Ich arbeite mich tot. Alles, was du verlangst. *Bitte.*«

»Also gut«, willigte Alex ein und nickte langsam. »Aber dein Geld will ich nicht. Nur eine Entschuldigung dafür, dass du dich wie ein Arsch aufgeführt hast.«

»Okay.« Rupes straffte sich. »Es tut mir leid«, sagte er mit einem langen Ausatmen.

»Dass du dich wie ein Arsch verhalten hast«, sagte Alex ihm vor.

»Dass ich mich wie ein Arsch verhalten habe«, brummelte Rupes.

»Okay, wann willst du anfangen?«

»So bald wie möglich.«

»Also gut, dann gleich«, sagte Alex. »Schreib heute Nachmittag einen Aufsatz, fünfhundert Wörter, wie man deiner Meinung nach Mobbing an Schulen verhindern kann und wie man die Täter bestrafen sollte. Ich korrigiere den Aufsatz und gehe dann die Fehler mit dir durch. Okay?«

Rupert bekam einen roten Kopf, nickte aber. »In Ordnung. Dann gehe ich jetzt besser wieder.«

»Ja. Bis später.«

»Liebling, jetzt hatte ich endlich Zeit, mich um die Schublade zu kümmern und sie zu öffnen«, sagte William, als er am Abend ins Schlafzimmer kam.

»Wirklich?« Erwartungsvoll drehte Helena sich zu ihm. »Und?«

»Ich fürchte, sie ist leer. Aber ich glaube, wir sollten den Schreibtisch gegen Holzwürmer behandeln lassen. Die halten sich bereits schadlos an ihm.«

»Ach«, sagte Helena enttäuscht. »Ich hatte so gehofft, dort etwas zu finden, das Aufschluss über Angus' verlorene Liebe gibt.«

»Na ja, immerhin ist es mir gelungen, sie zu öffnen, ohne das Schloss kaputt zu machen.« William warf einen Blick auf die Uhr. »Fertig? Es ist fast acht.«

»Jules, du siehst phantastisch aus! Stimmt's nicht, Helena?«, sagte William.

»Und ob«, pflichtete Helena ihm bei. Jules hatte in den vergangenen zwei Wochen eindeutig abgenommen, was ihr eine ganz neue Eleganz verlieh. Außerdem kamen nun ihre muskulösen, sonnengebräunten Beine besser zur Geltung. Die Sonne hatte rötliche Strähnchen in ihr mausbraunes Haar gefärbt, das ihr leicht gewellt ums Gesicht fiel. Ihre Wangenknochen traten ansprechend hervor, und in ihren Augen funkelte ein neu gewonnenes Selbstvertrauen.

»Alter Charmeur«, antwortete Jules kokett und führte sie auf die Terrasse. »Ich habe einfach wenig Appetit, offenbar ist Schock die beste Diät. Und völlig kostenlos obendrein«, fügte sie mit einem kleinen Lachen hinzu. »Chloë ist nicht mitgekommen?«

»Nein. Zur allgemeinen Überraschung ist sie mit Michel ausgegangen«, erwiderte Helena. »Sie haben nur noch zwei Abende, bevor Chloë nach Frankreich fährt.«

»Michel ist ein netter Kerl«, räumte Jules ein. »Er war vorhin hier, um die Klimaanlage zu reparieren. Möchtet ihr ein Glas Wein?«

»Guten Abend, Tante Helena und Onkel William.« Viola gab ihrem Patenonkel einen Kuss und umarmte Helena.

»Hallo, mein Schatz. Wie geht es dir?«, fragte sie.

»Mir geht's gut.« Sie nickte aufgeregt. »Stell dir vor, Mummy hat mir erlaubt, ein Kätzchen zu adoptieren!«

»Wirklich?«

»Nur für die Ferien, Viola«, warf Jules ein. »Nach unserer Abreise kümmert Alexis sich darum.«

»Kommst du sie dir ansehen?« Viola zog Helena an der Hand. »Sie schläft bei mir auf dem Bett, und sie ist so süß!«

»Aber gern, mein Schatz.«

»Ich habe sie Aphro getauft, nach der Göttin, und auch weil sie so schöne lange gekräuselte Haare hat«, erklärte Viola, als sie Helena an der Hand in die Villa führte.

Ein paar Sekunden später erschien Rupes in der Terrassentür. Er winkte Alex zu, der ihm ins Haus folgte.

»Also, William, was hältst du von dem Haus?«, fragte Jules und reichte ihm ein Glas Wein.

Er überquerte die riesige Terrasse, die offenbar erst vor Kurzem mit makellos cremefarbenen Steinen gepflastert worden war. »Der Blick ist fast noch schöner als von Pandora«, sagte er und betrachtete das Panorama, das sich ihm bot.

»Alexis hat das Haus eigens an dieser Stelle bauen lassen, um den großartigen Blick aufs Meer zu haben.« Jules deutete über das Tal hinweg. »Genau zwischen den beiden Bergen. Ich finde es traumhaft hier. Alles ist neu und frisch und komfortabel. Ich wünschte, ich könnte länger bleiben.«

»Wie sieht es denn aus?«, erkundigte William sich. »Ich habe von Sacha nichts gehört, seit er wieder in England ist, obwohl ich ihm ein paarmal auf die Mailbox gesprochen habe.«

»Wir sind per E-Mail in Kontakt. Er hat mir geschrieben, dass sie ihm sechs Wochen Zeit geben, um das Haus leer zu räumen und auszuziehen. Ich habe ihm mitgeteilt, dass ich ihm nicht dabei helfen werde. Um ehrlich zu sein, William, ich könnte es einfach nicht über mich bringen. Hätte er damals nur das Haus auch auf mich übertragen, dann sähe es jetzt vielleicht anders aus.«

»Sicher«, räumte William ein. »Und was passiert mit deinen ganzen Sachen?«

»Ich habe ihn gebeten, sie irgendwo einzulagern, bis ich weiß, wo wir drei wohnen werden.«

»Hast du schon irgendeine Vorstellung?«

Jules zuckte mit den Achseln. »Die Jury ist im Moment nicht anwesend. Ich hoffe immer noch, dass Rupes das Stipendium für Oundle bekommt – wenn er die Prüfung besteht, heißt das. Und wenn ich tatsächlich nach England zurückgehe, werde ich vermutlich eine Wohnung irgendwo in der Nähe seiner Schule mieten. Viola wird einstweilen in eine staatliche Schule gehen.«

»Das klingt alles sehr vernünftig.«

»Weißt du, einerseits möchte ich eigentlich nie wieder englischen Boden betreten, das kannst du vielleicht nachvollziehen. Es gefällt mir hier so gut, aber andererseits muss ich natürlich wieder zu arbeiten anfangen.«

»Was wirst du machen?«

»Früher war ich eine ganz erfolgreiche Immobilienmaklerin, erinnerst du dich? Bevor ich alles aufgab, um mich um Rupes zu kümmern. Ich bin mir ziemlich sicher, dass ich aufgrund meiner Erfahrung irgendwo eine Stelle bekomme.«

»Es freut mich zu hören, dass du in die Zukunft blickst, Jules«, sagte William. »Die letzten Wochen müssen ein Albtraum für dich gewesen sein.«

»Was bleibt mir denn anderes übrig? Friss oder stirb, würde ich sagen. Und Alexis ist einfach großartig. Es ist das absolute Gegenteil von Sacha, in jeder Hinsicht. Seit ich hier eingezogen bin, kümmert er sich um alles und scheut keine Mühe. Er kommt nachher auch, aber er musste heute nach Limassol, deswegen meinte er, es könne etwas später werden.«

»Mummy, Tante Helena liebt die kleine Katze«, sagte Viola, als sie und Helena wieder auf die Terrasse traten.

»Die muss man ja auch ins Herz schließen, sie ist so niedlich.« Jules sah lächelnd zu ihrer Tochter. »Also, sollen wir essen?«

Kurz vor Mitternacht machten sich William, Helena und Alex auf den Heimweg.

»Noch einen Brandy auf der Terrasse?«, fragte William, nachdem Alex gute Nacht gesagt und sich in sein Zimmer zurückgezogen hatte.

»Nein danke, aber ich leiste dir gern Gesellschaft, wenn du noch einen trinken möchtest«, antwortete Helena und ließ sich unter der Pergola nieder, während William im Haus die Flasche holen ging.

»Und wieder ein sternenklarer Himmel«, sagte sie, als er zurückkehrte und sich neben sie setzte.

»Ja, die Sterne sind hier wirklich unglaublich.«

»Jules war heute Abend anders. Sie wirkt irgendwie … weicher.«

»Ich weiß, was du meinst«, sagte William. »Ironischerweise verliert sie ihre Härte genau in dem Moment, in dem sie jeden Grund hätte, verbittert zu sein. Sie kam mir auch glücklicher und entspannter vor als seit Jahren. Hast du auch gesehen, was ich heute Abend gesehen habe?«

»Du meinst Jules und Alexis?«, fragte Helena.

»Ja. Sie scheinen sich miteinander sehr wohlzufühlen. Bei Alexis kann ich es nicht beurteilen, aber bei ihr habe ich stark den Eindruck, dass sie sich zu ihm hingezogen fühlt.«

»Wer weiß? Ein bisschen Liebe und Gesellschaft würde sicher beiden guttun.«

»Vor ein paar Wochen noch hätte ich den Gedanken absurd gefunden, aber jetzt nicht mehr«, meinte William nachdenklich. »Und selbst wenn es nur eine kleine Affäre ist, würde das keinem von ihnen wehtun.«

»Alexis ist nicht dazu fähig, jemandem wehzutun. Warten wir's ab, was passiert.«

»Und … und wenn es tatsächlich weitergeht«, sagte William, »wie fändest du das?«

Helena griff nach seiner Hand und drückte sie fest. »Es würde mir nicht das Geringste ausmachen, glaub mir.«

Alex' Tagebuch

9. August 2006

Jetzt verstehe ich, weshalb den Menschen, die das Sagen haben, die Macht zu Kopf steigt und sie irgendwann komplett abdrehen.

Heinrich VIII., der Gott abschaffte und beschloss, den Job selbst zu übernehmen.

Stalin, Hitler und Mao, die sich als wahre Teufel entpuppten.

Bush, der *seinen* Gott zum absoluten Obermacker erkor.

Und Blair, der Pudel, der unterwegs sowohl Haare als auch jegliche Orientierung verloren hat.

Als ich heute Abend Rupes' Aufsatz las, der, gelinde gesagt, grottenschlecht ist und mit dem er nicht mal in einen Kindergarten aufgenommen würde, ganz zu schweigen von einem der führenden Internate in England, bekam ich eine Ahnung davon.

Als er mich ansah und in meinem Gesicht verzweifelt nach einer positiven Reaktion suchte, wusste ich, dass ich ihn und sein Schicksal in der Hand hatte.

Ein Traum! Zumindest für ein paar Sekunden.

Dann tat er mir leid. Nur wegen meines mitfühlenden Herzens werde ich nie eine hohe Führungsposition innehaben, weil ich es nämlich nicht ertrage, jemanden leiden zu sehen. Ein mädchenhafter Zug, ich weiß, aber ich bin von Geburt an dazu verdammt, immer beide Seiten zu sehen.

Hätte ich den Vorsitz über Saddam Husseins ersten Prozess gehabt – ich weiß genau, was passiert wäre: Auch wenn ich den ruchlosen Massenmörder zutiefst verabscheue wegen des Leids, das er über so viele Menschen gebracht hat, hätte ich ihn als traurigen, verrückten, gebrochenen alten Mann vor mir sitzen sehen.

Und er hätte nur etwas zu sagen brauchen wie: »Meine Mutter hat mich nicht geliebt«, und ich hätte ihn wahrscheinlich in eine bequeme Gefängniszelle gesteckt, um den Rest seiner Tage Therapiesitzungen zu machen und Wiederholungen von *Friends* zu sehen.

Ich frage mich wirklich, ob mich das dazu prädestiniert, auf immer und ewig die ehemaligen Liberals zu wählen, unter welchem Namen sie auch gerade firmieren.

Aber egal, sogar Rupes, mein Erzfeind, der mir mehr Leid zugefügt hat als die chinesische Wasserfolter und Mücken zusammen, hat mich heute erweicht. Ich sah seine Verletzlichkeit.

Er ist ein geistig semibemittelter Schlägerarsch, der seine Zukunft in die Tonne treten kann, wenn ich ihm nicht helfe. Und natürlich helfe ich ihm.

Er muss *toute de suite* korrekte Rechtschreibung lernen. Ich habe ihn vergattert, sich ins Englisch-Wörterbuch zu versenken (wo er sich zweifelsohne *im* Wörterbuch versenken würde). Ich habe ihm eine Liste mit eindrucksvoll klingenden Adjektiven gegeben, die er auswendig lernen und nach Belieben in seine Aufsätze einstreuen soll, um sie aufzupeppen.

Sein Französisch ist der reinste Albtraum. Heute Abend war er auf dem Niveau von *un, deux, trois*, und ich glaube, ich muss um Verstärkung durch eine Fachkraft bitten, damit er auch nur den Hauch einer Chance hat. Ich werde also das größtmögliche Opfer bringen und Chloë bitten, ihm mit Pariser ... äh, Französischlektionen zu helfen. Allerdings nur, wenn sie gelobt, einen Niqab zu tragen, während sie ihn mit Befehls-, Möglichkeits- und Beugeformen traktiert. Sonst könnte seine Domina ihn zu sehr vom Spracherwerb ablenken.

Rupes, mein Lieber, du hast mir die Herausforderung des Jahrzehnts bereitet.

Und sosehr ich mich freuen würde, eines Tages an dir vorbeizugehen, wenn du als Obdachloser in der Gosse liegst und ein räudiger Hund dein einziger Gefährte ist, weiß ich doch, dass ich nicht an deinem Niedergang beteiligt sein kann.

Außerdem hege ich den Verdacht, dass sich »akademischer Tutor« nicht schlecht auf meinem späteren Lebenslauf machen wird.

Schließlich lege ich mich hin und versuche zu schlafen. Rupes kommt morgen um elf zum ersten Unterricht, und ich überlege mir, wie ich ihn gestalte. Unvermittelt bin ich meinem noch immer unbekannten Genpool dankbar, der mir zu einem Gehirn verhalf, das offenbar ziemlich mühelos funktioniert.

Das bringt mich zum Lehrstoff Geschichte, allerdings meiner eigenen. So schön die vergangenen zwei stressfreien Wochen waren, ich habe die Frage nicht vergessen, auf die ich eine Antwort bekommen möchte. Und ich wiederhole hiermit meinen Schwur, Pandora nicht den Rücken zu kehren, ehe ich sie bekommen habe.

Aufgepasst, liebste Mutter, du bist noch nicht aus dem Schneider! An dieser Frage kommst du mir nicht vorbei.

KAPITEL 20

»Guten Morgen, Dad.« Verschlafen schlenderte Chloë in die Küche und gab ihrem Vater einen Kuss. »Schöner Abend?«

»Ja, er war überraschend schön. Jules war richtig gut drauf.«

»Cool.« Chloë holte einen Karton Orangensaft aus dem Kühlschrank und trank direkt aus der Packung.

»Chloë, ich würde gern mit dir reden.«

Plötzlich munter wirbelte sie herum. »Und ich mit dir.«

»Gut, dann lass uns zusammen mittagessen gehen.«

»Nur du und ich?«

»Warum nicht? In zwei Tagen fährst du, und ich habe das Gefühl, dass ich dich in letzter Zeit kaum gesehen habe.«

»Ja, genau darüber möchte ich mit dir reden.«

»Worüber?«

»Dass ich weg ...«

»Hallo, Chloë, wo ist Mieschell?« Wie ein Wirbelwind stürmte Fred in die Küche und umklammerte liebevoll ihre Beine. »Er hat gesagt, er zeigt mir seine Pistole, eine richtige, und schießt Ratten tot.« Er sauste durch die Küche, erschoss mit einer eingebildeten Waffe eingebildete Nager und brüllte nonstop lauthals »Peng!«.

»Er kommt später, Schätzchen«, sagte Chloë über den Lärm hinweg.

»Lass uns doch gegen zwölf fahren, und dann unterhalten wir uns in Ruhe, ja?«, schlug William vor.

»Okay, aber um drei spätestens muss ich zurück sein, Michel will mit mir zu den Wasserfällen fahren.«

»Wir sind rechtzeitig wieder da«, versprach William, packte den aufgedrehten Fred um die Taille und setzte ihn auf einen Stuhl am Tisch. »So, junger Mann, und jetzt bekommst du dein Frühstück.«

William fuhr mit Chloë zu dem Lokal am Rand von Peylia, das er vor wenigen Wochen mit Helena besucht hatte. Er glaubte nicht, dass die Einwohner des kleinen Kathikas – die Chloë mittlerweile fast alle namentlich kannte – sie in Ruhe lassen würden, wenn sie dort äßen.

»Und was wolltest du mich fragen?« William trank einen Schluck von seinem Bier, Chloë nippte an ihrer Cola.

»Ob du mit Mum redest, dass ich den Rest der Ferien hierbleiben möchte.«

»Ah ja. Das ist eine ziemlich große Bitte.«

»Ich will nicht nach Frankreich. Mum ist mit dem schrecklichen Andy zusammen, es gibt dort nichts zu tun, außerdem kenne ich niemanden. Ich würde sooo viel lieber hier bei euch bleiben.«

»Mein Schatz, du bist fast schon einen ganzen Monat hier. Glaubst du nicht, dass deine Mutter sich freuen wird, dich zu sehen?«

»In den ersten paar Stunden schon, aber dann lässt sie mich wieder links liegen, und ich störe sie in ihrem Liebesnest. Andy mag mich nicht, abgesehen davon ist er ein fieser Typ. Du würdest ihn nicht leiden können. Mum hat einen grauenhaften Männergeschmack.«

»Danke!« William lachte.

»Daddy, dich habe ich nicht gemeint, das weißt du auch.«

Sie zuckte charmant mit den Schultern. »Wie auch immer – redest du mit ihr?«

»Um ehrlich zu sein, ein Gespräch mit deiner Mutter war für mich immer schon schwierig. Höchstwahrscheinlich knallt sie schon nach dem ersten Satz den Hörer auf.«

»Daddy, bitte, mir zuliebe«, bettelte Chloë. »Ich mag wirklich nicht fahren.«

William seufzte. »Weißt du, mein Schatz, das Szenario habe ich mit deiner Mutter schon zu oft erlebt. Sie wird mir emotionale Erpressung vorwerfen und sagen, ich wolle mich bei dir nur einschmeicheln und dir deinen Willen lassen. Es tut mir leid, Chloë, aber so ist es nun mal.«

»Das braucht dir nicht leidzutun. Ich weiß doch, wie schwierig sie ist. Ich meine, ich habe sie lieb – schließlich ist sie meine Mutter –, aber es wundert mich nicht, dass du dich von ihr hast scheiden lassen. So, wie sie ihre ganzen Männer behandelt, hätte ich das vermutlich auch. Sie muss rund um die Uhr sieben Tage die Woche im Mittelpunkt stehen.«

William verkniff es sich, ihr zuzustimmen. »Ich kann nur sagen, ich habe mein Bestes versucht, mein Schatz. Und bin gescheitert.«

»Ich weiß auch, wie schwer sie es dir gemacht hat, mich zu sehen, als du Helena geheiratet hast.«

»Nicht, dass ich es nicht immer wieder versucht hätte, bitte glaub mir das. Und in Gedanken war ich sehr oft bei dir.«

»Ach, was das betrifft, da habe ich sie irgendwann durchschaut. Einmal hast du mir zum Geburtstag geschrieben, aber sie hat die Karte zerrissen, und ich habe sie später im Papierkorb gefunden. Da wusste ich, dass du mich noch lieb hast und mich nicht vergessen hast. Aber ich musste Mums Spiel mitspielen. Du weißt doch, wie unbeherrscht sie ist, und sie war maßlos eifersüchtig auf Helena. Sie hat einen mordsmäßigen Tobsuchtsanfall hingelegt, bloß weil ich einmal sagte, dass ich sie richtig gern mag. Ich komme damit schon klar, Dad, wirklich.« Tröstend legte Chloë eine Hand auf seine.

»Ich komme damit nicht so ganz klar, Chloë«, sagte William und seufzte. »Ich hatte immer gehofft, dich aus unseren Schwierigkeiten heraushalten zu können, aber das ist mir nicht gelungen.«

»Ach, mir ist es egal, was zwischen euch passiert ist. Du bist mein Dad, und ich hab dich lieb, Punkt.«

»Und ich habe wirklich Glück, eine so vernünftige und schöne Tochter zu haben.« Vor Rührung versagte William fast die Stimme. »Du hast mir so gefehlt. Es hat mir regelrecht körperlich wehgetan, dich nicht heranwachsen zu sehen. Ein paarmal habe ich mir sogar überlegt, dich zu kidnappen.«

»Echt? Irre!« Chloë lachte leise. »Wie auch immer, Daddy, das ist jetzt vorbei. Demnächst bin ich fünfzehn und alt genug, meine Entscheidungen selbst zu treffen. Und eine ist, dass ich dich und meine Familie in Zukunft viel öfter sehen möchte – ob ihr das nun passt oder nicht.«

»Wir wissen beide, dass es ihr nicht passen wird.«

»Na ja, das hat nicht sie zu entscheiden, und wenn sie mir dumm kommt, dann drohe ich ihr damit, dass ich zu euch ziehe. Das sollte reichen«, sagte Chloë und grinste. »Außerdem, wenn sie Andy heiratet, dieses Arsch…«

»Chloë!«

»'tschuldigung, aber es stimmt. Und wenn sie ihn wirklich heiratet, dann will ich sowieso nicht mehr ständig bei ihr sein. Also, vielleicht können wir sie ja beide fragen, ob ich noch hierbleiben kann, anstatt nach Frankreich zu fahren?« Geschickt brachte Chloë das Gespräch wieder zu ihrem Anliegen zurück.

»Weißt du, es freut mich sehr, dass du dich bei uns so wohl-fühlst, Chloë, aber seien wir ehrlich, du willst ja nicht nur un-seretwegen auf Zypern bleiben, oder?«

»Das darfst du nicht sagen, Daddy.« Chloë sah gekränkt drein. »Es ist echt cool bei euch. Ich habe die Kleinen richtig lieb, und Alex ist süß, und Helena ist so unglaublich nett, und … na ja, es ist wie eine richtige Familie. Um ehrlich zu sein, zuerst fand ich die Aussicht nicht so toll. Ich dachte, es würde langweilig wer-den, aber es sind die besten Wochen meines Lebens gewesen.«

»Dass du Michel kennengelernt hast, hat seinen Teil dazu beigetragen.«

»Ja, natürlich«, räumte sie ein.

»Er ist auch wirklich nett«, sagte William. »Aber ich bin mir sicher, es wird in der Zukunft viele andere wie ihn geben.«

»Nein, das stimmt nicht.« Chloë schüttelte den Kopf mit Nachdruck. »Ich liebe ihn.«

William folgte Helenas Rat und widersprach nicht. »Ja, das glaube ich gern«, antwortete er matt. In dem Augenblick wur-den ihre Meze serviert. »So, und jetzt lass uns essen.«

»Soll ich Cecile anrufen oder nicht?« William saß am Rand von Helenas Sonnenliege. Er und Chloë waren noch keine fünf Minuten von ihrem Essen zurückgekehrt, als seine Toch-ter auch schon wieder auf dem Sozius von Michels Moped in einer Staubwolke davongebraust war.

»Das ist schwierig. Wenn du sie fragst, sagt sie garantiert Nein, nur um dich zu ärgern.«

»Genau.«

»Aber wenn du sie nicht fragst, hat Chloë das Gefühl, dass du sie hängen lässt. Wie wär's mit einem Kompromiss?«

»Wie würde der aussehen?«

»Du könntest Cecile anrufen und vorsichtig anfragen, ob Chloë am Ende des Frankreichurlaubs noch ein paar Tage zu uns kommen darf. So kann Cecile sie wie geplant sehen, dann hängt Chloë bei ihr und ihrem Freund herum, langweilt sich zu Tode und vergeht vor Sehnsucht nach Michel. Nach einer Weile wird Cecile heilfroh sein, Chloë wieder zu uns schicken zu können.«

»Brillant, Liebling!« Er drückte ihr einen Kuss auf jede Wange. »Danke, das sage ich Chloë.«

»Das wird zwar nicht genau das sein, was sie hören will, aber es ist wahrscheinlich für alle die beste Lösung.«

»Weißt du, Chloë ist wirklich großartig. Sehr vernünftig und sehr klug. Offenbar hat sie ihre Mutter durchschaut, und das ist mehr, als mir je gelungen ist.« William seufzte. »Und wichtiger noch, sie hegt offenbar auch keinen Groll gegen mich, was nun wirklich an ein Wunder grenzt.«

»Sie ist in den Wochen hier zweifellos reifer geworden.«

»Bitte nicht«, sagte William düster.

»So meine ich das nicht.« Helena setzte sich auf und schlang die Arme um die Knie. »Wir haben uns mal unter vier Augen unterhalten, und sie weiß, was sie tut. Mach dir keine Sorgen.«

»Mum, Telefon!«, rief Alex von der Terrasse.

»Ich komme, Schatz!«

Eine halbe Stunde später saß Helena in der Dorftaverne Sadie gegenüber. Nach deren SOS-Anruf hatte sie sich auf das Schlimmste gefasst gemacht – das Ende einer weiteren wunderschönen Beziehung, eine in Tränen aufgelöste Sadie. Aber ihre Freundin wirkte alles andere als unglücklich, ihre Augen funkelten, sie strahlte übers ganze Gesicht.

»Wo brennt's denn dann?«, fragte Helena verwundert.

»Süße, ich habe dir etwas zu berichten.«

»Das habe ich mir gedacht. Positiv oder negativ?«

»Das kommt darauf an. Vielleicht beides.«

»Dann komm schon, erzähl.«

»Ja, gleich. Einen Moment …«

Sadie wühlte in ihrer geräumigen Handtasche, aus der sie schließlich ein weißes Plastikstäbchen hervorkramte und Helena reichte.

»Schau dir das an. Was meinst du?«

»Das ist ein Schwangerschaftstest.«

»Das ist mir klar. Schau ihn dir an.«

»Da sind zwei rosafarbene Striche, das heißt … o mein Gott! Sadie!«

»Ich weiß!« Sadie klatschte in die Hände. »Es heißt wirklich positiv, oder? Du hast damit mehr Erfahrung als ich.«

»Na ja, sie unterscheiden sich alle ein bisschen, aber« – Helena studierte das Stäbchen wieder – »im zweiten Kästchen ist eindeutig auch ein Strich.«

»Das heißt also, ich bin schwanger.«

»Laut diesem Test, ja. Wow.« Helena versuchte, die Miene ihrer Freundin zu deuten. »Freust du dich?«

»Ich … Das weiß ich nicht. Ich meine, ich habe es erst vor ein paar Stunden erfahren. Es muss in der Nacht passiert sein, als wir nach der apokalyptischen Party in der Weinkellerei zum ersten Mal miteinander geschlafen haben. Wir waren beide ziemlich betrunken und haben nicht aufgepasst. Ich kann's einfach nicht glauben. Ehrlich, ich hatte schon die Hoffnung aufgegeben. Immerhin bin ich neununddreißig. Aber es ist passiert, es ist wirklich passiert!« Unvermittelt füllten sich Sadies Augen mit Tränen. »Ich bekomme ein Kind, Helena. Ich werde Mutter.«

Helena erinnerte sich an die Zeit, als sie beide junge Mädchen gewesen waren und von ihrem Märchenprinzen geträumt hatten, von dem hübschen Haus, in dem sie leben, und den Kindern, die sie bekommen würden. In den letzten Jahren hatte Sadie immer wieder von ihrem Kummer gesprochen, dass ihr Kinderwunsch nie in Erfüllung gegangen war. Aber dass er jetzt Wirklichkeit wurde, noch dazu in ihrer gegenwärtigen Situation, war eine völlig andere Sache.

»Und was ist mit Andreas? Was meint er dazu?«

Sadie zögerte. »Ich weiß es nicht. Ich habe es ihm noch nicht gesagt.«

»Ah so.«

»Ehrlich gesagt ...« Sadie holte tief Luft. »Ich weiß nicht, ob ich es ihm überhaupt sagen werde.«

»In ein paar Monaten wird er es womöglich selbst feststellen, meinst du nicht?«

»Nicht, wenn ich dann schon wieder in England bin.« Sadie fuhr mit dem Finger um den Rand ihres Glases.

»Habt ihr euch gestritten?«

»Aber nein. Sich zu streiten ist schwierig, wenn man keine gemeinsame Sprache spricht. Zwischen uns ist alles bestens.«

»Was ist dann das Problem?«

»Liegt das nicht auf der Hand? Er ist ein Zimmermann in einem winzigen Dorf auf Zypern, spricht kaum ein Wort Englisch und ist vierzehn Jahre jünger als ich. Ich meine, ich muss den Tatsachen ins Auge schauen. Kannst du dir wirklich vorstellen, dass wir zusammen auf glückliche Familie machen?«

»Liebst du ihn?«

»Nein.«

»Dann ist das ja schon mal geklärt.« Sadies ehrliche Antwort traf Helena völlig unvorbereitet.

»Ich mag Andreas wirklich gern, er ist ein richtig lieber

Mensch. Und was das Körperliche angeht, ist er der Beste überhaupt.«

»Das ist aus deinem Munde ein ziemliches Kompliment.«

»Die Sache ist, er ist wunderbar als Urlaubsflirt. Wie du nur allzu gut weißt, ging's mir ziemlich schlecht, als ich hier ankam, und Andreas hat mein Ego gewaltig aufgepäppelt. Aber mir war von vornherein klar, dass ich nach England zurückfahren würde. Nächste Woche fange ich ein großes neues Projekt an. Diese Affäre sollte ein wunderbares Souvenir sein.«

»Mein Schatz, wenn du das Kind wirklich bekommst, hast du den Rest deiner Tage ein lebendes Souvenir an diesen Urlaub«, warnte Helena. »Um ehrlich zu sein, stehe ich noch ein bisschen unter Schock. Ich weiß nicht, was ich dazu sagen soll.«

»Ich schon. Ich habe beschlossen, das Kind zu bekommen. Es ist vermutlich meine einzige Chance, jemals eins zu haben, und ich weiß, wie sehr ich es im Alter bereuen würde, wenn ich es abtreiben ließe.«

»Ja, das kann gut sein«, sagte Helena mitfühlend.

»Mein wirkliches Dilemma ist, ob ich Andreas vor meiner Abreise erzähle, dass ich schwanger bin. Ich habe doch nichts Illegales gemacht, oder? Er kann mich doch nicht dafür verklagen, dass ich sein Sperma gestohlen habe oder so was in der Art?«

»Ich habe keine Ahnung. Allerdings könnte er, wenn er es herausfindet, Besuchsrecht verlangen.« Helena trank einen Schluck von ihrem bitteren Kaffee. »Weißt du, ich will dir nicht die Freude verderben oder dich bevormunden, aber wie du weißt, habe ich das alles selbst erlebt.«

»Was?«

»Alleinstehend und schwanger zu sein. Es ist schwierig, in vieler Hinsicht.«

»Ich weiß nicht, wie es für dich war, Helena, du hast mir

nie viel von deiner Zeit in Wien erzählt, als Alex ein Baby war. Aber wie schwer kann es denn sein? Ich bin finanziell unabhängig, ich besitze mein eigenes Haus, ich bin freiberuflich tätig. Ich stelle ein Kindermädchen ein, so einfach ist das.«

Helena atmete tief durch. Sadie klang, als wäre ein Kind lediglich eine kleine Unbequemlichkeit, die sich durch die Anstellung von Hauspersonal leicht in den Griff bekommen ließe. Die Offenbarung ihrer Freundin wühlte sie innerlich auf, erinnerte sie sie doch an die dunklen Tage, die sie als Schwangere und dann als alleinstehende Mutter erlebt hatte.

»Sadie, es geht nicht nur um die praktischen Fragen, sondern auch um die emotionalen. Während der ganzen Schwangerschaft und der Geburt hast du niemanden, der dir zur Seite steht. Und wenn dann das Baby mitten in der Nacht schreit oder wenn es krank wird, bist ausschließlich du dafür zuständig, und zwar für sehr lange Zeit.«

»Ja, das stimmt. Aber Helena, ich bin schwanger! Was immer mir dieses Kind abverlangt, ich schaffe das! Das weiß ich genau.«

»Das glaube ich auch. Entschuldige, ich will dir keine Predigt halten. Es ist wunderbar, dass du dich so darüber freust, wirklich. Ich möchte dir nur raten, es dir genau zu überlegen, ehe du Andreas völlig außen vor lässt. Und wenn ich noch etwas sagen darf: Moralisch hat er meiner Ansicht ein Anrecht darauf, es zu wissen.«

»Vielleicht. Wenn ich wieder in England bin, mit ein bisschen Abstand zwischen uns, entscheide ich, ob ich es ihm sage oder nicht. Aber mein Leben mit jemandem zu verbringen, nur weil ich von ihm schwanger bin, wäre ein Rückfall ins finstere Mittelalter und völlig falsch für alle Beteiligten. Ich schaffe das auch allein, das weiß ich.«

»Na, dann viel Glück.« Helena brachte ein Lächeln zustande. »Du weißt, ich werde dir helfen, wo immer ich kann. Wann willst du zurückfliegen?«

»Angesichts der Umstände eher früher als später. Vielleicht bitte ich William, mich morgen zum Flughafen zu fahren, wenn ich ein Ticket bekomme.«

»Andreas wird am Boden zerstört sein.«

Sadie warf ihrer Freundin einen überraschten Blick zu. »Meinst du?«

»Natürlich!«

»Unsinn! Wahrscheinlich leidet er drei Tage an verletztem Stolz, aber sobald das nächste hübsche und zweifellos jüngere Gesicht auftaucht, hat er mich vergessen.«

»Da wäre ich mir nicht so sicher. Mein Eindruck war, dass er wirklich in dich verliebt ist.«

»Meinst du das im Ernst?« Panik breitete sich auf Sadies Gesicht aus. »O mein Gott, du glaubst doch nicht, dass er mir nach England nachkommt, oder?«

»Wer weiß?«

»Ist das nicht typisch? Offenbar ist es mein Los, mich in Männer zu verlieben, die mich nicht wollen. Und wenn mich dann einer will, dann will ich ihn nicht! Entschuldigung, ich muss auf die Toilette, mir ist schrecklich übel.« Sadie war tatsächlich grün im Gesicht geworden. »Bin gleich wieder da.«

Als Helena allein am Tisch saß, fragte sie sich, was sie so bedrückte, schließlich war Sadie eindeutig überglücklich.

Dann dämmerte es ihr: Sadie verhielt sich wie ein Mann.

Alex' Tagebuch

Die Kleenex-Polizei musste in Pandora heute eine Extra-schicht einlegen.

Sadie tauchte mit ihrem Koffer bei uns auf, und dann ging es mit der Heulerei los, als sie sich nämlich von Mum verabschiedete und Dad sie zum Flughafen fuhr. Ich kann nur vermuten, dass der Schreinermeister sein Ding nicht mehr gemeistert hat und Sadie nach London zurückfliegt, um sich eine neue Zukunft zu zimmern. Dann, als Mum Sadie nachwinkte, fing sie auch zu heulen an. Ich fragte sie, weshalb, und dann sagte sie, was sie in solchen Fällen immer sagt, nämlich: »Alles bestens«, obwohl ihr die Trä-nen übers Gesicht liefen und eindeutig nichts zum Bes-ten stand.

Chloë tropft das Haus seit Stunden voll. Sie ist tod-unglücklich, weil sie morgen zu ihrer Mutter nach Frank-reich fliegen muss und nicht hierbleiben darf. Sie hofft zwar, am Ende der Ferien noch einmal herzukommen, aber das ist offenbar kein Trost für sie. Außerdem ist es, ehrlich gesagt, eher unwahrscheinlich angesichts dessen, wie ihre Mutter so tickt.

Mittlerweile ist »Michelle« gekommen, um sich zu ver-abschieden, und die beiden haben sich in ihr Zimmer ein-geschlossen. Vor ihrer Tür sammelt sich schon eine kleine Pfütze.

Ich habe mich dazugestellt und selbst eine Träne hinein-vergossen. Chloë wird mir furchtbar fehlen.

Immy hat sich, als sie aus dem Pool kam, den Zeh so angestoßen, dass er geblutet hat. Das sowie der Umstand, dass keine Barbie-Pflaster im Haus waren, hat bei ihren Tränendrüsen ebenfalls zu einem Rohrbruch geführt.

Und Fred fühlte sich vermutlich ausgeschlossen angesichts der allgemeinen Stimmung und beschloss, einen seiner gigantischen Wutausbrüche hinzulegen. Niemand kennt den Auslöser, aber wir glauben, dass es mit einem Stück Schokolade zu tun hat. Mum hat ihn ins Bett verbannt, und da liegt er jetzt und schreit sich die Seele aus dem Leib.

Wie gesagt, alles ein einziger großer Spaß.

Im Moment sitze ich ganz allein auf der Terrasse. Mum ist oben und liegt in der Badewanne, und ich glaube, dass Dad – der gerade vom Flughafen zurückgekommen ist – bei ihr ist. Ich sitze über Rupes' Französisch-Aufsatz und korrigiere seine schauderhafte Grammatik. Ich bin zu dem Schluss gekommen, dass jetzt nicht der richtige Zeitpunkt ist, Chloë zu bitten, einen Abend seine Französisch-Domina zu sein. Also schiebe ich selbst Überstunden und versuche, nicht an ihre bevorstehende Abreise zu denken.

Ich lege den Stift beiseite und schaue zu den Sternen hinauf. Zwei ganze Wochen liegen noch vor uns, warum habe ich also das Gefühl, als gingen die Ferien zu Ende?

»Hallo, Alex.«

Ich zucke zusammen und sehe, dass es Mum ist. Wie eine Fee ist sie in ihrem weißen Kaftandingens herunter-geschwebt.

»Hallo, Mum.«

»Darf ich mich zu dir setzen?«

»Klar.«

Sie beugt sich über mich. »Was machst du da?«

»Ich helfe Rupes beim Lernen. Er muss eine Prüfung ablegen, um das Stipendium zu bekommen.«

»Das ist aber wirklich sehr lieb von dir«, sagt sie und setzt sich.

»Hat Fred inzwischen zu brüllen aufgehört? Auf jeden Fall höre ich ihn nicht mehr«, sage ich und versuche, das Gespräch neutral zu halten. Ich merke, dass sie wegen irgendetwas verstört ist.

»Ja. Irgendwann ist er schließlich eingeschlafen. Meine Güte, kann das Kind brüllen.« Sie seufzt. »Ist bei dir alles in Ordnung?«

»Die Frage sollte ich dir stellen.«

»Ich war bloß traurig, weil Sadie gefahren ist, mehr nicht.«

»Aber ihr seht euch doch in England wieder, oder nicht?«

»Doch. Wahrscheinlich hat es etwas damit zu tun, dass ich das Gefühl hatte, als würden die Ferien hier zu Ende gehen.«

»Genau dasselbe habe ich mir auch gerade gedacht. Dabei stimmt es überhaupt nicht.«

»Ja.« Sie mustert mich. »Und mit dir ist wirklich alles in Ordnung?«

»Ja. Nur Chloë wird mir fehlen.«

»Du magst sie gern, stimmt's?«

Ich nicke, greife nach dem Stift und tue, als würde ich weiter Rupes' Aufsatz korrigieren.

»Morgen kommt Fabio, mein früherer Tanzpartner, er

bleibt zwei Tage bei uns«, sagt sie unvermittelt. »Ich hole ihn mittags vom Flughafen in Paphos ab. Er ist ein sehr witziger Typ, zumindest war er das vor elf Jahren. Wahrscheinlich kannst du dich nicht an ihn erinnern, du warst zwei, als du ihn das letzte Mal gesehen hast.«

Ich rufe mir die vielen Gesichter und Bilder meiner Kindheit ins Gedächtnis. »Nein.«

»Er hat dir Bee geschenkt, deinen Hasen«, sagt sie und lächelt dabei.

Ich schlucke. »Ach, ehrlich?«

»Ja. Er hat uns nach deiner Geburt im Krankenhaus besucht und hat den Hasen neben dich in dein Bettchen gelegt.«

»Aber ich ... ich dachte ...«

»MUMMMYYYYY! Ich brauch dich!«

»Komm her, Immy, ich sitze mit Alex auf der Terrasse.«

»Kann nicht. Mein Zeh blutet wieder. HIIIILFEEE!«

Meine Mutter steht auf.

»Mum!«, protestiere ich.

»Tut mir leid, Alex, es dauert nicht lange.«

Verdammte Immy! Diese Chance darf ich mir nicht entgehen lassen. Ich packe sie am Arm, als sie an mir vorbeischwebt. »Ich dachte, mein Va...«

»MUMMMYYYY!«

»Ich bin gleich wieder da, mein Schatz.«

Und schon ist sie im Haus verschwunden. Ich weiß, dass sie Ewigkeiten fort sein wird. »Gleich wieder da« heißt Mitleid, Pflaster, ein Glas Milch und wahrscheinlich eine Geschichte. Wie ich Immy kenne, *Die vollständigen Werke Hans Christian Andersens*, Band eins bis sechzig.

Mist! Scheiße! Verdammt!

Aus lauter Frust streiche ich Rupes ein paar Fehler zusätzlich an.

Ich war wieder mal so nah dran. Ich bin mir ziemlich sicher, dass sie mir einmal sagte, der Hase sei von meinem Vater. Das ist auch der Grund, weshalb ich fast ertrunken wäre beim Versuch, sein nacktes Fell zu retten.

Wenn ich recht habe, dann sehe ich in wenigen Stunden das fehlende Puzzlestück im Rätsel meines Lebens: »Fabio.« Ziemlich tuntig, der Name, aber wenigstens heißt er nicht Archibald oder Bert.

Zu Hause hängt an der Wand ein Bild von ihm, auf dem er mit meiner Mum in irgendeinem Ballett tanzt. Sie hat ein Bein um seinen Rücken geschlungen und drückt ein Knie in seine Leisten. Ganz schön intim, muss ich sagen, andererseits ist er dicker geschminkt als sie, also kann man sein Gesicht nicht richtig erkennen. Abgesehen davon habe ich mir das Bild nie so genau angeschaut.

Aber morgen.

Allerdings stellt sich die Frage: Wenn Fabio mein Dad ist, warum hat sie mir das dann nie gesagt?

KAPITEL 21

Am nächsten Morgen war Helena vor lauter Aufregung bereits um halb sechs wach. Fabio hatte am Abend zuvor angerufen und gesagt, er werde mittags mit der Maschine aus Mailand in Paphos landen. Sie würde ihn abholen. Wieder einmal hatte sie kaum geschlafen und sich gefragt, was in sie gefahren war, als sie ihn nach Pandora eingeladen hatte.

Es war allein ihre Schuld, dass sie so lange keinen Kontakt gehabt hatten. Sie hätte ihn jederzeit durch das New York City Ballet ausfindig machen können, aber das hatte sie nie getan. Schlicht, weil es zu gefährlich war. Als sie aus Wien weggegangen war, hatte sie gleichzeitig ihre Vergangenheit hinter sich lassen wollen, und zu der hatte leider auch Fabio gehört. Einfach, weil er zu viel wusste.

Aber jetzt kam er nach Pandora, und Helena war hin- und hergerissen zwischen panischer Angst und Vorfreude.

Sie beschloss, nach seiner Ankunft gleich mit ihm essen zu gehen. Es gab so vieles, das sie ihm sagen wollte, Umstände, die er unbedingt erfahren musste, ehe er ihrer Familie begegnete. Er brauchte sich nur einmal zu versprechen, und …

Ja, es war ein Risiko, aber andererseits – sie wollte ihn so gern endlich einmal wiedersehen, den einen Menschen, der ihr zur Seite gestanden und sie unterstützt hatte, als sie ihn brauchte. Wahrscheinlich würde er kaum fassen können, was seitdem alles passiert war. Sie konnte es ja selbst kaum.

Auf dem Weg vom Schlafzimmer in die Küche hörte sie die rückwärtige Tür ins Schloss fallen, dann knirschten Schritte auf dem Kies.

Sie betrat die Küche und sah zu ihrer Überraschung Chloë weinend auf einem Stuhl sitzen.

Michel ging, wie sie mit einem Blick zum Fenster hinaus feststellte, mit schnellen Schritten den Berg hinauf.

Seufzend setzte sie den Wasserkessel auf. »Tee?«, fragte sie.

»Helena, wirst du es Daddy sagen?« Ängstlich schaute Chloë zu ihr.

»Dass Michel im Morgengrauen noch hier war? Also, *ich* habe ihn nicht gesehen.« Helena holte einige Teetassen aus der Spülmaschine.

»Ach, Helena, danke. Ich … Das haben wir vorher nie gemacht, aber es war unsere letzte gemeinsame Nacht, also hat Michel getan, als würde er abends gehen, er hat sein Moped oben am Berg zwischen den Weinstöcken versteckt, und dann ist er …«

»Ich will es lieber nicht wissen, Chloë. Dann muss ich deinen Vater nicht direkt anlügen.«

»Ach, Helena, er ist weg. Er ist weg, und ich weiß nicht, wann ich ihn wiedersehen werde.« Verzweifelt rang Chloë die Hände. »Wie soll ich ohne ihn leben? Ich liebe ihn. Ich liebe ihn so sehr.«

Helena ließ die Teekanne stehen, ging zu Chloë und nahm sie in die Arme. Das Mädchen schluchzte an ihrer Brust, und sie streichelte ihm über das lange, seidige Haar.

»Ich will nicht nach Frankreich. Ich will nicht wieder nach England. Ich will hier bei Michel bleiben«, klagte sie. »Bitte zwingt mich nicht zu fahren. Bitte!«

»Ich weiß, mein Schatz, ich verstehe das. Die erste Liebe ist immer die schlimmste.«

»Nein, sie ist die beste, und sie ist für immer, das weiß ich!«

»Wenn das wirklich stimmt und ihr euer ganzes Leben gemeinsam verbringt, dann kannst du doch ein paar Tage Trennung verwinden, oder nicht?« Helena setzte sich neben Chloë.

»Aber was ist, wenn der Sommer vorbei ist? Dann muss ich wieder in die Schule, und die dauert ... ewig!«

»Es gibt Ferien, und Michel wird dich doch sicher in England besuchen kommen.«

»Ja, aber Mum wird ihn nicht einmal bei uns übernachten lassen! Sie hält ihn bestimmt für einen zypriotischen Bauern. Sie will, dass ich einen Goldman heirate oder einen Sachs oder sonst jemanden mit ganz viel Geld!« Chloë sah Helena ins Gesicht. »Würdet du und Daddy ihn bei euch wohnen lassen, wenn er mich besuchen kommt?«

»Ich wüsste nicht, was dagegen spricht. Schließlich war Michel hier auch praktisch Dauergast.«

Chloë ergriff ihre Hände und drückte sie fest. »Danke, Helena. O nein!« Bekümmert schüttelte sie den Kopf. »Wie soll ich das nur überleben?«

»Du wirst daran denken, dass es Michel genauso schlecht geht wie dir. Und dass ihr euch, wenn es denn so sein soll, wiedersehen werdet.«

»Glaubst du wirklich, dass es ihm schlecht geht?«

»Aber ja. Glaub mir, Chloë, demjenigen, der zurückbleibt, geht es immer viel schlechter. So, und wie wär's jetzt mit einer Tasse Tee?« Sie wollte aufstehen, doch Chloë hielt sie fest umarmt. »Schade, dass du nicht meine Mutter bist, Helena. Ich finde dich wunderbar, wirklich.«

»Ach, Chloë.« Helena legte wieder die Arme um ihre Stieftochter und drückte sie an sich. »Ich wünschte mir auch, du wärst meine Tochter.«

Eine Stunde später weckte Helena William mit einer Tasse Tee.

»Du musst in einer Dreiviertelstunde zum Flughafen aufbrechen. Chloë duscht gerade.«

»Danke, Liebling. Hör, wenn ich schon am Flughafen bin – soll ich dann nicht gleich auf Fabio warten?«

»Nein danke. Ich muss in Paphos sowieso etwas besorgen, und ich dachte mir, vielleicht können Fabio und ich zusammen essen gehen und uns unterhalten, bevor wir nach Hause kommen. Wir haben uns so viel zu erzählen«, antwortete Helena ruhig.

»Gut.« William nickte. »Zumindest hast du ein bisschen Ruhe, bevor du fährst. Alle wollen mitkommen, um sich von Chloë zu verabschieden. Sogar Alex. Ich glaube, er hat sich in sie verknallt, was meinst du?«

»Ja, das hat er«, pflichtete Helena bei, während sie sich im Stillen dachte: Ach, ist dir das auch schon aufgefallen? Aber sie verkniff sich einen diesbezüglichen Kommentar, stattdessen sagte sie nur: »Es ist doch großartig, dass sie sie alle begleiten wollen. Sie ist ein liebes Mädchen.«

Am Flughafen checkte William seine Tochter ein, die sehr bedrückt wirkte, begleitet von ihrer ebenso bedrückt wirkenden Schar Halb- und Stiefgeschwister.

»Ich glaube, jetzt ist es so weit.« Chloë ging in die Hocke und umarmte Fred.

»Nich' gehen, Klo, bleib da. Wir haben dich lieb!«

»Ich hab dich auch lieb, Kleiner. Ich wünschte, ich könnte bei euch bleiben.«

»Und wer schaut jetzt mit uns Disney-Filme?«, fragte Immy vorwurfsvoll.

»Das macht jetzt Alex, oder?« Chloë drehte sich zu ihm.

»Äh, also, na gut, ich … ich versuch's mal.«

»Danke. Ciao, Alex, du wirst mir fehlen.«

»Ach, ehrlich?«, fragte er überrascht.

»Na klar. Du bist sooo cool und süß und schlau.«

»Echt?«

»Ja.« Chloë drückte ihm einen Kuss auf die Wange. »Und das weißt du auch.« Sie drehte sich zu William und umarmte ihn. »Ciao, Daddy. Es war super. Danke für alles.«

»Tschüs, mein Liebling. Du wirst uns allen fehlen, was meint ihr?«

»JAAA!«

»Wenn ich darf, komme ich wieder, aber ich glaube nicht, dass Mum mich fahren lässt«, sagte sie, und Tränen stiegen ihr wieder in die Augen. »Ciao, Leute.« Mit einem letzten Winken verschwand sie im Sicherheitscheck.

»Klo soll wiederkommen«, heulte Fred. Immy weinte ebenfalls, und Alex fuhr sich klammheimlich mit der Hand über die Wange.

»Also, Kinder«, sagte William, und seine Stimme war heiser vor Rührung, »wie wär's, wenn wir den nächsten McDonald's ansteuern?«

Mittags war Helena ebenfalls am Flughafen und wartete nervös, dass Fabio erschien.

»*Bella!* Helena!«

»Fabio!« Helena lief ihm entgegen, und er fing sie auf und wirbelte sie zur Begeisterung der Umstehenden durch die Luft. Lachend setzte er sie ab und schloss sie in die Arme.

»Es ist großartig, dich zu sehen«, sagte Helena. Tränen stiegen ihr in die Augen, als sie seinen vertrauten Geruch einatmete, ein Geruch, der eine völlig andere Zeit in ihrem Leben heraufbeschwor.

»Und es ist großartig, dich zu sehen, wirklich.« Fabio betrachtete sie prüfend aus seinen dunkelbraunen Augen. »Und du siehst phantastisch aus, *cara*, etwas schwerer als vor all den Jahren, als ich dich über die Bühne schleuderte, aber *puuh*!« – er zuckte mit den Schultern –, »wir werden beide alt. Können wir jetzt essen? Ich habe Hunger. Seit ich heute Morgen aus Mailand abgeflogen bin, habe ich nichts gegessen. Du weißt, das Flugzeugessen rühre ich nicht an.«

Sie fuhren nach Paphos hinein, parkten den Wagen und gingen zu einem Lokal am ruhigeren Ende des geschäftigen Hafens. Dort fanden sie einen Tisch mit herrlichem Blick auf das Meer und die Palmen, die entlang der Kaimauer wuchsen. Fabio bestellte eine Karaffe Chianti für sich und eine Cola für Helena, holte dann seine Lesebrille hervor und erörterte eine halbe Ewigkeit, was er essen sollte. »Ich hasse dieses zypriotische Essen! Sie haben einfach keine Ahnung vom Kochen«, beschwerte er sich für alle vernehmbar.

»Es gibt einen Salat, den können sie nicht verderben.«

»Du würdest dich wundern. Also! Ich habe mich entschieden.« Er schnippte nach dem Kellner und erläuterte ihm in aller Ausführlichkeit seine Wünsche.

Amüsiert beobachtete Helena ihn und erinnerte sich an seine vielen Eigenheiten, die nicht alle liebenswert waren. Er sah gut aus, war immer noch muskulös und fit vom täglichen Tanzen, aber sein Haaransatz, der ihm schon immer große Sorge bereitet hatte, war stark zurückgewichen.

»Warum starrst du auf meinen Kopf?«, fragte er, nachdem er den verwirrten Kellner entlassen hatte. »Dir fällt auf, dass ich meine Haare verloren habe?«

»Vielleicht ein bisschen. Entschuldige.«

»Das stimmt auch. Ich hasse es! Ich bin ein paranoider Mann

mittleren Alters und lasse nächstes Jahr eine Transplantation machen.«

»Wirklich, Fabio, so schlimm ist es auch wieder nicht. Du siehst fabelhaft aus.«

»Es ist wie die Flut, die zurückweicht, aber nie wieder hereinkommt. Also richte ich es selbst. Siehst du?« Er entblößte seine Zähne. »Ich habe letztes Jahr in L. A. neue bekommen. Sie sind schön, ja?«

»Sie sind ... beeindruckend weiß.« Helena bemühte sich, ein Lachen zu unterdrücken.

»Und auch meine Stirn.« Fabio deutete darauf. »Sie ist glatt, *sì?*«

»Sehr.«

»Botox. Helena, du musst dir welches spritzen lassen.«

»Warum? Habe ich es nötig?«

»Du musst es machen, bevor es anderen auffällt.«

»Gut«, sagte sie mit gespielter Ernsthaftigkeit. »Ich hatte vergessen, wie unglaublich eitel du bist.«

»Nun ja, alt zu werden ist viel schlimmer, wenn man, wie ich, ein hübscher Junge war. Wann immer ich in den Spiegel sehe, schmerzt es mich. Und jetzt, *cara*, trinke ich einen Schluck Wein, und wir erzählen uns von den Jahren, in denen wir getrennt waren.«

Helena legte über den Tisch hinweg eine Hand auf seine. »Fabio, bevor wir uns in den nächsten zwei Stunden in Erinnerungen verlieren und vom Hundertsten ins Tausendste kommen, musst du mir erst einmal zuhören.«

Er machte ein besorgtes Gesicht. »Ich sehe dir an, dass es ernst ist. Du bist doch nicht krank?«

»Nein. Aber bevor du meiner Familie begegnest, gibt es etwas, das du wissen musst.«

»Muss ich trinken?«

»O ja.« Helena nickte mit Nachdruck. »Und wenn ich nicht fahren müsste, würde ich auch trinken. Ich warne dich, du wirst aus allen Wolken fallen.«

Fabio trank einen großen Schluck Chianti. »Also gut«, sagte er und nickte. »Ich bin bereit.«

William lag entspannt am Pool, während die Kleinen im Haus einen Disney-Film sahen. Es herrschte brüllende Hitze.

Die vergangenen drei Wochen, nach den umwälzenden Offenbarungen der Chandlers und Helenas, waren wunderbar gewesen. So schwer es Helena gefallen war, ihm alles zu erzählen, war die Geschichte doch weit weniger dramatisch als manch anderes Szenario, das er sich ausgemalt hatte.

Natürlich war ihm klar, dass sie ihm keineswegs alles erzählt hatte. Schon damals, als er sie vor elf Jahren in Wien kennengelernt hatte, war sie von einer geheimnisvollen Aura umgeben gewesen. Was, so hatte er sich gefragt, machte diese wunderschöne, elegante Frau, deren gepflegte englische Aussprache ihre privilegierte Herkunft verriet, als Bedienung in einem Café? Schon auf den ersten Blick hatte er sich zu ihr hingezogen gefühlt.

Sie waren ins Gespräch gekommen, und aus einem Impuls heraus hatte er sie eingeladen, sich nach Feierabend mit ihm auf ein Glas Wein zu treffen. Wie erwartet, hatte sie abgelehnt, aber er hatte nicht lockergelassen. Wann immer Helena dort arbeitete, hatte er sich, anstatt Wien und die Sehenswürdigkeiten zu besichtigen, mit einem Buch ins Café gesetzt, und schließlich hatte sie doch eingewilligt, mit ihm etwas trinken zu gehen.

Sie erzählte ihm, dass sie früher Primaballerina gewesen sei und vor drei Jahren, als sie schwanger geworden sei, zu tanzen aufgehört habe. Offenbar hatte sie einen Sohn, und das Leuchten in ihren Augen, wann immer sie von ihm sprach, verriet William, dass sich in ihrem Leben alles um den kleinen Alex drehte.

Sosehr er sich auch bemühte, mehr zu erfahren, Helena gab ihm von Anfang an zu verstehen, dass sie nichts über ihre Vergangenheit und die Identität von Alex'Vater preisgeben wollte. Auch als William sie mit großer Entschlossenheit immer weiter umwarb und ihre Beziehung ganz allmählich enger wurde (wozu über Monate hinweg zermürbende Wochenend-Pendelflüge zwischen London und Wien gehörten), schwieg sich Helena beharrlich über ihr früheres Leben aus. Nach neun Monaten hatte er sie schließlich überredet, ihn nach England zu begleiten, und sie und Alex waren zu ihm in sein bescheidenes Cottage in Hampshire gezogen, das er nach der Scheidung hastig angemietet hatte.

An ihrem Hochzeitstag hatte sie in dem elfenbeinfarbenen Satinkleid hinreißend ausgesehen – die perfekte Braut, so die einhellige Meinung aller. Doch als sie zu ihm an den Altar getreten war und er am Ende der Zeremonie den Schleier gehoben hatte, um sie zu küssen, sah er in ihren Augen nicht, wie erwartet, Freude aufblitzen, sondern vielmehr Angst.

Jetzt hörte William Reifen auf der Kiesauffahrt knirschen und riss sich von seinen Erinnerungen los.

»Daddy, Mummy ist wieder da!«, rief Immy von der Terrasse.

»Daddy, er trägt ja rosa Shorts und so einen Schal um den Hals, und er geht wie ein Mädchen«, flüsterte sie, als sie um die Ecke zu dem Mann äugte, der gerade aus dem Wagen stieg.

»Das kommt daher, weil er Balletttänzer ist, Immy, und jetzt sei still«, trug William ihr auf, während Fabio auf sie zutrat.

»*Ciao*, William! Endlich, nach all diesen Jahren, lernen wir uns kennen. Es ist mir ein Vergnügen.« Fabio verbeugte sich respektvoll.

»Ganz meinerseits, Fabio.«

»*Ciao*, Kleines.« Fabio beugte sich vor und drückte Immy einen Kuss auf jede Wange. »*Prego*, du bist eine Miniaturausgabe deiner Mutter, ja? Ich bin Fabio. Und das muss Signor Frederick sein. Helena hat mir sehr viel von euch erzählt.«

»Es freut mich, Sie kennenzulernen, Mr. Fabio. Waren Sie und meine Mutter berühmt?«, fragte Immy und sah ihn aus großen blauen Augen an.

»Früher einmal waren wir nicht aufzuhalten, stimmt es nicht, Helena? Die nächsten Fonteyn und Nurejew ... aber nun ja«, sagte er mit einem Achselzucken. »Deine *mamma* hat etwas sehr viel Sinnvolleres mit ihrem Leben gemacht, als einem Traum nachzujagen. Sie hat eine wunderschöne Familie.« Fabio sah sich um. »Wo ist Alex? Beim letzten Mal, als ich ihn sah, war er noch ein Baby.«

»Irgendwo im Haus. Ich rufe ihn. Fabio, eine Tasse Tee?«, fragte William.

»Kaffee wäre schön, aber nur koffeinfrei für mich.«

»Ich glaube, irgendwo haben wir einen. Tee, mein Schatz?« William blickte zu Helena, die seiner Ansicht nach müde und angespannt aussah.

»Ja, bitte. Hallo, mein kleines Monster.« Lächelnd nahm sie Fred in den Arm. »Komm, Fabio, setz dich und genieß den Blick.«

»Er ist atemberaubend«, pflichtete er bei und ließ sich graziös auf einen Stuhl nieder. »William ist ein gutaussehender Mann. Ich kann ihn nicht leiden. Er hat mehr Haare als ich«, flüsterte er laut.

Immy stellte sich zu ihm. »Sind Sie wirklich ein Tänzer, Mr. Fabio?«, fragte sie scheu.

»Ja, das bin ich. Mein ganzes Leben tanze ich schon.«

»Haben Sie mit Mummy in Wien getanzt, als sie den Prinz kennengelernt hat?«

»Ah, der Prinz.« Er warf Helena ein Lächeln zu. »Ja, da habe ich mit ihr getanzt. *Giselle* war es, Helena, nicht wahr?«

»Nein, *La Sylphide*«, verbesserte sie ihn.

»Du hast recht«, sagte Fabio, bevor er seine Aufmerksamkeit wieder auf Immy richtete. »Und eines Abends bekam deine *mamma* ein Bouquet von ihm.«

»Was ist ein Bouquet?«, wollte Immy wissen.

»Das sind Blumen, die wunderschönen Damen geschenkt werden, wenn sie die Titelrolle tanzen. Aber in diesem Bouquet lag eine Diamantkette. Habe ich nicht recht, *mamma*?«

»Doch.«

»Und dann lädt er sie zu einem Ball in einem richtigen Palast ein.«

Immy war hingerissen. »Ooohh«, wisperte sie, »wie bei *Cinderella*.« Dann drehte sie sich zu Helena und stemmte vorwurfsvoll die Hände in die Hüften. »Und warum bist du dann jetzt nicht mit ihm verheiratet?«

»Du meinst, warum bist du nicht Prinzessin Immy, und warum wohnst du in einem einfachen Haus und nicht in einem Palast und musst dich mit mir als deinem alten Dad abfinden?«, fragte William lachend. Er trat gerade mit dem Tablett auf die Terrasse.

»Ich habe ihn nicht geliebt, Immy«, erklärte Helena.

»Ich hätte ihn wegen der Diamantkette und dem Palast geheiratet.«

»Ja, *du* hättest das wahrscheinlich schon«, stimmte William zu. »Fabio, dein Kaffee.«

»*Grazie*, William.«

»Habt ihr euch beim Mittagessen gut unterhalten?«, fragte William.

»Wir haben, wie man so schön sagt, nur an der Oberfläche gekratzt, nicht wahr, Helena?«

»Außerdem habe vor allem ich geredet, das heißt, vieles von Fabio weiß ich noch gar nicht.«

»Helena erzählte, dass du, kurz bevor ich sie kennenlernte, in die Staaten gegangen seist, oder?«, fragte William.

»Ja, und ich war fast zehn Jahre dort. Ich habe mit dem New York City Ballet getanzt, aber letztes Jahr sagte ich mir dann, Fabio, es ist Zeit, dass du nach Hause gehst. Und so bin ich jetzt wieder an La Scala. Ich gebe den Morgenunterricht und tanze die Charakterrollen, die für einen Mann meines Alters passend sind.« Er zuckte mit den Schultern. »Man muss Geld verdienen.«

»Fabio, du musst mehrere Jahre jünger sein als ich, aber du sprichst, als wärst du kurz vor der Rente«, sagte William mit einem kleinen Lachen.

»Das ist das Leben des Tänzers. Es ist sehr kurz.«

»Hast du Alex gesagt, dass er auf die Terrasse kommen und Fabio begrüßen soll, Schatz?«, fragte Helena.

»Ja. Er sagte, er komme gleich, aber du weißt, er hat seinen eigenen Kopf.«

»Ich sehe mal nach ihm, und dann kümmere ich mich gleich mal um das Abendessen.« Helena erhob sich und ging ins Haus.

»Ich habe erst neulich zu Helena gesagt, dass ich sie so gern tanzen gesehen hätte«, sagte William und trank einen Schluck Tee.

»Sie war exquisit! Und die beste Partnerin, die ich je hatte. Was für ein entsetzlicher Jammer, dass sie nach der Geburt von Alex glaubte, nicht weitertanzen zu können. Sie wäre eine der ganz Großen geworden, davon bin ich überzeugt.«

»Ich habe mich immer gefragt, weshalb sie aufgehört hat. Sicher können Frauen doch weiter tanzen, auch nachdem sie ein Kind bekommen haben?«

»Es war eine schwierige Geburt, William. Und sie war ganz allein und wollte für ihr Baby da sein.« Fabio seufzte. »Unsere Partnerschaft war etwas ganz Besonderes. So eine Gemeinsamkeit findet man selten. Und ich habe so etwas nie wieder gefunden, und auch nicht den Erfolg, den ich mit Helena hatte.«

»Du warst ein so großer Teil ihres Lebens. Ich muss zugeben, es ist ein merkwürdiges Gefühl, so gut wie nichts darüber zu wissen.«

»Genauso, wie ich von dir und euren Kindern nichts wusste, bis Helena mir neulich am Telefon von euch erzählte. Wir haben den Kontakt verloren, bald nachdem ich nach New York gegangen bin. Wenn ich sie in Wien anrief, ging sie nicht mehr ans Telefon. Niemand wusste, wo sie war. Aber natürlich«, sagte Fabio und zuckte wieder mit den Schultern, »sie war bei dir in England.«

»Wie hast du sie dann schließlich aufgespürt?«, fragte William.

»Das hat das Schicksal gefügt. Ich stehe in La Scala im Pressebüro, auf dem Schreibtisch liegt ein hoher Stapel von Briefen, die Vorankündigungen für die kommende Saison. Und obenauf liegt ein Umschlag, der an Ms. Helena Beaumont adressiert ist! Kannst du dir das vorstellen?«, berichtete Fabio aufgeregt. »Ich notiere mir die englische Adresse, und dann finde ich in einer Datei auf dem Computer von La Scala ihre Handynummer!« Er schlug sich klatschend auf den Oberschenkel. »Es war vorherbestimmt!«

»Helena erzählt wenig von früher«, sagte William nachdenklich. »Du bist der erste Mensch, den ich aus ihrer Vergangenheit kennenlerne, abgesehen von jemandem, den sie hier auf Zypern kannte. Also bitte entschuldige, wenn du dich von mir ausgefragt fühlst.«

»Manchmal ist es besser, einen Schleier über die Vergangenheit zu ziehen und einfach mit dem Leben weiterzumachen, *sí*?« Fabio tat, als müsste er gähnen. »Wenn es recht ist, ziehe ich mich auf mein Zimmer zurück. Ich musste heute Morgen sehr früh aufstehen.«

Als er sich erhob, trat Alex auf die Terrasse.

»Hallo, Fabio. Ich bin Alex. Schön, dich kennenzulernen.« Schüchtern trat er auf ihn zu und streckte die Hand aus, doch Fabio ignorierte sie, zog Alex an sich und drückte ihm auf beide Wangen einen Kuss.

»Alex! Mein Junge! So viele Jahre habe ich dich nicht gesehen, und jetzt bist du ganz erwachsen!«

»Na ja, nicht ganz«, antwortete Alex. »Zumindest das mit dem Wachsen lässt noch zu wünschen übrig.«

Fabio hielt seine Schultern umklammert, Tränen glitzerten in seinen Augen. »Erinnerst du dich an mich?«

»Äh … vielleicht«, murmelte Alex. Er wollte nicht unhöflich sein.

»Nein, du erinnerst dich nicht, du warst zu klein. Deine Mutter sagt, dass du sehr klug bist, aber vielleicht kein Tänzer.« Fabio musterte Alex' Körper. »Eher ein Rugby-Spieler?«

»Doch, Rugby mag ich«, räumte Alex ein.

»Jetzt müsst ihr mich entschuldigen, ich brauche meine Siesta. Nach dem Schlafen unterhalten wir uns und lernen uns wieder kennen, *sí*?«

Alex rang sich ein Lächeln ab. »*Sí*.«

Alex' Tagebuch

12. August 2006

Denke ich zuerst an die gute Neuigkeit oder die schlechte?

Vollführe ich jedes Mal einen Freudensprung, wenn ich an die letzten Worte denke, die Chloë zu mir sagte?

»Cool« ...

und ... »süß« ...

und »schlau«.

Wow!

Also, das ist die gute Neuigkeit.

Und jetzt die schlechte. Und die ist richtig schlecht.

Ich habe den Mann (den Begriff möchte ich im lockeren Sinn verstanden wissen) kennengelernt, der sich als mein Vater erweisen könnte. Geschenkt, dass er Italiener ist. Italienisch ist gut. Ich mag Pasta und Eis. Geschenkt, dass er Tänzer ist. Tänzer sind fit und stark und haben einen guten Muskeltonus.

Aber Folgendes ist nicht geschenkt: Alles an ihm, von seiner Kleidung über die Art, mit der er sich durch die spärlichen Überreste seiner Haare fährt, bis hin zu der Weise, wie er spricht und geht, deutet für mich auf eines und nur dieses eine hin:

Fabio ist ...

O Schreck ...

O Scheiße ...

SCHWUL! Und nichts wird mich vom Gegenteil überzeugen.

Ich bin bereit und willens zu akzeptieren, dass ein gewisser Grad an Weiblichkeit einen Mann nicht daran hindert, mit einer Frau das zu tun, was ein Mann tut, aber Fabio ist so tuntig wie ein Rudel Frisöre!

Ich versuche, diese Erkenntnis in aller Ruhe zu durchdenken, komme aber nur zu einigen ziemlich entsetzlichen Schlussfolgerungen.

Was, zum Beispiel, wenn Fabio vor langer, langer Zeit einmal sexuell zur Kategorie der Unentschlossenen gehörte?

Das heißt, er ist der Tanzpartner meiner Mutter, verbringt seine Tage damit, sich mit Teilen ihres Körpers vertraut zu machen, die sonst nur der Arzt kennt, dann verlieben sie sich und haben eine Beziehung. Meine Mutter wird schwanger mit mir, Fabio steht dazu, ist bei meiner Geburt an ihrer Seite und spielt den pflichtbewussten Vater.

Und dann, eines Tages, wie aus heiterem Himmel, wird Fabio klar, dass er vom anderen Ufer ist. Er ist hin- und hergerissen. Er liebt meine Mutter zwar noch und mich hoffentlich auch, kann aber keine Lüge leben. Also geht er in die Staaten, um ein neues Leben zu beginnen, und lässt meine Mutter einsam und verlassen mit mir in Wien zurück.

Was erklären würde, weshalb sie nicht mit ihm nach New York gegangen ist und auch nie wieder getanzt hat.

Und es erklärt auch die ganz große Frage, weshalb sie mir nie gesagt hat, wer mein Vater ist.

»Äh, Alex, mein Schatz, die Sache ist die, weißt du, dein

Vater, äh, nun ja, er ist stockschwul, um ehrlich zu sein, aber wenn du ihn und seinen Liebhaber am Wochenende besuchen und mit ihnen Liza-Minnelli-Filme ansehen willst, dann nur zu, ich habe nichts dagegen.«

Sie weiß, dass das für mich die ultimative Schande wäre. Wäre es für jeden Jungen. Allein bei der Vorstellung, was meine Klassenkameraden sagen würden, wenn Fabio zu einem Rugbymatch kommen und sich als mein Dad vorstellen würde, an der Seitenlinie schnell einen *entrechat* ausführt, während er zusieht, wie ich einen Versuch erziele, bricht mir der kalte Schweiß aus.

Das eigentliche Problem ist:

Ist Homosexualität genetisch bedingt? O Scheiße!

Wen kann ich fragen? Ich muss es wissen.

An diesem Punkt möchte ich nachdrücklich feststellen, dass ich nicht homophob bin. Ich habe kein Problem damit, dass andere Menschen ihr Leben so leben, wie sie es für richtig halten. Wenn's nach mir geht, können sie die Sau rauslassen, sooft ihnen der Sinn danach steht, und Fabio ist ein guter Typ, finde ich, witzig und klug und … na ja, schwul eben.

Er kann sein, wie er mag. Solange er nicht ist wie ich.

Oder ich wie er.

Kapitel 22

An dem Abend trafen sich alle – außer den Kleinen, die früh ins Bett gebracht wurden – zum Aperitif auf der Terrasse. Als Fabio erschien, war er frisch geduscht und trug ein pfauenblaues Seidenhemd und eine enge Lederhose.

»Dad, schwitzt er in der denn nicht?«, fragte Alex, als sie in der Küche Tabletts beluden.

»Als Italiener ist er die Hitze vielleicht gewöhnt«, antwortete William.

»Glaubst du, dass Fabio, na, du weißt schon …?«

»Dass er schwul ist?«

»Ja.«

»Das ist er. Das hat deine Mum mir gesagt.«

»Ach.«

»Stört dich das?«

»Nein. Und doch.«

»In welcher Hinsicht?«

»Ach, kein besonderer Grund«, antwortete Alex ausweichend. »Kann ich das Tablett jetzt raustragen?«

Nachdem Helena Fabio beim Mittagessen entsprechend instruiert hatte, konnte sie sich entspannen. Beim Essen schwelgten sie und Fabio in Erinnerungen, während Alex und William ihnen gebannt lauschten. Schließlich erfuhren sie Dinge aus Helenas Leben, die sie noch nie gehört hatten.

»Ihr müsst wissen, wir haben uns kennengelernt, als ich an die Oper in Covent Garden kam«, erklärte Fabio. »Helena war gerade zur Solotänzerin ernannt worden, und ich kam für eine Saison von La Scala nach London. Dort hatte sie diesen schaurigen Partner, der sie in die Luft wirft und dann vergisst, sie aufzufangen …«

»So schlecht war Stuart auch nicht. Er tanzt immer noch«, unterbrach Helena ihn.

»Also, ich komme als Gastkünstler, und Stuart liegt mit Grippe im Bett, und sie besetzen Helena und mich für eine Matinee von *La Fille mal gardée*. Und« – Fabio zuckte mit den Schultern –, »der Rest ist Geschichte.«

»Und dann bist du Fabio an die Scala gefolgt?«, fragte William.

»Ja«, sagte Helena. »Dort waren wir zwei Jahre. Dann hat uns das Wiener Staatsballett einen Vertrag als Erste Solotänzer angeboten, das konnten wir nicht ausschlagen.«

»Erinnere dich, am Anfang war ich nicht glücklich. Im Winter ist es dort sehr kalt, und ich bin krank geworden«, sagte Fabio und zitterte übertrieben.

»Du bist wirklich der schrecklichste Hypochonder, den ich kenne«, warf Helena lachend ein. »Wann immer wir mit der Truppe auf Tournee waren, hatte er einen ganzen Koffer voll Medikamente dabei«, erklärte sie William und Alex. »Widersprich nicht, Fabio, du weißt, dass es stimmt.«

»Ja, gut, du gewinnst, *cara*. Ich habe große Angst vor Bakterien«, stimmte er unbeeindruckt zu.

»Und, willst du jetzt an der Scala bleiben?«, fragte William und schenkte allen nach.

»Das hoffe ich, aber vieles hängt von meinem Partner ab, Dan. Er ist Bühnenbildner in New York. Er fehlt mir, aber er hofft, bald eine Stelle in Mailand zu bekommen.«

»Es freut mich sehr, dass du endlich deinen Seelenpartner gefunden hast, Fabio«, sagte Helena mit einem warmen Lächeln.

»Und ich, dass du deinen gefunden hast«, erwiderte Fabio galant und sah sie beide an. »Ich habe Fotos von Helena und mir beim Tanzen mitgebracht. Wollt ihr sie sehen? William? Alex?«

»Sehr gern, Fabio, bitte.«

»*Prego.* Ich hole sie.«

»Und ich mache Kaffee«, sagte William.

Als die beiden Männer im Haus verschwanden, warf Helena einen Blick zu Alex hinüber. »Du bist sehr still, mein Schatz. Ist alles in Ordnung?«

»Doch, alles bestens.«

»Was hältst du von Fabio?«

»Er ist, äh, sehr nett.«

»Ich freue mich so, dass er hier ist«, sagte Helena, als William mit dem Kaffeetablett wieder auf die Terrasse kam.

Ein paar Minuten später folgte Fabio, er wedelte mit einem dicken Umschlag. »Da wären wir.« Er setzte sich. »Hier, Alex, das sind deine Mutter und ich bei *L'Après-midi d'un faune.*«

»Der Nachmittag eines Fauns«, übersetzte Alex. »Worum geht's da?«

»Um ein Mädchen, das geweckt wird durch einen Faun, der durchs Fenster zu ihr ins Zimmer springt«, erklärte Helena. »Die Handlung ist nicht gerade atemberaubend, aber der männliche Tanzpart ist großartig. Du hast die Choreografie geliebt, Fabio, stimmt's?«

»O ja, sie gehört zu meinen liebsten – eine, in der der Mann angeben kann, nicht die Frau. Nijinsky, Nurejew – alle Großen haben die Rolle getanzt. Und hier, William, ist deine Frau in *La Fille mal gardée.* Ist sie nicht wunderschön?«

»Doch, das ist sie«, pflichtete William ihm bei.

»Und hier verbeugen wir uns zusammen nach *Schwanensee*.«

»Dad, das muss Immy sehen«, sagte Alex. »Da trägt Mum ein Krönchen und hat ganz viele Bouquets im Arm.«

»Und das sind wir in unserem Lieblingscafé in Wien mit … Helena, erinnerst du dich an Jean-Louis?«

»Ach, guter Gott, natürlich! Ein merkwürdiger Mensch – er hat nie etwas anderes gegessen als Müsli. Alex, reich mir das Foto«, bat sie.

»Und das ist Helena noch einmal im selben Café …« Mit einem Blick auf das Foto, das er William gerade reichte, wurde Fabio blass und versuchte panisch, es William wieder wegzunehmen. »Aber das ist nicht so gut, ich zeige dir ein anderes.«

William hielt das Bild fest. »Nein, ich möchte alle sehen. Das ist also Helena und …«

Voll Entsetzen sah Fabio zu Helena, seine Augen spiegelten die kommende Katastrophe.

William sah völlig perplex zu ihr. »Ich … Das verstehe ich nicht. Wann ist die Aufnahme entstanden? Wie … wie konnte denn *er* dort sein?«

»Wer?«, fragte Alex und beugte sich vor, um einen Blick auf das Foto zu werfen. »Ach ja – was hat er da mit dir zu suchen, Mum?«

»Aber … damals hast du ihn doch noch gar nicht gekannt, Helena. Wie konnte er mit dir und Fabio in Wien sein?« William schüttelte den Kopf. »Entschuldige, Helena, aber das verstehe ich nicht.«

Alle Blicke ruhten auf Helena, die ihren Mann und ihren Sohn schweigend anstarrte. Der Moment, vor dem sie sich immer gefürchtet hatte, der Moment, von dem sie gewusst hatte, dass er unausweichlich war, war schließlich gekommen.

»Alex, geh in dein Zimmer«, sagte sie leise.

»Nein, Mum, tut mir leid, aber ich will nicht.«

»Tu, was ich sage! Sofort!«

»Schon gut!« Alex sprang auf und marschierte davon.

»Helena, *cara*, es tut mir so unendlich leid.« Fabio rang die Hände. »Ich glaube, es ist besser, wenn ich mich zur Nacht zurückziehe. Ihr zwei müsst reden. *Buona notte, cara*.« Fabio sah aus, als wäre er selbst den Tränen nahe. Er küsste Helena auf beide Wangen und folgte Alex ins Haus.

William wartete, bis Fabio verschwunden war, dann deutete er auf die Flasche, die auf dem Tisch stand. »Brandy? Ich will auf jeden Fall noch einen.«

»Nein danke.«

»Also.« William schenkte sein Glas nach, nahm das Bild und wedelte damit herum. »Wirst du mir jetzt sagen, wie es dazu gekommen ist, dass du in die Augen meines ältesten Freundes blickst, und zwar mehrere Jahre, bevor du und ich uns kennenlernten?«

»Ich …«

»Ja, Helena? Jetzt komm schon, spuck's aus. Es muss einen nachvollziehbaren Grund geben, oder nicht?«

Helena starrte in die Ferne, ohne Antwort zu geben.

»Je länger du schweigst, desto mehr sehe ich Bilder vor mir, die … Himmel, die sind absolut unvorstellbar! Nicht zu ertragen!«

Sie schwieg weiterhin beharrlich, bis er schließlich sagte: »Jetzt frage ich dich noch einmal, Helena: Was hat *Sacha* mit dem Arm um dich da auf dem Bild zu suchen? Und warum in drei Teufels Namen hast du mir nie gesagt, dass du ihn kanntest, bevor wir uns trafen?«

Helena konnte kaum atmen. Schließlich gelang es ihr, die Lippen zu bewegen.

»Ich kannte ihn in Wien.«

»Das liegt, verdammt noch mal, auf der Hand. Und …?«

»Ich …« Sie schüttelte den Kopf, unfähig, noch ein Wort zu sagen.

William betrachtete das Foto noch einmal eingehend. »Er sieht ziemlich jung aus. Und du auch. Das muss vor Jahren entstanden sein.«

»Ich … Ja.«

»Helena, langsam verliere ich die Geduld. Verdammt noch mal, jetzt sag schon! Wie gut hast du ihn denn gekannt, und warum zum Teufel hast du mir nie davon erzählt?!« William schlug so heftig auf den Tisch, dass die Teller klapperten und eine Kaffeetasse auf den Boden fiel, wo sie zerbrach. »Himmel noch mal, ich kann's nicht fassen! Ich will eine Antwort, und zwar jetzt!«

»Und du bekommst sie auch, aber lass mich erst sagen, dass es mir so unendlich leidtut …«

»Das Foto macht mir klar, dass ich jahrelang betrogen worden bin, und zwar von meinem besten Freund und von meiner Frau! Großer Gott, wie viel schlimmer kann es denn noch werden! Kein Wunder, dass du immer so rumgedruckst hast mit deiner Vergangenheit. Schließlich hast du mit meinem besten Freund rumgevögelt und tust es vielleicht sogar immer noch!«

»So war es nicht, William, bitte!«

William rang um Selbstbeherrschung, als er zu ihr sah. »Dann sag mir … sag mir einfach, was für eine Beziehung du zu Sacha hattest. Und dieses Mal, Helena, behandelst du mich nicht wie den gehörnten Dummkopf, der ich eindeutig die letzten zehn Jahre gewesen bin!«

»William! Die Kinder! Ich …«

»Es ist mir scheißegal, ob sie hören, dass ihre Mutter mich

belogen und betrogen hat! Und dieses Mal kommst du nicht so leicht davon. Ich will alles wissen. Alles! Und zwar jetzt!«

»Ist gut! Ich sag's dir auch! Aber bitte, hör auf zu schreien.« Helena ließ den Kopf sinken und brach in Tränen aus. »Es tut mir leid, William, es tut mir so leid. Alles. Wirklich.«

William leerte seinen Brandy in einem Zug und schenkte sich nach. »Ich glaube nicht, dass es dieses Mal damit getan ist, deswegen kannst du dir deine jämmerlichen Entschuldigungen sparen. Jetzt ist mir auch klar, weshalb du Jules immer zur Seite gesprungen bist. Ich dachte, das geschähe aus reiner Freundlichkeit, aber dein schlechtes Gewissen hat dich getrieben, stimmt's?«

Helena schaute auf. »Hörst du zu, oder schreist du nur herum?«

»Ich höre.«

»Also gut.« Helena atmete zweimal tief durch. »Ich habe Sacha in Wien kennengelernt, ein paar Jahre bevor du und ich uns begegnet sind.«

»Himmelherrgott!« Unwirsch fuhr William sich durchs Haar. »Genau die Stadt, die er mir empfohlen hat, um über die Scheidung von Cecile hinwegzukommen. Und wie ein Trottel bin ich seinem Rat gefolgt. Er hat etwas gesagt in der Art: ›Da habe ich einmal die Liebe gefunden.‹ Und damit hat er dich gemeint, stimmt's?«

»William, wenn du das wissen willst, dann lass mich bitte ausreden. Ich erzähle dir alles, das verspreche ich dir.«

Er verstummte, und Helena begann zu erzählen …

September 1992
Wien

Konnte es überhaupt einen schöneren Ort auf der Welt geben?, fragte sich Helena, als sie auf dem Weg zum Café durch die eleganten Straßen Wiens schlenderte. Die für Ende September ungewöhnlich heiße Nachmittagssonne fiel schräg auf die hochherrschaftlichen Häuser und tauchte sie in ein goldenes Licht, das genau ihrer Stimmung entsprach.

Seit sie im Spätsommer nach Wien gekommen war, um ihre Stelle als Solotänzerin beim Wiener Staatsballett anzutreten, hatte sie ihre neue Heimat bereits ins Herz geschlossen. Von ihrem Apartment in der Prinz-Eugen-Straße, das aus einem einzigen großen Raum in einem prächtigen Haus bestand, mit großen, deckenhohen Fenstern und erlesenster Stuckverzierung, waren es zu Fuß zwanzig Minuten ins Zentrum. Und jedes Mal bewunderte Helena aufs Neue die ganze Pracht, die sich ihr unterwegs bot, ob die Alleen mit ihren hinreißenden klassizistischen und Jugendstilbauten oder die gepflegten Parkanlagen mit ihren alten Musikpavillons: Die gesamte Stadt war ein einziges Fest für die Sinne.

Es hatte viel Überzeugungsarbeit gekostet, bis Fabio bereit gewesen war, das Angebot Gustav Lehmanns anzunehmen, des künstlerischen Leiters der Wiener Staatsoper. Als gebürtigem Mailänder war es ihm ausgesprochen schwergefallen, die Scala zu verlassen. Aber man hatte sie mit dem Versprechen eines neuen, eigens für sie geschaffenen Balletts gelockt. Es sollte *Der*

Künstler heißen und auf den Gemälden Degas' beruhen. Fabio würde die Titelrolle übernehmen, Helena den Part seiner Muse, »Die kleine Tänzerin«. Mit der Premiere sollte die kommende Frühjahrssaison eröffnet werden, und sie beide hatten auch bereits den jungen französischen Choreografen und den recht avantgardistischen Komponisten kennengelernt. Es sollte ein modernes Werk werden, und beim Gedanken an die Herausforderungen, die das mit sich brachte, schauderte Helena vor Aufregung.

Und jetzt, gestand sie sich glücklich ein, beflügelte sie noch etwas anderes: Sie hatte sich verliebt.

Sie hatte ihn erst vor wenigen Wochen in der Gemäldegalerie kennengelernt, die der Akademie der bildenden Künste angeschlossen war und die sie einer Sonderausstellung wegen besucht hatte. Sie hatte vor einem besonders schrillen modernen Gemälde mit dem Titel *Albtraum in Paris* gestanden, ohne es zu verstehen.

»Wenn ich es recht sehe, trifft das Bild nicht ganz Ihren Geschmack.«

Helena drehte sich zu der Person um, die sie auf Englisch angesprochen hatte, und sah in die tief liegenden graugrünen Augen eines jungen Mannes, der direkt neben ihr stand. Mit seinem wirren rötlich braunen Haar, das sich über den Kragen seines verblichenen Samtjacketts lockte, und dem Seidentuch, das ihm nachlässig aus dem offenen Kragen seines weißen Hemds hing, musste sie sofort an den jungen Oscar Wilde denken.

Sie richtete den Blick wieder auf die Striche und Kleckse in leuchtendem Rot, Blau und Grün auf dem Bild vor ihr. »Sagen wir so, ich verstehe es einfach nicht.«

»Genau so ergeht es mir auch. Obwohl ich das über die Arbeit eines Kommilitonen eigentlich nicht sagen dürfte. Offenbar gewann er mit diesem Werk bei der Abschlussausstellung im vergangenen Jahr einen Preis.«

»Sie studieren hier?«, fragte sie überrascht und drehte sich wieder zu ihm, um ihn zu betrachten. Sein Akzent war unverkennbar englisch, und zwar geschliffen, wie ihre Mutter es genannt hätte, und er war nur wenige Jahre älter als sie, Helena, selbst.

»Ja, oder das werde ich zumindest, wenn ich Anfang Oktober mit dem Magisterstudium anfange. Ich habe eine große Vorliebe für Klimt und Schiele, deswegen habe ich mich für Wien entschieden. Ich bin vor drei Tagen angekommen, um vor Semesterbeginn eine Wohnung zu finden und mein ziemlich rostiges Deutsch aufzufrischen.«

»Ich bin schon sehr viel länger hier, aber ich glaube nicht, dass mein Deutsch auch nur um einen Deut besser geworden ist«, sagte sie mit einem Lächeln.

»Sie sind auch aus England?«, fragte er und starrte sie derart eindringlich an, dass sie errötete.

»Ja, aber im Moment arbeite ich hier.«

»Darf ich Sie fragen, was Sie machen?«

»Ich bin Tänzerin beim Wiener Staatsballett.«

»Ach, das erklärt alles.«

»Was?«

»Ihre Körperhaltung. Aus der Sicht des Künstlers sind Sie das perfekte Modell. Vielleicht wissen Sie ja, dass auch Klimt regelrecht besessen war von der Schönheit der weiblichen Gestalt.«

Helena errötete noch mehr, sie wusste gar nicht, wie sie auf ein derartiges Kompliment reagieren sollte.

»Ich frage mich, ob Sie eventuell Lust hätten, sich den Rest der Ausstellung mit mir zusammen anzusehen?«, fuhr er fort.

»Uns Künstlern tut es immer gut, die Meinung eines neutralen Betrachters zu hören. Und danach könnte ich Ihnen ein paar Meisterwerke aus der ständigen Sammlung zeigen. Die sind eher mein Stil, und ich vermute, auch der Ihre. Ach, ich heiße übrigens Alexander.« Er hielt ihr die Hand hin.

»Helena«, sagte sie und schüttelte ihm die Hand. Dabei überlegte sie, ob sie auf seine Einladung eingehen sollte. Derartige Annäherungsversuche von Männern waren nichts Neues für sie, und normalerweise lehnte sie ab, aber dieser Alexander hatte etwas an sich … Unvermittelt hörte sie sich mit »ja« antworten.

Nach dem Museumsbesuch waren sie einen Kaffee trinken gegangen und hatten sich zwei Stunden lang angeregt über Kunst, Ballett, Musik und Literatur unterhalten. Sie erfuhr, dass er in Oxford Kunstgeschichte studiert und sich dann in England als Maler versucht hatte. Aber nachdem er, wie er es ausdrückte, mit seinen Bildern gerade genügend verdient hatte, um sich die nächste Leinwand zu kaufen, hatte er beschlossen, seine Ausbildung fortzusetzen, seinen Horizont zu erweitern und in Wien weiterzustudieren.

»Schlimmstenfalls, wenn sich meine Bilder nicht verkaufen, kann ich mich mit einem Magister in Kunst bei Sotheby's um eine Anstellung bewerben«, hatte er erklärt.

Sie hatte eingewilligt, ihn am nächsten Tag wieder auf einen Kaffee zu treffen, und das war rasch zur täglichen Gewohnheit geworden. Seine Gegenwart war ausgesprochen unterhaltsam, er hatte einen ausgeprägten Sinn für Humor, dank dessen er bei praktisch allem im Leben die heitere Seite zu erkennen vermochte, und er lachte gern. Zudem war er hochintelligent, hatte einen hellwachen Verstand und interessierte sich derart leidenschaftlich für alles, was mit Kunst zusammenhing, dass sie häufig lebhaft über ein bestimmtes Buch oder Gemälde diskutierten. Immer wieder hatte Alexander sie gebeten, sie malen zu dürfen, und schließlich hatte sie eingewilligt.

Und damit hatte alles angefangen …

Als sie zur allerersten Sitzung in seine Wohnung ging, die ihm gleichzeitig als Atelier diente und im obersten Stockwerk eines alten Hauses in der Elisabethstraße lag, hatte sie vor Nervosität ebenso gezittert wie vor Aufregung.

»Herein, herein«, begrüßte er sie und führte sie in den großen Raum.

Helena konnte ein Lächeln nicht unterdrücken, als sie das Chaos in dem Mansardenraum sah. Jeder Quadratzentimeter war mit Pinselbehältern, Farbtuben, Bücherstapeln, benutzten Gläsern und leeren Weinflaschen übersät. An den Wänden und selbst am Holzrahmen des Doppelbetts, das eine Ecke des Raums einnahm, lehnten Leinwände. Neben dem großen geöffneten Fenster stand eine Staffelei.

»Du brauchst es nicht eigens zu sagen, ich weiß, es sieht hier aus wie ein Bühnenbild für *La Bohème*«, sagte er grinsend. Ihr amüsierter Gesichtsausdruck, als er sich vergeblich bemühte, rasch etwas Ordnung zu schaffen, war ihm nicht entgangen. »Aber das Licht bei Sonnenuntergang ist hier einfach zu schön.«

»Ich finde, es ist die perfekte Mansarde für einen mittellosen Künstler«, zog Helena ihn auf.

»Genau das bin ich«, sagte er zustimmend, kippte einen Berg Kleider von einem Stuhl, den er hier- und dorthin stellte, bis er den Platz gefunden hatte, an dem der Lichteinfall seinen Vorstellungen entsprach. »Jetzt setz dich hin«, forderte er sie auf. Er selbst ließ sich mit seinem Skizzenbuch auf dem niedrigen Fenstersims nieder. Dann bat er Helena, verschiedene Posen einzunehmen. »Leg deinen Arm auf die Rückenlehne … nein, heb ihn hinter den Kopf … stütz dein Kinn auf die andere

Hand ... schlag die Beine übereinander«, und so weiter, bis er zufrieden war und zu zeichnen begann.

Danach war Helena jeden Tag nach dem Vormittagsunterricht zu ihm gegangen. Sie hatten Wein getrunken, gelacht und sich unterhalten, während er unablässig zeichnete. Sie fühlte sich in seiner Gesellschaft entspannt und unbeschwert wie selten zuvor im Leben. Bei ihrem vierten Besuch hatte er unvermittelt das Skizzenbuch beiseitegelegt und frustriert geseufzt.

»So schön es ist, dich für mich allein zu haben, es funktioniert einfach nicht.«

»Was funktioniert nicht?«, fragte sie, und ihr Herz setzte einen Schlag aus.

»Das Bild. Irgendwie bekomme ich es nicht richtig hin.«

»Das tut mir leid, Alexander. Womöglich liegt es an mir. Ich habe keine Erfahrung damit, und ich weiß nicht, was ich anders machen könnte.« Seufzend stand sie auf. Sie fühlte sich steif, weil sie die Pose so lange gehalten hatte, und streckte sich unwillkürlich.

»Genau!«, rief er. »Du darfst nicht still sitzen – du bist eine Tänzerin! Du musst dich bewegen!«

Am folgenden Tag trafen sie sich auf Alexanders Wunsch hin im Schillerpark gegenüber seiner Wohnung, und Helena trug, ebenfalls auf seine Bitte hin, das schlichteste Kleid, das sie in ihrem Schrank finden konnte. Und dann bat er sie, für ihn zu tanzen.

»Tanzen? Hier?« Helena sah sich um, überall führten Leute ihre Hunde spazieren, andere saßen im Gras und machten Picknick, Paare schlenderten Arm in Arm vorbei.

»Ja, hier«, bestätigte Alexander. »Zieh dir die Schuhe aus, ich will dich zeichnen.«

»Was soll ich tanzen?«

»Was immer du magst.«

»Ich brauche Musik.«

»Ich würde ja summen, aber ich bin völlig unmusikalisch«, sagte er und holte seinen Zeichenblock hervor. »Kannst du die Musik denn nicht im Kopf hören?«

»Ich versuch's.«

Und dann stand Helena, die fast allabendlich vor ausverkauften Häusern über weite Bühnen schwebte, wie eine unbeholfene Fünfjährige vor ihm.

»Stell dir vor, du bist ein Blatt – wie das, das gerade von dem Kastanienbaum gefallen ist«, sagte Alexander. »Du wirst vom Lufthauch getragen, lässt dich hierhin und dorthin treiben … erfreust dich an deiner Freiheit. Ja, Helena, das ist wunderbar«, sagte er lächelnd, als sie kurz die Augen schloss und ihr graziler Körper sich zu bewegen begann. Mit rasch skizzierenden Zügen hielt er fest, wie sie die Arme über den Kopf hob und sich drehte und wiegte, so leicht und anmutig wie das Blatt, das sie in ihrer Vorstellung war.

»Großartig!«, flüsterte er, als Helena selbstvergessen zu Boden sank, ohne die Passanten zu bemerken, die stehen geblieben waren, um ihrer hinreißenden Darbietung zuzusehen. Er ergriff ihre Hände, um ihr beim Aufstehen zu helfen. »Mein Gott, Helena, du bist unglaublich. Absolut unglaublich.«

Er strich ihr ein Blatt aus dem Haar, seine Finger wanderten über ihre Wange hinab, um ihr Kinn zu seinem Gesicht zu heben. Sie sahen sich in die Augen, dann begegneten seine Lippen sehr langsam ihren …

Danach verstand es sich von selbst, dass sie in seine Wohnung zurückkehrten. Und dort liebten sie sich in ihrem ganz eigenen *Pas de deux*, der in einem leidenschaftlichen Crescendo gipfelte, als die Sonne über den Dächern Wiens versank.

Und nun war sie nach dem Unterricht auf dem Weg zu ihrem Lieblingscafé am Franziskanerplatz, einem hübschen gepflasterten Platz nur wenige Minuten vom Theater entfernt. Unwillkürlich klopfte Helenas Herz schneller, als sie Alexander vor dem Lokal sitzen sah.

»Mein Engel, da bist du ja.« Alexander stand auf, umfasste sie sacht an den Schultern und zog sie an sich, um sie auf den Mund zu küssen. Als sie sich setzten und ein Kellner kam, um ihre Bestellung aufzunehmen, hörte sie eine vertraute Stimme.

»Helena, *cara*!«, rief Fabio und kam über den sonnenbeschienenen Platz zu ihnen. Sein schwebender Gang und seine nach außen gedrehten Füße gaben ihn sofort als Tänzer zu erkennen. Wie immer war er auffällig gekleidet, heute in einem gelben Leinenanzug und dazu schokobraune Wildlederschuhe. Auf den Kopf mit dem zu seinem Leidwesen schütter werdenden Haar hatte er sich in einem kecken Winkel einen Panamahut aufgesetzt, um seinen Hals hing eine Kamera. »Ich dachte doch, dass du das bist.«

»Fabio, wie schön, dich zu sehen.« Helena stand auf und küsste ihn auf beide Wangen, warf ihm dabei aber nervöse Blicke zu, mit denen sie ihm zu verstehen geben wollte, dass der Moment sehr ungelegen war. Zwar hatte sie ihm beiläufig bereits von Alexander erzählt, doch wollte sie nicht, dass sich die beiden jetzt schon kennenlernten. Doch wie nicht anders zu erwarten, ließ Fabio sich nicht beirren.

»Und, Helena, willst du mich nicht deinem … Begleiter vorstellen?«

»Alexander, das ist Fabio, mein Tanzpartner. Fabio, das ist Alexander.«

»Guten Tag, Fabio.« Alexander erhob sich und gab ihm die Hand. »Möchten Sie sich nicht zu uns setzen?«, fragte er höfli

»Danke, gern, aber nur kurz. Ich habe gerade diese Kamera gekauft, also gebe ich heute den Touristen.«

Helena seufzte innerlich, als Fabio Platz nahm und herrisch nach dem Kellner schnippte. Ihr war klar, dass die beiden Männer sich irgendwann kennenlernen mussten, aber sie hätte den Zeitpunkt lieber selbst bestimmt.

Sie beobachtete die beiden, während sie sich unterhielten, und wand sich innerlich vor Unbehagen, als Fabio Alexander wie ein überfürsorglicher Vater ins Verhör nahm. Gerade wollte Helena ihn unterbrechen, als Fabio rasch das Thema wechselte – vielleicht spürte er ihren Unmut – und Alexander nach seiner Arbeit als Künstler fragte.

»Das Seminar hat noch nicht angefangen, aber es gibt hier in Wien auch so mehr als genug Inspiration«, antwortete Alexander und legte lächelnd eine Hand auf Helenas Arm.

»Das ist in der Tat wahr. Auch ich möchte Erinnerungen an diese schöne Stadt im Sonnenschein haben, deswegen die Kamera. Vielleicht sollte ich mit euch beiden anfangen?« Und schon richtete er das Objektiv auf sie.

»Fabio, muss das sein? Du weißt doch, ich werde nicht gern fotografiert«, bat Helena.

»Aber ihr seid ein hinreißendes Motiv, ich kann nicht widerstehen! Jetzt komm, *cara*, lächle für mich. Und Sie auch, Alexander. Ich schwöre euch, es tut nicht weh.«

Fabio drückte immer wieder auf den Auslöser, trug Alexander auf, den Arm um Helena zu legen, und schmeichelte ihnen derart übertrieben, dass sie bald herzhaft mit ihm lachten. Als Fabio seiner Ansicht nach genügend fotografiert hatte, trank er einen letzten Schluck Wein und lüftete den Hut. »Ich wünsche euch einen schönen Nachmittag. Und morgen sehe ich dich, Helena, zu unserer ersten Probe. Ich hoffe, du ziehst dich heute früh zum Schlafen zurück.« Mit einem Winken ging er über den Platz davon.

Als Helena und Fabio am folgenden Tag nach der Probe beim Mittagessen saßen, kam er auf Alexander zu sprechen.

»Dieser Mann, dieser Alexander ... ist es dir ernst mit ihm?«, fragte er.

»Ich ... ich weiß es nicht. Dafür ist es zu früh. Wir fühlen uns miteinander sehr wohl«, antwortete sie zurückhaltend.

Fabio machte eine wegwerfende Geste. »Helena, *cara*, es steht dir ins Gesicht geschrieben, dass du verliebt bist. Und auch wenn ich verstehe, dass du mit mir nicht über Einzelheiten sprechen magst, weiß ich, dass ihr euch eurer Leidenschaft bereits hingegeben habt.«

Helena wurde rot bis in die Haarspitzen. »Und wenn schon? Spricht etwas dagegen?«

Fabio seufzte dramatisch, tupfte sich mit der Serviette den Mund ab, lehnte sich im Stuhl zurück und musterte sie. »Natürlich nicht. Aber Helena, in manchen Dingen bist du naiv wie eine *bambina*. Ich mache mir Sorgen um dich. Was weißt du denn über diesen Mann?«

»Genug, danke«, sagte Helena trotzig. »Er ist als Maler sehr begabt, er bringt mich zum Lachen und ...«

»Aber ist dir aufgefallen«, unterbrach Fabio sie, »wie wenig er von sich preisgab, als ich ihn nach seiner Herkunft fragte? Er hat nur ausweichende Antworten gegeben. Ich muss dir sagen, er hat etwas an sich, dem ich nicht vertraue. Nenn es den Instinkt, den ein Mann für einen anderen hat. Ich sage, dass er ein Spieler ist. Und dass er etwas zu verbergen hat. Das sieht man in seinen Augen. Sie sind ...«, er suchte nach dem richtigen Wort, »... verschlagen.«

»Fabio! Jetzt hör auf! Du hast eine halbe Stunde mit ihm gesprochen! Wie kannst du das beurteilen?«

»Vertrau mir.« Fabio berührte einen Nasenflügel. »Bei Männern täusche ich mich nie.«

»Man könnte ja fast meinen, dass du eifersüchtig auf ihn bist«, sagte Helena wütend, stand auf und warf ihre Serviette auf den Tisch. »Außerdem geht es dich wirklich nichts an. Wenn du so freundlich wärst – ich will nicht mehr darüber reden.«

»Dann schweigen wir darüber.« Fabio zuckte nur lässig mit den Schultern. »Wie du willst, *cara*. Aber sag nicht, ich hätte dich nicht gewarnt.«

Helena war von Fabios Bemerkungen tief getroffen, und die folgenden Tage verhielt sie sich ihm gegenüber sehr reserviert. Die Proben für die neue Spielzeit waren in vollem Gang, und Fabio vermied bewusst das Thema. Außerdem musste Helena einräumen, dass sich Alexander tatsächlich recht zugeknöpft gab, was sein Leben in England betraf. Sie wusste, dass er irgendwo in Südengland in einem Cottage lebte und dass seine wohlhabenden Eltern nichts mehr mit ihm zu tun haben wollten, weil er keinen »anständigen« Beruf ergriffen hatte. Sie hatte sich gewundert, wie er sich unter diesen Umständen ein kostspieliges Kunststudium in Wien leisten konnte, und hatte ihn bei nächster Gelegenheit danach gefragt. Da hatte er erklärt, dass er das letzte Geld aus seinem Treuhandfonds dafür verwende und dass es für ihn bei diesem Magister-Studiengang um alles oder nichts ginge.

Sie wollte sich ihr Glück von Fabios Bemerkungen nicht trüben lassen und sagte sich, dass er nur aus übertriebener Fürsorge so reagiert habe. Und da sie ihm nie lange böse sein konnte, kehrten sie bald wieder zu ihrer üblichen Vertrautheit zurück.

Helena und Alexander sahen sich weiterhin so oft wie möglich, allerdings war es für beide schwieriger geworden, Zeit füreinander zu finden. Helena war beim Ballett voll eingespannt, und für Alexander hatte das Studium mit den vielen Vorlesungen, Seminaren und Hausarbeiten begonnen.

Trotzdem hatte sie nie zuvor jemanden gekannt, bei dem sie derart sie selbst sein konnte. Er seinerseits wirkte nicht minder glücklich, hinterließ in ihrer Wohnung kleine Briefchen, die sie später entdeckte, schrieb ihr Gedichte und sagte ihr ständig, wie sehr er sie liebe.

Als ihre Beziehung immer enger wurde, begann Helena fast wider Willen, über eine gemeinsame Zukunft nachzudenken. Auch wenn Alexander nie davon sprach und sich sehr bedeckt hielt, was seine Pläne nach dem Ende seines Studiums im Juli des kommenden Jahres betraf, gab sie sich Träumen hin, dass er in Wien bleiben könnte. Oder vielleicht könnte sie, wenn Fabio einwilligte, nach England und zum Royal Ballet zurückkehren, um in seiner Nähe zu sein.

Es war doch unvorstellbar, dass sie jetzt getrennt würden, oder nicht?

Sie lagen zusammen bei ihr im Bett, draußen ließ ein frischer Spätherbstwind die alten Fenster klappern, als er ihr sagte, dass er am nächsten Tag nach England fahren müsse.

»Leider gibt es ein familiäres Problem, um das ich mich kümmern muss. Mit etwas Glück bin ich in zwei Wochen wieder hier.«

»Aber wie kannst du jetzt das Studium unterbrechen?«, fragte Helena, stützte sich auf einen Ellbogen auf und sah verwundert zu ihm hinunter. »Das Semester ist doch in vollem Gang – kann das nicht bis zu den Weihnachtsferien warten?«

»Nein, das geht nicht. Es gibt … es gibt ein paar Dinge, um die ich mich sofort kümmern muss.«

»Was für ›Dinge‹, Alexander?«

»Nichts, worüber du dir Sorgen zu machen brauchst. Ich bin wieder da, bevor du überhaupt merkst, dass ich fort war, mein Engel, das verspreche ich dir.« Und er gab ihr einen Kuss.

Er weigerte sich, das »Problem« näher zu erläutern, und Helena musste sich mit seiner Versicherung begnügen, dass er bald wieder da sein werde. An dem Abend liebten sie sich mit besonderer Leidenschaft, und beim Einschlafen war sie glücklich und fühlte sich unendlich erfüllt.

Und wie sich herausstellte, hatte sie in den folgenden Wochen tatsächlich wenig Zeit, Alexander zu vermissen. Die Proben für die Inszenierungen von *L'Après-midi d'un faune, La Fille mal gardée* und *La Sylphide* verlangten ihren vollen Einsatz, zudem verbrachten sie und Fabio zwei Nachmittage pro Woche mit dem Choreografen und dem Komponisten, um an dem neuen Ballett *Der Künstler* zu arbeiten.

Als der Termin für Alexanders geplante Rückkehr nach Wien verstrich, ohne dass sie von ihm hörte, versuchte sie, nicht in Panik zu geraten. Doch wann immer sie an dem Notizbrett vorbeikam, auf dem im Theater persönliche Nachrichten für Ensemblemitglieder vermerkt wurden, schaute sie, ob in der Zwischenzeit nicht ein Anruf für sie eingegangen war. Sie besaß noch kein Mobiltelefon, und dummerweise hatte Alexander vergessen, ihr die Telefonnummer zu geben, unter der er in England zu erreichen war, obwohl er das versprochen hatte.

Als der November zu Ende ging, beschloss sie, seinen Fachbereich in der Kunstakademie aufzusuchen.

»Ich möchte mich nach einem Freund erkundigen, der hier

ein Magisterstudium macht. Ich muss erfahren, wann er zurückkehrt.«

Die Sekretärin sah Helena über den Rand ihrer Brille pikiert an. »Derartige Auskünfte erteilen wir hier nicht, Fräulein.«

»Bitte, es ist ein Notfall. Er musste überraschend nach England fahren, es ging um eine dringende Familienangelegenheit, und eigentlich sollte er mittlerweile wieder hier sein. Können Sie nicht in Ihren Listen nachsehen?«

Die Sekretärin verdrehte die Augen und seufzte gereizt. »Dann sagen Sie mir, wie er heißt.«

»Alexander Nicholls.«

»Ich versuch's. Nicholls, sagten Sie?«

»Ja.«

»Warten Sie hier.« Die Sekretärin war mehrere Minuten verschwunden. Als sie wiederkehrte, schüttelte sie den Kopf. »Nach unseren Listen gibt es hier keinen Studenten namens Nicholls.«

Verwirrt, aber auch voll Sorge – vielleicht hatte er einen Unfall gehabt, oder es hatte in der Familie einen Todesfall gegeben –, ging sie zu dem Haus, in dem er gewohnt hatte. Und erfuhr vom Pförtner, dass der junge Mann aus 14a vor fast einem Monat ausgezogen und die Mansardenwohnung bereits wieder vermietet sei.

Als sie davonging, zitterten ihre Beine so sehr, dass sie sich kaum aufrecht halten konnte. Benommen ging sie in den Park gegenüber, wo sie für ihn getanzt und er sie gezeichnet hatte, und ließ sich auf die nächste Bank sinken.

Der Kastanienbaum stand jetzt ohne Laub trostlos im fahlen Winterlicht.

Helena ließ den Kopf in ihre zitternden Hände sinken. Wie die Blätter des nun kahlen Baumes waren Alexander – und ihre Liebe – einfach davongeweht.

KAPITEL 23

»Ja«, sagte Helena, und vor Erschöpfung sackte sie in sich zusammen, »dann ist mir klar geworden, dass er nie zurückkommen würde. Und das war das Ende.«

Lange Zeit herrschte Stille, bis William schließlich das Schweigen brach. »Dir ist klar, dass du beileibe nicht die Einzige warst, oder? Bei hübschen Frauen war seine Aufmerksamkeitsspanne immer sehr begrenzt. Er ist verliebt ins Verliebtsein. Gib dich keinen Illusionen hin, Helena, ich kann dir versichern, du warst nur eine von vielen.«

»Das glaube ich sofort.« Sie weigerte sich, auf seine gehässige Stichelei einzugehen. Sie hatte es nicht anders verdient.

»Es wundert mich, dass er mir nie von dir erzählt hat. Normalerweise hat er brühwarm alle Details seiner außerehelichen Eroberungen vor mir ausgebreitet. Hätte ich dich damals gekannt, hätte ich dich warnen können. Aber ich kannte dich natürlich nicht. Und wenn ich dich gekannt hätte … tja, dann wären wir jetzt nicht hier. Das Letzte, was ich je wollte, war eine seiner abgelegten Frauen.«

Helena zog sich ganz in sich selbst zurück, um die Kraft aufzubringen, nicht vor Williams entsetzlichen Worten davonzulaufen. Er war derjenige, der sich verletzt fühlte, er durfte sagen, was er wollte.

»Ich verstehe.« Sie hielt den Blick auf ihre Hände gerichtet. »Vielleicht hat er es dir nicht gesagt, weil er sich schämte.«

»Sacha und sich schämen, weil er eine Frau flachgelegt hat?! Unmöglich. Das war für ihn der Sinn des Lebens. Warum in aller Welt hätte er sich schämen sollen?«

»Ich habe erfahren … sehr viel später war das, dass er offenbar nach Hause gefahren ist, weil Jules mit Rupes schwanger war.«

»Ah ja.« William nickte. »Das muss ein Schock für dich gewesen sein.«

»Ja.« Sie sah zu ihm. »Aber das wusste ich damals nicht und auch nicht, dass er verheiratet ist.«

»Ach, wie praktisch.«

»Er hat keine Silbe darüber verloren, das schwöre ich.«

»Und als du mich kennengelernt hast, bist du nie auf die Idee gekommen, dass dein Wiener Liebhaber ein und derselbe sein könnte wie mein ältester Freund?«

»William, als du das erste Mal von deinem besten Freund Sacha Chandler erzählt hast – der zugegeben mit dir in Oxford studiert und dir vorgeschlagen hatte, nach Wien zu fahren –, woher hätte ich wissen sollen, dass es sich um dieselbe Person handelte? Ich kannte ihn damals unter dem Namen Alexander Nicholls. So signierte er auf jeden Fall seine Bilder.«

»Wie ich dir bestimmt schon mal gesagt habe, ist Sacha sein Spitzname aus Kindertagen, und sein vollständiger Nachname lautet Chandler-Nicholls. Es fällt mir schwer zu glauben, dass du das damals nicht gewusst haben sollst, so« – in seinen Worten lag Abscheu – »nah, wie ihr euch damals wart.«

»William, unsere Beziehung dauerte keine zwei Monate. Wir waren zwei Fremde, die sich in einer fremden Stadt begegnet sind. Du magst mich ja naiv nennen, aber ich wusste wirklich sehr wenig über seine Herkunft. Und ich suche auch nicht nach Ausflüchten – aber woher hätte ich es wissen können, bevor ich ihn an unserem Hochzeitstag das erste Mal wiedersah?«

William warf ihr nur einen wütenden Blick zu, und Helena wusste, dass sie nichts sagen konnte, das den Schock für ihn erträglicher machen würde.

»Und dann? Er hat dich also sitzen lassen.«

»Ja.«

»Und was ist dann passiert? Hat er sich bei dir gemeldet, als er wieder in England war?«

»Nein, ich habe überhaupt nie wieder von ihm gehört. Heute weiß ich, dass er einen Job in London angenommen hat und dass Jules ein paar Monate später Rupes zur Welt brachte …«

»Moment mal!« Langsam setzte in Williams Gehirn das Denken wieder ein. »Verdammt!« Als der Gedanke allmählich zur Gewissheit wurde, zog ein Ausdruck abgrundtiefen Entsetzens über sein Gesicht. »Es gibt noch Schlimmeres als das, was du mir bislang erzählt hast, Helena, oder? Viel Schlimmeres?«

Sie schwieg. Was sollte sie schon sagen?

»Weil … Alex und Rupes sind gerade vier Monate auseinander … oder, Helena? Oder?«

»Ja.«

William sah in den funkelnden Nachthimmel hinauf, an dem Tausende von Sternen glitzerten. Sie hatten vergangene Nacht dort gestanden und die Nacht davor, und in der kommenden Nacht würden sie wieder dort stehen. Doch in seiner, Williams, Welt hatte sich an diesem Abend alles unwiderruflich verändert. Nichts würde mehr so sein wie zuvor.

Nach einer Weile stand er auf. »Jetzt schließlich ist mir vieles klar. Kein Wunder, dass du mir nie erzählt hast, wer Alex' Vater ist. Ich kann nur sagen, Gott steh *ihm* bei, wenn er das alles erfährt, Helena. Gott steh deinem armen Sohn bei. Herrgott noch mal!« Fahrig marschierte er auf der Terrasse hin und her. »Ich suche fieberhaft nach einem Weg, der von hier zurück-führt, aber im Moment sehe ich keinen.«Verzweifelt schüttelte er den Kopf. »Es gibt keinen Trost, nirgends.«

»Ich weiß. William, ich …«

»Entschuldige« – William streckte abwehrend die Hände vor sich –, »ich kann nicht, wirklich nicht. Ich muss hier weg.«

Er verschwand im Haus, und zehn Minuten später hörte Helena einen Wagen anspringen, dann über die Kiesauffahrt den Berg hinaufrasen. Kurz darauf sah sie, wie sich die Rücklichter in der Dunkelheit verloren.

Alex' Tagebuch

12. August, Fortsetzung

Ich sitze am Fußende meines Bettes ...

Und warte.

Ich warte, dass meine Mutter hereinkommt und mich weckt. Sie wird hereinkommen und mich in den Arm nehmen, wie sie es früher immer gemacht hat, wird mir über den Kopf streicheln und mir sagen, dass ich einen bösen Traum gehabt habe. Dass nichts davon wirklich passiert ist, dass ich die ganzen schrecklichen Sachen, die da vor meinem Fenster gesagt wurden, nicht gehört habe; dass mein Vater, der nicht mein Vater ist, nicht in seinem Wagen weggefahren ist und vielleicht nie mehr zurückkommt.

Wegen des Mannes, der mein richtiger Vater ist.

Gleich explodiert mein Gehirn. Es wird in Millionen kleiner Fetzen zerplatzen und über die Wände spritzen. Es kann das, was es weiß, nicht mehr fassen. Es weiß nicht, wie es die Information verarbeiten soll. Es ächzt und kracht und dreht sich im Kreis, aber es kommt nicht vom Fleck.

Es kommt nicht damit zurecht. Ebenso wenig wie ich.

Ich hämmere mit den Fäusten auf die Knie, damit der körperliche Schmerz größer ist als der seelische, aber es funktioniert nicht.

Nichts funktioniert.

Nichts kann mir meinen Schmerz nehmen.

Und das Schlimmste ist, dass diejenige, die immer alles heilen konnte, das alles angerichtet hat.

Also bin ich jetzt ganz allein. Im Dunkeln.

Wenn sich die Blockade in meinem Gehirn aufgelöst hat, wird es die Folgen all dessen, was ich gerade gehört habe, allmählich verarbeiten. Im Moment weiß ich nur, dass ich nicht mehr derjenige bin, der zu sein ich glaubte.

Und meine Mutter auch nicht.

KAPITEL 24

Mit zitternden Händen schenkte sich Helena ein Glas Brandy ein und leerte es in einem Zug. Die Wärme brannte ihr im Magen, aber natürlich konnte der Alkohol nicht das Grauen wegbrennen, das gerade über sie gekommen war. Sie stand auf, ging ins Haus und wanderte den Flur entlang zu Alex' Zimmer. Mit letzter Kraft klopfte sie an seine Tür.

»Darf ich reinkommen?«

Es kam keine Antwort, also ging sie hinein.

Im Zimmer war es dunkel, der fahle Mondschein fiel zu den offenen Fensterläden herein. Als ihre Augen sich an die Dunkelheit gewöhnten, sah sie am Fußende eine Gestalt sitzen.

»Können wir miteinander reden?«, fragte sie leise.

»Ist Dad weg?«

»Ja.«

»Kommt er wieder?«

»Das … das weiß ich nicht.«

Sie tastete sich zum Bett vor und setzte sich, ehe die Beine unter ihr nachgaben.

»Hast du uns gehört?«

Erst nach einer langen Pause sagte Alex: »Ja.«

»Alles?«

»Ja.«

»Also … dann weißt du jetzt, wer dein leiblicher Vater ist?«

Keine Antwort.

»Kannst du nun verstehen, warum ich es dir nie gesagt habe? Und auch niemand anderem?«

»Mum, ich kann nicht darüber reden … das geht einfach nicht.«

»Dad … William wollte die Gründe nicht hören, und ich kann verstehen, wenn auch du sie nicht hören willst. Aber ich möchte die Geschichte zu Ende erzählen und dir erklären, was passierte, nachdem er … Sacha, wie du ihn kennst, mich in Wien verlassen hatte. Bitte hör mir zu, Alex, es ist wichtig, dass du das weißt. Und mir ist es wichtig zu erklären, warum das ziemlich viel mit Alexis zu tun hat und mit dem, was hier passiert ist.«

Auch darauf bekam sie keine Antwort, und so redete sie weiter.

»Kurz nach Weihnachten stellte ich fest, dass ich mit dir schwanger war …«

Dezember 1992
Wien

Helenas Atem bildete in der eisigen Dezemberluft zarte weiße Hauchkringel, als sie von ihrer Wohnung zum Vormittagsunterricht ging.

Zu dieser Jahreszeit fand sie die Stadt ganz besonders entzückend. Die prachtvollen Häuser waren traditionell ge-
schmückt, überall hingen glitzernde Lichterketten, ihrerseits
verziert mit einer zarten Schicht Schnee, der über Nacht gefallen war. Es war der Tag vor Silvester, eine Atmosphäre freudiger
Aufregung lag in der Luft, alle Menschen waren beschwingt.

Alle außer ihr. Helena fragte sich, ob sie wohl jemals wieder
fröhlich, glücklich oder aufgeregt sein würde – ob sie überhaupt jemals wieder irgendetwas empfinden würde. Fast zwei
Monate waren seit Alexanders Abreise vergangen, und die Tage
der Verzweiflung und die Nächte, in denen sie sich in den Schlaf
geweint hatte, waren allmählich in eine dumpfe Taubheit übergegangen, die bis in die Tiefen ihrer Seele vordrang. Letztlich
hatte sie akzeptiert, dass Alexander aus welchen Gründen auch
immer nie nach Wien zurückkehren würde. Oder zu ihr.

Vor der Oper blieb Helena kurz stehen und sah an den goldenen Steinbögen empor, die abends prachtvoll erleuchtet sein
würden. Was für eine Ironie des Schicksals, dachte sie, dass ihre
Karriere genau dann, wenn sie persönlich einen Tiefpunkt erreichte, zum Höhenflug ansetzte. An diesem Abend würde sie
bei der Gala-Aufführung von *La Sylphide* die Titelrolle tanzen,

und das neue Ballett, *Der Künstler*, nahm Gestalt an und sollte die größte Produktion der kommenden Saison werden. Helena wusste, dass es ein weiterer Meilenstein in ihrer und Fabios Karriere sein würde, diese Rollen das erste Mal zu tanzen, doch im Moment konnte sie sich nicht im Geringsten darüber freuen.

Zumindest, sagte sie sich, als sie auf den Bühneneingang zuging, hatten die Disziplin und Strenge ihres Berufslebens sie davor bewahrt, vor Kummer den Verstand zu verlieren.

Sie begrüßte den Pförtner mit einem freundlichen Nicken und ging durch die verwinkelten Flure zu ihrer Garderobe, wo sie den Mantel durch ihr Übungstrikot ersetzte, die Beinstulpen überstreifte und in ihre heiß geliebte löchrige Wickeljacke schlüpfte, um nicht zu frieren, bis sich ihr zierlicher Körper aufgewärmt hatte.

Sie fasste ihre langen blonden Haare zu einem Knoten zusammen, schnürte die Seidenbänder ihrer Spitzenschuhe fest um die Knöchel und verließ die Sicherheit ihrer Garderobe.

Auf der riesigen Bühne hatten sich bereits mehrere Mitglieder des Ensembles eingefunden, sie standen plaudernd in kleinen Gruppen zusammen oder machten an der eigens dafür aufgebauten *barre* Dehnübungen. Ihrer gedrückten Stimmung zum Trotz musste Helena unwillkürlich lächeln, als sie die bunte Mischung der Übungsoutfits – einschließlich löchriger Leggings – und die ungeschminkten Gesichter der Tänzerinnen betrachtete und sich vorstellte, wie anders alle abends auf der Bühne wirken würden. Ein leichter Schauder erfasste sie, als sie einen Moment in den verwaisten, dunklen Zuschauerraum blickte, dessen funkelnde Lichter in wenigen Stunden die Pracht der vergoldeten Balkons erleuchten würden, bis zum letzten Platz mit einem erwartungsvollen Publikum von mehr als zweitausend Menschen besetzt.

Sie begrüßte ihre Mittänzer und nahm ihren Platz an der *barre* ein. Der Korrepetitor erschien, um den Unterricht zu leiten, der Pianist spielte das erste Stück, und die Stunde begann mit den üblichen *pliés*. Helena brauchte gar nicht nachzudenken, ihr Körper hatte die Bewegungen schon viele tausend Mal ausgeführt und war auf Autopilot gestellt, während er sich auf die anspruchsvolle Rolle der Fee in *La Sylphide* vorbereitete. Am Tag zuvor hatte die Kostümprobe stattgefunden, die sehr gut gelaufen war, doch da Helena den Part zuvor noch nie getanzt hatte, war sie nervös gewesen. Aus Erfahrung aber wusste sie, dass sie vor Publikum, unterstützt von einem Adrenalinstoß, noch besser sein würde.

»Guten Morgen, Helena, *cara*«, sagte eine Stimme hinter ihr. Fabio nahm seinen Platz an der *barre* ein.

»Du kommst schon wieder zu spät«, tadelte sie ihn, als alle sich umdrehten, um dieselbe Übung auf dem anderen Bein auszuführen.

»Das muss der Wecker sein, er ist eindeutig kaputt«, sagte er und verdrehte schelmisch die dunklen Augen.

Wie Helena wusste, war das Fabios Umschreibung für eine Affäre.

»Na, du wirst mir nach der Stunde sicher alles erzählen.«

Abends saß Helena in ihrer Garderobe und legte letzte Hand an ihr Make-up. Der Tag war sehr hektisch gewesen, nach dem Mittagessen im Anschluss an die Vormittagsstunden hatte sie mehrere Presseinterviews gegeben. So war ihr kaum Zeit geblieben, sich auszuruhen, und sie spürte die nervöse Anspannung, die ihren ganzen Körper erfasst hatte. Zur Ablenkung griff sie nach der Karte, die neben einem herrlichen Strauß weißer Rosen stand, der größte und üppigste mehrerer Blumengrüße, die im Raum verteilt waren.

Liebste Helena,

haben Sie noch einmal Dank für das Vergnügen Ihrer Gesellschaft beim Diner vergangene Woche und dafür, dass Sie mir morgen Abend beim Ball als Begleiterin Gesellschaft leisten. Viel Glück heute Abend, ich werde im Publikum sitzen und Ihnen zusehen.

Herzlichst, Ihr F.

Prinz Friedrich von Etzendorf

Dann erst bemerkte sie, dass sich zwischen den Blüten ein kleines, in Silberpapier gewickeltes Päckchen verbarg. Es enthielt ein Samtkästchen, und als Helena es öffnete, sah sie eine zierliche Halskette, an der drei funkelnde tränenförmige Diamanten an hauchdünnen Kettchen befestigt waren. Überwältigt lehnte sie sich im Stuhl zurück. Und als sie ihr Spiegelbild betrachtete, wusste sie nicht, ob sie angesichts der Ironie der Situation lachen oder weinen sollte.

Sie war Prinz Friedrich vor einigen Wochen bei einem Empfang anlässlich einer Aufführung vorgestellt worden. Jemand hatte ihr gesagt, dass er zu einer der ältesten und wohlhabendsten Familien Österreichs gehöre und sein besonderes Interesse der Kunst gelte. So gut aussehend und zuvorkommend er war, hatte sie das Gespräch mit ihm doch eher lustlos geführt. Er war eben nicht Alexander. Und irgendwie hatte die Tatsache, dass Friedrich – zumindest auf den ersten Blick – alles in sich vereinte, was eine Frau sich nur wünschen konnte, sie noch bedrückter gestimmt.

Am folgenden Tag hatte sie auf geprägtem Papier ein Briefchen von ihm erhalten, in dem er sie zum Essen einlud. Ihr erster Impuls war, sofort abzusagen, doch sie wusste, dass sie sich unbedingt wieder dem Leben zuwenden musste, nachdem

Alexander so abrupt daraus verschwunden war. Und als sie und Fabio in den Kulissen auf ihren Auftritt warteten, hatte sie ihm von der Einladung erzählt.

»Soll ich hingehen?«

»Helena, er ist ein Prinz wie aus dem allerschönsten Märchenballett! Natürlich musst du hingehen«, hatte er ohne zu zögern geantwortet.

Und so hatte sie die Einladung widerstrebend angenommen. Und es war … nett gewesen.

Seitdem hatten sie sich einige Male getroffen, wobei er sie gern weit häufiger gesehen hätte, als ihr Terminkalender es erlaubte. Und Friedrich schien in der Tat der Inbegriff des idealen Mannes zu sein: gut aussehend, kultiviert, sehr wohlhabend und bis über beide Ohren in sie verliebt.

»Was könnte eine Frau noch mehr wollen, Helena? Ich verstehe dich einfach nicht.« Fabio hatte, als er sie nach dem Stand der Beziehung fragte, angesichts ihrer mangelnden Begeisterung die Augen verdreht.

Nichts … dachte sie.

Es war, sinnierte Helena, während sie die Kette anlegte und feststellte, dass sie perfekt um ihren Hals lag, als wäre sie zu keinerlei Empfindung mehr fähig.

»Sie sind meine Grace Kelly«, hatte Friedrich beim letzten Essen gesagt, als er über den Tisch hinweg ihre Fingerspitzen geküsst hatte. »Ich möchte Sie zu meiner Prinzessin machen.«

Dann hatte er sie in aller Förmlichkeit darum gebeten, ihn zum Kaiserball zu begleiten, dem legendären Silvesterball in der Hofburg. »Ich möchte Sie allen vorführen«, hatte er hinzugefügt.

Zwar war ihr eigentlich nicht nach Feiern zumute, doch wollte sie nicht unhöflich wirken und die Einladung ausschlagen, zumal sie wusste, dass dieser Ball zu den begehrtesten gesellschaftlichen Anlässen in Wien gehörte. Und zumindest würde sie dann nicht allein zu Hause sitzen und sich die Augen ausweinen, wenn die Glocken der ganzen Stadt das neue Jahr einläuteten.

Erst nachdem sie die Einladung angenommen hatte, wurde ihr bewusst, dass sie zu einer derartigen Galaveranstaltung nichts anzuziehen hatte. Daraufhin hatte sie sich Klara, ihrer Garderobiere am Theater, anvertraut, und die hatte sie wie eine gute Märchenfee in die Kleiderkammer geführt, wo sie ein hinreißendes schulterfreies zartrosafarbenes Ballkleid gefunden hatten. Darin sah Helena, nachdem einige kleine Änderungen vorgenommen waren, tatsächlich wie eine Prinzessin aus.

Jetzt warf sie einen Blick zur Kleiderstange hinüber, wo das Kleid unter einem Plastikschutz hing, damit sie es heute nach der Vorstellung mitnehmen konnte. Wie aufs Stichwort kam Klara in die Garderobe geeilt, beladen mit dem duftigen Kostüm aus Bergen von weißem Tüll, Chiffon und Pailletten, das Helena an diesem Abend auf der Bühne tragen würde.

»Kommen Sie, Frau Beaumont, Sie müssen sich herrichten, wir haben nicht mehr viel Zeit«, befahl sie Helena auf Englisch mit starkem Wiener Akzent.

Und damit machte sie sich daran, Helenas Haar zu einem hochsitzenden Knoten zu frisieren und ihn mit Perlen und Diamantklammern zu schmücken, die im Licht der Scheinwerfer funkeln und schimmern würden. Zum Schluss besprühte sie ihr Werk mit so viel Haarspray, dass die Frisur auch einem Orkan standgehalten hätte, und half Helena in ihr Kostüm. Dabei gab sie Acht, dass nicht versehentlich Bühnenschminke daran geriet. Ihr aufmerksamer Blick fiel auf das offene Samtkästchen, das auf der Kommode stand.

»Ein Geschenk?«, fragte sie und deutete darauf.

»Ja.«

»Von wem?«

»Einem Freund.«

»Sie meinen den Prinzen?«

Helena nickte verschämt.

»Das braucht Ihnen gar nicht peinlich zu sein. Sie sind eine schöne Frau. Und ich weiß, dass er morgen mit Ihnen auf den Ball geht. Die Kette wird sich perfekt zu dem Kleid machen.«

»Ja, das denke ich auch.«

»Und Frau Beaumont, ich habe mir überlegt, ich komme morgen zu Ihnen und helfe Ihnen, sich herzurichten«, verkündete Klara, als wäre das bereits beschlossene Sache.

»Aber das ist doch wirklich nicht nötig«, widersprach Helena.

»Wie wollen Sie das Kleid ohne meine Hilfe schließen? Da sind im Rücken lauter kleine Perlenknöpfe. Außerdem kann ich Ihnen die Frisur machen, mit der Sie am schönsten aussehen.«

Helena gab nach, zumal sie aus Erfahrung wusste, dass bei Klara jede Widerrede zwecklos war. »Danke, das ist wirklich sehr lieb von Ihnen«, sagte sie.

Für ein weiteres Gespräch blieb keine Zeit, das erste Klingelzeichen erklang, in fünf Minuten würde die Vorstellung beginnen. Klara versprühte noch eine letzte Wolke Haarspray, ehe Helena aufstand und sich im Ganzkörperspiegel betrachtete. Das erlesene Kostüm mit dem perlenbesetzten Mieder und den fließenden weißen Röcken war das perfekte Sinnbild der ätherischen Gestalt, die sie in wenigen Minuten verkörpern würde.

»Sie sind fertig«, sagte Klara und bewunderte ihr Werk ebenfalls, während über die Anlage die »Anfänger« aufgerufen wurden. »Viel Glück«, fügte sie hinzu, als Helena die Garderobe verließ.

Zwei Stunden später führte Fabio Helena unter dem tosenden Applaus der Zuschauer an den Bühnenrand. Über der Aufführung hatte ein Zauber gelegen, das wussten sie beide. Das Publikum erhob sich und trampelte jubelnd mit den Füßen, während die beiden sich inmitten eines wahren Regens von Sträußen, die auf die Bühne geworfen wurden, immer wieder verneigten.

Nachdem der letzte Vorhang gefallen war, ging Helena in ihre Garderobe. Das Adrenalin schoss noch immer durch ihren Körper, und trotz ihrer gegenwärtigen persönlichen Probleme war sie in einer Art Rausch. Fast sofort klopfte es an der Tür, der erste einer ganzen Reihe von Gratulanten.

Ein ansprechendes Gesicht, umrahmt von hellblonden Haaren, sah zur Tür hinein.

»Ich hoffe, ich störe nicht«, sagte er.

»Aber gar nicht. Kommen Sie doch herein, Friedrich.«

Helena ging ihm entgegen und dachte sich, wie distinguiert er doch aussah in seinem Frack mit über seiner breiten Brust liegenden roten Schärpe, die sein Familienwappen trug. Friedrich gab ihr einen Handkuss.

»Mein Entzücken über Ihre Darbietung heute Abend lässt sich nicht in Worte fassen. Sie sind der Inbegriff einer Märchenfee. Und wie ich sehe, haben Sie meine Blumen erhalten«, sagte er und deutete mit dem Kopf auf die Rosen.

»Sie sind traumhaft. Und die Kette ist wunderschön, aber Friedrich, wirklich, das Geschenk ist viel zu großzügig ...«

»Still, liebste Helena, sie ist das Mindeste, was Ihnen zusteht. Bitte, ich wäre zutiefst betrübt, wenn ich glauben müsste, sie gefiele Ihnen nicht. Und ich hoffe sehr, dass Sie mein Geschenk morgen zum Ball anlegen werden.«

»Dann kann ich Ihnen nur von ganzem Herzen danken und Ihnen versprechen, die Kette morgen zu tragen.«

»Als einzigen Dank möchte ich, dass Sie morgen Abend an meinem Arm in die Hofburg schreiten.«

Helena wollte etwas erwidern, doch da klopfte es wieder an der Tür.

»Dann, Helena, werde ich mich für heute verabschieden. Und mich auf einen wunderschönen Silvesterabend freuen.« Damit verbeugte er sich tief und verließ den Raum, während eine Schar weiterer Gratulanten hereinströmte und sich um sie scharte.

Schließlich hatten alle die Garderobe verlassen, und Helena blieb allein zurück. Die Energie, die sie beschwingt durch den Abend getragen hatte, war verebbt, nun fühlte sie sich kraftlos und leer. Klara half ihr aus ihrem Kostüm, Helena schminkte sich ab und schlüpfte in ihre Jeans und den Pullover. Dann zog sie Mantel und Schneestiefel an, nahm das Ballkleid sowie die Kette und verließ das Theater.

Am folgenden Tag traf sich Helena mit Fabio zum Silvester-Lunch im Griechenbeisl.

»*Cara.*« Fabio erhob sich, als der Kellner sie an den Tisch führte. »Komm, setz dich, und lass uns auf den Erfolg der gestrigen Aufführung trinken.« Er griff nach der Flasche Champagner, die im Kühler bereitstand, und schenkte zwei Gläser ein.

»Auf uns! Und auf das kommende Jahr!« Er stieß mit ihr an. »Ich habe in den Morgenzeitungen die Rezensionen von *La Sylphide* gelesen, sie sind alle herausragend. Sie schreiben, dass du ein Stern bist, der zum Himmelsfirmament aufsteigt. Und nach der Premiere unseres neuen Balletts wird ihnen endgültig klar sein, dass wir ein Paar sind, mit dem man rechnen muss. Helena, wir sind auf dem Weg nach ganz oben. Das weiß ich.«

Helena versuchte, sich ähnlich begeistert zu geben wie Fabio, brachte aber nur ein mattes Lächeln zustande.

»Und ganz abgesehen von deinem Triumph gestern Abend auf der Bühne gehst du heute Abend mit dem schmucken Prinzen zum Ball in der Hofburg. Bist du nicht wahnsinnig aufgeregt, *cara*? Das muss doch der Traum einer jeden Frau sein. Und eines jeden Mannes«, fügte er lachend hinzu.

»Fabio, versteh doch, ich kann nicht einfach … ausblenden, was passiert ist.«

»Pfft!« Mit einer ungeduldigen Handbewegung wischte er ihren Einwand beiseite. »Du sprichst wohl immer noch von dem Schurken Alexander. Natürlich kann ich verstehen, dass er dich verletzt hat, aber es ist Zeit, dass du ihn vergisst und dein Leben weiterlebst. Ich dachte, der Prinz gefällt dir?«

»Ich … ja, das stimmt ja auch, aber … Ich weiß nicht, ob ich schon dafür bereit bin.«

»Vielleicht bist du einfach erschöpft.« Er beugte sich über den Tisch, um ihr Gesicht eingehend zu mustern. »Du siehst blass aus, Helena, und du hast noch keinen einzigen Schluck von deinem Champagner getrunken. Du wirst doch nicht etwa krank werden?«

»Nein, nein, ich … es ist nur … ich bin müde, das ist alles.« Sie biss sich auf die Unterlippe.

»Dann bestelle ich dir gleich nach dem Essen ein Taxi, das dich nach Hause fährt. Du musst dich hinlegen, um für den Ball ausgeruht zu sein. Ich möchte, dass du dich zur Abwechslung auch einmal vergnügst, Helena.«

»Ja, du hast recht.« Sie versuchte, ihn mit einem bemühten Lächeln zu beruhigen. »Wenn ich etwas geschlafen habe, geht es mir bestimmt viel besser.«

Fabio warf ihr einen argwöhnischen Blick zu, wechselte aber das Thema und erkundigte sich nach ihrem Ballkleid, um sie dann mit Klatsch über dieses und jenes Mitglied der Balletttruppe zu unterhalten. Als das Essen serviert wurde, bemerkte sie, dass er sie immer wieder prüfend ansah, da sie kaum einen Bissen zu sich nahm.

Es war, dachte Helena rückblickend, als hätte er bereits Bescheid gewusst.

Nach dem Mittagessen fuhr sie nach Hause, folgte Fabios Rat und legte sich aufs Bett. Doch so gern sie einschlafen wollte, die Gedanken wirbelten ihr durch den Kopf, und in ihrem Bauch rumorte es. Wieder einmal rechnete sie nach, zählte die Tage und fragte sich, ob es wirklich möglich war oder ob sie sich umsonst Sorgen machte.

Bald nachdem sie und Alexander das erste Mal miteinander geschlafen hatten, hatte der chaotische Alltag der Ballettsaison begonnen, und sie hatte wie die meisten Ballerinen die Pille ohne die übliche einwöchige Pause genommen, um die monatliche Blutung zu verhindern – eine notwendige Praxis, um auf der Bühne auftreten zu können.

Folglich wusste sie nicht genau, wann sie das letzte Mal »normal« geblutet hatte.

Aber dann … die Übelkeit, das Druckgefühl im Bauch, die Erschöpfung – lauter Symptome, an die sie sich nur allzu gut vom letzten Mal erinnerte.

Schließlich stand Helena wieder auf, Ruhe konnte sie ohnehin nicht finden. Wollte sie ihre Befürchtungen zerstreuen, gab es nur eine Möglichkeit: Sie musste sich Gewissheit verschaffen.

Um noch rechtzeitig in die Apotheke zu kommen, die an diesem Tag zweifellos früher als sonst schließen würde, warf sie sich rasch den Mantel über, griff nach ihrem Portemonnaie und lief hinaus. Nachdem sie das Nötige gekauft hatte, kehrte sie langsamer nach Hause zurück und sah unglücklich, dass Klara bereits vor der Haustür stand.

Verdammt! »Es tut mir leid, dass ich Sie in der Kälte habe warten lassen, Klara«, sagte sie. »Mir ist die … die Zahnpasta ausgegangen.«

Klara schürzte die Lippen, während Helena rasch die Tür aufschloss. »Wir müssen anfangen, sonst werden Sie nicht rechtzeitig fertig.«

In der Wohnung angekommen plauderte Klara unablässig über den bevorstehenden Abend, doch Helena schaltete innerlich ab und nickte nur bisweilen – an den passenden Stellen, wie sie hoffte. Im Kopf beschäftigten sie völlig andere Dinge.

Ich muss verrückt gewesen sein, die Einladung anzunehmen. Ich mache Friedrich falsche Hoffnungen … Was soll ich nur tun, wenn ich …?

Als Helena endlich zu Klaras Zufriedenheit hergerichtet war, konnte sie die Anspannung kaum noch ertragen. Sie stand auf und ging ins Bad, wo sie den Test beim Zurückkommen im Spiegelschrank versteckt hatte. Sie öffnete die Verpackung, nahm das Teststäbchen heraus und machte sich daran, die Plastikumhüllung zu entfernen. Ihr Herz raste.

Dann erstarrte sie. Die Türglocke hatte geläutet, keine Sekunde später klopfte Klara an der Badezimmertür.

»Frau Beaumont! Der Wagen ist da! Ihr Prinz wartet auf Sie!«, rief sie.

»Ich komme!« Einen Moment zögerte Helena noch, dann steckte sie das weiße Stäbchen in ihr mit Juwelen besetztes Täschchen und verließ das Badezimmer.

Klara wartete bereits mit einem hauchdünnen Seidencape in der einen und einem Paar langer Satinhandschuhe in der anderen Hand. Nachdem sie ihr diese übergestreift und den Umhang um ihre schmalen bloßen Schultern drapiert hatte, trat sie zwei Schritte zurück und begutachtete ihren Schützling. Das Mieder des zartrosafarbenen Kleids brachte Helenas makelloses Dekolleté perfekt zur Geltung und schmiegte sich um ihre schlanke Taille, ehe es in weite, weich fließende Röcke aus zartem Chiffon überging. Ihr blondes Haar war zu einem lockeren Knoten aufgetürmt, einige Strähnen lockten sich um ihr Gesicht, und die Diamantkette funkelte wie Eissplitter an ihrem Hals.

»Sie sehen wunderschön aus.« Klara seufzte zufrieden. »Und jetzt, meine Liebe, müssen Sie zu Ihrem Prinzen gehen.«

Klara scheuchte sie zur Wohnungstür hinaus und zum Lift.

»Einen schönen Abend!«, rief sie ihr nach, als sich die Türen schlossen.

Friedrich, der im Frack wieder eine großartige Figur machte, erwartete Helena im Foyer und schnappte sichtlich nach Luft, als sie aus dem Aufzug trat. Er ergriff ihre Hände und hielt sie einige Sekunden auf Armeslänge von sich, um sie zu bewundern, dann zog er sie an sich und küsste sie zart auf beide Wangen. »Sie sehen umwerfend aus, Helena«, flüsterte er. »Auf dem Ball ist mir heute Abend der Neid aller Männer gewiss.« Damit reichte er ihr seinen Arm, und sie gingen gemeinsam zur wartenden Limousine hinaus.

Im leise rieselnden Schneefall kam die imposant gerundete, hell erleuchtete Fassade der Hofburg in Sicht. Der Wagen fuhr unter einem hohen Bogen hindurch in einen großen, nicht minder hell erleuchteten Hof, wo ein roter Teppich über die Pflastersteine zum Eingang führte. Die Limousine blieb stehen, Helena stieg aus und ließ sich von Friedrich ins Gebäude und die prachtvolle Treppe hinauf in einen herrlichen Festsaal führen, wo der Champagnerempfang bereits in vollem Gang war.

Helena nahm vom Kellner ein Glas entgegen und trank einen Schluck, um ihre angespannten Nerven zu beruhigen und sich Mut für den bevorstehenden Abend anzutrinken. Ein schier endloser Strom von Menschen zog an ihr vorüber, um sie ehrerbietig zu ihren großartigen Auftritten im Opernhaus zu beglückwünschen und den Prinzen an ihrer Seite zu begrüßen.

Nach einer Weile gingen sie an ihren Tisch, wo weiterer Champagner bereitstand und Kellner Platte um Platte mit perfekt angerichteten Canapés reichten. Helena nahm keinen Bissen zu sich, doch der Prinz schien ihren mangelnden Appetit nicht zu bemerken, ebenso wenig wie ihre gedämpfte Unterhaltung.

Auf Aufforderung hin betraten die Gäste den großen Ballsaal, und staunend betrachtete Helena die korinthischen Marmorsäulen, die die prachtvolle Kassettendecke stützten, von der wiederum Dutzende Kristalllüster hingen. Das Orchester, auf einem erhöhten Podest platziert, spielte einen Walzer, darüber hing eine gewaltige Uhr, die die Stunden, Minuten und Sekunden bis Mitternacht zählte.

Unvermittelt breitete sich Stille aus, und in geordneten Reihen schritten junge Frauen in weißen Kleidern am Arm junger Männer in den Saal.

»Wer sind sie?«, fragte Helena.

»Das sind die Debütantinnen«, erklärte er leise. »Sie tanzen jetzt einen Walzer zum Zeichen ihres offiziellen Eintritts in die Wiener Gesellschaft.«

Als Helena dieses Ritual einer längst vergangenen Zeit verfolgte, fragte sie sich, ob sie nicht träumte. Und doch verspürte sie einen Anflug von Neid beim Anblick der nervösen jungen Frauen mit ihren unschuldigen Gesichtern, vor denen noch die ganze Zukunft lag und die keinerlei Sorgen kannten.

So war sie auch einmal gewesen.

Doch als sich die Debütantinnen unter Applaus wieder zurückzogen, kehrte sie abrupt in die Wirklichkeit zurück. Die roten Kordons, die die Gäste bislang zurückgehalten hatten, wurden entfernt, das Tanzen konnte beginnen. Helena verlor jedes Zeitgefühl, als Friedrich sie in den Arm nahm und Walzer um Walzer auf dem golden schimmernden Parkett mit ihr tanzte. Auch andere Herren forderten sie zum Tanz auf, und sie tat ihr Bestes, sich als die charmant lächelnde Prinzessin zu geben, die Friedrich sich an seiner Seite wünschte.

»Du siehst heute Abend einfach hinreißend aus, Helena. Mit deinem Zauber hast du mich und jeden anderen Mann hier betört«, flüsterte er, als die Kapelle schließlich einen langsameren Takt spielte und Friedrich die Gelegenheit nutzte, um sie an sich zu ziehen.

Helena hatte das eigenartige Gefühl, als würde sie sich und das Treiben ringsumher aus großer Höhe beobachten. Friedrich beugte sich vor, um sie am Nacken zu liebkosen. »Ich hoffe, dass du und ich im neuen Jahr noch sehr viel mehr Zeit miteinander werden verbringen können.«

»Das … das glaube ich sicher«, hörte sie sich erwidern.

Der Prinz verstand ihre Antwort als Ermutigung und

schmiegte seine Wange an ihr Haar, während sie sich elegant unter einem Lüster im Kreis drehten. »Bitte, Helena«, flüsterte er ihr ins Ohr, »sag, dass du heute Nacht zu mir nach Hause kommst.«

Bei diesen Worten kehrte Helena schlagartig auf den Boden der Tatsachen zurück. Sie schaute zu ihm hoch, und die Verehrung, die er für sie empfand, leuchtete in seinen Augen.

Was mache ich hier?, fragte sie sich panisch. Sie blickte zur Uhr, unvermittelt war ihr schlecht, die Knie wollten unter ihr nachgeben. In zehn Minuten würde es Mitternacht schlagen. Friedrichs Gesicht verzog sich besorgt.

»Helena, Liebling, fehlt dir etwas?«

»Ich weiß nicht. Ich … Mir ist etwas merkwürdig. Ich glaube, ich muss mich setzen.«

Fürsorglich führte Friedrich sie zu ihrem Tisch und ging davon, um ein Glas Wasser zu holen. Helena drehte sich der Kopf, sie wünschte inständig, ein paar Minuten allein zu sein. Sie stand auf und ging zu den Damentoiletten.

Dort spritzte sie sich kaltes Wasser ins Gesicht, was sie ein wenig beruhigte, dann betrachtete sie sich im Spiegel und griff nach ihrer Handtasche, um sich die Lippen nachzuziehen. Zitternd öffnete sie den Verschluss, und dabei fiel ihr die Tasche aus der Hand, der Inhalt verteilte sich über den Boden. Als sie alles wieder einsammeln wollte, fiel ihr Blick auf das weiße Plastikstäbchen.

Wie kann ich an eine Beziehung mit einem anderen Mann auch nur denken, während diese Ungewissheit wie ein Damoklesschwert über mir schwebt?, fragte sie sich vorwurfsvoll.

Friedrich wartete auf sie, und dies war kaum der richtige Moment, aber sie musste sich einfach Klarheit verschaffen, um wieder vernünftig denken zu können.

Was das neue Jahr für sie und ihre Zukunft bereithielt, hing von dem Stäbchen in ihrer Hand ab. Mit wild klopfendem Herzen ging Helena in eine Kabine.

Drei Minuten später wusste sie die Antwort.

Viele Menschengrüppchen bevölkerten das Foyer und achteten kaum auf die junge Frau, deren blassrosafarbene Röcke sich bauschten, als sie über den polierten Marmorboden lief.

Fast stolperte Helena auf der Treppe, die zum Eingang hinunterführte, und so blieb sie einen Moment stehen, streifte sich die hochhackigen Abendschuhe von den Füßen und ließ sie achtlos fallen, bevor sie in die frostige Nacht hinausfloh.

In dem Moment schlugen die Glocken des Stephansdoms zur Mitternacht und läuteten das neue Jahr ein.

Sie bemerkte kaum den eisigen Schnee unter den Füßen, als sie über den Hof und unter den Bogen hindurch auf die Straße lief. Durch das in ihren Ohren dröhnende Blut nahm sie vage eine Männerstimme wahr, die ihren Namen rief.

Sie hielt nicht inne, um einen Blick zurückzuwerfen.

KAPITEL 25

Helena sah zum Fenster hoch oben in Alex' Zimmer hinaus, wo am Himmel der Vollmond leuchtete. Wie in der Nacht, als sie aus der Hofburg gelaufen war. Wie viele Menschenschicksale, hatte sie sich oft gefragt, hatte dieser Mond nicht schon mit angesehen, ohne sich davon in seinem Lauf beirren zu lassen?

»Ja …«, sagte Helena und kehrte aus ihrer Erinnerung in die Gegenwart zurück, »und das ist meine Geschichte. Ich wünschte, ich könnte dir eine schönere erzählen, Alex, aber das kann ich nicht.«

Nach längerem Schweigen sagte er: »Nein, das kannst du nicht. Aber ich verstehe trotzdem nicht, was das alles mit Alexis zu tun hat.«

»Ich …« Helena zögerte. Sollte sie ihm das wirklich auch noch offenbaren? Er hatte ohnehin schon mehr gehört, als ein Sohn von seiner Mutter je erfahren sollte, ganz zu schweigen davon, dass er erst dreizehn war.

»Was immer es ist, Mum, noch schlimmer kann es nicht werden.« Alex schien ihre Gedanken zu lesen. »Jetzt komm, sag's schon.«

»Als ich damals hier in Pandora war, bin ich von Alexis schwanger geworden.«

»Aber … du warst doch erst fünfzehn.« Alex' Stimme war kaum mehr als ein ersticktes Flüstern.

»Ja. Und ich … ich habe es nicht bekommen. Ich glaubte,

keine andere Wahl zu haben. Und es war so entsetzlich. Was ich getan habe, habe ich mir bis heute nicht verziehen. Als ich also feststellte, dass ich mit dir schwanger war, konnte ich es einfach nicht noch einmal machen. Ich musste dich bekommen, was immer es mich kostete.«

Helena hörte Alex atmen, sonst nichts.

»Mit dem neuen Ballett, das auf dem Programm stand – es wäre einfach nicht fair gewesen, beim Ensemble zu bleiben. Ich hätte ja schlecht im März bei der Premiere die ›kleine Tänzerin‹ geben können, da wäre ich im sechsten Monat gewesen. Und es wäre auch nicht fair gewesen, es den anderen gegenüber zu verschweigen. Also sagte ich Fabio, er solle sich eine andere Partnerin suchen, und verließ die Truppe Ende Januar. Ich beschloss, in Wien zu bleiben. Nach England zurückzugehen kam für mich aus verschiedenen Gründen nicht infrage. Ich hatte noch etwas Geld, das meine Mutter mir bei ihrem Tod hinterlassen hatte, außerdem habe ich im Café Landtmann, ganz in der Nähe der Oper, als Bedienung angefangen. Ihnen gefiel, dass ich zusätzlich zu meinem rudimentären Deutsch gut Englisch sprach, sie waren dort sehr nett zu mir. Ich habe gearbeitet bis einen Tag vor der Geburt, als du ganz überraschend über einen Monat zu früh zur Welt kamst.

Aber du warst gesund, und du warst wundervoll.« Bei der Erinnerung spürte Helena einen kleinen Kloß im Hals. »Ich habe dich Alexander genannt, sowohl in Gedenken an das Kind, das ich nicht bekommen hatte – die englische Version vom Namen seines Vaters –, als auch nach deinem leiblichen Vater. Irgendwie schien mir dieser Name naheliegend.« Sie zuckte mit den Schultern. »Und deinen zweiten Vornamen Rudolf hast du natürlich von Nurejew, dem berühmten Tänzer, der so tragisch mit nicht einmal fünfundfünfzig Jahren starb, nur wenige Tage nachdem ich herausfand, dass ich mit dir schwanger war.«

Alex schwieg nach wie vor. Was sollte sie auch sonst erwarten? Also sprach sie weiter.

»Die Zeit nach deiner Geburt war sehr schwierig. Als Frühgeborenes brauchtest du besondere medizinische Betreuung, abgesehen davon ging es mir auch nicht gut. Ich hatte eine seltene Krankheit, die Postpartum-Eklampsie heißt. Ich will nicht dramatisch klingen, Alex, aber ich wäre beinahe gestorben, und deswegen habe ich sehr viel länger gebraucht, um wieder auf die Beine zu kommen. Wir waren beide über zwei Monate im Krankenhaus. Und danach war einfach nicht daran zu denken, dass ich wieder tanzte. Du magst lachen, aber eine Ballerina muss körperlich genauso fit sein wie ein Profifußballer, wenn nicht noch fitter. Gott sei Dank bin ich aber langsam wieder zu Kräften gekommen, und im ersten Jahr war ich einfach nur glücklich, dass es dich gab. Und Alex, Fabio war wunderbar zu dir. Er hat mit dir gespielt, er ist mit dir spazieren gegangen und war so sehr ein Vater für dich, wie ein Mann es nur sein kann. Und du weißt ja, er hat dir auch Bee geschenkt, deinen Hasen …«

Helena unterbrach kurz ihre Erzählung. Da sie im Dunkeln das Gesicht ihres Sohnes nicht erkennen konnte, war es unmöglich zu wissen, was in ihm vorging.

»Und dann gab es noch Gretchen, die in der Wohnung über uns lebte. Als ich wieder ins Café arbeiten ging – ich musste ja dringend Geld für uns verdienen –, hat sie auf dich aufgepasst. Du hast sie geliebt. Sie war dick und fröhlich und hat immer Apfelstrudel und Pfannkuchen für dich gebacken. Erinnerst du dich an sie?«

»Nein«, kam die knappe Antwort.

»Als ich also wieder zu Kräften kam, habe ich, ermutigt von Fabio, wieder Tanzunterricht genommen, wir dachten, dass ich vielleicht doch wieder als seine Partnerin tanzen könnte. Dann bekam er ein Angebot vom New York City Ballet und wollte unbedingt, dass ich ihn, gemeinsam mit dir, begleite. Er hatte Wien nie gemocht, aber Alex, ich wusste, dass ich nicht annähernd auf dem Niveau war, das dort verlangt wird. Bei kaum einem anderen Ensemble müssen die Tänzer so athletisch sein wie beim New York City Ballet. Ich wollte nicht als Fabios Partnerin angenommen werden und dann körperlich und seelisch nicht in der Verfassung sein, die Position auszufüllen. Das hätte ihn beruflich zurückgeworfen, und das wäre einfach nicht fair gewesen. Also sagte ich ihm, dass ich dir und mir keine derart drastische Veränderung zumuten wollte. Du kannst dir vielleicht vorstellen, wie unglücklich ich war, als er Wien verließ. Ich gab jede Hoffnung auf, wieder zu tanzen, und arbeitete weiter im Café. Dann mussten wir aus unserer schönen Wohnung ausziehen und Gretchen verlassen, einfach, weil ich mir die Miete nicht mehr leisten konnte, und wir zogen in eine eiskalte kleine Wohnung, eine Absteige eher, über dem Café, wo ich arbeitete. Ich war völlig mutlos und verzagt, als ich dann ein paar Monate später William kennenlernte.«

Helena schwieg kurz, um sich zu sammeln, bevor sie fortfuhr.

»William hat mich wieder ins Leben zurückgeholt. Wirklich, Alex. Er war so freundlich und beständig, ein durch und durch guter Mensch. Und allmählich habe ich mich in ihn verliebt. Das war keine Verliebtheit wie bei der ersten Liebe, wie bei Alexis, und auch nicht die verrückte, tollkühne Leidenschaft wie bei Sacha – es war ein tieferes und stärkeres Gefühl. Das erzähle ich dir alles, Alex, weil es die Wahrheit ist, aber auch, weil es gleichzeitig deine Geschichte ist. Ich erwarte nicht, dass du mich verstehst oder mir verzeihst.«

Helena betrachtete die Silhouette ihres Sohnes vor dem Mondlicht.

»Als William mich fragte, ob ich nicht mit ihm nach England zurückgehen wollte, habe ich erst nach einiger Zeit eingewilligt. Vorher musste ich mich vergewissern, dass ich mich nicht aus den falschen Gründen zu ihm hingezogen fühlte. Nicht, dass er damals besonders wohlhabend gewesen wäre, Cecile hatte bei der Scheidung das Haus bekommen, er wohnte in einem kleinen angemieteten Cottage. Aber wir waren dort so glücklich, Alex, und ich wusste, dass es das Richtige war. Dann hat er mir einen Heiratsantrag gemacht, und ich habe Ja gesagt. Bald darauf haben wir bei einer Auktion Cedar House ersteigert und es in unser Zuhause verwandelt. Wirklich, Alex, ich war nie so glücklich und zufrieden wie damals. Aber dann kam unser Hochzeitstag …« Helena brach die Stimme.

»Was ist da passiert?«, fragte Alex nach einer Weile brummelnd.

»William hatte mir von Sacha erzählt, seinem alten Studienfreund, der damals in Singapur lebte, aber eigens zu unserer Hochzeit mit seiner Frau nach England kommen würde. Es war im Standesamt, ich ging den Gang entlang nach vorn, da sah ich ihn, wie er mich entsetzt anstarrte. Später stellte William mir diesen Mann als seinen besten Freund Sacha vor – was, wie ich heute weiß, eine gängige Kurzform für Alexander ist. Als ich ›Ja‹ sagte, wäre ich beinahe in Ohnmacht gefallen, so schnell hat mein Herz geschlagen.«

»Hast du danach mit ihm gesprochen?«

»Nein oder zumindest nicht allein. William hat uns natürlich bekannt gemacht, aber du kannst dir sicher denken, dass Sacha sich in kürzester Zeit einen Vollrausch antrank und Jules ihn ins Hotelzimmer bringen musste. Aber davor hatte sie natürlich noch dich kennengelernt und mir von Rupert erzählt, ihrem Sohn, der vier Monate vor dir zur Welt gekommen war. Da war mir dann natürlich klar, weshalb Alexander nie nach Wien zurückgekommen war. Mein Gott, Alex.« Helena ließ den Kopf in die Hände sinken. »Es war grauenhaft, einfach grauenhaft. Ich habe den Großteil unserer wunderschönen Flitterwochen in Thailand damit verbracht, mir zu überlegen, ob ich William die Wahrheit sagen und reinen Tisch machen sollte. Dann hätte es an ihm gelegen zu entscheiden, ob er sich von mir trennt oder nicht. Aber ich hatte solche Angst, ihn zu verlieren. Ich habe ihn geliebt, Alex, ich war so glücklich, und *du* warst glücklich … Ich konnte mich einfach nicht dazu durchringen, es ihm zu sagen und das Märchen in einen Albtraum zu verkehren. Ich habe mich mit dem Gedanken getröstet, dass Sacha am anderen Ende der Welt lebte und sich unsere Wege nur selten kreuzen würden, auch wenn er und William beste Freunde waren. Und in den ersten Jahren war es ja auch so. Manchmal gelang es mir sogar wochenlang, alles zu vergessen.«

Wieder hielt Helena kurz inne und fuhr sich geistesabwesend durchs Haar. »Rückblickend ist mir natürlich klar, dass ich es William sofort hätte sagen sollen, gleich als ich Sacha sah. Alles wäre besser gewesen, als mit dieser schrecklichen Lüge zu leben. Und darauf zu warten, dass sie aufgedeckt wird. Wie du weißt, sind Sacha, Jules und die Kinder dann nach England zurückgekehrt. Zum Glück haben wir sie nicht allzu häufig gesehen. Manchmal haben sie uns für ein Wochenende besucht, und William und Sacha haben sich allein in London getroffen. Dann hat Jules gehört, dass wir hierher nach Zypern fahren, und hat sich und ihre Familie eingeladen, weil sie meinte, sie brauche dringend Urlaub. Ich konnte schlecht Nein sagen, aber ich hatte panische Angst. Ich hatte so eine ungute Ahnung. Und ich habe recht gehabt …«

Langsam schüttelte Helena den Kopf. »Und das ist eigentlich alles, mein Schatz. Mehr kann ich nicht sagen. Wenn ich dir nun völlig den Boden unter den Füßen weggezogen habe, Alex, kann ich mich nur von ganzem Herzen entschuldigen und dir sagen, dass ich dich mehr liebe als alles andere auf der Welt. Ich habe das Geheimnis für mich behalten, um dich, William und unsere Familie zu schützen.«

»Und dich selbst«, sagte Alex barsch.

»Ja, du hast recht, auch mich selbst. Ich weiß, es ist allein meine Schuld. Das Schlimmste ist, William war ein wunderbarer Vater für dich, und jetzt habe ich durch meine Dummheit und meine Selbstsucht das eine zerstört, was ich dir immer geben wollte. Mein Gott, was wünschte ich, er wäre wirklich dein Vater. Ich würde alles darum geben, die Uhr zurückzudrehen. Es tut mir unendlich leid, dass ich das alles verpfuscht habe. Ich weiß, William kann mir nie verzeihen. Es ist der schlimmste Verrat, den es gibt. Aber ich liebe ihn sehr, Alex, das habe ich immer und werde ich immer.«

»Weiß Sacha oder Alexander oder wer immer er in Wirklichkeit ist, dass ich …?« Alex verstummte.

»Ja. Das war ihm sofort klar, als er dich bei der Hochzeit sah. Um aller Beteiligten willen besteht zwischen uns ein unausgesprochenes Schweigeabkommen.«

»Wolltest du es mir je sagen?«

»Ich … Das wusste ich nicht. Ich konnte dir nicht die Wahrheit sagen, aber ich wollte dich auch nicht belügen. Er mag ja für deine Gene mitverantwortlich sein, Alex, aber er hat seitdem in deinem Leben keine Rolle mehr gespielt.«

»Liebst du ihn noch?«

»Nein. Wenn überhaupt, dann eher das Gegenteil. Ich …« Helena verbot es sich, mehr zu sagen, schließlich hatte Alex eben erst erfahren, dass Sacha sein leiblicher Vater war. Es wäre nicht richtig, schlecht über ihn zu sprechen. »Ein Teil von mir wünscht, ich wäre ihm nie begegnet, aber dann, mein Schatz, hätte ich dich nicht bekommen.«

»Gut. Und jetzt geh bitte«, sagte er.

»Ach, mein Schatz.« Helena unterdrückte ein Schluchzen und streckte zaghaft eine Hand nach ihm aus, bekam aber nur nasses Fell zu spüren. Die Tränen ihres Sohnes hatten seinen geliebten Bee durchnässt. »Es tut mir unendlich leid. Ich hab dich lieb, Alex.«

Dann stand sie auf und verließ den Raum.

Alex' Tagebuch

12. August, Fortsetzung

Ich
habe
absolut
nichts
zu
sagen.

KAPITEL 26

Helena saß auf der Terrasse. Sie hatte kein Auge zugetan, und nach der langen Nacht zog jetzt der Morgen herauf. Sie versuchte, sich mit dem Gedanken zu trösten, dass sie dieses Gefühl kannte, alles verloren zu haben; wenn sich das Leben auf einen Schlag veränderte und der bisherige Weg plötzlich versperrt war. Es würde einen anderen Weg geben, den gab es immer. Sie würde damit fertigwerden, sie würde überleben, das hatte sie immer.

Bloß mit dem Unterschied, dass es dieses Mal nicht allein um sie ging.

Sie konnte mit allem zurechtkommen, außer mit dem Gedanken, dass ihre Kinder leiden mussten. Schlimmer noch, dass sie selbst diejenige war, die ihnen Leid zufügte. Wenn sie daran dachte, wie unendlich traurig und verstört Alex sein musste, blutete ihr das Herz. Als Mutter war es ihre Aufgabe, ihn zu trösten, zu beschützen und ihm zur Seite zu stehen. Stattdessen hatte sie ihn tief verletzt.

Ebenso wie William.

Helena fühlte sich vollkommen ausgelaugt. Sie ging die Stufen zur Hängematte hinunter und legte sich hinein. Und als sie dort lag und in den heller werdenden Himmel hinaufsah, konnte sie zum ersten Mal verstehen, weshalb manche Menschen keinen anderen Ausweg sahen, als Selbstmord zu begehen. Vielleicht, dachte sie, hatte es nicht nur mit äußeren Ereignissen zu tun, sondern auch damit, wie man sich selbst wahrnahm. Denn letztlich zählte einzig und allein der Glaube, dass man ein guter Mensch war und seinen Mitmenschen mit Achtung und Liebe begegnete. Die Vorstellung, den Rest ihrer Tage mit dem Wissen leben zu müssen, dass sie bei den Menschen, die sie am meisten liebte, genau dabei versagt hatte, war unerträglich.

Helena wusste, dass sie die Kraft finden würde weiterzumachen. In diesem Moment aber war ihr, trotz der Schönheit der wärmenden Sonne, die gerade am Horizont aufging, so kalt, fühlte sie sich so trostlos wie an jenem Tag damals im Park in Wien, als sie begriff, dass Alexander für immer verschwunden war.

Schließlich schleppte sie sich nach oben in ihr Zimmer. Der Kleiderschrank stand offen. Williams Seite war leer geräumt, seine Reisetasche war fort. Unglücklich schloss sie die Türen, legte sich aufs Bett und schloss die Augen.

»Mummy, Mummy! Wo ist Daddy? Ich habe ein Bild für ihn gemalt von dir und Fabio beim Tanzen. Schau mal!«

Helena öffnete die Augen. Die Erinnerung an den vergangenen Abend traf sie unvorbereitet wie ein Schlag in den Magen, unwillkürlich traten ihr Tränen in die Augen.

»Mummy! Schau dir mein Bild an.« Immy hielt ihr das Bild unter die Nase.

Helena richtete sich auf. »Es ist sehr schön, mein Schatz. Gut gemacht.«

»Kann ich es Daddy geben? Ist er unten?«

»Nein, er musste für ein paar Tage wegfahren. Es hat mit seiner Arbeit zu tun.«

»In unseren Ferien? Warum hat er nicht Tschüs zu uns gesagt?«

»Er hat einen Anruf bekommen, als du schon im Bett lagst, und musste heute Morgen früh gleich weg.« Helena verabscheute sich dafür, schon wieder zu lügen.

»Ach. Kommt er bald wieder?«

»Das weiß ich nicht.«

»Mummy?«

»Ja?«

»Warum trägst du noch dasselbe Kleid wie gestern Abend?«

»Weil ich müde war, Immy, sonst nichts.«

»Aber wenn ich das sage, sagst du immer, dass ich trotzdem mein Nachthemd anziehen muss.«

»Ja, das stimmt. Da hast du recht.«

»Mummy, bist du wieder krank?«

»Nein, mir geht's gut.« Helena stand auf. »Wo ist Fred?«

»Der schläft noch. Soll ich dir Frühstück machen?«

»Nein, mein Schatz, es ist schon in Ordnung. Ich gehe mit dir nach unten.«

Irgendwie gelang es Helena, den Morgen zu überstehen. Sie ging mit Immy und Fred zum Pool, auch wenn es ihr das Herz zerriss, in ihre glücklichen, vertrauensvollen Gesichter zu sehen. Wie würde es ihnen ergehen, wenn sie erfuhren, dass die Familie, in der sie sich geborgen fühlten, von einem Tag auf den anderen nicht mehr existierte? Dass Daddy fort war und sicher nie zurückkommen würde? Und das alles durch ihre Schuld …

Gegen halb elf erschien Fabio in der Küche. Helena fand, dass er fast so schrecklich aussah wie sie.

Er nahm sie in die Arme und drückte sie an sich. »*Bella, bella*, es tut mir so unendlich leid. Das ist alles meine Schuld.«

»Versuch nicht, mich zu trösten, Fabio, sonst muss ich weinen. Außerdem ist es nicht deine Schuld, sondern ganz allein meine.«

»Helena, dein Mann – er ist ein guter Mensch. Und er liebt dich sehr. Er wird nachdenken, dann wird er alles verstehen und zurückkommen. Diese unglückliche Fügung, die euch passiert ist … das ist die grausame Hand des Schicksals.«

Helena schüttelte den Kopf. »Nein, er wird nicht zurückkommen. Ich habe ihn belogen, ich habe ihn unsere ganze Ehe hindurch getäuscht.«

»Aber, Helena, du hast es nicht gewusst!«

»Zuerst nicht, nein, aber ich hätte es ihm sofort sagen sollen, als ich es wusste!«

»Vielleicht. Aber später ist man immer schlauer, nicht wahr? Wo ist er jetzt?«

»Wahrscheinlich ist er nach England zurückgeflogen. Auf Zypern wollte er bestimmt nicht bleiben. Wie ich William kenne, hat er so viel Abstand wie möglich zwischen uns gebracht.«

»Dann musst du ihm folgen und ihm alles erklären.«

»Er will es nicht hören. Das habe ich gestern Abend schon versucht.«

»Das ist der Schock, *cara*. Lass ihm Zeit, bitte.«

»Wie können wir jetzt noch eine gemeinsame Zukunft haben? Er wird mir nie mehr vertrauen, und das kann ich ihm nicht einmal verdenken. Aber in Beziehungen ist Vertrauen alles, Fabio, das weißt du auch.«

»Ja, aber wenn Liebe da ist, gibt es immer eine Zukunft.«

»Hör auf, Fabio«, stöhnte Helena. »Mach mir nicht Hoffnung, wo keine besteht. Ich kann im Moment nicht klar denken. Und Jules … sie ist zurzeit auch hier! Was wird sie sagen, wenn sie das erfährt? William sagt es ihr bestimmt, das würde ich an seiner Stelle auch. Und sie hält mich für ihre Freundin!

445

O mein Gott, was für ein Durcheinander.« Sie ließ sich auf den nächsten Stuhl fallen und vergrub das Gesicht in den Händen.

»*Sí*, das ist ein Durcheinander«, sagte Fabio. »Aber so ist das Leben nun mal. Du musst wieder Ordnung schaffen.«

»Was meinst du – soll ich mit Jules reden? Es ihr sagen, bevor sie es von William erfährt? Das zumindest bin ich ihr doch schuldig, oder?«

»Nein, Helena. Im Moment braucht sie es nicht zu wissen. Du sagtest gestern, sie würde sich scheiden lassen?«

»Ja.«

»Warum willst du ihr noch zusätzlich Schmerz zufügen? Wenn William es ihr sagt, dann, nun ja« – er zuckte mit den Achseln –, »aber ich finde, dass sich alles erst wieder ein bisschen beruhigen muss.«

»Es war meine Schuld, weil ich dich so gern wiedersehen wollte. Ich habe das Schicksal herausgefordert. Ich hätte die Vergangenheit ruhen lassen sollen.«

»Ja – aber ist es nicht gut, dass Fabio jetzt hier ist, um dir wieder auf die Beine zu helfen? Und vergiss nicht den Kummer, den der böse Mensch dir bereitet hat. Was du durchgemacht hast, als er wegging. Er hat Schuld an dieser ganzen Situation. Ich habe es dir damals schon gesagt – auf den ersten Blick habe ich gesehen, dass er nichts Gutes bedeutet.«

»Das stimmt. Ich wünschte, ich hätte auf dich gehört.«

»Aber dann würde es Alex nicht geben, und Alexander hätte William nicht nach Wien geschickt, um sein Herz zu flicken, und du hättest nicht dein Leben mit ihm und deine wunderbaren Kinder auch nicht. Nein« – Fabio schlug mit der flachen Hand fest auf den Tisch –, »du darfst nichts in deinem Leben bereuen. Die Vergangenheit, ob gut oder schlecht, macht dich zu der, die du bist.«

Helena drückte seine Hand. »Ich hatte vergessen, wie klug du bist, Fabio. Danke.«

»Und was ist mit Alex? Wie geht es ihm? Er ist wahrscheinlich geschockt.«

»Er ist wie gelähmt. Vergangene Nacht habe ich versucht, ihm alles zu erzählen, aber jedes Wort muss ihn wie ein Pfeil mitten durchs Herz getroffen haben. Schließlich doch noch die Identität seines Vaters zu erfahren, ist schlimm genug, aber dann auch noch herauszufinden, dass die Mutter eine schreckliche Person ist, die ihre ganze Familie belogen hat … Ich liebe ihn so sehr, Fabio, und ich habe ihn enttäuscht und ihm wehgetan …«

Schließlich brach sie zusammen und weinte haltlos an Fabios Schulter.

»Helena, *cara*«, tröstete er sie. »Alex ist ein kluger Junge. Das weiß ich von damals, als er noch ganz klein war, er hat mit seinen zwei Jahren wie ein Erwachsener mit mir geredet! Am Anfang wird er dich vielleicht wirklich hassen, weil du ihm wehgetan hast. Aber das ist gut so, Wut gehört zum Heilungsprozess. Und dann wird sein großes, kluges Gehirn zu denken anfangen. Und er wird die Tatsachen erkennen und sie verstehen. Er wird daran denken, wie sehr du ihn liebst, dass du eine gute *mamma* bist und immer sein Bestes willst.«

»*Nein!* Ich bin eine entsetzliche Mutter! Kannst du dir vorstellen, hören zu müssen, was er vergangene Nacht zu hören bekommen hat? Ich habe ihm auch von meiner Abtreibung erzählt, weil ich fand, dass er wissen sollte, warum ich ihn unbedingt behalten wollte. Wie kann er mich da jemals wieder respektieren?«

»Helena« – Fabio fasste sie unters Kinn, damit sie ihn ansah –, »jetzt muss er begreifen, dass du nicht nur eine Mutter bist, sondern ein Mensch. Und der ist nicht vollkommen. Das muss jedes Kind früher oder später erkennen, und das zu akzeptieren ist nie leicht, schon gar nicht, wenn man so jung ist wie Alex. Aber er ist reif für sein Alter, er wird damit zurechtkommen. Gib ihm Zeit, *cara*, ich verspreche dir, er wird dich verstehen.«

»Und dann muss er auch noch mit den ganzen Konsequenzen zurechtkommen, zum Beispiel, dass er einen Halbbruder hat, den er nicht ausstehen kann.« Bei dem Gedanken schauderte Helena.

»Soll ich versuchen, mit ihm zu sprechen?«, fragte Fabio. »Vielleicht hilft es, wenn jemand anderes es ihm erklärt. Schließlich kenne ich Alex, seit er ein paar Stunden alt ist.«

»Du kannst es versuchen. Ich habe heute Vormittag dreimal an seine Tür geklopft, aber er hat mir jedes Mal gesagt, dass ich ihn in Ruhe lassen soll.«

»*Prego*, lass mich sehen, ob ich mit ihm reden kann.« Fabio warf einen Blick auf seine Uhr. »Aber um zwei Uhr muss ich nach Paphos fahren, um meinen Leihwagen abzuholen.«

»Musst du wirklich weg?« Helena griff nach seinem Arm. »Kannst du nicht etwas länger bleiben?«

»Helena, du kennst doch den Terminplan eines Tänzers. Ich würde liebend gern bleiben, aber es geht nicht. Vielleicht kannst du nächste Woche nach Limassol kommen, um dir die Vorstellung anzusehen, und dann können wir anschließend essen gehen. Jetzt muss ich mir aber das Taxi nach Paphos bestellen.«

»Nein, ich fahre dich. Ich glaube, es ist besser, wenn ich beschäftigt bin, und ich möchte ein paar Stunden weg aus Pandora. So schön das Haus ist, eigentlich hat es mir seit meiner Ankunft nichts als Unglück gebracht.« Fabio ging zur Tür. »Bitte sag Alex, dass ich ihn liebe und dass es mir unendlich leidtut …« Helena versagte die Stimme, hilflos zuckte sie mit den Schultern.

»Natürlich.« Fabio nickte, ging zu Alex' Zimmer und klopfte leise an. »Alex? Ich bin es, Fabio. Können wir uns unterhalten? Ich möchte mit dir reden über das, was passiert ist.«

»Lass mich in Ruhe. Ich will nicht reden. Mit niemandem«, kam die halb erstickte Antwort.

»Das kann ich verstehen. Also bleibe ich hier draußen stehen, und ich rede, und wenn du willst, kannst du zuhören, *sí?*« Schweigen.

»Gut … Es gibt nur eines, das ich dir sagen will, Alex, und das sage ich dir jetzt: Ich war da, als deine Mutter feststellte, dass sie dich in ihrem Bauch hat. Obwohl ich sie anflehte, das Kind nicht zu bekommen, zu erkennen, dass es keinen *papa* gibt, dass sie an ihre Karriere denken sollte und daran, dass sie ihr Leben zerstört, aber sie hat darauf bestanden. ›Nein, Fabio‹, hat sie gesagt, ›ich will dieses Kind bekommen.‹ Ihr war nichts anderes wichtig, als dich auf die Welt zu bringen. Und als du kamst, warst du ihre Welt. Die ganze Zeit gab es immer nur Alex.«

Fabio räusperte sich kurz.

»Ist das eine schlechte *mamma*? Nein, das ist eine *mamma*, die ihren Sohn so sehr liebt, dass sie sogar ihre große Leidenschaft zum Ballett aufgibt. Sie kümmert sich ganz allein um dich und beklagt sich nie. Und als dann ein guter Mann auftaucht, sieht sie eine Möglichkeit, euch beide glücklich zu machen. Sie wünscht sich Sicherheit für dich und das beste Leben, das sie dir geben kann, also geht sie mit dem Mann mit. Verstehst du das, Alex?«

Wieder kam keine Antwort, also fuhr Fabio einfach fort.

»Und als das Schicksal ihr einen bösen Streich spielt und sie den fiesen Alexander, der jetzt Sacha heißt, bei ihrer Hochzeit sieht, beschließt sie, das geheim zu halten. Alex, das war ein Fehler, aber sie hat es gemacht, weil sie dich so liebt. Das musst du verstehen. Ich bitte dich, es zu verstehen. Ja? Sie ist die tapferste Frau, die ich kenne, aber Alex, sie leidet auch! Und jetzt braucht sie dich, wie du sie damals gebraucht hast, als du klein warst. Du bist ein großer Junge mit einem großen Verstand. Du kannst verstehen, was passiert ist. Hilf ihr, Alex, hilf ihr.«

Fabio zog sein seidenes Taschentuch heraus und putzte sich geräuschvoll die Nase. »Ja, das ist alles, was ich dir sagen wollte. So Gott will, wird sich alles finden, und ich sehe dich bald wieder. Leb wohl, mein Freund, leb wohl.«

Nachdem Helena die Kleinen mit der Aussicht auf einen Besuch bei McDonald's bestochen hatte, fuhr sie Fabio nach Paphos, wo er seinen Leihwagen abholte. Sie war froh, das Haus verlassen zu können. Alex hatte sich noch immer geweigert, aus seinem Zimmer zu kommen, aber Angelina würde noch eine gute Stunde in Pandora mit Putzen beschäftigt sein und so zumindest ein bisschen auf ihn aufpassen.

»Versuchst du, nächste Woche nach Limassol zu kommen?«, fragte Fabio, als er sie zum Abschied umarmte.

»Ich werde mich bemühen, aber angesichts der Umstände kann ich wirklich nichts versprechen.«

»Nein, aber in einer Woche kann sich vieles ändern.« Er lächelte verständnisvoll. »Und durch all das haben wir zumindest unsere Freundschaft wiedergefunden. Vergiss nicht, ich bin immer für dich da, *cara*. Ruf mich an, Helena, wann immer du es brauchst. Und lass mich wissen, was passiert.«

»Fabio, danke für alles. Ich hatte vergessen, wie sehr du mir gefehlt hast.«

»*Ciao, cara, ciao*, ihr Kleinen.«

Sie winkten ihm nach, und obwohl Immy und Fred neben ihr standen, wusste Helena ganz plötzlich wieder, wie sich Einsamkeit anfühlte.

Alex' Tagebuch

13. August 2006

Als ich heute Morgen aufwachte, wusste ich, dass ich wegmuss. Egal, wohin, nur weg von diesem Schmerz … und von ihr.

Letzte Nacht lag ich auf dem Bett, nachdem Helena – ich kann sie im Moment einfach nicht »Mutter« nennen – gegangen war, und an mir zogen Bilder vorbei, in denen ich in einem Chevrolet über baumlose amerikanische Highways fuhr, bis ich irgendwann in irgendeinem Kaff landete, im einzigen Diner des Orts meinen Burger aß und im Motel übernachtete, nur um am nächsten Morgen weiterzufahren.

Dann fiel mir ein, dass ich noch zu jung bin, um Auto zu fahren. Und, wichtiger noch, dass ich noch zu unterentwickelt bin, um mir einen Bart wachsen zu lassen, was ein wesentliches Element aller Roadmovies ist, die ich je gesehen habe.

Also, wohin könnte ich verschwinden …?

Die Nächte unterm Sternenhimmel irgendwo im tiefsten Inneren Zyperns zu verbringen – oder auch in jedem anderen Landstrich – lockt mich nicht angesichts meiner Phobie vor Mücken und anderem Getier. Camping verabscheue ich, also ist der Plan auch hinfällig.

Da ich in einem Souvenirladen in Latchi eingefallen bin und sich mein Kontostand deshalb nur noch auf zwölf

Pfund und zweiunddreißig Pence beläuft, sind meine Optionen noch weiter eingeschränkt. Ich könnte versuchen, meine Schätze weiterzuverkaufen, aber ich bezweifle, dass ich für meinen Laserpointer und den Becher viel bekommen würde, selbst wenn ich die Zigarrenschachtel aus Holz mit der Inschrift *Love from Cyprus* als Zugabe drauflege.

Ein Weilchen döste ich wieder ein, dann wachte ich auf, und die Erinnerung lag mir schwer wie Zement in der Magengrube. Jetzt, im Moment, hasse ich sie, diese Frau, die ich seit meiner Geburt über alles liebe. Sie ist von ihrem Sockel gefallen und liegt jetzt zerbrochen am Boden. In meiner Vorstellung trampele ich auf dem Kopf herum und mache ihn noch kaputter. Danach geht es mir zwar etwas besser, aber das Problem mit ihrem schrecklichen Verrat ist dadurch noch nicht gelöst.

Allmählich kapiere ich, wie sehr ein Trauma gepaart mit Schlafmangel das Gehirn verstopfen kann. Ich weiß nicht einmal genau, ob ich noch eins habe. Mittlerweile habe ich rasenden Hunger und schrecklichen Durst, aber weil ich mein Zimmer nicht verlassen kann, ohne Gefahr zu laufen, einem meiner Halbgeschwister oder, schlimmer noch, Helena selbst über den Weg zu laufen, sitze ich in meiner Besenkammer fest. Immer wieder klopft sie an die Tür, und immer wieder verzichte ich auf eine Reaktion.

Ich will sie bestrafen.

Dann plötzlich ist es Fabio, der an die Tür klopft.

Er redet über sie, und ... ach, verflucht, meine Wut legt sich ein bisschen. Er wird es nie erfahren, aber ich war auf meiner Seite der Tür vollkommen in Tränen aufgelöst. Und als er weg war, fing ich an, etwas rationaler nachzudenken über das, was sie mir gestern erzählt hat.

Mein Verstand, der sich eine Auszeit genommen hatte und irgendwo auf den Bahamas am Strand in der Sonne lag, beschloss, den Urlaub zu verkürzen und zu mir zurückzukehren.

Und je mehr ich es mir überlegte, desto mehr erkannte ich, dass Fabio recht hat: Es ist nicht ihre Schuld. Ich brachte sogar ein mattes Lächeln zustande, als ich an ihre Geschichte mit dem Silvesterball dachte und mir überlegte, dass sie fast wie ein postmodernes Remake von *Cinderella* klingt. Immy wäre allerdings nicht glücklich, wenn die Disney-Version, die sie so liebt, ein ähnliches Ende gefunden hätte und das strahlende Prinzesschen einsam und allein zu seinem Ascheeimer zurückgekehrt wäre …

Zugegeben, die Vorstellung, dass die Frau, die mir das Leben schenkte, mit einem Mann dieses Hoch-Runter-Spiel spielte – zumal mit dem, der mich zeugte –, macht mich nicht so an, aber sie hätte mich auch umbringen können. Hat sie aber nicht.

Weil sie mich liebt.

Mittlerweile muss ich auch ganz dringend pinkeln. Als ich also höre, dass es still wird im Haus und danach Reifen auf dem Kies knirschen, sause ich nach oben ins Bad. Und dann fülle ich jeden Zahnputzbecher mit Wasser und sogar die Plastikgießkanne, mit der Fred in der Badewanne Immy piesackt. Auf halbem Weg zurück zu meinem Zimmer, beladen mit meinen Wasservorräten, höre ich das Tapsen von kleinen Füßen auf dem Gang.

»Hallo, Alex.«

Verdammt! Abrupt bleibe ich stehen, die Hälfte des Wassers spritzt auf den Boden und bildet Pfützen um meine Füße.

»Du bist ja wirklich da. Angelina hat gesagt, dass du hier bist.«

Es ist Viola. Genau das, was ich brauche. Sie kommt immer nur, um mir von ihren Problemen zu erzählen, und heute habe ich, gelinde gesagt, ein paar eigene. »Ja, bin ich«, sage ich.

»Alex, ist alles in Ordnung?«, fragt sie mich. Sie folgt mir zu meinem Zimmer und schaut zwischen mir und den Pfützen hin und her. »Gießt du Pflanzen?«

»Nein«, sage ich und sehe, dass sich ihr Blick auf Freds Gießkanne richtet. »Es tut mir leid, Viola, aber reden geht gerade gar nicht.«

»Schon in Ordnung. Ich bin nur gekommen, um dir zu sagen, dass Mummy und ich und Rupes am Ende der Woche nach England zurückfliegen. Sie möchte, dass wir uns in unserem neuen Haus einleben, bevor die Schule beginnt. Und ach ja, Rupes hat mir aufgetragen, dir zu sagen, dass er die Prüfung bestanden hat, und ich soll dir danke sagen für deine Hilfe. Er ist sehr glücklich.«

»Gut. Schön. Freut mich für ihn.«

Ich freue mich für Rupes. Meinen gerade entdeckten Halbbruder. Unvermittelt möchte ich laut lachen über die Absurdität der Situation und des Lebens im Allgemeinen.

»Na dann«, sage ich noch und trete einen Schritt in mein Zimmer. »Danke fürs Kommen, Viola.«

»Alex, Daddy ist hier, auf Zypern«, sagt sie unbeirrt. »Er hat gestern Abend Rupes zurückgebracht und wollte Mum überreden, es noch einmal zu versuchen.«

»Was hat sie gesagt?«

»Nein. Und dann hat sie noch gesagt, dass er ein Schuft ist und ein Säufer und hat ihn aus dem Haus geworfen.«

Viola biss sich auf die Unterlippe. »Ich mache mir Sorgen um ihn. Hast du ihn vielleicht gesehen? Ich dachte, vielleicht ist er zu euch gekommen, nach Pandora.«

Heiliger Strohsack! Diese Episode meines Lebens entwickelt sich zunehmend zu einer Farce. »Nein, Viola, tut mir leid.«

»Ach.«

Sie fängt gleich an zu weinen, und dann bekomme ich ein schlechtes Gewissen, weil ich so kurz angebunden bin. »Du hast deinen Dad wirklich sehr lieb, stimmt's?« Am liebsten hätte ich hinzugefügt: *Und das, obwohl er ein Schwein der übelsten Sorte ist und das Leben von dir und deinem Bruder und deiner Mutter und meiner Mutter kaputt gemacht hat. Und Dads – also Williams – und Immys und Freds auch. Und das meine obendrein, so ganz nebenbei gesagt.*

»Natürlich. Das hat er doch nicht absichtlich gemacht, dass sein Geschäft eingeht, oder? Er hat bestimmt sein Bestes versucht.«

Ach, Viola, wenn du nur wüsstest …

Und trotzdem rührt mich ihre treue Liebe. Vor allem angesichts dessen, dass sie nicht einmal blutsverwandt mit ihm ist. Was bei einigen von uns leider Gottes sehr wohl der Fall ist.

»Das hat er bestimmt, ja«, presse ich hervor. Schließlich kann ja Viola nichts dafür, dass jetzt alles so ist, wie es ist.

»Also, dann gehe ich jetzt«, sagt sie. »Ich bringe dir *Nicholas Nickleby* zurück. Es ist das allerbeste Buch, das ich je gelesen habe.«

»Ach, wirklich? Das freut mich.«

»Ja, und als Nächstes lese ich Jane Austen, wie du gesagt hast.«

»Gute Wahl«, sage ich und nicke.

»Ach, und hier ist etwas für dich von mir, falls ich dich nicht noch mal sehe. Nur, um danke zu sagen, weil du so nett zu mir warst.«

Sie tritt zu mir und reicht mir einen Umschlag, dann stellt sie sich auf die Zehenspitzen und gibt mir schüchtern einen Kuss auf die Wange. »Tschüs, Alex.«

»Tschüs, Viola.«

Ich sehe ihr nach, wie sie den Gang entlang davongeht, ihre zierlichen Füße berühren kaum den Boden. Sie gleitet eher, fast wie meine Mutt… wie Helena, meine ich.

Wahrscheinlich ist nur der Stress daran schuld, gepaart mit der Erschöpfung, aber als ich den Umschlag betrachte, der liebevoll mit Filzstiftblumen und -herzen bedeckt ist, könnte ich schon wieder losheulen. Es rührt mich, dass Viola so lieb ist, und als ich die Wassergefäße in mein Zimmer manövriere, wünsche ich mir, dass ich mit ihr verwandt wäre und nicht mit Rupes.

Ich trinke einen großen Zahnputzbecher voll Wasser auf einen Zug, setze mich aufs Bett und öffne das Kuvert.

»Lieber Alex, ich habe dir ein Gedicht geschrieben, weil ich weiß, dass du Lyrik magst. Ich glaube, es ist nicht besonders gut, aber es heißt ›Freunde‹. Und ich hoffe, dass du immer mein Freund bleibst. Liebe Grüße und danke für alles, Viola.«

Ich falte das Gedicht auf und lese es, und was jambische Pentameter und Reimpaare betrifft, ist es wirklich nicht so toll, aber es kommt von Herzen, und mir steigen schon wieder Tränen in die Augen. Ich habe in den letzten Stunden wahre Wasserfälle produziert, kein Wunder, dass ich Durst habe.

Ich gucke auf Bee, den Hasen, den mein neu gefundener Onkel Fabio mir vor all den Jahren geschenkt hat. Zumindest weiß ich jetzt, woher mein schauriger zweiter Name kommt – die Vorstellung, dass ich nach einem rotnasigen Rentier benannt sein könnte, war in den vergangenen dreizehn Jahren doch ziemlich erschreckend. Und dann denke ich an Viola und ihre bedingungslose Liebe zu dem Säuferidioten, der mich gezeugt hat.

Und zum ersten Mal seit gestern Abend dämmert mir, dass ich es schlimmer hätte treffen können. Mal abgesehen von dem furchtbaren Zufall, dass mein genetischer »Dad« und … na ja, »Dad« eben, beste Freunde sind, ist mein Genpool offenbar adeliger Abstammung. Und Sacha hat etwas in der Birne, wenn er nicht gerade einen sitzen hat. (Das ist etwas, worauf ich aufpassen muss, wird mir jetzt klar, denn erst letzte Woche habe ich gelesen, dass Sucht genetisch bedingt ist.)

Die andere gute Nachricht ist, dass mein leiblicher Vater groß ist, einen kräftigen Haarschopf hat und eine eindeutig als solche erkennbare Taille. Und schöne Augen …

O mein Gott! Ich stehe auf und schaue mich im Spiegel an. Und da sind sie, die Indizien, die all die Jahre über da waren, die Hinweise, die für jedermann erkennbar rechts und links von meiner Nase in den Augenhöhlen liegen. Es wollte nur niemand wahrhaben, was direkt *vor* seiner Nase war, einschließlich meiner Person.

Ich bin also nicht der Nachkomme eines Traubenpressers oder eines schwuchteligen Balletttänzers. Auch nicht eines Flugzeugpiloten oder eines Chinesen … Ich bin der Sohn eines akademisch gebildeten Engländers, den ich von klein auf kenne.

Der beste Freund meines Stiefvaters.

Dad ... der arme Dad. Plötzlich tut er mir wahnsinnig leid. Die Vorstellung, dass irgendein Mann mit seiner Frau du-weißt-schon-was gemacht hat, muss fast unerträglich sein, ganz zu schweigen, dass es sich dabei um seinen besten Freund handelt. Es war schlimm genug, als Chloë mit Rupes rumgemacht hat. Am liebsten hätte ich ihm seine selbstzufriedene Visage zu Brei geschlagen.

Die Frage ist: Kann Dad Helena je verzeihen?

Kann ich ...?

Da wird mir klar, dass Dad und ich im Moment im selben leck geschlagenen Boot sitzen. Ich frage mich, ob er wohl so viel geweint hat wie ich. Ehrlich gesagt kann ich mir das nicht vorstellen. Aber wenn es jemanden gibt, dem es im Moment genauso dreckig geht wie mir, dann ist er das.

Und dann wird mir klar, dass wir jetzt schließlich die Gemeinsamkeit gefunden haben, die uns verbindet. Es ist weder Fußball noch Cricket und auch nicht die Teekannen, die er kistenweise sammelt. Es ist Helena und der Schmerz, den sie uns beiden zugefügt hat.

Meine, äh, Erzeugerin, seine Ehefrau.

Beim Nachdenken versuche ich, den Restinhalt von Freds Gießkanne in meinen Mund zu leeren, womit ich mir aber eine erfrischende Gesichtsdusche verpasse. Und dann denke ich an das unterdrückte Schluchzen von der Terrasse gestern Nacht, nachdem ich ihr gesagt hatte, sie solle verschwinden.

Ich lasse mir noch mal durch den Kopf gehen, was sie mir erzählt hat.

Und dann überlege ich mir, dass sie ihre ruhmreiche

Karriere als berühmte Körperverdreherin im Tüllröckchen aufgegeben hat, nur um mich zu behalten ...

Und dann weine ich wieder. Ihretwegen.

Ein paar Minuten später habe ich einen Plan gefasst. Und mache mich daran, ihn in die Tat umzusetzen.

Kapitel 27

Ein Besuch am Strand füllte den restlichen Nachmittag. Zuvor hatte Helena mit Angelina gesprochen, um sich zu vergewissern, dass mit Alex alles in Ordnung war. Offenbar hatte Viola ihn besucht, er war aus seinem Zimmer gekommen, und die beiden hatten sich unterhalten.

Um sechs Uhr waren sie wieder in Pandora, und als Allererstes ging Helena zu Alex' Zimmer und klopfte an die Tür.

»Alex, ich bin's. Darf ich bitte reinkommen?«

Sie erhielt keine Antwort.

»Also gut, mein Schatz, ich kann das schon verstehen, aber du musst doch Hunger haben. Ich stelle dir etwas zu essen vor die Tür. Danach gehe ich die Kleinen baden, bringe sie ins Bett und lese ihnen eine Geschichte vor. Dann komme ich wieder.«

Um acht Uhr saß sie allein auf der Terrasse und lauschte auf die Stille im Haus, das bis zum vergangenen Abend von fröhlichem Lärmen erfüllt gewesen war. Sie ging hinein und sah, dass das Essen noch unberührt vor Alex' Tür stand. Sie klopfte wieder.

»Alex, mein Schatz, bitte komm raus. Die Kleinen sind im Bett, und niemand anderes ist hier. Können wir miteinander reden? Bitte«, flehte sie.

Nichts.

Helena setzte sich vor seine Tür, fest entschlossen, erst zu gehen, wenn sie eine Reaktion bekommen hatte.

»Bitte, Alex, sag einfach was, damit ich weiß, dass du da bist. Ich kann verstehen, dass du mich hasst und mich nicht sehen willst, aber das kann ich jetzt nicht ertragen. Bitte.«

Keine Antwort.

»Also gut, Alex, ich komme trotzdem rein.« Helena drehte am Knauf, der sich bewegte, doch die Tür ging nicht auf.

»Alex, mein Schatz, wenn's sein muss, schlage ich die Tür ein. *Bitte!* Sag etwas!« Mittlerweile war Helena in heller Aufregung. Entsetzliche Vorstellungen gingen ihr durch den Kopf, und Tränen der Verzweiflung rannen ihr über die Wangen. »Alex! Wenn du mich hören kannst, bitte, mach die Tür auf!«

Als auf ihr Schreien und Rufen weiterhin nur Schweigen folgte, lief sie auf die Terrasse, fand ihr Handy auf dem Tisch und wählte Alexis' Nummer.

Er hob sofort ab. »Helena?«

»Alexis!«

»Helena, was ist?«

»Ich … Ach, Alexis, bitte komm! Ich brauche dich.«

Zehn Minuten später war er da, sie stand bereits wartend am rückwärtigen Eingang.

»Was ist passiert?«

»Alex! Er macht seine Tür nicht auf! Ich habe Angst … o mein Gott …« Sie unterdrückte ein Schluchzen. »Vielleicht hat er sich etwas angetan … Bitte, komm!« Helena zog ihn am Arm ins Haus.

»Wo ist William?«, fragte Alexis sichtlich verwirrt.

»Weg. Er ist weg, aber wir müssen in Alex' Zimmer, sofort!«, schluchzte sie, als sie ihm voraus den Gang entlangeilte.

»Helena, beruhige dich. Natürlich kommen wir hinein.« Er drehte am Knauf, stellte aber, wie bereits Helena, fest, dass sich die Tür nicht bewegte. Auch als er sich mit seinem ganzen Gewicht dagegenstemmte, ließ sie sich nicht öffnen. Er versuchte es erneut, aber wieder erfolglos.

»Alex? Hörst du mich? Bitte antworte mir! *Bitte ...!*« Helena trommelte mit den Fäusten gegen die Tür.

Alexis zog sie fort, nahm Anlauf und warf sich mit voller Wucht dagegen, doch das Holz gab nicht nach.

»Also gut, ich versuche es durchs Fenster.«

»Ja, ja!«, rief Helena erleichtert. »Der Fensterladen ist offen, das habe ich vorhin gesehen.«

»Gut. Ich brauche etwas, auf das ich mich stellen kann. Das Fenster ist zu hoch, um ins Zimmer zu sehen.« Er ging auf die Terrasse und zog einen Stuhl unter das Fenster. »Kannst du mir sagen, was passiert ist, Helena?«, fragte er, als er hinaufstieg.

»Das erzähle ich dir gleich, aber bitte, schau doch, ob mein Sohn noch lebt!«

»Ja, das mache ich ja«, sagte er beruhigend. »Ich kann hineinsehen ... einen Augenblick.«

Helena stand daneben und konnte die quälende Spannung kaum ertragen. »Ist er da, Alexis? Ist er ... o mein Gott ... o Gott«, wisperte sie.

Dann drehte sich Alexis um und stieg mit einem erleichterten Seufzen vom Stuhl herunter. »Helena, das Zimmer ist leer.«

KAPITEL 28

»Sein Rucksack ist weg und Bee, sein geliebter Hase!«, sagte Helena, als sie panisch alles durchsuchte, was auf seinem Bett lag. Offenbar hatte Alex, als er gegangen war, die Tür hinter sich abgeschlossen. Mit Mühe war Helena durch das kleine Fenster in die Kammer gestiegen, nachdem Alexis die Scheibe eingeschlagen hatte.

»Aber warum ist Alex überhaupt weggelaufen?«

»Das ist eine lange Geschichte. Wir müssen das Gelände absuchen«, sagte sie und lief hinaus.

»Ich glaube kaum, dass Alex seinen Rucksack mitgenommen hätte, wenn er nur im Garten spazieren gehen wollte, Helena.«

»Ich schaue trotzdem, für den Fall, dass er sich irgendwo versteckt.«

Hektisch sah Helena in jeden Winkel des weitläufigen Gartens und der Außengebäude, ob Alex sich dort verborgen haben könnte. Alexis suchte unterdessen mit einer Taschenlampe die Weinfelder in der näheren Umgebung ab. Schließlich trafen sie sich auf der Terrasse wieder.

»Nichts, Helena. Ich bin überzeugt, dass er weggefahren ist.«

»Ich versuche noch mal, ihn auf dem Handy zu erreichen.« Helena wählte seine Nummer, aber wieder antwortete nur die Mailbox.

»Mein Schatz, hier ist Mum. Bitte, bitte ruf mich an, nur damit ich weiß, dass dir nichts fehlt. Tschüs.« Rastlos marschierte

Helena auf und ab und versuchte, sich zu beruhigen, damit sie wieder einen klaren Gedanken fassen konnte.

»Wenn du mir sagst, weshalb er weggelaufen ist«, sagte Alexis erneut, »könnte ich dir vielleicht helfen.«

Helena blieb stehen und drehte sich zu Alexis. »Er hat gestern Abend erfahren, wer sein Vater ist. Und William auch. Das ist der Grund, weshalb keiner von ihnen hier ist. Sie haben mich beide … verlassen.«

»Ich verstehe. Jetzt komm, Helena, du bist erschöpft. Bitte setz dich.« Er nahm sie an der Hand und führte sie zu einem Stuhl. »Jetzt hole ich dir etwas zu trinken.«

»Nein, ich mag nichts. Aber eine Zigarette.« Sie griff nach der Packung, die von der vergangenen Nacht noch auf dem Tisch lag, und zündete sich eine an.

»Und dieser Mann … Alex' Vater? Dein Sohn und dein Mann …« Alexis suchte nach den richtigen Worten, »finden ihn nicht gut?«

»Nein, überhaupt nicht. Du musst wissen, Alexis …« Seufzend kam sie zu dem Schluss, dass es ihr gleichgültig war, was er von ihr dachte. »Es ist Sacha, Jules' Mann, den ich früher einmal als Alexander kannte.«

»Mein Name und auch der von Alex.« Alexis sah sie an, sein Schock über diese Offenbarung stand ihm ins Gesicht geschrieben. »Nein, das war sicher keine willkommene Nachricht. Ich bin sicher, dass es eine Erklärung gibt, aber jetzt ist vielleicht nicht der richtige Zeitpunkt, darüber zu sprechen.«

»Nein.« Helena machte einen tiefen Zug. »Du glaubst doch nicht, dass Alex etwas … Dummes tun würde, oder?«

»Nein, das glaube ich nicht. Alex ist ein vernünftiger Junge. Vielleicht braucht er etwas Zeit, um in Ruhe nachzudenken. Das würde ich an seiner Stelle auch.«

»Ja, aber er ist auch ein Kind in einem fremden Land. Wo in aller Welt sollte er hingehen?«

»Das weiß ich nicht, aber wo immer er ist, Helena, er hat einen Plan.«

»Lass mich überlegen, lass mich überlegen.« Helena griff sich an die Schläfen und sah zu Alexis auf. »Er würde doch nicht zu Jules gehen, oder? Um es ihr zu sagen?«

»Ich war vorhin dort, da war Alex nicht bei ihr, aber ich bezweifle es sowieso.« Alexis zuckte mit den Schultern. »Sie haben keine enge Beziehung, und er mag Rupes nicht. Wenn du möchtest, kann ich sie anrufen.«

»Nein, du hast recht, zu ihr würde er nicht gehen. Sonst fällt mir niemand ein, den er hier kennt, außer dir und Angelina. Was, wenn er in Gefahr ist? Wenn er nur spazieren gehen wollte und dann …?«

»Helena, bitte, beruhige dich doch. Alex hat seinen Rucksack mitgenommen, er hat sich darauf vorbereitet wegzugehen. Die Frage ist, wohin.«

»Das … das weiß ich einfach nicht«, sagte sie seufzend und drückte die Zigarette aus. »So, wie ich Alex kenne, würde er dahin gehen, wo er sich aufgehoben fühlt.«

»Vielleicht nach Hause, nach England?«, fragte Alexis.

»Aber wie würde er dorthin kommen?« Abrupt setzte sie sich auf. »O mein Gott! Sein Pass! Lass mich nachsehen!« Sie stürzte in ihr Zimmer und öffnete die Schublade, in der sie die Pässe der Kinder und die Rückflugtickets aufbewahrte. Alex' Pass war nicht mehr da.

Sie lief wieder nach unten. »Er hat ihn mitgenommen. Er könnte überall sein, einfach überall …« Schluchzend ließ sie sich auf einen Stuhl fallen.

»Hat er Geld?«

»Er hat ein Bankkonto, von dem er mit einer Karte Geld abheben kann, aber wie viel drauf ist, weiß ich nicht. Nicht allzu viel, würde ich meinen. Geld rinnt ihm einfach durch die Finger.«

»Was ist mit William? Wo ist er?«

»Das weiß ich nicht!«, rief sie verzweifelt.

»Dann müssen wir das herausfinden. Helena, du musst ihn anrufen. Er muss erfahren, dass Alex verschwunden ist.«

»Wenn er sieht, dass ich anrufe, geht er nicht ans Telefon.«

»Dann rufe eben ich an.« Alexis holte sein Handy aus der Tasche. »Sag mir die Nummer.«

Alexis wählte Williams Nummer und hörte dann eine elektronische Stimme sagen, der Teilnehmer sei momentan nicht erreichbar und er möge es später noch einmal probieren. »Was ist mit eurem Haus in England? Könnte William nicht dort sein?«

»Wenn er nach England zurückgeflogen ist, wird er entweder dort sein oder in unserer kleinen Wohnung in London. Versuch beides«, bat Helena.

Unter beiden Nummern erreichte Alexis lediglich den Anrufbeantworter und hinterließ beide Male die Nachricht, William möge doch bitte zurückrufen.

»Möchtest du, dass ich ins Dorf fahre und dort herumfrage, ob jemand ihn gesehen hat?«

»Ja, bitte, Alexis.«

»Und du musst hierbleiben für den Fall, dass Alex zurückkommt. Weißt du, um wie viel Uhr er verschwunden ist?«

»Das muss irgendwann nach eins gewesen sein, da ist Angelina nach Hause gegangen. Ich hätte Fabio nicht nach Paphos fahren dürfen und auch nicht mit den Kindern an den Strand. Aber ich hätte nie gedacht, dass er weglaufen würde. Ich …«

»Helena, du musst Ruhe bewahren, dir und auch Alex zuliebe.« Er nahm ihre Hände in die seinen und drückte sie fest. »Wir finden ihn, das verspreche ich dir.«

Als Alexis eine gute Stunde später zurückkehrte, forschte Helena ängstlich in seinem Gesicht nach einem Hinweis.

»Niemand hat ihn gesehen. Wir suchen morgen weiter. Jetzt können wir nichts mehr machen.«

»Dann sollten wir jetzt aber die Polizei anrufen!«

»Helena, es ist nach Mitternacht. Auch die Polizei kann im Moment nichts unternehmen. Wir rufen morgen an.« Alexis streichelte ihr sacht über die Wange. »Liebste Helena, das Beste, was du tun kannst, ist zu schlafen. Morgen brauchst du wieder neue Kraft.«

»Aber ich kann nicht schlafen, Alexis. Unmöglich.«

»Mir zuliebe versuchst du es. Komm mit.« Er führte sie in den abgedunkelten Salon und bestand darauf, dass sie sich aufs Sofa legte.

»Bleibst du ein bisschen bei mir?«, fragte sie. »Nur für den Fall …«

»Aber natürlich. Ich bin hier. Wie immer«, sagte er leise.

»Danke.« Sie nickte matt. Und damit schlossen sich ihre Augenlider.

Während Helena schlief, saß Alexis still neben ihr. Er dachte an den Abend zurück – fünfzehn Jahre mochten es her sein –, als er sie im Amphitheater von Limassol mit dem Ballett der Scala den *Feuervogel* hatte tanzen sehen. Damals hatte er kaum glauben können, dass dieses außergewöhnliche Wesen, das dort auf der Bühne zweitausend Menschen in seinen Bann schlug, das junge Mädchen war, das er vor all den Jahren so sehr geliebt hatte.

Helena hatte natürlich nie erfahren, dass er dort war, er aber hatte den Abend nie vergessen. Und jetzt, als er mit ihr allein dort saß und auf ihr Gesicht hinabsah, wusste er, dass er sie, gleichgültig, was sie in der Zwischenzeit getan haben mochte, für den Rest seines Lebens lieben würde.

Mit einem Ruck wurde Helena wach und stellte fest, dass es Morgen war. Sie setzte sich auf und griff als Erstes nach ihrem Handy. Und sah, dass eine SMS gekommen war.

Das Herz schlug ihr bis zum Hals, als sie sie las.

Angesichts der Umstände möchte ich so bald wie möglich die Scheidung einreichen. Nenn mir bitte deinen Anwalt. W.

Verzweifelt ließ sie sich wieder aufs Sofa fallen.

Alexis rief bei der Polizei an, und Angelina, aufgelöst vor Sorge, holte die Kleinen ab und nahm sie zu sich nach Hause. Helena lief auf der Terrasse hin und her und wählte alle paar Minuten Alex' Handynummer, als könnte die ständige Wiederholung sie beruhigen.

William hatte auch auf Alexis' Nachrichten nicht reagiert. Helena hatte noch einmal die Nummern an beiden Wohnorten probiert, aber wieder hatten sich nur die Anrufbeantworter eingeschaltet. Dann rief sie bei Jules, Sadie und bei zwei Schulfreunden von Alex an.

Niemand hatte von ihm gehört.

Helena sah, wie Alexis einen Mann beim Aussteigen aus dem Wagen begrüßte und auf die Terrasse führte. »Helena, Kommissar Korda ist ein guter Freund von mir. Er wird alles tun, was in seiner Macht steht, um dir zu helfen, Alex zu finden.«

»Guten Tag.« Helena stand auf und versuchte sich zusammenzureißen. Sie wusste, sie könnte jederzeit laut zu schreien anfangen und nicht mehr aufhören. »Bitte setzen Sie sich doch.«

»Danke«, sagte er. »Ich kann etwas Englisch, aber wenn Alexis die Einzelheiten kennt, kann er mir alles auf Griechisch erklären, das geht schneller.«

»Natürlich. Darf ich Ihnen etwas zu trinken anbieten?«

»Wasser, gern.«

Helena holte Krug und Gläser aus der Küche und trug sie auf die Terrasse. Als sie hörte, wie Alexis auf Griechisch die Situation erläuterte, zog sie sich wieder in die Küche zurück und räumte auf – alles, um sich von ihren quälenden Gedanken abzulenken.

Schließlich ging sie wieder nach draußen. Korda machte bereits Anstalten zu gehen und empfing Helena mit einem Lächeln.

»Gut, ich weiß Bescheid. Wir brauchen ein Foto Ihres Sohnes, haben Sie eins?«

»Ja, in meinem Portemonnaie. Ich hole es.« Sie lief in ihr Zimmer, wühlte in ihrer Handtasche und stürzte wieder nach unten.

»Das Portemonnaie ist hier irgendwo«, sagte sie und durchsuchte die verschiedenen Fächer. »Ach, hier.« Als sie dem Kommissar Alex' Foto reichte, stiegen ihr Tränen in die Augen angesichts seiner geliebten Apfelbäckchen und des offenen Lächelns. »Das ist vor einem Jahr gemacht worden, sehr hat er sich in der Zwischenzeit nicht verändert.«

»Danke. Ich verteile eine Kopie an unsere Beamten.«

»Einen Moment …« Helena durchsuchte ihr Portemonnaie noch einmal. »Offenbar ist meine Debitkarte verschwunden.«

»Debit?« Korda sah fragend zu Alexis.

Alexis erläuterte die Bedeutung. »Sind Sie sicher, dass sie nicht mehr da ist?«

»Ja. Denken Sie, Alex könnte sie genommen haben?« Helena sah ihn an. »Er kennt die PIN, weil ich ihn manchmal bitte, Geld für mich abzuheben. Außerdem habe ich mein Portemonnaie gestern im Haus vergessen.«

»Das ist sehr gut«, sagte Korda und nickte bedächtig. »Wenn Ihr Sohn Ihre Karte verwendet hat, können wir herausfinden, an welchem Automaten er sie benutzt hat und wo eventuell noch. Bitte, schreiben Sie mir Ihre Bankverbindung auf.«

Helena kritzelte die Angaben auf den Notizblock, den der Polizist ihr reichte.

»Und außerdem Ihre Adressen in England. Ich werde auch mit den britischen Behörden sprechen. Wir werden alle Flüge überprüfen, die nach vier Uhr von Paphos abgeflogen sind. Und da Sie Ihren Mann in keinem Zuhause erreichen können, werden wir der englischen Polizei vorschlagen, zu beiden Ihrer Adressen zu fahren und nachzusehen, ob Alex sich dort aufhält.«

»Kommissar Korda, vielen Dank für alles«, sagte Helena, nachdem sie auch beide Anschriften notiert hatte und den Polizisten gemeinsam mit Alexis zu seinem Wagen begleitete. »Entschuldigen Sie den ganzen Ärger. Nichts davon ist die Schuld meines Sohn, sondern einzig und allein meine.«

Korda fuhr davon, und Alexis legte Helena tröstend einen Arm um die Schulter. »Ich muss jetzt ins Büro und meine E-Mails abrufen, mich duschen und etwas Frisches anziehen. Ich bin bald wieder da. Kommst du eine Stunde allein zurecht?«

»Ja, natürlich, Alexis. Hab vielen Dank für alles.«

»Du weißt, Helena, ich bin immer für dich da. Ich komme so bald wie möglich wieder.«

Sie sah ihm nach, wie er zu seinem Wagen ging, kehrte dann auf die Terrasse zurück und setzte sich. Erneut versuchte sie,

Alex, William, Cedar House und die Wohnung in London zu erreichen, aber vergebens.

Ihr Auge fiel auf eines von Alex' T-Shirts, das über der Leine hing. Sie ging es holen, und dabei stieg ihr ganz leicht der Geruch ihres Sohnes in die Nase. Sie schloss die Augen und sprach leise ein Gebet.

Ein paar Minuten später fuhr ein Auto vor, und Jules erschien auf der Terrasse.

»Ich schaue nur kurz vorbei, um zu hören, ob du in der Zwischenzeit etwas von Alex gehört hast.«

»Nein, nichts.«

»Ach, Helena, wie schrecklich für dich, es tut mir so leid. Bist du ganz allein hier?«

»Ja.«

»Wo ist William?«

»Ich weiß es nicht.« Helena war zu erschöpft, um zu lügen.

»Was meinst du damit?«

»Er ist abgereist«, sagte sie. »Ich habe keine Ahnung, wohin.«

»Und Alex ist auch einfach so verschwunden?« Jules warf ihr einen verwunderten Blick zu. »Da ist doch etwas passiert, Helena. Komm, erzähl schon.«

»Nicht jetzt, Jules, bitte. Es ist eine lange Geschichte.« Helena konnte es nicht ertragen, ihr ins Gesicht zu sehen.

»Dann muss ich mir wohl selbst einen Reim darauf machen. Du hast ihnen offenbar etwas erzählt, das sie nicht wussten, oder sie haben es durch Zufall erfahren. Welche der beiden Möglichkeiten war's?«

»Können wir es bitte dabei belassen, Jules? Ich fühle mich im Moment ziemlich überfordert«, sagte Helena flehentlich.

»Nein, das können wir nicht. Ich habe nämlich das Gefühl, dass ich weiß, worum es geht.«

»Das glaube ich nicht.«

»Na ja«, begann Jules langsam. »Wenn ich sage, dass mit großer Wahrscheinlichkeit mein abtrünniger Demnächst-Exmann etwas damit zu tun hat, läge ich doch nicht ganz falsch, oder?«

Helena hob den Kopf und starrte Jules fassungslos an.

»Ist okay, Helena. Ich habe immer Bescheid gewusst über dich und Sacha. Und natürlich Alex«, fügte sie hinzu.

Helena war zu benommen, um etwas zu erwidern. Erst nach einer ganzen Weile fragte sie heiser: »Woher?«

»Als er aus Wien zurückkam, war mir ziemlich klar, dass dort etwas passiert sein musste. Und so, wie ich Sacha kannte, hatte es etwas mit einer Frau zu tun. Zum einen hatte er sich aus Wien höchstens zwei-, dreimal bei mir gemeldet. Um ehrlich zu sein, unsere Beziehung stand auf der Kippe. Wir waren seit fünf Jahren verheiratet, und ich wusste von mindestens zwei Affären, die er in der Zeit gehabt hatte. Er war sehr unglücklich, weil sich seine Bilder nicht verkaufen ließen, und ich arbeitete Tag und Nacht im Büro. Also überlegte ich mir, dass wir beide etwas Abstand brauchten, und machte ihm dem Vorschlag, dass ich ihn ein Jahr lang finanzieren würde, wenn er in der Zeit den Magister machen würde. Zumindest bestünde dann die Chance, in einer Galerie angestellt zu werden oder vielleicht sogar als Lehrer. Außerdem kennst du ja das alte Sprichwort, Helena: Wenn du jemanden liebst, lässt du ihn ziehen. Das habe ich gemacht.«

»Da hast du ein großes Opfer gebracht, Jules.«

»Ja, aber ich wusste auch, wie Sacha tickt. Er kann nicht allein leben. Ich hatte gehofft, er würde in Wien merken, wie sehr er mich braucht, und mit eingezogenem Schwanz zu mir zurückkommen. Bevor er fuhr, sagte ich ihm, dass ich nicht mehr bereit sei, mich mit seinen Affären abzufinden. Ich habe natürlich nicht damit gerechnet, dass er dich kennenlernen würde. Oder dass ich bald nach seiner Abreise feststellen würde, dass ich mit Rupes schwanger war«, fuhr Jules fort. »Ich muss ehrlich sagen, ein paar Wochen habe ich hin- und herüberlegt, ob ich abtreiben lassen sollte, ohne Sacha überhaupt davon zu erzählen. Er hätte nie davon erfahren müssen. Aber wie du selbst weißt, Helena, je länger ich überlegte, desto realer wurde das kleine Ding in mir. Schließlich schrieb ich also Sacha nach Wien, er müsse nach Hause kommen, weil ein Kind unterwegs sei. Zu der Zeit war mir längst klar, dass es für mich kein Zurück gab, dass ich das Kind bekommen würde.«

»O mein Gott«, flüsterte Helena halb zu sich.

»In den ersten Wochen war es, als wäre ihm allein mein Anblick zuwider. Er war völlig benommen, er verbrachte die meiste Zeit in seinem Atelier, um zu malen. Ich war mir ziemlich sicher, dass er mich verlassen würde.« Sie sah zu Helena. »Ich habe Durst. Kann ich mir ein Glas Wasser holen?«

»Ja, natürlich«, sagte Helena leise. Jules verschwand im Haus, aber sie blieb reglos sitzen. Vor Schock war ihr Gehirn wie gelähmt.

»Ich habe es mir anders überlegt«, meinte Jules, als sie zurückkam. »Wir trinken beide ein Glas Wein. Es ist nach zwölf Uhr, also brauchen wir kein schlechtes Gewissen zu haben. Du kannst bestimmt auch eins vertragen.« Jules stellte ein Glas vor Helena, trank einen Schluck von ihrem und setzte sich.

»Danke.«

»Wie auch immer, eines Tages bin ich in sein Atelier gegangen, um ihn etwas zu fragen. Er war nicht da, er hatte einen seiner langen Spaziergänge unternommen – er war oft stundenlang verschwunden. Und auf seinem Schreibtisch lagen die wunderschönen Skizzen einer Tänzerin. Sie trugen alle den Titel *Helena*.«

Obwohl Helena übel war, trank sie einen großen Schluck Wein.

»Ich fürchte, ich habe sie alle zerrissen. Was eigentlich ein Jammer war, weil seine Zeichnungen von dir beim Tanzen wahrscheinlich die schönsten waren, die er je gemacht hat. Weißt du, großes Talent hatte er nie, aber die Verliebtheit hat ihn eindeutig inspiriert. An dem Abend war ich bereit für eine offene Aussprache. Die zerrissenen Zeichnungen musste er ja gesehen haben. Aber zu meiner Überraschung kam er zurück und hat mich in den Arm genommen. Er hat sich entschuldigt, weil er so distanziert gewesen sei, und hat gesagt, er habe etwas verarbeiten müssen. Wir haben nie mehr darüber gesprochen, aber uns war beiden klar, was – oder vielmehr, wen – er damit meinte.«

Eine Weile saßen die beiden Frauen schweigend da, verloren in ihren Erinnerungen an denselben Mann.

»Na ja«, fuhr Jules schließlich fort, »in den nächsten Tagen fingen wir an, über die Zukunft zu sprechen. Sacha wusste, dass er sich einen festen Job suchen musste, weil ich nach der Geburt zu arbeiten aufhören würde, zumindest eine Weile, und von seiner Malerei konnte er nicht einmal sich selbst ernähren, geschweige denn eine Familie. Also hat er ein paar alte Freunde aus Oxford angerufen und in London einige Vorstellungsgespräche vereinbart. Schließlich bekam er eine Stelle bei einer Firma von Börsenmaklern, bei der sein Vater jahrelang Kunde gewesen war. Dann kam Rupes zur Welt, und Sacha fand sich in seine Arbeit ein und war sogar ziemlich erfolgreich. Wie du dir vorstellen kannst, kam er mit seinem Charme und dem hübschen Gesicht gut an bei den reichen alten Damen, die Geld zu investieren hatten.«

Voller Abscheu verdrehte Jules die Augen und trank einen Schluck Wein.

»Wie dem auch sei, drei Jahre später, wir hatten gerade Viola adoptiert, bekam er das Angebot, nach Singapur zu gehen. Ich wollte unbedingt, dass er es annahm, ich hoffte, wir könnten dort völlig neu anfangen. Ich war sehr glücklich, und er auch. Alles war großartig, bis wir ein paar Monate später zu eurer Hochzeit nach England fuhren. Ich erkannte dich sofort von den Zeichnungen, und Sachas Miene, als er dich den Gang entlangkommen sah, war wirklich einmalig!« Jules lachte bitter. »Selbst wenn ich nichts gewusst hätte, der Ausdruck allein hätte mich davon überzeugt, dass zwischen euch etwas gewesen war.«

»O mein Gott, Jules, das tut mir unendlich leid«, brachte Helena hervor. »Mir war nie klar, dass du das wusstest.«

»Woher auch?«, sagte sie brüsk. »Dem Wenigen nach zu schließen, was ich auf der Hochzeit erfuhr, war mir klar, dass ich mich nicht täuschte. Einer der Gäste erzählte, dass du früher Balletttänzerin gewesen seist, und dann sagte William in seiner Rede, dass er dich in Wien kennengelernt hatte, weil Sacha ihm empfohlen hatte, nach Wien zu fahren, um dort die Liebe zu finden …« Jules schüttelte gequält den Kopf. »Beim anschließenden Empfang sah ich dann Alex, der sich wie ein verlorener kleiner Cherubim immer in deiner Nähe herumtrieb, und da wusste ich auch das. Obwohl er Sacha nicht sehr ähnlich sieht, aber er hat die grau-grünen Augen seines Vaters.«

»Ja, das stimmt.« Helena blickte zu dieser erstaunlichen Frau, die an ihrem Tisch saß und ihr seelenruhig erklärte, dass sie über alles Bescheid wusste; dass sie immer schon Bescheid gewusst hatte. »Ich weiß wirklich nicht, was ich sagen soll, Jules, außer dass es mir aufrichtig leidtut, welchen Kummer ich dir bereitet habe. Es ist keine Entschuldigung, aber Sacha hat mir nie gesagt, dass er verheiratet war. Er hat sich mir als Alexander vorgestellt. Um ehrlich zu sein, hat er mir überhaupt sehr wenig von seinem Leben in England erzählt.«

»Das wundert mich nicht«, meinte Jules trocken. »Wahrscheinlich fand er es großartig, sich ein neues Leben zu erfinden und praktischerweise zu vergessen, dass er verheiratet war.«

»Meinst du, Sacha wusste, dass ich die Frau war, die William heiraten wollte?«

»Ich sagte doch gerade, sein Gesichtsausdruck, als er dich bei der Hochzeit sah, war unbeschreiblich. Ich weiß noch, als wir die Einladung bekamen, sahen wir natürlich beide den Namen, der neben Williams stand – also deinen –, aber bestimmt dachte er, genau wie ich, dass diese Helena niemals im Leben dieselbe sein könnte.«

»Es ist ja auch ein unglaublicher Zufall. Ich habe mich immer gefragt, wenn er es wusste, weshalb er sich dann nicht bei mir gemeldet und mich gewarnt hat.«

»Also, hätte ich ihn – und dich – bestrafen wollen: Euer beider Gesicht bei deiner Hochzeit wäre Vergeltung genug gewesen. Und als Sacha an dem Tag dann Alex das erste Mal sah … tja.« Seufzend schüttelte Jules den Kopf. »Es muss entsetzlich gewesen sein, vor allem für dich, Helena. Ich habe es schließlich immer gewusst, aber William nicht.«

»Und du hast Sacha nicht gesagt, dass du ihn für Alex' Vater hältst?«, fragte Helena erstaunt.

»Dass Alex aller Wahrscheinlichkeit nach der Sohn meines Mannes war, hat mich natürlich hart getroffen, aber was hätte es gebracht, mich aufzuregen und die Scheidung einzureichen? Es lag auf der Hand – angesichts dessen, dass ich dich wenige Minuten nach deiner Hochzeit mit Sachas bestem Freund kennenlernte –, dass ich keine Angst zu haben brauchte, du würdest ihn mir wegnehmen. Außerdem habe ich gesehen, wie sehr du und William euch liebt.«

»Ja, das stimmt auch, oder zumindest …« Helena unterbrach sich. »Ich liebe ihn immer noch. Aber ich weiß wirklich nicht, wie du mit all dem zurechtgekommen bist, Jules, ehrlich nicht.«

»Selbstverständlich wäre es mir lieber gewesen, wenn du nicht eine heiße Affäre mit meinem Mann gehabt hättest, als ich einsam und verlassen und schwanger in England saß, aber du darfst nicht vergessen, ich habe es gewusst. Wissen ist Macht, und es war meine Entscheidung, bei ihm zu bleiben. Ein Leben als alleinstehende Mutter kam für mich schlicht nicht infrage, das habe ich dir überlassen«, erwiderte sie. »Ich wollte einen Vater für meinen Sohn, und zwar einen, der bei mir ist. Und wie ich dir schon sagte, damals habe ich ihn geliebt. Er war ein Mann mit vielen Fehlern und Bedürfnissen, aber man kann es sich nicht aussuchen, in wen man sich verliebt, stimmt's? Das solltest du wahrscheinlich besser als jede andere verstehen. Ich vermute mal, dass du Sacha auch geliebt hast?«

»Damals ja, sicher.«

»Eigentlich hast du mir immer leidgetan, Helena. Ich habe ja gesehen, dass du mit einer Lüge gelebt hast. Also, jetzt sag, wie hat William es herausgefunden?«

»Ich habe Fabio, meinen ehemaligen Tanzpartner, hierher eingeladen. Und auf einem Foto aus Wien, das er uns gezeigt hat, war Sacha mit mir zu sehen.«

»Mein Gott, ist er wütend? Das ist er doch bestimmt!«

»Er reicht die Scheidung ein. Das hat er mir heute Morgen per SMS mitgeteilt.«

»Aus dem Impuls heraus eine durchaus verständliche Re-aktion«, sagte Jules nüchtern. »Und wie hat Alex es aufgenom-men? Ist er entsetzt, dass Sacha sein Vater ist?«

»Ja. Deswegen ist er weggelaufen. Die Polizei war gerade hier, sie haben die Suche auf England ausgedehnt.«

»Alex taucht wieder auf. Er wird sich von dem Schock erholen und dir verzeihen. Er liebt dich über alles. Und was jetzt? Nachdem William und ich raus sind aus dem Spiel, könnt ihr zwei euch doch wieder in eure wilde Liebelei stürzen.«

»Nein, Jules, ich …«

»Helena, du kannst ihn haben, und zwar mit Handkuss. Ich hab's schon vor Ewigkeiten gecheckt, wie Rupes sagen würde. Diese Scheidung ist das Beste, was mir je passieren konnte. Rückblickend muss ich sagen, dass mir gar nicht klar war, wie unglücklich dieser egozentrische Schuft mich gemacht hat. Wenn du ihn willst, nur zu. Er war immer der Überzeugung, dass du die große Liebe seines Lebens bist, das erkenne ich an seinem Blick, wenn er dich ansieht. Obwohl ich mich ehrlich gesagt frage, ob Sacha überhaupt in der Lage ist, jemand anderen als sich selbst zu lieben.«

»Ich schwöre dir, Jules, Sacha ist der letzte Mensch, mit dem ich zusammen sein möchte. Er hat mich angelogen, er hat sich einfach aus dem Staub gemacht und mich in Wien sitzen lassen. Um ganz ehrlich zu sein, es fällt mir schwer, mit ihm in einem Raum zu sein. Ich liebe nur William und wünsche mir so sehr, er würde zurückkommen … Entschuldige.« Helena trocknete sich hastig die Tränen. »Ich habe absolut kein Recht zu weinen. Du musst mich zutiefst hassen.«

»Ich habe damals die Frau auf den Zeichnungen gehasst, das ja, aber wie könnte ich dich hassen, Helena? Du bist ein herzensguter Mensch, und du hast zufällig etwas an dir, weswegen Männer sich in dich verlieben. Aber Glück hat dir das eigentlich nicht gebracht, oder? Ehrlich gesagt habe ich eher den Eindruck, dass du dir damit nichts als Kummer eingehandelt hast.«

»Ich …« Helenas Handy läutete, und hastig griff sie danach. »Ja? William, hast du schon gehört? Alex ist verschwunden und … Wirklich? … Ach, Gott sei Dank! Gott sei Dank! … Ja, das mache ich. … Kann ich mit ihm reden? … Okay, ich verstehe. Grüß ihn einfach ganz lieb von mir. Tschüs.« Sie legte das Handy wieder auf den Tisch und ließ den Kopf in die Hände sinken. »Gott sei Dank, Gott sei Dank«, wiederholte sie und schluchzte vor Erleichterung.

»Alex ist wieder aufgetaucht?«, fragte Jules.

»Ja, er ist bei William in England. Ach, Jules, Gott sei Dank!«

Jules stand auf und legte die Arme um Helena. »Alles gut«, sagte sie beruhigend. »Ich habe dir doch gesagt, dass er wieder auftaucht. Er ist hart im Nehmen, genau wie sein Vater. Apropos Sacha – ich habe ihn gestern Abend rausgeworfen. Er kam einfach mit Rupes aus England hereingeschneit, sturzbesoffen wie immer, und hat mich angebettelt, ihn wiederaufzunehmen. Ehrlich gesagt war es eine ziemliche Genugtuung, ihm zu sagen, dass er verschwinden soll. Wahrscheinlich hat er die Nacht irgendwo zwischen den Weinreben verbracht. Mein Gott, Helena, er hat schauderhaft gerochen.« Jules rümpfte die Nase. »Er braucht wirklich Hilfe, aber zum Glück bin nicht mehr ich diejenige, die ihn dazu überreden muss.«

»Nein.« Helena hörte ihr nur mit halbem Ohr zu. Vor Erleichterung, dass Alex wohlbehalten bei William in England war, hätte sie am liebsten laut geschrien.

»Wir fahren also in zwei Tagen. Ich habe ein wirklich hübsches Cottage gefunden, ganz in der Nähe von Rupes' neuer Schule. Zugegeben, es ist gemietet und nicht ganz das, was wir gewöhnt sind, aber ich habe schon bei den Immobilienmaklern in der Umgebung die Fühler ausgestreckt und ein paar Vorstellungsgespräche vereinbart. Es wird mir guttun, wieder zu arbeiten. Und Viola kommt in die staatliche Schule, die auch sehr gut ist.«

»Ich dachte, es gefällt dir hier so gut?«

»Das stimmt auch, Helena, aber ehrlich gesagt, das wäre doch eine Flucht. Und ich muss an die Kinder denken.«

»Ja, das stimmt«, pflichtete Helena ihr bei. »Ich … Wirst du ihnen sagen, dass Alex Sachas Sohn ist?«

»Nein. Ich glaube, die beiden haben im Moment schon genug, mit dem sie fertigwerden müssen. Außerdem ist es Sachas Aufgabe, ihnen das zu sagen, obwohl er sich bestimmt davor drückt. Dafür ist er viel zu feige. Und jetzt«, meinte Jules mit einem Seufzen, »muss ich mich verabschieden. Danke für deine Unterstützung den ganzen Sommer über, Helena. Und vielleicht können wir ja jetzt, wo alle Karten auf dem Tisch liegen, wirklich Freundinnen werden? Lass von dir hören, wenn du wieder in England bist, ja?«

»Ja, aber natürlich. Obwohl mir schleierhaft ist, wo ich wohnen werde«, sagte Helena.

»Ach, da würde ich mir an deiner Stelle keine Sorgen machen«, sagte Jules beim Aufstehen leichthin. »Im Gegensatz zu Sacha liebt William dich viel zu sehr, um dich gehen zu lassen. Bis bald, *ciao*.«

Alex' Tagebuch

14. August 2006

Also, das war mal ein Abenteuer, anders kann ich das nicht nennen.

In den vergangenen vierundzwanzig Stunden ist aus mir, einem unbekannten, schwabbeligen Dreizehnjährigen ohne besondere Merkmale, ein Dieb und Ausreißer geworden, der in ganz Europa auf der Vermisstenliste steht.

Ob sie wohl Interpol eingeschaltet haben? Das hoffe ich doch sehr, das würde sich nämlich gut in meiner späteren Biografie machen.

Nachdem mir einmal klar geworden war, wie ich zwei Fliegen mit einer Klappe schlagen kann, ging alles sehr flott. Ich wusste, wo Mum meinen Pass aufhebt und auch ihre Debitkarte und einen Stapel zypriotischer Pfund. Dann habe ich das Taxiunternehmen angerufen, das sie immer nimmt, und einen sehr netten Fahrer erwischt, der auch etwas Englisch sprach, um mich zum Flughafen nach Paphos zu bringen. Unterwegs zog ich eine richtige Schau ab, dass ich wegen eines Notfalls dringend nach England fliegen müsse – als Ausrede habe ich die Gesundheit meiner bereits verstorbenen Oma, Gott hab sie selig, angeführt –, und als wir am Flughafen ankamen, war ich beinahe selbst davon überzeugt, dass sie nur noch wenige Stunden zu leben hätte. Und der Taxifahrer allemal.

Am Flughafen drückte ich ihm ein dickes Trinkgeld

in die Hand und fragte ihn, ob er mir helfen könne, am Schalter von Cypriot Airways ein Ticket für den nächsten Flug nach England zu kaufen, da ich kein Griechisch sprach. Ich sagte ihm auch, dass mein Vater, den ich dort treffen sollte, mir gerade gesimst habe, dass er sich verspäten werde und ich das Ticket schon mal ohne ihn kaufen solle. Ich hatte mich nämlich kundig gemacht, dass Kinder über zwölf bei den meisten Fluglinien allein fliegen können, bei anderen aber in Begleitung eines Erwachsenen sein müssen.

Dann spielte mir das Schicksal in die Hand. Vor dem Check-in-Schalter kam ich mit einer lieben alten Dame ins Gespräch, die vor mir in der Schlange stand. Ich hob für sie den Koffer auf die Waage und half ihr, als sie mit ihren knochigen, tattrigen Händen in einer Plastikmappe nach ihrem Ticket und Pass suchte. Die reichte ich der Dame am Schalter zusammen mit meinen Dokumenten, und so bekamen wir Sitzplätze nebeneinander. Während des langen Wartens in der Abflughalle freundeten wir uns dann richtig an, und beim Boarding verwendete ich denselben Trick, zeigte unsere Pässe gemeinsam vor und gab allen zu verstehen, dass ich mich um meine Begleiterin kümmerte. Die sie hoffentlich für eine ältere Verwandte von mir hielten. Omas – ob tot, im Sterben liegend oder lebendig – spielten eindeutig eine wichtige Rolle bei meiner Flucht nach England.

Nachdem wir unsere Sitzplätze eingenommen hatten, schlief meine »Leihoma« neben mir zum Glück sofort ein. Und so hatte ich auf dem Heimflug genügend Zeit zum Nachdenken. Über Dinge, über die ich nie zuvor nachgedacht hatte.

Bei meiner lebenslangen besessenen Suche nach meinem wahren Genpool hatte ich nicht gesehen, was direkt vor meiner Nase lag.

Und so bin ich jetzt wieder in England.

Ich bin meinetwegen hergekommen. Und ihretwegen.

Mir steht das wichtigste Gespräch meines bisherigen Lebens bevor.

Ich muss retten, was zu retten ist.

Weil ich meine Mutter liebe.

Und

meinen Vater.

Kapitel 29

William stellte den Wasserkocher an, um eine Kanne Tee zu machen, und starrte zum Küchenfenster hinaus auf den Garten. In einer Ecke standen Immys und Freds Schaukeln und das Klettergerüst. Freds geliebte Wasserpistole – fast so groß wie er – lag noch genau dort, wo er sie beim letzten Mal hatte fallen lassen.

Sie hatten Cedar House am Rand des Bilderbuchorts Beaulieu in Hampshire kurz vor ihrer Hochzeit in mehr oder minder baufälligem Zustand gekauft. Und ganz allmählich hatten er und Helena wieder Leben in das alte Gemäuer gebracht. Das war kurz nach seiner Scheidung gewesen und bevor er mit seinem Architekturbüro wirklich Erfolg hatte. Viel Geld hatten sie damals nicht gehabt, um das eher strenge und dunkle Backsteinhaus aus dem frühen 20. Jahrhundert in etwas Besonderes zu verwandeln, aber zum Glück stand das Haus nicht unter Denkmalschutz, sodass sie nach Belieben Änderungen vornehmen konnten. Er hatte für die Küche einen großen, hellen Anbau mit breiter Glasfront entworfen, der direkt auf die Terrasse und in den Garten hinausführte. Zudem hatte er zwischen den kleinen, dunklen Räumen mehrere Wände eingerissen, sodass mehr Licht einfallen konnte. Und nachdem einmal die Umbauten abgeschlossen waren, hatte Helena mit der Inneneinrichtung wahre Wunder gewirkt. Sie besaß großes Geschick, Farben und Stoffe zu kombinieren und die richtigen Möbel zu wählen, die sie im Lauf der Jahre auf Flohmärkten und bei verschiedenen Auslandsreisen immer wieder ergänzt hatte. Und so war es ihnen gelungen, einen Bau aus Ziegeln und Zement in ein wunderschönes, behagliches Zuhause zu verwandeln.

William schauderte. Sonst war er immer so stolz auf das, was sie hier geschaffen hatten, aber heute kam es ihm trostlos vor.

Aus dem Kühlschrank holte er die Milch, die er unterwegs an einer Tankstelle gekauft hatte. An der Kühlschranktür waren unzählige Zeichnungen von Immy und Fred mit Magnethaltern befestigt. Er vermutete, dass er das Haus, wie schon bei der letzten Scheidung, verlieren würde. Entweder würde Helena es bekommen, oder es würde an eine glücklichere Familie verkauft werden. Bei dem Gedanken zog sich ihm das Herz noch mehr zusammen.

»Tee, Alex!«, rief er nach oben.

»Komme, Dad!«, rief Alex zurück.

William durchquerte die Küche, öffnete die Terrassentür und trat in die Sonne hinaus. Im Halbschatten ließ er sich auf der schmiedeeisernen Bank nieder, die fast völlig von der uralten Glyzinie überwuchert war, daneben lag ein Beet duftender Rosen. In Abwesenheit ihrer Gärtnerin waren sie während des Sommers kräftig gewachsen, blühten üppig und mussten dringend beschnitten werden.

»Danke, Dad.« Alex setzte sich mit einem Becher Tee neben ihn.

»Komisches Gefühl, wieder zu Hause zu sein, oder?«

»Ja«, sagte Alex zustimmend. »Weil es so still ist. Mir ist erst heute klar geworden, wie laut wir alle sind.«

»Du bist nach deiner Odyssee bestimmt müde.«

»Eigentlich nicht. Irgendwie war's … aufregend.«

»Also, bitte mach das nicht noch mal. So schnell bin ich in

meinem ganzen Leben noch nie gefahren. Ich bin hier gerade mal zehn Minuten vor dir angekommen.«

»Du warst in der Wohnung in London, als die Polizei kam?«, fragte Alex.

»Ja. Als sie bei mir vor der Tür standen, habe ich ehrlich gesagt das Schlimmste befürchtet. Sie sagten, du seist in der Abendmaschine nach Gatwick gewesen, die kurz vor Mitternacht gelandet sei. Aber wohin du dann bist, wussten sie nicht.«

»'tschuldigung.«

»Schon in Ordnung. Ich dachte mir, dass du hierherkommen würdest.«

»Na ja, hätte ich gewusst, dass du in London bist, wäre ich gleich zu dir gefahren. So musste ich die Nacht am Bahnhof Waterloo verbringen, der letzte Zug nach Beaulieu war schon lange weg. Das war ganz schön gruselig«, sagte Alex. »Lauter Betrunkene und dazwischen ich.«

»Das glaube ich sofort.«

Schweigend tranken sie ihren Tee.

»Wie geht's Mum?«, fragte Alex schließlich.

»Besser, jetzt, wo sie weiß, dass dir nichts passiert ist, aber sie war völlig aufgelöst.«

»Es war auch ziemlich gemein von mir, aber ich hatte meine Gründe«, sagte Alex.

»Wie ging es ihr denn, nachdem ich weg war?«, fragte William vorsichtig.

»Grauenhaft. Sie kam zu mir, um mir alles zu erklären. Hat mir erzählt, was passiert ist, als ich zur Welt kam. Hast du gewusst, dass sie nach meiner Geburt fast gestorben wäre?«

»Nein, das habe ich nicht gewusst, aber ich bin auch nicht lange genug geblieben, um mir alles anzuhören.«

»Glaubst du, dass Mum ein schlechter Mensch ist?«

»Nein, eigentlich nicht.«

»Und dass sie dich ›belogen und betrogen‹ hat?«

William schaute zu Alex. »Du hast alles mitgehört?«

»Ja. Tut mir leid.«

»Nein, natürlich glaube ich das im Grunde nicht. Ich war nur … wütend. Wahnsinnig wütend. Und das bin ich immer noch.«

»Ich war auch sauer. Megasauer. Aber mittlerweile habe ich mich beruhigt.« Alex nickte.

»Wie das?«

»Weil ich's verstehen kann.«

»Du kannst verstehen, dass deine Mutter dich und mich jahrelang angelogen hat?«

»Also, fairerweise muss man sagen, sie hat mich nicht angelogen, sie hat … es mir einfach nicht gesagt.«

»Da magst du recht haben.«

»Als ich im Flugzeug saß, habe ich mir überlegt, was ich an ihrer Stelle getan hätte«, erinnerte sich Alex.

»Und?«

»Ich glaube, ich hätte auch gelogen. Was hättest du denn gemacht?«

William zuckte mit den Schultern. »Das weiß ich wirklich nicht.«

»Aber darum geht's doch, oder? Es weiß doch niemand, was er in einer bestimmten Situation tun würde, bis …«, er zuckte die Achseln, »bis er selbst drinsteckt.«

»Wahrscheinlich.« William seufzte. »Aber das spielt nun keine Rolle mehr. Es tut mir leid, dir das sagen zu müssen, Alex, aber ich habe deiner Mutter mitgeteilt, dass ich die Scheidung einreiche.«

»Schon in Ordnung. Kann ich verstehen.«

»Wirklich?«

»Doch, obwohl es irgendwie schade ist. Du liebst Mum, und sie liebt dich auch, sehr sogar. Und was Immy und Fred betrifft, na ja, für sie wird es auch nicht so toll sein. Aber ich kann's verstehen. Mir würde es an deiner Stelle vielleicht genauso gehen.« Alex stieß mit der Spitze seiner Turnschuhe gegen das Moos, das zwischen den Steinplatten wuchs. »Ich meine, bei uns Männern … das hat auch etwas mit verletztem Stolz zu tun, oder?«

»Na, ein bisschen sicher«, räumte William ein.

»Ziemlich viel sogar, wenn du es dir genau überlegst, Dad. Ich meine, das ist doch alles passiert, lange bevor ihr euch kennengelernt habt. Seit ihr verheiratet seid, hat Mum doch nicht mit einem anderen rumgemacht oder etwas anderes ganz Schlimmes angestellt, oder?«

»Meines Wissens nicht, nein. Allerdings ist es gut möglich, dass sie sich immer wieder mit … *ihm* getroffen hat. Womöglich liebt sie ihn noch, wer weiß?« William war überrascht, ein solches Gespräch mit einem Dreizehnjährigen zu führen.

»Wenn sie mit ihm zusammen sein wollte, meinst du nicht, dass sie dich dann schon längst verlassen hätte? Nein.« Alex schüttelte entschieden den Kopf. »Sie liebt nicht ihn, sie liebt *dich*.«

»Aber die Tatsache bleibt bestehen, dass sie mich unsere ganze Ehe hindurch angelogen hat, Alex.«

»Na ja, wir wissen doch beide, weshalb. Dad?« Er sah zu ihm. »Liebst du sie?«

»Das weißt du doch.«

»Warum lässt du dich dann von ihr scheiden?«

»Alex«, William seufzte ungeduldig. »Ich weiß, dass du sehr reif bist für dein Alter, aber wirklich, es gibt Dinge, die kannst du noch nicht verstehen.«

»Gut, mir ist klar, du hast die Möglichkeit, dich von meiner

Mutter scheiden zu lassen. Ich habe die nicht. Ich muss mich für den Rest meines Lebens mit ihr abfinden. Jetzt erklär mir doch mal, warum es für dich schlimmer ist als für mich? Ich muss obendrein damit zurechtkommen, dass Sacha mein leiblicher Vater ist.«

»Ich weiß.«

»Und dass er Mum sitzen gelassen hat, als sie schwanger war. Außerdem, gestern habe ich mir überlegt …«

»Ja?«

»Na ja, ich habe Mum sagen hören, dass er ihr erzählt hat, er hieße Alexander Nicholls.«

»Offenbar. Aber ehrlich gesagt heißt er ja eigentlich auch so.«

»Aber absolut jeder kennt ihn doch als Sacha Chandler. Und zwar immer schon. Warum sollte er das gemacht haben?«

»Das weiß ich nicht, Alex, wirklich«, sagte William und seufzte. »Vielleicht wollte er sich ein Künstler-Ego zulegen.«

»Also, ich glaube eher, dass er das bewusst gemacht hat, um Mum zu täuschen. Immerhin war er zu der Zeit schon mit Jules verheiratet. Ehrlich, wie hätte Mum da wissen sollen, dass er derselbe Mann ist wie dein ältester Freund? Bis sie es dann eben wusste.«

»Ich weiß, was du meinst, Alex, aber sie hätte es mir sagen sollen, sobald sie es wusste. Die Sache ist, sie hat mir nicht vertraut. Und um ehrlich zu sein, das hat sie nie.«

»Vielleicht nicht, aber ich bin mir nicht sicher.« Alex seufzte. »Vielleicht fällt es ihr einfach schwer, Menschen zu vertrauen. Ihre Kindheit war ja offenbar nicht so toll. Eine Mutter, die sie im Grunde nicht haben wollte. Sie war ganz auf sich allein gestellt.«

»Ja. Dem Wenigen nach zu urteilen, was sie erzählt hat, war es nicht schön.«

Eine Weile verfielen beide in Schweigen.

»Weißt du, was das Schlimmste ist?«, fragte Alex schließlich und sah zu William. »Dass Rupes mein Halbbruder ist! Das finde ich wirklich grenzwertig. Es macht mich ganz fertig, dass wir Blutsverwandte sind. Aber so ist es eben.«

»Gene sind was Komisches, Alex.«

»Ja, schon, aber wie gesagt, ich kann mich nicht von meiner Mutter scheiden lassen, also muss ich mich mit ihr abfinden. *Und* damit, dass Sacha mein leiblicher Vater ist. Du magst ja wütend sein, dass dein bester Freund eine Affäre mit Mum hatte, aber das war immerhin, bevor ihr euch kennengelernt habt. Und die Tatsache, dass er dein bester Freund ist – oder war –, heißt doch, dass auch gute Seiten haben muss. Und nur, weil ihr den gleichen Frauengeschmack habt, dadurch ist Sacha doch nicht über Nacht zu einem anderen Menschen geworden, oder? Er ist immer noch derselbe wie früher. Und Mum auch. Der einzige Unterschied ist, dass du – und ich – jetzt das Geheimnis kennen.«

Langsam drehte William sich zu ihm und schüttelte den Kopf. »Wie kommt es, dass du so klug bist?«

»Meine Gene. Oder – vielleicht auch nicht.« Alex lachte kurz auf.

»Wirst du ihn jetzt sehen wollen?«, fragte William.

»Du meinst, als meinen *Vater*? Eine Vater-Sohn-Beziehung zu ihm aufbauen und das alles?«

»Ja.«

»Keine Ahnung. Das muss ich mir überlegen. Im Moment hasse ich ihn für das, was er Mum angetan hat, aber vielleicht sehe ich das anders, wenn ich die ganze Sache erst einmal verdaut habe. Aber«, sagte Alex und seufzte, »das ist eigentlich völlig unwichtig. War es immer schon, bloß habe ich das erst jetzt herausgefunden.«

»Was meinst du damit?«

»Na ja … weißt du noch damals, als ich kopfüber vom Klettergerüst gefallen bin, und du bist wie ein Wahnsinniger mit mir ins Krankenhaus gerast?« Alex deutete auf den unteren Teil des Gartens.

»Aber natürlich. Mum war schwanger mit Immy. Als sie das ganze Blut sah, das aus deinem Kopf geschossen ist, dachte ich, dass gleich die Wehen einsetzen.«

»Und als du mir das Fahrradfahren beigebracht hast? Du bist mit mir zum Tennisplatz unten an der Straße gegangen und hast die Stützräder abmontiert. Und dann bin ich im Kreis gefahren, und du hast mich am Fahrrad festgehalten und bist keuchend und schnaufend mit mir im Kreis gelaufen, bis du irgendwann losgelassen hast, und dann bin ich allein davongeeiert.«

»Daran erinnere ich mich auch, ja«, sagte William.

»Und damals, als ich beim Rugby nicht ins Jahrgangsteam gekommen bin und so geknickt war. Dann hast du mir erzählt, dass du einmal nicht ins Cricketteam der Schule aufgenommen wurdest und es dir da genauso elend ging, aber dass sie dich im nächsten Jahr dann doch genommen haben?«

»Ja.« William nickte.

»Dad?«

»Ja?«

»Weißt du, die Sache ist …« Alex schob seine Hand in Williams und drückte sie fest. »*Du* bist mein Dad.«

KAPITEL 30

Jules war gefahren, bald nachdem sie gehört hatte, dass Alex wohlbehalten bei William angekommen war, und Helena beschloss, sich mit den gerade gehörten Enthüllungen erst später auseinanderzusetzen. Auch wenn ihr Leben gerade in Trümmern lag, wichtig war nur, dass Alex in Sicherheit war.

Nachdem sie alle Beteiligten über die frohe Botschaft informiert hatte, ging sie nach oben duschen. Erfrischt rief sie dann bei Angelina an und bat sie, die Kleinen möglichst bald zurückzubringen. Sie sehnte sich nach ihren Stimmen. Die Stille im Haus erinnerte sie unablässig daran, was sie verloren hatte.

Sie legte sich in die Hängematte, selbst zum Denken war sie zu müde. Sie brauchte wirklich dringend Ruhe, um ihre Gedanken zu ordnen. Sie schloss die Augen und döste, das sanfte Schaukeln lullte sie ein. Dann hörte sie einen Wagen vorfahren, und in der Vermutung, dass es Angelina und die Kinder waren, stand sie auf. Sie war auf halber Höhe der Treppe angekommen, als Sacha um die Ecke bog.

»Hallo, Helena.«

»Was willst du?« Helena ging an ihm vorbei ins Haus.

»Ein Glas Wein genügt, aber ein Whisky wäre besser«, scherzte er und folgte ihr in die Küche. »Hier herrscht bestimmt eitel Sonnenschein, seit die Katze aus dem Sack ist, was? Ich war gerade im Haus, um mich von den Kindern zu verabschieden, und Jules hat mir erzählt, dass William jetzt Bescheid weiß.«

»Wenn du es so sehen willst. Man könnte aber auch sagen, dass ich die schlimmsten vierundzwanzig Stunden meines Lebens hinter mir habe. Alex ist verschwunden, und dass ihm nichts passiert ist, weiß ich erst seit einer Stunde.«

»Ich habe gehört, dass er bei William in England ist.«

»Ja.« Helena reichte ihm ein Glas Wein.

»Danke.« Er stürzte es hinunter und gab es ihr sofort zurück, damit sie nachschenkte.

»Also, was willst du hier?«, fragte sie etwas scharf.

»Liegt das nicht auf der Hand? Ich bin deinetwegen hier«, antwortete Sacha, ging zu ihr, während sie die Weinflasche in den Kühlschrank stellte, und legte ihr die Arme um die Taille. »Wo sind die Kinder?«

»Die kommen jeden Augenblick mit Angelina wieder.« Helena versuchte, sich seinem Griff zu entwinden. »Sacha! Lass mich los!«

»Wehr dich doch nicht gegen mich, Helena.« Er küsste sie auf den Nacken. »Auf diesen Moment warten wir doch seit Jahren, oder etwa nicht, meine Schöne?«

»Nein! Hör auf!« Sie riss sich von ihm los. »Ich habe keine Ahnung, wovon du redest.«

»Dir muss doch klar sein, was ich die ganzen Jahre über für dich empfunden habe, Helena. Immer musste ich dich mit William sehen, und dabei wünschte ich mir ständig, du würdest mir gehören. Erinnere dich an Wien – das war die schönste Zeit meines Lebens. Und jetzt steht uns nichts mehr im Weg, jetzt können wir endlich zusammen sein. Mein Engel, wir sind frei.« Er näherte sich ihr, doch sie wich zurück.

»Ich erinnere mich nur an einen Mann, der versprochen hatte, zu mir zurückzukehren, und der nie kam.«

»Bist du deswegen so wütend? Nach all den Jahren noch?

Dir sollte doch klar sein, weshalb ich nicht kommen konnte. Jules war schwanger, ich konnte sie ja wohl kaum im Stich lassen, oder? Aber ich habe nie aufgehört, an dich zu denken, keine Sekunde.«

»Und ich habe nie aufgehört, daran zu denken, dass du irgendwie vergessen hattest, deine Ehefrau zu erwähnen.«

»Das habe ich bestimmt getan, du wolltest es nur nicht hören.«

»Nein! Untersteh dich, mir solchen Unsinn aufzutischen! Du hast es mir nicht gesagt. Und obendrein habe ich nach deiner Abreise kein Wort mehr von dir gehört.«

»Aber ich habe dir bestimmt geschrieben und dir alles erklärt.«

»Ach, Sacha, Himmel noch mal.« Helena schloss die Kühlschranktür mit einem Knall. »Du bist erbärmlich, wirklich.«

»Du liebst William doch nicht, Helena, sei ehrlich. Er war eine Notlösung.«

»Deine Meinung interessiert mich nicht.«

»Lässt er sich scheiden? Darauf würde ich wetten. Der gute alte Will, anständig und rechtschaffen bis auf die Knochen. Weiß Gott, weshalb er mich je als seinen besten Freund bezeichnet hat. Gegensätzlicher könnten wir gar nicht sein.« Er lallte leicht.

»Halt den Mund, Sacha. Ich werde ihn immer lieben, ob wir nun zusammen sind oder nicht.«

»Und Alex? Was ist mit ihm? Er ist immerhin mein Sohn. Bis jetzt habe ich mich ja von ihm ferngehalten, aus offensichtlichen Gründen, aber jetzt würde ich ihn gern besser kennenlernen.«

»Ich …« Helena zwang sich, ihre Wut zu zügeln. »Ich wüsste es sehr zu schätzen, wenn du darauf verzichten würdest, dich

494

bei Alex zu melden. Wenn er dich näher kennenlernen möchte, ist das seine Entscheidung.«

»Er ist mein Sohn. Ich kann tun und lassen, was ich will.«

Am liebsten hätte Helena mit der Faust ausgeholt, um ihm in das egoistische, aufgedunsene Gesicht zu schlagen, aber ihr war klar, dass es nichts brachte, ihn zu reizen.

»Also gut, dann bitte ich dich, ihn zumindest so lange in Ruhe zu lassen, bis er die ganzen Neuigkeiten etwas verarbeiten konnte. Darum bitte ich dich auch um unserer Familie willen. Wenn du es schon nicht meinetwegen tust, dann deinem ältesten Freund zuliebe, der sich entsetzlich betrogen und hintergangen fühlt.«

»Du stellst dich also immer noch schützend vor ihn.« Sacha applaudierte spöttisch. »Guter Auftritt, Helena. Du hast dich doch immer schon als Inbegriff der Vollkommenheit gesehen. Ich muss Jules natürlich die Wahrheit sagen.«

»Nur zu, sie weiß sie sowieso schon«, sagte Helena leichthin.

Sacha war wie vom Donner gerührt. »Woher?«

»Bei der Hochzeit war es ihr auf den ersten Blick klar. Sie sagt, Alex habe deine Augen.«

»Scheiße! Das wusste ich nicht.« Abrupt ließ Sacha sich auf einen Stuhl fallen. »Sie hat nie ein Wort darüber verloren.«

»Nein. Ehrlich gesagt ist deine Frau ziemlich erstaunlich. Sie hat dich genug geliebt, um über unsere Affäre hinwegzusehen und offenbar über mehrere andere auch. Im Grunde unvorstellbar.«

»Tja, jetzt komme ich mir wie ein richtiger Schuft vor. Wahrscheinlich stimmst du ihr da zu?«

Helena wollte sich von ihm nicht kriegen lassen. »Ich glaube, ich bin heute ein ganz anderer Mensch als damals in Wien. Das Problem ist, du bist noch ganz genau derselbe.«

Sacha fuhr sich durch die fettigen rotbraunen Locken. »Willst du mir damit sagen, dass du, auch wenn du ungebunden wärst, es nicht wieder mit mir versuchen wolltest?«

Helena musste sich zusammenreißen, um nicht hysterisch loszulachen. »Die Frage kann ich dir mit einem klaren Nein beantworten. Ich habe dir gesagt, ich liebe William. Ich habe ihn immer geliebt, punktum. Und selbst wenn nicht, würde ich trotzdem Nein sagen. Tut mir leid.«

»Komm schon, mein Engel, du bist doch nur noch so wütend, weil ich damals nicht zu dir zurückgekommen bin.«

»Sacha, du kannst denken, was du magst, aber für dich und mich gibt es keine Zukunft, weder jetzt noch später. Verstanden?«

»Ich höre, was du sagst«, antwortete er mit einem Nicken. »Es ist einfach noch zu früh. Ich hätte ein paar Tage warten sollen, bevor ich zu dir komme. Du stehst noch unter Schock.« Er stand auf. »So leicht gebe ich dich nicht auf, meine Schöne, glaub mir.«

»Tu, was du nicht lassen kannst, Sacha«, sagte sie matt. »Aber glaub mir, du bemühst dich umsonst. Du hast einen Sohn und eine Tochter, ganz zu schweigen von einer Ehefrau, deren Leben du gerade kaputt gemacht hast. Vielleicht wäre es für dich an der Zeit, endlich erwachsen zu werden und Verantwortung für sie zu übernehmen. Und für dich.«

»Also gut, Helena. Aber ich wette, sobald du zwei Wochen mutterseelenallein dasitzt, änderst du deine Meinung. Ohne Mann hältst du es doch nicht lange aus – ist nicht dein Stil, stimmt's?«

Helena ignorierte seine Gehässigkeit. »Ich glaube, es ist Zeit, dass du gehst.«

»Ich gehe ja schon.« Schwankend ging er zur Tür, blieb aber

noch einmal stehen und drehte sich um. Plötzlich wirkte er sehr reuevoll. »Verzeih mir, mein Engel, bitte.«

»Das habe ich schon vor langer Zeit.«

»Du musst wissen, ich liebe dich. Wirklich.«

»Leb wohl, Sacha. Ich wünsche dir alles Gute.«

Sie sah ihn mit unsicheren Schritten zu seinem Wagen gehen und einsteigen. »Ich glaube nicht, dass du Auto fahren solltest!«, rief sie ihm nach, doch die Warnung stieß auf taube Ohren. Die Wagentür fiel ins Schloss, und wenig später fuhr Sacha schlingernd den Berg hinauf.

Eine Woge der Erleichterung durchflutete Helena.

Was immer die Zukunft bringen mochte, mit der Vergangenheit hatte sie nun endgültig abgeschlossen.

Alex' Tagebuch

Ich habe Dad allein gelassen, damit er in Ruhe über alles nachdenken kann.

Nach unserem kleinen Gespräch wurde er sehr still.

Dann sagte er, er müsse Rasen mähen. Ich sah ihm von meinem Zimmer aus zu. Stundenlang saß er auf seinem kostbaren Gefährt, drehte in unserem Garten eine Runde nach der anderen, um noch dem letzten Grashalm einen Bürstenschnitt zu verpassen. Zum ersten Mal überhaupt empfand ich Mitleid mit dem Rasen. Dann kam Dad wieder ins Haus. Jetzt ist er irgendwo unten, aber ich habe das Gefühl, dass ich ihn nicht stören sollte. Draußen wird es langsam dunkel, und im Haus ist es still. Daran bin ich nicht gewöhnt, und es gefällt mir gar nicht.

Ich wünschte, er würde sich beeilen mit seiner Entscheidung, was er tun will.

Scheiden oder nicht scheiden lassen, das ist hier die Frage.

Dann könnte ich nämlich endlich nach unten gehen und mir eine Nudelsuppe warm machen. Bechersuppen sind das Einzige, was im Schrank ist. Ich habe am Vormittag mal nachgesehen – und mittlerweile bin ich am Verhungern!

Um mir die Zeit zu vertreiben, denke ich darüber nach, was es mit Männern und Gefühlen auf sich hat. Die schreckliche Wahrheit ist, dass die meisten Vertreter meines Geschlechts wahrscheinlich lieber tot umfallen als zugeben würden, dass sie Angst haben. Dann denke ich an die Schützengräben im Ersten Weltkrieg und das ganze lebende Kanonenfutter. Die Typen haben zum Sturmangriff geblasen, dabei aber so getan, als würden sie bloß zu einem morgendlichen Spaziergang in die freie Natur aufbrechen:

Ich gehe jetzt, Sir!

In Ordnung, Jones, alles Gute. Und wenn Sie den großen Boss sehen, legen Sie bei ihm ein gutes Wort für mich ein, in Ordnung?

Verstanden, Sir! Auf Wiedersehen, Sir!

Und damit zieht Jones von dannen, um sich über den Haufen ballern zu lassen. Oder mit viel Glück minus einem Arm oder Bein zu überleben und mit einem Verstand, der genauso lädiert ist wie sein Körper.

Ich möchte weinen, wenn ich an die armen Kerle denke, die sehenden Auges in den Tod gingen. Fast hundert Jahre später schaudert mich beim bloßen Gedanken, denn ich weiß, wäre ich an ihrer Stelle gewesen, hätte ich mir vor Angst in die Hose gemacht und Rotz und Wasser geheult. Wahrscheinlich hätten sie mich vorher mit Drogen ins Koma befördern müssen, und dann hätten sie mich irgendwo als Zielscheibe für ihre Schießübungen ablegen können.

Was mich zu meinem gegenwärtigen gedanklichen Hauptproblem zurückbringt:

Was wollen Frauen von uns?

Ich denke an Chloë, die große Liebe meines (bisherigen) Lebens, die den hirntoten Rupes mit seiner Protzerei und seiner Ganzkörper-Neandertalerhaftigkeit anschwärmt und keinen Moment bezweifelt, dass er ein Wollmammut mit einem Streich töten, sich über die

Schulter werfen und in ihre elegant eingerichtete Wohnhöhle tragen könnte.

Dann (nach einer kurzen Fummelei mit dem Flughafen-Typen) wendet sie ihre ganze Aufmerksamkeit im Handumdrehen »Michelle« zu. Der ist zwar ein netter Kerl, aber so, wie er mit seinem Moped immer den Kies spritzen lässt, ist er seinem mädchenhaften Namen zum Trotz jemand, den man durchaus als Macho und als Macker bezeichnen kann – während ich in der M-Kategorie höchstens als Memme durchgehe.

Ich bin ein gefühlsbetonter Mann. Und meine Gefühle würde ich Chloë nur zu gern zeigen, aber nicht bloß körperlich, sondern auch emotional.

Bin ich, weil ich mit anderen mitempfinde, unattraktiv?

Andererseits ... sämtliche meiner Informationsquellen zu diesem Thema – insbesondere ein Artikel mit der Überschrift »Die fünf wichtigsten Scheidungsgründe« (Copyright *The Daily Mail*), den ich gestern auf dem Heimflug las – bringen mich zu der Überzeugung, dass sich Frauen einen Mann wünschen, der sie emotional versteht.

So ähnlich, wie Sadie das mit Mum macht. Sprich, ihr Mann soll gleichzeitig ihre beste Freundin sein.

Aber wie können wir Männer beides sein? Wie können wir die wesentlichen Eigenschaften des Mannes und der Frau gleichzeitig verkörpern?

Ich habe den Eindruck, dass Frauen im Grunde nicht wissen, was sie wollen. Was bedeutet, dass wir Männer es ihnen nie recht machen können.

Und Dad ist zweifellos ein Mann durch und durch ...

Also hoffentlich, denke ich mir mit einem tiefen Seufzer, weiß wenigstens Mum, was sie will.

Und hoffentlich hat Dad verstanden, was ich sagen wollte. Zumindest denkt er darüber nach – das schließe ich aus der Zeit, die er auf seinem Rasenmäher gesessen hat. Er denkt nach über Mum und mich, über Immy und Fred und, hoffe ich, auch über Chloë.

Unsere Familie.

Sie mag ja etwas unorthodox sein, aber deswegen ist sie nicht schlecht oder falsch.

Wir sind die beste Familie, die ich kenne. Auf der Heimreise habe ich mir überlegt, wie viel Spaß wir miteinander haben. Wie viel wir lachen. Und wie sehr ich ihn liebe – meinen Dad. Erst mit einem »richtigen« ist mir klar geworden, wie schrecklich mir dieser sogenannte Ersatz-Dad fehlen würde, wenn er plötzlich nicht mehr da wäre.

Was durchaus möglich ist.

Wenn er sich für das Scheidungsszenario entscheidet.

Er hat mich die ganze Zeit wie seinen eigenen Sohn behandelt. Er hat mich weder bevorzugt noch benachteiligt. Gelegentlich findet er es schwierig, wenn ich eine meiner Launen habe, aber das hat nichts damit zu tun, dass ich nicht von ihm abstamme, sondern damit, dass ich sein Sohn bin und nervig sein kann. Und das nervt ihn, wie es jeden Vater nerven würde.

Er – William – ist nicht vollkommen. Er hat seine Macken. Wie alle Menschen, weil wir unvollkommen sind. Einschließlich meiner Mum.

Aber sie ist mehr gut als schlecht, ebenso wie er. Mehr kann man wahrscheinlich gar nicht erhoffen. Mir ist nämlich klar geworden, dass wir alle uns irgendwo auf einer Skala befinden, die an einem Ende schwarz und am anderen weiß ist. Die meisten von uns liegen irgendwo in der Mitte und tendieren mit sehr kleinem Spielraum in die eine oder andere Richtung.

Und solange sich keiner von uns zu sehr einem Extrem nähert, glaube ich, dass wir im Grunde ganz in Ordnung sind. Und ich und Mum und Dad und sogar Sacha und der verhasste Rupes (zumindest im Moment) treiben sich irgendwo in dieser Mitte herum.

Im Geiste füge ich die zerbrochene Statue meiner Mutter wieder zusammen, verzichte aber auf den Sockel. Von jetzt an steht sie auf ihren eigenen Beinen. Auf der Erde, weder Heilige noch Sünderin.

Ein Mensch, genau wie mein Dad.

Und wenn – falls, sollte ich sagen – er sich entschließt, seinen Stolz hinunterzuschlucken und meine Mutter zurückzunehmen, werde ich ihn fragen, ob er mich nicht adoptieren will. Dann machen wir das Ganze legal, und als Zeichen meiner Achtung und meiner Liebe nehme ich seinen Nachnamen an und bin dann – falls ich vorher nicht verhungere, ich habe nämlich seit gestern im Flugzeug nichts mehr gegessen – schließlich ein namentlich vollwertiges Mitglied unserer Familie.

»Alexander R. Cooke.«

Da habe ich also mein Leben lang nach etwas gesucht, von dem ich glaubte, es zu wollen, und jetzt habe ich es bekommen und will es nicht. Absolut überhaupt gar nicht.

Ich will nur das wiederhaben, was wir hatten.

Oh! Dad klopft an die Tür. Die Spannung steigt.

»Komm rein.«

Er steckt den Kopf zur Tür herein. »Hast du Hunger?«, fragt er.

»Und wie«, sage ich.

»Gehen wir zum Inder?«

»Klar, wieso nicht?«

»Ich dachte, solange wir die Möglichkeit haben, sollten wir die englische Küche genießen«, erklärt er.

»Wieso?«

Kurz schaut er beiseite, dann lächelt er und sieht wieder zu mir. »Weil wir morgen ins Land von Feta und Fischdreckpampe zurückfliegen. Ich habe gerade unseren Flug gebucht.«

KAPITEL 31

Es war ein weiterer strahlender Tag. Beim Aufwachen stellte Helena mit Erstaunen fest, dass sie gut geschlafen hatte. Und noch mehr erstaunte sie ihre innere Ruhe.

Sie stand auf, zog ihr Trikot und die Ballettschuhe an und ging auf die Terrasse. Sie begann mit den *pliés*, ihr Körper vollführte die Bewegungen von ganz allein, sodass sie den Kopf frei hatte, um nachzudenken.

Ihre Rückkehr in dieses Haus – Pandora ... Ihre innere Stimme hatte sie nicht getrogen. Die Büchse war tatsächlich geöffnet worden, alles Verstaubte, was sie geborgen hatte, war aus den dunklen Winkeln gewirbelt worden und hatte Chaos und Schmerz verursacht. Doch wie in dem alten Mythos blieb eines zurück: die Hoffnung. Es gab keine Geheimnisse mehr, nichts mehr, das sie zu verstecken brauchte, keine Schatten, die sie heimsuchten. Was immer jetzt kommen würde – und Helena ahnte, wie schrecklich eine Welt ohne William sein würde –, zumindest würde es ehrlich sein. Von nun an würde sie mit der Wahrheit leben oder untergehen.

Um zehn Uhr, Helena saß gerade mit Immy und Fred bei einem späten Frühstück auf der Terrasse, kam Alexis.

»Hallo, Lexis«, sagte Fred. »Hast du mir was mitgebracht?«

»Fred!«, sagte Immy vorwurfsvoll. »Das fragt er jeden, der kommt, das ist sehr unhöflich.«

Alexis küsste Helena herzlich auf beide Wangen. »Wie geht es dir?«

»Viel besser. Hab vielen Dank für deine große Hilfe. Es tut mir leid, dass ich neulich so durch den Wind war.«

»Was immer ›durch den Wind‹ heißen mag – ich kann dich gut verstehen. Nicht zu wissen, wo das eigene Kind ist, ist entsetzlich«, sagte er mitfühlend.

»Kaffee, Alexis?«, fragte Immy, ganz die Gastgeberin, und hielt die Kanne hoch.

»Gern, Immy, ja.«

»Ich hole dir eine saubere Tasse aus der Küche«, beschied sie und kletterte von ihrem Stuhl.

»Ich auch.« Fred tappte hinter ihr her.

»Deine Kinder sind entzückend, Helena, wirklich.«

»Ausnahmsweise gebe ich dir recht. In den vergangenen vierundzwanzig Stunden waren sie wahre Engel.«

»Vielleicht wissen sie, dass ihre Mutter Engel um sich braucht.«

»Die brauche ich in der Tat, das stimmt.«

»Wann kommt Alex wieder?«

»Ich weiß es nicht. Ich habe ihm gestern Abend eine SMS geschickt und gefragt, ob ich nach Hause kommen soll. Er hat noch nicht geantwortet. Bestimmt ist er immer noch wütend auf mich. Aber wenigstens weiß ich, dass es ihm gut geht.«

»Das heißt, womöglich fährst du sehr bald?«

»Wenn Alex mich in England braucht, dann fahre ich natürlich.«

»Helena, bevor du fährst, gibt es etwas, das ich dir zeigen muss.«

Sie betrachtete seine ernste Miene. »Alexis, was ist?«

»Ich bin schon öfter gekommen, um es dir zu sagen, aber ...«

Er machte eine hilflose Geste. »Es war nie der richtige Moment. Ist Angelina hier?«

»Ja, sie macht oben die Betten.«

»Könnte sie kurz auf die Kinder aufpassen? Ich möchte dich kurz entführen. Keine Sorge, es ist nicht weit.«

»Alexis, keine schlechte Nachricht, bitte. Die könnte ich wirklich nicht ertragen«, stöhnte sie.

»Nein.« Beruhigend legte er ihr eine Hand auf die Schulter. »Es ist keine schlechte Nachricht, nur etwas, das du wissen musst. Vertrau mir.«

»Also gut. Ich rede nur kurz mit Angelina, dann können wir los.«

»Wo um alles in der Welt willst du mit mir hin?«, fragte sie ein paar Minuten später, als Alexis ihr voraus die Stufen zum Pool hinabging.

»Das wirst du gleich sehen.« Er überquerte die Poolterrasse und ging bis zum Holzzaun, der den Garten vom angrenzenden Olivenhain trennte. An diesem Zaun löste er einen verborgenen Haken und entfernte dann ein breites Brett.

»Ach, diese Pforte ist mir nie zuvor aufgefallen«, sagte sie.

»Das sollte sie auch nicht, sie ist geheim.«

»Wer hat sie denn angebracht?«, fragte sie, während sie Alexis zwischen den Bäumen hindurch folgte.

»Geduld, Helena, bitte.«

Beim Weitergehen mussten sie sich immer wieder unter den Ästen der dichten Bäume ducken, bis sie schließlich auf eine kleine Lichtung gelangten. Dort standen sie nebeneinander und betrachteten die Berge rings um sich, die Olivenbäume, die sich unter ihnen bis ins Tal hinabzogen, und in der Ferne den schmalen, glitzernden Streifen des Meeres.

»Und das wolltest du mir zeigen, Alexis?«

»Dies ist die Stelle, ja.« Er drehte sich leicht nach rechts. »Aber was ich dir wirklich zeigen wollte, ist das.«

Helena ging in die Richtung, in die er wies.

»Ach, wie schön«, sagte sie, als sie davor stand. »Das ist eine Statue der Aphrodite, oder nicht?«

»Nein, nicht ganz.«

Sie sah zu ihm. »Wer ist es denn dann, und weshalb steht sie hier?«

»Schau auf den Fuß der Statue, Helena. Lies den Namen, der dort steht.«

Sie bückte sich. »Ich kann die Schrift nicht lesen, sie ist zu stark verwittert.«

»Doch, das kannst du schon, versuch's noch mal.«

Helena entfernte das Laub, das sich um den kleinen Sockel gesammelt hatte, und rieb mit dem Finger über die Inschrift.

»Das ist ein I und ein E … und ein N … und der erste Buchstabe ist ein V … Ich …« Verwirrt sah sie zu Alexis. »Da steht ja ›Vivienne‹.«

»Ja.«

»Aber Vivienne, so hieß doch meine Mutter.«

»Genau.«

»Was soll das bedeuten? Soll das sie sein? Als Aphrodite?« Helena fuhr mit der Hand sacht über das Alabastergesicht.

»Ja.«

»Aber warum, Alexis? Und warum hier?«

»Angus ließ die Statue nach ihrem Tod anfertigen«, antwortete er. »Dies war, wie meine Großmutter Christina mir sagte, die Stelle, die deine Mutter hier am meisten liebte.«

»Aber …« Helena fasste sich verwundert an die Stirn. »Ich weiß, dass sie regelmäßig auf Zypern war und sehr gern hier-herkam, aber ich …« Sie sah zu Alexis, und plötzlich dämmerte ihr, was das alles zu bedeuten hatte. »Soll das heißen, dass Angus in meine Mutter verliebt war? Stimmt das?«

»Ja, Helena. Vivienne war sehr oft in Pandora zu Gast. Alle hier kannten sie.«

»Wirklich? Ach … das ist also der Grund, weshalb so viele Einheimische gesagt haben, dass ich sie an jemanden erinnere! Angeblich sehe ich ihr sehr ähnlich.«

»Das stimmt auch. Meine Großmutter konnte die Ähnlichkeit nicht fassen, als sie dich neulich hier in Pandora sah.«

»Ich habe sie auf den alten Fotos gesehen, die wir in dem kleinen Raum gefunden haben. Das heißt« – in Helenas Kopf wirbelten die Gedanken wild durcheinander –, »die ganzen Briefe, die Alex gefunden hat, waren an sie gerichtet? War sie die geheimnisvolle Frau?«

»Ja, das war sie.«

»Aber woher weißt du das alles?«

»Helena – Christina hat fast dreißig Jahre hier gearbeitet. Sie hat alles gesehen. Und die Briefe – die hat dein Vater an Angus zurückgeschickt.«

»Er wusste also Bescheid?«

»Zweifellos, wenn er die Briefe zurückschickte.«

»Also«, sagte Helena und versuchte, sich einen Reim zu machen auf alles, was Alexis ihr erzählte. »Ehrlich gesagt hatte ich als Kind nie den Eindruck, dass sich meine Eltern besonders nahestanden. Mein Vater hat immer mehr Zeit in Kenia verbracht, ich habe ihn nur selten gesehen.«

»Vielleicht kam das Arrangement ihnen beiden entgegen. Schließlich ist jede Ehe anders«, meinte Alexis.

»Aber warum sind Angus und meine Mutter nie zusammengekommen? Den Briefen nach zu urteilen hat er sie vergöttert.«

»Helena, wer weiß? Wir wissen doch beide, dass es viele Gründe gibt, weshalb Menschen, die sich lieben, nie zusammenfinden«, antwortete er leise.

Helena schaute auf die abgestorbenen Olivenblätter auf dem Erdboden. Sie nahm eines in die Hand und befühlte die raue Oberfläche.

»Angus hat mir alles hinterlassen.«

»Ja.«

»Ich war sein Patenkind.«

»Das stimmt. Und …«

»Was?«

»Christina hat sich immer gefragt, ob du vielleicht mehr warst als nur das.«

»Was willst du damit sagen?«

»Helena, ich glaube, das weißt du.«

»Ja, das stimmt«, flüsterte sie.

»Die Briefe wurden bald nach deiner Geburt zurückgeschickt. Meine Großmutter erinnert sich ganz genau daran, sie fand Angus weinend an seinem Schreibtisch sitzen. Und deine Mutter ist danach nie mehr hergekommen.«

»Aber ich bin gekommen. Und zwar …« Helena überlegte. »Das war wenige Monate nach dem Tod meines Vaters.«

»Vielleicht war das die Art deiner Mutter, ihm ihre Liebe zu zeigen – indem sie dich hierhergeschickt hat.«

»Aber warum ist sie nicht selbst gekommen?«

»Helena, das weiß ich nicht. Vielleicht glaubte sie, es wäre besser, das Feuer nicht wieder zu entfachen. Vielleicht entsprach das Leben auf Zypern ihr nicht, ebenso wenig, wie es dir entsprochen hätte.«

»Vielleicht … aber jetzt kann ich sie nie mehr fragen. Und auch nicht herausfinden, wer wirklich mein Vater war.«

»Ist das wichtig? Angus hat dich wie seine Tochter geliebt. Er hat dir Pandora geschenkt. Aber ich hoffe, das zeigt dir, dass jeder Mensch Geheimnisse hat, Helena. Niemand ist so, wie man glaubt.«

»Ja, da hast du recht. Hast du welche?«, fragte sie mit einem Lächeln.

»Nicht vor dir. Aber vor meiner Frau, ja. Sie wusste nicht, weshalb ich sie nicht so lieben konnte, wie ich sollte. Ich habe deswegen immer noch ein schlechtes Gewissen. Aber komm, lass uns zurückgehen.« Er bot ihr seinen Arm an.

»Danke, dass du mir das gezeigt hast«, sagte sie, während sie langsam zum Haus zurückkehrten.

»Jetzt wissen wir beide, was es heißt, eine Frau auf den Sockel zu stellen«, sagte er lachend.

»Und das«, sagte Helena und seufzte, »ist außerordentlich gefährlich.«

Nachdem sich Alexis verabschiedet hatte, ging Helena in die Küche, wo Immy und Fred am Küchentisch saßen. Sie setzte sich zu ihnen, noch ganz verwirrt von dieser neuerlichen Offenbarung.

»Du bist wieder da! Ich habe was mit Honig gemacht, das ist ganz klebrig und hat Sesamstraßennüsse obendrauf!«, sagte Immy.

»Ich hab aber auch geholfen, Immy!«, protestierte Fred.

»Mummy, du guckst ja ganz komisch. Bist du komisch?« Immy kletterte auf Helenas Schoß und schlang die Arme um sie.

»Mummy guckt komisch, guckt komisch!«, wiederholte Fred im Singsang und versuchte auch, sie zu umarmen. Sie hob ihn auf das Knie, das Immy nicht besetzt hatte, und drückte beide an sich.

»Wir haben dich lieb, Mummy«, sagte Immy und küsste sie auf die Wange. »Stimmt's nicht, Fred?«

»Doch, ganz doll!«, bekräftigte er.

»Und ich habe euch auch lieb.« Sie küsste die beiden auf ihre klebrigen Gesichter. »Was haltet ihr von der Idee, an den Strand zu fahren?«

»Au jaaaa!«, riefen sie unisono.

Am Spätnachmittag waren sie wieder in Pandora. Helena machte den Kindern Abendessen, badete sie, und dann durften sie im Salon die DVD von *Cinderella* sehen.

Schließlich setzte sie sich mit einem Glas Wein auf den Balkon. Bald würde die Sonne untergehen, obwohl es gerade erst nach sieben Uhr war.

Der Sommer neigte sich dem Ende zu.

Sie fragte sich, ob sie wohl hier leben könnte, nachdem sie in Cedar House nicht mehr willkommen war.

Aber die Antwort auf diese Frage war eindeutig Nein. Wie sie – und womöglich auch ihre Mutter vor ihr – bereits vor all den Jahren gewusst hatte, war ihr bestimmt, ihr Leben woanders zu verbringen.

Wo und mit wem und wie, das wusste sie noch nicht …

Das Gefühl von Einsamkeit schnürte ihr die Kehle zu, und die Abwesenheit ihres Mannes und ihres Sohnes schmerzte sie beinahe körperlich.

Sie ging ins Schlafzimmer, schloss die Balkontür hinter sich und duschte, dann setzte sie sich an die Kommode und bürstete sich das Haar.

Als sie die Bürste zurücklegte, fuhr sie mit den Fingern über die schnörkeligen Perlmutt-Intarsien auf dem Deckel der Schatulle, die Alexis vor der Müllkippe gerettet hatte.

»Die Büchse der Pandora«, flüsterte sie.

Und dann sah sie:

Fast unsichtbar war in die Verzierung ihr Initial mit dem ihrer Eltern verwoben.

Ungebeten traten ihr Tränen in die Augen.

Schließlich ging sie nach unten, um nach den Kindern zu sehen. Sie waren in *Cinderella* vertieft, und ohne sie zu stören, trat sie auf die Terrasse hinaus. Als aus den Schatten zwei Gestalten auftauchten, die die Treppe vom Pool heraufkamen, fuhr sie vor Schreck zusammen.

»Guten Abend, Mum. Dad und ich dachten, dass uns eine kurze Erfrischung nach dem Flug nicht schaden würde.«

»Alex!«

»Ja, ich bin's. Du darfst mich aber nicht umarmen, ich bin ganz nass.«

»Das ist mir egal.«

»Also gut.« Er ließ sich in ihre ausgebreiteten Arme fallen, und sie drückte ihn fest an sich.

»Wie geht es dir?«

»Gut. Sehr gut.« Er sah sie an, und das leuchtende Grün seiner Augen sagte ihr, dass er die Wahrheit sagte. »Ich hab dich lieb, Mum«, flüsterte er.

»Ich dich auch, Alex.«

»Wo sind die Kleinen?«

»Sie sehen sich im Salon eine DVD an.«

»Ich habe Chloë versprochen, es mal mit Disney zu versuchen. Bis später.«

Sie rief ihm nicht nach, er solle sich nicht so klatschnass, wie er war, auf das empfindliche Damastsofa setzen. Weil es völlig egal war.

»Guten Abend, Helena.«

Vor Beklommenheit brachte sie kein Wort hervor.

William stand vor ihr, ebenfalls tropfnass.

»Wie geht es dir?«, fragte er.

»Gut.«

»Wirklich? Warum weinst du dann?«

»Weil, wenn du nur hier bist, weil du Alex zurückbringen wolltest, und gleich wieder fahren willst … dann kann ich es nicht ertragen, dich zu sehen.«

»Nein. Aber darf ich zumindest diese Nacht hierbleiben? Immy und Fred sehen?«

»Ja«, willigte sie unglücklich ein. »Natürlich.«

»Und morgen vielleicht auch? Und übermorgen?«

»Ich …« Sie sah ihn an, wusste noch immer nicht so recht, was er meinte.

»Helena, du hast … *wir* haben einen unglaublich fabelhaften Sohn. Er … Alex hat mir den Weg gewiesen. Und der führt zu dir.«

»Ach ja?«

»Ja. Und …« William versagte die Stimme. »Ich will nie mehr weggehen. Ich liebe dich.«

»Und ich liebe dich, mein Schatz. Bitte glaub mir das.«

Sie standen da, drei Meter voneinander entfernt, und beide sehnten sich danach, die Distanz zwischen sich zu überwinden.

»Aber eins musst du mir versprechen, Helena: keine Geheimnisse mehr. Bitte sag mir jetzt, wenn es noch etwas gibt, das ich wissen müsste.«

»Also«, sagte sie langsam, »vorhin ist wirklich etwas passiert.«

»Ach ja?« Williams Gesicht versteinerte.

»Ja.« Sie nickte. »Und es ist ein großes Geheimnis. Vielleicht das allergrößte. Und …«

»Du lieber Himmel! Was?«

Sie lächelte, und ihre blauen Augen strahlten, als sie langsam auf ihn zuging.

»Ich kann es gar nicht erwarten, es dir zu erzählen.«

Alex' Tagebuch

Morgen fahren wir nach Hause.

Mit »wir« meine ich unsere Familie.

Wir lassen Pandora und ihre Büchse oder ihr Kästchen oder was auch immer hinter uns.

Mum hat mir alles darüber erzählt – über das Kästchen, meine ich. Und hat mir die Statue meiner nackten Oma in den Oliven gezeigt.

Auch wenn es moralisch verwerflich ist, aber alle Beteiligten sind tot. Außer meiner Mutter, die damit offenbar kein Problem hat, also darf man sie ruhig schön finden.

Jetzt haben wir eine Gemeinsamkeit, meine Mutter und ich. Das gefällt mir.

Außerdem habe ich mit einem Los gleich zwei Preise ergattert:

Finde heraus, wer dein Vater ist, den Opa gibt's gratis dazu!

Es freut mich, dass Angus und ich wahrscheinlich verwandt sind. Er war ein richtiger Mann, der sich ziemlich machomäßig aufgeführt hat, sprich, er hat im Krieg gekämpft und Heere kommandiert. Und gleichzeitig hat er geheult wie ein Mädchen und die große Liebe gefunden.

Jetzt habe ich noch jemand anderen, dem ich nacheifern kann, nicht nur meinen Vater.

Die Namensetikett-Macher sind instruiert worden, ebenso wie die Anwälte. Von jetzt an heißt es »Beaumont-

Cooke«. Ich habe beschlossen, Vater und Mutter zu ehren. Angesichts der Umstände kam mir das nur richtig vor, sonst hätte Mum sich vielleicht benachteiligt gefühlt.

Offiziell werden Dad und ich erst in ein paar Monaten unsere neue Verbindung eingehen, das heißt, zu Schulanfang trage ich meinen neuen Nachnamen noch unrechtmäßig.

Ich überlege, ob ich es bedauere, nach Hause zu fahren. Und komme zu dem Schluss: Nein.

Richtige Ferien habe ich zwar nicht gehabt, eher war das Ganze ein emotionaler, mentaler und körperlicher Hindernisparcours. Aber schließlich hat unsere gesamte Familie einen schweißtreibenden Workout absolviert, der uns hoffentlich alle für die Zukunft gestählt hat.

Gestern Abend habe ich dann auch lange mit meinen Eltern über die ganze anstehende Sache mit der Schule gesprochen. Wie sich herausstellt, hat Mum einen Riesenbammel davor, dass ich weggehe. Und Dad ist einfach richtig stolz darauf, dass ich das Stipendium bekommen habe, und hält es für eine großartige Chance.

Beide dachten, dass ich wirklich auf die Schule gehen will. Ich erklärte ihnen, dass ich dachte, sie wollten, dass ich gehe. Das Fazit ist: Ich gehe. Zumindest für das erste Halbjahr. Und wenn es mir gar nicht gefällt, darf ich jederzeit aufhören.

Und jetzt, wo ich weiß, dass sie an dem Abend, an dem ich und mein Koffer sich in meine neue Besenkammer begeben, in meinem leeren Zimmer keine Party für all ihre Freunde und Verwandten feiern, sehe ich das Ganze etwas entspannter. Jetzt ist mir klar, dass sie wirklich mein Bestes wollen.

Ich bin an und in den vergangenen Wochen tatsächlich gewachsen. Im wahrsten Sinn des Wortes.

Als Mum für die grausige Schuluniform, die sie für mich bestellt, ein letztes Mal Maß an mir nahm, war ich gut 1,65 m.

Tja, so frage ich mich, was habe ich in diesen Ferien gelernt?

Dass es verschiedene Arten von Liebe gibt, und zwar in allen möglichen Formen und Farben.

Man kann sie verdienen, aber nicht bezahlen.

Man kann sie geschenkt bekommen, aber nicht kaufen.

Und wenn sie wirklich einmal da ist, dann bleibt sie auch.

Dieses Liebe-Dingens.

Alex

───◆───

13. Juli 2016
Pandora

Ich blättere um und sehe, dass die restlichen Seiten des Tagebuchs leer sind – weiße Blätter, bar jeglicher Details aus meinem Leben.

Was künftige Leser des Tagebuchs betrifft, hätte ich am folgenden Tag sterben können.

Ich sehe auf meine Uhr und stelle fest, dass es hier auf Zypern mittlerweile Mitternacht ist. Mit dem Tagebuch in der Hand gehe ich ins Haus zurück und schließe hinter mir sorgfältig die Läden. Diese schlichte Handlung erinnert mich daran, wie viel sich seit meinem letzten Aufenthalt hier verändert hat: Jetzt bin ich der Erwachsene, der Verantwortung übernimmt und dem sie übertragen wird.

Im Flur bleibe ich zögernd am Fuß der Treppe stehen, aber dann gehe ich doch weiter zu meiner Besenkammer, öffne die Tür und schalte das Licht und den Ventilator an. Nach den langen Jahren des Stillstands setzt er sich nur ächzend in Gang.

Auf dem Feldbett liegt kein Laken – und auch keine Strumpfhose mit Zwickel –, um mich vor irgendetwas zu schützen, das mich nachts stechen könnte.

Aber seit meinem letzten Besuch hier in Pandora war ich in Südamerika und habe am Amazonas geschlagene vier Nächte in einem Zelt übernachtet. Dort bin ich Spinnen in Esstellergröße begegnet und fliegenden Kakerlaken, die ein deftiges

Mahl für zwei abgeben würden. Im Vergleich dazu sind Mücken nicht mehr als ein lästiges Übel.

Ich ziehe mich aus, schalte das Licht aus und lege mich hin. Und ich merke, wie sich die Atmosphäre von Pandora um mich schließt. Hinter meinen geschlossenen Lidern defiliert ein Strom von Gesichtern aus der Vergangenheit vorbei. Sie erinnern mich daran, dass alle Beteiligten, die in jenem dramatischen Sommer vor zehn Jahren eine Rolle spielten, in weniger als achtundvierzig Stunden hier eintreffen werden.

Bis auf eine …

Dann schlafe ich tief und ruhig, und ausnahmsweise einmal habe ich keine Träume, an die ich mich beim Aufwachen erinnere.

Ich taste nach meinem Handy und sehe, dass es zehn Uhr ist. Also stehe ich auf, zwänge mich am Bett vorbei und gehe nach oben, um mich unter kaltem Wasser zu duschen. Nach dem Anziehen mache ich mir eine Tasse Kaffee, stelle mich mit ihr in die Terrassentür und blinzele kurzsichtig ins gleißende Sonnenlicht hinaus.

Danach beschließe ich, nach oben zu gehen und in den Schlafzimmern alle Fenster zu öffnen, damit frische Luft den Geruch des leerstehenden Hauses vertreibt. Es ist ja nicht so, als wären wir ganz bewusst zehn Jahre lang nicht hier gewesen … Es hat sich einfach so ergeben.

Während ich oben von Zimmer zu Zimmer gehe und die Läden und Fenster öffne, stelle ich erleichtert fest, dass die Betten schon frisch mit weißer Wäsche bezogen sind und am Fußende jeweils ein Handtuch liegt. Angelina hat ihre Aufgabe als Haushälterin von Pandora mit Hingabe erfüllt. Ich gehe auf die Terrasse und überlege mir, was ich als Nächstes tun soll. Dann höre ich Reifen auf dem Kies, und als ich mich umdrehe, sehe ich einen weißen Transporter vor dem Haus halten. Ein Mann und eine Frau steigen aus und kommen näher.

»Alex! Guter Gott! Bist das wirklich du?«

Ein Alexis, der geschrumpft zu sein scheint, tritt auf mich zu. Als er mich in die Arme schließt, stelle ich fest, dass ich ihm in die Augen sehe.

»Ja, ich bin's wirklich«, bestätige ich.

»Wie geht es dir? Es ist viel zu viel Zeit vergangen. Aber ich verstehe ja die Gründe«, sagt er und seufzt. »Und natürlich« – er bedeutet der Frau, die scheu hinter ihm steht, zu uns zu kommen –, »erinnerst du dich an Angelina?«

»Aber natürlich. Meiner Ansicht nach ist sie als Bäckerin nach wie vor unübertroffen.« Ich lächele sie an.

»Hallo, Alex«, sagt sie und drückt mir auf jede Wange einen Kuss. »Du bist ein sehr schöner Mann geworden. Du erinnerst mich an Brad Pitt!«

»Wirklich?«, frage ich und komme zu dem Schluss, dass sie mir noch besser gefällt als in meiner Erinnerung.

»Ja, aber genug. Im Transporter steht vieles zu essen, und ich muss jetzt in der Küche mit der Arbeit für morgen anfangen.«

»Alex, kannst du mir helfen, den Wein und die Gläser auszuladen?«

Wir gehen alle zum Transporter, und während wir die Lebensmittel in die Küche und die Weinkisten und Gläserkartons in den Lagerraum tragen, mustere ich Alexis. Die Jahre haben es gut mit ihm gemeint, die silbernen Strähnen, die jetzt sein dunkles Haar durchziehen, verleihen ihm etwas ungemein Distinguiertes.

»Gehen wir in die Küche und trinken ein Glas Wasser«, schlägt er vor, als wir die letzten der vielen Kisten verstaut haben. Wir sind schweißgebadet.

Angelina ist bereits am Kühlschrank zugange und verstaut Käselaibe und Salamis. Ich sehe überrascht, wie Alexis zu ihr geht, die Hände auf ihre Schultern legt und sie aufs Haar küsst, als er nach der Wasserflasche greift.

»Hier.« Er reicht mir ein gefülltes Glas.

»Danke.«

»Alex, du siehst verwundert aus. Ist etwas?«

»Ich … ihr zwei … seid jetzt zusammen?«

»Ja«, sagt er und lächelt. »Als Pandora Angelinas Hilfe nicht mehr brauchte, weil deine Familie fort war, habe ich sie bei uns als Haushälterin engagiert. Dann hat eines zum anderen geführt, und vor sechs Jahren haben wir geheiratet. Und vor zwei Jahren bin ich noch einmal Vater geworden, genau an meinem fünfzigsten Geburtstag!« Alexis grinst. »Ich habe einen weiteren Sohn bekommen.«

»Und ich lebe in einem Haus voller Männer!« Angelina lacht zufrieden. »Und jetzt möchte ich euch bitten, meine Küche zu verlassen, damit ich das Fest vorbereiten kann.«

»Und ich muss ins Büro zurück.« Alexis wirft einen Blick auf die Uhr. »Wenn du Zeit hast, komm doch zum Weinkeller hoch. Wir haben uns größenmäßig verdoppelt, und Dimitrios arbeitet jetzt mit mir in der Kellerei und im Verkauf.«

»Und Michel?«, frage ich zögernd.

»Er ist für den Verkauf per Internet zuständig. Wir sind also ein richtiges Familienunternehmen. Du wirst meine beiden Söhne später noch treffen, wir haben noch einiges in Pandora zu tun. Ruf mich an, wenn du etwas brauchst, Alex. Und ich freue mich schon darauf zu hören, wie es dir in den letzten zehn Jahren ergangen ist.«

Er wirft seiner Frau eine Kusshand zu, die ihm aus ihren dunklen Augen liebevoll nachsieht.

»Kann ich irgendetwas tun, Angelina?«, frage ich höflich.

»Nichts, Alex. Warum gehst du nicht im Pool schwimmen?«

Es ist offensichtlich, dass sie mich, wie jede viel beschäftigte Hausfrau, aus dem Weg haben will, und ich erfülle ihr den Wunsch. Als ich am tiefen Ende des Pools hineinspringe, erinnere ich mich an die grauenhafte Rettungsaktion für meinen armen ertrinkenden Hasen. Ich komme mir hier zunehmend wie Alice im Wunderland vor – irgendwie ist der Pool geschrumpft, ich bin nach fünf Zügen am anderen Ende und nicht erst nach zehn.

Hinterher ziehe ich mir in meiner Besenkammer eine trockene Shorts und ein T-Shirt an und hole die gesammelten Werke von Keats aus dem Regal. Dabei flattern einige Zettel aus den Seiten. Lächelnd sehe ich sie durch, aber bei einem treten mir Tränen in die Augen. Und als ich ihn lese, schlägt mein Herz wie wild gegen die Rippen.

Ob sie wohl kommt ...?

Ich weiß es einfach nicht.

Was hat Pandora nur an sich, frage ich mich, dass sich hier so viele Gefühle Bahn brechen? Als dringe eine starke Energie durch sämtliche schützenden Schichten bis zum tiefsten Inneren vor, um den Ursprung des Leids freizulegen. So, wie die Klinge eines Chirurgen mühelos bis zum befallenen Organ vordringt.

Du liebes bisschen, denke ich mir, wenn das jetzt schon so losgeht, dann werde ich morgen bestimmt die ganze Zeit vor mich hin heulen.

Ich stecke die Gedichte wieder in den Schuber und stelle ihn ins Regal zurück. Dann nehme ich das Tagebuch zur Hand. Und da es offenbar für mich nichts zu tun gibt, hole ich aus meinem Rucksack einen Stift und meine Sonnenbrille und aus der Küche ein kaltes Bier und setze mich draußen auf der Terrasse an den Tisch.

Dort schlage ich das Tagebuch bei der leeren Doppelseite nach dem letzten Eintrag auf. Einfach weil ich – so bin ich eben – nichts Unfertiges mag. Und wenn ich in fünfzig oder sechzig Jahren der Leser dieses Tagebuchs wäre, würde mich das abrupte Ende maßlos frustrieren.

Natürlich kann ich nicht mit Pepys und seinen ausführlichen täglichen Schilderungen über neun Jahre hinweg mithalten, ich bringe höchstens »Memoiren« zustande – eine Kurzfassung meines Lebens der vergangenen zehn Jahre. Aber das ist immerhin etwas. Was, wie jedermann weiß, mehr ist als nichts.

Oder doch nicht?

Das bleibt abzuwarten …

Alex' Memoiren

September 2006 – Juni 2016

Schule

Diejenige, wo man seine Frosties in Krawatte und Anzug zu sich nimmt. Viele Leute glauben zwar, Internate wären heutzutage ein Hort der Political Correctness – meine Erfahrungen im ersten Trimester kamen denen in einem Survival-Trainingscamp jedoch verdächtig nahe.

Seitdem das Schikanieren in derartigen Institutionen nicht mehr als unabdingbar zur Abhärtung des jungen Mannes angesehen wird – in alten Zeiten haben die Schulmeister die Tyrannen noch angefeuert –, wird es nur noch heimlich ausgeführt, dafür umso perfider.

Die Klassenzimmerdespoten sind wie abtrünnige Folterknechte einer militärischen Spezialeinheit: Sie fordern einen zu einer »freundschaftlichen« Kissenschlacht heraus, und während man sich selbst treuherzig mit Daunenfedern bewaffnet, zermatschen sie einem den Schädel mit einem Stoffsack voll Aktenordner. Oder schicken einem von einem Prepaid-Handy, das man niemandem zuordnen kann, per SMS Hassmails. Oder manipulieren dein Facebook-Profil und verändern deinen Status zu »Hat eine Beziehung mit einem Transvestiten«.

Nachdem ich auf Zypern durch Bees Kidnapping meine Lektion glücklicherweise gelernt hatte – so ungefähr das Einzige, wofür ich Rupes jemals dankbar sein werde –, hatte mein guter Freund mich, bestens vorbereitet, in einer kleinen Wiege begleitet, die ich mit Reißzwecken klammheimlich an der Unterseite meines Betts anbrachte. So konnte ich, auch wenn eine Matratze uns trennte, nachts meinen Arm nach unten strecken, die Sicherheit seines kahlen Fells spüren und durch den Lattenrost im Flüsterton mit ihm sprechen.

Ich muss zugeben, während der ersten entsetzlichen Wochen wäre ich beinahe wieder abgehauen. Allerdings gönnte ich Rupes nicht die Genugtuung, sich an meiner Flucht zu weiden, und abgesehen davon war der Unterricht wirklich großartig.

Und wie es gemeinhin der Fall ist, wurde alles besser, als ich an Körper und Geist wuchs. Und als ich schließlich in die Oberstufe kam, konnte ich nicht nur auf ein beeindruckendes Übergangszeugnis verweisen, sondern auch auf eine Schar jüngerer Schüler, die mir Kalfakterdienste zu leisten hatten.

»Kalfakter«: Neulich habe ich gelesen, dass das Wort (auch »Kalfaktor«) ursprünglich aus …

Ich halte im Schreiben inne und überlege mir, ob sich jemand, der dieses Tagebuch in fünfzig oder hundert Jahren liest, wirklich für die Herkunft des Wortes »Kalfakter« interessieren wird. Höchstwahrscheinlich sprechen wir bis dahin alle Mandarin als Weltsprache, zumindest der Anzahl der Chinesen an meiner Schule nach zu urteilen.

Guter Gott! Sie sind schlau, die Chinesen. Und unergründlich. Man kommt nicht so recht dahinter, was sie sich denken. Vielleicht sagen sie sich gerade: »Dieser Alex ist echt ein toller Typ, mit dem würde ich am Freitagabend gern mal im Pub ein paar Bier trinken«, aber so, wie sie einen ansehen, hat man den Eindruck, dass sie einen für einen Vollidioten halten, bei dem selbst Anspucken Energieverschwendung ist.

Wie auch immer, am Ende dieser fünf Schuljahre wurde ich in Oxford angenommen und begann Philosophie zu studieren.

Familie

Mums, Dads, Immys und Freds Leben ging parallel zu meinem weiter. Fred brachte das Kunststück fertig, meinen Goldfisch binnen zwei Wochen nach meiner Abreise ins Jenseits zu befördern. Als ich ihn fragte, ob er ihm wenigstens ein würdiges Begräbnis habe zukommen lassen, sagte er, er habe ihn im Klo runtergespült, weil er fand, er müsse im Wasser bestattet werden.

Mum wirkte glücklicher und entspannter, als ich sie je zuvor erlebt hatte. Offenbar zu entspannt, denn sobald Fred in die Schule kam, beschloss sie, selbst eine Schule zu eröffnen. Wie nicht anders zu erwarten, entwickelte sich die Beaumont-Tanzschule binnen kürzester Zeit zu einem multinationalen Konzern. Nur in finanzieller Hinsicht ließ die ganze Sache zu wünschen übrig – das Geld, das solche Unternehmen eigentlich erwirtschaften sollen, blieb aus. Wie es nun einmal Mums Art ist, unterrichtete sie die meisten ihrer Schüler kostenlos. Und wenn ich zu Ferienbeginn nach Hause kam, saß fast immer eine Person im Trikot schluchzend am Küchentisch und vertraute Mum ihren Kummer an.

Und zwar so lange, bis das eine grässliche Wort, das wohl jeder am meisten fürchtet, an ebendiesem Küchentisch ausgesprochen wurde. Und Mum sich um ihr eigenes Problem kümmern musste.

Mein Stift und ich halten inne. Ich bin immer noch nicht in der Lage, das Grauen, als sie und Dad es mir sagten, in Worte zu fassen. Ich hole mir aus dem Kühlschrank noch ein Bier, um die Erinnerung zu ertränken, und beschließe, diese Lücke später zu füllen.

Familie, Fortsetzung

Während Mums Problem verständlicherweise unser aller Leben gewaltig auf den Kopf stellte, wurden Immy und Fred still und leise allmählich erwachsener. Angesichts der Umstände blieb ihnen vielleicht auch nicht recht viel anderes übrig.

Und als Mum die Last nicht mehr tragen konnte, sprang Dad ein. Heute kann er den Wäschetrockner mit links bedienen und versteht sich darauf, eine Nudelsuppe aus frischen Zutaten zuzubereiten. Er ist echt ein guter Typ, mein Dad. Und ihn und seinen Nachnamen anzunehmen war das Beste, was ich je gemacht habe.

Und was meinen genetischen Vater betrifft, also, der ist ein gutes Jahr nach dem apokalyptischen Sommer kurz vor Weihnachten in Cedar House aufgetaucht und verlangte, mich, seinen »Sohn«, zu sehen. Mum kam mit dem besorgten Blick, den ich so gut von ihr kenne, zu mir ins Zimmer und sagte, Sacha sitze unten. Ich müsse ihn nicht sehen, meinte sie, aber ich sagte, sie solle sich keine Sorgen machen, ich würde kommen.

Als ich in die Küche kam, saß er am Tisch und kippte sich gerade irgendein alkoholhaltiges Getränk hinter die Binde, das mein Vater ihm vorgesetzt hatte. Er sah schaurig aus. Seine Hände zitterten, die papierene Haut spannte sich über die Knochen … Und so fest ich mir vorgenommen hatte, ihn zu hassen, empfand ich wie immer Mitleid.

Er wollte wissen, ob ich eine »Beziehung« zu ihm haben wolle.

Von allen Menschen auf dieser Welt stand dieser arme, traurige Mann nicht gerade ganz oben auf meiner Liste persönlicher Beziehungswünsche. Mit großer innerer Überwindung sagte ich also Nein. Und das sagte ich ihm nicht nur einmal, sondern so oft, als wäre es eine Beschwörungsformel. Bis Dad begriff, dass ich die Nase voll hatte, und Sacha aus der Küche in seinen Wagen bugsierte und zum Bahnhof fuhr.

Und danach sah ich ihn nicht mehr und hörte auch nicht wieder von ihm, bis …

Das überspringe ich.

Der Rest der Pandora-Truppe

Sadie bekam ihr Kind, ein süßes kleines Mädchen, das sie, typisch Sadie, Peaches nannte – andererseits hätte sie es ja auch nach einem anderen Obst benennen können – und machte mich zum Patenonkel!

Das war wirklich nett von ihr, obwohl es mir schwerfällt, ihren Namen laut auszusprechen, vor allem, wenn wir in der Öffentlichkeit sind. Es gibt nicht einmal eine pfiffige Kurzform. Aber sie ist ein liebes Kind und hat sich stoisch mit einer steten Abfolge von »Onkeln« abgefunden, da Sadie auch weiterhin ihre Liebhaber so oft wechselte wie ich früher meine Fußballkarten. In der Hinsicht war meine Kindheit vergleichsweise der reine Pappenstiel.

Andreas, der Schreiner, hat nie von seiner Tochter erfahren. Rückblickend frage ich mich, ob das der Grund sein könnte, weshalb Sadie mich zum Paten machte. Vielleicht glaubt sie, sie könnte, wenn Peaches dahinterkommt, dass das Verhalten ihrer Mutter nicht ganz einwandfrei war, ihre Tochter zum Beratungsgespräch zu mir schicken.

Was die übrigen Chandlers betrifft: Jules zog mit Rupes und Viola in ihr Cottage bei Oundle und schlug dort Wurzeln wie ein üppig wuchernder Efeu. Und laut ihres jährlichen Rundbriefs, der ihre ebenso jährliche Weihnachtskarte begleitet – die sie unweigerlich am ersten Dezember verschickt, sodass sie am vierten ankommt, wenn alle Normalsterblichen erste Überlegungen anstellen, welchen Leuten sie eine Weihnachtskarte schreiben sollten –, etablierte sie sich rasch als Vorsitzende jeder Eltern-Lehrer-Vereinigung und jedes Wohltätigkeitsbasars in der weiteren Umgebung, bei denen sie anderen Eltern Einsatz und Geld abschwatzte.

Im Grunde ging sie mit Rupes in die Schule (der zu guter Letzt Kapitän des ersten Rugbyteams war und damit glücklich) und hielt in der Zeit, die ihr das ließ, Leib und Seele der Familie zusammen, indem sie als Immobilienmaklerin arbeitete.

Das muss ich neidlos anerkennen, auch wenn Jules einer der enervierendsten Menschen ist, den ich kenne: Sie ist eine Macherin. Wenn ich's mir recht überlege, gäbe sie einen exzellenten Feldwebel ab.

Was die kleine Viola betrifft, wurde ihr Name immer in Jules' Weihnachtskarten erwähnt, also ging ich davon aus, dass sie noch lebte. Obwohl ich sie nicht mit eigenen Augen sah, bis …

An dieser Stelle muss ich mich beim Leser dieses Tagebuchs für die vielen Vertröstungen auf später entschuldigen. Es gibt vieles zu erzählen, und bei manchen Dingen fällt es mir sehr schwer, sie aufzuschreiben, darum bitte ich um ein wenig Geduld.

Und nicht zuletzt Chloë. Auf die eine oder andere Art habe ich sie in den vergangenen zehn Jahren relativ oft gesehen. Wie sich herausstellte, hielten unsere Schulen tatsächlich gemeinsame »Tanzvergnügen« ab, die sich allerdings weniger als förmliche Tanztees erwiesen denn als Fummelorgien auf einer improvisierten Tanzfläche in der Aula.

Da sie zu der Zeit immer noch in Michel verknallt war, erwählte sie mich, um sie vor den Aufmerksamkeiten anderer Jungen zu »beschützen«. Und dann saßen wir zusammen in einer Ecke und tranken unsere Limo, und sie schüttete mir ihr Herz aus und erzählte mir, wie sehr er ihr fehlte.

Sie war auch häufig bei uns in Cedar House und wurde ein richtiger Teil unserer Familie und ein wichtiger Teil, wie sich herausstellte, vor allem für die Kleinen.

Ich übte mich in Geduld und hoffte, ihre Fixierung auf Michel würde irgendwann verfliegen. Was nicht geschah. Aber ebenso wenig verflog meine Fixierung auf sie. Gleichzeitig standen wir uns sehr nahe, angeblich war ich ihr »bester Freund«.

Aber wie jeder beste Freund einer Frau weiß: Die Chancen, den Status quo der Beziehung in »das andere« zu verwandeln, von dem ich allnächtlich träumte, verblassten zusehends.

Nach der Schule nahm sie ein Jahr Auszeit und ging anschließend nach London, um Mode zu studieren.

Und als sie ihren Abschluss machte, löste sich auch der

Zauber, den Michel auf sie ausgeübt hatte. Sie weinte sich an meiner Schulter aus, schluchzte, sie liebe ihn immer noch, aber die Fernbeziehung habe sie beide überfordert, und es sei aus und vorbei zwischen ihnen.

Und ungefähr zu der Zeit änderte sich auch für mich alles …

Ich lege den Stift beiseite und strecke mich. Ich bin schläfrig von der Sonne und vom Bier und auch von der Anstrengung, die Ereignisse der vergangenen zehn Jahre Revue passieren zu lassen. Ich überfliege noch einmal, was ich geschrieben habe, überlege mir, ob ich jemanden vergessen habe, und stelle fest, dass tatsächlich jemand fehlt: ich. Oder zumindest meine restliche Geschichte bis heute. Aber mir ist zu heiß, ich bin zu müde und zu traurig, um weiterzuschreiben.

Außerdem sind gerade ein Auto und der weiße Transporter auf dem Kies vorgefahren. Aus dem einen steigen zwei Männer aus, in denen ich sofort Alexis' Söhne wiedererkenne. Und aus dem anderen Alexis selbst sowie ein Kleinkind, das nach seiner Hand greift, als sie auf mich zukommen.

Der kleine Junge – der Angelina wie aus dem Gesicht geschnitten ist – guckt mich schüchtern an.

»Sag ›Guten Tag‹, Gustus«, fordert Alexis ihn auf.

Aber Gustus versteckt sich hinter den langen Beinen seines Vaters. »Wir dachten, wir könnten ein paar Lichterketten über die Terrasse hängen und Laternen in den Olivenbäumen anbringen«, sagt Alexis.

»Gute Idee«, erwidere ich.

»Das wird ein richtiges Fest, oder?« Alexis schaut mich forschend an.

»Aber ja«, antworte ich mit Nachdruck. »Auf jeden Fall.«

Die nächsten Stunden verbringen wir wieder mit schweißtreibenden Aktivitäten, zu viert spannen wir Lichterketten von den Balkons im ersten Stock bis zur Pergola. Dabei reden wir über Belanglosigkeiten – Männergespräche eben –, vor allem über Fußball. Bei meinen Auslandsreisen habe ich festgestellt, dass ich allein aufgrund meiner englischen Staatsbürgerschaft – zumindest für Ausländer – ein Hort des Wissens über die erste Liga bin. Insbesondere über Manchester United, zu dessen Anhängern alle männlichen Lisles zählen.

Angesichts des Umstands, dass ich persönlich eher ein Faible für Rugby habe und mir der Zugang zum Schlafzimmer von Wayne und Colleen Rooney verwehrt ist, fällt es mir schwer, sie mit den gewünschten Informationen zu versorgen. Immer wieder werfe ich einen verstohlenen Blick zu Michel, der, sofern möglich, noch besser aussieht als damals. Ich würde ihn gern fragen, ob er eine Freundin hat, eine Verlobte oder eine Ehefrau gar, aber derart Persönliches wird mit keinem Wort angesprochen.

Angelina kommt mit einem Krug selbst gemachter Limonade und dem kleinen Gustus auf die Terrasse. Sobald wir uns setzen und durstig die Gläser leeren, klettert er auf den Schoß seines Vaters.

»Es ist doch seltsam, Alex, nicht wahr?«, fragt Alexis lachend. »Ich hatte so gehofft, Großvater zu werden. Und jetzt bin ich der Papa eines kleinen Jungen, und meine beiden Söhne haben immer noch keine eigenen Kinder.«

»Papa, ich bin erst Anfang dreißig, und Kassie ist neunundzwanzig«, tadelt Dimitrios ihn freundlich. »Wir haben noch jede Menge Zeit. Abgesehen davon nimmst du uns bei der Arbeit zu hart ran, um Zeit für Kinder zu haben«, fügt er lächelnd hinzu.

»Und du bist nicht verheiratet, Michel?«, frage ich.

»Nein«, antwortet er entschieden.

»Ich glaube, mein Sohn ist ein eingefleischter Junggeselle«, sagt Alexis und seufzt. »Offenbar gibt es keine Frau, die ihn ködern kann. Und was ist mit dir, Alex? Hast du seit unserer letzten Begegnung die Frau deines Lebens gefunden?«

»Ja«, antwortete ich nach kurzem Zögern. »Ja, das habe ich.«

»Papa.« Gustus zeigt mit dem Finger in seinen offenen Mund und sagt etwas auf Griechisch.

»Und jetzt verlangt Gustus nach seinem Abendessen. Wir müssen nach Hause«, dolmetscht Alexis. Er ruft Angelina, die zu uns herauskommt und mir Anweisungen erteilt, die letztlich darauf hinauslaufen, dass ich in der Küche und der Speisekammer nichts anrühren darf, bis sie morgen in aller Frühe wieder da ist. Als könnte ich die Dutzenden von Platten und Schüsseln über Nacht leer essen.

»Alex, möchtest du zum Essen zu uns kommen?«, fragt Alexis.

»Vielen Dank für die Einladung, aber morgen ist ein langer Tag, also bleibe ich wohl besser hier und gehe früh schlafen.«

»Ja«, sagt er verständnisvoll und nimmt den sich sträubenden Gustus in seine kräftigen, gebräunten Arme. »Dann wünschen wir dir eine gute Nacht.«

Die Familienmitglieder steigen in ihre Autos und fahren davon. Es wird dunkel, wieder einmal geht die Sonne über Pandora unter. Wie die vergangenen zehn Jahre auch, nur ohne dass ein Mensch Zeuge dieses schönen Anblicks gewesen wäre. Ich gehe in die Küche, wo überall mit Folien bedeckte Tabletts und Schüsseln stehen, und die Speisekammer ist nicht minder überladen mit geheimnisvollen Süßspeisen in allen Größen und Formen. Ich nehme mir von der Moussaka, von der mir Angelina für mein heutiges Abendessen widerstrebend eine Portion zugestanden hat.

Zu meinem einsamen Mahl setze ich mich auf die Terrasse und hoffe, dass Alexis nicht gekränkt ist, weil ich seine Einladung abgelehnt habe. Aber ich will allein sein, um meine Gedanken und meine Kraft für morgen zu sammeln.

Dann ziehe ich das Tagebuch zu mir und denke mir, dass es mir tatsächlich hilft, alles aufzuschreiben.

Alex' Memoiren

Ich, Fortsetzung

Ich gönnte mir ein Jahr Auszeit. In der ersten Hälfte verdiente ich Geld, um auf Reisen zu gehen, indem ich im Pub bei uns in Beaulieu Bier zapfte. Und die zweite Hälfte verbrachte ich damit, meine Ängste vor so ziemlich allem, was ich mir vorstellen konnte, zu überwinden.

Und einige andere Phobien zu erwerben. Z. B. Auslandsreisen.

Dann begann ich mein Philosophiestudium in Oxford, am ehemaligen College von Dad und meinem genetischen Dad. Als Dad drei Jahre später zu meiner Abschlussfeier kam und wir uns anschließend in einer dieser typischen Männerumarmungen versuchten, hatte er vor Stolz Tränen in den Augen.

Gestern Abend las ich in meinem zehn Jahre alten Tagebuch, ich könnte mir nicht vorstellen, ihn weinen zu sehen. Leider hat er das doch getan. Ziemlich oft sogar.

Ich blieb noch ein Jahr in Oxford und machte meinen Magister (mehr zu dem Jahr später). Und dann, gerade als ich jede andere Hoffnung hatte fahren lassen und mich mit einem Dasein als Akademiker anfreunden wollte, um zu promovieren und schließlich Professor für Philosophie zu werden, leitete mein Professor eine E-Mail an mich weiter.

Absender war eine Regierungsbehörde in der Mill-bank, die, wie ich wusste, direkt neben den Houses of Parliament lag. Die Kurzfassung: In der E-Mail wurde ich zu einem Bewerbungsgespräch für eine Stelle in einer Denkfabrik der neuen Regierung eingeladen.

Ich gebe zu, dass ich nach der Lektüre dieser Mail in meiner etwas verwahrlosten Unterkunft in Oxford auf mein schmales Bett fiel und mich vor lauter Lachen gar nicht mehr einkriegte. Offenbar verlangte es die seit einem Jahr bestehende Regierung, ich zitiere: »die klügsten jungen Köpfe an den Entscheidungen, die für die Zukunft Großbritanniens getroffen werden, teilhaben zu lassen«.

Genannt wurden unter anderem das EU-Referendum, die schottische Frage, das staatliche Gesundheitswesen, Einwanderungspolitik ...

Sprich, ALLES.

Tja.

Um ehrlich zu sein, ich bin nur aus Jux und Tollerei hingegangen, einfach, um sagen zu können, dass ich bei dem Gespräch war, und um auf Facebook und Twitter meine Freunde zu beeindrucken. Und insbesondere gewisse Freundinnen, die vielleicht zufällig, ohne mein Wissen, dort vorbeischauten.

Schließlich hatten wir beide genau davon geträumt ...

Da saß ich dann in dem schicken Büro – der Schaltzentrale der britischen Regierung – und hielt aufgeregt nach dem roten Knopf Ausschau, mit dem der Dritte Weltkrieg ausgelöst werden konnte. Dann verdrehte ich den Hals nach rechts, um zu sehen, ob es von hier eine direkte Signalverbindung zum M16-Gebäude gleich am gegenüberliegenden Themse-Ufer gab.

Sie stellten mir viele Fragen, bei denen es sich womöglich um Fangfragen handelte, weil sie so einfach waren. Zugegeben, es fiel mir schwerer als sonst, mich zu konzentrieren, weil ich mir ständig vorstellte, jeden Moment würde Daniel Craig hereinplatzen und mir sagen, dass ich hier zwei russischen Spionen hochvertrauliche Informationen ausplauderte. Und dazu den folgenden Schusswechsel, mit dem er mir meinen feigen Hintern rettete.

Leider handelte es sich bei Mark und Andrew − »nennen Sie mich Andy« − um zwei ziemlich dröge Beamte mittleren Alters, die meinen hastig zusammengestellten Lebenslauf studierten und mich dann um meine Ansicht baten, was die »jungen Menschen von heute« darüber dächten, dass wieder die Tories an der Macht waren. Und wie ich vorgehen würde, um deren offenbar negative Meinung zu verändern.

Ich verwendete nur wenige der großartigen Kant-Zitate, die ich aus dem Stegreif anführen kann. Stattdessen gab ich die Küchenphilosophie zum Besten, die ich instinktiv schon als Kind verstanden hatte, denn ich hatte den Eindruck, dass Mark und »Andy« eher an einem Mann aus dem Volk interessiert waren als an einem Lackaffen, der ihnen mit Psychojargon daherkam.

Auf dem Heimweg lachte ich in mich hinein. Eigentlich war ich immer ein Wähler der Liberals gewesen − unter welchem Namen sie jeweils auch firmieren mochten −, bis ich zusammen mit der gesamten Philosophischen Fakultät nach links gewandert war. Und jetzt wurde ich gebeten, für die gegnerische Seite anzutreten.

Nachdem ich draußen auf der Millbank ein Snapchat-Video gemacht und verkündet hatte, wo ich war und weshalb (wodurch ich vermutlich sofort aus dem Rennen schied, denn sicherlich muss man sich, wenn man für die Regierung arbeiten will, in vornehmer Zurückhaltung üben, aber das war mir ja egal), ging ich am Westminster-Palast vorbei zur U-Bahn-Station im sicheren Wissen, dass meine Chancen auf den Job plus/minus null waren. Denn wenn es etwas gibt, bei dem ich nicht bereit bin, auch nur einen Millimeter nachzugeben, dann sind das meine Grundüberzeugungen:

Gleichheit, Egalitarismus und freies Spiel der Märkte ...

Interessanterweise weiß ich noch, dass ich, als ich die Stufen zur U-Bahn hinunterging, dachte, dass dieser letzte Punkt der einzige war, der mit dem Wahlprogramm der gegenwärtigen Regierung übereinstimmte. FAKT: Wer hart arbeitet, soll belohnt werden. FAKT: Die kapitalistischen Staaten der Welt sind die reichsten. FAKT: Deswegen können sie den Schwächsten unter uns eine Ausbildung und soziale Absicherung bieten.

Oder das sollten sie zumindest. In Utopia ... und in meinen Träumen.

Niemand kannte mehr philosophische Lehrsätze als ich – das unglaublich Ärgerliche (und unglaublich Spannende) ist ja, dass es immer noch eine andere Sicht oder Meinung gibt, die der vorherigen widerspricht. Leider wurde mir im Verlauf der vier langen Jahre, in denen ich über die Menschheit und die Welt theoretisierte, auch klar, dass mein ganzes Papierwissen, das vermutlich so viel war, wie jemand in meinem Alter nur wissen konnte darüber, was seine Mitmenschen ausmacht, mir in meinem Privatleben keinen Deut weiterhalf. Denn das war im Moment, gelinde gesagt, ein Totalschaden.

Außerdem war ich mir nicht sicher, ob es auch rein praktisch irgendjemandem half. Als ich dieses Tagebuch wieder las, wurde mir klar, dass ich mich, auch wenn ich mein dreizehnjähriges Ich als nervtötenden Wichtigtuer bezeichnete, letztlich nur wenig verändert habe. Ich habe lediglich gelernt, meine kindlichen Gedanken und Gefühle auf akademische Art auszudrücken.

Eine Woche später lag auf dem Fußabstreifer ein Brief, in dem mir der Job angeboten wurde.

Und wieder ließ ich mich auf mein schmales Bett fallen und schlug mir vor Lachen auf die Schenkel.

Dann las ich den Brief ein zweites Mal, und zwar etwas aufmerksamer. Und verfiel, als ich das mir angebotene Gehalt sah, auf eine Sprache, die ich eigentlich nicht gutheiße.

Also. Ähmm … Boah Ey!

Und dann brach ich in Tränen aus. Mindestens zehn Minuten lang heulte ich und flennte und wischte mir den Rotz von der Nase.

Eigentlich dämlich, aber angesichts der Umstände doch verständlich.

Weil es nämlich einen Menschen gab, mit dem ich diesen Moment so gern geteilt hätte. Und der nicht da war. Und es wohl auch nie mehr sein würde.

Jetzt, ein paar Wochen später, sitze ich hier und überlege mir, dass ich wahrscheinlich einen Anzug werde tragen müssen – oder zumindest ein anständiges Jackett und Chinos –, wenn ich in knapp vier Wochen meinen neuen Job antrete.

Ich hoffe, ich kann mich dort für das Gute einsetzen – das stelle ich mir zumindest vor. Aber aus meinen Studien über die Menschen weiß ich, dass Politiker – und letztlich alle anderen auch – sich vornehmen, Gutes zu tun, dann aber von der Macht korrumpiert werden. Ich habe zwar keine Ahnung, ob man in einer Denkfabrik korrumpiert werden kann, aber für möglich halte ich alles. Erst letzte Woche bekam ich einen zweiten Brief – diesen aus dickem, cremefarbenem Velinpapier –, mit einer Einladung in die Downing Street Nr. 10 zu »einer Tasse Tee« mit dem Premierminister. Höchstpersönlich! Offenbar möchte er seine ganzen jungen Denkfabrikler persönlich kennenlernen.

Er möchte *mich* kennenlernen.

KAPITEL 33

Ich muss immer noch schmunzeln, als ich den Stift aus der Hand lege und ins Haus gehe, die Läden schließe und die Lichter lösche, deren Anzahl sich seit dem Nachmittag vervielfacht haben. Schließlich habe ich mich überzeugt, dass mir im Lauf der Nacht nicht das Haus um die Ohren fliegen wird aufgrund einer Überlastung der altersschwachen Stromleitungen, ziehe mich in meine Besenkammer zurück, schalte den Ventilator an und setze mich aufs Bett. Und greife in meinen Rucksack nach den Überresten von Bee.

»Kannst du glauben, dass ich demnächst den Premierminister des mehr oder minder Vereinigten Königreichs treffe? Ganz schön beeindruckend für einen Typen, der schlappe dreiundzwanzig ist, oder?«

Dann stecke ich ihn mir unter die Achsel.

Heute Nacht brauche ich seinen Beistand, um den morgigen Tag zu überstehen.

Ich bin gerade am Einschlafen, als mein Handy läutet. Mittlerweile habe ich mich fast an den aussetzenden Herzschlag gewöhnt, an den Horror, der mich packt, wann immer es klingelt.

»Hallo?«, frage ich heiser.

»Alex, ich bin's.«

»Ach, Immy. Hi. Wie sieht's zu Hause aus?«, frage ich ängstlich, wie immer seit ein paar Jahren.

»Gut. Ich meine, Fred und ich sind im Moment allein hier, aber Dad weiß über den morgigen Ablauf Bescheid.«

»Bei dir alles in Ordnung?«

»Ja, alles gut. Und in Pandora – alles cool?«

»Ich würde nicht gerade cool sagen, Immy, es ist brüllheiß. Aber doch, alles läuft bestens.«

»Cool«, wiederholt sie, und ich freue mich, dass zumindest ein Wort der englischen Sprache – so dämlich es auch sein mag – im Jargon fünfzehnjähriger Mädchen die Zeiten überdauert hat.

»Und das Taxi wird uns bei der Ankunft erwarten?«, fragt sie.

»Das sollte es auf jeden Fall, ja. Zumindest habe ich es gebucht«, sage ich. »Hat Fred gepackt?«

»Ansatzweise. Du kennst ihn doch – bestimmt vergisst er, frische Unterwäsche mitzunehmen. Aber ich habe es satt, ihn ständig an alles zu erinnern. Wie auch immer«, sagt Immy und seufzt leise, »wir sehen uns morgen.«

»Genau. Und, Immy?«

»Ja?«

»Es wird ein toller Abend werden.«

»Das hoffe ich, Alex. Wirklich. Gute Nacht.«

»Gute Nacht.«

Ich lege mich wieder hin, die Hände unter dem Kopf verschränkt, und denke mir, wie schwer die letzten Jahre für die beiden waren. Ich habe mein Bestes getan, genauso wie Chloë und Dad, aber die schwierigen Jahre können wir nie wieder wettmachen. Chloë und ich gingen sogar mit ihnen zu einem Therapeuten, und da sagten sie uns, wir dürften uns – was immer mit Mum passierte – kein schlechtes Gewissen machen, dass wir unser eigenes Leben weiterlebten und uns mit unseren eigenen Problemen beschäftigten, so unbedeutend sie im Vergleich auch erscheinen mochten.

Ehrlich gesagt half das mir wohl mehr als den beiden Jüngeren. Solche Sachen verfangen bei mir immer.

Deswegen wende ich mich gedanklich jetzt meinen eigenen Beziehungsproblemen zu. Und sofort verspannt sich mein ganzer Körper vor Schmerz bei der Vorstellung, dass sie morgen Abend nicht kommt. Natürlich hat sie eine Einladung erhalten, aber ich habe nichts von ihr gehört. Kein Wort.

Und wer könnte es ihr verdenken, wenn sie nicht käme?

Himmelherrgott! Warum ist das Leben so kompliziert?

Ja, technisch gesehen waren wir verwandt, und ja, es war wirklich schwierig, aber wir haben uns doch geliebt, zum Teufel!

Tja. Und jetzt bin ich hier, im selben Haus, im selben Bett, in dem alles begann. Und es muss doch einfach, trotz allem, weitergehen.

Einfach weil …

Es muss.

Wieder schlafe ich wie ein Toter – obwohl ich diesen Ausdruck aus verschiedenen Gründen zurzeit wirklich nicht verwenden sollte – und erwache zu einem weiteren strahlenden Morgen. Nach dem Duschen gehe ich in die Küche, wo Angelina bereits wieder eifrig zugange ist. Zumindest, denke ich, brauche ich nicht ängstlich zum Himmel zu blicken und mich zu fragen, ob es wohl im Lauf des Tages regnen wird.

Der Regen, Inbegriff des rachsüchtigen englischen Gottes aller Freiluftveranstaltungen. Jedes »fröhliche« Foto, das ich von Engländern bei Hochzeiten, Festen, Konzerten und ähnlichen Anlässen gesehen habe, bedeutet nicht unbedingt, dass sie vor lauter Glück in die Kamera strahlen, weil sie gerade ihre große Liebe geheiratet oder im Lotto gewonnen haben. Sie lächeln vor Erleichterung, weil der Wettergott ihrer Veranstaltung hold ist.

Vielleicht sollte ich auf Zypern heiraten, dann wäre ich wenigstens eine der Sorgen los, die einen solchen Tag begleiten.

Zumindest in meinem Fall …

Auch auf der Terrasse sind alle Mann schon im Einsatz. Dimitrios und Michel bauen die Klapptische für Bier, Wein und Gläser auf. Über dem langen gusseisernen Tisch unter der Pergola ist, um Angelinas Festbüfett einen gebührenden Rahmen zu geben, eine frisch gebügelte Decke gebreitet.

»Guten Morgen, Alex.« Alexis taucht wie aus dem Nichts auf und versetzt mir einen Schlag auf den Rücken. »Wann kommen die ersten Gäste?«

»Irgendwann am Nachmittag«, sage ich vage. »Hoffen wir, dass alle es schaffen.«

»Ja, hoffen wir mal.«

Den ganzen Tag bin ich beschäftigt, und zwischendurch schaue ich immer wieder auf mein Handy, Facebook, Twitter – als würde sie mir wirklich einen Tweet schicken! – und hoffe auf Nachricht von ihrer bevorstehenden Ankunft. Unbesehen der Kosten schalte ich das Data Roaming ein.

Aber es kommen keine Nachrichten. Nicht mal eine automatische Voicemail, die mir mitteilt, dass ich eine Schadensersatzzahlung für einen Unfall bekomme, den ich nie hatte.

Ich gehe kurz schwimmen, um mich von den anstrengenden Festvorbereitungen zu erholen. Als ich erfrischt herauskomme und auf die Uhr sehe, stelle ich fest, dass die ersten Gäste in weniger als einer Stunde eintreffen sollen. Als Nächstes stelle ich fest, dass mein rosafarbenes Hemd – zweifelsohne eine Mädchenfarbe und eine, die sehr an Rupes erinnert, aber auch eine, die meiner Erfahrung nach die meisten Frauen unwiderstehlich finden – zusammengeknüllt am Boden meines Ruck-sacks liegt. Dann suche ich verzweifelt im ganzen Haus nach einem Bügeleisen und einem Bügelbrett, Gerätschaften, mit denen ich zeit meines Lebens auf Kriegsfuß stehe.

Schließlich finde ich in der Speisekammer ein verrostetes Exemplar von beidem, und Gott sei Dank sieht Angelina das zerknüllte Stoffknäuel in meiner Hand und erbarmt sich mei-ner, und so überlasse ich das Hemd ihren fähigen Händen.

Und dann tigere ich wie ein hyperaktiver Wachposten durchs Haus. Alles ist bereit. Ich weiß, dass alles bereit ist. Aber das Umherwandern ist, wie der minütliche Blick aufs Handy, zum nervösen Tick geworden. Der Hall meiner Füße ist etwas, worauf ich mich konzentrieren kann, denn sonst konzentriere ich mich auf die Frage, wer heute Abend hier sein wird und wer nicht, und das kann ich nicht ertragen.

In ebendiesem Haus. In wenigen Stunden.

Ich bin außer mir – ein weiterer unsinniger Ausdruck, denke ich beiläufig – und beschließe, zur Ablenkung das letzte Kapitel meiner »Memoiren« zu schreiben. Obwohl ich den Ausgang meiner Erzählung erst am Abend erfahren werde.

Das erste Taxi fährt vor, und genau (oder fast genau) wie vor zehn Jahren steigen zuerst Jules und Sadie aus. Dann folgen Rupes und die kleine Peaches, Sadies Tochter. Mein Herzschlag stockt, doch ich hefte mir ein Lächeln ins Gesicht und gehe ihnen entgegen. Drei der Passagiere sehen fast genauso aus wie damals. Jules: verschwitzt und wütend. Sadie: unangemessen gekleidet. Rupes: stiernackig und rotgesichtig wie eh und je.

Dieses Mal immerhin wappne ich mich für seinen Hand-schlag, spanne sogar die Bauchmuskulatur und die Schulter-partie an, damit er mir nicht aus Versehen den Arm ausreißt.

»Mein Gott, die Fahrt hierher ist auch nicht besser geworden!«, sagt Jules stöhnend. »Und der Zustand des Hauses ist sicher noch schlimmer als damals. Es ist zehn Jahre älter und bestimmt noch verfallener.«

»Wir sind alle zehn Jahre älter, Jules«, erinnere ich sie und hoffe, dass sie die leise Anspielung versteht.

Sadie verdreht die Augen und schließt mich in die Arme. »Achte nicht auf sie«, flüstert sie mir zu. »Sie hat sich überhaupt nicht verändert. Komm, Peaches, Liebling, begrüß deinen Patenonkel«, fordert sie die zarte Gestalt auf, die neben ihr steht.

Ich bücke mich und drücke sie an mich. »Hallo, meine Süße, wie geht es dir?«

Sie kichert vor Vergnügen. »Mir geht's gut, Onkel Alex. Und dir?«

»Mir geht es auch sehr gut, Peaches, danke …«, lüge ich.

In dem Moment tippt Sadie mir auf die Schulter und deutet auf eine weitere Person, der Jules gerade beim Aussteigen hilft.

»Alex, ich warne dich. Wenn du Jules für nervig hältst, dann hast du ihren neuen Freund noch nicht kennengelernt«, flüstert sie mir zu.

Ich verfolge, wie sich ein Mann vom Beifahrersitz des Taxis hievt. Er hat einen Teint, der erschreckend an Rupes erinnert, die fehlenden Haare macht er mit einer leuchtend roten Chino und einem Karohemd wett.

»O mein Gott! Er sieht aus, als könnte er ihr Vater sein!«, flüstere ich Sadie zu, als der Mann Jules' Arm umklammert und über den Kies auf uns zukommt.

»Das ist er wahrscheinlich auch, aber offenbar gehört ihm die halbe Grafschaft Rutland, außerdem besitzt er einen ganzen Stall mit Vollblütern. Jules ist Pächterin auf seinem Landsitz, und sie haben sich kennengelernt, als er ihre zugefrorenen

Leitungen inspiziert hat«, raunt mir Sadie mit einem vieldeutigen Grinsen zu.

Jules stellt ihn mir als Bertie vor, während er entsetzt die Unterkunft in Augenschein nimmt.

»Du hast mich ja gewarnt, dass ich mich für das Schlimmste wappnen soll, aber wir machen sicher das Beste daraus«, sagt er affektiert. »Komm, Jules, altes Mädchen, zeig mir unsere Suite!« Damit versetzt er ihr einen Klaps auf den Hintern, und sie kichert wie ein junges Mädchen. Sadie und ich und sogar die kleine Peaches deuten derweil pantomimisch an, uns zu übergeben.

»Ist er nicht grässlich?«

Da wird mir erst bewusst, dass ich Rupes völlig vergessen habe, drehe mich um und sehe ihn mit den Händen in den Taschen hinter uns stehen. Keiner von uns sagt ein Wort, wir werden nur alle so rot, wie er von Natur aus ist.

»Ich habe Mum gesagt, dass sie fragen soll, ob er mitkommen kann. Und sie sagte, sie habe hier immer in einem Doppelbett geschlafen, also sei es bestimmt in Ordnung. Wie auch immer, Alex, wie geht's dir? Nach allem, was ich höre, läuft's für dich im Augenblick sehr gut.«

»Mir geht's prima, Rupes, danke. Und ich habe gehört, dass du jetzt Lehrer wirst?«

»Ja.« Er lacht laut. »Ein Witz, wenn man an unseren letzten Urlaub hier in Pandora denkt, stimmt's? Allerdings nicht gerade Sprachen, wie du dir denken kannst. Aber seit ich wegen meiner Knieverletzung nicht mehr professionell Rugby spielen kann, habe ich als Trainer angefangen, und ich muss sagen, es macht mir wirklich Spaß. Also dachte ich mir, warum nicht? Leider hat die Familie, wie du weißt, kein Geld, auf das ich zurückgreifen kann.«

»Also, Rupes, ich kann mir dich gut als Sportlehrer vorstellen«, sage ich und meine es auch so. Meine Sportlehrer hatten ihre Ausbildung alle bei den Triaden erhalten.

»Danke.«

»Lust auf ein Bier?«

»Warum nicht?«, sagt er.

»Entschuldige, wenn ich euch unterbreche, Alex, aber schlafen wir im selben Zimmer wie beim letzten Mal?«, fragt Sadie.

»Ja. Peaches, für dich hat Angelina ein Feldbett aufgestellt, genau wie das, auf dem ich in meiner Besenkammer schlafe.«

»Schläft du wirklich in der Besenkammer?«, fragt sie fasziniert.

»Nicht ganz. Wir nennen sie nur so, weil der Raum so klein ist«, erkläre ich ihr, als wir alle zusammen zum Haus gehen.

»Du bleibst hier unten bei Rupes, wir wissen, wohin wir gehen müssen«, sagt Sadie und steuert auf die Treppe zu.

»Miiister Rupes!« Angelina erscheint im Flur, und ich spreche ein Dankgebet, denn das Letzte, was ich jetzt brauche, ist ein Seelengespräch mit meinem Halbbruder, der nicht einmal weiß, dass er mein Halbbruder ist. »Wie geht es dir?«

»Gut, Angelina, danke«, sagt er und gibt ihr auf beide Wangen einen Kuss.

»Rupes, komm in meine Küche. Ich habe den Kuchen gebacken, der dir beim letzten Mal so geschmeckt hat.«

Ich folge ihnen in die Küche, und während Angelina ihn mit Fragen überschüttet, gebe ich ihm ein Bier. Dann höre ich höflich dem Gespräch zu und stelle fest, dass Rupes erheblich ausgeglichener geworden ist, seit wir uns das letzte Mal gesehen haben. Gut, damals hat er geweint, aber wahrscheinlich eher um seiner selbst willen, wie es bei solchen Anlässen oft der Fall ist.

Ich schaue auf die Uhr, es ist fast sechs. Nur eine gute Stunde bis zum offiziellen Beginn, wenn die Hauptdarsteller des heutigen Schauspiels ihren Auftritt haben.

»Rupes, du kommst zurecht? Ich würde gern noch kurz duschen«, sage ich.

»Ja, natürlich«, sagt er. »Wo schlafe ich?«

»Auf dem Sofa im Salon, fürchte ich. Wir haben heute Abend volles Haus.«

Ich verschwinde, bevor ich ihm die Frage stelle, die mir auf der Zunge brennt. Höchstwahrscheinlich weiß er die Antwort sowieso nicht, und womöglich gibt er mir die falsche Auskunft, und das wäre noch viel schlimmer.

Also halte ich den Mund und gehe nach oben ins Bad.

Als ich tropfnass aus der Dusche komme, lese ich eine SMS von Immy, die gerade eben erst durch die zypriotischen Leitungen geschlüpft ist.

Flug hat Verspätung. Landen um halb sieben.

Verdammt! Das heißt, dass sie frühestens um halb acht hier sein werden, wenn die Party schon in vollem Gang sein sollte. Was, wenn es noch später wird?

Unten sitzen Jules und ihr Begleiter an einem der kleinen Cafétische, die auf der Terrasse aufgestellt wurden. Sie haben sich auch schon jeder ein Glas Wein genehmigt, dessen Qualität Bertie lauthals beanstandet. Ich kann nur mit Mühe an mich halten, ihm nicht an die Gurgel zu gehen, als zum Glück Sadie durch die Terrassentür tritt.

»Guten Abend, mein Lieber. Alles so weit fertig?«

»Ich glaube schon. Uns fehlen nur noch eine ganze Reihe wichtiger Gäste.«

»Sie kommen ganz bestimmt. Ich finde es großartig, dass du das alles organisiert hast, wirklich.«

Spontan umarmt sie mich. Ich weiß, auch in ihr weckt das Haus viele Erinnerungen. »Übrigens« – sie senkt die Stimme, denn Peaches schießt gerade an uns vorbei und steuert auf die Schüssel mit Chips zu, die sie auf dem Tisch erspäht hat –, »du glaubst doch nicht, dass, äh, Andreas heute Abend kommt, oder?«

»Das weiß ich nicht. Du solltest Alexis fragen, er ist für die Liste der einheimischen Gäste verantwortlich.«

»Gut, werd ich machen.« Sie sieht zu Peaches, die sich gerade den Mund mit Chips vollstopft. »Er wird doch keinen Verdacht schöpfen, oder?«

Ich sehe ebenfalls zu Peaches – eine weibliche Version ihres Vaters in blond. »Das bezweifle ich«, lüge ich. »Aber wie gesagt, frag Alexis.«

Rupes schlendert auf die Terrasse, und im selben Moment höre ich einen Wagen vorfahren.

»Das sind Alexis und seine Familie«, sage ich. »Gut, Rupes, ich glaube, es ist Zeit, den Weißwein aus dem Kühlschrank zu holen, meinst du nicht?«

Um halb acht wimmelt es auf der Terrasse vor Menschen, an die ich mich kaum erinnere, die mich aber offenbar alle kennen. Ich fange gerade an, mir zu überlegen, wie sich ein Tod durch Umarmung anfühlt, als mich jemand an die Schulter stupst.

»Alex! Ich bin es! Ich bin hier!«

»Fabio! Du hast es geschafft!« Jetzt bin ich derjenige, der jemanden in die Arme schließt. In den letzten Jahren ist Fabio für uns alle zum Fels in der Brandung geworden, vor allem für meinen Vater.

»Siehst du? Und ich habe Dan mitgebracht. Jetzt kannst du ihn kennenlernen.«

Ein großer Mann mit dunklen Augen, der erschreckenderweise nur wenige Jahre älter aussieht als ich, tritt auf mich zu und küsst mich auf beide Wangen. »Es ist mir eine Freude, Ihre Bekanntschaft zu machen, Sir«, sagt er mit einem unverkennbar amerikanischen Akzent.

»Bitte, nenn mich Alex. Und es ist mir eine Freude, dass du hier bist.«

»Es ist mir eine Freude, hier sein zu dürfen.«

»Also.« Fabios Blick wandert über die Terrasse, ehe Dan und ich uns ein weiteres Mal unsere Freude bekunden können. »Wo ist der Rest deiner Familie?«

»Der Flug hat Verspätung. Ich hoffe, sie kommen, bevor alle anderen nach Hause gehen.« Nervös mache ich eine umfassende Geste auf die Terrasse und die kleine Band, die am Rand steht.

»Sie werden kommen, Alex«, beruhigt Fabio mich. »Und jetzt sollten wir beide den Wein probieren, den der Freund deiner Mutter macht und der mir bei meinem letzten Besuch so gut geschmeckt hat.«

Ich gehe mit ihnen zum Tisch mit den Getränken hinüber, und während ich mit Dan über seine langjährigen Schwierigkeiten spreche, Italienisch zu lernen, und mir überlege, ob ich ihn nach der Adresse seines Schönheitschirurgen fragen soll, klopft mir das Herz bis zum Hals.

Wo bleiben sie, verdammt?

Ich will mir ein Bier zur Nervenberuhigung genehmigen, werde aber ständig von Gästen abgefangen und von Angelina, die mich fragt, wann sie das heiße Essen auftragen und ob die Musiker jetzt zu spielen beginnen sollen.

Heiß, kalt oder tiefgekühlt, ist mir doch egal! Aber meiner Nervosität zum Trotz beherrsche ich mich.

Ich strecke den Arm nach einem Bier aus, als mich wieder jemand an der Schulter berührt.

»Alex, sie sind da.«

»Gott sei Dank«, sage ich erleichtert und folge Alexis durch die Menge. »Wie viele sind es?«

»Das konnte ich nicht erkennen.«

Wir eilen beide ums Haus zur Auffahrt, die mittlerweile mit Autos zugeparkt ist. Ganz hinten sehe ich schemenhaft Menschen aus einem Wagen aussteigen und zähle … ganze vier. Das Herz wird mir schwer, denn ich weiß, das war der letzte Flug, der heute aus England landet.

Immy ist als Erste bei mir. Sie sieht genauso angespannt und nervös aus, wie ich mich fühle.

»Es tut mir leid, Alex, aber ich konnte nichts machen. Ich musste mit ihnen in Gatwick sitzen und tun, als wäre es völlig egal, wenn wir uns verspäten. Fred war auch keine Hilfe. Wie immer.« Sie verdreht die Augen, während ein schlaksiger Teenager – mein kleiner Bruder – zu uns hinübergeschlendert kommt.

»Hi, Fred. Guten Flug gehabt?«

»Langweilig«, sagt er mit einem Achselzucken.

Das ist im Moment offenbar der ganze Umfang seines dreizehnjährigen Vokabulars. Ich kann mich nicht erinnern, dass das Wort in seinem Alter zu meinem gehörte.

»Also, dann sage ich den Gästen, dass ihr hier seid«, sagt Alexis, »und du, Alex, bringst sie auf die Terrasse.«

»Ja«, erwidere ich und schaue zu den beiden Neuankömmlingen, die langsam auf mich zugehen, ein Ausdruck der Verwunderung auf dem Gesicht.

»Hallo, Mum, hallo, Dad«, sage ich und schaue schuldbewusst hinter sie, ob nicht vielleicht doch noch jemand im Wagen sitzt.

»Was in aller Welt ist denn hier los?«, fragt William leise, während meine Mutter mich in den Arm nimmt.

»Tja … wart's ab. Mum, wie geht es dir?« Ich sehe sie forschend an und suche in ihrem Gesicht nach einem Indiz.

»Mir geht es sehr gut, Alex«, sagt sie und lächelt. Und es ist kein »Eigentlich nicht so gut, aber deinetwegen tue ich so als ob«-Lächeln, das ich in den letzten drei Jahren allzu oft gesehen habe. Es ist eines, dem ich glauben kann.

»Eure Mum hat gestern die Untersuchungsergebnisse bekommen – ohne Befund«, sagt William. Und wieder sehe ich Tränen in seinen Augen glitzern. »Es ist vorbei.«

»O mein Gott, Mum, das ist ja großartig! Einfach großartig!«

»Hast du gerade gesagt, dass die Ergebnisse ohne Befund sind?«, fragt Immy, die neben mir steht. Und sogar Fred spitzt die Ohren.

»Wir wollten es euch erst sagen, wenn wir alle zusammen sind. Aber es ist alles in Ordnung bei mir.«

»Ganz bestimmt, Mum?«, fragt Immy nach. Auch sie weiß, was falsche Hoffnungen bedeuten.

»Ganz bestimmt.«

»Für immer?«, fragt Fred, und seine Unterlippe bebt wie schon früher, als er klein war. Fürsorglich lege ich ihm eine Hand auf die Schulter, ich weiß, wie verletzlich er ist.

»Na, das wäre vielleicht etwas zu viel verlangt, aber heute Abend habe ich das Gefühl, dass es für immer sein könnte, mein Schatz«, sagt Mum und gibt ihm einen Kuss.

Dann umarmen wir uns zu fünft und müssen uns hinterher die Nase putzen, um wieder präsentabel zu sein.

»Also«, sage ich und räuspere mich. »Jetzt gehen wir mal. Schade, dass Chloë nicht hier sein kann. Sie hat es offenbar nicht geschafft«, sage ich.

»Sie hat gesagt, dass sie ihr Bestes versucht, aber du weißt ja, ihr Chef verlangt sehr viel von ihr«, sagt Mum, als ich ihnen zwischen den Autos hindurch zum Haus vorangehe.

»Zumindest bekommt sie kostenlos Designerklamotten, das ist mehr, als ich für mein Babysitten kriege«, meint Immy.

»Möchtest du denn ein kostenloses Baby, Im?«

»Fred, ehrlich, du bist ein Vollpfosten.«

»Alex, was genau geht denn hier vor sich?«, fragt meine Mutter.

»Ich sagte doch schon, wart's ab.«

»Immy, du hättest mir wirklich etwas sagen können, ich bin gar nicht passend angezogen.« Mum deutet auf ihre Jeans, die Flipflops und die weiße Seersuckerbluse.

»Alex hat mir mit Tod und Teufel gedroht, falls ich auch nur ein Wort sage. Das planen wir schon seit Ewigkeiten.«

Und mir wird bewusst, dass wir bestimmte Wörter wieder unbefangen laut aussprechen können.

»Ich bin so froh, Mum, wirklich«, flüstere ich ihr zu. »Das ist die beste Nachricht, die ich je gehört habe.«

»Du bist großartig gewesen, Alex. Danke.«

Dann umarmen wir uns noch einmal, nur wir zwei. Und ich rede mir ganz fest ein, dass das, was heute Abend nicht sein wird, angesichts des großen Ganzen eigentlich nichts zur Sache tun sollte.

»Also«, sage ich und reiße mich zusammen. Wir haben den Rand der Terrasse erreicht, von wo unterdrücktes Getuschel zu hören ist. »Mum und Dad, das ist ein Geschenk von euren drei Kindern. Alles Gute zum zwanzigsten Hochzeitstag!«

Dann führe ich sie auf die Terrasse, wo alle jubelnd und klatschend dasselbe auf Griechisch wiederholen. Champagnerkorken knallen, meine Eltern werden von Küssen und Umarmungen schier erstickt, und ich sehe das freudige Gesicht meiner Mutter, als sie Fabio und Sadie entdeckt.

Für mich war immer klar, dass ich das für sie organisieren würde. In den schlimmen Jahren nach der Diagnose, als wir nicht wussten, ob die Behandlung anschlagen würde oder nicht, habe ich oft daran gedacht. Meine Mum hat viele Erinnerungen an Pandora, einige weniger glücklich als andere, aber zumindest alle aus den Tagen vor Krankenhausbetten und Schmerzen.

Im Moment kann ich gar nicht fassen, dass das wirklich vorbei ist. Dass sie leben wird.

Und deswegen bemühe ich mich heute Abend, den anderen schrecklichen Schmerz zu vergessen, bei dem es nicht um Leben oder Tod geht, auch wenn es mir fast so vorkommt. Ich werde das Leben meiner Mutter feiern, im wahrsten Sinn des Wortes.

Der Abend schreitet voran, die Sterne leuchten auf die kleine Schar feiernder Menschen herab. Der Klang der Bouzouki trägt mich zu dem folgenschweren Abend vor zehn Jahren zurück, und ich hoffe, dass keine ähnlichen Offenbarungen die Feier stören werden, als Alexis wieder um Ruhe bittet und einen Toast anbringt. Ich trinke mehr Bier, als ich sollte, sowohl um auf die Gesundheit meiner Mutter anzustoßen, als auch um meinen persönlichen Kummer zu ertränken.

»Alex, mein Schatz, danke, dass du diese wunderbare Überraschung organisiert hast. Sie ist die schönste meines Lebens.«

Meine Mutter ist zu mir gekommen und stellt sich auf die Zehenspitzen, um ihre Arme um meine Schultern zu legen und mir einen Kuss zu geben.

»Das freut mich, Mum.«

»Dieser Abend könnte in keiner Hinsicht perfekter sein«, sagt sie und lächelt.

»Bist du sicher, dass du hundertprozentig wieder in Ordnung bist, Mum? Du würdest mich doch nicht anlügen, oder?«, frage ich sie wieder.

»Na ja, ich würde das vielleicht schon«, sagt sie und lächelt wieder. »Aber Dad würde da nicht mitmachen. Im Ernst, Alex, es geht mir sehr gut, wirklich. Endlich kann ich wieder mein Leben leben. Es tut mir so leid, dass ich in den vergangenen drei Jahren nicht so für dich da war, wie ich es gern gewesen wäre, aber du hast es eindeutig auch ohne mich sehr gut geschafft. Ich bin so stolz auf dich, mein Schatz, wirklich.«

»Danke, Mum.«

»Ach, Alex.« Mum dreht sich zur Seite. »Schau mal, wer da kommt! Komm, gehen wir sie begrüßen.«

Ich drehe mich ebenfalls um und blicke in das vertraute, geliebte Gesicht, das uns beide anlächelt, und mein Herz stellt wieder etwas Unsinniges an und hüpft herum, eine Mischung aus Aufregung und Angst.

Aber vor allem Liebe.

»Chloë! Ach, mein Gott, wie seid ihr jetzt hergekommen?«, fragt Mum, als wir vor ihr stehen.

»Frag nicht. Wir kommen aus Paris.« Chloë grinst und umarmt sie. »Alles Gute zum Hochzeitstag! Hi, Alex«, begrüßt sie mich und gibt mir einen Kuss auf beide Wangen. »Ich habe dir doch versprochen, dass ich dich nicht hängen lasse, oder?«

»Das stimmt«, antworte ich, obwohl ich eigentlich nur mit halbem Ohr darauf achte, was sie sagt, denn direkt hinter ihr steht das Objekt all meiner Träume und Albträume des vergangenen Jahres. »Du entschuldigst.«

»Natürlich.« Chloë zwinkert mir verständnisvoll zu.

Ich gehe die paar Schritte zu ihr, sie steht halb verborgen im Schatten des Hauses.

»Hallo«, sagt sie schüchtern und schaut dann mit ihren wunderschönen blauen Augen verlegen zur Seite.

»Ich habe nicht gedacht … ich …« Ich schlucke schwer, Tränen treten mir in die Augen, und ich befehle meinem Gehirn, ihnen sofort Einhalt zu gebieten.

»Ich weiß.« Sie zuckt mit den Schultern. »Es ist …« Ihr Blick schweift umher, nur nicht zu mir. »Es war schwierig.«

»Das kann ich verstehen.«

»Aber Chloë hat mir geholfen. Sie hat mich aus der Ecke rausgeholt, in die ich mich manövriert hatte. Sie war großartig. Ich glaube, Alex, wir haben ihr beide viel zu verdanken.«

»Wirklich?«

»Ja. Sie hat mich auch überredet, heute Abend mitzukommen. Und … jetzt bin ich froh, dass ich gekommen bin.« Sie reicht mir ihre schmale, blasse Hand, und ich ergreife sie. »Du hast mir gefehlt, Alex. Wirklich ganz schrecklich gefehlt.«

»Du hast mir auch gefehlt, mehr noch als ›ganz schrecklich‹, um ehrlich zu sein. Ich würde eher sagen, grottengrausam, herzzerreißend, lebensbedrohlich …«

»Ja.« Sie lacht leise. »Das würdest *du* sagen. Aber eigentlich ist es schon in Ordnung, oder nicht? Dass du und ich zusammen sind?«

»Na ja, es ist vielleicht nicht gerade die Norm, aber zumindest würden unsere Kinder keine sechs Zehen bekommen. Ich wusste einfach nicht, wie ich es dir sagen sollte …« Ich schlucke. »Es war alles so kompliziert. Und es tut mir so leid, dass ich es dir so lange verschwiegen habe.«

»Mir auch. Aber jetzt verstehe ich, warum.«

Die nächste Frage muss ich einfach stellen, bevor wir uns

weiter auf diesem holprigen Pfad vorantasten. »Bist du hier, weil du möchtest, dass wir es noch einmal miteinander versuchen?« Unwillkürlich bewegt sich meine eine Hand, die nicht die ihre hält, nach vorn, um ihr eine Strähne ihres wunderschönen tizianroten Haars aus dem Gesicht zu streichen.

»Na, ich hoffe ja, dass es mehr wird als nur ein Versuch.«

»Ist das in Viola-Sprache ein Ja?«

»Ja, aber du verstehst doch, warum ich Zeit brauchte, um das alles zu verarbeiten, oder? Ich war …«, sie seufzt tief, »… Ich konnte damit einfach nicht umgehen.«

»Ich weiß. Und natürlich verstehe ich es.« Ich nähere mich ihr, dann schließe ich sie in die Arme und ziehe sie an mich. Und spüre keinen Widerstand. Im Gegenteil, sie schmiegt sich an mich. Da küsse ich sie, und sie erwidert meinen Kuss, und ich spüre den Drang, jetzt und auf der Stelle Dinge mit ihr zu machen, die zu tun auf dem Fest zum zwanzigsten Hochzeitstag meiner Eltern höchst unangemessen wären.

»Meine sehr geehrten Damen und Herren«, tönt Alexis' Stimme von der Terrasse herüber.

»Komm.« Ich ziehe sie am Arm mit. »Bei den Reden sollten wir dabei sein. Und übrigens«, füge ich hinzu, als ich sie durch die Menschenmenge führe, die sich zum Zuhören versammelt hat, »meine Mutter ist wieder ganz gesund. Die letzte Untersuchung war ohne Befund.«

»Ach, Alex, das ist ja großartig!«

»Ja.« Ich sehe zu ihr. »Heute ist ein großartiger Tag.«

Alex' Memoiren

Viola

Alles hatte vor gut einem Jahr angefangen, als meine Mum mich anrief ...

»Alex, entschuldige, wenn ich dich während der Abschlussprüfungen störe, aber ich habe einen Brief von Sacha für dich.«

»Ach ja?«

»Ja. Er liegt in London im Krankenhaus. Vor ein paar Tagen hat Viola bei Dad angerufen und ihm ausgerichtet, dass Sacha ihn gern sehen möchte. Ich fürchte, es sieht nicht gut aus. Offenbar hat er einen schweren Herzinfarkt gehabt, und seine Leber ist natürlich jenseits von Gut und Böse ...«

Ich weiß noch, dass die Stimme meiner Mutter erstarb und ich mir dachte, dass ich in einem Jahr womöglich keinen leiblichen Elternteil mehr haben könnte.

»Was will er?«

»Er hat Dad gefragt, ob du ihn vielleicht bald besuchen würdest. Und ich glaube, das ›bald‹ ist wichtig. Wirklich, Alex, es liegt ganz bei dir. Ich weiß, du hast in den letzten zwei Jahren mehr als genug Krankenhausbesuche gemacht, und ...«

»Weißt du was? Ich notiere mir die Adresse des Krankenhauses und überlege es mir. In Ordnung?«

Ich hatte sie auch gebeten, mir den Brief weiterzuleiten. Zwei Tage später hielt ich ihn in der Hand, und obwohl ich geahnt hatte, was darin steht, und mir geschworen hatte, mich nicht davon berühren zu lassen, tat er's trotzdem. Sacha wollte sich verabschieden.

Am Sonntag direkt vor den Abschlussprüfungen, als jeder andere in Oxford im stillen Kämmerlein saß und entweder fieberhaft lernte, seinen Kater kurierte oder Selbstmord erwog, setzte ich mich in einen Zug nach London, fuhr mit der U-Bahn von Paddington nach Waterloo und ging von dort zu Fuß zum St. Thomas' Hospital.

Krankenhäuser waren an Wochentagen deprimierend genug, aber am Sonntag fand ich sie irgendwie noch schlimmer. Die dumpfe Stille wurde nicht von der üblichen Wochentagsbetriebsamkeit unterbrochen, überall hing der Geruch von gekochtem Rindfleisch und gedämpftem Kohl – dem traurigen Ersatz für den klassischen Sonntagsbraten – in der Luft.

Ich kann nicht behaupten, dass Sacha wesentlich schlechter aussah als bei unserer letzten Begegnung vor sechs Jahren, nur älter. Dabei war er genauso alt wie Dad, ganze fünfundfünfzig, nach heutigen Maßstäben quasi ein Teenager.

Er lag auf der Intensivstation und war an alle möglichen Infusionen und piepsenden Monitore angeschlossen. Er trug eine gewaltige Sauerstoffmaske mit einer großen Pumpe in der Mitte, durch die er wie ein entstellter Elefant aussah. Die freundliche Schwester hatte mir erklärt, dass er die Maske trug, weil sich nach dem Herzinfarkt Wasser in seiner Lunge gesammelt hatte, da sie nach dem Infarkt nicht mehr mit ausreichend Sauerstoff versorgt wurde und folglich nicht mehr richtig funktionierte.

Als ich das Zimmer betrat, schlief er, und so setzte ich mich still an sein Bett und betrachtete zum vermutlich letzten Mal den Mann, der mich gezeugt hatte.

Währenddessen sah ich eine junge Frau – oder sollte ich sagen, einen Engel der Vollkommenheit – durch die Station auf mich zukommen. Groß und anmutig; makellose Alabasterhaut und ein herzförmiges Gesicht mit einem Mund wie eine Rosenknospe und himmelblauen Augen. Ihr langes tizianrotes Haar floss ihr über die Schultern und erinnerte mich sofort an ein präraffaelitisches Gemälde. Eine Sekunde glaubte ich tatsächlich, sie wäre ein berühmtes Supermodel, dessen Gesicht – und Körper – ich von Plakatwänden im ganzen Land auf mich hatte herabblicken sehen.

Doch es war Viola Chandler, die da auf mich zukam. Die liebe kleine Viola mit den Hasenzähnen, den Sommersprossen und der Neigung, an meiner Schulter in Tränen auszubrechen.

»Guter Gott!«, murmelte ich unhörbar, als sie am Fußende des Betts stehen blieb und mich fragend ansah.

»Alex?«

»Ja«, brachte ich hervor. Immerhin hatte ich meinen Lippen in den vergangenen neun Jahren antrainiert, auch in der Gegenwart schöner Frauen sinnvolle Worte zu formen. »Ich bin es.«

»O mein Gott!«

Und dann kam dieses hinreißende Geschöpf auf mich zu und schlang die Arme um mich.

»Es ist wunderbar, dich zu sehen!«, sagte sie und vergrub

den Kopf an meiner Schulter – zugegeben nicht die übliche Reaktion schöner Frauen, wenn sie mich begrüßen. »Weshalb bist du hier? Ich meine«, verbesserte sie sich, »es ist wirklich sehr nett von dir und so, aber …?«

Als ich ihre Verwirrung bemerkte, wurde mir klar, dass vermutlich Jules ebenso wenig wie der Elefantenmann, der neben mir im Bett lag, ihr je von meiner genetischen Verbindung zu ihm erzählt hatte. In dem Fall aber waren weder Ort noch Zeit geeignet für eine solche Offenbarung. Vor allem auch, weil mein Hemd feucht von ihren Tränen war, als sie sich von mir löste. Und als ich ihr schönes Gesicht aus der Nähe betrachtete, sah ich die dunklen Ringe unter ihren Augen und den Kummer darin.

Ich überlegte mir, es ihr später beiläufig bei einem Kaffee oder was auch immer zu erzählen.

Im Flüsterton unterhielten wir uns darüber, wie schlimm es um ihn stand – aber dass sie die Hoffnung noch nicht aufgegeben hatte.

»Manchmal passiert doch ein Wunder, Alex, oder nicht?«

Und als sie mich derart verzweifelt ansah, wie schon vor all den Jahren, ein Blick, der den irrationalen Glauben barg, irgendwie würde es mir gelingen, alles zum Besseren zu wenden, alle Antworten zu kennen … da nickte ich.

»Ja, Viola, Hoffnung gibt es immer.«

Sie berichtete, dass Sacha seit zwei Tagen mehr oder weniger bewusstlos sei, nur hin und wieder aufwache, und dass sie ihre Mutter angerufen habe – die sich zu kommen weigerte – sowie Rupes, der »vielleicht« sagte.

»Aber das bezweifle ich«, sagte sie und seufzte. »Er hat Dad seinen Auftritt auf dem Fest damals nie verziehen. Mum derart bloßzustellen und uns dann praktisch ohne einen Penny stehen zu lassen«, fuhr sie fort, als wir auf einen Kaffee in die Cafeteria gingen. »Aber weißt du, was immer in der Vergangenheit war, ein Sohn sollte doch kommen, um seinen Vater am … am Sterbebett zu besuchen.«

»Ja.« Bei ihrer Bemerkung musste ich schlucken. Sie wusste ganz offensichtlich nicht Bescheid.

»Danke, dass du gekommen bist, Alex. Letzte Woche war dein Dad hier, aber sonst …« Sie zuckte mit den Schultern. »Sonst niemand. Nicht gerade viel für ein ganzes Leben, nicht?«

Dann erzählte sie mir, dass sie seit zwei Wochen im Krankenhaus war und im Zimmer für Angehörige schlief, weil sie ihn nicht allein lassen wollte.

»Das heißt zwar, dass ich kommende Woche an der Uni nicht die Erstjahresprüfungen machen kann, aber angesichts der Umstände haben sie sich bereit erklärt, mir eine geschätzte Note zu geben, ausgehend von meinen bisherigen Leistungen.«

»An welcher Uni bist du?«

»Am University College London, hier ganz in der Nähe. Ich studiere englische Literatur und Französisch. Zum Glück müssen wir viele Aufsätze schreiben, ich sollte also ganz gut durchkommen. Dir ist schon klar, Alex – das hat alles damit angefangen, dass du mir *Jane Eyre* empfohlen hast«, fügte sie leise hinzu, und zum ersten Mal verzogen sich ihre Lippen zur Andeutung eines Lächelns. »Eigentlich hatte ich dir das immer einmal schreiben wollen, aber …« Sie seufzte. »Das Leben geht einfach immer weiter, stimmt's?«

»Ja, da hast du recht«, sagte ich und nickte.

»Sogar unsere Familien haben im Lauf der Jahre den Kontakt verloren. Wahrscheinlich, weil Dad uns verlassen hatte, und es waren ja doch immer er und dein Dad, die die Verbindung aufrechterhalten haben. Und vielleicht wollte Mum nach der Scheidung einfach ganz neu anfangen.«

Sicher, aber mir wären auch noch einige andere Gründe eingefallen.

»Wie geht es deiner Mum?«, fragte ich aus Höflichkeit.

»Ach, wie immer.«

Eine Weile erzählte sie von den vergangenen neun Jahren, und ich hörte ihr zu, oder vielmehr, schaute sie an. Und merkte, dass mein Herz mit dieser blöden Hämmerei anfing wie damals bei Chloë.

»O Alex, ich habe von deiner Mum gehört. Das tut mir so leid. Wie geht es ihr?«

»Du kennst das doch, mal besser, mal schlechter. Die erste Behandlung hat nicht angeschlagen, und es ist an einer anderen Stelle wiedergekommen, aber dieses Mal sind die Ärzte ziemlich zuversichtlich, dass sie es kleingekriegt haben«, antwortete ich möglichst leichthin.

»Ach, Alex.« Viola biss sich auf die Unterlippe. »Wir sind schon ein Paar, meinst du nicht?«

Ach, Viola … ich wünsche mir wirklich sehr, dass wir das wären.

Ich nickte weise, und dann meinte sie, wir sollten besser wieder auf die Station gehen und nach ihrem Dad sehen.

Wir saßen an Sachas Bett, und ich hoffte inständig, dass er nicht aufwachen, mich sehen und ein großes Drama aufführen würde à la »O mein Gott, mein verlorener Sohn ist gekommen, um mir Lebwohl zu sagen«. Das war schon allein wegen Violas offensichtlicher Erschöpfung und ihres labilen emotionalen Zustands unerlässlich. Nach unendlich langen eineinhalb Stunden, in denen er reglos zwischen uns lag, stand ich schließlich auf.

»Es tut mir wirklich leid, Viola, aber ich muss jetzt gehen. Für mich fangen morgen die Abschlussprüfungen an, und …«

»Alex, das kann ich doch verstehen. Komm, ich begleite dich zur Tür.«

»Schön.«

Und ich beugte mich über den Mann, der technisch mein Vater war, küsste ihn auf die Stirn und versuchte, die Gedanken zu denken, die in einem derartigen Augenblick angemessen sind, denn ich wusste, dass ich ihn zum letzten Mal sah.

Aber die Gedanken blieben aus, weil in meinem Kopf nur Platz war für *sie*.

Mit einem letzten Blick auf ihn folgte ich Viola zur Station hinaus.

»Ich kann dir gar nicht sagen, wie dankbar ich dir bin, dass du gekommen bist«, sagte sie wieder, als wir vor dem Krankenhaus auf der bevölkerten Straße standen und sie sich mit leicht zitternden Händen eine selbst gedrehte Zigarette anzündete. »So etwas machst auch nur du, Alex. Ich habe nie vergessen, wie nett du in dem Sommer zu mir warst, als alles so schwierig war.«

»Aber ehrlich, Viola, so weit ist Oxford von London nun auch nicht entfernt«, sagte ich verhalten. Ich kam mir wie der letzte Schuft vor, weil sie glaubte, ich hätte Sacha aus reiner Herzensgüte besucht.

»Wenn er aufwacht, sage ich ihm, dass du da warst. Er

hat eine Schwäche für dich. Einmal habe ich ihm erzählt, dass du in Oxford studierst – du weißt doch, dass William mein Patenonkel ist, und er schickt mir zu Weihnachten immer einen Scheck und eine Karte, in der er mich über Neuigkeiten auf dem Laufenden hält –, und da war mein Dad richtig stolz! Ich dachte, gleich würde er in Tränen ausbrechen. Wie auch immer, du solltest gehen, sonst verpasst du deinen Zug.«

»Ja, stimmt.«

»Ich … würdest du mir vielleicht deine Handynummer geben? Dann könnte ich dir simsen und dir Bescheid geben …« Ihr versagte die Stimme. Sie wühlte mit gesenktem Kopf in ihrer Tasche, um die Tränen zu verbergen, die zweifellos in ihren wunderschönen Augen glänzten.

»Natürlich.«

Wir tauschten die Nummern aus und versprachen, in Kontakt zu bleiben.

»Ach, Alex, ich …«

Und da blieb mir nichts anderes übrig, als sie in meine Arme zu ziehen. Und sie festzuhalten. Und gegen jede Vernunft zu hoffen, es könnte für immer und ewig sein.

»Tschüs, Alex«, sagte sie schließlich.

Und ich ging davon und wusste, dass es um mich geschehen war.

Sobald ich wieder zu Hause in Oxford war, rief ich Dad an und sagte ihm, dass ich im Krankenhaus Viola getroffen hätte und dass Sacha in den vergangenen achtundvierzig Stunden nicht mehr richtig zu Bewusstsein gekommen sei. Und dann fragte ich, ob Sacha seinen Kindern wohl je erzählt habe, dass ich sein Sohn sei.

»Alex, das bezweifle ich«, sagte er. »Rupes kann ihn sowieso nicht leiden, und Viola, wie du weißt, liebt ihn von ganzem Herzen. Ich kann mir nicht vorstellen, dass Sacha sein Verhältnis zu ihnen noch weiter belasten wollte, und vor allem nicht das zu Viola. Sie war in den letzten Jahren mehr oder minder der einzige Mensch, den er noch hatte.«

»Und Jules? Glaubst du, dass sie etwas gesagt hat?«, fragte ich und hoffte zum ersten Mal im Leben, dass sie tatsächlich den Mund aufgemacht und Klartext geredet hatte. Denn dann würde mir das erspart bleiben.

»Da müsste ich Mum fragen, sie hat sich ja damals nach dem großen Knall auf Zypern mit ihr unterhalten. Aber auch das bezweifele ich. Jules mag schwierig sein, aber angesichts der Tatsache, dass die beiden gerade ihr Zuhause, ihr Geld und ihren Vater verloren hatten, glaube ich kaum, dass sie auch noch einen außerehelichen Halbbruder ins Spiel bringen wollte. Ach je, Alex, das tut mir jetzt leid«, entschuldigte er sich sofort für seine Unverblümtheit.

»Schon in Ordnung, Dad«, sagte ich. Ich wusste, dass er nie ein Blatt vor den Mund nahm.

»Aber ich werde mal Mum fragen. Und viel Glück kommende Woche bei deinen Prüfungen.«

Er fragte meine Mutter tatsächlich, und sie rief mich dann auch an und erklärte, Jules habe ihr damals gesagt, sie werde es Rupes und Viola nicht sagen.

»Wenn ich mich recht erinnere, sagte sie, es sei Sachas Aufgabe, ihnen die schlechte Nachricht beizubringen, nicht ihre, aber er werde sich sicher davor drücken, weil er dazu viel zu feige sei. Oder etwas in der Art«, erklärte sie.

»Meinst du, dass ich es Viola sagen sollte, Mum?«

»Im Moment nicht, nein. Es klingt, als hätte sie im Augenblick genug Sorgen am Hals. Es eilt doch nicht, oder?«

»Nein. Danke, Mum. Bis bald.«

An dem Abend beschloss ich, dass ich, sobald die Prüfungen vorbei waren, nach London fahren und Viola die Wahrheit sagen würde. Schließlich war das Ganze ja nicht meine Schuld.

Aber wie das Schicksal es will, spürte ich am Tag meiner letzten Prüfung morgens um fünf das Handy neben mir vibrieren. Es war ein entgangener Anruf von Viola, und die Voicemail teilte mir die Nachricht mit, die ich erwartet hatte. Ich rief Viola sofort zurück und hörte sie am anderen Ende herzzerreißend weinen. Auf meine Frage, wer bei ihr sei, sagte sie: »Niemand.«

»Rupes sagt, er hat zu viel zu tun«, klagte sie. »Und jetzt muss ich diese ganzen schrecklichen Dinge machen, die Sterbeurkunde besorgen, einen Bestatter finden und ...« Vom anderen Ende der Leitung hörte ich ein seltsames Geräusch, und ich wusste, dass sie sich die Nase abwischte. »Solche Sachen.«

»Weißt du was? Meine letzte Prüfung ist mittags vorbei, dann setze ich mich in den Zug und komme nach London, um dir zu helfen.«

»Nein, Alex! Du musst heute Abend feiern! Bitte, mach dir keinen Kopf ...«

»Ich schicke dir eine SMS, sobald ich im Zug sitze, und wir treffen uns vor dem Krankenhaus. So lange musst du noch durchhalten, in Ordnung?«

Anstatt also mit allen anderen Studenten meines Jahrgangs zwölf Stunden lang durch die Bars und Clubs von Oxford zu ziehen, war ich in London und kümmerte mich um die ganzen bürokratischen Dinge, die der Tod meines Vaters mit sich brachte, mit seiner untröstlichen Tochter an meiner Seite.

Die im Grunde gar nicht seine Tochter war. Und die nicht wusste, dass ich sein leiblicher Sohn war …

Und sie war in ihrem Kummer so entsetzlich dankbar und so erschreckend hinreißend. An dem Tag sah sie mich an, als wäre ich ihr Retter in der Not, ihr Fels in der Brandung, und das wiederholte sie ständig und immer wieder, bis ich mich am liebsten übergeben hätte, weil alles ein einziger Betrug war.

Obwohl es ja eigentlich kein richtiger Betrug war, denn ob Sacha nun mein Vater war oder nicht, ich wäre auf jeden Fall für sie da gewesen. Nichts war mir wichtiger, als sie zu beschützen – ein unwillkürlicher Impuls, an den ich mich nur allzu gut von unserer gemeinsamen Zeit in Pandora erinnerte. Und angesichts ihres Zustands wollte ich um keinen Preis auf meine Vernunft hören und ihr die Wahrheit sagen. Weil ich befürchtete, sie könnte daran zerbrechen. Und vielleicht wäre sie das auch.

Also sagte ich nichts.

Am Abend setzten wir uns in einen etwas heruntergekommenen Pub in Waterloo, und ich leerte drei Bier im Gegenzug zu Violas zwei Gläsern Weißwein. Sie ließ ihren Kopf in meine Armbeuge sinken, und ich versuchte, mich an die ganzen anderen Dinge zu erinnern, die am folgenden Tag anstanden.

»Warum bist du so nett zu mir?«, fragte sie unvermittelt und schaute aus ihrem wundervollen zartblassen (oder vielmehr verquollenen und fahlen) Gesicht zu mir auf.

»Ich … Das will ich einfach.« Plötzlich war ich um

Worte verlegen. »Noch einen Drink?«, fragte ich und stand auf.

»Gern.«

Als ich zum Tisch zurückkehrte, hatte ich schon ein Drittel des neuen Glases geleert, aber ich tröstete mich mit dem Gedanken, dass ich meine Leber wesentlich mehr geschädigt hätte, wenn ich diesen Abend in Oxford verbracht hätte. Sobald ich mich setzte, legte sie sich meinen Arm um die Schulter und schmiegte sich wieder an mich.

»Wir sind doch so gut wie eine Familie, Alex, oder nicht?«

Fast hätte ich mich an meinem Bier verschluckt.

»Ich meine, dein Vater ist mein Patenonkel, und Dad und er kannten sich seit der Schulzeit. Und als wir kleiner waren, haben wir uns doch oft gegenseitig besucht, oder? Alex, darf ich dich was fragen?«

Guter Gott! »Klar.«

»In dem Sommer in Pandora … warst du da in Chloë verliebt?«

Stirnrunzelnd sah ich sie an. »Woher weißt du das?«

Da lachte sie kurz auf. »Weil ich eifersüchtig war!«

»Eifersüchtig?«

»War das nicht offensichtlich? Ich war bis über beide Ohren in dich verknallt.« Sie drohte mir scherzhaft mit dem Finger, und da wurde mir klar, dass sie beschwipst war. Vermutlich hatte sie seit Tagen nichts mehr gegessen.

»Um ehrlich zu sein, Viola, das habe ich nicht gemerkt.«

»Nicht einmal, nachdem ich Stunden damit verbracht hatte, den Umschlag mit Blumen und Herzen zu bemalen? Ganz zu schweigen davon, wie lange ich brauchte, um dir das Gedicht zu schreiben.«

»Daran erinnere ich mich noch.« *War ich froh, dass ich mich wirklich erinnerte!* »Es hieß ›Freunde‹.«

»Ja. Aber konntest du denn nicht zwischen den Zeilen lesen?«

»Nein.« Ich schaute zu ihr hinunter. »Du warst damals erst zehn.«

»Um genau zu sein, war ich fast elf, gerade einmal zwei Jahre und vier Monate jünger als du«, gab sie gekränkt zurück.

»Du warst noch ein kleines Mädchen …«

»Genauso, wie Chloë dich vermutlich noch für einen kleinen Jungen hielt …«

»Ja«, sagte ich mit einem Seufzen. »Das stimmt wohl.«

»Das ist doch witzig, oder?«

»Findest du?«

»Doch, irgendwie schon. Du träumst von Chloë, und ich träume von dir.«

»Wahrscheinlich«, sagte ich im Versuch, sie zu überzeugen, dass dieser Teil meiner Biografie ersatzlos gestrichen werden müsste, weil er nicht mehr den Tatsachen entsprach.

Daraufhin setzte sie sich auf und schaute mich an. »Bist du immer noch in sie verliebt?«

»Nein.«

Leichter war mir eine Antwort noch nie gefallen.

»Aha.«

Daraufhin sah sie mich erwartungsvoll an, als sollte ich weiter ausholen. Das konnte ich aber nicht, ohne ihr zu gestehen, dass sie diejenige war, die den Bann gebrochen hatte, und zwar erst vor wenigen Tagen. Das zu sagen, wäre in diesem Moment wirklich das Allerunpassendste gewesen. Wenn in der Zukunft – nachdem sie schließlich die Wahrheit erfahren haben würde, weshalb ich urplötzlich wieder in ihrem Leben aufgetaucht war – auch nur ansatzweise ruchbar würde, ich hätte die Situation ausgenutzt, wären ich und mein armes Herz für den Rest aller Zeiten abgeschrieben.

»Es gibt nichts mehr zu sagen.«

Erleichtert spürte ich, dass sie sich wieder an mich kuschelte. »Gut. Ich meine, es ist doch etwas seltsam, in die eigene Stiefschwester verknallt zu sein, oder nicht?«

»Das finde ich eigentlich nicht«, sagte ich mit so fester Stimme wie möglich. Eine überzeugende Antwort war in diesem Fall dringend angeraten. »Ich meine, Chloë und ich sind ja nicht blutsverwandt, oder? Außerdem hat man früher in den meisten kleinen Gemeinschaften untereinander geheiratet, mal ganz abgesehen von den Adelsfamilien. Cousins und Cousinen, das war die Norm. Wie du bestimmt aus den ganzen Jane-Austen-Romanen weißt, die du sicher gelesen hast, seit wir uns das letzte Mal gesehen haben«, fügte ich sicherheitshalber noch hinzu.

»Ja, wahrscheinlich. Übrigens habe ich Chloë in letzter Zeit häufiger gesehen«, sagte sie unvermittelt.

»Ach ja?«

»Du weißt doch, dass sie jetzt hier in London bei der *Vogue* ein Praktikum macht? Und als ich hier zu studieren anfing, hat sie mich ganz lieb angesimst und gefragt, ob wir uns nicht mal zum Mittagessen treffen sollen. Ich glaube, dein Dad hat sie darum gebeten.«

»Ach«, sagte ich.

»Ja. Und ehrlich, Alex, jetzt kann ich verstehen, dass du so in sie verknallt warst. Sie ist einfach hinreißend schön.

Und noch dazu unglaublich nett. Kannst du dir vorstellen – sie hat mich tatsächlich gefragt, ob ich sie nicht mal bei der *Vogue* besuchen und die Moderedakteurin kennenlernen möchte. Sie hat gesagt, ich sei ein tolles Model. Ich meine, ich weiß, dass sie das bloß so dahingesagt hat, denn wer würde mich je für schön halten?« Bei dem Gedanken musste Viola lachen.

Ich, Viola, und ehrlich gesagt jeder andere Mann, der dir auf der Straße begegnet, und jede Frau auch.

Aber ich konnte verstehen, weshalb Viola Chloës Bemerkung nicht für bare Münze nahm. So ist das mit den hässlichen Entchen, die zum schönen Schwan werden.

»Im Herbst geht sie nach Paris«, erzählte Viola weiter. »Sie hat in irgendeinem Modehaus einen Job als Jungdesignerin bekommen. Ein neues mit einem unaussprechlichen Namen. Jean-Paul Irgendwie, glaube ich …« Plötzlich verstummte sie und seufzte schwer. »Ach je, jetzt ist es mir wieder eingefallen.«

»Was?«

»Entschuldige … Ich meine, ich habe es kurz vergessen, und das war schön. Aber heute Morgen ist doch Daddy gestorben, ach …«

Dann vergrub sie das Gesicht wieder in meiner Achsel, und ich hoffte und betete, dass ich genügend Deodorant hingesprüht hatte, um den Geruch von Abschlussprüfung plus Viola plus Tod meines genetischen Dads zu überdecken.

»Kann ich dir etwas zu essen holen?«, fragte ich im Versuch, etwas Praktisches vorzuschlagen, wie mein echter Dad es tun würde.

»Nein danke«, kam die Antwort aus meiner Achsel.

»Viola«, fuhr ich im gleichen Dad-Ton fort. »Ich glaube wirklich, dass du ein bisschen schlafen solltest. Du musst völlig kaputt sein.«

Bei diesen Worten tauchte sie aus meiner Achsel auf, sah mich an und versuchte, sich zusammenzunehmen. »Ja, das stimmt«, sagte sie und nickte. »Und du solltest nach Oxford zurückfahren.«

»Ich brauche nicht nach Oxford zurückzufahren, das hat bis September ein Ende. Ich schlafe heute Nacht in Dads und Mums Wohnung. Ich habe sie vom Zug aus angerufen und gefragt, ob das geht.« Ich schaute auf meine Uhr. »Ehrlich gesagt sollte ich mich auf den Weg machen. Die verrückte Alte, die den Schlüssel hat und im Souterrain wohnt, geht um zehn ins Bett, und dann komme ich nicht mehr rein.«

»Natürlich«, sagte sie wieder. »Wir müssen los.«

Sie leerte ihr Weinglas, aber als sie aufstand, verloren ihre Wangen die leichte Alkoholröte, und auf ihrer Stirn erschienen wieder Falten. Schweigend verließen wir den Pub.

»Also dann, Alex, hab noch mal vielen Dank. Du warst wunderbar.« Sie gab mir einen Kuss auf die Wange. »Gute Nacht.«

»Viola!«, sagte ich, als sie zurücktrat. »Wohin gehst du?«

»Nach Hause«, antwortete sie leise.

»Und ist jemand für dich da?«

Dieses Mal zuckte sie nur mit den Schultern.

»Hör mal, willst du nicht mit zu mir kommen? Ich meine, du musst doch heute Nacht jemanden bei dir haben.«

»Das ist wirklich lieb von dir, Alex, aber ehrlich, ich finde, du warst schon genug für mich da.«

Viola, ich werde niemals genug für dich da sein können …

Da nahm ich sie am Arm und hielt sie fest. »Sei nicht albern. Es kommt gar nicht infrage, dass ich dich heute Nacht allein lasse.«

Und dann war ich es, der sie in den Arm nahm, und als sie ihren Rosenknospenmund zu meinem Gesicht hob, war auch ich es, der tat, als bemerke er es nicht. Und ich war es, der unbeholfen meinen Mund an ihr zartes Ohr drückte, als ich sie an mich zog.

Als wir bei der Wohnung in Bloomsbury ankamen, die zufällig nicht weit von Violas Wohnheim entfernt lag, konnte ich die kleine alte Dame mit viel gutem Zureden dazu bewegen, an die Tür ihrer Souterrainwohnung zu kommen und mir durch den winzigen Spalt zwischen den vielen Sicherheitsketten hindurch den Schlüssel zu reichen. Bei ihrem knochigen Arm musste ich unweigerlich an das Zweiglein denken, das Hänsel im Märchen der Hexe hinhielt, um sie zu überlisten.

Ich zeigte Viola das Bad und holte gerade einen Pullover aus meiner kleinen Reisetasche, weil es in der Wohnung recht frisch war, als Viola ins Zimmer kam und aufs Bett plumpste.

»Entschuldige, Alex, aber … ich bin soooo müde …«

»Ich weiß.« Sie schloss die Augen. »Bist du dir sicher, dass du nicht doch etwas essen solltest?«, fragte ich und betrachtete sie, wie sie einer Nymphe gleich in ihrer ganzen Schönheit hingestreckt auf dem Bett lag – die Haare über das Kissen gebreitet, die langen Beine fotogen drapiert, dabei hatte sie sich einfach nur aufs Bett fallen lassen.

Es kam keine Antwort. Sie war eingeschlafen.

Also improvisierte ich ein Abendessen aus Baked Beans

und einer Dose Thunfisch, die ich im Schrank fand, und aß es im Wohnzimmer, wo ich im Fernsehen die BBC-Nachrichten sah (*warum?*). Und versuchte, in meinem Gehirn Ordnung zu schaffen und in meiner Seele nach einer Reaktion auf Sachas Tod zu forschen. Aber Viola hatte meinen Verstand außer Kraft gesetzt, und wann immer ich an meinen genetischen Dad dachte, der tot im Leichenhaus lag, und mir überlegte, wie es mir damit ging, schob Viola sich davor, und meine Gedanken schweiften in eine völlig andere Richtung ab.

Außerdem war die schreckliche Wahrheit, dass ich über die Trauer hinaus, dass ein Leben viel zu früh zu Ende gegangen war, gar nichts empfand.

Durch die dünne Wand hindurch hörte ich ein Wimmern und ging zu ihr.

»Was ist?«, fragte ich und tadelte mich sofort für die Unsinnigkeit meiner Frage.

Sie antwortete nicht, also tastete ich in der Dunkelheit nach einem freien Platz am Rand des Bettes, um mich nicht aus Versehen auf sie zu setzen.

»Ich habe … geträumt … dass er lebt …«

»Ach, Viola.«

»Ich weiß, dass er nicht mehr am Leben ist.« Ich spürte, wie sie sich mit dem Arm über das Gesicht fuhr, um sich die Tränen zu trocknen, und wünschte mir, ich könnte den gleichen Schmerz über den Tod unseres Vaters empfinden wie sie. Aber das konnte ich nicht. Und deswegen kam ich mir noch viel schäbiger vor.

»Es tut mir leid«, sagte ich beschwichtigend, »aber er ist gestorben.« Und in dem Augenblick verfluchte ich Jules und Rupes. Gleichgültig, was unser Vater getan oder nicht getan haben mochte, er war weder Saddam noch Stalin und auch nicht Mao. Nicht einmal ein wirklich schlechter Mensch ... nur ein mit Makeln behafteter und egozentrischer, schwacher Jammerlappen. Eine Mutter und ein Bruder – Adoptiv- hin oder her – sollten in diesem Moment doch wirklich zur Stelle sein, um das eine Familienmitglied zu trösten, das Sacha genügend geliebt hatte, um aufrichtig Trauer über seinen Tod zu empfinden. »Jetzt bin nur ich hier, tut mir leid.«

»Ach, Alex, das darfst du nicht sagen.« Die Hand, mit der sie sich die Tränen getrocknet hatte, tastete nach meiner, und in der Dunkelheit reichte ich sie ihr, und sie drückte sie sehr, sehr fest. »Von allen Menschen, die ich kenne, gibt es niemanden, den ich jetzt lieber bei mir hätte. Ich komme mir vor wie in einem surrealen Traum. Wirklich.«

Und beim letzten Wort drückte sie meine Hand besonders fest wie zur Bekräftigung.

»Alex?«

»Ja, Viola?«

»Würdest du ... würdest du mich bitte in den Arm nehmen?«

Guter Gott!

»Natürlich.« Und so stand ich auf und ging auf die andere Seite des Betts, wo ich wieder nach einem Platz auf der Matratze suchte, und legte mich neben sie. Sie schmiegte sich an mich, als wären wir zwei Teile eines Puzzles, die viel zu lange in getrennten Schachteln aufbewahrt waren und jetzt endlich zusammengefügt wurden. Mein Arm legte sich wie von selbst um ihre schmale Taille, und meine Knie beugten sich irgendwie und passten dann genau in ihre Kniekehlen.

»Danke«, sagte sie nach einer Weile, als ich gerade dachte, sie wäre eingeschlafen.

»Wofür?«

»Dass du hier bist. Dass du bist, wie du bist.«

»Das ist schon in Ordnung.« Dann dachte ich wirklich, dass sie eingeschlafen wäre, denn sie schwieg wirklich ewig. Und ich zählte die Sekunden.

»Alex?«, flüsterte sie halb im Schlaf.

»Ja?«

»Ich liebe dich. Klingt verrückt, aber ich habe dich immer schon geliebt. Und ich glaube, ich werde dich auch immer lieben.«

Das Schlimmste war, obwohl jede Gehirnzelle und jede Faser meines Körpers danach verlangte, dasselbe darauf zu antworten, hatte ich das Gefühl, es nicht zu dürfen. Denn ich dachte wieder daran, was sie wohl empfinden würde, wenn sie die Wahrheit erfuhr.

Diese Nacht war eine der qualvollsten meines bisherigen Lebens. Und nicht, weil ich gerade meinen Vater verloren hatte, sondern weil ich meine Zukunft gefunden hatte. Die ganze Nacht, als Viola unruhig in meinen Armen schlief, lag ich hellwach neben ihr. Wann immer sie unruhig wurde, streichelte ich ihr übers Haar, und dann schlief sie ruhig weiter.

»Ich liebe dich«, flüsterte ich unhörbar. »Ich liebe dich.«

Um gerecht zu sein: Ich möchte einen Mann sehen, der volle sechs Stunden mit einem der entzückendsten weiblichen Wesen der Welt in den Armen im Bett liegt, ohne unzulässige sinnliche Gelüste zu empfinden. Ganz abgesehen von der Unzulässigkeit meiner Beziehung mit Viola.

Viola … Irgendwann muss ich halluziniert haben, denn plötzlich schwebte ein Instrument durch mein Blickfeld, ein Instrument aus glänzendem nussbraunem Holz und mit Saiten bespannt.

Bratsche, Geige, Cello … Trompete! Vielleicht döste ich in der Nacht doch immer wieder ein, aber mein Schlaf war nicht sehr tief, denn ich weiß noch, dass ich mir irgendwann dachte, wir könnten unseren Erstgeborenen »Harp« wie »Harfe« nennen. Aber dann dachte ich mir, dass man nur ein »o« anzuhängen brauchte, um unserem Kind einen Namen zu geben, mit dem es vielleicht allzu sehr auf eine Rolle festlegt wäre.

Trommel? Oder vielleicht Fagott …?

Da muss ich dann doch richtig eingeschlafen sein, denn als Nächstes trieb mir der Duft von Kaffee in die Nase.

»Alex?« Meine tizianrote Muse stand über mir, die Haare nass vom Duschen, und reichte mir einen Becher. »Wach auf.«

»Ich bin doch wach! Ich meine, gleich.«

»Hier, ich habe dir einen Kaffee gemacht.« Sie stellte den Becher auf den Tisch neben mich, ging zur anderen Bettseite und setzte sich im Schneidersitz neben mich, einen Block auf dem Schoß und einen Stift in der Hand. »Also, was, sagtest du, müssen wir heute alles erledigen?«

Die Beisetzung wurde in der Kapelle von Magdalen abgehalten, Dads und Sachas altem College. Und jetzt meinem. Ich gebe zu, als Viola sehnsüchtig erwähnte, dass sie diesen Ort für die Feier am schönsten fände, ließ ich ein paar Verbindungen spielen. Angesichts dessen, dass Sachas Lebensleistung im Vergleich zu der anderer Absolventen nicht unbedingt herausstach, sprach ich dezent an den entsprechenden Stellen vor. (Es musste doch zumindest einen Vorteil haben, drei Jahre lang Philosophie studiert zu haben, wozu auch eine ganze Reihe unglaublich dröger Theologie-Vorlesungen des College-Kaplans gehörten.)

Mit vereinten Kräften gelang es uns, gut dreißig Trauergäste zusammenzutrommeln – im Grunde die Pandora-Truppe sowie eine Reihe alter Kommilitonen, die Dad zum Kommen überredet hatte, zweifellos mit der Aussicht auf ein anschließendes Besäufnis in der College-Bar als Überzeugungshilfe. Wer und wie auch immer, pflichtschuldig reisten sie alle an.

In der Kapelle wollte ich gerade zu meinen Eltern gehen, als Viola meine Hand nahm und darauf bestand, dass ich mich neben sie in die erste Reihe setzte. Rupes saß auf meiner anderen Seite, Jules neben Viola.

»Alex war großartig«, sagte sie zu den beiden.

Und so saß ich bei der Trauerfeier für meinen Vater in der vordersten Reihe, neben meinem Halbbruder – der wie ein Schlosshund heulte – und Viola, meine … tja, in welchem Verhältnis standen wir denn eigentlich?

Die meiste Zeit des Gottesdiensts hindurch grübelte ich über diese Frage. Und kam zu dem Schluss – obwohl ich mir vornahm, mich noch einmal im Internet schlauzumachen –, dass wir in gar keinem Verhältnis zueinander standen. Was zu meiner unendlichen Erleichterung hieß, dass sie mir in Zukunft alles bedeuten könnte. Danach ging es mir wesentlich besser.

Ich habe keine Ahnung, was Mum dachte, dass ich bei Sachas/Alexanders Beerdigung wie der sprichwörtliche

Kuckuck mitten im Chandler-Nest saß, sie äußerte sich nicht dazu. Sie hatte mit William, Chloë, Immy und Fred direkt hinter uns Platz genommen.

Beim anschließenden Leichenschmaus hielt ich mich im Hintergrund. Gelegentlich meinte ich Jules' Blicke zu spüren, obwohl ich mir das vielleicht auch nur einbildete. Irgendwann dankte sie mir allerdings, wie sehr ich Viola unterstützt hätte.

Nachdem sich Rupes die Tränen getrocknet hatte, fiel ihm nichts Besseres ein, als mich zu fragen, ob es wohl ein Testament gebe. Ich versicherte ihm, dass es keines gab. Das hatten Viola und ich bereits in Erfahrung gebracht und auch, dass Sacha (zum Glück) gar keines gemacht hatte.

Unser Vater hatte nichts mehr gehabt, das er jemandem hätte vererben können.

Bevor sie fuhren, kam meine Mutter zu mir. »Viola hat gesagt, wie großartig du dich verhalten hast.«

»Eigentlich nicht, Mum.«

»Du hast es ihr noch nicht gesagt, oder?«

Ich schüttelte den Kopf.

»Alex.« Sie nahm meine Hände in ihre entsetzlich knochigen, und ich dachte mit Schrecken, wie zerbrechlich sie aussah. »Bitte, lern aus meinen Fehlern. Je früher, desto besser ...«

Dann küsste sie mich mit aller Kraft, die sie aufbringen konnte. Was damals sehr wenig war.

Es war mir gelungen, für die Nacht zwei Zimmer im College zu bekommen – eines für mich und eines für Viola. Sie hatte viel zu viel getrunken, und der Alkohol im Verbund mit einem Übermaß an Gefühlen hatten eine prekäre Mischung aus Euphorie und Verzweiflung hervorgerufen.

Sie sagte ständig, dass sie ihre Mutter hasse – ja, hasse. Offenbar hatte Jules ihr einmal unter dem Einfluss von allzu viel Alkohol gesagt, dass es Sachas Wunsch gewesen sei, sie zu adoptieren.

»Von jetzt an kann sie mich mal«, hatte Viola gemurmelt. »Ich will sie nie wiedersehen – und meinen idiotischen Bruder auch nicht!«

Ich wusste, dass sie das nicht im Ernst meinte, dass da der Kummer und die Erschöpfung aus ihr sprachen, aber ich konnte es nachempfinden. Und dann war sie in *meinem* Zimmer aufs Bett gefallen, nicht in ihrem. Und wieder hatte sie jämmerlich geweint und gesagt, ich solle sie doch in den Arm nehmen.

Und meine Entschlossenheit, ihr die Wahrheit zu sagen, löste sich in nichts auf.

Morgen, dachte ich mir …

Doch dieses Morgen war nie gekommen. Ich hatte einfach nie den richtigen Moment gefunden. Und dann folgte die Nacht zwei Wochen später, als ich gemeint hatte, es könne ihr guttun wegzufahren, und ob sie nicht zu der grandiosen Party in Italien mitfahren wolle, die ein Freund aus Oxford dort veranstaltete. Der Gastgeber ging davon aus, dass wir ein Paar wären. Und dort, in unserem wunderschönen Zimmer in Florenz, schliefen wir das erste Mal miteinander.

Und dann … alles war so unglaublich perfekt gewesen, dass ich mich einfach nicht dazu durchringen konnte – wie damals meine Mutter –, ihr die Wahrheit zu sagen.

Und so ging es weiter und weiter … Und mein Schuldgefühl wuchs derart, dass ich von außen betrachtet ganz der alte Alex war, aber mich in Wirklichkeit wie ein kleiner, hässlicher, verlogener Betrüger fühlte.

Diese Monate waren in gewisser Hinsicht die schönsten meines Lebens. Ich arbeitete den Sommer über in London, ich hatte eine Praktikantenstelle an der British Library in King's Cross bekommen, wo ich die gebundenen und digitalisierten Ausgaben von philosophischen Werken dokumentierte und archivierte. Mum und Dad stellten mir für diese Zeit ihre kleine Wohnung in Bloomsbury zur Verfügung.

Tagsüber beschäftigte ich mich mit literarischen Kunstwerken und nachts mit Viola, die das vollkommenste Kunstwerk war, das ich mir vorstellen konnte.

Nachdem sie sich geweigert hatte, den Sommer bei ihrer Mutter im Cottage zu verbringen, da zwischen ihr und ihrer restlichen Familie Funkstille herrschte, besorgte sie sich einen Job im Supermarkt um die Ecke. Dann fragte sie zaghaft bei mir an, ob sie bei mir einziehen könne, weil sie keine Bleibe habe. Und ich hatte sofort eingewilligt.

Manchmal, wenn ich morgens die Euston Road zur Arbeit radelte – ja, auf dem Fahrrad –, kam ich mir vor wie eine Figur aus einem Roman. Meine Welt war perfekt.

Abgesehen davon, dass ich eine Lüge lebte …

Jeden Tag nahm ich im Souterrain der British Library Bücher voll kluger Gedanken in die Hand – und wusste, dass jedes von ihnen, von Sophokles bis zu den heutigen »Selbsthilfe«-Ergüssen, mir raten würde, die Wahrheit zu gestehen. Und jeden Abend, wenn ich wie ein Verrückter in die Pedale trat, um zu ihr nach Hause zu kommen, schwor ich mir, dass dieser Abend derjenige welcher sein würde.

Und dann kam ich an, und sie empfing mich mit einem leckeren Essen, das sie aus den Angeboten ihres Supermarkts, deren Verfallsdatum fast abgelaufen war, gekocht hatte, und sie sah so hinreißend und so zerbrechlich aus, dass ich es einfach nicht schaffte.

Und so kam es, dass eine zunehmend herbstliche Frische in der Luft lag, und Viola zog in das Kämmerchen, das sie als Studentenbude für das kommende Studienjahr gefunden hatte, und ich begann zu packen, um nach Oxford zurückzukehren und meinen Magister zu machen.

Bei der Vorstellung, dass unser Liebesidyll durch etwas so Banales wie das Leben ein Ende fand, waren wir beide zu Tode betrübt. Zu der Zeit hatten wir all unseren Kindern bereits Namen gegeben und unsere Hochzeit geplant, was gar nicht so abwegig war, schließlich war Viola einundzwanzig und ich fast dreiundzwanzig. Sprich: Es lag durchaus im Bereich des Möglichen. Eine Art unsichtbarer Kleister verband uns, und doch hatte keiner von uns allzu viele Worte über die neue, wunderbare Welt fallen lassen, die wir gemeinsam entdeckt hatten, aus Angst, sie zu zerstören.

Obwohl es nach Oxford keine Stunde Zugfahrt war und wir uns bereits darauf verständigt hatten, dass wir uns an den Wochenenden abwechselnd besuchen würden, war der letzte Abend in meiner Erinnerung so schmerzlich, als würde ich nach Westindien aufbrechen und erst in drei Jahren wiederkehren, wenn überhaupt. Wir wussten beide nicht mehr, was es bedeutete, ohne den anderen auszukommen.

Die Wochen bis zu den Weihnachtsferien vergingen in einem Nebel der Sehnsucht, und so konzentriert ich früher gearbeitet hatte, jetzt verlor ich mich bei Vorlesungen und Seminaren in einer traumartigen Leere. Tröstlicherweise erging es ihr ebenso, und als es Weihnachten wurde, fragte ich Mum und Dad, ob Viola mit mir nach Hause kommen könne, da sie es strikt ablehne, die Feiertage mit Jules und Rupes zu verbringen.

»Ich war immer bei Dad, um ihm Gesellschaft zu leisten«, erklärte Viola. »Jemand anderen als mich hatte er nicht.«

Gleich nach unserer Ankunft stürzte sich meine Mum – die sich zum Glück offenbar gut von ihrer letzten Behandlung erholte – auf mich und ermahnte mich wieder, Viola alles zu sagen. Und wieder versprach ich es, aber dann … Schließlich war es Weihnachten. Und Viola sah im Schoß unserer liebevollen Familie so glücklich und entspannt aus wie seit Sachas Tod nicht mehr.

Und so sagte ich wieder nichts.

Im neuen Jahr kehrten wir zu unserer Besuchsroutine zurück. Ich hatte schon beschlossen, dass ich alles daransetzen würde, nach der Magisterprüfung eine Arbeit in London zu finden. Letztlich war es mir egal, ob ich mich als Straßenfeger verdingen musste, Hauptsache, ich konnte Viola abends, wenn ich verschmutzt und übelriechend nach Hause kam, an mich drücken.

Es wurde Ostern, und Viola musste im Rahmen eines Literaturaustauschs für einen Monat nach Frankreich fahren. Den Abend vor ihrer Abfahrt verbrachten wir in der Wohnung in Bloomsbury. Sie fragte, ob sie meine Reisetasche borgen könne, und während sie packte, ging ich los, um uns zur Feier des Tages eine Flasche Wein und einen Imbiss vom Inder zu holen.

Als ich zurückkam, rief ich schon im Flur ihren Namen und ging weiter ins Wohnzimmer. Sie saß im Schneidersitz auf dem Boden, in der Hand den Brief, den Sacha mir kurz vor seinem Tod geschrieben hatte.

Das Herz rutschte mir in die Hose und dann weiter durch den ganzen Körper, bis es wild schlagend zu meinen Füßen lag.

»Ich … wo hast du den gefunden?«, fragte ich.

»Er steckte vorn in deiner Reisetasche.« Ihr Gesicht war tränenüberströmt und aschfahl. »Es war doch alles eine einzige Lüge, oder?«

»Nein, Viola, natürlich nicht!«

»Was mich betrifft, war es das sehr wohl«, flüsterte sie, eher fast zu sich selbst. »Und ich dachte, als du zu meinem Vater ins Krankenhaus kamst, dass es dir um ihn ging … mein Gott! Den ganzen Leuten, denen ich vorgeschwärmt habe, wie wunderbar du dich mir gegenüber verhalten hast … und dabei warst du seinetwegen da, nicht meinetwegen!«

»Das stimmt«, sagte ich. »Am ersten Tag bin ich gekommen, weil ich glaubte, ihn besuchen zu müssen. Aber das hat sich schlagartig geändert in dem Moment, als ich dich auf mich zukommen sah.«

»Bitte, Alex, hör auf zu lügen!«

»Viola, ich kann verstehen, dass das für dich ein Schock ist, aber das, was wir in den vergangenen Monaten miteinander erlebt haben – wie kann das eine Lüge sein? Wie?«

»Weil du nicht der bist, für den ich dich hielt. Der liebevolle, fürsorgliche Alex, der die ganze Zeit so tat, als wäre er für mich da … Und weißt du, was das Schlimmste ist?«

Mir fielen viele »schlimmste Dinge« ein, aber ich nannte keines davon.

»Nein.«

»Ich beneide dich. Weil du wirklich sein leibliches Kind warst, ich aber nicht.«

»Viola, im Ernst, er hat mir nichts bedeutet …«

»Danke!«

»So habe ich das nicht gemeint, aber ich war wirklich völlig entsetzt, als ich erfuhr, dass ich sein Sohn bin. Ich meine«, korrigierte ich mich, »ich stand unter Schock.«

»Wie ich jetzt.«

»Ja.« An dieser Rettungsleine hielt ich mich fest und ging auf sie zu. »Natürlich stehst du unter Schock. Es ist schrecklich, das herausfinden zu müssen, und Viola, es tut mir wirklich unendlich leid. Du kannst dir gar nicht vorstellen, wie oft ich es dir schon sagen wollte, aber dann warst du so unglücklich, dass ich es nicht übers Herz brachte. Und dann warst du … waren wir so glücklich miteinander. So glücklich, dass ich das nicht zerstören wollte. Kannst du das nicht verstehen?«

Sie wischte sich die Nase ab mit dieser unerträglich süßen Geste, mit der sie das immer machte, und schüttelte heftig den Kopf. »Im Augenblick verstehe ich überhaupt nichts. Außer dass ich eine Beziehung mit einem … Verwandten habe.«

»Viola, wir haben keinen Tropfen gemeinsames Blut, das weißt du genau.«

»Und mein Vater … wie konnte er bloß?! Guter Gott,

Alex, ich habe ihn so geliebt. Das weißt du genau. Kein Wunder, dass meine arme Mutter ihn hasst ...« Sie schaute zu mir. »Weiß sie Bescheid?«

»Offenbar ja.«

»Seit wann?«

»Das ist alles in den letzten Tagen in Pandora rausgekommen. Offenbar wusste sie es immer schon.«

»Guter Gott! Das ...« Sie schluchzte auf. »Mein Leben ist eine einzige Lüge!«

»Wirklich, Viola, ich kann gut nachvollziehen, dass es dir so vorkommt, aber ...«

»Und was ist mit deiner Mutter?«, fuhr sie mich an. »Was hat die heilige Helena, wie meine Mutter sie immer nannte, mit meinem Vater in einem Bett zu suchen?«

»Ach, Viola, das ist eine lange Geschichte. Lass mich doch die Flasche Wein aufmachen, und ...«

»Nein!« Sie sah mich mit einem Ausdruck abgrundtiefer Verachtung an. »Diese Sache kannst nicht einmal du richten, Alex. Und das Schlimmste ist, ich habe dir vertraut, mehr als jedem anderen, aber du hast mich genauso angelogen wie die anderen. Und zwar bei der Sache, die mir am wichtigsten im Leben ist! Ich habe gedacht, dass du mich liebst, Alex. Wie konntest du bloß die ganzen Monate mit mir zusammen sein und das wissen?«

»Ich ... Oh, Viola, es tut mir wirklich so unendlich leid. Bitte«, flehte ich, »bitte versuch zu verstehen, weshalb.«

»Ich muss hier weg. Ich ertrage das alles nicht mehr. Ich muss erst wieder einen klaren Kopf bekommen, um nachdenken zu können.«

Sie stand auf und griff nach der Reisetasche, die, wie ich zu meinem Entsetzen bemerkte, bereits gepackt war.

»Bitte, Viola, bitte! Lass uns wenigstens darüber reden.«

Sie ging direkt an mir vorbei zum Wohnzimmer hinaus und auf die Wohnungstür zu.

»Ich … kann nicht.« Ihre schönen Augen waren mit Tränen gefüllt. »Es geht nicht nur darum, dass du eine Lüge gelebt hast, es geht auch um mich. Ich weiß einfach nicht mehr, wer ich überhaupt bin.«

»Kommst du wieder?«, fragte ich sie. »Ich liebe dich, Viola, ich liebe dich über alles. Das musst du mir glauben.«

»Alex, ich weiß es nicht. Mach's gut.«

Und damit öffnete sie die Tür und ließ sie hinter sich ins Schloss fallen.

Das Einzige, was mich in der Nacht daran hinderte, mich bewusstlos zu trinken und zur Sicherheit vielleicht noch zwei Handvoll Tabletten einzuwerfen, war meine Mutter, die mich aus heiterem Himmel anrief, um zu hören, wie es mir gehe. Vielleicht ahnte sie etwas.

Wie üblich war sie der erste Mensch, den ich in der schrecklichen Stille nach Violas Fortgehen hatte anrufen wollen. Aber wie jedes Kind mit kranken Eltern weiß, hat man das Gefühl, sie nicht mit irgendwelchen Lappalien behelligen zu dürfen, etwa, wenn die ganze Welt um einen her einstürzt. Immerhin musste meine Mutter der Möglichkeit ins Auge sehen, dass ihr Leben von einem Tag auf den anderen zu Ende sein könnte.

Aber als sie anrief, weinte und schluchzte und jammerte ich in den Hörer. Und zwei Stunden später stand sie wie ein Engel der Barmherzigkeit vor der Tür. In der Nacht unterhielten wir uns sehr lange über die Parallelen zwischen ihrer Situation mit William und meiner mit Viola, und dabei hielt sie ihren großen Sohn die ganze Zeit im Arm. Natürlich übernahm sie die volle Verantwortung für mein Unglück, was ja, ehrlich gesagt, auch nicht ganz falsch war. Aber wenn ich immer noch Zweifel gehabt haben sollte, weshalb sie William nach der Hochzeit nie die Wahrheit gesagt hatte, waren die jetzt völlig ausgeräumt.

Man nannte das gemeinhin »Angst«.

»Möchtest du, dass ich mit ihr spreche?«, fragte sie.

»Nein, Mum, ich muss meine Kämpfe selbst ausfechten.«

»Selbst wenn dieser Kampf auf etwas zurückgeht, das ich getan habe?«

»Ich weiß es nicht«, sagte ich seufzend. »Ich weiß nur, dass ich sie liebe und dass ich den bloßen Gedanken daran, mein Leben womöglich ohne sie zu verbringen, nicht aushalte.«

»Alex, lass ihr Zeit. Sie muss ein paar ziemlich schwierige Erkenntnisse bewältigen, und vergiss nicht, sie trauert immer noch um ihren Vater. Der Aufenthalt in Frankreich wird ihr guttun. Da hat sie den Kopf frei. Und offenbar will sie in Paris auch Chloë besuchen.«

»O mein Gott, Mum.« Ich schüttelte den Kopf. »Wie soll ich damit zurechtkommen?«

»Weil du musst. Eine meiner Krankenschwestern sagte einmal zu mir, dass Menschen im Leben nur so viel aufgebürdet bekommen, wie sie ertragen«, meinte sie nachdenklich.

»Außer sie können es nicht ertragen, und dann bringen sie sich um«, sagte ich kummervoll. Ich lag mit dem Kopf auf ihrem Schoß, und sie streichelte mir übers Haar, als wäre ich noch ein kleines Kind.

»Also, ich glaube, dass sie recht hat. Nimm doch mich als Beispiel: Ja, ich habe Schmerzen und Kummer gehabt, aber ich weiß, dass ich dadurch zu einem besseren Menschen geworden bin. Und alle anderen in der Familie wahrscheinlich auch. Sicher war es für Fred und Immy am schlimmsten, aber langfristig gesehen denke ich, dass sie dadurch selbständiger und selbstbewusster geworden sind. Und dein Vater war natürlich großartig.«

Ich sah die Liebe in Mums Augen leuchten, und da musste ich an meine eigene verlorene Liebe denken, und mich überkam wieder das heulende Elend.

»Ich denke mir oft, dass das Leben wie eine Zugfahrt ist«, sagte Mum unvermittelt.

»Inwiefern?«

»Nun ja, wir sitzen im Zug und fahren der Zukunft entgegen, und bisweilen fährt der Zug in einen hübschen Bahnhof ein, wir dürfen aussteigen und uns eine Tasse Tee bestellen. Oder in deinem Fall, Alex, ein Glas Bier.« Sie lachte leise. »Und da sitzen wir dann und trinken den Tee, genießen den schönen Ausblick und die Ruhe und den inneren Frieden. Ich glaube, das sind die Momente, die die meisten Menschen als Glück bezeichnen würden. Aber dann muss man natürlich wieder einsteigen und die Fahrt fortsetzen. Aber diese Momente reinen Glücks wird man nie vergessen, Alex. Sie sind es, die uns die Kraft geben, uns der Zukunft zu stellen: der Glaube, dass solche Momente wiederkehren werden. Und es geschieht natürlich auch.«

Ich weiß noch, dass ich mir dachte: »Wow«, und dass ich meine philosophische Neigung vielleicht doch nicht nur von meinem Vater geerbt hatte. Für einen Amateurphilosophen war das gar nicht mal schlecht.

»Na ja, ich habe mit Viola in den vergangenen Monaten ungefähr tausend Gläser Bier geleert, und ich würde nur zu gerne hunderttausende mehr mit ihr leeren«, murmelte ich unglücklich.

»Siehst du?« Meine Mutter lächelte. »Die Hoffnung hast du schon, dass es dazu kommen wird.«

Kapitel 34

Während ich hier allein auf der Terrasse stehe – Viola ist mit Chloë nach oben gegangen, um sich frisch zu machen –, kann ich kaum fassen, dass das Leben mir wirklich eine zweite Chance gibt; dass *sie* wieder hier ist. Am liebsten würde ich in die nächste Kirche laufen, auf die Knie sinken und der Gottheit, die mir das gewährt hat, Dank sagen. Welcher auch immer. Und schwören, dass ich aus meinem Fehler lernen werde.

Mehr bleibt uns Menschen nicht zu tun.

Mir ist auch klar, dass mein persönliches Leid – und das aller anderen in der Pandora-Truppe – vernachlässigenswert ist im Vergleich zu dem Leid, das im Großteil der restlichen Welt herrscht. Keiner von uns hat einen Krieg, eine Hungersnot oder einen Genozid erlebt.

Mein jetzt vervollständigtes Tagebuch über die vergangenen zehn Jahre wirft lediglich ein Schlaglicht auf ein paar kleine Leben, die im großen Universum geführt werden. Aber für jeden von uns ist es *sein* Leben, und jedem kommen *seine* Probleme bedeutend vor. Wäre es anders, gäbe es die Menschheit vermutlich gar nicht mehr, denn, wie meine Mutter in ihrer Klugheit sagte (und Pandora würde ihr zweifellos recht geben), uns wurde das Geschenk der Hoffnung gewährt.

Die Musiker stimmen eine Party-Nummer an, und die Menge beginnt zu tanzen. Auf der Tanzfläche sehe ich Jules mit Bertie und Alexis mit Angelina. Und dann sehe ich einen der Gäste, der unverwandt die kleine Peaches anstarrt, die mit ihrer Mutter tanzt.

»Adonis« – wie Mum und Sadie ihn nannten –, ihren Vater.

Ich stutze und frage mich, ob ich gerade eine merkwürdige karmische außerkörperliche Erfahrung mache und den Moment nacherlebe, als Sacha bei Mums und Dads Hochzeit vor all den Jahren zum ersten Mal mich sah. Vielleicht sollte ich später mit Sadie reden. Vielleicht möchte sie ja von meinen Erfahrungen in diesem Bereich profitieren. Der »Bereich«, der den meisten der hier Versammelten (die nicht aus Zypern stammen) den größten Kummer bereitete.

Der Geist auf diesem Fest – derjenige, der nicht hier ist – ist natürlich mein Vater. Sacha oder Alexander – oder wie auch immer.

Nur ein Mensch, ein fehlbarer Mensch wie wir alle …

Ich gehe an den Rand der Terrasse, beuge mich über die Balustrade und schaue zu den Sternen empor. Und frage mich, ob er vielleicht doch von dort oben auf uns herabblickt, eine Flasche Whisky leert und über das Durcheinander lacht, das er hier auf Erden angerichtet hat.

Und zum ersten Mal regt sich in mir ein Gefühl. Ein Verständnis für ihn. Schließlich ist mein Leben vor gar nicht langer Zeit durch mein eigenes Zutun ins Schlingern geraten: Ich habe einen einfachen, überaus menschlichen Fehler begangen und darüber beinahe das mir Kostbarste verloren.

Ich weiß, ich werde mich den Rest meiner Tage bemühen, ein besserer Mensch zu werden, aber ebenso weiß ich auch, dass es mir nicht immer gelingen wird. Ich kann nur mein Bestes versuchen.

»Alex! Komm her!« Mum, Dad, Immy und Fred halten sich an den Händen und bilden einen kleinen Kreis.

»Gute Nacht, Dad«, flüstere ich in den funkelnden Nacht-himmel.

Ich gehe zu meiner Mutter und nehme ihre Hand, mit der anderen ergreife ich Immys, und so tanzen wir im Kreis, während die Band eine seltsame Bouzouki-Version eines Songs spielt, der angeblich ursprünglich einmal »Pompeii« hieß. Das erzählt mir zumindest Fred, denn dieser Tage ist er derjenige, der über solche Sachen Bescheid weiß.

Dann sehe ich Chloë auf die Terrasse treten.

Mum winkt sie zu uns, und in dem Moment bemerke ich, dass auch jemand anderes sie ansieht. Michel steht da wie gebannt, als wäre er vom Blick der Medusa in Stein verwandelt worden.

Fasziniert verfolge ich, wie Chloë auf uns zuschwebt, dann hält sie inne, als würde sie die Intensität seines Blicks im Rücken spüren. Langsam dreht sie sich um und sieht ihn an. Beide lächeln. Fast unmerklich nickt sie ihm zu, dann greift sie nach der Hand ihres Vaters und schließt den Kreis unserer Familie, und in dem Moment fängt die Band wieder zu spielen an.

Jetzt sehe ich Viola auf die Terrasse kommen. Sie trägt ein weißes Kleid, das eine Schulter frei lässt und in dem sie mich sehr an die Statue der nackten Oma/Aphrodite erinnert. Jules nähert sich ihr, Viola sieht zu ihrer Mutter, geht dann zu ihr und küsst sie auf beide Wangen.

Es ist keine Umarmung, aber ein Anfang. Ein Olivenzweig, der gereicht wird.

Der Anfang von Verständnis.

Und Vergebung.

Viola wendet sich uns zu und zieht Jules mit, die ihrerseits Rupes mit sich in den Kreis zieht. Und bald folgen Alexis und Angelina, dann Fabio und Sadie und Peaches und schließlich auch die anderen Umstehenden, bis wir alle eine lange Menschenschlange bilden, die sich unter den Sternen an der Hand hält und das Leben feiert.

Die Musik endet, und alle jubeln und klatschen. Und dann verlangen sie lauthals, dass Alexis und Helena ihren »Zorba« von vor zehn Jahren wiederholen.

»Hallo«, sage ich zu Viola, als sie sich zu mir gesellt. »Du siehst wunderschön aus.«

»Danke.«

Sie flüstert mir weiter etwas zu, doch ich bin abgelenkt – ich achte auf den Gesichtsausdruck meines Vaters, als meine Mutter zu Alexis geht und seine Hand ergreift. Dann, als sie in den Mittelpunkt des Kreises geführt wird, wirft sie Dad eine Kusshand zu, und Dad lächelt und wirft ihr eine Kusshand zurück.

Ich drehe mich zu Viola. »Entschuldige, was hast du gesagt?«

»Ich habe gesagt«, und sie lacht leise, »dass ich dich liebe, Alex. Ich habe dich immer schon geliebt, und ich glaube, ich werde dich auch immer lieben.« Sie macht eine verlegene Geste. »Das ist einfach so.«

Als die eindringliche Musik einsetzt, sehe ich sie an und erkenne, dass sie auf eine Antwort von mir wartet.

Immy packt mich an der Schulter und will mich und Viola drängen, uns in den Kreis der sich wiegenden Körper einzureihen.

»Alex, konzentrier dich!«, tadelt sie mich.

»Tut mir leid, Immy, das geht jetzt nicht.«

Und ich ziehe Viola mit mir fort. Wir lassen die Terrasse und den Menschenkreis, der sich sofort wieder schließt, hinter uns. Wie Diebe in der Nacht laufen wir in den von Laternen erleuchteten Olivenhain, um zusammen und allein zu sein. Ich nehme ihr Gesicht zwischen die Hände, und das Mondlicht fällt darauf.

»Ich liebe dich auch. Ich habe dich immer schon geliebt, und ich glaube, ich werde dich auch immer lieben.«

Und dann küsse ich sie, und sie erwidert den Kuss mit derselben Leidenschaft. Und als die Musik über uns zu einem Crescendo ansteigt, weiß ich mit absoluter Sicherheit, dass unser Tanz des Lebens erst beginnt.

Es ist einfach so.

DANK

Große Teile dieses Buchs schrieb ich vor zehn Jahren nach einem Familienurlaub auf Zypern, den wir in einer sehr schönen alten Villa am Ortsrand von Kathikas verbrachten. Dort spielt auch *Helenas Geheimnis*. Unsere fünf Kinder waren damals etwa so alt wie die Kinder in diesem Buch, und Familienfreunde kamen ebenfalls zu Besuch. Natürlich sind die Handlung und die Figuren vorwiegend frei erfunden, andererseits habe ich in keinem meiner Romane mehr auf meine Lebenserfahrung als Mutter, Stiefmutter, Ehefrau und ausgebildete Tänzerin zurückgegriffen.

Ich legte das Manuskript beiseite und entdeckte es erst wieder, als ich letztes Jahr in meiner Schreibtischschublade aufräumte. Natürlich waren die Kinder mittlerweile zehn Jahre älter geworden, und ich fand es ausgesprochen spannend zu lesen, wie ich sie beschrieben hatte, als sie kleiner waren. In gewisser Weise war es *mein* Tagebuch ihrer Kindheit, deswegen beschloss ich, den Roman abzuschließen. Und ja, es war für mich etwas völlig Neues: kein weitläufiger historischer Hintergrund, keine Zeitspanne von hundert Jahren – nur ein Monat, im selben Haus, mit wenigen Figuren. Beim Schreiben dieses Buchs habe ich wirklich sehr viel gelernt.

Mein allererster und größter Dank gebührt deswegen selbstredend meiner großartigen Familie: Olivia, Harry, Isabella, Leonora, Kit und natürlich meinem Mann Stephen, die mich überhaupt erst zu *Helenas Geheimnis* anregten.

Dank auch an meine großartige Clique internationaler Verleger, die mich ermutigten, das Buch fertig zu schreiben und es ihnen dann auch tatsächlich zu schicken: Jez Trevathan und Catherine Richards bei Pan Macmillan, Claudia Negele und Georg Reuchlein beim Goldmann Verlag, Knut Gørvell und Jorid Mathiassen bei Cappelen Damm sowie Donatella Minuto und Annalisa Lottini bei Giunti.

Und an alle im »Team Lulu«: Olivia Riley, Susan Moss, Ella Micheler und Jacquelyn Heslop. An meine Schwester Georgia Edmonds und meine Mutter Janet.

Und an all meine wunderbaren Leserinnen und Leser in aller Welt: Danke.

LUCINDA RILEY
Die sieben Schwestern
Roman

Maia ist die älteste von sechs Schwestern, die alle von ihrem Vater adoptiert wurden, als sie sehr klein waren. Sie lebt als Einzige noch auf dem herrschaftlichen Anwesen ihres Vaters am Genfer See, denn anders als ihre Schwestern, die es drängte, draußen in der Welt ein ganz neues Leben als Erwachsene zu beginnen, fand die eher schüchterne Maia nicht den Mut, ihre vertraute Umgebung zu verlassen. Doch das ändert sich, als ihr Vater überraschend stirbt und ihr einen Umschlag hinterlässt – und sie plötzlich den Schlüssel zu ihrer bisher unbekannten Vorgeschichte in Händen hält: Sie wurde in Rio de Janeiro in einer alten Villa geboren, deren Adresse noch heute existiert. Maia fasst den Entschluss, nach Rio zu fliegen, und an der Seite von Floriano Quintelas, eines befreundeten Schriftstellers, beginnt sie, das Rätsel ihrer Herkunft zu ergründen. Dabei stößt sie auf eine tragische Liebesgeschichte in der Vergangenheit ihrer Familie, und sie taucht ein in das mondäne Paris der Jahrhundertwende, wo einst eine schöne junge Brasilianerin einem französischen Bildhauer begegnete. Und erst jetzt fängt Maia an zu begreifen, wer sie wirklich ist…

LESEPROBE

Eins

Nie werde ich vergessen, wo ich war und was ich tat, als ich hörte, dass mein Vater gestorben war.

Ich saß im hübschen Garten des Londoner Stadthauses einer alten Schulfreundin, eine Ausgabe von Margaret Atwoods *Die Penelopiade* aufgeschlagen, jedoch ungelesen auf dem Schoß, und genoss die Junisonne, während Jenny ihren kleinen Sohn vom Kindergarten abholte.

Was für eine gute Idee es doch gewesen war, nach London zu kommen, dachte ich gerade in dieser angenehm ruhigen Atmosphäre und betrachtete die bunten Blüten der Clematis, denen die Hebamme Sonne auf die Welt half, als das Handy klingelte und ich auf dem Display die Nummer von Marina sah.

»Hallo, Ma, wie geht's?«, fragte ich und hoffte, dass mir die entspannte Stimmung anzuhören war.

»Maia, ich …«

Marinas Zögern verriet mir, dass sich etwas Schlimmes ereignet hatte.

»Ich weiß leider keine bessere Möglichkeit, es dir zu sagen: Dein Vater hatte gestern Nachmittag hier zu Hause einen Herzinfarkt und ist heute in den frühen Morgenstunden … von uns gegangen.«

Ich schwieg; lächerliche Gedanken schossen mir durch den Kopf, zum Beispiel der, dass Marina sich aus einem irgendeinem Grund einen geschmacklosen Scherz erlaubte.

LESEPROBE

»Du als Älteste der Schwestern erfährst es zuerst. Und ich wollte dich fragen, ob du es den andern selbst sagen oder das lieber mir überlassen möchtest.«

»Ich ...« Als mir klar zu werden begann, dass Marina, meine geliebte Marina, die Frau, die wie eine Mutter für mich war, so etwas nicht behaupten würde, wenn es nicht tatsächlich geschehen wäre, geriet meine Welt aus dem Lot.

»Maia, bitte sprich mit mir. Das ist der schrecklichste Anruf, den ich je erledigen musste, aber was soll ich machen? Der Himmel allein weiß, wie die andern es aufnehmen werden.«

Da erst hörte ich den Schmerz in *ihrer* Stimme und tat, was ich am besten konnte: trösten.

»Klar sag ich's den andern, wenn du das möchtest, obwohl ich nicht weiß, wo sie alle sind. Trainiert Ally nicht gerade für eine Segelregatta?«

Als wir diskutierten, wo meine jüngeren Schwestern sich aufhielten, als wollten wir sie zu einer Geburtstagsparty zusammenrufen, nicht zur Trauerfeier für unseren Vater, bekam die Unterhaltung etwas Surreales.

»Wann soll die Beisetzung stattfinden? Elektra ist in Los Angeles und Ally irgendwo auf hoher See, also dürfte nächste Woche der früheste Zeitpunkt sein«, schlug ich vor.

»Tja ...« Ich hörte Marinas Zögern. »Das besprechen wir, wenn du zu Hause bist. Es besteht keine Eile. Falls du wie geplant noch ein paar Tage in London bleiben möchtest, geht das in Ordnung. Hier kannst du ohnehin nichts mehr tun ...« Sie klang traurig.

»Ma, *natürlich* setze ich mich in den nächsten Flieger nach Genf, den ich kriegen kann! Ich ruf gleich bei der Fluggesellschaft an und bemühe mich dann, die andern zu erreichen.«

»Es tut mir ja so leid, *chérie*«, seufzte Marina. »Ich weiß, wie sehr du ihn geliebt hast.«

LESEPROBE

»Ja«, sagte ich, und plötzlich verließ mich die merkwürdige Ruhe, die ich bis dahin empfunden hatte. »Ich melde mich später noch mal, sobald ich weiß, wann genau ich komme.«

»Pass auf dich auf, Maia. Das war bestimmt ein schrecklicher Schock für dich.«

Ich beendete das Gespräch, und bevor das Gewitter in meinem Herzen losbrechen konnte, ging ich nach oben in mein Zimmer, um die Fluggesellschaft zu kontaktieren. In der Warteschleife betrachtete ich das Bett, in dem ich morgens an einem, wie ich meinte, ganz normalen Tag aufgewacht war. Und dankte Gott dafür, dass Menschen nicht die Fähigkeit besitzen, in die Zukunft zu blicken.

Die Frau von der Airline war alles andere als hilfsbereit; während sie mich über ausgebuchte Flüge und Stornogebühren informierte und mich nach meiner Kreditkartennummer fragte, spürte ich, dass meine emotionalen Dämme bald brechen würden. Als sie mir endlich widerwillig einen Platz im Vier-Uhr-Flug nach Genf reserviert hatte, was bedeutete, dass ich sofort meine Siebensachen packen und ein Taxi nach Heathrow nehmen musste, starrte ich vom Bett aus die Blümchentapete so lange an, bis das Muster vor meinen Augen zu verschwimmen begann.

»Er ist fort«, flüsterte ich, »für immer. Ich werde ihn nie wiedersehen.«

Zu meiner Verwunderung bekam ich keinen Weinkrampf. Ich saß nur benommen da und wälzte praktische Fragen. Mir graute davor, meinen fünf Schwestern Bescheid zu sagen, und überlegte, welche ich zuerst anrufen sollte. Natürlich entschied ich mich für Tiggy, die zweitjüngste von uns sechsen, zu der ich immer die engste Beziehung gehabt hatte, und die momentan in einem Zentrum für verwaistes und krankes Rotwild in den schottischen Highlands arbeitete.

Mit zitternden Fingern scrollte ich mein Telefonverzeichnis herunter und wählte ihre Nummer. Als sich ihre Mailbox meldete, bat ich sie lediglich, mich so schnell wie möglich zurückzurufen.

Und die anderen? Ich wusste, dass ihre Reaktion unterschiedlich ausfallen würde, von äußerlicher Gleichgültigkeit bis zu dramatischen Gefühlsausbrüchen.

Da ich nicht wusste, wie sehr mir selbst meine Trauer anzuhören wäre, wenn ich mit ihnen redete, entschied ich mich für die feige Lösung und schickte allen eine SMS mit der Bitte, sich baldmöglichst bei mir zu melden. Dann packte ich hastig meine Tasche und ging die schmale Treppe zur Küche hinunter, um Jenny eine Nachricht zu schreiben, in der ich ihr erklärte, warum ich so überstürzt hatte aufbrechen müssen.

Anschließend verließ ich das Haus und folgte mit schnellen Schritten der halbmondförmigen, baumbestandenen Straße in Chelsea, um ein Taxi zu rufen. Wie an einem ganz normalen Tag. Ich glaube, ich sagte sogar lächelnd hallo zu jemandem, der seinen Hund spazieren führte.

Es konnte ja auch niemand wissen, was ich gerade erfahren hatte, dachte ich, als ich in der belebten King's Road in ein Taxi stieg und dem Fahrer sagte, er solle mich nach Heathrow bringen.

Fünf Stunden später, die Sonne stand schon tief über dem Genfer See, kam ich an unserer privaten Landestelle an, wo Christian mich in unserem schnittigen Riva-Motorboot erwartete. Seiner Miene nach zu urteilen, wusste er Bescheid.

»Wie geht es Ihnen, Mademoiselle Maia?«, erkundigte er sich voller Mitgefühl, als er mir an Bord half.

»Ich bin froh, dass ich hier bin«, antwortete ich ausweichend und nahm auf der gepolsterten cremefarbenen Lederbank am

LESEPROBE

Heck Platz. Sonst saß ich, wenn wir die zwanzig Minuten nach Hause brausten, vorne bei Christian, doch heute hatte ich das Bedürfnis, hinten allein zu sein. Als Christian den starken Motor anließ, spiegelte sich die Sonne glitzernd in den Fenstern der prächtigen Häuser am Ufer des Genfer Sees. Bei diesen Fahrten hatte ich oft das Gefühl gehabt, in ein Märchenland, in eine surreale Welt, einzutauchen, die nichts mit der Wirklichkeit zu tun hatte.

In die Welt von Pa Salt.

Als ich an den Kosenamen meines Vaters dachte, den ich als Kind geprägt hatte, spürte ich zum ersten Mal, wie meine Augen feucht wurden. Er war immer gern gesegelt, und wenn er in unser Haus am See zu mir zurückkehrte, hatte er oft nach frischer Meerluft gerochen. Der Name war ihm geblieben, auch meine jüngeren Schwestern hatten ihn verwendet.

Während der warme Wind mir durch die Haare wehte, musste ich an all die Fahrten denken, die ich schon zu »Atlantis«, Pa Salts Märchenschloss, unternommen hatte. Da es auf einer Landzunge vor halbmondförmigem, steil ansteigendem, gebirgigem Terrain lag, war es zu Lande nicht erreichbar; man musste mit dem Boot hinfahren. Die nächsten Nachbarn lebten Kilometer entfernt am Seeufer, so dass »Atlantis« unser eigenes kleines Reich war, losgelöst vom Rest der Welt. Alles dort war magisch ... als führten Pa Salt und wir, seine Töchter, ein verzaubertes Leben.

Pa Salt hatte uns samt und sonders als Baby ausgewählt, in unterschiedlichen Winkeln der Erde adoptiert und nach Hause gebracht, wo wir fortan unter seinem Schutz lebten. Wir waren alle, wie Pa gern sagte, besonders und unterschiedlich ... eben *seine* Mädchen. Er hatte uns nach den Pleijaden, dem Siebengestirn, seinem Lieblingssternhaufen, benannt. Und ich, Maia, war die Erste und Älteste.

LESEPROBE

Als Kind hatte ich ihn manchmal in sein mit einer Glaskuppel ausgestattetes Observatorium oben auf dem Haus begleiten dürfen. Dort hatte er mich mit seinen großen, kräftigen Händen hochgehoben, damit ich durch das Teleskop den Nachthimmel betrachten konnte.

«Da sind sie», hatte er dann gesagt und das Teleskop für mich justiert. «Schau dir den wunderschön leuchtenden Stern an, nach dem du benannt bist, Maia.»

Und ich hatte ihn tatsächlich gesehen. Während er mir die Geschichten erzählte, die meinem eigenen und den Namen meiner Schwestern zugrundelagen, hatte ich kaum zugehört, sondern einfach nur das Gefühl seiner Arme um meinen Körper genossen, diesen seltenen, ganz besonderen Augenblick, in dem ich ihn ganz für mich hatte.

Marina, die ich in meiner Jugend für meine Mutter gehalten hatte – ich verkürzte ihren Namen sogar auf «Ma» –, entpuppte sich irgendwann als besseres Kindermädchen, das Pa eingestellt hatte, um auf mich aufzupassen, weil er so oft verreiste. Doch natürlich war Marina für uns Schwestern sehr viel mehr. Sie wischte uns die Tränen aus dem Gesicht, schalt uns, wenn wir nicht anständig aßen, und steuerte uns umsichtig durch die schwierige Zeit der Pubertät.

Sie war einfach immer da. Bestimmt hätte ich Ma auch nicht mehr geliebt, wenn sie meine leibliche Mutter gewesen wäre.

In den ersten drei Jahren meiner Kindheit hatten Marina und ich allein in unserem Märchenschloss am Genfer See gelebt, während Pa Salt geschäftlich auf den Sieben Weltmeeren unterwegs war. Dann waren eine nach der anderen meine Schwestern dazugekommen.

Pa hatte mir von seinen Reisen immer ein Geschenk mitgebracht. Wenn ich das Motorboot herannahen hörte, war ich über die weiten Rasenflächen und zwischen den Bäumen hindurch zur Anlegestelle gerannt, um ihn zu begrüßen. Wie jedes Kind war ich neugierig gewesen, welche Überraschungen sich in seinen Taschen verbargen. Und einmal, nachdem er mir ein fein geschnitztes Rentier aus Holz überreicht hatte, das, wie er mir versicherte, aus der Werkstatt von St. Nikolaus am Nordpol stammte, war eine Frau in Schwesterntracht hinter ihm hervorgetreten, in den Armen ein Bündel, das sich bewegte.

«Diesmal habe ich dir ein ganz besonderes Geschenk mitgebracht, Maia. Eine Schwester.» Er hatte mich lächelnd hochgehoben. «Nun wirst du dich nicht mehr einsam fühlen, wenn ich wieder auf Reisen bin.»

Danach hatte das Leben sich verändert. Die Kinderschwester verschwand nach ein paar Wochen, und fortan kümmerte sich Marina um die Kleine. Damals begriff ich nicht, wieso dieses rotgesichtige, kreischende Ding, das oft ziemlich streng roch und die Aufmerksamkeit von mir ablenkte, ein Geschenk sein sollte. Bis Alkyone – benannt nach dem zweiten Stern des Siebengestirns – mich eines Morgens beim Frühstück von ihrem Kinderstuhl aus anlächelte.

«Sie erkennt mich», sagte ich verwundert zu Marina, die sie fütterte.

«Natürlich, Maia. Du bist ihre große Schwester, zu der sie aufblicken wird. Es wird deine Aufgabe sein, ihr all die Dinge beizubringen, die du anders als sie bereits kannst.»

Später war sie mir wie ein Schatten überallhin gefolgt, was mir einerseits gefiel, mich andererseits jedoch auch aufregte.

«Maia, warte!», forderte sie lauthals, wenn sie hinter mir hertapste.

Obwohl Ally – wie ich sie nannte – ursprünglich eher ein unwillkommener Eindringling in mein Traumreich «Atlantis» gewesen war, hätte ich mir keine liebenswertere Gefährtin wünschen können. Sie weinte selten und neigte nicht zu Jähzornsausbrüchen wie andere Kinder in ihrem Alter. Mit ihren rotgoldenen Locken und den großen blauen Augen bezauberte Ally alle Menschen, auch unseren Vater. Wenn Pa Salt von seinen langen Reisen nach Hause zurückkehrte, strahlte er bei ihrem Anblick wie bei mir nur selten. Und während ich Fremden gegenüber schüchtern und zurückhaltend war, entzückte Ally sie mit ihrer offenen, vertrauensvollen Art.

Außerdem gehörte sie zu den Kindern, denen alles leichtzufallen schien – besonders Musik und sämtliche Wassersportarten. Ich erinnere mich, wie Pa ihr das Schwimmen in unserem großen Swimmingpool beibrachte. Während ich Mühe hatte, über Wasser zu bleiben, und es hasste unterzutauchen, fühlte meine kleine Schwester sich darin ganz in ihrem Element. Und während ich sogar auf der *Titan*, Pas riesiger ozeantauglicher Jacht, manchmal schon auf dem Genfer See fast seekrank wurde, bettelte Ally ihn an, mit ihr im Laser von unserer privaten Anlegestelle hinauszufahren. Ich kauerte mich im Heck des Boots zusammen, wenn Pa und Ally es in Höchstgeschwindigkeit über das spiegelglatte Wasser lenkten. Diese Leidenschaft schuf eine innere Verbindung zwischen ihnen, die mir verwehrt blieb.

Obwohl Ally am Conservatoire de Musique de Genève Musik studierte und eine begabte Flötistin war, die gut und gern Berufsmusikerin hätte werden können, hatte sie sich nach dem Abschluss des Konservatoriums für eine Laufbahn als Seglerin entschieden. Sie nahm regelmäßig an Regatten teil und hatte die Schweiz schon mehrfach international vertreten.

Als Ally fast drei war, hatte Pa unsere nächste Schwester gebracht, die er nach einem weiteren Stern des Siebengestirns Asterope nannte.

»Aber wir werden ›Star‹ zu ihr sagen«, hatte Pa Marina, Ally und mir lächelnd erklärt, als wir die Kleine in ihrem Körbchen betrachteten.

Weil ich inzwischen jeden Morgen Unterricht von einem Privatlehrer erhielt, wirkte sich das Eintreffen meiner neuen Schwester weniger stark auf mich aus als das von Ally. Genau wie sechs Monate später, als sich ein zwölf Wochen altes Mädchen namens Celaeno, was Ally sofort zu CeCe abkürzte, zu uns gesellte.

Der Altersunterschied zwischen Star und CeCe betrug lediglich drei Monate, sodass die beiden einander von Anfang an sehr nahe standen. Sie waren wie Zwillinge und kommunizierten in ihrer eigenen Babysprache, von der sie einiges sogar ins Erwachsenenalter retteten. Star und CeCe lebten in ihrer eigenen kleinen Welt, und auch jetzt, da sie beide über zwanzig waren, änderte sich daran nichts. CeCe, die jüngere der beiden, deren stämmiger Körper und nussbraune Haut in deutlichem Kontrast zu der gertenschlanken, blassen Star standen, übernahm immer die Führung.

Im folgenden Jahr traf ein weiteres kleines Mädchen ein. Taygeta – der ich ihrer kurzen dunklen Haare wegen, die wirr von ihrem winzigen Kopf abstanden wie bei dem Igel in Beatrix Potters Geschichte, den Spitznamen »Tiggy« gab.

Mit meinen sieben Jahren fühlte ich mich sofort zu Tiggy hingezogen. Sie war die zarteste von uns allen, als Kind ständig krank, jedoch schon damals durch kaum etwas zu erschüttern und anspruchslos. Als Pa wenige Monate später ein kleines Mädchen namens Elektra nach Hause brachte, bat die erschöpfte Marina mich gelegentlich, auf Tiggy aufzupassen, die oft an fiebrigen Kehlkopfentzündungen litt. Und als schließlich Asthma diagnostiziert wurde, schob man sie nur noch selten im Kinderwagen nach draußen in die kalte Luft und den dichten Nebel des Genfer Winters.

LESEPROBE

Elektra war die Jüngste der Schwestern, und obwohl ich inzwischen an Babys und ihre Bedürfnisse gewöhnt war, fand ich sie ziemlich anstrengend. Sie machte ihrem Namen alle Ehre, weil sie tatsächlich elektrisch wirkte. Ihre Stimmungen, die von einer Sekunde zur nächsten von fröhlich auf traurig wechselten und umgekehrt, führten dazu, dass unser bis dahin so ruhiges Zuhause nun von spitzen Schreien widerhallte. Ihre Jähzornsanfälle bildeten die Hintergrundmusik meiner Kindheit, und auch später schwächte sich ihr feuriges Temperament nicht ab.

Ally, Tiggy und ich nannten sie insgeheim »Tricky«. Wir behandelten sie wie ein rohes Ei, weil wir keine ihrer Launen provozieren wollten. Ich muss zugeben, dass es Momente gab, in denen ich sie für die Unruhe, die sie nach »Atlantis« brachte, hasste.

Doch wenn Elektra erfuhr, dass eine von uns Probleme hatte, half sie als Erste, denn ihre Großzügigkeit war genauso stark ausgeprägt wie ihr Egoismus.

Nach Elektra warteten alle auf die siebte Schwester. Schließlich hatte Pa Salt uns nach dem Siebengestirn benannt, und ohne sie waren wir nicht vollständig. Wir wussten sogar schon ihren Namen – »Merope« – und waren gespannt, wie sie sein würde. Doch die Jahre gingen ins Land, ohne dass Pa weitere Babys nach Hause gebracht hätte.

Ich erinnere mich noch gut an den Tag, an dem ich mit Vater im Observatorium eine Sonnenfinsternis beobachten wollte. Ich war vierzehn Jahre alt und fast schon eine Frau. Pa Salt hatte mir erklärt, dass eine Sonnenfinsternis immer einen wesentlichen Augenblick für die Menschen darstellte und Veränderungen einläutete.

»Pa«, hatte ich gefragt, »bringst du uns noch irgendwann eine siebte Schwester?«

LESEPROBE

Sein starker, schützender Körper war plötzlich erstarrt, als würde das Gewicht der Welt auf seinen Schultern lasten. Obwohl er sich nicht zu mir umdrehte, weil er damit beschäftigt war, das Teleskop auszurichten, merkte ich, dass ich ihn aus der Fassung gebracht hatte.

»Nein, Maia. Leider konnte ich sie nicht finden.«

Als die dichte Fichtenhecke, die unser Anwesen vor neugierigen Blicken schützte, in Sicht kam und ich Marina auf der Anlegestelle warten sah, wurde mir endgültig bewusst, wie schrecklich der Verlust von Pa war.

Des Weiteren wurde mir klar, dass der Mann, der dieses Reich für uns Prinzessinnen geschaffen hatte, den Zauber nun nicht mehr aufrechterhalten konnte.

Ende der Leseprobe
»Die sieben Schwestern«
von Lucinda Riley

Lucinda Riley

wurde in Irland geboren und verbrachte als Kind mehrere
Jahre in Fernost. Sie reist sehr gerne und ist nach wie vor
den Orten ihrer Kindheit sehr verbunden. Nach einer
Karriere als Theater- und Fernsehschauspielerin konzentriert
sich Lucinda Riley heute ganz auf das Schreiben – und das
mit sensationellem Erfolg: Seit ihrem gefeierten Roman
»Das Orchideenhaus« stürmte jedes ihrer Bücher die inter-
nationalen Bestsellerlisten. Lucinda Riley lebt mit ihrem Mann
und ihren vier Kindern an der englischen Küste in Norfolk
und in West Cork, Irland. Mehr zur Autorin unter
»http://www.lucinda-riley.de« und »http://lucindariley.co.uk«

<u>Von Lucinda Riley außerdem lieferbar:</u>

Das Orchideenhaus. Roman
Das Mädchen auf den Klippen. Roman
Der Lavendelgarten. Roman
Die Mitternachtsrose. Roman
Das italienische Mädchen. Roman
Der Engelsbaum. Roman
Der verbotene Liebesbrief. Roman
Das Schmetterlingszimmer. Roman
Die sieben Schwestern. Roman
Die Sturmschwester. Roman
Die Schattenschwester. Roman
Die Perlenschwester. Roman
Die Mondschwester. Roman
Die Sonnenschwester. Roman
(Alle Romane sind auch als E-Book erhältlich.)

GOLDMANN
Lesen erleben

Unsere Leseempfehlung

832 Seiten
Auch als E-Book
erhältlich

Reich, berühmt und bildschön: das ist Elektra d'Aplièse, die als Model ein glamouröses Leben in New York führt. Doch der Schein trügt – in Wahrheit ist sie eine verzweifelte junge Frau, die im Begriff ist, ihr Leben zu ruinieren. Da taucht eines Tages ihre Großmutter Stella auf, von deren Existenz Elektra nichts wusste. Sie ist ein Adoptivkind und kennt ihre Wurzeln nicht. Als Stella ihr die berührende Lebensgeschichte der jungen Amerikanerin Cecily Huntley-Morgan erzählt, öffnet sich für Elektra die Tür zu einer neuen Welt. Denn Cecily lebte in den 1940er Jahren auf einer Farm in Afrika – wo einst Elektras Schicksal seinen Anfang nahm …

www.goldmann-verlag.de
www.facebook.com/goldmannverlag

GOLDMANN
Lesen erleben

Unsere Leseempfehlung

680 Seiten
Auch als E-Book
und Hörbuch
erhältlich

Als der berühmte Schauspieler Sir James Harris in London stirbt, trauert das ganze Land. Die junge Journalistin Joanna Haslam begegnet auf der Beerdigung einer alten Dame, die ihr ein Bündel vergilbter Dokumente übergibt – darunter auch das Fragment eines Liebesbriefs voller mysteriöser Andeutungen. Doch wer waren die beiden Liebenden? Joanna beginnt zu recherchieren, doch noch kann sie nicht ahnen, dass sie sich damit auf eine gefährlich Mission begibt, die auch ihr Herz in Aufruhr versetzt – denn Marcus Harris, der Enkel von Sir James Harris, ist ein ebenso charismatischer wie undurchschaubarer Mann ...

www.goldmann-verlag.de
www.facebook.com/goldmannverlag

GOLDMANN
Lesen erleben

Unsere Leseempfehlung

576 Seiten
Auch als E-Book
und Hörbuch
erhältlich

Nach dem Tod ihres Vaters kehrt Ally d'Aplièse zum Familien-
sitz zurück, um den Schock gemeinsam mit ihren Schwestern
zu bewältigen. Sie alle wurden adoptiert und kennen den Ort
ihrer Herkunft nicht. Aber nun erhält Ally einen Hinweis: die
Biographie eines norwegischen Komponisten aus dem 19. Jahrhundert. Allys Neugier ist geweckt, und sie begibt sich auf die
Reise in das raue Land im Norden. Dort wird sie ergriffen von
der Welt der Musik, mit der sie tiefer verbundener ist, als sie es
je hätte ahnen können. Und Ally begreift zum ersten Mal im
Leben, wer sie wirklich ist ...

www.goldmann-verlag.de
www.facebook.com/goldmannverlag

Unsere Leseempfehlung

672 Seiten
Auch als
Hörbuch
und E-Book
erhältlich

Posy Montague steht kurz vor ihrem siebzigsten Geburtstag. Sie lebt alleine in ihrem geliebten »Admiral House«, einem herrschaftlichen Anwesen im ländlichen Suffolk. Eines Tages taucht völlig unerwartet ein Gesicht aus der Vergangenheit auf: ihre erste große Liebe Freddie, der sie fünfzig Jahre zuvor ohne ein Wort verlassen hatte. Nie konnte Posy den Verlust überwinden, aber darf sie nun das Wagnis eingehen, ihm noch einmal zu vertrauen? Freddie und das »Admiral House« bewahren indes ein lange gehütetes, düsteres Geheimnis – und Freddie weiß, er muss Posys Herz noch einmal brechen, wenn er es für immer gewinnen will …

www.goldmann-verlag.de
www.facebook.com/goldmannverlag

GOLDMANN
Lesen erleben

LUCINDA RILEY

Edel ausgestattete Sonderedition mit
Perlmutt-Einband und exklusiven Hintergrund-
informationen zu den jeweiligen Romanen

www.goldmann-verlag.de
www.facebook.com/goldmannverlag

 GOLDMANN
Lesen erleben